Problems in Marketing

McGraw-Hill Series in Marketing

CONSULTING EDITOR
Charles Schewe, University of Massachusetts

Problems in Marketing

Sixth Edition

E. Raymond Corey

Christopher H. Lovelock
Graduate School of Business Administration
Harvard University

Scott Ward
The Wharton School
University of Pennsylvania

McGraw-Hill Book Company
New York St. Louis San Francisco Auckland Bogotá Hamburg
Johannesburg London Madrid Mexico Montreal New Delhi
Panama Paris São Paulo Singapore Sydney Tokyo Toronto

PROBLEMS IN MARKETING

567890DODO8987654

Case materials of the Harvard Graduate School of Business Administration are designed as the basis for class discussion rather than to illustrate either effective or ineffective handling of administrative situations.

This book was set in Souvenir Light by Black Dot, Inc. The editors were Carol Napier and Elisa Adams; the design was done by Caliber Design Planning; the production supervisor was Dennis J. Conroy. New drawings were done by Burmar.
R. R. Donnelley & Sons Company was printer and binder.

Library of Congress Cataloging in Publication Data
Main entry under title:

Problems in marketing.

    (McGraw-Hill series in marketing)
    "Case materials of the Harvard Graduate School of Business Administration."
    Includes bibliographical references.
    1. Marketing—Case studies. 2. Marketing management—Case studies. I. Corey, E. Raymond. II. Lovelock, Christopher H. III. Ward, Scott, date IV. Harvard University. Graduate School of Business Administration.
HF5415.P724 1981   658.8'00722   80-26085
ISBN 0-07-013141-4

This edition of **Problems in Marketing** is dedicated to those members of the Harvard Business School Faculty who contributed so much to the early development of marketing as a field of study:

Neil H. Borden
Melvin T. Copeland
Malcolm P. McNair
Harry R. Tosdal

Their work was truly pioneering.

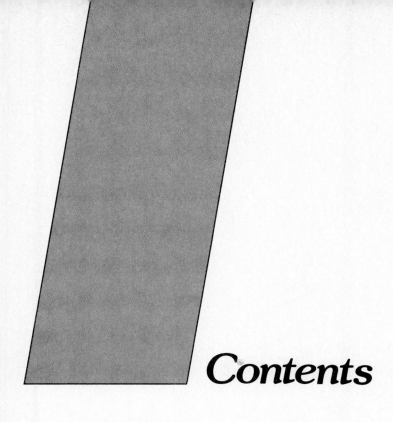

Contents

Preface

The development of casebooks in marketing has been a Harvard Business School tradition since 1920, when Melvin T. Copeland first published *Marketing Problems*. This sixth edition of *Problems in Marketing* continues many of the traditions of its predecessors, while introducing several distinctive changes from previous editions, including an expanded number of cases, greater diversity in the types of organizations presented, and a reduction in the average length of the cases.

Like all good marketing managers, we did some research before planning this new edition. In particular, we surveyed current users of the fifth edition, receiving responses from faculty members at over 60 different schools that had adopted the book. Their comments were very helpful, and we have tried to be responsive to them in selecting the materials included here.

The new edition features 51 cases, up from the 33 in the fifth edition. By offering a wider choice of materials, we hope to make it easier for instructors to tailor their courses to the educational focus desired, in terms of level of difficulty, types of problems addressed, and mix of application areas featured.

Fourteen cases have been retained from the fifth edition, but instructors should note that many of these have been pruned and edited to improve their pedagogical value still further. The balance of 37 cases includes, by request, several classics, as well as many new cases prepared during the last few years. In keeping with our custom, all have been classroom-tested at Harvard, and most have already achieved widespread use in MBA programs, advanced undergraduate courses, and executive development programs at many other institutions.

By increasing the number of cases in the book, we've been able to devote much greater coverage to three types of products that are attracting increased attention from marketing practitioners and academics alike: consumer services, goods and services sold to industrial (or institutional) buyers, and the services of public and nonprofit organizations. This has been achieved without reducing our traditional coverage of consumer goods and industrial goods marketing. As a result, the marketing problems presented depict a good cross-section of today's market economy.

In response to the concerns of those instructors who prefer to use less lengthy materials, especially in the early weeks of a case course, we've included a number of relatively short cases. We anticipate that these will be particularly helpful for instructors teaching courses in which many of the students are new to cases.

Many individuals have contributed to the development of the cases featured here. Our thanks are due, first, to our fellow case authors: Ralph M. Biggadike, Robert D. Buzzell, John F. Cady, Noel Capon, Darral G. Clarke, Craig E. Cline, Stanton G. Cort, Nancy J. Davis, F. Stewart DeBruicker, L. Frank Demmler, Steven L. Diamond, Albert H. Dunn, Richard W. Edelman, Paul W. Farris, Gary R. Garrasi, Stephen A. Greyser, Jeffrey S. Kahn, Jean-Louis LeCocq, Derek A. Newton, Dan E. Patterson, Edward T. Popper, Thomas S. Robertson, Walter J. Salmon, Benson P. Shapiro, Harvey N. Singer, Ralph Z. Sorenson II, Steven H. Star, Ralph G.M. Sultan, Cedric L. Suzman, Hirotaka Takeuchi, Ulrich E. Weichmann, and Lawrence H. Wilkinson.

We are also grateful for the cooperation of the organizations (sometimes disguised) that form the subjects of these cases, since nearly all the materials in this book were made possible only by the willingness of practicing managers to share experience and data. Equally important is the generosity of those who have contributed toward the costs of case development; in particular, we should like to thank the Associates of the Harvard Business School and the 1907 Foundation.

A great many people have helped us to bring the sixth edition to fruition. We are especially grateful to our secretaries, Marie Castro, Emily Feudo, Cathi O'Hara, and Louise Ringle, and to the staff of the Intercollegiate Case Clearing House under its director, Christopher E. Nugent. Additional help was provided by the editorial staff of the McGraw-Hill Book Company and by Karen Lindsey.

In contrast to some other methods of teaching, the use of cases requires the active participation of students, whose critical analysis in classroom discussions at Harvard and many other schools has served to shape and refine each of the cases included here. Much of the challenge and satisfaction of case teaching comes from the interaction between students and instructors. We hope that those who use this book will be equally stimulated by the process.

E. Raymond Corey
Christopher H. Lovelock
Scott Ward

To the Student

Marketing is a little-understood function. To the homemaker, it's often perceived as the TV commercial, the sales clerk behind the drugstore counter, and the cents-off coupon deals. To the average businessperson, marketing is simply sales and the people out there somewhere calling on the customers. To some in our society, marketing practices are manipulative, economically inefficient, and socially dysfunctional.

We hope that you will come to see marketing as being at the heart of what any organization, profit or nonprofit, does—what markets it serves, what products it produces, how it communicates. We also hope you will see marketing as *that function that relates an organization creatively and profitably to its environment.* If that strikes you as a broad definition, we would hasten to make clear that the marketing function, as we see it, is something the whole organization does, not just the sales and marketing departments.

But trying to relate our institutions to their environments was never more difficult. A current fact of corporate life is the increasing involvement of government in matters that affect product design, pricing, advertising, distribution systems, and, in fact, the way we go about making a sale. The values of the community are changing greatly, and the change is reflected in the public's multidimensional expectations of what our institutions, public and private, should deliver. At the same time public confidence in these institutions has seldom, if ever, been at a lower ebb.

If marketing is to function effectively it must, then, pick up its signals from a much wider range of sources—individual buyers, consumer groups, government agencies, and the community at large. The difficulties of charting a course in the midst of the often-conflicting pressures and influences are not to be underestimated.

The need exists for much-improved market-sensing devices, for better marketing decision-making processes, for more broadly conceived strategies, for marketing (corporate) objectives that distinguish the feasible from the impractical, for more sensitive performance measurement systems, and, indeed, for a set of values that may bring business and the publics it serves more closely in line. Adapting to these changes is a marketing challenge in the broadest sense. It is, in our view, the greatest challenge of all for management in the 1980s and 1990s.

About Cases

This is a book consisting almost entirely of case problems that you will be asked to solve. As you work your way through each one, your knowledge and understanding of marketing will build. Generally the cases become increasingly complex as you go along, and the concepts, analytical approaches, and factual information you pick up from each can be applied to help solve the cases ahead. By the time you have completed the course, the ideas coming out of studying the case problems in the book, together with any readings your instructor may assign, should add up to a comprehensive understanding of marketing no matter where you find it.

Since we rely so heavily on case problem analysis as a way of learning, it might be helpful here to talk about cases and what we can do with them. Cases describe actual business situations. In that respect, dealing with cases is very much like dealing with the kinds of problems that managers encounter daily.

Case studies are usually prepared by casewriters working under the supervision of teaching faculty members. It is a demanding process, calling for skills in interviewing and information collection as well as in writing. Casewriters have generally completed their Master of Business Administration or other advanced degree.

Case leads are developed by faculty members out of the needs they recognize to cover certain topics or problem areas in their courses. These needs are matched against their knowledge of many businesses and business situations, generated through their associations with managers and through reading current business literature. A faculty member will approach a company and ask for its cooperation in developing case material on a particular management situation. More often than not, the executive contacted is someone who has attended the Harvard Business School and is familiar with what cases are and the way they are used for educational purposes.

Having defined the case subject lead with a supervising faculty member, the casewriter interviews members of management who are familiar with the problem being studied, reviews memoranda, and gathers quantitative data—all relevant to the issue. He or she then prepares an initial draft, which is sent to company representatives for review. The review is intended to check the accuracy and completeness of the data and to provide the basis for deciding how the case should be disguised, if it is to be. Depending on the wishes of the company, its name and location, names of individuals, and figure data may be disguised, but not in a way that distorts the essence of the particular problem.

In spite of the realism we try to build into our cases, they are not, after all, actual business situations. First, the information comes to you in neatly written form. In contrast, managers in business and government accumulate facts through memos, conversations, statistical reports, and the public press.

Second, a case is designed to fit a particular unit of class time and to focus on a certain category of problems—say, marketing, or production, or finance. It may then omit elements of the real situation—people or organizational issues, for example—in order to focus attention on what the instructor would like his or her students to see.

Third, a case is a snapshot taken at a certain point in time. In reality, business problems are often seen as a continuum calling for some action today, further consideration, and more action tomorrow. It is very seldom that a manager can wrap up problems, put them away, and go on to the next "case."

A case may be lacking in reality in one final respect: while students of cases are called on (and, indeed, required) to make decisions, they don't have the responsibility for implementing their decisions.

We have discussed what a case is not. Let us look at the other side of the coin and consider the usefulness of cases for educational purposes.

Case studies cut across a range of companies, industries, and situations to provide an exposure far greater than what anyone is likely to experience in day-to-day routine. You can build your knowledge of a range of management subjects by dealing intensively with problems in each field. You will come to recognize that the on-the-job problems with which you will deal as a manager are not unique to your company, or even your industry. You will thus develop a more professional sense of management.

Perhaps the most important benefit that comes from using cases, however, is that they help us to learn how to ask the right questions. An able business leader once commented, "Ninety percent of the task of a top manager is to ask useful questions. Answers are relatively easy to find, but asking good questions—that is the more critical skill."

If discussion questions are suggested in connection with the preparation of a case, that does not preempt the task of identifying the key problems. You must still ask yourself: "What really are the problems this manager has to resolve?" So often, we manipulate facts and figures without defining the *problems* for which we seek solutions.

Cases help considerably to sharpen analytical skills. You will work with facts and figures to produce quantitative and qualitative evidence supporting recommendations and decisions. When challenged by both instructors and colleagues to defend your arguments, you develop increased ability to think and reason rigorously.

In addition, cases and case discussions provide a focal point for an exchange among students of the lessons of experience. Such discussions provide a vehicle for reassessing the lessons of experience and gaining increased learning from them.

Cases are useful for developing sets of principles and concepts that can be applied in practice. We consider each case by itself. But out of each will come important concepts and approaches. Taken together, a series of cases should develop for each of us some key ideas that can then be applied in specific managerial situations.

There is one final benefit we seek to achieve by using business case studies: to suggest the sense of fun and excitement that comes with being a manager. You may see a number of situations in businesses that you don't wish to be in! But you should come to sense that being a manager is a great challenge—intellectually, politically, and socially.

How to Prepare a Case

There is no one way to prepare a case. But to help you get started, we suggest the following approach. You can take it from there and develop your own methods.

1. Go through the case almost as fast as you can turn the pages, asking yourself, "What is the case about, and what types of information am I being given to analyze?" In particular, look at the first few and the last few paragraphs and glance over the exhibits.

2. Now read the case very carefully, underlining key facts as you go. Then ask yourself, "What are the basic problems this manager has to resolve?" Try hard to put yourself in the position of the manager in the case. Develop a sense of involvement in *the manager's* problems.
3. Note the key problems on scratch paper. Then go through the case again, sorting out the relevant considerations for each problem area.
4. Develop a set of recommendations supported by analysis of case data.

Let us expand on these steps for a moment.

Problem Definition.   Step 2, developing a statement of the questions that should be answered, is a critically important part of the analytical process. In cases, the explicit problems are often stated in the opening paragraphs and at the end. But you may find pieces of the problem scattered throughout the case. Sometimes the problem is crystal-clear; sometimes aspects of the problem may be implied in the middle of the case with a lead-in such as "Mr. X wondered, too, whether . . ." It is useful to pick these statements up, note them on your scratch paper, and then try to make some order out of them before you seek answers.

Problem definition is also a matter of delineating a suitable framework within which to deal with what may be posed in the case as an immediate question. For example, the manager in the case may be asking, "What should be our advertising strategy?" That could be the tip of the iceberg, and the more fundamental problem might be, "What should be our target market segment, and how do we develop an overall strategy for reaching it?" It becomes possible, then, to deal with the specific query regarding advertising strategy within the framework of the broader question. Thus, problems should be defined in a way that

- resolves the immediate (explicit) issues.
- deals with aspects of the business about which the immediate problem raises (implicit) issues.

The problem scope, however, should not be unrealistically and unmanageably broad. For example, it is tempting sometimes to raise the broad question: "Should we really be in this business at all—or in some other?" Much of the time, however, the manager in the case isn't in a position to redirect the company's business. Moreover, the case may not provide sufficient data to deal meaningfully with such a broad problem. In problem definition, then, it becomes important to take account of the scope of control and authority that the manager in the case has. That is, indeed, a relevant factor for you in laying out the questions to be answered.

Good problem definition, then:

- names the immediate issues and defines them in a way that calls for action-oriented answers.
- puts these issues in a proper marketing strategy context, that is, the broader issue.
- deals with these problems from the perspective of an individual manager, recognizing all the responsibilities and the scope of authority, as well as the limitations associated with that position.

Case Analysis   At this point in your preparation, it will be helpful to jot down relevant areas for analysis, one to a page. Areas for analysis are different from the problem statement. For example, if the problems are, "Should we introduce Product X? To whom should it be sold? What should be our advertising strategy?", the areas for analysis might include:

- trends in the marketplace
- buyer behavior
- competition
- break-even analysis

Facts in the case can then be marshalled to help you understand each area and to draw some meaningful observations and conclusions. These can, in turn, provide the basis for answering the questions that have been laid out. Inevitably, your analysis will generate arguments that seem to lead to different conclusions. All the evidence may not point in the same direction. It is important that you recognize conflicting considerations, weigh the evidence carefully, and decide what in your balanced best judgment is the best course of action.

Having arrived at a decision, you must be able to state your recommendations clearly and to support them with arguments developed from your examination of the analytical areas, using exhibits where it is helpful to back up your recommendations and proposed plan of action. Then, to complete the work, state any relevant ideas you may have regarding how your plan of action is to be implemented.

A good answer has these qualities:

- It deals explicitly with the specific problems posed in the case and within the context of the broader strategy issues.
- It is well supported by sound analysis and arguments that recognize the pros and cons of taking any recommended course of action.
- It includes ideas for implementation.

A good answer, in some cases, may also have another "plus": If, after sound analysis, you reject a course of action proposed by the manager in the case, it will be useful to suggest an alternative. There may not be one, of course. Even so, a complete treatment of the case problem will include a consideration of the alternative possibilities that might exist even if these, too, should be rejected.

Finally, one important characteristic of a good answer is that it seems to you to make sense. If it doesn't make sense, it is probably wrong!

Case Discussion. Up to now, your best results will come if you have worked by yourself. The next step is to meet with your discussion group, present your arguments to the members of this group, and hear theirs. The purpose of the discussion is *not* to develop a consensus or a group position. It is to help each member to refine, adjust, and fill out his or her own thinking. It is not necessary, or even desirable, that you agree.

The purpose of individual and group preparation is primarily to ready you to learn in class. The greater your command of the case facts and the more ideas you have about the case problems, the better prepared you are to take in, react to, and learn from the ideas of others in the class.

In class, your instructor will usually let you take the case where you wish. He or she will then prod you to explore fully the avenues of investigation down which you have started and will lead you into a consideration of other areas that you may have missed. Finally, if the case calls for it, the instructor will require you to make a decision. At the end, he or she may summarize the discussion and draw out the useful lessons and observations that come from the case problem and from class discussion comments—or ask some members of the class to do it.

The classroom is a place for you to express, support, and defend your conclusions and recommendations. We learn through controversy and discussion. The effective use of cases as a learning vehicle depends heavily on class participation. Through interchange and constructive controversy we build analytical skills, develop judgment, and gain conceptual understanding. There is, then, a burden of responsibility on each student not only for his or her education but for the learning of all other students as well.

Perhaps the greatest pedagogical benefit of the case method is that it generates a high degree of involvement in the learning process. People tend to learn the most from those things in which they are most deeply involved. But it follows, too, that there is little that can be learned from even the best cases without solid preparation.

Discussion in class is also an effective way for you to think rigorously and to develop skills in communicating, in thinking on your feet, and in responding to questions under pressure. Talking in class, expressing your own views, and defending them are all part of a distinctive experience. Seemingly rigorous and tension-building when you are doing it, class participation, in retrospect, becomes one of the most valued parts of the educational experience.

As important as talking is, however, listening is more important. It's easy to become so preoccupied with what we think that our minds close to the thoughts of other participants in the discussion. It is just as important in class to be open-minded and willing to shift positions as it is in business. The measure of your individual progress in any one case discussion is not based so much on your own after-class assessment of whether your ideas were "right." Instead it is more useful to ask, "How much did I take away from the class that I didn't know when I came in?"

E. Raymond Corey
Christopher H. Lovelock
Scott Ward

Problems in Marketing

I

The Marketing Process

Marketing is distinctive in that it is the management function which links the organization to its environment. This reflects marketing's concern with transactions—exchanges of value between the organization and its customers.

It's helpful to characterize marketing efforts according to *who* markets *what* to *whom*. For many decades, the study of marketing focused on the production, distribution, and sale of physical goods by firms in the private sector of the economy, emphasizing sales in consumer markets to individuals and households. Interest in studying marketing to industrial and institutional buyers did not emerge until later (although such transactions had, of course, long been an important aspect of the economy).

In recent years, the study of marketing has been broadened further to include several new fronts. It's now recognized that the ranks of marketers include not only private firms but also public and nonprofit organizations. The products marketed in today's economy are certainly not confined to physical goods; they include services (which now account for more than three-fifths of the American gross national product) and also ideas and behavior patterns—such as making donations to charitable organizations, voting for political candidates, and giving blood.

In this book, we shall emphasize situations in which there is an economic basis to transactions whereby the marketer sells a product (good or service) in exchange for a financial payment by the purchaser or by some third party.

Marketer Needs and Customer Needs

Marketing is the process by which organizations (1) select target customers or constituents, (2) assess the customers' needs and concerns, and (3) manage their resources to satisfy the customers. The objective for the private firm is to sell its goods or services in large enough quantities and at sufficient prices to cover all costs and yield a satisfactory profit. Public and nonprofit organizations, by contrast, frequently do not expect to cover their full costs from sales revenues and must depend on grants, donations, or tax revenues to make up the resulting deficits.

Looking at marketing in terms of exchange transactions forces us to consider the costs and benefits accruing to both parties. At one level, the marketing process is used by the organization to develop an overall product-market strategy: Which customers should we serve with what products in order to achieve our organizational goals? This view focuses on the costs and benefits accruing to the marketer.

At a second level, the marketing process should reflect the customer viewpoint: What specific combination of product features, delivery systems, information dissemination, and price will lead a specific customer (or group of customers) to purchase a particular product from us rather than from our competitors, or to purchase something from us rather than purchase nothing at all?

Unless the product's benefits to a prospective customer are perceived as outweighing its costs, the customer won't buy it. It's important to recognize that we're talking here about more than just value for money, since there are other costs, too, that the customer may incur, including time (a more precious resource for some than money) and psychic costs such as "hassle" and having to deal with strange or uncomfortable environments.

The task of the marketing manager should be as much concerned with determining and then alleviating these costs as it is with delivering the benefits most desired by customers.

Analysis and Strategy

The cases in this introductory section of the book introduce various analytical tools and techniques, including analysis of the market and its environment, customer buying behavior, competitive activities, and the needs and capabilities of marketing intermediaries. Understanding the economic implications of marketing decisions is particularly vital (and is discussed in depth in the Appendix, "Economic Analysis").

Implicit in the decisions of what customer groups to serve and how to combine marketing variables to appeal to a particular group of potential purchasers is the concept of market segmentation. This is based on the following propositions:

1. Consumers (or institutional buyers) are different.
2. Differences between consumers are related to differences in market behavior.
3. Segments of consumers can be isolated within the overall market according to such factors as their personal characteristics, their geographic location, their life-styles, the needs they seek to satisfy, and their buying behavior.

Market segmentation represents a middle way between a strategy of market aggregation, in which all customers are treated similarly, and one of market disaggregation, in which each consumer is treated uniquely.

In order for marketing managers to be able to develop an appropriate strategy in any given situation, they need to understand not only customer needs but also *buyer behavior:* How does a customer decide to buy a product and then go about the purchasing process? In a few instances, it may simply be an impulse purchase on the part of a single individual, such as buying a candy bar at a supermarket check-out counter. But most of the time more forethought and planning are involved. For larger purchases in a family or firm, a group of people—several members of a household or a buying committee in an institution—may constitute a *decision-making unit* (DMU) that arrives at the purchase decision collectively, even though a single individual may be charged with making the actual purchase. Additionally, others outside the DMU may offer advice. Consider, for instance, the process by which students arrive at the decision to enroll in college or graduate school. How many institutions do they consider? Do they visit any in advance? To whom do they turn for advice? What role do friends and family members play? If an applicant is accepted by more than one school, how does he or she make the final decision about which offer to accept? Now think about the process of buying a new stereo system, a ticket for an airline flight, a pack of cassette tapes, a meal in a fast-food restaurant, a box of detergent, or a postal money order. What do these purchases have in common, and what is different about them?

Many of the cases in this book challenge the reader's ability to understand buying behavior in industrial situations that may be unfamiliar—for example, situations concerning oil-drilling equipment, airfreight, industrial chemicals, and information-retrieval services. In these instances, the consumer is a corporation or some other institution rather than an individual, but organizations, too, have needs to meet and constraints on their resources. Like members of households, those involved in the purchase decision often have conflicting priorities; unlike members of households, they may have established formalized procedures for decision making.

Another major determinant of marketing strategy is the current and anticipated activities of competitors. The marketing manager first needs to identify both direct competitors (who market similar products) and indirect competitors (who market substitutes that satisfy the same basic customer need). Then answers to the following questions must be sought: What are our competitors' major strengths and weaknesses (financial, technical, marketing)? What market segments do they seek to serve? What specific marketing programs have they addressed to each segment? How well are they performing in terms of such measures as market share, sales volume, and profitability? How might they respond to any strategies of ours that threaten their market position? Finally, the manager needs to consider what new competitors might enter the market within a short- or medium-term period.

The Marketing Mix

As you will discover from the cases in this initial section, putting together a marketing plan requires that the manager make strategic decisions in several important areas, collectively referred to as the marketing mix.

Credit for coining this term is due to Professor Neil H. Borden. He developed the concept in 1948 after hearing a colleague at the Harvard Business School describe the marketing manager as a "mixer of ingredients." Borden's list of the ingredients available to the marketing manager was a long one; subsequent writers have simplified it to four basic components: (1) the product, (2) the delivery systems by which the product is made available to the customer, (3) the price at which the product is sold, and (4) the communications by which prospective customers are informed about the product.

Viewed in this way, marketing is seen to be a considerably broader function than is generally recognized by the lay person or casual observer. Marketing is much more than just advertising and selling. From the marketer's standpoint, the marketing mix provides a useful organizing framework for the development of strategy. Customers' needs for certain benefits can be determined from research and form the basis for decisions on which products to market and how they should be designed. Their need for convenience in purchasing and consumption (and sometimes for after-sales service, too) must be addressed through decisions on physical distribution channels (for goods) and delivery systems (for services). These must take into account not only locational decisions but also the scheduling of product availability—*when* consumers want to buy may be as important as *where* they wish to buy, particularly for services that are consumed as they are delivered. Customers' needs for information and reassurance require that the marketer consider the most cost-effective ways of communicating with customers. This involves decisions on brand names, advertising, personal selling, publicity, point-of-sale information, labeling, and instructional materials. Finally, the organization must determine how much prospective customers are able and willing to pay for the product in question; for expensive products, the pricing policy often incorporates credit procedures designed to help purchasers spread the cost over an extended period of time.

Use of Intermediaries

Because of the complexity of the marketing process and the physical separation of producers and consumers, certain marketing tasks are often delegated to intermediaries. Marketing research tasks may be handled on a confidential basis by a specialized research firm. The designing, planning, and implementation of advertising campaigns and publicity activities may be undertaken by advertising and public relations agencies. The physical distribution of manufactured products may involve transportation operators, warehousing firms, and wholesalers. The selling function may be handled by intermediaries such as distributors, manufacturers, and retail stores or service agencies. Finally, credit terms may be arranged through an independent financing organization.

Selecting, training, motivating, and controlling these intermediaries are all part of the marketing process. In a very real sense, these individuals or firms are also the marketer's customers, and other marketers may be competing for their custom.

Conclusion

The marketing process involves establishing an overall product-market strategy to meet organizational objectives and then developing detailed substrategies involving each element of the marketing mix. Decisions must be made concerning the nature of the product itself, how it is to be delivered to customers, how it is to be priced, and what information shall be communicated to potential customers. These decisions must be oriented toward the needs and characteristics of each of the market segments at which the product is targeted. They must also take into account the strategies employed by competitors.

A variety of different organizations are featured in this first part of the casebook—both for-profit and nonprofit, selling goods and services, in industrial and consumer markets, and in both domestic and international environments. Part of the learning task for you will be to understand the nature of the marketing process, together with the use of certain basic tools and concepts, in a variety of different contexts.

1

Gillette Safety Razor Division

Steven H. Star

Mr. Ralph Bingham, vice president–new business development of the Gillette Safety Razor Division (SRD), was considering a proposal for SRD to market a line of blank recording cassettes.[1] Like all Gillette divisions, SRD had received an earnings growth target as part of the corporate long-range planning process. SRD's forecast of demand for shaving systems implied that the division would not be able to achieve its earnings growth target several years out unless it added new product categories to its product lines. As vice president–new business development, it was Mr. Bingham's job to identify new business opportunities for the division, to assess their feasibility, and—working with functional managers in SRD—to develop plans for entering such new businesses.

Steven H. Star was formerly an associate professor at the Harvard Graduate School of Business Administration.

[1]Names of individuals and certain financial data have been disguised.

The Company

The Gillette Company was founded in 1903 to manufacture and market the safety razor and blade invented by Mr. King Gillette. The company grew very rapidly and had achieved sales of $60 million and profits before tax of $20.4 million by 1947. Until 1948, the company's product line was limited to safety razors, double-edge blades, and shaving cream.

In 1948, Gillette acquired the Toni Company, a leading manufacturer of women's hair preparations. This acquisition was Gillette's first effort outside the men's shaving business and was followed by acquisitions of the Paper Mate Corporation (1955), Harris Research Laboratories (1956), the Sterilon Corporation (1962), and the Braun Company (1967). Each of these acquisitions was intended as a diversification move, and the acquired companies were operated independently of the men's shaving business.

During this same period, Gillette had embarked on an extensive internal new-product development program. At first, such development had been limited to the shaving business, with introductions of the first blade dispenser in 1946, Foamy Instant Lather Shaving Cream in 1953, the Gillette adjustable razor in 1957, and the Super Blue Blade in 1960.

In 1960, Gillette had entered the toiletries business with the introduction of Right Guard Deodorant for men. In time, Right Guard had come to be positioned as a deodorant for the entire family and had obtained 28 percent of the $250 million deodorant market by 1968. During the 1960s, Gillette had also introduced an aftershave lotion, a men's cologne, a talc, and several men's hairgrooming products. The Gillette name had been prominently featured in the advertising and packaging of all these products, including Right Guard.

In 1967, it had been decided to split off the toiletries business from the razor and blade business, a move which was completed in 1968. Organizationally, a separate Toiletries Division, with its own headquarters, manufacturing plant, and sales force, was now responsible for Right Guard, Foamy, and Gillette's other toiletry products. The Gillette Safety Razor Division was now responsible for the development, manufacturing, and marketing of Gillette razors and blades in the United States, an activity which still accounted for a major share of corporate sales and profits.

In 1969, Gillette corporate sales were $609 million; profits before taxes were $119 million. Men's grooming products (razors, blades, and toiletries) represented 59 percent of sales, while women's grooming products represented 20 percent, Paper Mate 6 percent, and Braun 13 percent. According to the Gillette *Annual Report* for 1969, almost 50 percent of the corporation's assets were located outside the United States and Canada.

The Safety Razor Division

During the mid-1960s, as the toiletries business was in the process of being removed from its jurisdiction, the Safety Razor Division had concentrated on consolidating its position in the blade and razor business. In particular, it had responded vigorously and successfully to competitive threats from Wilkinson, Schick, and Personna with the introduction of the stainless steel blade in 1963, the Super Stainless blade in 1965, and the Techmatic shaving system in 1966. According to industry observers, these moves helped Gillette to maintain a high market share while significantly increasing the average selling price and unit profits of Gillette razors and blades.

The split-off of the Toiletries Division had, however, removed from SRD those product lines with the greatest potential for significant growth. By 1970, therefore, SRD was seeking new growth opportunities outside the blade and razor business.

In seeking new ventures for SRD, Bingham sought to identify "high growth markets where SRD's strengths would give it a competitive edge." Following discussions with other Gillette executives and trade sources, Bingham concluded that SRD was particularly strong in three areas: (1) shaving technology and development, (2) high-volume manufacturing of precision metal and plastic products, and (3) the marketing of mass-distributed packaged goods.

In the marketing area, distribution was generally considered to be SRD's most important strength. In 1968, Gillette razors and blades were sold by more than 500,000 retail outlets in the United States, including 54,000 chain and independent drugstores, 256,000 food stores, 21,000 discount and variety stores, and approximately 170,000 other outlets. Gillette razors and blades were stocked by 100 percent of the drugstores and discount stores in the United States, by 96 percent of chain and independent food stores, and by 83 percent of all variety stores. Wherever possible, SRD sought multiple displays of its products in a single outlet.

While SRD sold directly to large chain accounts, the majority of its retail accounts were served by 3,000 independent wholesalers. These wholesalers were of several types, including drug wholesalers, tobacco wholesalers, and toiletry merchandisers. The latter generally distributed to food and/or discount stores, often on a rack-jobbing[2] basis. According to SRD estimates, these wholesalers employed approximately 20,000 salespeople and were responsible for slightly less than 50 percent of SRD sales.

The SRD sales force consisted of four regional managers, a national accounts manager, 18 district managers, 109 territory representatives, and 27 sales merchandisers. Annual costs of operating this sales force (including compensation, expenses, and overheads) were estimated by industry observers to be between $5 million and $6 million. The territory representatives focused their attention on wholesalers and the headquarters of direct retail accounts but also called on the top 10 to 20 percent of the retail outlets served by wholesalers. The sales merchandisers confined their efforts to the retail level, where they supplemented wholesaler salespeople's efforts to obtain special displays and promotions.

According to industry sources, the SRD sales force was extraordinarily effective in working with chain headquarters and wholesalers to

[2]A rack jobber is essentially a wholesaler who sets up displays and keeps them stocked with merchandise. Rack-jobber personnel visit their retail accounts on a frequent basis. While in the store they replace defective or worn merchandise, add new items, set up promotional displays, and do other work designed to maintain the strength of the business. While retailers using rack jobbers generally retained formal authority to determine which products and brands they would carry and how they would be priced, in practice these functions were often delegated to the rack jobber. It was considered unlikely, however, that a rack jobber would undertake to add a new product category (e.g., blank cassettes) without first obtaining formal approval from the retailer's merchandising personnel.

achieve major impact at the retail level. As one observer put it:

> It's absolutely amazing, but when is the last time you went through a check out and didn't see a Gillette display? These things don't happen by themselves. Those guys [the SRD sales force] are great—well trained, aggressive, and supported by effective sales programming.

In addition to distribution, SRD's marketing department was considered exceptionally strong in the fields of sales promotion and media advertising. In working with the trade, SRD often offered free merchandise or display racks in return for orders above a specified level. Consumer promotions were often price-oriented, such as a free razor with a cartridge of blades, or vice versa. SRD's media advertising had historically emphasized the sponsorship of sports events, a policy which continued in 1970. In recent years, however, SRD had begun also to sponsor prime-time movies and network series in an effort to reach non-sports-oriented consumers. In 1970, SRD expected to spend approximately $10 million on media advertising, mainly on television.

The Blank Cassette Project

Bingham had become interested in the blank cassette market in early 1970. At that time, a number of trade journals had carried articles on the rapid growth of recording tape sales, which were expected to exceed $500 million in 1970. While tape cassettes (as distinct from reel-to-reel tapes or eight-track cartridges) represented only a part of this market, it was his impression that the cassette share of the market was large and growing rapidly. Moreover, on recent visits to outlets of large discount stores and drug chains, Bingham had noted that many of these outlets were now carrying blank cassettes. In his judgment, the packaging and display of such cassettes was rather weak, and no single brand

weakness

seemed to have obtained wide distribution. While admittedly not an avid viewer of television, Bingham could not recall having ever seen a television commercial for blank cassettes.

To learn more about the blank cassette market, Bingham hired a team of young consultants, all recent graduates of the Harvard Business School, to carry out a study of the industry. At the same time, he personally sought information from Gillette marketing and sales personnel and from his own contacts in investment banking and retailing. By October 1970, Bingham felt that he had obtained a reasonably good "feel" for the characteristics of the industry.

The Recording Tape Market

According to the consultants' report, the market for recording tapes of all types would be approximately $650 million (at retail list prices) in 1970. About $500 million of these sales would be for prerecorded tapes, while the remaining $150 million would be for blank tapes. Of prerecorded tape sales, 77 percent would be for eight-track cartridges (up 28 percent from 1969), 20 percent would be for cassettes (up 53 percent from 1969), and 3 percent would be for reel-to-reel tapes (up 5 percent from 1969). In the blank tape market, roughly 85 percent of the market was represented by cassettes, 10 percent by reel-to-reel tapes, and 5 percent by eight-track cartridges.

Bingham believed that the potential future market for blank cassettes would depend largely on two factors: (1) the equipment configurations selected by consumers and (2) how consumers chose to use their equipment. At present, consumers had three basic choices: reel-to-reel tapes, eight-track cartridges, and cassettes.[3] Reel-to-reel tape recorders were the earliest form of tape recorders. They tended to be relatively large, heavy, and complicated to operate. In recent years most sales of such recorders

had been at high price points (above $200). Bingham believed that reel-to-reel recorders were currently being used primarily for professional and business purposes and as components in elaborate home stereo systems. Reel-to-reel recording was thought to offer higher fidelity than either eight-track cartridges or cassettes and to have a very favorable image among serious audiophiles. In contrast to eight-track cartridges and cassettes, very large selections of prerecorded classical music were available on reel-to-reel tapes, although such "tape albums" tended to be relatively expensive.

Cartridge players, which had been introduced to the market in 1962, had rapidly gained a great deal of market acceptance. A cartridge was a continuous loop of tape enclosed in plastic. In contrast to reel-to-reel recorders, which required careful threading of the tape through recording heads and winding spools, cartridge systems were considered very easy to operate.[4]

In 1970, it was estimated that 6 million cartridge players were owned by consumers. Approximately 80 percent of these players were installed in automobiles, and 20 percent were used by consumers in their homes. According to the consultants' report, the heavy incidence of automobile use was attributable to two factors. First, the marketing strategy of the cartridge player industry had traditionally been automotive-oriented. Second, until 1969 cartridge equipment had been capable of playing prerecorded cartridges but not of making recordings. This lack of recording capability was believed to have restricted the sales of cartridge players for in-home use. In 1969 and 1970, however, numerous manufacturers had introduced eight-track recorder-players to the market. This equipment retailed for $79.95 to approximately $200. Advertisements for eight-track cartridge recorder-players generally carried this theme: "Now you can record your favorite

---

[3]See the Appendix (pp. 17–19) for illustrations of the three types of equipment.

[4]The eight-track player had a slot (generally on the front panel) into which the cartridge was easily inserted.

music at home, and listen to it both at home and in your car.''

Cassette recording had been developed by North American Philips (Norelco) in 1963 and introduced to the United States market by Norelco and numerous licensees in 1965. A *cassette* was essentially a miniature reel-to-reel system encased in plastic. The cassette was approximately one-third the size of an eight-track cartridge ($2\frac{1}{2} \times 4 \times \frac{1}{2}$ inches versus $5\frac{1}{2} \times 4 \times \frac{3}{4}$ inches) and had a capacity of up to 120 minutes of recorded sound (60 minutes on each side of the tape). Material recorded on a cassette could easily be erased, thus permitting subsequent recording of new material on the cassette. If handled carefully, a high-quality cassette had an expected life of approximately 1,500 hours of recording or playing versus 500 hours for a high-quality eight-track cartridge.

From the outset, cassette systems had been marketed as recording and playing systems. At first, the bulk of sales had been of relatively inexpensive ($19.95–$50) portable monaural cassette recorders, often of relatively poor design, construction, and reliability. More recently, however, higher-quality stereo cassette decks[5] ($100 and up) for use with home stereo systems had been introduced, apparently with considerable success. These systems, used in conjunction with newly developed tapes, were generally believed to produce fidelity equal to that of the best eight-track cartridge systems. Several very expensive models (above $200), which incorporated Dolby noise reduction principles,[6] had been introduced in early 1970. According to

audiophile magazines, these systems had sound reproduction capabilities comparable to those of all but the very best reel-to-reel recorders.

As of late 1969, it was estimated that 5.9 million cassette recorders had been sold in the United States. Virtually all these units were used as portables or as part of in-home stereo systems. The cassette system had not proved popular for automotive use, since the insertion of the cassette into the recorder required a considerable amount of attention by the user. Government agencies and consumer safety advocates had, according to trade sources, strongly discouraged the installation of cassette equipment in automobiles, apparently for safety reasons. Recent models of cassette equipment incorporated greatly simplified methods of cassette insertion and automatic reversal, however, and it was anticipated that cassettes would soon obtain a significant share of the automotive market.

In Bingham's opinion, portability, compactness, and ease of use were the primary reasons for the rapid market acceptance of cassette recorders. Typical portable cassette recorders had overall dimensions of $10 \times 5 \times 2\frac{1}{2}$ inches and weighed approximately 5 pounds; advances in electronic miniaturization had made possible even smaller units, which currently were intended primarily for the business dictation market.[7] According to the consultants' report, approximately 80 percent of the 1970 unit market would consist of portable units, ranging in price from $19.95 to $139.95. Some of the more expensive models included a built-in AM-FM radio, which facilitated off-the-air recording and was believed to increase the cassette recorder's attractiveness to young people. In the consul-

---

[5] In audio products terminology, a *deck* differed from a *player* in that it used the amplifier and loudspeakers of an independent high-fidelity system. A *player* contained its own amplifier and loudspeaker.

[6] A Dolby noise reduction system used advanced electronic techniques to reduce greatly the amount of mechanical and background sound which could be heard by the listener. Reel-to-reel and cassette recorders employing Dolby systems were generally used with specially coated tapes and cassettes. In early 1970, these tapes and cassettes were marketed exclusively by relatively small manufacturers of

expensive tape recorders and cassette equipment. List prices for 60-minute blank cassettes containing specially coated tape ranged from $3.95 to $4.95.

[7] The "business-type" dictating equipment market was forecast to reach $60 million (at manufacturers' prices) in 1970 by *Electronics* magazine. Bingham estimated that this market consisted of about 500,000 units, perhaps half of which utilized cassettes.

tants' judgment, portable cassette recorders selling for less than $50 frequently suffered from mechanical defects and offered only "minimum" sound quality, but the more expensive portable units generally provided fidelity equivalent to that of a good radio.

According to a study published by *Billboard* magazine, there was considerable variation in age between cassette equipment owners and cartridge equipment owners. (See Exhibit 1.)

While little was known about how consumers used cassette recorders, it was believed that they were used (1) by students for taking notes and recording lectures; (2) by businesspeople for dictating, recording conferences, and self-instruction; and (3) by households for live recordings (e.g., "baby's" first words) and for the recording and playing of music. While the music on virtually all new phonograph albums was also available on cassettes, prerecorded cassettes represented only $100 million (at retail prices) of the $3 billion recorded-music market. (Prerecorded eight-track cartridges were expected to have 1970 sales of $385 million.) The relatively low share of the prerecorded-music market held by cassettes was attributed to two major factors. First, prerecorded cassettes were considerably more expensive than phonograph records. A record which had a list price of $4.98 was cheaper than the $6.98 (list price) cassette or cartridge.[8] Second, the recording at home of

radio broadcasts (called off-the-air recording) was apparently quite prevalent among cassette recorder owners.

Trade sources estimated that 6 million to 7 million cassette recorders would be sold by retailers in 1970, with perhaps 50 percent of these sales during November and December. Blank cassette sales were expected to reach $130 million (at retail prices), a 60 percent increase over 1969.

The consultants forecast that blank cassette sales would grow at an average rate of 30 percent per year through the 1970s. They based this estimate on an extrapolation of historical trends and on the following considerations:

1. Cassette players were expected to represent a major share of automotive applications by 1975. As the cassette share of this market grew, the practice of making "tapes" at home for use in the automobile would create a huge new market for cassettes.
2. As the teen-age group which was around when cassettes were introduced moved into college and business, a revolutionary increase in the use of recorders in study and business activities was predicted.
3. The rapid growth of the teen sector of the population indicated continued interest in the portable and fun features of the cassette.
4. Improvement in equipment and tape quality would allow cassettes to capture an increased share of the serious audiophile market.
5. Some industry observers expected cassettes to be commonly used for "letter" writing,

[8]Records, cartridges, and cassettes were, however, all widely available at discounts of approximately 20 percent off list price.

EXHIBIT 1
OWNERSHIP OF CASSETTE AND
CARTRIDGE EQUIPMENT BY AGE GROUP

Age group	U.S. population	Cassette owners	Cartridge owners
0–19	23.9%	32%	17%
20–29	34.7	27	45
30–39	17.7	22	32
40+	23.7	19	6
	100%	100%	100%

home message centers, and a wide range of other consumer data storage and transmission purposes by the mid-1970s. In time, these observers believed, as many as 75 to 80 percent of the 65 million households in the United States would own one or more cassette recorders.

Products

Blank cassettes were produced in four basic capacity configurations: 30, 60, 90, and 120 minutes. Since all four configurations used the same cassette case, they could be used interchangeably with any standard cassette recorder. The most popular 60-minute size seemed to be available in three quality-price configurations: (1) professional quality, with a typical list price of $2.98; (2) standard quality, with list prices ranging from $1.75 to $2; and (3) budget quality, with list prices of about $1.[9] Professional quality and standard quality cassettes were generally sold under relatively well-known brand names (Sony, 3M, Mallory)[10] and were distributed through audio shops, the home entertainment departments of department stores, and

Competition

[9]Professional and standard quality cassettes utilized essentially similar cassette cases. The primary difference between the two types was in the materials used to coat the tape in the cassette. Generally, standard quality cassettes had red, blue, orange, or yellow labels, while professional quality cassettes used some combination of black, white, and silver.

Budget quality cassettes were believed to use inferior cassette cases and tape. They often had pastel or iridescent labels and were typically packed in blister packs (for pegboard display) rather than boxes. Budget quality cassettes were often promoted in newspaper advertisements and flyers by discount stores, occasionally at prices as low as two for 98 cents for the 60-minute size.

[10]Sony was a well-known manufacturer of television sets, reel-to-reel tape recorders, cassette recorders, and stereo systems. 3M manufactured a wide variety of consumer products (e.g., Scotch brand cellophane tape) and was well established as the leading brand in the blank reel-to-reel tape market. Mallory was well known as the manufacturer of long-life batteries, which were used primarily in electronic and photographic equipment.

some discount stores. According to the consultants' report, even the leading brands had done "a minimum of advertising" and had "limited distribution, poor display and packaging, and generally inferior merchandising." The consultants noted, however, that RCA and Capitol Records had recently entered the business and that Memorex, a leading supplier of tape to the computer industry, was about to do so. It was worth noting, the consultants believed, that Memorex had hired two former Procter & Gamble marketing executives to head its new blank cassette business.

Budget quality cassettes were believed to have captured 50 percent of the dollar market in 1970. These cassettes were sold under a large number of relatively unknown brands and under the private labels of several large mass-merchandising chains. Except for the private labels, it was rare for a particular brand to be stocked by a retailer on a regular basis.

In 1969 and 1970, the rapid growth of the cassette market had attracted a number of marginal firms into the industry. According to trade sources, 100 percent of the products of some of these firms were defective in some respect. While a superior quality cassette had an expected life of 1,500 hours of normal use, "the majority of cassettes produced in 1969 had on the average perhaps less than 50 hours of playing time. . . ." According to the consultants' report:

> Essentially, the problem boiled down to three parts: (1) oversize cassette cases which would not fit machines, (2) poor internal [cassette] construction in order to reduce costs, and (3) inferior quality tape resulting in poor recordings, limited high frequency response, and wear on machine recorder heads.

At the conclusion of their report, the consultants had attempted to ascertain the economics of the blank cassette industry. Using the 60-minute cassettes as their example, they noted that such cassettes typically had retail list prices of $1.95 (standard quality) and $2.95 (professional quality). Retailer discounts, if they bought direct from a manufacturer, were typically 50 percent off retail list price. Wholesalers and rack jobbers, who currently handled about 70 percent of professional and standard quality cassette volume, also received a 50 percent discount from retail list price, plus periodic promotional allowances. A retailer who purchased cassettes from a rack jobber or wholesaler received a 35 percent discount. The extent to which wholesalers passed promotional allowances on to retailers was not known.

In the course of their study, the consultants had interviewed a number of suppliers to the cassette industry. On the basis of these discussions, they estimated that high-quality unloaded cassette cases could be purchased in large lots for $0.159 each. Standard quality recording tape could be purchased for $0.08 per 100 feet; professional quality tape would cost $0.12 to $0.14 per 100 feet.[11] (A 60-minute cassette contained 268 feet of tape.) The cost of loading, packaging, and inspecting was estimated to be $0.20 per cassette.

While supplier cost data were difficult to obtain, the consultants estimated that manufacturers of unloaded cassettes obtained gross margins of approximately 25 percent on large-lot sales and that producers of tape realized gross margins as high as 50 percent. Despite the large increase forecast in cassette sales, the consultants believed that there was excess capacity in both unloaded cassette and tape manufacturing and that SRD would have no difficulty in contracting for whatever components and materials it might require.

The consultants had not investigated the feasibility of SRD's entering the blank cassette business from the standpoint of internal resources. Bingham had, however, held preliminary discussions on this subject with SRD sales and manufacturing executives. The SRD sales manager believed that his sales force could "squeeze cassettes in," that cassettes could get as much as 10 percent of his sales force's time during the first year, provided that SRD did not introduce any other major new products during this period. The manufacturing manager assured Bingham that his operation could assemble cassettes, although he thought it might take as long as a year to achieve a rate of 1 million cassettes per month. "On a very rough basis," he estimated that fixed manufacturing costs and overheads at this level of operations might be approximately $500,000 annually.

Developing a Program

While Bingham considered the data he had obtained to be "still pretty rough and incomplete,"[12] he had discussed the cassette market with several high-level SRD executives, who had shown considerable interest. On the basis of these discussions, Bingham had agreed to prepare a "hypothetical business plan" which could be used as a basis for deciding whether SRD should proceed toward entry into the blank cassette business. In developing his plan, he was especially concerned with the following considerations:

1. If SRD entered the blank cassette market, Bingham believed that it should initially limit its manufacturing activities to the assembly and packaging of purchased components. If the entry was successful, however, he believed that SRD should manufacture its own tape within 1 year of the introduction and its own unloaded cassettes within 2 years.

2. SRD's advertising agency had suggested that the use of the Gillette name would be a decided advantage, since *Gillette* had a high connotation of quality and reliability, and consumers had recently been "burned" by

---

[11]The new specially coated tapes for use in Dolby systems were not currently available from outside vendors.

[12]In particular, he felt that the trade estimates of blank cassette sales might be inflated, perhaps by as much as $30 million (at retail prices).

low-quality cassettes. In discussions with SRD executives, Bingham had suggested the name *Gillette Cassette,* which had received an enthusiastic response. He wondered, however, whether it would be a good idea to associate the Gillette name so directly with blank cassettes. While he was sure that SRD manufacturing expertise could ensure that cassettes marketed under the Gillette name would be of consistently high quality, such cassettes, at least initially, would have no functional advantages over other "quality" brands.

3. According to the consultants' report, blank cassette unit sales were divided among categories of retailers as follows:

Discount and department stores	40%
Electronics stores (one-third mail order)	18
High-fidelity stores	7
Drugstores	10
Variety stores	10
Stationery, TV, and appliance stores	5
Catalog stores (Sears, Wards)	7
Camera shops	3
	100%

Bingham knew that SRD's sales force and wholesalers called on discount stores, department stores, drugstores, variety stores, and catalog stores. He wondered whether it would be sufficient to distribute through these classes of outlets or whether electronics and high-fidelity stores should also be used. If he did seek to distribute through these outlets, he might wish to use audio products manufacturers' representatives, who received a 10 percent commission on the billed price to the stores. Bingham also wondered whether some of SRD's other retail outlets (e.g., supermarket chains), which did not presently sell blank cassettes, should be included in his distribution plan.

4. Bingham assumed that media advertising, while uncommon thus far in the blank cassette industry, would play an important role

in his marketing plan. In the past, SRD had spent more than $5 million to advertise the introduction of a new shaving system (e.g., Techmatic), but he doubted that such high expenditures would be required in a market where there was no significant competitive advertising. SRD's advertising agency, "on a very preliminary basis," had suggested a media budget of about $2 million for the first year and $1.2 million in ensuing years. While the agency's "thoughts on media" were "still pretty rough," the preliminary media advertising budget was based on the premise that virtual saturation of teen-oriented radio stations would be sought. Alternatively, the budget could be split (with reduced weight against each target) among teen-oriented radio, adult-oriented radio, and entertainment-oriented print media.

5. Most manufacturers of "quality" cassettes also marketed cassette accessories such as recording head cleaners and cassette storage cases. While Bingham doubted that such items would contribute significantly to profits, he wondered whether he should include them in his plan "in order to demonstrate to wholesalers, retailers, and consumers that Gillette is serious about getting into this business."

6. Bingham had not yet given much thought to pricing, but he felt that the Gillette image for quality might allow the *Gillette Cassette,* if that name were used, to command a premium price at retail. Competitive standard quality 60-minute cassettes (e.g., Sony, 3M, Mallory) had list prices of $1.95 but were typically discounted to $1.69–$1.75. He wondered whether a standard quality Gillette Cassette might not carry a higher list price.

7. Wholesale and retail discounts from list prices were somewhat higher in the cassette industry than they were in the razor and blade business. While Bingham doubted that retailers would accept lower margins than were common in the cassette industry, he won-

dered whether SRD's wholesalers might not be satisfied with normal health and beauty aid wholesale margins (about 15 percent). In this regard, he noted that SRD's wholesalers sold competitors' shaving products but did not presently carry blank cassettes.

8. Several weeks before, Bingham had asked selected members of the SRD sales organization "to check out this idea on a preliminary basis with trade sources." Excerpts from his notes on these investigations follow:

Competition is fierce, and completely price oriented. [Major off-brand suppliers] offer everyday margins up to 67%.

On the positive side, [many of our sources felt that] there is a real opportunity for an aggressive promoter to organize the market and assume a leadership position with the consumer.

Our investigation revealed that the absence of promotion against the consumer will not last long. Memorex, a West Coast firm, is building a 50-person sales force predominately staffed by ex-P&G people. They have also hired the Leo Burnett Agency to develop an ad campaign. Our information is that they plan to go in the direction of high quality audio shop distribution. It's difficult to imagine, however, that people with P&G backgrounds would refrain very long from attempting distribution in mass merchandising outlets.

Appendix

REEL-TO-REEL TAPE RECORDER-PLAYER

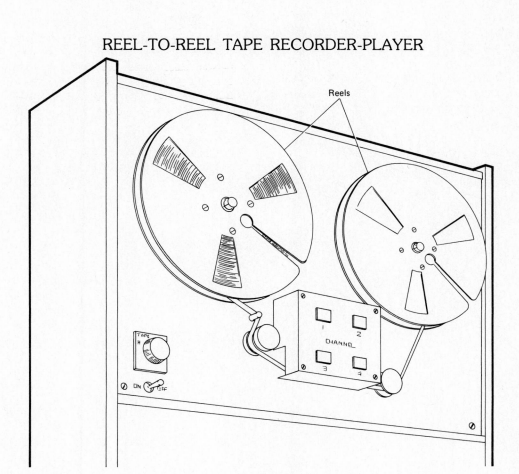

EIGHT-TRACK CARTRIDGE PLAYER

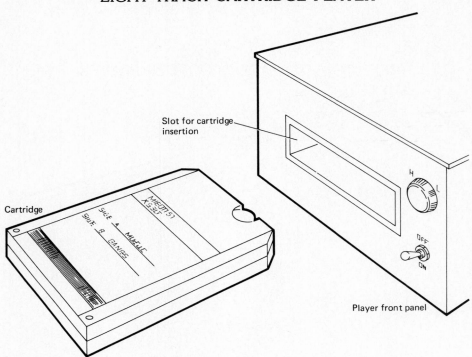

CASSETTE RECORDER-PLAYER

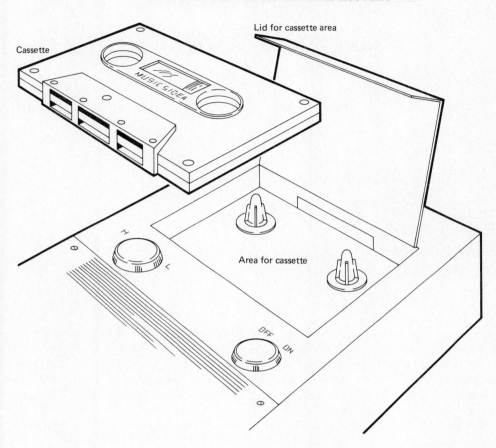

Cassette

Lid for cassette area

Area for cassette

Dominion Motors and Controls, Ltd.

2

E. Raymond Corey

Dominion Motors and Controls, Ltd. (DMC), had acquired over 50 percent of the available market for oil well pumping motors in the northern Canadian oil fields since these fields were discovered in 1973. While the company was a large supplier of motors and control equipment and had an excellent reputation for product quality, DMC executives believed the company had been especially successful in this market because of the work of one salesperson. This salesperson had been hired by DMC in 1974 when oil exploration had suddenly become active in northern Canada. He was both aggressive and capable, and he could "talk the oil people's language." He had come to DMC with a background of experience in electrical equipment sales and in oil field electrical application engineering which he had gained in Texas.

E. Raymond Corey is the Malcolm P. McNair Professor of Marketing at the Harvard Graduate School of Business Administration.

At this time none of DMC's competitors had salespeople in the northern Canadian oil fields who were similarly skilled. DMC had therefore been able to get a good foothold in this market at an early stage and develop a strong market position.

Early in 1980, however, DMC was threatened with the loss of this market because in tests performed by the Hamilton Oil Company the Dominion motor had been judged inferior to two competing motors for use in oil well pumping. The Hamilton Oil Company was the largest oil company active in Canada and owned and operated over 30 percent of the total producing wells. Mr. Bridges, the head of Hamilton's electrical engineering department, had been in charge of the motor testing program. He had concluded on the basis of the test results that DMC's motor should be considered the third choice behind the motors offered by Spartan Motors, Ltd., and the Universal Motor Company of Canada, respectively. Thus in March 1980,

EXHIBIT 1
SALES BY PRODUCT GROUP—1979

Product group	Dollar sales	Unit sales
Controls and panel boards	$12 million	Not available
Fractional horsepower motors	21 million	500,000
1- to 200-horsepower motors	12 million	22,000
250- to 2,000-horsepower motors	9 million	700

Source: Company records.

executives of DMC were faced with the necessity of deciding what action, if any, the company should take to maintain its share of the oil well pumping market.

Dominion Motors & Controls, Limited

DMC was a large Canadian motor manufacturer offering a line of motors ranging in size from small fractional horsepower units to large 2,000-horsepower motors. The company also produced motor control and panel-board units which would automatically control the operation of a motor and provide motor protection. In 1979, DMC sales approximated $54 million and were distributed among product groups as indicated in Exhibit 1.

About 80 percent of DMC sales were made directly by DMC salespeople to original equipment manufacturers (OEMs) and to large industrial users such as oil companies, paper mills, and mining concerns. Approximately 20 percent of sales were made to distributors for resale primarily to small users (small drilling contractors and others) and small OEMs. The discount schedule established for the various classes of purchasers is reproduced in Exhibit 2.

Oil Well Pumping Motor Market

Late in 1973, major oil fields were discovered in northern Canada. Following these major discoveries, a number of smaller fields were opened up in the area. By 1979, there were approximately 5,500 producing wells in these fields (see Exhibit 3). Hundreds of oil companies were active in the

EXHIBIT 2
DISCOUNT SCHEDULE BY CLASS OF PURCHASER

Purchaser	Discount	List price multiplier
OEM	45%	.55
Reseller	40	.60
Large user	38	.62
Small user	25	.75

Source: Company records.

EXHIBIT 3
NUMBER OF OIL WELLS IN NORTHERN CANADA 1973–1979

Year	Number of wells
1973	700
1974	1,300
1975	1,900
1976	2,750
1977	3,600
1978	4,650
1979	5,500

Source: Company estimates.

Canadian oil fields, but there were only about 25 who owned 50 or more wells.

According to industry estimates, an average of 1,000 new wells could be expected to be brought into production each year for the next 5 years. Estimators were careful to point out, however, the difficulty of making such forecasts with any degree of accuracy. Actually, many people intimately acquainted with the young Canadian oil industry believed that the estimate of 1,000 wells per year might prove to be low. Because of rapid changes in world economic and political conditions and in technology, forecasting such energy-related variables was most difficult.

DMC sales of oil well pumping motors had averaged approximately $360,000 per year from 1973 through 1979. Sales to this market were seasonal; over 80 percent of the total sales were made during the period April to September.

DMC's competition consisted of other well-known Canadian motor manufacturers[1] as well as a number of foreign competitors (particularly British and Japanese firms). All Canadian motor manufacturers maintained closely competitive pricing structures. Foreign competitors, however, usually sold motors at 10 to 20 percent less than the established prices of the Canadian manufacturers.

DMC executives indicated that company salespeople attempted to sell a motor and control unit as a package. Frequently, however, oil field customers bought the motor of one manufacturer and the controls of another. The majority of DMC's competitors did not offer motor controls. The main sources of motor control competition were control manufacturers.

During the 1973–1979 period, DMC sold about 15 percent of the control and panel-board units used in oil well applications. This market share represented an average annual sales income of about $90,000. The average pump installation installed to deliver oil from a proven well cost approximately $21,000. Approximately $3,000 of this total amount was invested in the electrification of the pumping installation (motor, controls, wiring, installation, and so forth). The motor itself accounted for approximately one-third of this $3,000 investment, and the control and panel-board units another 30 percent of the total.

Factors Affecting Specifications of Oil Well Pumping Motors

Approximately 80 percent of the motors sold for oil well pumping applications since 1973 had been 10-horsepower NEMA[2] design C (high starting torque, low starting current), totally enclosed, fan-cooled units with moisture-resisting insulation. The remaining 20 percent of sales consisted of motors of the same type but with higher or lower horsepower ratings.

Such factors as drilling depth, oil viscosity, water content of pumped fluid, underground pressure, and the government-controlled production allowables in the northern Canadian fields had determined the type of motor best suited for oil well pumping in this area.[3] One factor which had been a particularly important determinant of motor specifications in the Canadian oil fields had been the low winter tempera-

---

[1]Many United States motor manufacturers operated Canadian subsidiaries, and these companies were considered to be Canadian competition.

[2]National Electrical Manufacturers Association. NEMA was a nonprofit organization to which the great majority of electrical manufacturers in the United States and Canada belonged. This organization developed and promulgated standard specifications for electrical equipment. Adherence to these standards was entirely voluntary, and neither members of NEMA nor nonmembers were precluded from manufacturing or selling products not conforming to NEMA standards.

[3]It may be noted that the characteristics of oil fields that might be discovered in the future could easily differ from those of existing fields, and therefore other types of motors might be required in these new fields.

tures. Because of this, a motor with a high starting torque[4] was needed to start the pump in cold weather. To be assured of having sufficient starting torque, many oil companies were using 10-horsepower motors, even though motors of this size were larger than what was actually required to lift the oil to the surface. This practice was referred to as "overmotoring."

During 1979, two announcements were made by power companies serving the oil fields which could affect the specifications of oil well pumping motors. First, these power companies announced a change in their schedule of power rates. Prior to the middle of 1979, a flat rate for power usage had been charged regardless of the horsepower of the motors used on a pumping installation. In mid-1979, however, this flat rate was replaced by a graduated rate schedule based on the connected horsepower of an installation. This new schedule is shown below.

Horsepower of installation	Monthly base charge per horsepower*
5 hp	$15.00
7½ hp	13.50
10 hp	12.00

*The monthly base charge included payment for electric energy used in any month up to 400 kWh per horsepower of installation. All energy used in any month in excess of 400 kWh per horsepower of installation was billed at 3.0¢ per kWh. The vast majority of pumping installations did not use energy in excess of 400 kWh per month per horsepower.

Second, the power companies demanded that their customers stop overmotoring and that these customers improve the "power factors"[5] of

[4]Starting torque is the twisting or turning power of the motor which enables the motor to overcome the load resistance at the time of starting. Starting torque is expressed in pounds-feet.

[5]The "power factor" of an AC circuit is defined as the ratio of power-producing current to total current:

$$\frac{\text{Power-producing current}}{\text{Total current}} = \text{power factor}$$

In most AC circuits, the total current is composed of magnetizing current (which does no work) and power-

their installations. The power companies did not at this time, however, indicate what action, if any, would be taken to penalize companies for overmotoring.

Hamilton's Field Test Program

Following the change in the power rate schedule and the statement by power companies demanding higher power factors, Mr. Bridges, Hamilton's chief electrical engineer, had initiated field tests on oil well pumping motors. The objective of these tests was to define the specifications of a motor which could be used most economically for pumping. The tests, therefore, were designed to determine (1) the horsepower required to lift the fluid and (2) the maximum starting torque required to start the pumping units at the low winter temperatures experienced in the northern Canadian oil fields.

Although the tests were completed by early 1980, it wasn't until March 1980 that DMC executives became aware of Hamilton's testing program through the reports of a salesperson calling on this account. While the salesperson was not able to obtain a memorandum describing Mr. Bridges's test procedures and findings, DMC executives were able to piece together what they believed to be a fairly accurate picture

producing current. If no magnetizing current is present, the total current equals the power-producing current, and the power factor is unity or 100 percent. In the case of lightly loaded induction motors (motors working well below their rated capacity), a large amount of magnetizing current is present, and the power factor is quite low. The lighter the load relative to the capacity of the motor, the lower the power factor. The watt-hour meter used by a power company to determine a customer's bill records only the power-producing current. When a utility system must carry non-power-producing current, its ability to carry payload or power-producing current is reduced. Consequently, more facilities are required to serve a low-power-factor load than a high-power-factor load of the same kilowatt (payload) demand.

of the conclusions reached from his testing program.

According to their information, Mr. Bridges had arrived at the following conclusions: (1) fluid-lifting requirements dictated a 3- to 5-horsepower motor; (2) starting torques in excess of 70 pounds-feet would energize the pumping units at temperatures as low as −50°F; (3) in order to meet this starting torque requirement it would be necessary to use a 7½-horsepower motor; (4) since the Spartan 7½-horsepower motor had the highest starting torque of the motors tested (see Exhibit 4) and the Universal 7½-horsepower motor had the second-highest starting torque, these motors should be his company's first and second choices in the future. On the basis of these tests, DMC's 7½-horsepower motor was recommended as the third choice. It was also learned that Mr. Bridges planned to deliver a formal report of his findings to Hamilton's executives in May.

DMC executives believed that the tests performed by Mr. Bridges had not produced data which were extensive or intensive enough to form a conclusive body of evidence by which oil pumping requirements could be accurately defined. They did believe, however, that his findings had provided rather specific indications of pumping needs under a given set of operating conditions.

DMC personnel were extremely concerned, nevertheless, about the probable effect that Hamilton's endorsement of the Spartan and Universal motors would have on their company's market standing. Mr. Bridges was known to be very influential in establishing Hamilton's purchasing policy.[6] In addition, since the Hamilton Oil Company was the only firm operating in the Canadian oil fields which maintained an electrical engineering staff, Mr. Bridges's recommendations would probably carry a great deal of weight in the entire oil industry. It was the opinion of most DMC executives, therefore, that their company could not hope to stay in the oil well pumping market unless it met the specifications of the Spartan 7½-horsepower motor immediately and thus gained Hamilton's endorsement.

Possible Solutions to DMC's Problem

Dominion executives reasoned that there were four alternative courses of action—and perhaps more—from which the company could choose

[6]All oil well pumping motors used by Hamilton Oil Company were procured through the company's Production Department, and most of the motors purchased by this department were for oil well pumping. Other departments of the company independently purchased large numbers of motors, and these motors were procured either directly from the manufacturer or through contractors. Motors used in refineries, for example, were typically acquired as original equipment through the contractors who built the refineries. Motors for an average oil refinery in Canada, it may be noted, cost between $225,000 and $750,000.

EXHIBIT 4
MAXIMUM STARTING TORQUES (IN POUNDS-FEET) OF MOTORS TESTED BY HAMILTON OIL COMPANY, LIMITED

Horsepower	Starting torque, by motor manufacturer			Minimum starting torque required by NEMA standards
	Spartan	Universal	Dominion	
5	68	65	60	57.7
7½	102	97	89	76.5
10	110	109	105	101.5

in dealing with the marketing problem which might be created for the company as a result of Mr. Bridges's findings. They further believed that each alternative should be considered in the light of the 5-year market estimate noted earlier, which had been made by oil industry experts. These alternatives were outlined as follows:

1. Reduce the price of DMC's 10-horsepower motor to the price of the 7½-horsepower motor.
2. Reengineer DMC's present 7½-horsepower motor in an effort to raise the starting torque of the motor to a level at least equal to that of the Spartan 7½-horsepower unit.
3. Undertake the design of a definite-purpose motor for the oil well pumping market. Such a motor would ideally be a basic 5-horsepower motor with the starting torque of a 10-horsepower motor.
4. Talk with Mr. Bridges and executives of the Hamilton Oil Company in an effort to persuade them that the conclusions reached from their test program results placed an undue emphasis on obtaining the *maximum* amount of starting torque available.

Alternative 1

The possibility of reducing the price of DMC's 10-horsepower motor to the price level of the company's 7½-horsepower unit was advocated by several executives as a quick means of initially meeting the product problem which faced their company. Such a pricing move, they thought, could be taken either immediately or as late as May 1980. These executives pointed out that the oil well motor market was rapidly becoming active after its usual winter slump and that if DMC wanted to share in the 1980 sales to this market, management must place the company in a competitive position immediately. It was recognized that lowering the price of DMC's 10-horsepower motor would not be a long-run solution to the company's product problems. It did appear, however, that since the savings which resulted from the use of a 7½-horsepower motor instead of a 10-horsepower motor were not large and no oil company had yet been penalized for maintaining low power factors, a 10-horsepower motor could continue to be acceptable at least on a short-run basis. Exhibit 5 shows the price-cost relationships which existed among the small motors in DMC's line.

Some executives argued that there was no need to reduce the price of the company's 10-horsepower motor until May, since Mr. Bridges was not scheduled to deliver the formal report of his findings to Hamilton's executives until that time. It was doubtful, they thought, that many oil companies would hear of the results until this formal report was delivered. Therefore,

EXHIBIT 5
COST-PRICE RELATIONSHIPS AMONG SMALL INTEGRAL MOTORS

Horsepower	Manufacturing cost*	Commercial cost†	List price	Prices to large users‡
5	$300.90	$336.00	$ 990.00	$ 613.80
7½	390.30	420.00	1,140.00	706.80
10	480.00	534.00	1,500.00	930.00
15	723.00	807.00	2,190.00	1,357.80

*The manufacturing cost includes the cost of direct labor, the cost of materials, and manufacturing overhead.

†The commercial cost includes the manufacturing cost; charges for engineering, transportation, sales service, and advertising; administrative overhead; and depreciation. The commercial cost does not include salespeople's salaries and commissions, which amounted, on all sales, to approximately 8 percent of net sales billed.

‡These prices are based on the discount schedule shown in Exhibit 2.

Mr. Bridges's findings and recommendations might not have much influence on the type of motor purchased for oil well pumping for another 2 or 3 months. During this time DMC could continue to sell its 10-horsepower motor at the usual price; it would cut the price only when objections were encountered and when the market had become aware of Hamilton's endorsement of the Spartan 7½-horsepower motor.

Executives who favored this alternative summarized their position by saying that they believed that this alternative would provide an immediate means of combating Hamilton's endorsement of the Spartan 7½-horsepower motor. It would serve as a useful temporary competitive measure until Mr. Bridges's test results could be obtained and completely studied and questioned. Then a more satisfactory and reasoned decision could be reached regarding what steps DMC should take. They believed that an adequate appraisal of Mr. Bridges's tests, results, and conclusions might require as much as 1 year to complete, especially if company executives wanted to check Mr. Bridges's results against tests performed by DMC's own engineers.

Alternative 2

Several company executives believed that DMC's best opportunity to stay in the oil well market lay in the reengineering of the company's present 7½-horsepower motor so that its starting torque would be equal to or greater than that of Spartan's 7½-horsepower motor.[7] Initial investigations into this alternative revealed that there were two ways of increasing starting torque.

First, at least 105 pounds-feet of starting torque could be obtained by modifying the existing internal motor components. The new

[7]Under this alternative DMC's present 7½-horsepower motor with a starting torque of 89 pounds-feet would continue to be manufactured and sold to customers who had no need for or interest in high starting torques.

motor would have the same frame size (i.e., mounting dimensions) as the existing 7½-horsepower motor, but the temperature rise of the motor would be greater than that permitted by NEMA standards. This departure from NEMA standard specifications would not, according to DMC personnel, significantly alter the safety or operating characteristics of the motor, since special high-temperature insulation was to be used. DMC executives were uncertain, however, as to how oil field users might react to the idea of using a motor having a higher operating temperature than NEMA-standard motors. A commercial cost of $465 would be incurred in the manufacture of this motor.

A second way of obtaining at least 105 pounds-feet of starting torque was to use a larger-size motor frame. The motor would continue to meet or exceed all of NEMA's minimum standard performance specifications, but not NEMA mounting dimensions for this rating. It was believed, however, that standard motor mounting dimensions were not important in oil well pumping applications. It was also believed that a motor with non-NEMA mounting dimensions would meet with less customer resistance than a motor which exceeded NEMA's maximum temperature rise. The commercial cost of this motor, utilizing a large motor frame, would be $510.

Neither of the two alternative methods of increasing the starting torque of the company's existing 7½-horsepower motor would involve an additional investment in plant or equipment. It was believed that approximately 3 months would be necessary to enable DMC to begin shipment of a modified 7½-horsepower motor.

Advocates of altering the company's existing 7½-horsepower motor to increase the starting torque believed that this alternative was the answer to the company's product problem. They pointed out that by "souping up" its 7½-horsepower motor the company could go to the market with a motor which would have the highest starting torque of any 7½-horsepower motor then available.

Not all the DMC executives agreed that it would be desirable to increase the starting torque of the company's 7½-horsepower motor. Those who disagreed pointed out that such a move would invite a "torque war" which could lead to unbalanced motor designs.[8] This situation would cause confusion in motor-buying practices and would be detrimental to the motor industry as a whole. It had long been DMC's policy to support industry standards by not publicizing or claiming operating characteristics in excess of NEMA standards. The company had excellent testing facilities which enabled engineers to design motors close to NEMA standards and thus reduce costs. One executive stated, "There is no point in building more margin into our motors than required by the NEMA standards . . . it is because of our better testing facilities that we are able to design closer to NEMA standards than our competitors. . . . There is no point in building a large margin into our motors."

Alternative 3

A number of DMC's executives supported a move to design a definite-purpose motor for the oil well pumping market. They felt that this was the only way their company could effectively regain product leadership after Hamilton's endorsement of the Spartan motor. They pointed out that the tests performed by Hamilton personnel indicated that the specific motor to meet the oil company's needs would be a motor with the running characteristics and rating of a 5-horsepower unit but with the starting torque of a 10-horsepower motor. Such a motor would exceed minimum NEMA specifications. If DMC would produce a motor with these characteristics, they reasoned, then the company could offer a motor to this market which would have unquestioned competitive superiority. A preliminary examination of this proposal indicated that such a motor could be produced at a commercial cost of approximately $390.

Executives believed that such a motor could be successfully sold at a net price of $615 or $630 to large users. Executives reasoned that the definite-purpose motor should be priced close to the price of the 5-horsepower general-purpose motor, since it was actually a 5-horsepower motor. Also, they thought that it would be priced below the 7½-horsepower general-purpose motor in order to give DMC a price advantage over 7½-horsepower motors competing in the oil well market. An investment of $45,000 was believed adequate to provide for the engineering and testing required to bring a definite-purpose motor into production. Executives believed that only minor expenditures for plant and equipment would be necessary to produce the new motor. Engineers estimated that 4 to 5 months would be required before production of the definite-purpose motors could begin.

Those who favored this alternative summarized the merits of such a move by calling attention to the fact that DMC would be offering the market just *exactly* what the market wanted. Furthermore, they believed that the first manufacturer to offer a definite-purpose motor tailored to the needs of the market would have an important tactical advantage over competitors which could be expected to last a long time. They believed that with such a motor DMC could increase its share of the oil well pumping market to approximately 60 percent.

It is significant to note that with few exceptions the Canadian motor industry had adhered to a general-purpose motor philosophy. Under such a policy, motors were designed to be acceptable for a number of applications. As a general rule, the performance characteristics of such motors exceeded the specific motor requirements of an individual application. Some motor industry executives believed that the general-purpose motor philosophy (based on NEMA standards) had been the salvation of the Canadian motor industry. They pointed out that

[8]Such a state of affairs was described by one executive as "technical inflation."

the Canadian motor market was only about one-tenth the size of the United States market. Since the total market was small, it had been economically difficult for motor manufacturers to justify small production runs of special-purchase motors. Manufacturers had concentrated on standard, general-purpose motors in order to achieve unit costs which would enable them to compete with low-cost imported motors on a satisfactory basis.

Alternative 4

Several members of DMC's management group believed that the conclusions drawn by Mr. Bridges were not completely accurate. They argued that before company personnel begin to consider changes in product and market strategy, an attempt should be made to persuade Mr. Bridges and the executives of the Hamilton Oil Company that there was another set of conclusions which could be drawn from the test results. Several DMC executives knew Hamilton's purchasing vice president socially and believed that perhaps they could approach him concerning this matter.

It was pointed out that all 7½-horsepower motors tested by Hamilton Oil's personnel had starting torques in excess of 80 pounds-feet (see Exhibit 4) and therefore should have been satisfactory, since Mr. Bridges concluded that 70 pounds-feet of torque was capable of "breaking" a pump under the most extreme cold-weather conditions. Mr. Bridges had apparently reasoned that since starting torque was the most important feature in oil well pumping motor applications, he should get as much starting torque as possible. As a consequence he had endorsed the Spartan motor as the first choice, since it had the highest starting torque. Most DMC executives believed that the number of instances when 80 pounds-feet of torque would not start a motor would be extremely low, but, as one executive expressed it, "engineers love big margins whether they use them or not."

Many company executives believed that there

was real reason for questioning the conclusions drawn by Mr. Bridges, but they did not know how they might present different conclusions. It was known that Mr. Bridges was scheduled to present a paper on his test results and conclusions early in May 1980 to the top management of the Hamilton Oil Company. Several DMC executives close to the situation reported that Mr. Bridges was convinced of the validity of his conclusions and evidenced an intense pride of authorship in his test efforts. They believed it would be very difficult to approach him directly. There was some feeling among DMC executives that nothing but ill will could be generated by any attempt to alter Mr. Bridges's conclusions.

DMC executives were united in their concern over the fact that although Mr. Bridges had begun his tests in October, they had not known of his efforts until March 1980. Most of the company's management personnel believed that the present problem with oil well motors would never have come into existence had they known of Mr. Bridges's testing activities in October 1979. Although most executives were not in favor of encouraging a trend toward definite-purpose motors, they did feel that when it was indicated that a customer was attempting to define his or her motor needs precisely, DMC personnel should attempt to work with him or her so that the company could be in on the ground floor of subsequent developments.

Some executives believed that DMC personnel should go one step further and begin testing and defining the motor needs of the company's various market segments in preparation for the day when a customer company (such as the Hamilton Oil Company) might decide to conduct such an investigation itself. Executives who supported this policy believed that such work could be looked on as a long-term investment in the maintenance of the company's future market position. Company engineers, however, were already overburdened with work assignments, and such a program would necessitate the hiring of additional engineering personnel.

3 Polaroid France (S.A.)

Robert D. Buzzell • Jean-Louis Le Cocq

In July 1967, M. Jacques Dumon, general manager of Polaroid France (S.A.), was preparing a preliminary marketing plan for 1968. M. Dumon was scheduled to present his proposals to the marketing executives at the headquarters office of the American parent firm, Polaroid Corporation, in September. Following this review, a final version of the plan would be adopted as a basis for Polaroid's operations in France during the forthcoming year.

In preparing his recommendations for 1968, M. Dumon was especially concerned with problems of pricing and promotion for the Model 20 Swinger camera. The Swinger had been introduced in France during the fall of 1966 and was the first Polaroid Land Camera available to French consumers at a retail price under fr.300.[1] Sales of the Swinger during 1966 and early 1967 had not reached expected levels, and M. Dumon was aware that the basic attitude of headquarters management toward overseas operations in 1968 was cautious, because Polaroid's unconsolidated foreign subsidiaries had incurred a combined loss of $907,000 in 1966. He recognized, therefore, that all proposals for 1968 would be subject to extremely careful scrutiny.

Company Background

Polaroid Corporation, with headquarters in Cambridge, Massachusetts, produced a wide line of photographic and related products for household and business uses, including cameras, film, photographic equipment, polarizing products, and X-ray products. Total 1966 sales in the United States amounted to $316.5 million,

Robert D. Buzzell is a professor at the Harvard Graduate School of Business Administration. Jean-Louis Le Cocq is the directeur des études at the École Supérieur de Commerce et d'Administration des Entreprises de Rouen.

Note: Certain data have been disguised.

[1] In 1967, 1 franc equaled approximately US$0.20.

more than three times the amount of business done in 1962. Worldwide sales in 1966, including Polaroid's 13 subsidiaries, totaled $363 million.

The company was founded in 1937 by Dr. Edwin H. Land to produce polarizing products, including sunglasses, photographic filters, and glare-free lamps. By 1941, sales had reached $1 million. Following World War II, Dr. Land developed a new method for developing and printing photographs. The Polaroid Land Camera was announced in 1947, and the first models were sold in November 1948. The Polaroid Land Camera utilized a "one-step" process, in contrast with the "three-step" process required for conventional photography. In conventional still photography, the sequence involved in producing a black-and-white picture is as follows:

1. A photosensitive material (film) is exposed to light. The light converts grains of silver bromide into specks of silver, the amount of silver deposited in a given area depending on the amount of light reaching that area.
2. The film is developed by immersing it in a chemical solution which converts the exposed grains into black silver. The unexposed grains are then dissolved with a second solution and washed away. This yields a finished negative in which all the natural tones are reversed; i.e., black appears as white, and vice versa.
3. The negative is placed in contact with a sheet of light-sensitive paper and exposed to light. The developing process is then repeated to produce a finished positive print.

The second and third steps of conventional photography require that exposed film be processed in a commercial laboratory or in a home darkroom. For most amateur photographers, this means a delay of several days between taking a picture and receiving a finished print of it.

The technique developed by Dr. Land yielded finished prints from the *camera itself*, with no delay for processing. Basic discoveries in photographic chemistry, and new materials based on these discoveries, permitted the entire process to be completed in 60 seconds (later, in 10 seconds) with no equipment other than the camera and film.

The Polaroid Land Camera was commercially successful almost from the beginning. In 1949, sales of cameras and film amounted to over $5 million.

Product Line

Between 1949 and 1964, research and development activities at Polaroid provided the basis for a continuous improvement and diversification of Polaroid's camera product line.

The earliest versions of the Polaroid Land Camera produced sepia-colored prints of a quality inferior to that of conventional films. Subsequent improvements in the film permitted clear black-and-white photographs and, beginning in 1963, color pictures as well. Another major innovation in 1963 was the introduction of the Automatic 100 Land Camera. The Model 100 utilized a film pack rather than the film roll which had been used in all earlier Polaroid cameras. With a film pack, the camera could be loaded more easily and quickly, since it was not necessary to wind the film around a series of rollers. Instead, the user simply opened the camera, inserted the pack, and closed the camera. In addition to the pack-loading feature, the Model 100 incorporated several other improvements over the earlier models. It weighed less than earlier models and had a better exposure control.

Following the introduction of the Model 100, Polaroid introduced three lower-priced pack cameras: The Model 101 in 1964 and Models 103 and 104 in 1965. In early 1967, a redesigned line of five pack cameras was introduced. Thus, in mid-1967, the models offered and their suggested retail prices in the United States were as follows:

Model 250	$159.95
Model 240	124.95
Model 230	94.95
Model 220	69.95
Model 210	49.95

All these cameras produced both black-and-white and color photographs in a 3¼ × 4¼ inch format, and all had electric-eye mechanisms for automatic exposure control. The main differences among the various models were in lens qualities and in materials. For example, the Model 250 featured a Zeiss rangefinder-viewfinder, a three-piece precision lens, an all-metal body, and a leather carrying strap. The Model 210 had a plastic body, a nylon strap, a less expensive focusing system, and a two-piece lens, and it was not designed to accommodate the accessories (such as a portrait lens) which could be employed with the higher-priced models.

In late 1965, Polaroid introduced the Model 20 Swinger Land Camera in the United States. The Swinger was a roll-film camera, capable of taking black-and-white photos only, in a 2¼ × 3¼ inch format and with a 15-second development time. It was made of white plastic; the suggested retail price, emphasized in national advertising, was $19.95. The introduction of the Swinger enabled Polaroid to compete for the first time in the large-volume market for inexpensive cameras; around three-fourths of all still cameras purchased each year sold for less than $50 at retail. Thus, the launching of the Swinger was a major contributing factor in the dramatic growth of the company's sales during 1965 and 1966 (see Exhibit 1). According to company reports, by "sometime in 1967" over 5 million Swinger cameras had been sold by Polaroid.

All Polaroid cameras were produced for the company by outside contractors. The company itself manufactured black-and-white and color

EXHIBIT 1
SALES AND NET EARNINGS OF POLAROID CORPORATION IN THE UNITED STATES AND CANADA, 1950–1966

| | Sales ($ thousand) | | Net earnings ($ thousand) | |
Year	U.S. only	U.S. & Canada	U.S. only	U.S. & Canada
1950	NA	$ 6,390	NA	$ 726
1951	NA	9,259	NA	512
1952	NA	13,393	NA	597
1953	NA	26,034	NA	1,415
1954	NA	23,500	NA	1,153
1955	NA	26,421	NA	2,402
1956	NA	34,464	NA	3,667
1957	NA	48,043	NA	5,355
1958	NA	65,271	NA	7,211
1959	$ 89,487	89,919	$10,750	10,743
1960	98,734	99,446	8,838	8,813
1961	100,562	101,478	8,008	8,111
1962	102,589	103,738	9,872	9,965
1963	122,333	123,459	11,078	11,218
1964	138,077	139,351	18,105	18,323
1965	202,228	204,003	28,872	29,114
1966	316,551	322,399	47,594	47,963

Source: Company annual reports.

film rolls (for pre-1963 cameras), film packs for pack cameras, and film rolls for the Swinger.

In addition to amateur cameras and film, Polaroid produced one camera (the Model 180) for professional photographers and highly skilled amateurs, as well as several different types of industrial photographic equipment and supplies. Special-purpose industrial products included a system for producing identification cards and badges; X-ray equipment and film; and the MP-3 Industrial View Land Camera, designed for such applications as photomicrography.

Polaroid Corporation did not publish sales figures for individual products. According to the company's annual reports, photographic products accounted for between 93 and 97 percent of sales during the 1950s and 1960s. The remaining 3 to 7 percent of total volume was derived from sunglasses, polarizers, and other nonphotographic products. Trade sources estimated that cameras represented about 55 to 60 percent of Polaroid's sales volume in the mid-1950s and around 40 percent in the mid-1960s.

The United States Camera Market

The market for still cameras in the United States expanded dramatically during the early 1960s. According to trade estimates, some 14 million still cameras were sold in 1966, three times as many as in 1960. Estimates of total industry sales and of Polaroid's market share (in units) are shown in Exhibit 2. According to trade estimates, Polaroid camera sales in 1966 represented approximately 50 percent of the total *dollar value* of United States retail camera sales.

The rapid growth of the camera market was due, in the opinion of industry observers, to rising levels of consumer income and to the introduction of new products by Polaroid and by the Eastman Kodak Company. As described in the preceding section, Polaroid had introduced a series of new models in 1963, 1964, and 1965

EXHIBIT 2

Year	Industry sales,* million units	Polaroid market share,* percent
1954	4.5	4–5
1958	4.9	
1960	4.6	8
1962	5.3	
1964	8.4	11
1965	11.0	
1966	14.0	30–35

*Industry sales estimates published in annual statistical reports, prepared by Augustus Wolfman of *Modern Photography* and *Photo Dealer* magazines. Polaroid market share estimates from various trade sources; for 1964, from Duncan M. Payne, *The European Operations of the Eastman Kodak Company*. Institut d'Etudes Européenes de Geneve, 1967, p. 28.

at progressively lower prices and with various improvements in operating features.

In 1963, Kodak had introduced its new line of Instamatic cameras. Instamatic cameras used pack-in film rolls, like Polaroid's earlier models. Instamatic cameras were designed to use 35-mm film enclosed in a special cartridge produced only by Kodak. Thus, although Kodak licensed other companies to manufacture cameras using Instamatic film, it was the only source of film for all such cameras.

Kodak's own line of Instamatic cameras included simple, fixed-focus models selling at retail for around $12 and more sophisticated models priced as high as $100. Thus, Instamatics competed in virtually all price segments of the camera market except the under-$10 category. According to trade estimates, Instamatics accounted for around a third of all still cameras sold in the United States in 1964 and 1965.

Still cameras were purchased primarily by "amateur" users for personal recreational use. In 1966, 70 to 75 percent of all United States households owned one or more still cameras. Some cameras, and a significant proportion of all film, were bought by business, institutional, and governmental users for use in research, sales promotion, record keeping, etc. The principal objective of Polaroid's marketing programs was, however, the sale of Polaroid Land Cameras to household consumers.

Household consumers used several different types of cameras, ranging from very simple, inexpensive "box" cameras up to very complex 35-mm instruments. According to Polaroid estimates, 35-mm cameras (exclusive of Instamatics) represented only about 5 to 7 percent of total camera purchases in 1965. In terms of retail price categories, around 15 percent of all cameras were sold at retail prices under $10, between 60 and 65 percent were priced between $10 and $49, and 20 to 25 percent cost $50 or more. Nearly half of all cameras were for the purchasers' own use, over 40 percent were purchased as gifts, and almost 10 percent were obtained as prizes, as premiums, or in return for trading stamps.

Because of the importance of gift giving, camera sales were highly seasonal. November and December accounted for over 50 percent of total annual retail sales. The second most important selling season, May to July, accounted for nearly one-fourth of annual sales.

Up to 1963, the dominant type of customer for still cameras costing over $10 was the relatively affluent family with small children. The introduction of the Instamatics, the Swinger, and the relatively inexpensive Models 104 and 210 pack cameras resulted in a substantial broadening of the household market. The estimated distribution of purchasers by income groups and age groups in 1965–1966 is shown in Exhibit 3.

Polaroid Marketing in the United States

Polaroid had no direct competition in the instant-photography field. Although the patents on the original version of the Polaroid Land Camera had expired in 1965, Polaroid still held some 750 unexpired patents on various improvements in film chemistry and camera design that had been developed during the 1950s and 1960s. The company's products were, however, in active competition with many conventional types of cameras and films.

Polaroid Advertising

At the time of its introduction in 1948, the first Polaroid Land Camera was a radical product innovation in photography. According to *For-*

EXHIBIT 3

| | Purchasers of: | | | |
Income group	All still cameras	Polaroid pack cameras	Polaroid Swingers	All U.S. households
Under $3,000	4%	1%	3%	17%
$3,000–$4,999	11	9	20	18
$5,000–$6,999	21	16		20
$7,000–$9,999	31	31	38	26
$10,000 or more	34	43	39	19

Age of principal user				All U.S. individuals
19 or younger	30%	23%	26%	22%
20–49 years	53	63	65	50
50 years or more	16	14	9	28

tune magazine,[2] "Land's revolution was at first derided by all the experts . . . (including) virtually every camera dealer in the country, every 'advanced' amateur photographer, and nearly everyone on Wall Street." To overcome the skepticism of consumers and dealers, Polaroid placed considerable emphasis on national advertising. According to trade estimates, the company's advertising expenditures increased during the 1950s and 1960s as shown in Exhibit 4.

Especially during the introductory phases of Polaroid marketing, the Land Camera lent itself ideally to the medium of television, where the method of operation and its results could be demonstrated. The company was among the first major sponsors of "big-time" network television programs in the 1950s, such as the Garry Moore and Perry Como music-variety shows. Advertising trade publications estimated that around 45 percent of Polaroid's total advertising budget was devoted to network television in the mid-1960s, about 30 percent to magazines, and less than 5 percent to newspapers.

Early Polaroid advertising in the United States was designed to acquaint consumers with the basic idea of instant photography. An illustrative advertisement from the mid-1950s is shown in Exhibit 5. Later, after the majority of prospective buyers were familiar with the concept of "a

[2]Francis Bello, "The Magic that Made Polaroid," *Fortune,* April 1959.

picture in a minute," the company's advertising efforts were devoted to announcements of successive changes in product features, such as color film and pack-loading cameras, and to publicizing the availability of lower-priced cameras. An example of a 1966 Swinger advertisement is given in Exhibit 6.

Distribution and Pricing

In the United States, Polaroid sold its cameras and film directly to around 15,000 retailers. Pack cameras were sold primarily by specialty photographic stores, department stores, and general-merchandise discount stores. Swinger cameras and Polaroid films were carried by a greater number and variety of outlets, including many drugstores. Sales were made to many of the smaller outlets via wholesalers, but the bulk of Polaroid sales was made directly to stores and to buying offices of chain and mail-order firms.

Polaroid Corporation established "suggested" retail prices for cameras and film, but there were no legal or other restrictions on the freedom of dealers to set their own resale prices. The suggested retail prices provided gross margins for the retailers of around 33⅓ percent on the Model 250, 28 percent on the Model 210, 33⅓ percent on the Swinger, and 33⅓ percent on pack films. Because Polaroid Land Cameras were regarded by the larger retailers as attractive products to feature in discount promotions, the prevailing retail prices were often well below suggested levels. In mid-1967, consumers in large metropolitan areas could buy the Model 250 at a discount price of around $129.95, the Model 210 for around $39.95, and the Swinger for as little as $14. The smaller conventional photographic stores sold Polaroid cameras and films at lesser discounts and, often, at full list price. Polaroid films were also often sold at prices significantly below the suggested or list figures (Exhibit 7).

Discounting by retailers was also common in the sale of competing cameras. Some of the larger and more aggressive discount stores sold

EXHIBIT 4

Year	Estimated advertising expenditures*	
1954	$ 1,700,000	
1957	3,000,000	
1958	4,000,000	
1960	7,500,000	
1963	8,000,000	(Color film and pack
1964	8,500,000	cameras introduced)
1965	12,000,000	(Swinger introduced)
1966	18,000,000	

*Estimates by *Advertising Age* and other trade sources.

EXHIBIT 5
MAGAZINE ADVERTISEMENT FOR POLAROID
LAND CAMERA, UNITED STATES, MID-1950S

How to take a picture 1 minute and see it the next! Today's Polaroid Land Camera is a magnificent photographic instrument that not only takes beautiful pictures—but develops and prints them as well. With this camera in your hands, you are a magician, who can produce a finished print in 60 seconds. You are a professional photographer, fully equipped to produce expert pictures—clear, sharp, lasting black and white prints—on the spot. Whether you own several cameras or have never even owned one, you will have to own a Polaroid Land Camera. Ask your dealer to show you this remarkable instrument. There are three to choose from, including a new smaller, lower-priced model. *the amazing* **POLAROID** *Land* **CAMERA**

EXHIBIT 6
MAGAZINE ADVERTISEMENT FOR SWINGER
CAMERA, UNITED STATES, 1966

American Girl July 1966 Pg. B/W Bld
This Advertisement prepared by DOYLE DANE BERNBACH, INC
For Polaroid Corp. Job no. PO 611

EXHIBIT 7

Film type	Suggested retail price	Discount price
107: Black-and-white pack	$2.85	$1.99–$2.49
108: Color pack	5.39	3.99– 4.99
20: Black-and-white Swinger	2.10	1.49– 1.79

cameras at prices very slightly above cost, and the smaller conventional stores found it very difficult to compete with such outlets. Partly for this reason, a substantial proportion of total retail camera sales were made by a relatively small number of dealers. For example, 40 percent of Polaroid's total sales were accounted for by 10 percent of its total number of sales accounts, and 60 percent of total sales by 20 percent of the accounts.

Sales were made to dealers by Polaroid's field sales force of some 55 salespeople, who were responsible for calling on dealers periodically, setting up displays in the stores, training retail salespeople, assisting dealers in planning retail advertising of Polaroid products, and introducing new products. From time to time, the salespeople conducted special promotional campaigns, such as used-camera trade-in campaigns. For these programs, Polaroid would provide display and advertising materials for the dealers, and the salespeople would assist them in promoting the sale of new Polaroid cameras via special trade-in allowances on used Polaroid cameras.

The frequency of sales calls depended on a dealer's size and location. Small dealers located in remote areas were visited only once every 4 to 6 months. Large dealers located in major metropolitan areas were visited weekly. Dealers' orders were almost always placed by telephone or mail to one of Polaroid's six regional warehouses.

Polaroid sales representatives were compensated on a salary basis. A typical sales territory included about 300 regular dealers, along with wholesalers and other types of accounts.

Polaroid Overseas Operations

Up to 1964, Polaroid's sales outside the United States and Canada were relatively small. Cameras and film were exported from the United States and were subject to high tariffs which most countries imposed on photographic products. As a result, prices of Polaroid products were so high as to make them virtually luxury items.

Beginning in 1965, Polaroid undertook a more aggressive program of developing international markets. Mr. Stanford Calderwood, marketing vice president of Polaroid, commented on this development at an international distributors' meeting in September 1966:

> In 1965, things began to change somewhat and the international curve began perking up as we introduced the Models 103 and 104. . . . In 1966, international sales began to climb very sharply because of the introduction of the Swinger. It is our goal—and we think it is an achievable goal—that in the next decade we can make the international business grow so it will be equal in size to the U.S.A. total.

According to the company's annual reports, sales to dealers by Polaroid's overseas subsidiaries in 1966 amounted to $36 million, compared with $18.2 million in 1965. Beginning in 1965, the company had adopted a policy of pricing cameras and film "as if they were being made behind the Common Market and Commonwealth tariff barriers." Also in 1965, Polaroid established manufacturing facilities for Swinger film at Enschede, The Netherlands, and at the Vale of Leven, Scotland. Swinger camera production in the United Kingdom commenced in late 1965 at a plant set up by one of Polaroid's American camera suppliers.

Along with the establishment of manufacturing facilities, Polaroid

. . . embarked on a program designed to stimulate increased demand for its products overseas. Margins were adjusted downward to bring prices to the foreign consumer more in line with those to U.S. consumers. . . . Greatly expanded magazine and newspaper advertising, as well as commercial television where available, carried the Polaroid instant-picture message in many languages.[3]

The costs of the expanded marketing program, coupled with delays in providing Swinger cameras from the new overseas factory, contributed to an operating loss of $907,000 by Polaroid's unconsolidated subsidiaries (excluding Canada) in 1966.

The general managers of the European subsidiary companies reported to a European coordinator, located at the Polaroid International headquarters in Amsterdam, who in turn reported to Polaroid's vice president–sales, Mr. Thomas Wyman. Mr. Wyman and his assistant manager for international sales also had frequent contact with the subsidiary managers by mail and through periodic visits.

Advertising policies were established by the company's vice president–advertising, Mr. Peter Wensberg, in consultation with representatives of Doyle Dane Bernbach, the company's advertising agency. The agency was also charged with directing the work of its subsidiary and affiliate agencies in other countries. Thus, advertising campaigns for European markets were developed by the overseas agencies within broad guidelines established by Mr. Wyman and by DDB–New York. Mr. Wensberg stated that "we are great believers in the power of advertising" and that "most of the success of our advertising efforts over the years has been due to the fact that we have what we feel is the world's best advertising agency—Doyle Dane Bernbach, in New York."

[3]Polaroid *Annual Report* for 1966, p. 13.

International Planning and Control

During 1965, Polaroid's marketing executives had developed a new planning and control system for overseas marketing operations. This system included a standardized format for financial accounting, standardized monthly performance reports, and annual operating plans for each subsidiary company. The system required that an annual operating plan be developed and submitted to Cambridge headquarters each fall, covering proposed operations during the next calendar year. The format of the plan called for:

1. A review of market conditions, including trends in total industry sales, competitive developments, distribution, and changes in consumer buying habits
2. A statement of objectives for the year, expressed in concrete terms (e.g., "increase distribution by adding at least 20 more department stores and 100 more photographic stores")
3. A summary of planned marketing activities, including sales force, advertising budget and media, publicity, market research, and customer service
4. Estimated operating results for the year, including monthly sales forecasts for each major product, operating expenses, estimated profits, and cash flow

Monthly reports to Cambridge indicated actual results in comparison with the plan, and significant discrepancies were explained via accompanying correspondence.

Polaroid France (S.A.)

Polaroid France (S.A.) was established in November 1961 as a wholly owned subsidiary of Polaroid Corporation. Up to 1964, sales in France were relatively small. With the introduction of the Models 103 and 104 cameras in 1964 and 1965, followed by the Swinger in late 1966, sales of Polaroid France increased rapidly.

M. Dumon became general manager of Polaroid France early in 1966. During 1966, he was responsible for making preparations for the introduction of the Swinger, which took place in September. The addition of the Swinger involved a significant expansion of sales volume, advertising and promotional efforts, and retail distribution for Polaroid France. Consequently, M. Dumon had devoted most of his efforts during 1966 to discussions with the major advertising media, hiring additional personnel, and working with retailers to obtain distribution and promotional support for the new camera.

In mid-1967, Polaroid France employed 86 persons. The company's headquarters office and warehouse were located at Colombes, a suburb of Paris. Reporting to M. Dumon were the sales manager, the advertising manager, and the administration manager.

The French Camera Market

The market for still cameras in France was about one-tenth as large as that in the United States. According to estimates by Polaroid's marketing research department, total camera sales to household and business users in France had increased slowly since 1963 (see Exhibit 8).

In comparison with the United States market, cameras selling for less than fr.50 ($10) constituted a large proportion of total camera sales—around one-third. These inexpensive cameras were primarily simple, fixed-focus "box" cameras, many of which were imported. In France and elsewhere in Europe, Kodak offered less expensive models in the Instamatic line than those available in the United States. According to one source, Kodak sales represented about half the French camera market in 1965–1966.

Altogether, there were some 11,000 retail outlets for cameras in France.[4] Specialty photographic stores sold around three-fourths of all still cameras bought by France household consumers. Other important types of outlets included department stores (5 to 10 percent of total sales), supermarkets (5 percent), and opticians (2 percent). There were fewer general-merchandise discount retailers in France than in the United States, and this type of outlet sold only 1 to 2 percent of all still cameras.[5] Some of the larger photo retailers were aggressive discounters, however, especially in the Paris metropolitan area. The large department stores, such as Galeries Lafayette and Au Printemps, also sold cameras at substantial discounts from suggested retail prices. Outside Paris, smaller conventional photo stores dominated the retailing scene. These smaller stores typically had markups on photographic products of 25 to 30 percent, while the larger stores operated on margins of around 20 percent. As in the United States, the dealers earned their highest margins on film processing (35 to 40 percent).

Market studies by Polaroid indicated that about one-third of total camera sales were made in Paris, although only 17 percent of the population lived in the region. An additional 15 percent

EXHIBIT 8
STILL CAMERA SALES
(THOUSAND UNITS)

Year	Total	Over $50	Under $10
1963	1,200	210	390
1964	1,350	220	390
1965	1,300	220	400
1966	1,350	230	420

[4]Payne, op. cit., p. 98.

[5]Some French "supermarkets" carried diversified lines of general merchandise in addition to food, however, and were essentially combinations of United States food supermarket and discount department store types of outlets.

of camera sales were accounted for by other major cities (population over 100,000).

In France, about a third of all still cameras were purchased to be given as gifts. This compared with a gift proportion of nearly half in the United States. Because gift giving played a lesser role in the market, Christmas season sales naturally represented a smaller percentage of annual industry volume than in the United States. The peak selling season in France was during the spring and summer: May, June, and July accounted for more than half of annual camera sales, and November-December represented less than 15 percent.

According to Polaroid estimates, sales of Kodak Instamatic cameras amounted to over a fourth of the French market; 35-mm cameras, including the Agfa Rapid line manufactured in Germany and designed to compete with Instamatics, had a market share of over 20 percent.

Camera purchases were relatively concentrated in the higher-income groups (see Exhibit 9). About two-thirds of all French camera users were men. Among both men and women, persons under 24 years of age accounted for 34 percent of all camera users.

Among Polaroid Swinger buyers nearly 20 percent were under 21 years of age, and another 20 percent were between 21 and 30. The corresponding figures for all cameras selling for less than fr.100 were 30 percent and 35 percent.

Polaroid Marketing in France

Prior to the introduction of the Models 103 and 104 pack cameras, Polaroid products were distributed in France on a limited scale. In 1963, only around 400 outlets carried Polaroid cameras. During 1965 and 1966, the marketing program had undergone a complete transformation. A broadened product line, lower prices, increased distribution, and more aggressive promotion all contributed to the company's growth.

Distribution and Sales Force

The number of outlets handling Polaroid products increased steadily from 1,300 in 1964 to 1,600 in 1965 and 3,400 in 1967. By mid-1967, M. Dumon estimated that Polaroid accounts represented around two-thirds of total retail camera sales among all photographic specialty stores, and 60 percent in the department store category. The largest 15 percent of Polaroid's accounts represented about 80 percent of the company's total sales.

Polaroid's sales force, which consisted of 10 men in mid-1966, had grown to 22 by July 1967. On the average, each salesperson made eight calls per day. The salespeople were compensated on a straight salary basis. They called on the dealers, took orders, arranged for in-store promotions of Polaroid cameras, and handled

EXHIBIT 9

Annual income, francs	All still camera buyers, %	Individuals over 15 years, %	Polaroid buyers, % All French	
			Pack	Swinger
≤6,000	3	17	1	1
6,001–8,400	14	17		
8,401–12,000	29	26	1	1
12,001–24,000	36	30	4	9
>24,000	18	11	94	89

dealer problems relating to camera repairs, deliveries, etc.

Pricing

While Polaroid Corporation did not release cost figures for individual products, Polaroid France's gross margin on total sales (cameras and film) was approximately 30 percent (see Exhibit 10).

According to industry sources, Polaroid France's gross margin on the Swinger was probably slightly less than that earned on other cameras. These sources also indicated that gross margins on cameras were typically about twice what they were on film. If Polaroid was typical of the French camera industry, these sources added, it probably sold about eight rolls of film for each camera during the first year in the user's hands.

Experience with other cameras suggested that the Swinger would probably have a useful life of 5 to 6 years.

Because cameras were easily shipped from one country to another, Polaroid felt that it was essential to coordinate prices on an international level. Consequently, all selling prices for Polaroid France were prescribed within narrow limits by management in Cambridge. Following the changes in Polaroid's marketing policies in 1965, prices to dealers were reduced substantially. The price paid by a dealer depended on quantities ordered. On the average, dealer costs for Polaroid pack cameras and film provided gross profits for the retailer of about 33 percent if the retailer resold at full list price. Typical retail selling prices for Polaroid cameras and film and for major competing products in the United States and France are shown in Exhibit 11. These prices were from 15 to 20 percent below suggested retail prices.

When the Swinger was introduced, it was believed that small dealers would be reluctant to handle it unless there was some kind of guarantee of obtaining adequate margins. Resale price maintenance was permitted in France only when specifically authorized. Polaroid applied for, and received, permission to establish a retail price of fr.99 ($19.90) for the Swinger; under French

EXHIBIT 10
CONDENSED OPERATING STATEMENT AND UNIT SALES OF CAMERAS, 1966–1967, IN THOUSANDS OF DOLLARS

	1966 actual	1967 original plan	1967 revised estimate
Net sales	$ 5,640	$ 8,800	$ 7,300
Cost of goods sold	3,950	6,170	5,150
Gross margin	$ 1,690	$ 2,630	$ 2,150
Advertising and promotion costs	800	750	630
Selling costs	150	370	370
General and administrative costs	1,000	850	750
Operating profit	($ 260)	$ 660	$ 400
Unit sales:			
Pack cameras	25,000	30,000	25,000
Swinger cameras	85,000	115,000	95,000

EXHIBIT 11
RETAIL PRICES OF POLAROID CAMERAS AND FILM AND OF MAJOR COMPETING PRODUCTS, UNITED STATES AND FRANCE, 1967

Camera model or film type	U.S. typical prices	France* Typical prices	France* Lowest discount prices
Cameras:			
Polaroid Swinger	$17.00		$19.08
Polaroid Model 104	40.00	$70.04	67.40
Kodak Instamatic 104	13.50	15.00	
Films:			
Polaroid Type 20	1.77	2.01	
Pack Film, color	4.49	5.03	
Pack Film, black and white	2.09	2.48	
Kodak Instamatic color film:			
Per pack (12 prints)	1.24	0.97	
Per finished print	0.44	0.45	

* French prices include taxes on "value added" of approximately 20 percent of retail price.

law, dealers were permitted to deviate from this price by up to 5 percent, and the prevailing price in larger retail outlets was quickly established at fr.94. The price paid by the dealer to Polaroid was fr.84.

Advertising and Promotion

During 1966, Polaroid France spent some $600,000 on advertising, of which slightly over half was devoted to the introduction of the Swinger. The budget for 1967 was somewhat lower at around $550,000. About 40 percent of the total was devoted to magazines, 50 percent to newspapers, and 10 percent to cinema advertising.[6]

Because Polaroid cameras were much less well known in France than in the United States, a major objective of Polaroid advertising was to

[6]Total advertising expenditures by all photographic manufacturers in France were estimated at $1.8 million in 1965.

increase consumers' awareness and understanding of the "instant picture" idea. According to studies by the company's marketing research department, in early 1966 fewer than 5 percent of French consumers demonstrated "proved awareness" of Polaroid Land Cameras, and the level of awareness had increased only slightly by early 1967. A consumer was classified as having "proved awareness" if he or she (1) indicated knowledge of the Polaroid brand name *and* (2) knew of the instant-picture feature. The French level of awareness compared with an estimated 85 percent in the United States, 70 percent in Canada, 15 percent in Germany, and 26 percent in the United Kingdom. An illustrative Swinger advertisement from the 1966 introductory campaign is shown in Exhibit 12.

A major obstacle to increasing awareness of Polaroid was the fact that commercial television was not available in France. Polaroid marketing executives believed that television had been a major factor in the growth of Polaroid sales in

EXHIBIT 12
ADVERTISEMENT FOR THE POLAROID SWINGER
(*TELE 7 JOURS* MAGAZINE, SEPTEMBER 1966)

"POLAROID" est la marque déposée de Polaroid Corp. Cambridge, Mass., U.S.A.
"SWINGER" est la marque déposée de Polaroid Corp. Cambridge, Mass., U.S.A.
"POLAROID" (France) S.A. 110 Rue des Champarons 92 - Colombes

Maintenant
vous pouvez avoir une photo en 15 secondes
avec un appareil Polaroid qui ne coûte que
99 F

Le nouveau "Swinger" Polaroid, c'est vraiment autre chose.

Pour 99 F seulement, voilà un appareil qui vous donne des photos noir et blanc parfaites, bien contrastées, des gros plans et des scènes rapides sensationnels.

Et vous avez en main l'épreuve terminée en 15 secondes.

C'est à peine croyable. Si vous n'avez pas vécu ces 15 secondes, ces 15 "interminables" secondes, vous ignorez encore tout du vrai plaisir de la photo !

Et c'est si facile. Visez, tournez le bouton de temps de pose : quand le mot YES apparaît dans le viseur, déclenchez.

Tirez le film hors de l'appareil et comptez jusqu'à 15 · Détachez l'épreuve du négatif. Et voici, terminée, votre épreuve sur papier.

Le "Swinger", c'est un appareil comme vous n'avez jamais rêvé d'en posséder pour seulement 99 F.

Ne vous privez pas de ce plaisir. Offrez-vous le nouveau "Swinger" Polaroid. Il est sensationnel.

SWINGER POLAROID

15 secondes après, la voici.

the United States, and in other countries where commercial television was available—such as Germany and the United Kingdom—it was used extensively.

To demonstrate the concept of instant photography to French consumers, Polaroid placed considerable reliance on in-store sales demonstrations. The company encouraged dealers to perform demonstrations by offering a free roll or pack of film (eight exposures) for each 14 demonstration photos taken by the dealer. To qualify for this partial reimbursement, the retailer had to send the negative portions of 14 film exposures to the company.

In-store sales demonstrations were also conducted by Polaroid demonstrators. These demonstrators, who were paid fr.35 per day, visited retail stores on prearranged schedules to conduct demonstrations of Polaroid cameras before groups of potential customers. Polaroid France provided the films for the demonstrations, provided that the dealer ordered cameras in advance. For example, if the dealer ordered 15 pack cameras, the company provided six packs of black-and-white film and three packs of color film for use in the demonstrations.

Total expenditures for promotion in 1966 amounted to $200,000, and approximately the same amount was budgeted for 1967. Polaroid marketing executives were not satisfied with the dealers' participation in the promotion program. Mr. Wyman, vice president–sales of Polaroid Corporation, wrote to M. Dumon in May 1967, stating that "it appears that the dealer is not demonstrating cameras as frequently and as skillfully as we should like."

1966–1967 Results and 1968 Prospects

Sales and profits of Polaroid France during 1966 and the first half of 1967 had not lived up to expectations. As shown in Exhibit 10, a net loss was incurred in 1966. Moreover, by July it was apparent to M. Dumon and to the Polaroid headquarters marketing staff that the goals set for 1967 would not be attained. Hence, a revised plan was prepared calling for a lower sales volume and lower levels of expenditure.

Polaroid's other European subsidiaries were also below the levels planned for 1967, but not to the same degree as in France. In several countries, including Italy, Switzerland, and Belgium, Polaroid's estimated share of the camera market was significantly higher than in France. Polaroid's market penetration was about the same in France, Germany, and the United Kingdom, however, despite much higher levels of consumer awareness in the latter countries. In some other countries, the company's advertising expenditures were proportionately higher than in France; with the French 1966 expenditure per camera sold set as 100, indexes of cost per unit for Germany, the United Kingdom, and Italy were 112, 133, and 120, respectively.

For 1968, it was anticipated that the French camera market would grow very slightly, if at all. No major competitive new-product introductions were anticipated. Polaroid was contemplating the introduction of a new camera model in the United States around midyear, but production would probably not be adequate to meet worldwide demand until the end of the year. Consequently, M. Dumon's plans for 1968 were to be based on the same basic product line as in 1967.

In considering his marketing program for 1968, M. Dumon was especially concerned with the problems of pricing and promoting the Swinger. With regard to pricing, he wondered whether he should recommend that the company apply for a 1-year continuance of government approval for resale price maintenance. The current approval was due to expire on August 1, 1967, and M. Dumon felt that there might be some advantages in allowing completely free pricing after that date. On the other hand, he did not want to lose any of the distribution which had been so carefully built up during the preceding year, on account of "cutthroat" price competition by the discount stores.

The problem of promotion was a chronic one

for Polaroid. Awareness of the Polaroid name and instant-picture feature had increased only slightly between early 1966 and early 1967, and even Polaroid camera owners displayed a lack of full understanding of some important features. For example, among a group of 100 Swinger owners interviewed in June 1967, nearly half did not realize that it was possible to obtain duplicates of Polaroid pictures from the company's print copy service.

Although the need for further consumer education about Polaroid photography seemed great, it was also clear that advertising had played a very important role in building demand during 1966 and 1967. Among a sample of Swinger owners interviewed in November 1966, 53 percent mentioned advertising as their original source of information about the camera, 5 percent mentioned conversations with photo dealers, and 5 percent in-store demonstrations.

M. Dumon wanted to recommend a program which would contribute to the company's longer-term marketing goals in France. At the same time, he was aware of the need to improve current operating results. He had recently received a letter from Mr. Wyman indicating that "we must be in a position, with a prepared advance plan, to reduce expenditures and limit our activities to insure that we are producing a profit for the year."

4 *Hood College*

Christopher H. Lovelock

"Welcome to Hood, Chip—it's good to have you with us!" Dr. Martha E. Church, president of Hood College, shook hands with Alfred W. (Chip) Brown, Hood's new director of admissions. It was July 1, 1976, and Chip Brown's first day in his new position.

"Hood is at a significant point in its history," said Martha Church as the two sat down in the president's comfortable but unostentatious office in Alumnae Hall. "My predecessor turned the college around, committing Hood firmly to women's education and reversing an admissions decline that threatened to destroy the institution. Now we have a rising enrollment and a projected housing shortage on campus, which means that we're going to have to try and attract more commuting students. On the other hand, census statistics project a long-term drop in the number of 18-year-olds, we've just had a significant

Christopher H. Lovelock is an associate professor at the Harvard Graduate School of Business Administration.

increase in fees, and our day student facilities are not as good as they might be."

Background to Hood College

An independent liberal arts college for women, Hood College was located on an attractive, neo-Georgian campus in Frederick, Maryland. Frederick (population 25,000) is about 45 miles northwest of Washington, D.C., and a similar distance west of Baltimore (Exhibit 1). In 1975–1976 the college had about 1,000 under-graduates and some 300, mostly part-time, graduate students. A partial organization chart of Hood's administrative officers is shown in Exhibit 2.

History

Hood College was founded in 1893 as the Women's College of Frederick, leasing the facili-

EXHIBIT 1
MAP OF WESTERN MARYLAND AND SURROUNDING AREA

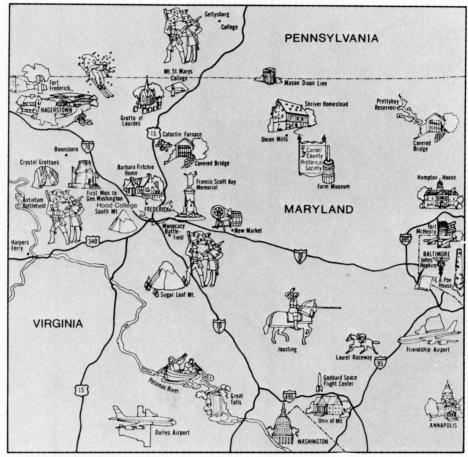

Source: Hood College brochure.

ties of an earlier institution, the Frederick Female Seminary, which dated from 1845. The name was changed to Hood College in 1913 to honor an early benefactor.

From the outset, the college sought to provide "quality education for women." Instruction emphasized both traditional liberal arts and preparation for careers. In 1915, the education depart-

ment was initiated in response to the need for college-trained teachers; meanwhile the new department of home economics began offering a B.S. degree. Both departments stressed practical experience as a complement to classroom education.

By the mid-1920s, the percentage of students enrolled in the teaching program had increased

EXHIBIT 2
PARTIAL ORGANIZATION CHART, HOOD COLLEGE, 1976–1977

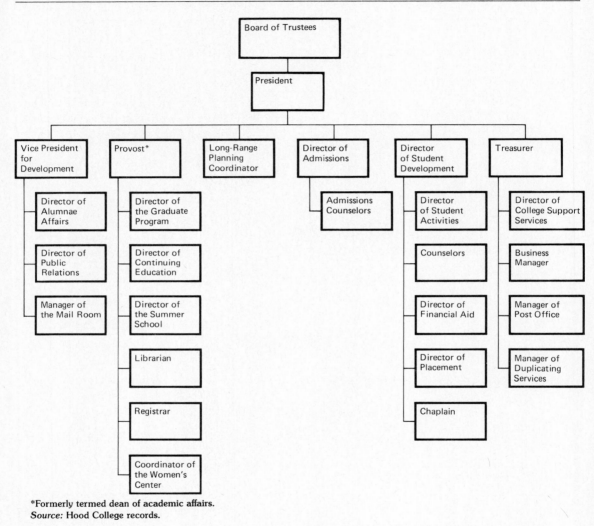

*Formerly termed dean of academic affairs.
Source: Hood College records.

significantly. Some faculty members questioned whether this might weaken the liberal arts program. The outcome of this debate was an expansion of both the liberal arts and professional curricula. Following World War II, rapid growth in enrollment facilitated a further increase in course offerings. Between 1942 and 1962, Hood's student body grew from 397 to 661, subsequently reaching a high of 753 in 1966. During the 1960s two new dormitories were built and a Junior Year Abroad at Strasbourg University was introduced for French majors. In 1971 a graduate program was initiated in the human sciences, and male day students enrolled for the first time as undergraduate degree candidates.

Growing Difficulties

The middle 1960s was a boom period for applications and admissions at Hood; then both began a steady decline. From a peak of 948 in 1964–1965, applications dropped by more than half in 6 years, despite a doubling of the admissions office budget. In July 1971, the director of admissions wrote in his annual report:

> The important problem of attracting greater numbers of applicants is still not solved as the College has now experienced seven consecutive years of declining applications. The situation is critical and the institution will soon realize, I hope, that while the College has an admissions problem, the problem is not in admissions. It will take the total commitment of all toward a more realistic, stimulating academic environment to enable the admis-

sions office to be more successful in the function it performs for the college.

This was a difficult period administratively for Hood. The president resigned in May 1971, and an interim successor was appointed. Despite another increase in the admissions office budget, applications fell again in 1971–1972. In an attempt to maintain the size of the entering class, a higher proportion of applicants was accepted. In 1971–1972, the number of new students enrolling was only 188 (Exhibit 3), down from an average of 220 a year in the 1960s. Freshmen SAT scores and high school ranks also dropped (Exhibit 4).

The Turnaround at Hood

In August 1972, the trustees appointed Dr. Ross Pritchard as the sixth president of Hood College. Pritchard, then age 47, had a varied back-

EXHIBIT 3
HOOD COLLEGE:
ADMISSIONS OFFICE STATISTICS, 1968–1976*

Academic year	Inquiries	Applications	(Yield)†	Acceptances	(Yield)†	New students	(Yield)†
1967–1968	NA	677	(NA)	473	(69.9%)	203	(42.9%)
1968–1969	NA	603	(NA)	465	(77.1%)	196	(42.2%)
1969–1970	1,601	490	(30.6%)	418	(85.3%)	212	(50.7%)
1970–1971	1,472	441	(30.0%)	384	(87.0%)	193	(50.3%)
1971–1972	2,267	410	(18.1%)	352	(85.9%)	188	(53.4%)
1972–1973	2,889	368	(12.7%)	307	(83.4%)	174	(56.6%)
Freshmen	2,279	258	(11.3%)	219	(84.8%)	112	(51.1%)
Transfers	610	110	(18.0%)	88	(80.0%)	62	(70.5%)
1973–1974	4,017	694	(17.1%)	603	(86.8%)	366	(60.6%)
Freshmen	3,405	589	(17.2%)	518	(87.9%)	310	(59.8%)
Transfers	612	105	(17.1%)	85	(80.9%)	56	(65.8%)
1974–1975	7,285	851	(11.7%)	656	(77.1%)	345	(52.6%)
Freshmen	6,966	724	(10.4%)	555	(76.7%)	291	(52.4%)
Transfers	319	127	(39.8%)	101	(79.5%)	54	(53.5%)
1975–1976‡	6,374	728	(11.4%)	602	(82.7%)	308	(51.2%)
Freshmen	6,044	607	(10.0%)	504	(83.0%)	254	(50.4%)
Transfers	330	121	(36.7%)	98	(80.1%)	54	(55.1%)

*Figures are exclusive of continuing education totals but include transfers.
†"Yield" in each case is defined as a percentage of the figure in the preceding column.
‡Projected (as of June 30, 1976).
Source: Hood College admissions office.

EXHIBIT 4
HOOD COLLEGE: PROFILES OF NEW
UNDERGRADUATE STUDENTS

(A) SAT means and high school ranks for freshmen

	SAT means		High school class rank	
Class of	**Verbal**	**Math**	**Top 1/5**	**Top 2/5**
1972	569	566	61%	89%
1973	542	541	45%	81%
1974	535	532	50%	80%
1975	524	530	54%	77%
1976	521	524	56%	79%
1977	497	506	51%	81%
1978	498	508	55%	86%
1979	504	513	60%	88%
1980	500	510	62%	88%

(B) Home state of freshmen

Class of

	1974	1975	1976	1977	1978	1979	1980
Maryland	32	31	33	44	88	107	79
Pennsylvania	43	33	25	22	34	56	49
New Jersey	41	32	24	13	70	52	53
New York	24	20	23	9	37	19	24
Connecticut	14	5	5	5	13	16	12
Massachusetts	9	9	5	6	13	9	18
Virginia	7	5	6	4	10	8	4
West Virginia	3	1	1	NA	6	4	1
Delaware	1	2	1	NA	4	4	5
District of Columbia	–	1	–	NA	6	2	2
Florida	–	–	2	NA	7	2	1
Other/Foreign	16	13	10	NA	24	12	6
Total Freshmen	188	154	135	112	304	291	254

(C) Home state of transfers

	Entering college in		
	1974	**1975**	**1976**
Maryland	33	38	43
Pennsylvania	5	4	4
New Jersey	5	4	5
New York	3	–	1
Connecticut	–	5	–
Virginia	2	2	3
Other states	4	3	2

(D) Type of college previously attended by transfers

Community and junior colleges	23	32	36
4-year colleges and universities	29	25	22

Source: Hood College admissions office.

ground. He had taught economics and coached football at Southwestern College in Memphis, worked with a private development corporation building hydroelectric projects in underdeveloped countries, and spent 6½ years overseas as a senior executive in the Peace Corps.

Looking back, a senior administrator at Hood recalled:

> In August 1972 the College was at a decision point. It had been drifting for a number of years and it was just a matter of time before the College would go under. The whole atmosphere was negative, frightened. Hood was ready for leadership—and that was good for getting things done.

Hood's Mission

After making some new appointments, Dr. Pritchard set out to encourage a reexamination of the college's mission. An institutional self-study, required as part of the reaccreditation procedures for the Middle States Association was already under way and served as a catalyst.

The question of coeducation was discussed at some length. Admissions office surveys showed that many applicants turned down acceptances from Hood because of its single-sex status. Some used this fact to argue for going coed. Others, however, strongly disagreed, asking "What's the point of becoming like every other campus?" Advocates of remaining a women's college felt that there were opportunities for an institution which appealed to "the more ambitious, self-identified type of woman."

Dr. Patricia E. Cunnea, appointed as dean of academic affairs just a month before Dr. Pritchard arrived on campus, argued:

> Women are afterthoughts and second-class citizens on most coed campuses. Let's build a place that's really for *women*—the whole curriculum, all the attitudes, the extra curricular activities available in the dorms. Let's make it clear that this is a place where women are encouraged to be their best selves. . . .

Finally, the decision was taken that Hood would remain a women's college, committed firmly to the concept of women's education. The institutional self-study continued with this in mind. Attention was focused on the curriculum, with a view to taking the traditional liberal arts base and making it more responsive to the career interests of women. As one administrator put in, "A liberal arts education ought to be an education for life, not just ostentatious leisure." Recalled Dean Cunnea:

> We started on a series of conversations with the departments and I think this was the next essential ingredient. You've got to have a concept that has some validity and also is appropriate for the particular institution. You have to find some key people with ideas, with whom you can start producing results very rapidly, so that these provide examples—you have to start a bandwagon going.

Department chairpeople were invited to submit curriculum changes compatible with Hood's new concept. Many faculty members enthusiastically made proposals they had had in mind for some time. Others hung back initially, but eventually they followed suit when they saw that innovation was rewarded with administration support, including enlarged budgets. While Dean Cunnea spent her time speaking with individual department chairpeople, President Pritchard had meetings with the whole faculty in each department. Inevitably, there were difficulties, and some expressed fears that Hood was becoming a "trade school," but most concerns were amicably resolved. Administrators also met with students and spoke to Hood alumnae clubs.

Between 1972 and 1974, some 400 changes were made in the instructional program. These had two major thrusts. The first was to add more career preparation to Hood's traditional liberal arts curriculum. For example, they began to prepare women for work in health science occupations instead of simply offering a major in biology. And they changed the home economics course—described as previously little more than "how to be a good housewife"—to include consumer affairs and the type of nutrition studies that could lead to a career as a dietitian.

The second move was to develop internship programs at nearby government, research, and health institutions. Examples included internships at nearby Fort Detrick (a cancer research center) for biology students, at a county institution serving the handicapped for psychology students, at Johns Hopkins Hospital in Baltimore for home economics majors studying dietetics, at local newspaper and public relations firms for journalism students, and with government agencies in Washington for political science students. Said Dr. Pritchard:

> We've changed the way we view ourselves. Instead of taking the traditional view of Hood as an attractive retreat—a place where nice girls went, isolated from the hurly-burly of the outside world—we now see the College as being right in the middle of things.

A New Approach to Admissions

Having redefined Hood's role and initiated evolving changes in curriculum, career counseling, and placement, Ross Pritchard turned his attention to admissions.

Matters had continued to deteriorate during 1972–1973, with application acceptances and enrollments dropping to new lows (Exhibit 3). The freshman class (1977) was again sharply down in numbers and SAT scores; on the other hand, transfer enrollments had more than doubled, from 23 the previous year to 62 in 1972–1973. Although total inquiries (including transfers) were up 75 percent over the preceding year and almost double the level of 2 years earlier, this was ascribed to more "shopping around" by prospective students because they knew that more colleges were available to them.

Several steps were attempted in 1973 to improve the admissions situation. First, the college retained a Chicago educational consulting firm, Stuart Weiner & Associates, to review the admissions picture at Hood and prepare appropriate recommendations. In a related step, a market research firm undertook a telephone survey. The subjects were two key groups of "lost prospects," comprising 108 "lost contacts" (those who had contacted Hood for materials but did not apply) and 75 "lost acceptances" (those who were accepted by Hood but gave no deposit). The firm also surveyed current Hood freshmen and seniors. Meanwhile, a Baltimore consulting firm, Interpreting Institutions, was retained to reshape Hood's publications. Another change came with the appointment of a new director of admissions.

"Lost Prospect" Survey Findings

The telephone survey findings were presented in August 1973. Over 80 percent of the lost prospects indicated that they would be enrolling in a 4-year college, divided roughly equally between private and public institutions. Only one in four would be attending an all-women's school, but "lost acceptances" were more than twice as likely to be going to a single-sex college as "lost contacts" (38 percent versus 15 percent).

Hood's main disadvantages were seen as:

"It is not coed; there are no boys; no social life." (44 percent)
"It is too far in the country; far from the city; too small a town." (20 percent)
"It is too expensive." (17 percent)

Advantages of attending Hood were seen as:

"Small, more personal, friendly." (32 percent)
"Good reputation; good scholastic reputation." (20 percent)
"Small, good student-teacher ratio." (18 percent)
"Location, climate, atmosphere." (12 percent)
"Beautiful campus." (10 percent)
"All-women's college." (8 percent)

The main answers to the question about why

a female student might prefer attending an all-women's college were:

"Study habits easier, few distractions." (40 percent)

"Looking for education, not husband." (15 percent)

"Less competition, feel more comfortable in class." (12 percent)

"Girls are under less social pressure." (11 percent)

The market research firm concluded its review of the survey findings with the following recommendations:

It would seem advisable to immediately develop a communications program outlining the virtues of an "all women's" college if the school intends to maintain an all female enrollment. Such a program would also have to "play up" the positive aspect of the "social life" at Hood, in the surrounding community, and with surrounding coed institutions.

Consultants' Evaluation

The consultants' report began with a look at Hood's admissions statistics since the early 1960s. It then moved to an evaluation of the situation facing the college at the beginning of the 1973–1974 academic year. Extracts from the report follow below.

THE EXTERNAL SITUATION

The external situation for Hood College . . . presents a dismal outlook. Let us look at some of the important factors:

(1) The total number of students attending undergraduate colleges is increasing at a less rapid rate in the 1970's than occurred in the 1960's. . . .

(2) The number of high school graduates will increase at a much slower rate during the 1970's. This lower growth rate will level off in the late 1970's and show decreases beginning in the early 1980's.

(3) The Office of Education projects only very slight increases for the next ten years in the number of students attending college. The growth, if any, for the private college will be very small. It is, in fact, likely that the private college enrollment level will decrease substantially over the next ten to fifteen years.

. . . .

The result of the external situation is a *highly competitive* atmosphere among colleges in attracting students.

Although *all* institutions of higher education are feeling the "pinch" from external factors, the private women's college is in more serious difficulty than the coeducational private college. The women's college market is limited to less than 3% of the college bound market and has been "shrinking" for the last thirteen years.

Women's colleges have decreased from 300 in 1960 to 146 in 1973. In a recent E.T.S. survey only 96 of the 146 women's colleges indicate they plan to remain single-sex institutions. The *Chronicle of Higher Education* in a recent report states that "Indications are that the marketplace may not even be able to sustain the 96 colleges that want to remain women's institutions."

. . . .

Although the challenge of the future for a women's college such as Hood will be more difficult than that of other private and public institutions, it is important to note that there still is a market large enough to support the future enrollment goals of the college.

. . . .

INTERNAL PROBLEM AREAS

The following areas are perceived to be . . . inhibiting the enrollment growth of Hood College. [These factors] are controlled by the administration and faculty of the college and can be changed to improve the results of the admissions recruiting program. . . .

Three important questions were asked:

(1) Why didn't more than the 2,700 potential students who made inquiries express an interest in Hood College?
(2) Why didn't more of [those making inquiries] complete an application to the college?
(3) Why didn't more than 57% of the students who were accepted to the college this year deposit and matriculate at the college?

The consultants' report went on to identify a number of specific problem areas in recruitment and admissions procedures. These included poor coverage of key market areas by admissions office personnel; limited resources directed at prospective transfer students from both 2- and 4-year colleges; ineffective publications that presented the college in a dull and unexciting way; a badly designed mailing program; poor follow-up of interested prospects and applicants; ineffective use of alumnae in the recruitment program; failure to set clear objectives and then measure and evaluate subsequent performance; disorganized and inadequate admissions office facilities; poor communication in both directions between the admissions office and the rest of the college; and poor training of admissions representatives.

Developing a Master Plan for Admissions

Based on research and planning undertaken jointly by consultants and the admissions staff, a master plan was prepared for 1973–1974. This established program objectives for the admissions office (Exhibit 5); created flow charts detailing each step in the inquiry, preapplication, and postapplication stages of the admissions process; established realistic timetables for each step; determined what communications were needed and how the alumnae and other constituents of the college could participate in the program; checked costs against budgetary allotments; and created control and review procedures that would keep the program on target.

At the president's urging, a target of 250 new

students was set for fall 1975, comprising 150 freshmen and 100 new transfers—figures considered highly optimistic. Targets were also set for the number of inquiries, applications, and acceptances. These figures excluded the newly instituted continuing education program, designed for women and men aged 25 and over who wanted to start or complete their undergraduate educations. Recruiting for this program, like that for the graduate program, was administered separately.

During the summer, the admissions staff underwent extensive training—their first formal training in counseling prospects. Sessions included round table discussions, lectures, and videotaped practice presentations. An admissions counselor job manual was also prepared.

The college's new admissions publications were built around the theme "A new dimension in higher education for today's woman." A logo was designed using the college name, with the second "O" transformed into the universal female symbol: .These graphics were used throughout Hood's published materials.

Since the master plan divided the application process into three phases, communications were tailored to these same categories. The key pieces during the *inquiry* phase were a poster and a mailer (or general information folder). Both were printed in eye-catching orange and red, with return cards coded so that they could be traced to their source. The direct-mail folder was sent to students on selected lists (such as National Merit commended students and semifinalists) and to individuals referred by alumnae and other students.

The key publication for the *preapplication* period was the 32-page student prospectus. Its text built a case for attending a women's college, arguing with some conviction that women still had second-class status at coeducational colleges. The academic program was described on a department-by-department basis with emphasis

EXHIBIT 5
ADMISSIONS OFFICE PROGRAM OBJECTIVES

A. Promotion Objectives
1. To change the image of the college from a good traditional girls' school to an exciting, high-quality college for women, which emphasizes the new women's concerns and careers in a personable atmosphere.
2. To more effectively communicate the "new" image of the college to a targeted audience in particular market segments.
3. To improve the publications program—better appeals and more information, expanded use of printed materials.
4. To expand the inquiry base through increased mailings, posters, advertising special events, career workshops, counselor luncheons, and alumnae.
5. To better promote financial aid, early acceptance, transfer programs, and career-oriented curricula.

B. Field Objectives
1. To improve services to high school seniors, transfer students, and counselors.
2. To increase amount of time spent with potential students and make better use of territory management.
3. To increase total number of high school interviews by better promotion of high school visits.
4. To triple the number of campus visits by potential students.
5. To increase the frequency of high school visits to at least two times per year.
6. To develop a counselor rapport with the potential students through systematic, personal contact.
7. To improve the effectiveness of each counselor through the use of a continuous training program.
8. To develop strong articulation programs with community colleges.

C. Office and Support Staff Objectives
1. To improve data collection capabilities.
2. To develop a manual of procedures detailing the technical parts of the office and its functions.
3. To improve procedures that will provide improved efficiency in the office.
4. To improve the facilities used by the admissions office in interviewing and work areas.

Source: **Master plan for 1973–1974, Hood College admissions office.**

---

on the practical experience offered by Hood and career opportunities open to majors in each field. Other "nuts and bolts" folders described Hood policies and procedures in such areas as financial aid and transfer admissions. Planned for 1974 were a series of four-page academic discipline folders describing in "a warm, friendly manner" the offerings of each department, its faculty and facilities, and the career opportunities open to graduates in this field. These folders were originally prepared by department faculty members and then edited by Hood's director of public information to ensure consistency of style.

For the *postapplication* period, the primary publication was the catalog. Since the 1973–1974 version had already been printed, a new edition had to wait until the following year. Another publication was a "viewbook" designed and written by students to promote extracurricular activities.

To provide greater focus for both personal and printed communications, each of the five admissions counselors was assigned territories categorized as primary, secondary, or tertiary.

Maryland and other nearby states were usually divided up by counties and cities. Primary areas included all or most of Maryland, New Jersey, Pennsylvania, Washington, D.C., Connecticut, Massachusetts, and Florida, plus northern Virginia and southern New York State. Secondary areas included the balance of the above states, West Virginia, Delaware, Maine, Ohio, and Illinois. Exhibit 4 shows the home states of freshmen and new transfer students in recent years. More than 75 percent of the freshmen were drawn from just four states—Maryland, Pennsylvania, New York, and New Jersey. Transfer students were even more concentrated geographically, with the great majority coming from Maryland. They transferred from both 2- and 4-year institutions.

Results

The response to the new admissions procedures among prospective freshmen during 1973–1974 was dramatic. Freshmen inquiries for the Class of 1978 rose by 49 percent over the previous year's figure, applications by 128 percent, and acceptances by 137 percent; matriculations were up by no less than 276 percent. Transfers, by contrast, were marginally below the previous year's level. New students in the fall of 1974 numbered 366, an all-time high and up from 174 the previous year (Exhibit 3). The attrition rate among students dropped to 14 percent from a historical average of 20 percent. SAT scores and the high school class ranks of new freshmen showed a slight increase (Exhibit 4).

The extent of this turnaround, in an otherwise dismal recruiting year for private colleges, drew national attention. Personal letters and news releases from the director of public information attracted reporters from the *Washington Post* and *Baltimore Sun* to campus and led to substantial publicity for Hood College.

Buoyed by this success, the trustees voted in October 1974 to seek 310 new undergraduate students each year, with a view to raising residential enrollment to between 1,100 and 1,200 students. With this directive, the admissions office moved into another vigorous recruiting year, revising the master plan after careful evaluation of the previous year's efforts.

Despite the praise Hood was receiving, not everyone approved the new directions the college was taking. Some alumnae were uneasy at the greater career emphasis in the curriculum, or at Hood's more strongly feminist orientation. And some faculty members disliked what they perceived as Hood's new "hard sell" approach. One administrator criticized the admissions staff for too much "hand-holding" in its efforts to be "warm and friendly" toward prospective students.

A momentary flurry was caused by an October 1974 editorial in *The Blue and Grey,* the campus newspaper. This pointed to an alleged gap between what prospective students were told by recruiters and what they found on enrolling. Subsequent issues carried several pages of letters, mostly supporting the editorial. The *Morning Herald* in nearby Hagerstown picked up the story, running it under the headline "Hood Freshmen Attack Recruitment Policies." Some students, stated the *Herald,* "said that they expected Hood would be a hotbed of radical feminism and liberal thought, but have found instead that most of the women attracted here are actually quite conservative." One student reported that "campus life is not as stimulating outside the classroom as some recruiters may have suggested." Others complained that recruiters overemphasized small class sizes, since several freshmen student classes had a hundred or more students.

College officials were reported as "strenuously defending" Hood's recruiting techniques. The story noted that despite their complaints, none of the discontented freshmen planned on leaving Hood, citing their general satisfaction with the quality of the academic program.

During the 1974–1975 year, Dr. Pritchard was offered the presidency of Arkansas State

University. A native Arkansan, he decided to accept. A search was therefore initiated for a new president of the college.

A New President

In May 1975, the board of trustees elected Dr. Martha E. Church as seventh president of Hood College and the first woman to hold this position. A graduate of Wellesley College, Dr. Church had obtained an M.A. from the University of Pittsburgh and her Ph.D. from the University of Chicago. In 1960, she returned to Wellesley as assistant professor of geography, moving in 1965 to Wilson College in Chambersburg, Pennsylvania, where she became dean of the college and professor of geography. From 1971 until her appointment at Hood, Dr. Church served as associate executive secretary of the Commission on Higher Education of the Middle States Association.

In an introductory message to alumnae, the new president gave her view of Hood's role in the education of women:

Academically, Hood is on the cutting edge of women's education. . . . Hood has earned a national image as a forerunner in women's education.

Today . . . the College faces a rapidly-changing public attitude—an attitude that is becoming more receptive to women but that is still somewhat uncertain about what women can really do. Women applying for what once were considered "men's jobs" are still being asked about their typing skills. Even when women reach executive status, they find it difficult to get past the personal secretaries of their male counterparts. Fortunately all this is changing.

And Hood is helping to bring about the change. . . .

Your College is *not* an adherent of militant feminism. This would be self-defeating—contrary to the very goals of the College. But *Hood is for women!* We constantly are examining—and re-examining—what the College can do to assure that

Hood students go out into a changing world as confident, well-equipped women who can hold their own in any profession, any career.

Dr. Church was especially proud of the fact that 65 percent of all faculty members at Hood College were female, with each rank having at least 50 percent women. She believed this to be the highest ratio for any women's college not run by Catholic sisters.

To review all the facets of Hood's operations, the president appointed a long-range planning task force. In the spring of 1976, input was being sought from all segments of the college community.

Financial concerns were receiving attention, since Hood had been drawing down its unrestricted funds in recent years (Exhibit 6). On the other hand, faculty salaries were below average, and enlargements to Hood's physical facilities were required to meet the needs of an expanding student body. Following a $150 increase in tuition in 1975–1976, annual fees were being increased by another $220 in 1976–1977. The admissions office stated that as a result of this last move, Hood had lost several potential applicants to state schools.

A number of people were concerned about the position of day students on campus. The director of student development observed:

We really need to do something for the day students at Hood. Relationships between day students and resident students aren't as good as they might be. Hood is still basically a residential school and some of the day students are resentful. They don't go out of their way to get involved; events aren't necessarily scheduled at convenient times for them; and parking is miserable. Many of them have spent two years at Hagerstown or Frederick Community Colleges, and tend to come from somewhat lower income families.

Exhibit 7 shows, for the spring semester of 1976, the number of students, as well as the breakdown between the four undergraduate classes. In recent years, approximately half the

EXHIBIT 6
HOOD COLLEGE: STATEMENT OF CURRENT FUND REVENUES, EXPENDITURES, AND TRANSFERS

	Years ending June 30 ($000)					
	1973	**1974**	**1975**	**1976 (budget)**	**1976 (actual)**	**1977 (budget)**
Revenues:						
Student tuition and fees	2,008	2,066	2,746	3,497	3,388	3,867
Endowment income	242	262	281	255	227	220
Interest income	56	85	80	80	50	25
Gifts and grants	603	580	777	838	774	942
Bookstore sales	81	87	125	153	153	162
Summer conferences	94	105	91	143	115	143
Other	71	35	42	43	42	41
	3,154	3,220	4,141	5,007	4,749	5,400
Expenditures:						
Instructional	877	1,020	1,310	1,551	1,527	1,817
Physical, plant, dining, hall, health services	765	827	1,123	1,220	1,259	1,428
General and administrative	807	924	1,074	1,185	1,222	1,356
Student aid	214	205	305	304	271	285
Bookstore	84	88	112	141	141	151
Summer conferences	66	87	73	108	98	105
Library	82	81	104	108	112	120
Other	55	51	54	59	41	46
	2,949	3,281	4,154	4,676	4,671	5,308
Net surplus (deficit)	204	(61)	(13)	331	78	92
Net transfers (to) from other funds	(133)	(122)	(183)	(323)	(380)	(469)
Net increase (decrease) in unrestricted current funds	71	(183)	(196)	8	(302)	(377)

Source: Hood College records and CPA reports.

new transfer students enrolling had been commuters, versus only 4 to 7 percent of each freshman class. Virtually all graduate students, most of whom were part-time, commuted to campus.

Looking ahead at the future of the college, Martha Church commented:

> The whole thrust of my administration currently is attempting to get the College ready for the 1980's. These are going to be extraordinarily difficult years for private colleges to get through. The census statistics predict that, beginning in 1978–1979, we are going to start seeing a significant drop in the number of 18 year olds, which is projected to last to the end of the century.

Data collected by Dr. Church facilitated the evaluation of Hood against other, closely comparable women's liberal arts colleges. These data showed that from 1972–1973 onward, the costs of attending Hood had fallen progressively behind the costs of 16 similar institutions. By 1975–1976, Hood's annual costs were $1,000 below the median of these other institutions. The 1976–1977 tuition increase narrowed the gap somewhat but still left Hood some $750 below the median level (Exhibit 8).

EXHIBIT 7
HOOD COLLEGE: UNDERGRADUATE ENROLLMENT, SPRING 1976

	Full-time		Part-time		Total		Total F.T.E.	
	M*	F*	M	F	M	F	M	F
Degree								
Residential								
Freshmen	0	263	0	0	0	263	0	263
Sophomores	0	234†	0	0	0	234	0	234
Juniors	0	97†	0	0	0	97	0	97
Seniors	0	106	0	0	0	106	0	106
Total residential	0	700	0	0	0	700	0	700
Nonresidential/traditional								
Freshmen	3	20	0	0	3	20	3	20
Sophomores	6	25	0	0	6	25	6	25
Juniors	6	25	0	3	6	28	6	26.58
Seniors	6	28	3	3	9	31	7.41	29.41
Unclassified	0	1	0	0	0	1	1	1
Nonresidential/continuing education								
Freshmen	0	0	0	1	0	1	0	0.25
Sophomores	2	5	0	3	2	8	2	6.25
Juniors	3	12	2	15	5	27	4	20.17
Seniors	5	11	4	17	9	28	6.91	20.58
Unclassified	0	0	1	3	1	3	0.50	1.33
Total nonresidential	31	127	10	45	41	172	35.82	150.57
Total degree								
Freshmen	3	283	0	1	3	284	3	283.25
Sophomores	8	264	0	3	8	267	8	265.25
Juniors	9	134	2	18	11	152	10	143.75
Seniors	11	145	7	20	18	165	14.32	155.99
Unclassified	0	1	1	3	1	4	0.50	2.33
Total	31	827	10	45	41	872	35.82	850.57
Total enrollment (degree)	858		55		913		886.39	
Nondegree								
Traditional	2	8	22	39	24	47	8.50	17.91
Continuing education	0	1	2	14	2	15	0.66	4.75
Total nondegree	2	9	24	53	26	62	9.16	22.66
Total undergraduate	869		132		1,001		918.21	
Total nonresidential and nondegree	64	136	34	98	67	234	44.98	173.23

*M = male; F = female.
†Includes one continuing education student.
Source: Hood College records.

On the other hand, admissions data for the same colleges showed Hood to be well matched and improving relative to most others on such statistics as the percentage of applicants offered admission, average SAT scores for new students, and the percentage of students enrolled as freshmen who graduated from the same institution 4 years later. Statistics showed Hood ranking third out of 17 on this last-mentioned statistic, with 62.5 percent of the original fresh-

EXHIBIT 8
HOOD COLLEGE: TUITION AND OTHER EXPENSES FOR COMPETITIVE COLLEGES, APRIL 1976

| | Tuition and board | | | | Total expenses,* |
	1972–73	1973–74	1974–75	1975–76	1976–77
Agnes Scott College (has largest endowment of group)	$3,350	$3,450	$3,650	$3,950	$4,650
Cedar Crest College	3,580	3,940	3,995	4,200	5,100
Chatham College	3,735	4,050	4,200	4,500	5,050
Elmira College	3,970	3,970	4,420	4,850	5,650
Goucher College	3,900	4,150	4,595	4,900	5,455
Hollins College	3,750	3,975	4,315	4,675	5,650
Mary Baldwin College	3,750	3,900	4,150	4,450	5,400
Mills College	3,885	4,095	4,300	4,725	5,775
Randolph Macon College	3,775	3,950	4,200	4,475	5,275
Salem College, N.C.	3,300	3,400	3,600	3,900	n/a
Scripps College	4,025	4,225	4,675	5,130	$6,130
Skidmore College	4,390	4,590	4,890	5,290	6,755
Sweetbriar	3,800	4,050	4,250	4,600	5,455
Wells College	3,950	4,150	4,500	4,835	5,550
Wheaton College	4,230	4,530	4,930	5,450	6,400
Wilson College	3,640	3,640	3,700	4,060	4,710
Median	3,775	4,013	4,323	4,675	5,400
Hood College†	3,500	3,500	3,500	3,650	4,645

*Including Transportation. From *Chronicle of Higher Education*, Apr. 26, 1976.
†As listed in *Chronicle of Higher Education*.
Source: President's office, Hood College.

man class of 1975 graduating 4 years after its first enrollment at the college.

Admissions

The new president inherited a continuing success story in admissions. Figures for 1974–1975 showed a 75 percent increase in inquiries, a more than 25 percent increase in applications, and slightly more acceptances; however, yields were down in each category, and the number of new students had dropped from 366 to 345 (Exhibit 3). SAT scores and class ranks among freshmen had increased again. Biology (including medical technology), education (comprising special education—for the handicapped—and early childhood education), and home economics together accounted for over half the majors

selected by entering freshmen. Education was easily the most popular major among transfers, followed by biology.

During 1975–1976, it appeared that the college would fall behind its projected target of 950 applications. This was ascribed, in part, to a cut in the number of admissions counselors from five to four. However, in the spring of 1976 active follow-up procedures, including a newsletter announcing new programs and activities, resulted in a sudden surge of applications. The outcome was that Hood actually exceeded its applications target.

Wendy Zimet, a 1971 graduate of Hood, had been the director of admissions since her predecessor's promotion to a new position in January 1975. Previously she had spent 6 months as associate director and 2½ years as an admissions counselor. However, she planned to leave at the end of the academic year.

Admissions activities required close coordination with several administrators at Hood, including the director of financial aid and the director of public information. Ms. Zimet also worked with a number of faculty members, who participated in Campus Open Days and sometimes wrote or telephoned applicants having questions about a particular department.

Wendy Zimet spent much of her time working with the admissions counselors. They were responsible for interviewing, visiting high schools, working with alumnae who assisted in recruitment, phoning applicants, and reading admissions folders. Ms. Zimet was trying to delegate more of the clerical "busy work" in the office to student assistants, to make better use of the counselors' time.

She stressed the importance of training counselors to become critical readers of admissions folders, which, she said, included "some of the greatest works of fiction!" she added:

> The admissions counselors tend to *like* the applicants and to want to help them. They have to realize that there's no point in having a student come to Hood if she's not going to be happy. It doesn't do anything for either the student or the institution.

The admissions staff attempted to have a representative at College Nights at every high school in Hood's "primary" area. The plan was to train alumnae to handle some College Nights

so that the staff was not spread too thinly. Experience with untrained alumnae had been unsatisfactory, with many reverting to a "Well, when I was there . . ." syndrome when counseling prospective applicants.

Problems identified by the admissions office in a spring 1976 report to the trustees included (1) a need to update the publications, (2) a lack of receptivity by some high school guidance counselors toward Hood's admissions counselors, and (3) the impact of the 1976–1977 fee increase.

The New Admissions Director

After an intensive search, President Church announced the appointment of Alfred W. Brown, Jr., as director of admissions. "Chip" Brown was selected as the most qualified applicant from a large field. Previously he had been director of admissions and financial aid at Bard College in New York State, where he had reversed a 6-year history of declining enrollments. On July 1, 1976, he took up his new position at Hood College.

Dr. Church asked Chip Brown to meet with her in her office. She wanted to share with him her thoughts on the directions that Hood would be taking in the future, the admissions strategy that would be appropriate for 1976–1977 and subsequent years, and the implications of this strategy for both the admissions office and other college administrators.

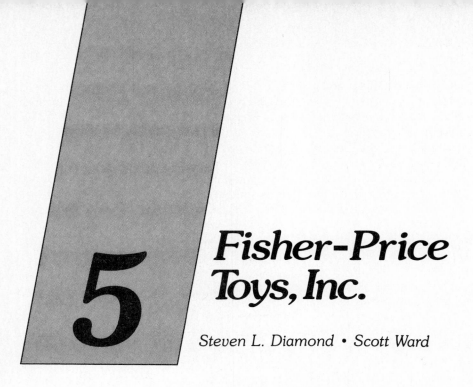

5

Fisher-Price Toys, Inc.

Steven L. Diamond • Scott Ward

Over the past four decades, the Fisher-Price toy company had distinguished itself by producing a wide line of quality toys for preschool children at moderate prices. Jack Asthalter, Fisher-Price's marketing vice president, was therefore confronted with a difficult situation in August 1971 when his production staff announced that mold costs for the new ATV Explorer toy would make the intended $12 retail price impossible to meet. In fact, according to the production people, the ATV Explorer could not be profitably distributed at the wholesale level for less than $9.20 per unit, thereby calling for an $18.50 retail price after markups. While concept tests had promised a substantial demand for the new riding vehicle at the $12 price, Mr. Asthalter was unsure that the potential consumers would remain interested at the new price. Moreover, because the Fisher-Price product line was generally priced below $5 retail, Asthalter believed there would be considerable internal resistance to introducing the ATV Explorer.

Industry Background[1]

Industry sources estimate that toy sales at the retail level in the United States were $2 billion to

Scott Ward is a professor of marketing at the Wharton School, University of Pennsylvania. Steven L. Diamond was formerly a research associate at the Harvard Graduate School of Business Administration.

[1]This section is based on *Note on the Toy Industry*, University of Minnesota Graduate School of Business Administration (Boston, Mass.: Intercollegiate Case Clearing House, 9-514-060).

$3 billion in 1968. A study by the A. J. Wood Corporation divided total consumption as follows:

EXHIBIT 1
TOY SALES BY CATEGORY

	Approximate percentage of dollar sales at retail
Riding toys (including bicycles)	22
Dolls, doll clothing, and accessories	13
Nonriding transportation	12
Sporting goods	12
Games, puzzles, magic sets	6
Educational and scientific	5
Musical	5
Toy guns	5
Handicraft and models	4
Novelty toys	3
Activity toys	3
Stuffed Toys	2
Child-size furniture	2
Preschool	2
All others	4
	100

Approximately one-sixth of the items purchased accounted for almost two-thirds of the total dollars spent on toys:

EXHIBIT 2
TOY SALES BY RETAIL PRICE CLASS

	Percentage of unit sales	Percentage of dollar sales
$15.00 and over	4	33
$10.00–$15.00	3	13
$ 5.00–$ 9.99	10	20
$ 3.00–$ 4.99	14	16
$ 2.00–$ 2.99	12	8
$ 1.00–$ 1.99	20	6
$ 0.50–$ 0.99	16	3
Under $ 0.50	18	1
Not classified	3	–
TOTAL	100	100

The A. J. Wood study showed that parents accounted for the bulk of toy purchases:

EXHIBIT 3
PERCENTAGE OF UNIT SALES OF TOYS, BY PURCHASER

Parents	73
Grandparents	11
Uncle/aunt	5
Brother/sister	2
Friends	4
Other (including purchases made by children themselves)	6

The toy industry is composed of a few large firms and several hundred small manufacturers. In 1967, there were over 1,000 toy manufacturers in the United States, but the eight largest manufacturers together accounted for 35 percent of sales, and the 20 largest firms accounted for 58 percent of sales. Foreign manufacturers accounted for only 9 percent of toy sales in the United States (at manufacturers' prices), but foreign imports were growing, particularly for less expensive toys.

The toy industry was highly seasonal in nature. At the retail level, 53 percent of all dollar sales and 45 percent of unit sales were made in November and December. Toys were sold through approximately 10,000 retail outlets, distributed as follows:

EXHIBIT 4
PERCENTAGE DISTRIBUTIONS OF SALES AND STORES

Type of retail outlet	Percentage of dollar sales	Percentage of total stores
Department	18	13
Discount	17	18
Chain discount	11	9
Catalog	9	5
Variety	9	21
Auto supply	7	3
Toy	7	8
Hardware	4	2
Drug	3	5
Hobby	2	2
Supermarket	2	4
Sporting goods	2	1
All others	9	9
TOTAL	100	100

Toy retailing had become more concentrated in recent years, and industry sources expected this concentration of more sales through few outlets to continue. For example, the Census of Business indicated that the number of hobby and toy and game shops had declined 18 percent between 1963 and 1967, although total sales of these shops increased by more than one-fourth. A Stanford Research Institute study predicted that chain stores, particularly discount and variety chains, were likely to continue to be major vendors of toys.

Recently, two major discount chains opened stores which sell only toys. Both managements believed that their chains could do a specialized year-round business in toys because (1) year-round promotion by toy manufacturers and retailers could create a year-round demand, (2) the youth population (10 and under) was growing, with a 27 percent gain projected until the late 1970s, and (3) American affluence was increasing, with personal income increasing 72 percent between 1960 and 1968.

Toy industry observers broke down the types of toys available into four categories:

1. *Prestige items.* Most of these were European imports. They offered high margins (40 to 60 percent) to retailers, with little advertising but elaborate point-of-sale promotions.
2. *Staple nondiscount toys.* These included basic items such as clay sets, doctor kits, and building blocks. Many "educational" toys fell into this category. Some advertising was done for these toys, but themes stressed quality and were directed primarily toward women.
3. *Semidiscount items.* These included push-and-pull toys, riding toys, and games. Some national advertising was done, but it was essentially "awareness" promotion to keep the names of the product and firm before the consumer.
4. *Extreme discount toys.* These included items which were fads, as well as a few perennial favorites. Most imported toys from the Far East fell into this category; were sold through jobbers to discount, department, and toy stores; and offered low (less than 10 percent) margins.

Company Background

Fisher-Price Toys, Inc., was founded in East Aurora, New York, in 1930 with the concept that solid wood blocks with lithographs applied would sell as toys for preschool children. Herman G. Fisher, the president and one of the three founders of the firm, believed that "kids not only want toys to play with, but toys to play with them." Accordingly, he saw in wood lithographing the opportunity to make action toys which would walk, crawl, whine, and generally "respond" to children.

In order to survive the difficult Depression years, Mr. Fisher established as a corporate creed that each Fisher-Price toy must have (1) intrinsic play value, (2) ingenuity, (3) strong construction, (4) good value for the money, and (5) action. These guidelines for toy making, still observed today, led to the relatively successful operation of the company in its early years. While avoiding head-on competition with the mainstream of the toy business, Fisher-Price continued to make specialty toys of the wood lithograph variety, and by 1947 the firm had reached the $1 million sales level.

The next decade was marked by moderate but steady growth under the continuing conservative management of Mr. Fisher. In 1959, however, significant changes in Fisher-Price's product line and pricing policies were instrumental in transforming the firm into a major factor in the toy industry. First, Fisher-Price enjoyed a highly significant breakthrough in the toy industry as the first successful producer of a line of music box toys. While other manufacturers had developed similar toys, they had been either too fragile or too expensive to attract substantial consumer acceptance. The Fisher-Price line, however, could withstand a good deal of punish-

EXHIBIT 5
TYPES OF STORES IN WHICH TOYS ARE PURCHASED

Question: How often Do you Buy Preschool Toys in the Following Places?

	Usually	Sometimes	Never	No answer
Discount stores	43.0%	36.8%	7.1%	13.1%
Department stores	23.6	50.3	12.7	13.5
Variety stores	8.3	52.5	19.3	19.9
Toy stores	14.7	38.4	26.5	20.5
Mail-order catalog	5.1	25.9	46.2	22.8
Supermarkets	1.2	29.5	45.1	24.3
Military base stores	2.3	1.0	–	–
Drugstores	0.6	1.2	–	–
Baby stores	0.3	1.0	–	–
Other	0.6	1.5	–	–

Note: These results were derived from 2,341 valid returns of a four-page questionnaire mailed to 6,000 female *Redbook* subscribers, chosen randomly on an *n*th name basis from the complete listing of *Redbook* subscribers (*n* = 2,339).

Source: *"Redbook*'s Baby Products Study," June 1971.

ment and yet was available at moderate prices. Accordingly, sales of the new line were extremely high, thereby providing the resources and the incentive for further new-product introductions.

The changing retail structure of the toy business prompted a second vital decision of Fisher-Price. While Mr. Fisher had always advocated price maintenance, the coming of age of large discounters made such a policy impractical (Exhibit 5). Faced with the threat of losing the growing market share serviced by high-volume discount chains, Fisher-Price departed from its stringent pricing policies in 1959.

These fundamental product and pricing strategy changes led Fisher-Price into a decade of substantial growth in the 1960s. During that period Mr. Fisher set aside his policy of promoting solely from within the organization and began hiring professional management from other industries. The impact of the new management team was first evident in the expansion of Fisher-Price's product line, with an average net increase of six new toys yearly. Moreover, the purchase mix changed over the decade, reflecting the increased volume in $3 to $5 toys and a relative reduction in the proportion of $1 and $2

toys sold by Fisher-Price. By 1969, Fisher-Price had become a major factor in the toy industry. Sales increased to a respectable $32 million in that year (Exhibit 6), and three-fourths of all toy purchasers recognized Fisher-Price as a leading producer of preschool toys (Exhibit 7). Nonetheless, under the guidance of Mr. Fisher, the firm continued in its conservative ways in terms of both financial and marketing policies. Accordingly, it was not surprising that the Quaker Oats

EXHIBIT 6
SALES HISTORY OF FISHER-PRICE TOYS

Year	Sales (in $ millions)
1960	$ 7
1961	9
1962	12
1963	15
1964	16
1965	18
1966	22
1967	26
1968	30
1969	32
1970	52 (est.)

EXHIBIT 7
UNAIDED BRAND AWARENESS SURVEY
Question: What Brands of Preschool Toys Can You Name?

	1962	1969
Fisher-Price	50%	75%
Playskool	85	86
Creative Playthings	NA	36
Mattel	78	87

(n=2,000)

Source: "Redbook's Baby Products Study," June 1971.

Company of Chicago saw great potential in Fisher-Price and purchased the firm from Mr. Fisher for $50 million in cash.

While Quaker tended to be a far more aggressive concern than had been Fisher-Price under Mr. Fisher's direction, Quaker's management was hesitant to meddle in the concerns of the toy manufacturer. They recognized Fisher-Price as a well-run organization and sought to ensure continuity of management. At the same time, however, Quaker encouraged Fisher-Price executives to adopt a less conservative posture, specifically in their marketing and advertising programs. Advertising especially took on a dimension of importance with the impersonalization of the retail selling process, creating the need for a shift from a push to a pull strategy within the toy business. To accompany this desired change in outlook, Quaker made it clear that it stood ready to provide whatever resources would be necessary to ensure a more substantial growth rate.

Product Testing and Marketing Programs

Fisher-Price's steady and respectable growth rate was in great measure attributable to the very effective product testing and marketing programs. Unlike other toy manufacturers, Fisher-

Price generated virtually all its new toy ideas internally. While the impetus for such toy introductions had traditionally come from the research and development department, marketing executives were increasingly providing the direction for new-product design. Accordingly, a review of the Fisher-Price product line and of the preschool toy market often led to recognition of a potential toy to fill a market niche. This suggestion was then passed on to designers, who provided a dozen or so sketches and, given encouragement from top management, would proceed to develop a prototype of the new toy.

Unique within the industry, Fisher-Price operated a licensed on-premise nursery school for local preschool children at which toy prototypes could be tested. Classes were conducted at two age levels—2 to 3 years and 4 to 5 years—by trained teachers, and each met twice weekly for 3-week periods. While classes were in session, corporate engineers and behavioral scientists, the creators of the Fisher-Price toy line, could watch children playing with new-toy prototypes as well as already proven toys. By noting children's reactions to toys through such measures as average attention span time and repeat toy usage, these toy designers could effectively pretest new toys and ensure maximum interest, safety, education, durability, and the like.

After this pretest phase, however, Fisher-Price's marketing staff geared its promotions almost exclusively to adult purchasers rather than to child consumers. Because mothers and grandmothers purchased about three-quarters of all preschool toys (Exhibit 8), corporate advertising was carried in women's magazines such as *Good Housekeeping*, *Parents' Magazine*, and *Woman's Day*. While advertising copy recognized that toys should be enjoyable, parental concerns for safety, durability, and quality were always taken into account (Exhibit 9). As Jack Asthalter explained, "The real success of this company lies in our ability to think as a mother would."

Fisher-Price also differentiated itself from competitors by promoting an entire product line

EXHIBIT 8
PURCHASERS OF CHILDREN'S TOYS

Question: Who Usually Buys Most of Your Child's Preschool Toys?

Wife	63.2%
Grandparents	30.7
Other friends or relatives	12.4
Husband	11.3
No answer	5.0

(n=2,339)

Note: Percentages total more than 100 percent because of multiple responses.

Source: "Redbook's Baby Products Study," June 1971.

rather than pushing single items, as was customary in the toy industry. While other manufacturers would introduce a variety of new toys each year in the hope that one or two would become best sellers, Fisher-Price maintained most of its product line year after year, adding only a few new toys annually. Advertising and promotion efforts were all designed around this umbrella strategy of selling an entire product line and company image, rather than attempting to ride the crest of an occasional fad. Accordingly, each Fisher-Price toy was boxed in a familiar red and blue package, and displays were designed to show the toys as a collection of playthings rather than an unrelated group of items. To further promote this umbrella strategy, a catalog of all Fisher-Price toys was included with each toy, inducing parents and children alike to make further purchases in the Fisher-Price family.

With the attraction of new management to the corporation in the mid-1960s, Fisher-Price's marketing efforts began to take on a more aggressive dimension. In dealing with the trade, Fisher-Price had traditionally presented its product line and taken orders for each upcoming Christmas season. More aggressive merchandising at trade shows and an increased number of sales representatives in the field, however, led to a substantial sales increase in the late 1960s.

Also, prior to 1969, corporate advertising was confined to the print media, and advertising budgets were unrealistically small; in 1965 the budget was $202,000. Fisher-Price abandoned its no-TV advertising policy in 1969, and (with the added resources and encouragement provided by Quaker) the advertising budget was increased substantially, to $643,000 that year. Plans called for a spending level of $1.1 million in 1970. The effect of television advertising in well-supervised test markets indicated the magnitude of its potential impact. While Fisher-Price maintained its insistence on selling a product line rather than individual toys, the line was broadened substantially to accommodate the new demand which television appeared to capture. By 1970 the firm's advertising budget was more than twice the 1968 level, with a high proportion of this investment directed to mothers through daytime television talk shows and soap operas. In determining its marketing strategies, corporate executives kept in close touch with relevant public opinion studies (Exhibit 10).

The effect of these new marketing policies became evident in Fisher-Price's sales statistics almost immediately. With a greater number of products and higher-volume sales on the already existing product line, it was not long before Fisher-Price's production capacity proved inadequate. In 1970, therefore, a new factory was added in Medina, New York, and a new shipping facility was built in Albion, New York, to accommodate the new sales levels.

Pricing Policies and Product Line

While Fisher-Price underwent substantial change as it grew from a small toy producer to a major factor in the industry, executives who had grown up within the firm continued to cling to one unwritten rule of thumb throughout the company's history—namely, that a toy priced at over $5 retail would not sell in the marketplace. Despite inflationary pressures and increasing

EXHIBIT 9
EXAMPLE OF MAGAZINE ADVERTISING, 1965

EXHIBIT 10
ATTITUDES TOWARD TOYS

Question: Considering Toys in General, Please Indicate Which of the Following Statements You Agree or Disagree With.

	Agree	Disagree	No answer
Toys are good for children.	97.0%	0.6%	2.5%
Toys are good value for the money.	33.1	60.3	6.5
Toy prices have held the line.	12.4	80.2	7.4
There is a wide choice of toys.	96.7	1.5	1.9
Toys are more fun than ever.	70.5	24.7	4.8
It's difficult to shop for toys.	47.1	48.8	4.1
Toys are made better than ever.	31.6	62.9	5.5
Toys are safer than ever.	44.8	49.0	6.2
You spend too much on toys.	54.9	39.7	5.4
Toys last longer than they used to.	27.6	65.5	6.8
Toys are more educational than ever.	92.4	5.0	2.6

(n=2,339)

Source: "*Redbook*'s Baby Products Study," June 1971.

levels of disposable income, the old guard at Fisher-Price believed that its success had come from a moderately priced product line in the past, and they were hesitant to deviate from this proven track record.

Accordingly, when Mr. Asthalter and sales manager Chuck Weinschreider were brought into the firm in the mid-1960s to take over Fisher-Price's market efforts, many of their new ideas met with considerable resistance. Both Asthalter and Weinschreider saw the American toy consumers as being affluent and willing to spend substantial sums on preschool toys if they could be assured of quality and good value for their money. The Fisher-Price image and product line were strong enough, they reasoned, to command higher prices for larger and more intricate toys (Exhibit 11). Clearly, a company which had spent decades earning a reputation unequaled in the toy industry was not going to jeopardize the quality of its products in order to keep prices below the $5 level. At the same time, many exciting new-product ideas could not be followed through if this imaginary $5 barrier were to be strictly enforced.

Unfortunately, Fisher-Price's single excursion into the over $5 price level in the early 1960s had been a dismal failure. Specifically, in 1962 the company had introduced the Fisher-Price Circus—a snap-together set of circus animals, ladders, rings, and the like—at a price of $6.83 to the trade and $13.95 retail (Exhibit 12). The

EXHIBIT 11
BEST-KNOWN BRAND ASSESSMENT

Question: Which Do You Consider the Best-Known Brand of Preschool Toys?

Brand	Percentage of respondents
Fisher-Price	64.7
Playskool	13.0
Mattel	3.2
Creative Playthings	2.3
Childcraft	0.6
Kenner	0.4
Tonka	0.4
Tupperware	0.4
Romper Room	0.3
Child Guidance	0.3
Hasbro	0.1
Kohner	0.1
Remco	0.1
Other	0.7
Don't know/no answer	17.4

(n=2,339)

Source: "*Redbook*'s Baby Products Study," June 1971.

EXHIBIT 12
FISHER-PRICE CIRCUS

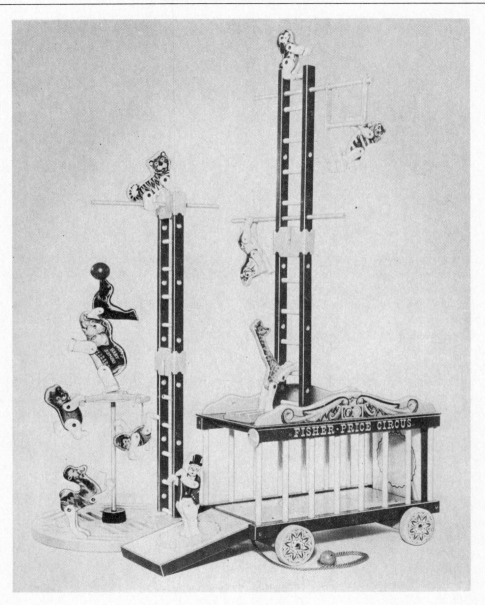

Circus had commanded an average attention span of 45 minutes from Fisher-Price's nursery school youngsters, compared with the 10- or 15-minute playing times which the children allotted to most of the other toys in the product line. Accordingly, the Circus was introduced into a line of 50 other toys all priced at $5 or less. While initial sales to the trade were reasonable, sales at the retail level were so poor that the toy was eventually dropped from production completely (Exhibit 13).

Against this backdrop, many Fisher-Price executives stood firm on their insistence that toys could not be priced at more than $5. Specifically, they pointed out that Fisher-Price sold a line of products to the trade and that most buyers purchased Fisher-Price toys sight unseen because of the company's reputability and fine track record. Certainly Fisher-Price could not endure more failures such as the one that occurred with the Circus toy and still command the respect and confidence of the trade.

After considerable controversy within the company, Messrs. Weinschreider and Asthalter did venture forth in 1964 with another toy which broke through the price barrier. This toy, called the Creative Coaster, was the first significant riding toy marketed by Fisher-Price and was priced at $3.33 to the trade (a price still modest by industry standards) and $6.95 retail. Unlike the Circus, the Creative Coaster was a simple wooden toy, solidly built but lacking a stylish design (Exhibit 14). It was positioned within Fisher-Price's product line (then 72 products) to compete directly with Playskool's similarly con-structed preschool riding toys. Despite the head-on nature of the competition, the Creative Coaster met with great success; 226,000 units were sold in 1964 and 332,000 units by 1970, when the price had been raised to $5.25 cost and $10 retail.

While many corporate officials were convinced that the Creative Coaster experience was a fluke and that the $5 price barrier remained a valid one, Asthalter and Weinschreider continued to pursue attractive toy concepts at a variety of price levels. In 1968 they introduced the Family Farm, which pretested well in their nursery school and was expected to hold significant appeal to parents as well as children. The Family Farm was priced at $6.50 cost and $13 retail, and orders for it exceeded production capacity from the start. It continued to sell well in following years. The next higher-priced toy, the Play House, was introduced in 1969 at $7 wholesale and $14 retail and enjoyed similar success. Nonetheless, a considerable number of executives at Fisher-Price continued in their insistence that the firm should limit its product line to below the $5 level.

Development of the ATV Explorer

As Fisher-Price continued to meet with success on new-toy introductions, as well as on its existing product line, Messrs. Asthalter and Weinschreider began seeking new opportunities within the preschool market. The well-established acceptance of the Creative Coaster by 1969 led them to believe that additional riding toys held considerable promise for Fisher-Price. Discussions with sales representatives and with buyers for major retail chains reinforced this belief, and accordingly Ashthalter requested that the engineering and product design people prepare prototypes of riding toys for product testing.

After considerable experimentation, a prod-

EXHIBIT 13
SALES HISTORY OF THE FISHER-PRICE CIRCUS

Year	Unit sales of circus
1962	57,000
1963	17,000
1964	13,000
1965	10,000
1966	20,000
1967	27,000
1968	27,500
1969	22,000
1970	Discontinued

EXHIBIT 14
CREATIVE COASTER

uct was developed which appeared to hold great promise as an addition to the Fisher-Price line. The toy—called the ATV (All-Terrain Vehicle) Explorer—was a stylish, multicolored plastic vehicle, durable enough to carry as much as 200 pounds. It could be steered; came equipped with a horn, a motor-noise lever, and two small, removable passengers; and provided a storage space to carry additional toys. Designs on the side panels conveyed a moon exploration theme and included an American flag and a model space-tracking screen (Exhibit 15).

By early 1970 the ATV Explorer was enjoying substantial success in the Fisher-Price nursery school, commanding a respectable 20-minute average attention span and a high level of repeat usage among youngsters from 2 to 5 years old. Furthermore, the toy showed itself to be safe, durable, and educational, satisfying all the Fisher-Price guideposts.

Concept tests among prospective purchasers proved similarly encouraging. In a series of market research sessions, parents of 2- to 5-year-olds were asked to anticipate their children's reactions to the toy and were then asked to assess the probability that they would purchase the ATV Explorer were it available at a $12 retail price. On the basis of the results of

EXHIBIT 15
ATV EXPLORER

these interviews, Weinschreider estimated that Fisher-Price could sell about one million units of the toy annually, a volume equaled by only six other products in the Fisher-Price line. At this volume, the ATV would have accounted for higher sales than any other Fisher-Price toy by a wide margin.

While initial reactions were generally quite favorable, the ATV Explorer was not without its drawbacks. Fierce competition in the riding toy area was thought by some Fisher-Price sales representatives and executives to justify scrapping the toy. Playskool, a major factor in the preschool toy industry, had long dominated the riding toy market and was offering six riding toys in 1970. Industry gossip, however, led Fisher-Price executives to believe that Playskool was

losing a substantial share of this market to small, unknown firms which were using new blow molding processes to produce riding toys for as little as $3 or $4 retail. While these blow-molded vehicles could not compare in quality, strength, durability, design, and complexity to the Playskool or Fisher-Price entries, their low price apparently held substantial appeal to many toy purchasers. Accordingly, many of the more conservative members of the Fisher-Price staff believed the ATV Explorer was far too risky a venture to pursue.

Nonetheless, Asthalter insisted that the gamble was well worth the risk which it carried. He pointed out to other executives that the entire Fisher-Price product line had been enjoying remarkable acceptance both within the trade

EXHIBIT 16
BRAND PREFERENCE MEASURE FOR PRESCHOOL TOYS
Question: Do You Buy One Brand of Preschool Toys Most Often?

Response	Percentage of respondents
Buy one brand most often *(Loyalty)*	60.5
Do not buy one brand most often	30.1
No answer	9.4

(n=2,339)

Question: Which Brand of Preschool Toys Do You Buy Most Often?

Brand	Percentage of respondents
Fisher-Price	82.7
Playskool	11.3
Creative Playthings	4.3
Mattel	1.4
Childcraft	0.5
Tonka	0.5
Child Guidance	0.2
Kenner	0.2
Remco	0.2
Other	1.4
No answer	0.7

(n=1,414)

Source: "*Redbook*'s Baby Products Study," June 1971.

and among parents (Exhibit 16). Moreover, Fisher-Price's higher-priced entries—with the singular exception of the Circus—were all selling quite well, a factor which Asthalter attributed in great measure to a highly effective television advertising campaign. Finally, while projections of market size showed a decreasing number of children under 6 years of age in upcoming years, there was some reason to believe that the more optimistic forecasts for the number of first births were a more relevant market index, given Fisher-Price's image as a maker of "hand-me-down" toys which last from one child to the next. For all these reasons, the decision was made to go ahead with the ATV Explorer, and in June 1970, Asthalter directed the production department to begin tooling up for the 1971–1972 season.

The New Pricing Dilemma

Within a month after the Asthalter directive had gone to the production department, Fisher-Price's vice president of manufacturing turned up in Asthalter's office with some unfortunate news. He explained that as his manufacturing design people pursued the ATV Explorer a bit more, they discovered that initial costs on the toy would be considerably higher than expected. Specifically, the initial investment in the mold from which the plastic toy would be made was to be $161,000, while special tooling costs would run another $18,000. The company traditionally amortized its investments over a 1-year period. The direct costs were $4.21 for materials and $0.73 for labor. Thus, if Fisher-Price were to take its standard markup on cost, the toy would have to sell for $9.20 to the trade (about 17 percent of which would represent selling and administrative expenses, which generally meant an $18.50 retail price. Suddenly, the ATV Explorer, which looked like an attractive investment at $12 retail, began to appear increasingly marginal.

Accordingly, Asthalter called in Chuck Weinschreider to discuss their new problem. As Fisher-Price's sales manager, Weinschreider suggested that they immediately get in touch with the company's 30-person sales force, as well as the six major corporate buyers of Fisher-Price toys. These people were thought to be most sensitive to retail buying habits and were expected to offer much-needed advice on how to proceed with the ATV Explorer.

Contacting the sales representatives and buyers, however, proved inconclusive. Many Fisher-Price sales reps, themselves solid believers in the company's product line, felt that customers would recognize value and pay for the new toy accordingly. Others, generally optimistic, were hesitant to push the toy. While they recognized that a success with the ATV Explorer might mean inroads into a whole series of riding toys, they focused their concern on relations with the trade. As one of Fisher-Price's leading sales reps summed it up:

> We've spent years building a product line that we know will sell. And we've also spent years establishing a rapport with the trade, so that each time Fisher-Price comes out with its annual product line these buyers give us orders with no hesitation. If we come out with this Explorer and it bombs, those retailers will be stuck but good. Stuck with a toy that sells for $18.50, not with a little $3 toy. That could mean a lot of inventory to carry, especially when you do almost all your business at Christmas time [Exhibit 17]. All we need is one failure—all we need to do is to hurt those retailers one time—and they're going to be afraid to take our advice for years to come. I think we should find a way to sell it for $12 or $13 or scrap it for good!

Reactions among major buyers were similarly mixed. Of the six national chains which accounted for a substantial percentage of Fisher-Price's volume, two buyers commented that at any price the ATV Explorer would not be a good

EXHIBIT 17
MONTHLY SALES PERCENTAGES

Month	Percentage of sales to consumers	Percentage of sales to the trade
January	1.8	3.6
February	2.6	3.2
March	3.5	8.9
April	3.5	8.2
May	3.3	7.1
June	5.1	8.8
July	4.7	12.0
August	4.1	10.1
September	3.9	12.0
October	5.6	14.5
November	20.6	7.0
December	41.3	4.6

seller because the moon theme which it conveyed was outdated. Nonetheless, one of these buyers and three of the other four felt that the Fisher-Price name coupled with the attractive design and engineering of the toy would assure reasonable sales at the $18.50 level, and accordingly they said they would order the toy if Fisher-Price decided to include it in its 1971–1972 product line. However, the remaining two buyers said they would refuse to order the Explorer, pointing to adverse economic conditions and expressing the belief that people will pay only so much for good quality toys.

Asthalter and Weinschreider were confused about how to proceed. In order to get any definitive reading from the trade or the marketplace they would have to commit themselves to mold and tooling costs. And even at that, a single mold would only be capable of producing 500,000 units of the Explorer. Perhaps the market would be price-insensitive and the demand would come closer to the initial forecasts. If that should happen, Fisher-Price would be unable to meet the demand and could accordingly generate substantial ill will among the trade. At the same time, however, an investment in two molds on a toy which remained a mystery seemed highly risky.

As they continued to discuss their alternatives, Asthalter and Weinschreider recognized still other options. For one, they could cheapen the product a bit, removing a horn or a plastic "passenger" or a secret compartment from the toy. While such an action would be totally inconsistent with the Fisher-Price policy of never sacrificing quality in toys, it would allow the Explorer's price to be brought into line with the prices of competitive riding toys.

Another thought was to depart from corporate advertising policies and push the Explorer on television as a single item. Fisher-Price management had always insisted that they sold a line of toys rather than separate items, and their advertising had always reflected this philosophy.

EXHIBIT 18
PROPOSED TELEVISION STORYBOARD FOR ATV EXPLORER

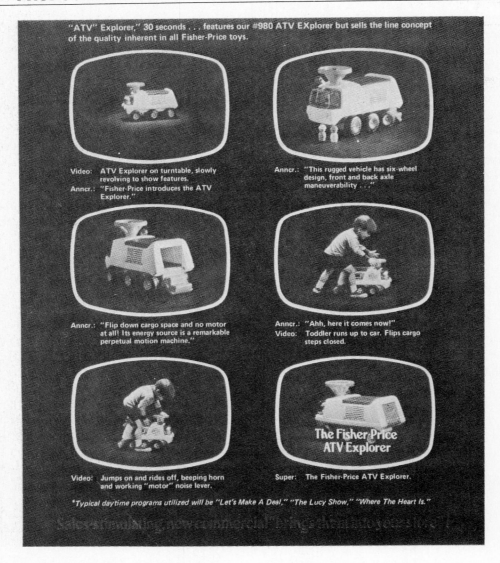

"ATV" Explorer," 30 seconds . . . features our #980 ATV EXplorer but sells the line concept of the quality inherent in all Fisher-Price toys.

Video: ATV Explorer on turntable, slowly revolving to show features.
Anncr.: "Fisher-Price introduces the ATV Explorer."

Anncr.: "This rugged vehicle has six-wheel design, front and back axle maneuverability . . ."

Anncr.: "Flip down cargo space and no motor at all! Its energy source is a remarkable perpetual motion machine."

Anncr.: "Ahh, here it comes now!"
Video: Toddler runs up to car. Flips cargo steps closed.

Video: Jumps on and rides off, beeping horn and working "motor" noise lever.

Super: The Fisher-Price ATV Explorer.

The Fisher-Price ATV Explorer

"Typical daytime programs utilized will be "Let's Make A Deal," "The Lucy Show," "Where The Heart Is."

Television advertising effectiveness to date, however, indicated that this medium was extremely effective and that it could perhaps create a demand for the Explorer, even at the $18.50 level. In giving this idea consideration, Mr. Asthalter even went so far as to have television "storyboard" themes developed and to assess the costs of such a campaign (Exhibit 18) at $250,000.

The final series of options revolved around the price of the toy. Fisher-Price had always taken a fixed markup on direct costs for all its toys. Possibly by reducing its margin in this one instance it would begin to bring the wholesale cost and ultimately the retail price of the Explorer into line with the costs and prices of competitive products. At the same time, however, both Weinschreider and Asthalter were reluctant to start a precedent which would permit the production department to relax its cost-cutting efforts with the thought that marketing could always lower its margins if costs got out of line.

On the other side of the fence, there was some consideration of milking the Explorer. Namely, Weinschreider felt that a toy which would sell at $18.50 would also sell at $19.50.

Accordingly, he suggested that perhaps Fisher-Price should actually increase its price by 50 cents or $1 and use the added revenues to support increased promotion, either to the trade or at the retail level.

With all these possibilities in the air, Asthalter realized that a decision would be necessary almost immediately if Fisher-Price were to have the Explorer in its 1971–1972 line. Because of the seasonal nature of the toy business and the lead times required, Fisher-Price had to go into production on its toys by August in order to ensure adequate distribution to meet the Christmas rush of the following year.

II

Market Selection and Product Planning

The single most important decision any company makes is what markets it elects to serve with what products. Market-product choices are the basis for building and enlarging the business. They represent long-term commitments to sets of customers, sets of competitors, fields of technology, manufacturing processes, and distribution systems. Moreover, one enters the race seldom knowing the extent of the commitment in terms of capital investments in plant, equipment, technology, and human resources.

It goes without saying that product-market decisions ought to be approached judiciously, with careful analysis and considerable caution. Yet often they are not. Decisions to move into new markets with new products seem, all too frequently, to emerge as answers to short-term problems: How can we fill excess plant capacity? What will we do with a new technical development coming out of the R&D laboratory? What else can we give the sales force to sell? What's new that could be featured in our advertising?

The cases in this section of the book seek to develop for the student a direct and rational framework for dealing with market selection–product planning decisions. There is the conviction that through objective analysis, the firm considerably improves its chance of succeeding in the marketplace.

Market selection begins with market segmentation. The marketing manager must first divide the field into sets of customers (segments) who are alike in the way they perceive the product, value it, buy it, and use it. Sometimes it's useful to divide the market in broad terms by the purpose for which the purchase is to be made. For example, an item may be purchased for personal use or as a gift. Also, an item may be purchased for incorporation into the product an industrial buyer makes and sells, or it may serve as production equipment. Some market segments may be defined demographically (e.g., by age, sex, marital status, income bracket, level of education, and occupation). Some may be delineated geographically (e.g., the South, the West, Western Europe, the Far East). For consumer products, in particular, psychographic segmentation is relevant. Psychographic segmentation is based on people's life-styles and their attitudes toward work, the family, the community, and the home.

The important thing to keep in mind is that a segmentation scheme is simply a way of grouping like buying units for the purpose of determining what products to offer them and what marketing strategies to formulate to assure success in turning potential demand into sales and profits. Market segmentation schemes thus provide the frameworks for formulating strategies.

The choice of a market segment is based on both identifying a significant pocket of demand and assessing the strength of competitive entries in that segment or space. If competitors have staked out strong positions in a space, it is clearly less attractive than spaces where there are no entrants or where the entrants are weak—that is, they are not satisfying market needs as well as it could be done. In market selection, then, one is always concerned with identifying market opportunities—i.e., sets of potential buyers with needs that are not being fully satisfied by competitors in the market.

As markets grow and mature, segmentation changes. Often there is a proliferation of market segments. Total demand becomes increasingly segmented, with product offerings and strategies for each segment being highly tailored to that segment's needs and buying behavior.

In a mature state, consumer goods markets in particular tend to be segmented psychographically, with subtle differences among segments regarding the meaning of the product. The car market is a case in point, with market segmentation based to a large extent on such matters of consumer psychology as status, life-style, and self-image.

Product Planning

Product planning and market selection go together in that the product form has to respond to the needs of a target market. Similarly, how we present the product in advertising and through personal selling serves to position it as being intended for certain types of potential buyers. By differentiating the product physically and by creating a certain image of it in the minds of buyers we may carve out for ourselves a market niche in which we enjoy a competitive edge.

Companies like Wang Laboratories and Digital Equipment Corporation that make and sell small computers design their products for particular applications in offices, plants, and laboratories. They tend to avoid competing head on with International Business Machines by preempting certain market niches in which they may take leading positions and leaving others to their giant competitor.

In the beer market some companies position their product in the higher-volume segments (e.g., "The beer to have when you're having more than one"). Other product offerings are targeted to those who are concerned about being overweight, those who associate beer drinking with social gatherings, or those who see it as a relaxant after hard physical work. To some extent such positioning is achieved by physical differentiation (e.g., light beer, regular beer, dark beer); to an even greater extent it may be achieved through advertising imaging which shows the product being consumed in one context or another.

The product—whether it is for industrial market or household consumption, whether it is a physical good or a service—must be perceived as a package of benefits which the buyer receives when he or she makes the purchase. The package of benefits includes the basic function which the product performs, the psychological needs it fulfills, the service that goes with it, and even the experience of shopping for it (for better or worse).

It is the *buyer's* perception of that package of benefits which is important, and different types of purchasers may place significantly different values on one dimension of the product package or another. The technical service, for example, that a large chemical manufacturer may offer its customers might have more value to its small accounts than to larger companies that have their own laboratories.

Moreover, how customers perceive the product package and value each of its several elements will change over time. As they become experienced in buying and using the product, the perceived value of product service, technical service, brand image, status appeals, and price will shift. They may become more or less important.

Perceived values will change, as well, with market conditions. A company buying stainless steel sheets, let's say, to make restaurant kitchen equipment may value highly the overnight delivery which a local steel warehouse distributor might offer when supplies are plentiful. In the face of steel shortages, however, that service may pale in importance compared with having some assurance of supply through buying direct from the steel mill.

We have focused so far on addressing product line offerings to market segments having certain identifiable needs, usage patterns, and buying behavior characteristics. The other side of the coin is that the product-market choice must be a right one for the seller. Does the company have the requisite resources to enter the market and compete successfully? Can it fund product development work, plant investments, advertising, and field sales and service? What does it "bring to the party" that competitors don't offer and may not be able to contribute?

Product-market choices must also be made with a concern for their impact on the company's total business. Will offering some new product or service cut into sales of our more profitable items? If that is so, is it important to go ahead to hold a market position against competitors who are ready to offer comparable new products? Will adding the new product help to build sales for other products we offer by attracting new customers? Will the new product maximize the utilization of our scarce resources, such as shelf space, factory capacity, or the skilled professionals that we have on our staff?

These are the kinds of questions managers might find it useful to ask to assess the product-market-company fit. The product might be right for the market but not for us; the product might be right for us, but the market may be limited and hard to find; the company-market match may be favorable, but the product may not meet a definable need.

Market selection and product planning decisions are crucial to the success of any organization. For this reason, it is often useful to invest money in market research to find out how markets may be usefully segmented, to determine buyer needs, and to assess competitors' strengths and weaknesses. (Market research is the subject of a later section in this book.) With or without the benefit of market research, these are the areas in which the hard questions lie—questions which the marketing manager must answer.

6

Gould, Inc.: Graphics Division

Ulrich E. Wiechmann • Ralph Z. Sorenson II

Mr. Willard C. Koepf, national sales manager of the Graphics Division of Gould, Inc., had been asked by corporate headquarters to review the marketing possibilities for the electrostatic printer Gould 4800 and to formulate a marketing plan for the 1969–1970 fiscal year. The printer, which was the division's only product, had been introduced 3 months earlier with high expectations at the Spring Joint Computer Conference in Boston. "Our feelings ranged from the belief that customers would break our door to take the device from our hands to the opinion of the engineers that the product was almost too good to be put on the market," Mr. Koepf commented.

So far, no orders for the printer had been received. During the computer show, however, potential end users had examined the product with interest, and the printer had found an extensive coverage in the trade press. Leading

Ulrich E. Wiechmann is an associate professor at the Harvard Graduate School of Business Administration. Ralph Z. Sorenson II is the president of Babson College.

original equipment manufacturers (OEMs), such as IBM, Honeywell, Burroughs, and Univac, had been equally interested in the product. None, however, had made a commitment to promote it to end users and to provide the necessary interfacing and software support. As he was thinking about the most suitable marketing approach for the printer, Mr. Koepf wondered particularly whether he should concentrate his marketing efforts on the OEMs or whether the Graphics Division should try to sell the product directly to end users.

Company Background

The Graphics Division in Cleveland, Ohio, was one of 26 quasi-independently operating divisions of Gould, Inc., a diversified concern resulting from a merger effective July 31, 1969, of Gould National Battery, Inc., and the Clevite Corporation.

Prior to the merger, the Graphics Division had been a department of Brush Instruments

Division of the former Clevite Corporation. Clevite, an old, well-established company, was manufacturing and marketing such diverse products as copper foil for printed circuits, engine bearings and bushings, hearing aids, and torpedos, as well as a wide array of high-precision data display instruments for scientific, industrial, and aerospace applications, such as oscillographs, biomedical recorders, and plotters.

The merger of Clevite and Gould National Battery, Inc., had been initiated by Gould's president, Mr. William T. Ylvisaker. He had been appointed chief executive of Gould National Battery late in 1967. Gould National Battery, founded in 1905, had relied mainly on the manufacturing and marketing of automotive and industrial batteries, with a minor part of its revenues coming from the sale of engine parts and air-oil-fuel filters to machinery manufacturers and the automotive aftermarket. In 1967, the company was generally considered an ailing member of a stagnant industry, facing a declining market share and a fall in earnings of 25 percent between 1962 and 1967.

To turn the company around, Mr. Ylvisaker looked for opportunities to broaden the base of Gould through a strategy of planned acquisitions of compatible businesses and emphasis on new-product development. "We sat down and asked ourselves: 'What is this company?' " one company officer said.

> The definition we came up with was not one of products or markets; we define our business in terms of technology. We thought that if we defined our business in terms of markets or products, we might finally find ourselves in a lot of unrelated technologies and be unable to stay in a leadership position. Since technology is usually the basis for new products, this could be most serious. I think it is harder to develop good technology than to revise a distribution system and a marketing organization. If you define your business in terms of technologies, you have a sounder basis for growth.
>
> This is really why the Clevite Corporation was attractive for us. While there was some similarity in

terms of markets served and products produced between Gould and Clevite, they were not serious direct competitors and were really different. . . .

> We are all committed to building a business on a good, sound, solid basis. Our financial goals are to maintain a 15 per cent growth in earnings per share over the next ten to fifteen years. To reach this goal requires two key things. (1) You must be willing to invest at that rate in new products and engineering, fixed assets and working capital. We are willing and able to do this. (2) You must be in markets that are growing at a rate of 15 per cent a year. But we aren't yet and we must be. Our major thrust, therefore, will most likely be in the electronics field in order to get that growth. Statistically, we stand a better chance if we emphasize the electronics. Certainly, one of the problems is to get into these growing markets.

The new electrostatic printer was seen by Gould's management as a way to enter the rapidly growing computer peripheral market. Gould envisaged the development of a complete line of computer peripheral devices and was prepared to invest up to $10 million in developing this line. Management was prepared to forgo immediate profits on new investments but expected that such investments should become profitable within at least 5 years.

The Electrostatic Printer

The Gould 4800, a machine of about the size of a teletype console, was a nonimpact printer using the technology of electrostatic printing.[1] It was designed as an output printing device for data from computers, magnetic tape, punched-card readers, cathode ray tube (CRT) memories, or telecommunication lines. It could print both alphanumeric characters and graphs at a speed of 4,800 86-character lines per minute, or the equivalent of one 8½ × 11 inch page per second. Exhibit 1 shows a picture of the Gould

[1] For details on printing technologies, see the appendix to this case.

EXHIBIT 1

GOULD® 4800

Gould 4800   electrostatic printer

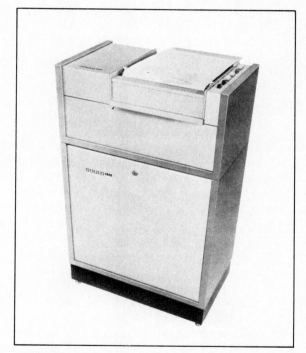

FEATURES

- 4800 lines/minute

- alphanumerics and graphics
- versatility of application
- built-in character generator-controller
- built-in control lines
- electrostatic printing—silent operation

- high-contrast smudge-proof hard copy
- programmed control of output forms
- minimum maintenance
- reliable low voltage operation

4800 together with some product information from Gould's sales catalog.

The printer was a "by-product" of the Brush Division's activity in the field of data display instruments. In the course of the development of high-speed oscillographs, Brush engineers had gotten the idea that the oscillograph technology they were working on could be used in the creation of a high-speed printer for which, they thought, a wide market would exist in view of the fact that the existing computer printing devices were working at a much lower speed than the data-processing units to which they were connected. Indeed, one of the most widely discussed problems in the computer industry was the relative slowness of print-out equipment compared with the speed of computers themselves.

Development work on the electrostatic printer was started in 1963. Initially, two engineers were engaged in it full time; in 1966 the development group was enlarged to four engineers. No formal budget had been established for the development work. Management's attitude, as one executive described it, had been "Just work on it and see what can be done." Total development costs, up to the market introduction in May 1969, amounted to roughly $500,000.

In 1968 a prototype of the printer had become ready, and shortly afterward the development group was separated from the Brush Division to form the Graphics Division, headed by a general manager, Mr. Koeblitz, who had been the engineering manager of the Brush Division for approximately 12 years. A national sales manager, Mr. Koepf, was hired. He had worked in computer-related industries for approximately 4 years.

With its printing speed of 4,800 lines per minute, the Gould 4800 was at least four times faster than conventional line printers used for computer output. In contrast to these conventional line printers, the Gould 4800 could also print any kind of graphic output, such as charts, graphs, line drawings, curves, and vectors. Exhibit 2 gives a sample of the range of possible output. Graphic output for engineering and scientific purposes was typically produced on high-precision, high-price *XY* plotters. The Gould 4800 printed graphic output 200 to 400 times faster than these plotters.

The major elements in the printing process of the Gould 4800 were an electromagnetic printing head and specially coated paper. Gould had applied for patents for both, but management of the Graphics Division thought that the process was not so unique that the patents could not be circumvented by competitors with similar technologies in less than 2 years.

The printing head contained a row of 600 styluses that could be selectively charged to 300 volts. As a web of the special paper passed beneath the styluses, the coating acquired an opposite electrical charge beneath each charged stylus. The charge then attracted a dark toner in a liquid suspension to form the characters as an array of black dots. The liquid evaporated, and the printed output came out dry. Since there were few moving parts and no printing hammers as in a conventional line printer, the Gould 4800 operated noiselessly and presented relatively fewer maintenance problems.

Like all nonimpact printers, the Gould 4800 produced only single copies at a time. Since specially coated paper had to be used, the output could not be printed on preprinted forms. The copies from Gould's printer were brilliant white with a high-gloss surface, like the paper used in oscillographs and Brush analog recorders. They had the standard letter size of 8½ × 11 inches, which the design engineers believed to be the most acceptable format. The cost of the paper to users was set at 4.2 cents per 8½ × 11 inch page. This compared with the 0.14 cent per page of plain one-ply tab paper used in conventional impact printers.

The paper supply for the Gould 4800 was from a 300-foot roll. The paper-feeding mechanism moved the paper at a continuous speed of 10 inches per second on the average. The

EXHIBIT 2
SAMPLE OUTPUT OF THE GOULD 4800

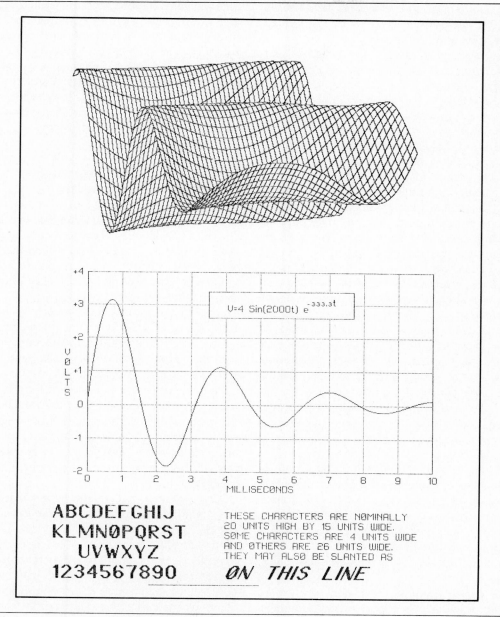

$$V = 4\,\sin(2000t)\,e^{-333.3t}$$

VOLTS

MILLISECONDS

ABCDEFGHIJ
KLMNØPQRST
UVWXYZ
1234567890

THESE CHARACTERS ARE NØMINALLY
20 UNITS HIGH BY 15 UNITS WIDE.
SØME CHARACTERS ARE 4 UNITS WIDE
AND ØTHERS ARE 26 UNITS WIDE.
THEY MAY ALSØ BE SLANTED AS

ØN THIS LINE

dominant form of paper supplied in conventional line printers came packaged "fanfolded," that is, in accordian fashion, with each sheet easily torn from every other sheet at the perforated creases that connected them.

The paper used in the Gould 4800 was unperforated, and so far, engineers had not developed a paper-output collecting, folding, or cutting device.

For use of the printer on-line with a computer, a translating or interface device was necessary to bring the data output of the computer into the format or arrangement desired by the user. The commercial utilization of the Gould 4800, therefore, required the creation of appropriate interfaces for computers of many manufacturers. It could also become necessary to create interfaces for different computer languages within each computer manufacturer's equipment. In addition, an extensive programming effort was required to develop software or application packages for various industry users. The prevailing experience in the computer industry had been that the end users of a particular piece of peripheral equipment like a printer or a card puncher were usually not willing to develop the necessary software or interfacing themselves. They expected this to be included in the "package." In addition, they were not favorably disposed to making modifications in existing programs to be able to run with a particular new peripheral device.

Production of the Gould 4800 was primarily an assembly operation and required the same technology as used in the Brush Instruments Division. Brush had free capacity available for up to 200 units per year which the Graphics Division could use to make the new product. Direct manufacturing costs amounted to roughly $4,500 per unit.

The paper used in the Gould 4800 was regarded as equally as important to the printing process as the hardware. Management therefore wanted to control the production of the paper to ensure reliability. A pilot paper coater had been built, but management had already started ordering items for a paper coater with a capacity of 50,000 rolls per shift. Completion of the facility, requiring an investment of roughly $450,000, was planned for February 1970. The present paper costs to users of 4.2 cents per sheet reflected the Graphics Division's own manufacturing costs. With the larger paper coater, management expected to reduce manufacturing costs to 3 cents per sheet.

The Market for Computer Peripheral Equipment

The computer peripheral market which the Graphics Division was about to enter had grown faster than the computer main-frame market in recent years. Although forecasts differed widely, the market was expected to continue its growth for some time to come.

The market was characterized by intense competition and rapid technological development. The major computer manufacturers, notably IBM, Honeywell, RCA, CDC, and NCR, were selling their own peripheral devices, competing against each other and against a number of smaller manufacturers such as Mohawk Data Sciences and Digitronics and against special-purpose terminal houses like Sanders Associates and Bunker-Ramo. Many new companies had recently been attracted to the peripheral equipment field.

Compatibility of the peripheral device with the communicating computer was a necessity and had been a major stumbling block to many of the smaller companies. To overcome this difficulty, a number of smaller companies with limited resources, e.g., Mohawk, had found it desirable to sell through one of the main-frame computer manufacturers. This approach relieved the peripheral company of the maintenance and marketing burden and enabled it to rely on the well-established customer relations of the computer manufacturer. It was realized, though, that total reliance on the marketing effort of the main-frame manufacturer might make it difficult for the peripheral company to establish an identity of its own in the end-use market.

Peripheral-equipment purchase decisions among end users were normally made by the data-processing department manager or an executive with similar functions. The orientation of this group, according to a recent study, was strongly toward their traditional suppliers, the computer manufacturers, among which IBM held the dominant position. Reluctance to "experiment" was widespread, notably with regard to devices that might present compatibility problems. A survey among 1,600 computer users conducted by The Diebold Group[2] revealed a decided preference for a single vendor of both the computer and peripheral equipment for 31 percent of the respondents, but 19 percent mentioned multivendor preference, and 50 percent remained uncommitted. As stated in the survey report, however, in cases where the main-frame manufacturer had all the desired peripheral equipment available, the user's expression of preference to use multiple vendors had to be taken with some precaution. Still, the rate of development of useful new peripheral products by new or non-main-frame manufacturers was so great that computer users generally felt it necessary to give serious consideration to these product sources.

The Market for Electrostatic Printers

Little market research had been undertaken prior to or during the development work for the Gould 4800. "The engineers relied more on their own feelings," one executive observed.

"Maybe they talked to some of the . . . people who service our own computer; but on the whole contacts with the computer industry have been minimal."

Even after the prototype had become ready, very little market information was gathered before the printer was introduced in 1969. Mr. Koepf explained:

> We are a very small division. From the very beginning, we were running the division almost like our own little business. We don't have the time and the money to do much research. There is no planning group, no research group like in some of the larger divisions of Gould. All the planning and budgeting work splits essentially between Bill Koeblitz, our General Manager, and myself. In early 1968, The Diebold Group made a study for us on the printer market. They had data on conventional printers but when it came to electrostatic printers, they had to guess. Electrostatic printing is entirely new. Ours is not a "me-too" product. So, it's very difficult to say anything really firm about the market. But everybody knows that existing printers are much too slow.

The Diebold Group had undertaken to estimate the market potential for high-speed nonimpact printers for the period 1968 to 1972. Their estimate, which was based on extensive industry surveys, amounted to a total of 14,000 units for the 1968–1972 time period and included thermographic, electrostatic, and electrographic equipment.[3] Direct-ink printers were not included because of their low speed. This forecast posed the question of what portion of the potential market for high-speed nonimpact printers could be expected for electrostatic devices. As noted by the consultants, the factor that was most likely to affect this determination was the degree of support that major OEMs would give to the electrostatic printing technology. The consultants were confident that at least one major OEM would complement its product line

---

[2]A major consulting company in the computer field.

[3]See the appendix to this case.

with an electrostatic printer. On the basis of this belief, they predicted that at least one-half the forecasted 14,000-unit market potential for high-speed nonimpact printers would be for electrostatic printers. The consultants assumed that 50 percent of the electrostatic market would subsequently go to this innovating OEM and thought it reasonable for Gould to obtain about 20 percent of the remaining market with an aggressive marketing policy.

So far, the Graphics Division had only one direct competitor, Varian Data Products, a smaller but well-known company manufacturing an electrostatic printer which was very similar in all its functional features to the Gould 4800. Varian had introduced its product in 1968 and tried to market it at prices between $15,000 and $18,000 direct to end users, with discounts of 30 and 40 percent offered to OEMs. Mr. Koepf thought that manufacturing costs for the Varian printer were higher than those for the Gould 4800. Paper costs to users were identical, i.e., 4.2 cents per 8½ × 11 inch page. Mr. Koepf believed that Varian was not an important factor in the market and that its product had serious operational problems. Mr. Koepf thought that Varian had sold only a few units.

The Graphics Division saw the Gould 4800 as a potential entrant into five basic functional areas of the information terminal market and into one broad area of miscellaneous new application not yet served by other devices: (1) computer line printer; (2) hard-copy printer of cathode ray tube (CRT) displays; (3) proof-copy or hard-copy printer for computer output to microfilm (COM) systems; (4) high-speed communications printer replacing teletype machines; (5) quick plotter from a computer-plotting program; and (6) in the miscellaneous area, servicing a multiplicity of scientific, medical, military, and commercial applications (like proofreading for computerized typesetters). Little information existed on the particular requirements for this last-mentioned market segment.

Line Printer Market

The line printer market represented by far the largest market segment under consideration. The Graphics Division estimated that about 8,000 line printers had been installed during fiscal year 1969, equivalent to a shipment value of $160 million, and that the market was growing at a rate of 10 to 15 percent per year.

Virtually every traditional computer installation used a line printer as its main print-out device, and all the OEMs carried such printers as part of their product line. The purchase price of these machines ranged from $11,500 (Mohawk, 750 lines per minute) to $64,000 (Mohawk, 1,250 lines per minute). They could be rented for a monthly fee including full maintenance ranging from $315 to $1,020; IBM, for example, charged $875 per month for its 1403/3 model (1,100 lines per minute).

The existing printers were usually capable of printing up to six copies simultaneously on ordinary tab paper. They could also easily accommodate special-purpose preprinted forms of different sizes and thicknesses. The most common paper width used was 14⅞ inches. Most users of line printers required multiple copies of their output, and, for cost reasons, these had to be simultaneously produced, rather than serially or off-line on copying machines. Preprinted forms were used extensively, especially by organizations such as banks, insurance companies, credit card companies, and magazine publishers. Programming a printer to produce forms was generally not regarded as an alternative to the use of preprinted forms.

The speed of all existing line printers was many times slower than the rate at which the computer processor could generate data. Multiprogramming techniques had been developed, however, permitting the processor to activate more than one printer at a time and thus reduce the users' problem with jobs previously limited by printer speed.

CRT Hard-Copy Market

The market for the Gould 4800 as a device for printing permanent copies of data displayed on CRT screens was regarded as one of the fastest-growing segments with an estimated annual growth of 30 to 40 percent. Shipments of CRT hard-copy printers in fiscal year 1969 were estimated at 700 units, or $5 million. Among the users of CRT hard-copy printers were banks, stockbrokers, insurance companies, and high-technology companies like aerospace firms that used CRTs for engineering purposes. In management's view, the almost perfectly silent operation of the Gould 4800, allowing its use in an office environment where the noise level had to be kept at a minimum, and the high printing speed, constrained only by the CRT or the telephone line, made the Gould 4800 well suited for application as a CRT hard-copy printer.

A number of CRT hard-copy printers were currently marketed by main-frame manufacturers and some of the larger computer peripheral manufacturers (IBM, 3M, Litton Industries, Beta Instruments Corporation). These machines used a thermographic or photographic process and were selling at user prices from $6,000 (3M) and $12,600 (Litton/Datalog) to $33,000 for a high-precision IBM machine. The printing costs of these devices were considerable, since specially coated paper had to be used; they ranged from roughly 12 cents (3M) to about 18 cents (IBM, Litton/Datalog) per copy. The machines currently being marketed generally gave a higher resolution[4] than the Gould 4800, which was of particular interest in engineering applications.

CRT Microfilm Market

The market for CRT microfilm printers was still a small segment of the computer peripheral market, but it was growing at a rate of 30 to 40

[4]That is, dots per inch, determining clarity and accuracy of output.

percent annually. In fiscal year 1969, about 100 units had been shipped, representing a value of roughly $15 million. The manufacturers of these machines were Kodak, 3M, and Datagraphics. The Gould 4800 was not a substitute for these devices but rather a supplement for high-speed paper output. Some of the CRT microfilm machines were also equipped for paper output, which they printed at the same speed as or at an even higher speed than the Gould 4800.

Communications Printer Market

The market for communications printers was dominated by the familiar teletypes, manufactured by a sizable number of specialized companies. More recently the traditional impact teletype had been supplemented by the Inktronic, using direct-ink printing technology. In fiscal year 1969, an estimated 30,000 teletypes had been shipped, representing a value of about $35 million. Management expected this market to grow by 10 to 15 percent annually.

Impact teletypes reaching a speed of 10 characters per second were selling for roughly $1,000 to users. There was at least one faster unit available, operating at 37 characters per second and priced at $3,600. Direct-ink printers had a speed of 250 characters per second and ranged between $5,000 and $7,000 in price. Both impact teletypes and direct-ink printers printed on ordinary paper. The average cost per page to users was 0.5 cent for impact printers and 0.8 cent for the Inktronic. The impact teletype could also be equipped for multiple copies.

Theoretically, the Gould 4800 could print several thousand characters per second as a communications printer. Printing at such a speed required, however, that a communications line be available which could transmit data at such a speed. So far, no equipment existed, either from a private company or from the Bell system, for transmitting faster than 2,000 bits per second, i.e., 250 characters per second, on dial-up lines. The smallest telephone charge for a dial-up line was for 3 minutes; thus at printing speeds of 250 characters per second, the telephone charges for one and ten pages (60 lines with 80 characters each) were the same, since neither took more than 3 minutes (for example, 65 cents for transmission between New York and Philadelphia at a rate of 65 cents for the first 3 minutes and 15 cents for each additional minute). An increase in the speed of transmission for dial-up lines to 3,600 bits per second (450 characters) by the end of 1969 and to 4,800 bits per second (600 characters) in 1971 was expected.

Privately leased transmission lines were available for transmitting up to 9,600 bits per second (1,200 characters). The cost of a private line was proportional to the length of the line and was a fixed monthly fee independent of usage. For example, the cost for a private line from New York to Philadelphia was about $350 per month.

Plotter Market

The sales volume of plotters in fiscal year 1969 had been estimated by management at $10 million, equivalent to shipments of roughly 500 units. It was expected that this segment would show an annual growth of 30 to 40 percent. In the judgment of Mr. Koepf, the Gould 4800 offered a number of advantages over the conventional digital _XY_ plotters, such as higher speed, more versatility because of symbol-plotting and character-printing ability, and less service requirements, since no ink and no moving pens as in _XY_ plotters were used. The Gould 4800, however, did not offer the precision of conventional plotters: the smallest plotting increment possible with the Gould 4800 was 12.5 milli-inches compared with 0.01 milli-inch obtainable from conventional plotters. Many plotter users also required a wider paper web than 8½ inches and the flexibility to use different plotting surfaces, e.g., translucent paper.

Users of plotters fell into two broad categories: (1) scientific and engineering users and (2) nonscientific or commercial users.

1. Scientific and engineering users were the most important group requiring computer graphics and plotting techniques. Companies and institutions in this group included automobile companies, aircraft and aerospace manufacturers, universities, and scientific laboratories. Computer-aided plottings were required in the generation of high-accuracy engineering designs or in the solution of complex problems such as the plotting of missile trajectories. Most of these users had considerable computer experience and close contact with computer main-frame manufacturers. They required high accuracy and extensive software support for the plotter to meet these frequently changing, sophisticated plotting needs. The initial purchase price of the plotter was a less important consideration for them than accuracy, versatility, and having an extensive software library. A number of large companies were currently serving this user group with digital _XY_ plotters. Among them IBM marketed plotters manufactured by California Computer Products, Inc., as part of IBM's full line of computers and peripheral devices.

2. Nonscientific, commercial users included companies and organizations requiring a plotter for fairly simple graphic representations of mathematical functions or time series (e.g., histograms, weekly or monthly sales and profit curves, line fitting). Minute accuracy was of less concern to this group of users. Their plotting needs appeared to be relatively stable over time and of limited sophistication. Consequently, it was expected that only a modest software library would be necessary. In the judgment of The Diebold Group, graphic output among commercial users of data-processing equipment was still in its very infancy, amounting to less than 1 percent of

total printing output. Commercial users seemed to be largely unaware of the potential applications for a plotting device. The Diebold Group expected, however, an increasing popularity in graphic data output, primarily due to the emergence on the market of graphic CRT terminals.

Initial Marketing Plans

Management of the Graphics Division believed that most printing and plotting would ultimately be nonimpact to meet "instant information" requirements, to keep down sound pollution, and to provide absolute reliability. The Gould 4800, in management's view, met these needs completely, and it was expected that the design would receive rapid technical acceptance in its first year of exposure.

Management's sales forecast provided for a total volume of $800,000 in fiscal year 1970, $2.5 million in fiscal year 1971, and $5 million in fiscal year 1972. Exhibit 3 shows a breakdown of sales expectations in 1970 by market segments.

The price to end users for the Gould 4800 had been set at $15,000 plus $4,000 for a character generator which was required to prevent excessive burdening of expensive computer memory space with output format instructions. Manufacturing costs of the character generator

EXHIBIT 3
SALES FORECAST FOR FISCAL YEAR 1970 BY MARKET SEGMENTS

Segments or application	Graphics Division sales volume	
	Dollars	**Units**
Line printer	420,000*	34
CRT hard copy	45,000	5
CRT microfilm	0	0
Teletype	40,000	4
Plotter	180,000	20
Miscellaneous	115,000†	10
Total	800,000	73

* Includes 34-character generators.
† Includes paper and supplies.
Source: Company records.

amounted to roughly $750. The price to OEMs was $9,900 for one to nine units of the Gould 4800 plus $3,200 for the character generator. Quantity discounts were available to OEMs, as shown in Exhibit 4. Mr. Koepf explained:

> When we initially priced the product we didn't really know what to charge and what the market would bear. We thought that a larger spread between the users' price and the OEM price than was usually available for peripheral equipment would get us the interest of the OEMs for the product.

EXHIBIT 4
OEM PRICE LIST

	Yearly unit quantity regularly scheduled	Unit price
Printer	1–9	$9,900
	10–19	9,158
	20–34	8,910
	35–49	8,663
	50–99	8,415
	100–499	8,168
	500–999	7,920
	1,000–up	7,670
Character generator		3,200

EXHIBIT 5
CONSULTANTS' ESTIMATE OF AVERAGE ANNUAL MARKETING AND SUPPORT COST SELLING DIRECT TO END USER MARKET

Sales considerations

Salaries of 20 salespeople (excluding commissions)	$200,000	
Employee benefits	50,000	
Overhead	150,000	
Travel and business expenses	120,000	
Recruiting costs (including relocation)	18,000	
Training program	20,000	
Trade shows	80,000	
Advertising	50,000	
Total average annual sales considerations		$ 688,000

Support considerations

Programming:		
Programmers salaries	$145,000	
Employee benefits	36,000	
Overhead	109,000	
Recruiting costs (including relocation)	13,000	
Total average annual programming considerations*		$ 303,000
Maintenance:		
Maintenance engineers salaries	$108,000	
Employee benefits	27,000	
Overhead	81,000	
Recruiting costs (including relocation)	4,000	
Training program	6,000	
Travel and business expenses	43,000	
Revenue from maintenance contracts	(70,000)	
Total average annual maintenance considerations		$ 199,000
Total average annual marketing and support costs		$1,190,000

*Cost of computer time required to test and "debug" program not included.
Source: The Diebold Group.

So far, no rental arrangements had been considered for the Gould 4800.

One of the major issues facing management was whether to concentrate the sales effort for the Gould 4800 on end users or on the OEMs.

The Diebold Group had prepared estimates for the required annual marketing expenditures for both approaches. A summary of their calculations is given in Exhibits 5 and 6. On the basis of the assumption that for direct selling to end users

EXHIBIT 6
CONSULTANTS' ESTIMATE OF AVERAGE ANNUAL MARKETING AND SUPPORT COSTS SELLING TO OEMS AND SYSTEMS HOUSES

Sales considerations:

Salaries of five salespeople, employee benefits, overhead, travel and business expenses, recruiting costs (including relocation), training program	$140,000

Programming considerations:†

Salaries, benefits, overhead, and recruiting costs	$ 60,000

Maintenance considerations:‡

Salaries, employee benefits, overhead, recruiting costs, training program, and travel	$ 54,000
Total average annual marketing and support costs	$254,000

* Based on the assumption that five salespeople would incur about 20 percent of costs shown in Exhibit 5.

† Based on 20 percent of programmers' expenses in Exhibit 5.

‡ Based on 20 percent of maintenance engineers' expenses (excluding revenue from maintenance contracts) in Exhibit 5.

Source: The Diebold Group.

a total sales force of 20 would be needed and that the Graphics Division would do all its programming, interfacing, and equipment maintenance itself, the consultants arrived at a figure of $1.19 million as the total annual marketing and support cost for selling direct to end users. For the approach of selling through OEMs and systems houses, they came up with a figure of $254,000 as the average annual marketing and support cost. This estimate was based on the assumption that a sales force of five would be sufficient and that the OEMs would shoulder a large part of the programming, interfacing, and maintenance burden. The consultants concluded that it would be advisable for the Graphics Division to concentrate its marketing effort on the OEMs and systems houses.

Management's initial thinking essentially followed this recommendation. Mr. Koepf explained:

> We just wanted to sell the machine; if you go directly to end users you must have all the answers on programming, cost, and interfacing. We aren't quite ready for this. We thought that our product is so good that the OEMs would take it and run with it. We wanted them to do our homework for us, that is, provide users with interfacing, software, and maintenance.

The initial market response had been slower than expected. End users, in spite of a high expressed interest, remained hesitant, and first discussions with OEMs had shown signs of reluctance to push the product before end user pull had built up. "It seems to be one of these fantastic, successful products which nobody wants to buy," one executive at Gould's headquarters commented. Mr. Koepf remarked:

> People don't like to be the first ones to try a new product. The problem is, the OEMs already sell printers and plotters.
>
> Our product doesn't do anything they can't do with their existing equipment; the only advantage we have is that we can do it faster. The OEMs we have talked to see that our printer may have market potential, but they don't see enough of it so that they would want to put the printer into their line. Perhaps we also weren't convincing enough in selling the product to them; we used to be an instruments company and we didn't have all the information on possible applications of the printer.
>
> Maybe we should concentrate more on end users. The OEMs told us: "Great, this is a wonderful machine; when you get some of our users interested come back and see us." It seems that you have to create a desire for your product among the end users to bring pressure on the OEMs to take it.

Appendix

Diagram of Printing Technologies

PRINTERS

IMPACT PRINTERS

Operation:
Each character printed separately as a hammer
strikes against an inked surface and the paper

Advantages:
Multiple copies printed simultaneously
Specially coated paper generally not required
Preprinted forms may be used

Disadvantages:
Noise
Maintenance problems because of many
moving parts

SERIAL PRINTERS

Operation:
Character types on hammer or
drum transverse paper;
columns printed sequentially

Speed:
10 to 37 characters per second

Principal application:
Telecommunication,
time–sharing,
low–cost computers

PARALLEL PRINTERS (line printers)

Operation:
Each column to be printed has
its own set of character types,
which allows simultaneous
printing of columns

Speed:
330 to 1650 characters
per second

Principal application:
Most widely used printing device
for high-speed computers

ELECTROGRAPHIC PRINTER

Operation:
Electric current is passed
through chemically treated
paper to burn in the image of
each character

Speed:
N. A.

Note: The technique has fallen
into disfavor because the
burning of paper produces
odor and hazardous gases

NONIMPACT PRINTERS

Operation:
Various nonmechanical printing techniques
(see below)

Advantages:
Generally faster than impact printers
Little or no noise
No or few moving parts; fewer
maintenance problems

Disadvantages:
Multiple copies not produced simultaneously
With one exception, special
(more expensive) paper needed

DIRECT INK PRINTER ("Inktronic")

Operation:
Each character is written on the
page by a burst of magnetically
deflected ink dots; special paper
not needed

Speed:
120 to 250 characters per
second; may still be increased

Principal application:
Telecommunication

ELECTROSTATIC PRINTER

Operation:
Characters are written by
bringing electrostatic charges
on dialectrically coated paper

Speed:
6900 characters per second
(Gould)

Principal application: ?

THERMOGRAPHIC PRINTER

Operation:
Characters are printed by
heating to between 120° and
200°F; specially treated paper

Speed:
300 characters per second; may
be increased to 3200 characters
per second without major
development work

Principal application:
CRT: hard copy output

7

Coolidge Bank and Trust Company

Christopher H. Lovelock

Mr. Milton Adess, president of the Coolidge Bank and Trust Company of Watertown, Massachusetts, was debating whether or not his bank should introduce NOW accounts.

Although modest in size, Coolidge had gained a national reputation for its innovative approach to banking. Among other things, it had pioneered in the development of no-service-charge checking accounts. In 1972, however, a mutual savings bank in Worcester, Massachusetts, had begun offering negotiable order of withdrawal (NOW) accounts, which were effectively interest-bearing checking accounts. This concept was soon adopted by a number of other banks in Massachusetts. In the spring of 1974, Coolidge management recognized that some of their bank's large personal checking depositors

Christopher H. Lovelock is an associate professor at the Harvard Graduate School of Business Administration.

were taking their business to NOW accounts at competing banks.

Banking in Massachusetts

Studies by the Federal Bank of Boston identified the existence of eight major banking markets in Massachusetts in the early 1970s. The largest of these, the Boston market, covered nearly all of eastern Massachusetts, extending from a few towns in southern New Hampshire, whose residents worked in the Boston area, down to the neck of Cape Cod. The wide geographic expanse of this market reflected Boston's position as the cultural and economic hub of New England as well as its role as the governmental center of the Commonwealth of Massachusetts.

Observers described the Boston retail banking market as "very competitive." This growing market had been the scene of active developments in recent years. The city of Boston was the home of a number of large and powerful banking organizations, headed by the First National Bank of Boston, the nation's tenth largest correspondent bank. As commuting into metropolitan Boston from the outlying areas had increased, banks located in this area had become alternative sources of banking to more people.

While the population of metropolitan Boston was approximately 2.8 million in 1974, that of the Boston banking market was estimated by the Federal Reserve Bank at 3.8 million. The total population of Massachusetts was 5.8 million.

State banking laws in Massachusetts restricted the operations of individual commercial banks to a single county. Banks were not allowed to open new branches or merge with other banks outside the county in which the home office was located. However, subject to regulatory approval, a bank holding company could acquire another bank anywhere in the state. This provided a means of circumventing the county-branching restrictions. Many large Boston-based banks had recently formed holding companies which allowed them to take advantage of this situation, although subsidiary banks retained separate identities in each county. In the long run, observers anticipated that banking laws would be amended to permit statewide branch banking in Massachusetts.

The Boston banking market covered major portions of five of Massachusetts' 14 counties. Suffolk County comprised the cities of Boston, Revere, Winthrop, and Chelsea; Essex County comprised the so-called "North Shore" communities running up to the New Hampshire border; Middlesex, the most populous county in the state, included Cambridge, Watertown, and a large number of towns and cities west of Boston; gerrymandered Norfolk County included Brookline and many communities south and west of Boston; while Plymouth County extended south

of Norfolk down toward Cape Cod (Exhibit 1).

Although not direct competitors in all commercial bank services, thrift institutions[1] in Massachusetts competed vigorously with commercial banks for savings deposits and were also important lenders of consumer credit. The introduction of NOW accounts by mutual savings banks in 1972 had enabled them to offer a substitute for commercial-bank demand deposits (checking accounts). In January 1974, the right to offer NOW accounts was extended to savings and loan associations, cooperative banks, and also commercial banks.

In mid-1974, there were 167 mutual savings banks operating in Massachusetts, plus 179 savings and loan associations and cooperative banks. These institutions controlled approximately $18.8 billion in total deposits, exceeding the total deposits of the state's 153 commercial banks.

Competition in Retail Banking

Prior to the advent of "free" checking in the mid-1960s, retail banking institutions in Massachusetts and other states had avoided any significant price competition.

It was generally assumed that customers selected their banks primarily on the basis of convenience and, to a lesser extent, image. An article in the *New England Economic Review* noted:[2]

[1]The term *thrift institutions* comprised mutual savings banks, savings and loan associations, and cooperative banks. These were distinguished from commercial banks in that only the latter had authority to accept demand deposits (i.e., checking accounts) or make commercial loans. The three types of thrift institutions fulfilled essentially similar banking functions, and the primary differences between them lay in the source of their charters and whether they were regulated and insured by state or federal authorities.

[2]Steven J. Weiss, "Commercial Bank Price Competition: The Case of 'Free' Checking Accounts," *New England Economic Review*, September–October 1969.

EXHIBIT 1
CITIES AND COUNTIES IN EASTERN MASSACHUSETTS

Many banks have found that they can draw a larger volume of customers by increasing the accessibility of their facilities, for example by establishing branch offices in convenient locations, by adding parking space or opening drive-in windows, or by extending banking hours. Advertising is also an important mode of competition. Through creative use of the media, some banks have achieved an attractive image, stressing their friendly or personal services, or their status as a small bank underdog—trying harder, of course. Advertising campaigns are often combined with such gimmicks as baby photo contests, washing the windshields of customers' cars, or a wide variety of promotional giveaway offers to new customers, ranging from flatware to thermal blankets. Building attractive offices, adopting modern logos and offering "beautiful" checks are other items in the repertoire of appeals to retail customers.

Price competition, by contrast, was rare. In any given region, the prices of retail banking services (e.g., loan rates, checking account service charges, and other fees) had tended to settle at a competitive rate that was relatively uniform among all banks in the area, with only minor deviations in evidence. Price competition on a broad scale was restrained not only by a plethora of state and federal regulations designed to protect bank solvency but also by customary industry practices and widespread distaste for "price-cutting" in banking circles. Coolidge Bank had shattered this situation in 1964 by introducing, and vigorously promoting, the concept of no-service-charge checking accounts.

The Growth of Coolidge Bank

The Coolidge Bank and Trust Company[3] received its charter from the Commonwealth of Massachusetts in July 1960. It was founded by a

[3]The bank was named after one of the seventeenth-century founders of Watertown.

group of merchants and businesspeople who, dissatisfied with the quality of service provided by the local bank in Watertown (a suburb of Boston), resolved to start their own.

The leader of this group, Mr. Milton Adess, became the president of the new bank. Mr. Adess himself had no previous banking background. As a young man during the Depression, he had worked as a Fuller Brush salesperson. From there, he went into retailing and subsequently built up a successful hardware business.

Coolidge Bank opened for service in a former store in December 1960 with a staff of 12 people. Initially, the operation was managed by the executive vice president, a former Rhode Island banker with 21 years' experience who had been recommended by one of the large Boston banks. However, after a year, this individual left Coolidge, and Mr. Adess, in his own words, "offered to come in and just watch the store."

Looking back, many years later, Mr. Adess discussed the background he brought to banking.

> I didn't know a thing about banking. I took a few AIB courses at night and learned a little bit about the language, but I certainly don't claim—even today—to have a strong banking background. I know a little about operations, but my forte is really marketing and loans. It's more of a straight businessman's view of what should be done.

Over the years, the president said, Coolidge had built up a strong professional management group with skills complementing his own. Regarding the bank's philosophy, he observed:

> We look at banking as another business and money as another commodity. We have one color to offer—green. And it's very much like selling any other commodity: we're selling money. And I've always been convinced that the individual or company who brings the best product to the public at the lowest possible price usually does very, very well.

The challenge during the bank's first years

was to develop an asset base since—as Mr. Adess noted—the bank's lending ability was limited by the size of its capital.

> I devoted half my time in the first formative year to just making cold calls. Strangely enough, a couple of my directors who are among our largest customers came as a result of those cold calls. We went out and knocked on doors, we got all our friends and cousins and everyone we could possibly grasp by the lapels and drag into the bank to open up an account of one sort or another, either savings or business.
>
> For the convenience of the public, we immediately started opening at 8 o'clock in the morning, rather than 9. And we extended the hours of banking. We were the first commercial bank to open Saturday mornings. We felt that Saturday mornings were times when the public, as a whole, had their leisure hours and were able to do their banking or sit down and talk to a bank loan officer.

Other early innovations for Coolidge included becoming the first bank in the Boston area to pay interest on Christmas Club accounts as well as the first to pay postage both ways for bank-by-mail accounts. Coolidge also reduced service charges for business checking accounts by one-third. Reproductions of billboards advertising these and later innovations are shown in Exhibit 2.

No-Service-Charge Checking

From total assets of $4 million at the end of its first year, "which was quite amazing to our friendly competitors and bankers in Boston," Coolidge Bank's asset base grew steadily, reaching some $12 million by the end of 1964. However, this still left Coolidge a very small bank by the standards of the major Boston banks, whose assets were in the hundreds of millions and higher.

During 1964, Coolidge began testing a radical departure in banking practice: no-service-charge (NSC) personal checking. Coolidge management had decided that the way to compete

with the giants was, in Mr. Adess's words, "by trying to use our old hardware efforts—bring the best product to the people at the lowest possible cost." Commented the president:

> After doing an in-depth statistical study, we decided that service charges on personal checking accounts were really not necessary to operate a bank successfully. I didn't think that the profit picture of a bank required service charges—and still don't!
>
> I thought it was a little unusual, really, that for all these years banks had been charging you for the privilege of leaving your money in their bank so that they could lend it out and make money on it. Now if you're going to be good enough to deposit your money with us, and we can make money on your money, why should we charge you for that privilege?
>
> Well, I thought of a plan in 1963 and it took me close to a year and a half to convince my Board, because it was really breaking all existing banking principles. And when our friendly competitors in Boston heard about our plan, their reaction was one of amazement. I received many telephone calls with gloomy forecasts that eliminating service charges on personal checking accounts would result in disaster. They said, "Do you realize what service charges amount to in banks?" And my response was, "Look, I don't know what your service charges amount to, but I know that mine don't mean too much because we haven't got very many customers!"

After preliminary testing, Coolidge adopted NSC checking for all personal checking accounts in 1965, requiring a $100 minimum balance. After promoting this concept through billboards and newspapers, a limited advertising budget was assigned to WEEI, a talk-show radio station. The response to the radio advertising was described as "astounding." Coolidge Bank started getting accounts from "every city, town and hamlet in the state" and at one point, before the competition began following suit, was opening up to 200 accounts a day.

Many other banks soon followed Coolidge's lead, and within a few years NSC checking had become widespread in the Boston area. In 1969,

EXHIBIT 2
COOLIDGE BANK BILLBOARDS, 1960–1970

Source: Coolidge Bank, Annual Report 1970.

Coolidge went one better, becoming the first to offer genuinely free checking by dropping its $100 minimum balance requirement.

A subsequent survey by the Federal Reserve Bank of Boston indicated that Coolidge's success in attracting new accounts as a result of its NSC plan had been replicated by many other banks in New England, mostly fairly new ones, which had been the first to offer NSC accounts in their local area.

Other Marketing Activities at Coolidge

Other innovations promoted by the bank included a program to market the American Express Gold Card—which carried a $2,000 credit line and was issued only through banks—to graduating M.B.A. students with verified job offers. Coolidge promoted this concept to business school students nationwide (and later to medical and dental students) and before long became the second largest retailer of such cards in the United States.

Beginning in late 1971, Coolidge introduced its *Cool Cash* concept by installing automated banking consoles, termed *Cool-O-Mats*, outside certain branches. These machines effectively provided 24-hour, 7-day banking transaction services for customers and were more sophisticated than existing cash-dispensing machines (which had been in use in Britain since 1967 and in the United States since 1969). Coolidge was the first bank in the Boston area to install automatic "total tellers," capable of performing the same range of banking transactions as a human teller. It promoted them aggressively, and by 1973 its Harvard Square machines were the most heavily used in the country.

Despite some early mechanical problems, later resolved, the Coolidge machines had generally performed well. Mr. Adess conceded that there had been occasional vandalism. "We've had some strange people in the Harvard Square area who poured bottles of Coke into the machines, but security has not been a problem." In an overall view, he saw automatic tellers as a major opportunity to offer the public greater convenience.

Over the years, Coolidge had experimented with a number of communications approaches, including on-campus representatives, direct mail ("very expensive"), television ("outlandishly expensive"), newspapers, billboards, and radio. Commented Mr. Adess:

> I found that the greatest response came from radio. We checked this. Every new account was asked, "How did you happen to open an account at Coolidge?" And the greatest response came from talk programs. At one time, we were on three or four stations in the Boston area.
>
> We haven't had a direct mail piece now for

EXHIBIT 3
COOLIDGE BANK AND TRUST COMPANY: YEAR-END DEPOSITS ($ MILLION), 1960–1973

	Demand deposits*	Time deposits*	Total deposits†
1960	0.4	0.2	0.8
1961	1.9	1.0	3.5
1962	2.7	1.9	5.7
1963	3.8	3.0	8.0
1964	4.2	3.9	10.2
1965	6.7	5.4	13.9
1966	9.3	7.6	18.9
1967	16.2	10.7	29.8
1968	24.2	15.8	44.3
1969	25.4	11.1	44.3
1970	27.9	22.5	61.2
1971‡	43.1	29.9	84.8
1972	51.7	32.5	94.2
1973	54.5	46.1	113.6

* Deposits of individuals, partnerships, and corporations.

† Total deposits included deposits of the U.S. government ($1.7 million in 1973), of states and political subdivisions ($9.6 million in 1973), and of commercial banks, as well as certified and officers' checks.

‡ Coolidge acquired two other banks in 1971.

Source: Year-end reports by Coolidge Bank to FDIC.

years. We went out of the newspaper business. Our response from local newspapers has been minimal. Large Boston newspapers are very expensive and you're competing with some very big people in there.

When you buy that minute on the radio, that's yours. And if that man—or woman—is driving in his car, or listening to that program at home, you've got his ear. And the results for us have been really great. Very, very good.

Stimulated by a combination of innovative approaches to banking and aggressive advertising. Coolidge's deposits and assets grew rapidly (Exhibit 3). Although a holding company, First Coolidge Corporation, had been organized in 1970 to acquire the assets of Coolidge Bank and Trust Company, no attempt had been made to acquire subsidiaries outside Middlesex County. Nevertheless, Coolidge had succeeded in drawing some deposits not only from other parts of

Massachusetts but also from throughout the United States and even from depositors resident abroad.

Partly responsible for the growth in Coolidge assets and deposits were two mergers and the addition of several new offices. Branches were opened in Watertown in 1962 and in Cambridge in 1964, 1967, and 1970. In 1970 the bank also opened an attractive new four-story headquarters in Watertown Square, replacing its existing office there. The year 1971 was a particularly busy year for expansion. In April, Coolidge acquired the Industrial Bank & Trust Company of Everett, and in July it acquired the Arlington National Bank, with offices in Arlington, Lexington, and Bedford. In that same year, the bank moved its Harvard Square, Cam-

bridge, office from a temporary location in a large trailer into a gaily painted former garage. In Milton Adess's words, this was all part of Coolidge's attempt to "get away from that cold, granite-faced banker image that banking seems to have acquired over the years."

Coolidge Bank in 1974[4]

By mid-1973, the First Coolidge Corporation ranked as the ninth largest commercial banking organization in the Boston banking market (Exhibit 4). Its operating income in 1973 exceed-

[4]Certain nonpublished data in the balance of the case are either disguised or approximations.

EXHIBIT 4
BOSTON BANKING MARKET, JUNE 30, 1973

	Organization	No. of offices	Total deposits		Demand deposits <$20,000 (6/30/72)	
			$ million	%	$ million	%
1	First National Boston Corp.	42	3,137.8	30.7	202.3	15.3
2	Shawmut Association, Inc.	104	1,520.5	14.9	191.3	14.5
3	State Street Boston Financial Corp.	34	1,169.2	11.4	103.8	7.9
4	Baystate Corp.	125	1,138.4	11.1	239.9	18.2
5	New England Merchants Company, Inc.	17	921.2	9.0	72.7	5.5
6	Arltru Bancorporation	14	242.5	2.4	26.0	2.0
7	Multibank Financial Corp.	35	199.1	1.9	46.5	3.5
8	Essex Bancorp	14	118.2	1.2	26.4	2.0
9	First Coolidge Corp.	9	94.9	0.9	28.5	2.2
10	UST Corp.	9	93.3	0.9	21.6	1.6
11	Framingham Financial	15	87.2	0.9	19.4	1.5
12	Charterbank, Inc.	13	78.2	0.8	19.4	1.5
13	Atlantic Corp.	5	73.2	0.7	7.9	0.6
14	Hancock Group	14	68.3	0.7	21.5	1.6
15	Rockland Trust	15	68.2	0.7	22.7	1.7
16	Massachusetts Bay Bancorp	8	67.5	0.7	10.4	0.8
17	Security National Bank	9	66.1	0.6	14.4	1.1
18	Harbor National Bank	3	65.1	0.6	4.4	0.3
19	Commonwealth National Corp.	8	57.9	0.6	11.3	0.9
20	New England Bancorp.	15	53.4	0.5	12.9	1.0
	Next 60 banking organizations	150	491.0	8.8	220.8	17.0
	Total	658	10,220.7	100.0	1328.4	100.0

Source: Federal Reserve Bank of Boston, *Research Report* 59.

ed $9 million and net income was some $668, 000 (Exhibit 5), while year-end assets stood at $127 million (Exhibit 6).

In early 1974, the Coolidge Bank and Trust Company had a total staff of 201. There were 37 officers of the bank, headed by the president and executive vice president. Most of the senior officers had over 15 years' professional banking experience.

Five of the bank's nine offices were located in the densely populated cities of Cambridge and

Watertown. Although five-sixths of its personal checking account holders in the Boston area resided in Middlesex County, Coolidge also drew a number of accounts from residents of neighboring counties, notably Suffolk. This was true of savings accounts too.

Coolidge had about 100,000 accounts of all categories. About 70 percent of these were personal checking accounts, while 23 percent were regular savings accounts held by individuals. There were no charges for transactions in

EXHIBIT 5
FIRST COOLIDGE CORPORATION: CONSOLIDATED STATEMENT OF INCOME FOR THE YEARS ENDED DECEMBER 31, 1973 AND 1972

	1973	1972
Operating income:		
Interest on loans	$7,952,215	$6,210,930
Interest and dividends on securities:		
U.S. government securities	304,233	277,300
Obligations of state and political subdivisions	199,672	332,103
Other securities	59,601	10,331
Other operating income	732,947	587,376
Total	9,248,668	7,418,040
Operating expenses:		
Salaries	1,895,640	1,705,963
Other employee benefits	159,723	203,117
Interest	2,471,277	1,790,298
Occupancy expense of bank premises	435,340	461,532
Loan loss provision (Note 4*)	626,228	451,860
Other operating expense	2,476,142	2,268,194
Total	8,064,350	6,880,964
Income before income taxes and securities gains	1,184,318	537,076
Less applicable income taxes (Note 6*):		
Current	178,299	(508,588)
Deferred	340,169	425,703
	518,398	(82,885)
Income before securities gains	665,920	619,961
Securities gains, less applicable income taxes of $2,158 and $41,785	1,843	35,737
Net income	$ 667,763	$ 655,698
Earning data per common share (based on 1,435,180 shares):		
Income before income taxes and securities gains	$ .83	$ .37
Applicable income taxes	(.37)	.06
Income before securities gains	.46	.43
Securities gains, less applicable income taxes	.01	.03
Net income	$ .47	$ .46

* Notes to financial statement not shown here.
Source: First Coolidge Corporation, *Annual Report,* 1973.

EXHIBIT 6
FIRST COOLIDGE CORPORATION: CONSOLIDATED
STATEMENT OF CONDITION, DECEMBER 31, 1973
AND 1972

	1973	1972
Assets:		
Cash and due from banks	$ 14,175,427	$ 12,911,111
Investment securities (Note 2*):		
U.S. government obligations	5,009,926	5,049,377
Obligations of state and political subdivisions	8,949,981	3,516,426
Other securities	1,237,556	686,252
Total investment securities	15,197,463	9,252,055
Loans	89,803,957	78,335,088
Federal funds sold		800,000
Bank premises and equipment (Note 3*)	4,247,813	4,254,904
Customers' liability under letters of credit	2,528,392	3,404,040
Accrued interest receivable	657,558	375,564
Other assets and deferred charges	558,277	1,726,388
Total	$127,168,887	$111,059,150
Liabilities and capital:		
Demand deposits	$ 60,944,902	$ 57,722,105
Time deposits	52,576,676	36,186,015
Federal funds purchased		2,000,000
Unearned income	1,965,975	1,804,323
Letters of credit outstanding	2,528,392	3,404,040
Other liabilities	804,708	1,637,124
Total liabilities	118,820,653	102,753,607
Reserve for loan losses (Note 4*)	882,989	882,989
Capital funds:		
Capital debentures (Note 5*)	190,000	241,000
Stockholders equity:		
Common stock, $0.60 par value, 2,000,000 shares authorized, 1,435,180 shares issued and outstanding	861,108	861,108
Surplus	5,645,020	5,645,020
Undivided profits	769,117	675,426
Total stockholders' equity	7,275,245	7,181,554
Total capital funds	7,465,245	7,422,554
Total	$127,168,887	$111,059,150

* Notes to financial statement not shown here.
Source: First Coolidge Corporation, *Annual Report,* 1973.

either type of account. Savings account holders maintained a small passbook which was updated every time they made a deposit or withdrawal, and they received 5 percent interest on the outstanding balance. Management believed that a high proportion of their savings account holders also maintained checking accounts at Coolidge. Other types of consumer deposits included 90-day notice savings accounts and longer-term savings certificates of deposit, all of which paid higher interest rates. Coolidge was more retail-oriented than most commercial banks, and accounts held by businesses represented only a small proportion of the total; however, the value of their deposits was quite substantial (Exhibit 7).

One significant difference between demand and time deposits was the reserve requirements.

EXHIBIT 7
COOLIDGE BANK AND TRUST COMPANY: DISTRIBUTION OF ACCOUNTS BY TYPE AND DEPOSIT VOLUME, MID-1974

Category	Percent of accounts	Percent of dollar deposits
Checking:		
Government	*	2
Business	4	22
Personal	70	26
Savings:		
Regular savings	23	24
Notice savings	*	3
Savings certificates of deposit	3	11
Commercial certificates of deposit	*	12
	100	100

* Less than 1 percent.
Source: Coolidge Bank records (disguised data).

Under Massachusetts law, not more than 85 percent of demand deposits (i.e., checking accounts) could be reinvested by banks, whereas they were free to reinvest 100 percent of time and savings deposits.[5] NOW accounts were treated as time and savings deposits. Like most banks, Coolidge maintained cash balances and deposits with other banks exceeding this legal minimum. The treasurer indicated that as of mid-1974, Coolidge was realizing an average yield on loans and securities of around 9½ percent.

The Competitive Situation

Coolidge was one of 32 commercial banks and some 60 thrift banks in Middlesex County. Management saw the principal competition as banks with branches in the southeastern part of the county. A 1973 survey showed that Coo-

[5]Demand deposit reserve requirements were 20 percent in the city of Boston. Commercial banks which were members of the Federal Reserve System (Coolidge was not) had a 3 percent reserve requirement on time and savings deposits.

lidge and two other commercial banks—Harvard Trust Company ($264 million in assets, 13 branches) and Middlesex Bank N.A. ($302 million in assets, 29 branches)—each had approximately 11 percent of the personal checking account market in Middlesex. Another significant competitor was Newton-Waltham Bank & Trust Company ($236 million in assets, 21 branches), with an estimated 8 percent of this market. These three competing banks were all subsidiaries of the Baystate Corporation, a Boston-based bank holding company. A fourth competitor, County Bank N.A. (11 branches, $171 million in assets), was a subsidiary of the Shawmut Association, Inc. Profiles of the personal checking customer base served by Coolidge and other selected Middlesex banks are shown in Exhibit 8.

Where savings accounts were concerned, competition was much stronger, coming from both thrift institutions and other commercial banks. Coolidge's market share of regular savings accounts was believed to be 1 to 2 percent for the county as a whole. Thrift institutions had an advantage in that they could pay 5¼ percent on passbook savings versus the 5 percent legal

EXHIBIT 8
CONSUMER ACCOUNT HOLDER PROFILES OF BOSTON AREA BANKS, COOLIDGE BANK, AND SELECTED COMPETITORS

	Income, $ thousand					Age					
	<5	5-10	10-15	15-25	>25	18-24	25-34	35-44	45-54	55-64	65+
All Boston area checking accounts	9.5%	25.4%	32.1%	24.4%	8.7%	12.6%	27.3%	20.2%	18.7%	11.5%	9.7%
Individual bank profiles:											
Coolidge Bank	13.6	21.4	31.4	25.7	7.9	19.1	47.1	15.3	10.2	5.7	2.5
Harvard Trust	12.0	28.0	22.7	28.7	8.7	17.9	31.5	19.1	14.2	8.6	8.6
Middlesex Bank	10.2	32.3	37.8	17.3	2.4	10.6	17.7	25.5	20.6	14.2	11.3
Newton-Waltham Bank	4.0	20.8	29.7	30.7	14.9	11.7	20.7	26.1	19.8	9.9	11.7
All Boston area savings accounts	10.9	26.7	31.6	23.0	7.8	12.8	25.5	19.4	18.9	12.6	10.9

	Marital status			Education				
	Married	Single	Other	Some high school	High school graduate	Some college	College graduate	Postgrad work
All Boston area checking accounts	70.3%	18.4%	11.3%	6.8%	25.5%	25.3%	21.3%	21.0%
Individual bank profiles:								
Coolidge Bank	57.6	32.9	9.5	3.8	14.0	17.2	23.6	41.4
Harvard Trust	64.6	26.8	8.5	3.0	12.2	23.8	19.5	41.5
Middlesex Bank	77.3	10.6	12.1	10.0	40.0	23.5	13.6	12.9
Newton-Waltham Bank	73.2	13.4	13.4	7.2	17.1	23.4	27.9	24.3
All Boston area savings accounts	69.5	18.3	12.1	9.1	27.6	24.9	19.9	18.6

Source: Survey conducted for Coolidge Bank and Trust Company, mid-1973.

maximum payable by commercial banks. Many of the thrift banks had multiple branches, and a number were active in marketing their services.

Most of the locations served by a Coolidge branch were populated by several competing banks. The extreme example was at Harvard Square in Cambridge, where, including Coolidge, four commercial banks and three thrift banks could be found within a 200-yard radius.

Bank Consumers

A large-scale consumer survey in the Boston area found that nearly 82 percent of the respon-

dents maintained a checking account, while some 87 percent had savings accounts. However, there were significant variations in the pattern of checking and savings account ownership among households with different demographic characteristics (Exhibit 9).

In general, the survey found that the respondents were more satisfied with their savings account bank than they were with their checking account bank. "Need better hours" and "poor personnel" were the principal complaints for both types of bank. About 10 percent of the respondents had switched their accounts to different banks during the past year, but moving

EXHIBIT 9
POSSESSION OF CHECKING AND SAVINGS ACCOUNTS IN THE BOSTON AREA BY DEMOGRAPHIC SEGMENTS

Do you and your family currently have a checking account/savings account?

	Percent responding yes	
	Checking account	**Savings account**
All Boston area	81.8	86.9
Age:		
19–24	78.1	83.8
25–34	87.7	86.7
35–44	85.6	87.2
45–54	82.6	88.9
55–64	78.7	90.8
65+	69.0	83.9
Marital status:		
Married	84.9	89.1
Single	79.1	84.0
Other	69.5	80.2
Education:		
Not high school graduate	55.1	78.0
High school graduate	72.6	83.6
Some college	85.5	88.9
College graduate	92.6	91.6
Postgraduate work	96.7	90.7
Income:		
<$5,000	59.8	73.2
$5,000–10,000	73.2	81.6
$10,000–15,000	87.3	91.2
$15,000–25,000	95.1	94.7
$25,000+	98.8	94.7

Source: Survey conducted for Coolidge Bank, mid-1973.

to a new house was given as a reason more frequently than dissatisfaction or ability to obtain a "better deal" at another bank. "Good service" was the most frequently cited reason for recommending a checking account bank, while "good rates" was cited most often for savings account banks (Exhibit 10).

In terms of location, branches close to home were preferred to those nearer to work. Of the respondents with personal checking accounts, 50 percent said that the branch they used most often was closer to home than to work, 24 percent said the opposite, 16 percent said it was about equidistant, while 10 percent said they banked by mail. People in lower income and educational brackets were somewhat more likely to use a branch nearer home, while single people showed a greater tendency to patronize a bank near their work or to bank by mail than the sample as a whole.

The Advent of NOW Accounts

Negotiable order of withdrawal (NOW) accounts originated as a device to expand the ability of mutual savings banks to attract deposits.

The first attempt to obtain regulatory approval of NOW accounts in the United States was made in July 1970 by the Consumers Savings Bank of Worcester, Massachusetts. The bank filed a plan with the state banking commissioner to allow its savings account customers to withdraw funds by means of a negotiable order, similar to a check, instead of presenting a passbook. Although the commissioner denied this application, a suit brought by Consumers Savings later resulted in a ruling in the bank's favor by the Massachusetts Supreme Judicial Court.

On June 12, 1972, Consumers Savings began offering NOW accounts, paying the maximum legal interest rate of 5¼ percent and charging 15 cents for each withdrawal order. Ten other mutual savings banks followed suit in August 1972. The following month, after it had been established that New Hampshire law was similar to Massachusetts law, savings banks in New Hampshire began offering their own version of NOW accounts, paying a 4 percent interest rate but making no charge for withdrawals.

NOW accounts were soon adopted by the other mutual savings banks in the two states and attracted significant deposits. However, commercial banks saw these accounts as an unfair advantage in competing for household deposits, especially since they were prohibited by federal law from offering NOW accounts themselves. Although the commercial banks lobbied hard for abolition, state and federal regulatory agencies were unable to reach an agreement on control of NOW accounts.

The issue was then brought to Congress, where, after further debate, a compromise was reached. Public Law 93-100, signed in August 1973, extended authorization to issue NOW accounts to commercial banks, savings and loans, and cooperative banks but limited such accounts to Massachusetts and New Hampshire.

The various regulatory agencies then authorized commercial banks, savings and loans, and cooperative banks to begin offering NOW accounts from January 1, 1974, setting a maximum interest rate of 5 percent on these accounts for all institutions, including mutual savings banks. Advertising efforts were limited to media aimed primarily at residents of the two states. Although individuals and nonprofit organizations were allowed to hold NOW accounts, businesses were prohibited from doing so.

Coolidge Bank and NOW Accounts

Coolidge management had followed the development of NOW accounts closely. Despite the bank's reputation for innovation, Mr. Adess's attitude toward them had, initially, been quite negative. As he explained, "To take away service charges, pay postage both ways, and give everything free—that's one thing. But to

EXHIBIT 10
COOLIDGE BANK: SELECTED RESPONSES TO BOSTON AREA CONSUMER BANKING SURVEY

	Checking acct. bank	Savings acct. bank
What would you say is the most irritating characteristic of your checking account bank/savings account bank?		
Need better hours	4.2%	3.8%
Poor personnel	4.0	2.3
Want free checking	3.8	0.1
Long lines	2.2	2.0
Hidden charges	2.0	0.5
Bookkeeping errors	1.8	0.5
Slow bookkeeping	1.7	0.2
Low interest	0.1	1.0
Bad location/parking	0.8	0.5
Other complaints	5.2	2.7
No complaints cited	74.2	86.4
	100.0%	100.0%
Have you switched your account from another bank within the last year?		
Yes	10.3%	9.3%
No	89.7	90.7
	100.0%	100.0%
If yes, what was the major reason you switched your account?		
Moved	35.6%	35.1%
Dissatisfied with former bank	23.0	26.0
Better deal at new bank	9.2	15.6
Proximity to home or work	6.0	9.1
Other	25.3	14.3
	100.0%	100.0%
Why would you recommend this bank for checking accounts/savings accounts?		
Own experience*	10.7%	9.9%
Proximity*	8.6	10.6
Good service	35.1	24.0
Helpful, friendly personnel	10.5	10.6
Word of mouth	3.4	2.7
Good rates (Chkg. or Svgs.)	14.1	28.2
Full service	5.1	3.9
More branches	2.6	1.4
Liberal on loans	0.5	0.4
Large, stable	1.5	1.9
Good hours	1.5	1.4
Other	6.4	5.1
	100.0%	100.0%

* If respondent answered "own experience" or "proximity," interviewer was instructed to probe why the experience was good and circle another category if valid.

Source: Survey conducted for Coolidge Bank, mid-1973.

start paying 5 percent on top of that—now that's something else. That could become a real financial problem."

Coolidge held back in January 1974 when commercial banks first became entitled to issue NOW accounts. In that month, 11 of the 153 commercial banks and 12 of the 179 savings and loans and cooperative banks in Massachusetts began offering the accounts. Some 75 mutual savings banks in the state already offered NOW accounts prior to 1974, and by the end of January the figure had jumped to 85, more than 50 percent of all such banks in the state. Data

collected each month by the Federal Reserve Bank of Boston showed a steady increase in the number of banks offering NOW accounts, as well as in new accounts opened and the volume of deposits (Exhibit 11). By May 1974, 13 percent of all commercial banks offered NOW accounts, as compared with 45 percent of all thrift banks. However, not all commercial banks offering NOW accounts advertised the fact, although thrift institutions did so vigorously. The only commercial banks actively promoting these accounts in the Boston area were some small- and medium-sized banks in Essex County.

EXHIBIT 11
NOW ACCOUNT ACTIVITY IN MASSACHUSETTS BY TYPE OF BANK, 1974

	Jan.	Feb.	Mar.	Apr.	May
Commercial banks:					
No. of new accounts:					
Existing customers	917	409	478	799	461
New customers	347	557	642	613	774
No. of accounts closed	5	18	34	37	89
Total no. of accounts at month end	1,259	2,207	3,293	4,668	5,814
Deposits ($ million)	2.5	2.3	4.0	6.0	6.7
Withdrawals ($ million)	0.2	0.8	1.9	3.5	5.9
Balance at month end ($ million)	2.3	3.8	5.9	8.4	9.2
Mutual savings banks:					
No. of new accounts:					
Existing customers	4,660	4,061	4,960	4,784	5,033
New customers	3,360	3,715	4,157	4,021	4,860
No. of accounts closed	1,379	1,753	1,489	1,599	1,730
Total no. of accounts at month end	95,677	101,701	109,365	116,618	124,822
Deposits ($ million)	57.0	49.0	62.7	72.7	76.5
Withdrawals ($ million)	59.8	45.9	53.8	70.8	75.9
Balance at month end ($ million)	134.8	138.5	147.8	150.3	151.5
Savings & loans, cooperatives:					
No. of new accounts:					
Existing customers	784	809	1,242	1,499	1,355
New customers	464	763	1,043	739	1,077
No. of accounts closed	8	8	27	36	57
Total no. of accounts at month end	1,240	2,804	5,062	7,264	9,639
Deposits ($ million)	1.0	2.3	4.3	7.3	8.8
Withdrawals ($ million)	0.1	0.8	2.4	4.7	6.9
Balance at month end ($ million)	0.9	2.4	4.3	6.9	8.8

Source: Research Department, Federal Reserve Bank of Boston.

Many of the new accounts were opened by existing customers of the same bank, and quite a significant volume of funds deposited in these NOW accounts represented transfers from existing demand deposits or time and savings deposits at the same institution.

At commercial banks, two-thirds of internal transfers to NOW accounts came from checking accounts and one-third (by value) from savings accounts.

By June, Mr. Adess had noticed "quite a few decent-size, personal checking accounts" leave Coolidge for NOW accounts at nearby competing thrift institutions. He had also received "more than a few" calls from long-standing Coolidge customers who had historically carried "decent balances" in their personal checking accounts. They explained the dilemma that they faced. Although they felt kindly disposed toward Coolidge for the innovative banking services that it had provided for them over the years, they were nevertheless strongly tempted to move their checking business to other banks offering interest-bearing NOW accounts. The president felt that the time had come for the board to reassess the bank's position.

If Coolidge management decided to offer such accounts, then one issue would be what terms to offer. It was evident from the Federal Reserve Bank reports that significant variations existed between banks in the terms attached to NOW accounts, especially in the service charges levied per draft. Although most commercial banks charged 15 cents per draft, many thrift banks charged only 10 cents, and fully one-third of them made no charge at all.

There were other inputs to this decision, too. Management knew the size distribution of existing demand and time deposits at Coolidge (Exhibit 12). The treasurer estimated that the direct cost to the bank of servicing a checking account transaction averaged around 10 cents, with overhead costs about the same. Costs for savings account transactions were substantially higher, due to the greater labor input required, not least by tellers. However, the number of

EXHIBIT 12
COOLIDGE BANK AND TRUST COMPANY: DISTRIBUTION OF PERSONAL CHECKING AND SAVINGS ACCOUNTS BY SIZE OF AVERAGE MONTHLY BALANCE

Average monthly balance	Personal checking accounts		Regular savings accounts	
	Percent of accounts	Percent of deposits	Percent of accounts	Percent of deposits
$50 and under	22.4	1.4	4.4	0.1
$51–100	29.9	5.6	2.1	0.2
$101–250	16.4	7.2	2.2	0.7
$251–500	11.3	10.6	13.2	7.3
$501–1,000	11.2	21.1	70.5	59.3
$1,001–2,500	7.6	30.3	4.0	7.0
$2,501–5,000	0.7	7.1	1.8	6.3
$5,001–10,000	0.4	7.0	1.3	9.7
$10,001–20,000	0.1	5.6	0.4	6.3
$20,001+	*	4.1	0.1	3.1
	100.0	100.0	100.0	100.0

* Denotes less than 0.1 percent.
Source: Coolidge Bank records (disguised data).

EXHIBIT 13
VOLUME OF DRAFTS ISSUED BY HOLDERS OF NOW ACCOUNTS IN MASSACHUSETTS, 1974

	Jan.	Feb.	Mar.	Apr.	May
Commercial banks:					
Total volume of NOW drafts, thousands	3.2	4.7	11.1	19.2	25.1
% distribution of NOW accounts by no. of drafts per account:					
0 drafts	51.8	55.0	47.8	43.9	44.5
1–9 drafts	46.1	34.7	39.1	41.4	39.6
10–20 drafts	2.0	9.0	10.7	11.7	12.2
> 20 drafts	0.2	1.3	2.5	3.0	3.7
Average no. of drafts per active account	5.4	4.7	6.4	7.3	7.7
Mutual savings banks:					
Total volume of NOW drafts, thousands	493.7	498.2	598.5	708.8	757.5
% distribution of NOW accounts by no. of drafts per account:					
0 drafts	25.1	27.2	26.9	27.2	26.6
1–9 drafts	56.5	55.7	56.3	53.2	52.9
10–20 drafts	14.6	13.2	13.5	15.3	15.5
> 20 drafts	3.8	3.9	3.3	4.3	4.9
Average no. of drafts per active account	6.8	6.7	7.4	8.3	8.2
Savings & loans, cooperatives:					
Total volume of NOW drafts, thousands	2.1	9.9	25.5	46.8	66.4
% distribution of NOW accounts by no. of drafts per account:					
0 drafts	59.5	30.0	36.0	25.7	20.0
1–9 drafts	37.6	57.5	44.0	47.2	49.1
10–20 drafts	2.9	11.2	15.9	20.7	23.1
> 20 drafts		1.3	4.1	6.4	7.8
Average no. of drafts per active account	4.2	5.0	7.7	8.5	8.4

Source: Research Department, Federal Reserve Bank of Boston.

savings account transactions each month was only a tiny fraction of those by checking accounts.

Also available was additional Federal Reserve Bank data on NOW account activity concerning the number of drafts issued by individual accounts each month (Exhibit 13).

"The priority," Mr. Adess told his fellow directors at the executive committee meeting called to discuss the NOW account issue, "is to hold the accounts that we have. We've taken a good hard look at every account that we've lost or are afraid of losing, and it's been the better ones—like those with an average monthly balance of over $1,000—not the 'garbage' accounts averaging $50."

8 *The Boston Globe*

John F. Cady

Advertising the Krugerrand

Ms. Anne Wyman, editorial editor of *The Boston Globe*, set aside her memorandum to the executive editor concerning an upcoming meeting at which they would discuss whether or not *The Globe* would carry controversial Krugerrand coin advertisements in the spring of 1978. Ms. Wyman was concerned about the criteria *The Globe* should use in making this decision. She also wondered what impact the Kruggerand decision would have on future advertising and editorial policies at the paper.

Krugerrands

Krugerrands are coins consisting of one troy ounce of pure 22-carat gold. Named for the first president of the South African Republic, the

John F. Cady is an associate professor at the Harvard Graduate School of Business Administration.

coins were struck at the South African mint with the likeness of President Paul Kruger on one side and the antlered African springbok on the other.

Because several million Krugerrands had been sold between 1974, when they were introduced, and late 1977, the coins were not particularly valued by coin collectors. Rather, Krugerrands were a medium for the exchange of gold on a worldwide basis.

Krugerrand Marketing Program

The marketing program for the Krugerrand had been developed by the International Gold Corporation, Ltd. (InterGold), a subsidiary of the South African Chamber of Mines, which represented South Africa's gold mining companies. The principal purposes of InterGold were to promote the industrial use of gold and to promote consumer investment in gold.

In 1974 InterGold had begun marketing Krugerrands in Europe, and sales had been immediately described as "brisk." Between August 1975 and September 1976, 4.8 million Krugerrands, accounting for 21 percent of South Africa's gold output, were sold. Relatively low gold prices in 1975 further stimulated European gold sales, and by mid-1976, 45,000 Krugerrands per week were being sold in Germany and Switzerland alone.

In the fall of 1975 InterGold began to test-market in the United States, and 1 year later the Krugerrand was being sold in 25 major United States metropolitan markets. InterGold had retained Doyle, Dane, Bernbach, a New York advertising agency, and the Rubenstein, Wolfson public relations agency for its United States promotional campaign. The initial 1976 advertising budget for the United States was estimated to be $3 million. Estimates of the 1977 budget for Krugerrand advertising ran as high as $7 million. Advertisements appearing in newspapers (the principal print medium) and on television (the principal broadcast medium) featured the value of gold as an investment and the historical appreciation in gold pieces (Exhibit 1).

Three agents represented InterGold in the United States. These agents purchased Krugerrands from the Chamber of Mines and sold them to United States retail dealers. These consisted of several hundred coin dealers, banks, and stock brokerage firms such as Merrill Lynch. Retail dealers in the United States could buy Krugerrands from the three agents, from European dealers, or "off the street" from individual owners. The names of local Krugerrand retail dealers were featured in newspaper advertisements.

The retail price of the Krugerrand was tied to the daily price of gold on the world gold exchanges. The retail price of the Krugerrand equaled the market price for gold for the day, plus an additional charge to cover the costs of minting, shipping, insurance, and the dealer commission. For example, when the price of gold was $130.20 on the London exchange in late 1976, First National Bank of Chicago sold one Krugerrand for $144, or ten Krugerrands for $139 each.

Krugerrand purchasers in the United States were described as "older individuals who are sophisticated and often professionals." Most customers were investors concerned about inflation and the recent lackluster performance of the stock market. Many Krugerrand purchasers believed that despite the sometimes volatile fluctuations in prices, gold provided a hedge against inflation and dollar devaluation. A relatively few purchasers were interested in purchasing Krugerrands as gifts, and some coins had been sold as pendants.

By November 1977 the price of gold had reached $160 per ounce. Gold purchasing by United States citizens had accelerated, and $100 million in Krugerrands had been sold in the United States during the year.

South Africa

South Africa is a country situated at the southern tip of the African continent. Rich in natural resources such as timber, gold, and diamonds, it was first populated by Europeans during the seventeenth and eighteenth centuries as a colony controlled by the Dutch East India Company. During the 1700s the colony was settled by German immigrants and French Huguenots seeking religious freedom. These immigrants, who became known as Afrikaners, or Boers, had been excluded from government, education, and politics by the British who seized South Africa in 1795. The principal reason why the Afrikaners were excluded from these activities was that they did not speak English. During the 1830s thousands of Afrikaners migrated to the interior of South Africa, and sporadic warfare broke out between these migrants and black natives who migrated throughout the interior in search of grazing land. The discovery of gold in the interior in 1886 led to a large influx of English-speaking settlers and constant conflict

EXHIBIT 1
KRUGERRAND NEWSPAPER AD

© International Gold Corporation, Ltd.

This coin,
unlike paper money,
is backed by gold.

The coin is called the Krugerrand and it contains one ounce of pure gold.

So if you own a few Krugerrands you, in effect, have money backed by gold.

You could look at this as a kind of *personal reserve*—a hedge against inflation or the devaluation of paper money. And that's not only what millions of individuals do, it's what *most of the world's nations* do as well.

For although countries no longer back their currencies with gold, it is, in fact, something they prize *above* money. They do not use up their gold and hold money in reserve. They *use money* and *hold their gold* in reserve.

You maybe don't realize how rare gold really is—all that exists would make a cube only *18 yards* on each side!

But countries own only half the gold. The rest is held by companies, banks, religious groups —and by individuals.

Today many Americans are buying gold coins. And the coin they're buying most is the South African Krugerrand.

There is no other coin like it.

Instead of a fractional percentage of gold, it contains *exactly one troy ounce.*

And unlike standard gold coins, it's not sold at premium prices for rarity or aesthetics but at a price *based on its gold content.* (The only extra charge you pay is for coinage and distribution.)

You can easily figure your Krugerrand's value just by checking the world gold-ounce price in your daily

newspaper. And because it is the world's most sold gold coin, there is a broad market for you to buy and sell them. They are available at many banks, brokerage firms and coin dealers.

Krugerrands are about the size of a half-dollar (though thicker, and heavier). So you can slip one, two, or quite a few into your regular safe deposit box.

At some point you should be cautioned that the gold price is subject to fluctuations and there is no guarantee that it will not go down as well as up.

On the other hand, paper money, too, can lose value.

In the last twenty-two years there have been more than 400 currency devaluations by over one hundred nations.

The Krugerrand
The world's best way to own gold.

between Afrikaners and the British, which finally ended with the defeat of the Afrikaners in the Anglo-Boer War of 1899–1902. After the Boer War, Afrikaners maintained their culture, language, and religion and worked to obtain political power in South Africa.

In 1909, the British withdrew the rights of all nonwhites to sit in parliament, and when the Afrikaner government came to power in 1948, legislation extending a policy of apartheid (apartness) of the races was expanded. Since that time over 300 pieces of legislation, ranging from laws banning intermarriage across racial lines to "pass" laws which controlled the movement of blacks, were adopted by the South African parliament. Apartheid had both economic and social dimensions. Blacks, who constituted 71 percent of the population, and "coloreds" (individuals of mixed racial heritage), who constituted almost 10 percent of the population, generally held the more dangerous, menial, and lower-paying jobs. Blacks employed in mining, for example, earned 22 percent of the average wage of their white counterparts.[1] "Petty apartheid," which included segregated beaches, buses, lunch counters, and hotels, had been likened to segregation in the United States South prior to the 1960s.

Recent Developments in South Africa

Racial tensions increased in the mid-1970s, with occasional outbreaks of violence. In particular, the black city of Soweto, outside Johannesburg, was the scene of black and white confrontation in 1975 and 1976. The dissension centered on black working and living conditions and the use of the Afrikaans language in black schools. These recent racial tensions coincided with the most serious financial recession to occur in South Africa in over 30 years. By 1976 real

growth in the GNP had slowed to 2 percent.[2] Unemployment among the 18 million members of the black work force rose to 1.2 million.[3]

Partially as a result of the South African economic slowdown, new investment by foreign corporate affiliates slowed markedly. Among the 300 United States corporate affiliates which had a combined $1.5 billion investment in South Africa, virtually no new investments were made in 1976.[4]

On March 1, 1977, 12 major United States corporations with business interests in South Africa expressed support for equal employment rights for blacks and nonwhites. These companies developed programs which provided for nonsegregation of employees in work areas and dining halls and called for equal pay for all employees doing equal and comparable work.

The implementation of such programs had increased during 1977. Stockholders had brought considerable pressure to bear on management to avoid any policies which might support South African apartheid. Mobil Oil, General Electric, Ford Motor Company, and Citibank, among others, had had stockholder resolutions submitted for discussion at annual meetings on the issue of apartheid.

By mid-1977, South African black unemployment had reached almost 2 million, and black trade union members were being laid off at the rate of 12,000 to 15,000 per month.[5] The GNP was rising at a rate of less than 1 percent.

Foreign loans became difficult for the South African government to obtain. Chase Manhattan Bank had decided not to lend to gold or diamond mines because of the poor wages and

[1]"An Ounce of Love?" *More: The Media Magazine*, December 1977, p. 25.

[2]"South Africa: Wary Investing Policy—Until Reform," *Business Week*, Feb. 14, 1977, p. 67.
[3]"South Africa Tightens Its Grip on Capital," *Business Week*, Apr. 18, 1977, p. 54.
[4]"South Africa: Wary Investing Policy—Until Reform," *Business Week*, Feb. 14, 1977, p. 67.
[5]"Why Struggle for Peace Is Losing in South Africa," *U.S. News & World Report*, May 9, 1977, p. 71.

working conditions found in those industries. Wells Fargo Bank and some other financial institutions had decided not to lend to South Africa at all under existing circumstances. Citibank and five German banks scaled down a requested $300 million South African government loan to $110 million to be repaid over 5 years.[6]

To meet increased expenditures on black housing, black education, and defense and national security, the government imposed a tax surcharge on one-third of all imports and limited the amount of money that South African emigrants could ship out of the country.[7] It had been reported that on the average 1,500 professionals per month were leaving the country. The government also increased train fares and removed subsidies on bread in an attempt to meet budget increases. Even with such measures, the government planned to borrow $2.4 billion from local sources to finance the budget. Banks, insurance companies, and pension funds in South Africa were urged to invest in government securities.[8]

Racial tension and international concern peaked in mid-September of 1977, when it was learned that a popular black leader of the Black People's Convention, Stephen Biko, had died in a Pretoria jail.

On October 19, 1977, the South African police implemented a new policy under the strict South African security laws. Eighteen black and biracial organizations were "banned,"[9] among them the Black People's Convention. Also

[6]"South Africa: Wary Investing Policy—Until Reform," *Business Week,* Feb. 14, 1977, pp. 67, 68.

[7]"Why Struggle for Peace Is Losing in South Africa," *U.S. News & World Report,* May 9, 1977, p. 71.

[8]Ibid. p. 72, and "South Africa Tightens Its Grip on Capital."

[9]Under South African law, organizations which are banned may not operate. The banning of individuals is a form of "near solitary confinement which can include house arrest." "The Defiant White Tribe," *Time,* Nov. 21, 1977, p. 52.

banned were seven white journalists who had spoken out for black causes in South Africa. The country's largest black newspaper was banned and its editor jailed without charges. At the same time security forces were deployed to Soweto to prohibit public demonstrations against the government actions. Approximately 150 blacks and Indians were arrested in protests that followed the government's action.[10]

The Boston Globe

The Boston Globe was a wholly owned subsidiary of Affiliated Publications, Inc., and had total revenues of just over $100 million in 1977. It was the largest daily newspaper in New England. *The Globe* published a morning and evening edition Monday through Friday and a morning edition on Saturday and Sunday. Daily circulation was estimated at 468,000, including 82 percent of the newspaper-reading households with incomes over $15,000. *The Globe* was read by 75 percent of those who owned their own home.

Advertising at The Boston Globe

Advertising at *The Boston Globe* was departmentalized along three lines: retail store, classified, and general or national advertising. The total advertising revenue was $80 million in 1977. Each of these three departments was supervised by an advertising manager. All three departments were managed by the advertising director, who reported to the director of sales and marketing.

Each of these three departments had a sales force responsible for making sales calls on potential accounts and servicing accounts once they began advertising in *The Globe.*

[10]"Burning Bridges between Races," *Time,* Oct. 31, 1977, pp. 46, 51, and "The Defiant White Tribe."

The Globe and five other newspapers owned a system of advertising sales representation called "Million Market Newspapers, Inc.," which solicited advertising accounts. Million Market Newspapers maintained offices in New York, Philadelphia, Detroit, Chicago, Los Angeles, and San Francisco. The Krugerrand coin account had come to *The Boston Globe* through the Million Market Newspapers service unsolicited.

Mr. Millard Owen was the advertising director for *The Boston Globe*. Mr. Owen described the policy of the paper with respect to controversial or sensitive advertisements:

All of the advertising salesmen and the personnel at the display desk (where ads that come in are written up for publication) are aware of what types of ads are "sensitive." Anything potentially sensitive would be taken to the general ad manager for an opinion. Advertisements deemed to be very sensitive might be taken up the organization to the President, Mr. William O. Taylor, or to the Publisher, Mr. Davis Taylor, for a decision on whether to print an ad in modified or unmodified form, or whether to print an ad at all.

Mr. Owen noted that four topics were generally considered "sensitive," thus requiring extra caution: those affecting ethnic groups, racial groups, and religious groups and those dealing with moral (sexual) material. The general rule that *The Globe* followed with respect to all advertising material, including those four sensitive areas, was that so long as the advertisements were not obscene, fraudulent, slanderous, or libelous, or a direct incitement to violence, or advocations of illegal actions, the advertising would be run.

The Boston Globe had no formal board of review for potentially controversial advertising, and there were frequently disagreements among personnel in the general advertising department, as well as between the advertising staff and the news staff, as to the appropriateness of particular advertisements.

Other newspapers, notably *The New York Times*, did employ a review board for screening advertising. This board, which was independent of any department with the paper, had the power to edit or veto any advertising deemed inconsistent with the policies of *The New York Times*.

Mr. Owen believed such a board of review was appropriate for *The New York Times*, which, because of the size and scope of circulation, received advertising from lobbying organizations and foreign governments with constituencies in the United States. *The Boston Globe* seldom received such advertising, and Mr. Owen believed its current informal review procedures were preferable to any rigid and formal system of advertising review. He cited two principal reasons for these beliefs: the inflexibility of such a procedure and changing community standards.

To give an example of the former, Mr. Owen noted that both *The New York Times* and *The Los Angeles Times* had recently imposed stringent requirements on advertisers of "X"-rated movies in an attempt to preclude explicit sexual material from the movie pages. However, "R"-rated movies were not covered by any such requirements, and in Mr. Owen's opinion "R" advertisements were as explicit as "X"-rated movie advertisements.

To give an example of changing community standards, Mr. Owen noted that the advertising of birth control clinics and abortion referral clinics had at one time been prohibited but were now accepted.

"Things change daily. Attitudes change, politics change. Because we advertise a product," continued Mr. Owen, "it doesn't mean we endorse it. We don't approve of the South African government, but we publish their ads. It's the same with many products, like cigarettes. We don't express approval or disapproval through our advertising policy so long as the ads meet our general guidelines."

The Editorial Department at *The Boston Globe*

The editorial staff under Anne Wyman was generally responsible for presenting to readers the position of *The Globe* on matters of local, regional, national, and international importance. The editorial staff also took positions for *The Globe* on such matters as support of local politicians, local referenda, local busing problems, and national issues such as defense and foreign policy.

The editorial position of *The Globe* was generally considered "liberal" but balanced. In the past, *The Globe* had supported the Equal Rights Amendment, court-ordered busing, gun control, and Senators Edward Brooke and Edward Kennedy.

When the first full-page advertisement for the Krugerrand ran in *The Globe* on October 2, many of the editorial staff members became concerned that the advertisement conflicted with editorial policies denouncing apartheid in South Africa. After a quarter-page advertisement ran on October 11, *The Globe*, along with other members of the Boston media, received a letter from a consortium of black community groups denouncing Krugerrand advertising and calling for the ads to be stopped. The letter indicated that a continuation of the advertising program served to support the South African government. (Exhibit 2 is a copy of this letter.) By the 18th of October, when the third Krugerrand advertisement ran in *The Globe*, several of the editorial staff members had become convinced that the paper should no longer carry the advertisements. The Massachusetts House of Representatives had passed a resolution condemning the advertising and sale of the coin. Several phone calls were received by the paper calling for an end to the advertisements, and black groups opposed to Krugerrand advertising had threatened to picket WBZ-TV, a local NBC-affiliated television station carrying the advertisements.

The issue came to a head on Thursday, October 20, with the news that South Africa had arrested black leaders, shut down newspapers, and "banned" several antiapartheid organizations. That morning Ms. Wyman wrote an editorial condemning the actions, but not mentioning *The Globe's* policy on the Krugerrand ad.

The editorial went to the president, Mr. William O. Taylor, who called an informal meeting in his office to discuss the paper's policy in the light of the editorial and the new developments in South Africa. Present were John Giuggio—treasurer; Richard C. Ockerbloom—vice president, marketing and sales; Millard Owen—advertising director; Paul Liahy—assistant general advertising manager; Robert Healy—executive editor; and Anne Wyman. The publisher, Mr. Davis Taylor, and the editor, Mr. Thomas Winship, were out of town.

The completed editorial was cleared to run the next day, October 21 (Exhibit 3). But discussion centered on a future editorial that should be tied to a fourth Krugerrand advertisement, scheduled to run on Tuesday, October 25.

Several points were agreed upon at the outset of the meeting:

1. The policies of other newspapers with respect to the Krugerrand advertisements were not to be considered relevant to *The Globe's* decision.
2. The revenue loss from the cancellation of the account would be small as a percentage of total advertising revenues. The 11 scheduled advertisements resulted in about $40,000 in gross revenues.
3. The October 19 crackdown indicated that the South African situation was much more serious than had been indicated. In Ms. Wyman's opinion the event constituted a clear declaration of the abandonment of civil rights in South Africa.

In addition, in the background were some other critical issues. The advertising staff noted

EXHIBIT 2
LETTER FROM THE STEVE BIKO MEMORIAL COALITION

October 13, 1977

Dear Member of the Boston Media:

We are the Steve Biko Memorial Coalition, named after the Black South African anti-apartheid leader who was murdered not too long ago in a South African jail. We organized out of concern for the Black South Africans who struggle to survive under racist, oppressive conditions.

Recently, it has come to our attention that several local media outlets, specifically The Boston Globe, and television stations WCVB, WMAC, and WBZ, are running advertisements for the sale of Krugerrands, which are South African gold coins. The coins, worth roughly $159, are about the size of a Kennedy half-dollar. The Krugerrand ads extol the virtues of owning solid gold coins in these economically unstable times. They also stress their "beauty," their relative inexpensiveness, and their accessibility.

What the ads *don't* tell you is that monies from the sales of these Krugerrands go directly to the South African government. That government needs the money to buy arms to help it maintain apartheid. In short, one who invests in Krugerrands is, in effect, helping to fortify a repressive economic, social and political system, the likes of which has not been seen since Nazi Germany.

We are campaigning to get these Boston media outlets to remove the ad from the airwaves and from print. So far, these outlets have refused, saying that they could be sued by the ad agency they contracted with (Doyle, Dane and Bernbach) for breach of contract, and that unless the ad is offensive, obscene or misleading, it must continue to run.

We feel that the ad is offensive, obscene and misleading, and we feel we can prove it, legally. And we feel that the moral issue here is so great that these media outlets *must* remove the ad even if it means they will lose millions in ad revenue or risk a law suit.

We ask that you, member of the local media, assist us in our endeavor. We urge you to talk to your general manager, editors, heads of advertising and business departments, and tell them to stop supporting the South African government; stop running the Krugerrand ad!

Sincerely,

The Steve Biko Memorial Coalition:

Action for Black Media
National Conference of Black Lawyers
Black American Law Students Association
Africa-National Congress
Boston Community Media Council Community Caucus

EXHIBIT 3
SOUTH AFRICA'S TRAGIC MOVE

The climate of repression in South Africa has steadily worsened since the rioting in Soweto of June 1976. But, until the death in prison of Stephen Biko last month, there had also been some reason to hope the Afrikaaner government of Prime Minister John Vorster was moving in some degree to deal with the realities of a political entity in which 4 million whites made the laws for a population of 25 million. Now, in the wake of Biko's death, all that has changed.

On Wednesday the South African government shut down three newspapers, raided the offices of black and white professionals, arrested 70 black leaders and banned nearly every major black organization in the country, including the racially-mixed Christian Institute of South Africa. Banning means that individuals under the order may not be quoted; they may meet with no more than one other person at a time; and their movements are strictly restricted. In effect it amounts to a state of non-existence.

Such grossly abusive measures, in violation of every concept of civil liberties, can only backfire on South Africa. Most of the victims were moderates, seeking to alter the pervasive system of apartheid without recourse to violence. Without their calming influence, violence can only worsen.

Rational and humane people everywhere have watched the events build with growing concern. Many had hoped that continued political and commercial dealings with South Africa could help preserve discourse and provide avenues of change. In the United States, arguments for forcing an end to apartheid by breaking commercial ties had been outweighed by the view that new provisions sanctioning more equitable practices at least in foreign-owned corporations made the maintaining of ties a more positive course. Clearly that may no longer be wise or even possible.

The Carter Administration has denounced the Vorster government's move as "a very serious step backwards" and warned that this country will reexamine its relations with South Africa in the light of the move. Six congressmen have asked for the recall of our ambassador and for steps to "disentangle" the United States from South Africa, economically and otherwise. The time may have come when there is no other way to protect America's long-range interests and to express the basic philosophy of this nation toward repression on such a scale.

America's views on human rights are clear. Our obligation to humanity and to our own minority population demands that we act to uphold them. Our views include respect for other nation's rights to hold different goals and pursue different solutions to their internal problems. Our aim is persuasion rather than pressure. In this, as in any other arena, preserving ordinary channels of intercourse is preferable to disengagement. But the South African government's behavior, reportedly considered for three weeks prior to this action, is so repugnant to everything America stands for, so insusceptible to persuasion that it compels a drastic response, however reluctant. We cannot sit by while the basic rights of 20 million people are threatened and actively violated in South Africa.

From *The Boston Globe* editorial page, Oct. 21, 1977.

that while *The Globe* refused up to 10 potential advertisements per week, this usually occurred only because the advertisements were deemed questionable or fraudulent. They also noted that there was a clear precedent for accepting advertisements from Eastern European countries which had oppressive regimes, as well as from the Soviet Union, which had imposed sanctions on dissident Jews. The question was raised as to whether cancellation of the Krugerrand advertisements on moral grounds meant an implicit endorsement of every other advertisement carried by the paper. Several staff members of both departments noted the responsibility of the paper under the First Amendment[11] to provide access to all points of view.

Among those on the staff who were in favor of discontinuing the ads, several arguments were proposed. One staffer noted that it was a

[11] The First Amendment to the United States Constitution guarantees freedom of speech and the press, although considerable legal debates center on the extent to which First Amendment privileges extend to commercial speech, such as advertisements and paid political announcements.

requirement of corporate responsibility to make arbitrary decisions. "The corporation has as much discretion as a person to say 'this just won't do.' The issue of black linkage in the U.S. makes this advertisement unique. The U.S. has a history of racial tension, and Boston in particular has had a recent period of racial turmoil. *The Globe* has a substantial stake in taking a strong stand." In view of the South African government's policies of October 19, some of those on the staff now viewed the advertisements as immoral and exceeding the limits of ordinary propriety.

It was decided that *The Globe* should run the fourth advertisement as scheduled and on the same day run an editorial explaining to the readers (1) *The Globe's* position on South Africa and (2) its reasons for continuing to take the advertisement (Exhibit 4).

Although there was still disagreement over what policy should be implemented, staff responses to Ms. Wyman's editorial convinced her that the important issues had been clearly exposed (Exhibits 5 and 6).

EXHIBIT 4
CONSIDERING THE KRUGERRAND

On another page of today's Globe readers will find the fourth in a series of 11 scheduled advertisements for a South African gold coin called the krugerrand. In the light of the South African government's new policy of repression, the decision to continue publishing this ad is a difficult one. The lives and safety of some 20 million black South Africans are now in jeopardy. Our own industry is threatened by the closing of three South African newspapers and the silencing of their editors. Nevertheless, it is the essence of a newspaper to present information, without fear or favor, not only for its friends but for its enemies, not only in its news columns but also in its advertising columns.

We deplore the apartheid policy of the South African government and its denial of human rights. And we urge any would-be buyers of the krugerrand to recognize that the purchase of these coins will help perpetuate the inhumane and suicidal policies that government is now pursuing.

But though we reserve the right to criticize or condemn on our editorial page, we defend the right of others to promote their wares or air their views through the medium of this newspaper, so long as the advertisements that result are not obscene or fraudulent or a direct incitement to violence or illegal action. The advertisements for the krugerrand do not fall into any of these categories.

Some may argue it is hypocritical for The Globe to maintain financial ties with South Africa while urging other businesses to pull out. Payment to The Globe for the ads amounts to an estimated one twentieth of 1 percent of our yearly advertising revenues. Far more significant in making the distinction between this and other businesses is the unique role of a newspaper in providing open access.

This newspaper has taken advertisements for many causes and commodities that run counter to editorial policy. These include promotions on both sides of the Mideast issue. They include ads for commodities we feel are foolish or unwise investments. They include political statements by candidates with whom we clearly disagree. We do not want to give our paid advertising columns the power of this newspaper's endorsement. To reject the krugerrand ads would have that effect.

If The Globe pursued its long-felt sympathies in this case, we would drop the South African government's ads for the krugerrand. But to do that would be to pursue the same course of censorship and repression that we condemn in South Africa.

From *The Boston Globe* editorial page, Oct. 25, 1977.

EXHIBIT 5
STAFF MEMORANDUM

TO: Anne

RE: South Africa question

I think we should continue to press to have The Globe drop the Krugerrand ads. I've tried to think the thing through and put my thoughts on paper.

1. Is it a First Amendment question? No. The First Amendment says that government can't tell a paper what to print and not to print. It doesn't have anything to do with a paper's own decisions on what it runs.

2. Then what's bothering us? It is, I think, the somewhat vague notion of "press

responsibility." Despite its vagueness, I don't underestimate its importance. As newspapers have consolidated and monopolies or near monopolies have been created there has been a growing obligation on the press to be "responsible." This responsibility should be exercised, I think, through the news columns primarily. Stories should be "fair"; all points of view should be represented. This effort is supplemented by letters to the editor and op ed columns. The responsibility is to provide a full airing of points of view on issues of public interest; it is not the responsibility of the press to help anybody make a profit—either in the sale of dipsticks or Krugerrands.

3. But what about providing open access to the advertising columns? First of all, of course, neither The Globe nor any other major paper provides open access to advertising columns. Advertisers have got to be able to pay the bill (life is hard; life is earnest). At this point we have reached the "commercial" side of the operation, but a commercial operation still tinged with the notion of press "responsibility." So how can The Globe say we will run these ads but not those. It is hard to hit upon a firm guideline, but I think we ought to be able to agree on some generalized standards.

And I think we can look back to the standards on the "press" side of the operation. We should allow all advertisements that involve an exchange of ideas. That is, if South Africa wants to take an ad defending its apartheid policies, we should run it. The whole idea of the exchange and airing of points of view is that the truth will win out. But the paper has no responsibility to be an agent for the economic strengthening of South Africa—or the local pizza shop. When it's a straight business ad, it's a free market economic situation. If we don't take the ad, we don't get the advertising revenue. Within this rather loose framework I would think The Globe could deny the Krugerrand ad but accept ads on all sides of all political questions.

But how do we decide to accept the pizza shop ad and reject the Krugerrand ad? Here I think we simply have to examine the proposed advertiser and weigh its standards against our own. We may not like chemical additives in pizzas but their presence certainly does not violate deeply felt political or moral principle. We may not like Mobil's energy policy, but the profits they will reap if it is adopted will not be truly "immoral" (only, really, excessive).

4. In the end, then, I don't really think it's so much a "press" question as a question of "corporate responsibility" not much different than that faced by GM or GE in deciding whether to deal with South Africa. And if that's the case, I suppose its really not my position to advocate policy. Having said that, I will, of course, now do so.

First I think the crackdown on South African moderates ends any hope of subverting them from within—a la the Sullivan approach of having American companies with American employment policies set up shop in South Africa. I think our running ads is the overseas equivalent of that approach. And I think it should be abandoned, at least until the most recent government policy decisions there are reversed.

Second, while I think the Krugerrand issue comes down finally to a "commercial" rather than a "press" question, I think a newspaper, whose business is public policy, should be a corporate leader in these affairs. And I think the proper direction to lead now is away from any dealings with a racist, oppressive government that shows no willingness to end its deprivation of human rights.

EXHIBIT 6
STAFF MEMORANDUM

Memo to Anne on Krugerrand:

To refuse the ad on the grounds that accepting it implicates The Globe in the crimes of South Africa reminds me of the McCarthy liberals who wouldn't support Hubert Humphrey in 1968 because he had supported Johnson and the war up to the end: They were more interested in their abstract moral purity than in the practical consequences of their actions.

If we really want to fight the South African gold sale, the Jeffersonian method is the best way; namely, to apply the principle that the best way to defeat a bad idea is to allow it complete exposure. By exposure, I don't mean simply allowing the ad to appear, but exposing it in the active sense: exposing it for what it is, what it represents, and also exposing it as a bad investment. In other words, not only saying that buying gold bolsters immoral policies, but that it is a waste of money.

In taking this approach we reap three benefits: (1) we can fight the gold sale far more effectively than we could by simply refusing to soil our hands with the ad, (2) we can maintain the newspaper's traditional detachment from policy making, as opposed to policy advocating, thereby not inviting the charge which we're always denying: that the media actually control events, and (3) in opposing the gold sale with all the editorial clout we've got, we're meeting in a practical way the charge (see Mel King letter Thursday) that we are helping South Africa.

It is a risky business, in terms of our editorial independence, to couple our economic clout (via joining the boycott) with our editorial clout. Moreover, it would have little or no practical effect and would serve only to make us look like Aborezk in leaving the Senate: "You're so nasty that I won't have anything to do with you."

D.M.

9 *Federal Express: I*

Christopher H. Lovelock

It was one o'clock in the morning at Memphis International Airport. The lights of an approaching aircraft grew brighter as it descended toward the runway, while more lights could be seen in the distant sky. "They'll be landing every few minutes from now on," said Heinz J. Adam to the visitor he was showing around the Federal Express distribution "hub." Mr. Adam, Federal's director of marketing administration, was referring to his company's fleet of 32 Falcon jet "minifreighters," which flew into Memphis, Tennessee, every weeknight from all over the country.

Moments later, a small twin-engined jet taxied noisily up to the huge shed housing Federal's distribution center. Painted a brilliant purple, red, and white, the jet rolled to a stop under the

Christopher H. Lovelock is an associate professor at the Harvard Graduate School of Business Administration.

arc lights, parallel to half a dozen identical aircraft. Before the pilot had even cut the engines, an electric truck towing a train of small cargo bins had emerged from the distribution center and pulled alongside. The jet's cargo door was thrown open, revealing a cabin crammed with small packages. While mechanics checked the jet's exterior and an avionics engineer conversed with the captain, a crew of young men went rapidly to work unloading the little aircraft by hand. The unloading was completed within a matter of minutes, by which time another Falcon had parked alongside and been met by a second crew.

Mr. Adam led his visitor back inside the busy distribution building, which contained an 800-foot-long conveyor system. Packages were being unloaded from one of the trains, deposited on moving conveyor belts, and sorted according to destination cities. There were boxes in a variety of sizes, large metal cans, cardboard tubes, envelopes, and an occasional sturdy package marked with the distinctive black and yellow symbol for radioactive materials.

"We're carrying 19,000 packages a day now, and have stations in 75 cities throughout the U.S.," said the director. "There's tremendous growth potential ahead for Federal Express, but we'll need to focus our efforts more carefully." He leaned over the conveyor belt and plucked up a large purple, red, and white envelope. "This is what we call a Courier Pak," he said. "You can put anything you like in it up to two pounds in weight, and for $12.50 we'll guarantee overnight delivery directly to the addressee before noon the next day anywhere in our system. Right now, we're averaging about 1,300 Courier Paks a day, but we've never put any real marketing effort behind it. I see no reason why we shouldn't increase that number to at least 6,000 daily."

The Genesis of Federal Express

Federal Express was the brainchild of Frederick W. Smith, Jr., who had incorporated the company in 1971 at the age of 27. After combat service as a highly decorated U.S. Marine Corps pilot and 2 years' successful operation of a business buying and selling used jet aircraft, Smith set about putting into practice a new concept for air transportation of packages. He was convinced that there was significant market potential for a small-package air service, flying primarily at night, on routes which met the needs of freight shippers. Most package airfreight at that time flew on commercial passenger flights.

Mr. Smith believed that there were major differences between passengers and packages, requiring totally different treatment of the two. Most passengers were moving between major business centers and wanted the convenience of daytime flights, whereas shippers needed night-time service to coincide with late-afternoon pickups. Additionally, most people flew round trip, whereas any given shipment of goods flew in only one direction.

Consulting firms were retained to study the nature of the market for small-package air service. The resulting reports established that a mere 10 percent of the airline fleet was flying after 10 p.m. and that over 60 percent of all airline movements occurred between the 25 largest geographic markets. By contrast, over 80 percent of small, urgent shipments originated or terminated *outside* the 25 top markets. The reports also found the number of such shipments to be growing rapidly.

Encouraged by the consulting firms' optimistic growth projections for airfreight, Mr. Smith subsequently recruited several of the consultants as officers of the new corporation and set about raising almost $90 million in financing. This included his entire personal worth, $8 million from his family, a $40 million equity capital package from six major corporate investors, plus another $40 million in bank loans. The privately owned Federal Express Corporation (FEC) thus became the largest single-venture capital start-up in the history of American business.

The Federal Express Concept

The company flew small jet freighters over a unique route system, similar to the spokes of a wheel. The hub of this system was a sophisticated sorting facility located in Memphis, Tennessee. Memphis was chosen because it was relatively close to the "center of gravity" of package movements within the United States; its airport's excellent weather record also made it a reliable base point.

Aircraft stationed throughout the United States left their home cities every weeknight with a load of packages and flew into Memphis, often making one or two stops en route. At Memphis, all packages were unloaded, sorted by destination cities, and reloaded. The aircraft then returned to their home cities in the early hours of the morning. Packages were picked up and delivered within a 25-mile radius of the airport by FEC couriers driving company vans and working to a tight schedule. From door to door, each package was in Federal Express hands.

To facilitate handling, Federal Express limited packages to 70 pounds, with a maximum length plus girth of 108 inches. In its use of the hub system and limited package size, FEC borrowed heavily from the experience of United Parcel Service (UPS), a successful surface package carrier. Many of the new firm's operations managers were recruited from UPS.

For its fleet, Federal Express settled on the French-built Dassault Falcon, a twin-engined executive jet. FEC converted it into a "mini-freighter" with a cargo-carrying capacity of 6,200 pounds. The use of these small aircraft qualified Federal Express as an air taxi operator and enabled it to avoid restrictive regulation by the Civil Aeronautics Board.

Operations began in April 1973. Although losses were initially high, the volume of packages increased steadily. In mid-1975, Federal Express passed the break-even point. For the fiscal year ended May 31, 1976, the company achieved a net profit of $3.7 million on revenues of $75 million, after paying $65.3 million in operating expenses and $6 million in interest.

In the early summer of 1976, FEC operated 32 Falcons of its own (nine other aircraft were operated under contract by supplemental carriers) and 500 vans leased from Hertz. It had over 2,000 employees and boasted an average daily volume of close to 19,000 packages. Its flights served 75 cities directly, and pickup and delivery service was provided for 130 cities in the United States. Because of the growth in volume, the company had established a second "minihub" in Pittsburgh and also operated a shuttle service between Boston, New York, Washington, and intermediate cities. Some aircraft flew more than

one trip per night. Federal Express had 31,000 customers, of whom about 15,000 used the service in any one month.

The Airfreight Industry

A 1975 study estimated that some 1.5 billion tons of freight was shipped annually in the United States by rail, boat, truck, barge, and air. However, air's share of this total was less than 2 percent, the main reason being that airfreight cost a great deal more than surface freight.

Airfreight offered several advantages in addition to speed. Packaging requirements were less and damage and loss rates usually lower. Airfreight shippers also had a lower volume of goods in transit or inventory at any one time than when surface transportation was used.

Typical users of airfreight were producers of time-sensitive, high-priced, finished goods going to widespread locations. Bulk products and commodity goods were rarely sent by air. Indeed, most air shipments were rather small; 55 percent weighed less than 50 pounds, while 90 percent of all shipments were composed of individual pieces weighing under 70 pounds.

Airfreight usage had grown faster than any other segment of freight transportation. Domestic airline freight revenues nearly doubled between 1965 and 1970. By 1975, it was estimated that the airfreight market was producing nearly $1 billion in revenue to the airlines, without including the retail markup charged by intermediaries.

Only one-fifth of all airfreight was delivered to airports by the shipper or picked up by the consignee. The bulk of the remaining 80 percent was accounted for, in roughly equal proportions, by three major intermediaries.

Air Cargo, Inc., was a trucking service, wholly owned by 26 airlines, which performed pickup and delivery service for the airlines' direct customers. The service was provided by 520 contract truckers at 480 of the 522 airports served by the airlines in the United States.

Freight forwarders were trucking carriers who consolidated cargo going to the airlines. Basically, they purchased "wholesale" cargo space from the airlines and retailed this in small amounts. Forwarders catered to small-shipment customers, providing pickup and delivery services in most cities, either in their own trucks or through contract agents. Whereas it cost the airlines about $10 in 1975 to handle a 50-pound shipment on the ground, forwarders' costs were around $6.80. The freight forwarder industry grew at an average rate of 20 percent annually between 1965 and 1975. There were some 250 firms, with the largest 25 accounting for over 90 percent of the business. Most forwarders were not profitable, and only a few of the top firms consistently earned profits. Emery Air Freight was the largest and most profitable, with 1975 domestic billings totaling $164 million and an operating income of $17.9 million.

The *United States Postal Service* used air services for the transportation of long-distance letter mail and air parcel post. It had recently introduced expedited transportation of letters and packages up to 40 pounds in weight through its Express Mail concept. This offered guaranteed overnight delivery or money back (Exhibit 1). For a 2-pound package, the USPS charged a flat rate of $2.25 from post office to post office, or $6.25 from post office to addressee.

Since most airfreight was carried in the bellies of passenger aircraft, the operations of these intermediaries were constrained by the airlines, which flew routes and schedules designed to meet the needs of people rather than packages.

Shipping Decisions

Even in the mid-1970s, the purchase of transportation services had yet to receive the same management attention devoted to such company functions as manufacturing, purchasing, engineering, finance, or marketing; it was rare for a traffic executive to rise to top management in any company.

In most organizations, the responsibility for selecting a carrier to handle a specific freight shipment rested with an individual whose title typically was traffic manager, mailroom supervisor, shipping clerk, or dispatcher. Often this person was restricted to the use of firms on an "approved carriers" list. Sometimes, others in the organization insisted upon the use of a particular shipping method and even specified the carrier for packages they were sending. Federal Express had found that for one shipment in four, it was the consignee who specified that FEC service be used.

Competitive Activity

Competition in the airfreight business was intense. It was believed that there were close to 1,000 airfreight forwarder salespeople across the country, to which could be added the representatives of the airlines and of couriers and messenger firms that provided high-cost special pickup and delivery services, using both scheduled and charter airlines. Every *Yellow Pages*[1] in the larger cities had extensive listings under "Air Cargo Service" (Manhattan had 240 entries), "Delivery Service," or "Messenger Service."

In general, the industry lacked marketing expertise, relying heavily on personal selling efforts. Brochures, sales materials, rate sheets, and routing guides were used to support the sales force. Direct mail was often used to generate sales leads. Only the biggest carriers, such as Emery and Shulman, advertised regularly on a large scale. One reason for the limited use of advertising was that most airfreight forwarders had few competitive advantages to offer. Emery

[1]The *Yellow Pages* is a directory of goods and services suppliers organized by product category and published in each city by the local telephone company.

EXHIBIT 1
EXTRACT FROM U.S. POSTAL SERVICE BROCHURE ON EXPRESS MAIL, "HERE TODAY . . . THERE TOMORROW"

You can send almost anything by Express Mail.

Anything that's mailable up to 40 pounds—letters, reports, magnetic tapes, merchandise, you name it. And insurance coverage is included at no extra cost. What's more, you can combine letters and merchandise in the same package. For example, you could include regular letters, or data processing runs in the same carton with spare parts, or other merchandise. The Express Mail cost for the entire carton would be the normal weight-and-distance charge with no extra charge for the letters.

Guaranteed overnight delivery.

We will deliver it by 3 P.M. *next day* or, if you prefer, your shipment can be picked up as early as 10 A.M. We will get it there or you get your money back.

It's so easy to use Express Mail.

Just bring your shipment to any Postal facility with an Express Mail window by 5 P.M. Check the enclosed insert for the location nearest you.

You'll get a special Express Mail address label at the window, so there's no need to make out your own shipping label.

You get a receipt for each shipment and a record of delivery is kept at the destination Post Office, if you ever need confirmation.

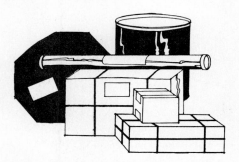

Programmed service too

If your business depends on quick, *regularly scheduled* intercity shipments of information, financial documents or merchandise, we'll *custom-tailor* a special Express Mail program for you. Pickup and delivery time will be arranged to meet your precise requirements. Service is also available to some foreign countries. For more information, write to: Express Mail, P.O. Box 23555, Washington, DC 20024.

EXHIBIT 2
AMERICAN AIRLINES PRIORITY PARCEL SERVICE ADVERTISING

We're American Airlines. Doing what we do best.

If they left out the research report for tomorrow's meeting...

...you can have it tonight. Tell them to get it on American's Priority Parcel Service.

It's just that simple and just that fast.

When you have a small parcel that has to get somewhere *fast,* just get it on American's Priority Parcel Service and it'll get there...fast.

How small? Pretty big, as a matter of fact. Your parcel can weigh up to 50 pounds and its size can total 90 inches in length, width and height.

With Priority Parcel Service you can ship to 50 cities on American's U.S. and Canadian routes plus San Juan, St. Thomas and St. Croix. Through our interline agreements you can ship practically anywhere in the U.S.

It's easy to get it on American. Just take your parcel to any American airport ticket counter at least 30 minutes prior to the departure time of the flight you want it on. Naturally, American can arrange for pick-up and delivery.

So, when you need to ship a parcel fast, use American's Priority Parcel Service.

American Airlines Freight System
633 Third Avenue, New York, N.Y. 10017 U.S.A.

Get it on American
AMERICAN'S PRIORITY PARCEL SERVICE

Source: Advertisement in *American Way,* July 1976

Air Freight, by contrast, had spent millions on the development of a systemwide computer tracing capability called EMCON and had promoted this in its advertising.

The Small-Package Market

The market for the domestic transportation of small packages could be divided into four groups, categorized by order of speed desired.

Emergency service received maximum speed and was the most costly. This category catered to "panic" shippers and was not price-sensitive. It included courier services, airline baggage services, and aircraft charter (Exhibit 2). Companies active in this field included Purolator Courier Corporation, Shulman Sky Cab, Delta Dash (a service of Delta Airlines), and other airlines, some air taxis, and many expeditors. This category was generally known as "same-day service."

Rush service could be described as "fast, within certain limits," was only somewhat price-sensitive, and generally involved next-day delivery. Competition included many airfreight forwarders, some airlines, and United States Postal Service Express Mail.

Routine Air was the largest airfreight category. Price-competitive, it was often referred to in the trade as "2 + 1" (want it there in 2 days but can live with 3). Competition included Air Parcel Post (United States Postal Service), UPS "Blue Label" service, and some airfreight forwarder activity.

The *Routine* category included all other freight services and involved mostly surface transportation. It was by far the largest segment of the market and highly price-sensitive. Major carriers were the United States Postal Service (fourth-class Parcel Post) and United Parcel Service.

The estimated size of the three air markets in 1974 was:

Market	Number of shipments (millions)	Average cost per shipment	Total $ volume (millions)
Emergency	2.5	$30	$ 75
Rush	15.5	10	155
Routine Air	122.3	4	490

All three markets had been growing rapidly since 1974, together averaging an estimated 20 percent increase each year. The higher-priority services were believed to be growing even faster.

Federal Express Service in 1976

The majority of FEC's shipments were for next-day delivery. *Priority One* provided overnight service for packages, with deliveries before 12 noon on the next business day. Special handling, at an extra charge of $2.50, was available for hazardous materials or, at a $5 surcharge, for *Signature Security*. The latter was designed to provide continuous responsibility for the custody of high-security packages (such as confidential documents or exceptionally high-value shipments). Another overnight delivery service was *Courier Pak*. This provided transportation of documents or other items up to 2 pounds in special waterproof, tearproof envelopes that were 12 inches by 15½ inches. On the average, the contents of a Courier Pak weighed about 1 pound. Courier Paks could be shipped individually or in containers holding about 30 each. Pak envelopes cost $12.50 each for shipment anywhere in the Federal Express system and had to be purchased in advance in quantities of five or more at a time.

For shippers who were in less of a hurry, Federal Express offered its less expensive *Standard Air Service*, with deliveries guaranteed on the second business day after pickup. A service of even lower priority, *Economy Air*, offering third-day delivery, had been discontinued in

January 1975 when it was found to be losing money.

Rates for Priority One (P-1) and Standard Air Service (SAS) were based on weight and distance traveled, with discounts being granted on a sliding scale for the consignment of multiple shipments on a single day. As a result, shipping costs per package varied widely, but analysis showed that in 1976 the average P-1 package cost the shipper $23.56 to send, while the average SAS package cost $12.62.

Various restrictions discouraged the shipment of large packages with a high volume-to-weight ratio, since the carrying capacity of the Falcons usually "cubed out" (i.e., filled the aircraft interior) before it "grossed out" (i.e., reached the maximum loaded weight allowable). The average P-1 or SAS package weighed about 14 pounds. A rough rule of thumb at FEC was that 10 pounds of cargo took up about 1 cubic foot of space.

Marketing at Federal Express

At the outset, FEC's main problem had been to find any shippers willing to use its services. It took a long time to break into major accounts, although an early commitment from the Department of Defense and other United States government agencies provided needed volume, as well as credibility.

Several "blitz teams" of four or five salespeople canvassed different cities prior to FEC's start-up, working a few weeks in each city to presell the service. Selling continued after start-up, while "blitz" efforts were extended to other areas as the system expanded. Advertising was limited to an opening announcement in local newspapers and to direct mail.

As the organization matured, contact with customers came to be made by three types of employees. The first were sales representatives, called customer service representatives or senior account managers. The second were the couri-

ers, who delivered and collected packages. And then there were the customer service agents, who worked at the stations, handling customers queries by phone and arranging for special pickups of packages.

In 1974, J. Vincent Fagan was appointed senior vice president–marketing. He quickly determined that an aggressive advertising policy was necessary. Focus group interviews with shipping managers had shown them to be somewhat "timid" individuals. For the most part, they were neither well educated nor particularly ambitious, and their basic job strategy seemed to be one of avoiding problems with their supervisors. One way was to use a reliable, well-regarded carrier such as Emery Air Freight, which enjoyed very high awareness. In Vince Fagan's words, "They could use Emery forever and never be criticized."

The New York firm of Carl Ally, Inc., was selected in October 1974 as the company's advertising agency, since it had a reputation of being a "bomb thrower" in the advertising business. The first advertising, in early 1975, used both press and TV and was a 4- to 5-week introductory campaign designed to stimulate awareness.

In April 1975, Federal Express commissioned the Opinion Research Corporation to conduct an impartial test of relative delivery speeds and costs for FEC, Emery, and two other well-known carriers. The results, after rotating shipments among different city pairs and different days of the week, showed that 93 percent of Federal Express Priority One packages arrived the next day, versus only 42 percent for Emery and even lower percentages for the other two. These results were used as the basis for the 1975–1976 TV and print advertising campaign (Exhibit 3), which positioned FEC firmly against Emery.

In March 1976, Mr. Fagan established a new position—director of marketing administration. To fill this he recruited Heinz J. Adam, a marketing executive with the American Can Company in New York. Mr. Adam was evaluat-

EXHIBIT 3
FEDERAL EXPRESS: LOCAL NEWSPAPER ADVERTISING IN THE
LOS ANGELES AREA, 1975–1976

IF YOU'RE USING EMERY, DON'T LET YOUR BOSS SEE THESE FIGURES.

TEST RESULTS

Percentage of packages delivered
the next day at regular rates.

EMERY 42%

FEDERAL EXPRESS 93%

Test conducted by Opinion Research Corporation, involving hundreds of
identical packages sent door to door. Summaries and other information available
upon request from Vincent Fagan, Senior V. P., Federal Express Corporation.
AMF Box 30167, Memphis, Tennessee 38130.

The word is out.

Federal Express is faster and cheaper than Emery.

At least, in a recent test we were faster and cheaper than they were, and the test was as fair and as realistic as could be devised.

We hired an independent research organization to send identical packages between 47 cities via Emery and Federal Express at each company's regular rates.

To be fair, we told our employees nothing of this test.

And also in the interest of fairness, we told Emery nothing of it either.

The numbers above tell the story.

Emery, for years regarded as the best in the business, delivered an average of 42% of their packages by the next day.

Federal Express' average: 93%.

REGULAR RATES FOR NEXT DAY DELIVERY

City Pairs	Emery	Federal Express
70 Pound Package		
Los Angeles to Seattle	$46.05	$39.07
Los Angeles to Philadelphia	51.14	47.26
Seattle to Los Angeles	47.07	39.07
50 Pound Package		
Los Angeles to New York	47.95	40.03
Los Angeles to Portland	38.58	34.56
Memphis to Los Angeles	42.47	40.03
25 Pound Package		
Los Angeles to Detroit	33.00	31.24
Los Angeles to Memphis	32.25	31.24
Los Angeles to Miami	35.41	34.55
Los Angeles to Denver	31.63	31.22
Cleveland to Los Angeles	34.20	31.24
15 Pound Package		
Los Angeles to Cleveland	29.13	26.92
Los Angeles to Atlanta	29.04	26.92
Los Angeles to Kansas City	29.07	28.72
Dallas to Los Angeles	29.88	25.95
10 Pound Package		
Los Angeles to Dallas	26.21	22.37
Los Angeles to Boston	25.96	22.51
Los Angeles to Houston	26.21	24.75
Chicago to Los Angeles	26.41	22.51
5 Pound Package		
Los Angeles to New York	17.82	17.32
Los Angeles to San Antonio	18.61	17.86
New York to Los Angeles	17.82	17.32

Source: Federal Express Rate Schedule effective September 1, 1975 Current rates also less
than Emery. Emery Air Freight — (CAB No. 58 General Commodity Tariff) (CAB No. 65 Pick-Up
and Delivery Tariff)

And we were cheaper, and still are.

Confronted with figures like these, any reasonable person would switch to Federal Express.

And with the time and money saved in doing so, any reasonable person would then hit the boss up for a raise.

Burbank 842-2141, Long Beach 595-4364

ing FEC's various services, with a view to developing strategies for future growth. Working with other staff members, he had begun an in-depth analysis of the market potential for Courier Pak.

The Situation in June 1976

The early summer of 1976 saw Federal Express management looking ahead to continued growth. With the average flight carrying 4,900 pounds of freight and loaded to 85 percent of volume capacity, the company was seeking legislation in Congress to allow it to operate larger aircraft. However, it was recognized that this might take a long time to achieve.

A January 1976 survey showed that awareness of FEC among prime prospects (i.e., airfreight shippers not presently using FEC) had increased significantly, with FEC ranking third out of 10 airfreight companies. Among these prospects, 75 percent recalled the Federal Express name on prompting. However, prompted awareness of Emery was close to universal, and for Airborne (a large airfreight forwarder) it was 85 percent. Unprompted recall figures were Emery, 61 percent; Airborne, 22 percent; and FEC, 12 percent.

At this point, Heinz Adam had been with Federal Express just 3 months. While still adjusting to the move to Memphis, after some 20 years living in New Jersey and working in New York City, he was enthusiastic about his new position, which he described as demanding but very stimulating. "It's the first time I've really had fun in a job!" he remarked.

Mr. Adam termed Federal Express "a very people-oriented organization: people are what make things work here; the loyalty of its employees has been very important to the company." In addition to offering high wages and good benefits, FEC operated a profit-sharing scheme for employees. A recent attempt by the Team-

sters to unionize Federal Express employees had been voted down by a four-to-one margin. On the other hand, Adam did not see Federal Express as a customer-oriented business. "It's operations-oriented," he said, "and as a marketing man this drives me up the wall sometimes."

Courier Pak

As he reviewed the company's performance since the beginning of 1975, Heinz Adam became increasingly convinced that Courier Pak had unfilled potential. Sales had almost doubled in the past year (Exhibit 4) but still represented less than 10 percent of the total overnight package volume for Federal Express and barely 5 percent of the overnight dollar volume. Studies by the cost accounting department showed that the variable costs associated with the average Priority One package totaled $10.60; for the average Standard Air Service package they were $9.21, and for Courier Pak, $4.25.

An analysis of Courier Pak usage by customer type produced the profile shown in Exhibit 5. Experience suggested that the decision to use a Courier Pak was often made by executives (or their secretaries) rather than by shipping managers. For instance, an advertising executive might rush advertising proof sheets to a client by Courier Pak, bypassing the shipping department altogether.

A spring 1976 survey of Priority One (P-1) and Courier Pak (CP) usage by FEC's top 1,400 customers found that 24 percent used both CP and P-1 and less than 1 percent used only CP, while the rest used only P-1. The key attribute separating Courier Pak from Priority One service in the customer's mind was the expectation that packages sent by the former would be delivered to the addressee and not just to the receiving dock. Another analysis showed that 57 percent of CP volume came from the top 14 FEC stations and 20 percent from the top three; the figures for P-1 were 44 percent and 15

EXHIBIT 4
FEDERAL EXPRESS: VOLUME/REVENUE TREND ANALYSIS, 1974–1976

Week ended	Average daily package volume				Average daily revenue ($000)			
	P-1	SAS	EA	CP	P-1	SAS	EA	CP
1974[1]								
1/4[2]	2,096	–	1,001	140	28	–	5	< 1
2/1	2,986	–	1,571	195	39	–	7	< 1
3/1	3,436	–	2,365	268	45	–	11	1
4/5	4,115	–	3,430	481	53	–	14	2
5/3	4,010	–	3,991	411	55	–	17	2
6/7	4,451	–	4,850	481	64	–	20	2
7/5[2]	3,952	–	4,159	525	56	–	18	3
8/9	4,950	–	5,436	527	70	–	23	3
9/6[3]	5,955	2,825	3,617	547	97	33	18	5
10/4	6,350	2,465	4,229	502	103	28	20	4
11/8	6,745	2,003	4,466	511	107	23	21	4
12/6	6,694	2,351	3,033	534	111	28	18	5
1975								
1/10[4]	6,599	2,556	–	559	119	38	–	5
2/7	7,033	2,395	–	575	129	35	–	6
3/7	7,630	2,266	–	592	140	34	–	6
4/4	7,116	2,056	–	661	132	30	–	7
5/2	7,553	2,204	–	764	140	31	–	8
6/6	7,663	2,252	–	794	153	31	–	8
7/4	7,489	2,257	–	805	148	30	–	8
8/1	8,076	2,159	–	745	161	30	–	7
9/5	9,372	2,142	–	859	200	33	–	8
10/3[5]	10,032	2,289	–	982	215	34	–	10
11/7	10,384	2,203	–	987	221	32	–	10
12/5	11,177	2,600	–	1,034	238	36	–	10
1976								
1/9	11,128	2,772	–	1,090	232	32	–	11
2/6	11,065	2,918	–	1,156	230	33	–	11
3/5[6]	11,248	3,053	–	1,194	248	35	–	12
4/2	12,820	4,979	–	1,370	287	48	–	13
5/7[7]	13,400	6,022	–	1,304	298	65	–	16

[1]Courier Pak volumes tended to be higher in the first and last weeks of the month than at midmonth.
[2]Four-day week.
[3]Priority One prices increased; Standard Air Service was introduced; Courier Pak prices increased from $5 to $8.50.
[4]Economy Air was discontinued; Courier Pak prices increased to $10.
[5]Standard Air Service prices were reduced.
[6]Courier Pak prices increased to $12.50.
[7]Figures were inflated by the United Parcel Service strike.

EXHIBIT 5
USAGE PROFILE OF COURIER PAK CUSTOMERS
May 1976 Statistics

Category	Number of accounts*	Number of Courier Paks used monthly	Percentage of total usage
Manufacturing and distribution	639	4,945	17.1
Advertising industry	140	2,285	8.2
Printing and publishing	80	1,558	5.6
Data processing and sales	125	1,160	4.1
Office and business equipment (Xerox = 862)	22	1,024	3.7
Marketing research	61	886	3.2
Mortgage and investment banking	98	733	2.6
Computer service bureau	50	686	2.5
Electronic parts and components	76	679	2.4
Communications (telephone and electronics)	34	631	2.3
Law firms	94	598	2.1
Insurance companies and agents	38	568	2.0
Service and leasing	76	537	1.9
Medical/dental/optical equipment and supplies	41	476	1.7
Aviation manufacturing and sales	57	448	1.6
Internal Revenue Service	36	443	1.6
Freight forwarders and transport	51	380	1.4
Engineering firms	44	346	1.2
Construction	37	318	1.1
Pharmaceuticals manufacturing	28	304	1.1
Subtotal	1,727	19,005	68.0
Next 15 categories	360	2,375	8.3
Miscellaneous categories	NA	946	3.6
Unclassified†	NA	5,632	20.1
Total	NA	27,958	100.0

*Some companies had more than one account, representing several departments at a single location or several locations of the same company.

†These were sales by users without an FEC account (either infrequent users or new users not yet assigned an account number).

Source: Company records.

---

percent, respectively.[2] On the average, users sent 0.45 Courier Pak per day.

A review of the market size for "emergency," "rush," or "special handling" delivery of documents or other small items suggested that the market was almost 870,000 pieces per day (Exhibit 6).

Although Federal Express management was pleased with the company's progress, they knew that the competitive climate had toughened. The better carriers had improved their service and were becoming more aggressive, while Express Mail was believed to be doing well. A few days earlier, Mr. Adam had opened his *Wall Street Journal* and had been greeted by a double-page

[2]In rank order, the 14 largest airfreight markets in the United States were New York, Los Angeles, Chicago, San Francisco, Boston, Philadelphia, Detroit, Atlanta, Dallas, Milwaukee, Minneapolis, Cleveland, Houston, and Miami.

EXHIBIT 6
MARKET STATISTICS FOR SPECIAL-HANDLING PACKAGES

	Pieces per day	Estimated average charge per piece
Express Mail (United States Postal Service) (Specially handled packages, separated from ordinary mail, with guaranteed delivery by 3 P.M. next day or money back. Available at major post offices in 410 cities nationwide. The sender had to take the package to a specified post office, but USPS would make a special delivery at the other end.)	4,400*	$ 6.00
Registered Mail (USPS) (Special security for valuable packages, separated from ordinary mail, but no advantages on speed of delivery. Available at most post offices.)	256,960†	$ 3.00
Certified Mail (USPS) (Mail is handled in the ordinary way, but the sender receives proof of delivery. Available at all post offices.)	295,156†	$ 0.50
Special Delivery Mail (USPS) (Mail is handled in the ordinary way until it reaches the destination post office, when it is delivered immediately to the addressee without having to wait for the next regular mail delivery. Available at all post offices.)	301,232†	$ 1.50
Airline Over-the-Counter (See Exhibit 2 for details of typical service.)	11,000‡	$50.00
Skycab and VIP (These services were usually provided by firms that specialized in picking up packages, shipping them by whatever airline or charter service offered the fastest transportation, and then delivering them at the opposite end.)	1,000‡	$90.00

*FEC estimate. The USPS was known to be expanding this service rapidly.
†Actual figures are from the 1974–1975 *Annual Report* of the Postmaster General, p. 52.
‡FEC estimates.
Source: These data were prepared by FEC management as an aid to evaluating the market potential for Courier Pak service.

advertisement for Emery Air Freight. He planned to make a proposal soon to Mr. Fagan on the future strategy for Courier Pak and would have to take this overall situation into account in deciding how to proceed.

The 911 Emergency Number in New York

Jeffrey S. Kahn • Christopher H. Lovelock

The calls were pouring in at an unusually high rate at Police Headquarters yesterday about how hot it was, how the water wasn't running, how a big dog was after a cat again, and, occasionally, about a shooting or a suicide.

It was the fifth anniversary of the 911 system, the consolidation of the police, fire department and ambulance services through a single phone number, and it appeared that city residents, by the thousands, were ignoring Mayor Lindsay's appeal last week not to dial 911 except in a true emergency.[1]

So began a story in *The New York Times* in July 1973 describing some of the problems surrounding New York City's 911 emergency telephone number. Flooded with calls which were often quite inconsequential, the Police

Jeffrey S. Kahn was a member of the Harvard M.B.A. class of 1975. Christopher H. Lovelock is an associate professor at the Harvard Graduate School of Business Administration.

[1]Pranay Gupte, "Calls to 911 Show That One Man's Vexation Is Another Man's Dire Emergency," *The New York Times,* July 10, 1973, pp. 43, 83.

Department found itself unable to respond promptly to genuine emergencies.

Rising public criticism of such delayed responses had convinced Major John V. Lindsay and his advisers that a public education campaign should be developed to discourage the use of 911 for nonemergency calls. The problem was how to devise a campaign which would differentiate emergencies from nonemergencies without reducing citizen confidence in the 911 system. As the mayor stated, "We're suffering from success."

Development of the 911 Concept

In March 1967, the President's Commission on Law Enforcement and Administration of Justice recommended that "wherever practical a single [emergency] number should be established, at least within a metropolitan area and preferably over the entire United States." By dialing a simple, easily remembered series of digits, any citizen would be able to summon a quick response to an emergency.[2]

At that time, most American cities had innumerable different numbers for fire, police, and ambulance service. The St. Louis telephone directory listed 161 emergency numbers on a single page; Washington, D.C., had at least 45 emergency numbers; and Los Angeles County had 50 numbers for police alone. The existing numbers were hard to memorize and rarely duplicated in other cities.

Hence the suggestion for a simple, universal emergency number. The concept was not new, having already been implemented in a number of other countries. Great Britain had used the number 999 ever since 1937 to call for police, fire, or ambulance service. Although skeptics argued that the services desired could be reached just as simply by dialing zero for the operator, studies showed that going through the operator took longer and that every second counted in achieving an effective response to emergencies.

The rising crime rate and civil unrest of the late sixties lent urgency to the Presidential Commission's recommendation. The American Telephone and Telegraph Company announced in January 1968 that it would make the digits 911 available as the single emergency telephone number throughout the nation.[3] However, the decision on whether or not to use this facility was left up to individual local governments.

Implementation in New York

In New York City, which was often regarded as a magnification of the good and bad points of American city life, the 911 concept seemed ideal to the city administration and the Police Depart-

ment. Mayor Lindsay's promise of a "Fun City" depended to a great degree on removing the fear of crime which affected both resident and visitor alike. Although New York had had a single emergency police number since November 1964, the seven digits (440-1234) were less easily remembered than 911 and took longer to dial.

The idea of easy access to police protection and emergency help was viewed not only as a solution to lawlessness but also as a cure for citizen alienation. Inspector Anthony Bouza (later assistant chief and commander of the Police Communications Division) pointed out that 911 was to be "a police-extended offer to participate in the solution of a citizen's problems . . . to overcome cultural and psychological barriers to these contacts" [between citizen and police officer].[4]

This reduction in citizen alienation was especially important to the New York City Police Department, the largest municipal police force in the nation. With 32,000 officers protecting 8 million New Yorkers in five boroughs, the department provided one of the highest police-to-citizen ratios in the world. The organization of the force was divided along both functional and geographic lines. Functionally, there were detective, public affairs, communications, and other divisions; geographically, the department was split into 75 precincts and seven field-service-area commands (the five boroughs, plus Manhattan and Brooklyn divided north/south). Over the years the NYCPD had been responsible for a number of innovations in police methods and technology, and at this time (summer 1968) New York was the first major American city, and only the third city in the nation, to initiate the 911 system. Nevertheless, the city continued to be regarded as a crime center.

The same commission which advocated 911 had also produced a report which showed a

---

[2]J. Edward Roush, "911—A Hot Line for Emergencies," *Readers' Digest,* December 1968, pp. 211–219.

[3]"AT&T Units Plan '911' Emergency Number Nationwide: Cost Will Exceed $50 Million," *Wall Street Journal,* Jan. 15, 1968, p. 3.

[4]Anthony V. Bouza, "911 = Panacea or Nostrum?" *Bulletin* (Associated Public Safety Communications Officers), March 1972, pp. 8ff.

significant relationship between police response time to a crime and the probability of an arrest. By instituting 911, the police hoped to increase citizen participation in crime detection, speed police response time, and reduce crime. Reducing crime would increase public confidence in the force and, it was hoped, produce greater community support for the police—thus improving the probability that even more citizens would use 911 to notify police of emergencies.

The Emergency Communications Center

A centralized communications system had been recommended several years earlier, but it was only after several "hot" summers and AT&T's announcement of 911's availability that the mayor gave the go-ahead for the multi-million-dollar project.

Technologically the project was almost totally handled by the New York Telephone Company in coordination with the police. Previously there had been five separate "communications centers" in each of the city's five boroughs. Each answered calls to the "old" police emergency number, 440-1234, dialed from its portion of the city, and each had its own method for dispatching officers to the scene. Now there was to be one communications center handling all emergency calls via "automatic call distributors" (ACDs), which would continuously and evenly feed incoming calls to 48 switchboard positions.[5] These positions would in turn be linked by a 12-channel color-coded conveyer belt to the radio dispatch consoles for each borough. An ACD operator would receive a call, fill out the appropriately colored dispatch form, and place it on the belt, via which it would be whisked to the appropriate dispatcher.[6]

The dispatchers were linked to more than 500 radio motor patrol (RMP) cars and to an increas-ing number of walkie-talkie-equipped foot patrol officers. Each dispatcher covered about a dozen precincts with a separate radio frequency for that area.

Planning the Communications Campaign

The complex task of informing New Yorkers about 911 was shared by the mayor's office, the New York Telephone Company, and the police department. The mayor would be in charge of the operation and would provide press releases at timed intervals. The police would distribute the message on all department forms and stationery and the large mobile "billboards" provided by the doors and trunks of their radio cars. The New York Telephone Company would, in coordination with its advertising agency, develop and disseminate the marketing message.

The mayor wanted the 911 campaign to be a highly visible symbol of his administration. Even more important, if the system were to succeed, it would have to be understood and used by a population which represented a wide range of educational and ethnic backgrounds. A message simultaneously bold and simple was required, and after some discussion the campaign slogan became "DIAL 911." This logo, with the number written large inside a square frame, was to be endlessly repeated throughout the city, often in conjunction with an additional message (Exhibit 1).

Most critical was the timing of the campaign. To create the maximum awareness desired, it was felt that the campaign had to peak all at once, but if it were premature and people began using the system before it was ready, then they might quickly condemn it as simply another publicity flop. And so, in the week of June 24, 1968, after the last of a series of publicity releases on the forthcoming project had been reprinted in the *Times, News,* and *Post,* a publicity blitz covered the city. All telephone booths[7]

[5]Marce Eleccion, "Electronics in Law Enforcement," *IEEE Spectrum,* February 1973, pp. 33–40.

[6]David Burnham, "Police Emergency Center Dedicated by Mayor," *The New York Times,* July 2, 1968, p. 43.

[7]Pay telephone booths were converted to make it possible to dial 911 without first inserting a dime.

EXHIBIT 1
THE 911 SYMBOL AS USED IN PRINT ADVERTISING, SUMMER 1968

received a bright red decal; police cars sported the symbol; subways and billboards urged the message, too. Newspapers carried advertising, and end-of-the-month telephone bills displayed the logo. It was a saturation campaign.

Inauguration of the System

The following Monday, on July 1, 1968, Mayor Lindsay made the first "official" call inaugurating the system. After several false starts, caused by dialing 911 on an inside line, the mayor finally got through, identified himself, and suggested that a squad car be sent to lock up the City Council. In his dedication speech, Mr. Lindsay said:

This is, perhaps, the most important event of my administration as Mayor. The miraculous new electronic communications system we inaugurated this morning will affect the life of every New Yorker in every part of our city, every hour of the day. No longer will a citizen in distress risk injury to life or property because of an archaic communications system.[8]

After less than 4 weeks of operation, the Police Department reported that emergency telephone calls had risen from 12,000 daily under the old 440-1234 number to 18,000 (including 2,000 for ambulances and 200–300 for fire emergencies) for 911. "The big thing we're doing is building up the public's access to us," commented Deputy Chief Inspector William J. Kanz of the Communications Division. Officials claimed that police cars typically arrived at

[8]Burnham, loc. cit.

the scene of a complaint within 2 minutes of a telephone call, more than a minute faster than under the previous system.[9]

Despite several complaints of slow response, the initial reaction was generally one of jubilation and acclamation. It was felt that 911 was bringing about a better relationship between citizen and government by overcoming the reluctance of many people to call the police. As Inspector Bouza pointed out:

> The implication of . . . [overcoming inhibitions] is tremendous because it reveals that the police are not dealing with a known volume of work, but rather with a flexible volume, the size of which depends on the accessibility and efficiency of the police.[10]

Concern over Delayed Responses

Yet this "accessibility and efficiency" were the very points which soon began to trouble both citizen and police officer alike, not to mention Mayor Lindsay. The original criteria for 911 operations had emphasized speed in answering: 90 percent of all calls were to be answered within 15 seconds of the first ring, and 95 percent within 30 seconds. At first these standards were met and exceeded. However, as 18,000 calls per day began pouring in, the 5 percent acceptable delay rate meant that almost a thousand calls took longer than half a minute to be answered, during which time many people hung up in frustration and lost confidence in the system.

Articles began appearing in the city's three dailies questioning the efficacy of the 911 system or more pointedly, the efficiency of the New York City Police Department itself. 911 became the butt of some "New York City life" jokes, drawing guffaws from local TV and radio personalities as they called the emergency number on the air for the amusement of their viewers and listeners.

9"911 Busy Number, Police Here Find," *The New York Times,* July 27, 1968, p. 25.

10Bouza, op. cit.

In response, the Police Department and telephone company consultants turned to improving the mechanics of the system. They eliminated the secondary pool of operators which handled overflow calls in order to increase the number of operators to answer primary demand. Since there was an unexpectedly large number of Spanish-speaking callers, more bilingual operators were put on the line. Yet even as goals for fast response were met and exceeded, the press and public continued to criticize the police.

Much of the souring of public response resulted from people's perception of the success or failure of the police in terms of visible response, which meant prompt arrival "on the scene." Unfortunately, the rising volume of calls at peak times (such as Saturday nights) placed a heavy strain on the NYCPD's squad-car resources. Too often police responded to a call only to discover that the "emergency" actually did not demand a squad car and two officers. Fewer such problems had arisen when an experienced precinct sergeant had handled calls; he might know that Mrs. Smith's "missing" husband was in fact sitting in the bar on the corner, and he might be able to calm Mrs. Smith over the phone. Now Mrs. Smith called 911 with her problem, and operators, answering within 15 seconds, dispatched a patrol car to her door.

Facing these difficulties, the department first requested additional patrol calls from the mayor. Communications also set up a screening process which identified those calls which, in the operator's judgment, did not require a dispatch. A computer system was installed to direct reception and dispatching. All these improvements meant that calls were answered faster and patrol cars arrived sooner.

Yet as crime in the country at large—and in New York City in particular—continued to rise, more and more people dialed 911. In 1972 the Police Department, having made continuous use of technology to keep up with demand, now began to wonder if perhaps another approach was needed. In particular, many involved with

911 felt that there should be some way of cutting down on the nonemergency calls which were entering the system—not only the "Mrs. Smith's husband" types of calls, which ought by rights to still go to the precinct, but also those which the police had never handled and were not equipped to handle.

How to Eliminate Nonemergency Calls?

The situation finally came to a head in the summer of 1973, when hot weather helped push the total number of calls to well over 20,000 a day. Many of these calls were relatively inconsequential, such as requests for police officers to fix a malfunctioning air conditioner. "What may be an emergency for a lot of people," said Sergeant Albert Lucci, a supervisor in the communications center, "isn't necessarily an emergency for the police. A lot of people just don't realize this."

As a result, the 48 emergency phone circuits were often jammed with nonemergencies. "Sometimes," added Sergeant Lucci, "it takes a while for people with real emergencies to get through to us." Studies had shown that out of a daily average of 18,000 calls, only 7,100 were real emergencies to which police cars were dispatched. Other calls concerned such diverse problems as Medicaid information, marriage licenses, open hydrants, street potholes, and even VD information.

The rising volume of complaints about slow police response to the initial 911 call (delays of 5 to 45 minutes were cited) and subsequent tardy follow-up was a matter of serious concern to both the police and the city administration. The problem was particularly acute on weekends and on weekday evenings.[11]

The question was, What to do? An appeal by Mayor Lindsay in early July not to dial 911 except in a genuine emergency had no apparent impact. A *New York Times* editorial noted that "it is too easy for New Yorkers to make use of the emergency system, it costs too little in time and trouble, and therefore the temptation to dial '911' for trivial reasons has apparently become more irresistible." The editorial thereupon suggested that dialing 911 be "made a little more bothersome"—perhaps by turning 911 into a seven-digit number like 911-1000.[12] Others argued that the problem could be resolved by charging for 911 calls from pay phones.

After discussions between the Police Department, the telephone company, and the mayor's office, it was eventually decided that some form of educational campaign was needed. At issue was the form the campaign should take. What organization(s) should sponsor it? At whom should it be directed? What media should it use? And what should the message say?

Watching the situation in New York City with some interest was adjacent Nassau County on Long Island, which was about to introduce its own 911 service. The Nassau County Police Department was very anxious to avoid a repetition of the problems which had plagued New York City and wondered which strategy it should employ.

[11]Pranay Gupte, "Delays Are Cited on Calls to 911," *The New York Times*, July 23, 1973, p. 1.

[12]"Emergency Calls . . ." *The New York Times*, Aug. 14, 1973, p. 32.

11 Hecht Company

Hirotaka Takeuchi

"We seem to have a 'problem child' within the Domestics Merchandise Group," said Allan Bloostein, president of Hecht Company in Washington, D.C., and Baltimore, Maryland. He was concerned that the Bedsheets Department was achieving an average gross margin[1] approximately 10 percentage points lower than the margins of the three other departments within the Domestics Merchandise Group—Towels, Table Linens, and Bed Covers. "In fact," Bloostein said, "the gross margin percentage of the Bedsheets Department has been declining in the last three years. If anything, I would have thought that gross margin would be going up with the influx of designer-name bedsheets into the market."

Hirotaka Takeuchi is an assistant professor at the Harvard Graduate School of Business Administration.

Certain statistical data have been disguised to preserve confidentiality.

[1]Gross margin, as used in this case, is defined as retail selling price less cost of goods less markdowns less cash discount.

"As you well know, Allan, bedsheets have long been used as a promotional item to draw customer traffic into the store," said Jerry Politzer, vice president and general merchandise manager in charge of the Domestics Merchandise Group. "And the trouble is that we are still using bedsheets as a promotional item when our customers are beginning to perceive bedsheets as a fashion item and not necessarily a commodity."

"Hecht, too, used to be perceived as a promotional store," said Bloostein, "until we launched the 'excitement' program several years ago. We adopted the slogan 'Where the Excitement Is' and tried to project an image of an upgraded, updated, exciting store. I personally feel the transition from a promotional store to a more fashion-oriented department store has already taken place in the minds of our customers. I was wondering, Jerry, if the same thing couldn't be done with the Bedsheets Department."

"It's not going to be easy, but we may have

some hope in an exciting new product called Comfortcale," replied Politzer. "Comfortcale, which is made by Cannon, is the first major new product introduction in the bedsheet industry since the introduction of the permanent press sheets over 10 years ago. It has a higher cotton content (60 percent cotton and 40 percent polyester) than the usual 50/50 blends. We've been test marketing Comfortcale in 18 of our 19 stores for the past 6 months. As I recall, the buyer was really excited about Comfortcale."

Industry Background

In 1977, 15.5 million dozen bedsheets and 13 million dozen pillowcases were shipped by the textile mills. In wholesale dollars, these shipments amounted to $605 million and $172 million for sheets and pillowcases, respectively. Compared to 1967 figures, unit shipments of sheets and pillowcases combined (referred to as "bedsheets" in the case) remained stable, while dollar shipments almost doubled, as shown below:

Mills' Shipments of Bedsheets

	Units	Wholesale dollars
1967	28.0 million dozen	$438 million
1973	31.9 million dozen	$667 million
1977	28.5 million dozen	$777 million

Source: *Seidman News Bulletin*, Oct. 10, 1977, and Apr. 24, 1978.

Cotton was still the predominant bedsheet fabric in the mid-1960s. But permanent press bedsheets, which were made of blended fabrics, took over the market by the turn of the decade. The switch from all cotton to blended fabrics enabled the mills to produce more colorfully patterned bedsheets. As shown below, patterned sheets (e.g., florals, lettered designs, abstracts, scenics, and geometric designs) increased their share of total dollar shipments threefold between 1967 and 1977.

Sheet category	Percentage of total dollar shipments of bedsheets	
	1967	1977
Whites	62	17
Solid colors	14	9
Patterns	24	74
	100	100

Source: *Seidman News Bulletin*, Oct. 10, 1977, p. 1.

The emphasis on fashion was further enhanced through the use of designer names. Burlington was one of the first mills to move successfully into the designer trend with its Vera brand name. Other mills soon followed with bedsheets and towels bearing such designer names as Bill Blass (Springs Mills), Yves St. Laurent (J. P. Stevens), Halston (Fieldcrest), Giorgio Sant' Angelo (Wamsutta), Jean Cacharel (J. P. Stevens), Oscar de la Renta (Cannon Mills), and Barbara Brody (Martex). More recently, celebrity names such as Suzanne Pleshette (J. P. Stevens), Dinah Shore (J. P. Stevens), and Mary Martin (Fieldcrest) have been added to the list of designer names for bedsheets and towels. There were more than 30 designer and celebrity names on the market in 1977. But according to *The New York Times* (June 3, 1977) Vera and Bill Blass were the only designer brands to exceed annual wholesale sales of $10 million.

Despite the continued trend toward more fashion-oriented bedsheets, unit shipments dropped by over 3 million dozen between 1973 and 1977. One reason offered for this decline was the fact that blended bedsheets lasted longer than all-cotton bedsheets.

Another reason for the decline in unit shipments, according to an industry source, "was due to customers having loaded up the linen closet with sale-priced bedsheets." The so-called "White Sale" period had increased from the traditional once-a-year January sale period to three times a year—January, May, and August. As a result, the number of sale-period weeks increased to 20 or 25 a year. Among department stores, the three sale periods were believed to account for 60 percent of their bedsheet sales. Five years before, the comparable figure was believed to have been below 35 percent.

Bedsheets versus Towels

In 1977, there were eight major mills producing bedsheets. Five of these mills also manufactured towels (i.e., bath towels, hand towels, and washcloths). Their 1977 shares of bedsheet and towel production (in dollars) were estimated as follows:

	Share of bedsheet production	Share of towel production
J. P. Stevens	20%	15%
Springs Mills	20	–
Cannon Mills	18	35
Martex	12	20
Wamsutta	10	–
Burlington	10	5
Fieldcrest	8	25
Dan River	2	–
	100%	100%

Source: **Company data.**

Cannon Mills had the highest share of towel production because of its strength in the institutional market (i.e., sales to hotels, hospitals, schools, and others). Fieldcrest, which *Forbes* called "The Kingpin of Upstairs Linen," was generally regarded as the leader in the towel business. Its 27-year-old Royal Velvet towel was, "despite a $10 price tag for the bath size, the world's best-selling towel."[2] Springs Mills and Wamsutta marketed towels under their own names but did not manufacture them. They bought towels from Fieldcrest and J. P. Stevens.

"The mills are making money on towels but are suffering from overproduction and de-

[2]*Forbes,* Oct. 1, 1977.

pressed prices on bedsheets," said one department store buyer. Other differences between the two businesses included the following:

Unit shipments of towels dropped more sharply than unit shipments of bedsheets in the last 10 years, from 78.4 million dozen in 1967 to 68 million dozen in 1977.

Dollar shipments of towels increased more sharply than dollar shipments of bedsheets in the last 10 years, from $272.5 million in 1967 to $618 million in 1977.

Average prices of towels increased twice as fast as those of bedsheets between 1967 and 1977.

White towels and solid-color towels combined made up 65 percent of the 1977 dollar shipment, as compared with 26 percent for white and solid-color bedsheets.

Forty percent of the towels sold in department stores were bought during the three White Sale periods in 1977, as compared with 60 percent for bedsheets.

Most of the better-selling towels had a very high cotton content (e.g., Royal Velvet had a 90 percent to 10 percent blend of cotton and polyester, respectively) or an all-cotton content.

Retail Distribution

Bedsheets were sold in four types of retail outlets. General merchandise chain stores (such as Sears, J. C. Penney, and Montgomery Ward) had the largest dollar volume of bedsheet sales in 1977, with 34 percent of the dollar market. Discount stores and variety stores[3] were second, accounting for 29 percent of 1977 dollar sales of bedsheets. Department stores closely followed the discount and variety stores with 27 percent

[3]Variety stores, which were also known as "5¢, 10¢, and 25¢" stores, carried limited-price "convenience" goods, while discount stores usually carried a wider assortment of general merchandise, including "shopping" goods.

of bedsheet dollar sales. Most department stores carried an "upstairs" or regular line as well as a "basement" or irregular line.[4] All other stores accounted for 10 percent of dollar sales.

Discount and variety stores accounted for the largest retail dollar volume of towels in 1977, followed by department stores, general merchandise chain stores, and all other stores:

1977 Dollar Sales in Bedsheets and Towels

	Bedsheets		Towels	
General merchandise chain stores	34%		22%	
Discount and variety stores	29	85%	34	85%
Department stores	27		25	
All other stores	10		19	
	100%		100%	
Institutional	15		15	
	100%		100%	

Source: Company data.

Department stores tried to differentiate themselves from other retailers in the bedsheets market by carrying a wider assortment of higher-quality items. Almost all the bedsheets carried in department stores were made from a top-quality fabric called "percale," which had a thread count of 180 per square inch. Large proportions of the chain and discount store lines, however, consisted of lower-grade bedsheets known as "muslins." With a lower thread count of 130 per square inch, muslins were not as soft and comfortable as percales.[5]

[4]Most mills had separate brand names for their basement lines, such as St. Mary's (Fieldcrest), Monticello (Cannon), Lady Pepperell (Martex), Tastemaker (J. P. Stevens), and Pacific (Wamsutta).

[5]Percales and muslins commanded different prices. J. C. Penney, for example, listed its twin-size muslin patterns in the 1978 fall-winter catalog at $3.45 to $4.45 and its twin-size percale patterns in the same catalog at $5.45 to $7.95.

Most retailers carried a larger number of bedsheet sizes. One bedsheet pattern usually came in 10 different sizes (i.e., four basic sheet sizes—twin, full, queen, and king—broken down into fitted and flat, plus two pillowcase sizes). In contrast, towels had only three basic sizes (i.e., bath and hand towels plus washcloths). Among the four basic sheet sizes, full-size sheets had the highest unit shipments, as shown in the table below:

Unit Shipments of Bedsheets by Size as of April 1, 1978

	Fitted	Flat	Total
Twin	8.1%	9.2%	17.3%
Full	11.2	12.8	24.0
Queen	4.4	5.8	10.2
King	1.8	2.7	4.5
Subtotal			56.0%
All pillowcases			44.0
Total			100.0%

Source: Seidman News Bulletin, May 22, 1978.

Company Background

Hecht Company was one of 11 department store companies owned and operated by The May Department Stores Company. In 1977, sales of the 11 department store companies accounted for 81 percent of The May Department Stores Company's total retail sales of $2.37 billion and 87 percent of its operating earnings of $212 million. Besides the department store business, The May Department Stores Company (hereafter referred to as May) operated 27 discount stores (Venture) and 17 shopping centers. See Exhibit 1 on the following pages for a 10-year performance record of May.

May was the second largest department store chain in the United States in 1977. The largest

EXHIBIT 1
10-YEAR PERFORMANCE RECORD
*The May Department Stores Company and Subsidiaries**

	Jan. 28, 1978	Jan. 29, 1977	Jan. 31, 1976
Operations			
Net retail sales‡	$ 2,355,409	$ 2,170,946	$ 2,002,487
Rental revenues	14,872	13,938	13,105
Earnings before income taxes	164,354	138,002	134,344
Percentage of sales and revenues	6.9%	6.3%	6.7%
Net earnings	83,963	69,209	66,523
Percentage of sales and revenues	3.5%	3.2%	3.3%
Dividends on common stock	25,659	24,776	23,838
Earnings retained in the business	57,949	44,077	42,230
Capital expenditures	97,051	91,964	86,008
Depreciation and amortization	54,316	47,370	42,566
Operating lease rentals of real property	14,822	13,731	12,012
Interest and debt expense, net	34,485	32,141	29,992
Per common share:			
Net earnings	$3.71	$3.05	$2.93
Dividends	1.15	1.10⅔	1.06⅔
Common stockholders' equity (book value)	28.10	25.51	23.60
Return on common stockholders' beginning equity	14.5%	12.9%	13.5%
Financial position			
Accounts and notes receivable, net	$ 519,049	$ 472,030	$ 427,293
Merchandise inventories	298,353	271,584	261,247
Working capital	504,489	416,007	372,165
Property, plant, and equipment, net	670,594	630,732	586,346
Long-term debt			
Real estate and finance subsidiaries	296,808	301,356	249,507
Parent company	151,168	110,804	114,419
Capitalized lease obligations	42,311	41,441	42,774
Common stockholders' equity (book value)	625,095	568,980	527,300
Store facilities			
Number of stores			
Department and discount stores	145	137	129
Catalog showroom stores	70	68	58
Number of square feet of store space	31,600,000	30,600,000	29,400,000

*The 11 May Department Stores companies included May Co. of California, Hecht Company, Famous-Barr (St. Louis), The May Co. of Cleveland, Kaufmann's (Pittsburgh), G. Fox & Co. (Hartford), The M. O'Neil Co. (Oregon), May-D&F (Colorado), Strouss (Youngstown), Meier & Frank (Oregon), and May-Cohens (Florida). The catalog showroom stores were sold in 1978. The 10-year performance record for years prior to fiscal year 1977 has been restated to reflect, on a retroactive basis, the adoption of the provisions of a recently issued accounting standard relating to capital leases.

†Dollars in thousands, except per share data.

‡Net retail sales have been restated to include finance charge revenues.

Source: Annual report.

EXHIBIT 1
Continued

Fiscal years ended:†

Feb. 1, 1975	Feb. 2, 1974	Feb. 3, 1973	Jan. 29, 1972	Jan. 30, 1971	Jan 31, 1970	Feb. 1, 1969
$ 1,740,407	$ 1,561,890	$ 1,460,406	$ 1,318,984	$ 1,197,735	$ 1,165,047	$ 1,114,422
11,140	10,806	9,896	7,123	6,482	6,149	5,672
93,357	97,918	97,438	86,957	63,898	61,533	71,680
5.3%	6.2%	6.6%	6.6%	5.3%	5.3%	6.4%
46,617	48,046	47,716	41,830	31,722	28,791	33,880
2.7%	3.1%	3.2%	3.2%	2.6%	2.5%	3.0%
23,883	24,064	24,148	24,104	24,111	24,164	23,856
22,237	23,485	23,071	17,229	7,113	4,129	8,980
96,128	75,704	56,724	52,338	51,898	60,500	42,500
35,804	31,705	29,738	27,827	26,820	24,999	22,853
11,269	8,433	7,056	6,466	6,216	5,781	5,157
26,277	20,956	17,771	16,505	16,416	13,907	9,821
$2.05	$2.10	$2.08	$1.83	$1.38	$1.25	$1.46
1.06⅔	1.06⅔	1.06⅔	1.06⅔	1.06⅔	1.06⅔	1.06⅔
21.74	20.71	19.65	18.67	17.96	17.64	17.47
9.9%	10.7%	11.1%	10.2%	7.8%	7.2%	8.8%
$ 407,261	$ 377,497	$ 324,709	$ 293,566	$ 279,810	$ 280,227	$ 260,472
213,693	207,617	195,519	186,370	172,483	176,338	166,847
354,912	330,537	326,047	280,566	290,545	255,005	240,879
552,918	494,321	453,851	434,804	413,091	391,955	359,015
237,598	193,999	199,897	153,780	151,934	99,447	57,538
118,041	123,543	78,403	90,711	101,107	105,826	112,597
35,824	33,693	34,759	32,806	33,764	31,695	32,534
484,461	463,781	444,099	421,183	404,981	398,314	395,905
118	109	102	97	89	85	84
57	53	–	–	–	–	–
28,000,000	26,800,000	25,200,000	24,500,000	23,300,000	22,600,000	21,500,000

department store chain was Federated Department Stores, which operated such stores as Filene's, Bloomingdale's, I. Magnin, and Abraham and Straus. Dayton Hudson Corporation was the third largest chain, followed by Allied Stores Corporation (Jordan Marsh, Bon Marche, etc.) and Carter Hawley Hale Stores (The Broadway, Neiman-Marcus, etc.).

Hecht Company was the second largest May department store company, with 19 stores (3.9 million square feet of total store space) and 1977 sales of approximately $290 million. It was the largest department store operation in the Washington, D.C./Baltimore market. Of the 19 stores, 12 were located in the Washington SMSA[6]; the other 7 were in the Baltimore SMSA. Sales of approximately $215 million were generated by the 12 Washington stores and $75 million by the 7 Baltimore stores in 1977.

As shown in Exhibit 2, the oldest of the 19 Hecht stores was opened in 1895 on Howard Street in downtown Baltimore. The following year saw the opening of the Washington downtown store on F Street. Except for these two stores and two additional stores in downtown Baltimore, all subsequent stores were opened in shopping centers or malls.

Hecht's Domestics Merchandise Group, which accounted for approximately 5 percent of total store sales in 1977, consisted of a staff of nine people—four buyers, four assistant buyers, and a divisional merchandise manager. There was a buyer and an assistant buyer for each of the four departments (Bedsheets, Towels, Table Linens, and Bed Covers). The members of the buying group were in their mid-to-late-20s and had college degrees. A typical job progression for a buyer would be the following: (1) an

initial training program, (2) work in the store as a manager of a department, (3) appointment to the position of assistant buyer, and then (4) promotion to the position of buyer. The promotion to buyer usually took between 2 and 4 years, depending on the person's past retailing background and other factors.

The buyers were responsible for two major functions—buying and merchandising. Buying involved such tasks as "shopping the market" for new products, ordering and reordering the merchandise on the basis of inventory checks and demand forecasts, establishing retail prices, making sure that deliveries were made on time, initiating markdowns, and planning and implementing the promotional and advertising programs. Buying necessitated spending a considerable amount of time with outside resources (for example, textile mills in the case of bedsheet buyers). Merchandising, on the other hand, required buyers to work closely with the store personnel by providing them with product information, display suggestions, and point-of-sale materials.

The buyers reported to Ray Dashow, the divisional merchandise manager for the Domestics Group, as shown in Exhibit 3. Dashow reported to Jerry Politzer, who was responsible for the Domestics Group as well as other divisional merchandise groups (Home Furnishings, Furniture and Major Appliances, and Floor Coverings). Politzer reported to Irwin Zazulia, vice chairman in charge of five general merchandise groups, who in turn reported to Allan Bloostein.

Allan Bloostein was the president of a major department store in New York from 1965 to 1968 prior to joining the Hecht Company, Washington,[7] in 1970 as president. When he became the president of the New York store at the age of 35, Bloostein was described as "the

---

[6]SMSA stands for Standard Metropolitan Statistical Area and was designated by the Census Bureau. The Washington SMSA is made up of the District of Columbia, three surrounding counties from Maryland, and seven surrounding counties from Virginia. The Baltimore SMSA was separate from that of Washington. It included the city of Baltimore and five surrounding counties.

[7]Hecht, Washington, and Hecht, Baltimore, were run as two separate divisions of May when Allan Bloostein became president. The two companies were merged in 1973.

EXHIBIT 2
HECHT STORES IN WASHINGTON AND BALTIMORE

	Total gross sq ft	Sales per sq ft index*	Date opened
Washington, D.C.:			
F Street	571,204	62	1896
Silver Spring	221,014	87	1947
Parkington	285,139	96	1951
Prince Georges	197,550	133	1958
Marlow Heights	196,240	137	1960
Laurel	92,716	132	1964
Landmark	162,378	170	1965
Montgomery Mall	216,217	150	1968
Tysons Corner	234,444	179	1968
Landover Mall	154,584	125	1972
Columbia Mall	160,398	111	1975
Manassas	106,233	75	1976
Baltimore:			
Howard Street	439,810	41	1895
Annapolis	26,567	106	1950
Northwood	185,948	69	1954
Edmondson	182,035	49	1956
Reisterstown	185,988	100	1961
Salisbury	89,390	91	1968
Golden Ring	149,982	146	1974
Total	3,857,837	100	

*The index was established by (a) calculating the average sales per square foot data for all the Hecht stores and setting it equal to 100, then (b) dividing the individual store's sales per square foot data into the average Hecht data and multiplying the quotient by 100.

Source: Company records.

city's youngest department store head." During his presidency of that store, he converted an ailing downtown department store into an "avant-garde department store emphasizing newness, imports, and 'different' merchandise."[8]

Bloostein tried to apply a similar strategy at Hecht Company in Washington and Baltimore. To support his effort in converting the image of Hecht Company from "just another department store" to "an exciting, living store," Bloostein and his management team adopted a contemporary company logo and a new advertising format

[8]*Forbes,* Aug. 1, 1966.

(see Exhibit 4). Once the customer was inside the store, Bloostein tried to sustain the "excitement" concept by conducting special fairs (e.g., craft fairs, Oriental fairs, and houseware fairs), by utilizing eye-catching visual presentations (e.g., blowup photographs and lighted displays), and by developing what he called "ego-intensive" shops throughout the store. Examples of such shops included the "I Gotta Be Me" shop, a youth-oriented shop displaying decorative home furnishings and accessories and the newest novelty items, and the "Bazaar," a women's ready-to-wear and accessories shop offering international merchandise.

EXHIBIT 3
HECHT COMPANY ORGANIZATION CHART

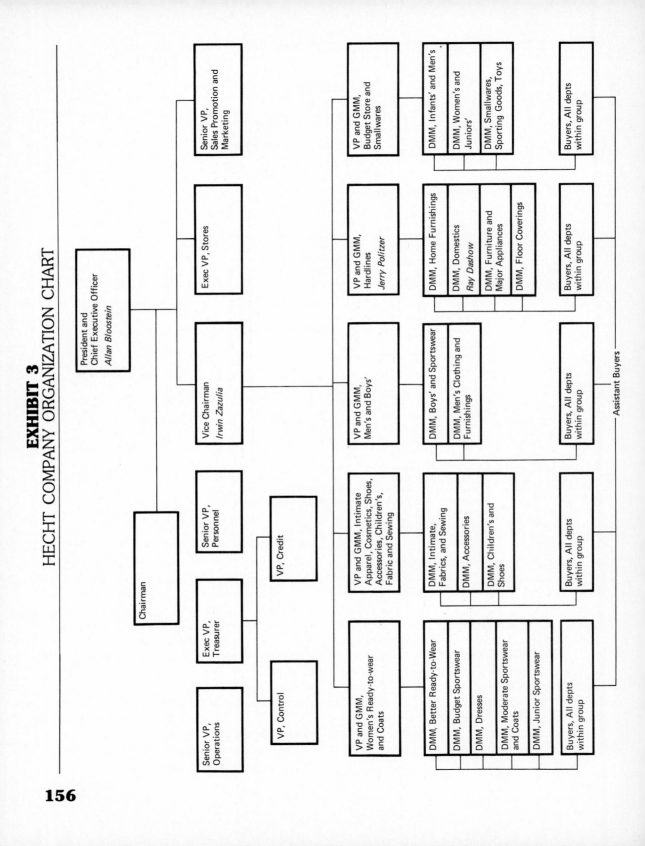

Chairman

President and Chief Executive Officer
Allan Bloostein

Senior VP, Operations

Exec VP, Treasurer

Senior VP, Personnel

Vice Chairman
Irwin Zazulia

Exec VP, Stores

Senior VP, Sales Promotion and Marketing

VP, Control

VP, Credit

VP and GMM, Women's Ready-to-wear and Coats

VP and GMM, Intimate Apparel, Cosmetics, Shoes, Accessories, Children's, Fabric and Sewing

VP and GMM, Men's and Boys'

VP and GMM, Hardlines
Jerry Politzer

VP and GMM, Budget Store and Smallwares

DMM, Better Ready-to-Wear
DMM, Budget Sportswear
DMM, Dresses
DMM, Moderate Sportswear and Coats
DMM, Junior Sportswear

DMM, Intimate, Fabrics, and Sewing
DMM, Accessories
DMM, Children's and Shoes

DMM, Boys' and Sportswear
DMM, Men's Clothing and Furnishings

DMM, Home Furnishings
DMM, Domestics
Ray Dashow
DMM, Furniture and Major Appliances
DMM, Floor Coverings

DMM, Infants' and Men's
DMM, Women's and Juniors'
DMM, Smallwares, Sporting Goods, Toys

Buyers, All depts within group

Buyers, All depts within group

Buyers, All depts within group

Buyers, All depts within group

Buyers, All depts within group

Assistant Buyers

156

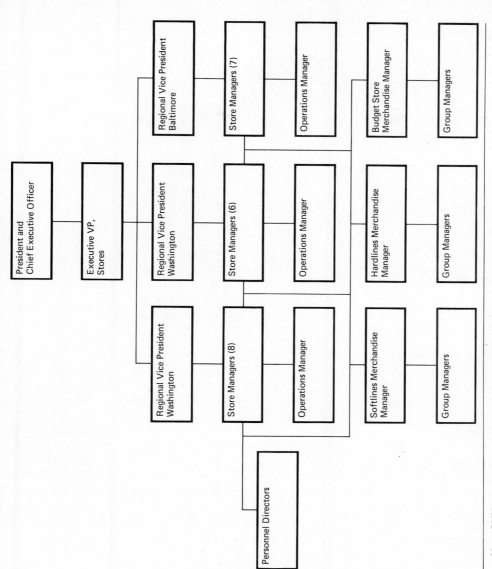

President and
Chief Executive Officer

Executive VP,
Stores

Regional Vice President
Baltimore

Regional Vice President
Washington

Regional Vice President
Washington

Store Managers (7)

Store Managers (6)

Store Managers (8)

Operations Manager

Operations Manager

Operations Manager

Personnel Directors

Budget Store
Merchandise Manager

Hardlines Merchandise
Manager

Softlines Merchandise
Manager

Group Managers

Group Managers

Group Managers

Note: GMM = general merchandise manager; DMM = division merchandise manager.

EXHIBIT 4
ADVERTISEMENT

COMPANY LOGO

Old: the Hecht co

New: ▐▌HECHT'S
where the excitement is

Chenille. A new feeling for fall. Get in touch with the sensuous soft texture. Rows and rows of luscious plush shaped by a swing of dolman sleeve, secured by a twisted rope tie. Pure cotton in mauve. By the Dress Division. Sizes 6-14, \$43. Metropolitan Dresses, F Street, Parkington, Landmark, Montgomery Mall and Tysons Corner.

HECHT'S
where the excitement is

Competition

One factor that influenced Allan Bloostein's decision to try to alter the image of Hecht Company using the "excitement" campaign was the growing competitive pressure in the Washington metropolitan market. In September 1976, Bloomingdale's opened a large store (243,000 square feet) in the Tysons Corner Mall in the Washington suburb. According to *Forbes,* the new store was furnished with "ultra-chic decorations and display cases" and was promoted to project a "Manhattan-youthful-trendy" image.

Besides Bloomingdale's, other national department stores and large specialty stores such as Lord and Taylor, Saks Fifth Avenue, and Neiman-Marcus had penetrated the Washington metropolitan market. But Hecht's major competitor was Woodward and Lothrop, a local department store chain referred to as "Woodies" by the local people. Opened in 1887, Woodies had long been perceived as the "traditional" depart-

ment store by most Washingtonians. Woodies currently operated one large downtown Washington store (within three blocks of Hecht's downtown store) and 11 suburban stores. Nine of these 11 Woodies suburban stores were situated in the same malls as Hecht stores, as shown in Exhibit 5. In Washington alone, the combined sales of Hecht and Woodies accounted for approximately 15 percent of GAF sales (general merchandise, apparel, and home furnishings) of \$2.9 billion[9] in 1977.

[9]GAF data for the Washington SMSA was taken from "1978 Survey of Buying Power," *Sales and Marketing Management,* July 24, 1978. The breakdown of GAF sales was as follows:

General merchandise	\$1,646 million
Apparel	668
Home furnishings (including furniture and appliances)	597
Total GAF	\$2,911 million

Total GAF sales in Baltimore were \$1,576 million.

EXHIBIT 5
HECHT'S COMPETITION

Washington

F Street:	Woodward and Lothrop, Raleigh's,* Garfinckel's†
Silver Spring:	J. C. Penney
Parkington:	J. C. Penney, Sears (1 mile)
Prince Georges:	Woodward and Lothrop, Raleigh's
Marlow Heights:	K Mart, Woodward and Lothrop, Montgomery Ward
Laurel:	Montgomery Ward
Landmark:	Woodward and Lothrop, Sears, Raleigh's
Montgomery Mall:	Woodward and Lothrop, Garfinckel's, Raleigh's, Sears
Tysons Corner:	Woodward and Lothrop, Garfinckel's, Raleigh's, Bloomingdale's
Landover Mall:	Woodward and Lothrop, Garfinckel's, Sears, Raleigh's
Columbia:	Woodward and Lothrop
Manassas:	Montgomery Ward
Gaithersburg:‡	Woodward and Lothrop, Garfinckel's, Sears, J. C. Penney, Montgomery Ward

Baltimore§

Howard St.:	Three local retail stores
Annapolis:	Woodward and Lothrop, Sears, Montgomery Ward
Northwood:	One local retail store
Edmondson:	Two local retail stores
Reisterstown:	Two local retail stores
Salisbury:	One local retail store
Golden Ring:	Montgomery Ward and one local retail store

*Raleigh's is a local specialty store chain.
†Garfinckel's is a local department store.
‡To be opened in September, 1978. This store projects an "ultra-modern sophisticated" image.
§The names of local retail stores in Baltimore are not identified.

Hecht was also facing increased competition from other types of retailers. General merchandise chains such as Sears, J. C. Penney, and Montgomery Ward, according to Bloostein, were pursuing "sharp pricing policies on commodity-type merchandise." These policies were in direct competition with the "value image" for which Hecht Company had previously been known. As shown in Exhibit 5, six Sears stores were located in the same malls as the Hecht stores. J. C. Penney and Montgomery Ward operated three and six stores, respectively, in the same malls as the Hecht stores. Increased competition was also forthcoming from specialty stores that targeted their merchandising efforts toward selective segments of the market.

The Washington/Baltimore Market

The intense retailing competition that existed in the Washington metropolitan area was a reflection of the economic attractiveness of the area. The Washington SMSA was the nation's eighth largest SMSA as measured by number of households. Among the 10 largest SMSAs, Washington was the second most affluent market, with a median spendable income per household of $20,213 in 1977 (Detroit was first with a median spendable income per household of $20,366).[10] Washington's spendable income was 31 percent higher than the national median. Washington ranked second in general merchandise store sales per household ($1,543) among the top 10 SMSAs.[11]

The Washington area had grown in size from 911,500 households in 1970 to 1,066,800 households in 1977. This increase represented a growth rate of 17 percent, the third highest for this period among the 10 largest SMSAs. Washington was also known as a transient market—approximately 35 percent of the population turned over every 5 years.

The Baltimore SMSA was not as affluent as Washington. In 1977, the median spendable income per household was $15,395 (2.5 percent above the United States median), and general merchandise store sales per household were

[10]These trade market data were taken from "1978 Survey of Buying Power," *Sales and Marketing Management, July 24, 1978.*

[11]According to the Standard Industry Classification (SIC) published by the United States government, general merchandise stores included traditional department stores, limited-price variety stores, general merchandise chains, and discount stores.

EXHIBIT 6
DEMOGRAPHIC CHARACTERISTICS OF WASHINGTON AND BALTIMORE

	Washington SMSA	Baltimore SMSA
Population (1977)	3.07 million	2.16 million
Age:		
18–24	13.7%	13.3%
25–34	18.1	15.6
35–49	17.8	17.3
50 and over	19.3	24.3
Education:		
Attended/graduated from college	50.0%	24.8%
Graduated from high school	35.4	40.6
Did not complete high school	14.6	34.6
Occupation:		
Professional/managerial	32.1%	13.0%
Clerical/sales/craft/foreman	18.9	27.1
Other employed	13.4	17.6
Household income:		
$25,000 or more	29.9%	14.4%
$20,000 to $24,999	10.9	8.1
$15,000 to $19,999	27.1	21.9
$10,000 to $14,999	22.2	26.5
Less than $10,000	9.9	29.1

Source: 1977 Target Group Index (TGI) data, published by Axiom Market Research Bureau, Inc.

$1,331 (0.5 percent below the United States average). But Baltimore had grown nearly as fast as Washington. The number of households grew from 630,700 in 1970 to 732,300 in 1977, an increase of 16 percent.

There were other demographic differences between Baltimore and Washington. As shown in Exhibit 6, twice as many people surveyed[12] attended or graduated from college in Washington as in Baltimore. Also, more than twice as many people surveyed were employed in professional or managerial positions in Washington, and more than twice as many households in Washington earned over $25,000 a year.

But despite these differences in demograph-

ics, buying patterns for bedsheets in the two cities were quite similar. For example, the share of "white" sheets was estimated to be only a few percentage points higher in Washington than in Baltimore (20 percent versus 17 percent). Similarly, the percentage of bedsheets sold during White Sale periods was estimated to be only slightly higher in Washington than in Baltimore (62 percent versus 57 percent).

Performance of the Domestics Group

The buying office of the Domestics Group for the 19 stores in Washington and Baltimore was located on the third floor of the Washington downtown store on F Street. Soon after returning from his meeting with Allan Bloostein on the

[12]The data were obtained through the 1977 *Target Group Index* (TGI), published by Axiom Market Research Bureau, Inc.

EXHIBIT 7
1977 DEPARTMENTAL PERFORMANCE OF HECHT'S DOMESTICS MERCHANDISE GROUP

	Departments			
	Bedsheets	**Towels**	**Table linens**	**Bed covers**
Sales ($000)	$6,600	$3,400	$1,700	$3,000
Annual rate of sales growth (1977 vs. 1974)	7.8%	9.1%	11.5%	24.4%
Gross margin	37.8%	48.8%	51.0%	47.0%
Stockturns	3.5	3.1	2.2	3.0
Selling space (000)	44 sq ft	29 sq ft	17 sq ft	34 sq ft
Sales per sq ft	$150	$117	$100	$88
Direct departmental profit:*				
Percentage	5.2%	16.8%	14.3%	10.7%
Dollars (000)	$343	$571	$243	$321

*Direct departmental profit is calculated as follows: gross margin less all direct costs and other departmental costs. (See Exhibit 9 for a detailed description of direct costs.)

Source: Company records.

fifth floor of the same building, Jerry Politzer called a meeting with Ray Dashow and Tom Schulz, buyer for the Bedsheets Department.

Dashow came to the meeting with two tables relating to departmental performance which he had compiled from several computer printouts. The first table, reproduced in Exhibit 7, showed that in 1977, the Bedsheets Department outperformed the other Domestics departments in terms of sales volume, sales per square foot, and stockturns. But the table also showed that other departments outperformed the Bedsheets Department in terms of sales growth, gross margin percentage, and departmental profit percentage.

The second table that Dashow had prepared (see Exhibit 8) compared the performance of the Hecht Bedsheets Department with the average performance of the same department in all May stores. Hecht's Bedsheets Department had a higher-than-average record on sales per square foot and stockturns, but it had a lower-than-average record on growth, gross margin percentage, and departmental profit percentage.

"We don't seem to have much of a problem

generating sales," commented Politzer, "but we sure aren't making a good rate of return on Bedsheets. How do the direct expenses[13] for

[13]Direct expenses included (1) merchandising and buying expenses, (2) selling expenses, (3) advertising and sales promotion expenses, and (4) merchandise handling cost. See Exhibit 9 for details.

EXHIBIT 8
PERFORMANCE OF THE BEDSHEETS DEPARTMENT (1977)
Hecht Company vs. All May Department Stores

	Hecht	May
Annual rate of sales growth (1977 vs. 1974)	7.8%	9.8%
Gross margin	37.8%	40.2%
Stockturns	3.5	3.2
Sales per square foot	$150	$131
Direct departmental profit	5.2%	10.7%
Sales as percentage of Domestics Merchandise Group	44.9%	42.0%
Sales as percentage of total store sales	2.3%	1.6%

Source: Company records.

EXHIBIT 9
1977 DEPARTMENTAL OPERATING STATEMENT
In Percentages

	Bedsheets	Towels	Table linens	Bed covers
Sales	100.0	100.0	100.0	100.0
Gross margin	37.8	48.8	51.0	47.0
Total merchandising and buying	4.2	4.3	5.6	4.4
Merchandising	1.8	1.6	1.7	1.8
Buying	1.6	2.3	3.2	1.9
Merchandising and buying clerical	0.8	0.4	0.7	0.6
Total selling	8.1	8.4	9.5	9.0
Selling salaries and commissions*	5.7	6.1	7.4	6.9
Selling supervision	1.6	1.6	1.5	1.6
Mail and telephone orders	0.3	0.2	0.2	0.2
Merchandise adjustment	0.2	0.2	0.1	0.2
Other selling services	0.3	0.3	0.3	0.1
Total advertising and sales promotion	5.2	4.8	4.2	6.1
Net newspaper advertising	3.1	2.2	2.0	4.2
Advertising preparation	0.5	0.5	0.2	0.3
All other advertising	0.9	1.5	1.4	0.9
Display and signs	0.7	0.6	0.6	0.7
Total merchandise handling	3.2	3.3	4.7	2.9
Receiving, checking, and marking	1.4	1.6	2.6	1.3
Transfer hauling	0.4	0.3	0.4	0.3
Stock maintenance	0.7	0.8	0.6	0.7
Wrap and pack	0.3	0.3	0.4	0.4
Delivery	0.4	0.3	0.7	0.2
Total direct expenses	20.7	20.8	24.1	22.3
Total other expenses	11.6	10.9	12.1	13.5
Telephone and security	1.6	1.5	1.5	1.5
Space and fixed asset	6.0	5.2	6.6	7.7
Control and accounting	0.8	0.9	0.9	1.0
Other general expenses	3.2	3.3	3.3	3.3
Credit and interest (income less expense)	0.3	0.3	0.5	0.5
Direct departmental profit	5.2	16.8	14.3	10.7

*Sales personnel in the Domestics Group were compensated entirely by salary. In some other departments such as Furniture and Major Appliances, compensation was part salary and part commission.

Source: Company records.

Bedsheets compare with the other departments?"

"Bedsheets had the lowest direct expenses as a percentage of sales in 1977," replied Dashow. "It was 20.7 percent as compared to 20.8 percent for Towels, 22.3 percent for Bed Covers, and 24.1 percent for Table Linens."

Schulz, who had remained silent in the meeting thus far, felt than an opportune time had arrived for him to "defend" the Bedsheets Department. He commented that its performance should not be evaluated only in terms of its ability to generate profits. "I believe that the 44,000 square feet of selling space allocated to the Bedsheets Department can be justified on the basis of the traffic generated for the entire store," he said. "Besides, I don't think we're so different from our competitors. They are also using bedsheets as traffic builders. They carry a broad assortment of patterns and have as many

EXHIBIT 10
NUMBER OF BEDSHEET PATTERNS CARRIED BY HECHT, WOODIES, AND BLOOMINGDALE'S AS OF AUGUST 1978

	Hecht*	Woodies	Bloomingdale's
Springs Mills	12	0	2
J. P. Stevens	6	6	10
Burlington	6	0	0
Cannon Mills	3	0	4
Martex	2	4	4
Wamsutta	2	6	10
Fieldcrest	0	6	2
	31	22	32

*Sales of these 31 branded "upstairs" bedsheets accounted for approximately two-thirds of Hecht's bedsheet sales. The remaining one-third was accounted for by the "basement" line, which consisted of irregulars and closeouts.

Source: Company records.

sale periods as we do. I found out that Bloomies carries 32 different patterns, Woodies carries 22, and we carry 31. The only difference, of course, is that Bloomies and Woodies carry Fieldcrest and we don't."[14] (See Exhibit 10 for a breakdown of the number of patterns carried by competing stores, Exhibit 11 for a finer breakdown by price points, and Exhibit 12 for a list of patterns carried by Hecht.)

"Now that Fieldcrest allowed some of our stores to carry its Karastan brand of carpets, there's a good chance we'll be carrying the Fieldcrest towel and bedsheet lines in the near future," said Politzer. "But in the meantime, we've got to work with what's available. . . . Tom, do we have any 'stars' in the making?"

"I'm still convinced that Comfortcale is going to have a long-run potential of becoming a 'star,'" Schulz replied. "But the results of the

[14]For years, Fieldcrest had refused to sell its products to Hecht because of the store's alleged promotional posture. The absence of Fieldcrest was believed to be a major drawback to Hecht's image and, more specifically, to the Domestic Group's profit level.

first few months since its introduction don't look all that good."

Comfortcale Line of Bedsheets

Comfortcale was introduced in 40 major markets throughout the United States in February 1980. Retail distribution was limited to one or two major department stores in each market. For example, distribution was limited to Bloomingdale's in New York and Filene's in Boston. In Washington, Comfortcale was carried only in the 19 Hecht stores,[15] and later by two Bloomingdale's stores. Most of the stores introduced the five Comfortcale patterns (one white, two geometric prints, and two Oscar de la Renta prints) at premium prices. Twin-size Comfortcales (flat and fitted), for example, were initially priced at $5.99 for the basic white and $7.99 for the Oscar de la Renta prints. Considerable retailer support was offered in the form of a special 10-minute sales training film for the store salespeople and a 5-minute point-of-sale visual aid for the customer. Comfortcale ads, featuring "the very cotton sheet" theme, appeared in such magazines as *Ladies' Home Journal, The New Yorker, Better Homes and Gardens, The New York Times Magazine, Sunset,* and *Southern Living.* They were also aired on two TV morning shows, NBC's "Today" and ABC's "Good Morning America." Trade publications and local newspapers also carried free publicity for Comfortcale.

The name "Comfortcale" was derived by combining the words "comfort" and "percale." Comfortcale was developed jointly by Cannon and Cotton Incorporated[16] in one of the indus-

[15]The president of Cannon Mills later admitted that he had some reservations about going with Hecht because of its past promotional image but decided to do so because Hecht was building a new image through its "excitement" campaign.

[16]Cotton Incorporated, commonly known as Cotton Inc., was a trade association representing cotton producers.

EXHIBIT 11

NUMBER OF BEDSHEET PATTERNS* CARRIED BY HECHT,† WOODIES, AND BLOOMINGDALE'S AS OF AUGUST 1978

Prices of twin-size bedsheets	Springs Mills			Stevens			Burlington			Cannon			Martex			Wamsutta			Fieldcrest			Total		
	H‡	W‡	B‡	H	W	B	H	W	B	H	W	B	H	W	B	H	W	B	H	W	B	H	W	B
$ 3.00–$3.99	3	–	–	–	–	–	1	–	–	1	–	–	–	–	–	–	–	–	–	–	–	4	0	0
$ 4.00–$4.99	3	–	–	1	2	5	–	–	–	–	–	1	1	1	–	–	2	9	–	1	–	6	6	15
$ 5.00–$5.99	9	–	1	6	–	9	3	–	–	–	–	3	–	1	1	1	3	2	–	1	–	19	5	16
$ 6.00–$6.99	–	–	–	3	4	5	–	–	–	–	–	1	–	1	–	–	–	–	–	1	4	4	6	10
$ 7.00–$7.99	–	–	–	–	1	–	1	–	–	2	–	3	–	2	2	–	–	–	–	1	–	3	4	5
$ 8.00–$8.99	–	–	–	–	1	–	–	–	–	–	–	–	1	–	1	–	2	3	–	–	1	1	3	5
$ 9.00–$9.99	1	–	–	–	–	–	–	–	–	–	–	–	–	–	–	1	–	–	–	–	–	2	0	0
$10.00 and above	–	–	–	–	–	–	–	–	–	–	–	–	–	–	–	–	–	2	–	1	2	0	1	4
Total	16	0	1	10	8	19	6	0	0	3	0	8	2	5	4	2	7	16	0	5	7	39	25	55

*Patterns are broken down further in this exhibit on the basis of colors.

†Price points of all bedsheets in the Washington stores were equivalent to those in the Baltimore stores.

‡H = Hecht, W = Woodward and Lothrop, B = Bloomingdale's.

Source: Company records.

EXHIBIT 12

PRODUCT ASSORTMENT OF BEDSHEETS BY STORE

Mill and pattern	No. of colors	Washington Stores												Baltimore Stores						
		F	SS	PK	PG	MH	LA	LK	MM	TC	LO	CM	MA	HO	NO	ED	RE	SA	GR	AN
Springs Mills:																				
Queen Anne's Lace	1	x	x	x	x	x	x	x	x	x	x	x	x	x	x	x	x	x	x	x
Peignoir Pastels	3	x	x	x	x	x	x	x	x	x	x	x	x	x	x	x	x	x	x	x
Earth Tones	2	x	x	x	x	x	x	x	x	x	x	x	x	x	x	x	x	x	x	x
White Wondercale	1	x	x	x	x	x	x	x	x	x	x	x	x	x	x	x	x	x	x	x
Gallop	1	x	x	x	x	x	x	x	x	x	x	x	x	x	x	x	x	x	x	x
Whoo	1	x	x	x	x	x	x	x	x	x	x	x	x	x	x	x	x	x	x	x
Whispur	1	x	x	x	x	x	x	x	x	x	x	x	x	x	x	x	x	x	x	x
Newburyport	1	x	x	x	x	x	x	x	x	x	x	x	x	x	x	x	x	x	x	x
Mariposa	1	x	x	x	x	x	x	x	x	x	x	x	x	x	x	x	x	x	x	x
Fresh Daisy	2	x	x	x	x	x	x	x	x	x	x	x	x	x	x	x	x	x	x	x
Challis Rose	1	x	x	x	x	x	x	x	x	x	x	x	x	x	x	x	x	x	x	x
Metropolis	1	x	x	x	x	x	x	x	x	x	x	x	x	x	x	x			x	x
J. P. Stevens:																				
Country Lace	3	x	x	x	x	x	x	x	x	x	x	x	x	x	x		x	x	x	x
Pipeline Solids	3	x	x	x	x	x		x	x	x	x	x	x	x	x		x	x	x	x
Federal Stripe	1	x	x	x	x	x	x	x	x	x	x	x	x	x	x		x	x	x	x
Boxes	1	x	x	x	x	x	x	x	x	x	x	x	x	x	x	x	x	x	x	x
Island Fresco	1	x	x	x	x	x	x	x	x	x	x	x	x	x	x	x	x	x	x	x
Narcissus	1	x	x	x	x	x	x	x	x	x	x	x	x	x	x	x	x	x	x	x
Burlington:																				
Nairobi	1	x	x	x	x	x	x	x	x	x	x	x	x	x	x	x	x	x	x	x
Cameroon	1	x	x	x	x	x	x	x	x	x	x	x	x	x	x	x	x	x	x	x
Lion	1	x	x	x	x	x	x	x	x	x	x	x	x	x	x	x	x	x	x	x
Celestial	1	x	x	x	x	x	x	x	x	x	x	x	x	x	x	x	x	x	x	x
China Trade	1	x	x	x	x	x	x	x	x	x	x	x	x	x	x	x	x	x	x	x
Doug Wilson cases	3	x	x	x	x	x	x	x	x	x	x	x	x	x	x	x	x	x	x	x
Martex:																				
Pageantry	1	x	x	x	x	x	x	x	x	x	x	x		x	x	x	x	x	x	
Autumn Bouquet	1	x	x	x	x	x		x	x	x	x	x	x	x	x		x		x	x
Wamsutta:																				
Tomorrow's Rainbow	1	x	x	x	x	x	x	x	x	x	x	x	x	x	x	x	x		x	x
Supercale	1	x	x	x	x	x	x	x	x	x	x	x	x	x	x					
Cannon Mills:																				
Windrush	1	x	x	x	x	x	x	x	x	x	x	x	x	x	x	x	x	x	x	
Dimensions	1	x	x	x	x	x	x	x	x	x	x	x	x	x	x	x	x	x	x	x
Whites	1	x	x	x	x	x	x	x	x	x	x	x	x	x	x	x	x	x	x	x

The letter "x" denotes the availability of the pattern in the store.

F = F Street   PG = Prince Georges   LK = Landmark   LO = Landover Mall   HO = Howard Street   RE = Reisterstown   GR = Golden Ring
SS = Silver Spring   MH = Marlow Heights   MM = Montgomery Mall   CM = Columbia Mall   NO = Northwood   SA = Salisbury   AN = Annapolis
PK = Parkington   LA = Laurel   TC = Tysons Corner   MA = Manassas   ED = Edmondson

try's most closely held secrets. When the news of the introduction was released in November 1977, most of the mill spokespersons expressed surprise but "were supportive of the move to a newer product, viewing any break from the traditional product mix as a plus for the industry." In exchange for developing the new 60 percent cotton/40 percent polyester blend and a special finish which enabled the new blend to retain its permanent press characteristics, Cannon was promised advertising and sales promotion support of $1 million in the first year by Cotton Incorporated. Cotton Inc. also agreed to give exclusive merchandising and promotional support to Cannon for the first year and a half.

Cannon's decision to develop and market the new product line was supported by the findings of a two-stage consumer study sponsored by Cotton Inc. In the first stage, 805 personal interviews were conducted in the summer of 1976 by an independent marketing research firm. Respondents were asked to rate products made of "all cotton or mostly cotton" fabric and products made of "all or mostly polyester" fabric on comfort and quality. Seventy-nine percent of the respondents perceived cotton products to be comfortable as compared with 53 percent for polyester products. Similarly, 76 percent of the respondents perceived cotton products to be of high quality as compared with 54 percent for polyester products.

The second stage of the consumer research conducted by Cotton Inc. was designed to evaluate consumer intent to purchase the 60/40–blend bedsheet. Personal interviews with 454 women were conducted in large shopping malls in 10 major markets throughout the country by another independent research firm. Respondents were first shown written product descriptions of the 60/40–blend bedsheet and the 50/50–blend bedsheet and then asked to rate their interest in buying each type of bedsheet. The results were as follows:

	60/40–blend bedsheet	50/50–blend bedsheet
1. Definitely buy	25%	22%
2. Probably buy	47	48
3. Might, might not	21	20
4. Probably not buy	6	8
5. Definitely not buy	1	2
	100%	100%

Respondents were next asked which of the two types of sheets they would rather buy. Sixty-one percent of the respondents preferred the 60/40 blend, and 39 percent preferred the 50/50 blend. The demographic profile of respondents who preferred the 60/40–blend bedsheet was younger, more affluent, and more highly educated than the profile of respondents who preferred the 50/50–blend bedsheet. Asked whether one bedsheet would cost more than the other, two-thirds of the respondents answered "yes." Of those who responded "yes," two-thirds thought the 60/40–blend bedsheet would be priced higher.

Hecht's Decision

Schulz was excited about the introduction of Comfortcale for a number of good reasons. First, the product was a "breath of fresh air in the weary and overproduced industry" and was consistent with the store's "excitement" campaign. Second, Hecht would have a jump on its competitors, especially Woodies. Third, Comfortcale could attract a segment of the market favorably disposed to the so-called "natural" movement;[17] this segment might be a good match with the kind of segment that Hecht wanted to attract. Finally, Hecht would have an opportunity to improve its profit picture in the Bedsheets Department.

[17]Manifestations of the "natural" movement could be seen in the rising popularity of natural food and beverages, natural fibers in clothing, and natural childbirth.

By the end of August 1978, the combined 6-month sales of Cannon's Comfortcale sheets were $42,000. Of the three Comfortcale prints that Hecht carried since February 1978, "White" had the highest sales ($22,500). Oscar de la Renta's "Windrush" and a geometric pattern called "Dimensions" followed with sales of $12,300 and $7,200 respectively. The gross margins averaged 42.3 percent for White, 48.8 percent for Windrush, and 49.8 percent for Dimensions. (See Exhibit 13 for existing retail prices of Comfortcale patterns in Washington and Exhibit 14 for a comparison of Comfortcale's performance record with the records of the three best-selling bedsheet patterns and the three worst-selling bedsheet patterns in the months of June, July, and August.) Although these margins were among the highest in the Bedsheets Department, Tom Schulz was somewhat disappointed with the sales level of Comfortcales. Part of the problem he attributed to Hecht's decision not to pursue aggressively the point-of-purchase display which Cotton Inc. prepared.

EXHIBIT 13
ACTUAL RETAIL PRICES OF COMFORTCALE
As of August 1978

	Hecht	Bloomingdale's
Whites:		
Twin	$ 4.99	$ 4.99
Full	6.99	6.99
Queen	10.99	10.99
King	13.99	13.99
Standard cases	5.99	6.50
King cases	6.99	7.50
Patterns:		
Twin	7.99	7.99
Full	9.99	9.95
Queen	13.99	14.50
King	16.99	17.50
Standard cases	7.99	7.50
King cases	8.99	8.50

Source: Company records.

Schulz, however, knew from Cotton Inc.'s past experience with the successful launching of the 60/40 fabric in the men's dress shirt industry that it took time (over half a year or so) for a new product to be adopted to any great extent by the consumers. Cotton Inc. was continuing its TV and magazine advertising on Comfortcale, and as more and more stores began carrying the product line, Tom Schulz believed that consumer awareness and acceptance of Comfortcale would pick up.

In August 1978, Tom Schulz circulated a short questionnaire to all store managers asking what the Comfortcale fabric blend meant to their customers. The consensus of the respondents was that most customers were not aware of the new fabric and that even if they were, the type of pattern seemed more important than the blend of the sheet fabric to their purchase decision.

In the same questionnaire, Tom Schulz also asked the 19 store managers to evaluate all the existing patterns, using a five-point scale, on whether or not each pattern should be continued through the winter White Sale. As shown in Exhibit 15, the ratings of the two patterned Comfortcales were below the average rating, while the rating of the white was equal to the average rating.

Just as the questionnaire responses were coming in, a Cannon salesperson gave Schulz a preview of the five new patterns Cannon was adding to the fall line (see Exhibit 16). The package was also changed to highlight the higher cotton content of Comfortcale. Schulz was very enthusiastic about the new patterns and the improved package. He believed that the new Comfortcales had a winning combination of good looks and the natural, comfortable feel.

Schulz also believed that the trend of the bedsheet business toward a higher cotton content would not be short-lived. Although there were no immediate plans for setting up production facilities, Springs Mills had been experimenting with a 60 percent cotton and 40 percent

EXHIBIT 14
PERFORMANCE RECORDS OF SELECTED BEDSHEET PATTERNS AT HECHT
June–August 1978

	Comfortcale*	Three best sellers			Three worst sellers		
		Brand A (geometric)	Brand B (novelty)	Brand C (white)	Brand X (animal)	Brand Y (animal)	Brand Z (floral)
Sales (3 months)	$27,000	$75,000	$55,000	$40,000	$ 5,000	$4,000	$ 3,000
Inventory†	$23,000	$28,300	$24,300	$18,300	$14,000	$6,700	$12,700
Gross margin	46.5%	43.0%	44.7%	45.5%	34.7%	40.5%	35.1%
Markdown	0	0	0	0	10%	5%	10%
Stockturns	1.2	2.7	2.3	2.2	.4	.6	.2
Price points (twin size)	$4.99‡	$5.99	$5.99	$4.99	$5.99	$5.99	$5.99
	7.99						
Co-op advertising allowance	11%	5%	9%	10%	9%	10%	8%

*All patterns combined (i.e., one white, four prints).
†Average monthly inventory for 3 months.
‡$4.99 for white and $7.99 for patterns.
Source: Company records.

EXHIBIT 15
RESULTS OF STORE MANAGERS' EVALUATION OF BEDSHEETS
July 1978

Evaluation criteria: 4—**Excellent, should be continued through the winter White Sale**
3—**Good, should probably be continued**
2—**Fair, no opinion as to keeping**
1—**Poor, should be discontinued**
0—**Very poor**

Overall average rating: 2.7

Mill and pattern	Average points	Mill and pattern	Average points
Springs Mills:		Burlington:	
Queen Anne's Lace	2.2	Nairobi	2.8
Peignoir Pastels	2.8	Cameroon	1.2
Earth Tones	2.8	Lion	1.9
White Wondercale	3.9	Celestial	3.7
Gallop	1.6	China Trade	3.1
Whoo	2.9	Cannon Mills:	
Whispurr	3.2	Windrush	1.8
Newburyport	3.6	Dimensions	2.3
Mariposa	3.6	Whites	2.7
Metropolis	3.4	Martex:	
Fresh Daisy	3.3	Pageantry	2.4
Challis Rose	3.4	Autumn Bouquet	3.4
J. P. Stevens:		Wamsutta:	
Country Lace	2.2	Tomorrow's Rainbow	3.9
Pipeline Solids	2.6	Supercale	1.9
Federal Stripe	2.7		
Boxes	2.8		
Island Fresco	1.3		
Narcissus	3.0		

Source: Company records.

polyester fabric for some years. *Retailing Home Furnishings* reported that Dan River was continuing research on the development of a 100 percent cotton sheet with no-iron characteristics.

On the other hand, Schulz was also aware that Burlington had recently introduced a silkier, smoother sheet called Caresse which was made of a blend of 70 percent Dacron[18] polyester and 30 percent cotton. Caresse only came in solid

[18]Dacron is a Du Pont trade name.

colors with decorative hems. Caresse commanded a higher retail selling price and gross margin than Comfortcale.

Summary

As the buying decision for the winter merchandising was drawing closer, Tom Schulz had to decide which of the Comfortcale patterns, if any, should be carried. More broadly, he had to

EXHIBIT 16
NEW COMFORTCALE PATTERNS

HERITAGE LACE

TARASCON BORDIER

 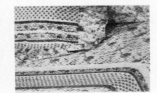

MOHAVE IMPRESSIONS

PAISLEY PROVINCALE

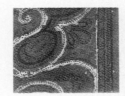 

FLEUR AVIGNON

 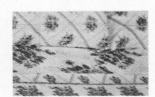

determine the "right" product assortment for each of the 19 stores and the "right" prices and advertising for each product. "Let me see what I can do to improve the bottom line," he said as he thumbed through the reams of computer printouts.

Jerry Politzer was more concerned with the long-run strategy of the Bedsheets Department. Should the department continue to serve as the traffic builder for the entire Domestics Group, or should steps be taken to change that role? How important would Bedsheets be in bringing about the change in store image from a "promotional" store to an "upgraded, updated, exciting store?" Would Bedsheets ever become a "star"?

"I'd better have some answers before my next meeting with Allan," Politzer said as he thumbed through his calendar. "I know what Allan's first three words are going to be when we meet next week," he said. "'Anything exciting, Jerry?'"

12 KCTS
Channel 9, Seattle

Christopher H. Lovelock • Lawrence H. Wilkinson

The difference between transmission and broad-casting is that the latter requires an audience. Transmitter operators simply mind their machines. You don't become a broadcaster until you relate to the people in your audience and are concerned about how they respond to your programs.

—A PBS executive

"The response has been fantastic!" ex-claimed Burnill F. Clark, director of program-ming and operations at KCTS, as he surveyed the ballots submitted for Channel 9's "Viewers' Choice 1976." "We've received sacks of mail from members and nonmembers, regular and occasional KCTS/9 viewers, all anxious to state

Christopher H. Lovelock is an associate professor at the Harvard Graduate School of Business Administration. Lawrence H. Wilkinson was a member of the Harvard MBA class of 1976.

what kind of programs they want to see on television."

Channel 9, the Seattle area's major public television station, had developed a strong repu-tation for its community orientation. Mr. Clark saw the innovative "Viewers' Choice" project, conducted in February 1976, as a way to increase the viewing public's input into program-ming decisions. He planned to use the ballot responses as one of several inputs when making purchases of program series from the PBS[1] Station Program Cooperative.

Program selection and scheduling, the direc-tor indicated, was a complex process involving a great many trade-offs. He would have to decide how much emphasis to give the viewers' ballots in making his selection.

[1]Public Broadcasting Service.

Public Broadcasting in the United States

In the mid-1970s, the United States was unusual in having a commercially dominated broadcast industry. In some countries—such as Britain and Canada—long-established, state-owned broadcasting corporations financed by receiver license fees or by tax monies faced highly regulated commercial competitors. But in most countries the state broadcasting system had a monopoly.

Public broadcasting in the United States presented a very different picture. Although noncommercial broadcasters had operated in some numbers since the first "sign-on," nationally organized public broadcasting was a relative newcomer. The federal government provided partial funding but did not own or operate any facilities.

Historically, all noncommercial TV in the United States had been termed "educational television" regardless of its purpose. Until the 1960s there was no networking, and most programming was locally produced. In 1958, the federal government became involved in funding, awarding substantial grants for research and experiments in educational TV. In 1962, it authorized $32 million for the construction of educational stations in the form of 50–50 matching grants against funds provided by state and local sources. That same year, the National Educational Television and Radio Center (NET) established a national program service during prime-time evening hours for all 57 existing stations.

In 1967, after intensive study, the presidentially appointed Carnegie Commission on Educational Television concluded:

> A well-financed and well-directed educational television system substantially larger and far more pervasive and effective . . . must be brought into being if the full needs of the American public are to be served.

The report distinguished two types of noncommercial operations, "public" and "instructional," and centered its recommendations on the former. It proposed the establishment of a federally financed Corporation for Public Broadcasting (CPB) to facilitate both local and national programming, encourage technical and personnel development, and provide network interconnection.

In November 1967, Congress passed the Public Broadcasting Act, establishing CPB as an independent, nonprofit corporation funded by yearly congressional appropriations. CPB established a national TV landline interconnection and created the Public Broadcasting Service (PBS) to manage this distribution system. National Public Radio was formed in 1970 along similar lines. PBS took responsibility for running the interconnection and also for scheduling and coordinating national programming, subject to joint review with CPB. It also provided other support services, including legislative lobbying. In 1975 CPB provided some 40 percent of PBS's $25 million budget.

The total budget for public broadcasting in the United States in 1975 was $353 million. Funding came from federal, state, and local appropriations, plus foundation grants and corporate and individual donations. The Ford Foundation's decision to phase out its long-standing grants to public TV, together with the budgetary constraints facing local school boards, emphasized the need for station fund raising. Corporate funding was often sought for underwriting specific programs ("made possible by a grant from Mobil Oil"), while many stations pursued an aggressive and frequently criticized policy of on-the-air fund raising.

By late 1975, 26 percent of the 962 television stations on the air in the United States and 31 percent of the 2,571 FM radio stations were operating noncommercially. About 40 percent of the TV stations transmitted on VHF (Channels 2–13), where the commercial network stations were generally located; the balance transmitted on UHF (Channels 14–38), which was often difficult to receive, although increasing use of cable TV was helping to resolve this problem. It was estimated that public TV signals reached about 84 percent of the nation's homes.

There were four types of licensees—community-supported (36 percent of the total), colleges and universities (34 percent), state agencies (17 percent), and public school systems (12 percent). Community stations tended to be quite audience-conscious, reflecting both their community governance and their dependence on viewer donations for financial support. Some of the stations licensed to colleges and universities had adopted a broader community mandate and reflected that in their operations policies and fund-raising activities. Seattle's KCTS was such a station.

The Seattle Area

Seattle, seat of King County and the largest city in the Pacific Northwest, had a metropolitan population of some 1.4 million in 1976, making it the twentieth largest metropolitan area in the United States. The nonwhite population represented about 14.4 percent of the total, comprising blacks, Chicanos, American Indians, and Asian-Americans of Chinese and Japanese descent.

An attractive city, Seattle was built on seven hills between Puget Sound on the west and some large freshwater lakes on the east. Travel around the area afforded striking views of both mountains and shorelines; on a clear day, one could see the snow-capped summit of Mount Rainier over 50 miles away. Local residents enjoyed excellent fishing and sailing all year long, and Seattle boasted the highest per capita boat ownership of any major city in the country. Water skiing was invented there, and snow skiing was a popular winter sport, with good slopes as close as 1 hour's drive from the city. Seattle had achieved international prominence with its 1962 World's Fair. One legacy was the Seattle Center, a 74-acre convention and family entertainment center dominated by the 607-foot Space Needle and connected to the downtown area by monorail service.

The city was home to a number of arts organizations, including the Seattle Symphony Orchestra, Seattle Opera Association, Seattle Repertory Theatre, Seattle Art Museum, and ACT Theatre. College and amateur groups provided a variety of other cultural offerings. Spectator sports in the area included major league baseball, soccer, football, and horse racing. With the opening of the huge Kingdome (King County domed stadium) in early 1976, there was a new site for large spectator events.

Seattle Area Media

Greater Seattle was well served by print and broadcast media. The city had two major dailies, the *Seattle Times* (circulation 219,000) and the *Seattle Post-Intelligencer* (circulation 183,000), as well as numerous local papers and periodicals. There were 21 AM and 19 FM radio stations on the air in the region, including four public FM stations.

Viewers had a good choice of television stations, although reception was uncertain in some locations. Eight stations were broadcasting in the Seattle-Tacoma television market in early 1976, six on VHF and two on UHF. According to the 1975 edition of *Broadcasting Yearbook,* there were 768,400 TV households in the "Area of Dominant Influence"; 606,000 of these were located in King County and in adjoining Pierce and Snohomish Counties.

The Seattle/Tacoma TV market was dominated by the three commercial network affiliates operating in Seattle. The oldest station in the area was an NBC affiliate, KING-TV (Channel

5), which had begun operation through an earlier license in 1948. The owner, King Broadcasting Co., also operated stations in Spokane and Portland. KOMO-TV, an ABC affiliate, dated from 1953 and was operated on Channel 4 by a company which also owned a station in Portland. The CBS affiliate, on the air since 1958, was KIRO-TV (Channel 7). This station was a subsidiary of the Bonneville International Corporation, owned by the Mormon church, which administered numerous other broadcast properties. The fourth commercial station in this market was KSTW (Channel 11) in Tacoma, an "independent" owned by the Oklahoma Publishing Company.

In addition to KCTS, there were three other public TV stations in the Seattle-Tacoma area. Two of these were licensed to the Clover Park School District in Lakewood Center, south of Tacoma. Clover Park had operated a UHF station, KPEC-TV (Channel 56), for a number of years; recently it had also acquired the license for Channel 13, an independent commercial station, redesignated as KCPQ. Although this station's resources were limited, it had a strong signal and was seen as a potential competitor by Channel 9 management. Another UHF station, KTPS (Channel 62), was licensed to a Tacoma school district and specialized in educational programming.

The Development of KCTS

KCTS was licensed to the University of Washington, a state institution, and transmitted a powerful signal on Channel 9. Aided by microwave links and cable systems, its signal extended from the Oregon border in the south up through British Columbia in the north and from the Cascades in the east to the Pacific Ocean (Exhibit 1). KCTS had an authorized power of 275 kW visual and 55 kW aural, exceeding that of two of the three commercial TV network affiliates in Seattle. Although reception was generally good, Seattle's hilly terrain made it difficult to view KCTS transmissions from some parts of the city.

In many respects, KCTS epitomized the evolution of public television over the years. From a low-budget, local educational outlet, Channel 9 had developed into a technically sophisticated station with a high community profile, broadcasting more national than local material and ambitious to see its own productions achieve nationwide distribution.

KCTS History, 1954–1972

KCTS first went on the air in December 1954 and was the eighth noncommercial television station to begin broadcasting in the United States. Its initial objective was to provide educational broadcasting for the schools of Seattle and surrounding King County. The station's offices and studios were housed by the University of Washington, while monetary support came initially from public schools and institutions of higher education.

During its early years, Channel 9 employed a dozen staff members—all state employees—and broadcast 20 hours weekly, Monday through Friday. Most of the programs were locally produced, although some films were obtained from outside agencies. Daytime instructional programming for use by teachers was combined with limited evening broadcasts of "telecourses" and community-oriented programs.

In 1962, NET's establishment of national program service during prime evening time increased KCTS's programming hours and broadened the range of programs available. A more powerful transmitter improved Channel 9's geographic coverage, as did the growth of cable and microwave links. In 1969, the PBS interconnection further extended the station's programming capabilities. Despite these improvements, Channel 9 operated only on week-

EXHIBIT 1
KCTS COVERAGE MAP FOR WASHINGTON STATE AND BRITISH COLUMBIA

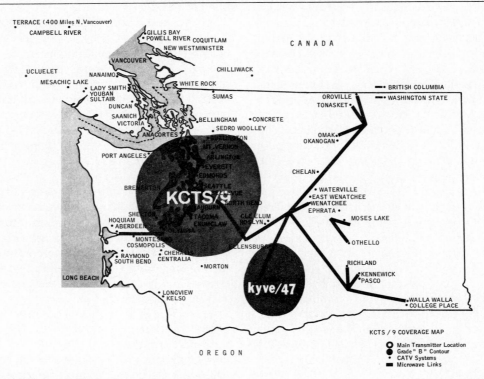

Note: KCTS also reached the Vancouver, B.C., area by cable.

Source: KCTS records.

days and was perceived by most people as a local educational station.

New Management

In 1972, Channel 9's first station manager retired after 17 years. Later characterized by a journalist as a "quiet, don't-rock-the-boat sort of man who tended to think of educational TV as dealing with academic education," this individual had consistently maintained a low personal profile.

His successor, who joined the station in July 1972, was entirely different. Dr. Richard J. Meyer, then aged 38, came to KCTS from WNET in New York, one of the best-known public TV stations in the country, where he had been a producer and vice president.

Richie Meyer, portrayed by a local journalist as "bearded, curly haired, exuberant and energetic," inherited what some described as "a stodgy and stuffy old educational television station, the channel nobody watched [unless they wanted] to sit through god-awful panel discussions featuring erudite but inarticulate professors or watch [someone] explain the intricacies of hemstitching under water."[2]

When Meyer arrived in Seattle, he immediately set about making changes: canceling much of Channel 9's local programming, making staff changes, and seeking the active involvement of the local community.

His credo, he said, was to involve public television in all areas of contemporary life: "The public is what public TV is really all about and that is why I like it." Commenting on his ambitions for the station, he observed:

The background of Channel 9 is fascinating because it was one of the first public TV stations in the nation, starting out on a par with WNET in New York, WGBH in Boston and KQED in San Francisco. But while they progressed, Channel 9 stayed just about the same. My goal is to try to make it equal again. I would like to make Channel 9 one of the nation's flagship stations for public broadcasting.

Initiating an aggressive fund-raising policy in the fall of 1972, he took the station from zero to 25,000 supporters in less than 2 years. By the end of 1975, KCTS boasted some 30,000 individuals and families in the state of Washington and British Columbia who gave annually toward the station's operating expenses. About one-third of these "members" were Canadian. On the average, 80 percent of current members renewed again the following year.

The staff also grew rapidly as new technical and managerial expertise was added. In September 1975, many of the staff members were rehoused in another building owned by the university, freeing up additional production space at the studios. By early 1976, KCTS employed a staff of 50.

The general manager hoped to give KCTS the capacity to produce programs of a high

[2]Ed Sullivan, "The Old Place Ain't What It Used to Be," *Seattle Business*, Feb. 11, 1974.

enough quality and caliber so that the station could market them nationally through PBS. "We're not likely to receive any production grants," he said, "until we have the equipment that will allow us to do a first rate job. We already have the talent."

Color transmissions of films and slides started in December 1973, and in late 1975, KCTS began purchasing the new equipment long coveted by Dr. Meyer. This included state-of-the-art color cameras and recorders, a mobile unit and microwave equipment to permit live outside telecasts, plus major improvements in studio lighting and audio systems. Meyer saw these improvements as central to his goals of technical excellence, local programming which reflected Seattle's needs and problems, and the development of major production capabilities. An 18-month installation period was anticipated. Financing came from public contributions, a capital grant from the university, and matching federal funds.

Organization and Financing

The upper levels of the KCTS organization reflected the station's dual identity as both a university station and a community station. Since the license was held by the University of Washington, all legal authority and responsibility rested with this institution through its vice president for university relations.

As a practical matter, executive authority rested with a 30-member advisory board. Ten of these individuals represented institutions providing financial support for the station while the remaining 20 were drawn from the community at large. In the language of its bylaws:

The present board is charged to make recommendations and to advise on matters relating to finance, development, ascertainment and education.

These bylaws specifically excluded programming from the board's domain.

Station Management

After Meyer was hired as general manager, he initiated a reorganization of the station's management, upgrading the position of director of programming and adding a director of development. Exhibit 2 shows a partial organization chart. It reflects a further reorganization in early 1976, when the director of programming, Burnill F. Clark, assumed additional responsibilities in operations and was named assistant general manager.

Clark had joined KCTS in May 1975 after 10 years' experience with Nebraska Educational Television, a state network, where his most recent position had been assistant network program manager. At Channel 9, he handled local program conceptualization and studio operations. He also worked closely with the station's research director.

The development director, Hope S. Green, had first come to KCTS in 1974, after 6 years at WGBH in Boston. She headed up fund-raising activities for Channel 9; these included membership solicitation on the air and by mail, foundation and government development, and corporate underwriting. Green also coordinated the activities of Channel 9's volunteer group.

Other senior staff members at Channel 9 who reported to the general manager included the directors of administration, engineering, and community involvement.

Financial Matters

Funding for KCTS had historically come from public school districts and from the University of Washington. Beginning in 1972, fund raising was directed toward the community at large.

Public contributions had jumped from $215,000 in 1972–1973 to a projected $600,000 for 1975–1976. Also from 1974 onward, efforts had been made to attract local underwriting for specific programs. Four local firms donated $43,000 in 1974–1975, and in 1975–1976 seven firms—including the telephone company, a local restaurant, a department store, a regional oil company, and the *Seattle Post-Intelligencer*—had collectively donated almost $70,000 to underwrite programs on Channel 9. Exhibit 3 shows the growth and changing composition of KCTS's operating income and expenditures from 1970–1971 through 1975–1976.

The fiscal year 1976 budget projected an annual deficit of almost $360,000,[3] as compared with a $178,000 surplus the previous year. Underlying this change in financial circumstances were increased operating expenses, noncapital equipment purchases, and a projected $250,000 cut in the school district levies payable to KCTS. Station management was concerned about the implications of this cut for the future of school programming.

University support was being increased in the present budget, but some members of KCTS management expressed frustration at the relative inflexibility imposed by Channel 9's relationship to the University of Washington. The latter's biennial funding, voted by the state's legislature, was one problem. Another was the slow, complicated process of hiring personnel. It involved civil service salary regulations and other procedures. Only a few station personnel were exempt, and management was concerned that these procedures made it difficult not only to hire and fire but also to pay competitive salaries.

Development activity was seen as an important means of improving the station's financial situation and its flexibility. Said Hope Green, "I'm interested in increasing the percentage of viewers who are donors." Her goal was to obtain

---

[3]This deficit, made possible by the size of the station's reserves, was planned as a one-time-only situation. By February 1976, it appeared that the deficit would, in fact, be much smaller than originally projected.

EXHIBIT 2
KCTS: PARTIAL ORGANIZATION CHART, MARCH 1976

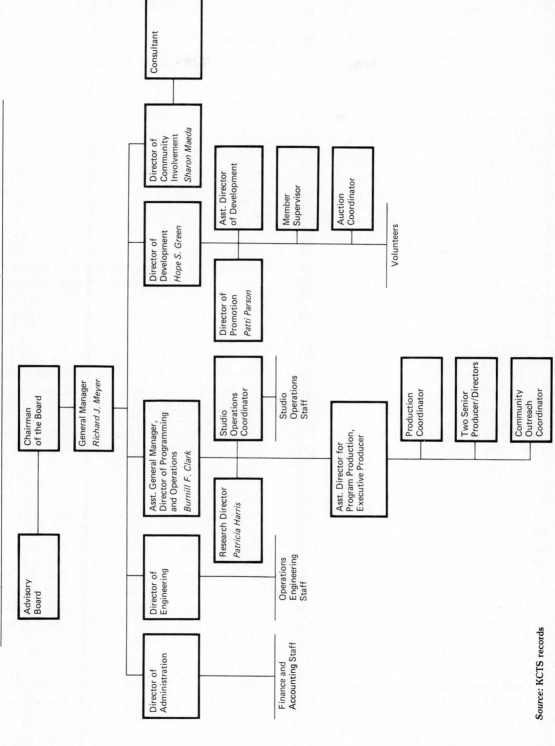

Source: KCTS records

EXHIBIT 3
KCTS: INCOME AND EXPENSE STATEMENT, FY 1971–FY 1976

	1970–71	1971–72	1972–73	1973–74	1974–75	Budget 1975–76
Revenues						
University of Washington	$225,050	$133,797	$135,855	$ 142,606	$ 162,426	$ 267,432
Schools, institutions of higher education	412,248	347,799	353,612	348,194	446,521	133,000
Public contributions	0	0	215,856	348,627	467,267	600,000
Grants	0	0	180,289	173,873	201,829	165,000
Interest	0	0	0	16,325	18,610	10,000
Underwriting	0	0	0	0	43,609	69,500
Other	53,364	80,857	31,824	73,361	29,828	11,000
Total revenues	$690,662	$562,453	$917,386	$1,102,986	$1,370,190	$1,255,932
Expenses						
Programming, education, development, and administration	$203,156	$199,920	$253,346	$ 298,804	$ 410,380	$ 568,666
Engineering	164,477	124,283	168,934	242,693	280,792	418,562
Other operating expenses	187,391	145,337	299,526	333,334	494,982	419,488
Total operating expenses	$555,024	$469,540	$721,806	$ 874,831	$1,186,154	$1,406,716
Noncapital equipment purchases*	0	0	15,574	212,276	6,347	208,646
Total expenses	$555,024	$469,540	$737,380	$1,087,107	$1,192,501	$1,615,362
Net increase (decrease) in funds	$135,638	$ 92,913	$180,006	$ 15,879	$ 177,689	$ (359,430)
Beginning fund balance	104,343	239,981	332,894	512,900	528,779	706,648
Ending fund balance	$289,891	$332,894	$512,900	$ 528,779	$ 706,468	$ 347,038

*In 1975, KCTS planned to use $1.8 million in specially earmarked funds (of which $1.5 million was coming from the University of Washington) for the purchase of new capital equipment.

Source: KCTS Records.

10 percent of the viewing audience as subscribers. Nielsen research data indicated that approximately 280,000 households in the Seattle-Tacoma area (about 40 percent of the total) watched a KCTS program for at least 15 minutes in any given week.

Green conceded that there had been some negative reaction to KCTS's increased emphasis on fund raising. "There's a large faction," she remarked, "not only in this station, but everywhere, that considers fund raising 'philistine.'"

Pledge weeks, known in 1975–1976 as "Festival Weeks" at most PBS stations, occurred four times annually; previously fund-raising evenings had been scattered throughout the year. Green indicated that an effort was made to include particularly high-quality programs during Festival Weeks. "What we try to do," she said, "is to get all those people who tune in just once in a while to tune in during pledge week." A station auction was also planned, beginning in November 1976. Burnill Clark felt strongly that individual programs should not be interrupted for pledge breaks, and Hope Green agreed: "I really think that what we're selling is uninterrupted service."

Programming

In early 1976, KCTS was broadcasting daily, 100 hours a week. In addition to presenting nationally distributed shows from PBS and some local-interest programs, KCTS devoted more than a third of its air time to instructional programming. Meyer discussed the broader interpretation of "educational" broadcasting shown by public television in recent years:

There's nothing that says that educational or public television has to be dry and uninteresting. I feel that if we can inform and educate in an interesting way we should do it. Today's television viewers look for good quality entertainment and fine productions. My philosophy is that our programming should be just as excellently produced and just as entertaining.

Everything we do is educational in some way, but it's no longer the old and deadly image of Miss Johnson standing in front of her blackboard and throwing an eraser at someone. . . .

What we have to remember is that public television tends to be a collection of "minority" programs that commercial stations can't afford to run. For instance, in summer 1973, we carried the Spassky-Fisher "world championship" chess match, and we had viewers watching that thing on little portable sets all over the city. That's one example of what I mean by a "minority" program, appealing to a minority or numerically small audience. There are many other examples.

However, KCTS was also interested in broadening its appeal. Burnill Clark emphasized that one of his programming objectives was to increase public awareness of Channel 9:

Public television involves the public. It is *their* station and we've got to have large numbers of people watching us in order to meet the mandate that I see.

In analyzing the situation when I arrived here, it occurred to me that the best way to make people aware of us and what we're trying to do is to get the best damn schedule we can. So we want to do a number of high visibility programs at this stage in our development.

As an example of high visibility, Clark cited an upcoming program on "redlining" in the Seattle area, which coincided with a mayor's task force investigation of that problem in the city.[4]

Sources of Programming

In-school programming on KCTS originated locally. Approximately one-third was produced at KCTS or at another station supported by an overlapping school district. The balance came from instructional programming services, such as American Instructional Television and the Great Plains National Instructional Television Library.

Public programming, which accounted for some 60 broadcast hours weekly, was "sourced" in several ways. About 5 percent consisted of programs produced locally at KCTS, mostly focusing on topics of interest to one or more segments of the Seattle community. Other programs came from public TV stations in the state, independent distributors, the Eastern Educational Network, or PBS. In a typical week, PBS-distributed materials accounted for 50 broadcast hours.

Programs taken from the PBS national interconnection were made available to stations in one of four ways. Shows which had been underwritten—i.e., covered in advance by a foundation, a corporation, CPB, or a government agency—were offered to affiliates "free of charge." A station's decision on whether or not to carry them was based on their content.[5]

[4] Redlining is a practice allegedly followed by many banks whereby red lines are drawn on a map around certain urban neighborhoods that are considered poor loan risks. Refusal to make loans for home purchases or improvements in the "redlined" areas thus contributes to urban decay.

[5] Examples of such underwritten programs in 1976 included "Masterpiece Theatre" (underwritten by Mobil Oil) and "Black Journal" (Pepsico).

Many unfunded or only partially underwritten shows were offered through the Station Program Cooperative. The SPC was an arrangement whereby PBS affiliates "bid" the programming dollars they intended to spend next year through PBS on series or individual programs.[6] Many of the shows offered were still only in pilot or concept form; they were submitted by the producing stations in the hope that their costs would be spread. Since 1976 marked the cooperative's third year, the upcoming effort was referred to as "SPC III." There were several rounds of SPC bidding; after each one shows with insufficient "votes" were dropped. The costs of those shows which survived the entire process were apportioned among the stations that bid. SPC bids thus involved a commitment to pay an unknown amount (subject to a predetermined maximum). The amount for specific programs was determined after each round by the number of stations bidding on the programs. These shows could only be carried by the stations which had previously bid on and paid for them.

The SPC III offerings totaled some 1,000 hours of programming. It was planned that the first round of bidding should take place in early March. Clark's goal was to purchase 500 to 550 hours. His budget for SPC use was $102,700, of which $36,000 was nonmatching funds contributed by the Ford Foundation and CPB.

The Station Acquisition Market (SAM) was another PBS vehicle for station programming. SAM was created to deal in existing programs (e.g., a BBC series packaged for American distribution). SAM shows were offered at a fixed price, keyed to the size of the station, and program directors had only to vote "yes" or "no."

[6]The SPC bidding process was actually somewhat more complex than depicted in this case, involving bidding rounds to determine the level of support, elimination rounds to get rid of the least popular programs, and, finally, purchase rounds. The explanation of the SPC selection process has been simplified here for the purposes of case analysis.

The fourth source of PBS programming was the Station Independence Project (SIP). This was a PBS service which in 1975–1976 provided special shows for 2 weeks each year that were aimed at helping participating stations with fund raising and membership drives.

Program Selection and Scheduling

Balancing content and cost to fill the desired number of broadcast hours was a complicated task, Clark indicated.

It's a tough choice when I have limited dollars to spend and three 90-minute shows of the caliber of "American Musical Theater" will cost me $30,000, versus ten series of thirty programs each for the same price. Everyone says "buy quality," but then you have to fill up that schedule.

I think there are a lot of misconceptions among people within public television stations—as well as among the general public—as to what it really costs to do a local show, what it costs to buy a program. It's expensive!

I'm not sure that the people who watch us really understand that it costs us $1,500 a week to have "Nova" in the schedule. So we told them, "The program you just watched costs $1,500 a week. We have to have your support in order to show those kinds of programs." I think that sort of honesty will pay off in the long run.

To me, it's tremendously important to clear up some misconceptions, not only on their part, but also on ours. Our overhead at this station for the programming department is $200,000 in salaries, and we pay $100,000 for SPC programs and $30,000 more for acquisitions. So that's a third of a million already without producing one show out of that studio ourselves!

It was necessary, Clark emphasized, to invest a certain amount of money in acquisitions.

We have to give our program schedule variety. We need to get a number of acquisitions so that we don't duplicate constantly what Channel 13 and Channel 62 are airing.

Research, he indicated, played a significant

role in deciding not only what programs to broadcast but also *when* to schedule them. It was vital to promote the program schedule and specific shows so that viewers would know what KCTS would be offering and would be encouraged to watch.

Promotional Activities

Patti Parson, promotion director, reported to the director of development. However, she noted that half her time was spent on production and program promotion—"anything that helps production helps fund raising."

Her activities comprised a range of promotional, PR, and communications tasks. In a typical week she prepared 10 to 15 press releases and distributed them to 160 periodicals and appropriate special interest groups. Almost all were related to special programs, but general station activities were mentioned too. She also prepared the monthly news and program guide, *Nine*, which was mailed to all subscribers, and compiled program listings for *TV Guide* and daily and weekly newspapers. Parson was critical of PBS's frequent failures to send out press materials on time for national shows, and she noted that underwriters' advertising agencies could not always be relied upon to promote their clients' shows in local media.

Listings and press releases were supplemented by newspaper advertising and by on-the-air promotion on KCTS. Advertising had several objectives in addition to encouraging people to watch a specific show. For instance, the promotion of specific programs tended to help fund raising, while advertisements in smaller newspapers were believed to generate goodwill and to improve the station's chances of receiving editorial coverage in these papers' entertainment sections.

On-the-air promotion of a forthcoming show was seen as an excellent way to increase viewing. Said Parson, "It doesn't build a new audience, but it solidifies the audience you already have. Instead of getting them for one show, you get them to watch your schedule." Recent rating improvements at KCTS were ascribed in part to heavy on-the-air promotional activity, and there were plans to conduct new research to test this hypothesis.

Other promotional activities included parties to introduce new shows to the press and local underwriters. These often included a visit from one of the stars of the show in question. Meantime, leaflets were used to reach specific target segments. For example, an insert promoting "Classic Theatre" was put in the printed programs of a local theater group.

Although no scientific attempt had been made to measure the effectiveness of promotional efforts, some insights were obtained from a review of clippings, the level of mail and phone calls received, the amount of donations, and the trend of Nielsen ratings.

For local productions, Parson made suggestions on the choice of title and general tone. Clark also sought her input when considering schedule changes, with a view of determining their implication for promotional activities.

Research

Research at KCTS was the responsibility of the programming department. The staff used ratings and internally generated data to assess the station's effectiveness at reaching general and specific audiences and to plan future programming strategy.

For the past 3 years, KCTS had selected a part-time research director from among doctoral candidates at the University of Washington School of Communications. This individual worked 20 hours a week (and often more) at the station and was paid through a CPB grant at the standard rate for a graduate assistant.

Patricia Harris, research director in 1975–1976, was working closely with Burnill Clark on a number of studies as well as interpreting research data and presenting it in an intelligible form for other station personnel. KCTS subscribed to the Nielsen Station Index rating service. Each rating period, Pat Harris digested the data received and distributed them in a format which included the ratings obtained for the same time slot in the same week of the previous year (Exhibit 4).

The rating data were used to evaluate the performance of individual shows and to make scheduling decisions. Attempts were made to maximize "audience flow" by juxtaposing programs in such a way that an audience attracted to one show would find it followed by another calculated to appeal to them. The Nielsen indexes provided some insights into Channel 9's success in building and holding audiences in this way.

The ratings of competing shows were another input used for making decisions, especially when the shows being compared were similar. In such instances, Clark sometimes "counterprogrammed." For instance, he placed an entertainment show on Channel 9 in the time slot when Channel 7 presented the CBS News magazine, "60 minutes," anticipating that a KCTS public affairs program would be wasted in that slot. On the other hand, like the programming directors at many public TV stations, he often scheduled movies at the "network standard" time of 9 P.M.; viewers expected movies to start then and were believed to evaluate all the films offered by different stations before choosing one of them.

In addition to purchasing syndicated research, KCTS collected its own data. Using a CPB grant, the station had, over the past 3 years, conducted "viewer profile" research; this involved detailed studies of KCTS viewer characteristics and a comparison between viewers' program interests and those of non-KCTS viewers. In the 1975 study, which involved a mail survey, the sample was segmented into (1) KCTS members in the state of Washington and in British Columbia, (2) KCTS viewers who were not members, and (3) non-KCTS television viewers. Demographic findings are summarized in Exhibit 5, while Exhibit 6 highlights program interests for the different segments.

Harris had instituted other, more specialized studies. Convinced, for instance, that Nielsen figures did not adequately represent the viewing habits of the college and teen audience, she conducted a simple poll of students in three area schools. These were the university (specifically an undergraduate psychology class); a high school located in predominantly white, middle-class neighborhood; and a high school containing a large percentage of black and Asian-American students from relatively low socioeconomic backgrounds.

The subject of her study was KCTS's Tuesday night schedule, which was planned by Clark to attract and hold younger viewers. Her findings suggested that the schedule was somewhat successful but that this success was not reflected in the Nielsen ratings. (The Nielsen research techniques were not used to measure such phenomena as viewing in college dorms.) One unexpected finding was the discovery that Channel 9 reception was poor in the neighborhood of the minority high school.

Harris regularly evaluated unsolicited mail and phone comments from viewers. She also participated in the station's ascertainment efforts, helping Channel 9 to identify community problems and needs. In this, she was joined by Sharon Maeda, the director of community involvement, who worked with a consultant to ensure that KCTS obtained inputs from all segments of the Seattle community. Maeda spent much of her time with representatives of ethnic and other groups to determine their programming concerns and interests.

"Viewers' Choice 1976"

In late 1975, Channel 9 conceived the idea of seeking viewers' opinions of program offerings. Arrangements were made to preempt all regular programming on the evening of Friday, Febru-

EXHIBIT 4
DIGEST OF NIELSEN DATA FOR KCTS PROGRAMS

4-WEEK PERIOD ENDING NOVEMBER 26, 1975

	MONDAY	TUESDAY	WEDNESDAY	THURSDAY	FRIDAY	SATURDAY	SUNDAY
6:30–7	HUMAN SEXUALITY $(-.3)1^{10}$	COSMOLOGY $(-.3)^{-.3}$	HUMAN SEXUALITY $(-.3)1^{6}$	COSMOLOGY $(-.3)^{-.3}$	PEACE-MAKERS $(-.3)^{-.3}$	SCENE 1 TAKE 1 $(1)^{-.3}$	CHAPLIN SHORTS $(1)2^{15}$
7–7:30	CLASSICAL PREVIEW $(-.3)1^{6}$	LILIAS YOGA $(1)^{-.3}$	LILIAS YOGA $(-.3)^{-.3}$	ASCENT OF MAN $(1)3^{21}$	FIRING LINE $(-.3)2^{11}$	WASHINGTON WEEK $(-.3)2^{13}$	WORLD PRESS $(1)2^{11}$
7:30–8	WORLD PRESS $(1)^{-.3}$	VARIOUS $(1)1^{5}$	BOOK BEAT $(-.3)1^{7}$	ASCENT OF MAN $(2)3^{24}$	FIRING LINE $(1)1^{11}$	WALL ST. WEEK $(-.3)1^{8}$	LOWELL THOMAS $(2)2^{16}$
8–8:30	VARIOUS (WOLF TRAP) $(2)2^{13}$	VARIOUS $(3)2^{12}$	TRIBAL EYE $(1)2^{15}$	ROMANTIC REBELLION $(1)1^{9}$	WASHINGTON WEEK $(2)3^{20}$	RIVALS OF SHERLOCK HOLMES $(1)2^{23}$	SYMPHONY $(2)2^{17}$
8:30–9	VARIOUS (WOLF TRAP) $(2)3^{25}$	RIVALS OF SHERLOCK HOLMES $(2)2^{14}$	TRIBAL EYE $(1)2^{18}$	CLASSICAL PREVIEW $(1)1^{10}$	WALL ST. WEEK $(2)2^{18}$	RIVALS OF SHERLOCK HOLMES $(2)2^{23}$	SYMPHONY $(5)1^{8}$
9–9:30	VARIOUS $(1)2^{20}$	RIVALS OF SHERLOCK HOLMES $(2)2^{19}$	JENNIE $(2)6^{41}$	CLASSICAL THEATRE $(-.3)3^{24}$	MASTERPIECE THEATRE $(2)2^{20}$	SILENT YEARS $(1)1^{7}$	MASTERPIECE THEATRE $(5)3^{29}$
9:30–10	VARIOUS $(1)2^{17}$	MONTY PYTHON $(1)4^{26}$	JENNIE $(2)5^{40}$	CLASSICAL THEATRE $(-.3)3^{24}$	MASTERPIECE THEATRE $(2)2^{19}$	SILENT YEARS $(1)1^{5}$	MASTERPIECE THEATRE $(3)4^{26}$
10–10:30	FIRST CHURCHILLS $(1)2^{12}$	SOUNDSTAGE $(1)2^{14}$	SAY BROTHER $(2)1^{7}$	CLASSICAL THEATRE $(1)3^{20}$	VARIOUS $(1)1^{5}$	SILENT YEARS $(1)^{-.3}$	ASCENT OF MAN $(1)1^{9}$
10:30–11	FIRST CHURCHILLS $(1)2^{14}$	SOUNDSTAGE $(2)2^{11}$	SAY BROTHER/ JAZZ $(1)1^{4}$	CLASSICAL THEATRE $(-.3)3^{19}$	VARIOUS $(-.3)1^{9}$	SILENT YEARS $(1)^{-.3}$	ASCENT OF MAN $(1)1^{9}$

KEY: $(1)2^{14}$ —— TOTAL NO. OF HOUSEHOLDS
— CURRENT RATING
— NOV. 1974 RATING

Note: The large number (current rating) and the small subscript in parentheses (November 1974 rating) represent the percentage of Seattle area homes watching TV in that time slot which are tuned in to Channel 9. The convention −.3 is traditionally used to denote a viewership which is too small to measure. The small superscript denotes the number of homes (in thousands) actually watching Channel 9 at the time.

Research conducted for PBS in 1974–1975 showed that *nationally*, public TV achieved an average rating of 1.0. Ratings nationally varied from an average of 1.5 for "arts" programs to 0.7 for "public affairs." A rating of 5 was considered extremely good.

Source: KCTS records.

EXHIBIT 5
DEMOGRAPHIC CHARACTERISTICS OF KCTS VIEWING GROUPS

	Non-KCTS viewers (n=93)	KCTS viewers (n=211)	American KCTS members (n=243)	Canadian KCTS members (n=236)
Education of respondent:				
12 years or less	49.5%	28.4%	13.2%	24.6%
13–15 years	20.4	23.2	20.6	22.0
16 years or more	30.1	48.3	66.3	54.5
Age of respondent:				
Under 30 years	26.9%	27.0%	12.3%	6.8%
30–59 years	43.0	46.4	53.9	59.7
60 years or over	30.1	26.5	33.7	33.5
Sex of respondent:				
Male	50.0%	52.4%	50.0%	56.0%
Female	50.0	47.6	50.0	44.0
Occupation of respondent:				
Blue- or white-collar worker	30.8%	22.5%	12.7%	18.5%
Skilled worker, business	20.9	25.0	19.1	24.0
Professional	9.9	18.1	28.0	19.7
Housewife	11.0	12.7	16.1	12.0
Student	22.9	28.6	3.0	4.3
Not working	18.7	16.7	21.2	21.5
Child under 12 years old in household:				
No	52.7%	65.4%	65.4%	65.7%
Yes	47.3	34.6	34.6	34.3
Race:				
White	88.9%	96.6%	98.8%	98.7%
Black	4.4	1.0	0.4	0.0
Other	6.7	2.4	0.8	1.3
Daily hours of TV viewing:				
0–2 hours	17.1%	16.6%	18.5%	21.9%
3–5 hours	44.7	55.6	50.6	54.8
Over 5 hours	37.8	28.3	30.7	23.4

	Nonmembers (viewers + nonviewers) (n=279)	Members (n=226)	Canadians (n=223)
Weekly hours of KCTS viewing by adults in household:			
0 hours	15.8%	2.2%	0.9%
1–5 hours	56.6	41.1	41.7
Over 5 hours	27.7	56.7	57.3
Weekly hours of KCTS viewing by children in household*:			
0 hours	47.2%	26.3%	21.4%
1–5 hours	29.1	35.6	37.1
Over 5 hours	23.7	38.1	51.5

*Includes only those households who reported having children in the family.
Source: KCTS records.

EXHIBIT 6
PROGRAM INTERESTS OF KCTS VIEWING GROUPS

Programs on KCTS/9 that respondents enjoy viewing: open-ended responses[*]

KCTS/9 program titles	Category	American KCTS members (*n* = 243)	Canadian KCTS members (*n* = 236)	Nonmember KCTS viewers (*n* = 211)
"Masterpiece Theatre"	Drama	63.3%	77.5%	34.1%
"Ascent of Man"	Instructional/cultural affairs	33.7	42.0	18.9
"Washington Week in Review"	News/public affairs	29.9	19.5	12.2
"Nova"	Documentary (science)	28.4	30.0	19.9
"Bill Moyers"	News/public affairs	25.8	13.9	11.3
"Wall Street Week"	Public affairs (economics)	22.6	16.1	9.0
"Firing Line"	News/public affairs	21.8	21.1	10.9
"America"	Instructional/cultural affairs	15.6	21.2	11.2
"Evening at Pops"	Music	14.4	21.5	11.3
"Sesame Street"	Children's	12.0	6.3	14.1
Classical music (unspec.)	Music (classical)	9.8	10.9	13.2
"Theater in America"	Drama	9.3	7.6	3.3
"World Press"	News/public affairs	9.1	5.9	5.2
"Romantic Rebellion"	Instructional/cultural affairs	8.9	16.9	5.8
"Electric Company"	Children's	8.1	5.0	7.5
"Mr. Rogers"	Children's	7.8	3.3	7.5
Public affairs (unspec.)	News/public affairs	7.7	5.8	9.9
"In Performance at Wolf Trap"	Music	7.0	4.2	1.9
Movies (unspec.)	Movies	6.8	8.4	9.8
"Zoom"	Children's	6.1	5.0	4.7
"Feeling Good"	Health	6.0	2.0	3.8
"The Japanese Film"	Movie	5.6	6.3	5.6
Plays (unspec.)	Drama	4.9	9.7	6.6
Popular music (unspec.)	Music	4.4	5.9	6.1
"Book Beat"	Cultural affairs	4.0	3.7	0.9
"The Silent Years"	Movie	4.0	3.3	1.9
"Nana"	Drama	4.0	2.4	2.4
"Behind the Lines"	News/public affairs	3.2	1.2	1.0
"Yoga"	Health (yoga)	2.8	3.7	2.9
"Bridge"	Recreation	2.8	2.5	3.2
"Watergate"	News/public affairs	2.4	2.9	1.9
Science-nature (unspec.)	Instructional/science	2.4	2.8	4.6
"Hollywood TV Theater"	Drama	2.4	2.0	0.9
"Roads to Freedom"	Cultural affairs	1.6	3.6	1.4
Contemporary scene (unspec.)	Instructional/cultural affairs	1.6	2.4	3.7
"Black Journal"	Public affairs (black)	1.6	0.8	1.9
Health programs	Health	1.6	2.1	5.1
"Assignment America"	News/public affairs	1.6	0.0	0.9
Ballet	Cultural affairs performance	0.8	4.2	1.4
"Soundstage"	Music (rock and jazz)	0.4	0.0	1.9
"Great Performances"	Drama	1.2	1.6	0.0
"Evening at Symphony"	Music (classical)	0.4	0.4	0.9

EXHIBIT 6

Continued

Commercial programs respondents enjoy viewing: open-ended responses*

Commercial program category	American KCTS members (*n* = 243)	Canadian KCTS members (*n* =236)	Nonmember KCTS viewers (*n* = 211)	Non-KCTS viewers (*n* = 93)
News-public affairs	58.4%	38.1%	41.2%	24.7%
Situation comedy	43.6	42.8	43.1	32.3
Documentary	37.4	38.1	30.8	15.1
Drama	29.2	13.1	32.2	30.1
Sports	27.2	24.6	26.5	18.3
Travel-nature	24.7	25.8	24.6	12.9
Movies	21.8	24.6	29.9	11.8
Crime	19.3	26.3	31.8	26.9
Game	14.4	7.2	15.6	15.1
Variety-talk	9.9	5.5	13.7	8.6
Music	8.5	9.3	10.4	4.3
Variety-comedy	8.5	9.7	7.0	7.1
Children's	2.1	1.7	2.8	1.1
Western	1.6	0.8	4.3	2.2
Soap	1.6	0.4	3.3	8.6
Religion	0.4	0.0	0.5	2.2
Other	11.5	36.4	8.5	3.2

*Open-ended responses, multiple responses permitted.
Source: KCTS records

ary 2, 1976. Between 7 P.M. and 10 P.M. that night, pilot segments of 18 potential new series for Channel 9's fall season were shown. These shows were a representative sampling of programs which public TV stations across the country were thinking of purchasing through the PBS Station Program Cooperative. At 10 P.M. there followed a half-hour "kaleidoscope" of 22 series previously shown on KCTS which could be purchased again for rebroadcast in the fall.

Ballots were printed in *Nine, TV Guide,* and the two major Seattle newspapers (Exhibit 7). Further publicity was generated by press releases. Viewers were reminded to complete and return their ballots through on-the-air promotional messages (Exhibit 8). Additionally, 450 community leaders and organizations were contacted individually and urged to participate. To complement this activity, Channel 9's consultant for community involvement hosted a preview of ethnically oriented SPC programming at his home on February 1; national programs available to PBS stations were grouped into four ethnic categories and shown to individuals and representatives of interested organizations.

The results of "Viewers' Choice" greatly exceeded expectations. Within less than 2 weeks, over 4,500 completed ballots had been returned. To the station's surprise, $3,800 was received in unsolicited donations—more than covering the $3,000 cost of "Viewers' Choice." Another side benefit was the generation of many new names for Channel 9's mailing list. The overall feeling at the station was that considerable goodwill and favorable publicity had been generated by this project.

Planning the Fall Program Schedule

Within a few weeks, all "Viewers' Choice" ballots had been tabulated and the responses analyzed. Exhibit 9 shows the percentage of respondents voting for each program pilot. Burnill Clark had earlier given each pilot the rank he expected viewers to give. Although the rank orders were quite closely correlated, there were a few significant discrepancies. "World Press" and "Prism" (a science program) had been ranked by viewers rather higher than Clark had predicted. By contrast, "Sesame Street"— which, according to Nielsen data, had consistently been the station's most popular program— was ranked fourteenth by the viewers. The profile of "Viewers' Choice" respondents indi-

EXHIBIT 7
BALLOT FOR "VIEWERS' CHOICE 1976"
(Actual Size as Published on TV Listings
Page of Seattle Times, Monday, Feb. 2, 1976)

WHAT DO YOU WANT TO SEE ON PUBLIC TV 9?

Tonight, from 7-10:30 p.m., KCTS/9 airs VIEWERS' CHOICE 1976, a look at 40 series proposed for purchase. Put a check next to those you want to see in the fall; put 2 checks if you REALLY like the show. Mark the space "N" if you did not watch the segment. If you want to see the entire show of the current series, note broadcast time.

BALLOTS MUST BE RETURNED BY FEBRUARY 9 TO BE COUNTED.
Mail ballots to: KCTS/9, 4045 Brooklyn Ave. N.E., Seattle, Wash. 98105

7:00-10:00 p.m.
Pilots of proposed series
AUTO TEST '77 _____
BLACK FILM FESTIVAL _____
DOCTORS AND PATIENTS _____
DOCUMENTARIES _____
EVENING ON DOCK STREET _____
EVENING EDITION WITH
    MARTIN AGRONSKY _____
FICTIONARY GAME _____
INTERNATIONAL ANIMATION FEST. _____
LIFETIME MAGAZINE _____
LOOK AT ME _____
MONEYWATCH _____
OUTDOOR ADVENTURE _____
PRISM _____
SMITHSONIAN FESTIVAL OF
    AMERICAN FOLKLIFE _____
WRAP AROUND _____
CROCKETT'S VICTORY GARDEN _____
IN SEARCH OF REAL AMERICA _____
WALSH'S ANIMALS _____
. . . .

10:00-10:30 p.m.
Excerpts
ANYONE FOR TENNYSON (2/3, 7:00) _____
AUSTIN CITY LIMITS (2/3, 7:30) _____
BILL MOYERS' JOURNAL (2/8, 10:00) _____
BOOK BEAT (2/5, 10:30) _____
CONSUMER SURVIVAL KIT (2/4, 7:30) _____
ELECTRIC COMPANY (2/3, 5:30) _____
EVENING AT SYMPHONY _____
GRAND PRIX TENNIS _____
GREAT PERFORMANCES (2/4, 9:00) _____
LOWELL THOMAS REMEMBERS
(2/6, 8:00) _____
MARK RUSSELL COMEDY SPECIALS _____
NOVA (2/8, 8:00) _____
REALIDADES (2/8, 5:30) _____
SAY BROTHER _____
SESAME STREET (2/3, 4:30) _____
SOUNDSTAGE (2/3, 10:00) _____
WALL STREET WEEK (2/6, 8:30) _____
WASHINGTON WEEK IN REVIEW
(2/5, 8:30) _____
WHAT'S COOKING (2/4, 7:00) _____
WOMAN ALIVE! (2/7, 5:30) _____
WORLD PRESS (2/8, 6:30) _____
ZOOM (2/3, 6:00) _____

Optional: Age_____ Sex_____ No. in household_____
I watch KCTS/9_____hrs. in average week.

(Ad paid for by PBS and CPB)

PBS PUBLIC BROADCASTING SERVICE

KCTS

EXHIBIT 8
ON-THE-AIR PROMOTION FOR "VIEWERS' CHOICE"

Production: VIEWERS' CHOICE 1976—Opening Segment (3:30)   Producer/Director: Lee Olson

VIDEO	AUDIO
FADE UP ON SLIDE: Logo	For the next 3½ hours, we are pre-empting all regular programming to bring you VIEWERS' CHOICE 1976. This special presentation will give you an opportunity to say what you want to see on Public TV 9. With VIEWERS' CHOICE 1976, we become one of the first television stations in the country to give its viewers a chance for input into programming decisions.
	Starting in a few minutes, we will show you excerpts of 40 national programs available for purchase by Public TV 9.
DISSOLVE TO SLIDE: Ballot in NINE Magazine—NINE logo and date	You will be able to mark your preference on ballots which can be found in the February issue of NINE magazine . . .
CUT TO SLIDE: Ballot in TV GUIDE—logo and date	The January 31st issue of TV GUIDE . . .
CUT TO SLIDE: Ballot in newspaper—PI and TIMES logos and dates	And the February 2 editions of the SEATTLE POST-INTELLIGENCER and the SEATTLE TIMES.
DISSOLVE TO SLIDE: Station Program Cooperative	The programs you can select from are national series that Public TV 9 is considering buying from the Station Program Cooperative. This cooperative is made up of all Public Broadcasting Service member stations who wish to acquire PBS programs for local use. Each station is invited to submit programs, and then to purchase from the pool.
	If enough buyers are found for a specific show, it becomes part of the PBS broadcast schedule. However, each station can air only those programs that it has purchased specifically.
DISSOLVE TO SLIDE: CU (close-up) of left side of ballot	The first selection of segments you will see tonight is listed on the left side of your ballot. They are short pilots of 18 potential new series to air in the fall. This is not the complete list of program pilots which will be offered to Public TV 9 for consideration. But it is a representative sampling of those pilots available for broadcast at this time. Your reaction to them will tell us the kinds of programs you are interested in. This group of pilots will run for 3 hours.
DISSOLVE TO SLIDE: CU of right side of ballot	Then, from 10:00 to 10:30 tonight, we will broadcast a sample of 22 series that are listed on the right side of the ballot. These are shows that have been carried recently, or are currently on Public TV 9. And they are available again to be purchased for broadcast in the fall. Not included in this list are certain PBS shows, like MASTERPIECE THEATRE, which we do not buy through the Station Program Cooperative.
DISSOLVE TO SLIDE: CU hand with pen making check marks on ballot	We invite you to watch each of these segments, and then to vote by putting a check next to those you want to see on Public TV 9 this fall. Put 2 checks if you really like the show. For your convenience in identifying the program pilots, we will give the name of the program both before and after each segment.
DISSOLVE TO SLIDE: CU hands cutting out ballot over table top. Addressed envelope seen on table	After you have voted, cut out your ballot, and mail it to the address given.
DISSOLVE TO SLIDE: mailing address	If you do not have a ballot, write down your preferences on a piece of paper, and mail it to: KCTS/9 Box 5028 Seattle, Washington 98105
DISSOLVE TO SLIDE: "Deadline: February 9"	In order to process your choices, we must have the ballots in our hands by February 9. So please get them ready, so they can be mailed first thing in the morning.
DISSOLVE TO SLIDE: "Pilots of Proposed New Series"	Now we begin VIEWERS' CHOICE 1976 with the 18 pilots of proposed new series.

EXHIBIT 9
RESULTS OF "VIEWERS' CHOICE 1976"
Percentage of Respondents Voting for Each SPC Pilot

Program	Category	Percentage of respondents
"Nova"	Documentary (science)	78.7
"Documentaries"	Documentary (miscellaneous)	69.5
"Great Performances"	Drama	67.3
"Evening at Symphony"	Music (classical)	64.8
"Bill Moyers' Journal"	News/public affairs	63.2
"Washington Week in Review"	News/public affairs	53.8
"World Press"	News/public affairs	50.5
"Outdoor Adventures with Lute Jerstad"	Documentary (nature)	49.6
"Crockett's Victory Garden"	Nature	48.9
"Evening Edition: Martin Agronsky"	News/public affairs	46.1
"Walsh's Animals"	Nature/children's	45.4
"Prism"	Documentary (science)	45.4
"Wall Street Week"	Public affairs (finance)	44.8
"Sesame Street"	Children's	44.4
"Moneywatch"	Public affairs (economics)	44.2
"Book Beat"	Public affairs (books)	43.0
"Lowell Thomas Remembers"	Public affairs (travel)	42.2
"Evening at Dock Street"	Drama	42.1
"Doctors and Patients"	Health	41.9
"Smithsonian Festival"	American cultural heritage	41.7
"Consumer Survival Kit"	Public affairs (economics)	40.0
"Anyone for Tennyson?"	Drama (poetry)	38.9
"International Animation Festival"	Movies	38.1
"Autotest '77"	Consumer report/automobiles	38.0
"In Search of the Real America"	Public affairs (commentary)	34.1
"Lifetime Magazine"	Programming for elderly	30.3
"Soundstage"	Music (rock and jazz)	30.3
"Electric Company"	Children's	28.8
"Mark Russell Comedy Specials"	Variety-comedy	27.5
"What's Cooking?"	Cooking	27.4
"Wraparound"	Life-style "magazine"	27.1
"Fictionary Game"	Game show (adults)	25.6
"Grand Prix Tennis"	Sports	22.8
"Zoom"	Children's	21.0
"Look at Me"	Public affairs (parents)	20.7
"Black Film Festival"	Movies (black)	18.2
"Woman Alive"	Public affairs (women)	17.8
"How We Got Here"	Documentary (ethnic immigrants)	16.7
"Realidades"	Spanish-language programming	14.0
"Austin City Limits"	Music (country)	10.3
"Say Brother"	Programming for blacks	7.2

EXHIBIT 10
PROGRAM CATALOG FOR SPC III, APRIL 1976

Series title	Category	Format (minutes)	Number of programs	Total hours
"Washington Week in Review"	News/public affairs	30	52	26
"Evening at Symphony"	Music	60–90	13	15
"Wall Street Week"	News/public affairs	30	52	26
"Sesame Street"	Children's	60	130	130
"Great Performances"	Drama	60–180	25	37½
"Electric Company"	Children's	30	130	65
"Nova"	Documentary (science)	60	20	20
"The Age of Uncertainty"	Documentary (economics)	60	13	13
"Consumer Survival Kit"	Public affairs (economics)	30	26	13
"Soundstage"	Music (rock and jazz)	60	12	12
"Black Perspectives on the News"	News/public affairs	30	52	26
"Anyone for Tennyson?"	Drama (poetry)	30	15	7½
"Woman Alive"	Public affairs (women)	30	46	23
"Special Events"	News/public affairs	30–60	40	25
"Mark Russell Specials"	Comedy	30	4	2
"Crockett's Victory Garden"	Gardening	30	34	17
"Lowell Thomas Remembers"	News/public affairs (nostalgia)	30	39	19½
"The Best of Ernie Kovacs"	Variety-comedy (nostalgia)	30	10	5
"Opera Theatre Presents"	Music/drama	60–150	5	10
"World Press"	News/public affairs	30	52	26
"Parent Effectiveness"	Public affairs (parents)	30	13	6½
"Scenes from a Marriage"	Drama	60	6	6
"Zoom"	Children's	30	66	33
"Book Beat"	Public affairs (books)	30	45	22½
"Lilias, Yoga and You"	Health (yoga)	30	52	26
"Bill Moyers' Journal"	News/public affairs	60	6	6
"Front and Center"	Public affairs (pollution)	30	20	10
"Walsh's Animals"	Children's	30	10	5
"Studio See"	Children's	30	26	13
"At the Top"	Music (jazz)	60	13	13
"International Animation Festival"	Movies	30	11	5½
"Austin City Limits"	Music (country)	60	10	10
"Evening Edition: Martin Agronsky"	News/public affairs	30	60	30
"Mother's Little Network"	Variety-comedy	30	10	5
"Say Brother"	Public affairs (black)	30	13	6½
"Max Morath: Illustrious Past"	Music (nostalgia)	30	10	5
"Autotest '77"	Consumer report/automobiles	60	3	3
"The Highest Court"	Public affairs (law)	30	20	10
"Mancini"	Music	30	12	6
"What's Cooking?"	Cooking	30	13	6½

*Since large stations were assessed at a higher rate for program costs, they had a greater purchasing power than small stations. The "purchasing power percentage" was thus a more significant measure of the support for a program (and its chances for success) than the total number of stations bidding. Mr. Clark believed that a program which commanded less than 25 percent in purchasing power support at this time was unlikely to survive and that a program with less than 45% had at best an even chance.

Purchasing power percentage*	Number of stations selecting	Estimated cost to KCTS (max.)— $000
97	150	2.3
95	148	2.1
94	146	2.5
93	145	16.7
92	142	8.5
91	142	9.7
86	134	11.3
80	120	6.3
80	132	4.2
75	124	2.9
75	112	3.3
66	112	2.7
65	104	2.0
65	92	10.6
64	102	0.6
62	96	2.1
60	96	9.0
54	88	2.6
53	80	4.4
51	82	5.0
50	76	2.3
48	65	6.6
46	70	4.1
46	75	2.7
45	82	1.5
44	66	12.2
37	51	7.6
37	56	4.7
35	60	3.9
35	63	3.7
32	51	5.3
27	47	4.4
23	41	17.9
23	30	15.9
22	28	7.1
17	27	5.1
15	20	4.9
13	18	36.2
10	16	43.7
10	16	5.6

cated that they were primarily evening viewers of public TV and tended to be older and living in one- or two-person households. Hence their relative lack of interest in children's programming. Clark also recognized that the interests of minorities and those who watched public TV would be underrepresented in the ballot results. To compensate for this, he had received inputs from the special preview of ethnically oriented SPC III programs; among those which had been particularly well received by representatives of ethnic groups were "Realidades," "Black Film Festival," and "Black Perspectives on the News."

In early March, 83 program proposals had been presented to member stations for the preliminary "bidding" round in the SPC III selection process. Some of these programs were subsequently withdrawn. Underwriting had been obtained for "In Search of the Real America" and "Grand Prix Tennis" so that they could be distributed by PBS free of charge, while CPB had decided to fund "Realidades" and "Black Film Festival" to make them widely available. By April, a number of programs which had fared poorly in the preliminary rounds of SPC bidding had been eliminated; there had been a lack of sufficient station support.

In mid-April 1976, Clark and Harris were reviewing the list of programs remaining in the SPC III catalog (Exhibit 10). Less than half of the original offerings remained, and Clark believed that many of these did not command sufficient support to survive. In a few days, KCTS would be asked to make its selection for an SPC "purchase" round. Program selections made on this occasion would become irrevocable purchase commitments if prices did not increase beyond the predetermined maximum.

In addition to making SPC selections for KCTS's fall schedule, Clark had to decide how to address the programming concerns voiced by ethnic minority groups, as well as the criticism raised by some observers that Channel 9 still did not provide enough local programming.

A related concern was the competition posed by KCPQ (Channel 13) in Lakewood Center, now that this public TV station was operating with its powerful new VHF transmitter. Clark wondered what programming and scheduling strategy his own station should adopt toward Channel 13. As far as SPC III selections were concerned, he believed that KCPQ had a budget of about $50,000, was seeking to buy about 500 hours of SPC programming, and would only have to pay about 60 percent of the program prices charged to KCTS. He could foresee three basic options: to ignore KCPQ completely, to compete directly, or to work with the station in planning complementary schedules.

As he reviewed the overall situation, Clark recognized that KCTS had many different constituencies. A strategy directed at satisfying the needs of one group might result in losing the support of others. In the light of past experience and recent research findings, he had to decide where his station should place its priorities in making programming selections for the current year.

13 Levi Strauss & Company

Benson P. Shapiro

Mr. Mel Bacharach, vice president–marketing of Levi Strauss & Company, was considering what action the firm should take with regard to the manufacture and distribution of boys' wear in the early 1970s. The company was the largest (by several times) manufacturer of nationally branded boys' wear of high quality and was the "Cadillac of the industry" with a strong brand reputation. While the production and sale of such merchandise had constituted a sizable portion of the total Levi's business over the years, the company had consciously limited the resources allocated to the Boys' Department because of its low profits, the demands of other parts of the business, and chain store dominance of the boys' market.

Benson P. Shapiro is a professor at the Harvard Graduate School of Business Administration
Certain information in this case has been disguised.

Levi Strauss & Company

In 1971, the company was one of the largest firms in the apparel industry, with sales in 1970 of $327 million (Exhibit 1). It manufactured a wide variety of jeans, slacks, shorts, and related apparel for men, boys, and women in the United States and overseas.

In the spring of 1971, Levi Strauss & Company was due to issue stock for public ownership. Of the proceeds of the stock sale, $32 million were to be spent for facility expansion, one-half in calendar 1971 and the remainder in calendar 1972.

went public

Current Product Line

The product line and the marketplace had undergone substantial change in the years since World War II. Just after the war, Levi Strauss &

EXHIBIT 1
CORPORATE FINANCIAL DATA

Income statements, in millions of dollars

	Nov. 27, 1966 (52 weeks)	Nov. 26, 1967 (52 weeks)	Fiscal year ended Nov. 24, 1968 (52 weeks)	Nov. 30, 1969 (52 weeks)	Nov. 29, 1970 (52 weeks)
Net sales	147.8	159.0	196.2	250.7	327.8
Cost of goods sold	106.1	112.9	133.3	171.0	222.4
Gross profit	41.7	46.1	62.9	79.7	105.4
Marketing, general, and administrative expenses	26.3	30.8	35.4	46.8	63.9
Operating income	15.4	15.3	27.5	32.9	41.5
Other income expenses and taxes	7.5	7.5	15.4	18.4	23.1
Net income after tax	7.9	7.8	12.1	14.5	18.4
Net income per share	0.81	0.80	1.24	1.50	1.92

Balance sheet, in millions of dollars

Current assets		Current liabilities and equity	
Cash	8.1	Payable to banks	32.5
Accounts receivable	47.2	Accounts payable	34.5
Inventories	95.6	Accrued liabilities	10.5
Other	5.5	Other	6.6
	156.4		84.1
Property plant and equipment (net)	27.5	Long-term debt	25.2
Other Assets	11.2	Other	1.3
		Stockholders' equity	84.5
	195.1		195.1

Notes: (1) Figures may not add because of rounding. (2) These are incomplete summaries, since they do not include the necessary notes.

Company manufactured a short product line of basic blue jeans and related items mainly for the working man. During World War II, however, jeans started to become popular for general wear. In the fashion revolution of the early 1950s, the shift continued to more informal and diverse wearing apparel. Manufacturers responded with cotton (chino) pants and later with men's slacks with a buckle in the back. Many of these casual pants were made like jeans (an inexpensive, durable construction), looked like sportswear, and were of washable fabrics. Levi's responded to the needs of the marketplace with a new department—Levi's Lighter Blue—which offered the highly successful faded blue denim jeans.

During the late 1950s the fashion boom began to gain momentum, with male teenagers leading the way. At the end of the fifties white jeans became popular, and in 1961 Levi Strauss successfully introduced its White Levi's line of pastel jeans. In 1964, the first true permanent press slacks ever made were introduced by the firm under its Sta-Prest label, and they created a revolution in the garment industry. With no initial competition, the company significantly increased its sportswear penetration and distribution.

Male dress became increasingly fashion-oriented throughout the 1960s. The marketplace demanded pants of new designs in an increased range of fabrics, patterns, and color. Style numbers became obsolete at an accelerated rate. Levi Strauss and its competitors were forced to offer a wider variety of faster-changing styles. By 1971, Levi Strauss & Company was selling a broad line of jeans, slacks, and shorts for men, women, and boys and some related apparel such as shirts and jackets.

As Levi Strauss grew, it also changed organizationally. There was a general move toward departmentalization and, later, adoption of the product manager concept. During the late 1960s more and more merchandising personnel had been added, and the line divided into finer and finer departments. In January 1968 the women's operation, Levi's For Gals, was made into a separate division, and in very early 1971 the men's sportswear operation had been made a division.

The new sportswear operation provided a typical example of a specific product line. It was divided into three segments: Mr. Levi's, Young Men's Casuals, and Rugged Sportswear. The sportswear line differed from the original Levi's in that sportswear was manufactured by a more expensive process resulting in a more "finished" garment. In addition, sportswear was typically, but not always, made of more expensive and more colorful fabrics and was "dressier."

The Mr. Levi's line was designed to appeal to the "more mature man," with the major segment probably being sold to consumers in the mid-twenties to early forties age range. The pants were sized to accommodate the changes in body configuration which typically took place during the twenties. The young men's line was designed to appeal to the male from the mid-teens to mid-twenties and was sized for the trimmer build and styled for the younger tastes.

The Mr. Levi's line consisted of four models. Exhibit 2 describes each model and shows the number of fabrics and colors for each model. Each model-fabric-color combination was manufactured in 55 different primary sizes.

The Product Manager's Function and Product Planning

The company had adopted the product manager form of organization in the fall of 1969. Although product managers had a wide range of responsibilities, they were not directly responsible for profits. They did not control the sales force or manufacturing facilities but were responsible for designing, pricing, and planning the production and distribution of a segment of the product line.

Models in the men's and boys' lines tended to change relatively infrequently. Most of the season-to-season product variation was in fab-

EXHIBIT 2
THE MR. LEVI'S LINE

	Model name			
	Traditional/Classic	**Saville**	**Cavalero**	**Sportster**
Nature of styling	Ivy league (basic taper)	Ivy league but sportier	Quite fashionable	Continental (no belt)
Active fabrics	3	6	11	5
Active fabric-color combinations	9	12	30	18
Range of suggested retail prices	$11–13	$12–15	$13–15	$13–15
Average suggested retail price	$11 +	$15 –	$14.50	$14.00

rics and colors, the choices of which were the responsibility of product managers. Product managers actually purchased the piece goods (fabrics) and accessories (ornaments, etc.), prepared sales estimates, and determined the timing of product production. They set dates for the expected delivery of garments to retailers and were also responsible for designating merchandise for closeouts (merchandise left after a style went out of fashion) and seconds.

The complexity and timing of the product-planning function had changed rather abruptly over the preceding few years. While there were still two major seasonal lines—fall (or back-to-school) and spring—there were now more "sweeteners" introduced between the regular lines. These products were designed to exploit current fashion trends. In the past retailers had committed themselves to purchasing goods 5 months before the merchandise would be placed on sale in their stores. By 1971, retailers would commit themselves only 2 to 3 months in advance of retail sales, forcing a basic change in the product-planning function. While previously the sales force had gone into the field and received orders upon which the product manager relied in purchasing piece goods, this practice had changed over the years. By 1971 the product manager had to purchase piece goods and order the garments into production before

the salespeople had called on the retailer. Thus, rather than producing upon receipt of orders, the firm was producing in anticipation of orders.

Because the style of piece goods was rapidly changing, the choice of fabrics was critical. The cost of the fabric averaged about 40 to 45 percent of the total cost of a garment. Levi Strauss produced garments only in large quantities. Its normal minimum purchase of a fabric (in one color) was 75,000 yards, worth about $100,000. It was necessary to produce at least 15,000 pairs of a model-fabric-color combination to break even, since about 3,000 to 4,000 pairs per model-fabric-color combination would become closeouts sold at reduced prices.

Advertising

Levi Strauss & Company's advertising program could be divided into five segments. The most important and largest advertising program was designed to change the consumer's image of the firm from that of a manufacturer of jeans to that of a manufacturer of a variety of fashion pants in addition to jeans. The primary media for the program were network TV and radio. Management believed that TV reached a wide range of prospective consumers and offered the opportunity for creative, action-oriented advertising. Radio was used to obtain additional teenage impact in the metropolitan markets. Both media were used on a seasonal basis, with peak advertising during the heavy retail selling periods of early spring, fall (back-to-school), and Christmas.

The second segment was cooperative advertising, which emphasized retail sales generation. The firm paid about 50 percent of media costs, with the store paying the remainder. As part of the cooperative program the company provided advertising copy for all media.

Levi Strauss & Company had a trade advertising program which was used primarily to develop more sales from existing retail accounts. It was directed at enhancing the retailer's image and at promoting Levi Strauss as a manufacturer of fashion pants. Some executives believed that the company had a fashion-oriented consumer image, while consumer perceptions of Levi Strauss's retailers were not at all clear. Levi Strauss wished to generalize its image to retailers.

The fourth segment of the firm's advertising was that run by the Levi's For Gals Division. This cooperative advertising effort was partly a print advertising program in the nation's major fashion magazines to support the brand image. However, the program was also designed to gain more extensive distribution for a relatively new line. An attempt was being made to encourage the division's salespeople to emphasize cooperative advertising with prestige accounts because it was believed that association with prestige stores could be used to improve the image of the firm.

The fifth segment of advertising activity consisted of dealer support, including point-of-purchase displays and other sales aids.

Management believed that the firm had an unusually large, well-established advertising program for an apparel manufacturer.

Sales Force

Levi Strauss had a sales force of about 365 persons, 50 of whom were account executives. Account executives were very competent, experienced salespeople who managed the firm's relationship with between one and three large existing accounts, providing intensive sales contact with major accounts. The other salespeople covered geographic territories, calling on potential and existing accounts.

The Levi's For Gals sales force was separate from the rest, since management had felt earlier that many salespeople might emphasize the easy-to-sell basic jeans line to the detriment of the more fashion-oriented apparel which had great potential but took more time to sell. More important, sales management was concerned about the length of time it took a salesperson to present the whole line. The retail buyer was bound, some believed, to lose interest during a long sales presentation. A separate sportswear sales force was introduced in California in the early 1970s. Later, the Eastern sales force was partially divided, with special sportswear salespeople designated for the nine largest metropolitan areas. The sportswear salespeople sold both men's and boys' sportswear. All salespeople, except those just getting started, were compensated solely on commission and paid their own expenses. Arrangements with account executives varied.

Distribution

The company had approximately 15,000 retail accounts comprising more than 25,000 separate stores in the United States and Canada. These accounts could be classified in two groups: primary and secondary distribution. Included in primary distribution were department and specialty stores. In the secondary group were Army-Navy stores and basement divisions of department stores. These were solicited for basic jeans business but not for the more fashion-oriented business.

The distribution system used by the firm had changed in recent years to reflect changes in the product line. In the mid-1960s, when a decision was made to upgrade the sportswear line to a maximum retail price of $25, a decision was also made to upgrade distribution to stores more capable of selling such goods and better able to contribute to the firm's image. Some executives believed in the early 1970s that in spite of high total sales the firm was not selling enough to outlets which would lend an image of prestige and fashion to the company.

The company had an explicit policy of not selling to discounters or private-label[1] chain operations such as Sears, Roebuck; Montgomery Ward; or J. C. Penney in the continental United States. Most executives of the firm believed that more money could be made selling branded merchandise through department and specialty stores and that there was a significant risk in allocating a large share of the firm's business to any single retail organization. In 1971, no single customer accounted for as much as 4 percent of the company's sales.

The firm did not solicit business from discount stores—in spite of their keen interest—because its executives believed discounters would have a negative effect on the image of the Levi's brand and upon the support of established accounts.

Levi Strauss & Company management was aware of the interest which both the chain stores and the discount stores had in the firm's products.

Pricing

Prices of Levi Strauss & Company merchandise were based upon fabric and manufacturing costs. Most of the firm's merchandisers believed that company prices were exceptionally reasonable for the garments offered and that the consumer who purchased a Levi Strauss garment was not very price-conscious. Some felt

that Levi's prices were too low for the quality provided. On the other hand, several executives were concerned with the increasing competition. Many small new firms had recently entered the men's fashion pants market because of its rapid growth.

The more fashionable items in the line were typically priced higher than the staple goods for three reasons: (1) higher fabric cost (more stylish fabric with more complex treatments), (2) higher labor input because of more intricate construction and changeover costs as new models were introduced, and (3) higher inventory losses due to faster obsolescence and a higher percentage of clearance goods. The Levi's For Gals line was a good example of the relationship among prices. The basic jean in the line retailed for $6. The more fashionable women's jeans retailed for $10 to $20, and the women's sportswear pants retailed for $12 to $24. As more fashionable items had been added to the line, the upper price limit had been rising. The division's margins on the higher-priced items, furthermore, were greater than on the lower-priced items.

Exhibit 3 shows average wholesale prices and suggested retail markups for a variety of lines from 1965 to 1970.

Production

The company supplemented its own production with that of contractors. In 1970 it had used more than 40 independent contractors, who manufactured about 17 percent of its unit volume—a slightly higher proportion than the senior manufacturing executive would have preferred. Contractors were used to provide flexibility in capacity, although they had serious disadvantages (higher costs, greater difficulty in maintaining quality standards, and inaccurate delivery schedules).

In recent years Levi Strauss & Company had consistently sold more goods than it could produce. The anticipated availability of funds from the public offering of stock was expected to

[1]These chains typically sold merchandise only under their own brand names.

EXHIBIT 3
INDEX* OF AVERAGE WHOLESALE PRICES AND SUGGESTED RETAIL MARKUPS

	1965	1966	1967	1968	1969	1970
Basic Blue Jeans:†						
Av. wholesale price	93	94	100	108	117	117
Retail markup, %	32	32	39	39	40	42
Boys' Double-Knee Jeans:						
Av. wholesale price	80	85	100	105	104	108
Retail markup, %	40	40	40	41	41	42
Stretch Jeans:†						
Av. wholesale price	97	95	100	108	108	108
Retail markup, %	44	44	44	44	44	44
Classic Fashion Jeans:†						
Av. wholesale price		90	100	106	109	109
Retail markup, %		45	46	47	48	49
Young Men's Casual Sportswear:						
Av. wholesale price		99	100	106	120	124
Retail markup, %		46	46	47	48	49
Mr. Levi's:						
Av. wholesale price			100	107	109	116
Retail markup, %			47	48	50	50

* Note that 1967 prices = 100 percent.
† Includes boys' sizes.

alleviate that problem by providing increased production capacity.

Product Integrity

Quality assurance was an exceedingly important function at Levi Strauss & Company. The director of product integrity reported to the president and was a director of the corporation. He had personnel working in all factories and had the authority to stop production or reject incoming raw materials. Typically, quality problems arose when the factories and textile mills were working at capacity. It was at these times that the product integrity department was most criticized by merchandising and production personnel who believed that the product quality standards were overly strict. Product integrity personnel, however, thought that the maintenance of a reputation for high quality was crucial

to the long-term growth of the firm. Although some managers believed that the women's and boys' product lines did not require the stringent quality standards of the men's lines, the product integrity department enforced nearly the same high-quality standards for all product lines. Some managers felt that the quality standards were too high and resulted in overly high prices for the consumer and in overly low profits for the company.

The Boys' Wear Operation

The question of what to do with the boys' wear operation had been discussed over many years. In the mid-1960s a statement of policy (see Exhibit 4) ranked future market development in the following order: (1) slacks for young men, (2) women's jean-type sportswear, and (3) boys'

EXHIBIT 4
POLICY STATEMENT, 1966

Today Levi Strauss & Company stands as the largest manufacturer of our type of apparel in the world. We are recognized as leaders in our field. It is our desire to conduct our affairs as business statesmen, recognizing our obligations to our communities and to our country so that we will not only maintain but reinforce this position of leadership. We will remain an ethical manufacturer providing customers with full value and maintaining a reputation for fair and honest business practices. Our major objective in the next few years is to obtain an increasing share of the popular priced pants market both here and overseas.

We will strive to establish a solid base in most of the important areas of the pants apparel business. This will include expansion of present markets by age groups, sex, and price lines. There are tremendous opportunities for growth beckoning in several fields, but we must establish priorities so that the desired growth can be obtained without straining our resources, both financial and otherwise.

Regardless of new opportunities, it is our purpose and desire to maintain the distinctiveness of brand and company identity of Blue Levi's. The tradition and identity of the original Levi's jeans are a unique and invaluable asset and must not be diminished in importance. Levi's is one of the strongest brand names in the apparel and consumer products field.

Regarding new merchandising opportunities, our present view would rank them in the following order: (1) Mr. Levi's—slacks for the young men; (2) women's jeans-type sportswear (eventually as a separate division); and (3) a separate department to concentrate on boys' and juveniles' pants. Each of these fields will only be entered in turn after we have assurance that our objectives of superior quality and service have been established in our present lines and can be assured in the new merchandise.

Although as we expand individual ability and efficiency will be demanded and recognized, we must never lose sight of our basic philosophy of responsibility to our own personnel at all levels. We are aware of the need for any progressive business to be increasingly responsive to a wide range of social responsibilities in all areas in which it operates and we have long been considered a leader in these matters. We will continue to plan, insofar as possible, so as to provide steady employment throughout the year for our production workers. We must maintain relationships with everyone working for Levi Strauss & Company in a manner that will encourage the loyalty and interest which have been among our most unique and valuable assets. We want to provide a productive, satisfying, and challenging work environment for employees, regardless of position or department, so that anyone who applies himself will be assured of security as well as career opportunities for personal development and advancement.

---

and juveniles' pants. By the early 1970s several of these policies had been implemented; the Levi's For Gals Division had been formed in 1968, and in very early 1971 the Sportswear Division had been created. In June 1970 a unified boys' wear merchandising group had been organized. A major marketing research and planning study had been prepared. Excerpts are in appendix A of this case. Appendix B includes general information available on the apparel market.

Many executives thought that the boys' wear

operation had been treated as an "orphan" or "afterthought." The most commonly stated examples were that when either textiles were hard to obtain or production facilities were in great demand, the boys' wear operation was neglected in favor of other areas. Other issues also concerned marketing management. Although sales of boys' wear were substantial (in the same range as sales for the Levi's For Gals Division) and contributed significant gross profit dollars to the company, the cost of goods sold averaged about 5 percent higher than in the remainder of the firm. Thus, the dollar gross margin per unit was significantly lower because of the combination of a relatively low unit price and lower percentage margins.

Several alternatives were open to management. First, the whole operation could be discontinued. Second, it could be made into a full-fledged division. Finally, the boys' operation could continue to be included in the men's basic, dress, and casual jean area and in the men's sportswear division. If the boys' wear operation were to be continued in any form, there were major decisions to be made concerning product line, advertising, and distribution.

With regard to the product line, some executives favored emphasizing only a few basic items, each of which would generate a large volume and, they felt, higher profits. Other executives believed that if Levi Strauss & Company were to be in the business, it should be committed to it with a full line which could fill all of a retailer's needs. The boys' line for spring 1971 retail sales is enumerated in Exhibit 5. A major innovation was to be introduced in the fall 1971 line. The garment looked like sportswear and was made of a fabric typically used for sportswear, but it was of jeans-type construction so that it could retail for about $2 less than the same garment in sportswear-type construction.

The advertising issues were quite involved. One boys' wear merchandiser believed that because the Levi's line was known primarily as a teenage line, substantial advertising was needed to convince both the retailer and the consumer that Levi Strauss was an important supplier of boys' wear. There was also concern about whether the major portion of the advertising budget should be devoted to consumer advertising or to trade advertising. The most appropriate target for consumer advertising was not clearly evident. One group felt that the emphasis should be on advertising directed toward the child. If this were done, the reasoning went, the child could be made more aware of his clothing and would want to become involved in the choice of it. He could be interested in style and fashion and would be likely to emulate the teenagers in their loyalty to Levi's.

Other executives stressed the importance of advertising to mothers. Since they were already the decision makers, it would be easier to convince them to buy Levi's than to stimulate young boys to take an interest in clothing. These executives reasoned, furthermore, that if mothers could be made more aware of Levi's, they would tend to buy Levi's for their husbands. One theory regarding the teenage strength of Levi's proposed that while males were aware of Levi's and purchased them during the teenage years when they bought their own clothes, females were not as aware and did not tend to purchase Levi's for their children or husbands.

With regard to distribution, the key issue involved whether or not to solicit sales from chains and discounters. One group of executives was in favor of this approach because they believed it to be the only way to develop a large business in boys' wear. Other executives were categorically against the idea because it offered too much control to too limited a number of retailers and might threaten the support of established outlets. These executives were, furthermore, against selling goods under a private label. Finally, they doubted that Levi's could earn as high a margin as it desired by selling through these outlets.

EXHIBIT 5
BOYS' WEAR LINE—SPRING 1971

Model	Description	Number of fabrics	Number of fabric-color combinations	Suggested retail price (price depends on size and fabric)
Hopster Flares*	Sportswear	10	37	$7.50–11.00
Cordova Flares*	Sportswear	7	25	8.00–11.00
Trimcuts*	Cuffed sportswear	2	11	5.50– 9.00
Trimcuts*	Cuffless sportswear	1	4	6.50– 7.50
Swinger Flares*	Sportswear	3	11	6.00– 9.00
Levi's Bell Bottoms*	Jeans	4	8	5.50– 7.50
Levi's Flares*	Jeans	4	15	6.00– 8.50
Levi's Dress Flares†	Jeans	3	6	10.00
Blue Levi's	Jeans	1	1	6.00
Saddleman Boot Jean	Jeans	1	1	6.00– 7.00
Super Slims	Jeans	1	1	5.50
Boys' Double-Knee Levi's	Jeans	2	6	4.50– 5.50
Authentic Levi's Jacket	Denim jacket	1	1	7.50
Stretch Levi's	Jeans	1	3	4.98
Levi's Slim Fits	Jeans	1	3	5.50
Sta-Prest Levi's	Jeans	1	4	6.50– 7.50
Sta-Prest Slim Fits*	Jeans	1	4	5.50
Nuvos	Jeans	1	3	6.50
Levi's Jeans Shorts	Shorts	2	5	4.00
Frayed Shorts	Shorts	1	2	4.00

* Available in boys' sizes (6–12) and students' sizes (25–30 waist).
† Available only in students' sizes (25–30 waist).
No designation means available only in boys' sizes.
This listing does not include the Little Levi's line which was available in juvenile sizes 2–7. There were seven models in that line, with 32 model-fabric-color combinations, and retail prices ranging from $3.98 to $6.00 for the pants.
Source: Spring 1971 catalog.

Many of the executives believed that it was exceedingly difficult to obtain exposure and shelf space in boys' wear departments. They knew that many people in the department store trade believed that boys' wear departments were weak because top-level department store managers were not willing to invest heavily to meet the chains and discounters in a price-sensitive area.

Appendix A
Boys' Wear Market Review

Boys' Pants Market

The boys' pants market covers boys from ages 2 to 14, including juveniles (sizes 2–7), boys (sizes 6–14), and students or preps (waists 25–30). Primary consumers for Levi's boys' wear are wearers of boys' and students' sizes.

Population

U.S. Department of Commerce population projections indicate that the primary market (5–14 year-olds) will decline slightly (−3.8 percent) from 1969 to 1975 because of the recent low birthrate. The 5–9-year-old segment will decline by nearly 1 million persons, while the 10–14 group will rise nominally (see Table 1).

Boys' Pants Production

Projections of boys' pants production in the United States are shown in Table 2. Growth in total produc-

tion of boys' pants (18.6 percent from 1969 to 1975) will result primarily from increased per capita purchases, since population will remain relatively stable.

Distribution Channels and Available Market

Of the total boys' market, a substantial portion is sold through non-Levi's channels (chains, discount houses, and variety stores). Only the remaining portion is available to Levi's boys' wear, as represented in Table 3.

Competition

The chains (Penney, Sears, and Ward) are the major forces in the boys' pants market. In 1968, these three chains accounted for 47 percent of total jeans unit sales and 33 percent of total slacks unit sales.

Table 4 details approximate 1968 market shares for the major boys' pants manufacturers. Penney, Sears, Ward, the discounters, and variety outlets base their appeal largely on reasonable quality at attractive

TABLE 1
Boys' Population Projections, United States, Thousands

	1969	1970	1971	1972	1973	1974	1975
Age group:							
0–4	9,545	9,571	9,746	9,996	10,261	10,540	10,835
5–9	10,626	10,507	10,209	9,939	9,747	9,623	9,649
10–14	10,411	10,500	10,654	10,709	10,718	10,701	10,580
Total 0–14	30,582	30,578	30,609	30,644	30,726	30,864	31,064
Total 5–14	21,037	21,007	20,863	20,648	20,465	20,324	20,229
% change from 1969 5–14		−0.1	−0.8	−1.8	−2.7	−3.4	−3.8

TABLE 2

Projected Domestic Boys' Pants Production, Millions of units

	1969	1970	1971	1972	1973	1974	1975	% change 1969–1975
Jeans	76.8	79.0	81.2	83.4	85.5	87.7	89.9	17.1
Slacks	67.4	69.6	71.8	74.0	76.1	78.3	80.5	19.4
Shorts	8.5	8.9	9.3	9.6	10.0	10.3	10.7	25.8
Total	152.7	157.5	162.3	167.0	171.6	176.3	181.1	18.6

TABLE 3

Total and Available Market—Boys' Sizes, Millions of units

	Jeans		Slacks and shorts	
	1970	1975	1970	1975
Sold through chains and discount stores	54	65	38	45
Sold through department and specialty stores	25	25	41	46
	79	90	79	91

TABLE 4

Market Shares in 1968, Ages 6–13

	Jeans			Slacks		
Brand	% total units	% total dollars	Brand	% total units	% total dollars
Penney	21.4	20.7	Sears	17.7	16.5
Sears	19.8	18.9	Penney	10.9	10.7
Levi's	6.0	9.3	Brand B	5.0	6.8
Ward	6.0	5.8	Ward	3.9	3.4
Brand A	3.3	3.5	Levi's	2.7	3.4
Brand B	2.8	3.5	Brand D	2.4	3.1
Brand C	2.2	2.8	Brand E	2.4	NA
Brand D	1.8	2.2	Brand F	1.9	NA
Others	36.7	33.3	Brand A	1.5	1.7
Total	100.0	100.0	Others	51.6	54.4
			Total	100.0	100.0

prices, and they emphasize special price promotions. Boys' wear retailers in leading department and specialty stores generally believe that they should not engage in direct price competition with the chains and discounters but rather should base their appeal on quality, fashion, and brand strength.

Consumer Purchase Decision

Consumer surveys indicate that 6–13-year-old boys buy less than 10 percent of the total pants purchased for their use, while over 75 percent are bought by the boys' mothers, and 15 percent by other family members or groups. A consumer study conducted for Levi Strauss & Company indicated that the degree of influence exerted by the boy on his mother's purchase decisions is a product of two factors: (1) his age and (2) his interest in the product being purchased. The study concluded that until the boy reaches the age of 8–10, he has little interest in pants and exerts minimal influence on his mother's purchase decisions. Around the age of 10, a boy begins to show some interest in his appearance and the pants he wears, and his influence on his mother's pants purchase decisions becomes evident. Thereafter it increases with his age.

Appendix B
Data Gathered by the Marketing Planning Department

Store Shares

	Age of wearer				
	6–13*	14–18	19–24	25–34	35 & over
Male $8–$15 permanent press slacks					
Department stores	31%	46%	39%	42%	39%
Specialty stores	16	42	45	37	32
Chains	31	7	9	16	18
Discount stores	14	4	2	2	4
All others	8	1	5	3	7
	100%	100%	100%	100%	100%
Male $5–$12 jeans					
Department stores	24%	48%	47%	40%	31%
Specialty stores	8	37	38	40	36
Chains	45	6	6	9	21
Discount stores	14	7	8	8	10
All others	9	2	1	3	2
	100%	100%	100%	100%	100%

*All prices

Brand Preference for Male Pants, Based on a Sample of United States Males

	Age of wearer				
	6–13	14–18	19–24	25–34	35 & over
Levi's	8%*	21%	20%	13%	7%
Farah	7	10	12	11	7
Penney	16	9	8	12	11
Sears	16	8	5	11	10
Blue Bell	2	4	3	2	1
H.I.S.		3	3	1	1
Haggar		2	2	5	5
Don't know or other	51	43	47	45	58

*To be read: "8 percent of those respondents aged 6 to 13 preferred Levi's."

A GROWING MARKET: UNITED STATES POPULATION

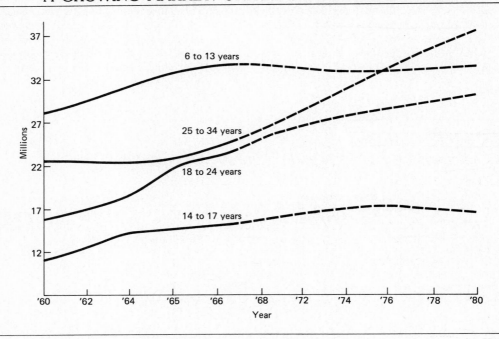

14 FTC v. Levi Strauss

John F. Cady

As Peter E. Haas, president of Levi Strauss & Co., emerged from a meeting with the corporation's general counsel, he wondered what action the firm should take as a result of a complaint issued by the Federal Trade Commission (FTC). Two years earlier the FTC had charged Levi Strauss with a number of violations of the Federal Trade Commission Act (Appendix A). Levi's management would have to review its entire domestic distribution strategy before deciding how to respond to the Commission complaint. Several alternatives were open to Levi's management:

1. Levi could enter into a consent agreement with the FTC. This meant that the firm would not admit to having violated the law but would refrain in the future from engaging in any of the activities outlined in the complaint.

John F. Cady is an associate professor of business administration at the Harvard Graduate School of Business Administration.

This case was developed from public sources and a Levi Strauss *Annual Report.* Statements concerning management's beliefs have been inferred from these sources.

The advantages of this alternative were that it could be carried out quickly and help to minimize any adverse publicity the firm might receive as a result of being involved with an antitrust lawsuit. It would also not require a large time commitment from top management, as antitrust suits generally did.

2. Levi could attempt to negotiate a consent agreement concerning some parts of the complaint but, at the same time, attempt to persuade the FTC to drop other parts. Mr. Haas's attorneys had noted that if the firm could demonstrate the necessity of some of its practices, or demonstrate their procompetitive effects, the FTC might not press these issues in trial.

This alternative was attractive to Mr. Haas because he believed that certain practices alleged in the complaint, notably resale price maintenance agreements, had already been discontinued by the firm. On the other hand, Levi's policy of selling to selected retailers only was believed by management to have accounted, in part, for its traditional sales and earnings growth. However, the apparel market had changed dramatically in the past few years, and Mr. Haas was uncertain as to what a review of Levi's selective distribution policy would reveal.

3. Levi could respond to the complaint in court. A trial would be held by an FTC administrative law judge, and either party could appeal the outcome to the federal courts.

   This alternative would be costly in management time, direct legal costs, and possible adverse publicity. Some observers had estimated that the total cost of a suit would be $5 million. Mr. Haas knew that such suits rarely required less than 3 years' time and considerable expense. Still, this might be the only way that Levi Strauss could maintain its current distribution policies.

Levi Strauss & Company

When young Levi Strauss, a Bavarian immigrant, landed in San Francisco in 1850, he intended to sell canvas to gold miners for tents and wagon covers. However, he discovered a greater need for durable men's pants. He quickly decided to turn his material and a simple design for pants over to a tailor. With that decision, Strauss entered the apparel business.

More than 120 years later, Levi Strauss & Co. had grown tremendously. In 1970, the firm had "gone public" and issued its first public annual report. Sales were $328 million, and earnings were $18.5 million. (Exhibit 1 provides sales and earnings data for 1971, 1973, and 1977). In 1971, Levi Strauss adopted a divisionalized organization in order to facilitate the attainment of sales and earnings growth objectives. The divisions created in 1971 were Jeans, Sportswear, Levi's For Gals, and Levi Strauss International. By 1977, these divisions had expanded to five domestic divisions (Jeanswear, Youthwear, Sportswear, Womenswear, Diversified Products) and an International Group of four divisions

(Europe, Canada, Latin America, Far East). Its combined worldwide operations in 1977 established Levi Strauss as the largest apparel manufacturer in the world, with sales of $1.56 billion.

Distribution Policies of Levi Strauss

From the time that Levi Strauss entered the apparel business, its strategy had always been to produce goods that were of very high quality and to closely monitor changes in the needs and demands of consumers and meet those demands. Walter Haas, chairman of Levi Strauss, noted, "We try to find out what the public wants and react to it quickly. . . . If there's a trend away from jeans to kilts, we'll make kilts."

The firm's management believed that in order to maintain quality control standards, a policy of selective distribution was most appropriate. Management desired to distribute its products only in outlets that were physically appealing, that had attractive display areas, that provided sales assistance, and that carried full lines of apparel items, including Levi's. They reasoned that such services and amenities complemented Levi products. The company also believed that its products should be sold through retailers that had good local reputations and stable financial structures and that specialized to some extent in the sale of clothing produced by high-quality, recognized manufacturers.

Accordingly, Levi Strauss focused its distribution through specialty stores, traditional department stores, and departmentalized specialty stores. The firm did not sell through the three major department store chains—Sears, Ward, and Penney—nor did it generally sell through mass merchandisers. By 1976, Levi sold through 16,000 accounts that operated approximately 30,000 stores. These 30,000 outlets represented 43 percent of the potential accounts which nominally met the criteria of not being chains or mass merchandisers.

Levi Strauss distributed directly to its retail accounts and did not use wholesalers or apparel

EXHIBIT 1
FINANCIAL SUMMARY
Levi Strauss & Co. and Subsidiaries
(Dollar Amounts in Millions Except Per Share Data)

	Year ended November:		
	1977	**1973**	**1971**
Net sales	$1,559.3	$653.0	$432.0
Gross profit	$ 562.6	$184.4	$129.6
Interest expense	20.0	10.1	4.4
Income before taxes*	270.0	33.8	35.7
Provision for taxes on income	140.2	22.0	16.0
Net income	$ 129.8	$ 11.9	$ 19.7
Earnings retained in the business	$ 108.0	$ 6.6	$ 16.3
Cash flow retained in the business†	128.7	17.7	22.5
Income before taxes as percentage of sales	17.3%	5.2%	8.3%
Net income as percentage of sales	8.3%	1.8%	4.6%
Net income as percentage of beginning stockholders' equity	35.8%	7.0%	23.2%
Current assets	$ 694.2	$305.5	$202.8
Current liabilities	263.5	155.7	67.9
Working capital	430.7	149.8	134.9
Ratio of current assets to current liabilities	2.63/1	1.96/1	2.99/1
Long-term debt‡	$ 80.6	$ 48.1	$ 28.4
Stockholders' equity	463.9	176.4	148.8
Capital expenditures	$ 31.4	$ 28.8	$ 15.6
Depreciation	13.7	8.3	5.1
Property, plant and equipment—net	119.3	68.0	39.6
Number of employees	37,170	29,141	21,383
Per share data			
Net income	$ 5.87	$ 0.54	$ 0.93
Cash dividends declared	1.00	0.24	0.16
Book value (on shares outstanding at year end)	21.32	8.10	6.84
Market price range	31⅝–24¼	24⅞–8⅜	32⅛–16⅝
Average common and common equivalent shares outstanding	22,128,673	21,760,160	21,172,000

*Net of minority interest in net income of consolidated subsidiaries.
†Working capital provided by operations minus dividends declared.
‡Excludes current maturities.

jobbers. This strategy was believed to benefit the firm in two ways. First, it allowed Levi to enforce its policy of selective distribution. Because there was great interest among chains and mass merchandisers in carrying the Levi Strauss line (or at least Levi's jeans), management reasoned that some wholesalers might divert some denim products to those retailers. Management believed that this would have the effect of damaging the image of Levi's as a quality product and would deprive traditional retail accounts of the products for which their efforts had helped create demand. Management also feared that if mass merchandisers obtained Levi's merchandise, they would "loss leader" it. This would damage Levi's image as well as sales by traditional accounts. In the past some of Levi's retail accounts had engaged in "bootlegging" Levi's jeans. This practice occurred when retailers resold Levi's jeans to mass merchandisers. In such situations Levi Strauss unilaterally refused to deal with retailers who resold to mass merchandisers or other unauthorized outlets.

A second reason for Levi's policy was to maintain maximum control over inventory. Fashion apparel items were frequently subject to rapid changes in sales volume due to changes in consumer tastes. By selling directly to selected retailers, Levi's management believed that it was able to detect changing tastes and respond to them quickly. A principal activity of the sales force was developing and maintaining strong ties with retailers in order to facilitate Levi's product planning and new-product development. The 1975 *Annual Report* clearly described the Levi Strauss emphasis on distribution and control. "Our managers the world over emphasized the importance of control over assets—particularly inventory and receivables . . . this control, coupled with effective merchandising, substantially reduced markdowns for the year and caused the growth rate in earnings to substantially exceed the sales growth rate." To achieve its growth and control objectives, Levi's had introduced a number of cooperative programs with its retail-

ers. One such program involved linking Levi's computers with retailers' computers. The purpose of this was to enhance the capacity of the firm to forecast fashion trends, improve inventory turnover, and reduce markdowns.

A number of specialty store chains that carried only denim apparel had developed during the mid-1970s. Some of these chains, such as The Gap, which was the nation's largest blue jeans specialty chain, carried only Levi's brand. These specialty stores provided Levi with a substantial number of new distribution outlets. By late 1977, The Gap, for example, had become Levi's third largest customer. Management believed that competition from these stores had led to even more aggressive merchandising in traditional department stores. In particular, many department stores had established specialty jeans shops within the stores and increased the display area devoted to Levi Strauss products.

Personal Selling, Sales Promotion, and Advertising

Levi's distribution strategy was carried out and monitored through the company's sales force. By 1973 Levi employed over 500 salespeople. Each salesperson was responsible for the sale of Levi Strauss products in a single division. In 1973, about 60 percent of the sales force was assigned to the Jeans Division.

Within the sales force, there were four types of positions: stocktaker, trainee, salesperson, and account executive. Stocktakers were usually part-time employees; their function was to monitor unit sales in retail outlets and report these to sales management. Trainees were "apprentice" salespeople who worked with a regular member of the sales force, learning the division's products and policies and the needs of retail customers. As sales territories opened up, trainees were assigned low-sales-volume territories and were provided with financial incentives to build Levi sales volume. Salespeople were encouraged to actively promote all products in their divisional line and to assist in the development of promotions that featured a number of division products. A successful salesperson could be promoted to account executive. An account executive was responsible for no more than six very large Levi accounts. Usually these accounts were multiple store groups such as Macy's, May Co., Gimbel's, Abraham & Straus, and Marshall Field. The account executives were expected to develop good relationships with these retail accounts.

By the mid-1970s one function had become very important to maintaining good account relations. Denim jeans were frequently in short supply due to strong demand. The sales force was responsible for allocating available denim jeans among retail accounts. Retailers were anxious to avoid stock-outs on Levi's jeans and frequently attempted to obtain assurances of a steady supply from the sales force.

Levi provided retailers with promotional materials, displays, and ideas for the in-store promotion of Levi Strauss products. These promotions were developed for retailers through the account executives and salespeople. Levi also generated publicity for itself which frequently featured a retail account. In such cases publicity releases would be sent to major media in a retailer's market area.

Until the late 1960s, the bulk of Levi's advertising dollars had been spent on cooperative advertising with retail accounts. The firm paid 50 percent of media costs for its co-op advertising, and the participating retailer paid the remainder. Levi's assumed all costs associated with the development of advertising copy for its cooperative advertising program. Levi's sales force discouraged the use of Levi's brand names in retail advertisements or irregular or discontinued Levi Strauss products. Management believed that this policy was consistent with its desire to promote an image as a quality apparel manufacturer.

Since 1971, Levi had placed relatively more of its advertising budget into media advertising designed to develop and support a strong consumer brand franchise. A number of Levi's television advertisements had won "Clio" awards for advertising creativity. The firm had contracted to spend $8 million on advertising during the 1980 Olympics and had been designated as the designer and manufacturer of uniforms for the 1980 Olympic team.

Distribution Margins and Retail Prices

Levi Strauss management believed that in order to obtain adequate and appropriate retail display space, sales effort, in-store promotion, and retail advertising support, retailers must obtain adequate margins. The firm maintained a policy of suggesting retail prices to its retail accounts. If retailers followed Levi's suggested prices, they received a margin of approximately 50 percent. Thus, if the suggested retail price for one style of denim jeans was $16, Levi's selling price was approximately $8. Discounting by Levi's accounts was discouraged, since management believed the practice could hurt its quality image and reduce the amount of retailer effort that would be exerted on its behalf. Adherence to suggested retail prices was generally maintained by retail accounts. One reason for this was the fact that throughout the late 1960s and into the mid-1970s the demand for Levi's products, particularly its jeans, exceeded supply. Exhibit 2 shows the relative retail prices for various brands of denim jeans in 1975.

Competition for Levi's Britches

Levi Strauss faced competition from a number of branded and private-label manufacturers of blue jeans, as well as branded and private-label manufacturers of men's, women's, and chil-

EXHIBIT 2
ESTIMATED RELATIVE RETAIL PRICES OF BLUE JEANS (1975)*

Levi Strauss	1.20
Blue Bell	1.00
H. D. Lee	1.14
Sears	
Ward	
Penney	0.89

*These relative prices were estimated as follows: The estimated average selling price of blue jeans for all manufacturers in 1975 was divided into the average selling price for each manufacturer. Thus, the retail selling price for Levi Strauss blue jeans was estimated to be 20 percent higher than average. The prices are not adjusted to reflect the quantities sold by each manufacturer.

Source: A variety of published materials.

dren's apparel and accessories. Levi's share of denim jeans was between 30 and 40 percent.

There were two other major United States manufacturers of branded jeans—Blue Bell and H. D. Lee. Blue Bell, which produced under the "Wrangler" brand, was a large and diversified company. In 1977 two-thirds of Blue Bell's sales of $874 million were from nonjean items. However it was generally believed that almost half of Blue Bell's profits was derived from the sale of jeans. Blue Bell's distribution strategy utilized traditional department stores, departmentalized specialty stores, mass merchandisers' discount stores, and its own franchised Wrangler Wranch outlets. About 65 percent of Wrangler Wranch sales were from Blue Bell products. By 1977 Wrangler Wranches accounted for approximately $6 million in sales. Wrangler's share of denim jean unit sales was believed to have remained stable, between 50 and 60 percent of Levi's unit sales.

H. D. Lee produced under the "Lee" brand. Lee manufactured leisure apparel such as shirts and slacks but was not as diversified as either Blue Bell or Levi Strauss. Lee distributed its apparel through the same types of retail outlets as did Blue Bell. It was estimated to have a unit

share of jeans sales equal to about 40 percent of Wrangler's share. Market analysts believed that Lee's share had declined somewhat in recent years.

There were a larger number of low-volume manufacturers of branded jeans. These brands, such as Cowboy, Saddle Itch, and Cheap Jeans, had proliferated during the early 1970s as the demand for denim jeans grew rapidly. These brands varied considerably in construction quality, style, price, and availability.

Each of the three department store chains—Sears, Roebuck; Montgomery Ward; and J. C. Penny—had developed its own brand of denim jeans. These brands were available only through each firm's branch stores. Collectively, these merchandisers were believed to account for approximately 20 percent of the denim jeans sales.

The Denim Connection: The Development of International Operations

In 1969, Levi began to formulate a strategy for its European operations that was dramatically different from the strategy in the United States and elsewhere. Peter Coombs, vice president for European operations, decided that Levi Strauss should expand rapidly to attain as large a share of the European jeans market as possible. Only after this would the company impose its usual financial and management controls. Mr. Coombs reasoned that it would be much easier to gain a position in Europe before competitors become entrenched. He believed that if competition were allowed to entrench, it would be more difficult for Levi to develop a leading position in Europe. In addition, since the demand for jeans and related denim items exceeded the supply substantially, there appeared to be no need for developing an extensive inventory control system.

Levi began buying factories for European production and ordering goods from other Levi plants around the world in an attempt to meet demand. In 1970, Levi's European inventory turned over seven times, compared to a normal turnover rate of four times.

In order to achieve satisfactory distribution, Levi acquired the firms that had been its national distributors in 10 European countries and turned them into sales subsidiaries. It was believed that these subsidiaries would provide the same type of close relationships with retailers that the Levi Strauss sales force provided in the United States. It became apparent, however, that it was extremely difficult to integrate the 10 previously independent subsidiaries into a consistent distribution system. Each had its own accounting and inventory control system, and each had its own method of reporting sales information from its retail accounts back to Levi Strauss.

As a result of these acquisitions, the potential for inventory control problems had multiplied by 10. Such problems were also a concern as a result of two other trends. First, only about one-quarter of Levi's products sold in Europe were produced in Europe. Due to a chronic lack of European manufacturing capacity, most products were shipped from the United States, Puerto Rico, Mexico, and Hong Kong. Frequently, it took 6 months from the production order to delivery. Second, the number of styles, fabrics, and product items being sold by Levi had grown rapidly. As a result the number of inventory reports required of the sales subsidiaries increased considerably.

In 1972, European production increased dramatically, and shortages began to decline. However, Levi's management was unable to accurately monitor the reduction in shortages, due to the reporting incompatibilities with the sales subsidiaries. Fashion preferences changed rapidly, and in a matter of several months the demand for straight-legged jeans dropped as the demand for bell-bottom jeans sharply increased.

Most of the orders for straight-legged jeans that had been placed months earlier by retailers were refused when they arrived in Europe. A similar switch in preferences occurred when European consumers changed from bell-bottom corduroy pants to bell-bottom denim jeans. A number of the sales subsidiary managers believed that these changes were temporary, however, and continued to order straight-legged jeans and bell-bottom corduroys.

The changes in preferences turned out not to be temporary, however, and in a relatively short period of time a very large inventory of Levi Strauss products had built up. By the time management learned the true nature of the problem and cut back new orders, competitors had begun reducing their own inventories through markdowns. One Levi executive described the European price-cutting that occurred between late 1972 and mid-1973 as "our Kamikazi dive." In Germany, for example, the wholesale prices for bell-bottom corduroy pants fell from $6 to $1.50. Retail prices fell from $10 to $3.

The company lost $12 million in its European operations, and this resulted in a 1973 fourth-quarter deficit of $7.2 million. This was the first quarterly loss registered by Levi since 1932. In 1974 strict inventory controls were introduced. The *Annual Report* noted that "important personnel reassignments have already been made to give our foreign operations full advantage of our domestic depth of experience." By 1975 Levi Strauss had obtained a profitable 15 percent share of the Eastern European market. Blue Bell held 9 percent, and H. D. Lee 4 percent.

Overseas operations in Japan had also resulted in a number of changes in distribution policies over time. The traditional Japanese distribution channels for manufacturers of consumer goods involved a complex of intermediaries, from import agents through a number of wholesalers to final retailers. "Costs are high," noted one industry observer, "and along the way you frequently lose control of how your product is sold."

Because of unaggressive promotion by wholesalers, Levi Strauss had established its own sales force to distribute directly to retailers. Initially, the company lost 300 Tokyo department stores and shops because those retailers did not want to alienate their wholesalers. In time, most of these accounts returned, primarily because Levi Strauss was a well-known American firm and its products were considered a status symbol. One Levi Strauss manager noted that the company could never have achieved any success in Japan if it had not gained control over distribution channels. And it could not have gained control over distribution without a strong name and product quality. "Without the Levi name we'd be just another jeans company."

By 1977 the sales of Levi Strauss International totaled $518 million.

Recent Developments in the United States

From 1971 through 1976, the demand for denim jeans and casual apparel increased tremendously. Many of Levi's (and competitors') most popular denim items were put on customer allocation, and inventories of manufacturers and retailers turned over rapidly. Jeans manufacturers and denim producers expanded capacity to meet demand. By 1975, however, the rate of demand growth had declined, and by mid-1976 there was an ample supply of jeans and denim.

In 1976, denim producers lowered their prices by 2 percent, and Levi Strauss responded by increasing the amount of jeans allocated to its customers. In June of 1977, the County Seat, a specialty chain, began discounting two lines of Levi's denim apparel and one line of corduroy. The Gap specialty chain soon followed by discounting Levi's jeans. Major retailers cut prices on some Levi jeans from a suggested retail price of $16 to $12.50. Sears and Penney discounted their brands to under $10. Retailers of Wrangler, Lee, and other branded denim jeans cut prices on those brands as well.

In response to pressure from retailers and in an attempt to maintain its market share, Blue Bell reduced prices to retailers by 6 percent. Lee made similar reductions. Levi Strauss, however, maintained its prices to retailers. Unit sales of Levi's products and 1977 sales and profits increased.

By 1978, however, the retail discounting began to have an adverse effect on operations. Consumers had apparently "loaded up" on denim jeans. Retailers began reducing orders from manufacturers in order to reduce their inventories. Blue Bell reduced its price to retailers once again in order to maintain its market share. Levi maintained its prices but was forced to reduce its production in many plants to 4 days in order to manage inventories. By mid-1978, however, production was back at a full 5-day schedule, and the Levi market share had increased slightly over the 1977 figure.

By July of 1978 denim jeans accounted for about 33 percent of Levi's domestic sales volume and about 45 percent of worldwide sales.

Appendix A
United States of America
before Federal Trade Commission

COMPLAINT

Pursuant to the provisions of the Federal Trade Commission Act (U.S.C. Title 15, Section 14 et seq., as amended), and by virtue of the authority vested in it by said Act, the Federal Trade Commission, having reason to believe that Levi Strauss & Co., a corporation, hereinafter referred to as "respondent," has violated the provisions of Section 5 of said Act, and it appearing to the Commission that a proceeding by it in respect thereof would be in the public interest, hereby issues its complaint, stating its charges in respect thereto as follows:

For purposes of this complaint, the following definitions shall apply:

"Product" is defined as any item of wearing apparel and any related accessory which is manufactured, offered for sale, or sold by Levi Strauss & Co.

"Dealer" is defined as any person, partnership, corporation or firm which purchases any product from Levi Strauss & Co. for resale.

"Prospective Dealer" is defined as any person, partnership, corporation or firm which may desire to purchase any product from Levi Strauss & Co. for resale but has not been accepted by Levi Strauss & Co. as a dealer.

PARAGRAPH ONE: Respondent Levi Strauss & Co. is a corporation organized, existing and doing business under and by virtue of the laws of the State of Delaware, with its principal office and place of business at 2 Embarcadero Center, San Francisco, California 94106.

PARAGRAPH TWO: Respondent is now and has been for many years engaged in the manufacture, sale and distribution of a wide variety of wearing apparel for men, women and children, including but not limited to jeans, slacks, shorts, shirts, jackets and related items. Gross sales by respondent for the 1975 fiscal year exceeded $1,000,000,000. Respondent claims to be the largest apparel manufacturer in the world.

PARAGRAPH THREE: Respondent sells and distributes its products directly to more than 15,000 retail dealers located throughout the United States who in turn resell respondent's products to the general public.

PARAGRAPH FOUR: Respondent maintains a comprehensive and integrated manufacturing, sales and distribution system throughout the United States. Sales of respondent's products are effectuated through seven regional sales offices located in New York, New York; Atlanta, Georgia; Chicago, Illinois; Dallas, Texas; Los Angeles, California; San Francisco, California; and Seattle, Washington. More than 500 salesmen working under control of these regional sales offices sell respondent's products throughout the United States.

Respondent also maintains manufacturing plants located in the States of California, New Mexico, Texas, Tennessee, Arkansas, Mississippi, Georgia, Virginia, North Carolina, Missouri, and Louisiana. Respondent transports its products, either directly from its manufacturing plants. . .located in the aforementioned States to dealers or from these manufacturing plants to warehouses located in California, Texas and Kentucky, and from there, distributes such products to its dealers located in every State of the United States and the District of Columbia. . .There is now and has been at all times mentioned in this Complaint, a pattern and course of commerce in respondent's products which is in and affects interstate commerce, as "commerce" is defined in the Federal Trade Commission Act.

Appendix A

Continued

complaint

PARAGRAPH FIVE: Except to the extent that competition has been hindered, frustrated, lessened and eliminated as set forth in this Complaint, respondent has been and is now in substantial competition with other corporations, individuals and partnerships engaged in the manufacture, sale and distribution of wearing apparel similar to that listed and described in PARAGRAPH TWO hereinabove.

PARAGRAPH SIX: In the course and conduct of its business as above described, respondent has for some time past effectuated and pursued a policy throughout the United States, the purpose or effect of which is and has been to fix, control, establish, manipulate and maintain the resale prices at which its dealers advertise, offer for sale and sell its products.

PARAGRAPH SEVEN: By various means and methods, respondent has effectuated and enforced the aforesaid practice and policy by which it can and does fix, control, establish, manipulate and maintain the resale prices at which its products are advertised, offered for sale and sold by its dealers. To carry out said practice or policy, respondent adopted and employed, and still employs, the following means and methods among others:

(a) It requires prospective dealers as a condition of becoming dealers, or requires dealers as a condition of remaining dealers, to enter into oral agreements or understandings with respondent, or to give oral assurances to respondent, that they will adhere to those resale prices established or suggested by respondent for its products.

(b) It requires prospective dealers as a condition of becoming dealers, or requires dealers as a condition of remaining dealers, to enter into oral agreements or understandings with respondent, or give oral assurances to respondent, that they will not advertise any of respondent's first-line quality products, whether or not in conjunction with any of respondent's trademarks, at resale prices other than those respondent had established or suggested.

(c) It requires prospective dealers as a condition of becoming dealers, or requires dealers as a condition of remaining dealers, to enter into oral agreements or understandings with respondent, or to give oral assurances to respondent, that they will not advertise any of respondent's second-line quality or irregular products as having been manufactured by respondent.

(d) It requires prospective dealers as a condition of becoming dealers, or requires dealers as a condition of remaining dealers, to enter into oral agreements or understandings with respondent or to give oral assurances to respondent, that they will not resell respondent's products to any retailer not authorized by respondent to sell its products.

(e) It has established and employed, and still employs, a surveillance system, the purpose of which is to ascertain whether any dealer, prospective dealer, person or firm is engaged in any of the following activities:

(1) offering for sale or selling any product at a price other than that which respondent has established or suggested.

(2) advertising any first-line quality products, whether or not in conjunction with any of respondent's trademarks, at a price other than that which respondent has established or suggested.

(3) advertising any second-line quality or irregular product as having been manufactured by respondent.

Appendix A
Continued

       (4) reselling any product to any retailer not authorized by respondent to sell its products.

   (f) As part of the surveillance system as set forth in Subparagraph "(e)" hereinabove, respondent has:

       (1) Solicited and encouraged the cooperation and assistance of dealers to identify and report any dealer, prospective dealer, person or firm who engages in any of the activities set forth in Subparagraph "(e)(1)–(4)" hereinabove.

       (2) Shopped retailers not authorized by respondent to sell its products who are selling *any* product in order to ascertain from which dealer said retailers obtained said product.

   (g) It warns, intimidates, harasses and uses various forms of coercion and discipline, including but not limited to delaying order shipments, restricting the availability of products, limiting the frequency of salesmen's visits, and threatening termination, against dealers engaged in, or suspected of engaging in, any of the activities set forth in Subparagraph "(e)(1)–(4)" hereinabove.

   (h) It terminates dealers engaged in, or suspected of engaging in, any of the activities set forth in Subparagraph "(e)(1)–(4)" hereinabove.

   (i) It refuses to deal with certain prospective dealers for the reason that respondent believes that such prospective dealers will engage in any of the activities set forth in Subparagraph "(e)(1)–(4)" hereinabove.

   (j) It prohibits any dealer from being reimbursed pursuant to respondent's cooperative advertising program for any advertisement offering any product at a price other than that which respondent has established or suggested.

   (k) It misrepresents to dealers that its products are fair traded and that dealers must, as a matter of law, adhere to respondent's established resale prices.

The above are among the various means and methods which have been used, and are now being used, by respondent in the enforcement of its system of maintaining resale prices, all with the result that said prices have been and are generally observed and maintained by dealers handling respondent's products.

PARAGRAPH EIGHT: The aforesaid acts and practices have had and still have the capacity, tendency and effect of hindering, suppressing or eliminating competition between or among all dealers selling respondent's products, by requiring them to resell the same at prices fixed or controlled by respondent as aforesaid; such practices prevent dealers from selling these products at prices of their own choosing; hinder and suppress price competition in the resale of such products in the various States of the United States and the District of Columbia, thus tending to obstruct the free and natural flow of commerce and the freedom of competition in the channels of interstate commerce.

PARAGRAPH NINE: In the course and conduct of its business as above described, respondent has refused to sell and continues to refuse to sell its blue denim jeans to dealers and prospective dealers desirous of purchasing said products unless said dealers and prospective dealers also purchase certain other products manufactured by the respondent.

Further, through the use of an allocation program, respondent has refused to and continues to refuse to increase the allotments of its blue denim jeans to dealers unless said dealers also purchase or increase their purchases of certain other products manufactured by respondent.

Appendix A
Continued

PARAGRAPH TEN: The aforesaid acts and practices of the respondent have the tendency to unduly hinder competition; have injured, hindered, suppressed, lessened or eliminated actual and potential competition, and thus are to the prejudice and injury of the public; and constitute unfair methods of competition in or affecting commerce or unfair acts and practices in or affecting commerce, in violation of Section 5 of the Federal Trade Commission Act.

WHEREFORE, THE PREMISES CONSIDERED, the Federal Trade Commission on this 5th day of May, A.D., 1976, issues its complaint against said respondent.

The following is the form of order which the Commission has reason to believe should issue if the facts are found as alleged in the complaint. If, however, the Commission should conclude from record facts developed in any adjudicative proceedings in this matter that the proposed order provisions as to Levi Strauss & Co. might be inadequate fully to restore and protect competitive conditions in the retail sale of wearing apparel, the Commission may order such other relief as it finds necessary or appropriate.

ORDER

For purposes of this Order, the following definitions shall apply:

"Product" is defined as any item of wearing apparel and any related accessory which is manufactured, offered for sale, or sold by Levi Strauss & Co.

"Dealer" is defined as any person, partnership, corporation or firm which purchases any product from Levi Strauss & Co. for resale.

"Prospective Dealer" is defined as any person, partnership, corporation or firm which may desire to purchase any product from Levi Strauss & Co. for resale but has not been accepted by Levi Strauss & Co. as a dealer.

IT IS ORDERED that respondent Levi Strauss & Co., a corporation, its successors and assigns, and respondent's officers, agents, representatives and employees, directly or indirectly, or through any corporation, subsidiary, division or other device, in connection with the manufacture, offering for sale, sale, distribution or advertising of any product in or affecting commerce, as "commerce" is defined in the Federal Trade Commission Act, shall forthwith cease and desist from:

I

a. Fixing, establishing, controlling, or maintaining, directly or indirectly, the price at which any prospective dealer or dealer may advertise, promote, offer for sale or sell any product.

b. Establishing, exacting assurances to comply with, continuing, enforcing, or announcing the terms of any contract, agreement, understanding, or arrangement with any prospective dealer or dealer which has the purpose or effect of fixing, establishing, maintaining or enforcing, directly or indirectly, the price at which any product is to be resold or advertised.

c. Publishing, disseminating, circulating or providing by any means, any suggested resale price for a period of three (3) years after the date on which this Order

Appendix A
Continued

becomes final; *provided, however,* that after said three (3) year period, respondent may suggest resale prices if it is clearly and conspicuously stated on those pages of any list, book, advertising or promotional material or other similar document where any suggested resale price appears:

"THE PRICES QUOTED HEREIN ARE SUGGESTED ONLY. YOU ARE FREE TO DETERMINE YOUR OWN PRICES."

and *provided further, however,* that after said three (3) year period, respondent may suggest resale prices on any tag, ticket or comparable marking affixed or to be affixed to any product, if it is clearly and conspicuously stated in connection therewith the following:

"THIS PRICE IS SUGGESTED ONLY. RETAILERS ARE FREE TO DETERMINE THEIR OWN PRICES."

and *provided further, however,* that after said three (3) year period, if respondent suggests any resale price, respondent shall mail to all its dealers a letter stating that no dealer is obligated to adhere to any suggested resale price and that such suggested resale price is advisory only.

d. Refusing to sell or threatening to refuse to sell to any prospective dealer or dealer who desires to engage in the sale of any product for the reason that such prospective dealer or dealer will not enter into any contract, agreement, understanding or arrangement with respondent to advertise or sell any product at respondent's established or suggested resale price.

e. Securing or attempting to secure any promise or assurance from any prospective dealer or dealer regarding the price at which such prospective dealer or dealer will or may advertise or sell any product, or requesting or requiring any prospective dealer or dealer to obtain approval from respondent for any price at which such prospective dealer or dealer may or will advertise or sell any product.

f. Threatening to withhold or withholding earned cooperative advertising credits or allowances from any dealer or limiting or restricting the right of any dealer to participate in any cooperative advertising program because said dealer advertises or sells any product at any retail price other than that which respondent has established or suggested.

g. Requiring, soliciting or encouraging any prospective dealer or dealer to report the identity of any prospective dealer, dealer, person or firm who does not adhere to any resale price which respondent has established or suggested for any product, or who advertises any product at any retail price other than that which respondent has established or suggested, or acting on any reports or information so obtained by threatening, intimidating or coercing any prospective dealer or dealer, or by terminating any dealer.

h. Conducting any surveillance program to determine whether any dealer, prospective dealer, person, or firm is advertising, offering for sale or selling any product at any price other than that which respondent has established or suggested.

i. Terminating, coercing or taking any other action to restrict, prevent, or limit the sale of any product by any dealer because said dealer has sold, is selling, is suspected of

Appendix A

selling or contemplates selling such product at any price other than that which respondent has established or suggested.

j. Terminating, coercing or taking any other action to restrict, prevent, or limit the sale of any product by any dealer because said dealer has advertised, is advertising, is suspected of advertising or contemplates advertising, whether or not in conjunction with any of respondent's trademarks, such product at any price other than that which respondent has established or suggested.

k. Threatening, intimidating, or coercing any prospective dealer, person or firm because said prospective dealer, person or firm has sold, is selling, is suspected of selling or contemplates selling any product at any price other than that which respondent has established or suggested.

l. Threatening, intimidating, or coercing any prospective dealer, person or firm because said prospective dealer, person or firm has advertised, is advertising, is suspected of advertising or contemplates advertising, whether or not in conjunction with any of respondent's trademarks, any product at any price other than that which respondent has established or suggested.

m. Taking any action to hinder or preclude the lawful use by any dealer, prospective dealer, person or firm of any of respondent's trademarks in conjunction with the sale or advertising of any product at any price.

n. Refusing to sell to or deal with any prospective dealer because respondent believes that said prospective dealer has the reputation or potential for selling or advertising any of respondent's products at any price other than that which respondent has established or suggested.

II

IT IS FURTHER ORDERED that respondent shall forthwith cease and desist from:

a. Controlling or restricting in any manner the customers or classes of customers to whom any prospective dealer or dealer may sell any product.

b. Establishing, exacting assurances to comply with, continuing, enforcing, or announcing the terms of any contract, agreement, understanding or arrangement with any prospective dealer or dealer which have the purpose or effect of establishing, controlling or restricting in any manner the customers or classes of customers to whom said prospective dealer or dealer may sell any product.

c. Refusing to sell or threatening to refuse to sell to any prospective dealer or dealer for the reason that such prospective dealer or dealer will not enter into any understanding or agreement with respondent to establish, control or restrict in any manner the customers or classes of customers to whom said prospective dealer or dealer may sell any product.

d. Securing or attempting to secure any contract, agreement, understanding or arrangement with any prospective dealer or dealer which has the effect of establishing, controlling or restricting in any manner the customers or classes of customers to whom said prospective dealer or dealer may sell any product.

e. Requiring, soliciting or inviting any prospective dealer or dealer to report the

Appendix A
Continued

identity of any prospective dealer, dealer, person or firm who has not or is not restricting or limiting the customers or classes of customers, approved by respondent, to whom said prospective dealer, dealer, person or firm is selling any product.

f. Conducting any surveillance program to determine whether any prospective dealer, dealer, person or firm is offering for sale or selling any of respondent's products to any customer or class of customer not approved by respondent.

g. Threatening, intimidating, coercing, or taking any other action to restrict, prevent, or limit the sale of any product by any prospective dealer, dealer, person or firm because said prospective dealer, dealer, person or firm has sold, is selling, is suspected of selling, or contemplates selling such product to customers or classes of customers not approved by respondent.

h. Terminating any dealer because said dealer has sold, is selling, is suspected of selling, or contemplates selling any of respondent's products to customers or classes of customers not approved by respondent.

i. Refusing to sell to or deal with any prospective dealer because respondent believes said prospective dealer has the reputation or potential for selling any of respondent's products to customers or classes of customers not approved by respondent.

III

IT IS FURTHER ORDERED that respondent shall forthwith cease and desist from:

a. Selling, making or attempting to make any contract or agreement for the sale of any product on the condition or understanding that any prospective dealer or dealer must or will purchase a full line of any of the products manufactured or sold by respondent.

b. Selling, making or attempting to make any contract or agreement for the sale of one or more products on the condition or understanding that any prospective dealer or dealer must or will also buy one or more other products.

c. Terminating, coercing or taking any other action to restrict or prevent the sale of any product by any dealer because said dealer will not purchase any product respondent offers to sell said dealer.

d. Utilizing any allocation program for any particular product or products which has the effect of influencing in any manner any dealer to purchase any other product or products not being allocated by respondent.

15 Parker Brothers

John F. Cady

Parker Brothers manufactured and sold a broad line of toys and games—including highly popular board games under such trademarks as Monopoly, Clue, and Risk; children's games such as Peter Rabbit and Winnie the Pooh; and card games such as Rook. In addition, Parker Brothers produced action games, Nerf toys and balls, electronic toys, and strategy games for older children and adults. In 1978 Parker Brothers produced over 75 toy and game items and reached sales of just over $82 million. The company was the seventh largest game and toy company in the United States, following Mattel, Fisher-Price, Milton-Bradley, Kenner, Hasbro, and Ideal. The company was generally regarded as an industry leader with respect to product quality, product innovation, and financial performance.

It took Parker Brothers 95 years to reach its leadership position in the industry. The company was founded in 1883 by George Augustus

John F. Cady is an associate professor of business administration at the Harvard Graduate School of Business Administration.

Parker (then a high school boy), who invented, developed, and sold a board game called Banking. The game was a success, and before he graduated from high school George Parker brought out an additional successful board game called Famous Men.

As an adult, Mr. Parker continued to develop new games; he keyed each new addition to his product line to topical subjects of the day. The Spanish American War period, for example, spurred the development of Military Game, War in Cuba, The Seige of Havana, and Hold the Fort. The excitement of the Yukon gold rush led to the introduction of Klondike. Between 1900 and the Great Depression in the 1930s, Mr. Parker introduced puzzles and board games, invented Ping-Pong, and popularized Mah-Jongg. By 1932 Parker Brothers had reached $500,000 annually.

In 1933 Charles Darrow, an unemployed heating engineer, invented a real estate board game for his own diversion that ultimately had a major impact on Parker Brothers. Parker Brothers purchased the rights to the game in exchange for sales royalties, developed the game further, and put it on the market under the trademark Monopoly. The game was an immediate success. By 1979 Monopoly was the largest-selling board game in the world and had been for many years.

New-product development and product introductions continued on a regular basis through the 1940s and 1950s and into the 1960s. In 1968 Parker Brothers's annual sales reached $21 million. In that year, a combination of heavy cash needs to finance further growth and tax considerations (the company was completely family-owned) led to the merger of Parker Brothers with General Mills, Inc.

The purchase of Parker Brothers by General Mills marked the latter company's second acquisition in the large industry of games, crafts, and toys. Earlier, General Mills had purchased the Kenner Toy Company, a leading producer of promotional toys, and both companies were a part of the General Mills Fun Group. While the Kenner Company's line of toys generally had very short life cycles, Parker Brothers's product strategy focused on stable game products with long-term sales potential.

Parker Brothers's new-product development efforts for board and card games continued after the General Mills acquisition, and several new games were introduced each year. In addition, Parker Brothers's research into "nongame" toy areas resulted in the development and successful introduction of Nerf balls (soft polyurethane balls for indoor use) and a line of preschool polyurethane toys during the early 1970s. Nongame toy development continued to play a major role in total development efforts, and by the mid-1970s the company was developing a new line of electronic toys.

Research and Development at Parker Brothers

During the early years of Parker Brothers most new games were developed by George Parker himself. In recent years, most of the games published by Parker Brothers had been submitted to the company by outside inventors. During the late 1960s, for example, Parker Brothers received as many as 3,000 unsolicited game ideas annually. By 1970 the tremendous volume of new toy ideas, coupled with the creation of professional toy design firms, led management to discourage the direct submission of ideas by amateurs and to deal almost exclusively with the professional design firms.

Parker Brothers's research and development staff was responsible for the identification and initial screening of attractive new ideas provided by the design firms. Each year the staff screened approximately 150 promising ideas; these were evaluated for their play and interest value on the basis of comparisons with other Parker Brothers products as well as the products of other firms. New ideas that appeared to be of exceptional appeal were further developed in conjunction with the marketing department, which was responsible for undertaking all necessary concept testing, panel testing, and use testing prior to commercialization.

Development costs for new ideas varied considerably. For some new board games, for example, no consumer testing was undertaken, and little new production equipment was required. On the other hand, for some plastic toys manufacturing molds costing over $200,000 were required, and the total precommercialization development and testing costs might have exceeded $500,000. This latter figure did not include the costs of initial introductory advertising or other direct marketing costs; nor did it include indirect costs such as an allocation of the sales force budget or administrative costs.

The Construction Toy Business

The construction toy business was one of the fastest-growing portions of the toy industry. Contrasted to the 11 percent growth in the industry overall, construction toys grew 25 percent between 1976 and 1977 and reached $132 million. Although a portion of this growth resulted from price increases, most industry analysts believed that the construction toy business could grow at a compound rate of 20 percent per year if the business was developed aggressively.

The largest manufacturer of construction toys was Lego, which held a 42 percent share in 1977. Lego manufactured plastic interlocking block construction sets for children between the ages of 3 and 6. Other major producers in the construction toy business were Tinkertoy, which held a 15 percent share, Playskool, with an 11 percent share, and Erector with a 9 percent share.

The construction toy business was generally divided into segments according to the age of children for whom products were developed. Preschool (2–5) construction toys were produced by Lego and Playskool. Playskool specialized in preschool toys and produced a broad line of products for these younger children. Upper-age construction toys were produced by Erector, and by Lego. Erector, which produced metal and motorized construction sets, was the oldest construction toy specialist in the market and accounted for approximately 20 percent of the upper-age construction toy market.

Parker Brothers's Entry into the Construction Toy Business

In early 1975 Parker Brothers's management believed that the age segment between 6 and 12 was not fully satisfied by the current construction toy product lines. Specifically, there was no toy which allowed children to advance from the relatively simple preschool construction sets to the more sophisticated metal sets. Parker Brothers's management sought to capitalize on this gap in the construction toy market through the introduction of a new construction toy called the Riviton.

The concept of Riviton was that of a flexible construction set: easier and faster to build with than the Erector set; safer than Erector due to the use of plastic rather than metal parts; more colorful, and less expensive than Erector based on equivalent building capacity. The Riviton was targeted to children in the 6–12 age group.

The Riviton construction toy utilized plastic pieces of various shapes and dimensions that were joined by means of a small, reusable, soft, flexible rubber rivet. The rivet was inserted between two plastic pieces by means of a rivet "gun." The gun did not propel the rivet into the plastic pieces. Rather, when the trigger on the gun was pulled, the pulling action stretched the rubber rivet so that it would fit into the holes of the plastic construction pieces. When the trigger was released the rubber rivet expanded to join the pieces together. Exhibit 1 shows four versions of the Riviton toy as it was sold during 1978.

The Development of the Riviton

The development of the Riviton concept for commercialization began in 1975 with two main program research components: the "play-and-use" component and the "communications" component. The play-and-use component was initially formulated to determine if Riviton generated enough interest with children to warrant continued development. Riviton was tested for play value and children's interest against competing construction sets. The communications component of the development process focused primarily on the identification of purchaser and user demographic and life-style characteristics and the evaluation of alternative product-positioning strategies for Riviton. Exhibit 2 presents an outline of the overall Riviton development program. Development and testing costs totaled approximately $250,000 in fiscal 1976 and $139,000 in fiscal 1977.

Riviton Marketing Plans

On the basis of the very favorable reaction of children and parents to the Riviton during its 2 years of testing Parker Brothers coordinated an aggressive and comprehensive marketing pro-

EXHIBIT 1

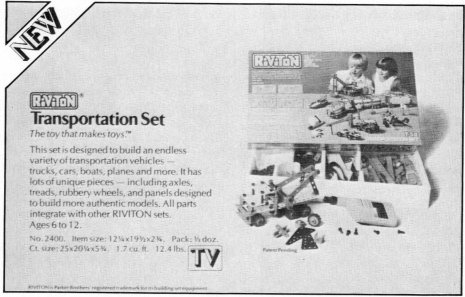

gram. The principal objective of the program was to capture a 10 percent share of the upper-age construction toy business in 1977 and generate a pretax contribution of $2.3 million.

The Riviton was positioned as an integrated system that would be extended through new product offerings in the future.

Initially, management introduced Riviton in

EXHIBIT 1
Continued

Basic Set 100

The toy that makes toys.™

The Basic Set comes with the RIVITON hand tool, 103 flexible plastic shapes of varying sizes and colors, and over 90 reusable rubber rivets. Includes 4 wheels for making cars and trucks and assembly instructions for 15 different creations. It's more than just one toy.

No. 2100. Item size: 12¼x15¾x2¾. Pack: ½ doz. Ct. size: 16x12½x16. 2.0 cu. ft. 13.0 lbs.

Expanded Set 200

The toy that makes toys.™

This edition has all the advantages of the basic set with 129 plastic shapes, over 140 reusable rubber rivets, a large dome for making bugs and radar units, a platform for trucks, a cube and channel system and assembly instructions for 25 different constructions.

No. 2200. Item size: 12¼x19½x2¾. Pack: 4 pcs. Ct. size: 20x13x10¾. 1.7 cu. ft. 12.0 lbs.

Master Set 300

The toy that makes toys.™

This set offers everything found in sets 100 and 200 plus more. Children may choose to assemble the 31 different constructions found in the instruction booklet or create their own. Comes complete with 171 durable plastic shapes, over 185 reusable rubber rivets plus additional panel sizes, more flexible and rigid brackets, a large platform, and special corner brackets for large and complex creations.

No. 2300. Item size: 12¼x23¼x2¾. Pack: 4 pcs. Ct. size: 23½x12½x10¾. 2.0 cu. ft. 16.0 lbs.

three versions: the Riviton 100, the Riviton 200, and the Riviton 300. Extensions of the product soon followed. These versions differed in the number of pieces, the assortment of shapes and pieces, and price. Parker Brothers management initially thought the Riviton 100 set would sell for approximately $12 retail, the Riviton 200 for $16, and the Riviton 300 for $20. However,

EXHIBIT 2
RIVITON DEVELOPMENT

PLAY EVALUATION—APRIL 1975

OBJECTIVE: Lab test to determine if Riviton generates enough interest with children to warrant continued development (tested vs. Erector and Lego)

RESULTS: HIGH LEVEL OF INTEREST—continue development
Set should include wheels—starting point
Determined approximate mix of parts

IN-HOME PLAY EVALUATION—SEPTEMBER 1975

OBJECTIVE: Evaluate the performance of the Riviton set under longer-term usage and aid design of introductory sets

RESULTS: SETS PERFORMED QUITE WELL
Gun should be redesigned to allow for improved insertion of rivets in tight places
Determined relative importance of parts (mix and quantity) and needed improvements in design of parts

PRODUCT DEVELOPMENT—Completed product exploration and development
New tool/two-piece rivet
Lengthened nose of original tool
Cubes and channels
Improved one-piece rubber rivet

FOCUS GROUPS—DECEMBER 1975

OBJECTIVE: Determine what consumers expect from building sets (background to develop questionnaire for mail-out consumer survey)
Feedback on Riviton positionings for copy development

RESULTS: GENERAL FINDINGS ABOUT BUILDING SETS
Great baby-sitter
Traditional toy
Used often/long periods of time
Worthwhile activity
Good price/value perception
Multiple ownership common
Specifics on competitive sets and Riviton

MAIL-OUT CONSUMER SURVEY—JANUARY 1976

OBJECTIVE: Develop sophisticated background on building set purchasers/users

RESULTS: Guidelines on purchasers/users

MARKETING DEVELOPMENT:
Improved positionings for Riviton
Further development of competitive background information

IN-HOME II PLAY EVALUATION—MARCH 1976

OBJECTIVE: Compare two insertion systems and evaluate improved parts, mix, etc.

RESULTS: One-piece rivet system preferred
Like "look" of big gun/operation of pistol grip (smaller tool)
In general, mix of parts is satisfactory

EXHIBIT 2
Continued

PRODUCT DEVELOPMENT:

Developed "Big Gun" that is shorter, simpler, lighter and has pistol grip (still retains Rivet Gun look)

MARKETING DEVELOPMENT:

Evaluated market, competitive creative, pricing, volume, etc.
Developed alternative positionings for Riviton

POSITIONING TEST—MARCH 1976

OBJECTIVE: To test consumer appeal of three positionings ("comparative," "system," and "tool for boys") and three tools (big gun, small gun, awl)

RESULTS: Big gun/system positioning for both parents and children. (All three sets appeared to have good potential.)

CONCEPT TEST—APRIL/MAY 1976

PURPOSE: Volume projection for Riviton line

METHOD: Similar to "action game" study
Parents *with* children
Videotape presentations
Competitive set
Lego
Erector
Girder and Panel
Lincoln Logs
Tinkertoy

FIELD: Late April

---

management discovered that many retailers frequently sold the popular, fast-selling toy at discounts far below their usual margins to increase retail store traffic. The average gross margin for retailers, for all products, was estimated by Parker Brothers management to be 25 to 30 percent of the retail selling price.

Parker Brothers spent $1 million in fiscal 1978 to introduce the Riviton and support retail promotion. In addition the company had spent almost $200,000 on promotional materials such as point-of-purchase displays (Exhibit 3) and brochures. At the end of fiscal 1978 management estimated that spending on promotional materials would continue at around $1 million per year for the foreseeable future.

Parker's retail accounts included the mass merchandisers (Sears, Roebuck; Montgomery Ward; J. C. Penney), discount stores (Zayre, K-Mart), toy specialty stores, and department stores. Initial Riviton plans called for the toy to be sold in stores in 1977 that represented 86 percent of Parker Brothers's 1976 total volume. Those plans had been met and complete distribution coverage had occurred within 1 year. Exhibit 4 shows the financial performance of the Riviton product through the first 6 months of fiscal 1979. Because of these early results, the Riviton promised to be one of Parker Brothers's most profitable products.

November 1978

On Thursday, November 16, 1978, Mr. Randolph Barton, president of Parker Brothers,

EXHIBIT 3

19"

15"

18"

4'

RIVITON promotion kit is available free and contains full-color header, shelf-talker and window streamer for maximum consumer impact.

received a telephone call from a New Jersey newspaper reporter. The reporter told Mr. Barton that a 9-year-old boy in Keasbey, New Jersey, had suffocated on one of the rubber rivets of the Riviton.

This was the second time in 7 months that Mr. Barton had been informed of a Riviton-related death. After the first death (the suffocation of an 8-year-old boy) a review of the safety of the Riviton had been conducted by Parker Brothers. This review confirmed that the toy met all industry safety specifications, exceeded all requirements of the Voluntary Toy Industry Safety Standards, and met all standards imposed by the Federal Hazardous Substances Act. The Con-

sumer Product Safety Commission also conducted a hazard evaluation of the Riviton after the first Riviton-related death. After the evaluation the commission did not recommend that action should be taken to change the Riviton product or its promotion or distribution. Following these evaluations Parker Brothers's management had concluded that the first child's death, although tragic and unfortunate, was an isolated accident and that no additional special action by the firm was required.

However, on Monday, November 20, when the second Riviton-related death was confirmed, Parker Brothers's top management met to review and analyze this new situation. Essentially the known facts were these:

Two deaths had resulted from misuse of the Riviton.

Riviton met all voluntary and industry and federal safety standards.

Parker Brothers was under no pressure from any person, group, or government agency to take action.

There had been no known fatality or serious accident resulting from the use or misuse of a Parker Brothers product in the previous 95 years.

The two deaths had occurred only 7 months apart, and both appeared to involve the same part from the same product—a rubber rivet from the Riviton.

A general study published by the Consumer Product Safety Commission, *Hazard Identification and Analysis,* concluded that two deaths from suffocation among children was highly significant. Among 8- and 9-year-old children, it was very rare.

As management saw the situation, there were four basic alternatives facing the company:

1. The company could do nothing. Both accidents had occurred as a result of product misuse. The children had put the Riviton rivets in their mouths.
2. The company could issue a warning state-

EXHIBIT 4
RIVITON FINANCIAL PERFORMANCE

	1977	1978	1979 (6 months)
Shipments	–	$5,404	$4,320
Less variable cost	–	2,226	1,780
Gross margin	–	$3,178	$2,540
Less allocated overhead	–	535	428
Manufacturing margin	–	$2,643	$2,112
Less:			
Media	–	$1,000*	$ 663
Development cost	$ 86	54	40
Testing cost	53	–	–
Other marketing costs	198	100*	105
Tooling and printing plates	260	232	67
Fixed equipment	15	–	–
Total expenses	$612	$1,386	$ 875
Net contribution	($612)	$1,257	$1,237

*These costs are estimates for the fiscal year. Fiscal years run from July to June. The fiscal year 1977 ran from July 1976 to June 1977.

ment to the consumer and put a warning label on the package pointing out the hazards of misuse.

3. The product could be modified after a thorough product evaluation, research, and testing.

4. The product could be recalled from retail distributors and final consumers.

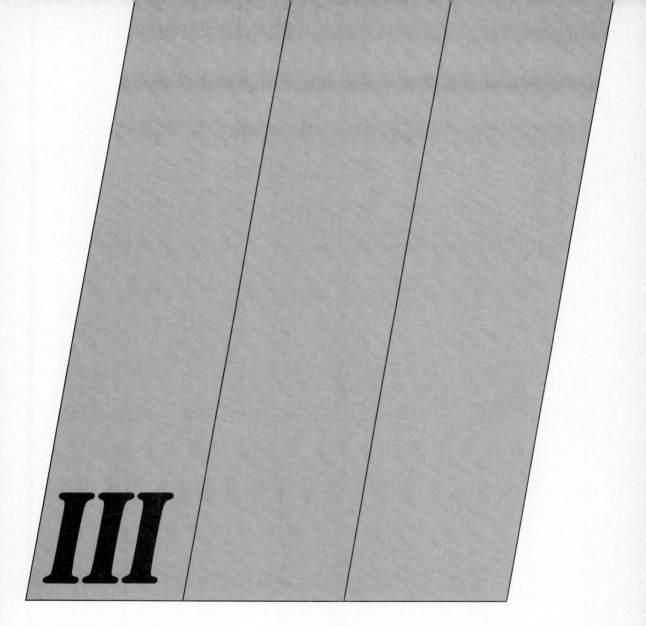

III

Marketing Systems

A marketing system is a chain of business units or other organizations that take the product from its inception to its ultimate markets. It may include the retailers, wholesalers, jobbers, and agents in the company's channels of distribution. For companies like McDonald's or Dunkin' Donuts, it includes franchisees. For high-technology companies such as Amicon, it may include licensees. And for producers of basic materials such as plastics, an important element of the marketing system is the fabricators who purchase the materials and make them into end products. Our concern in this section of the book is with planning marketing systems, understanding how they work, identifying the needs of each element in the chain, and learning how to manage marketing systems effectively.

What will become apparent is that marketing systems perform a wide range of functions, such as maintaining stocks of products at locations convenient for customers; displaying merchandise; offering point-of-sale information; influencing the customer's choice among competing product lines; granting credit, delivery, and after-sale service; and in some cases assembling components into end products and/or designing systems for particular applications, such as heating or air conditioning.

A key part of planning any system for taking products to market is to determine which of these functions can be performed most economically and effectively at each particular level of manufacture and distribution. A closely related consideration is what kinds of fabricators and resellers are best equipped by virtue of their resources, expertise, and market access to perform these functions.

Another major aspect is the rewards they expect—and, indeed, demand—for performing the essential functions that are required of them to meet the needs of the market. Will it take high margins to compensate resellers for carrying stock, committing display space and sales personnel, and promoting the product line? Will the supplier need to help create local market demand by advertising? Is sales training needed for the reseller's sales personnel? Is it important to give favorable credit terms to resellers to encourage them to carry ample stocks of the manufacturer's products?

Finally, we are concerned about interfirm relationships in marketing systems and about the power of each unit to influence the way the total system operates.

Ultimately these relationships are based on a sense of mutual dependency tempered by strong individual concerns for advancing each member's self-interests. The power of any individual manufacturer, fabricator, or reseller to shape the system, control it, and maximize its share of the total system's profitability depends on the uniqueness and differentiability of the product itself and on the way in which people buy the product. (For example, is point-of-purchase service important? Is the manufacturer's brand name of key significance? Is advertising a key factor in the purchase decision?) Another condition affecting the balance of power among elements in the marketing system is the economic power of each relative to the economic power of the others—that is, its relative size, its resources, the extent to which it dominates technology, its reputation in the markets it serves, and the breadth of its customer base. In addition, a key consideration is the legal framework which significantly regulates systems' relationships and the extent to which any one business entity in a chain can exercise control over the actions of others. These are all factors which will be explored in the cases in this section.

The Need for Change

Marketing systems are, of course, designed in response to conditions at a point in time—product technology, market segmentation, buyer behavior, the availability of a marketing infrastructure including channels of distribution and promotional media, and the geographic locations of potential customers. As these original base points for formulating a marketing system change, the system itself may become increasingly ineffective in serving customers and holding a market position against newer competing systems. Or the system may continue to serve its original market segments well but be less well suited to compete effectively for new sets of customers.

But change is difficult; once a system is put together, it generates commitments to relationships that are hard to break. To restructure the marketing system is to risk losing a market position with no assurance that the anticipated gains in sales volume and profits from going after some new market segment will, in fact, materialize. These are calculated risks, and given the personal relationships that build up around any marketing system, there are typically strong tendencies to preserve the status quo as long as possible. Consequently, obsolete marketing systems usually fall victim to the new, more efficient ones that are better designed to serve the needs of new groups of customers. Adaptation to changing market conditions is, at best, a painful process, but it must be confronted and undertaken by marketing managers if a system is to maintain its competitive edge, or even survive at all.

16 *American Standard, Inc.: I*

Stanton G. Cort • Walter J. Salmon

Mr. William Eberle, president of American Standard, Inc., was reviewing his company's distribution policies. His concern was whether the distribution systems used by American Standard's two largest product divisions (the plumbing and heating and air-conditioning divisions) were congruent with the short- and long-term requirements of their respective markets.

The Company

By 1967, American Standard had established itself worldwide as the largest manufacturer of plumbing fixtures, plumbing fittings, and heating equipment. In 1966 it had generated $19.7 million in pretax profit on worldwide sales of $569 million. Domestic business had accounted

Stanton G. Cort is an associate professor of marketing at the Case Western Reserve School of Management. Walter J. Salmon is the Stanley Roth, Jr., Professor of Retailing at the Harvard Graduate School of Business Administration.

for $369 million of total sales and returned pretax profits of $13.2 million.

The company had eight domestic divisions. Three of these accounted for about $280 million, or 76 percent of corporate domestic sales in 1966.[1] They were the plumbing and heating division, with sales of $163 million; the air-conditioning division, with sales of $22 million; and the Amstan division, with $94 million in sales. The first two of these divisions manufactured and marketed plumbing, heating, and air conditioning products, while the third, Amstan, was a wholesaling organization for these products.

In a normal year 50 percent of domestic volume was accounted for by sales to the residential housing market, including single-family and multifamily housing units. Most of the balance went to the commercial and industrial construction markets.

[1]The remaining 24 percent of sales were mainly of industrial products.

The Plumbing and Heating Division

The plumbing and heating division (P&H) was American Standard's oldest, largest (in sales volume), and most profitable division. In 1966, P&H earned pretax profits of $11.6 million on sales of $163 million.

P&H consisted of six operating departments: chinaware, brass fittings, enamelware, hydronics, seats, and resale. The resale department purchased products which American Standard did not manufacture (e.g., steel bathtubs and shower receptors) from other companies and resold them in order to fill out the P&H product

line. Selected operating results of P&H and its departments are shown in Exhibit 1.

P&H competed in virtually all segments of the plumbing products industry and in the hydronic heating segment of the heating products industry. The following paragraphs describe the products, competitive structures, and markets of each of these industries.

Plumbing Products

Plumbingware was generally divided into three product classifications: plumbers' brass fittings, water boilers, and plumbing fixtures.

Plumbers' brass fittings included faucets,

EXHIBIT 1
PLUMBING AND HEATING DIVISION SELECTED DATA
Net sales and pretax income by department ($000)

Department	1964 Net sales	1964 Pretax income	1965 Net sales	1965 Pretax income	1966 Net sales	1966 Pretax income
Chinaware	$ 51,481	$ 6,265	$ 49,503	$ 6,042	$ 51,538	$ 6,321
Enamelware	50,231	3,361	48,040	3,221	45,943	3,039
Brass fittings	31,589	2,499	31,610	2,466	31,066	2,410
Toilet seats	7,505	421	7,658	429	6,204	348
Hydronics	29,638	119	29,298	117	25,528	104
Resale	8,063	(1,841)	2,665	(603)	2,891	(654)
Total P&H	$178,507	$10,824	$168,774	$11,672	$163,170	$11,568

1966 income statement by department
(Expressed as percentages of sales)

	Chinaware	Enamelware	Brass fittings	Toilet seats	Hydronics	Resale
Net sales	100.0	100.0	100.0	100.0	100.0	100.0
Cost of goods sold*	78.0	83.1	81.3	81.0	82.6	97.0
Gross profit	22.0	16.9	18.7	19.0	17.4	3.0
Operating expenses:†						
Administrative and general	3.8	3.6	4.7	5.2	5.0	NA
Selling	4.6	5.0	5.1	7.2	9.9	NA
Advertising and promotion	1.4	1.6	1.1	1.0	2.1	NA
Total	9.8	10.2	10.9	13.4	17.0	25.6
Pretax income	12.2	6.7	7.8	5.6	0.4	(22.6)

*Fixed costs constitute the following percentages of the cost of goods sold: chinaware, 26 percent; enamelware, 27 percent; brass fittings, 34 percent; toilet seats, 21 percent; hydronics, 33 percent; and resale, 6 percent.

†Division total is allocated to departments.

shower heads, drains, and various accessories. Such fittings typically varied considerably in design concept (e.g., utilitarian versus high style), depending mainly on the markets for which they were intended (e.g., hospitals, country clubs, homes).

Water boilers were used to heat water for household use; they were also used for hydronic central heating systems. Depending upon the intended use, they differed considerably in capacity, pressure limits, temperature ranges, etc.

Plumbing fixtures included toilets, lavatories, bathtubs, sinks, and miscellaneous fixtures such as towel racks, soap dishes, and toilet seats. These products were made mainly of either porcelain-enameled iron or vitreous china. The use of steel and enameled steel for sinks and tubs, however, had increased rapidly since World War II and now accounted for slightly more than 20 percent of annual industry dollar sales.

Nevertheless, historically, product innovation had not been characteristic of the plumbingware industry. Rather, design emphasis since the 1930s had been placed on the use of color in plumbing fixtures, with colored fixtures accounting for 15 percent of industry unit sales in 1966. Industry sources, however, expected colored fixtures to decline in importance. Consumer color preferences changed rapidly, thus "dating" colored fixtures, and colored fixtures complicated the task of choosing the overall color scheme of a kitchen or bathroom.

Hydronic Heating Products

The three primary heating methods used in the United States were warm-air heating, in which air was heated and then distributed through ducts; hydronic heating, in which hot water or steam was forced through pipes and radiators after water was heated in a boiler; and resistance heating, in which electricity was passed through heat-generating resistance cables. With the exception of resistance heating, any common fuel (oil, gas, coal, electricity) could be used for any type of heating system. While hydronic heating had been the most common method in the late nineteenth and early twentieth centuries, it represented only approximately 11 percent of new heating installations in 1964 (versus 70 percent for warm-air).[2] Moreover, resistance heating and heat pumps (both using electricity) were becoming increasingly popular and were expected to erode hydronic heating's market share even further.

Hydronic heating products included furnaces, boilers, radiators, valves, pipes, and similar items.

Competition

The plumbing products industry was dominated by a few large companies. The need to maintain modern production facilities, coupled with severe operating losses, had driven most smaller competitors out of the business during the 1930s. In 1966 four companies accounted for more than three-fourths of the industry's dollar sales. These were American Standard, Crane, Kohler, and Wallace-Murray. Other important companies in the industry were Universal-Rundle, Sterling Brass, and Price Pfister. None of these companies, including American Standard, produced complete plumbing systems for any major market segment (e.g., new residential, residential renovation, new commercial, and commercial renovation).

Heating products were manufactured by many companies. Some were large, diversified corporations which produced a number of heating systems. Others were small, specialized operations producing perhaps one or two systems in a limited range of sizes, or perhaps only the burner, boiler, or ductwork components of a system. No single company was dominant. As in the plumbing industry, no company produced a

---

[2]Remaining installations included electrical resistance heating, heat pumps, and fuel conversions.

complete product line for all means of conduction, fuels used, and sizes required.

Markets

The construction industry was the primary market for plumbing and hydronic heating products. This market could be segmented in several ways. The first distinction was between large projects, which often required custom-engineered systems, and small projects, which generally used stock components. A second distinction was between residential construction (single-family and multiunit buildings) and commercial construction (factories, office buildings, stores, hotels, schools, hospitals, etc.). In general, the commercial segment was primarily interested in functionality, while the residential segment placed greater emphasis on aesthetic qualities. Finally, all these segments could be subdivided into new construction and renovation. Industry sources believed that the renovation market tended to be more interested in higher quality than the new construction market because the ultimate users were often involved in the purchasing decisions.

The commercial market, which typically involved large-volume orders, was extremely competitive but nevertheless attractive. Although discounts were prevalent, the commercial market provided higher average margins for manufacturers than the residential market. The reason was that functionally designed toilets, sinks and tubs, water fountains, and urinals and the special fixtures and fittings required by hospitals carried higher margins than the stylishly designed products suitable for residential use.

The residential plumbing market included segments which offered the lowest and the highest potential margins. The lowest factory margins prevailed on the low-priced end of the residential plumbing product lines. Builders of speculative residential projects, who were primarily interested in reducing their costs, typically chose to install these products. If these builders were buying in large quantities, margins were likely to be particularly slim.

On the other hand, the residential market also consumed the high-priced, stylishly designed products which carried the highest margins. These products were sold for installation in custom-built homes and in residential renovation projects.

The Purchasing Decision

According to industry sources, the purchasing decision was typically based on (1) the desired performance, reliability, and cost criteria of a particular product and (2) the product's desired appearance.

The relative importance of the two parts of the decision varied. For example, in large commercial projects, the overriding consideration normally was grade and quality, while in custom home building, appearance often was the key factor. The importance of appearance varied also with the visibility of the product. The design and color of plumbing fittings and fixtures, for instance, was more important than the appearance of furnaces. Finally, the involvement of the long-term owner of the project also influenced the importance of appearance. Architects and builders were heavily influenced by cost and performance criteria, while long-term owners would often pay premium prices for installations which they considered attractive.

Customers

Installing contractors purchased most of the components and subsystems in the plumbing and hydronic heating industry. These installers, working as subcontractors for general contractors or builders, created the final product by assembling and installing the various components of the sanitary (e.g., plumbing) and heating and ventilating systems. In large commercial or residential projects, *mechanical contractors* were normally the installers. In small projects, *plumbing and heating contractors* were normally the installers.

The installing contractors' purchasing decision was affected by various people: architects, who designed projects; consulting engineers, who were experts on specific types of projects or certain aspects of projects; general contractors or builders, who owned the project during construction; and long-term owners. Although their involvement in the purchasing decision varied depending upon circumstances, these "influentials" typically placed some constraints on the installing contractors' decision-making freedom.

Mechanical contractors were responsible for the purchase of plumbing and hydronic heating products for large construction projects. They had the required engineering skills, personnel, and financing to design and install complete systems which required sophisticated engineering and the handling of large quantities of products. They were often consulted during the design phase of a project to aid the architects and consulting engineers. In the construction phase, they accomplished the installation using their own personnel or subcontractors. All mechanical contractors had union shops.

Plumbing and heating contractors typically ran small operations and lacked the skills required to design large-scale systems. They were used by general contractors to install relatively simple, more or less standard systems.

The plumbing contractor had an important influence on brand choice. According to industry sources, the architect, owner, or builder typically determined the quality and color of the product, but not the brand name.

The plumber was a very important subcontractor to the builder because of the length and intricacies of local building codes. These codes had originated to protect the public against dangerous building practices. The plumber, as an expert on these codes, was needed to ensure approval of the plumbing and hydronic heating systems when they were inspected by the building inspector.

Because of their importance in the construction process, plumbers had been able to establish a strong fraternity. Actions by an owner, builder, architect, wholesaler, or manufacturer that were viewed as detrimental to one or a few plumbers had frequently led to retaliatory strikes, slowdowns, or boycotts. Industry observers believed that there was little chance of winning a battle with plumbers and plumbing and heating contractors if they decided to use their unions or trade associations to retaliate.

Plumbers considered themselves to be intermediaries as well as installers. Therefore, in addition to payment for installation labor, they received a 20 to 25 percent margin on all products they installed. On larger projects, however, they were often willing to accept margins as low as 10 percent.

According to industry sources, plumbers were not aggressive merchandisers. While they might suggest a particular product, they would readily accept countersuggestions from the builder or owner. Plumbers earned a profit on the complete installation (including labor) and were reluctant to jeopardize the installation contract in order to sell a particular product. Because of their powerful position, however, plumbers could negate a manufacturer's merchandising efforts by advising against a product or, in extreme cases, refusing to install it.

Most small builders subcontracted all plumbing and hydronic heating installations and purchased components from the plumbing contractor. The large builders, however, sought to buy directly from manufacturers. To overcome opposition from distribution channels (especially the plumbers), the largest builders (e.g., Levitt & Sons, Larwin, and Ryan Homes) used plumbers who contracted to work exclusively for them and agreed to accept either a very small margin or no margin on the products they installed.

Channels of Distribution

Plumbing and hydronic heating products were sold by manufacturers to plumbing and heating equipment wholesalers, who then sold them to plumbing and heating contractors. In 1966, approximately 96 percent of these wholesalers were small, independently operated businesses with one, or perhaps a few, outlets. Purchases by these independents, who maintained their own stocks, sales representatives, and showrooms, accounted for about 90 percent of all manufacturers' dollar sales of plumbing and hydronic heating products. The remaining wholesalers included the four or five independent chains, which had more than 20 outlets, and the company-owned outlets operated by American Standard, Inc., and the Crane Company. Exhibit 2 shows the number of independent wholesalers in 1959 and 1962 classified by number of employees.

These wholesalers were the targets of most of the manufacturers' selling efforts for the small-construction market. Because wholesalers performed the stocking function, it was considered essential that they carry large inventories in order to offer an extensive variety of styles to the plumber.

The plumbing and heating equipment whole-salers' activities varied from merely maintaining inventories and filling plumbers' orders to aggressive and creative selling and promotion. One of the larger independent chains, for example, maintained extremely attractive showrooms staffed by sales representatives. These rooms attracted architects, builders, and some homeowners to see what new products were available. In addition, the chain's counter clerks were trained to suggest new products. Industry sources were happy to see this kind of merchandising but indicated that it was the exception rather than the rule.

In addition to directing selling efforts to wholesalers, manufacturers' sales reps called on architects, consulting engineers, builders, and plumbing and mechanical contractors to encourage them to specify particular brands and grades. Although architects and engineers were sometimes willing to write detailed specifications citing brand names and model numbers, more often they wrote broader specifications citing a brand preference and minimum grade or quality level. For example, a toilet specification for a hotel might read "American Standard 'Cadet' or equivalent."

Exhibit 3 is a schematic diagram of the distribution channels used by the plumbing and hydronic heating industry. The following pages provide additional information on the P&H division, especially with regard to distribution.

Products

P&H's product line, which was the broadest in the industry, included the following:

Plumbing products	Heating products
Bathtubs, shower receptors, lavatories, dental lavatories, toilets, toilet seats, bidets, urinals	Residential cast-iron boilers: electric, gas, oil Baseboard panels, convectors, radiators

---

EXHIBIT 2
NUMBER OF PLUMBING AND HEATING EQUIPMENT WHOLESALERS*

Number of employees	Number of wholesalers	
	1962	1959
0–7	3,383	3,158
8–19	1,689	1,620
20–49	655	575
50 or more	132	124
Total	5,859	5,477

*Excluding company-owned branches.
Source: U.S. Department of Commerce, Bureau of the Census.

EXHIBIT 3
THE PLUMBING, HEATING, AND AIR-CONDITIONING INDUSTRY— LARGE-CONSTRUCTION PROJECT MARKET

Flow of Selling Effort, Orders, and Products— Plumbing and Hydronic Heating

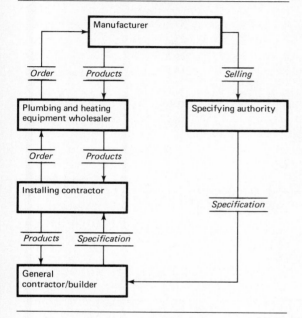

Faucets, shower
 heads, fittings for
 all fixtures
Kitchen sinks, pantry
 sinks, service sinks,
 food waste
 disposers
Drinking fountains,
 laundry trays,
 water softeners
Specialized hospital
 and medical
 fixtures and fittings,
 bath lifts

Within these product categories, P&H products

covered virtually all price and quality segments. In general, however, P&H had elected not to produce the "faddish" or low-quality items, characteristic of certain short-line manufacturers, which recently had entered the industry.

Performance

As the leading factor in the industry, P&H had been able to maintain its market share[3] and profitable operations during the early 1960s, when sales growth was limited and many fixtures and fittings manufacturers were having difficulty achieving profits. Nevertheless, members of division and corporate management were concerned about the division's pretax returns in 1966 on average gross assets of 6.7 percent.

A further concern was the tendency for the low end of the P&H product lines to account for a large proportion of sales. Exhibit 4 shows how

[3]See Exhibit 5 for P&H market share by product line and Exhibit 6 for P&H sales of each product category to the various market segments.

EXHIBIT 4
PLUMBING AND HEATING DIVISION

Gross Margin Percentages on Factory Selling Price
(Ranges by Product Category, 1966)

Product category	Margin percentages on factory selling price		
	High	Average	Low
Plumbing products:			
Toilets	47	24	20
Bathtubs	44	19	14
China lavatories	60	39	25
Iron lavatories	47	26	11
Steel kitchen sinks	32	26	25
Iron kitchen sinks	33	22	22
Fittings	38	15	(16)
Toilet seats	42	25	8
Hydronic heating:			
Gas boilers	29	25	18
Oil boilers	36	23	12

EXHIBIT 5
PLUMBING AND HEATING DIVISION
Share of Market by Product Line, 1965–1967

Product line	Percentage of industry unit sales		
	1965	1966	1967 (est.)
Enamelware:			
Iron tubs	23.2	24.9	26.3
Iron lavatories and sinks	19.4	18.3	19.4
Steel tubs	3.7	3.2	3.3
Stainless fixtures	0.9	1.3	2.3
All enamelware	13.8*	14.4	15.2
Chinaware:	27.8*	29.1	29.5
Brass fittings	NA	20.1	NA
Seats and molded products	NA	NA	NA
Hydronics:			
Gas boilers	19.1	16.8	18.6
Oil boilers	28.7	26.7	28.2
Cast-iron radiators	27.4	27.4	28.4
Baseboard convectors	14.1	14.1	15.3
All hydronics	21.4	20.1	21.1

*P&H's share of the 1965 dollar market for plumbingware had been just under 30 percent. In a few local markets, however, the division's share was as high as 75 percent.

EXHIBIT 6
PLUMBING AND HEATING DIVISION
Product Line Sales by Market Segment: 1966

Product line	Percentage of product line sales to:				
	Residential Market		Commercial Market		
	New construction	Reno-vation	New construction	Reno-vation	Export
Enamelware (enameled tubs, sinks, lavatories, etc.)	54	27	9	8	2
Chinaware (vitreous china tubs, sinks, lavatories, etc.)	43	28	17	9	3
Plumbing fittings (faucets, shower heads, drains)	35	36	16	11	2
Toilet seats	30	38	17	12	3
Hydronic heating	40	39	15	4	2

Source: P&H records.

factory margins vary among products in different categories and price ranges.

P&H Distribution

The P&H distribution division had three important distribution policies. First, all division sales were made through wholesalers. There had been rare cases of direct sales to contractors, but in these instances permission was first asked of the affected wholesalers. Second, distribution was through independent wholesalers whenever possible. Division management believed that the use of independent wholesalers was necessary for P&H to maintain its market share. Amstan Supply Company branches were used only when equally suitable independents were unavailable. Finally, P&H did not determine formally the boundaries of any wholesaler's territory. Territories overlapped, and in some large metropolitan areas, up to 10 and 11 wholesalers competed with each other.

The first two policies were designed to maintain a strong, loyal wholesaler organization, consisting of 900 plumbing and heating equipment wholesalers. According to management, support and loyalty to wholesalers brought rich returns in terms of wholesaler loyalty and quality of selling effort. Management admitted, however, that loyalty had been waning in the last 5 to 10 years as many wholesalers diversified their product lines and plumbing products became a smaller component of their total sales.

The third distribution policy of nonexclusive wholesalers and unconfined territories furthered market penetration because the more aggressive wholesale firm was not blocked in its expansion efforts. Moreover, when several wholesalers competed in a market area, they could specialize in serving specific market segments (e.g., tract residential construction, institutional construction, and custom home building). Division management continually evaluated wholesalers to determine which were the most aggressive merchandisers and provided the best customer service. Special selling efforts were programmed for those not performing well. If there was no improvement over several years, the wholesaler was replaced. In 1966, 32 wholesalers were eliminated and 26 added.

The P&H division's independent wholesalers each typically operated a single warehouse. These wholesalers assembled inventories of plumbing and heating equipment from various manufacturers in order to respond to the varied demands of plumbing contractors. Normally a wholesaler carried competing lines of products, like fixtures and fittings, in which brands differed significantly in styling or price. Because of the variety of plumbing and heating equipment items and accessories required, the typical wholesaler stocked 8,000 different items.

Most independents were small-business owners doing primarily a walk-in business with plumbers. Sales were primarily handled by counter clerks dealing with plumbing contractors. The counter clerks filled the plumbers' orders from stocks on hand or took special orders when the plumbers would not take an alternate choice. In most cases, the wholesalers then used their trucks to deliver the products to the plumbers.

According to company records, total sales of all the products P&H wholesalers carried averaged $725,000 in 1966; 58 percent of the wholesalers employed fewer than eight people.

Although plumbers bought from several wholesalers, they normally preferred a particular wholesaler. Typically the plumbers believed they received better prices, credit terms, stocking services, and technical assistance from their preferred wholesalers.

Wholesaler margins averaged about 17 percent, although they varied considerably on individual items and therefore with the mix of products carried. Industry executives stated that a determination of representative wholesaler margins was difficult in view of the general "softness" of prices at all levels of distribution.

P&H management believed that wholesalers

generally saw themselves as stockers, assemblers, and sources of credit but not as merchandisers. Only a few maintained showrooms or conducted promotion programs. Although most engaged in some outside selling to solicit new business, usually the sales representatives concentrated on persuading builders and plumbers to trade with the wholesaler, and did not promote P&H products aggressively.

Noland Co., a large chain operation in the Eastern United States which handled P&H and other manufacturers' plumbing products, was an exception to this rule. This chain merchandised both itself and P&H division products aggressively. All Noland outlets were similarly designed to convey a bright, modern, "Noland" image. They contained modern, attractive showrooms staffed by competent salespeople who were trained to explain the features of new products. Even Noland counter clerks suggested new items to plumbers presenting routine orders.

Noland's success was proved by the company's growth and profitability. In 1965 and 1966, 12 new outlets were opened, and several unprofitable outlets closed. The company's after-tax return on sales was higher than the industry average of 1.5 percent.

The Amstan Supply Company was an important part of P&H's distribution system. Sixty-eight of P&H's wholesalers were Amstan branches. These generally were concentrated in the North Central United States, although Amstan outlets were also located in the South Central United States and on the West Coast. In 1966, Amstan accounted for 12 percent of P&H's sales.

The division's policy was to use existing Amstan branches but to recommend against opening another Amstan branch unless absolutely necessary. In other words, only in areas where adequate existing or obtainable independent distribution was unavailable would P&H encourage Amstan to establish a branch. Amstan, in turn, would judge the area market potential against its sales and profit criteria and make a decision.

In areas where Amstan acted as a P&H wholesaler, the relations between it and the P&H division were the same as those between the division and any independent wholesaler. Amstan, for example, carried products which competed directly with P&H products and was not given exclusive territories or special services by P&H. Nevertheless, Amstan was P&H's only wholesaler in nearly half the market areas where it had branches.

Competitive Distribution Policies

The three other major competitors—Crane, Kohler, and Wallace-Murray (Eljer)—maintained distribution policies similar to P&H's. These three firms sold their products through wholesalers to plumbing and heating contractors. Crane's entire organization consisted of approximately 60 company-owned branches and some independent wholesalers. In addition, Crane had manufactured two special retail brands for sale through lumberyards and J. C. Penney. According to P&H management, neither had shown much success. Kohler and Wallace-Murray concentrated on independent wholesalers. All three maintained sales forces which were charged with duties similar to those of the P&H sales force. (See below.)

No competitor had as many wholesalers or sales representatives as P&H. In the opinion of P&H management, competitors' wholesalers offered stocking, credit, and delivery services inferior to those of P&H's wholesalers. This inferiority was allegedly recognized by large purchasers in the construction industry.

While many manufacturers also used traditional channels, some had begun to develop new means of distribution. These included selling directly to builders and homeowners and selling to mail-order houses, department and hardware stores, lumberyards, and building supply dealers.

Pricing

P&H published two prices, the distributor's net price and the suggested list price. The former was the factory price to the wholesaler, while the latter was, in effect, the ceiling from which the installer made discounts in quoting installed prices to the builder or owner. This price also provided contractors with a guide to various grades and qualities of products. For any particular product, there was wide variation in the price, depending on the features and quality level the buyer wanted. For example, the suggested list price for bathtubs ranged from $70 to $415, and wholesaler prices ranged from $40 to $222.

Prices quoted by P&H and its competitors were "soft" prices; that is, they were starting points from which wholesalers and installing contractors estimated materials costs for projects on which they were bidding. Depending on the competitive situation (e.g., the size of the project, the prices quoted by competitors, the importance of the customer, and services required by the customer), the contractor, wholesaler, and/or factory allowed discounts from the published prices.

P&H adhered to its published distributor's net price primarily when wholesalers purchased products to be stocked and sold over the counter to plumbers for small projects. Products sold for larger projects were sold at discounts. When the wholesalers bid on these larger projects, they normally quoted discounts from their published prices and requested similar discounts from P&H so that they could maintain their margins. P&H granted discounts only to meet prices which had been quoted by competing manufacturers for materials to be used for similar projects in the wholesaler's area. Before granting a discount, P&H verified the competing manufac-

turers' prices from trade sources. If P&H decided to grant a discount to the wholesaler who requested it, the division also offered the same discount to all wholesalers in that wholesaler's market area.

Field Sales

The 221-person P&H sales force performed two basic functions. It provided service for current customers and prospected for new sales. One hundred fifty-eight general line sales representatives were responsible for selling the entire P&H line to wholesalers and providing the services they required. Sixty-three special representatives were responsible for calling on architects, mechanical contractors, mechanical engineers, and hospital consultants, who were key influencers in the buying decision. Each of P&H's 26 sales offices was staffed with both types of sales reps.

The primary duty of the general line sales representatives was to sell an adequate variety and quantity of products to enable a wholesaler to respond to the plumbing and heating contractor's order for "a pink toilet by tomorrow." The sales reps also spent considerable time solving logistical problems between the factory and wholesalers. These problems ranged from misshipments or late deliveries to disputes over special orders. A special order for a pink toilet or some other piece of chinaware, for example, required a lead time of 8 weeks. The sales reps were often under pressure from the plumbers who wanted it tomorrow and the wholesalers who were embarrassed because they had not stocked it.

The general line sales representative was also responsible for the surveillance of orders resulting from specifications secured by a special representative in another area. For example, in persuading a hospital consultant in Chicago to specify American Standard products for a proposed Savannah hospital, a special representative would use the assurance of on-time delivery as a key argument. The general line sales representative in Savannah was then responsible for helping the local wholesaler secure the order and then for making sure the wholesaler ordered the items in time to meet the construction schedule.

Although the general line sales reps inevitably spent considerable time helping the wholesalers improve their operations, their principal function was not to be consultants to the wholesalers. The sales reps were measured on net sales in their territories and whether the distributor had enough P&H products to respond effectively to plumbers' orders. Additionally, the sales reps were expected to visit local plumbing contractors and builders to stimulate interest in P&H products.

Special representatives were responsible for the specification of P&H products in large construction projects through missionary work with architects, consulting engineers, and other persons likely to influence plumbing and heating specifications on major projects. The sales appeals used by special representatives were the quality of P&H division products, their trouble-free performance, P&H's reputation for on-time delivery, and the convenience of having the products at nearby wholesalers during construction. Special representatives had been particularly successful in obtaining the specification of P&H plumbing fixtures and fittings in most new-hospital construction.

Potential Distribution Problems

The P&H division was reluctant to risk injuring its strong distribution system by experimenting with controversial ideas. Thus, the division had failed to counter some recent developments in the industry.

In the 1960s a number of manufacturers had introduced, under new brand names, new lines of plumbing fixtures and fittings. P&H executives asserted that the products included in these new lines were frequently of inferior quality or of faddish designs. Nevertheless, they had achieved some success through aggressive promotion and direct distribution through hardware and department stores and lumberyards. P&H managers believed that most sales through these outlets were to homeowners who installed the products themselves. P&H had failed to adopt similar merchandising and distribution policies because (1) the executives considered it uneconomical to commence production of low-quality fad items and (2) the introduction of new distribution methods risked alienating members of the existing distribution system. Also, management had been unable to estimate the dollar volume of plumbing fittings and fixtures sold through the 22,000 hardware and department stores and lumberyards in the United States.

The growth of mass builders was another development which might affect distribution policies. Mass builders included prefabricated home manufacturers, who accounted for 200,000 houses in 1966, and the mobile home manufacturers, who built an additional 200,000 housing units during the year. (These mobile homes were not counted as housing starts in federal government figures.) P&H had received several requests from mass builders to buy plumbing products direct from the factory. Large tract builders, such as Levitt & Sons, Inc., and Ryan Homes, were making similar requests. The merger of some of these large tract builders with larger, publicly held companies would undoubtedly intensify these requests.

P&H could not accept these requests without changing its policy of selling exclusively through distributors. Other manufacturers, including Borg-Warner and Briggs, acceded to some of these requests, although most of their sales were still through distributors who provided logistical support for the sales. According to P&H spokespersons, these relatively small competitors in the industry could discard the tradition of selling through wholesalers and plumbing contractors without arousing much opposition. If American

Standard followed suit, however, these intermediaries might view the move as a dangerous precedent. Management feared retaliation from wholesalers and plumbers.

Finally, P&H management was eager to improve market penetration in the Central United States but did not want to add wholesalers in the area. They felt that the division's wholesaler organization was already sufficiently large. Nationwide the wholesaler network had declined by 100 outlets in recent years because of both unsatisfactory performance and P&H management's desire to streamline the distribution system. P&H executives preferred to increase penetration in the Central United States, therefore, by stimulating the existing wholesalers to improve their market penetration and consequently increase their purchases from P&H.

The Air-Conditioning Division

American Standard's air-conditioning division (ACD) manufactured and sold two related product lines: warm-air heating equipment and air-cooled air-conditioning equipment. In 1966 division sales were $21.8 million, with adjusted profits before taxes of $1.7 million. (For selected operating data see Exhibit 7.)

The division's warm-air heating equipment included gas-fired and oil-fired furnaces with capacities ranging from 45,000 BTU to over 200,000 BTU.[4] Filling out the line of warm-air heating equipment were electric furnaces, gas-fired unit heaters, a variety of electric element heaters, heat pumps, and a limited selection of baseboard electric heaters.

The division's air-conditioning line included

[4] BTU = British thermal unit. The term is defined as the quantity of heat required to raise the temperature of 1 pound of water 1 degree Fahrenheit. A furnace of about 45,000 BTU provided sufficient heating capacity for a small residence. Small commercial establishments, such as stores, small plants, and motels, required furnaces with heating capacities at the 200,000-BTU level.

EXHIBIT 7
AIR-CONDITIONING DIVISION
Market Share by Product Category

	Percentage of total units sold by industry	
	1965	**1966**
Warm–air heating:		
Gas heating	6.5	6.9
Oil heating	4.7	5.0
Electric furnaces	13.7	8.7
Total	6.3	6.6
Residential cooling:*		
Rooftop units	1.0	0.6
Packaged units	1.2	1.2
Split systems	4.5	4.7
Heat pumps	1.2	1.0
Total	3.6	3.7

*ACD's only entry into the commercial cooling market in 1965 and 1966 was in split systems, in which the heat exchanger was outside the building. ACD's share of split system sales was 0.2 percent in 1966 and less than 0.1 percent in 1965.

Source: Company records.

24 models of central air conditioners. They ranged in capacity from about 18,000 BTU for small residences to about 120,000 BTU for small commercial establishments. In addition to central systems, the division also produced such special-purpose equipment as conversion air conditioners for adapting forced warm-air furnaces to air conditioning.

There were three basic types of air-conditioning equipment: (1) large custom-engineered central systems serving large office buildings, hotels, hospitals, apartment houses, and industrial plants; (2) small standard central systems of varying cooling capacity for homes, small apartment houses, and small business establishments; and (3) room air conditioners. Division sales by major product groups are shown in Exhibit 8.

The market for warm-air heating products and air-conditioning products could, like the market for plumbing fixtures, be divided into several segments. These were large and small construction projects, new residential construc-

EXHIBIT 8
AIR-CONDITIONING DIVISION SALES BY PRODUCT CATEGORY

Product category	1965		1964	
	$000	Percentage of total	$000	Percentage of total
Heating:				
Gas heating	7,508	37.6	7,591	34.9
Oil heating	2,155	10.8	2,119	9.7
Electric furnaces	357	1.8	333	1.5
Unit heaters	202	1.0	353	1.6
Parts and accessories	713	3.6	768	3.5
Total heating	10,935	54.8	11,164	51.2
Cooling:				
Rooftop units	274	1.4	282	1.3
Packaged units	250	1.2	271	1.2
Split systems	5,963	29.8	6,948	31.9
Heat pumps	318	1.6	196	0.9
Parts and accessories	2,225	11.2	2,915	13.5
Total cooling	9,030	45.2	10,622	48.8
Total ACD sales	19,965	100.0	21,786	100.0

Source: Company records.

tion and residential renovation, and new small commercial construction and renovation.

In contrast to warm-air heating, the air-conditioning business was young and rapidly growing. Consequently, product-development efforts had been directed at producing materially improved equipment. ACD was initiating an extensive research and development program to maintain its competitive position. An example was the development of a competitive rooftop air-conditioning unit for small commercial establishments.

In 1965, engineered central systems, standard central systems, and room units accounted for 37, 38, and 25 percent, respectively, of the industry's total dollar sales.

Recent demonstrations that air conditioning could enhance productivity, patient treatment, and learning had led to increased interest in installing systems in industrial buildings, hospitals, and schools.

Strong demand for air-conditioning systems for residences, small apartment houses, and small commercial establishments reflected both the rising scale of living and price reductions. Substantial sales of such systems had been made for new construction and modernization projects.

Sales of room air conditioners were extremely sensitive to weather, with the majority of units being sold in the hottest 9 to 20 weeks of the year.

Competition

Competition in the air-conditioning industry was very intense. Over 100 companies were active in at least one segment of the market. These companies, which included some of the largest in the nation, sought continually to increase their market share by reducing prices, promoting product features, and developing new products. The importance of production innovation was signified by the fact that the majority of the models produced in 1966 had been developed in the last 5 years.

Large engineered and small standard central air-conditioning systems were produced by Carrier, Crane, Borg-Warner, and Worthington. Several other companies, including American Standard, Buffalo Forge, General Electric, Hupp, McQuay, and Weil-McLain, also competed for this market.

In room air conditioning, Fedders, a specialist in room units, was the recognized leader. Nevertheless, most of the major appliance producers like General Electric, RCA, Whirlpool, and Westinghouse made room air conditioners.

ACD's Marketing Position

ACD's objective was to increase its share of the air-conditioning market and to maintain its share of the warm-air heating market. (Share data are shown in Exhibit 7.) This meant reaching some of the same customers who were important to the P&H division because the most lucrative market for warm-air heating and air conditioning was the residential construction market. Sixty percent of total industry unit sales of warm-air heating systems in 1966 were made to the new residential construction market. In the same year, 53 percent of central air conditioning sales were made to this market. The remaining sales were split between the residential and commercial renovation market and the new, small commercial construction market.

Channels of Distribution

Although the channels for the distribution of warm-air heating and air-conditioning products were similar to those for hydronic heating and plumbing products (wholesalers, installers, builders), certain differences existed. In contrast to the installation of plumbing and hydronic heating equipment, which required plumbing contractors' skills, warm-air heating and air-conditioning products required the skills of sheet metal contractors for the fabrication and installation of ducts as well as air-conditioning specialists for the installation of refrigeration apparatus. Air-conditioning dealers who performed these tasks had developed as the primary installers of warm-air heating and air-conditioning equipment.

Although some plumbing and heating equipment wholesalers had been able to expand into warm-air heating and air conditioning, many wholesalers had not obtained personnel with the technical skills to serve air-conditioning dealers.

The dealer's position in the market was less powerful than the plumber's. Sheet metal work had become important in construction relatively recently; entry into the trade was easier than entry into plumbing, and no trade organization comparable in power to that of the plumbers had been formed. Consequently, the dealers did not always obtain a margin on products installed in addition to reimbursement for their labor.

In other respects the role of the heating and air-conditioning dealers was very similar to that of the plumber.

At the wholesale level, small, independent heating and air-conditioning equipment wholesalers had operations very similar to those of the plumbing wholesalers. Although there had been very few independent chains, company-owned branches had been maintained by American Standard, Borg-Warner, and Crane Co. Exhibit 9 shows the number of independent heating and air-conditioning wholesalers in 1959 and 1962

EXHIBIT 9
NUMBER OF HEATING AND AIR-CONDITIONING EQUIPMENT WHOLESALERS*

Number of Employees	Number of wholesalers	
	1962	**1959**
0–7	1,609	1,571
8–19	540	512
20–49	210	131
50 or more	53	42
Total	2,412	2,256

*Excluding company-owned branches.
Source: U. S. Department of Commerce, Bureau of the Census.

by size (as indicated by the number of employees). Exhibit 10 is a schematic diagram of distribution channels in the warm-air heating and air-conditioning industry.

To reach the air-conditioning market, ACD used three types of wholesalers: plumbing and heating equipment wholesalers, including Amstan, which had taken on warm-air heating and air-conditioning products; air-conditioning equipment wholesalers; and ACD factory branches. In addition, the division sold direct to two installing contractors.

ACD sold through 112 independent plumbing and heating equipment wholesalers, 91 of whom also handled P&H division products, and 44 Amstan branches. Amstan was used when management determined that it would provide better service than independents.

EXHIBIT 10
THE PLUMBING, HEATING, AND AIR-CONDITIONING INDUSTRY
Distribution Channels for Warm-Air Heating and Air-Conditioning Products

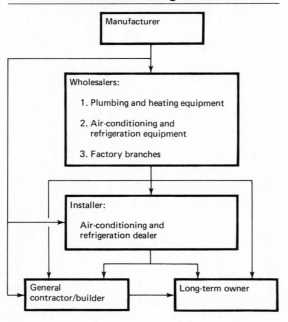

ACD sold through 26 air-conditioning and refrigeration wholesalers. They were usually small, independent operations which specialized in air conditioning and had close contacts with sheet metal contractors. Many were new in the industry and financially weak. Therefore, ACD, like its competitors, extended long-term credits so that they could carry adequate inventories.

The wholesalers, in turn, specialized in selling one manufacturer's products. If, as in the case of ACD, the manufacturer did not produce a full range of equipment, the wholesalers completed their lines through purchases from other manufacturers.

ACD opened its own branches only when, after a careful search of an area, it could not find a wholesaler, including Amstan, who seemed capable of providing the technical assistance and carrying the inventory needed by air-conditioning dealers. In 1967, 4 of the 186 distribution points used by the division were ACD factory branches. These were located in Cleveland, Phoenix, Los Angeles, and Sacramento. Throughout the industry, distribution through factory branches had become increasingly prevalent. Lennox maintained 37 factory branches; Chrysler, 22; and Bryant, 22. And General Electric distributed entirely through factory branches except for the "three or four independents it had left." Carrier, Crane, Fedders, Rheem, and Payne all financed wholesaler inventories to a large extent.

Although air-conditioning dealers tended to concentrate their business with one wholesaler in hopes of securing more credit and technical service, the dealers were not very brand-loyal. Most, according to ACD management, carried more than one line of basic equipment.

ACD's 31-person sales force was organized into four geographic regions, to cover the East, South, Central, and Pacific areas. It included 19 field sales reps, nine field warehouse sales reps, and three technical representatives. The field warehouse sales reps sold to dealers out of the four ACD-owned factory branches, while the three technical representatives provided technical assistance wherever it was needed. Each of the 19 field sales reps had an assigned territory.

ACD management considered the selling effort provided by the field sales force to be a key element in strengthening the division's distribution system. The field sales reps, who, in accordance with division policy, made sales to wholesalers whenever possible, performed a dual role. Their primary job was to encourage the wholesalers to carry sufficient inventories and to make every effort to penetrate their market areas by selling aggressively to local air-conditioning dealers, builders, and specifying agents. The sales reps also made sure that the wholesalers were aware of ACD's national advertising and promotion programs and encouraged them to participate in the division's cooperative promotions aimed at local areas. Furthermore, in any area where the wholesaler had shown weakness, the sales rep acted virtually as a marketing consultant, studying operating methods, formulating plans for market development, and setting specific targets.

In playing the second part of their dual role, the sales reps stimulated market penetration in the wholesalers' areas by calling directly on dealers, builders, and specifying agents. The objectives of this activity were to develop dealer accounts for the wholesaler and to develop preference for ACD products among the specifiers. The ACD sales reps' efforts essentially complemented those of the wholesalers and their sales reps. ACD sales reps took orders directly from dealers and builders only when no ACD wholesaler was established in the area.

17 American Standard, Inc.: II

Stanton G. Cort • Walter J. Salmon

As part of his review of American Standard's distribution policies,[1] Mr. William Eberle, the company's president, had solicited the views of a number of American Standard executives. These views could be categorized as follows:

Viewpoint 1. The current distribution organization was performing the proper functions for the major traditional customer group, installing contractors, and was organized correctly, assuming that all the channel members performed their selling functions. Only improved coordination and an intensified merchandising effort were required.

Stanton G. Cort is an associate professor of marketing at the Case Western Reserve School of Management. Walter J. Salmon is the Stanley Roth, Jr., Professor of Retailing at the Harvard Graduate School of Business Administration.

[1]See "American Standard, Inc.: I."

Viewpoint 2. To perform different functions for different customer groups, more flexibility was needed. Efforts of builders to buy direct from manufacturers strengthened the belief that different functions were important to different purchasers. Supporters of this viewpoint argued that purchasers should receive and be charged for only those services that they wanted. Therefore, wholesalers and installing contractors should be part of the distribution channel only when needed. The Amstan Supply Division should act as one of the traditional wholesalers, serving customers who wanted full service. A direct-selling organization would be established which would handle orders to large builders and others who needed minimum service and wanted maximum discounts.

Viewpoint 3. The functions performed by the

present organization and the flexibility central to viewpoint 2 could be obtained by expanding the Amstan Supply Division into a nationwide system of company-owned wholesalers. Over time, as financial and managerial resources permitted, Amstan branches would replace all the independent wholesalers. All plumbing and heating division and air-conditioning division distribution would be conducted through Amstan. The branches would be traditional wholesalers as well as operating bases for servicing direct accounts.

Viewpoint 4. Distribution should be entirely through independent wholesalers, and the Amstan Supply Division should be liquidated. American Standard would concentrate on manufacturing and marketing but stay out of distribution.

To determine what role Amstan should play in American Standard's future distribution strategy, Mr. Eberle decided to review the history and recent performance of the Amstan division.

Amstan Supply Division

The Amstan Supply Division had several origins. During the corporation's early growth through mergers, factory branches of acquired companies were maintained. In addition, during the Depression, the corporation took over several independent wholesalers who went bankrupt. Finally, since the Depression, Amstan branches had been established where suitable independent wholesalers for P&H division products were unavailable.

Amstan outlets were called branches, but they had never functioned as factory branches—that is, they had never been exclusively outlets for American Standard products. The division had always been a full-line plumbing and heating equipment wholesaler. Therefore, branches carried a variety of products complementary to those produced by American Standard, and in rare cases they carried competing products in order to provide complete assortments. The average Amstan branch stocked approximately 5,000 to 7,000 items, including different sizes and colors of the same item.

In 1966, the Amstan Supply Division included 68 branches operating in 20 states. It had sales of over $94 million and pretax profits of $2 million. Selected operating data are presented in Exhibit 1.

Amstan sales of corporate products accounted for about 30 percent of its sales, while 2.5 percent of sales were in products competing with P&H products. No sales were made of products competing with ACD lines. According to P&H division sources, the low percentage of competitive sales indicated a concentration of selling effort on American Standard products. Exhibit 2 shows competitive product sales by product line for both Amstan and independent wholesalers.

Amstan was the largest single customer for both P&H and the air-conditioning division. Between 10 and 15 percent of P&H sales and about 21 percent of ACD sales were to Amstan.

In 20 of P&H's 300 recognized marketing areas, Amstan was its only wholesaler. Moreover, as Exhibit 3 shows, in 1964 Amstan accounted for a substantial proportion of P&H sales in a total of 55 areas. P&H sales to Amstan in 1965 were double those of the largest independent chain. Exhibit 4 shows Amstan's gross purchases from P&H, classified by product category for the years 1959 to 1965.

Amstan was the exclusive distributor for ACD products in 44 of ACD's 170 market areas. The share of total division sales to Amstan had declined since 1961 (Exhibit 5). ACD managers blamed this decline on Amstan's failure to penetrate its markets as well as the independent wholesalers. ACD executives thought that the 44 Amstan markets, which covered 27 percent of the estimated potential dollar market, should account for 27 percent of division sales, not the

EXHIBIT 1
AMSTAN SUPPLY COMPANY: SELECTED DATA

Net sales and pretax income ($000)

	1964	1965	1966
Net sales	91,653	91,880	94,343
Pretax income	1,301	1,553	2,060

1962–1966 income statements expressed as percentages of sales

	1962	1963	1964	1965	1966
Net sales	100.0	100.0	100.0	100.0	100.0
Cost of goods sold	86.0	86.2	85.7	85.7	84.8
Gross profit	14.0	13.8	14.3	14.3	15.2
Operating expenses:					
Administrative and general	0.6	0.5	0.5	0.6	0.4
Selling	11.3	11.3	11.5	11.3	11.7
Advertising and promotion	0.1	0.1	0.1	0.1	0.1
Corporate charge*	0.5	0.5	0.8	0.7	0.8
	12.5	12.4	12.9	12.7	13.0
Pretax income	1.5	1.4	1.4	1.6	2.2

Amstan average gross investment ($000)

	3-year average (1964–1966)†	1967 (est.)†
Cash	3,705	3,640
Receivables	11,202	11,200
Inventory:		
Branch	14,475	14,300
In-transit	3,005	2,500
Total	17,480	16,800
Real estate	8,064	7,160
Other	1,541	1,200
Gross investment	41,992	40,000
ROI	3.89%	1.75%

*Corporate administrative service charge.
†Based on 68 branches.

EXHIBIT 2
SALES OF COMPETITIVE PRODUCTS BY AMSTAN
AND BY INDEPENDENT WHOLESALERS
USED BY AMERICAN STANDARD, INC. (1964)

Product line	Amstan		Independent wholesalers	
	Percentage of outlets selling competitive lines	Percentage of product-line sales realized in products competing with P&H lines	Percentage of outlets selling competitive lines	Percentage of product-line sales realized in products competing with P&H lines
Cast-iron boilers	1.4	–	23.3	19.7
Cast-iron fixtures	8.7	0.5	28.0	4.1
Steel fixtures	24.6	10.1	56.0	47.8
Stainless sinks	76.8	36.7	84.7	76.0
Chinaware	2.9	0.1	72.0	11.9
Brass fittings	58.0	8.1	94.0	25.5

Source: P&H biannual distributor evaluation.

current 21 percent. Furthermore, they pointed out that ACD's market share was greater in markets where Amstan existed, but was not ACD's distributor, than in markets where Amstan was the distributor (Exhibit 6). Thus they justified not using Amstan in the 24 remaining markets where Amstan operated and, in fact, justified operating ACD factory branches in Los Angeles, Chicago, and Cleveland, where Amstan also operated branches.

Amstan Operations

The primary responsibility of the Amstan division central management group was to develop overall strategy and to translate the strategy into

EXHIBIT 3
AMSTAN DISTRIBUTION OF PLUMBING PRODUCTS
FOR PLUMBING AND HEATING DIVISION, 1964

Percentage of P&H division sales in area generated by Amstan	Number of trading areas*	Amstan plumbing products purchased from P&H
100	20	$ 2.8 million
50–99	18	5.6 million
25–49	16	7.7 million
Under 25	1	0.5 million
Total	55	$16.6 million

*Market areas were defined by the individual divisions.
P&H had 300 areas nationwide, while ACD had 170.
Source: P&H sales records.

EXHIBIT 4
AMSTAN GROSS PURCHASES OF P&H DIVISION PRODUCTS, 1959–1965

Year	Plumbing products		Hydronics		Water heaters		Total purchases	
	$ millions	Percentage of total	$ millions	Percentage of total	$ millions	Percentage of total	$ millions	Percentage of total
1959	19.8	75.8	3.6	13.8	2.7	10.4	26.1	100
1960	17.9	77.8	3.1	13.5	2.0	8.7	23.0	100
1961	15.3	73.9	3.5	16.9	1.9	9.2	20.7	100
1962	16.2	75.4	3.4	15.8	1.9	8.8	21.5	100
1963	17.5	78.5	3.1	13.9	1.7	7.6	22.3	100
1964	16.6	78.3	3.0	14.1	1.6	7.6	21.2	100
1965	15.2	83.5	3.0	16.5	*	–	18.2	100

P&H discontinued the manufacture of water heaters.
Source: P&H sales records.

goals for the branches. Division strategy typically set very specific levels for Amstan net sales, return on sales (ROS), and return on investment (ROI) for each branch. In these determinations, Amstan management considered the potential of each branch's market area and the branch's historic performance. Although Amstan, P&H, and ACD discussed desirable levels of sales of corporate products through Amstan, no quotas were set for individual branches. Branch performance throughout the year was measured against the net sales and ROS and ROI goals set by divisional management.

In addition to establishing goals, division management provided branches with some market information as well as accounting and personnel services. Data on construction trends, market potential, and competitive activity were

EXHIBIT 5
AMSTAN GROSS PURCHASES OF
AIR-CONDITIONING DIVISION PRODUCTS,
1961–1965

Year	Amstan purchases of ACD products		Total ACD sales, $000
	$000	Percentage of total ACD sales*	
1961	3,267	23.1	14,121
1962	3,938	23.0	17,084
1963	4,318	22.6	19,135
1964	4,302	20.8	20,685
1965	4,252	21.3	19,965

*Remaining sales were to independent wholesalers.
Source: ACD sales records.

EXHIBIT 6
AIR-CONDITIONING DIVISION 1965 SHARE OF DOLLAR MARKET
Amstan vs. Non-Amstan Market Areas

Market area group	Furnaces	Air conditioning
Total U.S.	8.0%	5.2%
Amstan areas	5.7	4.9
Non-Amstan areas	8.9	5.3
Amstan states*	6.4%	5.3%
Amstan areas	5.7	4.9
Non-Amstan areas	7.1	6.0
Non-Amstan states†	10.2%	5.1%

*States in which Amstan-served market areas are located.
†States in which no Amstan-served market areas are located.
Source: ACD distributor analysis.

collected at the division level for use by branch managers who wanted them. The controller kept central records of branch operations to determine comparative sales, accounts receivable, and return on investment performance by branch. Further, the controller provided a central source of data for assessing credit risks on large contracts.

Central personnel services included recruiting new sales and management personnel, administering the employee compensation programs, and maintaining performance records for review in considering salary increases and promotions. Typically the division chose managers for small branches from among branch salespeople who showed potential management skills. Managers for large branches were selected from the ranks of small-branch managers. There was no division-level training program for branch management or sales personnel.

The average Amstan branch had sales of $1.4 million in 1966. It was staffed by a branch manager, four outside salespeople, four warehouse workers, and five office employees. In this, according to Amstan management, the Amstan branch was similar to independent wholesalers of comparable size.

The Amstan branch managers, six of whom had college degrees, were responsible for day-to-day management and for attaining the sales and profit goals established for their branches. Performance ratings and bonuses were based on the attainment of these goals and on dollar profits. The bonus, which was computed as a percentage of the branch's dollar profit, averaged 12 percent of the managers' total compensation in 1966. Merit increases in base salary were also awarded, if the managers were judged to be doing an excellent job. Total compensation in 1966 averaged $12,000, and reimbursable expenses were kept at an absolute minimum. In a typical independent chain, the average branch manager's earnings were about $15,000, of which over 40 percent was incentive compensation.

According to management, the Amstan branch manager's best route to higher earnings was through promotion to a larger branch. Base salaries were higher in branches with higher sales volumes, and dollar profits were also likely to be higher.

Amstan branch managers planned their marketing effort within the guidelines set by the division plan. They had, subject to policies on inventory size, significant freedom in allocating their financial and personnel resources. Each manager to a large degree decided what items to stock, how best to use floor space, how best to serve over-the-counter customers, and which outside customers (e.g., architects and builders) to seek through personal selling.

The typical Amstan outside salesperson had no college education or formal technical training. At the end of 1966, 63 of the division's 252 salespeople had been with Amstan only 9 months. The average total compensation for an Amstan salesperson was $7,100, about 28 percent of which was incentive compensation based on a percentage of the branch's gross margin on the sales produced. Reimbursement for expenses averaged $1,000. The salesperson for a typical independent chain earned $7,200, of which 22 percent was added compensation, and was reimbursed for $2,100 in expenses.

The Amstan branch building itself was considered only a location for servicing orders. Warehouse workers maintained warehouse stocks and drove delivery trucks. Office employees maintained inventory, sales, and billing records. Because counter clerks were necessary only irregularly to take over-the-counter orders from plumbers, one or two of the warehouse workers or office employees served part-time as counter clerks. When a customer entered, these employees left their work and filled the customer's order. Many branches also had showrooms for the display of plumbingware and related products.

Typically the manager tried to maximize dollar sales by selling to large-volume markets. Thus outside branch salespeople concentrated on large contractors and specifying authorities for commercial construction and multiunit residential projects. The results are shown in Exhibits 7 and 8.

Amstan Performance Problems

Amstan dollar sales had been relatively stable, while independent distributors had made impressive gains. From 1958 to 1963, while sales

EXHIBIT 7
AMSTAN BRANCHES CLASSIFIED BY PERCENTAGE OF DOLLAR SALES REALIZED FROM THEIR FIVE LARGEST ACCOUNTS, 1965

Percentage of sales	Number of branches
Under 20	7
20–30	17
30–40	20
40–50	18
50 and over	6

Source: Amstan records.

of all plumbing and heating distributors had increased 14 percent and the sales of other manufacturers' branches had increased 30 percent, Amstan sales had grown only 3 percent.

Some American Standard executives urged Amstan to increase its selling effort and service in the residential market. They believed the increase in cost would be covered by additional sales. Amstan management hesitated to accept this suggestion, since in the residential market long-standing personal contacts between the distributor and the plumbing and heating contractor were very important. Amstan was at a disadvantage in these cases, they claimed, because Amstan personnel normally moved to

EXHIBIT 8
SALES TO THE CONSTRUCTION MARKET BY TYPE OF CONSTRUCTION
Amstan vs. Independent Wholesalers, 1965

Type of construction	Amstan (Percentage of dollar sales)	Independents (Percentage of dollar sales)
New residential	42.0	48.7
Residential renovation	13.0	20.0
New commercial	38.5	23.0
Commercial renovation	6.5	8.3
Total sales to construction market	100.0	100.0

Source: P&H 1965 distributor evaluation.

larger branches when they were promoted. Thus, promotable branch managers had difficulty in developing the same kinds of relationships with plumbing contractors as the independent wholesalers had.

Some P&H division and ACD managers had also been critical of Amstan's penetration of the markets for their products. Using the penetration data in Exhibits 6 and 9, these critics showed that Amstan had not kept up with independents. Amstan argued that its geographic area of concentration, the Central United States, was weak with P&H and that in this area Amstan had done as well as the independents. Furthermore, Amstan managers alleged that they were unaware that their primary responsibility was to push P&H and ACD products.

Amstan's recent pretax profit had also been questioned. A study conducted in early 1965 had shown that Amstan's profits were lower than for two independent chains, the average for members of Central and Eastern United States trade associations, and the United States average as computed by Dun and Bradstreet. Furthermore, the Amstan gross profit was lower

EXHIBIT 9
PLUMBING AND HEATING DIVISION, 1964 MARKET PENETRATION
Amstan vs. Non-Amstan Market Areas

Market area group	Penetration index*
Total U.S.	3.0
Amstan areas	2.3
Non-Amstan areas	3.4
Amstan states†	2.4
Amstan areas	2.3
Non-Amstan areas	2.4
Non-Amstan states‡	4.1

*Market area penetration index =

$$\frac{\text{P\&H plumbing sales (at manufacturer's price)}}{\substack{\text{total sales of plumbing and heating wholesalers}\\ \text{(at wholesale price)}}}$$

†States in which Amstan-served market areas are located.
‡States in which no Amstan-served markets are located.
Source: P&H sales records and Census of Trade.

than industry averages. Thus, in spite of Amstan's low expense ratios, pretax profit suffered in comparison with that of other wholesalers. Exhibit 10 shows the results of the 1964 study.

EXHIBIT 10
AMSTAN PROFITS COMPARED WITH DATA FOR INDEPENDENT WHOLESALERS, 1964
Percentage of Net Sales

	Pretax profit	Gross profit	Expenses
Amstan	1.4	14.3	12.9
Hajoca* (estimates)	2.9	16.3	13.7
Noland* (estimate)	3.8	NA	NA
Typical or average data provided by:			
Central Supply Association†	2.5	19.5	17.0
Mid-Atlantic Association	2.2	19.7	17.5
N.Y. plumbing and heating wholesalers	1.7	21.7	18.8
Dun and Bradstreet‡	2.7	19.8	16.9

*Independent chain.
†Association of independent wholesalers operating in more or less the same area as Amstan.
‡Industry average.
Source: Comparison prepared by American Standard.

EXHIBIT 11
ANNUAL PRETAX PROFIT OF 28 BRANCHES THAT OPERATED AT A LOSS FOR AT LEAST ONE OF THE LAST 5 YEARS

Branch	Percentages					Range
	1961	1962	1963	1964	1965	
1	(1.2)	(2.1)	1.8	2.8	2.6	(2.1)– 2.8
2	(0.9)	2.6	4.4	3.4	3.6	(0.9)– 4.4
3	*	1.1	(0.9)	2.3	1.3	(0.9)– 2.3
4	(2.1)	0.5	1.0	2.0	2.5	(2.1)– 2.5
5	(4.0)	(2.0)	0.4	0.9	1.4	(4.0)– 1.4
6	0.8	0.3	0.5	0.5	(1.3)	(1.3)– 0.8
7	1.3	(0.6)	0.5	*	2.6	(0.6)– 2.6
8	1.5	(0.8)	(1.5)	0.2	1.4	(1.5)– 1.5
9	(3.2)	1.3	2.2	3.2	1.8	(3.2)– 3.2
10	(0.8)	1.0	1.5	3.3	0.5	(0.8)– 3.3
11	(3.6)	0.3	(0.2)	0.4	5.0	(3.6)– 5.0
12	1.0	(0.4)	0.8	0.1	2.8	(0.4)– 2.8
13	(0.5)	1.6	2.1	2.8	1.8	(0.5)– 2.8
14	2.9	3.6	(0.5)	3.3	5.3	(0.5)– 5.3
15	(0.3)	3.1	2.9	4.3	(2.3)	(2.3)– 4.3
16	3.2	3.2	2.1	(*)	(1.6)	(1.6)– 3.2
17	1.0	1.6	(1.9)	0.9	(1.6)	(1.9)– 1.6
18	2.4	3.3	(1.0)	(4.0)	1.7	(4.0)– 3.3
19	2.7	1.2	0.7	0.5	(0.7)	(0.7)– 2.7
20	3.3	3.8	2.0	3.1	(1.0)	(1.0)– 3.8
21			0.5	0.2	(0.5)	(0.5)– 0.5
22				(6.3)	(3.7)	(6.3)–(3.7)
23	2.4	0.4	*	0.2	(0.7)	(0.7)– 2.4
24	(1.3)	0.2	(0.8)	(2.3)	(1.0)	(2.3)– 0.2
25		(13.2)	(3.7)	0.8	(1.4)	(13.2)– 0.8
26	0.7	(2.5)	(4.0)	(2.1)	(2.8)	(4.0)– 0.7
27	(1.7)	(2.0)	0.4	1.8	2.8	(2.0)– 2.8
28	2.7	3.3	2.4	(1.4)	*	(1.4)– 3.3

*Less than 0.1 percent.
Source: Amstan branch operating statements.

Pretax profits for individual branches varied from a 6.3 percent loss to a 6.2 percent profit.

Individual branches' pretax profits varied significantly from year to year. For example, in studying the 28 branches that had operated at a loss for at least 1 year between 1961 and 1966, Amstan management concluded that a branch often showed satisfactory results one year and a loss the next, or vice versa. Exhibit 11 shows pretax profit data for 28 branches for a 5-year period.

The 28 branches included units which varied widely in sales volume. Exhibit 12 shows pretax profits for branches classified by sales volume.

Finally, Amstan's return on investment had been criticized by corporate management. The supply company's ROI was not keeping pace with that of the manufacturing divisions. In 1966 Amstan's pretax ROI was 4.8 percent versus 6.7 percent for P&H, 16.6 percent for ACD, and a corporate goal for United States operations of 12.4 percent. This low return raised the question

EXHIBIT 12
AMSTAN BRANCH PRETAX PROFIT BY SALES VOLUME, 1964

Branch volume ($000)		Pretax profit							Total branches
	Loss	Under 1.0	1.0– 1.9	2.0– 2.9	3.0– 3.9	4.0– 4.9	Over 5.0		
Under 500	2	2	–	–	–	–	–		4
500–750	1	1	–	4	–	1	1		8
750–1,000	–	5	3	4	1	–	1		14
1,000–1,250	2	1	1	3	3	1	–		11
1,250–1,500	–	1	–	2	–	2	–		5
1,500–1,750	–	–	1	4	1	–	1		7
1,750–2,000	–	–	2	2	1	–	–		5
2,000–2,250	–	–	1	–	–	–	–		1
2,250–2,500	–	1	2	1	–	–	–		4
2,500–2,750	1	2	1	–	–	–	–		4
2,750–3,000	–	–	–	–	–	–	–		–
Over 3,000	–	–	2	1	1	–	–		4
Total branches	6	13	13	21	7	4	3		67

Source: Amstan branch operating statements.

of whether Amstan funds could be better invested elsewhere.

EXHIBIT 13
SALES RECOVERY IN AMSTAN MARKETS

Years after Liquidation	Percentage of former sales volume	
	P&H	ACD
1	50	30
2	70	40
3	85*	50*

*Recovery of 100% of sales would require 5 to 7 years.
Source: P&H and ACD sales managers.

P&H management had estimated that if Amstan were liquidated, 3 years would be required to rebuild P&H sales to preliquidation levels in the markets formerly served by Amstan. The ACD sales recovery would require 5 to 7 years, according to division management. Exhibit 13 shows sales recovery estimates for the first 3 years following Amstan liquidation.

Mr. Eberle realized that action on Amstan's problems could also affect the P&H and ACD divisions. He planned, therefore, to evaluate the needs of all three divisions and of the corporation as a whole. Then he intended to establish a distribution strategy to fulfill the immediate and long-term needs of the corporation.

18 *Dunkin' Donuts: I*

Hirotaka Takeuchi

"It's said America runs on oil, but America also runs on coffee," wrote *California Business.*[1] Aware of this heavy reliance of Americans on cars and coffee, William Rosenberg, chairman and founder of Dunkin' Donuts, opened his first roadside coffee and doughnut shop in Quincy, Massachusetts, in 1950. Five years later, he began licensing his retail operation to independent franchise owners. By 1978 the number of Dunkin' Donut shops had expanded to 956 in the United States, of which approximately 90 percent were operated by independent franchise owners.

Robert Rosenberg, son of the founder, became president in 1963 at the age of 25, soon after his graduation from the Harvard Business School. William Rosenberg assumed the role of chairman of the board. By 1963, the company,

which had started on an initial investment of $5,000, was operating four subsidiaries:

1. Industrial Cafeterias, which operated in-plant cafeterias
2. Menumat, which provided full-line vending services for smaller plants
3. Howdy Beefburgers, which competed with McDonald's in the New England region
4. Dunkin' Donuts, which consisted of a basic coffee and doughnut shop operation as well as a luncheonette-type food and doughnut shop operation

Since 1963, all operations other than the basic coffee and doughnut shops had either been phased out or sold. The franchising of additional Dunkin' Donuts combination food/doughnut shops was discontinued in 1963. The franchising of Howdy Beefburgers was deemphasized in 1968, resulting in the decline in the number of Howdy Beefburgers outlets from a peak of 27 in 1968 to 6 in 1978. Industrial Cafeterias and Menumat were sold in 1969. The company also experimented with a franchised

Hirotaka Takeuchi is an assistant professor at the Harvard Graduate School of Business Administration.

Certain statistical data have been disguised to preserve confidentiality.

[1]*California Business,* Feb. 3, 1977, p. 6.

EXHIBIT 1
HISTORICAL DATA ON DUNKIN' DONUTS STORE OPERATIONS
Number of Shops

	1978	1977	1976	1975	1974	1973	1972	1971	1970	1969
Beginning-year shops	901	851	820	780	736	698	651	543	426	334
New shops opened*	65	59	37	40	45	61	76	129	135	96
Number of shops closed	(10)	(9)	(6)	–	(1)	(23)	(29)	(21)	(18)	(4)
Total year-end shops	956	901	851	820	780	736	698	651	543	426
Number of company-owned shops operated on a permanent basis†	85	85	76	48	19	8	6	–	–	–

*Does not include previously closed shops that were reopened after remodeling or other changes.

†Some stores were operated by the company on a temporary basis. These were formerly franchised shops which were reacquired by the company and then made available to prospective franchise owners.

Source: Company records.

seafood operation called Charlie Goodlight in 1969 but terminated its operation the following year.

After going public in 1968, Dunkin' Donuts vigorously pursued an expansion program of its coffee and doughnut shops. The number of these shops almost doubled in a 3-year period between 1969 and 1972 (see Exhibit 1). All new shops had been standardized in terms of seating capacity (20 seats) and stores design (see Exhibit 2).

A large number of Dunkin' Donuts shops

EXHIBIT 2
EXTERIOR OF DUNKIN' DONUTS
PROTOTYPE SHOP

EXHIBIT 2
Continued

INTERIOR OF DUNKIN' DONUTS PROTOTYPE SHOP*

*This shop has a lighted menu board and a muffin counter.

were open 24 hours a day, 7 days a week. Customer traffic was heaviest between 7 A.M. and 11 A.M. and between 7 P.M. and 11 P.M. Eat-in customers generated 70 percent of the traffic and 35 percent of sales, while takeout customers generated 30 percent of the traffic and 65 percent of sales. Each shop did continuous on-site production of doughnuts (52 varieties) and other pastry items. One of the company's advertising copy themes was "We pledge to make our Dunkin' Donuts fresh every four hours and our coffee fresh every 18 minutes."

The company encountered several difficulties in attempting to grow so rapidly. In an effort to acquire more franchises, "Dunkin' Donuts wasn't as choosey as it had been"[2] about site

[2]*Forbes,* July 15, 1977, p. 78.

selection. As a result, numerous newly opened Dunkin' Donuts shops proved unsuccessful. As shown in Exhibit 1, 91 shops were closed between 1970 and 1973.

In addition, because of the company's reliance on debt to finance rapid growth, its financial condition deteriorated. Debt soared to some 65 percent of total capitalization[3] as the company added approximately $10 million in long-term debt between 1970 and 1973. Interest expense rose from $734,000 in 1970 to $2.3 million in 1973. The company suffered an after-tax loss of $1.7 million in 1973 (see Exhibit 3).

Dunkin' Donuts also encountered extensive

[3]Total capitalization is defined here as the sum of long-term debt and stockholders' equity.

EXHIBIT 3
HISTORICAL DATA ON DUNKIN' DONUTS FINANCIAL PERFORMANCE
In Thousands of Dollars

	1978	1977	1976	1975	1974	1973	1972	1971	1970
Systemwide sales*	$249,357	$221,636	$210,533	$193,864	$169,474	$141,757	$126,693	$106,312	$87,368
Average sales unit	269	251	241	237	219	195	185	176	170
Gross revenue†	57,097	51,767	43,256	34,465	26,719	23,993	22,251	17,676	17,594
Net income	3,764	3,100	2,492	1,881	1,311	(1,720)‡	1,069	949	1,720
Total assets	51,980	47,925	45,166	43,624	42,226	40,275	39,413	36,926	27,339
Total liabilities	29,679	28,987	29,024	29,997	30,382	29,742	27,160	27,871	19,163
Stockholders' equity	22,301	18,938	16,142	13,627	11,844	10,533	12,253	9,055	8,176

*Includes sales of company-operated and franchised donut shops and Howdy Beefburgers but excludes sales of donut shops in Japan.
†Excludes sales of franchised stores but reflects income flows from these stores to Dunkin' Donuts.
‡Includes a $3,167,000 provision for future losses.
Source: Annual Report of the company.

EXHIBIT 4
DUNKIN' DONUTS ORGANIZATION CHART
PRIOR TO 1973

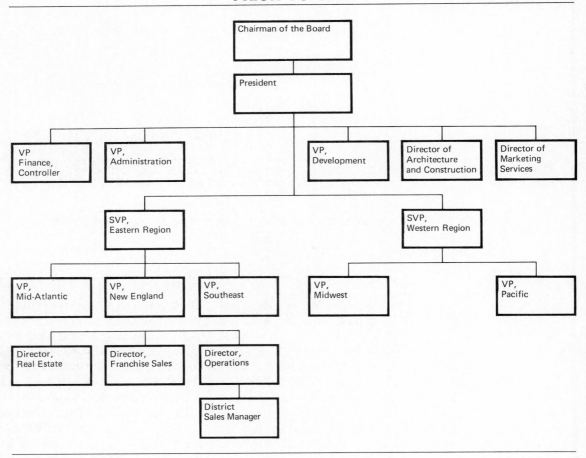

legal difficulties during the expansion period. Litigation came from prosperous franchise owners who wanted more favorable contract terms, as well as from marginal franchise owners who wished to terminate their contracts and collect punitive and compensatory damages based on various charges of having been misled about the opportunities of franchise ownership. In 1972, there was a class action suit filed in the U.S. District Court for the Eastern District of Pennsylvania by a group of 13 current and former franchise owners (*Rader, Ungar, et al. v. Dunkin' Donuts Incorporated et al.*). The plaintiffs charged Dunkin' Donuts with antitrust violations, misrepresentation in the sale of franchises, and breach of fiduciary duties. In addition, private lawsuits were filed in Michigan and Texas and by the state attorney in North Carolina, all alleging antitrust violations by virtue of tying the acquisition of real estate, equipment signs, and supplies to the granting of the franchise. Dunkin' Donuts's management denied all charges and

EXHIBIT 5
DUNKIN' DONUTS ORGANIZATION CHART AFTER 1973*

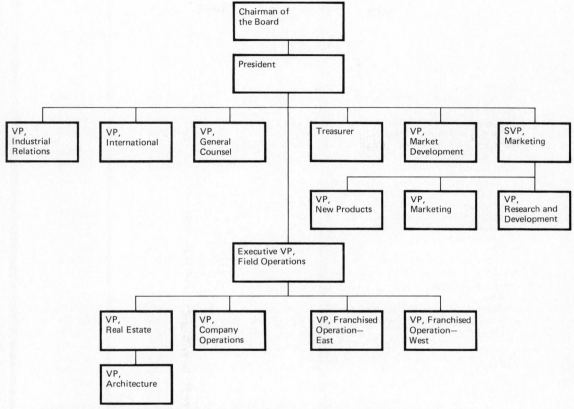

*Further reorganization was carried out in 1978, making the organization chart more centralized. Tom Schwarz was promoted to executive vice president, and five vice presidents reported to him. These vice presidents were in charge of franchised operations, company operations, development (including real estate and construction), marketing, and architecture. Various staff personnel (e.g., the controller) reported to the five vice presidents.

proceeded to litigate each charge vigorously. By 1978, all major suits had been successfully resolved from Dunkin' Donuts's point of view, except for the class action suit, which was still pending.

The company's stock prices reflected the difficult days during the "crisis of 1973." Its stock had sold for 10 when it had gone public in 1968, had climbed steadily to 33, and then dropped rapidly to 1¾ by 1973.

Since the "crisis of 1973," Dunkin' Donuts's management had pursued a consolidation strategy which was reflected in the following developments:

1. Field operations, which had formerly been decentralized on a geographic basis under five regional vice presidents (see Exhibit 4), became centralized under Thomas Schwarz, executive vice president (see Exhibit 5).

EXHIBIT 6
STATEMENT OF CONSOLIDATED INCOME
Dunkin Donuts Incorporated and Subsidiaries

	Fiscal year ended	
	October 28, 1978	October 29, 1977
Gross revenues:		
Sales by company-operated shops	$27,317,000	$24,807,000
Rental income	15,699,000	14,579,000
Continuing franchise fee income	10,965,000	9,729,000
Initial franchise fee income	1,215,000	990,000
Gain on sales of property, plant, and equipment at existing locations	613,000	724,000
Interest and other income	1,288,000	938,000
	$57,097,000	$51,767,000
Costs and expenses:		
Company-operated shops:		
Food and paper	$ 9,033,000	$ 8,664,000
Depreciation and amortization	1,007,000	860,000
Interest expense	436,000	492,000
Rent	1,187,000	1,191,000
Other operating expenses	12,936,000	11,999,000
	$24,599,000	$23,206,000
Rental properties:		
Rent	$ 6,138,000	$ 5,832,000
Depreciation and amortization	1,334,000	1,203,000
Interest expense, less amounts capitalized	1,372,000	1,554,000
Other expenses	345,000	257,000
	$ 9,189,000	$ 8,846,000
Selling, general, and administrative expenses	$15,854,000	$13,373,000
Total costs and expenses	$49,642,000	$45,425,000
Income before income taxes	$ 7,455,000	$ 6,342,000
Provision for income taxes	3,691,000	3,242,000
Net income	$ 3,764,000	$ 3,100,000
Net income per share of common stock	$1.75	$1.46
Average shares outstanding	2,151,000	2,125,000

Schwarz, 42, was also a graduate of the Harvard Business School.

2. A new division called Company Operations was formed to supervise the development of company-owned shops. These shops were seen by management as vehicles for testing systemwide marketing and operating programs and for improving the overall profitability of the company.

3. A formal corporate budgeting and planning process was introduced. The profit plans of all individual shops were consolidated to formulate a "corporate profit plan."[4]

4. National advisory councils, which were composed of franchise owners and Dunkin' Donuts representatives, were formed to develop common goals and standards for conducting business and to develop programs aimed at improving store performance.

[4]A more detailed description of the process is provided in "Dunkin' Donuts: II."

EXHIBIT 7
CONSOLIDATED BALANCE SHEET
Dunkin' Donuts Incorporated and Subsidiaries

Assets

	October 28, 1978	October 29, 1977
Current assets:		
Cash (including $1,710,000 of certificates of deposit in 1978, $2,196,000 in 1977)	$ 3,335,000	$ 2,606,000
Short-term investments, at cost (which approximates market)	2,200,000	2,700,000
Accounts receivable, principally from franchise owners, less allowance of $356,000 in 1978 and $295,000 in 1977 for doubtful accounts	3,490,000	2,986,000
Current portion of notes receivable	315,000	363,000
Food, supplies, and equipment inventories	998,000	789,000
Prepaid rent, deposits, and other current assets	813,000	1,005,000
Construction costs reimbursable under financing arrangements	878,000	1,504,000
Total current assets	$12,029,000	$11,962,000
Property, plant, and equipment, at cost:		
Land	$ 7,250,000	$ 5,958,000
Buildings	28,350,000	26,373,000
Leaseholds and leasehold improvements	4,875,000	4,511,000
Restaurant and other equipment	7,567,000	6,928,000
	$48,042,000	$43,770,000
Less accumulated depreciation and amortization	13,366,000	11,286,000
	$34,676,000	$32,484,000
Other assets:		
Net investment in leases	$ 2,901,000	$ 1,305,000
Notes receivable	397,000	262,000
Lease acquisition costs	1,614,000	1,571,000
Other	363,000	341,000
	$ 5,275,000	$ 3,479,000
	$51,980,000	$47,925,000

5. Management focus shifted from opening new shops to improving the sales of existing shops. New sales promotion programs and new products were introduced to generate store traffic.

The consolidation strategy appeared to have been successful. For example, the following improvements occurred between 1973 and 1978:

Systemwide sales increased from $135 million to $249 million.

Average annual sales per shop increased from $195,100 to $268,700.

After-tax earnings rose from a loss of $1.7 million to $3.8 million.

The debt-to-total capitalization ratio dropped from 65 percent to 36 percent.

The number of company-owned shops operated on a permanent basis increased from 8 to 85.

Stock prices jumped from a low of 1¾ to a range of 8 to 18.

Exhibit 6 shows Dunkin' Donuts's income statement for 1977 and 1978, and Exhibit 7 shows its balance sheet.

EXHIBIT 7

Continued

Liabilities and stockholders' equity

	October 28, 1978	October 29, 1977
Current liabilities:		
Accounts payable	$ 5,026,000	$ 3,869,000
Accrued expenses	2,696,000	2,239,000
Income taxes	1,263,000	1,208,000
Current portion of notes and mortages payable and capital lease obligations	1,761,000	2,642,000
Current portion of estimated future losses	177,000	311,000
Total current liabilities	$10,923,000	$10,269,000
Notes and mortgages payable	$12,625,000	$13,969,000
Capital lease obligations	$ 2,777,000	$ 1,157,000
Deferred liabilities and credits:		
Estimated future losses associated with permanently closed locations	$ 1,166,000	$ 1,575,000
Income taxes	667,000	646,000
Income on notes receivable	558,000	458,000
Security deposits by lessees	963,000	913,000
	$ 3,354,000	$ 3,592,000
Stockholders' equity:		
Common stock, par value $1—authorized 4,000,000 shares; issued 2,104,575 shares in 1978, 2,101,175 shares in 1977	$ 2,105,000	$ 2,101,000
Capital in excess of par value	2,339,000	2,328,000
Retained earnings	17,960,000	14,607,000
	$22,404,000	$19,036,000
Less treasury stock, at cost (47,300 shares in 1978 and 46,800 shares in 1977)	103,000	98,000
	$22,301,000	$18,938,000
Commitments, pending litigation, and contingent liabilities	$51,980,000	$47,925,000

"It was only a few years ago that Tom Schwarz and I spent 15-hour days traveling throughout the country in a small plane, evaluating and closing shops," recalled Bob Rosenberg. "In hindsight, it was helpful for young managers like us to have the opportunity to live through a time like that and still retain stewardship of the company," he said. He noted that the average age of the present top management team was a little over 40.

Bob Rosenberg predicted that "the momentum we gained since the turnaround will continue to grow in the future." A 1978 report from a major Wall Street firm supported his prediction:

We believe that Dunkin' Donuts can continue to extend its favorable earnings progression of recent years for many years into the future and look for per share profits to compound at an average annual rate of about 20 percent.

19 Dunkin' Donuts: II

Hirotaka Takeuchi

"We're in the people business," said Bill Rianhard, district sales manager (DSM) of Dunkin' Donuts for the greater Boston district. "I see myself being like the cream of an Oreo cookie. I put the two sides—that is to say, the franchisor and the franchisee—together. I can't be too hard; nor can I be too soft. If you are, then the two sides won't stick together."

"Not only that," added Dan O'Neil, DSM for the metropolitan Boston district, "you can't be hard on one side and soft on the other. You have to be fair and honest."

"I believe that our relationship with franchise owners is now at its all-time high," said Rianhard. "We were at our all-time low in the early '70s, when we had to close a large number of stores. I'd like to think we had some part in turning this relationship around."

Dan O'Neil continued:

There's a sense of belongingness now—like the

company and franchise owners being part of a Dunkin' Donuts family. To give you an idea, there's a franchise owner in Bill's district who started out ten years ago with a single shop. Eventually, his brothers, nephews, and in-laws opened up franchised shops so that the entire family now operates about 40 shops. To foster this idea of a Dunkin' Donuts family, we're inviting all franchise owners and their families to attend a national seminar in Reno this August.[1]

In the four remaining months before the national seminar, each DSM had to resolve a sticky franchise situation. Bill Rianhard was in the process of negotiating the best deal for a disgruntled franchise owner, Tommy, who was "thinking of better things to do." Tommy's shop was only a mile away from the Dunkin' Donuts corporate headquarters in Randolph, Massachusetts, and was considered an eyesore by Dunkin' Donuts executives. According to periodic evalu-

Hirotaka Takeuchi is an assistant professor at the Harvard Graduate School of Business Administration.

[1]Franchise owners would pay for transportation and accommodation expenses.

ations, it consistently operated below Dunkin' Donuts standards.

Dan O'Neil was in the process of determining which of two existing franchise owners (Herman or Benito) would be allowed to open a second shop on Harvard Street, which stretched through the adjoining Boston communities of Brookline and Allston. Herman had made a bid to open a shop on Harvard Street in Brookline a few months before Benito but was having some difficulty acquiring a permit from the Town of Brookline, partly because the property was located right next to a Catholic church. In the meantime, Benito had bought an abandoned gas station 1.5 miles away on Harvard Street in Allston and came to Dan with a sale and purchase agreement for the newly acquired property. Their past performance records indicated that Herman qualified "with flying colors" as a multiunit operator. Benito, on the other hand, was a borderline case. In any case, the locations were too close for Dunkin' Donuts location standards.

Both DSMs wanted these situations resolved amicably prior to leaving for Reno. They feared that if they didn't resolve the problems, the 4-day seminar would be an ideal place for adverse criticism to spread among the franchise owners.

Field Organization

Dunkin' Donuts had 46 DSMs throughout the country in 1979. Each DSM covered an average of 20 franchised shops in each district. Five or six DSMs reported to a director of sales and operations (DSO), which meant that a DSO was responsible for approximately 100 to 120 franchised shops in a given area. Eight DSOs reported directly to Ralph Gabellieri, senior vice president of franchised operations, who in turn reported to Tom Schwarz, the company's executive vice president. "With close to 90 percent of our stores being operated by franchise owners,

you can understand the importance we attach to the DSM organization," said Schwarz. (See Exhibit 1 for an organization chart of franchised operations.)

The remaining 10 percent of Dunkin' Donuts stores were company-owned. Five directors of company operations reported to a senior vice president in charge of company operations, who in turn reported to Tom Schwarz.

Bill Rianhard and Dan O'Neil

Bill Rianhard, 30, joined Dunkin' Donuts as a DSM in 1976 after working for a large restaurant chain. A born-again Christian, Bill decided to move to Dunkin' Donuts because he saw an opportunity to be closer to his family and be in close contact with a larger number of people. Looking back to his interview with Dunkin' Donuts, Bill said, "I saw honesty, fairness, and a good feedback system written all over the place within this organization."

Dan O'Neil, 29, had been a DSM for only a few months. Before that he had worked for 4 years as a controller in the corporate office. He applied for a transfer a year earlier, approximately the same time that he enrolled in an MBA evening program. Before assuming full responsibility as a DSM, Dan went through 6 months of training. He traveled with Bill Rianhard and other DSMs, took a 5-week course at Dunkin' Donuts University in Braintree, Massachusetts, and ran a company-owned store for 9 weeks. (During 7 of those weeks he baked doughnuts every night.) Reflecting on his yet short tenure as a DSM, Dan recalled:

> The biggest problem for me these few months as a DSM has been personal organization. Most of my time is taken up on the road . . . visiting stores and talking with franchise owners. In the meantime, the mail, paperwork, and filing keep piling up. I now have an office in my own house (like most other DSMs) where I do most of my administrative work. You really have to know how to manage your own time.

EXHIBIT 1
ORGANIZATION OF DUNKIN' DONUTS FRANCHISED OPERATIONS

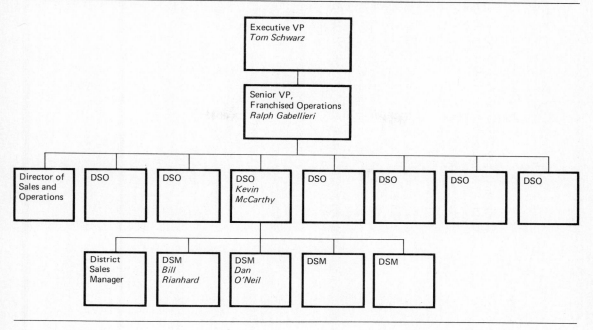

Like Dan, Bill did most of the paperwork and phoning at his home office. He usually spent 10 to 20 hours a week at his home office. As Bill's "Weekly Activity Report" (see Exhibit 2) shows, it was not unusual for him to work late hours and on weekends. Bill, like all other DSMs, received a straight salary and was eligible for an incentive award. There was no overtime pay.

Working with Franchise Owners

Dan O'Neil recalled his first business meetings with his franchise owners:

> Most of the franchise owners were very easy to get to know. Some even took me out to lunch. But a few of them were hard to get along with. One franchise owner had a mind-your-own-business attitude and kept on asking me, "Why do you want

to know that?" Another tried to go over my head and told me, "You don't know what you're doing. Let me call your boss." Yet another tried to use a scare tactic by telling me, "The last time a DSM started monkeying around with my cash register, I told him to get out. I called the police to tell him how serious I was."

Dan found out quickly that working with franchise owners required skills quite different from those required in the controller's office.

Although no two franchise owners were alike, Dan found some common traits. Franchise owners were, first of all, very independent. Most of the current franchise owners started with Dunkin' Donuts because they wanted to be their own bosses. Second, they were willing to spend long hours at the shop. Some franchise owners were still working 16 hours a day, 7 days a week. Third, they were highly motivated. Many of the franchise owners were "from the old country"

EXHIBIT 2
WEEKLY ACTIVITY REPORT

Name: William Rianhard   **Title: DSM**   **Week Ending: January 13, 1972**

Day/date	Time	Location	Contact	Purpose/result
Mon 1/8	8:45 a.m.– 5:15 p.m. / 6:30 p.m.– 9:00 p.m.	Home Office		Weekly phone calls; follow up CSG Letters; expense report, weekly activity record; shop status cards; P&L analysis for Oct.; BEP
Tues 1/9	8:30–10:00 a.m.	Weymouth Landing	Irene Botsdis	Discussed Mike's condition; operations of the shop; wholesale prices; promotions; changes on inventory procedures
Tues 1/9	10:15 a.m.–10:45 a.m.	S. Weymouth	Bob Jefferies	Discussed fund raising program with Bob and George
Tues 1/9	11:00 a.m.– 1:00 p.m.	Braintree Office	Neil Guanci / Tony Andrade	
Tues 1/9	1:30 p.m.– 2:00 p.m.	S. Weymouth	Hilprist	Dropped off sample of coupon to be printed for the fund raising program
Tues 1/9	2:15 p.m.–3:30 p.m.	Norwood	George Glaropoulos	Discussed P&L statements from Plymouth and Norwood; checked on the percentage rent bill for year ending; discussed hot coffee roll program; Easter promotion; wholesale form
Tues 1/9	4:15 p.m.– 4:45 p.m.	Boston	General Bakeries	Picked up nomogette base for Wareham
Tues 1/9	7:45 p.m.– 9:30 p.m.	Home Office		Weekly activity record; phone calls with Hy Swartz; Manny Pita; Carlos Andrade; District Digest
Wed 1/10	8:30 a.m.– 9:30 a.m.	Home Office		
Wed 1/10	10:35 a.m.–12 noon	Falmouth	Amos Corrcia	Reviewed promotions coming up; discussed sales; fund raising; coffee by the pound; reviewed P&L statement for Nov.; discussed installing souper soup; Go-for-Dough tickets
Wed 1/10	12:40 p.m.–12:50 p.m.	Hyannis	F/O not at shop	
Wed 1/10	1:15 p.m.– 2:15 p.m.	S. Yarmouth	Mike Sullivan	Check on new F/O and how shop was operating: made suggestions on improvements; discussed finishing & donut case; baking scheduling; Go-for-Dough tickets
Wed 1/10	2:45 p.m.– 5:00 p.m.	Wareham	Harry Costa	CSG taken; discussed up-coming promotions; reviewed P&L statements; discussed hostess scheduling; fund raising; testing of New Family Labels; Go-for-Dough tickets.
Wed 1/10	5:30 p.m.– 6:30 p.m.	Plymouth	John Stavropoulus	Discussed John's brother buying out George's share of the business; promotions coming up; hot coffee roll program; improvement needed in the shop
Wed 1/10	9:00 p.m.–10:15 p.m.	Home Office		Paperwork
Thur 1/11	8:40 a.m.– 9:15 a.m.	Home Office		Planning the day
Thur 1/11	9:50 a.m.–12:30 p.m.	Quincy S. Artery	Hy Swartz	Completed equipment inventory for Hy & Tony Andrade
Thur 1/11	12:40 p.m.–12:50 p.m.	N. Quincy	F/O not at shop	
Thur 1/11	1:15 p.m.– 2:15 p.m.	S. Weymouth	G. Mandell	Dropped off contract agreement on equipment for the Brockton shop—Discussed Marshfield deal
Thur 1/11	2:30 p.m.– 2:30 p.m.	Braintree Office		Checked mail
Thur 1/11	3:00 p.m.– 3:30 p.m.	South Shore Bank		Certified checks
Thur 1/11	3:30 p.m.– 4:30 p.m.	Randolph	Tommy M.	Discussed buy-out option
Thur 1/11	5:15 p.m.– 5:30 p.m. / 6:30 p.m.–10:00 p.m.	Home Office		Mail reports due—phone calls T. Andrade—Hy Swartz—John Stavropoulus—District Digest
Fri 1/12	8:45 a.m.– 5:00 p.m.	Randolph	Tommy M.	Outlined sell-out options and ran the numbers with Tommy
Sat 1/13	11:30 a.m.–12 noon	Randolph	Tommy M.	Outlined sell-out options and ran the numbers with Tommy

and were believers in the American dream of "a small guy making it big."

Despite these similarities, the backgrounds of franchise owners varied considerably. One franchise partner in Bill Rianhard's district was only 22 years old. He had started working for a Dunkin' Donuts shop when he was 15, had accumulated $3,000 in initial investment, and had become a part owner in the last year. Other franchise owners included an ex-taxi driver, an ex-construction worker, an ex-hardware store owner, an ex-office manager for a utility company, and an ex-gasoline station operator.

Whatever their backgrounds, all owners had to complete successfully a 5-week training program at Dunkin' Donuts University to qualify as a franchisee. The program was divided into a 3-week course in production methods and techniques and a 2-week course in business management. At the end of the first 3 weeks, prospective franchise owners were required to pass two exams. They took (a) a production exam in which they had to demonstrate the ability to produce 175 dozen doughnuts within an 8-hour period, 80 percent of which had to be of salable quality, and (b) a troubleshooting exam in which they had to identify the causes of any deficiency in the quality of doughnuts. At the end of the fifth week, prospective franchise owners had to pass a comprehensive exam covering such topics as personnel management, cost control, production scheduling, marketing, profit and loss statements, and sales and cash flow budgeting.

Asked by the casewriter what was the most difficult aspect of their business, most franchise owners said personnel management. "It's so hard to get good people working for you," said one franchise owner. "And just when you think you trained them well, they leave you."

Another franchise owner said, "My biggest problem is all the stealing that goes on by my employees. They make deals with friends, hide money in their shoes, and find all kinds of ways to cheat you."

"I didn't mind it too much when I was younger," said a third franchise owner, "but it really bothers me now when the night production crew decides to call in sick. That means I've got to get out of bed and get into the kitchen."

Participative Management

To enable the company and franchise owners to work together toward the common objective of improving the system's sales and profitability, an "advisory system" had been in operation for some years. Advisory councils were established at the district level (46 districts) and the zone level (five zones)[2] in 1965 and at the national level in 1971. All advisory council members were franchise owners who were elected to the council by their peers for 2-year terms.

Ten franchise owners (two from each zone) made up the National Advisory Council Chairmen's Committee (NACCC). The NACCC met every quarter with Bob Rosenberg, Tom Schwarz, and Ralph Gabellieri to devise and approve plans for every aspect of the business. In addition, NACCC members usually headed ad hoc committees formed to investigate certain proposed programs. In the past, these committees investigated and reported on such matters as advertising programs, new-product introductions, frozen-food production, sanitation, and in-store training.

Most franchise owners believed in the advisory system. "It's good to know that a group of our own guys is running the show," said one franchise owner.

"It also works like a court system when it comes to settling grievances," said another franchise owner. "If our grievance is not resolved with the DSM, then we can make written appeals to the District Advisory Council and so on up the ladder."

[2]The five zones consisted of the Northeast zone, headquartered in Braintree, Mass.; the Southeast zone (Atlanta); the Mid-Atlantic zone (Edison, N.J.); the Midwest zone (Park Ridge, Ill.); and the West zone (Dallas).

District Meetings

A number of franchise owners had the opportunity of working with company executives through advisory councils and committees, but for the rest of the franchise owners, the major interface came during district meetings. Held once in about 2 months, these meetings were usually attended by franchise owners and their spouses.[3] Meetings were usually held at local hotels or restaurants for about 3 to 4 hours. Approximately half of this time was devoted to reviewing past records and future plans, and the rest of the time was given to open discussion.

The liveliest part of a recent meeting in Bill Rianhard's district came after a few drinks when the floor was opened up for free discussion. One franchise owner asked Roy Jemison, vice president of franchised operations, why muffins were in some stores but not in others. Another franchise owner asked why frozen donuts never took off from the testing stage. Some other complaints:

> The apple and raspberry fillings I've been getting are so inconsistent. They're hard as jello one day but soft as tomato juice the next day.
>
> Dunkin' Donuts coffee mugs are selling at a nearby discount store for 39 cents apiece. That's 20 cents less than what I'm charging my customers! How can a thing like this happen?
>
> I find the paper boxes are becoming too thin. If they become any thinner, I could even use them to blow my nose.

Bill Rianhard promised to look into each such situation and report back. The meeting room was still filled with lively discussion and loud laughter long after the meeting was adjourned at 4:30 P.M.

---

[3]Spouse involvement in these meetings was encouraged because most Dunkin' Donuts shops were run by husband-wife teams.

Control of Franchised Operations

To pursue the objective of maximizing sales and profitability among franchised outlets, Dunkin' Donuts's management maintained tight controls over store standards as well as financial standards. Dunkin' Donuts's management knew that these controls, if not administered properly, could be construed by franchise owners as being autocratic. Said Dan O'Neil:

> That's where district sales managers play an important role. You've got to convince franchise owners that you're not out there to rule with an iron hand or to harass them. You've got to convince them that they'll come out ahead if they'd adhere to the standards we suggest. In other words, controls would not work without a sense of trust between you and the franchise owner.

Store Standards

A major procedure for maintaining quality control within the store was an unannounced inspection known as the Customer Satisfaction Guide (CSG). Conducted by district sales managers, a Customer Satisfaction Guide was completed at least once a year per store. This quality control mechanism was so named because a DSM would evaluate the entire store from the customer's point of view. "We ask ourselves, will the customers be satisfied with the quality and variety of our products, the cleanliness of our store, and the quality of our in-store service," Bill Rianhard explained.

Some 250 inspection items were grouped into eight categories:

1. Quality and freshness of doughnuts[4]
2. Quality and freshness of coffee

---

[4]For each item in the doughnut line, for example, such factors as flavor, volume, weight, shape, color, shortening absorption, texture, and freshness were individually rated.

3. Maintenance and cleanliness of the store (exterior and interior)
4. Variety of products offered and in-store merchandising
5. Quality of service by store personnel
6. Quality of Souper Soup program
7. Sanitation tests
8. Other regulations

A DSM wrote in a numerical point within a certain preassigned range for each of the 250 checklist items, added up the points in each category, and calculated a category score by dividing the sum of "earned" points into the maximum number of available points. Any score below 80 percent was considered unsatisfactory.

The written portion of the CSG, which also included open-ended remarks, usually took DSMs 2 to 3 hours to complete. As soon as the scores were tallied and the percentages calculated, the DSM went over the CSG with the franchise owner. According to Rianhard:

I try to emphasize the point that the CSG is a tool or a guide that franchise owners can use to upgrade their operation. If some categories are below the minimum passing score of 80 percent, we try to work out some improvement plans. If the composite score for the entire store is below 80 percent, I try to conduct another CSG within a month. In some rare cases, I've done as many as four CSGs a year for a substandard operator. But patience usually pays off in the long run.

Besides the Customer Satisfaction Guide, about a dozen other standards improvement programs were in operation (see Exhibit 3). Except for two evaluative programs (i.e., "Best Foot Forward" and "Mystery Shopper" programs), all the other programs were designed to help franchise owners to improve their CSG scores.

Financial Standards

The DSM played different roles as a budget planner, a collection agent, a firing officer, and a financial analyst in trying to control the financial condition of franchised operations. As financial planners, DSMs established sales forecasts for every store in the district (based on past sales records, planned promotions in the coming year, and guidelines set forth by the corporate office). For example, one of the subobjectives in 1979 was to increase same-shop sales by at least 8 percent. When actual monthly sales reports were submitted by franchise owners, DSMs compared actual sales and budgeted sales and prepared variance reports. Said O'Neil:

Whenever I see a negative variance, I try to find out if it was due to a forecasting error, some uncontrollable events like the blizzard we had last year, or something which the franchise owner and I could have controlled for. Let's face it. Meeting the budget is serious business for me personally because my bonus is partly dependent on it.[5] It's also serious business for the company because its income from franchise fees will fluctuate with the store's sales volume. So, there's every incentive in keeping a close eye on the store's ability to meet the budget.

As a collection agent, the DSM was responsible for helping to control the receivables (i.e., rents and commissions) due from franchise owners. When payments were delayed, DSMs worked with franchise owners to develop reconciliation plans that would remedy the problem.

As a firing officer, the DSM recommended that franchise owners be disenfranchised when budgeted plans were repeatedly not met and when all attempts for standards improvement were exhausted. Bill Rianhard knew that he could possibly be in such a position with the Randolph case. As financial analysts, DSMs conducted break-even, cash flow, and return on investment analyses for new-store development or for remodeling. Dan O'Neil knew that he would soon be analyzing numbers in trying to

---

[5]Yearly bonuses for DSMs, which were determined by their immediate supervisors, ranged from zero to $5,000.

EXHIBIT 3
STANDARDS IMPROVEMENT PROGRAMS

1. *Customer Satisfaction Guide (CSG)*
   A 14-page inspection report covering all aspects of the operation. Used as a tool in assisting franchise owners in recognizing deficiences in the operation so that positive changes can be made.
2. *LaBelle Audio-Visual System*
   An audio-visual projector and cassettes used to train and retrain shop employees. Currently the library consists of three films on customer service and satisfaction and a film on product finishing. The cost of the mutual program is approximately $400 and is paid by the franchisee.
3. *Technical Assistance Program*
   A program whereby a DSM or technical adviser will review production techniques with an individual donutman or a group of donutmen to improve product quality.
4. *Applied Sanitation System*
   A program which encourages the use of not only cleaning products but also sanitizing agents to prevent the growth of bacteria. The program also includes the use of a swab testing program to measure the amount of bacteria.
5. *Best Foot Forward Program*
   A program involving franchise owner evaluations of other franchise-owned shops. The program's objective is to emphasize good standards by examples and to use peer group influence. The shop with the highest average score is awarded a 3-day trip, paid for by the company.
6. *Operation Facelift*
   A paint-up/fix-up repairs and maintenance program costing at least $1,500.
7. *Mystery Shopper*
   A program whereby an operator or a group of operators may pay an outside service to make unannounced visits to their shops to conduct evaluations.
8. *Dunkin' Donuts University Refresher Training*
   A program whereby existing franchisees or their representatives return to DDU for reviews and updating in product quality and profit training.
9. *Landscaping Program*
   Improvements to a shop's landscaping in excess of $300 are done by a professional or shop employee.
10. *Linestriping Program*
    A program whereby shops' parking lot lines are restriped at least annually or as often as necessary.
11. *Pavement Sealing*
    A program whereby shops' parking lots are patched and resealed with asphalt products to improve appearance and prevent deterioration.
12. *Remodeling*
    Changing of the interior and exterior of a shop to fit the current image. The cost usually exceeds $30,000 and is paid by the franchisee.
13. *Improved Production Scheduling—6 P.M. and 8 P.M.*
    A program whereby the hours of production are extended to 6 P.M. and 8 P.M. to improve product freshness.

determine whether the Harvard Street expansion should be awarded to Herman or to Benito.

The Randolph Decision

A little over 2 years remained in the franchise contract of Tommy, the operator of the Randolph store near corporate headquarters. A franchise owner for more than 17 years, Tommy was looking for a change, especially since he had just finished putting his third and last child through school. Rianhard's reaction:

> It was a relief for us to learn that Tommy wasn't thinking of renewing his contract with us. From our point of view, the Randolph store was a big headache. The store was dirty and standards were extremely low. His composite Customer Satisfaction Guide score was consistently below 80. Tommy used to freeze his doughnuts and we'd have a stack of letters from customers complaining about stale doughnuts. Fees were often not paid on time or in the correct amount. Cash register tapes weren't retained so we weren't sure if his sales reports were accurate. And because it was an old contract, Tommy operated a food section that served breakfast items (other than doughnuts) and hamburgers, which he claimed generated about half of his sales. With all these things going against him, there was no way the company was going to renew his contract.
>
> Tommy feels that he's being harassed by the company. When I took over the store about a year ago (as a DSM), he told me his side of the story. He told me that a DSM walked into his store at midnight one night and started conducting a CSG. He also told me that nobody from Dunkin' Donuts visited his store or sent in any company mail for a period of three years or so. He also had this idea that the company was trying to rip him off. He told me how the company was misusing advertising money and rebates for its own benefit, not for the franchise owners. Tommy, incidentally, was one of the 12 plaintiffs who filed the class action suit against Dunkin' Donuts in 1972.

Despite poor store standards and a disgrun-

tled owner/operator, business thrived in the Randolph store. Average weekly sales reached $6,150 in 1978, reflecting an increase of 12 percent over 1977 sales. The store had good visibility from both directions of traffic, good accessibility, and ample parking space (24 cars). The site also had population and traffic counts higher than the Dunkin' Donuts norms. "There's no reason why this store cannot ring up $6,000 in weekly sales even without breakfast items and hamburgers," said Bill. "That's if good store standards are maintained."

Bill had spent months discussing various options available to Tommy. Explained Bill:

> Tommy was first interested in buying out the franchise from Dunkin' Donuts. He would take down the Dunkin' Donuts sign and continue to operate the shop under a new store name of his choice. He would also negotiate a direct lease with the landlord instead of leasing the building and land from Dunkin' Donuts.[6] The company's original asking price was $50,000, which stood firm under several negotiations. Tommy told me recently that he was no longer interested in pursuing this option.
>
> We also discussed the option of Dunkin' Donuts buying out the franchise from Tommy. The company, in turn, had the options of operating a company-owned store at Randolph or selling the franchise to a new or existing franchise owner. After several negotiations, Tommy seemed agree-

[6]Under the current arrangement, Dunkin' Donuts leased the building and land from the landlord or investor and then leased them back to the franchise owner. This type of arrangement, known as a three-party case, accounted for about half of all Dunkin' Donuts real estate arrangements. Other arrangements included the following:

1. The company purchased the land and constructed the building.
2. The company leased the land from the landlord or investor but built and owned its own building.
3. The franchisee owned or leased the land and building approved by the company (franchisee-developed shops).

The fastest-growing real estate arrangement was the franchisee-developed option. Over half of the new-store openings in 1979 were expected to be developed by franchise owners.

able to selling the business to Dunkin' Donuts for $80,000.

A few months ago, Tommy was also approached by Royce, a highly qualified Dunkin' Donuts franchise owner operating several shops. Royce wanted to buy the franchise directly from Tommy. The company encouraged Tommy and Royce to work out a deal between themselves. But Tommy was somewhat reluctant in pursuing this option, since it would most likely mean a lower selling price than $80,000.

In recent weeks, however, two new developments had complicated the negotiation process. To Bill's surprise, Tommy bought the Randolph store's building and land from the current landlord and became its new landlord. He then doubled the price to Dunkin' Donuts from $80,000 to $160,000. "Even if we bought Tommy's bluff and paid him $160,000, we would have possession of his franchise, signs, and equipment, but we would still have to deal with him as our landlord," said one company official.

Given these new developments, there was some sentiment within the company that current negotiations with Tommy should be dropped immediately and management should confront him with "We will disenfranchise you now for poor standards" or "We will wait two years and not renew your contract." Bill was not sympathetic to either approach because "it almost assures litigation.[7] What we need to know now is whether or not his offer of $160,000 is economically acceptable to us."

Whether Dunkin' Donuts was interested in opening a company-owned store or another

franchised store, an additional investment of $90,000 was required for leasehold improvements ($65,000), new sales-area equipment ($20,000), and a new sign package ($5,000). The company would pay all incremental costs under the option of opening a company-owned store but only for leasehold improvements under the franchised store option.

Bill estimated Dunkin' Donuts's profit margin for operating a company store at the Randolph site to be 13 percent:

Sales		100.0%
Variable costs		65.0
Food	27.8%	
Payroll	29.2	
Supplies	4.0	
Advertising	4.0	
Gross margin		35.0
Operating costs*		22.0
Operating profit		13.0

*Includes all fixed operating expenses, such as insurance, professional fees, repairs, telephone, and utility, but does not include selling, general, and administrative (SG&A) expenses at store and corporate levels.

Bill also calculated the revenue generated by franchising the store to a new or existing franchise owner as follows:

1. Initial franchise fee of $32,000 for a new franchise owner or $25,000 for an existing franchise owner opening up an additional store
2. Continuing franchise fee of 4.5 percent of sales in the first year and 4.9 percent thereafter
3. Flat rental fee of $3,000 per year and an additional override rental fee of 7.0 percent of sales beyond annual sales of $165,000

Bill estimated operating expenses (excluding SG&A expenses at store and corporate levels) to run about 3 percent of sales.

"The numbers aren't hard to handle," said Bill Rianhard, "but what I don't have a good handle on is figuring Tommy out." Thinking out loud, Bill continued, "Now, what do you sup-

[7]In the last Congress, Representative Abner Mikva introduced a bill aimed at protecting existing franchisees from "arbitrary and unfair" termination and failure to renew their franchise contracts. According to *Restaurant Business* (Mar. 1, 1979), "The major objection franchisors find with the Mikva bill [which is still pending] centers around its definition of 'good cause' for termination and nonrenewal, which they claim is used arbitrarily and thus would become a source of friction and litigation."

pose Tommy's motive was for buying the real estate? He told me it just made good accounting sense, but I'm not even sure now whether he's serious about getting out of the business. I can easily figure out what's best for the company, but I really am not sure what's best for Tommy."

The Harvard Street Decision

Dan O'Neil had two applications from existing franchise owners wanting to develop (i.e., buy the building and land) a second shop. Each had been a Dunkin' Donuts franchise owner since the early '70s. Each was a first-generation American who had constructed a solid financial base for himself. Each had picked a gasoline station of about the same size as a potential site. Both sites were located on a heavily trafficked street (25,000 to 30,000 cars per day) surrounded by retail stores and office buildings. Both sites were located in very densely populated areas capable of generating a large walk-in business. The problem, however, was that both sites were located on Harvard Street, only 1.5 miles apart from each other. Dan, therefore, could give a franchise agreement to only one of the two applicants in this case.

Herman and Benito were the two applicants. Herman, 50, operated one of the highest-volume shops (over $9,000 in average weekly sales) in downtown Boston. Herman used to be a store manager for a Dunkin' Donuts company-owned store before becoming a franchise owner. He consistently scored high on Customer Satisfaction Guides. Besides a doughnut shop, he owned two apartment complexes and held a one-half interest in two more apartment complexes in the Boston area. His personal assets were believed to approach a million dollars.

Benito, 41, operated an average-volume store in a suburb of Boston. His brother, whom Benito lured into the business, owned a Dunkin' Donuts shop in "uptown" Boston. Although Benito had no ownership interest in the Boston

store, he actually spent most of his time operating his brother's shop. Both of the shops managed to pass the CSG, but not consistently nor with high scores. His personal assets, a large part of which was in unlisted securities, were believed to approach half a million dollars.

Herman first applied to open a store on Harvard Street (Brookline) about 2 years prior to the current events. Herman and the proposed site location passed Dunkin' Donuts guidelines "with flying colors."[8] But the location was rejected by town officials because the North Brookline Neighborhood Association objected to fast-food establishments "downgrading the neighborhood." A writer for a Brookline paper wrote:

> It could ultimately lead to the destruction of the neighborhood we call North Brookline and the destruction of one of our major commercial areas.

Moreover, the location was next to a synagogue.

Herman then applied for another Harvard Street location in a different precinct in Brookline. An attorney for Dunkin' Donuts presented the new shop plan to the Brookline Village Citizens Work Group at a Town Hall meeting on November 21, 1978. Several objections to the planned opening were voiced in the meeting:

> The Harvard Street intersection is busy enough, and it's too close to the Pierce Elementary School.

> It's bad for the precinct because the store will attract undesirable people, especially late at night.

> If the shop was opened, it would certainly increase traffic. I'm afraid we're going to hear more screeching brakes with kids running around this area.

> We don't have enough police protection in the

---

[8]In addition to conducting an in-depth analysis of the applicant's background and personal finances, the company assessed the probable results from a proposed site location using a sophisticated computer model. Input to the computer model came from a detailed seven-page questionnaire which collected some 300 pieces of data per location.

area. Besides, everybody wants a drugstore on that location.

The fact that the second proposed site was located next to a Catholic church did not help Herman's cause, either. A meeting with the Town Planning Board was scheduled in 3 weeks. The public was invited to attend the meeting.

In early November of 1978, Benito purchased an abandoned gasoline station located on Harvard Street in Allston. A formal request for site approval reached Dan O'Neil through Benito's attorney on November 15. Dan explained the pending Brookline situation to Benito and asked that he wait until a final decision was reached by the Town of Brookline. Benito did not expect any difficulty in obtaining a permit from the Town of Allston, where neighborhood groups were not as active as in Brookline.

Four months had elapsed since Benito submitted his application, and Dan could tell that his patience was fast disappearing. Benito was also not pleased to hear that he needed to meet several requirements to qualify as a multiunit operator. These requirements were:

1. Passing three CSGs in all categories between April and May
2. Submitting profit and loss statements within 30 days after the end of the month on a continuing basis
3. Disassociating himself from the Boston store if the Allston site became available

"I'm sure Benito would comply with these requirements," said Dan. "But can you imagine what he'll say if Brookline comes through with Herman's permit?"

Dan ran some numbers on the two potential sites. The numbers—which included cash outlays on the part of the franchise owner (Exhibit 4), break-even projects (Exhibit 5), and sales forecasts (Exhibit 6)—seemed to indicate a lower risk on the Allston store alternative.

With the Brookline Planning Board meeting only 3 weeks away, Dan was wondering if the entire presentation should be handled by the same attorney who met with the Citizens Work Group last November. In that meeting, the attorney was asked why Dunkin' Donuts selected the particular Harvard Street site. "I don't know what prompted the company to choose the particular site," said the attorney. "I'm a

EXHIBIT 4
COMPARISON OF CASH OUTLAYS: BROOKLINE VS. ALLSTON

	Brookline	Allston
Land	$125,000	$100,000*
Building construction (including landscape)	135,000	125,000
Equipment	45,000	40,000
Signs	10,000	6,000
Professional fees (legal, architecture)	9,000	6,000
Working capital	10,000	7,000
Franchise fee	25,000	25,000
Total	$359,000	$309,000
Cash payment	$100,000	$ 70,000
Bank financing†	$214,000	$199,000
Dunkin' Donuts financing†	$ 45,000	$ 40,000

*Already paid for.
†Interest rate of 12 percent.

EXHIBIT 5
BREAK-EVEN CALCULATIONS:
BROOKLINE VS. ALLSTON

	Brookline	Allston
Fixed operating costs:		
Bakery and kitchen	$ 300	$ 300
Cash—short and over	300	500
Cleaning	1,800	1,800
Insurance	6,700	4,000
Laundry and uniform	600	500
License and permits	100	100
Office expense	300	300
Payroll: fixed*	28,600	28,600
Professional fees	2,400	2,000
Rent—fixed mortgage	29,729	23,869
Repairs and maintenance	1,500	1,500
Telephone	300	200
Utility	10,500	10,500
	$ 83,129	$ 74,169
Variable costs:		
Food costs	27.0%	27.0%
Supply costs	4.0	4.0
Franchise fee	4.5	4.5
Advertising expense	4.0	4.0
Payroll	29.0	27.0
	68.5%	66.5%
Breakeven points:		
Annual	$263,902	$221,400
Weekly	5,075	4,258

*Includes franchise owner's draw.

EXHIBIT 6
SALES PROJECTIONS:
BROOKLINE VS. ALLSTON

	Brookline	Allston
January 1980	$ 25,600	$ 27,500
February	26,800	28,800
March	33,400	35,900
April	26,800	28,800
May	27,200	29,300
June	34,100	36,600
July	27,200	29,300
August	27,700	29,700
September	34,500	37,000
October	27,700	29,700
November	25,600	27,500
December	32,000	34,400
Total	$348,600	$374,500

lawyer, not a marketing expert." Dan felt that he could ask the company to organize a special task force headed by a marketing expert to prepare a strong case for Herman and to appear in the town meeting. "I know what's best for the franchise owners," said Dan, "but I'm not sure what's best for the company."

20 Dunkin' Donuts: III

Hirotaka Takeuchi

"MURPHY'S LAW: IF ANYTHING CAN GO WRONG, IT WILL (AT THE WORST TIME)" reads a sign in one of Dunkin' Donuts's corporate offices in Randolph, Massachusetts. "That sign, I guess, best describes those difficult days we experienced several years ago," said Bob Rosenberg, president of the company. "Those difficult days" referred to the "crisis of 1973" when "Dunkin' Donuts had to close 56 money-losing stores . . . and take a $1.7 million write-off"[1] as a result of an overzealous expansion program in the late '60s and early '70s.

But since 1973, Dunkin' Donuts had made an impressive turnaround. Earnings had increased for 5 consecutive years at a compounded annual rate of over 30 percent. A recent investment report stated that "the company had reached a stage of development in which earnings increases are visible for several years ahead."

"It's about time we replaced Murphy's Law with a new sign like 'WHEN YOU'RE HOT, YOU'RE HOT,'" said Rosenberg with a grin.

Given these recent developments, Rosenberg was planning to accelerate the company's growth strategy. He saw three areas of opportunity. The first was to accelerate new-shop openings, but he was concerned about whether the new shops should be primarily franchised or company-owned. "Historically, we developed the stores and leased them to franchise owners," said Rosenberg. "The question we're facing now is whether to shift our emphasis towards company-owned stores and/or franchisee-developed stores."

The second opportunity was to expand the existing product line. Dunkin' Donuts introduced eight varieties of soups (called Souper Soups) in 1977. The company also started testing muffins on a regional basis in 1978. Initial test results were starting to come in, and management faced the immediate question of whether or not to expand the introduction of muffins nationally.

Hirotaka Takeuchi is an assistant professor at the Harvard Graduate School of Business Administration.

[1] *Forbes*, July 15, 1977, p. 78.

The third opportunity was to "pull" more customers into the stores by utilizing network television ads. The company had embarked on the "Network TV" program in the fall of 1978. Eighty percent of the franchise owners contributed an additional 2 percent of sales to this new program. Encouraged by sharp increases in average weekly sales in the fourth quarter of 1978 (compared with sales of the previous year), management decided to extend the Network TV program into the 1980s. To its surprise, the sign-up rate for the second round of Network TV was slower than expected. Of immediate concern was whether enough franchise owners would sign up (a sign-up rate of approximately 80 percent was needed) to enable this program to continue.

Business Definition

After the "crisis of 1973," Dunkin' Donuts's management had established formal corporate planning procedures at all levels of the firm. Top management wanted an answer to the question "What business are we in?" as a basis for long-range planning. Tom Schwarz, executive vice president, recalled the discussion at that time:

Someone would argue that we are in the "franchising" business since a large portion of our revenue comes from fees collected from franchisees.

Others would argue that we are in the "fast-foods" business, since the distinction between retail shops serving meals and those serving snacks seemed to be fading away. McDonald's, for example, started to serve a breakfast line known as "Egg McMuffin" and snack items such as sundaes and pies two years ago. Mister Donut, on the other hand, recently introduced a new line of sandwiches. If this trend were to continue, we should be capitalizing on the growing eating-out market by extending our menu to include meals.

When it was all said and done, however, we agreed that we were basically in the high end of the "bakery and snack" businesses. Three considerations led us to this conclusion. First of all, we noticed that we had a competitive advantage in this business. Independent "mom and pop" neighborhood bakeries were fast disappearing from the market, being replaced by bakery departments within supermarkets.[2] But most people buying from supermarkets were buying because of convenience, not quality. Since not many supermarkets were baking their products from scratch, customers weren't getting the "top of the line." Fast-foods chains, at the same time, were keeping their hands off bakery items because they couldn't very well automate the labor-intensive nature of the baking production process.

Secondly, customers perceived Dunkin' Donuts shops as some place to stop by to acquire "handmade," "fresh" products at all times of the day. A lot of the customers came into the store on impulse. It wasn't the same as planning a trip to McDonald's for a meal. In the minds of most customers, we were a nationally known neighborhood bakery shop serving refreshments 24 hours a day.

Thirdly, the "bakery and snack" business was compatible with our company's strength. We established a smooth production operation run by trained bakers and equipped with the right kind of machinery. We also operated a relatively small store in which quick product turnover was the key to success. We displayed all our finished products, which served to encourage customers to try a variety of items.

On the basis of this definition of the "business," top management established a corporate mission by the end of 1974. The mission was "to be the dominant worldwide retailer of high-

---

[2]According to *Chain Store Age—Supermarkets* (July 1978), some 12,000 supermarkets, which represented 30 percent of all supermarkets, had in-store bakeries in 1977. Some 1,700 new in-store bakeries were added throughout the country in 1977 alone. Of all existing supermarket in-store bakeries, only 38 percent baked their products on the premises from scratch. The remaining 62 percent of the stores used a bake-off process. In the bake-off process, bakery products were prepared by outside suppliers and delivered to the supermarkets (often frozen) in finished or semifinished forms.

quality donuts and compatible high-quality bakery and fresh snack products and beverages." This mission remained unchanged in 1979.

Shop Development

In the heyday of the expansion program in the late '60s to early '70s, over 100 new shops were opened in a year. In 1970, for example, 135 new shops were opened, all of which were leased to franchise owners (i.e., franchised shops). But during the consolidation period of the mid-1970s, new openings of franchised shops declined drastically. For example, only 13 new franchised shops opened in 1976. Exhibit 1 shows the mix of company-owned, franchised, and franchisee-developed stores in the 1974–1978 period.

The company objective was to increase new-shop openings to 90 in 1979 and to 150 by 1982. Now that the company was planning an accelerated program again, Jim Dangelo,[3] senior

[3]At age 34, he was the youngest senior vice president in the company. He had joined Dunkin' Donuts 10 years earlier as a district sales manager and worked his way up through the ranks. Two department managers from real estate and construction reported to Jim Dangelo, who in turn reported to Tom Schwarz, executive vice president.

vice president of the Development Division, had to recommend a "shop portfolio" that maximized growth potential and minimized risk.

Competitive Pressure

One of the reasons for Dunkin' Donuts's renewed interest in a more aggressive expansion program was the competitive pressure exerted by other doughnut chains. Mister Donut, a subsidiary of International Multifoods, had 678 shops in 1978—427 in the United States, 49 in Canada, and 202 in Japan. It had announced plans for opening 500 new shops in the next 5 years in the United States and Canada. "Our objective is to be the largest donut operation in the world, and we hope to accomplish this in the next five years," said Ronald Stebleton, vice president and controller of Mister Donut.[4]

Winchell's, which was a regional doughnut shop franchisor in the West, had begun to expand as far eastward as Chicago. In 1978, Winchell's had 850 shops in 16 states. Its president, Verne Winchell,[5] boasted that Winchell's was the "first in profitability of any

[4]*Bakery*, August 1978.

[5]Mr. Winchell was the chairman of the board and president of Denny's, which owned Winchell's.

EXHIBIT 1
NEW-SHOP OPENINGS

Year	Company-owned	Franchised	Franchisee-developed*	Total new
1974	12	33	–	45
1975	15	25	–	40
1976	12	13	12	37
1977	12	20	27	59
1978	15	24	26	65

*A franchise owner who developed his or her store could make one of the following arrangements:
1. Purchase his or her own land and construct the building
2. Lease the land and construct the building
3. Have a landlord or investor purchase the land, construct the building and lease it back to him or her

EXHIBIT 2
COMPARISON OF THREE MAJOR DOUGHNUT
CHAINS, 1976

	Dunkin' Donuts	Winchell's	Mister Donut
Number of units:			
Company	98	681	7
Franchised	753	–	536
Total	851	681	543
New units added:			
Company	12	71	–
Franchised	25	–	62
Total	37	71	62
Sales ($000):			
Company	$ 17,535	$80,787	$ 1,391
Franchised	187,814	–	80,350
Total	$205,350	$80,787	$81,741
Average unit sales ($000)	$241	$126	$178
Average seating capacity	20	limited	28–30
Average shop size (sq ft)	1,500	1,200	NA
Sales per square foot	$161	$105	NA

Source: Company records.

doughnut chain in the world."[6] He expected Winchell's to accelerate its expansion into the Eastern and Midwestern areas of the country where Dunkin' Donuts had historically been the dominant doughnut chain.

Mister Donut and Winchell's represented two contrasting approaches toward chain store development. As of 1978, all Mister Donut shops, except for six company-owned shops in Omaha, were franchised. In contrast, all Winchell's shops were company-owned.[7] Company-owned shops served as test stores where new products and new equipment were tested for Mister Donut. Company-owned shops served as money-makers for Winchell's. "They serve both as test stores and as money-makers for us," said Dunkin' Donuts's Jim Dangelo. See Exhibit 2 for comparative data on these three major doughnut and coffee chains.

Company-Owned Stores

The number of Dunkin' Donuts company-owned stores had increased steadily since they first appeared in 1972. By 1978, company-owned stores accounted for over 10 percent of all the stores. "We believe, to be a good franchisor, you also have to be a good operator, so you have to run some percentage of the stores yourself," said Bob Rosenberg.[8]

According to Dangelo:

Company stores are attractive for several reasons. First of all, it's a lot easier to control your own managers than some of the independent-minded franchise owners. Secondly, company stores provide an ideal testing ground for new products, new

[6]*Bakery*, August 1978.

[7]Other food chains that owned 100 percent of their shops included Sambo's, Friendly's, and Gino's. As of 1977, large hamburger chains such as McDonald's and Wendy's owned less than one-third of their stores.

[8]*Bakery*, August 1978.

marketing programs, or new production facilities. Thirdly, we don't have to worry about legal problems with company stores. And lastly, the profit potential from company stores seems much greater than from franchised stores.

Dangelo was also mindful of some criticisms directed at company-owned stores:

Controllers look upon company stores as a drain on the balance sheet. Since all developments are bank-financed, it's no big surprise to see the debt-equity ratio rise. Also, some franchise owners fear that the small guys are going to be driven out of the system with companies trying to buy back franchised units and converting them to company-owned stores. Finally, some executives are concerned at the high turnover and low morale among company store managers. Store managers, on their part, see limited opportunities for further internal promotion.

Moreover, according to a recent investment report, Dunkin' Donuts's company-owned stores had not yet attained management's targeted margins:

Because this program is in the relatively early stages of development, central selling, general and administrative expenses attributable to company-operated shops are still high relative to the gross profits generated by these units. Hence, the relative contribution of company-operated outlets is nominal.[9]

Exhibit 3 shows the relative performance of the Franchise Division and the Company Operations Division in the period 1974–1978.

Franchisee-Operated Stores[10]

All the shops that William Rosenberg, the founder and chairman of Dunkin' Donuts, had operated in 1955 were owned by himself and a partner. "My father then bought out his part-

---

[9]Blyth Eastman Dillion investment report, *Dunkin' Donuts Inc.*, March 1978.

[10]Includes both franchised stores and franchisee-developed stores.

ner[11] and decided to franchise, selling his first franchises to associates and friends," said Bob Rosenberg. "From then on, it was franchising all the way until the problems we encountered in the early '70s."

Having survived the crisis of 1973, the company was looking again to expansion. But this time, the company was encouraging franchise owners to operate multiple shops and to develop their own real estate. "If the trend continues," said Dangelo, "about half of the new shops projected to open in the next three years will be developed by franchise owners."

By developing their own real estate, franchise owners would be "getting a bigger share of the pie," since they would no longer be required to pay rental charges. "That's fine with us," said Dangelo, "because franchising offers us benefits we could not expect from company-owned stores." According to Dangelo, franchising offered the following advantages:

1. A relatively risk-free means of expanding market coverage, since franchise owners provide the capital
2. A group of highly motivated owners who play a large part in the day-to-day operation of the store
3. Longer store hours, since most franchise owners are willing "to put in the time"
4. An opportunity to upgrade store operations (e.g., new menu boards, remodeling, and an audiovisual training program) with little financial burden on the company, since the incremental investments are paid for by franchise owners
5. An improved balance sheet which would make the company more attractive to investors

"I asked a recent MBA graduate to study the alternative development options and to recommend a plan compatible with our business

---

[11]His partner went on to open his first Mister Donut shop that year.

EXHIBIT 3
PERFORMANCE OF FRANCHISED STORES VS. COMPANY-OWNED STORES
(1974-1978 Fiscal Years)

Franchise division [1] (000 omitted)	October 28, 1978	October 29, 1977	October 30, 1976	October 25, 1975	October 26, 1974
Revenues:					
Rental income	$15,699	$14,579	$14,106	$13,329	$12,168
Continuing franchise fee income	10,965	9,729	9,260	8,701	7,745
Sales by temporarily operated shops	2,722	3,052	2,604	2,396	2,056
Other	1,657	1,637	1,082	904	1,232
Total revenues	31,043	28,997	27,052	25,330	23,201
Expenses:					
Expenses related to rental properties	9,189	8,846	9,366	10,540	10,267
Expenses related to temporarily operated shops	2,636	3,147	2,617	2,455	2,131
Selling, general, and administrative expenses directly related to Franchise Division	4,434	4,080	4,068	4,069	3,703
Total expenses	16,259	16,073	16,051	17,064	16,101
Contribution to income before income taxes and prior to corporate selling, general, and administrative expenses	$14,784	$12,924	$11,001	$ 8,266	$ 7,100

Company operated shop division (000 omitted)	October 28, 1978	October 29, 1977	October 30, 1976	October 25, 1975	October 26, 1974
Revenues:					
Sales	$24,595	$21,755	$14,931	$ 8,214	$ 2,671
Other	328	227	117	42	21
Total revenues	24,923	21,982	15,048	8,256	2,692
Operating costs and expenses	21,963	20,059	13,130	7,025	2,503
Gross profits from operations	2,960	1,923	1,918	1,231	189
Selling, general, and administrative expenses directly related to Company Operated Shops Division	2,044	1,791	1,487	1,043	634
Contribution to income before income taxes and prior to corporate selling, general, and administrative expenses	$ 916	$ 132	$ 431	$ 188	$ (445)

Summary (000 omitted)	October 28, 1978	October 29, 1977	October 30, 1976	October 25, 1975	October 26, 1974
Contribution by Franchise Division	$14,784	$12,924	$11,001	$ 8,266	$ 7,100
Contribution by Company Operated Shops Division	916	132	431	188	(445)
Interest and other income	1,131	788	1,156	879	826
Less corporate selling, general, and administrative expenses	9,376	7,502	7,314	5,562	4,780
Income before income taxes	$ 7,455	$ 6,342	$ 5,274	$ 3,771	$ 2,701

Source: *Annual Report* of the company.

[1]Includes franchised stores and franchisee-developed stores.

definition and corporate objective," said Jim. The report was due in a few days.

New-Product Introductions

Prior to 1977, Dunkin' Donuts had had a limited product line, consisting of doughnuts, coffee, and drinks. The company added Souper Soups in 1977 and hot coffee rolls in 1978. "We're also planning to add muffins and other bakery products in the next few years," said Sid Feltenstein, Jr.,[12] senior vice president of marketing.

Souper Soup

In early 1977, Dunkin' Donuts started to roll out eight varieties of soups (called Souper Soups) on a regional basis. Souper Soups were available in three sizes:

Cup size: 7 ounces of soup with two crackers for a suggested price of 45 cents

Bowl size: 11 ounces of soup with bread and butter and a free soup refill for a suggested price of 79 cents

Special size: 11 ounces of soup with bread and butter, a free soup refill, a cup of coffee, and a doughnut for a suggested price of 99 cents

The primary objective of the soup introduction was to increase shop patronage during lunch hours, which had been a slack time for most shops. The soups, which were positioned as a "hearty snack," were served at the counter at all hours except between 6 A.M. and 10 A.M.

By 1979, 80 percent of all shops had adopted the Souper Soup program. In these shops, soups accounted for about 4 percent of total shop sales.[13] Most franchise owners found that about 40 percent of soup sales occurred during lunchtime, 10 percent during the late afternoon and evening, and the remaining 50 percent after midnight.

Most franchise owners considered the Souper Soup program a financial success. With an investment of $2,000 in equipment and installation, the payback period for most franchise owners was very short. Soup sales averaged $225 per week, while variable costs averaged 62 percent[14] of sales for the three sizes combined.

Many franchise owners attributed the success of the Souper Soup program to (a) the increased patronage it created during slack hours, (b) the ease with which the installation was executed,[15] and (c) the heavy promotional campaign backing the introduction. "Besides," added Feltenstein, "no additional labor was required to serve soups. Soups also improved employee morale by virtue of being the first major introduction of a higher priced item in recent history."

Testing Muffins

Just as Souper Soup was being rolled out nationally in 1977, muffins entered the consumer testing stage of the new-product development process. Prior to 1977, muffins had been screened among a variety of bakery products (through focused group interviews) and had also undergone an extensive evaluation of various production possibilities, including a make-or-buy option. From these studies and a preliminary market study, Feltenstein had acquired the following information concerning muffins by mid-1977:

Muffins enjoyed greater popularity in the Northeastern part of the country.

---

[12]Feltenstein joined Dunkin' Donuts in 1972 at age 31. Among other responsibilities, he had worked as a brand manager for Proctor & Gamble prior to joining Dunkin' Donuts.

[13]Doughnuts and fancy pastries normally accounted for 70 percent of store sales. Coffee and soft drinks accounted for the rest of store sales.

[14]Variable costs included the cost of goods sold (soups were bought ready-made from a subsidiary of the Kellogg Company), the cost of supplies, the cost of utilities, franchise and rental fees, and advertising fees.

[15]An under-the-counter soup warmer, which took only about 2 feet of space, was installed by an electrician in a matter of 2 or 3 hours.

Muffins were more adult-oriented than child-oriented.

Muffins had a more "substantial" image than doughnuts; they had an image somewhere between bread and cake.

Muffins usually sold for 50 percent more at retail than did doughnuts. (For example, most of the doughnut prices at Dunkin' Donuts ranged from 20 cents to 25 cents per unit, with up to one-third off per dozen purchased.)

Muffins had virtually the same gross margin percentage as doughnuts (i.e., approximately 30 percent).

In June 1977, a 2-day consumer taste test was conducted in four Massachusetts Dunkin' Donuts shops. Three varieties of muffins (blueberry, corn, and bran) were tasted by 326 Dunkin' Donuts shoppers. Feltenstein was encouraged when he found that over 90 percent of the buyers rated the taste as either "excellent" or "good" and that over 90 percent said they would most likely purchase muffins in Dunkin' Donuts shops. But he was concerned by the fact that 40 percent of the shoppers stated that they would buy fewer doughnuts at Dunkin' Donuts if muffins were offered for sale and by the fact that the median prices shoppers expected to pay for muffins were only 25 percent higher than the median prices of doughnuts sold at Dunkin' Donuts.

In March 1978, an independent research firm conducted a small-scale telephone interview to obtain additional buyer information. The sample consisted of 74 Dunkin' Donuts customers who had purchased muffins in two Danvers, Massachusetts, shops. Among other things, the survey found that 67 percent of the customers ate muffins at the counter and 77 percent of the purchases were made in the morning.[16]

By late 1978, 11 test stores in the Providence, Rhode Island, market were selling muffins at 30 cents each.[17] Some test stores were realizing sales of over $500 per week on muffins alone. "As soon as these figures became known, many franchise owners called us to ask if their shops could start carrying muffins right away," said Feltenstein.

One franchise owner explained why he was enthusiastic about muffins:

> Say a shop rings up $400 per week in muffin sales. That's over $20,000 a year in sales. And if the gross margin percentage is the same as doughnuts (i.e., 30 percent) we're talking over $6,000 margin in a year just on muffins. We'd pay back the $4,000 investment[18] in no time!

Another franchise owner saw other attractions to carrying muffins:

> Muffins are going to make my life a lot easier. With muffins, even if the price of cooking oil skyrockets, you can relax. Besides, it takes me close to four hours to produce a yeast doughnut[19] from start to finish. With muffins, you're cutting down your time in the kitchen by one-fourth. This means that I'll have more time to devote to supervising the shop.

Other franchise owners, however, were not as convinced. One multistore owner explained:

> We just spent $2,000 per shop installing the soup warmer. Now it's another $4,000 per shop for a new oven. With two shops, that's an $8,000 investment. I can think of a lot of better ways of spending $8,000. The way we are adding machinery into our shops, pretty soon we're going to be automated like McDonald's. Being like McDonald's isn't bad, but what's going to happen if a

---

[16]Recall from "Dunkin' Donuts: I" that 70 percent of the customers ate doughnuts at the counter and that about half the doughnut purchases were made in the morning.

[17]A discount of 10 to 15 percent was offered for the purchase of a dozen muffins during the introductory period.

[18]The investment of $4,000 included machinery, tools, electrical and plumbing charges, audiovisual training tape, and other up-front charges.

[19]"Yeast doughnuts" referred to doughnuts made from a yeast mix as opposed to cake doughnuts, which were made from a cake mix. Yeast doughnuts were "spongier" than cake doughnuts (e.g., old-fashioned doughnuts and twists). It took about an hour and a half to produce cake doughnuts from scratch. At Dunkin' Donuts, yeast and cake doughnuts each accounted for about half of doughnut sales.

personal financial crisis arises and you have all your money tied up in equipment?

Besides, baking muffins means having to go through production training all over again. Then once you master the skill, you'll have to spend time teaching your crew. Keep it simple—that's how I like to operate.

The initial results of the Providence test stores indicated that muffin sales accounted for 8 percent of overall weekly store sales of $6,000. Doughnut sales in these stores, however, were about $200 lower per week than those of matching control stores.

Encouraged by these results, Feltenstein expanded the scope of the test marketing in 1979 to include 60 other test stores (in seven test markets) throughout the country. These markets were added to test the extent to which such factors as media advertising, price-off coupons, and prices (30 cents versus 35 cents) would affect muffin sales. "We want to test as many factors as we can, so that when it's time to go national, we know exactly what's the best way to go," said Feltenstein. He continued:

It's critical that we do everything right with muffins. If franchise owners accept the muffin program, then we are one step closer to becoming a "national neighborhood bakery." We can utilize the same oven to produce other bakery products. It's not inconceivable for us to be testing cakes, cookies, brownies, macaroons, bread products, and other baked items in the near future.

Network TV

Elliot Karlin, director of advertising, came out of the studio with his thumbs up. He had just finished reviewing a new TV commercial produced by Ally and Gargano, Dunkin' Donuts' advertising agency. The new 30-second commercial (entitled "Competition") was the fourth institutional ad developed for the Network TV program. "It's dynamite," said Karlin, "and I'm sure the franchise owners are going to love it."

Management proposed the Network TV program to the National Advisory Council Chairmen's Committee (NACCC)[20] in 1977 as a means of increasing average weekly sales of existing Dunkin' Donuts shops. The annual growth rate of average weekly sales was on the decline then, as shown in Exhibit 4.

Management proposed that all shops contribute an additional 2 percent of their sales (total of 4 percent) for a period of 18 months to the new Network TV program. The additional 2 percent, if approved, would be allocated solely to purchasing program time on national television networks. The increase was seen as "a matter of survival" by one executive, who cited two danger signs for Dunkin' Donuts at that time. First of all, McDonald's introduced its breakfast menus in 1976, and Burger King was expected to do the same soon. In 1976, McDonald's and Burger King had television advertising budgets of $80 million and $22 million, respectively. In contrast, Dunkin' Donuts spent about $2 million on television advertising (all of it on local spot TV) that year. Secondly, media costs were increasing at a much faster rate than Dunkin' Donuts's average weekly sales (Exhibit 5). If this trend continued, Dunkin' Donuts would be acquiring less advertising impressions per dollar expended.

[20]The committee was composed of 10 elected franchise owners; they had the responsibility of helping to shape company policies in conjunction with company top management.

EXHIBIT 4
AVERAGE WEEKLY SALES GROWTH, 1973–1976

	Average weekly sales	Actual growth rate
1973	$3,752	–
1974	4,215	12.5%
1975	4,559	8.2
1976	4,631	1.8

EXHIBIT 5
GROWTH RATE INDEX (1974=100)

	1974	1975	1976	1977*
Spot TV	100	102	129	142
Newspaper	100	115	128	141
Radio	100	107	115	120
Dunkin' Donuts	100	108	110	112

*Estimated in 1976.
Source: Company records.

Management proposed to switch from local spot TV to national network TV because the latter was a more cost-effective medium. Elliot Karlin[21] calculated that the costs of purchasing 2,200 household gross rating points[22] would equal $4.8 million for network TV and $6.8 million for spot TV. He also knew that in 1976, major fast-food chains were allocating large portions of their television budgets toward network TV (Exhibit 6). "Besides, when you come right down to it," Karlin added, "network TV carries more clout, more prestige."

The NACCC endorsed Network TV in early 1977 and encouraged franchise owners to give

[21]Karlin had started his advertising career as a media buyer for Procter & Gamble in a large advertising agency prior to joining Dunkin' Donuts 5 years ago. He had also worked as an account supervisor for the Burger King account in another large advertising agency.

[22]Gross rating points are calculated by multiplying the percentage of the target households an advertiser expects to reach (e.g., 55 percent reach) by the number of times the ads will be exposed (e.g., 40 exposures). That is to say, $55 \times 40 = 2,200$.

the program an 18-month test run. "Deciding to go ahead with the Network TV program was one thing, but convincing franchise owners to contribute an extra two percent of store sales was another story," said one district sales manager. "To most franchise owners, this increase meant an out-of-pocket expense of over $5,000 a year. That's asking a lot."

The company, therefore, employed several "hard sell" techniques in order to accumulate the necessary funds. Among other things, the company prepared a 45-minute multimedia presentation on the benefits of the new program, handed out an 11-page booklet containing 22 questions and answers regarding Network TV, and arranged for company executives to visit skeptical franchise owners who hadn't signed up for the program. After 1 year of these and other efforts and the constant urging of district sales managers (DSMs), almost 80 percent of the franchise owners signed an agreement to contribute an extra 2 percent for Network TV.

The first flight of commercials was shown in the fall of 1978. The commercials were targeted toward women takeout buyers between the ages of 18 and 49. After extensive consumer research, Ally and Gargano produced three 30-second commercials carrying one major theme—"It's Worth the Trip." The ads sought to persuade customers to make a special trip to a Dunkin' Donuts shop because its freshly made and handcrafted doughnuts were superior to those sold by supermarkets and other retail stores. (See Exhibit 7 for the storyboards of the two most frequently shown TV ads.)

EXHIBIT 6

	Spot TV (million $)	Network TV (million $)	Total TV Advertising (million $)
McDonald's	$47.7	$32.3	$80.0
Kentucky Fried Chicken	17.8	14.0	31.8
Burger King	4.5	17.4	21.9
Pizza Hut	2.5	5.0	7.5

Source: Company records.

EXHIBIT 7
"KIDS"

"KIDS"

LENGTH: 30 SECONDS   COMM'L NO.: QDBF 7301

(MUSIC THROUGHOUT)

ANNCR: (VO) You could save yourself a little extra time

by buying donuts in the supermarket, | and you could save yourself a little extra trouble | by buying donuts at the first place you see.

But if this isn't worth driving a couple of extra blocks for, | what is? | SINGERS: DUNKIN' DONUTS. IT'S WORTH THE TRIP.

EXHIBIT 7 *Continued*
"WHAT YOU GET"

"WHAT YOU GET"

LENGTH: 30 SECONDS   COMM'L NO.: QDBF 7303

(MUSIC UNDER THROUGHOUT)
SPOKESMAN: (VO) The donuts you find
in a supermarket

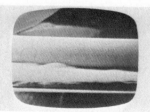

are usually made by machine.

At Dunkin' Donuts, we make ours by
hand.

In the store you have 5 or 6 varieties to
choose from.

We give you 52.

In the supermarket, you don't really
know

how old the donuts are.

We make donuts night and day. Why do
we do all this?

Because it's easier for you to buy
donuts in the supermarket

than to make a special stop at Dunkin'
Donuts.

So we make it worth the trip.

(MUSIC OUT)

The commercials went on the air for 6 weeks in the fall of 1978 and for another 4 weeks in April 1979. The agency also booked the third flight of commercials during the fourth quarter of 1979. During the first two flights, "It's Worth the Trip" ads appeared on (a) prime-time shows, including "Happy Days," "Incredible Hulk," "Dallas," "Soap," "Hawaii Five-0," "What's Happening," "Laverne and Shirley," and weekend movie shows; (b) late-night shows, including "Saturday Night Live" and "The Tonight Show"; and (c) about 15 morning and daytime shows.

Interim Results

All indications pointed to a successful start of the Network TV program. DSMs reported a remarkable improvement in the morale of franchise owners, as well as the morale of store employees. "The ads offered something to talk about— among themselves and with their customers," said one DSM. "I'm sure there was also a sense of prestige attached to being a sponsor of the top-rated TV programs in the country," he added. There were reports that some stores went as far as displaying the media schedule at the counter or hanging an autographed picture of TV star Johnny Carson[23] on the wall.

The advertisements and media program developed by the ad agency also produced positive preliminary results. In several day-after recall tests, Dunkin' Donuts advertisements scored at above-average levels in awareness and content recognition. Recent Nielsen ratings[24] also showed that the combined ratings of the programs selected for Dunkin' Donuts surpassed the original projection.

---

[23]All shops received an enlarged photo of Johnny Carson with the handwritten words "To My Friends at Dunkin' Donuts" on it in early September 1978. (See Exhibit 8.)

[24]By using an audimeter, which is an electronic device attached to the television sets of cooperating households, A. C. Nielsen Company estimates the percentage (and number) of all TV households viewing a given TV show at a particular time. Nielsen ratings refer to the percentages.

The most gratifying feedback thus far had been the sharp increases in average weekly sales since the ads were first shown in the fourth quarter of 1978. Compared with sales of the previous year, average weekly sales increased by approximately 10 percent for the three quarters combined (i.e., fourth quarter of 1978 and first two quarters of 1979). "Of course, not all sales increases are due strictly to advertising," said Elliot Karlin. "But I don't know what else to blame."

Future Plans

Encouraged by these interim results, the company decided to extend its Network TV program into the 1980s. The basic program would remain the same, except that "Network TV '80" would be in effect for 3 years instead of 18 months. When the program was officially announced in May 1979, one optimistic executive predicted that "franchise owners will be beating down our doors to renew their ad agreements."

By July 1979, however, many franchise owners had not signed up for Network TV '80. "I'm somewhat disappointed," admitted Elliot Karlin. "The second time around, we expected a higher renewal rate. We thought the results of the past three quarters would speak for themselves. The franchise owners know that they'll be breaking even with only a four percent increase in average weekly sales."[25]

Field reports from DSMs revealed that the franchise owners were less concerned with the profit issues of the new program than with issues relating to fairness and equity. Listed below are some of the criticisms voiced by franchise owners:

> Why should I be paying $6,000 a year when three guys in our district are taking a free ride? They get as much from the program as myself without paying a penny for it. Next time around, it's either 100 percent participation or no participation at all.

---

[25]See Exhibit 9 for a hypothetical economic calculation sent to all franchise owners in the fall of 1978.

EXHIBIT 8

EXHIBIT 9
"NETWORK TV" ECONOMICS

	Percentage of sales increase							
	2%		4%		6%		8%	
	$	%	$	%	$	%	$	%
Average weekly sales	5,000	.0	5,200	.0	5,300	.0	5,400	.0
Total annual sales	260,000	100	270,400	100	275,600	100	280,800	100
Food cost	75,400	29.0	78,416	29.0	79,924	29.0	81,432	29.0
Payroll	62,400	24.0	62,400	23.1	62,400	22.6	62,400	22.2
Supplies	10,400	4.0	10,816	4.0	11,024	4.0	11,232	4.0
Franchise fee	12,740	4.9	13,250	4.9	13,504	4.9	13,759	4.9
Advertising fee	5,200	2.0	10,816	4.0	11,024	4.0	11,232	4.0
Percentage rent	6,650	2.6	7,378	2.7	7,742	2.8	8,106	2.9
Cost of sales	172,790	66.5	183,076	67.7	185,618	67.4	188,161	67.0
Gross profit	87,210	33.5	87,324	32.3	89,982	32.6	92,639	33.0
Operating expenses	64,370	24.8	64,370	23.8	64,370	23.4	64,370	22.9
Net operating profit	22,840	8.7	22,954*	8.5	25,612	9.3	28,269	10.1

*If sales increased 4 percent, then a store would have approximately the same net operating profit, even if the advertising fee increased from 2 to 4 percent.

And you can bet on my being the last one in the district to sign up.

It's not fair for my shop to be paying the same percentage of sales as another shop in downtown Boston. My customers here on Cape Cod don't watch as much TV. And even if they wanted to, it's hard getting a good reception on all the channels.

Do you know what these institutional ads are going to do? They're going to make the company really known to millions of people. And sure enough, some of these people are going to be interested in opening a Dunkin' Donuts franchise. That's why I think the company should pay more to this program than it has in the past.[26] After all, the company probably gets more out of the program than we do.

District sales managers were also confronted with numerous suggestions on how the program should be modified. One franchise owner sug-

gested an "equitable" program in which non-participants of Network TV '80 would not be allowed to take part in local sales promotion programs.[27] Another franchise owner suggested a "no-fault" program in which franchise owners whose shop sales did not increase beyond the break-even point would be reimbursed by the company. A third franchise owner suggested a "differential" program in which certain markets would pay a higher or lower percentage of sales than others. Other franchise owners suggested an "annual" program in which they would have the option of renewing the contract each year instead of committing themselves over a 3-year period.

"I'm not certain whether these criticisms and suggestions are serious allegations or whether they are part of the normal belly-aching that goes on," said Elliot. "But what I do know for certain is that the new program will not fly unless

[26]Besides the 2 percent that each company-owned store contributed, Dunkin' Donuts contributed $150,000 for the production of the ads used in Network TV and $15,000 for every 1 percent beyond the 70 percent sign-up rate.

[27]Prior to Network TV, sales promotion accounted for about one-fourth of the entire promotional budget. In 1979, sales promotion was estimated to account for one-eighth of the year's promotional budget of $8 million.

80 percent of the franchise owners are signed up by our deadline on September 30."

Elliot Karlin asked his secretary to order 50 copies of the newly produced "Competition" ad and to send them to all 46 DSMs in the country via Federal Express.[28] "If this isn't going to accelerate the sign-up rate, I don't know what will," he said. The deadline was less than 3 months away.

Environmental Changes

Tom Schwarz came to work on Monday, July 16, with three newspaper clippings he had collected over the weekend. The first article, entitled "Gas at $1.00: Squeeze on Retailers," predicted a slowdown of fast-food sales as a result of escalating gasoline prices. The second article, entitled "The Real Estate Spiral and Small Business," described how spiraling costs of developing real estate constrained "mom-and-pop" operators from starting their own businesses. The third article, entitled "Children, Advertising and Nutrition," argued that advertising of presweetened foods (cereals in particular) should be banned from television.

He ordered copies of these articles to be distributed to Bob Rosenberg and all the senior vice presidents. The attached memo read: "Is our growth strategy still viable given these environmental changes?"

---

[28]The new ad featured children walking past Dunkin' Donuts's competitors and finally eating doughnuts from a Dunkin' Donuts shop.

21 *Amicon Corporation*

Noel Capon

"It's five and a half years since we were awarded a patent on our blood filtration technology, and so far we don't have a dollar to show for it. We must decide on the best way to generate revenue from our invention or the patent will expire and our research and development effort will have been wasted," said Mr. Norman Jacobs, president of Amicon Corporation, to a meeting of the senior management committee in January 1978.

The United States Patent Office had granted Amicon a patent in December 1972 on a new and superior method of separating blood plasma from whole blood. The patent claims had recently been confirmed in a 2-year laboratory study conducted by the American National Red Cross,[1] the largest single blood collection organization in the United States. However, Mr. Jacobs

Noel Capon is an associate professor at the Columbia University Graduate School of Business.
[1]The American National Red Cross is a federally chartered nonprofit organization.

was unsure how to turn ownership of the patent into profit for Amicon over the remaining 11½-year life of the patent. He thought that Amicon might produce and market products itself, possibly find a joint-venture partner, or maybe even grant licenses to other manufacturers.

The Company

Amicon was founded in 1962 by Dr. Alan S. Michaels, a professor of chemical engineering at Massachusetts Institute of Technology, and some of his former students. In 1971, Norman A. Jacobs, who was administrative vice president, treasurer, and one of the founders, was appointed president when Dr. Michaels left.

Originally Amicon concentrated on performing contract research for industrial clients in the areas of chemical separation, surface chemistry, and polymer chemistry. The arrangements with clients were typically on a joint-venture basis rather than on a cost-plus-fee basis, so that Amicon retained an ownership interest in the technology which it developed. Resulting products (or processes) outside the client's field of interest could then be manufactured (or employed) by Amicon or licensed to other companies.

In 1977 Amicon's profits exceeded $500,000, on sales of over $11 million. Over the past 2 years sales growth had averaged 22 percent per annum, and Mr. Jacobs confidently expected revenues to reach $20 million by 1980. Income statements and a balance sheet for the years 1974–1977 are shown in Exhibits 1 and 2.

Amicon's sales and profits were derived from three basic businesses—polymer products, scientific systems, and research services and licensing. The Polymer Products Division produced a range of epoxy adhesives and electrical insulating compounds and sold them to the automotive and electronics markets. By 1977 its sales of $4.2 million were 38 percent of corporate sales and accounted for 39 percent of corporate profits. The Scientific Systems Division pro-

duced a range of membrane filters and associated equipment and sold them to medical research laboratories. By 1977 its sales of $6.7 million were 59 percent of corporate sales and accounted for 64 percent of corporate profits. Revenues from research services and licensing were only 3 percent of corporate sales and represented a 3 percent operating loss in 1977. The sales and profit history of the business segments for 1973–1977 are shown in Exhibit 3.

Mr. Jacobs said that whereas in Amicon's early years there had been an emphasis on developing and licensing technology, growth in recent years had come almost entirely from products which Amicon manufactured and sold. While much of the growth had resulted from Amicon's own research, in the past 3 years Amicon had acquired a small line of related epoxy products, technology for additional membrane filters, and distribution rights in the United States and Japan for a line of British laboratory products. The company was increasingly active in foreign markets, and by late 1977, over one-third of Amicon's sales were made outside the continental United States.

EXHIBIT 1
INCOME STATEMENTS
Thousands of dollars

	1977	1976	1975	1974
Income:				
Sales	11,232	8,873	7,435	7,141
Expenses:				
Cost of goods sold	4,891	3,688	3,138	3,021
General sales, and administrative	4,621	3,651	3,085	2,841
Research and development expense	647	592	574	570
Interest expense	115	107	113	94
Currency loss (gain)	33	(42)	19	(13)
Total	10,307	7,996	6,929	6,513
Net income before taxes	925	877	506	628
Provision for taxation	352	395	222	234
Net income	573	482	284	393*

*In 1974 and 1975, Amicon recorded losses from discontinued operations to bring its net income to $122,000 and $365,000, respectively, in those years.

EXHIBIT 2
BALANCE SHEETS
Thousands of dollars

	1977	1976	1975	1974
Current assets:				
Cash	454	413	362	77
Accounts receivable	1,949	1,440	1,335	1,185
Inventories	1,702	1,533	1,263	1,360
Prepaid expenses and deposits	229	163	155	118
Deferred taxes	–	–	90	–
Net assets from discontinued operations	–	–	23	208
Total current assets	4,334	3,549	3,228	2,948
Fixed assets:				
Land	161	161	142	142
Buildings, machinery, and fixtures	2,976	2,476	2,286	2,128
	3,137	2,637	2,428	2,270
Less accumulated depreciation	(1,259)	(1,054)	(869)	(686)
	1,878	1,583	1,558	1,584
Investment in affiliates	511	540	360	333
Deferred preoperating costs	23	–	–	–
	6,746	5,672	5,146	4,867
Current liabilities:				
Notes payable and current installment on long-term debt	119	38	31	996
Accounts payable	692	441	366	480
Income taxes	235	137	73	41
Accrued expenses and other liabilities	591	468	461	317
Total current liabilities	1,637	1,084	931	1,834
Long-term debt	1,652	1,606	1,687	620
Deferred income taxes	34	36	95	106
Stockholders' equity				
Common stock outstanding	188	187	187	187
Additional paid-in capital	1,102	1,088	1,088	1,085
Retained earnings	2,128	1,611	1,157	1,036
Total stockholders' equity	3,418	2,886	2,433	2,308
	6,746	5,672	5,146	4,867

Background to Blood Filtration

Amicon was involved in two quite different types of blood filtration applications, the separation of blood plasma from whole blood and the removal of toxic molecules from blood. Both of these applications had been developed as an outgrowth of research on ultrafiltration membranes, the main business of Amicon's Scientific Systems Division.

EXHIBIT 3
PERCENTAGE OF CORPORATE SALES AND OPERATING PROFITS BY BUSINESS SEGMENT, 1973–1977

	1977		1976		1975		1974		1973	
	Sales	Operating profit	Sales	Operating profit	Sales	Operating profit	Sales	Operating profit	Sales	Operating profit
Scientific Systems Division	59	64	61	66	62	73	58	70	60	72
Polymer Products Division	38	39	36	33	31	17	35	20	32	16
Research services and royalty income	3	(3)	3	1	7	10	7	10	8	12

The products which the Scientific Systems Division sold were of two basic types: disposable membrane filters, which were essentially thin plastic films with pores, and the laboratory equipment in which the membranes were placed. The filters had been developed by Amicon in the mid-1960s as a result of contract research financed in part by Dorr-Oliver Corporation. Named ultrafiltration membranes, for the first time they enabled molecules of size 10–150 angstroms[2] to be filtered successfully. Thus, for instance, water and salt molecules, whose size was less than 10 angstroms, could pass through an ultrafiltration membrane, but viruses, enzymes, and protein molecules which were over 10 angstroms in size could not.

The use of ultrafiltration membranes fulfilled two functions. First, a solution containing extraneous large molecules could be cleansed of these impurities; second, protein and other biological molecules could be obtained in a more concentrated form.

Amicon's agreement with Dorr-Oliver specified that Dorr-Oliver could use the new technology to manufacture products for industrial applications, whereas Amicon was free to manufacture products and sell them to the research laboratory market. Each firm paid the other royalties on the basis of 5 percent of membrane sales, but not on sales of the associated equipment which each of them made.

Amicon sold its ultrafiltration products to the life science and medical research laboratories of universities, hospitals, and pharmaceutical companies for a variety of research applications. Sales were made to approximately 3,000 accounts[3] in the United States by a 10-person sales force, backed by a small internal marketing and technical service staff. In addition, Amicon employed resident salespeople in several countries and sold through distributors in others. Mr. Jacobs estimated that Amicon's sales accounted for over 75 percent of the world market for ultrafiltration membranes and associated laboratory equipment in research laboratories. Amicon manufactured all its ultrafiltration membranes. Historically, equipment parts had been manufactured for the most part by outside suppliers to Amicon specifications and assembled in Amicon's shops. In recent years, however, Amicon had become more involved in machine-part production, and currently almost 50 percent of parts were manufactured in house.

---

[2]An angstrom is a unit of length. One angstrom is equivalent to 0.00000001 cm, or 10^{-8} cm.

[3]Orders for supplies and small pieces often came in by telephone and mail as well as through paid sales representatives.

In the late 1960s, Amicon's management became dissatisfied with Dorr-Oliver's progress in developing industrial applications for ultrafiltration membranes and initiated a renegotiation of the license agreement. Under the new agreement both Amicon and Dorr-Oliver were free to address any market which they chose, each agreeing to pay the other a 5 percent royalty on sales. In 1969 Amicon established a new group to design, develop, manufacture, and sell industrial ultrafiltration equipment. However, after 3 years of modest sales and heavy start-up losses, management decided that the company could not support this program on its own. In 1972, a joint venture with Rohm & Haas, called Romicon, was formed in which Amicon held an equity interest of slightly under 20 percent. In forming Romicon, Amicon provided its patents, production knowhow, plant, inventory, and key personnel, while Rohm & Haas supplied the start-up capital. Romicon, which had its own plant and administrative offices, sold ultrafiltration membranes and associated equipment for industrial applications through a small sales force to customers in the United States and Europe. Mr. Jacobs said that industrial applications had been more difficult to develop than had been anticipated but that good progress had been made in three specific applications: paint recovery in the electrocoat paint process widely used in the manufacture of such products as automobiles and appliances, protein extraction for cheese waste, and water purification. Sales had just reached the $2 million level, and although Romicon had not made a profit, Mr. Jacobs said it had approached a break-even level. He anticipated that 1978 would be a profitable year overall.

Blood Filtration for Toxin Removal

A recent technical breakthrough by Amicon was in the removal of toxins from blood, a function performed in the human body by the kidneys.

The artificial-kidney field was one of the fastest-growing areas of medicine in the United States, Western Europe, and Japan. Mr. Jacobs believed that for certain patients Amicon's system was superior to existing artificial-kidney systems.

Existing artificial kidneys worked by dialysis, in which the patient's blood flowed in a continuous manner on one side of the membrane and a wash fluid flowed on the other side. During the process, toxins in the blood traveled through the membrane and were carried away in the wash fluid, while the cleansed blood was returned to the patient. Although thrice-weekly artificial-kidney treatments were sustaining 100,000 patients worldwide[4] the treatment did not fully duplicate the natural kidney function and had undesirable side effects for most patients.

Amicon's breakthrough was the development of ultrafiltration membranes to filter blood in a manner similar to the operation of the human kidney. When blood flowed over an ultrafiltration membrane surface, toxins passed through the membrane, while the blood, cleansed of the toxins, was retained and could be returned to the patient. The Amicon system provided a simple method of removing excess fluid from the patient, as well as reducing the incidence of the side effects of hypertension and buildup of fat molecules for certain patients.

In 1978, the use of Amicon's ultrafiltration membranes for blood cleansing was being tested clinically to generate data on the safety and efficacy of the process for submission to the Food and Drug Administration (FDA). FDA approval was required before the Amicon device could be manufactured in the United States and sold commercially here or abroad. However, interest from Western Europe, particularly Germany, had been so enthusiastic that Amicon was building a plant in Ireland to serve the European market. Initial sales efforts were planned for European countries where Amicon presently

---

[4]Of approximately 20 centers using the Amicon process which were sustaining a total of 75 patients without normal kidney function, 85 percent were located in Europe and 15 percent in the United States.

had subsidiaries. Sales would be made direct to hospitals and kidney treatment centers by newly trained salespeople specializing in sales of artificial-kidney systems.

Separation of Blood Plasma from Whole Blood

Amicon's development of filtration technology for separating blood plasma from whole blood was a direct result of solving an existing problem in ultrafiltration—the buildup of a filter cake on the membrane surface, which reduced membrane efficiency by reducing the flow rate through the membrane. Amicon had developed a method for flowing the solution to be filtered through thin channels in a direction parallel to the membrane to ensure continuous circulation on the membrane surface. Having developed the parallel-flow technique in ultrafiltration, Amicon scientists investigated the possibility of employing the same technique elsewhere. In particular, they investigated *microfiltration*,[5] for molecules in the size range 4,000–6,000 angstroms. When whole blood was filtered by the Amicon process over a microfiltration membrane, blood plasma was successfully separated from whole blood. Blood plasma, which consists of water, a variety of salts, and many types of protein, passed through the membrane, while the blood cells (red and white) flowed on. Previous to the application of Amicon's parallel-flow technique it had been impossible to separate blood plasma from whole blood by a filtration process without rupturing the blood cells, which then contaminated the blood plasma.

On the basis of its discovery, Amicon applied for a patent on a new apparatus and process for the separation of blood plasma from whole blood, and in December 1972, the U.S. Patent

Office granted patent number 3,705,100, which protected Amicon's discovery. Amicon was subsequently granted patents on the invention in Canada, Japan, France, West Germany, and the United Kingdom.

A key advantage of the Amicon filtration system over existing technology was the continuous nature of the filtration process. The existing method for obtaining blood plasma involved a number of complex stages. First, whole blood was collected from the patient or donor. Second, the whole blood was placed in a centrifuge and spun at moderate velocity to effect a separation of blood plasma from the blood cells. Third, the blood plasma was removed from the separation vessel, and fourth, in certain applications, the blood cells were returned to the patient or donor. Use of the Amicon filtration system permitted whole blood to be withdrawn from the patient or donor and filtered to remove blood plasma and the blood cells to be returned in one continuous operation.

Because of a long history of unsuccessful attempts to separate blood plasma from whole blood using microfiltration membranes and conventional filtration processes, suppliers of products to the blood-plasma collection industry, and some government funding agencies, had expressed skepticism over the practical value of Amicon's process. However, as the result of a study funded by the National Institutes of Health (NIH),[6] researchers at the American National Red Cross had concluded that Amicon's process claims were fully justified. Further, Red Cross technical staff personnel were actively promoting the concept of blood-plasma collection by filtration.

The Red Cross had subcontracted a portion of this study to Amicon, and as a result of Amicon's work, two new patent applications, generally known as improvement inventions, had been filed in early 1978. One, coauthored by Red Cross and Amicon personnel, specified

---

[5]Although the production of ultrafiltration membranes was limited to Amicon, Dorr-Oliver, and Romicon, since the original patents were still in force, the production of microfiltration membranes was not controlled by patents, and they were available from many suppliers.

[6]A division of the U.S. Department of Health, Education, and Welfare (HEW).

the exact conditions under which a commercial-size plasma separation system would have to operate; the second, authored solely by Amicon personnel, specified a particular filter design which would allow blood plasma separation in commercial quantities. Should these two patent applications be granted, however, the patents would be owned by NIH, since it had funded the study which gave rise to them.[7] For an optimum commercial system to be manufactured and used, however, all three patents (including Amicon's patent number 3,705,100) would probably be required.

Mr. Jacobs said that there were four major applications for which the separation of blood plasma from whole blood might offer considerable benefits: three human applications—blood plasma collection, blood plasma analysis, and blood plasma therapy—and animal blood plasma collection. Of these applications, human blood plasma collection offered the greatest immediate potential.

Human Blood Plasma Collection[8]

In 1978 the United States led in the production and distribution of blood plasma fractions, a series of natural drug products which were obtained by secondary processing of human blood plasma.[9] Sales of blood plasma fractions by United States organizations in 1977 were estimated at $240 million and were 96 percent of total world volume. Approximately 20 percent of this amount was exported. United States market leadership had resulted from a number of factors: technological leadership, more liberal laws relating to blood than in some other countries,[10] and a general inability of other countries to meet local needs because of the high growth in demand for blood plasma fractions. For example, Japan imported over 40 percent of its plasma needs in 1977. Because of the growth of demand abroad, several United States plasma processors had been acquired by Japanese, German, and French companies.[11]

While the centrifuge process was the sole method by which blood plasma was separated from whole blood, two distinct plasma collection systems existed.

In one system whole blood was obtained from *unpaid donors*. Typically donors gave one-half liter of blood in a 30-minute session, a maximum of once per month. Donated blood was either distributed to hospitals for blood transfusions or sent to contract processors who separated off the blood plasma and then extracted the blood plasma fractions. From ½ liter of whole blood, slightly over 300 milliliters of blood plasma could be obtained. Typically the blood collection agency distributed the blood plasma fractions along with the whole blood for blood transfusions.

Blood collection and distribution were dominated by the American National Red Cross, which accounted for over 50 percent of volun-

---

[7]For many years the United States government had granted no-fee, nonexclusive licenses to anyone interested in operating within the claims of one of its patents. Thus, government-owned patents essentially had the status of scientific publications. However, more recently HEW had begun to release patent rights to nonprofit organizations such as the American National Red Cross and to encourage such organizations to collect fees for licenses to use such patents. HEW had not yet decided whether it would release the two improvement inventions on blood separation technology if the patent applications were granted.

[8]Much of the data for this section was obtained from an article in *Business Week*, Sept. 11, 1978.

[9]Any particular blood plasma fraction consists of a defined molecular weight range of protein molecules.

[10]For example, the separation of blood plasma from whole blood was banned in Italy; in Japan payment for blood was not allowed, and French law forbade profiting from the sale and processing of human blood.

[11]There were significant advantages to using blood plasma fractions rather than whole blood if the patient's condition allowed its use. First, blood plasma, unlike whole blood, was not "typed" and thus a matching of donor to recipient was not required. Second, blood plasma could be stored for up to 2 years after collection, whereas whole blood had only a 30-day shelf life.

tary blood donations.[12] Hospitals and independent blood collection agencies accounted for the remainder. The Red Cross had a network of 57 regional blood centers and almost 4 million donors. Industry observers estimated that over 50 percent of the whole blood collected by the Red Cross was sent to contract processors for blood plasma fraction production. The Red Cross was reported to have paid contract processors $9.1 million for blood plasma fractions in 1977, which it then sold for $29.4 million.

In the second system whole blood was obtained from paid donors for the specific purpose of producing blood plasma. As with the former system, ½ liter of blood, the maximum allowable under federal law, was withdrawn from the donor. However, in this system the blood was immediately centrifuged, and the blood cells were reintroduced to the donor. The effect of this procedure was to allow a second ½ liter of blood, which in turn was immediately centrifuged for blood cell reintroductions, to be collected in the same session. Thus, in a single 2-hour session approximately 625 milliliters of blood plasma could be obtained. An additional feature of the blood cell reintroduction procedure was that a donor, who was typically paid $7 to $10, could give blood plasma up to twice per week.

Blood plasma was obtained from donors in 500 to 600 commercial blood plasma collection centers nationwide, mostly located near universities or in the low-income areas of urban centers. A typical center collected 10,000 liters of blood plasma annually, the range being 3,000 to 20,000 liters. Independent commercial centers sold blood plasma either under long-term contract for between $47 to $50 per liter or in the spot market at between $50 and $55 per liter. Approximately 65 percent of the commercial centers were independent operations; 20 per-

cent were owned and operated by Maynard-Smith Inc., and 10 percent by Jackson Industries.[13]

Both Maynard-Smith and Jackson Industries were involved in other aspects of the blood collection and processing industry. Maynard-Smith produced disposable blood collection kits consisting of catheters, tubing, storage vessels, and anticlotting chemicals, most of which were supplied to its own plasma collection centers. It also processed blood plasma into blood plasma fractions. Maynard-Smith had recently been acquired by a large European pharmaceutical company.

Jackson Industries, a billion dollar company, also produced disposable blood collection kits; it was estimated to have a 90 percent share of the sales of kits to the independent plasma collection centers, the Red Cross, and other centers which collected just whole blood. Jackson Industries was also a major processor of blood plasma into plasma fractions and accounted for 25 percent of United States fractionating capacity. It was the major customer of the independent plasma collection centers for blood plasma and the major contract processor for the Red Cross and other voluntary blood collection organizations.

A furor had erupted in the industry in early 1978 with the announcement that Jackson Industries and the American National Red Cross planned to build a 1-million-liter blood plasma fractionating plant in a $40 million to $50 million joint venture. Such a plant would account for about 20 percent of industry fractionating capacity. By controlling the fractionating of its own blood, the Red Cross believed that it could achieve better quality control and reduce the $18-per-liter fractionating price by $5 per liter. However, independent companies in the industry had charged that the American National Red Cross was trying to drive them out of business, and the joint-venture proposal was under review by the Justice Department at the request of the Red Cross.

[12]Nearly half of the Red Cross's 1977 revenues of $350 million was accounted for by blood-related activities. For its non-blood-related activities the Red Cross was the leading beneficiary of United Way funds, receiving a total of $126 million in 1977.

[13]Fictitious names.

The Amicon Process

Mr. Jacobs believed that the Amicon filtration process offered considerable benefits to both the voluntary blood collection agencies and the commercial plasma collection centers.

The critical feature of the Amicon process was its continuous nature. It would permit blood plasma to be collected directly from a donor, while the blood cells were simultaneously reintroduced to the donor. In this manner 625 milliliters of blood plasma could be collected in a 30- to 45-minute session, and a donor could give plasma up to twice a week.

To the voluntary agencies the Amicon process opened up the possibility of direct blood plasma collection. Such collection had not previously been possible, since the voluntary agencies felt they could not expect a volunteer donor to spend the 2 hours required by the centrifuge technique.

To the commercial plasma collection center the key advantage was the elimination of any possibility of the donor receiving someone else's blood cells. Despite careful checks in the present system, there was always the possibility of a slip-up which could have disastrous consequences for the donor. Second, the time saving inherent in the continuous process would significantly increase the capacity of a blood collection center and greatly reduce donor inconvenience.

On the other hand, the cost to the collection centers of disposable items would increase from $12 to $20 per application.[14] The difference would be partially offset by a $2 to $3 labor cost savings. In addition, centers would also have to purchase electronic control systems (one per bed) to monitor blood flow rates. Mr. Jacobs thought, however, that the cost of these systems would be equivalent to that required for centrifuges, which would no longer be required.

---

[14]The $8 increase was a net figure. A disposable filtration device, consisting of a specially designed microfiltration unit embedded in a plastic casing, would be required. However, some of the other disposable items (catheters, tubing, storage vessels, anticlotting chemicals) would no longer be needed.

The overall attractiveness of increased safety and shorter plasma collection times versus higher total costs for disposables was subject to much debate. Some industry representatives had told Mr. Jacobs that plasma collection centers would willingly pay the higher cost to eliminate the risk of returning the wrong cells to a donor and to attract more donors by shortening the time required. Others said that the centers' low profit margins would severely restrict the number which could pay the added cost of the new system.

Mr. Jacobs estimated, however, that if all commercial collection centers in the United States adopted the Amicon process, there would be an annual requirement for 4 million filtration units (the microfiltration membranes embedded in plastic casings). Further, should the American National Red Cross and the other voluntary organizations switch a significant proportion of their whole-blood collection programs to blood plasma collection, there would be a considerably increased demand there for filtration units. However, before the Amicon process could be used commercially in the United States, FDA approval would be needed. No such impediment existed for sales to overseas markets, provided that the filtration units were manufactured abroad. Mr. Jacobs believed that demand from overseas could be substantial.

Mr. Jacob's belief that considerable sales potential existed had been confirmed in a recent confidential study issued by a California-based investment company. The author had estimated that in 1983, 1.8 million filtration units could be sold worldwide, approximately 50 percent in the United States and 50 percent in Europe.

Human Blood Plasma Analysis and Therapy

Two additional human applications for the Amicon process were blood plasma analysis and blood plasma therapy. Many blood analyses were more efficiently carried out on blood plasma than on whole blood. Under the present system, samples of blood were drawn from a patient in a hospital or doctor's office and subsequently centrifuged in a laboratory to obtain blood plasma. Mr. Jacobs believed that the small quantities of plasma required for analytic purposes could be obtained more simply by using the Amicon filtration technique.

Although he was unsure of the potential demand for filtration units in the analytic market, Mr. Jacobs believed that it might be substantial because of the advantages of the continuous system. This was especially true for automated blood analyses, where the centrifuge stage represented the only discontinuous step in an otherwise continuous operation. He believed that hospitals represented the most likely customer group, but he did not rule out the possibility of sales to physicians, particularly group practices or clinics where patient throughput was high. FDA approval would also be required for this application, but diagnostic devices required significantly less testing than medical devices.

Many blood disorders required the hospital treatment or replacement of blood plasma. The current therapeutic process called for the collection of whole blood and the separation of blood plasma from blood cells by centrifuge. Then, either the patient's plasma was treated by exposure to enzymes or other active chemicals, recombined with the blood cells, and reintroduced to the patient, or the patient's own plasma was discarded and his or her blood cells combined with donor-supplied plasma and then reintroduced to the body. The Amicon separation technique would permit the whole process, regardless of whether the plasma was treated or discarded, to be performed continuously and would considerably reduce both the treatment time and patient trauma associated with the current therapeutic process. Amicon was currently working with one doctor who was very excited about the potential of its process. However, Mr. Jacobs said that commercial development was many years away, since much more research was necessary and, again, FDA approval would be required. He was unable to put a

figure on the potential market size but thought that it, as well as the size of the analytic market, might be considerable. He anticipated that hospitals would represent the major customer group.

Animal Blood Plasma Collection

A final application for Amicon's blood plasma separation process had recently been identified by Dr. Solomon, Amicon's director of research. An industry had developed for the production of antibodies for use in medical research and diagnostic tests. These antibodies were grown in specially kept sheep, pigs, and goats, housed in farms devoted entirely to antibody production. The antibodies grew in the animal's blood plasma, and periodically the animals were bled and the blood plasma obtained by a centrifuge technique, similar in concept to that used for human donors. It appeared that Amicon's process, which allowed for continuous plasma collection and blood cell reintroduction, could offer considerable benefits to farm owners. Although a prototype product for animal blood plasma separation had not yet been developed, Dr. Solomon said that he was being besieged by telephone calls from farm owners willing to pay very high prices for a working system. In contrast to the human blood plasma collection application, there was a possibility that filtration devices could be sold in the United States without FDA approval.

Alternative Courses of Action for Amicon

With each of the four fields of use presenting important opportunities for Amicon, Mr. Jacobs had to determine which seemed most promising for purposes of directing Amicon's market development effort. Direct entry, licensing, and joint ventures were all possibilities. Even within these options there were further choices to be made.

Human Blood Plasma Collection

Mr. Jacobs said that the large potential market for human blood plasma, together with the anticipated growth, made direct entry, which would include manufacturing and selling the filtration units, a tempting proposition. Since Amicon would be protected by its patents for another 11 years, it could, by 1989, build up a dominant position. On the other hand, he was concerned about the resource commitment entailed. Amicon would have to perform the engineering development work necessary to turn its prototype filtration units into commercial products. Second, it would have to set up a production line to manufacture high-volume, low-cost plastic parts.[15] Further, outside plastics engineers would be required to design the molds, since Amicon did not have the expertise in house.

Mr. Jacobs said that Amicon would probably purchase the microfiltration membranes from an outside supplier but would have to set up two assembly operations: one to construct filtration units from the membranes and plastic parts, and a second to connect the filtration units to the auxiliary plastic tubing sets to produce blood plasma collection kits. The tubing and other components would be purchased from outside suppliers. A clean-room manufacturing facility would have to be constructed to create the dust- and bacteria-free environment required for the molding of parts, as well as the assembly and packaging of medical devices. A sterilization system would also be required. He estimated the total capital cost at $1 million to $2 million, although a small-scale operation might be put in place for only $500,000.

Finally, Amicon would have to develop a sales force to visit blood collection centers and a service operation to solve in-use problems and to ensure that the plasma separation was being

[15]Plastic materials used for this purpose would have to meet medical-grade specifications. These materials were particularly difficult to mold.

properly carried out. In particular, a service facility would be required to assure prompt maintenance, repair, and/or replacement of control systems components. The cost to Amicon of having a sales representative or service person in the field was approximately $40,000 per annum, $20,000 for compensation and an additional $20,000 for travel and expenses. Mr. Jacobs estimated that at a minimum five sales representatives, a sales manager, and three service personnel would be required. If Amicon did enter directly, Mr. Jacobs estimated that it could obtain sales revenues of $20 for a blood plasma collection kit, while the direct manufacturing cost would be approximately $10.

Mr. Jacobs was unsure how Maynard-Smith and Jackson would react to Amicon's entry. Since Maynard-Smith produced all the tubing sets and collection vessels for its own blood collection centers, it might be unwilling to purchase the completed kits from Amicon. Further, in dealing with the independent centers and the Red Cross, Amicon would be competing head-to-head with Jackson, which currently supplied the disposable kits to the major portion of the market. An even more critical consideration was that Amicon's direct entry into the plasma collection market would almost certainly stimulate efforts by Maynard-Smith and Jackson to "invent around" the Amicon patent and develop their own filtration device.

A second alternative which Mr. Jacobs was considering was a joint venture, but he was unsure whether Amicon's patent by itself was sufficient for a joint-venture partner to be interested. Further, there was the problem of whom to approach to be a joint-venture partner. Should it be Maynard-Smith, Jackson, or some third party not currently directly involved with blood plasma production? Indeed, since the Red Cross was planning to enter the plasma fractionating business, perhaps it would be interested in becoming a partner in the production of filtration units.

Finally, Mr. Jacobs was considering the possibility of licensing. The major advantage of this approach was that Amicon could receive royalty payments for little additional investment of money or people. However, in 1989, all royalty payments would cease. Further, Amicon would no longer be at the cutting edge of blood plasma separation technology. Licensing presented a number of other serious problems.

The most serious problem revolved around the nature of the rights to be granted by the licensor, Amicon, to a licensee. In particular there was the question of "field of use." While Mr. Jacobs might be interested in making license agreements in the human blood plasma collection application, he might wish to exclude any licensee or licensees in this application from the analytic, therapeutic, and animal blood plasma collection applications. Though simple in principle, in practice it was very difficult to separate fields of use. For instance, if a hospital purchased a filtration device for blood plasma collection, there was nothing to stop it from using this device for therapeutic purposes, too, if it was suitable. Mr. Jacobs thought it might also be very difficult to draft language which clearly delineated applications.

The agreements would also have to avoid carefully the implication that they represented a "carving up" of markets among competitors, which would be a violation of antitrust law. Although the Justice Department had recently acknowledged informally that field-of-use licensing was not automatically an antitrust violation, certain agreements had been challenged on such grounds.

Furthermore, if another competitor produced and sold devices covered by the patent and Amicon filed suit to stop such activity, the infringer would be certain to examine carefully any license agreement, hoping to find a possible antitrust violation which would prevent Amicon from enforcing the patent. There was, however, a possibility that the filtration devices designed for different applications would be sufficiently unique that product specifications could be written into a license agreement, thus, in effect, delineating fields of use.

A second problem was what sort of license to grant. There were four types: exclusive, exclusive but for Amicon, limited exclusive, and nonexclusive. If Amicon granted an exclusive license, just one licensee would enjoy all rights under the patent that currently accrued to Amicon. If a license which was exclusive but for Amicon was granted, the one licensee and Amicon would be the only companies able to enjoy the patent rights. If limited exclusive licenses were granted, Amicon would specify how many companies could enjoy the patent rights at the time the first company signed a license agreement. (It could not subsequently increase the number of licensees beyond that stipulated number.) Finally, if nonexclusive licenses were granted, Amicon could offer licenses to whomever it chose. If Amicon entered into a nonexclusive license arrangement, the value of the agreement to a licensee would, of course, be lower and the price which Amicon could command would be less than if an exclusive license was granted. Further, Mr. Jacobs was not certain whether the protection of exclusivity was required to encourage a potentially strong licensee to make the investment necessary to commercialize the product. On the other hand, by granting more than one license, Amicon might encourage competition and thus hasten market development.

If a license or licenses were granted, Mr. Jacobs would have to decide how to charge for the license and how much to charge. As a rule of thumb he believed that licensors typically received between 10 and 35 percent of the profits that the licensee made during the life of the license. However, if the license fee was set at some percentage of the profit, Mr. Jacobs was concerned that there would be serious accounting problems in determining the true "profit" from which the royalty would be computed. If Maynard-Smith was a licensee, the problem would be doubly complicated, since the price at which the filtration units were sold would be an administered transfer price from one division to another and not a market-determined price. Finally, to the extent that any licensee sold the filtration unit as one part of a blood plasma collection kit, there would be a problem in determining the value of the filtration unit.

Regardless of the basis on which the license fee was determined, there was the question of how high the fee should be set. A high fee might bring in a good return of royalties to Amicon, but too high a fee might discourage companies from taking up a license and might lead them to attempt to develop alternative filtration devices outside the patent. Further, Mr. Jacobs was concerned about whether any licensee would in fact commit sufficient resources to bring products to market under the terms of the license. Therefore, he had to find some way of ensuring that any licensee would move quickly to gain FDA approval and place products on the market so that Amicon could start to receive earned royalty payments. Mr. Jacobs thought that a minimum royalty payment might be the way to solve this problem. If he did institute a minimum royalty payment, Mr. Jacobs would have to decide how much it would be and whether it should be constant or based on an ascending or descending scale.

Mr. Jacobs also had to take into account the possibility of patent infringement or circumvention. Under patent law, if the optimal system involved operation within the patent and the process was used just outside the patent claims in a clear attempt to get around the patent, then it would be deemed an infringement. However, the possibility of a legal infringement was reduced the further outside the claims that the process was operated. While Amicon's scientists had assured Mr. Jacobs that the patent was "watertight" and that operation outside the patent was impossible, he was nevertheless concerned about this issue after learning that one or more companies were already conducting tests similar to Amicon's.

In the light of all these considerations, Mr. Jacobs would have to decide whom to license if he decided to license. The major candidates for a license were Jackson, Maynard-Smith, and a German company, Behrstein.[16] While Mr. Jacobs believed that an exclusive license, which provided a monopoly for the licensee, would be attractive, neither Behrstein nor Maynard-Smith had shown a strong interest in this. Jackson, however, had indicated that it would be interested in an exclusive arrangement.

The major advantage of making an agreement with Jackson was its dominance in the market. It was closely tied to the independent commercial blood collection centers and to the Red Cross. If it decided to push the Amicon filtration process, Mr. Jacobs had little doubt that impressive sales would be forthcoming, although it would take significant sales force and service efforts from Jackson to persuade the independent centers to adopt the invention. If Maynard-Smith took up the license, the adoption of the invention might be extremely fast, since Maynard-Smith owned its own blood collection centers. However, it accounted for only 20 percent of the blood plasma collected directly on an individual basis from paid donors. On the other hand, for years Maynard-Smith had tried to lessen Jackson's hold on the independent centers with very little success, and the new filtration process might enable it to do so.

Behrstein was a major company in the supply of blood collection kits to blood plasma collection centers in Germany, and it saw a license under the Amicon patent as a way of gaining a foothold in the blood plasma business in the United States as well. However, Mr. Jacobs thought it unlikely that Behrstein would achieve significant penetration in the next few years, even if it had exclusive rights under the Amicon patent. Its strength in Germany, however, raised the question in Mr. Jacob's mind as to whether he should put territorial restrictions on licenses.

[16]Fictitious name.

He knew that although Jackson and Maynard-Smith were active in the blood plasma business abroad, other locally based companies might be significantly stronger. He guessed that the potential for Amicon's process in blood plasma collection overseas might be considerable.

Human Blood Plasma Analysis and Therapy

Mr. Jacobs said that he had had extended discussions with representatives of a small Boston company about granting a license to exploit the analytic market. This potential licensee was anxious to sign a patent agreement, and Mr. Jacobs knew from experience that an enthusiastic potential licensee could easily lose interest if negotiations were long and drawn out. Therefore, he knew that he had to make a decision quickly. He was concerned, however, about the implications that granting a license in the analytic market could have on licensing in the blood plasma collection market. His concern was about the issue of division of exclusive rights in a patent, for it was as yet unclear whether different products would be used in the two applications. Further, since the customers for blood plasma analysis devices were largely concentrated in the hospitals which Amicon salespeople now visited, he wondered if perhaps Amicon should undertake to develop this market itself.

Commercial development of the blood plasma therapy market was some years away, but Mr. Jacobs wanted to retain the rights in this field for Amicon. He saw a good fit between this application and the blood filtration application for artificial kidneys which the company was developing. Further, he anticipated that NIH would be willing to fund research and clinical testing in conjunction with outside medical researchers, as it had done in the kidney field.

Mr. Jacobs realized, however, that he should decide now how this market should be approached if the technical development efforts were successful. Otherwise he might foreclose his options with decisions made regarding other applications. He thought that Amicon might wish to enter the market directly, although a joint venture might also be a possibility. He had already been approached by some large drug companies about the possibility of entering into joint-venture arrangements.

Finally, there was the possibility of licensing, which raised the question of whom to license. He considered Jackson as one possibility but thought that one complicating factor regarding other potential licensees was that Jackson's management, apparently aware of the one doctor's research efforts, might wish to include access to the therapeutic application in any license which it negotiated.

Animal Blood Plasma Collection

The identification of the animal application was so recent that Amicon executives had given little thought to how to proceed. Amicon's executives were fairly confident, however, that they could successfully insulate this application from the human applications and that providing for field-of-use restrictions would not be difficult, whichever commercialization route they chose.

U.S. Pioneer Electronics Corporation

22

Hirotaka Takeuchi

Bernie Mitchell, president of U.S. Pioneer Electronics, placed an ad featuring a portrait of William Shakespeare in several trade magazines. The ad was an open letter from William Shakespeare and Bernie Mitchell to several "dissident" dealers who were franchised to sell Japanese-made Pioneer products in the United States. The advertisement, shown in Exhibit 1, alleged that "a few dealers" had resorted to "the practice of disparagement of Pioneer products and 'bait and switch' advertising" and threatened dealer investigations to protect Pioneer's reputation.

Bernie Mitchell hoped that these "unjustifiable practices" were the sporadic misconduct of only "a few unwise" dealers which could be dealt with on a case-by-case basis. But if these practices represented an overall erosion of dealer support for Pioneer products, Mitchell was determined to (a) take immediate steps to

Hirotaka Takeuchi is an assistant professor at the Harvard Graduate School of Business Administration.

prevent further erosion and (b) establish a new long-run distribution strategy that would ensure U.S. Pioneer's continued leadership in the hi-fi industry.

The Hi-Fi Industry

The United States hi-fi industry was started in the 1960s by a few men who, according to industry legend, decided to leave their engineering positions (mostly in the aerospace industry) and pursue their hobby of building amplifiers and speakers in the garages and basements of their homes. The origin of the hi-fi industry is told as follows:

Once upon a time, there was a Mr. Fisher, and a Mr. Marantz and a Mr. Grado and a Mr. Karman and a Mr. Bogan, and together they made a high fidelity component industry. They held audio fairs, and the faithful from near and far flocked in not only to see and hear their amplifiers, loudspeakers,

EXHIBIT 1

AN IMPORTANT MESSAGE FROM WILLIAM SHAKESPEARE AND PIONEER.

The Granger Collection

"Who steals my purse steals trash . . .
But he that filches from me
my good name
Robs me of that which not
enriches him
And makes me poor indeed."

The Immortal Bard said it over three hundred years ago. It's still true today.

It has come to our attention at Pioneer that a few dealers of high fidelity products, acting in what they believe to be their best interest, have taken up the practice of disparagement of Pioneer products and "bait and switch" advertising, often using Pioneer's hard earned reputation in the industry as the "bait."

This tactic hurts Pioneer, hurts the consumer and ultimately hurts all dealers since it will damage the credibility of our high fidelity business in the eyes of consumers. To protect our legitimate dealers, Pioneer will conduct frequent investigations of this practice, and we will take appropriate steps to protect and defend our reputation on behalf of the great majority of our dealers against the unjustifiable practices of an unwise few.

Respectfully,

William Shakespeare, *Stratford-upon-Avon*
Bernie Mitchell, *U.S. Pioneer Electronics*

cartridges and other audio equipment, but to talk to the men themselves. [*Merchandising Week*, Aug. 25, 1969]

In the early days of the industry, retailers[1] had very little choice of products to carry. According to *Merchandising Week*:

> If you were a retailer selling high fidelity components,[2] you had to carry Mr. Fisher's products—and Mr. Scott's—and Mr. Stanton's—and Mr. Shure's—and so on.

By the late 1960s, the largest component manufacturers were beginning to broaden their product lines. For instance, Scott, a name which had been previously identified solely with electronics, was building its reputation in the speaker business. Sherwood, which also had started out as an electronics manufacturer, introduced an automatic turntable in 1969. KLH, which had started out making speakers, turned to stereo compacts[3] about the same time.

The late 1960s also saw the entry of Japanese hi-fi manufacturers into the United States market. The subsequent success of such companies as Pioneer, Kenwood, Sansui, Teac, and others from Japan coincided with the transition in electronic circuitry from vacuum tubes to transistors (i.e., solid-state electronic devices). Explained Bernie Mitchell:

> I think that Scott and Fisher, who were The Establishment, were slow and not very decisive in the changeover. The interlopers, the Young Turks (Pioneer, Kenwood, Sansui and others), were far less conservative. They had a far smaller market share, had good engineering capability and a good understanding of solid-state devices, and made that transition quickly. [*The Boston Phoenix*, Aug. 30, 1977]

By the late 1960s, too, most of the men who had originally founded the hi-fi companies and had operated the business within a "club-like" atmosphere were either "retiring, selling out, merging or generally disappearing." (*Electronics Retailing*, October 1975)

The 1970s saw a new attitude develop among hi-fi manufacturers. As Bernie Mitchell told one trade magazine reporter:

> Six years ago we had this attitude that we only wanted to sell our product to a certain select group of people who had to qualify somehow intellectually and technologically. We didn't want to sell our stuff to kids or to ordinary people, only to super people. It was a real elitist attitude, and terribly dangerous. We've changed it from an elitist business that didn't really want to grow to an industry that has some pride in itself and its products and says, "These products are so good we won't be happy until we tell everybody." [*Crawdaddy*, July 1976]

Company Background

Pioneer Electronics Corporation was founded by Nozomu Matsumoto, chairman and director, in Tokyo in 1938. According to Bernie Mitchell, the parent company in Japan

> . . . is not part of the banking, the trading company, or the manufacturing cartels. Pioneer is a little independent company that got started when an inventive guy was converted to Christianity . . .

---

[1]The words "retailers" and "dealers" are used interchangeably in this case.

[2]Components are combinations of different audio equipments which reproduce sound highly faithful to the original record or tape (thus, high fidelity or hi-fi sound). Consumers create component systems of their choice by combining the following units: (*a*) an inlet source such as a turntable, tape deck, or FM tuner; (*b*) a control center such as an amplifier or a receiver, which is an amplifier and FM tuner combined into one unit; and (*c*) an outlet, such as speakers. In audio terminology, receivers and amplifiers are referred to as "electronics."

[3]Compacts are preassembled audio systems which usually consist of two units—one unit containing a turntable, receiver, and/or tape player and the other consisting of a pair of speakers. A compact system is usually lower in price and smaller in size than a component system. It reproduces stereo sound (i.e., sound reproduced through two separate channels) but does not necessarily reproduce high fidelity sound.

and he actually started to build loudspeakers to put in churches. He made the speakers and the public-address systems and his wife delivered them on her bicycle and installed them. [*The Boston Phoenix*]

In fact, Pioneer Electronics Corporation's original company name was Fukuin Denki (translated: "Gospel Electronics").

Matsumoto's operation, which started out with capital of $235, had expanded to $843 million in worldwide sales in 1977. As shown in Exhibit 2, overseas sales surpassed domestic sales in 1974 and, in 1977, accounted for 65 percent of total worldwide sales.

U.S. Pioneer was established in March 1966 in New York State[4] with capital of $50,000 under the leadership of Ken Kai, vice president of U.S. Pioneer, who was then 26 years old. He had joined the parent company in Tokyo after

[4]The company moved its main office to Moonachie, New Jersey, in 1970.

EXHIBIT 2
PIONEER ELECTRONICS CORPORATION AND CONSOLIDATED SUBSIDIARIES: 5-YEAR SUMMARY OF OPERATIONS
Year Ended September 30

	U.S. dollars (in thousands of U.S. dollars except per share information)				
	1977	**1976**	**1975**	**1974**	**1973**
Net sales:					
Domestic	$297,670	$315,620	$256,220	$213,449	$159,204
Overseas	545,665	421,143	268,196	225,363	147,976
Total	$843,335	$736,763	$524,416	$438,812	$307,180
Net income	$ 60,641	$ 56,665	$ 28,702	$ 18,731	$ 18,653
Net income as a percentage of sales	7.2%	7.7%	5.5%	4.3%	6.1%
Per Curaçao depositary share:					
Net income	$7.13	$7.08	$3.87	$2.56	$2.76
Cash dividends applicable to earnings of the period	$0.98	$0.79	$0.44	$0.41	$0.37
Per American depositary share:					
Net income	$1.42	$1.42	$0.78	$0.51	$0.55
Cash dividends applicable to earnings of the period	$0.20	$0.16	$0.09	$0.08	$0.07
Weighted average number of shares outstanding (in thousands)	85,057	80,079	74,070	73,099	67,554
Net working capital	$217,678	$155,298	$105,951	$ 79,837	$ 57,396
Total assets	$603,416	$534,445	$378,996	$361,033	$242,220
Bank loans and long-term debt	$134,237	$130,033	$119,563	$146,061	$ 69,943
Shareholders' equity	$319,563	$229,061	$152,955	$126,049	$ 97,898
Number of employees	7,604	7,317	6,691	7,156	6,800

Per share amounts are based on the weighted average number of shares outstanding during each period, appropriately adjusted for free share distributions.

The U.S. dollar amounts in this report represent the translation of Japanese yen for convenience only at the rate of Y245 = US$1. Curaçao depositary share and American depositary share represent common stock of 10 shares and 2 shares, respectively.

Source: Annual report.

graduating from college in 1963 and was sent to New York in 1964 to act as Pioneer's United States liaison. In 1966, U.S. Pioneer had less than $200,000 in sales and fewer than 30 dealers.

Bernie Mitchell joined the company in 1970. He was an economist by training and a music buff, as well as a member of the board of directors of the New Jersey Symphony and the Metropolitan Opera. He had worked previously with Westinghouse, Toshiba, and Concord Electronics.

Bernie Mitchell and Ken Kai realized that if U.S. Pioneer was to grow, it had to take on the task of developing the market by making more people aware of and knowledgeable about h-fi products in general. U.S. Pioneer sponsored hi-fi shows on college campuses and became the first hi-fi company to advertise in such magazines as *Playboy*, *National Lampoon*, and *The New Yorker*. In its ads, Pioneer featured such celebrities as Elton John; Blood, Sweat, and Tears; the Allman Brothers; Walt Frazier; and Andy Warhol.

The market expansion strategy was accompanied by a strengthening of the distribution network for Pioneer products. U.S. Pioneer was supplied by its parent company in Japan. It used sales representatives on commission to sell to its retail dealers. In 1972, U.S. Pioneer had six sales representative offices, all of which were independently run companies, each with its own president. They agreed to carry and sell only Pioneer products (with the exception of accessories, cartridges, blank tapes, and other complementary items, as well as very high-priced lines of electronics which did not directly compete with Pioneer). Each sales representative office had its own sales force and served hi-fi dealers within a given region. Every office had from four to seven salespeople, each of whom was paid an average annual salary of approximately $20,000. They provided retailers with assistance on merchandising and display, store operations, and sales training. By 1975, U.S. Pioneer had added 10 independent sales representative offices and four exclusively owned sales representative offices in New York; Washington, D.C.; Florida; and Missouri. The "captive" offices were paid the same commission as the independent sales representatives[5] but were not allowed to carry product lines of direct and indirect competitors.

By 1975, the number of retail outlets carrying Pioneer products had grown to almost 3,000, up from approximately 500 in 1970. To carry Pioneer products, a retailer had to sign a franchise agreement with U.S. Pioneer. Retailers, Bernie Mitchell thought, did not hesitate to sign the agreement, since a considerable amount of consumer pull was created through U.S. Pioneer's strong national and local cooperative advertising programs. Five percent of U.S. Pioneer sales was allocated to local ads featuring Pioneer products. In addition, U.S. Pioneer offered dealers attractive gross margins and credit terms.

The FTC Consent Decree

Just as the market expansion and distribution building strategies were starting to generate a higher sales level for U.S. Pioneer ($80 million in 1974), U.S. Pioneer and three other competitors were issued a complaint by the Federal Trade Commission. According to the complaint, Sansui, Sherwood, Teac, and U.S. Pioneer granted dealerships to retailers only if they agreed to maintain suggested retail prices, directed their sales representatives to report on retailers who failed to maintain such prices, and delayed shipments to retailers if they cut prices. The FTC charged that these practices were in violation of the provision of Section 5 of the Federal Trade Commission Act, which prohibited "unfair methods of competition . . . and unfair or deceptive

---

[5]Prior to 1974, U.S. Pioneer sales representative offices received a 10 percent commission rate. In 1974, the commission rate was reduced to 5 percent, a rate comparable to that of other manufacturers.

acts or practices in commerce." The effect of these practices, the FTC charged, was to inflate prices paid by consumers.

In August 1975, the four companies signed consent decrees with the FTC. Although not admitting guilt, the four companies promised not to engage in the alleged practices. Specifically, they were prohibited from fair-trading[6] their products for 5 years in states where the practice was still permitted (there were 21 such states then) and from using suggested list prices for 2 years in any part of the country. The consent decree also prohibited the practice of using a warranty registration form which asked the consumer the price of the purchased product. In addition, the four companies were required to distribute copies of the consent order to all their dealers and to give any dealer whose franchise was formerly terminated an opportunity to regain his or her franchise.

Asked why U.S. Pioneer decided not to

[6]Fair-trade (or resale price maintenance) laws permitted a manufacturer or distributor of trademarked products to determine a resale price for each product. Although on the surface such laws seemed to support a manufacturer's desire to influence prices at the retail level, their initial development had been advocated by small, independent retailers who had sought protection from threats of direct price competition by the large chains. The first state resale price maintenance law was passed by California in 1931, and by 1941 all but three states had resale price maintenance laws on their books. In 13 of the states, a "nonsigner clause" was in effect, binding all retailers selling a "fair-traded" product to the contract if one retailer within the state signed an agreement. The national resale price maintenance legislation was first introduced in Congress in 1914 but did not become law (Miller-Tydings Act) until 1937. The passage of this act enabled resale price maintenance to apply to interstate commerce.

By 1952, some 1,600 manufacturers fair-traded their products. The percentage declined steadily. By 1975 fair trade was being used for only certain brands of hi-fi equipment, television sets, jewelry, bicycles, clothing, cosmetics, and kitchenware. The number of states enforcing fair trade also declined over the years. Nebraska became the first state to repeal its fair-trade law in 1957, but the major efforts to repeal state laws did not start until 1974. In December 1975, President Ford signed the Consumer Goods Pricing Act, which terminated interstate utilization of fair trade.

contest the FTC's consent decree, Bernie Mitchell replied:

I don't mind being a crusader. In fact, I kind of enjoy it. But I like to crusade for something that makes some long-term sense.

The FTC is asking us not to violate the law. It has never been our intention to violate the law. They are asking that we no longer fair trade our products. We had already unilaterally made the decision that fair trade wasn't viable anymore anyhow, and that we had to extricate ourselves from fair trade lest it die around us and make more problems than solutions. The third thing they are asking us is that we not conspire to fix prices, either among dealers or among ourselves, and we had no intention of doing that.

We did try to fix retail prices at the dealer level as long as fair trade lasted; that was the purpose of fair trade statutes. When we fair traded, we did it pretty darn well. But when we decided to go off fair trade, we decided we were going to be the best there was at free market practices and that became our new goal. [*Electronics Retailing*]

To implement this new goal, Pioneer replaced the price sheet which was in effect during the fair-trade days (see Exhibit 3) with a new price list (see Exhibit 4). On the new price list the words "fair trade resale" were replaced with "approximate nationally advertised value," and seven columns of optional retail prices were added under gross margins of 15, 20, 25, 30, 35, 40, and 45 percent.

According to *Home Furnishings Daily* (August 27, 1975), "most of the dealers and manufacturers contacted scorned [Pioneer's] list because they felt it was, in the words of one manufacturer, 'an open invitation to cut the hell out of prices.'" Bernie Mitchell said in the same article that the initial response to Pioneer's price list was one of fear and that dealers did not understand the significance of the change from fair-trade prices to free-market prices.

Too often, under the fair-trade environment, dealers felt, "If we have a very fine mix of products, and people come in and we tell them wonderful

EXHIBIT 3
PRICE LIST OF SELECTED PRODUCTS
April 22, 1975

Stereo receivers	Description	Fair trade resale	1-3 pcs.	4-more	Case	Shipping weight
SX01010	AM/FM stereo receiver	$699.95	$466.60	$420.00	1	60 lb
SX-939	AM/FM stereo receiver	599.95	400.00	372.00	1	51 lb
SX-838	AM/FM stereo receiver	499.95	333.40	310.00	1	44 lb
SX-737	AM/FM stereo receiver	399.95	266.60	248.00	1	35 lb
SX-636	AM/FM stereo receiver	349.95	233.30	217.00	1	29 lb
SX-535	AM/FM stereo receiver	299.95	200.00	186.00	1	27 lb
SX-434	AM/FM stereo receiver	239.95	160.00	148.80	1	22 lb

U.A. Series	Description	Fair trade resale	1-3 pcs.	4-more	Case	Shipping weight
Spec 1	Stereo pre-amplifier	$499.95	$333.40	$300.00	1	30 lb
Spec 2	Stereo power amplifier	899.95	600.00	540.00	1	60 lb
SA-9900	Integrated stereo amp.	749.85	500.00	450.00	1	50 lb
SA-9500	Integrated stereo amp.	499.95	333.40	300.00	1	44 lb
SA-8500	Integrated stereo amp.	399.95	266.60	240.00	1	32 lb
SA-7500	Integrated stereo amp.	299.95	200.00	180.00	1	30 lb
SA-5200	Integrated stereo amp.	138.95	93.30	84.00	1	23 lb
TX-9500	AM/FM stereo tuner	399.95	266.60	240.00	1	24 lb
TX-7500	AM/FM stereo tuner	249.95	166.70	150.00	1	21 lb
TX-6200	AM/FM stereo tuner	139.95	93.30	84.00	1	18 lb
RG-1	RG dynamic expander	179.95	120.00	108.00	1	15 lb
SR-202W	Stereo reverb. amp.	139.95	93.30	84.00	1	12 lb
SF-850	Electronic crossover	199.95	133.30	120.00	1	16 lb
SD-1100	Quad/stereo display	599.95	400.00	360.00	1	34 lb
WC-UA1	Walnut cabinet*	34.95**	23.30	21.00	1	11¼ lb

Turntables	Description	Fair trade resale	1-3 pcs.	4-more	Case	Shipping weight
PL-71	2-Speed, DC brushless servo motor, anti-skating, direct-drive	$299.95	$200.00	$180.00	1	33 lb
PL-55X	2-Speed, DC brushless servo motor, anti-skating, direct-drive automatic turntable	249.95	166.60	150.00	1	31 lb
PL-A45D	2-Speed, automatic turntable 2-motor, belt-drive, anti-skating	169.95	113.30	105.40	1	26 lb
PL-15D/II	2-Speed, automatic turntable with hysteresis synchronous motor, belt-drive, anti-skating	129.95	87.10	83.20	1	20 lb
PL-12D & PL-12D/II	2-Speed, hysteresis synchronous motor, belt-drive, anti-skating	99.95	70.00	66.00	1	19 lb

*Walnut cabinet for SA-8500, SA-7500, TX-9500, and TX-7500 only.
**Suggested resale.

EXHIBIT 4
PRICE LIST OF SELECTED PRODUCTS
July 1, 1975

Stereo receivers	Description	Dealer cost 1-3 pcs.	Dealer cost 4-more	Case	Shp. wt.	15% margin	20% margin	25% margin	30% margin	35% margin	40% margin	45% margin	Approx. nationally adv. value	Your price	Model number
SK-1010	AM/FM stereo rec.	$466.60	$420.00	1	60 lb	$494.00	$525.00	$560.00	$600.00	$646.00	$700.00	$764.00	$700.00	_____	SX-1010
SX-939	AM/FM stereo rec.	400.00	372.00	1	51 lb	438.00	465.00	496.00	531.00	572.00	620.00	676.00	600.00	_____	SX-939
SX-838	AM/FM stereo rec.	333.40	310.00	1	44 lb	365.00	388.00	413.00	443.00	477.00	517.00	564.00	500.00	_____	SX-838
SX-737	AM/FM stereo rec.	266.60	248.00	1	35 lb	292.00	310.00	331.00	354.00	382.00	413.00	451.00	400.00	_____	SX-737
SX-636	AM/FM stereo rec.	233.30	217.00	1	29 lb	255.00	271.00	289.00	310.00	334.00	362.00	395.00	350.00	_____	SX-636
SX-535	AM/FM stereo rec.	200.00	186.00	1	27 lb	219.00	233.00	248.00	266.00	286.00	310.00	338.00	300.00	_____	SX-535
SX-434	AM/FM stereo rec.	160.00	148.80	1	22 lb	175.00	185.00	198.00	213.00	229.00	248.00	271.00	250.00	_____	SX-434

U.A. series	Description	Dealer cost 1-3 pcs.	Dealer cost 4-more	Case	Shp. wt.	15% margin	20% margin	25% margin	30% margin	35% margin	40% margin	45% margin	Approx. nationally adv. value	Your price	Model number
Spec 1	Stereo pre-amplifier	$333.40	$300.00	1	30 lb	$353.00	$375.00	$400.00	$429.00	$462.00	$500.00	$545.00	$500.00	_____	Spec 1
Spec 2	Stereo power amp.	600.00	540.00	1	60 lb	635.00	675.00	720.00	771.00	831.00	900.00	982.00	900.00	_____	Spec 2
SA-9900	Integ. stereo amp.	500.00	450.00	1	50 lb	529.00	563.00	600.00	643.00	692.00	750.00	818.00	750.00	_____	SA-9900
SA-9500	Integ. stereo amp.	333.40	300.00	1	44 lb	353.00	375.00	400.00	429.00	462.00	500.00	545.00	500.00	_____	SA-9500
SA-8500	Integ. stereo amp.	266.60	240.00	1	32 lb	282.00	300.00	320.00	343.00	369.00	400.00	436.00	400.00	_____	SA-8500
SA-7500	Integ. stereo amp.	200.00	180.00	1	30 lb	212.00	225.00	240.00	257.00	277.00	300.00	327.00	300.00	_____	SA-7500
SA-5200	Integ. stereo amp.	93.30	84.00	1	23 lb	99.00	105.00	112.00	120.00	129.00	140.00	153.00	140.00	_____	SA-5200
TX-9500	AM/FM stereo tuner	266.60	240.00	1	24 lb	282.00	300.00	320.00	343.00	369.00	400.00	436.00	400.00	_____	TX-9500
TX-7500	AM/FM stereo tuner	166.70	150.00	1	21 lb	176.00	189.00	200.00	214.00	231.00	250.00	273.00	250.00	_____	TX-7500
TX-6200	AM/FM stereo tuner	93.30	84.00	1	18 lb	99.00	105.00	112.00	120.00	129.00	140.00	153.00	140.00	_____	TX-6200
RG-1	RG dyn. expander	120.00	108.00	1	15 lb	127.00	135.00	144.00	154.00	166.00	180.00	196.00	175.00	_____	RG-1
SR-202W	Stereo reverb. amp.	93.30	84.00	1	12 lb	99.00	105.00	112.00	120.00	129.00	140.00	153.00	150.00	_____	SR-202W
SF-850	Electronic crossover	133.30	120.00	1	16 lb	141.00	150.00	160.00	171.00	185.00	200.00	218.00	200.00	_____	SF-850
SD-1100	Quad/stereo display	400.00	360.00	1	31 lb	424.00	450.00	480.00	514.00	554.00	600.00	655.00	600.00	_____	SD-1100
WC-UA1	Walnut cabinet†	23.30	21.00	1	11 lb	25.00	26.00	28.00	30.00	32.00	35.00	38.00	35.00	_____	WC-UA1
WC-UA2	Walnut cabinet‡	26.70	24.00	1	11 lb	28.00	30.00	32.00	34.00	37.00	40.00	44.00	40.00	_____	WC-UA2

EXHIBIT 4
Continued

Turn-tables	Description	Dealer cost		Case	Shp. wt.	Dealer's gross margins at various retail prices							Approx. nationally adv. value	Your price	Model number
		1-3 pcs.	4-more			15% margin	20% margin	25% margin	30% margin	35% margin	40% margin	45% margin			
PL-71	2-Sp., DC brushless servo motor, anti-skating, direct drive	$200.00	$180.00	1	33 lb	$212.00	$225.00	$240.00	$257.00	$277.00	$300.00	$327.00	$300.00	———	PL-71
PL-55X	2-Sp., DC brushless servo motor, anti-skating, direct drive, auto. turntable	166.60	150.00	1	31 lb	176.00	188.00	200.00	214.00	231.00	250.00	273.00	250.00	———	PL-55X
PL-A45D	2-Sp., auto turntable 2-motor, belt drive, anti-skating	113.30	105.40	1	26 lb	124.00	132.00	141.00	151.00	162.00	176.00	192.00	175.00	———	PL-A45D
PL-15D/II	2-Sp., auto. turntable w/hysteresis synch. motor, belt drive, anti-skating	87.10	83.20	1	20 lb	98.00	104.00	111.00	119.00	128.00	139.00	151.00	125.00	———	PL-15D/II
PL-12D & PL-12D/II	2-Sp., hysteresis synch. motor, belt drive, anti-skating	70.00	66.00	1	19 lb	78.00	83.00	88.00	94.00	102.00	110.00	120.00	100.00	———	PL-12D PL-12D/II

†Walnut cabinet for SA-8500, SA-7500, SA-7500, TX-9500, and TX-7500 only.
‡Walnut cabinet for SA-9900, and SA-9500 only.

324

stories about each of those products, they will tell us which products they want. They'll sort of self-sell in an enlightened environment."

I don't really think that's a very good way to run a business. Dealers have to identify what needs the consumer has, acquaint him very quickly with his options, suggest an option they think he ought to take and bear down very hard to lead him to take that option. That's called selling.

Impact of the Consent Decree

The immediate impact of the consent decree, according to *Home Furnishings Daily*, was a "price war which lowered dealer profit margins to five or six percent in many parts of the country." The newspaper also said that "many retailers began to criticize manufacturers for 'abandoning' them and called for them to control the fluctuating markets." Some softening of the market, according to an FTC spokesperson, was expected as a "backlash to the many years when dealers were forced to sell at prices mandated to them." But, said the spokesperson, "prices won't stay as low as they are now and higher margins will eventually return. [In the meantime] I expect to see greater sales at discount prices and the good dealers will survive."

In 1976 there were significant increases in retail dollar sales as well as unit sales, as indicated below (see Exhibit 5).

| Year | Annual percentage increase over previous year's figures | |
	Dollar sales	Unit sales
1975	1.6	2.2
1976	12.6	9.4

According to Ken Kai, the small percentage increase between 1974 and 1975 was probably due to the recession and consumer decisions to delay purchases until fair-trade laws were repealed. In New York and New Jersey, repeal of

the fair-trade laws had been rumored as early as August 1975.

In the meantime, U.S. Pioneer sales increased from $80 million in 1974 to $87 million in 1975. In addition, Pioneer's market share within the different hi-fi product categories increased between 1974 and 1975, with the exceptions of the market shares for turntables and speakers (see Exhibit 6). All of Pioneer's market share percentages in 1976 were equal to or higher than those of 1974.

Whether it was due to the demise of fair trade or simply the maturing of the hi-fi market, the market was growing, and there was evidence, as well, that buyer profiles for component parts were changing. As shown in Exhibit 7, there were:

More men
More young adults between the ages of 18 and 24
More residents in the Pacific area
More college graduates
More households with incomes of $25,000 and over

purchasing stereo component parts in 1975 than in the previous year.

The Post–Fair-Trade Era

Realizing that there was a shift in buyer demographics, U.S. Pioneer embarked on an extensive research program to determine (a) the market potential of hi-fi products vis-à-vis that of low-fi products such as compacts or consoles[7] and (b) the purchasing behavior of hi-fi component buyers.

Through an independent research firm, U.S.

[7]Consoles are preassembled, all-in-one audio systems which resemble a sideboard in outward appearance. They are larger in size and higher in price than most component systems. But the sound reproduced by consoles is generally considered of lower fidelity compared with the sound reproduced by components.

EXHIBIT 5
UNIT AND DOLLAR SALES OF HI-FI COMPONENTS
1974–1977

	1974	1975	1976	1977
Unit sales (in thousands)				
Total components	7,799	7,971	8,719	9,539
Receivers	960	970	1,050	1,185
Amps, preamps, tuners	231	263	275	320
Turntables (exec. OEM)	1,767	1,709	1,866	2,015
Speakers	2,500	2,550	2,800	3,125
Tape decks (cassette and open reel)	341	399	428	494
Headphones	2,000	2,080	2,300	2,400
Dollar sales (in millions)				
Total components	1,056	1,073	1,208	1,390
Receivers	336	306	341	392
Amps, preamps, tuners	69	76	81	97
Turntables (exc. OEM)	168	179	222	252
Speakers	300	319	350	416
Tape decks (cassette and open reel)	113	120	133	147
Headphones	70	73	81	86

Source: Merchandising, March 1978, p. 51.

Pioneer found that sales of components were growing faster than sales of compacts and consoles. But in sheer volume, compacts outsold components and consoles by a wide margin. In 1975, 3.5 million units of compacts were sold in the United States, as compared with 1.5 million component systems and 400,000 consoles. To Bernie Mitchell, this meant that 3.9 million buyers in the United States were taken off the hi-fi market. Once they had purchased compacts and consoles, these customers were not expected to consider replacing them with hi-fi components for several years.

"Also, every time a compact or console is sold, you lose the potential of an additional speaker, add-on tape deck, upgraded receiver,

EXHIBIT 6
U.S. PIONEER MARKET SHARE DATA*

Product category	1971	1972	1973	1974	1975	1976
Receivers	7%	15%	23%	22%	25%	25%
Tuners	3	5	25	18	23	18
Amplifiers	3	5	8	9	12	10
Turntables	3	3	3	11	10	11
Speakers	2	1	4	5	3	7
Headphones	10	5	4	7	9	9
Cassette decks	–	–	4	11	26	20
Open reel tape decks	–	–	–	5	9	9

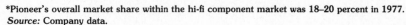

*Pioneer's overall market share within the hi-fi component market was 18–20 percent in 1977.
Source: Company data.

EXHIBIT 7
DEMOGRAPHIC PROFILE OF BUYERS
OF STEREO COMPONENT PARTS*

	1974		1975	
	U.S. (n = 139,778)	Stereo components buyers (n = 3,400)	U.S. (n = 141,622)	Stereo components buyers (n = 2,788)
Sex:				
Men	47.3%	73.4%	49.6%	76.4%
Women	52.7	26.6	50.4	23.6
Age:				
18–24	18.1%	42.5%	18.5%	47.6%
25–34	20.6	31.8	21.2	26.9
35–49	24.6	18.0	24.2	15.0
50–64	22.4	6.8	21.7	9.9
65 or over	14.2	1.0	14.4	0.5
Residence:				
New England	3.9%	4.4%	5.9%	6.6%
Middle Atlantic	22.2	18.6	20.6	18.8
East Central	13.1	16.9	14.2	15.1
West Central	16.5	19.8	15.2	16.6
Southeast	18.0	14.0	19.1	14.9
Southwest	10.6	10.4	10.1	7.1
Pacific	15.6	15.9	14.8	20.8
Education:				
Graduated from college	11.9%	16.3%	12.5%	25.6%
Attended college	14.0	30.8	14.7	27.5
Graduated from high school	37.7	39.5	38.0	36.2
Did not graduate from high school	36.4	13.4	34.8	10.7
Household income:				
$25,000 or more	8.8%	11.5%	11.3%	20.9%
$20,000–$24,999	7.5	9.3	8.4	9.1
$15,000–$19,999	17.1	21.4	18.6	22.7
$10,000–$14,999	24.1	21.5	23.2	21.1
$ 8,000–$ 9,999	9.2	9.8	8.7	8.5
$ 5,000–$ 7,999	14.4	10.8	13.3	11.3
Less than $5,000	18.8	15.7	16.5	6.4
Family life cycle:				
Single	16.2%	38.8%	17.3%	41.9%
Married	69.5	50.4	67.9	52.2
Widowed/divorced/separated	14.3	10.8	14.9	6.0
(Parents)†	(43.7)	(36.0)	(42.4)	(37.6)

*Buyers of stereo component parts within the past year.

†Figures indicate percentage of *n* shown above.

Source: 1975 and 1976 issues of *Target Group Index*, published by Axiom Market Research Bureau, Inc. Approximately 30,000 interviews were conducted in both Feb.–Dec. 1974 and Feb.–Dec. 1975 to derive the percentages in the columns with the heading "Stereo components buyers."

tuner, turntable, and more, . . ." said Bernie Mitchell. The research revealed that this add-on market was a larger segment than expected. In 1975, add-on sales were found to account for 55 percent of total dollars spent on hi-fi components, with new-system sales making up the remaining 45 percent.

Research on consumer buying behavior revealed that buyers of different audio systems were influenced by different factors. In the order of importance, they were:

Component buyers
1. Lifelike reproduction of sound
2. Superior electronics
3. Add-on capability
4. Status symbol

Console buyers
1. Aesthetics
2. Adequate electronics
3. No involved hookup
4. Get a lot for the money

Compact buyers
1. Lower price
2. Saves space
3. No involved hookup
4. Ease of operation

The same research also found that component buyers:

Depended heavily upon the advice of family and friends in the information-gathering stage of the buying process.

Thought they knew just enough about hi-fi components to get by. (Only 8 percent thought they knew a lot.)

Shopped around, especially in the case of the initial purchase.

Paid either $350–$400 or $650–$750 for their initial purchase of a hi-fi component system.

Replaced or upgraded the components approximately 1 to 2 years after the initial purchase.

On the basis of the results of the market and consumer research, Bernie Mitchell established the goal of "doubling the number of people owning and buying *any* brand of hi-fi components next year." In announcing this goal to the dealers, he said:

> We'd rather see a consumer buy a Marantz, Sansui . . . yes, and even a Technics than a fancy fruitwood console, or plastic compact, both of which deliver less than true high fidelity.

To implement this goal, Bernie Mitchell asked the dealers to persuade prospective compact or console buyers to consider lower-priced hi-fi components. He argued that such an effort could be best accomplished by prominently displaying low-end components in the store and by pointing out their advantages over compacts and consoles to the customers. "Taking initial purchases away from compacts and consoles would mean a higher chance of the customers returning to the store for add-ons or replacements," added Bernie Mitchell. To support this dealer effort, Pioneer had introduced component products at lower prices. It also allocated $6 million toward national advertising for 1976. Of this amount, $2 million was earmarked for educating consumers about the fact that only hi-fi components produced true high fidelity sound. One of the ads carried this head copy: "Bad Sound Is an Unnecessary Evil." The ad named some of Pioneer's competitors— Marantz, Kenwood, and Sansui—and referred to them as dedicated companies that were trying to reproduce high-quality sound.

Bernie Mitchell also asked the dealers to use direct-mail advertisements to tap the replacement and add-on markets. These ads were mailed to customers who had purchased audio systems 1 to 2 years ago.

Results of the New Strategy

Bernie Mitchell and Ken Kai were very satisfied with their new strategy as they saw Pioneer's sales increase from $87 million in 1975 to $135 million in 1976. Although their goal of doubling the number of hi-fi owners and buyers was not achieved, they felt that more people were buying components than compacts and consoles. Data published in a trade journal showed that the number of compact systems sold in the United States increased from 3.5 million in 1975 to 3.6 million in 1976, whereas the total number of component *units* (not systems) increased from about 8 million in 1975 to 8.7 million in 1976 (see Exhibit 8).

Bernie Mitchell and Ken Kai were also impressed by the findings of a consumer survey undertaken by the Gallup Organization[8] for U.S. Pioneer. The survey, which was conducted in the first half of 1977, measured consumer brand preference for different hi-fi component categories (i.e., receiver, FM tuner, amplifier, turntable, speaker, and tape deck). Almost 200 prospective component purchasers (constituting a national probability sample) were interviewed. As shown in Exhibit 9, Pioneer was preferred over all other brands in every hi-fi component category except tape decks.

[8]The Gallup Organization was an independent research firm which specialized in survey research and gained its reputation primarily through its work on political polls.

Retailer Dissidence

Just as Pioneer's "franchise" with consumers was strengthening, Bernie Mitchell came across a number of reports which suggested that Pioneer's relationships with its franchised dealers were starting to deteriorate. In particular, he was concerned about reports from his sales representatives regarding such practices as (a) disparagement of Pioneer products in the form of misrepresenting product specification sheets or manipulating sound demonstrations and (b) the use of an illegal and unethical tactic known as "bait and switch."[9]

Disparagement of Pioneer products was spotted as a result of continuous field work carried out by Pioneer employees (mostly part-timers)

[9]"Bait and switch" referred to the trade practice of advertising a product at a bargain price for the purpose of drawing customers into the store in order to sell them something similar to, but more expensive than, the advertised item.

Pioneer products served as good "baits" because of the strong consumer pull created through national advertising and favorable "word-of-mouth" communication. In one survey conducted by Pioneer, 98 percent of Pioneer components owners interviewed said they were satisfied with their Pioneer products and would buy the same brand again.

EXHIBIT 8
UNIT SALES OF COMPACTS VS. UNIT SALES OF COMPONENTS, 1974–1977

In Thousands

	1974	1975	1976	1977
Compact systems				
Cassette tape recorder bimode	32	36	38	44
Cassette tape recorder trimode	103	190	197	233
8-Track tape player bimode	652	528	525	527
8-Track tape player trimode	1,234	798	843	910
8-Track tape recorder bimode	549	590	555	569
8-Track tape recorder trimode	480	1,024	1,100	1,183
Changer bimode	377	325	324	337
Total	3,427	3,491	3,582	3,803
Component parts (total)	7,799	7,971	8,719	9,539

Source: Merchandising, March 1978, p. 51.

EXHIBIT 9
BRAND PREFERENCE DATA FOR HI–FI COMPONENTS

Source: Gallup Organization
Date: July 12, 1977
Sample: National probability sample of 196

Brand of receiver	All prospective purchasers (%)	Brand of FM tuner	All prospective purchasers (%)
Pioneer	26	Pioneer	28
Marantz	15	Marantz	18
Sony	13	Sansui	14
Sansui	12	Fisher	6
Kenwood	7	Kenwood	6
Fisher	2	Dynaco	3
Harman-Kardon	2	Technics	1
Technics	1	Sherwin	0
Sherwood	1	Rotel	0
Other	2	Other	1
Don't plan to buy	5	Don't plan to buy	5
Don't know	14	Don't know	18
Total	100	Total	100

Brand of amplifier	All prospective purchasers (%)	Brand of turntable	All prospective purchasers (%)
Pioneer	29	Pioneer	24
Marantz	17	Garrard	19
Sansui	9	Dual	12
Kenwood	8	BSR	8
Harman-Kardon	5	Technics	6
Superscope	3	Sansui	5
Crown	1	Bang & Olufsen	2
Dynaco	1	B.I.C.	1
Technics	1	JVC	1
Other	2	Other	3
Don't plan to buy	6	Don't plan to buy	4
Don't know	18	Don't know	15
Total	100	Total	100

Brand of speaker*	All prospective purchasers (%)	Brand of tape deck	All prospective purchasers (%)
Pioneer	32	Teac	21
Jensen	11	Pioneer	17
JBL	11	Sony/Superscope	15
AR	5	Sansui	9
Infinity	5	Fisher	6
KLH	4	Akai	5
B.I.C.—Venturi	3	Bekorder	1
Technics	3	Harman-Kardon	1
Dynaco	1	Technics	0
Other	3	Other	2
Don't plan to buy	4	Don't plan to buy	9
Don't know	18	Don't know	14
Total	100	Total	100

*Among the different component parts, speakers usually offered the highest gross margin to dealers. One industry source estimated the margin spread between speakers and other components (branded products) to be 10 to 20 percentage points. This spread differed by brand and by type of retail outlet.

who visited Pioneer's franchised stores, played the role of interested shoppers of Pioneer products, interacted with store personnel, and prepared "shopping reports" for Pioneer. Included in a shopping report was such information as:

Salesperson's and/or store's attitude toward Pioneer

Pioneer product(s) the salesperson disparaged; competing products pushed

Unfavorable comments about Pioneer; favorable comments about competing brands

Display of Pioneer's products in comparison with display of competing brands

In one of the shopping reports, a U.S. Pioneer employee told about a visit to a Midwestern hi-fi specialty store. The employee had asked for a Pioneer tape deck but was persuaded by the store salesperson to buy a competing brand. Excerpts from the report are reproduced in Exhibit 10. In the report, the employee noted that (a) the store salesperson commented that "he could produce copies of letters that dealers had written to Pioneer complaining about service"; (b) Pioneer's tape deck (CT-F7272) was missing from Pioneer's display area; (c) the store salesperson, when asked for a CT-F7272 specification sheet, handed him a competing brand's specification sheet but did not have one in stock for Pioneer; and (d) the store salesperson set the playback sound control at maximum volume for the competing brand but at less than maximum for Pioneer.

To counter these objectionable practices, Pioneer placed the aforementioned William Shakespeare ad (Exhibit 1) in major trade publications. The ad was designed to appeal directly to the dealers.

Pioneer also organized a meeting with the presidents of all its sales representative offices (16 independent sales representative offices and four exclusive Pioneer sales representative offices). Pioneer asked the presidents to identify the "most blatant, most persistent" offenders practicing disparagement and bait-and-switch tactics within their market territories.

As a result, Pioneer took one of the most "blatant and persistent" offenders to court in July 1977. U.S. Pioneer filed a suit against Audio Warehouse, a five-store chain with sales of $10 million in 1977, and its advertising agency, both of Akron, Ohio. It charged them with using bait-and-switch tactics, advertising without sufficient inventory, and disparaging Pioneer products to customers. U.S. Pioneer won a temporary restraining order barring Audio Warehouse from engaging in these practices.

Ed Radford, the 34-year-old president of Audio Warehouse, told *Retail Home Furnishings* (Sept. 26, 1977):

Yeah, we're being sued [by U.S. Pioneer], but we're not taking this lying down—we're going to fight it. Pioneer surprised me because they got a temporary restraining order, and within one day, they had it in every newspaper in my state. As far as I'm concerned, Pioneer's trying to make me look bad. The public doesn't understand that a temporary restraining order doesn't mean anything. Anybody who puts up a bond can get one.

To prove his point, Ed Radford (who was called "Fast Eddie" because of his hurried speech and quick rise to fortune[10]) placed a full-page advertisement in two Ohio newspapers. The ad, whose head copy read "Legal Beagle," showed a Sherlock Holmes–type dog (with deerstalker hat and mantle) reading a book entitled *Guidelines for Intimidation* and holding a magnifying glass over the Audio Warehouse logo (see Exhibit 11). The ad contained Audio Warehouse's

---

[10]According to *The Sunday Tribune* (Feb. 12, 1978), Ed Radford, who was orphaned at the age of 5, was planning a "fast" retirement at age 49. He had started his business in 1973 with his life savings of $10,000. In 1978, "Fast Eddie" was a millionaire who still came to work in jeans and an "exploding blond Afro."

EXHIBIT 10
SHOPPING REPORT

1. *Shopper's name*: John Smith*
2. *Store visited*: ABC Sounds*
3. *Salesman and/or store attitude toward Pioneer*. Store's attitude generally negative. Salesman was not really negative but went along with negative comment by another salesman.
4. *Products they tried to get you to buy and discouraged*: Pushed Sankyo STD-1900 (a tape deck on sale for $218) and discouraged Pioneer CT-F7272 (a tape deck on sale for $208).
4. *Unfavorable statements toward Pioneer*. The salesman made no derogatory remarks about Pioneer to me but became involved in a conversation with another store salesman and prospective customer during which the other salesman stated that he could produce copies of letters that dealers had written to Pioneer complaining about service.
6. *Favorable statements toward competition*: Sankyo unit had much better frequency response and much cleaner sound. Sankyo was the second largest manufacturer of tape decks and manufactured components for Teac.
7. *How were Pioneer products displayed in comparison to competition?* I did not see any of the Pioneer equipment that was advertised in the paper displayed in the normal manner. Specifically, CT-F7272 was missing from where all other Pioneer decks were displayed. It was in another room with a Sankyo unit sitting on top of it.
8. *Other comments*: When the salesman set up to play the tapes back I noted that the Sankyo playback control was set at maximum volume and that he adjusted the Pioneer control to about 6. He began playing the tapes back, switching from one deck to the other and commented on the very audible difference of sound due to the higher frequency response of the Sankyo deck. I made no comment but asked to see the spec sheets on the two units. He left and came back with the spec sheet on the Sankyo but not the Pioneer.

    During the time I spent in the store I overheard no less than six customers ask specifically for one of the Pioneer products that were advertised in the paper. In each case the customer was told that the particular item had been sold out but that they had lesser or better products in the Pioneer line or comparable products in other lines. I also heard another customer ask if ABC Sounds could order Pioneer's HMP-100s for him. The salesman replied, "No, we can't." The customer dropped the idea at that point.

    *Disguised names.

Source: Company data.

version of the suit filed by U.S. Pioneer and, at the same time, offered sharply reduced prices on a number of Pioneer products.

Ed Radford contended that "many dealers around the country were having difficulty maintaining margins on Pioneer equipment" and charged that Pioneer didn't "seem to care whether we make a profit or not" (*Retail Home Furnishings*).

Although Bernie Mitchell was confident that the suit would be settled in Pioneer's favor (especially because the attorney general of Ohio joined Pioneer in the suit as a co-plaintiff), he was concerned about the impact of the "Legal

EXHIBIT 11
AUDIO WAREHOUSE ADVERTISEMENT

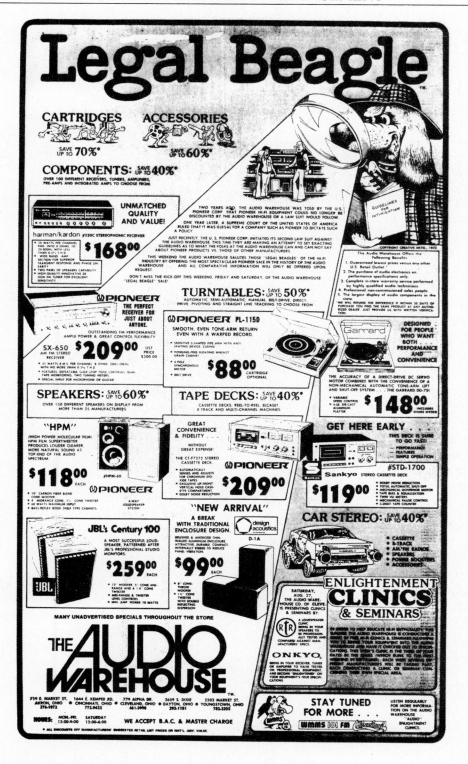

Beagle" publicity on Pioneer's 3,600 dealer outlets. At the same time he wondered whether he should initiate legal action against other offenders and/or terminate their franchises.[11]

Dealer Communication Program

The suggestion was also made in the sales reps' meeting that U.S. Pioneer organize an extensive dealer communication program. The objectives of such a program would be to convince dealers that Pioneer was concerned with their well-being and to demonstrate how an effective selling job for Pioneer products could improve their profit pictures. A need for such a program was felt by the sales reps, who were increasingly confronted with complaints from dealers such as:

> Most of my customers ask for Pioneer. But I can't make money with Pioneer.

> How can we compete with discounters or mail-order guys who are selling Pioneer for as low as 10 percent above cost?

> We'd be better off selling products of smaller manufacturers like Advent and Bose, which still sell at list prices.

> I'm making a 50 percent to 60 percent margin on house brands; why should I push Pioneer?

Such comments were of considerable concern to Bernie Mitchell, since dealer support was crucial for U.S. Pioneer. When asked "What factors had the greatest influence in your most recent purchase of hi-fi products?" in a recent consumer survey, 27 percent of the respondents replied "dealers/salespersons." As indicated below, only "recommendations of friends" was considered to be more influential by those interviewed.

[11]Most of these dealer franchise agreements (see Exhibit 12) had been signed during the "fair-trade" days and did not fully reflect the changes in the relationship between the dealers and U.S. Pioneer brought about as a result of the FTC consent order.

	Percentage of respondents[*]
Recommendations of friends	29
Dealers/salespersons	27
Advertising by manufacturers	15
Recommendations by family members	12
Advertising by dealers	8
Store display	7
All others	14
No answer	(n = 1,290)

[*]Percentages add to over 100 percent because of multiple answers.

In the meeting, Bob Gundick, president of an exclusive Pioneer sales representative company in Florida called Sunshine Audio Sales, displayed a sales presentation package which he had used with success among his dealers. The package consisted of a set of flip charts and a handout. The flip charts were shown to the dealers during regular visits from U.S. Pioneer salespeople and the handout (which was similar in content to the clip charts) was left with the dealers after the presentation. As shown in Exhibit 13, the sales presentation package suggested ways in which the dealers could (a) cope with their competitors, (b) determine their product mixes, (c) creatively sell Pioneer products in combination with other brands, and (d) improve their businesses in general. Bob Gundick was willing to have his package adopted on a nationwide basis.

Other suggestions made during the meeting on how the dealer communication program could be carried out included the following:

1. Sending out direct-mail brochures to all the dealers
2. Hiring more salespeople to increase the frequency of visits to the dealers
3. Offering cash rebates to the dealers throughout the country or creating other incentive programs (e.g., a contest of some sort)
4. Organizing a "national dealers conference" at some resort area and inviting all the dealers to attend the conference

EXHIBIT 12

Dealer Franchise Agreement

AGREEMENT made _____ this _____ day of _____ 19____, by and between U. S. PIONEER ELECTRONICS CORP. a Delaware Corporation, having its principal place of business in Moonachie, New Jersey (hereinafter called "PIONEER"), and

hereinafter called "Dealer"

Signer's name: _____

Corporate name: _____

dba _____

Address _____

City_____ State _____ Zip _____

Telephone No. (_____) _____

WITNESSETH:

WHEREAS Pioneer is the Distributor of certain quality products which are sold under the Pioneer brand name and trade marks (hereinafter referred to as "Products"); and

WHEREAS, Dealer desires to engage in the sale of Products at retail.

NOW, THEREFORE, Pioneer and Dealer mutually agree as follows:

1. Pioneer hereby appoints Dealer one of its Franchised Dealers in the continental limits of the United States only, and Dealer hereby accepts such appointment and agrees conscientiously and diligently to promote the sales of the above mentioned products.

2. Dealer shall purchase from Pioneer such Products for resale but all sales or agreements by Dealer for the resale of Pioneer Products shall be made by Dealer as principal and not as agent of Pioneer.

3. Prices to Dealer for such Products shall be set forth in the Pioneer Dealer Cost Schedules issued from time to time by Pioneer. Pioneer shall have the right to reduce or increase prices to Dealer at any time without accountability to Dealer in connection with Dealer's stock of unsold products on hand at the time of such change. When a new price schedule is issued by Pioneer it shall automatically supersede all such schedules on and after its effective date.

4. Dealer has represented to Pioneer, as an inducement to Pioneer for entering this agreement, that Dealer is at the time of entering into this agreement solvent and in a good and substantial financial position. Dealer shall from time to time when requested by Pioneer furnish such financial reports and other financial data as may be necessary to enable Pioneer to determine Dealer's financial condition.

5. Pioneer shall have the right to cancel any orders placed by Dealer or to refuse or to delay the shipment thereof if Dealer shall fail to meet payment schedules or other credit or financial requirements established by Pioneer and the cancellation of such orders or the withholding of shipments by Pioneer shall not be construed as a termination or breach of this agreement by Pioneer.

6. Pioneer will use its best efforts to make deliveries with reasonable promptness in accordance with orders accepted from Dealer, but it shall not be liable for any damages, consequential or otherwise, for its failure to fill orders or for delays in delivery or for any error in the filling of orders.

7. No territory is assigned exclusively to Dealer by Pioneer. Pioneer reserves the absolute right, for any reason whatever, to increase or decrease the number of Franchised Dealers in Dealer's locality or elsewhere, at any time without notice to Dealer.

8. Pioneer shall have the right at any time to discontinue the manufacture or sale of any or all of its Products and parts without incurring any liability to Dealer.

9. Pioneer is at liberty to change its service policies, its financial requirements and the design of its Products and parts thereof at any time without notice, and the Dealer shall have no claim on Pioneer for damage by reason of such change or changes.

10. Dealer agrees to forward promptly to Pioneer information concerning all charges, complaints or claims involving Products, by customers or accounts, that may come to its attention.

11. Dealer shall at no time engage in any unfair trade practices and shall make no false or misleading representations with regard to Pioneer or its Products. Dealer shall make no warranties or representations to customers or to the trade with respect to Products except such as may be approved in writing by Pioneer. Dealer shall hold Pioneer harmless from all damages caused by Dealer's violation of this paragraph. Any written representations respecting Pioneer products must first be submitted to Pioneer for its written approval.

12. Dealer will use its best efforts to resell Products purchased from Pioneer.

13. Dealer shall have no rights in the names or marks owned, used, promoted by Pioneer or in the names or marks of Products, except to make reference thereto in selling, advertising and promoting the sale of Products, which right shall be completely terminated upon the termination of this agreement.

14. Nothing herein contained shall be deemed to establish a relationship of principal and agent between Pioneer and Dealer, Dealer being an independent contractor, and neither Dealer nor any of its agents or employees shall be deemed to be an agent of Pioneer for any purpose, whatsoever and shall have no right or authority to assume or create any obligation of any kind, express or implied, on behalf of Pioneer except as specifically provided herein, nor any right or authority to accept service of legal process of any kind on behalf of Pioneer nor authority to bind Pioneer in any respect whatsoever.

15. All negotiations, correspondence and memoranda which have passed between Pioneer and Dealer in relation to this agreement are merged herein and this agreement constitutes the entire agreement between Pioneer and Dealer. No representations not contained herein are authorized by Pioneer and this agreement may not be altered, modified, amended, changed, rescinded or discharged, in whole or in part, except by a written memorandum executed by Pioneer and Dealer in the same manner as is provided for the execution of this agreement, except that the agreement may be terminated by either party as herein provided.

16. This agreement shall become effective only upon its execution by Pioneer in its executive offices at Moonachie, New Jersey, and no changes, additions or erasure of any printed portion of this agreement shall be valid and binding unless such change, addition or erasure is initialled by both Pioneer and Dealer.

17. This agreement supersedes and terminates any and all prior agreements or contracts, written or oral, if any, entered into between Pioneer and Dealer as of the effective date of this agreement with reference to all matters covered by this agreement.

EXHIBIT 12

Continued

18. Dealer is appointed a Franchised Pioneer Dealer by reason of Pioneer's confidence in Dealer, which appointment is personal in nature, and consequently this agreement shall not be assignable by Dealer, nor shall any of the rights granted hereunder be assignable or transferable in any manner whatsoever without the consent in writing of Pioneer.

19. This agreement shall be governed and construed in accordance with the laws of the State of Delaware. In the event of the provisions of this agreement, or the application of any such provisions to either Pioneer or Dealer with respect to its obligations hereunder, shall be held by a court of competent jurisdiction to be contrary to any State or Federal Law, the remaining portions of this agreement shall remain in full force and effect.

20. Either Dealer or Pioneer may terminate this agreement at any time by giving five days' written notice to the other and such termination may be made either with or without cause. Neither Dealer nor Pioneer shall be liable to the other for any damages of any kind or character whatsoever on account of such termination. Pioneer, at its option, shall have the right to repurchase from Dealer any or all Products in Dealer's inventory within a reasonable period from said notice of termination, at the net prices at which such Products were originally invoiced to Dealer less any allowances which Pioneer may have given Dealer on account of such Products: If such option to repurchase is exercised by Pioneer, Dealer agrees to deliver the inventory of Products so purchased to Pioneer, Moonachie, New Jersey, immediately after receipt of the exercise of such option.

21. Any notice which is required to be given hereunder shall be given in writing and shall either be delivered in person or sent by registered letter via United States mail to the respective addresses of the parties appearing above. If mailed, the date of the mailing shall be deemed to be the date such notice has been given.

22. Dealer shall not return merchandise without Pioneer's prior written authorization; and Pioneer shall assume no responsibility for returns made without prior written authorization.

IN WITNESS WHEREOF, the parties hereto have caused these presents to be executed the day and year first above written.

DEALER:

BY: _____   U. S. PIONEER ELECTRONICS CORP.

Title: _____   BY: _____

Although the exact format of the dealer communication program was yet to be determined, Bernie Mitchell felt that the program was important enough to receive a promotional budget of $3 million. He was uncertain, however, about whether it should be an incremental budget or whether some funds should be transferred from the consumer advertising program.

Long-Run Strategy

Citing the broad changes taking place in the hi-fi industry, several sales reps argued in the meeting that the existing situation provided a timely opportunity for U.S. Pioneer to reconsider its long-run distribution strategy.

One possible strategy was to shift Pioneer's retail distribution away from specialty stores and toward department stores and catalog showrooms. Currently, 75 percent of U.S. Pioneer's dollar sales were being accounted for by hi-fi specialty stores, 5 percent by department stores, 7 percent by catalog showrooms, and 13 percent by appliance/TV/hardware/furniture stores.[12] Department stores and catalog showrooms did not generally offer the extensive customer services provided by specialty stores, including professional sales assistance, demonstration, extended store warranty,[13] on-the-premises repair service, home delivery and installation, and loaner component programs. They usually had, however, extensive credit facilities, strong consumer "pull" advertising, and lower prices. Industry sources predicted a substantial increase in the market shares held by department stores and catalog showrooms in the future.

[12]In terms of the number of existing retail outlets for U.S. Pioneer products, 69 percent of the stores were classified as hi-fi specialty stores, 2 percent as department stores, 3 percent as catalog showrooms, and 26 percent as other stores.

[13]Many specialty stores extended the 2-year guarantee on parts and labor offered by Pioneer on its electronics guarantee to 3 years.

EXHIBIT 13
SUNSHINE AUDIO SALES PRESENTATION PROGRAM

MOST OF MY CUSTOMERS ASK FOR PIONEER!!!
I CAN'T MAKE MONEY WITH PIONEER!!!

HOW OFTEN HAVE WE HEARD, OR HAVE YOU MADE, THESE VERY STATE-
MENTS?

IF YOU ARE INTERESTED IN INCREASING YOUR OVERALL BUSINESS AND YOU
WANT TO INCREASE YOUR OVERALL PROFIT DOLLARS—READ ON.

You and Your Competitor

Your business is really not that different from the man down the street. You both sell hi-fi,
you both are after the same consumer, you both have to make a profit, you both want your
business to grow and you are both competing against each other. Why?

View your competitor as an ally and see what happens to your perspective of the
business. You are both fighting to get the consumer's disposable income dollar from the T.V.
dealer, the motorcycle dealer, the travel agent, the car dealer, and any number of places he
can spend that extra $300–700. You and your hi-fi retailers should run ads to make the hi-fi
market in your town grow—not to "get the other guy" with a low ball price. Think about
it—how many people in your market know that a RZ105 receiver at $136 is a good buy
(cost, in fact), but much less what a receiver is?

You and Your Sales

Think about this for a minute. Most of your business should be in systems—about 70%.
Single piece sales account for the 30% balance. 15% are high margin pieces or accessory
sales and 15% are low margin promotional pieces. Now, think about that margin. If you only
sell 40% margin products and you are not a "discount" house, how come your balance
sheet only shows your gross margin between 28% and 32%? Interesting.

You and Pioneer

Now for the sales pitch. When you put a Pioneer piece in a system you will sell more systems
(better brand name recognition) at your usual system margin. Pioneer has plenty of products
that sell at full margin all the time—SG-9500, RG-1, turntables with cartridges, component
ensembles, RT-2022, etc. Of course, we have promotional pieces too, CTF 2121, Project
60, 100A, etc. But, how low a margin is a CTF 2121 at a cost of $124—with an advertised
price of $139—when you sell the deck and its case for $179? This makes the margin 26%;
sell tape and your margin is higher. I can't make money on Pioneer. Don't believe it! How
about the SX1250 at $595—only a $50 profit. With the $50 rebate recently offered your real
profit dollars is $100. Sell an extra 3 SX1250/week and we added over $15,000 profit
dollars to your bottom line in a year. Even without the $50 rebate, the contribution to profit
is still $7,500 in one year.

Instead of using your energy for not selling, down selling, or selling off Pioneer, what
would happen if you put that effort into creatively selling it?

EXHIBIT 13

Continued

You and Your Business

Some suggestions:

— Put together systems with brand name products that can't be duplicated by any dealer in your market.
— Sell the accessories with the promotional pieces or make them part of a system to increase profitability.
— Sell brand name goods that customers want.
— Think in terms of profit dollars, not always gross profit margin.

You and the Industry

Pioneer will spend close to 7 million dollars in advertising. Take advantage of this tremendous support. Without advertising and without brand names your business would dry up. Most hi-fi dealers have some exclusive lines. But limited distribution can be limited market and limited growth. Pioneer in a system will help sell more JVC receivers, Bose, JBL, or Advent speakers, Technics turntables, or whatever your exclusive is, and your business will grow. Pioneer has a product and a model that will fit almost any system you can design. The quality has never been questioned. Sandy Ruby from Tech HiFi in a recent *Home Furnishings Daily* was quoted as saying "We're actually not doing as much business in limited distribution lines as we were a few years ago. We've tried to look more toward what the market wants. We see surveys of what people are buying or what they say they plan to buy around the country . . . and then we get that equipment. You can't just look at your sales figures. Sure, you may be selling a lot of private brand equipment, but what about the people who didn't buy from you?" What brand do they want? You've got to have a handle on the customers who walked. Pretty interesting stuff. How many of your customers walked? How many did your salesmen's paranoia scare away?

We can help.

Some sales reps suggested that one way U.S. Pioneer could take advantage of the trend toward more mass-oriented retail outlets and, at the same time, "keep specialty stores reasonably happy" would be to adopt a multiple branding strategy. Under this strategy, U.S. Pioneer would offer several product lines of varying quality levels and price points under separate brand names. These product lines would be expected to be carried in different retail outlets. For example, there could be a "regular" line carried by hi-fi specialty stores and a "department store" line. The latter, with a distinctive brand name, would presumably be lower in quality and price points than a "regular" line. Supporters of multiple branding pointed out that such a strategy had been used in other industries in the past[14] and that it would enable U.S. Pioneer to adapt most effectively to changes in

[14]Multiple branding, for example, was used in the watch industry. The Bulova Watch Company had three brand names—Bulova, Accutron, and Caravelle—which differed in quality level and price points. The Bulova line was intended for jewelry and department stores and the Accutron line for the best of stores which carried the Bulova line. The Caravelle line was predominantly in quality drugstores and specialty gift shops. In fact, Bulova had experienced considerable difficulty in maintaining discrete channels for these lines.

EXHIBIT 14
INCOME STATEMENT OF A HI-FI SPECIALTY STORE* (1976)

Income	$680,069	Heat, light, and power	1,242
Cost of sales	$509,182	Bad checks	4,108
Expenses:		Recruiting expenses	889
Advertising	$ 34,803	Store supplies and expense	3,055
Salespeople's commissions (4 salespeople)	36,048	Selling and promotion	115
Payroll, home office (administration)	12,875	Cleaning and rubbish removal	45
Payroll, home office (clerical)	767	Cash over and short	442
Payroll taxes	1,770	Office supplies and expense	1,058
Rent	18,780	Group insurance	257
Depreciation	1,831	Interest expense	857
Insurance	2,937	Legal and accounting	3,648
Taxes—other	237	Auto and truck expense	2,070
Freight out	2,017	Rental commissions	130
Store security	1,168	Computer service expenses	44
Outside labor	3,374	Bank service charges	147
Travel and entertainment	1,336	Officers' life insurance	193
Bad debts	3,313	Miscellaneous	916
Repairs and maintenance	579	Total expenses	$146,120
Repairs to merchandise	57	Operating income before federal taxes	$ 24,767
Credit plan service charges	872		
Telephone	5,318		

*One of the stores of a four-unit chain.

future retail distributions.[15] Others were concerned that such a strategy would tarnish Pioneer's reputation for selling only products as "top of the line."

Another strategic option available to U.S. Pioneer was to move toward operating its own retail stores. Some retailers in the low-fi market (such as Radio Shack and Sears) had been marketing their own "house brands" for some time. More recently, house brands were also starting to make inroads into the hi-fi market. For example, house brand sales within Pacific Stereo (a CBS subsidiary operating a chain of 80 stores on the West Coast) were estimated to be 25 percent of the total unit sales. In other hi-fi specialty stores, house brands were believed to account for 5 to 10 percent of total unit sales.

[15]Should discount stores become a major force in hi-fi components sales, a "discount store" line (with a new brand name) could be added. Pioneer Electronics of America, which was a separate, wholly owned subsidiary of Pioneer Electronics Corporation of Japan, currently sold compacts and car stereos to discount stores under the brand name Centrex.

Some sales reps felt that the growth of house brands would pose a serious threat to U.S. Pioneer in the future. Since the primary promoters of house brands in the hi-fi industry were large specialty store chains (such as Pacific Stereo), Pioneer ran the risk of being "squeezed out" of the larger chains.

One possible means of countering this threat would be for U.S. Pioneer to start operating its own retail stores by acquiring existing one-unit or two-unit family-owned stores or by converting nonaudio stores into "Pioneer shops."

The initial fixed investment for starting up, say, a 5,000-square-foot hi-fi store was estimated by U.S. Pioneer to be about $50,000.

Given the operating data for a comparable existing specialty store (one of the four stores operated by an East Coast retail chain), shown in Exhibit 14, the initial investment appeared to be recoverable in a short period of time. (U.S. Pioneer's income statement is provided in Exhibit 15.)

A few months after the sales rep meeting, Bernie Mitchell met with Ken Kai in his head-

EXHIBIT 15
STATEMENT OF INCOME AND RETAINED EARNINGS FOR U.S. PIONEER (000s OMITTED)

	1976*	1975*
Net sales	$134,836	$87,105
Other operating revenue	258	235
Total revenue	$135,094	$87,340
Cost of goods sold (primarily purchases from the parent company)	$ 91,707	$60,470
Selling, general, and administrative expenses	30,608	23,409
Total CGS and SG&A	$122,315	$83,879
Income before income taxes	$ 12,779	$ 3,461
Provision for income taxes	6,530	1,716
Net income	$ 6,249	$ 1,745
Retained earnings at beginning of year	4,985	3,240
Retained earnings at end of year	$ 11,234	$ 4,985

*Fiscal year ended September 30.
Source: Company data.

quarters office. They tried to decide what action, if any, should be taken in the short run and the long run to ensure U.S. Pioneer's growth and profitability. As they evaluated the various alternatives, the sound of "The William Tell Overture" echoed through the four-way speaker system installed in the office.

23 L'eggs Products, Inc.

Harvey N. Singer • F. Stewart Debruicker

Jack Ward sat down at his desk to resolve a problem which required a decision that week. As group product manager of L'eggs Products, Inc., he had to decide what supplemental advertising and promotional activities, if any, to employ for L'eggs Pantyhose during the coming fall season.

L'eggs Products, Inc., was a subsidiary of the Hanes Corporation, producers of hosiery, knitwear, and foundation garments. L'eggs Pantyhose was the first major nationally branded and advertised hosiery product distributed through food and drug outlets. It had been remarkably successful since its first test market introduction in 1970, through market-by-market roll-out, and now was distributed through grocery stores and drugstores in 90 percent of the country. By mid-1973 it accounted for over 25 percent of the hosiery volume done by food and drug outlets. These outlets represented between 20 and 25 percent of total United States hosiery sales. The

resulting 5 to 6 percent overall market share made L'eggs Pantyhose the largest-selling single brand in the hosiery industry.

With success, however, had come increased competitive efforts from other major manufacturers and from private-label brands. In response, and in keeping with the L'eggs philosophy of aggressive marketing utilizing packaged goods techniques to reinforce consumer purchase behavior, L'eggs was considering various types of advertising and promotional activities for the fall season of 1973. These would coincide with the back-to-school season and the advent of cooler weather, both traditional stimuli to hosiery sales.

Developing the L'eggs Strategy, 1969–1972

L'eggs was the first brand in the hosiery industry to utilize a "packaged goods" marketing program to advertise, promote, display, and sell hosiery to the consumer through food and drug

Harvey N. Singer was formerly a research associate at the Harvard Graduate School of Business Administration. F. Stewart Debruicker is an assistant professor at the Wharton School, University of Pennsylvania.

outlets. This represented a departure from the traditional methods used to merchandise hosiery.

Before the introduction of L'eggs, branded hosiery sales by major industry producers (including Hanes) were made exclusively through department and specialty stores. Starting in 1965, however, sales of private-label hosiery through supermarkets and drugstores had grown dramatically and by 1969 represented a significant share—6 percent for drugstores and 12 percent for supermarkets—of the $1.5 billion retail hosiery market.

Noting these trends, Hanes investigated possible entry into these mass-merchandising outlets on a branded basis. Extensive market, consumer, and product research studies were made to determine (1) the actual size, composition, and nature of the market; (2) consumer attitudes and behavior toward hosiery in general and supermarket hosiery in particular; (3) whether new products developed by Hanes would fulfill planned advertising promises and the consumer expectations these generated.

Market information received from the A. C. Nielsen Company store audits in 1969 verified the existence of a substantial market but indicated problems to be overcome if food and drug hosiery sales were to reach full potential. (In the case of health and beauty aid products, for example, mass outlets accounted for 50 percent of industry volume.) Further channel research isolated these problems:

1. A very fragmented market. Over 600 different hosiery brands were sold in mass outlets, and no brand had more than a 4 percent share.
2. Advertising and promotion to stimulate sales were based on price only—rather than informing the consumer about product qualities or why she should consider buying in a particular outlet.
3. Stock-outs ran as high as 25 percent—manufacturers did not anticipate needs, keep

stocks in balance, or provide necessary service.
4. Retail turnover lagged behind the average of all food and drug products—the retailer's return on investment was unattractive.

Consumer research provided insights into what had to be done to establish a permanent branded franchise:

1. The consumer felt that supermarket and drugstore hosiery had a low-quality image.
2. There was no brand loyalty.
3. Products lacked consistency from package to package.
4. Frequent stock-outs diluted the consumer's confidence in product availability and drove her back to traditional hosiery outlets where such problems did not exist.

Despite these problems, the research indicated a strong desire by consumers to purchase hosiery regularly in convenience outlets if they could develop a lasting confidence in the product.

Hanes concluded that the trade and consumers needed a completely new hosiery product and a marketing program which would build consumer loyalty by virtue of unique product benefits: a distinctive name, package, and display; heavy advertising to build awareness of the brand name, the product's benefits and consistency, and where the product was to be available; and promotional techniques to stimulate both trial and repeat purchases.

The company had developed a new and superior product (preferred over any product tested against it, including the consumer's own brand). It was a one-size, superstretch pantyhose which had no shape until placed on the woman's leg and which then shaped itself to conform to her leg structure, thereby providing an excellent fit for 70 percent of all wearers. This product was more expensive to manufacture than conventional pantyhose. However, with only one size required, Hanes could drastically reduce the inventory and display space required at retail and could consider major innovations in packaging and display.

Hanes sought to develop an integrated hosiery program for food stores and drugstores in which all elements—including name, package design, display configuration, advertising, and promotion—would complement each other. The name, package, and display would have to be dramatic and different if they were to attract the consumer's attention in the store. Other objectives were (1) a package which would differentiate the Hanes product from competitive offerings, minimize pilferage, simplify consumer choice, and facilitate stocking and (2) a display which would hold an adequate amount of inventory to minimize stock-outs while utilizing the smallest practical amount of costly square footage and the greatest practical amount of "free" vertical space. In addition, it was hoped that the display could be designed in such a way that it would be of use to Hanes but not to competitive brands and that the display would be able to provide service and education for the consumer via information panels, literature racks, etc. In essence, Hanes management hoped to use display and packaging techniques to duplicate, in self-service channels, the personalized service available in department and specialty stores.

Working with a package design consultant, the Hanes new-product group developed the brand name *L'eggs*. The name, in turn, suggested the package, an actual plastic egg held in color-coded cylinders (for various colors and styles) that was modular and distinctive from the packages of competitors. They developed a plastic display (called the *L'eggs Boutique*) that carried through the egg concept. It had only a 2-foot diameter, carried 24 dozen pairs, lent itself to placement in high-traffic locations of a store, and proved to be a highly effective point-of-purchase devise.

The L'eggs program was supported by advertising and promotion spending equal to that for a new cigarette or detergent introduction. Introductory advertising was at the rate of $10 million nationally, a level twice as high as total advertising expenditures for the entire industry in support of name brands. Media included daytime and prime-time (7 P.M. to 11 P.M.) television, magazines, Sunday supplements, and local newspapers. In L'eggs's test market cities, two out of three hosiery advertisements seen by consumers were for L'eggs—a brand available only in supermarkets and drugstores. As Mr. David Harrold, the original marketing director of L'eggs Products, explained:

> Given the unstructured market, the nonexistent brand awareness of food and drug hosiery, and the need to reinforce brand permanency to the consumer and the trade, we wished to: (*a*) build strong brand awareness and recognition of our logo and package; (*b*) let the consumer know where L'eggs was available, that it was new and different, and that it would become a permanent grocery and drugstore fixture; (*c*) stress our major product attribute, that L'eggs fit better than any other hosiery product—our theme was "Our L'eggs fit your legs"; (*d*) show the display and package in all advertising to make them synonymous with the L'eggs program.

In addition to media advertising, a $5 million market-by-market consumer promotion plan was tested, using introductory direct-mail coupons worth 25 or 35 cents off the purchase price of one pair, as the products were introduced in each test market. This was the hosiery industry's first heavy use of coupons as strategic trial-generating devices to increase consumer awareness and product experience.

The L'eggs marketing strategy also included a major innovation in the distribution system offered to the trade. L'eggs hosiery was delivered through the front door of the store directly to the retail display by L'eggs sales personnel, who traveled in distinctive trucks. These salespeople saw that a full range of styles and colors was always in stock. They ensured the attractiveness and cleanliness of the display. They rotated and balanced inventory for each store's display rack to maximize sales velocity at each location. Accordingly, the displays had excellent turnover. The company estimated that L'eggs dollar sales per square foot were more than seven times the retailer's average for all goods, and since the products were consigned,[1] the retailer had no investment. The sales-route force also acted as a detail force to implement promotions and other merchandising events at the store level.

Another innovation was a computerized, on-line marketing and sales information network to support the distribution system. It tracked product movement for each display, and through its reports L'eggs could assure balanced product availability on every route van, in every warehouse, and along the pipeline from factory to each market. An outside management consulting firm was hired to design and implement this information and control system. In use, it coordinated manufacturing, warehouse distribution, retail inventory balancing, sales and market analysis, and billing and accounts receivable. Each sales call to a display unit provided a body of inventory and sales information for the system. This information was then assembled by display, by account, by route, by market, and by branch warehouse on a weekly basis and constituted an excellent and timely data source for the analysis of sales performance. In addition, extensive marketing information was routinely gathered in all markets via store audits and diary panels purchased from syndicated information sources. Special field survey research in specific markets conducted by outside research contractors plus concept tests and focus group interviews conducted by the company's own market research personnel supplemented the routine syndicated information.

Sales Results through 1972

Test marketing was conducted from March to October of 1970. After the first 6 months of test

marketing, 40 percent of all potential women users had tried L'eggs at least once. Over two-thirds of those triers repeated with one or more subsequent purchases. Brand awareness and advertising awareness exceeded 80 percent after only 7 weeks of advertising in the test markets. L'eggs became the leading brand of pantyhose, regardless of outlet, in the test markets. At the end of 6 months, almost 25 percent of all women listed L'eggs as their regular brand.

Market-by-market roll-out commenced in the fall of 1970. At its introduction into each geographic market, L'eggs was accompanied by high levels of advertising, demonstration, introductory coupons, and cents-off deals to induce initial trial. This introductory program was often continued for 13 weeks or more, until the product group felt that the introductory objectives had been met. Additional coupon promotions in specific markets were generally repeated several times per year. The L'eggs brand quickly became the dominant factor influencing the entire industry's approach to consumer marketing of hosiery products.

In 1970, L'eggs retail sales were $9 million, representing only 9 months' sales experience in test markets accounting for 3½ percent of the United States and 2 months' sales in the first roll-out market. In 1971, retail sales were over $54 million. L'eggs became firmly established as the best-selling hosiery brand in the country, regardless of outlet, with over a 3 percent share of the total $1.6 billion market. This level was reached with distribution which in 1971 covered only 33 percent of the United States, on the average.

The L'eggs program dramatically expanded hosiery sales through food and drug outlets. Prior to the introduction of L'eggs, only one out of four women had purchased hosiery in these outlets. After 6 months in test markets, over 40 percent of all women had tried L'eggs, which were available only through food and drug outlets. Nielsen data confirmed that total hosiery sales through convenience outlets had expanded

---

[1] That is, the retailer was not billed for the product until after it had been purchased by a consumer.

substantially; L'eggs sales were thus primarily "add-on" sales. Trade acceptance and distribution levels in all market areas equaled the penetration that an established marketing company such as Procter & Gamble or General Foods would expect to achieve on a major new-product introduction—even though this was Hanes's first exposure to mass-merchandising channels.

By the end of 1972, the program had expanded into 75 percent of all retail markets. Fifty major markets had been opened in the span of 18 months. About 45,000 stores were under contract to display the L'eggs Boutique in prominent, high-traffic locations.

1973: Marketing Organization and Strategy

As of mid-1973, the success of the L'eggs program had continued. As market-by-market roll-out proceeded and L'eggs attained deeper penetration of each successive market, retail sales climbed to over $110 million in 1972 and were projected to top $150 million for the fiscal year ending December 31, 1973. By mid-1973, L'eggs had achieved distribution in over 90 percent of the United States and was represented in every major market except New York City. The company's goal was to become fully national by late 1973.

The marketing organization had expanded from an in-house group that in 1969 consisted only of a marketing director, one product manager, an assistant, and one merchandising manager. The present structure included product managers for each of L'eggs's major product extensions; assistants and merchandising managers for each; managers for new products and market development; and a marketing research group. This was in addition to some 700 sales and administrative personnel. An organization chart is shown in Exhibit 1.

Since introducing the original L'eggs Pantyhose and stockings, the company had introduced several successful product extensions under the L'eggs brand: Sheer From Tummy to Toes pantyhose, Queensize pantyhose, Sheer Energy (a support-hosiery product positioned toward nonsupport-hose wearers), and L'eggs Knee Highs. All these product extensions cannibalized the original L'eggs brand to some extent, but the majority of sales were pure incremental sales—coming at the expense of competitors in the marketplace and expanding the total unit and dollar sales of L'eggs Products, Inc.

The use of packaged goods marketing techniques continued to receive the same emphasis in 1973 as it had during the original test-market period. Now that L'eggs was approaching 100 percent national distribution, the initial test-market advertising and promotion spending of $15 million on an equivalent national basis had evolved to an annual spending level of nearly $20 million for advertising, promotion, market research, and new-product development.

The sales effectiveness of this strategy was readily apparent, as detailed in Exhibit 2.

The Industry

L'eggs was introduced into a mature, stable industry. After some expansion in the 1960s with the widespread introduction of pantyhose, the industry had stabilized at a dollar volume of about $1.5 billion and was not expected to increase. Unit sales had increased moderately over the previous several years, but this increased demand had not expanded dollar volume, since the increased sales had only come in the wake of decreased prices. Many purchasers had merely shifted from name-brand department store hosiery at an average price of around $3 to discount hosiery sold in food and drug outlets at prices typically ranging from $0.99 to $1.39. Trade publications had estimated that up to 50 percent of food and drug private-label hosiery sold at prices as low as $0.39 per pair.

Grocery and drugstore outlets represented the fastest-growing hosiery channel. Estimates in

EXHIBIT 1
ORGANIZATION CHART

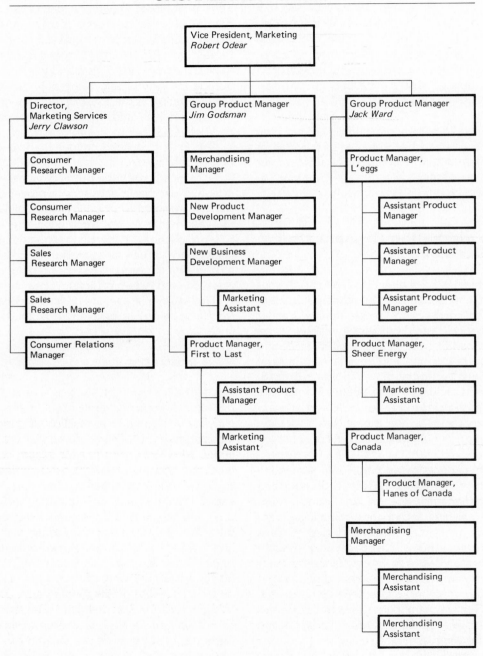

EXHIBIT 2
L'eggs SHARE OF TOTAL HOSIERY SOLD
THROUGH FOOD AND DRUG OUTLETS

Unit Basis, Pairs

	Jan.–Feb.	Mar.–Apr.	May–June	July–Aug.	Sept.–Oct.	Nov.–Dec.
1972	20%	22%	25%	27%	27%	27%
1973	29%	30%	31%	29%		

Source: Nationally syndicated retail audit service.

the trade were that these outlets had accounted for only 5 percent of the units (pairs) sold in 1968. They accounted for 22.1 percent of unit sales in 1972 and were expected to account for as much as 50 percent of unit sales by 1976. L'eggs Products, Inc., had prepared its own estimates of distribution channel changes (see Exhibit 3).

The major companies in the industry appeared to be hastening this trend with huge amounts of marketing spending to advertise and promote food and drug hosiery. Estimates of industry spending ran as high as $33 million in 1972 and the same amount in 1973 by three companies alone, although this figure was probably based on announced intentions, not actual spending.

Competition

Although there were almost 600 different brands of hosiery competing in food and drug outlets, many were private-label and house brands, and the large majority of these were distributed only locally or in a grocery chain's own outlets. L'eggs's only identifiable branded competition in 1972 and 1973 consisted of those products marketed by the Hanes Corporation's major competitors in the hosiery industry: Kayser-Roth Corporation and Burlington Industries. These companies, like Hanes, witnessed the stagnation of hosiery in department store outlets, and soon after L'eggs appeared, they brought out their own heavily advertised and promoted brands for food and drug outlet distribution. Kayser-Roth's entry was called *No Nonsense Pantyhose*, and Burlington called its product *Activ Pantyhose*.

These competitors were companies with considerable financial resources in comparison with those of the Hanes Corporation. Hanes's 1972 sales were $245 million, of which women's hosiery accounted for about $140 million. Hanes's other divisions manufactured and marketed men's and women's knit outerwear and underwear, foundation garments, and swimwear. Kayser-Roth had sales of $519 million in 1972, of which women's hosiery was estimated to account for less than 20 percent. Kayser-Roth also manufactured men's sportswear and clothing, women's sportswear and swimsuits, textiles, and Supphose, the industry's leading support-hosiery brand. Burlington Industries was even larger, with 1972 sales of $1.8 billion, of which women's hosiery sales were $101 million. Burlington also manufactured many other products, such as fabrics, yarns, hosiery for private-label marketers, carpets, furniture, sheets and pillowcases, and industrial textiles. Additional financial information for the three companies is given in Exhibit 4.

These competitors each utilized a somewhat different marketing strategy for hosiery products sold through food and drug channels. Kayser-Roth marketed its No Nonsense brand through supermarket warehouse distributors, who delivered to the back door inventory area of the

EXHIBIT 3
WOMEN'S HOSIERY UNIT SALES
*1971–1973 Estimated, 1974 Forecast**

	All hosiery			Pantyhose		
	Total volume	In food and drug outlets	Percentage of change	Total volume	In food and drug outlets	Percentage of change
1971	123	28.0		82	20.8	
1972	121	29.5	+5	92	24.4	+17
1973	114	29.9	+2	85	25.6	+5
1974	110	30.5	+2	79	25.0	−2

(All hosiery Percentage of change: 1972 −2, 1973 −6, 1974 −4)
(Pantyhose Percentage of change: 1972 +12, 1973 −8, 1974 −7)

*Units: millions of dozens of pairs.
Source: Company estimates.

EXHIBIT 4
COMPANY FINANCIAL DATA*

	Hanes	Kayser-Roth	Burlington
1972 total sales	245	579	1,816
1972 women's hosiery sales (est.)	142	80–100	101
1972 total net income	8.2	11.9	49.6
1971 total sales	176	467	1,727
1971 women's hosiery sales (est.)	88	70–95	115
1971 total net income	3.5	12.3	40

*All figures in millions of dollars.
  Source: Annual reports; corporate 10-K forms filed with the Securities and Exchange Commission.

store—a system typical for packaged goods products. To compensate the store or chain for stocking and cleaning retail displays, No Nonsense offered a retail margin of 42 percent versus L'eggs's 35 percent. The No Nonsense retail prices started at $0.99 versus $1.39 and up for L'eggs.

Burlington distributed its Activ brand in a manner similar to that used by L'eggs. Activ salespeople and vans delivered via the "front door" to the Activ display fixture in food and drug outlets. In addition, Burlington distributed Activ through the General Cigar Corporation, which placed the product in cigar stores and newsstands to achieve a retail base beyond food and drug outlets. Like the retail price of No Nonsense, Activ's suggested retail price of $1 was substantially below that of L'eggs.

L'eggs responded to this price competition neither with direct price-cutting policies of its own nor by permitting the retailers to reduce normal L'eggs prices at the store level. L'eggs was a fair-trade item, and indeed the maintenance of the fair-trade policy was strictly enforced by the company. Management had not hesitated to drop individual stores or even chains from the retail network when it became aware of discounting and the abuse of suggested prices for L'eggs products (via information gathered by the route salespeople during store visits). Retail price maintenance was an important part of L'eggs's overall marketing strategy.

The L'eggs response to competitive price differences was to continue the original strategy of competing in food and drug channels on bases other than price, particularly superior fit. L'eggs management believed that higher prices were necessary and justified because the product was more expensive to produce, due to specially developed high-quality yarn and 100 percent inspection. L'eggs management preferred over the long run to pursue a strategy of maintaining prices and using the resulting margins to support product improvements and advertising to the consumer. In 1973, L'eggs contribution was about $5 per dozen pairs.

An additional reaction to branded price competition came in 1971 when L'eggs Products, Inc., test-marketed its own $0.99 brand, First To Last. The First To Last marketing strategy did not utilize price as the primary sales quality differentiating the product—because there were numerous house brands and private-label pantyhose in all retail outlets that sold at prices considerably below $0.99. Rather, the durability and long-lasting qualities of the product were stressed. Advertising and promotion for First To Last made a conscious effort to minimize any linkage in the consumer's mind between First To Last and L'eggs brands, thereby reducing the degree of cannibalization. The First To Last roll-out proceeded cautiously, with the objective of profitable penetration before further expansion, and in mid-1973 First To Last was distributed in less than 10 percent of the United States.

Although Activ and No Nonsense each announced at their respective introductions planned advertising and promotion spending levels of $10 million nationally, the actual figures were much less. Industry estimates were that No Nonsense would spend no more than $3 million and Activ no more than $1.5 million in 1973. This was partially due to a slower distribution growth than originally planned. While Kayser-Roth had announced that No Nonsense would be distributed in 60 percent of the United States by the end of 1973 and 100 percent by 1974, Mr. Ward estimated that actual distribution had reached less than 15 percent of the country by mid-1973 and would be no more than 40 percent by the end of the year. Similarly, while Burlington had planned for Activ to be distributed in 35 percent of the United States by the end of 1973 and 50 percent by 1974 or 1975, Mr. Ward estimated that actual distribution had reached less than 10 percent of the country by the summer of 1973 and would be no more than 30 percent by late fall.

Market shares for No Nonsense and Activ reflected this lack of national distribution and penetration in comparison with the distribution and penetration of L'eggs. In the late summer of 1973, the national market share in food and drug outlets was 1 percent for both No Nonsense and Activ, compared with 29 percent for L'eggs Pantyhose. Mr. Ward noted, however, that actual spending levels indicated that these competitors could be major factors in geographic markets where they had achieved distribution.

Developing a Supplemental Program for Fall 1973

In considering various supplemental advertising and promotion programs for the fall season, Mr. Ward was acutely aware of the fact that L'eggs seemed to have at least two distinct types of markets characterized by different levels of consumer response to its products. Like many mass marketers, L'eggs used as a measure of this responsiveness a quantity called the BDI (brand development index). For L'eggs, the BDI was defined for each geographic market as the number of L'eggs pairs sold per thousand target women per week divided by the national average number of L'eggs pairs sold per thousand target women per week, then multiplied by 100. An area with a BDI below 100 was an area where L'eggs lagged in penetration versus its national average. Exhibit 5 presents a listing of markets, their BDIs, and the share of L'eggs sales accounted for by each.

In certain regions of the country, the BDIs were consistently less than 80. Mr. Ward's rationale was that these areas had longer warm seasons that might explain lower pantyhose sales. Consumer surveys and panels conducted frequently by L'eggs's market research group, by the advertising agency, and by hired outside research organizations had shown that these low-BDI markets almost uniformly had low—and unsatisfactory—L'eggs trial rates. Typical comparisons between markets are shown in Exhibits 5 and 6. Thus, a major objective in low-BDI areas was to increase trial rates.

In other areas of the country trial rates had peaked at around 50 percent in 6 to 12 months after markets were opened. The brand group did not feel that trial rates in these areas could be increased profitably or at least sustain increases long enough to generate profitably long-run sales. The major problem in high-BDI areas, therefore, was to increase the repurchase rate among L'eggs purchasers.

From different sources of research data, Mr. Ward inferred that much brand switching was taking place. In consumer market surveys, typically 20 to 30 percent of consumers would *say* that L'eggs was their usual brand. However, actual sales figures taken from the company's sales-tracking system and from syndicated store audits indicated that L'eggs had achieved only

EXHIBIT 5
1972 PERFORMANCE IN MARKETS OPENED
DURING 1971 AND EARLIER

Markets	BDI	Share of sales, %	Markets	BDI	Share of sales, %
Portland	80	1	Binghamton	110	1
Sacramento	60	1	Springfield	140	1
Milwaukee	90	2	Hartford/New Haven	90	2
Kansas City	70	1	Erie	160	*
Chicago	110	6	Buffalo	100	2
Los Angeles	120	7	Rochester	110	1
Eugene	80	*	Syracuse	150	2
Medford	60	*	Utica	50	*
Klamath Falls	80	*	Columbia/Jefferson City	90	*
St. Joseph	80	*	Macon	60	*
Topeka	60	*	Chattanooga	70	1
Madison	40	*	Grand Junction	170	*
Rockford	70	*	South Bend/Elkhart	100	1
Santa Barbara	70	*	Cincinnati	120	2
Philadelphia	130	9	Dayton	100	2
Reno	80	*	Indianapolis	110	2
Chico/Redding	90	*	Harrisburg/York	120	2
San Francisco	90	6	Green Bay	60	1
Salinas/Monterey	120	1	Terre Haute	60	*
San Diego	90	1	Eureka	130	*
Detroit	140	6	Las Vegas	130	*
Flint/Saginaw	150	2	Grand Rapids/Kalamazoo	150	2
Lansing	180	1	Fort Wayne	100	1
Boston	130	8	Boise	100	*
Providence	100	2	Twin Falls	110	*
Cleveland	110	5	Idaho Falls/Pocatello	130	*
Youngstown	90	1	Fresno	80	1
Atlanta	90	2	Phoenix	100	1
Denver	150	2	Tucson	60	*
Colorado Springs	100	1	Salt Lake City	80	1
Cheyenne	200	*	Miami	50	1
Toledo	90	1	Tampa	80	1
Columbus	150	2	West Palm Beach	60	*
Lima	110	*	Fort Myers	60	*
Zanesville	120	*	Pittsburgh	100	1
					100%

*Less than 0.5 percent.

about a 10 percent share of the total market in high-BDI areas. Therefore, the most important objectives in these areas were to change users (even repeaters) from casual users to loyal users, to increase their repurchase rate, and to load users with the product to decrease the probability that they would switch to competitive brands. Both Activ and No Nonsense were running

introductory promotions as part of their roll-outs *competitors' activities* in many market areas during the fall season.

The Alternatives

Mr. Ward was considering two basic approaches to accomplishing L'eggs's marketing objectives. On the one hand, he could boost L'eggs's

EXHIBIT 6
PENETRATION MEASURES IN HIGH- AND LOW-BDI AREAS

Market	Kansas City (low BDI)			Philadelphia (high BDI)		
Time after introduction	13 weeks, %	6 months, %	12 months, %	13 weeks, %	6 months, %	12 months, %
Brand awareness	90	90	90	100	100	100
Advertising awareness	60	60	60	80	70	70
Trial	20	20	30	30	40	50
Repurchase rate*	60	70	70	60	70	80
Product satisfaction	70	70	70	90	90	90
L'eggs is usual pantyhose brand	10	10	10	10	20	20

*Defined as percentage of purchasers who bought more than once in last 3 months.
Source: Company data.

planned media advertising expenditures for August through October from the currently planned level of approximately $2.5 million to, perhaps, $3.5 million. Such an increase in media advertising would ensure media dominance in all markets and would be expected to have a significant positive effect on both trial and repurchase. Advertising copy would stress L'eggs quality advantages (especially fit and durability) and subtly carry the message "You get what you pay for." If spot TV rather than national television were used (at a cost penalty of about 20 percent), separate campaigns could be run in high-BDI and low-BDI areas, or expenditures could be concentrated in selected markets.

On the other hand, Mr. Ward was attracted by the idea (developed by the product group) of maintaining media advertising expenditures at the planned level but using in-store price promotions as a direct means of inducing consumer trial and/or repurchase. The product group had developed two such promotions: (1) a 40-cents-off twin-pack offer (see Exhibit 7) and (2) a 20-cents-off single-pack offer (see Exhibit 8).

In focusing on these alternatives, the product group had reasoned as follows about their likely effects. The 40-cents-off twin pack probably would achieve the objective of loading the consumer in high-BDI areas (for her next pair the consumer would have the second pair of

L'eggs in the twin pack already and would have no need to go out and purchase, perhaps, a competitive brand). It was hoped that more product use and experience with two pairs rather than one would predispose the consumer to repurchase L'eggs the next time she needed hosiery. However, Mr. Ward thought the twin pack might not be effective in low-BDI areas because with the low trial rates and low market shares in these areas, sufficient numbers of consumers might not purchase the twin pack often enough to make the promotion effective. Besides, the consumer, not a L'eggs user anyway, might balk at having to purchase two pairs in order to try L'eggs.

The 20-cents-off single pack seemed to have a good potential in both types of markets. In low-BDI areas, consumer take-away for the promotion (the number of consumers purchasing) would presumably be higher because the new trier would not be forced to purchase two pairs. In high-BDI areas, the consumer might buy two or more single packs, satisfying the objectives of consumer loading and raising repeat rates. There was nothing, however, to encourage the consumer (or force the consumer, as did the twin pack) to purchase more than one pair.

Under either alternative, L'eggs would bear 65 percent of the cost of the price reduction and

EXHIBIT 7
40-CENTS-OFF TWIN-PACK

the retailer would bear 35 percent (the same ratio as the retailer's gross margin). For example, for the 20-cents-off single pack, the retailer would absorb 7 cents (35 percent of 20 cents) and L'eggs would absorb 13 cents (65 percent of 20 cents).

Since L'eggs was a fair-traded item, Mr. Ward knew that it could not appear in any store under a cents-off deal except for a limited time only and that it could not appear in any store under two different prices for the same quantity (such as the regular price for the boutique pack and 20-cents off for the promotional single pack) simultaneously. This meant that to implement the single-pack offer, L'eggs would have to move all existing inventory out of stores at the beginning of the promotion, replace them with

special 20-cents-off single packs, remove all special packs at the promotion's end, and move all regular inventory back in.

A possible solution was for L'eggs to make the special single pack a simple variation of the regular pack. At the promotion's start all existing store packs could have a flag inserted; it would be removed at the promotion's end. (Exhibit 8 shows a discount flag inserted into a regular L'eggs pack.) Because the L'eggs route persons were fully occupied with their normal stocking, accounting, and boutique-cleaning operations in over 70,000 outlets, a temporary work force would have to be hired to travel with the route persons to insert flags. Mr. Ward estimated that each of the 600 L'eggs route persons would need a temporary assistant for one 3-week cycle.

EXHIBIT 8
20-CENTS-OFF SINGLE PACK

These temporaries could be hired from well-known agencies at the rate of $30 per day per person. After the promotion was begun, the temporary labor would be replaced by factory labor because flags would be inserted in boutique-destined replacement packs at the factory. The product group recommended that the route persons be used for unflagging boutique packs at the promotion's end, even though their route schedules could be delayed considerably by the extra work.

To supplement the boutique in the stores during the promotion, the factory would also make up special "shippers"—self-contained cardboard floor displays that would be packed at the factory to minimize setup time at the retail store but which (if accepted by the retailer) would require allocating additional floor space to L'eggs. Mr. Ward estimated that the cost of the single-pack shippers, freight, point-of-sale material, etc., would average out to $0.35 per dozen pairs. The shippers could simply be removed at the promotion's conclusion.

The twin-pack promotion required no such expensive field labor for implementation. Because the quantity in the promotional twin packs would differ from the quantity in the regular boutique packs (one pair each), the twin-pack shipper display could be utilized to implement the promotion without boutique flagging. The shipper and promotional packs for it could be completely factory-made and placed in the store to coexist with regular-priced boutique packs, then simply removed at the promotion's conclusion. Fair-trade laws would not be violated, since the cents-off promotional twin packs would hold different quantities than the regular-priced boutique packs. Mr. Ward estimated the cost of making up these shippers, freight, point-of-sale material, and twin packs at $0.38 per dozen hosiery pairs.

He anticipated a bit of increased trade resistance to the twin-pack alternative, since the shippers were absolutely necessary in the case of the twin packs, and thus the retailer would have to devote roughly 6 more square feet of selling space to L'eggs during the promotion. In contrast, the 20-cents-off single-pack alternative could be accomplished solely via flagged boutique packs if the retailer refused the additional single-pack shippers. However, Mr. Ward expected this resistance to be minimal because of L'eggs's outstanding sales velocity. In addition, retailer acceptance for the twin-pack alternative might be greater. The retailer could be shown that because the boutique packs at regular prices (and margins) were still in the store, consumers could elect to purchase a single pack at the normal price and margin instead of the twin pack with its commensurately lower margin per pair.

Mr. Ward recognized, of course, that it would theoretically be possible to use both the 40-cents-off twin-pack promotion in high-BDI markets and the 20-cents-off single-pack promotion in low-BDI markets. While conceptually attractive, such an option would be undesirable, in his view, because of increased costs and the difficulty of implementation. Under either in-store price promotion alternative, for example, L'eggs planned to devote a substantial portion of its *normal* media advertising budget to advertising the promotion on television and in local newspapers. If the 20-cents-off single pack were used in some markets and the 40-cents-off twin pack in others, it would be necessary to switch from national network advertising to local spots at a considerable additional cost.

Moreover, the mechanics of implementing two promotions simultaneously would cause headaches for L'eggs production and warehouse personnel, who would have to produce and ship several different types of point-of-sale materials, special packages, and shipper displays of merchandise. Finally, selling a "mixed" promotion to national and regional accounts, with stores in both high-BDI and low-BDI markets, would be exceedingly difficult. As Mr. Ward explained, "How do you convince Safeway's national buyer to take the promotion when you also have to tell him why his Little Rock stores have to take single-packs and his Los Angeles stores have to take twin-packs?"

Estimating Sales Response to Promotion

Relying on his personal judgment and his experience gained during the national roll-outs, Mr. Ward estimated some of the sales response effects of the 20-cents-off single-pack promotion and the 40-cents-off twin-pack promotion. For the 20-cents-off single pack, he reasoned that during the 4 weeks the promotional packs were actually in stores, about 80 percent of what would have been L'eggs purchases at normal prices would be made instead at the reduced price. The other 20 percent would represent stores that did not accept the promotion, lost flags, and similar factors. Since normal L'eggs volume was running at 150,000 dozen per week, or 600,000 dozen per 4 weeks, Mr. Ward estimated that normal purchases at reduced prices would thus total 80 percent of 600,000, or 480,000 dozen.

It was more difficult, of course, to estimate the effect of a promotion on incremental business. Mr. Ward made the working assumption that the single-pack promotion would generate a 10 to 11 percent net cumulative sales increase[2] over

---

[2] That is, sales during the 20 weeks would be 10 to 11 percent greater (in the aggregate) than they would have been without the promotion.

EXHIBIT 9
POSSIBLE ADVERTISING COPY FOR
FALL 1973 SUPPLEMENTAL CAMPAIGN

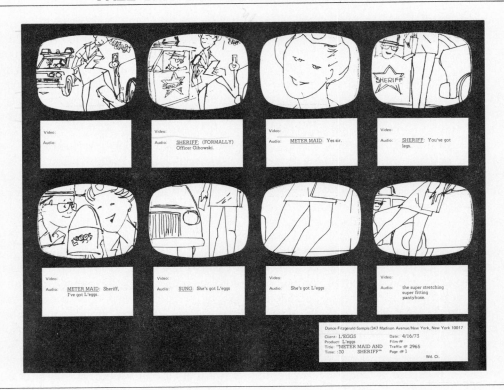

an immediate period of 20 weeks during and following the promotion, plus a 10 percent long-term (sustained) sales increase.

For the 40-cents-off twin-pack alternative, Mr. Ward judged that during the 4 weeks the packs were actually in the stores, about 60 percent of what would have been L'eggs purchases at normal prices would be made instead at the reduced price. This estimate was lower than the 20-cents-off single-pack figure because:

1. Single pairs at regular prices would be coexisting in the stores with promotional packs, and women—even L'eggs users—who did not want two pairs would still have the opportunity to purchase one pair at the regular price.

2. Mr. Ward expected the twin-pack alternative to have less of an effect with nonloyal L'eggs users, who might resist buying two pairs at a time but might pick up one pair, even at the regular price.

3. Some stores might not accept the promotion.

Taking these factors into account, Mr. Ward estimated that the twin-pack alternative would generate a 10 percent net cumulative sales increase over the immediate 20-week period during and following the promotion but would produce no long-term increase in sales.

EXHIBIT 9
Continued

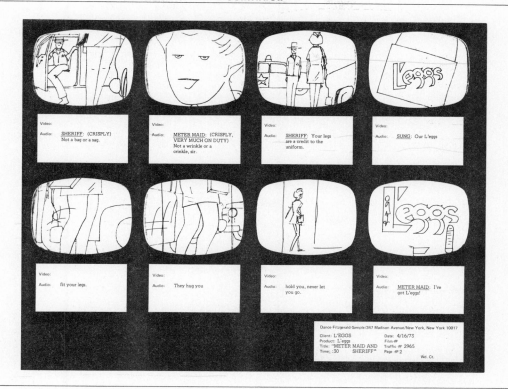

Video:
Audio: SHERIFF: (CRISPLY) Not a bag or a sag.

Video:
Audio: METER MAID: (CRISPLY, VERY MUCH ON DUTY) Not a wrinkle or a crinkle, sir.

Video:
Audio: SHERIFF: Your legs are a credit to the uniform.

Video:
Audio: SUNG: Our L'eggs

Video:
Audio: fit your legs.

Video:
Audio: They hug you

Video:
Audio: hold you, never let you go.

Video:
Audio: METER MAID: I've got L'eggs!

Dance-Fitzgerald-Sample/347 Madison Avenue/New York, New York 10017
Client: L'EGGS   Date: 4/16/73
Product: L'eggs   Film #
Title: "METER MAID AND   Traffic # 2965
Time: :30   SHERIFF"   Page #2
                        Wd. Ct.

The consumer response to an increased media advertising budget was exceptionally difficult to estimate, Mr. Ward believed, but would almost certainly not be as great (in the short run) as the response to either of the cents-off promotional alternatives. Nevertheless, he was strongly attracted to the ease of implementation of this alternative and to the possible strategic advantages of not focusing the consumer's attention on price at this point in the development of competition in the market. At his request, the L'eggs advertising agency had prepared rough copyboards for a series of 30-second vignettes which stressed L'eggs's superior quality, especially with regard to fit. (See Exhibit 9 for an example of the proposed copy.)

Conclusion

As he reviewed the alternatives, Mr. Ward remained convinced that some form of supplemental advertising or promotion should be employed during the fall of 1973. While L'eggs had had considerable market success during the 3 years since it had first begun test marketing, he considered it imperative that actions be taken to sustain that success, especially in the face of increasing competition. Moreover, he remained concerned about those low-BDI markets where L'eggs's apparent penetration was well below its national average.

Since the fall season was rapidly approaching, Mr. Ward knew that he would have to make a firm decision as to what course to follow before the end of the week.

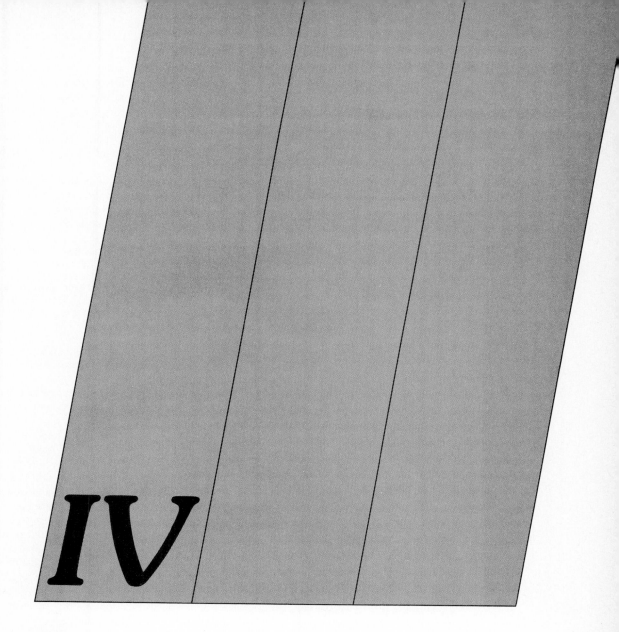

IV

Communications
Strategy

The term "communications strategy" often evokes thoughts of mass media advertising, since we all are exposed to a good deal of it. Consumer goods marketers spend over $25 billion per year on media advertising, and for some companies media advertising might represent as much as 15 to 20 percent of the total sales revenue. Industrial marketers spend over $1 billion per year on trade advertising (not including "image" advertising in consumer-oriented media). Such are the costs of reaching large segments of buyers through mass media such as television, radio, magazines, and newspapers.

But "communications strategy" also includes the personal selling effort which might be required to implement marketing strategy. An industrial salesperson is the key link between a selling organization and a buying organization. An industrial sales call might cost $75 or more depending on the industry, the product, the relative concentration of customers in a sales territory, and the particular salesperson.

The elements of communications strategy included in the communications mix are as follows:

1. Advertising, including mass media campaigns, direct mail, and mail order advertising
2. Sales promotion, including merchandising tools such as point-of-sale displays, cents-off coupons, and trade show exhibits
3. Personal selling

In general, the cases in this section are intended to provide students with experience in formulating, implementing, and evaluating communications strategies across a wide variety of products and services.

One objective is to assess the different roles which various elements in the communications mix play in the marketing strategy and to examine various ways of setting the communications budget.

Communications decisions follow from marketing objectives, and it is important to formulate communications strategies in concert with product, price, and distribution decisions. But how does the manager determine the optimal proportions of the communications budget to be allocated among advertising, personal selling, and sales promotion? Can a company ever do without any advertising—or, for that matter, without some other element of the communications mix? Allocating resources requires that managers understand the functions that various forms of communications perform for different consumer segments, for different products or services, at different points in time. For example, consumer needs for information are greatest when a new product is launched—particularly when that new product is truly innovative. If the market is large, mass media advertising might be the most cost-effecient way to reach the greatest number of consumer segments. On the other hand, a new industrial product might require the more targeted and detailed information best communicated by a salesperson, perhaps after trade show promotions and trade advertising have made industrial customers aware of the product, and the selling company.

Just as there is no formula for allocating resources to the elements of the communications mix, there is no simple way to set the communications budget in the first place. This is because it is quite difficult to know with certainty the profit impact of promotion. One cannot trace a certain level of sales to, say, three or four full-page magazine ads, since many other influences affect sales, such as past advertising, competitive activity, distribution, and sales force activities. Often marketers simply take a percentage of past or anticipated sales as the promotion budget, although the logic of such an approach is questionable.

A second objective of the cases in this section is to illustrate issues in planning and managing personal selling. What role does the salesperson play in the marketing process, and how can the personal selling function be planned, evaluated, and improved? Often, such questions depend heavily on the salesperson's abilities to understand and respond effectively to the buying decision process in customer organizations.

A final objective is to provide experience in making tactical decisions for implementing communications strategy. Should you have more salespeople? Should you spend over $200,000 for a 30-second commercial on "Monday Night Football"? Should you buy a page in the *Wall Street Journal* or advertise on prime-time television? Should you run one ad 3 times, 5 times, or 20 times? Should you make implicit or explicit comparisons with your competition in advertising? These are tactical issues in managing the communications mix, and as in making allocation and budgeting decisions, there are no easy answers to questions regarding the optimum mix of print versus broadcast media, media advertising versus increased sales force spending, or message decisions. The manager might wish to test various levels and mixes of communications in a few cities or regions, assuming one can control extraneous factors which might bias results. Most often, however, tactical decisions are based on the cumulative experience of marketing managers and advertising specialists. The crucial need is to base tactical decisions on carefully planned communications objectives; these, in turn, must be based on clear marketing objectives and strategies.

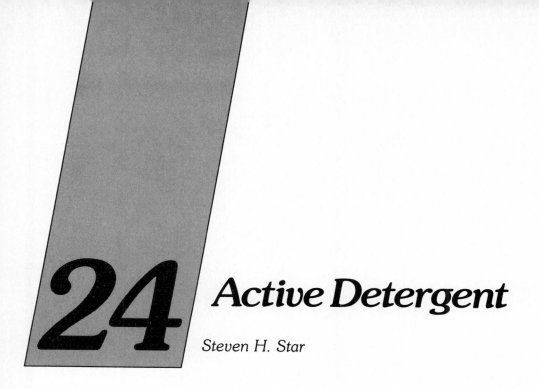

24 Active Detergent

Steven H. Star

The Witco Chemical Company of Paterson, New Jersey, announced that it was introducing *Active*, a new, "nonadvertised national brand" of laundry detergent in the New England and Washington-Baltimore markets. According to Dr. Marvin Mausner, vice president of Witco's Ultra Division, laundry detergents were one of the most heavily advertised product categories in the United States, with 1974 industry media advertising expected to reach $80 million, 8 percent of industry sales (at manufacturers' prices). Since detergents were a mature product category, such high advertising expenditures were unwarranted in Dr. Mausner's view, especially in an era when consumerism and intense concern over inflationary price increases were so pronounced. In the light of this analysis, Witco planned to position Active as a detergent which

This case has been written from published sources, an address by Dr. Mausner to the Marketing Club of the Harvard Business School, and a number of industry sources who prefer to remain anonymous.

Steven H. Star was formerly an associate professor at the Harvard Graduate School of Business Administration.

was "as good as" the nationally advertised brands, but which would sell at a lower price because no money would be spent on consumer advertising. To acquaint consumers with its new product, Witco planned to rely on a public relations program, package copy, and visible shelf locations in supermarkets.

Company Background

The Witco Chemical Corporation was one of the world's larger manufacturers of specialty chemical products, with 1974 sales of slightly more than $550 million. Witco's product line covered a wide range of industrial and consumer applications, from private-label laundry detergents to diatomaceous earth and urethane chemicals and systems. In 1973, "consumer" markets represented between 18 and 19 percent of Witco's sales. Witco's major consumer products included the Amalie® and Kendall® brands of motor oil, private-label detergents, and lubricants.

Witco had been a major manufacturer of

detergents and ingredients used in the manufacture of detergents for many years. In 1973, Witco had detergent sales of approximately $28 million, most of which represented sales of private-label detergents to such major retailers as Stop & Shop, Jewel, and Shop Rite. The remainder was sold to other detergent manufacturers. According to industry sources, Witco was by far the largest manufacturer of private-label detergents in the United States.

Witco's decision to enter the branded detergent business had the twin objectives of increasing Wicto's detergent volume and increasing Witco's profit margin. While a manufacturer of private-label detergents (such as Witco) received only about 27 cents per pound (including transportation) for packaged detergents, a national brand manufacturer (such as Procter & Gamble, Lever Brothers, or Colgate) received between 33 cents and 37 cents per pound. No matter how they were marketed, detergents cost from 19 cents to 21 cents per pound to manufacture in late 1974 (including transportation and packaging).

Dr. Marvin Mausner was in charge of the technical aspects of the Active project. A Ph.D. in chemistry, Dr. Mausner had specialized in detergents research and development for many years and had—in his own words—"seen and cleaned more piles of dirty laundry than any woman in the room." By late 1974, Witco had hired several persons with extensive packaged goods marketing experience to develop the Active marketing program.

The United States Detergent Market

The United States laundry detergent market was estimated at $1.105 billion (at retail prices) in 1974, up 1.4 percent over 1973. While product category unit sales had grown by as much as 5 percent per year in the late 1960s, this rate of growth had slowed considerably in the early 1970s. According to industry observers, this reduction in the industry's growth rate could be attributed to a tendency by consumers (1) to use less detergent in each wash load, (2) to wash more clothes in each load, and (3) to form households later and have fewer children than they had during the 1960s.

The detergent industry was dominated by three large multinational companies: Procter & Gamble, Lever Brothers (a subsidiary of Unilever), and Colgate-Palmolive. These three companies accounted for 91.9 percent of the United States market in 1974, up 1.5 percent from 1973. Private-label laundry detergents were estimated to account for less than 5 percent of the United States market in 1974, a notably lower percentage than in most other household-product categories.

The three industry leaders pursued marketing strategies based on multiple products aimed at individual market segments and on heavy advertising and promotion expenditures. In 1974, Procter & Gamble, with 54 percent of the total market, marketed nine brands of laundry detergent; Lever Brothers (22 percent share) marketed seven brands; and Colgate (15.9 percent share) marketed six brands. During that year, only seven brands had more than a 4 percent market share: Tide (P&G), 27.3 percent; Cheer (P&G), 9.3 percent; All (Lever), 9.3 percent; Wisk (Lever), 8 percent; Fab (Colgate), 5 percent; Cold Power (Colgate), 4.7 percent; and Bold (P&G), 4.5 percent. Comparative data on the leading detergent brands are shown in Exhibit 1.

In 1974, P&G, Colgate, and Lever were the first, sixth, and seventh largest advertisers in the United States, allocating the vast bulk of their advertising expenditures to television. According to industry estimates, P&G spent $42.7 million on laundry detergent advertising in 1974, Lever spend $18 million, and Colgate spent $17.2 million. While all three firms used nighttime television to advertise some of their products, the majority of their detergent advertising was

EXHIBIT 1
LEADING LAUNDRY DETERGENTS:
MARKET SHARES AND MEDIA ADVERTISING, 1974

Manufacturer	Brand	U.S. market share, %	New England market share, %	Measured media advertising, $ million
Procter & Gamble	Tide	27.3	18.3	11.5
Lever	All (powder & liquid)	9.3	13.3	7.8
Procter & Gamble	Cheer	9.3	4.8	10.0
Lever	Wisk (liquid)	8.0	13	8.4
Colgate	Fab	5.0	6.2	3.8
Colgate	Cold Power	4.7	6.6	4.0
Procter & Gamble	Bold	4.5	4	4.0
Procter & Gamble	Gain	3.6	1.7	3.3
Procter & Gamble	Dash	3.0	3.8	4.7
Colgate	Ajax	3.0	4	3.2
Procter & Gamble	Oxydol	2.7	3.1	3.2
Colgate	Dynamo (liquid)	2.0	2.6	5.6
Procter & Gamble	Duz	2.0	NA	1.2
Lever	Breeze	1.5	NA	0.7
Lever	Drive	1.3	NA	1.0
Colgate	Punch	1.0	NA	nil
Procter & Gamble	Bonus	1.0	NA	0.1
Church & Dwight	Arm & Hammer	NA	4.9	NA
All others		NA	NA	7.5
		100	100	80

Source: Advertising Age, April 7, 1975; Leading National Advertisers, January–December, 1974; SAMI (courtesy of a supermarket chain which prefers to remain anonymous).

on daytime television, expecially the so-called "soap operas." (See Appendix A for examples of detergent advertising.) It was estimated that the leading manufacturers in the detergent category spent approximately as much on consumer promotion (e.g., cents-off coupons) and trade promotions (e.g., allowances for special displays) as they did for media advertising.

The vast bulk of laundry detergent sales was through food stores. Detergents were an important product category to food retailers, which frequently sold them at relatively low margins to reinforce their low-price images with consumers. One large supermarket chain in New England devoted 24 linear feet (48 square feet of floor space) to laundry detergents in a "typical" store. During the fourth week of October 1974, this "typical" store sold 384 units of powdered

laundry detergents and obtained $522.89 in sales and $61.93 in gross margins from the powdered laundry detergent product category. (See Exhibit 2 for a detailed analysis of an average week's laundry detergent sales in this store and Exhibit 3 for a "Plan-O-Gram" showing the shelf locations of individual brands and sizes in this store.) According to the groceries merchandising manager for this chain, detergents were a stable product category which required little management attention.

During recent years, there had been trends in the industry toward low phosphate or nonphosphate detergents, toward larger package sizes, and (most recently) toward phosphate-free liquid detergents. Looking ahead, industry observers believed that the laundry detergent product category would grow very little, if at all, in unit

EXHIBIT 2
SALES OF POWDERED LAUNDRY DETERGENTS IN ONE "TYPICAL" SUPERMARKET: OCTOBER 21–26, 1974

Item	Cost/ unit	Retail/ unit	Weekly sales units	Weekly sales dollars	Weekly gross profit	Approx. linear feet
Tide:						
20 oz.	$0.47	$0.53	56	$ 29.68	$ 3.36	3.4
49 oz.	1.12	1.27	39	49.53	5.85	7.2
84 oz.	1.87	2.13	18	38.34	4.68	2.4
All:						
49 oz.	$0.99	$1.15	32	$ 36.80	$ 5.12	7.2
157 oz.	2.97	3.29	11	36.19	3.52	2.4
320 oz.	5.95	6.29	6	37.74	2.04	3.0
Cheer:						
49 oz.	$1.12	$1.27	18	$ 22.86	$ 2.70	2.4
84 oz.	1.87	2.13	6	12.78	1.56	1.8
Fab:						
20 oz.	$0.47	$0.53	26	$ 13.78	$ 1.56	1.8
49 oz.	1.12	1.27	15	19.05	2.25	3.0
84 oz.	1.87	2.13	6	12.78	1.56	1.8
Cold Power:						
49 oz.	$1.12	$1.27	18	$ 22.86	$ 2.70	2.4
84 oz.	1.87	2.13	8	17.04	2.08	1.8
Bold:						
84 oz.	$1.87	$2.13	7	$ 14.91	$ 1.82	1.8
Gain:						
49 oz.	$1.12	$1.27	9	$ 11.43	$ 1.35	1.8
Dash:						
49 oz.	$0.99	$1.15	8	$ 9.20	$ 1.28	2.4
157 oz.	2.97	3.29	5	16.45	1.60	1.8
Ajax:						
49 oz.	$1.12	$1.27	9	$ 11.43	$ 1.35	2.4
84 oz.	1.87	2.13	1	2.13	0.26	1.8
Oxydol:						
49 oz.	$1.12	$1.27	9	$ 11.43	$ 1.35	2.4
Duz:						
50 oz.	$1.35	$1.47	4	$ 5.88	$ 0.48	2.4
Miracle White:						
49 oz.	$1.08	$1.27	3	$ 3.81	$ 0.57	1.8
Instant Fels:						
49 oz.	$1.13	$1.27	5	$ 6.35	$ 0.70	1.8
Arm & Hammer:						
30 oz.	$0.47	$0.54	15	$ 8.10	$ 1.05	1.8
70 oz.	1.08	1.25	16	20.00	2.72	1.8
115 oz.	1.68	1.99	6	11.94	1.86	3.0
Private label:						
49 oz.	$0.82	$1.05	12	$ 12.60	$ 2.76	5.4
84 oz.	1.38	1.62	12	19.44	2.88	8.4
160 oz.	1.86	2.09	4	8.36	0.92	1.8
Total			384	$522.89	$61.93	83.2

EXHIBIT 3

PLAN-O-GRAM OF LAUNDRY DETERGENTS SECTION:
ONE "TYPICAL" SUPERMARKET, OCTOBER 1974

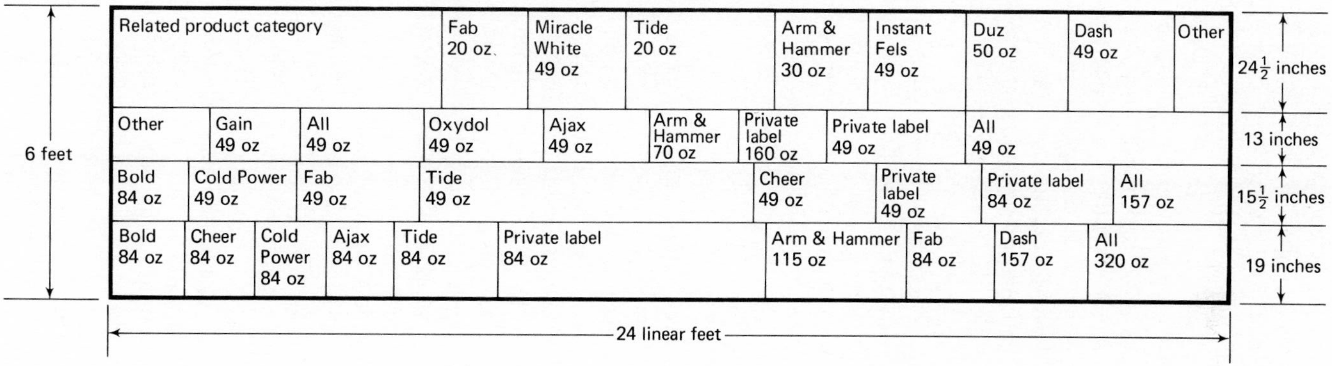

Related product category								Other
Other	Gain 49 oz	All 49 oz	Fab 20 oz	Miracle White 49 oz	Tide 20 oz	Arm & Hammer 30 oz	Instant Fels 49 oz	Duz 50 oz / Dash 49 oz
Bold 84 oz	Cold Power 49 oz	Fab 49 oz	Oxydol 49 oz	Ajax 49 oz	Arm & Hammer 70 oz	Private label 160 oz	Private label 49 oz	Private label 49 oz / All 49 oz
Bold 84 oz	Cheer 84 oz	Cold Power 84 oz	Ajax 84 oz	Tide 49 oz / Tide 84 oz	Private label 84 oz	Cheer 49 oz	Private label 84 oz	Private label 84 oz / All 157 oz
						Arm & Hammer 115 oz	Fab 84 oz	Dash 157 oz / All 320 oz

Shelf heights (right side, top to bottom): 24½ inches, 13 inches, 15½ inches, 19 inches

Overall dimensions: 6 feet (height) × 24 linear feet (length)

volume, although dollar sales might increase as a result of inflation. The new category of liquid laundry detergents was expected to increase in market share, but low-phosphate and nonphosphate powdered detergents, such as Arm & Hammer, were not expected to make further inroads. While P&G and Colgate had each increased their market share by about 1.5 percent in 1974 (Lever and "others" had each lost about 1.5 percent in 1974), no major changes in manufacturers' market shares were anticipated for 1975. It was expected, however, that increased pressure on retail inventories and shelf space might cause major supermarkets to reduce their numbers of stockkeeping units (a single size of a specific brand) in 1975.

The major new branded detergent on the market in 1974 was P&G's Era, a nonphosphate heavy-duty liquid positioned to compete with Lever's Wisk. P&G introduced Era in Oklahoma City and in Portland, Oregon, in November 1972 and gradually expanded east into Kansas City, Wichita, St. Louis, Milwaukee, Chicago, Cincinnati, Cleveland, and Pittsburgh. In each of these markets, it did massive sampling and couponing programs, gave dollar allowances to the trade, and ran saturation TV advertising. Lever countered with a "buy one, get one free" promotion on Wisk, but according to P&G's sales literature, Era still beat it handily. In some markets, Era became the best-selling liquid detergent 2 months after its introduction and the best-selling of all competitive powders and liquids within 3 months. P&G sources said Era had leveled off to a 6 percent share in its test markets. In October 1974, P&G had begun to introduce Era into New York and New England markets.

Industry sources would not speculate on P&G's total introductory expenditures for Era, but it was known that P&G had spent as much as $25 million to launch Bold detergent in 1965. During the first half of 1973, according to measured media figures, P&G spent $236,400 on Era in Oklahoma City and Portland ($204,400 in spot TV and $32,000 in Sunday newspa-per supplements). Measured media sources put spot TV expenditures on Era through the first 6 months of 1974 at about $800,000, but that did not include subsequent outlays for Chicago, Cincinnati, Cleveland, and Pittsburgh. In Milwaukee, during a 1-week period, TV advertising expenditures came to $7,000. According to P&G sources the TV spots reached "nine out of ten women every four weeks with an average of six Era spots." All spots were 60 seconds. Their theme was "The new detergent that could make your present one obsolete. New Era. Outpowers the powders." P&G did not emphasize the fact that Era did not contain phosphates, largely, it was thought, because P&G still asserted that a small amount of phosphorus was necessary to make an effective powdered detergent.

For the introduction of Gain, P&G had distributed about 40 million samples door to door across the country. The total Era sampling was not expected to be as large, however, because only major metropolitan areas got free samples. Smaller towns got free coupons via mail. In Chicago the sampling consisted of about 1.2 million samples of 16-ounce-size Era (55 cents retail) in sealed bags containing a sales brochure, a 25-cents-off coupon for Downy fabric softener, and a 10-cents-off coupon for two bars of Zest. The Milwaukee distribution was estimated at over 1 million.

Active

Witco's marketing strategy for Active was based on the premise that a significant segment of consumers would be attracted to a new detergent positioned as equivalent to the nationally advertised brands in ingredients and performance but considerably less expensive to purchase. According to Dr. Mausner, a homemaker who used Active would receive a performance at least as good as that of such national brands as Tide, Cheer, and All. As a mature product category, Dr. Mausner continued, detergents were all essentially the same in performance, although they could differ significantly in color, fragrance, and density. With regard to density and performance, Active was formulated to be "virtually identical" to the best-selling brands.

The package for Active was brightly colored (red, yellow, and blue) to attract consumer attention and contained more body copy than was typical on detergent packages. The Active message, "As good as the advertised brands; less expensive because it is not advertised," was featured in the body copy, as was this promise: "double your money back guarantee if not completely satisfied." According to Dr. Mausner, the Active package was intended to induce consumer trials and to reinforce the Active message once it was in the consumer's home.

Active was to be distributed as intensively as possible through supermarkets and independent grocers. The manufacturer's selling price was to be $9.45 per case of ten 49-ounce packages. Most supermarkets were expected to sell Active for $1.10 to $1.15 per unit. Supermarkets typically obtained 5 to 12 percent gross margins on advertised brands of detergents, which they sold at retail from $1.25 to $1.35 for the 49-ounce size. While supermarkets could obtain gross margins of more than 20 percent on their private-label laundry detergents, such private labels, as noted above, accounted for only a small share of industry volume.

Witco planned to use food brokers to sell to retailers, beginning in the New England and Washington-Baltimore markets. These two areas were believed to account for approximately 8 to 10 percent of the laundry detergent market. Food brokers did not take title to the merchandise they sold and typically acted as agents for a number of noncompeting manufacturers. They received compensation in the form of a commission on their sales, usually 5 percent of the manufacturer's selling price. In recent years, food brokers had increased in importance in many product categories. While most of the lines they carried were specialty products manufac-

tured by companies which could not afford their own sales forces, there had been a recent tendency for large packaged-food manufacturers to use food brokers for some of their products and their own direct sales forces for others. In following this course, such manufacturers seemed to value highly the long-standing relationships between leading food brokers and major supermarket accounts and to believe that food brokers could give more focused attention to certain brands than their own multiproduct sales forces.

In the laundry detergent product category, none of the leading manufacturers utilized food brokers. P&G was believed to have the strongest sales force in the packaged-goods industry, while Colgate's and Lever's sales forces were considered very effective. Witco had been able to sign up the leading food brokers in the New England and Washington markets, both of which were highly enthusiastic about having an entry in the detergent product category. On the basis of early indications from the food brokers, it was anticipated that Active would achieve 80 percent distribution in the New England and Washington-Baltimore markets by mid-1975.

While Active would not be advertised to the consumer, Witco planned some trade advertising in late 1974 and early 1975. These advertisements, which would be placed in such trade publications as *The Griffin Report of New England* and *Food World*, would stress the benefits of the product to the retailer. Among the major benefits to be cited were higher gross margins, a better value to the consumer during a period of rapid inflation, and an image of being responsive to the consumerism movement.

Public relations was to be the primary instrument for acquainting consumers with the fact that Active was on the market. Dr. Mausner and other Witco personnel were to speak to women's groups, educational institutions, trade associations, and consumerist groups throughout the Washington, D.C., and New England markets, to be interviewed by newspaper and magazine "consumer affairs" reporters, and to appear on radio and television talk shows. On the basis of previous experience, the public relations firm employed for this purpose estimated that as many as 1 million persons would be exposed to Active through the news media by the end of the first quarter of 1975. In support of this projection, they explained that high prices and consumerism issues in general were very topical in early 1975 and that newspapers were always looking for interesting material for their weekly food sections.

Appendix A
Audio Text of Television Commercials
(All Major Brands)

1. "Tide" Detergent (60-second commercial)

WOMAN:	Did you ever watch your little boy when he's helping his father?
MAN SINGS:	Gary is daddy's little helper. You can tell by his knees how hard he's tried. You get a lot of dirt with children. You get a lot of clean with Tide. Helping dad, a kid gets hungry, and his shirt gets covered with cherry pie. You get a lot of dirt with children. You get a lot of clean with Tide.
WOMAN:	Somehow Gary gets twice as dirty as his father. And the dirt's not only on his clothes, it's in them. Ground right through to the inside. Kids' dirt's the worst kind of dirt, but it's the kind of dirt I depend on Tide to get out. See. The shirt's nice and clean. And look how clean Tide got the pants—outside and inside. All ready for Gary to help his father again.
MAN SINGS:	Tide was designed with mothers in mind. It gets out the dirt kids get into. You get a lot of dirt with children. You get a lot of clean with Tide.
ANNCR:	Get Tide. 'Cause Tide gets out the dirt kids get into.

2. "All" Detergent (30-second commercial)

MAN:	Where you going?
WOMAN:	To that laundry test.
MAN:	But that's my favorite shirt.
WOMAN:	Well, it's my favorite laundry problem, greasy oil.
MAN:	Move over. If my shirt goes, I go. Look at these problems.
WOMAN:	But our greasy oil is the toughest.
ANNCR:	Let's see. We're dropping greasy oil into three leading detergent solutions.
MAN:	Hey, a demonstration.
WOMAN:	Don't get excited. Nothing's—
MAN:	Hey, this one's breaking up.
WOMAN:	And the others aren't.

Appendix A
Continued

ANNCR:	What did it? "All" with Bleach, Borax, and Brighteners.
WOMAN:	Look.
MAN:	The greasy oil's gone. "All's" what you need to clean the tough stains.
WOMAN:	It's what I need to clean everything.

3. "Liquid All" Detergent (30-second commercial)

MAN:	She's all set. Here's your warranty, and here's a surprise. I call it the out-cleaner.
WOMAN:	Thanks, but I use this.
MAN:	The leading all-temperature powder? Liquid All out-cleans that in hot, warm, and cold water.
WOMAN:	Even this greasy shirt?
MAN:	Watch. Liquid All is penetrating. It's lifting out the dirt now. See? Liquid All out-cleans your powder.
WOMAN:	Mine. Yours. I'll take the out-cleaner.
ANNCR:	Liquid All—the out-cleaner. In hot, warm, and cold water.

4. "Cheer" Detergent (60-second commercial)

BOY:	Hey Mom! Look at Dad's old sweater. 1960, what an antique!
WOMAN:	Hey Jeff. I was class of '60 myself.
BOY:	Unbelievable. You wear stuff like this too?
WOMAN:	Back then your dad and I looked keen!
BOY:	Keen?
WOMAN:	Groovy.
BOY:	Huh?

Appendix A
Continued

WOMAN:	Uh, out of sight.
BOY:	Right. Can I wear it?
WOMAN:	Not till we wash it.
BOY:	Okay.
WOMAN:	Jeffrey, that's hot water. That's a cold thing.
BOY:	Cold thing?
WOMAN:	Look at the Cheer. See? Different clothes need different temperatures.
BOY:	Right. Hot or cold?
WOMAN:	Uh huh. Cheer's made for all temperatures. Hot for whites, warm for permanent press.
BOY:	And cold for old stuff.
WOMAN:	Cold's for the bright stuff; to protect it from fading. Three temperatures. One detergent.
BOY:	Far out!
WOMAN:	Permanent press, whites.
BOY:	And these colors. Wow!
WOMAN:	Jeff, those aren't just colors. That's old pomegranate and puce.
BOY:	Pomegranate and puce? Far out!
ANNCR:	All-temperature Cheer. For the way you wash now. All-Tempa Cheer.

5. "Wisk" Detergent (30-second commercial)

MAN:	(SINGS) You are doing fine. Now watch your shoulder. Oh, you've got a ring. Ring around the collar! Ring around the collar!
ANNCR:	Those dirty rings. You try scrubbing, soaking, and you still have . . .
MAN:	(VO) Ring around the collar!
ANNCR:	Now try Wisk. Liquid Wisk sinks in and starts to clean before you start to wash.
MAN:	(SINGS) Here's a man with everything. Pretty wife and no more ring.

Appendix A
Continued

MAN:	No more ring.
ANNCR:	Wisk around the collar beats ring around the collar every time.

6. "Fab" Detergent (30-second commercial)

ANNCR:	Who can resist them. Clothes so fresh you know they're deep-down clean. The kind you get from Fab with Lemon-Freshened Borax. Lots of things get clothes clean. But only Fab gets all your wash that lemony fresh clean. Come home to Fab with Lemon-Freshened Borax.
CHORUS:	Oh Fab, we're glad, there's Lemon-Freshened Borax in you.

7. "Cold Power" Detergent (30-second commercial)

MEADE:	This is Julia Meade in Milwaukee, Wisconsin, with the William Paluzzi family. They're concerned about the energy crisis, too.
MAN:	We're turning our thermostat down. Not using as much electricity.
WOMAN:	And I'm washing in cold water with Cold Power. I've done so much washing with Cold Power. I'm really convinced clothes come out clean and bright without fading.
MAN:	Not using hot water cuts fuel costs, too.
MEADE:	Wash with Cold Power. The detergent specially formulated to get your clothes really clean in cold water.

8. "Bold" Detergent (60-second commercial)

MAN:	Engine trouble, eh Joey?
BOY:	No. Adjusting the carburetor.

Appendix A
Continued

MAN:	Dual carburetors?
BOY:	Of course, Grandpa. All racing cars have dual carbs.
(MUSIC)	
CHORUS SINGS:	He's the bold one.
MAN:	Your mom's gonna love me when she sees all this dirt.
BOY:	Race you to the house, Grandpa.
CHORUS SINGS:	He's the bold one. He's the one for Bold.
MAN:	Joey sure got dirty.
WOMAN:	He always gets dirtier than anyone in the family. But fortunately there's—
MAN:	Bold, huh?
WOMAN:	Bold's got so much cleaning energy, I think they made it special for your grandson.
MAN:	Enough for this, I hope.
WOMAN:	The next time Joey wears that shirt he'll look as nice as anyone in the family. You watch. Thank you. Well?
MAN:	It's dandy.
BOY:	Want to go to the moon?
MAN:	The moon?
BOY:	In my rocket.
CHORUS SINGS:	He's the bold one. He's the one for Bold.
ANNCR:	Try Bold.
CHORUS:	Bold can make the bold one bright.

9. "Gain" Detergent (60-second commercial)

GIRL:	I hate Norman Brown.
1ST WOMAN:	What happened?
GIRL:	He tripped me.
1ST WOMAN:	He sure did.

Appendix A
Continued

GIRL:	I wanted to wear this to the movies, and now it's had it. I never want to see him again.
1ST WOMAN:	Norman Brown's form of courtship.
2ND WOMAN:	Gain? I thought we both used—
1ST WOMAN:	I switched.
2ND WOMAN:	Switched?
1ST WOMAN:	It smells nice but it's not why I switched.
2ND WOMAN:	This dirt, gravy stains, ground-in dirt, and grass stains? Come on, no detergent will get all this out.
1ST WOMAN:	No detergent gets out everything. But Gain's dynamite on dirt and on tough stains like these. You'll see.
2ND WOMAN:	The dirt came out! And the gravy and the grass stains.
1ST WOMAN:	But that's not why I switched to Gain.
GIRL:	You got it clean!
2ND WOMAN:	Oh, Molly, she noticed the wash.
1ST WOMAN:	That's why I switched.
ANNCR:	Gain gets clothes so clean, people actually notice the difference.

10. "Dash" Detergent (60-second commercial)

WOMAN:	Richard, I thought the wife did the laundry?
MAN:	Momma. While Joan's in school we share the housework.
WOMAN:	Well, you sure didn't learn that from your father. Well, I'll wash later.
MAN:	Oh, no. You're our guest. You just have a few things. I'll throw them in with my regular load. This is a big machine.
WOMAN:	Are you sure the whole load will get clean?
MAN:	Uh, huh.
WOMAN:	Your apron is mighty dirty.
MAN:	Momma. That's Joan's. Don't worry. Joan got Dash. With Dash you can wash a big load and still get it clean. It's concentrated. Here. Feel.

Appendix A
Continued

WOMAN:	Wow!
MAN:	Yeah!
WOMAN:	You were right about Dash. My extra stuff got really clean. And look how clean your apron is now.
MAN:	Momma, I told you. That's not my apron. This is my apron.
ANNCR:	Try it yourself. Get more clothes really clean. With big machine Dash.

11. "Ajax" Detergent (30-second commercial)

WOMAN:	Give me strength.
ANNCR:	You've got it when you put your wash in Ajax. (MUSIC)
WOMAN:	Oh, give me strength.
ANNCR:	You've got it when you put your wash in Ajax. Ajax Laundry detergents. Whiteners, brighteners, sure. But above all Ajax cleaning strength to really dig dirt. Next time you think . . .
WOMAN:	Give me strength.
ANNCR:	Think Ajax. Ajax gives you strength.

12. "Oxydol" Detergent (60-second commercial)

JENNY:	Ah. There. You can carry this easily.
WOMAN:	Sure Jenny. When it's empty.
MAN:	Well, you can practice by carrying these home.
WOMAN:	Oh, no. We're not buying white jeans.
MAN:	Why not?
WOMAN:	Do you know how dirty they'll get?
JENNY:	Oh, what's a little dirt. Where's your pioneer spirit?

Appendix A
Continued

WOMAN:	What pioneer spirit? I can't get white clean.
JENNY:	Well chances are you're not getting colors clean either. Ever try Oxydol?
MAN:	You mean you sell detergent too?
JENNY:	No. But I do sell clothes. And that's why I tell folks about Oxydol with bleach. Bleach whitens. And that's not all. Oxydol bleach actually helps break up dirt. Sort of like this. While the detergent washes it away.
WOMAN:	Bet even Oxydol couldn't get this clean.
JENNY:	You lose. This smock was as dirty as that.
WOMAN:	Okay. Pack up the white.
JENNY:	I'll even pack up the Oxydol. Oxydol. For the white that says the wash is clean.

13. "Dynamo" Detergent (30-second commercial)

(SILENT)

WOMAN:	Oh. Motor oil on your shirt.
WOMAN:	You'll never get that clean.
WOMAN:	(LAUGHS) Dynamo will, mother.
WOMAN:	A liquid?
WOMAN:	Uh, huh. A quarter cup cleans the whole wash. And gets out these oily stains on Clarence's shirt. No powder can do all that.
WOMAN:	Sounds expensive.
WOMAN:	Uh, uh. Wash for wash costs the same as powders. See. A quarter cup cleaned the whole wash.
WOMAN:	Dynamo does more than powders do.
ANNCR:	For the whole wash.
WOMAN:	Right, mother.
ANNCR:	With greasy stains Dynamo works better than powders.

Appendix A
Continued

14. "Duz" Detergent (30-second commercial)

WOMAN: Know what a wool sweater costs now? Frank could work almost six hours just to pay for a sweater for a ten-year-old. So I learned to knit. When you don't have money, it pays to know little tricks like knitting. Like Duz. Duz is famous for getting things clean. It costs a little more, but there's a pretty blue glass in every box. So I don't have to buy glasses. I'm smart to buy Duz. Even Frank thinks so.

15. "Breeze" Detergent (30-second commercial)

DOLLY: Folks, I've got something for you. A surprise package. That's right. A surprise package. Because this season, Breeze Detergent is full of new surprises. New rose towels, new solid-color towels, and even new candy-stripe towels. Nine colorful towel surprises. And you can mix 'em or match 'em, but you can't buy 'em. You can only get them in boxes of Breeze. And that's no surprise. You always collect beautiful towels in Breeze.

16. "Drive" Detergent (30-second commercial)

(GIRLS GIGGLING)

MOTHER: Oh no! Lipstick! How'll my detergent wash that out?

LADY: Relax. We'll use Drive with Stain Eraser. (PULLS OUT STICK) Ta da!

MOTHER: Drive's Stain Eraser?

LADY: Puts extra cleaning power where you need it . . . right on the stain.

MOTHER: You rub it on?

LADY: Yeah . . . It's got concentrated stain fighters. Then Drive's powder does the rest. They team up to fight tough stains.

LADY: Ta da!!!

MOTHER: Lipstick's gone! It's clean!

Appendix A
Continued

ANNCR:	Only Drive has Stain Eraser. Puts extra cleaning power where you need it.

17. "Bonus" Detergent (60-second commercial)

WOMAN:	Okay, open your eyes.
GIRL:	Oh mom, the bathroom looks so pretty.
MAN:	It's all red, white, and blue.
WOMAN:	I just did a few things here and there.
GIRL:	Look, we got new towels. Oh, red, white, and blue ones.
MAN:	Sara, they really cheer up the old bathroom. But they look so expensive. They're textured.
WOMAN:	Honey, they're the new red, white, and blue towels you get from Bonus Detergent.
GIRL:	It's so soft.
BOY:	Smells good too.
WOMAN:	You get a fluffy red, white, and blue one in every box of Bonus.
MAN:	In the Bonus we use?
WOMAN:	That's right. The same Bonus that gets Jimmy's baseball shirt really white.
BOY:	Yeah, it was really dirty.
MAN:	That's terrific. And the red, white, and blue towels are great too.
GIRL:	They really are pretty, Mom.
BOY:	Yeah. Now at least it'll be fun to take a bath.
ANNCR:	From Bonus. New red, white, and blue towels.

25 Southwest Airlines: I

Christopher H. Lovelock

"Y'all buckle that seat belt," said the hostess over the public address system, "because we're fixin' to take off right now. Soon as we get up in the air, we want you to kick off your shoes, loosen your tie, an' let Southwest put a little love in your life on our way from Big D to Houston." The passengers settled back comfortably in their seats as the brightly colored Boeing 737 taxied down toward the takeoff point at Dallas's Love Field airport. Moments later, it was accelerating down the runway and then climbing away steeply into the Texas sky on the 240-mile flight to Houston.

On the other side of Love Field from the airport terminal, executives of Southwest Airlines ignored the noise of the departing aircraft, which was clearly audible in the company's modest but comfortable second-floor offices next to the North American–Rockwell hangar. They were about to begin an important meeting

Christopher H. Lovelock is an associate professor at the Harvard Graduate School of Business Administration.

with representatives from their advertising agency. In just 2 weeks'. time, on July 9, 1972, the airline would be raising its basic fare from $20 to $26. One problem was how to break the news of this increase to the public. This issue had to be resolved within the context of developing future advertising and promotional strategy for the airline as it moved into its second year of revenue operations.

Company Background

Southwest Airlines Co., a Texas corporation, was organized in March 1967. The founder, Rollin W. King, had obtained his M.B.A. in 1962 and was previously an investment counselor with a San Antonio firm. From 1964, Mr. King (who held an airline transport pilot's license) had also been president of an air taxi service operating from San Antonio to various smaller south Texas communities.

From the middle 1960s onward, Rollin King

and his associates became increasingly convinced that there was an unmet need for improved air service within Texas between the major metropolitan areas of Houston, Dallas–Fort Worth, and San Antonio. These four cities were among the fastest growing in the nation. By 1968 the Houston standard metropolitan statistical area had a population of 1,867,000. Dallas's population was 1,459,000, San Antonio's 850,000, and Forth Worth's 680,000. The cities of Dallas and Fort Worth were located 30 miles apart in northeastern Texas but were frequently thought of as a single market area. Although each had its own airport—with Dallas's Love Field the busier of the two and the only one served by the airlines—construction had recently begun on the huge new Dallas–Forth Worth Regional Airport, located midway between the two cities and intended to serve both.

Air service between these market areas was provided primarily by Braniff International Airways and Texas International Airlines. In 1967, Braniff operated a fleet of 69 jet and turboprop aircraft on an extensive route network, with a predominantly north-south emphasis, serving major United States cities, Mexico, and South America. Total Braniff revenues in that year were $256 million, and it carried 5.6 million passengers. Texas International Airlines (then known as Trans-Texas Airways) was a regional carrier serving Southern and Southwestern states and Mexico. In 1967, it operated a fleet of 45 jet, turboprop, and piston-engined aircraft on mostly short-haul routes, carrying 1.5 million passengers and generating total revenues of $32 million. Both Braniff and TI were headquartered in Texas.

Service by these two carriers within Texas represented legs of much longer, interstate flights, so that travelers flying from Dallas to San Antonio, for example, might find themselves boarding a Braniff flight which had just arrived from New York and was calling at Dallas on its way to San Antonio. Local travel between Dallas and Houston (the most important route) aver-

aged 483 passengers daily in each direction in 1967, with Braniff holding an 86 percent share of this traffic (Exhibit 1).[1] Looking back at the factors which had first stimulated his interest in developing a new airline to service these markets, Mr. King recalled:

> The more we talked to people, the more we looked at figures of how big the market was and the more we realized the degree of consumer dissatisfaction with the services of existing carriers, the more apparent the opportunities became to us. We thought that these were substantial markets, and while they weren't nearly as large as the Los Angeles–San Francisco market, they had a lot in common with it. We knew the history of what PSA had been able to do in California with the same kind of service we were contemplating.[2]

On February 20, 1968, the company was granted a Certificate of Public Convenience and Necessity by the Texas Aeronautics Commission, permitting it to provide intrastate air service between Dallas–Fort Worth, Houston, and San Antonio, a triangular route structure with the legs ranging in length from roughly 190 to 250 miles (Exhibit 2). Since the new airline proposed to confine its operations to the state of Texas, its executives maintained that it did not need certification from the federal Civil Aeronautics Board.[3]

The following day, Braniff and Texas International asked the Texas courts to enjoin issuance of the Texas certificate. These two airlines already offered service on the proposed routes

---

[1] Local travel figures excluded passengers who were traveling between these cities as part of a longer journey.

[2] Pacific Southwest Airlines (PSA) had built up a substantial market share on the lucrative Los Angeles–San Francisco route, as well as on other intrastate operations within California.

[3] The Civil Aeronautics Board regulated the activities of all interstate airlines in matters such as fares and routes but had no authority over airlines operating exclusively within a single state. [The CAB should not be confused with the Federal Aviation Administration (FAA), which regulated safety procedures and fight operations for all passenger airlines, including intrastate carriers.]

EXHIBIT 1

SOUTHWEST AIRLINES AND COMPETITORS: AVERAGE DAILY LOCAL PASSENGERS CARRIED IN EACH DIRECTION, DALLAS-HOUSTON MARKET*

	Braniff†		Texas Int†		Southwest		Total market passengers
	Psgrs.	% of mkt.	Psgrs.	% of mkt.	Psgrs.	% of mkt.	
1967	416	86.1	67	13.9			483
1968	381	70.2	162	29.8			543
1969	427	75.4	139	24.6			566
1970:							
First half	449	79.0	119	21.0			568
Second half	380	76.0	120	24.0			500
Year	414	77.5	120	22.5			534
1971:							
First half	402	74.7	126	23.4	10	1.9	538
Second half	338	50.7	120	18.0	209	31.3	667
Year	370	61.4	123	20.4	110	18.2	603
1972:							
Jan.	341	48.3	105	14.9	260	36.8	706
Feb.	343	47.6	100	13.9	277	38.5	720
Mar.	357	47.5	100	13.3	295	39.2	752
Apr.	367	48.3	97	12.8	296	38.9	760
May	362	48.5	84	11.3	300	40.2	746
June‡	362	46.8	81	10.5	330	42.7	773
First half	356	48.0	93	12.5	293	39.5	742

* The numbers should be doubled to yield the total number of passenger trips between the two cities.
† These figures were calculated by Mr. Muse from passenger data which Braniff and TI were required to supply to the Civil Aeronautics Board. He multiplied the original figures by a correction factor to eliminate interline traffic and arrive at net totals for local traffic.
‡ Projected figures from terminal counts by Southwest personnel.
Source: Company records.

and considered the market insufficiently large to support the entry of another airline.

The resulting litigation proved extremely costly and time-consuming, eventually reaching the U.S. Supreme Court. But the case was finally decided in Southwest's favor.

During the summer of 1970, Rollin King was approached by M. Lamar Muse, an independent financial consultant, who had resigned the previous fall as president of Universal Airlines—a Detroit-based supplemental carrier—over a disagreement with the major stockholders on their planned purchase of Boeing 747 jumbo jets. Mr. Muse had read of Southwest's legal battles and told Mr. King and his fellow directors that he

would be interested in helping them transform the company from "a piece of paper" into an operating airline.

The wealth of experience which Lamar Muse could bring to the new airline was quickly recognized. Before assuming the presidency of Universal in September 1967, he had served for 3 years as president of Central Airlines, a Dallas-based regional air carrier. Prior to 1965, Mr. Muse had served as secretary-treasurer of Trans-Texas Airways, as assistant vice president–corporate planning of American Airlines, and as vice president–finance of Southern Airways. After working informally with Southwest for a couple of months, Mr. Muse became

EXHIBIT 2
SOUTHWEST AIRLINES ROUTE MAP

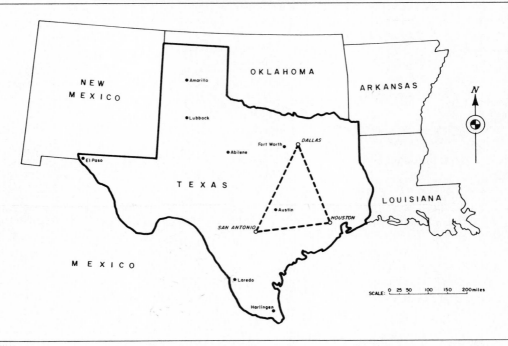

an employee of the company in October 1970 and was elected president, treasurer, and a director on January 26, 1971. Mr. King was named executive vice president–operations at the same time.

One of the reasons why he was attracted to Southwest, Lamar Muse explained, was that:

I felt the interstate carriers just weren't doing the job in this market. Every one of their flights was completely full—it was very difficult to get reservations. There were a lot of cancelled flights; Dallas being Braniff's base and Houston TI's base, every time they had a mechanical problem it seemed like they always took it out on the Dallas-Houston service. From Dallas south to San Antonio and Houston is the tag end of Braniff's system; everything was turning around and going back north to Chicago or New York or wherever. There was so much interline traffic that most of the seats were occupied by those people. While Braniff had hourly service, there really weren't many seats available for local passengers. People just avoided flying in this market—they only went when they had to.

Mr. Muse added that Braniff's reputation for punctuality was so poor that it was popularly referred to by many travelers as the "world's largest unscheduled airline."

Optimistic about the outcome of Southwest's legal battles and content to leave such matters to the company's lawyers, Messrs. Muse and King spent many weeks on the West Coast in late 1970 and early 1971 prospecting for new aircraft. There was a recession in the airline industry at the time, and prospective aircraft purchasers were being courted assiduously.

High-pressure negotiations were therefore initiated by Southwest with representatives of McDonnell-Douglas, Boeing, and several airlines for the purchase of new or used jet aircraft.

Finally, the Boeing Company, which had overproduced its Boeing 737 twin jet (in a speculative assessment of future orders which had failed to materialize), offered both a substantial price reduction and very favorable financing terms. In March 1971 the Southwest executives signed a contract for three Boeing 737–200 aircraft, and some months later they increased their order to four. The total purchase price for the four 737s was $16.2 million, compared with a previous asking price for this aircraft of approximately $4.6 million each.

Mr. Muse and Mr. King regarded the 737s as better aircraft for their purposes than the McDonnell-Douglas DC-9s operated by Texas International or the larger tri-jet Boeing 727s that required more crew members and were flown by Braniff on its Texas routes.

Preparing for Takeoff

Back in Texas, Muse and King faced some urgent problems and an extremely tight deadline. The start of scheduled operations had been tentatively set for June 18, a little over 4 months away. During this period, Southwest had to raise additional capital to finance both start-up expenses and what might prove to be a prolonged period of deficit operations. The existing skeleton management team had to be expanded by recruiting several new specialist executives, while personnel had to be hired and trained for both flight and ground operations. Meantime, numerous marketing problems had to be resolved and an introductory advertising campaign developed to launch the new airline. Finally, Braniff and Texas International were continuing their legal battles to stifle Southwest.

Once again, legal matters were left to the company's lawyers while the Southwest executives moved quickly to attend to financial, personnel, and marketing problems. An urgent need was to improve the airline's financial position, since at the end of 1970 the company had a mere $183 in its bank account (Exhibit 3). Between March and June 1971, Southwest raised almost $8 million through the sale of convertible promissory notes and common stock. The cover of the stock prospectus carried a warning in heavy black type: "These securities involve a high degree of risk."

Vacancies on the existing management team were soon filled by four executives with many years' airline experience. Three of them had previously worked for either Braniff or TI and had recently been fired by those carriers—a fact which Mr. Muse considered one of their strongest recommendations for employment with Southwest.

Decisions on route structure and schedules had already been made. Initially, two of the three Boeing 737s would be placed in service on the busy Dallas–Houston run, and the third would fly between Dallas and San Antonio. For the time being, Southwest did not plan to exercise its rights to operate service on the third leg of the triangle, between Houston and San Antonio.

Schedule frequency was constrained by aircraft availability. Allowing time for turning around the aircraft at each end, it was concluded that flights could be offered in each direction between Dallas and Houston at 75-minute intervals and between Dallas and San Antonio at intervals of every 2½ hours. Both services were scheduled for 50 minutes. The Monday–Friday schedule called for 12 round trips daily between Dallas and Houston and six round trips daily between Dallas and San Antonio. Saturday and Sunday schedules were more limited, reflecting both the lower travel demand at weekends and the need for downtime to service the aircraft.

The pricing decision, meantime, had been

EXHIBIT 3
SOUTHWEST AIRLINES: BALANCE SHEET AT DECEMBER 31, 1971 AND 1970

Assets

	1971	1970
Current assets:		
Cash	$ 231,530	$ 183
Certificates of deposit	2,850,000	
Accounts receivable:		
Trade	300,545	
Interest	35,013	
Other	32,569	100
	368,127	283
Less allowance for doubtful accounts	30,283	283
	337,844	
Inventories of parts and supplies, at cost	171,665	31
Prepaid insurance and other	156,494	314
Total current assets	3,747,533	
Property and equipment, at cost:		
Boeing 737-200 jet aircraft	16,263,250	
Support flight equipment	2,378,581	
Ground equipment	313,072	9,249
	18,954,903	9,249
Less accumulated depreciation and overhaul allowance	1,096,177	
	17,858,726	9,249
Deferred certification costs less amortization	477,122	530,136
	$22,083,381	$539,699

Liabilities and stockholders' equity

	1971	1970
Current liabilities:		
Notes payable to banks (secured)	$ 355,539	$ 30,819
Accounts payable	54,713	79,000
Accrued salaries and wages	301,244	
Other accrued liabilities		
Long-term debt due within 1 year	1,500,000	
Total current liabilities	2,211,496	109,819
Long-term debt due after 1 year:		
7% convertible promissory notes	1,250,000	
Conditional purchase agreements— Boeing Financial Corporation (1½% over prime rate)	16,803,645	
	18,053,645	
Less amounts due within 1 year	1,500,000	
	16,553,645	
Contingencies:		
Stockholders' equity:		
Common stock, $1.00 par value, 2,000,000 shares authorized, 1,108,758 issued (1,058,758 at Dec. 31, 1971)	1,058,758	372,404
Capital in excess of par value	6,012,105	57,476
Deficit	(3,752,623)	
	3,318,240	429,880
	$22,083,381	$539,699

Notes to financial statement not shown here.
Source: Southwest Airlines Company *Annual Report,* 1971.

arrived at after talking with executives of Pacific Southwest Airlines. PSA had revolutionized commuter air travel in California in the 1960s with the aid of reduced fares and aggressive promotion. Rollin King recalled:

> What Andy Andrews [President of PSA] said to Lamar and me one day was the key to our initial pricing decision. Andy told us that the way you ought to figure your price is not on how much you can get, or what the other carriers were charging or anything, but that you had to sort of go back and forth. He said, "Pick a price at which you can break even with a reasonable load factor, and a load factor that you have a reasonable expectation of being able to get within a given period of time, and that ought to be your price. It ought to be as low as you can get it without leading yourself down the primrose path and running out of money."

After estimating the amount of money required for preoperating expenditures and then carefully assessing both operating costs and market potential, Muse and King settled on a $20 fare for both routes, with a break-even point of 39 passengers per flight. This compared with existing Braniff and TI coach fares of $27 on the Dallas–Houston run and $28 on the Dallas–San Antonio service.[4] The two executives felt that an average of 39 passengers per flight was a reasonable expectation in the light of the market's potential for growth and the frequency of flights Southwest planned to offer, although they projected a period of deficit operations before this break-even point was reached. They anticipated that while Braniff and TI would probably reduce their own fares eventually, Southwest could expect an initial price advantage.

Immediately after returning from Seattle, Lamar Muse got together with Dick Elliott, vice president–marketing, to select an advertising agency. (The company already employed a public relations agency to handle publicity.) The airline's account was given to The Bloom Agency, a large regional advertising agency conveniently headquartered in Dallas. The assign-

ment: Come up with a complete communications program—other than publicity—within 4 months. "We've got no hostesses and no uniforms and no airplanes and no design and no money," Mr. Muse told the agency people. "But we're going to have an airline flying in 120 days!"

The account group at Bloom approached Southwest Airlines "as though it were a packaged goods account." Their first task was to evaluate the characteristics of all American carriers competing in the Texas markets. To facilitate comparisons, they prepared a two-dimensional positioning diagram, rating each airline's image on "conservative-fun" and "obvious-subtle" dimensions (Exhibit 4). This was based primarily on a content analysis of recent airline advertising, with a view to determining the image conveyed by each carrier.

Texas International was immediately dismissed as dull and conservative, with a bland image. (Exhibit 5 shows typical TI advertisements of that period.) Braniff's advertising, however, presented an interesting contrast in styles. From 1965 to 1968, Braniff had employed the New York agency of Wells, Rich, Greene, which had developed an innovative marketing and advertising strategy for its client, with a budget that exceeded $10 million in 1967. Braniff's aircraft were painted in a variety of brilliant colors that covered the entire fuselage and tail fin. Hostesses were outfitted in "couture costumes" created by an Italian fashion designer, while the advertising sought to make flying by Braniff seem a glamorous and exciting experience.

This strategy was believed by many observers to have been an important factor in Braniff's rapid growth during the second half of the 1960s. However, in 1968 Wells, Rich, Greene resigned the Braniff account following Mary Wells's marriage to Harding Lawrence, the airline's president, and a new agency took over. Bloom executives concluded that by 1971 Braniff's image was changing; the airline had abandoned its initial fun image in favor of a more

---

[4]Braniff also offered first-class service at a higher fare.

EXHIBIT 4
ADVERTISING AGENCY'S POSITIONING DIAGRAM
OF U.S. AIRLINES ADVERTISING/COMPETING
IN TEXAS MARKETS

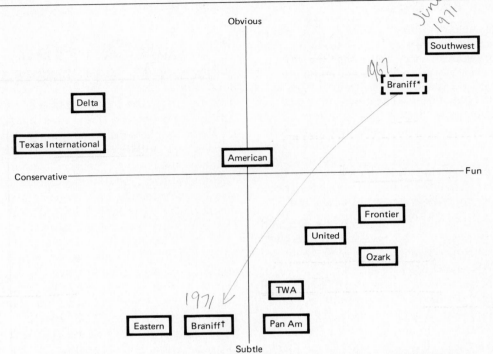

*Former advertising by Wells, Rich, Greene ("The End of the Plain Plane," "The Air Strip") 1965–1968
†Clinton Frank advertising, 1971
Source: Bloom Agency (2/11/71)

conservative style (Exhibit 6), with an advertising budget reduced to approximately $4 million. This left a vacuum into which Southwest could move. So the agency decided to position Southwest even further out on the "fun"-"obvious" side of the old Braniff image.

With this in mind, the account group developed what they termed "an entire personality description model" for the new airline. The objective was to provide the agency's creative specialists with a clear understanding of the image that Southwest should project so that this might be reflected consistently in every facet of the communications campaign they had to design. This personality statement, which was

also used as a guideline in staff recruiting, saw Southwest as "young and vital . . . exciting . . . friendly . . . efficient . . . dynamic."

While copywriters were busy developing advertising themes, other specialists at The Bloom Agency were working feverishly on projects which included research, overall marketing plans, and media evaluation. Personnel from Ernest G. Mantz & Associates, industrial designers, flew out to Seattle to work with Boeing on designing the aircraft interior. Mr. Mantz, who had been retained to develop the exterior color scheme and all related corporate image collateral material, worked closely with the agency people. The result was a striking-looking aircraft,

EXHIBIT 5
EXAMPLES OF TEXAS INTERNATIONAL
NEWSPAPER ADVERTISING, 1970–1971*

if we listed all the 66 cities in the 9 states and mexico that we jet to it would take up this entire costly page. we'd rather spend the money getting you there on time.

Texas International
We run an intelligent airline.

we don't run big expensive ads.

we run big expensive jets instead.

serving 9 states and mexico
Texas International
We run an intelligent airline.

*The original of each advertisement occupied only a small corner of the newspaper page.

painted in red, orange, and earth tones with bold white lettering; the same colors gave a bright, cheerful appearance to the cabin. Meantime, fashion specialists at Bloom were designing uniforms for the airline personnel.

At one point, as many as 30 different people at Bloom were working on the Southwest account, which had a first-year budget of $700,000. Looking back, one member of the Bloom account group observed, "It was almost as if we were an arm of the airline."

One constraint which restricted marketing activities in the months and weeks prior to passenger operations was the planned issue of over $6 million worth of Southwest stock on June 8. The company's lawyers had advised that a media campaign promoting the airline prior to the stock issue might violate Securities and Exchange Commission regulations against the promotion of stock. Virtually the only advertising conducted prior to this date, therefore, was for personnel.

Recruitment advertising in one area proved outstandingly effective, with over 1,200 young women responding to advertisements placed in national media for positions as air hostesses with Southwest. Forty applicants were selected for training, and while airline officials made no secret of the attractive looks of the successful candidates, it was also pointed out that their average scores on the required FAA proficiency test placed them among the highest ranked in the nation.

The prohibition on advertising did not keep Southwest entirely out of the news. The airline's continuing legal battles with Braniff and TI received wide press coverage in the mass media, while its public relations agency put out a number of press releases which subsequently appeared as news or feature stories.

Inauguration of Service: The First 6 Months

On June 10, 1971, The Bloom Agency's advertising campaign for Southwest finally broke. It began modestly with small "teaser" advertisements in the newspapers. The ads contained provocative headlines such as "The 48-Minute Love Affair," "At last a $20 ticket you won't mind getting," "Love can change your ways,"

EXHIBIT 6
EXAMPLE OF PRESS ADVERTISING FOR
BRANIFF INTERNATIONAL, 1970

Welcome to "747 Braniff Place." The most exclusive address in the sky.

Braniff's new 747 is more than flight. It is a place to live well in flight. We put in contoured chairs, not straight-backed seats. Three of six lounges are in Coach. The menu was created by Braniff's International Board of Chefs. In all, we've made this the most exclusive address in the sky. Join our first 747 Braniff Place non-stop flights between Dallas/Fort Worth and Hawaii starting January 15. For reservations and connections to Dallas/Fort Worth, call Braniff or your travel agent.

Come up to the International Lounge.

Our upstairs Lounge is like an intimate club overlooking the world. You'll find superb beverages. And an hors d'oeuvre buffet that's going to be a legend.

Relax in one of our six Lounges.

No more gathering in the aisles. We have lounges for everyone—three in coach alone. More lounges than any other 747. And they are furnished handsomely, with comfortable chairs and couches.

You reserve a chair, not a seat.

No ordinary straight-back airplane seat. You're wrapped in a contoured chair that curves forward for privacy. And from Pucci, another flight of fancy. New hostess ensembles. Inside each, a young lady to pamper you outrageously.

We set a beautiful table.

You'll appreciate the gleaming linens, fine china and crystal. Select your six-course meal from an international menu. Coach cuisine? The best you've ever savored. With a choice of entrees, too.

747 Braniff Place
The most exclusive address in the sky.
BRANIFF INTERNATIONAL

and "A Fare to Remember." The ads were unsigned but contained a telephone number for the reader to call. On phoning, a caller in Dallas would hear the following message:

> Hi. It's us. Southwest Airlines. Us with our brand new, candy-colored, rainbow powered Boeing 737 jets. The most reliable plane flying today. And we start flying June 18, to Houston or San Antonio. You choose—only 45 minutes non-stop. In that time, we'll be sharing a lot of big little things with you that mean a lot. Like love potions, a lot of attention and a new low fare. Just $20. Join us June 18. Southwest Airlines. The somebody else up there who loves you.

There were approximately 25,000 telephone calls as a result of these teaser ads.

On Sunday, June 13, all newspapers in the three market areas ran a four-color double-truck[5] advertisement for Southwest (see Exhibit 7). On each succeeding day for the next 2 weeks, full-page newspaper ads were run in all markets, each one focusing on the various advantages Southwest Airlines offered the traveler, including new aircraft, attractive hostesses, low fares, fast ticketing, and inexpensive, exotically named drinks. Television advertising was also heavy and included 30-second spots featuring the Boeing 737, the hostesses, and what was referred to as the "Love Machine" (Exhibit 8). Whereas the competition used traditional, handwritten airline tickets, the Southwest counter staff accelerated the ticketing process by using a machine to print out tickets and a pedal-operated tape recorder to record the passengers' names for the aircraft manifest as they checked in—both these ideas having been copied from PSA. Rounding out the advertising campaign were strategically located billboards containing painted displays at the entrances to all three airports served by Southwest. Nearly half the year's promotional budget was spent in the first

month of operations. (Exhibit 9 shows a media breakdown of expenditures in 1971 and 1972.)

Scheduled revenue operations were inaugurated in a blaze of publicity on Friday, June 18, but it soon became evident that the competition was not about to take matters lying down. In half-truck and full-page newspaper ads, Braniff and TI announced $20 fares on both routes. The CAB had disclaimed authority over intrastate fares, and Texas law barred jurisdiction by TAC over carriers holding Federal Certificates of Public Convenience and Necessity; thus, the CAB carriers were free to charge any fare they wanted. Braniff's advertising stressed frequent, convenient service—"every hour on the hour," hot and cold towels "to freshen up with," beverage discount coupons, and "peace of mind" phone calls at the boarding gate; it also announced an increase in the frequency of service between Dallas and San Antonio (Exhibit 10). TI, meantime, announced that on July 1 it would inaugurate hourly service on the Dallas–Houston route, leaving Dallas at 30 minutes past each hour. TI also introduced "extras" such as free beer, free newspapers, and $1 drinks on those routes competing with Southwest (Exhibit 11). Southwest then countered with advertising headlined "The Other Airlines May Have Met Our Price But You Can't Buy Love."

Initial results for Southwest, however, were hardly spectacular; between June 18 and 30, there were, on the average, 13.1 passengers per flight on the Dallas–Houston service and 12.9 passengers on the Dallas–San Antonio route (Exhibit 12). Passenger loads during the month of July showed only a marginal improvement. Southwest management concluded that it was essential to improve schedule frequencies to compete more effectively with those of Braniff and TI. This became possible with the delivery of the company's fourth Boeing 737 in late September 1971. Effective October 1, therefore, hourly service was introduced between Dallas and Houston and flights every 2 hours between Dallas and San Antonio.

---

[5]*Double truck* is a printer's term used to describe material printed across two full pages. A *half-truck* ad is one printed across two half-pages.

EXHIBIT 7
SOUTHWEST AIRLINES INTRODUCTORY ADVERTISING

At last, there's somebody

The planes are new. The pilots are not. We've talked to, tested, and evaluated very good, reputable, reliable pilots that any major airline would hire. Out of them all we've selected a group — maybe an elite — of the very best in the business, with an average of 15,200 hours in the air.

Our ground crew is no small potatoes, either. They're well-trained in dozens of skills that insure your comfort aboard Southwest Airlines.

It's us, Southwest Airlines.

Us, with our brand new Boeing 737's.

We fly to Dallas/Ft. Worth, Houston and San Antonio. Your choice, all flights non-stop.

In that time you're going to feel there really is somebody else up there who loves you.

By sharing a lot of little things with you. Big, little things that mean a lot to travelers.

Three years ago the Boeing 737 was introduced to the public all over the world. Today — as of this morning — the Boeing 737's have accumulated 1,000,000 flight hours, carrying nearly 70 million passengers approximately 430 million miles. The Boeing 737 is the super reliable jet specially designed for short haul traffic. Obviously, it is more than just a beautiful body. No other airlines will be flying 737's on these routes. And Southwest Airlines won't be flying anything else.

And we give trading stamps. Not the ordinary kind. Ours are Love Stamps. You get one from our hostess if for any reason she finds you unhappy in any way with our service. The basic idea is that we want you to trade in your bad feelings for good ones. The Love Stamp hopefully will make amends — with a free drink or something, and then you'll feel better about us right away. And want to ride our airplanes again, and again.

JUNE 18

LOVE STAMP
GOOD FOR ONE FREE LOVE POTION ON YOUR NEXT FLIGHT

Dallas/Ft. Worth to Houston (and back)
Dallas/Ft. Worth to San Antonio (and back)
All flights non-stop.

Dallas/Ft. Worth to Houston		Houston to Dallas/Ft. Worth	
Depart	Arrive	Depart	Arrive
7:30 a*	8:18 a	7:30 a*	8:18 a
8:45 a*	9:33 a	8:45 a	9:33 a
10:00 a	10:48 a	10:00 a*	10:48 a
11:15 a*	12:03 p	11:15 a	12:03 p
12:30 p	1:18 p	12:30 p*	1:18 p
1:45 p**	2:33 p	1:45 p	2:33 p
3:00 p	3:48 p	3:00 p**	3:48 p
4:15 p**	5:03 p	4:15 p	5:03 p
5:30 p	6:18 p	5:30 p**	6:18 p
6:45 p**	7:33 p	6:45 p	7:33 p
8:00 p	8:48 p	8:00 p**	8:48 p
9:15 p**	10:03 p	9:15 p**	10:03 p

Dallas/Ft. Worth to San Antonio		San Antonio to Dallas/Ft. Worth	
Depart	Arrive	Depart	Arrive
7:00 a*	7:50 a	8:15 a*	9:05 a
9:30 a	10:20 a	10:45 a	11:35 a
12:00 n	12:50 p	1:15 p	2:05 p
2:30 p	3:20 p	3:45 p	4:35 p
5:00 p	5:50 p	6:15 p	7:05 p
7:30 p**	8:20 p	8:45 p**	9:35 p

* Except Sunday
** Except Saturday

EXHIBIT 7
Continued

else up there who loves you.

By paying attention to you, giving efficient service, and getting you there on time.

And, if for some reason, you don't get all the love we've got to give, we'll make it up by giving you a Love Stamp. Why are we doing all this? Because we need your love, too. And we know we won't get it unless we give it.

She will not plee-aze you. Plee-aze is stiff, formal and very affected English for please. It is usually accompanied by a gleaming toothpaste smile. People who say plee-aze are trying very, very hard to be nice to you. Too hard. And it isn't real. It's like plastic flowers vs. real flowers. You can feel the difference. That's why in our hostess school we haven't taught our girls how to be nice to you. We figure if they didn't already know, they weren't for us. In our school we teach other things. Mostly how to take care of you. Then we dress them in our exciting new hot pants designed for Southwest Airlines by Lorch of Dallas. That really ought to please you.

$20

Save from $14 to $16 per round trip. Eventually, the other airlines may meet our price, but remember, you can't buy love.

Love Potions for the very weary. Order by numbers 1-10, and they're only $1.00 each, not $1.50. That's what happens when you have somebody else up there who loves you.

A love machine which issues you tickets in under 10 seconds. Another way we prove our love: love machines in two great locations — at the ticket counter and at the departure gate, take your pick. Then you give your $20 (or any one of five charge cards) to our people stationed behind the love machines and you're on your way.

DALLAS 826-8840 • HOUSTON 228-8791
SAN ANTONIO 224-2011 • FORT WORTH 283-4661

This is another Southwest Airlines exclusive — our phone number. Keep it on file in your head or elsewhere because it's not in the phone book yet! Use this number to call ahead for reservations if you want to. If you don't want to, that's o.k. too. You don't need reservations to board the plane. Just come, plunk down $20 and out pops your ticket from our Love Machine. We plan to make waiting in line a thing of the past.

SOUTHWEST AIRLINES
The somebody else up there who loves you.

EXHIBIT 8
SOUTHWEST AIRLINES INTRODUCTORY
TV ADVERTISING, JUNE 1971

SOUTHWEST AIRLINES | CODE NO: SWA-3-30-71 | TELEVISION STORYBOARD
TITLE: "TV Love Machine" | THE BLOOM AGENCY

1. (Natural sfx, people talking up and under)...

2. ...

3. ...

4. ...

5. (Wm Anncr VO) If you're standing in line...

6. ...you're not flying...

7. ...Southwest Airlines.

8. Because our Love Machine gives you a ticket...

9. ...in under ten seconds.

10. HOSTESS: Have a nice flight.

11. (Sfx: music and jet engine) 12 flights each day to Houston...

12. ...6 to San Antonio, for a loveable $20...

13. ...on Southwest Airlines.

14. "The somebody else up there...

15. ...who loves you."

BRY CHICAGO

EXHIBIT 9
SOUTHWEST AIRLINES: ADVERTISING AND PROMOTIONAL EXPENDITURES, 1971 AND 1972

| | 1971 | | | 1972 |
	Preoperating	Operating	Total	(budgeted)
Advertising:				
Newspaper	$139,831	$131,675	$271,506	$ 60,518
Television	36,340	761	37,101	127,005
Radio	5,021	60,080	65,101	95,758
Billboards	26,537	11,670	38,207	90,376
Other publications	710	20,446	21,156	28,139
Production costs	52,484	43,483	95,967	83,272
Other promotion and publicity:	29,694	27,200	56,894	48,366
	$290,617	$295,315	$585,932	$533,434

Source: **Company records.**

Advertising and promotional activity continued with regular television advertising and frequent publicity events, usually featuring Southwest hostesses. A direct-mail campaign was targeted at 36,000 influential business executives living in Southwest's service areas. Each of these individuals received a personalized letter from Lamar Muse describing Southwest service, and a voucher good for half the cost of a round-trip ticket was enclosed. About 1,700 of the vouchers were subsequently redeemed.

Surveys of Southwest passengers departing from Houston showed that a substantial percentage would have preferred service from the William P. Hobby Airport, 12 miles southeast of downtown Houston, rather than from the new Houston Intercontinental Airport, 26 miles north of the city. Accordingly, arrangements were completed in mid-November for 7 of Southwest's 14 round-trip flights between Dallas and Houston to be transferred to Hobby Airport (thus reopening this old airport to scheduled commercial passenger traffic). Additional schedule revisions made at the same time included a reduction in the number of Dallas–San Antonio flights to four round trips each weekday; the inauguration of three round trips daily on the third leg of the route triangle, between Houston (Hobby) and San Antonio; and the elimination of the extremely unprofitable Saturday operation on all routes. These actions contributed to an increase in transportation revenues in the

EXHIBIT 10
BRANIFF'S RESPONSE TO SOUTHWEST INTRODUCTION:
ADVERTISING IN DALLAS NEWSPAPERS, JUNE 1971*

*Prepared by Clinton E. Frank, Inc.

EXHIBIT 10
Continued

Houston
(every hour on the hour)

(a) with the experience of Braniff's million-mile Captains.
(b) with Braniff's big 3 & 4 engine jets.
(c) in Braniff's reclining seats.
(d) and because you have a choice of either 1st class or coach service.
● **Special Service Representatives At The Boarding Area** . . . to help speed and ease things up.
● **Peace-Of-Mind Phone Calls** . . . made for you at the last minute.
● **Hot or Cold Towels** . . . to freshen-up with in the morning and afternoon.
● **Local Newspapers and The Oil Daily or Other Special Interest Journals Available** . . . because you requested them.

● "747 Braniff Place" Hors D'Oeuvre Sampling . . . on selected flight.
● **Commuter Refreshment Discount Book Available** . . . to save you money on any Braniff flight.

*Braniff Style Commuter Service: On the hour flights to Houston from 7 am to 9 pm and on the hour flights to San Antonio from 7 am to 7 pm (San Antonio on the hour flights start July 1, 1971). Coach fare —tax included. $20 fare effective June 18.

You'll like flying
Braniff Style.

. . .Braniff Style.

EXHIBIT 11
TEXAS INTERNATIONAL RESPONSE TO SOUTHWEST INTRODUCTION: ADVERTISING IN DALLAS NEWSPAPERS, JUNE 1971

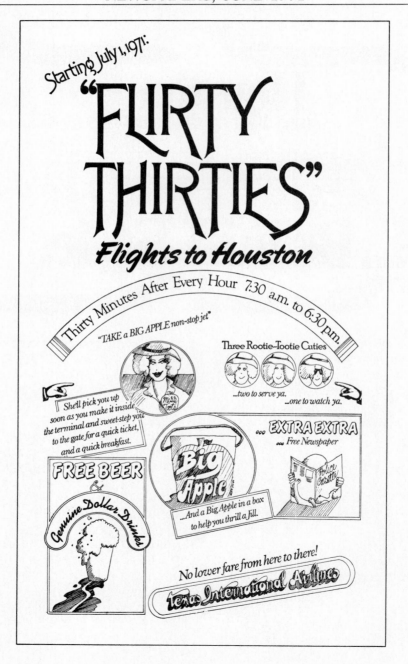

(handwritten annotations: "assume only 1 way / double effect for 2nd 6 mths.")

EXHIBIT 12
SOUTHWEST AIRLINES
MONTHLY FLIGHTS AND PASSENGER COUNTS
ON EACH ROUTE

Month	Dallas–Houston		Dallas–San Antonio		San Antonio–Houston	
	# psgrs.	#flights	# psgrs.	# flights	# psgrs.	# flights
June 1971*	3,620	276	1,910	148		
July	10,301	642	5,158	346		
Aug.	11,316	672	4,805	354		
Sept.	11,674	612	4,766	327		
Oct.	14,522	764	6,492	382		
Nov.	14,060	654	4,167	240	888	72
Dec.	14,665	687	4,004	165	1,707	134
1971 total	76,568	4,307	31,302	1,962	2,595	206
Jan. 1972	16,122	634	2,788	141	1,954	128
Feb.	16,069	640	2,755	142	2,088	134
Mar.	18,285	669	4,270	209	2,803	146
Apr.	17,732	605	4,617	189	2,301	130
May	18,586	584	4,254	198	2,461	138
June†	19,782	521	5,198	201	2,628	140
First half total	106,576	3,653	23,882	1,080	14,235	816

(handwritten numbers in margins: 13.1, 12.9, 11046 5, 17.8, 16, 12.6, 20864, 9.97, 29.1, 22.1, 17.4, 2(144693), 289386, 39.5, 7684, 2894, 144693, Total MCF = 1465246)

* Part-month only
† Projected figures
Source: Company records.

final quarter of 1971 over those achieved in the third quarter, but Southwest's operating losses in the fourth quarter fell only slightly, from $1,006,000 to $921,000 (Exhibit 13). At the end of 1971, Southwest's accumulated deficit stood at $3.75 million (Exhibit 3).

The Second 6 Months

In February 1972, Southwest initiated a second phase of the advertising campaign, hired a new vice president–marketing, and terminated its public relations agency (hiring away the agency's publicity director to fill a newly created position as public relations director at Southwest).

The objective of this new phase was to sustain Southwest's presence in the marketplace after 8 months of service. Heavy-frequency advertising,

employing a wide variety of messages, was directed at the airline's primary target, the regular business commuters. Surveys had shown that 89 percent of Southwest's traffic at that time was accounted for by such travelers. Extensive use was made of television in this campaign, which featured many of Southwest's own hostesses.

Mr. Elliott, whom the president described as having performed a "Herculean task" in getting Southwest off the ground, had resigned to take a position with a national advertising agency. The new vice president–marketing, Jess R. Coker, had spent 10 years in the outdoor advertising business after graduating from the University of Texas. He now became responsible for all marketing functions of the airline, including advertising, sales, and public relations. Jess Coker typically met with the account executive from The Bloom Agency to discuss not only

EXHIBIT 13
SOUTHWEST AIRLINES: QUARTERLY INCOME STATEMENTS

Income statements, $ thousand	1971 Q3	1971 Q4	1972 Q1	1972 Q2 (projected)
Transportation revenues*	887	1,138	1,273	1,401
Operating expenses:				
Operations & maintenance	1,211	1,280	1,192	1,145
Marketing & gen. admin.	371	368	334	366
Depreciation & amortiz.	311	411	333	334
Total	1,893	2,059	1,859	1,845
Operating profit (loss)	(1,006)	(921)	(586)	(444)
Net interest revenues (costs)	(254)	(253)	(218)	(220)
Net income (loss) before extraordinary items	(1,260)	(1,174)	(804)	(664)
Extraordinary items	(571)†	(469)†		533‡
Net income (loss)	(1,831)	(1,643)	(804)	(131)

* Includes both passenger and freight business.
† Write-off of preoperating costs.
‡ Capital gain on sale of one aircraft.
Source: Company records.

media advertising but also the numerous other small activities handled by the agency. These included the preparation and execution of pocket timetables, point-of-sale materials for travel agents, and promotional brochures.

Although the majority of ticket sales were made over the counter at the airport terminals, sales were also made to travel agents and corporate accounts. Travel agents, who received a 7 percent commission on credit card sales and 10 percent on cash sales, would often arrange package deals for travelers, such as a weekend in San Antonio, including airfare, hotel, and meals. Corporate accounts—companies whose personnel made regular use of Southwest Airlines—received no discount but benefited from the convenience of having their own supply of ticket stock (which they issued themselves) and receiving a single monthly billing. Jess Coker was responsible for a force of six sales representatives, whose job was to develop and service both travel agents and corporate accounts, encouraging maximum use of Southwest through the distribution of point-of-sale

materials, the development of package arrangments, the distribution of pocket timetables, etc. The sales representatives also promoted the availability of Southwest's airfreight business, which featured a special rush delivery service for packages. Each representative, as well as most company officers, drove a company car strikingly painted in the same color scheme as Southwest's aircraft.

Also reporting to Mr. Coker was Southwest's new public relations director, Camille Keith, formerly publicity director of Read-Poland, Inc., the public relations agency which had up till then handled the airline's account. Ms. Keith's responsibilities focused on obtaining media coverage for the airline and also included the publication of Southwest's in-flight magazine and the development of certain promotions jointly with the advertising agency.

Between October 1971 and April 1972, average passenger loads systemwide increased from 18.4 passengers per flight to 26.7 passengers. However, this was still substantially below the number necessary to cover the total costs per trip flown, which had been tending to rise. Management recognized that the volume of traffic during the late morning and early afternoon could not realistically support flights at hourly intervals. It also knew that most Houston passengers preferred Hobby Airport to Houston Intercontinental. Over time, the number of Southwest flights to Hobby had been steadily increased, and the decision was now taken to abandon Houston Intercontinental altogether.

On May 14, a new schedule was introduced which reduced the total number of daily flights between Dallas and Houston from 29 to 22, primarily by reducing service in the 9:30 A.M. to 3:30 P.M. period from hourly to every 2 hours. Eleven flights daily continued to be offered on the Dallas–San Antonio route and six between San Antonio and Houston, with some minor schedule modifications. Hobby Airport was to be used exclusively for all flights to and from Houston. Braniff quickly retaliated by introducing its own service from Dallas to Hobby and undertaking an extensive publicity promoting this airport.

From a financial viewpoint, the most significant aspect of Southwest's actions was that the new schedule made it possible for the company to dispose of its fourth Boeing 737. Experience had shown that the 737s could be turned around (i.e., loaded and unloaded) at the gate in as little as 10 minutes. This meant that an hourly schedule on the Dallas–Houston run could be maintained with only two aircraft instead of three. With the slack provided by the reduced midday frequencies and a schedule which involved periodically flying an aircraft around all three legs of the route triangle, management concluded that a total of three aircraft would suffice and that the fourth could be sold. By mid-1972, the airline industry had recovered from its 1970–1971 slump, and aircraft manufacturers had waiting lists for their more popular models. Southwest had no trouble finding a ready buyer for its now-surplus 737 and made a profit of $533,000 on reselling it. The combina-

tion of this capital gain, lower operating costs, and a continued increase in revenues resulted in a reduction of the quarterly net loss from $804,000 to $131,000 between the first and second quarters of 1972 (Exhibit 13).

For some months, Southwest had been experimenting with a $10 fare on Friday evening flights after 9 P.M. In May, this reduced fare was extended to post–9 P.M. flights on a daily basis. The result was sharply higher load factors on these discount flights relative to the average achieved on standard-price flights.

higher load.

June 1972 saw Southwest Airlines celebrating its first birthday. This provided Camille Keith with an opportunity for more of the publicity stunts for which the airline was already becoming renowned. Posters were hung inside the aircraft and in the waiting lounges; the aircraft cabins were decorated; and there was an onboard party every day for a week, with birthday cake for the passengers and even balloons one day for the children. This activity, promoted by newspaper advertising, generated considerable publicity for the airline and, in management's view, reinforced Southwest's image as the plucky, friendly little underdog which had now survived an entire year against powerful, entrenched competition. Discussing her job, Ms. Keith observed:

promo.

> One good point was that Mr. Coker and I didn't have airline backgrounds. Our backgrounds were in the areas that we're serving—public relations and marketing and sales. Nobody had ever told me "You can't have a flying birthday party" and I didn't know you're not supposed to have Easter bunnies on airplanes. So we did things that other people who'd been brought up in the [airline] business never did. We went out and tried things and if they didn't work, then we tried something else. And we had more flexibility in that area to do it. We were new, we knew all our employees and everybody knew that if the company went under we were all out of a job. Mr. Muse has been great and let me do a lot of crazy things. And our really great bunch of hostesses has made it easy. How many airline stewardesses would dress up in

Halloween costumes on a flight and pass out trick-or-treat candy? Or wear bunny costumes at Easter or reindeer horns at Christmas?

Not all public relations activity was just hoopla, Ms. Keith stressed, mentioning that she worked quite closely with the advertising agency to coordinate the airline's mass communication strategy.

I keep them informed and I sit in on their meetings and they sit in on some of our brainstorming sessions, because it has to go together. I can't do one kind of PR campaign if they're doing an opposite advertising campaign. Neither can we have advertising running that I'm unaware of, in case the media should ask me about it.

One example of a specialized promotional campaign involving inputs from both Camille Keith and The Bloom Agency was the Southwest Sweetheart's Club. Through the use of a specialized mailing list, a direct-mail piece was sent to executive secretaries in Southwest's market area; it offered them membership in this club. For each reservation on Southwest that she made for her boss, the secretary received a "sweetheart stamp," and for each 15 stamps, she obtained a free ride on Southwest. Additional bonuses for members included a twice-yearly drawing for a big Mexico City vacation.

While recognizing that interesting, well-written press releases could generate some publicity, Ms. Keith believed that for Southwest to get far more than its fair share of media coverage, the airline had to be constantly alert to opportunities for newsworthy stories or incidental coverage. She noted:

The unusual is what's going to get covered. The standard thing that we flew everyday on time (which is what we're supposed to do), and that we didn't lose any bags (which is an obligation under our certificate), and that the passengers were happy (which is our responsibility to them), is not news. It's supposed to happen. The news is that Senator Bentsen flew on Thursday afternoon and the girls knew him and spoke to him, and that I was

in Houston when he landed and had a nice talk with him . . . Lots of times, PR is getting the TV people to pan your airplane when someone like this gets off, instead of just taking his picture inside the terminal building.

On several occasions, Southwest had been featured in articles appearing in such national media as *Business Week*. Ms. Keith stressed that, typically, these articles did not just "happen" but were often the result of a long-term selling effort on her part to interest the editors of a particular publication.

Planning Ahead

After a year of operation, Southwest management decided it was time to take a hard look at the fare structure and its relationship to costs and revenues. They soon concluded that the airline could no longer afford a $20 fare on daytime flights. New tariffs were therefore filed with the Texas Aeronautics Commission, effective July 9, 1972, which raised Southwest's basic one-way fare from $20 to $26, provided for a round-trip fare of $50, and offered a $225 Commuter Club Card providing unlimited transportation for the purchaser on all routes for a 30-day period.

One problem was how to break the news of the increased fares to the public. A meeting was therefore called to discuss appropriate strategy. An important consideration was how the competition would react. Braniff and TI offered $20 fares on routes served by Southwest, but it was not certain that they would necessarily follow suit with increases to $26; however, Southwest management knew that both airlines were losing money on these routes.

At this meeting, Southwest executives also planned to discuss future marketing communications strategy. Mr. Muse felt that it was an appropriate time to take stock of the airline's position in the market and formulate a strategy for its second year of operations.

26 Honeywell Information Systems

Nancy J. Davis • Steven H. Star

There is no way that we can continue to increase awareness of Honeywell as a computer manufacturer without maintaining a high level of advertising exposure. We have managed to stake out the number two awareness position over the years, but we can't afford to let up or we'll find the rest of the pack breathing down our necks.— *director of advertising*

Inflation has driven our marketing costs out of line. We've got to cut costs across the board, and that includes advertising. Besides, our market is primarily our present customers. We don't need to blanket the country with advertising to tell our customers about our new line.—*director of finance*

This new product announcement is our most important event since we took over General Electric's computer operation. It will do more for our image than anything else we can advertise. We need to get this story across not only to prospects,

Nancy J. Davis was formerly a research associate at the Harvard Graduate School of Business Administration. Steven H. Star was formerly an associate professor at the Harvard Graduate School of Business Administration.

but to the financial community.—*corporate vice president*

This new product announcement is important, but we have to make our '74 goals with our current product line. Our total ability to satisfy our customers' needs is the story we must get across. This capability is enhanced by the new line, but it's only part of the story.—*branch manager*

These were the arguments facing Christopher J. Lynch, vice president of marketing, and Daniel E. Callanan, director of communications, for the data-processing operations of Honeywell Information Systems in September 1973 as they pondered the advertising budget and creative format for 1974.

They recognized the need for continuing to stress Honeywell's overall capabilities and ability to achieve results in a marketplace dominated by one competitor. Further, they had a new product line that would require a major promotional investment. They felt it was important in this promotion to position the new line as an enhancement to the existing product line, which would have to continue to generate revenue and profits for some time. But inflation was beginning to squeeze profits, and there were increasing pressures to slash costs wherever possible.

Company History

In 1973, Honeywell Information Systems was a division of Honeywell, Inc., an international industrial corporation whose worldwide sales totaled $2.39 billion. The information systems division accounted for $1.177 billion, or 49 percent of sales, and $93 million, or 41 percent of corporate earnings before interest and taxes. It controlled about 8 percent of the United States computer market as measured in dollars. While Honeywell's corporate headquarters was located in Minneapolis, the main offices for the North American operations of Honeywell Information Systems were on Route 128 in Waltham, Massachusetts.

Honeywell Information Systems traced its origins to Datamatic, a joint venture with Raytheon established in 1955 when Honeywell, Inc., recognized that evolving computer (or digital) technology would have a profound effect on the controls business—the primary thrust of the company.[1] In 1957 Honeywell bought Raytheon's 40 percent, and Datamatic became a division of Honeywell. In 1963 Honeywell introduced a medium-size computer, the Model 200, which it called the *Liberator* because it was designed to be compatible with IBM's 1401 system and therefore was able to free the customer from having to stay with IBM. The Model 200 was expanded into a full series of computers and proved to be the backbone of Honeywell's computer line throughout the sixties. Despite its success, however, company management decided that Honeywell could not stay in the computer business without a larger market share and a broader customer base. Therefore, in 1970 Honeywell, Inc., acquired General Electric's computer operations,[2] merged it with its own, and formally created Honeywell Information Systems. (Hereafter *Honeywell* refers to Honeywell Information Systems, not to the total corporation.)

General Electric's line of large and small computers, when combined with the Series 200, made Honeywell a full-service computer company with a range of computers and services as wide as that of any competitor and a customer base equal to a 10 percent share of the worldwide market. Since General Electric's computer operations extended throughout the world, Honeywell's computer business immediately became a worldwide concern. In all, it reached into the 58 countries which constituted 97 percent of the worldwide data-processing market. It had production and engineering facilities in the United States and five other countries. It was divided into four operating units, each responsible for marketing and financial control in its geographic territory and with certain manufacturing, design, and development activities. This case is concerned only with the North American operations unit, which was responsible for all business in the United States and Canada.

Between 1970 and 1973, a great deal of time, effort, and money was spent merging the two lines and building a functioning operation out of the two organizations. Especially, current General Electric and Honeywell customers had to be reassured that they would not need to switch or reprogram their entire systems and that

---

[1]Various control systems, especially heating, air conditioning, and process control systems, had been the basis for Honeywell's formation and early growth. By 1973, the control systems division, the counterpart of the information systems division, manufactured sophisticated monitoring and control systems for the environment, guidance systems for the United States space program, industrial process control systems, and cameras.

[2]The General Electric computer business included its own domestic operations as well as those of two computer businesses it had acquired abroad, Machines Bull in France and Olivetti in Italy.

any improvements developed by Honeywell would be compatible with their systems. Honeywell management stated that the customers' concerns were justified, since immediately after the merger Honeywell had 10 different product lines, 12 major operating-systems software packages, and 157 different kinds of peripheral equipment.

By 1973 the product lines had been consolidated so that Honeywell marketed essentially five lines of general-purpose computers. These ranged from the Series 50 family of small computers, which were aimed primarily at small businesses, up to the Series 6000, which were giant computers used by such diverse organizations as Ford Motor Company, Pillsbury, and the Department of Defense's Worldwide Military Command and Control System. Small systems rented for about $2,000 a month, medium-size systems for about $20,000, and large systems for about $100,000 per month. Sale prices ranged from $50,000 to $7 million. Honeywell was planning to introduce a new line, known as the Series 60, during 1974—ideally in April. This line would include the full range from mini- to supercomputers and would be Honeywell's major product for the future. It was designed to be compatible with equipment currently used by

the customer base, which Honeywell had acquired from General Electric (including the Machines Bull and Olivetti computer businesses), as well as by its own original customer base. Thus it was the next generation of computers to which each of the four original customer groups could upgrade. Its development had cost more than $300 million.

The Computer Industry

The computer industry got started during World War II when the United States government initiated several research projects oriented toward rapid data processing. The first commercial installation was in 1954 when Univac delivered a computer to General Electric. By 1956 the competitive structure of the industry was emerging. Though about 15 companies were manufacturing computers, IBM had captured about 80 percent of the market. (See Exhibit 1 for worldwide market share data, 1953–1973.)

Over the next several years, the industry was characterized by rapid growth in demand, intense competitive activity, and rapidly changing technology. Several solid companies such as RCA, Bendix, Raytheon, Philco-Ford, and Gen-

EXHIBIT 1
COMPUTER INDUSTRY SHARE OF MARKET WORLDWIDE

	1953 $150 million	1958 $650 million	1963 $4.1 billion	1968 $7 billion	1970 $7.1 billion	1971 $7.2 billion	1972 $8 billion	1973 $9 billion
IBM	36%	73.7%	78.7%	69.7%	71.1%	67.9%	64.2%	63.9%
Honeywell		0.6	1.7	4.3	7.3	9.6	10.6	10.5
GE			1.2	4.0				
Univac	49	13.7	6.5	5.9	5.9	7.8	8.0	7.5
Burroughs		3.1	2.0	3.2	3.2	4.3	4.6	4.7
Control Data			2.7	4.3	4.2	4.0	4.4	4.2
RCA		1.5	2.5	3.4	2.3			
NCR			1.6	2.2	2.1	2.1	2.5	2.5
Others	15	7.4	3.1	3.0	3.9	4.3	5.7	6.7
	100%	100%	100%	100%	100%	100%	100%	100%

Source: International Data Corporation.

eral Electric had gotten into the computer business but were either unwilling or unable to invest the necessary funds in research, development, and marketing and eventually dropped out of the industry. Technological changes had indeed been enormous. During the fifties, relatively slow, limited-memory-capacity computers were used primarily for massive, often repetitive calculations in scientific application. Beginning in the early sixties, significant strides were made in increasing computers' speed and memory capacity, and manufacturers began to distinguish more between computers for businesses and those for scientific applications. Later in the sixties, solid-state technology, remote terminals, improved programming, and other innovations were introduced, making much of the earlier equipment obsolete.

In 1964, IBM introduced the Series 360, whose development costs were estimated to be $5 billion. This was followed 6 years later by the Series 370, which, though recognized as a technological leader, was not nearly as revolutionary. Customers proved to be less ready to switch from their present computers than they had been in the past. In 1973, Honeywell was making plans to introduce its new Series 60 during 1974. Other than this, most new products being introduced by the industry were peripheral accessories rather than main computer-processing units.

By 1973 almost all organizations were considered potential computer customers. Customers could either purchase or rent the equipment. Sales of large computers which cost over $1.5 million generally required 6 to 12 months of selling and negotiating, and top management was almost always involved. Medium-size units—i.e., those which sold for $200,000 to $1.5 million—were also usually purchased by experienced and sophisticated managers in companies which were expanding their operations. When small units (purchase value $40,000 to $200,000) were sold to large organizations for specific purposes which their larger computers did not perform, a data-processing executive

who was a sophisticated buyer usually made the purchase decision.

In smaller organizations that were buying small computers, however, the purchase decision almost always involved top management, which usually was not at all sophisticated in computers. Often, it was the company's initial computer purchase, and it represented a substantial financial commitment. In such situations, the salesperson had to understand the customer's business well enough to explain clearly how the computer would be installed and used. However, the limited revenue from a small-computer sale did not justify as large a selling effort as did the revenue from larger units, and the sale of a small computer was expected to be consummated within 2 months.

Once customers purchased a particular computer, they usually stayed with that brand because there was little compatibility among different manufacturers' hardware and software. In fact, from 1971 through 1973 roughly 80 percent of Honeywell's shipments were delivered to firms that already had some type of Honeywell equipment installed.

Competition

In 1973 IBM, Honeywell, Sperry-Rand/Univac, and Burroughs were the leading full-line computer companies. IBM was by far the market leader, with about 70 percent of the market. While IBM was strong in every area, it was considered especially strong in medium-size computers. Its 6,000-person sales force and $2.2 million space advertising[3] budget (plus an estimated $5 million in TV and radio) were also the largest in the industry. Honeywell management expected IBM's advertising expenditures to increase in the near future, particularly to promote its small computers. The increase was expected to be evident in the pages of general news and general business publications, the media IBM

[3]Space advertising referred primarily to magazine and newspaper advertising.

already utilized most. IBM had not previously advertised in key market publications such as those edited for manufacturing, distribution, financial, and education audiences (as Honeywell had been doing); nor had IBM advertised to any extent in computer publications. As had been the case with many other computer companies, IBM had changed its advertising theme fairly often and had used a wide variety of formats.

Sperry-Rand/Univac controlled about 8 percent of the market, primarily with large computers. However, its medium-size computers appeared to be increasing in popularity. Its advertising expenditures were second only to IBM's. Its advertisements in general publications such as *Business Week* and *Fortune* usually consisted of human interest stories in which a computer played a significant role. In key market and computer publications, human interest stories were sometimes used, but more often the ads consisted of pictures and descriptions of computers.

Burroughs, perhaps best known for its strong line of office machines for routine bookkeeping chores, was strong in both large and small computers. Its smaller computers were sold by its office machine sales force and its other computers by a special sales force. It usually concentrated on selected markets, such as banking and retailing, where it had strength. It controlled about 6 percent of the United States market. It traditionally had confined its advertising largely to product announcements consisting of pictures of equipment with nontechnical functional descriptions.

Honeywell considered three other companies—Control Data, National Cash Register, and Digital Equipment Corporation—as competitors, even though they did not market full lines of computers. Control Data specialized in very large special-purpose computers for scientific and government applications, areas in which it had early demonstrated competence. National Cash Register (NCR) marketed a broad line of computers and was especially strong among

retailers. Digital Equipment Corporation (DEC) had been extremely successful in producing minicomputers, many of which were sold to other manufacturers to be incorporated into their products. DEC had recently begun to sell small computer systems for educational, scientific, and general-purpose uses.

According to data which Honeywell had compiled from the magazines and newspapers in which it regularly advertised, from 1970 through 1973 computer manufacturers' space advertising expenditures had been fairly erratic. Generally speaking, the introduction of a new line or special emphasis on an old line was accompanied by very large expenditures, which might well drop off sharply the next year. NCR, for example, had spent over $1 million in both 1971 and 1972, but in 1973 it had spent only $385,000. Sperry-Rand/Univac, which had dropped from over $1 million in 1970 to $85,000 in 1971, had jumped to $972,000 in 1973. Except for 1971, IBM's expenditures had consistently been over $2.2 million, though its 1973 level was below its 1970 level. In recent years, Honeywell had been spending approximately $1 million per year. (See Exhibit 2 for sample advertisements of Honeywell's competitors.)

Structure of the Organization

In September 1973, Honeywell's North American operations (NAO) was headed by Mr. Robert P. Henderson, vice president and general manager. Reporting to Mr. Henderson were the vice presidents of finance, administration, field engineering, and manufacturing, and four marketing executives—two concentrating on federal government and Canadian accounts, plus Mr. Christopher J. Lynch, vice president of marketing for the data-processing operations, and Mr. Richard R. Douglas, vice president of marketing operations and planning. (See Exhibit 3 for an abbreviated organization chart of data-processing operations.)

EXHIBIT 2
TYPICAL COMPETITIVE ADVERTISING

Computers and Growth

Agribusiness

"Every week we have 14 shiploads of bananas coming at us—maybe one million 40-pound boxes. If we don't get those bananas fanned out across the country within days after they arrive, we could be facing huge reductions in revenue. Bananas don't keep forever, you know."

Marketing perishable agricultural products is a tricky proposition, as the people of Chiquita Brands, Inc. can tell you. High-volume production, high-velocity shipping schedules, daily fluctuations in demand, varying prices in different geographical areas and the constant threat of spoilage have all made the distribution of perishables as much of an art as a science.

At Chiquita Brands, a subsidiary of United Brands Company, a computer system keeps management up to the minute on all orders nationwide, on one hand, and on all incoming cargoes on the other. This makes it far easier to match supply and demand, since distribution decisions can now be based on current, centralized information.

The system uses an IBM System/370 computer at Boston linked to terminals at eight ports and six sales centers. When a ship arrives at a port, customers' trucks are loaded in accordance with orders previously entered in the system. Bananas not sold at the ports can be routed to areas of greatest demand as indicated by the nationwide data furnished by the computer.

The system allows Chiquita Brands' customers to place orders farther in advance, with deliveries guaranteed. At any time, they can get quick answers as to the status of their orders. And computer-produced reports provide management with clearer insights into buying patterns by season and area.

In businesses where supply and demand are subject to constant fluctuation, the computer can promote orderly growth by helping keep those forces in balance.

IBM

Think of the computer as energy. As mental energy. Power to get things done. **IBM**

EXHIBIT 2
Continued

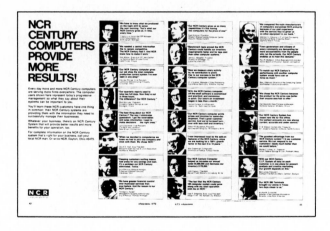

EXHIBIT 2
Continued

EXHIBIT 2
Continued

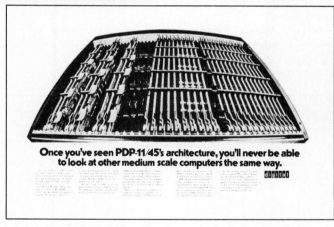

EXHIBIT 3
ABBREVIATED CHART OF DATA-PROCESSING OPERATIONS, 1973

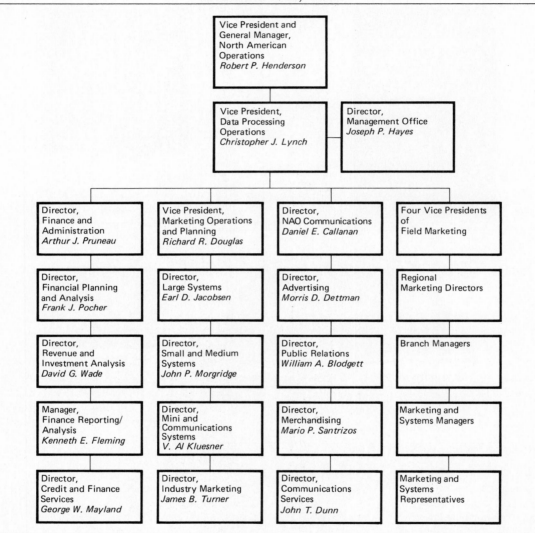

The Field Marketing Organization

The line sales organization for United States commercial accounts was headed by four vice presidents of field marketing. They were responsible for different geographic sections of the country and reported directly to Mr. Lynch. They managed 12 regional marketing directors, who in turn supervised over 2,000 people in 50 branch offices. This organization accounted for more than 75 percent of NAO's computer revenues. (The remaining 25 percent was derived from various Canadian and United States federal government accounts, which were handled by other NAO sales organizations.)

Some branch offices, especially those in large metropolitan areas, were organized by customer industry, while others were organized geographically. Some salespeople specialized by customer type, while others covered a wide variety of industries. Salespeople were committed to serving customers' needs and were paid on a commission basis according to a formula which considered both rental and sales revenue.

In 1973, Mr. Lynch instituted a formal program of account management, a system that called for each salesperson to investigate and record each customer's future needs for information systems. This system included the current system, the next system, when it should be ordered, when it should be installed, and so forth. This was an important step in assuring customer continuity when making the transition from present systems to the new Series 60. It also aided the marketing organization in planning priorities and recommending factory schedules and helped define the promotional and educational requirements that would be needed at announcement time. It was a key tool in defining the total capability that Honeywell planned to stress in launching the new product line.

The Home Office Marketing Organization

Honeywell's home office marketing functions included marketing operations and planning, NAO communications, and finance and administration. Marketing operations and planning, under the direction of Mr. Douglas, helped develop broad strategies for the company with regard to product lines, pricing, industry specialization, market research, competitive evaluation, and so forth. Specialists within this department worked closely with internal departments, outside sources, and progressive customers to develop information systems for specific industries. They also staffed exhibits at trade shows and actually assisted in much of the company's high-level selling.

NAO communications, directed by Mr. Daniel E. Callanan, consisted of four well-defined functions: merchandising, public relations, communications services, and advertising.

The merchandising function was concerned with assisting the marketing activity by developing promotional programs and materials such as brochures, product briefs, visual aids, and other items used by the sales force in sales calls and presentations. A key activity was producing case histories of customer success stories. The staff also provided the editing, illustrating, and composing and much of the writing for the technical literature required by customers for the operation, installation, and maintenance of Honeywell information systems. Others activities included planning and conducting national sales conferences and seasonal motivational meetings, administering special incentive sales contests, publishing a weekly newsletter, and videotaping a 15-minute news program which was distributed every other week to branch offices.

The public relations function was conducted by four resident employees and the full resources of Carl Byoir & Associates, an independent firm which handled public relations for all of Honeywell, Inc. This group was responsible for counseling management on public postures, establishing press relations, conducting press conferences, generating articles, and writing press releases and executive speeches. It also helped produce films and various programs and promotional pieces designed to communicate a positive Honeywell image to the general public.

The communications services department was created initially to be the production facility for NAO communications. It included the print shop and offices which purchased outside printing and warehoused, distributed, and invoiced all literature used by field marketing and its customers. Manuals were sold to customers. With its extensive distribution, list maintenance, and billing facility, it gradually took over the marketing of basic supplies such as magnetic tape reels, disk packs, and printer ribbons.

Communications services also included the marketing of items such as animal posters (described below), pewter replicas, coffee mugs, place mats, decals, and book matches—all featuring the same animals used in Honeywell advertising and illustrated in an animal "gift catalog" sent to all marketing personnel. Honeywell marketing people liked to present token gifts to their customers as contracts were signed, equipment was installed, or leases were renewed. Customers who wanted additional items and employees who wanted items for personal use were encouraged to order directly by sending personal checks. In 1973, sales of animal items totaled $98,000; nearly half of the items were ordered by individuals. Communications services was a self-financing operation—all its costs were recovered either from customers or from Honeywell departments and individuals.

The advertising function came under the direction of Mr. Morris D. Dettman, a 25-year Honeywell employee, who had established his reputation as an ad executive in Minneapolis before his 1956 transfer to the computer group in Boston. Dettman's organization handled Honeywell's exhibits, direct mail, and media advertising. Exhibits were the responsibility of an exhibits manager who set up displays and equipment at various trade shows. Frequently these exhibits featured a selection of the original computer component sculptures. Honeywell normally avoided general computer conventions which catered to a wide range of computer-specialist audiences and required massive budgets. It preferred to concentrate more directly on the specific needs of an audience. Direct mail was used to communicate with customers when new products were announced, to elicit responses from prospects for specific products, and to respond to inquiries generated by media advertisements and editorial items.

Honeywell's Advertising Philosophy

Honeywell's current media advertising program dated back to 1962, when the industry was, in the words of one executive, "like Snow White and the Seven Dwarfs—IBM led with an 80 percent share and the rest of us little guys tagged along behind." A survey of several financial executives that year had revealed that only 31 percent were aware that Honeywell sold computers, only 11 percent could recall any Honeywell advertising, and only 14 percent said they would consider investigating Honeywell as a supplier if they needed equipment. Until this time, Honeywell's advertising, like that of most computer companies, had consisted of straightforward pictures of computers with copy describing their capabilities.

Company executives and Honeywell's advertising agency, Batten, Barton, Durstine, and Osborn (BBDO), then decided that the company's advertising aimed at managerial and financial personnel should be switched from solely promoting computer hardware to putting more direct emphasis on creating awareness of Honeywell as a computer manufacturer. The idea was that an increase in share of mind had to precede growth in share of market. The BBDO creative staff then went to work on a new campaign format. They came back with the idea of using four-color illustrations of animals sculpted out of computer parts. This idea had several advantages. The electronic sculptures related to the product. They could be used with a wide variety of subjects—hardware, software, applications, even philosophy. They provided a continuity for all advertising, so the program would build as more and more ads were produced. Most important, they resulted in advertising uniquely different from anything else in the industry. Parts for the animals were selected from assembly lines and scrap bins and were bona fide computer components. (See Exhibit 4

EXHIBIT 4
TYPICAL HONEYWELL COMPUTER-COMPONENT SCULPTURE ADVERTISEMENT

When you haven't got all the customers, you fight for all the customers you've got.

The way we see it, the only way to get ahead in this business is to do right by the business you've got.

So we make sure our customers are happy customers. We make sure our computer systems are doing what our customers expect them to do: solving the right problems—faster, better, more economically.

We've got a world-wide force of support specialists who make sure your investment in a Honeywell computer system pays off for you. Now. And in the future.

And best of all, Honeywell offers basic software, systems support, application packages, and education at no extra cost.

Sure, we'll fight for new customers. More aggressively than any other company in the business.

But after we get the business, we knock ourselves out.

for a typical computer component ad.) Once a sufficient stable of animals had been created, fewer and fewer new animals were necessary, since the established ones could be used in different ads for different publications and modified slightly with props or accessories and re-used. Some animals had been used in as many as eight different advertisements.

In 1968 Mr. Dettman began looking for a theme line for the company. In a conversation he had with a customer in Chicago, the customer commented, "You know, you really are the only logical alternative to IBM." Mr. Dettman seized the line as the basis for a theme or positioning statement. The agency's creative team took it and came back with the line "The Other Computer Company: Honeywell." After testing, this line was installed as Honeywell's advertising signature. (See Exhibit 5 for sample advertisements.)

The function of the animals in Honeywell advertising was twofold. First, they had proved to be uniquely effective attention getters. (Honeywell advertising executives considered getting attention the first objective of any advertisement.) Second, they had provided continuity

---

EXHIBIT 5
EXAMPLES OF PRINT
ADVERTISING CAMPAIGNS

MANAGEMENT CAMPAIGN

Objective: To build awareness of Honeywell as a computer manufacturer that:

- Is the logical alternative to IBM
- Is committed to delivering results
- Has a total capability that combines people, products, and services
- Is dedicated to the long-range continuity of its customer's investments in information systems

Target audience: Middle and top managements of present and potential computer user organizations.

KEY MARKET CAMPAIGN

Objective: To emphasize Honeywell's commitment and communicate its industry-specific capabilities to selected key markets.

Target audience: Operating and top management personnel in selected industries.

DATA-PROCESSING PROFESSIONAL CAMPAIGN

Objective: To build awareness of Honeywell's technological expertise among data-processing professionals.

Target audience: Managers of data-processing installations, key systems personnel, and consultants (specifiers of computer equipment).

EXHIBIT 5
Continued

Management

Management

Management

Management

Key Market – Banking

Key Market – Manufacturing

Key Market – Hospitals

Key Market – Education

Key Market – Distribution

and identity for Honeywell advertising and helped to set the tone or personality of Honeywell.

The campaign proved to be quite successful. Studies of financial officers revealed that many more of them began to recognize Honeywell as a computer company, and if they needed equipment, more were likely to consult Honeywell than had been the case in 1962. (See Exhibit 6 for historical trends.) Similarly, the ads ranked high in advertising recall studies done by *Business Week*, and the magazine reported that the campaign had consistently scored better than any other ad campaign ever run in the weekly. (See Exhibit 7 for sample *Business Week* reports.) Moreover, in 1970, color reproductions of four sculptures were offered for $1 in ads in *Computerworld* and *Datamation*. During the first week of the offer, Honeywell received 2,000 orders. One industry observer commented, "When people start paying for your advertising illustrations, your ads must be pretty damn good."

Mr. Callanan commented as follows:

One strength of our print campaign is its consistency. The longevity of the theme has built a strong, widely recognized reputation for us. Our customers and our prime prospects immediately think of Honeywell when you say "The Other Computer Company" or when they see animals sculpted from computer parts. If we switch our format or theme now, we'll be wasting all the money Honeywell has spent to develop its present image. At today's prices, launching a new advertising campaign in 1974 would cost at least twice as much as we're spending in 1973 to maintain our present program.

EXHIBIT 6
RESEARCH TRENDS

	1962	1964	1966	1968	1970	1972
Number surveyed	**400**	**410**	**300**	**302**	**300**	**378**
	100%	**100%**	**100%**	**100%**	**100%**	**100%**

When asked to name the leading computer manufacturers, a sample of executives gave the following responses:

	1962	1964	1966	1968	1970	1972
IBM	93%	97%	98%	97%	98%	96%
Honeywell	31	55	66	67	75	68
Univac	56	58	51	49	49	44
NCR	42	41	42	42	41	35
Burroughs	39	39	39	32	41	33
RCA	29	37	39	32	41	
GE	14	21	33	27	40	
Control Data	7	23	30	30	38	28

When asked what manufacturers they would consult if they were seeking new computer equipment, the executives responded as follows:

	1962	1964	1966	1968	1970	1972
IBM	83%	89%	92%	91%	90%	87%
Honeywell	14	32	46	43	48	44
Univac	33	36	30	20	19	17
NCR	24	23	24	29	31	22
Burroughs	19	19	17	20	20	20
RCA	16	14	20	14	21	
GE	5	9	16	12	16	
Control Data	2	5	7	10	12	9

Source: Financial Executive Benchmark Studies conducted annually by BBDO.

EXHIBIT 7
BUSINESS WEEK ADVERTISING READERSHIP
RESEARCH SCORES, 1971–1973

Issue	Ad subject	% recalling	Issue norm	Rank	Cost efficiency index	Rank
1/20/70	Small computers (frogs)	20	14	3	176	3
2/17/70	Cost effectiveness (bull)	32	9	1	440	1
3/17/70	Maintenance (owl)	38	14	1	266	3
4/14/70	Maintenance (owl)	25	7	1	408	1
5/12/70	Small computers (frogs)	34	8	1	687	1
6/09/70	Maintenance (owl)	27	7	2	676	1
7/07/70	Small computers (frogs)	34	9	1	387	1
8/04/70	Small computers (frogs)	33	13	1	246	1
9/01/70	Maintenance (owl)	27	10	1	289	1
9/29/70	Cost effectiveness (bull)	25	9	1	357	1
10/27/70	Maintenance (owl)	24	8	2	310	2
3/20/71	Time-sharing (tub)	32	7	3	226	2
4/17/71	Time-sharing (tub)	31	8	2	247	2
5/15/71	Responsiveness (St. Bernard)	25	11	3	209	4
6/05/71	Responsiveness (St. Bernard)	31	9	1	179	5
7/10/71	Complete line (steer)	43	11	1	425	1
8/07/71	Complete line (steer)	36	10	1	430	2
10/02/71	Complete line (steer)	38	9	1	628	1
10/30/71	Time-sharing (tub)	23	8	3	249	2
1/22/72	Response 2000 (eagle)	36	11	1	321	2
4/15/72	Customer support (kangaroo)	23	9	3	400	2
5/13/72	System 700 (bees)	26	7	2	474	2
6/24/72	System 700 (bees)	31	9	1	452	2
7/08/72	Responsiveness (poodle)	40	12	1	165	5
8/05/72	Cost effectiveness (grizzly)	21	11	4	182	3
10/28/72	Responsiveness (poodle)	28	7	1	468	1

Source: "Multimeasure Proved Advertising Recall Studies," conducted for *Business Week* by Opinion Research Corporation, Princeton, N.J. Studies show ability of readers of publication to recall (unaided) advertisements appearing in each issue. Note that the Honeywell ad ranked first in 16 of the 26 insertions listed, based on recall percentage, and first 11 times based on cost efficiency.

Honeywell segmented its potential audiences into three categories and designed media advertisements to appeal to each. The first category consisted of general managers and financial officers earning more than $15,000 per year and working in companies which employed more than 100 people. Advertisements for this group were run in general business publications such as *Forbes, Fortune, Business Week,* and *The Wall Street Journal* and in news weeklies such as *Times, Newsweek,* and *U.S. News & World Report.* They were designed to make executives aware of Honeywell as a major computer manufacturer. Mr. Eustis Walcott, Honeywell's account supervisor at BBDO's Boston office, commented on advertising to this market as follows:

Ads for general managers and financial officers are not designed to promote hardware directly. Rather, they are designed to sell Honeywell's concept of data processing, and this encompasses hardware, software, and knowhow. We want the ads to stop the reader and establish in his mind that Honeywell is different from any other computer company and is a logical alternative to IBM. Even if he doesn't read the whole ad, he is made aware that Honeywell is a computer company. He will remember Honeywell the next time he is asked to approve a computer recommendation or needs to install or change a system.

The second audience category was referred to as key-market prospects, and it included senior and operating management in fields such as finance, manufacturing, government, hospitals, distribution, and education. This was essentially the program which supported the industry marketing specialists. Ads aimed at this category focused on specific applications of Honeywell's equipment and were designed to make managers aware of Honeywell's interest and capabilities in specific industries. Unlike ads for general managers and financial officers, these contained somewhat more technical information, particularly with respect to software designed for specific industries. Typical publications used included *Iron Age*, *Banking*, *Modern Hospital*, *Nation's Schools*, *The American City*, and *Electrical Wholesaling*.

The third category consisted of data-processing professionals. Ads for this category emphasized technical facts about the different systems. They were run in magazines such as *Computerworld*, *Datamation*, and *Computer Decisions* and often involved multiple-page units due to the amount and level of detail incorporated.

Mr. Dettman commented as follows on this philosophy:

We realize that eyeball-to-eyeball contact provided by a salesperson is what sells computers, not advertising. Nevertheless, our program for general managers and financial executives serves two important purposes. First, it makes prospects aware that Honeywell is a computer company so that when a salesperson visits the prospect, he or she is not walking into totally uncharted territory. Second, after the sale is made, our advertising program helps keep customers aware of what is going on with Honeywell. It projects the image of a growing, dynamic company which the customer can be proud to associate with. Hopefully, this will make him less susceptible to rival products.

In addition, our advertising to data processing professionals does go into more technical detail for those who are looking for, and can appreciate, detailed product information.

Of our three major programs, the management campaign essentially sells Honeywell as a computer company worthy of consideration. Our key market program sells our capability and dedication to meeting needs of specific industries. Our data processing manager program sells our technological capability to computer professionals.

Traditionally we spend about half our budget to reach our management target, one-third on key markets, and one-sixth to reach the data processing professional. This particular emphasis is due more to the size of the audience (which determines costs) than it is to the relative importance of the categories.

Proposed Campaigns for 1974

Honeywell's advertising department and BBDO assumed a maximum budget of $1 million and prepared the following two alternative recommendations:

1. To achieve maximum impact for the new product announcement, no advertising will run in 1974 prior to the late April announcement date. Starting with the press conference, two-page "announcement advertising" will run in management publications (*Business Week*, *The Wall Street Journal*, *Newsweek*, *Fortune*, and *Forbes*), and "announcement advertising" will continue with one-page units for the balance of the year. This advertising will emphasize features, functions, and benefits of the new product line as distinguished from the more general capabilities (responsiveness, cost effectiveness, time sharing) which were subjects of prior

management advertisements. This effort will use approximately $250,000 of the $1 million annual budget.

Space advertising will be supplemented with a 13-week spot television campaign on network golf and news programs to provide additional impact and coverage of middle and top management executives on behalf of the new line. This will cost $500,000 or half the annual budget.

The final $250,000 will be invested in a major exhibit at the National Computer Conference which happens to coincide closely with the announcement date. The conference tends to attract data processing professionals and will take the place of space advertising normally addressed to this audience.

Under this proposal, there will be no funds available for key market advertising during 1974, and the full budget will be spent to maximize the market impact of the new product line—75 percent aimed toward the management audience and 25 percent toward data processing professionals.

2. We will continue to advertise to traditional management and key market audiences from January to April, emphasizing customer success stories and deemphasizing hardware and software specifics.

At announcement time, we will produce major "announcement advertising" (2-page units) for management publications and continue to emphasize the new product line with follow-up one-page units for the balance of year. This will require $500,000 or half the annual budget. We will use the same product announcement advertisements in key market publications.

Under this plan, we will hold back on advertising addressed to the data processing professional until announcement time and then produce an 8-page supplement on the new line for two computer publications, *Computerworld* and *Datamation*. Then we will follow with 2-page semitechnical units for the balance of the year.

This proposal will result in an expenditure of $500,000 or one-half the total budget to reach the management audience, and the remaining half to reach key markets and data processing professionals, with key markets getting the larger share. From an emphasis standpoint, this proposal devotes roughly one-third of the total budget to results-oriented capability advertising and two-thirds to the new product announcement.

Objectives of the 1974 Advertising Program

In September 1973, Mr. Lynch outlined the broad objectives for the 1974 advertising program as he saw them:

A computer-buying decision is generally looked on as a significant long-term relationship. For this reason, the stature and commitment of the supplier can be as important as the performance of the system. Moreover, as the marketplace becomes more sophisticated, our users become increasingly concerned with a system's ability to achieve an overall result and less interested in the specifications and performance of bits and pieces of the system. As a result of these conditions in the marketplace, we want to be known as a company fully committed to satisfying the information system needs of its customers, and we will continue to position our company as a fully-capable contender and logical alternative to IBM. Moreover, rather than emphasizing specific hardware and software features, we want to stress the overall results which our systems can achieve. In doing this, we can capitalize on the acceptance we have achieved at major, well known companies.

Many users have had traumatic experiences in converting from one computer system to a newer generation or even a newer model. Our new line has been designed to make the transition as painless as possible. In announcing it, we must stress that it enhances the continuity of our users' past and present investments in information systems.

Our objectives must be accomplished within a budget that recognizes the tremendous pressures for profitability in a lackluster, if not deteriorating, national economy. We'll have to do the job with no more, and perhaps less, money than we had last year. Fortunately, we've got a lot going for us. Our signature, "The Other Computer Company: Honeywell," is well-recognized and right on target as a corporate positioning statement. And we've got a device in the computer component animals that is a proven attention-getter and identifier.

It was with these objectives in mind that Mr. Lynch and Mr. Callanan would review the proposals which the advertising department had presented and decide how to build a successful advertising campaign for 1974.

year. Fortunately, we've got a lot going for us. Our signature, "The Other Computer Company: Honeywell," is well-recognized and right on target as a corporate positioning statement. And we've got a device in the computer component animals that is a proven attention-getter and identifier.

It was with these objectives in mind that Mr. Lynch and Mr. Callanan would review the proposals which the advertising department had presented and decide how to build a successful advertising campaign for 1974.

27 Lawford Electric Company

Derek A. Newton

On February 2, 1979, Robert Allen, a field sales engineer for the Systems and Controls Division of the Lawford Electric Company, was notified by a letter from Bayfield Milling Company that Bayfield had decided to purchase the drive system for a new shearing line from one of Lawford's competitors. The news was a bitter disappointment to Mr. Allen. This sale, which he had been working on for over a year, would have been a $871,000 order for him. He decided to review his call reports to see whether his failure to secure the order was caused by any flaw in his sales presentation to Bayfield personnel. He was sure that the Lawford equipment was equivalent, if not superior, to that manufactured by his competitors—A G Corporation, Kennedy Electric, and Hamilton Electric. He was

just as certain that Bayfield personnel had been scrupulously fair in their decision.

Background Information

Lawford was one of the oldest, largest, and most respected firms in the electrical equipment industry. It manufactured a broad line of electric motors, generating equipment, and control devices. Its products and service backup were widely regarded for quality and reliability. Lawford's sales volume in 1978 was in excess of $200 million, second only to that of Kennedy Electric in this segment of the electrical equipment industry.

Lawford sales executives considered Mr. Allen an above-average sales engineer. His background was similar to that of most of Lawford's 37 field sales engineers. He held a bachelor's degree in electrical engineering and

Derek A. Newton is the Olsson Professor of Business Administration at the Colgate Darden Graduate School of Business Administration, University of Virginia.

was working on his master's degree in a night program at a local university. He had joined Lawford directly after college graduation in 1968 as an assistant sales engineer, handling routine telephone sales inquiries and processing and following up on customer orders. He had been promoted to his present position in 1970. A lifelong resident of Buffalo, N.Y., Mr. Allen considered himself fortunate to be assigned to the Buffalo sales territory, the site of his company's headquarters. He was married, had two young children, and was active in community affairs—Junior Chamber of Commerce, Rotary Club, and the local chapter of the Institute of Electrical and Electronic Engineers.

The Bayfield Milling Company was located in upstate New York, not far from the Lawford headquarters in Buffalo. Bayfield converted strip steel purchased from large steel producers into a variety of forms for sale to steel supply houses and end users. The company also engaged in a limited steel supply business for its own. Bayfield sales in 1978 were in excess of $80 million.

Mr. Allen had been calling on Bayfield regularly during the past 8 years. Given the size of his territory, which included the metropolitan areas of Albany, Syracuse, and Rochester, and the importance of Bayfield, whose annual purchases from Lawford occasionally totaled as much as $50,000, Mr. Allen attempted to call on Bayfield at least once a month. During this 8-year period Mr. Allen had formed close business friendships with Bayfield's purchasing agent, Mr. George Gibson, and with several of the company's engineers and operations personnel.

The shearing line recently ordered by Bayfield from Magna Machinery Corporation would add a new capability to Bayfield's mill operation, enabling the firm to convert rolled strips of steel into steel sheets of various dimensions. The shearing line would unroll strips of steel at high speed. Because the new equipment could control the speed and tension of the strip at several points along the line, it could trim, flatten, and shear the strip into sheets of precise dimensions. The machinery could then convey the finished sheets to a stacking device and ultimately to a pallet for transfer to a warehouse, truck, or flatcar. The cost of the mechanicals—including uncoiling rolls, pinch rolls, and drag rolls to control tension, plus side trimmers, shears, and conveyors—was about $2 million. The drive system would be about another $900,000.

Allen's Sales Activity

From his call reports Mr. Allen reconstructed his activities during the period between January 13, 1978, when he learned of Bayfield's need for the new drive system, and February 2, 1979, when he learned that he had lost the sale.

January 13, 1978

"Called on Gibson. Learned from him that Bayfield was soliciting bids on a drive system for a new shearing line. The line was to be purchased from Magna Machinery Corporation for delivery and installation in January 1980. Preliminary bids on the drive system for the line were due on July 14, 1978. Final bids were due on December 29, 1978, the award to be announced on February 2, 1979. Gibson got very businesslike with me and said that *no* supplier sales personnel—including staff and management—were to contact Bayfield engineering personnel to discuss product specifications ['specs']. He said that the operations vice president did not want the engineering people bothered, since they would be too busy working on other problems connected with the new shearing line. Instead, all supplier personnel were to work through Gibson, although contact was to be permitted with operations personnel. Gibson gave me the name of the Magna engineer to contact for details of the new line. Gibson said that judging from the preliminary bids, he would choose four or five suppliers to submit final bids. The final decision would be a joint one made by Gibson, purchasing; Lorenz, chief engineer; Mainwaring, plant superintendent; and Vogel, operations vice president—also not to be contacted in person. Gibson suggested that Lawford would be a cinch to be one of the finalists, but that Vogel and Lorenz would be 'pretty hardnosed' about the final decision. I took this to mean that cost would be an important factor.

"Returned to the office and wrote the Magna engineer in Cleveland for the specs on the shearing line. Wrote to Albany Fabricators for a testimonial letter about the drive system I sold them last year for their slitting line. Told the boss [Fred Webster, Lawford regional sales manager] about the situation. 'Anything I can do to help, . . .' he said. Took home for review our general specifications on various Lawford drive components."

January 23, 1978

"Received specs from Magna [see Exhibit 1]. Took them to Pollack [Lawford's systems design engineer] and asked him to put together a tentative system for the Magna line. Called Mainwaring at Bayfield and made a luncheon date for next week.

February 2, 1978

"Spent all morning with Gibson. Found out that operations and engineering are in a bad hassle over the drive system specs, but Gibson didn't understand the technicalities of the dispute. Showed him Pollack's tentative ideas. He seemed impressed. Spent about an hour going over the features of our variable voltage speed drives, stressing our static regulators for accurate speed control and our portable control panels.

EXHIBIT 1
GENERAL DESCRIPTION OF MAGNA SHEARING LINE DRIVE MACHINERY REQUIREMENTS

Entry System, consists of:

Processor uncoiler, 100 kw, to operate as a drag generator. It is powered from a current-regulated static power supply. The motor field is controlled by a CEMF* regulator. The combination of the two regulator systems will ensure constant horsepower control over the full range of coil diameter.

Processor, 500 hp motor powered from a voltage-regulated static power supply.

The No. 1 Loop regulator controls processor speed.

No. 1 Pinch Roll, two 30 hp motors powered from a current-regulated static power supply.

Side Trimmer, 250 hp motor, and side trimmer Pinch Roll. 30 hp, powered from a voltage-regulated static power supply.

No. 2 Pinch Roll, two 30 hp motors powered from a voltage-regulated static power supply.

The No. 2 Loop regulator controls the side trimmer and No. 2 Loop Pinch Roll speed.

Temper Mill System, consists of:

The No. 1 Bridle, three 120 hp and one 200 hp motors to be powered from a current-regulated static power supply. These motors are to operate as drag generators, with tachometer generator for speed indication.

EXHIBIT 1
Continued

Temper Mill, Top—600 hp, Bottom—600 hp, powered from a speed-regulated static power supply. One tachometer generator for speed indication and another for speed regulation.

No. 2 Bridle, one 200 hp, one 120 hp, two 250 hp, powered from a static power supply which will be current-regulated if the temper mill is used, and speed-regulated when the temper mill is not used. A tachometer generator will provide the speed signal for regulation.

A voltage-regulated static power supply will be used to power No. 3 Loop Pinch Roll, two 20 hp motors when shearing. It will also be used to power a deflector roll, 7.5 hp, and an oiling machine, 20 hp, when the line is run for coiling.

The No. 3 Loop regulator, used only when shearing, controls the entire mill system speed.

The No. 1 Bridle is always used whether shearing or recoiling, and is current-regulated for tension control.

The temper mill may be open or closed when either recoiling or shearing. If mill is closed, the No. 2 Bridle is current-regulated. If mill is open, the rolls will not touch the strip and the No. 2 Bridle is speed-regulated.

If the mill is closed, it sets the speed of the mill system. If open, the No. 2 Bridle sets mill system speed.

Tension Reel—Hallden Shear System, consists of:

Tension Reel, 500 hp motor, powered from a current-regulated static power supply. The motor field is controlled by a CEMF regulator. The two-regulator combination will regulate for constant hp through the entire coil buildup.

Hallden Shear, 400 hp motor, powered from the same static power supply as the tension reel, except that now it will be voltage-regulated. The speed signal provided by a tachometer generator, driven by the shear leveler, will be the reference to the conveyor section.

The maximum line of speed when shearing is 350 f.p.m.† at a rated voltage.

When recoiling, the system's line speed can be increased by field weakening on some of the drives from 500 to 1000 f.p.m., as outlined earlier. A selector switch on the main desk can preset the speed at 500 or 1000 f.p.m. Interlocking will be provided to prevent change while the line is running.

When shearing, the Hallden Shear is the keynoter for the section beyond the shear. However, the line reference for the line as either a recoiling or shearing up to and through the shear is provided by the line reference motor-operated rheostat.

Conveyor and Leveler System, consists of:

The drives beyond the shear through Prime Pinch Roll (excluding the leveler), as shown on the single line, powered from a voltage-regulated semiconverter static power supply.

The strip leveler, 400 hp motor, powered from a speed-regulated static power supply. This section will have a fixed minimum speed of 75 f.p.m.

The drives are geared at 400 f.p.m., with field weakening to 450 f.p.m. on all those drives beyond the McKay Leveler.

*Counter electromotive force.
†Feet per minute.

Left him a mountain of literature, including the Albany Fabricators' testimonial letter.

"Spent $30 on lunch with Mainwaring and his assistant, Hughes. Told Hughes about a good place to buy a boat. Mainwaring denied that his people and engineering were having a hassle; the problem seemed to be that nobody had a clear understanding of what was needed. He added that 'maybe the preliminary specs will give us a few ideas.' He seemed to feel that engineering would draw up specs with whatever features his operations people wanted. Made a mental note to concentrate my sales efforts on Mainwaring.

"After lunch I went over the same ground with Mainwaring and Hughes that I covered with Gibson, only in more detail. They both seemed concerned with reliability: 'Down-time kills you.' I reminded them that Lawford, being a neighbor, so to speak, was in the best position to provide prompt and regular service. They agreed. Left them with the testimonial letter, a mountain of literature, and a copy of Pollack's proposal.

"At home that evening I formulated my strategy. Decided to concentrate on Mainwaring at first, emphasizing our service capability and product reliability. After Lawford had passed the preliminary bid stage, I would shift my major effort to Lorenz in order to get a crack at influencing the final specs. Gibson would be 'kept on board' throughout."

February 17, 1978

"Stopped by to check progress with Gibson. Nothing new from him, so I spent some time talking about our mutual activities in Rotary. Arranged a lunch with him, Lorenz, Mainwaring, and my boss, Fred Webster, for the middle of next month.

"Went to see Mainwaring, but he was out for the day. Hughes and I discussed some developments in systems design that improve reliability. Spent about an hour with the foreman on the cutting floor. He seemed to want a line that would allow fine tolerances in cutting accuracy. Talked to him about the advantages of the Lawford regulator systems as aids in controlling tolerances, due to their high-speed response capabilities. Discovered that two of their four splitting lines are powered by Lawford drive systems, one by a Kennedy system, and one by an A G. The two Lawford systems were the oldest and the newest. Checked with several operators and they were unanimous in their praise of the Lawford machinery, although one man liked the A G because of the case steel motor enclosure. When I pointed out that this feature made the motor bulky and harder to secure access for service, he remarked that he didn't have to service it but he 'sure liked a big, heavy motor.' Bought him a Coke and we parted friends."

March 14, 1978

"Webster bought us all—Lorenz, Mainwaring, Gibson, Hughes, and myself—a magnificent lunch at the country club and made a great pitch about Lawford quality and service. This was the first time that I had met Lorenz—he joined Bayfield less than six months ago. He seemed a sour individual, but he loosened up after the second martini. After lunch I got Gibson aside and asked him about new developments. He now believed, as Mainwaring had previously indicated, that the difficulty seemed to center on uncertainty as to what was needed in the drive system, and not on a dispute about features. He indicated that engineering had stopped working on the specs until after Bayfield had had a chance to look over the preliminary bids."

April 10, 1978

"Spent the morning with Mainwaring discussing the trade-off between the inertia in a heavy machine, which can provide for an even feed, and the speed of response in a light machine, which allows more precise cutting tolerances.

Left him with some additional literature describing Lawford's latest developments in regulator systems, and a paperweight [a scale model of an experimental automobile powered by a Lawford electric motor]. Stopped by to see Gibson and closed a $2,500 order for circuit breakers.''

May 19, 1978

"Spent the day with Pollack working out the details of our tentative bid. His idea, based on my input, was a complete drive system that would include d.c. adjustable voltage drive motors and control equipment, a.c. motors, a static d.c. constant potential power supply, and a static master regulator system. All components would be Lawford-made—a servicing advantage to Bayfield—and would include a one-year warranty and a service contract. Judging by the Magna line specs, I thought that the system offered a perfect compromise between even feed and cutting precision. Webster approved the pricing of $895,000, and I mailed out the bid later that week.''

May 30, 1978

"Checked with Gibson, who grinned when I asked him how our bid looked. He said not to bother him until after July 17. We both laughed and I left for a brief visit on the cutting floor with the foreman. Found him grumbling about the regulatory instability on the older Lawford slitting line drive system. Good-naturedly reminded him that regulators are temperature sensitive and that a drive system of that age deserves congratulations, not criticism. He laughed and said that maybe we should replace it with another. I said that if he meant that Bayfield should replace it with another Lawford, I would take it up immediately with Mainwaring. He laughed again and said that the machine was O.K.; he was only pulling my leg. On the way out I saw my old friend, the A G booster, and I bought him another Coke.''

July 17, 1978

"Gibson telephoned and said that a letter was in the mail inviting Lawford to bid on the final specifications. The other firms invited to bid are Kennedy, A G, and Hamilton. I dug up price lists and specs on our competitors' systems and took them home to study that evening.

"The Kennedy product line is almost identical to Lawford's. Felt that Kennedy's has about a 5 percent price advantage over Lawford, item for item. But, on the other hand, their reputation for quality and service is not as good as Lawford's. Unlike both Kennedy and Lawford, A G and Hamilton don't manufacture all their own components. Lacking unit responsibility, neither of these two companies can offer an extensively field-tested, integrated package. A G could offer more capacity in its regulator system than any of the other companies. This incremental capacity, however, would come at considerable additional cost to Bayfield. I felt that Bayfield would need add-on benefits only if they found themselves in the unlikely circumstance of buying another shearing line. Hamilton equipment I consider over-priced.''

July 19, 1978

"Stopped by to see Gibson. He suggested that our tentative bid was 'a little high.' Assured him that Lawford would be 'rock bottom' once we had the final specs to bid on. Asked him about the committee's thinking on regulator capacity, and he told me to go see Lorenz, but reminded me that supplier personnel could not bother anyone else in the engineering section. Lorenz was free, and I spent about an hour with him talking about our components. He did not seem as concerned about add-on capacity in the regulator system as he did about the system's stability. He said that the operating people were concerned about temperature sensitivity. Since this feature is one of Lawford's strong points, I went into considerable detail with him about our temperature stability. Left him some additional highly technical literature to supplement the literature I had left with Gibson and Mainwaring, which apparently had found its way to Lorenz's desk."

August 2, 1978

"Gibson told me over the phone that the committee had made no progress on the specs, nor did he expect any progress during August because of vacation schedules. He suggested that I check back after Labor Day."

September 12, 1978

"Had lunch with Gibson and Lorenz. Both men agreed now that the committee had been in a bind over the specs. From the considerable experience that Bayfield personnel had had with drive systems for smaller lines, such as the slitters, the committee had proceeded on the belief that this experience would be transferable and would therefore make a decision about a drive system for the shearing line relatively easy, despite the increased size and complexity of the operation.

"Apparently the problem had been a lack of criteria upon which the specs could be developed. Mainwaring had finally recognized this fact after the tentative bids had been opened. Implicit in all the tentative proposals were assumptions about criteria that were, in turn, manifested in a variety of specs. Accordingly, Mainwaring had requested technical assistance from Magna engineers to develop criteria for Bayfield's installation. Mainwaring had just made a two-day visit to Magna headquarters, and had brought these criteria back with him. Bayfield operating and engineering personnel were just beginning to study them. Lorenz expected the final specs to be ready by early November.

"This news elated me, because I felt that I was now in a position to go to work on Lorenz. I wanted to make sure that the specs included certain features standard with our constant

potential power supply and our control panels. Incorporating these features into the final specs would, I felt, give Lawford a big price advantage in the bidding. Since Lorenz was busy that afternoon, I made an appointment to see him the following week."

September 20, 1978

"Had lunch with Lorenz and spent two more hours with him that afternoon. Covered thoroughly all aspects of our system, with heavy emphasis on standard features in our power supply sets and control panels that reduce the incidence of generator breakdown and control component failure. He listened attentively throughout and asked very few additional questions. He seemed sold on the Lawford benefits."

October 4, 1978

"Had lunch with Hughes, who told me that Mainwaring had left Bayfield for another job and that he had been promoted to Mainwaring's former position as plant superintendent. Neither Hughes nor Gibson, with whom I talked later that afternoon, cared to go into details. Discussed with Hughes the reliability features that I had discussed with Lorenz, only this time I stressed the benefits from the user's point of view, instead of the cost savings. Over dessert and coffee we discussed the merits of our respective boats. After lunch Gibson and I talked price, but he managed to talk a lot without telling me much. Got the feeling that the operations vice president, Vogel, was upset about 'some of the trimmings' that the engineers wanted to write into the specs."

November 6, 1978

"Received final specs for the drive system in the mail from Gibson. Also got an invitation to make a formal presentation on our bid to Vogel, Lorenz, Hughes, and Gibson on December 27. The specs were a surprise. Bayfield has gone along with our power supply and control features, but is also specifying some special wiring, which is no problem, and a significant amount of additional capacity in the master regulator—which could be a problem. I put Pollack to work drawing up the final proposal and arranged for him and Webster to participate in the formal presentation."

November 8, 1978

"Called Gibson on the phone to verify the December 27 presentation date. Lawford is to be given one hour for a presentation, as are our three competitors. The alphabet gives us a break; ours will be the last presentation on that day. All four suppliers are expected to hand in their bids at the conclusion of their respective presentations. Asked him a few questions about the specs, and he suggested that I see Lorenz."

November 13, 1978

"Spent two hours in the morning going over specs with Lorenz, who, it turned out, was a stickler for attention to small details. Gave him a brief pitch on every detail, and he seemed satisfied with my assurances that Lawford could deliver on all its promises. Stopped by to see Hughes, who was quite busy, so I left after ten minutes. Neither he, Gibson, nor Lorenz was available for lunch."

December 27, 1978

"Our presentation went very well. Webster did a great job on Lawford's reliability and service. Pollack covered thoroughly the technical aspects of our proposed drive system, matching them with all Bayfield's specifications. I concluded with a summary and handed the sealed bid to Vogel. The bid, which Pollack, Webster, and I had agonized over for hours, was a 'rock bottom' $871,000."

February 2, 1979

"After opening Gibson's letter and learning that A G had won the bid, I called Gibson on the phone. He said that all bids had been in the 'plus or minus ten thousand dollar range' and that A G had just edged out Lawford. I asked him on what basis. He replied that Vogel, Lorenz, and Hughes had felt the A G system 'fitted in better' with the new shearing operation, but each gave different reasons for thinking so. He strongly suggested that holding a postmortem with the three men, either individually or collectively, would be a waste of time, since all Bayfield personnel concerned in the purchase were relieved that the decision was over and done with. He congratulated me on Lawford's showing and said that he hoped that I did not feel too bad about 'coming in second.'"

28 / Aurora-Baxter Corporation: I

E. Raymond Corey

Mr. Jack McGowan, chairperson of the Aurora-Baxter Corporation (ABC) Audit Committee, called the meeting of his committee to order promptly at 9:30 A.M. and opened with:

> Our first item of business is one that's not on the agenda you've received. It has to do with a "questionable payments" situation that the auditors have uncovered in the Construction Materials Division. I'll ask Arnie Gates [ABC controller] to give you the background.

Aurora-Baxter Corporation, with sales in 1976 of $557 million, was a diversified manufacturer of industrial products. Its Construction Materials Division sold such products as pipe (concrete, iron, and plastic), cement, sand, asphalt, tile (roofing, floor, and wall tile), and a

E. Raymond Corey is the Malcolm P. McNair Professor of Marketing at the Harvard Graduate School of Business Administration.

All names, locations, and quantitative data not publicly available have been disguised.

limited line of protective coatings. Its customers included large commercial contractors as well as state and federal government agencies.

Present at the meeting were the members of the Audit Committee: four outside directors; ABC's president; the controller; the director of the internal audit staff; and three representatives of the company's outside auditing firm, Bixby, Lyons and Bolton (BLB).

Arnie Gates, the controller, spoke:

> As you know, Construction Materials does a lot of business with state governments. Among our big accounts for pipe and tile is Missawba [a large Midwestern state].
>
> A couple of years ago, following a scandal in the awarding of highway contracts, they enacted some very stiff legislation forbidding state purchasing officers and buyers from accepting any gifts—even free lunches. Since then our relations with Missawba buyers have gotten a little awkward in certain respects. When our marketing guys are in the middle of negotiations with them or when

they've concluded a big contract, it's natural to go out with the buyers, maybe for drinks and a nice meal. Everybody knows that each person there is supposed to pay for his or her own meal. Our guys are told that they have to make that clear. So at some point one of them will say, "OK, everybody, chip in. You know the rule." Maybe there are five of them and three of us and say the bill is $100. When the meal's over they've put in $2 each and we pick up the rest of the tab.

In fact, on one recent occasion our sales rep for the Missawba State Highway Department had concluded a big sale and our guys and the buyers went out to a restaurant to celebrate. The ABC rep put a big bowl in the middle of the table and made sure everybody saw him drop in 15 one-dollar bills. When we counted the money after dinner there were 8 one-dollar bills! He mentioned it to a senior buyer for the state, and the response was, "ABC is a big company; you ought to be able to find some way to buy me a dinner!"

On each occasion our account representative submits an expense voucher recording the amount, the place, the time, and the names of those attending. Now, the practice they've been following in Construction Materials is that when the voucher is approved and the claim for entertainment expenses paid, the supporting documentation is destroyed.

Ms. Rachel Stuart, a member of the Audit Committee and a lawyer, spoke:

If you do that, you can't take it as a tax deduction; and, up to certain limits, entertainment, if it is properly documented, is still a deductible expense. How much money is involved anyway?

Gates responded:

It amounts to $3,840 for the last fiscal year, and if we do document it for tax purposes, we expose the buyers. If they're caught accepting favors, they could lose their jobs.

Jack McGowan turned to Mr. Ralph Dominick, senior BLB auditor on the ABC account:

Ralph, what do you think?

Dominick replied:

There's no reason for us to take any exception. In the first place, the expense is not being claimed as a deduction on either state or federal tax returns. Second, it's being recorded on ABC books. There's been no effort to conceal anything.

Mr. Warren Phelps, ABC's president, spoke up:

Ralph, maybe BLB doesn't have a problem with it, but we surely have. I think we're "between a rock and a hard place," and we really have to do something. Our salespeople do a lot of business over lunches and probably get more useful information on what competition is doing and what's going on in the customers' shops than at any other time. I don't want us to cut that off. But I also don't want our salespeople being compromised.

As he spoke, Mr. Phelps had in mind the ABC Corporate Responsibility Statement, which had been promulgated less than a year before. It read in part as follows:

The Corporation intends to comply strictly with all domestic and foreign laws which apply to its business. Employees will not be permitted to violate any law relating to the conduct of business or to engage in unethical business practices. Although customs and standards of conduct may vary from country to country, the Corporation will, at all times, conduct its business with integrity and honesty. In cases where laws or business practices are subject to interpretation, management will obtain legal advice from the General Counsel.

Failure to adhere to ethical and legal standards of conduct may result in disciplinary action, including immediate suspension and eventual discharge.

A complete list of illegal or unethical practices is impossible. However, areas where practices inconsistent with accepted standards commonly occur are:

Personal Gifts. The giving or receiving of gifts, loans, favors or other services by an employee acting on behalf of the Corporation directly or indirectly to or from anyone outside the Corporation is strictly forbidden. Such gifts are not limited to tangible or cash gifts or loans but include intangibles such as promises for the future, valuable "tips," advantageous purchases or other opportunities.

Excluded from this prohibition are the exchange of normal business courtesies such as luncheons or dinners, when they are proper and consistent with regular business practice. Also excluded are advertising or promotional materials of nominal value as well as the exchange of gifts or favors because of kinship, marriage or social relationships provided they do not violate Corporate Policy 4, *Conflict of Interest*. The criteria for deciding what is proper and reasonable is based on the judgment a disinterested third party would make under the same circumstances.

29

Aurora-Baxter Corporation: II

E. Raymond Corey

Mr. Jack McGowan, chairperson of the Aurora-Baxter Corporation (ABC) Audit Committee, was meeting with ABC's president, Mr. Warren Phelps to discuss the agenda for the September 1977 Audit Committee meeting. Phelps opened the conversation with:

> Jack, the BLB [Bixby, Lyons and Bolton] auditors have come up with what appears to be a serious questionable payments situation in our Venezuelan subsidiary. They've found substantial discrepancies between freight bills paid on the importation of fiber glass scrim and the amounts paid to our customs broker to cover those charges. It looks as though we may have been paying off the Venezuelan customs agents to the tune of about $123,000 over the past three years.

ABC's Venezuelan company manufactured and sold a wide range of industrial products.

E. Raymond Corey is the Malcolm P. McNair Professor of Marketing at the Harvard Graduate School of Business Administration.

All names, locations, and quantitative data have been disguised.

One of its largest-selling lines was fiber glass reinforced plastic (FRP) pipe for oil field applications. The fiber glass scrim used as the reinforcing material was imported from the United States.

In late 1974, when many materials were in short supply, ABC de Venezuela (ABC-V) had suffered a loss of sales in FRP pipe because of late deliveries of scrim. Sr. Valdez, the managing director of the company, had expressed his keen dissatisfaction with these delays and was severely critical of the performance of ABC-V's purchasing manager, Sr. Rodriguez.

Sr. Rodriguez then began to import fiber glass scrim by airfreight to expedite the shipments. As was customary, he contracted for the services of a customs broker, in this case Gomez y Cie, to move the shipments as rapidly as possible through the airport at Caracas. Sr. Gomez billed ABC-V for freight charges and import duties, which he paid out to the air carrier and government customs officials. He was in turn reimbursed for these payments and was given a commission amounting to 5 percent of the value of the shipments. As supporting documentation, he submitted the original freight bills and his statement of duties paid, his commission, and any incidental charges.

In April 1975, Gomez informed Rodriguez of the strong possibility that fiber glass scrim would be reclassified by Venezuelan customs officials from category 17, unfinished materials, to category 77, industrial components. The reclassification would cause the duty to increase from 25 percent to 110 percent. He assured Rodriguez that he could arrange to have ABC-V shipments of fiber glass scrim remain in category 17 for duty purposes if Rodriguez would permit him to pay fees to certain agents at the Caracas airport. These fees would amount to approximately a third of the difference between the category 17 rate and that of category 77.

Thereafter, Gomez included the additional payments as part of the freight item on his submissions to Rodriguez. Rodriguez instructed Sra. de Failla, a clerk in the import department, to ignore the discrepancies between this item and the attached freight bills and simply approve the statements as rendered by Sr. Gomez.

In October 1975, a member of the ABC internal auditing staff on a routine visit to the Venezuelan subsidiary noted the discrepancies in Gomez's statements. He reviewed the matter with Rodriguez and was told that this "arrangement" had "management approval." Nevertheless, in his work papers the internal auditor attributed the unusually high freight costs to the use of air shipment. When questioned later about this notation, he commented that he had understood the real reason for the high freight charges but that "he didn't want to put that sort of thing in writing." He did state that he had informed his superior of what he had discovered. When questioned, the superior did not recall such a conversation.

In December 1976, Sr. Rodriguez directed that all incoming air shipments of fiber glass scrim be routed through the Maracaibo airport.

He had learned that this material was still classified in category 17 by the government customs agent at that location.

In February 1976, an ABC-V tax accountant questioned the subsidiary's controller about the freight payments. He was concerned about deducting them as an expense. If he did so, it would reduce tax payments to Venezuela but would result in a corresponding increase in United States tax liabilities for the parent corporation.

Sr. Valdez happened to come into the controller's office at the time. All present agreed that the matter was really past history and should be dropped. Sr. Valdez, in that conversation, expressed some concern about jeopardizing ABC's excellent relations with the Venezuelan government if past years' tax returns had to be reopened because of freight and duty payments.

In May 1977, shipments of fiber glass scrim by ocean freight were resumed. However, because of certain deficiencies in the import license a large shipment of fiber glass scrim which arrived in the port of La Guaira was impounded by Venezuelan customs officials as contraband. From La Guaira it was taken to a government warehouse at the Caracas airport. Through Sr. Gomez's efforts, arrangements were made for ABC-V personnel to withdraw the scrim from storage in small amounts.

It was at that point that Sr. Valdez decided to initiate litigation in the Venezuelan courts to enjoin government customs agents from classifying fiber glass scrim in category 77. While the suit was pending, ABC-V was allowed to pay the 25 percent duty and to give customs officials bank letters of credit for the difference between that amount and the 110 percent rate for category 77.

Warren Phelps concluded his account of the questionable payments situation in Venezuela by saying:

What troubles me, in particular, is that Enrique Valdez is one of the very best managers we have anywhere. He's increased his sales and profits more than fivefold in eight years, and he has by far the largest market shares for the products we sell in Venezuela.

Jack McGowan had listened intently. He was concerned about what action ABC's management ought to take. He wondered what the Audit Committee could and should do. In particular, he was concerned about whether the matter should be reported to the U.S. Securities and Exchange Commission and the Internal Revenue Service.

30 Federal Express: II

Christopher H. Lovelock

Heinz J. Adam, director of marketing administration for the Federal Express Corporation (FEC), was reviewing a significant marketing challenge facing his company.

It was June 1976, and Mr. Adam had to decide what strategy would be most appropriate to achieve a 350 percent increase in sales of Courier Pak—one of several package express services offered by FEC—within the next 6 months.

The Company and Its Product Line

Federal Express was founded by Frederick W. Smith, Jr., as the nation's first airline devoted exclusively to the transportation of small packages weighing 70 pounds or less. Operations began in 1973.

The company flew small jet freighters over a

Christopher H. Lovelock is an associate professor at the Harvard Graduate School of Business Administration.

unique route system, similar to the spokes of a wheel. The hub of this system was a sophisticated sorting facility located in Memphis, Tennessee. Aircraft stationed throughout the United States left their home cities every weeknight with a load of packages and flew into Memphis, often making one or two stops en route. At Memphis, all packages were unloaded, sorted by destination cities, and reloaded. The aircraft then returned to their home cities in the early hours of the morning. Packages were picked up and delivered within a 25-mile radius of the airport by FEC couriers. From door to door, each package was in Federal Express hands.

At the outset, Federal Express faced widespread skepticism from shippers. Recalled one senior executive:

We initially served 22 cities. So, we had to go to a shipper who had never heard of us and who had been inundated by fly-by-night operations promising the moon and gone the next day. The shipper is very careful about changing. He's learned the hard way. We came in and said we were flying our own planes and could take certain sized packages of certain weight going to certain cities. About halfway through our presentation, eyes would start rolling and skepticism became pretty evident. It took a long time to break into major accounts.

Volume increased steadily as additional Falcons were delivered and new cities added, but the company continued to lose money heavily. At one point, Federal Express was technically bankrupt. While top management worked desperately to renegotiate loans, couriers deposited their watches as security when obtaining gas for company trucks, the president sold his personal aircraft, and base personnel hid the Falcons to keep sheriffs from serving attachment papers and chaining the little jets to the ramps. Looking back at the fledgling airline's early difficulties, Smith observed ruefully, "The biggest asset we had going for us was our naiveté. God takes care of fools, you know."

In mid-1975, the company finally became profitable. By mid-1976 FEC boasted an average daily volume of almost 19,000 packages and over 2,000 employees. It operated 32 Dassault Falcons of its own—plus nine other aircraft flown under contract by supplemental carriers—and 500 leased vans. Its flights served 75 cities directly, and pickup and delivery service was provided in 130 cities in the United States. Because of the growth in volume, the company had established a second "minihub" in Pittsburgh and also operated a shuttle service between Boston, New York, Washington, and intermediate cities. FEC had 31,000 customers, of whom about 15,000 used the service in any one month.

Federal Express offered three basic services:[1] Priority One, Standard Air Service, and Courier Pak.

Priority One (P-1) provided overnight service for packages, with deliveries before noon the next business day. Rates were based on weight and distance traveled, with discounts for multiple shipments on a single day. The average daily

sales volume in May 1976 was 13,400 packages with revenues of $298,000.

Standard Air Service (SAS) guaranteed delivery on the second business day after pickup. The average daily sales volume in May 1976 was 6,022 packages with revenues totaling $65,000.

Courier Pak (CP) provided overnight transportation of documents or other items weighing up to 2 pounds in waterproof, tearproof envelopes that were 12 inches by 15½ inches. CP envelopes cost $12.50 each for shipment anywhere in the Federal Express system and had to be purchased in advance in quantities of five or more at a time. Average daily sales in May 1976 totaled 1,304 Courier Paks versus 764 daily in May 1975 and 411 in May 1974. Studies by FEC's cost accounting department showed that the variable costs associated with Courier Pak averaged $4.25 per unit.

A spring 1976 survey of Priority One (P-1) and Courier Pak (CP) usage by FEC's top 1,400 customers found that 24 percent used both CP and P-1 and less than 1 percent used only CP, while the rest used only P-1. The key attribute separating Courier Pak from Priority One service in the customer's mind was the expectation that packages sent by the former would be delivered to the addressee and not just to the receiving dock. Another analysis showed that 57 percent of CP volume came from the 14 top FEC stations and 20 percent from the top three; the figures for P-1 were 44 percent and 15 percent, respectively.[2] On the average, users sent 0.45 Courier Pak per day.

Local Operations and Sales

A sense of what took place at the end of one of the "spokes" thrusting out from the Memphis "hub" was provided by a visit to the Boston

---

[1]Special handling was available at extra charges for hazardous materials or high-security packages.

[2]In rank order, the 14 largest airfreight markets in the United States were New York, Los Angeles, Chicago, San Francisco, Boston, Philadelphia, Detroit, Atlanta, Dallas, Milwaukee, Minneapolis, Cleveland, Houston, and Miami.

station, considered representative for its size of FEC station operations.

Federal Express operations in the Greater Boston area were based at Hanscom Field in Bedford, about 15 miles west of downtown Boston. Federal leased half a large hangar for light maintenance and package-sorting operations; adjoining offices housed the station manager, Denis Spina, the sales staff, and a radio-dispatch facility.

One senior FEC executive described the job of station managers as "the key to company operations." These individuals, he said, had profit and loss responsibility for a business that might amount to as much as $5 million in large stations. They had to watch costs carefully, supervising performance in both the station office and the field.

Each weekday morning, a Federal Express Falcon "minifreighter" flew into Hanscom Field from Memphis, being scheduled to arrive at 7:30 A.M. Two supplemental carriers, operating under contract to FEC, flew in packages from the recently established Pittsburgh "minihub" and from several East Coast cities.

At 7:25 one summer morning, a crew of Federal Express couriers could be seen busily unloading the Pittsburgh supplemental flight, a white Hansa jet. This task was almost completed when, at 7:40, the second supplemental flight, an old-fashioned, propeller-driven Twin Beech, arrived at the end of its "milk run" from Washington, via Baltimore, Philadelphia, and Newark. There was still no sign of the Memphis flight, and a check over the Teletype established that it had been delayed half an hour before leaving its home base. Mr. Spina indicated that such a delay occurred about once every 3 weeks. Finally, at 7:55 the purple-colored Falcon touched down and taxied quickly over to be unloaded.

In the hangar, two lines of vans, all painted in FEC colors, had been backed up against a line of rollers. As the packages trundled along the rollers, each courier picked out those destined

for consignees on his or her route and positioned them carefully inside the vehicle. About 7 percent of the packages were marked "Hold at Airport" for individual collection by the consignees.

The station manager noted that there was an imbalance between outbound and inbound loads in the Boston area. A check of the previous day's totals yielded the following figures, described as "fairly typical."

Sample Daily Operating Statistics, Boston Area, Summer 1976

	Package category			
	Priority 1	Standard Air	Courier Pak	Total
Packages outbound	911	227	39	1,177
Packages inbound	539	133	22	694

However, the couriers had actually made more delivery stops (363) than pickup stops (326). The daily report indicated that 151 of these pickup stops were regular daily visits to frequent shippers, while the remaining 175 had been scheduled in response to telephone calls by customers. About 12 percent of the outbound packages were brought directly to the airport by the shipper.

Because of the imbalance in loads, there were four flights out of Hanscom Field in the evening, which required routing a second FEC Falcon into Boston at night. Flights left for Memphis at 6:30 and 10 P.M., for Pittsburgh at 10:30, and for the East Coast "milk run" at 10:55 P.M.

A Morning with a Courier

Working fast, the couriers had loaded all the vans by 8:35 A.M. and had made up some of the time lost by the late arrival of the Memphis flight. Ken Barlow, a cheerful man in his early thirties, jumped into the driver's seat of his van and within minutes was pulling out of the main gate of Hanscom Field onto the road to Lexington. His regular route covered five suburban towns near Boston. He made a delivery run in the morning and a pickup run in the afternoon and usually finished work around 6:30 P.M.

Barlow's first stop, at 8:45, was to deliver a small package at the suburban plant of a large chemical company. It was signed for by the head shipper at the plant's loading dock. As the courier got back in the van, his radio crackled, asking his estimated time of arrival at a particular address. Ken responded that it would be in about an hour.

Five minutes later he was pulling into the receiving dock of a well-known office machinery firm. He delivered two boxes and a Courier Pak to the receiving dock. At 9:02, another radio call came through.

"Do you have a package for Raytheon there, Ken?"

"Yeah, I've got it, Jean. Should be in Waltham around 11:30." There was a pause, then:

"What's your next stop?"

"I'm on the way to Xerox, then Hewlett-Packard in 20 minutes."

"He'll meet you there."

At 9:05 Ken stopped at the Xerox plant and delivered a package downstairs at the receiving office and a Courier Pak to the receptionist in the office upstairs. Leaving the parking lot, the van was met by a green car. The driver waved Ken to a stop. He was the man from Raytheon. He signed quickly for a small package and explained that it was a product part long overdue from the suppliers.

The morning continued with stops every few minutes, typically at newish suburban plants and office buildings. Most deliveries consisted of one or two small packages. Two of the larger boxes in the van, both relatively light, were delivered to a major computer firm and bore labels showing that they had been dispatched from the same company's plants in Pennsylvania and California.

Ken exchanged a cheery word or two with many of the shipping clerks, traffic managers, and receptionists who signed for his packages, but he never dallied at any location. At one plant, the traffic office was empty. "The receiver here's an old-timer—he's never around," muttered Ken, looking around quickly for somebody else to accept delivery. By 11 he was driving through a run-down industrial area of Watertown and expressing concern that he might not be able to complete all his deliveries before noon. He was annoyed that his route that morning included two deliveries in Arlington, 20 minutes' slow driving time away. For the first time, he had to use his handcart to transport several bulky parcels from the van. At another stop, he dropped off 10 new Courier Paks which were needed for forthcoming shipments of engineering prints.

It was past 12 before the courier arrived in Arlington for his last two shipments. At 12:15 he delivered a package to a Datsun dealer and 5 minutes later a box marked "laboratory specimens" to a doctor's office, but neither the dealer nor the doctor showed any awareness that the delivery had been made after the twelve o'clock standard. Heaving a sigh of relief, Ken walked across the street to a small restaurant and bought a large submarine sandwich and a soft drink. He had driven about 30 miles, made 37 stops, and delivered some 60 packages, including three Courier Paks.

An Afternoon with a Sales Representative

John Griffin had been with Federal Express since June 1973. Then an undergraduate at Boston University, he had taken time out from school to earn extra money by working as a courier for the fledgling Boston operation. Persuaded to stay on, he had been promoted to lead courier and made responsible for assigning the areas to be covered by individual couriers. Next came a year and a half as night operations supervisor. In 1975, he had accepted a position as a customer service representative (CSR), feeling that its long-term opportunities outweighed the immediate sharp drop in salary. His optimism appeared justified by a promotion to senior account manager (SAM) 11 months later. In his new position he reported to the regional sales manager, whereas he had previously reported to the local station manager.

Mr. Griffin explained that he was in a transition between his old and new jobs. His future assignment would be to focus on 70 key accounts in the Boston/Worcester area. Presently, he had 101 accounts in the Boston area alone and would be transferring the smaller ones to other CSRs. Although he described Federal Express as an "easy product to sell," he believed that more effort was needed to develop the market. In particular, he felt that CSRs should report to SAMs rather than to station managers. It was difficult, he said, to get support for a better CSR program, improved secretarial assistance, and more information on who was shipping what to whom.

Griffin's first call after an early lunch was to the corporate headquarters of a large eastern retailing firm, located just outside Boston. The previous week, he and the regional sales manager had made a 1½-hour presentation to the firm's traffic manager and three traffic supervisors. Their interest in Federal Express lay in obtaining rapid transportation of small rush orders—"where we needed delivery yesterday"—from vendors and the firm's own warehouses to its numerous stores. Among the concerns raised at this first meeting was that some vendors and stores were located more than 25 miles from a Federal Express station, and hence outside the normal pickup and delivery area. What extra charges, they asked, would be incurred for the use of a supplementary carrier to serve these out-of-area locations?

Griffin parked his car, entered the attractive modern building, and gave his name to the receptionist. A secretary came out and led him to the traffic manager's office, where a well-dressed man in his late thirties shook hands and waved him to a seat. The sales representative had

researched store and vendor locations and was able to identify for his prospective client which stores and vendors were located "out-of-area." For the next hour they discussed the costs and logistics of servicing these locations and how to resolve the stores' preference for paying COD rather than being billed separately. Griffin said that he'd raise the COD issue with Federal's accounting office. The meeting concluded with the traffic manager's requesting a complete proposal within a month.

From the suburbs, John Griffin drove into Boston for his next appointment. A traffic manager had called the Federal Express office asking that a sales representative visit; since Griffin already had a later appointment in the immediate area with an existing client, he had agreed to take this call.

The address turned out to be a gloomy warehouse building, with boxes of all sizes stacked in tall racks. The prospect's office was in a small, green, hutlike structure built out from one of the walls. A middle-aged man, tieless and in shirtsleeves, could be seen through the cracked glass door working at a cluttered desk. Spotting the sales representative, he waved him in, and Griffin introduced himself. For a moment, the other looked puzzled; then his face cleared. "Oh, yeah," he said. "You're the people with the purple planes. Tell me all you know, kid!"

Griffin began by asking about the company's business, what its products were, where they were shipped, how important delivery times were, and to what extent airfreight was presently employed. Shipments went in spurts, the manager indicated; the company used several airfreight firms, most shipments went to Texas and the Midwest, and second-day delivery was usually sufficient. As he spoke, he was sorting waybills into piles on his desk, pausing only to flick ash from his cigarette onto the worn linoleum floor.

"How much do you know about Federal Express?" asked the sales representative.

"I watched you on the TV versus Emery."

The traffic manager raised his hands, palms down, one a foot above his desk and the other high above his head. Griffin remembered the TV commercial which had last run in Boston some 4 months ago. (Exhibit 1 shows a print advertisement from the same campaign.)

"Is that how you found out about us?"

"Yeah."

The manager went back to his sorting while the sales representative briefly described the Federal Express operation and how it worked, outlining the procedures for calling a courier, billing arrangements, and FEC size limitations. The latter would evidently be restrictive, since many of the shipper's packages exceeded Federal's maximum limits, but the traffic manager just shrugged and stubbed out his cigarette in a dirty saucer. When the sales representative offered to have a courier call that afternoon, the traffic manager said that he didn't need anything today, thanks, but he'd be calling.

John Griffin shook hands and saw himself out. "That was a rum one," he murmured to himself as he walked out onto the street again. "But I think we'll be seeing some business from him."

His 3:15 appointment was with the operations manager of a medical firm which ran a number of specialist treatment centers around the country. The corporate offices in Boston were responsible for most of the financial work; management apparently placed great importance on shipping financial and statistical reports quickly to local treatment centers for immediate review. The firm had been using Federal Express since 1974 for shipping boxes of reports; it had tried several airfreight forwarders and settled on Federal as providing the best service. In late 1975, finding special delivery mail increasingly unreliable after cutbacks in airlines' schedules, the firm began using Courier Paks for shorter reports. It currently sent 50 Courier Paks and 30 packages each month by Federal Express.

Mr. Griffin made a point of calling on this account once every 2 or 3 months, following up any problems, and explaining any changes in

EXHIBIT 1
FEDERAL EXPRESS:
PRINT ADVERTISING, 1975–1976

FEDERAL EXPRESS. TWICE AS GOOD AS THE BEST IN THE BUSINESS.

EMERY 42%   **FEDERAL EXPRESS 93%**

Percentage of packages delivered the next day at regular rates.

If you've been fairly satisfied with Emery Air Freight, you'll be completely satisfied with Federal Express.

Because in a test, we were faster and cheaper than they were, and the test was as fair and as realistic as could be devised.

We hired an independent research organization to send identical packages between 47 cities via Emery and Federal Express at each company's regular rates.

To be fair, we told our employees nothing of this test.

And also in the interest of fairness, we told Emery nothing of it either.

The numbers above tell the story. Emery, for years regarded as the best in the business, delivered an average of 42% of their packages by the next day.

Federal Express' average: 93%.

And we were cheaper.

Let's see, faster and cheaper than who you're using now.

Kinda makes you want to pick up the phone and call us, doesn't it?

Test conducted April, 1975, by Opinion Research Corporation, involving identical 9½-lb. packages sent door to door. Summaries and other information available upon request from Vincent Fagan, Senior V.P., Federal Express Corporation, AMF Box 30057, Memphis, Tennessee 38130

Federal Express service or prices. On this occasion, he brought a supply of new Courier Paks with him. The operations manager was a woman in her thirties. Her office was a large, windowless room with stacks of boxes, documents, and computer print-outs. She and the sales representative spent about 20 minutes discussing the implications of her firm's planned move to the new John Hancock Tower in central Boston. Griffin mentioned that Federal Express was thinking of installing a drop box for Courier Paks on the ground floor of the new building so that the courier could make a late afternoon collection after the offices had closed.

Leaving the building at 3:40, the sales representative sought out a pay phone and called his office to check if there were any messages. A prospective customer, located about 10 minutes' driving time away, had phoned asking for a presentation, he was told. Griffin obtained the name, address, and phone number, called the prospect, and set up an appointment for 4 o'clock.

The new prospect was the director of office services for an advertising agency. The decor of the office was arty, modern, and expensive, with several prize-winning advertisements in frames on the walls. The director, a smartly dressed woman in her fifties, shook hands and thanked the SAM for responding to her inquiry so promptly. She paid all the agency's bills, she said, and used airfreight for shipping items like films and artwork, research materials, and even office stationery. Recently, she had noticed that the research department had been receiving packages shipped by Federal Express and returning materials to its clients via this carrier. Her interest had been stimulated by Federal's recent TV advertising—"I know you have your own planes," she remarked.

Griffin explained the nature of FEC service and emphasized the importance of having one's own aircraft. He then showed her a Courier Pak and fielded several questions about billing and insurance. Told that the agency frequently shipped film insured for $5,000, he explained that the maximum insurance on a Courier Pak was currently only $200 but that arrangements for higher coverage could be made with Priority One. When the director mentioned that Delta Dash charged $26.50 for express document handling between Boston and New York, he told her that using Courier Pak service would save her $14. She appeared impressed.

The interview concluded with the sales representative's leaving a booklet containing information on rates and billing, as well as a supply of airbills (combined bills and shipping orders), and explaining the procedures for completing the latter. He also sold the director five Courier Paks. Descending in the elevator, John Griffin checked his watch. It was 4:40. With luck, he'd be on the turnpike and heading back to his office before the traffic built up too badly.

Marketing Activities in 1976

FEC's efforts to promote its services made use of both personal selling and media advertising.

Personal Contact with Customers

In the summer of 1976, Federal Express had some 35 senior account managers (SAMs) and 75 customer service representatives (CSRs). About 50 percent of the SAMs had been recruited from sales positions with airfreight forwarders, and 10 percent had been promoted from among Federal's own CSRs, while the remaining 40 percent had other sales experience. By contrast, four-fifths of the CSRs had been recruited from the ranks of the company's couriers and customer service agents.

SAMs reported through regional sales managers to Craig Bell, vice president–sales, and through him to J. Vincent Fagan, senior vice president–marketing (both of whom were located in Memphis). By contrast, customer service representatives, customer service agents, and couriers reported to their local station managers, who were part of the operation's chain of command. Exhibit 2 shows how these personnel were described in a customer brochure.

Mr. Bell saw the task of CSRs as focusing more on account maintenance than on selling. They should, he said, be able to generate new leads and to assist station operations by such activities as following up on missing or damaged packages, checking on billing problems and procedures, and ensuring that delivery and pickup schedules were satisfactory for the customer. These tasks were more appropriately included under operations than sales, he believed. On the average, CSRs made 8 to 10 calls daily by phone and in person, and they were

EXHIBIT 2
FEDERAL EXPRESS: EXTRACT FROM CUSTOMER BROCHURE

Our people.
Although there are over 2000 people employed by Federal Express to help you with your shipping needs, there are just a few key people and departments you should know about.

Your Federal Express Sales Representative. His job is more than simply introducing us to you. Whenever you have any questions about us, or our services, he's there to help. He's an expert in the air package express business, and he is always available to discuss your special shipping needs or problems.

Your Federal Express Courier. He is your day-to-day contact with Federal Express. Each Federal Express Courier is trained to answer your questions about proper labeling, preparation of shipping documents and even how to cut shipping costs. He can also give you advice on special packaging and shipping situations such as Hazardous Materials, Signature Security, Courier Paks and Saturday Deliveries. Our Couriers will stop by regularly or on an on-call basis (please call us as early in the day as possible).

Your Federal Express Customer Service Agent. If you need to call for a special pick-up, have tariff questions or require package delivery information on the day of scheduled delivery, our local Customer Service Agents are ready to serve you. They can also help you with additional insurance requirements and with questions not answered in the "Features of Service" section of this guide.

Your Federal Express Station Manager. Locally, he is the person responsible for making sure that you receive good service. He is available at any time to answer any questions that you may have, and to solve any immediate problems.

Delivery Information Service. When you call Federal Express for delivery information, you get it fast—without annoying busy signals or "holds." For calls initiated the day *following* scheduled delivery, our toll-free Delivery Information Hotline . . . will provide you with the necessary information within 30 minutes. If you should need delivery information the same day delivery is scheduled, contact your local Federal Express Customer Service Agent for assistance.

Customer Service Department. Should you have any additional questions or problems, our Customer Service Department is always available to help you with anything from service to billing, and to assist you in any way they can. To contact this department, use our Customer Service Hotline.

paid $11,000 to $13,000 a year, plus a bonus. The total annual cost of maintaining a CSR in the field, including a salary, expenses, and overheads, averaged about $18,000.

The role of the SAM he saw as more sophisticated. Identifying the decision maker in a large firm was often a difficult task, Bell noted. Clarifying what had to be done to win the business (or a greater share of an existing customer's business) might require skillful probing and analysis. It could involve, among other things, working with shippers to determine their long-term needs and providing advice in such areas as packaging and logistics.

SAMs typically earned a base salary of $15,500 to $22,000. Bonuses added an average of 10 percent to this base and were calculated on the individual's performance in three areas—improving volume on present accounts, generating new business, and accurately forecasting account volumes. Mr. Bell placed a lot of emphasis on forecasting ability:

> Once an individual is able to forecast his business accurately, that tells you that he understands his customers and their business. Once he knows about his basic accounts, then he knows the questions that should be asked.

The total annual cost of maintaining a SAM in the field averaged $31,000. Typically, a SAM was expected to make five to eight customer calls daily.

Additional customer contact took place in person through the couriers and by telephone through the customer service agents who were based at FEC offices and who provided information on services as well as scheduling pickups.

Advertising

During 1975–1976, Federal Express had run an intensive TV and print advertising campaign, which had been rolled out on a market-by-

market basis in selected cities across the country. This positioned FEC firmly against the nation's leading airfreight forwarder, Emery Air Freight, emphasizing Federal's faster delivery record and cheaper rates.

It proved possible to measure the impact of this advertising by running it only in selected markets. Changes in package volumes in these test cities were then compared with those in the remainder of the system. One wave of advertising was run in the New York and Los Angeles areas between late June and early September 1975. By mid-March of the following year, the average daily package count in these two areas was up 89 percent over the April-May 1975 base, versus a 48 percent increase in the rest of the system. A second wave of advertising appeared between early October and mid-November 1975 in Detroit, Cleveland, Philadelphia, and Dallas. By mid-March 1976, the average daily count in these cities was 46 percent higher than the August-September 1975 base, versus a 34 percent increase in the rest of the system over the same period.

The company's advertising plan for 1976–1977 included TV commercials promoting Federal's overall competitive advantages (Exhibit 3). Press and magazine advertising would include two different full-page advertisements for use in *Business Week, U.S. News & World Report, Time, Newsweek,* and the *Wall Street Journal,* as well as in various trade publications. One of these two ads mentioned Courier Pak in the text and showed a small picture of it (Exhibit 4). An advantage of advertising, Mr. Fagan believed, was that the company maintained complete control, whereas attempting to communicate through couriers or the sales force was subject to the human element.

Ms. Teri Romines, FEC's director of advertising, reported to Mr. Fagan. She planned to inform employees at the 75 Federal Express stations about the objectives, scheduling, and content of the 1976–1977 advertising program.

EXHIBIT 3
FEDERAL EXPRESS: TV ADVERTISEMENTS IN 1976–1977*

Carl Ally Inc.
437 Madison Avenue, New York, N.Y. 10022
Murray Hill 8–5300

CLIENT:	Federal Express
PRODUCT:	Federal Express
TITLE:	"Overnight"
COMMERCIAL NO.:	QFAS6304—30 seconds
DATE APPROVED:	6/28/76

ANNCR: When a freight forwarder like Emery or Airborne promises to deliver your packages overnight, he's relying on the passenger airlines. But 80 percent of their planes spend the night on the ground. When Federal Express promises to deliver your packages overnight, we're relying on no one but ourselves. Because we own our own planes. And they fly when we say so, overnight.
(SFX: VVVVRRRROOOOMMMM.)
ANNCR:
(VO) Federal Express. Take away our planes, and we'd be just like everybody else.

CLIENT:	Federal Express
PRODUCT:	Federal Express
TITLE:	"Reliable"
COMMERCIAL NO.:	QFAS6302—30 seconds
DATE APPROVED:	6/28/76

ANNCR:
If Federal Express misplaces a package, there's only a few places it can be. For instance, here in one of our trucks, or here, in one of our own planes. If one of our competitors misplaces a package, it's either on his truck, or on American, United, TWA, Delta, Braniff, PSA, Western, National . . .
(FADES OUT.)

Note: Only the audio portion of the ads is reproduced here.

Her aim was to enable the field offices to coordinate their own promotional and sales activities with the company's national advertising campaign.

Competitive Activity

The market for domestic transportation of small packages by air, estimated at 140 million packages annually in 1974, was growing by some 20 percent a year. The "Emergency" and "Rush" segments of the market (same-day and next-day delivery, respectively) accounted for some 12.8 percent of the total unit volume in 1974 and were believed to be growing at an even faster rate than the total market.

Competition in the airfreight business was intense. It was believed that there were close to 1,000 airfreight forwarder salespeople across the country, to which could be added the representatives of expeditors, couriers, messenger services, REA Air Express, UPS "Blue Label" service, and the airlines themselves. Every *Yellow Pages* in the larger cities had extensive

EXHIBIT 4
FEDERAL EXPRESS: PRINT ADVERTISING FOR 1976–1977

TAKE AWAY OUR PLANES, AND WE'D BE JUST LIKE EVERYBODY ELSE.

Take away our planes and we'd be just another air freight forwarder.

And since there're already 250 of them, the world didn't need one more.

What the world did need when we went into business 3 years ago was a fast, low cost, dependable way to get packages delivered from one city to another overnight.

A ROUTE SYSTEM FOR PACKAGES, NOT PEOPLE.

So instead of shipping packages on airlines designed for people, we created a system especially for packages.

With a route structure designed for packages. To and from big cities like New York and Los Angeles. And smaller cities like Macon and Albuquerque, and 5,000 other combinations, many of them impossible to connect with on the passenger airlines.

And we fly when packages need to fly, overnight, when more than 80% of the passenger planes are "asleep" on the ground.

It's a totally enclosed system. The packages are picked up by our trucks, flown on our planes, and delivered by our trucks.

Unlike the air freight forwarder/passenger airline system, *the package never leaves our hands.*

This is why our claim rate is so low: two hundredths of one percent.

And in a test conducted by an independent research organization, our delivery rate was twice as good as Emery's.*

Not only that, our prices are the same and sometimes less than theirs.

But Federal Express is more than the best way to send a package.

It's also the best way to send an envelope.

DELIVERED VIRTUALLY ANYWHERE IN THE COUNTRY OVERNIGHT FOR $12.50.

The Federal Express COURIER PAK™ is a waterproof, tearproof envelope that holds up to 2 lbs. of documents, contracts, tapes, etc. And anything you put in it can be almost anywhere in the country overnight, for only $12.50.

Another application of our system is the Federal Express PartsBank.

It does away with the need for a lot of regional warehouses and the expensive inventory that's had to go into them. Located in Memphis, the "air center" of the country, it's a warehouse and an airline combined. And once you put your parts there, there's no faster, more efficient way for machines scattered all over the country to get the parts they need.

If you took away our planes, none of this would be true.

We'd be just another "me too" system of sending packages.

We'd have to come up with some jingle, or some clever line in our advertising like, "Here today, there tomorrow" or something equally vague.

The planes are the whole idea behind Federal Express.

Take them away and you might as well call somebody else.

FEDERAL EXPRESS

*Test conducted April, 1975, by Opinion Research Corporation, involving identical 9-lb. packages sent door to door. Summaries and other information available upon request from Vincent Fagan, Senior V.P., Federal Express Corporation, AMF Box 30167, Memphis, Tennessee 38130.

EXHIBIT 5

SELECTED LISTINGS FROM THE 1976 BOSTON *YELLOW PAGES* FOR
THREE CATEGORIES—"AIR CARGO SERVICE,"
"DELIVERY SERVICE," AND "MESSENGER SERVICE"

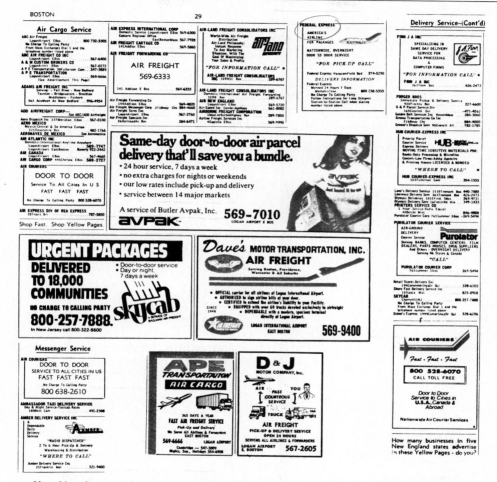

Note: Many firms were listed in two or all three of these categories. In 1976–1977, Federal Express would be listed under "Air Cargo" in 575 *Yellow Pages* directories throughout the United States, at a total cost of $80,000. The format of its listings would be similar to, or smaller than, that shown in column 4 above.

Source: 1976 Boston *Yellow Pages*. Reproduced by permission.

listings under "Air Cargo Service," "Delivery Service," or "Messenger Service." Exhibit 5 shows extracts from the 1976 Boston area *Yellow Pages* in these three categories.

In general, the industry lacked marketing expertise, relying heavily on personal selling efforts. Brochures, sales materials, rate sheets, and routing guides were used to support the sales force. Direct mail was often used to generate sales leads. Only the biggest carriers, such as Emery, Shulman, and REA Air Express, advertised regularly on a large scale. One reason for the limited use of advertising was that most airfreight forwarders had few competitive advantages to offer. Emery Air Freight, by contrast, had spent millions on the development of a systemwide computer tracing capability called EMCON and had promoted this in its advertising.

Air Transport World characterized the airfreight industry as "an aggressive, even seamy business." According to a 1974 marketing study prepared for Federal Express by a consulting firm:

> The techniques of selling air freight services vary from strictly ethical to outright bribery. Techniques vary from discrediting the competition to kickbacks and payoffs. _____ [name deleted] supports a penthouse and a yacht in New York City.

Some of the forwarding firms focused their attention on shipping for particular industries. Alternatively, salespeople within a given airfreight organization might elect to follow a strategy of industry specialization in their choice of customers and prospects.

Passenger airlines were making greater efforts to promote their small-package rush services, often through advertising in their own in-flight magazines. Meantime, the United States Postal Service was promoting Express Mail through its customer representatives in the field, through the use of limited advertising, and through lobby displays and brochures in the large post offices that offered this service.

Developing a Marketing Plan for Courier Pak

Mr. Adam had discussed the future of Courier Pak with Mr. Fagan, senior vice president–marketing. The two men had agreed that seeking a 350 percent increase in Courier Pak sales volume, to 6,000 Paks daily by January 1977, would not be an unrealistic objective.

The task now facing Mr. Adam was one of developing an appropriate marketing strategy to reach this sales target. In particular, he had to decide what type and level of advertising and sales effort to put behind Courier Pak.

An analysis of Courier Pak usage by customer type produced the profile shown in Exhibit 6. Experience suggested that the decision to use a Courier Pak was often made by executives (or their secretaries) rather than by shipping managers. For instance, an advertising executive might rush advertising proof sheets to a client by Courier Pak, bypassing the shipping department altogether.

Apart from mentioning Courier Pak in some of the magazine advertising (Exhibit 4), one other effort had already been planned to promote this product specifically. This was an advertisement on the cover of FEC's upcoming July/August routes and tariffs brochure (Exhibit 7). Would this suffice, Mr. Adam wondered, or should a more aggressive policy be adopted, involving additional advertising, sales activity, and other promotions?

One possibility was to install a nationwide "Hotline" for Courier Pak information, using an "800" area code telephone number which would be free to callers. The estimated monthly costs, including WATS rental at $1,670 and employee wages, totaled $4,770.

To help evaluate alternatives, Mr. Adam's assistant had collected data on advertising rates for a number of periodicals (Exhibit 8) and for leading daily newspapers and TV stations in certain large cities (Exhibit 9).

EXHIBIT 6
DETAILED COURIER PAK USAGE PROFILE BY CUSTOMER CATEGORY
May 1976 Statistics

	Number of accounts*	Number of Courier Paks used monthly	Percentage of total usage
Manufacturing and distribution—general	639	4,945	17.1
Advertising industry	140	2,285	8.2
Printing and publishing	80	1,558	5.6
Data-processing equipment—manufacturing and sales	125	1,160	4.1
Office and business equipment	22	1,024†	3.7
Marketing research	61	886	3.2
Mortgage and investment banking	98	733	2.6
Computer service bureaus	50	686	2.5
Electronic parts and components	76	679	2.4
Communications (telephone and electronic)	34	631	2.3
Law firms	94	598	2.1
Insurance companies and agents	38	568	2.0
Service and leasing	76	537	1.9
Medical/dental optical equipment and supplies	41	476	1.7
Aviation manufacturing and sales	57	448	1.6
Internal Revenue Service	36	443	1.6
Freight forwarders and transport	51	380	1.4
Engineering firms	44	346	1.2
Construction	37	318	1.1
Pharmaceuticals manufacturing	28	304	1.1
Medical/dental laboratories	16	252	0.9
Motion picture/film industry	30	238	0.8
Real estate	48	233	0.8
Chain stores	42	225	0.8
CPA—accounting	45	222	0.8
Consultants (management and research)	53	196	0.7
Import/export brokers	13	190	0.7
Banks	23	181	0.6
Stocks and bonds brokers	14	147	0.5
Record industry	18	120	0.4
Architects and designers	14	114	0.4
Medical care (hospitals)	15	90	0.3
TV stations	16	83	0.3
TV broadcasting	8	47	0.2
Trade associations	5	37	0.1
Subtotal	2,187	21,380	76.3
Miscellaneous categories	NA	946	3.6
Unclassified‡	NA	5,632	20.1
Total	NA	27,958	100.0

*Some companies had more than one account, representing several departments at a single location or several locations of the same company.

†Xerox accounted for 862 of these Courier Paks.

‡These were sales by users without an FEC account (either infrequent users or new users not yet assigned an acocunt number).

Source: Company records.

EXHIBIT 7
FEDERAL EXPRESS: COURIER PAK PROMOTION ON CUSTOMER BROCHURE, SUMMER 1976

COURIER PAK®
When you'd give a million to get something somewhere overnight... we'll do it for $12.50.

Our regular services, Priority One and Standard Air Service were designed for the shipper in a hurry.

Then we developed Courier Pak*. For the businessman in a hurry.

Here's how it works.

Courier Paks are sold at $12.50. You simply keep the prepaid envelopes in your office. Whenever you have sales orders, contracts, blueprints, tapes, samples or anything weighing up to two pounds, just put them in the Courier Pak envelope, fill out the label and give us a call. Your Courier Pak will be delivered next morning anywhere in our nation-wide system.

Courier Paks are fast, low-cost and safe. The 15½" x 12" waterproof envelope can't be torn and will hold bulky reports and data printouts.

There are just a few minor restrictions. You must comply with U.S. Postal regulations and apply the proper amount of postage covering any first-class (letter) material contained in the Courier Pak. Courier Paks are prepaid (like postage) and must be purchased in minimum quantities of five at a time. No service is provided outside the 130 major metro areas served by Federal Express.

That's all there is to it. For $12.50 we'll pick up, fly and deliver your important business documents next morning, anywhere in our nation-wide system.

If you're using Federal Express on your shipping dock, chances are your front office or mailroom will have a need for Courier Pak.

Your local sales representative can give you more information.

Courier Pak is the Registered trade mark of Federal Express Corporation.

EXHIBIT 8
COST OF ONE-PAGE ADVERTISING IN SELECTED PUBLICATIONS, 1976

Vertical publications	Cost of one full-page insertion	Circulation
Advertising Age	$ 5,200	68,063
Broadcasting	2,800	32,267
Journal of Marketing	520	16,669
Graphic Arts Monthly	3,350	76,245
Banking	2,390	43,816
Savings & Loan News	3,200	63,174
ABA Journal (law)	5,000	200,755
Insurance Magazine	725	14,256
Journal of Accountancy	1,890	186,382
The Secretary	950	49,135

General publications	Cost of one full-page insertion	Circulation
Newsweek	$22,650	3,028,000
Wall Street Journal	27,972	1,733,000
Time	31,925	3,502,000
Business Week	11,920	1,564,000
U.S. News & World Report	15,690	1,885,000
Sports Illustrated	20,290	2,353,000

EXHIBIT 9
PRESS AND TV ADVERTISING COSTS IN SELECTED MAJOR MARKET AREAS

(A) Cost of one-page advertisement in leading daily newspapers, 1976

Newspaper	Cost of one full-page insertion	Circulation
The New York Times	$12,192	806,495
Chicago Tribune	10,769	750,707
Washington Post	8,207	534,400
Los Angeles Times	9,840	1,000,866
San Francisco Chronicle	8,211	457,310

(B) Cost of 30-second TV spot on leading stations in selected cities, 1976

TV station	City	Prime time Cost	Prime time Audience men, 18–49	Late evening Cost	Late evening Audience men, 18–49
WAGA	Atlanta	$ 900	108,000	$ 340	77,000
WNAC	Boston	1,500	212,000	750	94,000
WFAA	Dallas	2,200	365,000	550	100,000
WPLG	Miami	1,222	160,000	540	87,000
WCCO	Minneapolis	900	86,000	450	111,000
WCBS	New York	6,050	964,000	1,500	398,000
WCAU	Philadelphia	1,500	216,000	1,200	137,000
WTOP	Washington, D.C.	1,500	189,000	550	79,000
WCPO	Cincinnati	450	63,000	275	63,000
KHOU	Houston	1,150	107,000	1,000	127,000

Source: Company records.

31 Jim Thompson for Governor

*Richard W. Edelman • Dan E. Patterson •
Paul W. Farris*

It was May 1976, and Illinois gubernatorial candidate "Big Jim" Thompson sat in the Chicago office of Citizens for Thompson wondering what action he should take before the general election in November. Thompson, the Republican candidate and United States Attorney, was particularly concerned about the formulation of his communications strategy and the problems of raising funds to support his campaign. Although he currently enjoyed a 15 percent lead in the polls over his Democratic opponent, Mike Howlett, Thompson believed that his situation was far from secure.

Thompson had become famous because of a stream of convictions he had won against major public figures, Democrats and Republicans alike.

Paul W. Farris is an associate professor of marketing at the Colgate Darden Graduate School of Business Administration, University of Virginia. Richard W. Edelman and Dan E. Patterson were formerly students at the Harvard Graduate School of Business Administration.

Several prominent Democrats, including former Governor Otto Kerner, City Council leader Thomas Keane, and County Clerk Ed Barrett, were behind bars as a result of Thompson's energetic prosecutions.

Thompson's image as a young, aggressive, crime-busting United States Attorney was certainly advantageous in the post-Watergate days and had made him something of a media darling. Physically, he was impressive—with an attractive face and an imposing height. His weight of 237 pounds was distributed on a 6-foot 6-inch frame. Hailing originally from the west side of Chicago, Thompson had never run for public office. Perhaps as a result of this inexperience, he was just beginning to develop the personal touch so important for effective campaigning. At first he had a hard time meeting people, but later he grew quite fond of "pressing the flesh." His speaking style, though earnest, was still somewhat wooden and sometimes overly professorial. At 39, Thompson was not married but had just gotten engaged for the first time, and the wedding was set for June 1976.

The Democratic Primary

The primaries[1] had been held over a month ago. Illinois voters had rejected the incumbent Democratic Governor, Dan Walker, in favor of Mayor Daley's favored candidate, Michael Howlett. Chicago's Mayor Daley and Governor Walker had been on less than friendly terms since 1972, when Walker had narrowly upset the Chicago Democratic organization's candidate for Governor, Paul Simon. Walker went on to win the general election, and the much publicized Walker-Daley feud had grown worse, with each man jockeying for leadership of the Democratic party in Illinois. Daley's influence with the Illinois legislature was used to thwart many of Walker's initiatives, and consequently, Walker's record of accomplishment as Governor had suffered. This intraparty struggle culminated in a very bitter Walker-Howlett primary campaign. Howlett had won by a narrow margin (51 percent versus 49 percent), but the split within the Democratic party had not been healed. Many Walker supporters were embittered by the outcome.

Michael Howlett was the secretary of state and a household name in Illinois, due largely to the presence of his name on every driver's license and license plate application. He had worked his way up in the party through a host of lesser offices, and so he had extensive support within the Democratic party. This was in contrast to Thompson's experience. As a relative newcomer to politics, Thompson had no real cadre of supporters within the Republican organization.

Howlett had gained a reputation for integrity

[1]A primary election is used by individual political parties to select their nominee for the statewide elections.

during his 35 years of public service and showed remarkable strength in the usually Republican areas outside Chicago. He had been the biggest vote getter on the Democratic ticket in the Nixon landslide of 1972 and was considered a very strong opponent. Although Howlett was rarely seen in public without a three-piece suit, he was an experienced campaigner who used humor and impromptu speeches effectively.

The Republican Primary

Almost relegated to the shadows was the comparatively uninteresting Republican primary. Thompson had resigned from his post as United States Attorney for the Northern District of Illinois in June 1975 to run for governor. His primary opponent, Richard Cooper, was a Chicago-area businessman who had made a fortune as the founder of Weight Watchers. Cooper promised a businessman's approach to government problems but never generated much voter enthusiasm.

Thompson spent most of his efforts during the primary campaign in an attempt to increase his name recognition downstate—through personal campaigning and editorial board sessions with local newspapers. He had decided to concentrate his primary campaign downstate for two reasons: (1) prior to the primary elections, he was not well known there, and (2) he thought that with the media preoccupation with the Walker-Howlett-Daley controversy, he had little chance of making the Chicago 6 o'clock news.

Thompson's victory margin of 80 percent had been accomplished with a relatively small advertising budget. Of the $500,000 in funds that had been raised during the primary campaign, less than $100,000 had been spent for advertising. Thompson had been prepared to spend more, but the relatively poor showing of Cooper in the polls had prompted him to cut back on the original budget of $282,000. Over 90 percent of the budget had been spent downstate; about 60 percent of the funds were for TV, and the remainder were for spot radio and brochures.

State of Illinois

Illinois, a Midwestern state with almost 12 million people, stretched 450 miles from Wisconsin to Kentucky, (Exhibit 1). It was well known that the people of southern Illinois were closer to Mississippi both geographically and philosophically than they were to Chicago. This diversity spread across occupation lines as well. Chicago, in the north, was the largest manufacturing center in the nation. Champaign, on the other hand, in central Illinois, was representative of the numerous agricultural centers that together made Illinois the nation's leading exporter of farm products.

The voters of Illinois could be divided into four segments. The first segment, Chicago, with 3.5 million people, comprised about one-half of Cook County and voted heavily along Democratic lines. The second, Cook County suburbs, had 2.5 million residents. These voters cared little for party loyalties, tending toward ticket splitting. The third—the five "collar"[2] counties of DuPage, Will, McHenry, Lake, and Kane—had 1.5 million residents, voted mainly along Republican lines, and in a good year could bring in as large a plurality as Chicago could. The fourth, downstate Illinois, comprised 96 counties and five media markets. The 4 million downstate residents had a little of each of the above characteristics, with the strongest party loyalties being exhibited in the most southern part of Illinois as well as in Madison and St. Clair Counties (East St. Louis), where the local Democratic organizations were still powerful.

Appendix A contains the results of a survey measuring the historical voting patterns and

[2]These five heavily populated counties surround the Chicago and Cook County area.

intentions of the Illinois population. To be successful, Republican candidates had historically concentrated on minimizing their almost inevitable defeat in Cook County and attaining wide victory margins in other parts of the state.

One of the reasons for Democratic strength in Cook County was the effectiveness of Chicago Mayor Daley's political organization in this area. Daley was the most prominent political figure in Cook County and managed his organization in a way that consistently produced a large Democratic voter turnout in Cook County. The size of this vote was considered relatively immune to the effects of inclement weather, issues, or voter apathy.

Illinois Political Issues

Illinois was not a happy place at present, Thompson mused. It was not getting its share of federal transit money—some believed because of the Daley-Walker bickering that prevented the formation of an effective lobby. Much of the state's vaunted economic muscle was aging, and slowly Illinois companies were moving factories to the Sunbelt. Their major complaint, it seemed, was taxation. The recession had hit business quite hard, and many of them could no longer afford to pay the state income tax. In addition, a generous worker's compensation bill had recently passed through the Legislature, over Walker's veto, and the combined influence of these problems was accelerating the outflow of business.

The financial picture from the state's side was equally gloomy. Three years of record budget deficits had eroded the state's savings to the point where Illinois faced the serious threat of bankruptcy. It was also rumored that the state's credit rating might be lowered. Walker had been reluctant to raise the personal income tax, however. Indeed, it was widely speculated that the tax issue had toppled Richard Ogilvie, Walker's predecessor. Thompson knew that the

EXHIBIT 1
STATE MAP OF MEDIA MARKETS (WITH POPULATION)

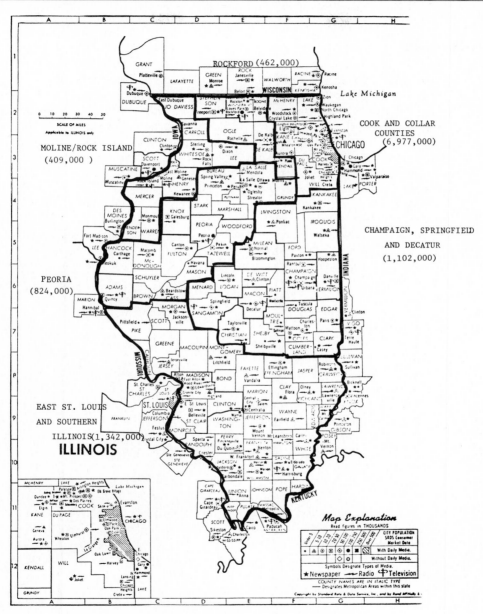

voters didn't want a tax increase, but he was unwilling to make a promise not to raise taxes when he wasn't sure that such a promise could be kept.

Thompson believed that inefficiencies and poor management by the Walker administration had raised other issues. The state welfare, social security, and unemployment compensation systems were notoriously ineffective in getting the checks out on time or in the right amounts or to the right people. Medicaid reimbursements for doctors, for example, sometimes trailed billings by as much as 8 months. In addition, the recent upsurge of crime had caused such a strong public reaction that state judges, who were elected in Illinois, began issuing more and longer sentences. But the prisons were already overcrowded and could do little expanding to handle the influx of inmates. These were some of the major issues thought to be concerning Illinois voters.

Thompson's Decision

The fundamental question facing Thompson was what kind of campaign would maximize votes and at the same time generate sufficient funds to support the campaign effort. Although Thompson had managed to spend under $100,000 on advertising in the primary race, after the primary he spent an additional $75,000 on 4½-minute biographical programs in downstate Illinois in an effort to boost name recognition. Thompson spent $50,000 on a series of 30-second spots to attract the disgruntled Walker supporters. He was pleased with the results but now had more immediate concerns as he realized that he had a monthly payroll and overhead expenses of about $60,000 to meet. The money that he had raised for the primary, about $500,000, was essentially gone.

With the help of Bailey, Deardourff, and Eyre, Inc., a consulting firm specializing in providing assistance for "moderate" Republican candidates for public office, Thompson had worked out a tentative budget of $1.25 million for the remainder of the campaign (see Exhibit 2). Although the budgeted $1.25 million was felt to be reasonably attainable, Thompson was determined that the campaign wasn't going to be run in the red. "If the money isn't raised and in the bank, it won't be spent," he said. There were two major sources for these campaign funds. The first was individual contributions—primarily, but not exclusively, from Republican party members. These were solicited by direct

EXHIBIT 2
TENTATIVE GENERAL ELECTION BUDGET
Prepared by
Bailey, Deardourff, and Eyre, Inc.*

Salaries (and taxes)		$ 275,900
Fund raising (clerical supplies, support funds, computerization)		17,000
Advertising		
Handout production (see Exhibit 4)	$ 65,475	
Television (see Exhibit 5)	486,900	
Radio (see Exhibit 5)	43,500	
Print (see Exhibit 5)	32,100	
Agency fee	47,700	675,675
Polling		37,500
Consultant's fee		15,000
Operations		
Rent and furniture	$ 15,200	
Telephone, duplicating, supplies, postage	70,000	
Photography, press, TV, and radio	5,000	
Insurance	2,000	
Travel for advance men, candidate, and staff	32,000	
Rallies	10,000	
Field organization†	91,900	
Miscellaneous	5,000	231,100
Total		$1,252,175

*A national consulting firm that specializes in providing campaign advice for candidates for public office.

†Overhead expenses for Chicago headquarters of Citizens for Thompson.

mail, fund-raising dinners, and personal calls. However, this source had just about dried up after the primary, largely because of the enormous victory margin which seemed to indicate that he didn't need the money. He knew he could count on the Republican contributors in a pinch, but probably not for more than $1 million.

Thompson's only other source of money would be organized lobby groups such as unions, professional organizations, and ethnic groups. Union money was largely committed by past professional and personal ties to Howlett. Ethnic groups' money, which in past years had gone chiefly to the Democratic party, was also largely committed to Howlett. In the past, professional organizations whose members did business with the state (e.g., road builders) had been more likely to wait to see which candidate emerged as a clear favorite before contributing. Thompson's 16 percent lead over Howlett was not believed by these groups and therefore was not quite large enough to attract money with the election still 7 months away. Thompson felt that if he could get his margin up to around 25 percent, then he would begin to get some more funds from these groups.

As Thompson thought, it seemed that he had two choices: (1) make a strong media push early and hope for favorable polls to attract group contributions, but run the risk of failing to achieve the 25 percent margin and losing momentum toward the end of the campaign, or (2) count on the limited Republican money to finance a low-budget campaign with the hope of saving enough money for a respectable media campaign in October.

Communications Decisions

In addition to dealing with the broad strategy considerations described above, Thompson would have to decide on the most effective use of his resources to implement his campaign strategy. Especially important in the evolution of the plan were three issues: the purchase of media time and space, budgeting his own time, and the selection of a communications approach.

Purchase of Media Time and Space

Thompson estimated that his total remaining budget for advertising would be approximately $675,000. Three principal decisions were to be made with respect to media purchases. These were as follows:

1. How much of each major medium to buy. Alternatives included TV spots at various times, newspaper space in varying amounts, radio spots of various lengths, and billboard space. Exhibit 3 presents costs and audience measures for selected media vehicles.

   The above did not, of course, exhaust the possibilities. Thompson could also allocate various amounts from the total budget to buttons, bumper stickers, and posters to be distributed by volunteer organizations. (See Exhibit 4.) Volunteer organizations required financial support, however, to cover office overheads and supervision.

2. Just as important as the amount of the budget allocated to media vehicles were decisions about the geographic concentration of the media campaign. Thompson was certain that more media weight would have to be given to some areas than others. Unfortunately, it was not always possible to match media coverage to voter regions.

3. The timing of media expenditures was also critical. They could be spread out fairly evenly over the period remaining before the election, concentrated in initial weeks to build an even larger lead, or saved until the end for a last-minute blitz.

   The economy was starting to recover, and

EXHIBIT 3
REPRESENTATIVE RATE AND AUDIENCE DATA

	Cost*	Audience size (18 or older)	
Chicago			
TV (WBBM)	$ 3,000		700,000
Radio (WGN)†	260		160,000
Newspapers (*Tribune*)			
Daily	9,600	City	279,000
		Suburbs	374,000
		Outside Chicago SMSA	101,000
		Total	757,000
Sunday	13,500	City	393,000
		Suburbs	606,000
		Outside Chicago SMSA	156,000
		Total	1,155,000
Peoria			
TV (WMBD)	$ 140		61,000
Radio (WMBD)	24		18,000
Newspapers (*Journal Star*)			
Daily	1,632		106,000
Sunday	1,632		122,000
Champaign			
TV (WCIA)	$ 200		86,000
Radio (WPGU)	17		15,000
Newspapers (*News Gazette*)			
Daily	963		41,000
Sunday	963		44,000
East St. Louis			
TV (KMOX)	$ 2,100		378,000
		(31% of the audience are Illinois residents)	
Radio (KMOX)	125		179,500
		(31% of the audience are Illinois residents)	
Newspapers			
East St. Louis			
(*Metro East Journal*)			
Daily	1,008		37,000
Sunday	1,008		40,000
		(Almost all of the readership is in Illinois)	
St. Louis (*Post Dispatch*)			
Daily	4,728		68,694
		(All in Illinois)	
Sunday	6,240		182,000
		(All in Illinois)	

*Cost data are as follows: TV—30-second spot in prime time (7 P.M.–10 P.M.)
radio—30-second spot in drive time (6 A.M.–10 A.M.)
newspapers—full page

†Radio stations selected tend to have listenerships that are broad in terms of age distribution.

EXHIBIT 3
Continued

	Cost*	Audience size (18 or older)
Moline/Rock Island		
TV (WHBF)	$ 150	87,000
		(46,800 in Illinois)
Radio (WHBF)	19	15,500
		(8,800 in Illinois)
Newspapers (*Moline Dispatch/ Rock Island Argus*)		
Daily	1,324	60,000
		(All in Illinois)
Sunday	1,324	61,000
		(All in Illinois)
Rockford		
TV (WIFR)	$ 80	41,000
Radio (WROK)	18	11,500
Newspapers (*Rockford Register Star*)		
Daily	1,491	80,000
Sunday	1,491	80,000

Please note that the media costs and rates provided in this exhibit are only representative of costs in each area. Other media may have higher or lower costs and larger or smaller audiences. The relationships between time or space prices and audience size are comparable to those of other major media opportunities in the same localities. Political candidates are always offered the lowest rates for radio and TV time quoted for that time slot during the entire year to any advertiser. They rarely receive additional discounts for the quantity of time or space purchased.

Additional media considered, but rejected, included outdoor advertising. A "100 showing" in the Chicago area would cost $48,000 for a month and would reach 89% of the adults with an average frequency of 31 times (*Ayer Media Facts*, 1974).

EXHIBIT 4
HANDOUT PRODUCTION*

Item	Quantity	Date	Cost
Summer leaflet	500,000	6/1	$ 10,000
Fall brochure	1,000,000	9/1	20,000
Door hanger	500,000	9/1	7,500
Lights-on flyers	500,000	8/15	7,500
Bumper strips	100,000	6/1	4,000
Buttons	250,000	6/1	4,250
Home headquarters signs	1,000	6/1	2,000
Posters	10,000	6/1	2,500
Thompson/O'Neil			
Brochure	200,000	7/1	4,000
Strips	15,000	7/1	900
Buttons	50,000	7/1	1,500
Home headquarters signs	200	7/1	500
Posters	2,500	7/1	825
			$ 65,475

*To be distributed by volunteer organizations.

national demand for advertising space and time was growing. There was, however, no guarantee that TV or radio time would be available on short notice near the end of the campaign. Because broadcast media were required by the government to sell political candidates time at the lowest price quoted for that time slot over the year (adjusted for variation in audience size), they were not anxious to book time for candidates when demand was heavy. Typically the fall session was busiest in terms of demand for media time.

Doug Bailey, a principal of Bailey, Deardourff, and Eyre, had prepared a tentative media budget (see Exhibit 5) which, it was hoped, addressed these key issues, but Thompson wanted to think this through himself. As Thompson reflected in his office, he recognized

EXHIBIT 5
PROPOSED MEDIA BUDGET

	Production	Media costs and fees
Television		
Postprimary	$10,000	$ 36,000
½-hour coffees (Chicago, Rockford, St. Louis, and Springfield)	2,000	5,400
Lights-on fund	3,000	16,200
5′	1,800	27,000
Cinema verite	21,000	117,000
Man in street	12,000	148,500
Endorsements	6,000	81,000
	$55,800	$431,100
Radio		
Bridge, man in street	$ 2,000	$ 22,500
Endorsements	1,000	18,000
	$ 3,000	$ 40,500
Newspapers		
Tribune fund	$ 600	$ 7,200
Last week	800	18,000
Weeklies	1,000	4,500
	$ 2,400	$ 29,700

Addendum to Exhibit 5

Television

Postprimary	These were 30-second spots which were extracted from the 5-minute biographical programs. The 30-second spots were not biographical but intended to prevent the disheartened Walker supporters from returning to Howlett.
½-hour coffees	The idea was to host a TV talk show in a coffee-hour setting. In addition to conversing with the participants Thompson would answer phone inquiries from viewers on any pertinent issue.
5′	These were biographical programs and were actually 4½ minutes long.
Cinema verite	Cinema verite is a style of filming in which nothing is scripted. Spontaneous conversations between Thompson and voters were to be filmed and the commercials edited from this material.
Man in street	As with cinema verite, nothing is scripted. Instead, private citizens are asked their opinion of Thompson, and their response is filmed. Thompson was not to appear in these commercials.

EXHIBIT 5
Continued

Radio	
Bridge, man in street	These were radio spots similar to TV's "man in street." They were to be used to bridge the time between TV blitzes.
Newspapers	
Tribune fund	Coordinated with the TV commercials, this was a newspaper solicitation. Readers would be asked to mail in contributions.
Last week, weeklies	The same newspaper appeal for votes was to be used in each. The ad emphasized Thompson's public service as a United States Attorney, and the banner was to read: "Now He Needs Your Help."

that he would have to determine the amount of money to spend in the various media servicing the six distinguishable media markets. Cost efficiency, he realized, meant more than the traditional cost per thousand. How he defined his target audience would have a major impact on his cost figures. To complicate matters further, he understood that there were "feedback" effects. For example, were he to commit more advertising dollars to a traditional Republican stronghold, he might elicit greater effort from the party regulars, eager to elect the local candidates who often ride on the coattails of the statewide candidates.

Of the six major markets, Chicago was clearly the dominant one. The city itself had more than 3.5 million residents and the surrounding area 4 million more. Chicago's three newspapers, the *Tribune*, the *Daily News*, and the *Sun Times*, were major forces in both and had considerable reach downstate (see Exhibit 3), particularly in nearby counties. The impact of the adult radio stations, with the exception of WGN, was more localized and limited to the metro area.

Champaign, in the eastern part of the state, was the home of the University of Illinois. Its permanent population was oriented to servicing the university and the farm community and tended toward a strong Republican affinity. Voters were not concentrated and could be hard to reach through traditional means. Springfield, also in this market, was the state capital and more politically conscious, but otherwise it was similar to Champaign and Decatur.

East St. Louis, Illinois, as the name suggests, was right across the Mississippi River from St. Louis, Missouri, and was part of the currently economically depressed area of southern Illinois. Thompson wondered if it would be worth paying the St. Louis rate for media in order to reach a small Illinois subgroup of the total audience.

Moline/Rock Island, on the border of Iowa and part of the Quad Cities group (the other two were on the Iowa side), also shared its media with its Iowa sister cities. A swing district, it was dependent on the financial strength of the farmers, in addition to the area's largest employer, John Deere.

Peoria, in the central part of the state, was a more manufacturing-oriented city—the home of Caterpillar Tractor. Its immediate residents leaned toward the Republican side, and its metropolitan area was more suburban than farm. Self-sufficient in terms of media, it was a microcosm of Chicago.

Rockford, 90 minutes from Chicago to the northwest, was the second-largest city in Illinois. Politics in Rockford were dominated by the sometimes fragmented Republican party. Like Peoria, it was self-sufficient in media, but due to its proximity to Chicago, there was considerable fallout, particularly in the print and radio areas.

As Thompson approached his decision, he felt that he should consider the following issues. First, should he ignore the waste factor and advertise in the areas which were not self-sufficient in media but depended on sister cities for coverage? Were certain media better for this task than others? Also, in the same vein, how could he get to the traditional Republican voters, who tended to be dispersed, in the most cost-effective manner? Third, what were the trade-offs in greater frequency versus reach? Was there some threshold to be passed in order to gain credibility, or would the first one or two exposures be sufficient?

Targeting his media campaign to specific areas was also a major concern. In the primary, Walker had shown strength downstate that Thompson felt was primarily due to Walker's success in exploiting the distaste of downstate voters for Chicago politicians. He thought the last thing the voters wanted was a Governor with Mayor Daley's "hand on his collar." Now that he was facing Howlett, Thompson wondered whether he might be able to exploit this issue downstate as well.

Alternatively, he could try to make some inroads into the powerful Chicago Democratic bloc. Thompson felt that if he could break even with Howlett in the city, a formidable goal, then it wouldn't matter what else happened around the state; the Cook County suburbs would carry him.

Finally Thompson could campaign in the collar counties, where he was already well known but where the voters tended to pick and choose across the ballot, voting for the candidate, not the party.

Budgeting the Candidate's Time

Another scarce resource which Thompson had to allocate was his own time. He could concentrate on the county fair circuit downstate to improve his standings further in the rural and southern areas or spend more time in the north.

Appearances at functions such as county fairs were almost guaranteed to result in local media coverage, but they were likely to be before nonpartisan crowds and result in little additional funds. On the other hand, they did serve to enhance existing support. Exhibit 6 outlines a

EXHIBIT 6
THOMPSON'S PROPOSED TIME COMMITMENTS

May 15–June 30

Top priority	Chicago fund raising
	Downstate media market fly-arounds*
2d priority	Meetings with unions, ethnic leaders, and other organized groups
	Opening of county headquarters for Citizens for Thompson

July 1–September 15

Top priority	County fairs, small downstate media
	Media market fly-arounds
	Downstate fund raising
2d priority	Chicago independent/GOP wards
	TV coffees

September 16–October 15

Top priority	Public campaigning—Cook County and collar county suburbs
	Newspaper endorsements
	Chicago fund raising
2d priority	Work with volunteer organizations

October 16–October 23

Top priority	Downstate media appearances
	Newspaper endorsements
2d priority	Campus visits
	Work with volunteer organizations

October 24–November 1

Top priority	Cook County and collar county media appearances
	First-day media market fly-around

*A fly-around is a 1-day tour of all major media markets. Starting in Chicago, the candidate and his press staff fly from place to place; they stay just long enough to deliver a personal message at the airport and then move on to the next stop. It requires exact timing and an early start to make the media deadlines in seven cities in 1 day. (The deadline for a story in the afternoon paper is 11 A.M., and for the evening TV news the deadline is 3 P.M.) The advantage of a fly-around is that it generally guarantees media exposure, while press releases seldom do. The disadvantages of a fly-around are that it is expensive and time-consuming. Moreover, if a candidate gets a reputation for lack of substance in the press conferences, the reporters will stop coming.

tentative schedule for Thompson's personal appearances up to the election.

Campaign Approach

Thompson was still uncertain about the type of campaign which would be most effective. Some advisers argued that in the post-Watergate era it was less important to concentrate on specific issues than it was to convey his record of public service, personal integrity, and professional competence. These attributes, they reasoned, would be more important to the general voting public than necessarily complex statements of his positions on issues such as the environment, energy, ethics, and taxes. The same advisers pointed to Carter's strong showing in the primaries and the polls as support for this approach.

Thompson did not, however, want to be accused of not addressing the most important issues. Indeed, he had strong positions on excessive government spending, business incentives, prison reform, ethics legislation, and Medicaid fraud. Thompson was anxious to make these positions a part of his campaign. Some mix of the two approaches would have to be used, he thought.

Other Strategic Considerations

As he sat in his Dearborn Street office, Thompson knew that there were other considerations that would influence his decision. In the first place, he knew that in a state like Illinois, where there are so many different factions vying for control of the legislature, it made a great deal of difference if a statewide candidate won by a narrow margin or by a large margin. A clear and visible mandate from the people was a powerful asset. Thompson calculated that he would need 60 percent of the vote in order to have that mandate.

Another issue revolved around what Walker would do. Rumors were floating that he might run as an independent Democrat. Walker wouldn't have to decide for another month, and in the meantime, Thompson didn't know how advisable it would be to spend valuable resources trying to attract Walker's natural constituents downstate.

As Thompson reviewed the latest poll results, he began to wonder how secure his 49 to 33 percent lead was, especially with Jimmy Carter gaining momentum. Strong performance by the Democratic national ticket had always meant trouble for a Republican statewide candidate.

Appendix A

Results of Statewide Survey of Registered Illinois Voters (Conducted May 3–May 18, 1976)

Table of Contents

If the election for Governor were today,* how would you be voting? As of today, which way do you lean?

	Total sample	Under 34		34–54		55+	
		Noncollege	College	Noncollege	College	Noncollege	College
1. Thompson (R)	395 ‡	46	79	59	81	87	37
	49.	46.	56.	46.	63.	40.	55.
2. Howlett (D)	262	39	50	53	27	73	17
	33.	39.	35.	41.	21.	34.	25.
9. Refused	33	2	3	2	8	11	5
	4.	2.	2.	2.	6.	5.	7.
0. Don't know	110	13	10	16	13	45	9
	14.	13.	7.	12.	10.	21.	13.

	Total sample	Voter type			Chicago	
		Rep.	Ticket splitter	Dem.	Nonblack	Black
	656 †	129	279	212	162	70
	100.	100.	100.	100.	100.	100.
1. Thompson (R)	395	114	191	63	95	25
	60.	88.	69.	30.	58.	36.
2. Howlett (D)	262	15	87	149	67	45
	40.	12.	31.	70.	42.	64.

*These responses are to questions that did not list Daniel Walker as an independent candidate.
†Numbers don't add across because of some voters who couldn't be classified.
‡Decimal points stand for "percent" throughout this exhibit.

Appendix A
Continued

If the election for Governor were today,* how would you be voting?
As of today, which way do you lean?

Union		Religion		Sex		Ticket splitter	
Union	**Nonunion**	**Catholic**	**Protestant**	**Male**	**Female**	**Male**	**Female**
123	264	99	231	204	190	108	83
45.	52.	42.	56.	50.	49.	58.	55.
113	146	102	118	138	124	52	35
41.	29.	43.	28.	33.	32.	28.	23.
9	20	8	11	15	18	3	9
3.	4.	4.	3.	4.	5.	2.	6.
29	75	28	56	55	55	23	25
10.	15.	12.	13.	13.	14.	12.	17.

Political areas					Media markets			
Bal. of Cook County	**Collar Counties**	**North**	**Central**	**South**	**Chicago**	**Springfield Decatur Champaign**	**St. Louis**	**Peoria**
93	67	174	78	12	430	46	50	37
100.	100.	100.	100.	100.	100.	100.	100.	100.
67	45	117	42	4	257	35	18	26
72.	67.	67.	53.	35.	60.	75.	36.	71.
26	22	57	36	8	173	11	32	11
28.	33.	33.	47.	65.	40.	25.	64.	29.

Appendix A
Continued

**If the election for Governor were today,
how would you be voting? As of today, which way do you lean (with Walker as an alternative)?**

	Total sample	Voter type Rep.	Ticket splitter	Dem.	Chicago Nonblack	Black
Total vote	800 100.	145 100.	339 100.	246 100.	201 100.	84 100.
1. James Thompson (R)	333 42.	99 69.	169 50.	44 18.	87 43.	19 22.
2. Michael Howlett (D)	219 27.	13 9.	72 21.	126 51.	62 31.	35 42.
3. Daniel Walker (I)	132 16.	18 12.	51 15.	48 20.	21 10.	18 21.
9. Refused	29 4.	1 1.	9 3.	4 2.	10 5.	1 1.
0. Don't know	87 11.	13 9.	39 11.	24 10.	22 11.	11 14.

**If the election for Governor were today,
why would you be voting for—James Thompson?**

	Total sample	Voter type Rep.	Ticket splitter	Dem.	Chicago Nonblack	Black
Total	333 100.	99 100.	169 100.	44 100.	87 100.	19 100.
Honest/integrity	48 15.	18 18.	23 14.	5 11.	13 15.	4 21.
Republican	43 13.	26 26.	13 8.		4 5.	1 4.
Don't like other candidates—Walker/Howlett	39 12.	8 6.	21 13.	8 18.	7 8.	3 15.

Appendix A
Continued

**If the election for Governor were today,
how would you be voting? As of today, which way do you lean (with Walker as an alternative)?**

Political areas					Media markets			
Bal. of Cook County	Collar Counties	North	Central	South	Chicago	Springfield Decatur Champaign	St. Louis	Peoria
118 100.	79 100.	205 100.	97 100.	15 100.	526 100.	58 100.	64 100.	41 100.
63 53.	44 55.	87 42.	31 32.	3 19.	233 44.	31 54.	12 18.	17 42.
24 20.	21 26.	41 20.	31 32.	6 42.	147 28.	9 16.	28 43.	10 24.
7 6.	7 9.	54 26.	22 23.	2 14.	67 13.	10 17.	14 21.	8 19.
6 5.	2 3.	6 3.	3 3.	2.	18 3.	4 6.	1 2.	1 2.
18 15.	5 7.	17 8.	10 10.	3 22.	61 12.	4 6.	10 15.	5 13.

**If the election for Governor were today,
why would you be voting for—James Thompson?**

Political areas					Media markets			
Bal. of Cook County	Collar Counties	North	Central	South	Chicago	Springfield Decatur Champaign	St. Louis	Peoria
63 100.	44 100.	87 100.	31 100.	3 100.	233 100.	31 100.	12 100.	17 100.
16 25.	7 17.	7 9.	1 3.		43 18.	1 3.		1 6.
6 9.	3 8.	20 23.	8 27.		18 8.	9 30.	2 17.	5 30.
9 14.		13 15.	6 20.	1 46.	20 9.	6 20.	3 28.	3 16.

Appendix A

Continued

**If the election for Governor were today,
why would you be voting for—James Thompson?**

	Total sample	Rep.	Ticket splitter	Dem.	Chicago Nonblack	Chicago Black
Own man—not influenced/Daley machine	38 11.	4 4.	22 13.	10 23.	19 22.	2 11.
Best man/better man	35 10.	11 11.	18 11.	4 9.	8 9.	1 5.
Past record/ Experience/background	34 10.	8 8.	18 11.	2 5.	13 15.	
Good U.S. Attorney	31 9.	8 8.	18 11.	4 9.	9 11.	3 15.
Like him/like what I know about him	30 9.	10 10.	16 10.	2 5.	7 8.	
Change/new face	22 7.	6 7.	13 8.	3 7.	6 7.	1 5.
Howlett—Daley man/ machine politician	13 4.	4 4.	6 4.	3 6.	4 5.	2 11.
Good man	8 2.	2 2.	4 3.		1 1.	1 5.
Concerned about people/ more for the people	8 2.	2 2.	4 2.		4 4.	
Young/young blood	7 2.	2 2.	3 2.	1 2.	6 7.	
Energetic/dynamic/ hard worker	7 2.		5 3.	1 2.	4 4.	
Walker ineffective in what he has done	6 2.	1 1.	4 2.	1 2.	2 2.	1 5.
For law and order	6 2.	2 2.	4 2.	1 2.	2 2.	
Like his ideas/ programs	6 2.	5 5.	1		1 2.	
Intelligent/knowledge	5 2.	3 3.	2 1.			1 5.
Other positive Thompson-related responses	11 3.		6 4.	3 6.	2 2.	1 4.
Other negative Howlett/ Walker–related responses	5 1.	1 1.	1 1.	1 2.	2 2.	
Don't know	24 7.	5 5.	15 9.	4 8.	6 7.	2 9.

Appendix A

Continued

**If the election for Governor were today,
why would you be voting for—James Thompson?**

Political areas					Media markets			
Bal. of Cook County	Collar Counties	North	Central	South	Chicago	Springfield Decatur Champaign	St. Louis	Peoria
5 8.	5 11.	4 5.	3 8.		31 13.	1 3.	2 13.	2 10.
6 10.	7 17.	7 8.	5 15.		26 11.	6 20.	1 4.	
10 16.	8 19.	3 3.	1 2.	12.	31 13.	1 3.	1 7.	
11 18.	2 5.	5 6.	1 3.		27 12.	1 3.		1 6.
3 5.	4 9.	13 15.	3 8.	1 25.	16 7.	5 15.	1 4.	3 21.
1 1.	5 11.	7 8.	2 5.	1 34.	14 6.	1 3.	1 4.	3 16.
1 2.	1 2.	3 3.	1 4.	12.	9 4.	1 2.	1 7.	1 6.
3 6.	1 2.	1 2.	1 2.		7 3.		1 4.	
1 2.	1 2.	2 2.	1 2.		6 2.		1 4.	
	1 2.				7 3.			
1 2.	3 6.				7 3.			
2 3.	2 4.				6 3.			
1 2.		3 3.	1 2.		4 2.		1 4.	1 6.
1 2.		3 3.		1 25.	5 2.			
2 3.	1 2.	1 1.			4 2.			
	1 2.	4 4.	3 8.	1 25.	4 2.	2 6.	1 4.	1 4.
		2 2.	1 3.		2 1.		1 7.	1 6.
2 3.	2 5.	8 10.	3 10.	1 17.	16 7.	1 2.	2 17.	2 12.

Appendix A

Continued

What is the name of the republican candidate for Governor? Jim Thompson—how much do you feel you know about him and what he stands for/ is your general impression of him favorable or unfavorable?

	Total sample	Rep.	Ticket splitter	Dem.	Nonblack	Black
			Voter type		**Chicago**	
Total	800	145	339	246	201	84
	100.	100.	100.	100.	100.	100.
Name of the Republican candidate for Governor						
1. Named Jim Thompson	423	81	204	109	129	25
	53.	56.	60.	44.	64.	30.
2. Named other	40	4	16	15	8	5
	5.	3.	5.	6.	4.	6.
0. Don't know	336	60	119	121	65	54
	42.	41.	35.	49.	32.	64.
Thompson—how much feel you know about him						
1. A great deal	82	22	35	22	30	4
	10.	15.	10.	9.	15.	5.
2. A moderate amount	240	52	113	56	70	16
	30.	36.	33.	23.	35.	19.
3. Very little	387	58	164	128	83	48
	48.	40.	48.	52.	41.	57.
0. Don't know	91	12	27	40	18	16
	11.	8.	8.	16.	9.	19.
Thompson—general impression of						
1. Favorable	428	102	202	97	129	26
	53.	70.	59.	39.	64.	31.
2. Unfavorable	69	4	26	34	17	11
	9.	3.	8.	14.	9.	13.
0. Don't know	303	39	112	115	56	47
	38.	27.	33.	47.	28.	56.

If the election for Governor were today, why would you be voting for—Michael Howlett?

	Total sample	Rep.	Ticket splitter	Dem.	Nonblack	Black
			Voter type		**Chicago**	
Total	219	13	72	126	62	35
	100.	100.	100.	100.	100.	100.
Democrat	67	1	12	50	26	13
	31.	8.	17.	39.	42.	36.
Past record/proven himself/experience	27	1	10	15	11	1
	12.	8.	15.	12.	17.	2.
Best man/better man	23	1	5	18	7	3
	11.	8.	7.	14.	12.	8.
Like him/like what I've heard	23	2	7	12	6	5
	11.	14.	10.	10.	9.	13.
Know him more	19	2	10	7	6	3
	9.	14.	14.	6.	11.	8.

What is the name of the republican candidate for Governor? Jim Thompson—how much do you feel you know about him and what he stands for/ is your general impression of him favorable or unfavorable?

	Political areas					Media markets		
Bal. of Cook County	Collar Counties	North	Central	South	Chicago	Springfield Decatur Champaign	St. Louis	Peoria
118	79	205	97	15	526	58	64	41
100.	100.	100.	100.	100.	100.	100.	100.	100.
77	48	102	38	5	306	29	21	18
65.	60.	50.	39.	35.	58.	50.	33.	45.
3	2	12	9	1	19	6	5	6
3.	2.	6.	10.	7.	4.	10.	7.	14.
38	30	91	50	9	201	23	39	16
32.	37.	44.	52.	58.	38.	40.	60.	40.
18	11	15	4		69	3	2	1
15.	14.	7.	4.		13.	5.	2.	2.
51	34	49	17	2	188	15	6	10
44.	43.	24.	18.	12.	36.	25.	10.	24.
40	28	120	61	7	220	36	39	27
34.	35.	59.	63.	45.	42.	63.	60.	67.
8	6	21	15	7	49	4	18	2
7.	7.	10.	16.	43.	9.	7.	27.	6.
80	51	102	37	3	311	31	15	17
68.	64.	50.	38.	18.	59.	54.	23.	42.
8	9	16	7	1	46	4	4	6
7.	12.	8.	7.	7.	9.	8.	7.	15.
30	19	86	53	12	169	22	45	18
26.	24.	42.	55.	76.	32.	39.	70.	44.

If the election for Governor were today, why would you be voting for—Michael Howlett?

	Political areas					Media markets		
Bal. of Cook County	Collar Counties	North	Central	South	Chicago	Springfield Decatur Champaign	St. Louis	Peoria
24	21	41	31	6	147	9	28	10
100.	100.	100.	100.	100.	100.	100.	100.	100.
9	3	6	8	3	49	2	10	1
37.	15.	14.	26.	44.	34.	21.	36.	8.
	3	8	4		16	1	3	3
2.	15.	19.	12.	6.	11.	8.	10.	31.
2	2	4	5	1	16	1	4	1
8.	10.	9.	15.	15.	11.	11.	12.	8.
3	2	6	1		16	3	1	2
12.	12.	16.	3.		11.	29.	4.	18.
2	2	2	3	2	14	1	1	
8.	8.	5.	8.	23.	9.	11.	4.	

Appendix A

Continued

If the election for Governor were today, why would you be voting for—Michael Howlett?

	Total sample	Voter type			Chicago	
		Rep.	Ticket splitter	Dem.	Nonblack	Black
Don't like other candidates—Walker/Thompson	15 7.	1 8.	5 7.	9 7.	1 2.	2 6.
Good man	11 5.	1 8.	4 6.	3 3.	2 4.	
He's a Daley man	10 5.		4 6.	5 4.	4 7.	3 8.
Gets things done/ gets results	9 4.		3 5.	6 5.	3 4.	2 5.
Need a change/ Give him a chance	8 4.		4 5.	5 4.	2 3.	2 6.
Don't know Thompson	5 2.		3 5.	2 1.	1 2.	1 3.
Make a good governor	3 1.		2 2.	1 1.		
Other positive Howlett-related responses	14 6.		5 7.	8 6.	4 6.	2 6.
Other negative Thompson/ Walker–related responses	3 1.		1 1.	2 2.	1 2.	1 3.
Don't know	20 9.	6 48.	5 7.	7 6.	1 1.	2 6.

Voter type within political area

	Total sample	Vote intention governor			Ticket splitters		
		Thompson	Howlett	Undecided	Thompson	Howlett	Undecided
Total	800 100.	395 100.	262 100.	143 100.	191 100.	87 100.	61 100.
Chicago	285 36.	120 30.	112 43.	53 37.	58 30.	29 34.	18 30.
Republican	25 3.	21 5.	1 *	3 2.			
Ticket splitter	105 13.	58 15.	29 11.	18 13.	58 30.	29 34.	18 30.
Democrat	128 16.	28 7.	80 31.	20 14.			
Marginal	27 3.	14 3.	2 1.	11 8.			

Appendix A

Continued

If the election for Governor were today, why would you be voting for—Michael Howlett?

	Political areas					Media markets		
Bal. of Cook County	Collar Counties	North	Central	South	Chicago	Springfield Decatur Champaign	St. Louis	Peoria
4	1	4	1	2	8		2	2
17.	5.	11.	3.	29.	5.		6.	18.
1	1	6	1		4	3	1	
4.	4.	14.	3.		3.	29.	3.	
	1	2			10			
	5.	4.			7.			
2	1	1	1		7			1
7.	5.	2.	3.		5.			10.
1	1		2		6		1	
4.	5.		7.		4.		4.	
		2	1		2		1	
		5.	2.	6.	1.		3.	
2		1			2			1
8.		2.	1.		1.		1.	8.
2	1	2	3	1	9		3	1
8.	5.	5.	9.	8.	6.		12.	10.
		1			2			
		2.			1.			
2	4	6	5		10	2	4	2
8.	22.	14.	16.	6.	7.	21.	15.	18.

Voter type within political area

Democrats			Soft vote		Age		Walker primary voters
Thompson	Howlett	Undecided	Thompson	Howlett	Under 35	35+	
63	149	34	156	119	244	542	102
100.	100.	100.	100.	100.	100.	100.	100.
28	80	20	56	46	91	188	42
44.	54.	60.	36.	38.	37.	35.	41.
			7	1	6	19	2
			5.	1.	2.	4.	2.
			26	15	30	75	18
			17.	12.	12.	14.	18.
28	80	20	13	28	45	81	21
44.	54.	60.	8.	24.	18.	15.	21.
			9	2	11	12	1
			6.	1.	4.	2.	1.

Appendix A

Continued

	Total sample	Vote intention governor			Ticket splitters		
		Thompson	**Howlett**	**Undecided**	**Thompson**	**Howlett**	**Undecided**
Balance of Cook County	118	67	26	25	36	10	12
	15.	17.	10.	17.	19.	11.	20.
Republican	25	23	1	1			
	3.	6.	*	1.			
Ticket splitter	58	36	10	12	36	10	12
	7.	9.	4.	9.	19.	11.	20.
Democrat	20	5	11	4			
	3.	1.	4.	3.			
Marginal	15	4	4	7			
	2.	1.	1.	5.			
Collar counties	79	45	22	12	17	9	3
	10.	11.	8.	8.	9.	11.	5.
Republican	28	21	2	5			
	3.	5.	1.	4.			
Ticket splitter	30	17	9	3	17	9	3
	4.	4.	4.	2.	9.	11.	5.
Democrat	14	3	11				
	2.	1.	4.				
Marginal	7	4		4			
	1.	1.		3.			
North	205	117	57	31	57	25	16
	26.	30.	22.	22.	30.	29.	27.
Republican	52	37	10	4			
	6.	9.	4.	3.			
Ticket splitter	98	57	25	16	57	25	16
	12.	14.	10.	11.	30.	29.	27.
Democrat	47	21	19	7			
	6.	5.	7.	5.			
Marginal	8	2	2	3			
	1.	1.	1.	2.			
Central	97	42	36	19	21	11	10
	12.	11.	14.	13.	11.	13.	16.
Republican	15	12	1	2			
	2.	3.	*	1.			
Ticket splitter	42	21	11	10	21	11	10
	5.	5.	4.	7.	11.	13.	16.
Democrat	32	6	23	2			
	4.	2.	9.	2.			
Marginal	8	2	1	5			
	1.	1.	*	4.			

Voter type within political area

Appendix A

Continued

Voter type within political area

Democrats			Soft vote		Age		Walker primary voters
Thompson	Howlett	Undecided	Thompson	Howlett	Under 35	35+	
5	11	4	18	14	33	79	8
8.	8.	12.	11.	12.	13.	15.	8.
			6	1	5	17	
			4.	1.	2.	3.	
			8	5	16	41	6
			5.	4.	6.	8.	6.
5	11	4	3	7	7	13	2
8.	8.	12.	2.	6.	3.	2.	2.
			1	1	6	7	
			*	1.	2.	1.	
3	11		15	11	24	56	10
5.	7.		9.	9.	10.	10.	10.
			4	1	3	25	
			3.	1.	1.	5.	
			6	7	11	19	6
			4.	6.	5.	3.	6.
3	11		3	3	6	8	4
5.	7.		2.	3.	2.	1.	4.
			2		4	4	
			1.		2.	1.	
21	19	7	48	29	63	142	28
33.	13.	20.	31.	24.	26.	26.	28.
			8	7	13	9	
			5.	6.	5.	7.	
			29	13	36	62	9
			19.	11.	15.	11.	9.
21	19	7	9	7	11	36	19
33.	13.	20.	6.	6.	4.	7.	18.
			1	2	3	5	1
			1.	1.	1.	1.	1.
6	23	2	17	16	30	66	13
10.	16.	7.	11.	14.	12.	12.	13.
			7	1	7	8	1
			4.	1.	3.	1.	1.
			·9	6	12	30	5
			6.	5.	5.	5.	4.
6	23	2	2	9	9	23	7
10.	16.	7.	1.	7.	4.	4.	7.
				1	2	5	1
				*	1.	1.	*

Appendix A
Continued

		Voter type within political area					
	Total sample	**Vote intention governor**			**Ticket splitters**		
		Thompson	**Howlett**	**Undecided**	**Thompson**	**Howlett**	**Undecided**
South	15	4	8	3	3	2	1
	2.	1.	3.	2.	2.	3.	2.
Republican	*		*				
Ticket splitter	6	3	2	1	3	2	1
	1.	1.	1.	1.	2.	3.	2.
Democrat	5		4	1			
	1.		2.	*			
Marginal	4	1	1	2			
	*	*	*	1.			

		Area—political				
	Total sample	**Voter type**			**Chicago**	
		Rep.	**Ticket splitter**	**Dem.**	**Nonblack**	**Black**
Total	800	145	339	246	201	84
	100.	100.	100.	100.	100.	100.
Chicago	285	25	105	128	201	84
	36.	17.	31.	52.	100.	100.
Balance of Cook County	118	25	58	20		
	15.	17.	17.	8.		
Collar counties	79	28	30	14		
	10.	19.	9.	6.		
North	205	52	98	47		
	26.	36.	29.	19.		
Central	97	15	42	32		
	12.	10.	12.	13.		
South	15		6	5		
	2.		2.	2.		

Appendix A
Continued

Voter type within political area

	Democrats			Soft vote		Age		
Thompson	Howlett	Undecided	Thompson	Howlett	Under 35	35+	Walker primary voters
	4	1	3	4	4	11	1
	3.	1.	2.	3.	2.	2.	1.
				*		*	
			2	1	2	4	
			1.	1.	1.	1.	
	4	1		1	1	4	1
	3.	1.		1.	*	1.	1.
			1	1	1	2	
			1.	1.	1.	*	

Area—political

Political areas					Media markets			
Bal. of Cook County	Collar Counties	North	Central	South	Chicago	Springfield Decatur Champaign	St. Louis	Peoria
118	79	205	97	15	526	58	64	41
100.	100.	100.	100.	100.	100.	100.	100.	100.
					281			
					53.		1.	
118					117			
100.					22.		1.	
	79				79			
	100.				15.			
		205			47	25		41
		100.			9.	43.		100.
			97		1	33	52	
			100.			57.	81.	
				15			12	
				100.			18.	

Thinking about all elections, how many of them have you voted in over the past few years?

	Total sample	Voter type			Chicago	
		Rep.	Ticket splitter	Dem.	Nonblack	Black
Total	800	145	339	246	201	84
	100.	100.	100.	100.	100.	100.
1. All of them	258	52	95	100	74	34
	32.	36.	28.	41.	37.	40.
2. Most of them	303	56	145	83	71	23
	38.	39.	43.	34.	35.	27.
3. About half of them	147	26	67	40	35	14
	18.	18.	20.	16.	17.	17.
4. Less than half of them	55	8	30	12	9	5
	7.	5.	9.	5.	4.	6.
5. None of them	18	2	2	2	4	4
	2.	1.	1.	1.	2.	5.
0. Don't know	19	1	1	8	10	4
	2.	1.		3.	5.	5.

Area—ADI

	Total sample	Voter intention (governor)			Ticket splitters		
		Thompson	Howlett	Undecided	Thompson	Howlett	Undecided
Total	800	395	262	143	191	87	61
	100.	100.	100.	100.	100.	100.	100.
Chicago	526	257	173	96	125	54	38
	66.	65.	66.	67.	65.	62.	62.
Peoria	41	26	11	4	13	6	3
	5.	7.	4.	3.	7.	7.	5.
Davenport/Rock Island/Moline	30	16	12	3	7	7	2
	4.	4.	4.	2.	4.	8.	3.
Rockford	31	20	6	5	10	4	1
	4.	5.	2.	4.	5.	4.	2.
Springfield/Decatur/Champaign	58	35	11	12	17	2	5
	7.	9.	4.	8.	9.	2.	9.
Quincy/Hannibal	16	11	2	2	5		2
	2.	3.	1.	2.	3.		3.
St. Louis	64	18	32	15	9	7	6
	8.	5.	12.	10.	5.	9.	10.
Terre Haute	11	3	6	3	2	4	3
	1.	1.	2.	2.	1.	5.	5.
Evansville	4	2	2		1	1	
	*	*	1.		1.	1.	
Paducah/Cape Ginadeau	19	7	8	4	2	2	1
	2.	2.	3.	3.	1.	2.	2.

Thinking about all elections, how many of them have you voted in over the past few years?

	Political areas					Media markets			
	Bal. of Cook County	Collar	North	Central	South	Chicago	Springfield Decatur Champaign	St. Louis	Peoria
118	79	205	97	15	526	58	64	41	
100.	100.	100.	100.	100.	100.	100.	100.	100.	
36	20	57	33	4	178	19	19	14	
31.	26.	28.	34.	28.	34.	33.	29.	34.	
50	32	82	36	9	197	18	25	13	
43.	41.	40.	37.	57.	37.	32.	39.	33.	
16	21	44	18		92	15	10	8	
13.	26.	22.	18.		17.	25.	16.	21.	
10	6	17	7	1	29	3	6	5	
8.	7.	9.	8.	9.	6.	6.	10.	12.	
4		4	1	1	13	2	2		
3.		2.	1.	6.	2.	3.	3.		
2		1	2		17	1	1		
2.			2.		3.	2.	2.		

(Column assignment note: the header row order is Bal. of Cook County, Collar, North, Central, South, Chicago, Springfield Decatur Champaign, St. Louis, Peoria.)

Democrats			Soft vote		Age		Walker primary voters
Thompson	Howlett	Undecided	Thompson	Howlett	Under 35	35+	
63	149	34	156	119	244	542	102
100.	100.	100.	100.	100.	100.	100.	100.
38	106	27	100	80	166	348	62
61.	71.	80.	64.	67.	68.	64.	61.
6	3	1	10	4	14	27	6
9.	2.	3.	6.	4.	6.	5.	6.
2	2		4	4	6	24	4
3.	1.		3.	3.	2.	4.	4.
3	2	1	5	4	7	24	5
5.	1.	2.	4.	3.	3.	4.	5.
7	6	2	13	7	21	36	6
11.	4.	5.	8.	6.	9.	7.	6.
2	1		8	1	4	12	2
3.	*		5.	1.	2.	2.	2.
3	22	2	7	14	20	44	11
5.	15.	7.	4.	12.	8.	8.	11.
	2		2	2	1	10	
	1.		1.	2.	*	2.	
	1		2	1	1	3	
	1.		1.	1.	*	1.	
2	5	1	4	3	6	13	4
3.	3.	3.	3.	2.	2.	2.	4.

Appendix A

Continued

	Voter type			Chicago		Political areas					Media markets			
	Total sample	Rep.	Ticket splitter	Dem.	Nonblack	Black	Bal. of Cook County	Collar Counties	North	Central	South	Chicago	Springfield Decatur Champaign	St. Louis	Peoria
Total	800 / 100.	145 / 100.	339 / 100.	246 / 100.	201 / 100.	84 / 100.	118 / 100.	79 / 100.	205 / 100.	97 / 100.	15 / 100.	526 / 100.	58 / 100.	64 / 100.	41 / 100.
Chicago†	526 / 66.	92 / 63.	217 / 64.	171 / 69.	197 / 98.	84 / 100.	117 / 100.	79 / 100.	47 / 23.	1 / 1.		526 / 100.			
Peoria	41 / 5.	8 / 6.	22 / 7.	10 / 4.	4 / 2.				41 / 20.						41 / 100.
Davenport/ Rock Island/ Moline	30 / 4.	9 / 6.	16 / 5.	4 / 2.					30 / 15.						
Rockford	31 / 4.	6 / 4.	15 / 4.	6 / 2.					27 / 13.						
Springfield/ Decatur/ Champaign	58 / 7.	13 / 9.	24 / 7.	15 / 6.					25 / 12.	33 / 34.			58 / 100.		
Quincy/ Hannibal	16 / 2.	5 / 3.	7 / 2.	3 / 1.					16 / 8.						
St. Louis	64 / 8.	6 / 4.	23 / 7.	27 / 11.	*		*			52 / 54.	12 / 76.			64 / 100.	
Terre Haute	11 / 1.	1 / 1.	8 / 2.	2 / 1.						11 / 12.					
Evansville	4 / *		2 / 1.	1 / *							4 / 24.				
Paducah/ Cape Ginadeau	19 / 2.	6 / 4.	5 / 1.	8 / 3.					19† / 9.						

*Numbers don't always add across to the total because of voters who couldn't be classified.

†This tabulation was mistakenly included in the northern region. In fact, these observations should be grouped under "South."

The Federal Trade Commission In Re: Firestone

Steven H. Star

Mr. Robert Hughes, hearing examiner for the Federal Trade Commission, was considering the recent FTC complaint against the Firestone Tire & Rubber Company. In this complaint, the FTC had alleged that Firestone had engaged in deceptive advertising practices during 1966, 1967, and 1968. Hearings had been held in March, April, and May of 1971, and final arguments had been filed in June. It was now

Steven H. Star was formerly an associate professor at the Harvard Graduate School of Business Administration.

This case was prepared from published sources and legal documents filed in the actions described in the case. It is intended for discussion by graduate students of business administration and simplifies many of the legal issues under consideration. In addition, considerable evidence and certain arguments have been omitted for the sake of brevity. Consequently, this case should not be viewed as a complete summary of the actions it describes.

In several instances, the sequence of events has been modified; paraphrases and summaries of testimony are often presented as direct quotations. The hearing examiner described in the case is purely fictitious, as are the thought processes and opinions attributed to him.

Mr. Hughes's responsibility to decide whether Firestone had engaged in deceptive advertising and, if he found that it had, to determine what remedies should be ordered.

Mr. Hughes's task was complicated by the intervention in the case of Students Opposed to Unfair Practices (SOUP) and the Association of National Advertisers (ANA). SOUP had argued that the FTC's traditional remedy, a cease and desist order, was inadequate in this case, since the effects of Firestone's allegedly deceptive advertising would continue to be felt even after the cessation of such advertising. To mitigate these long-term effects, SOUP had contended, Firestone should be required to "affirmatively disclose" its previous alleged deceptions in future advertisements. ANA, on the other hand, had argued (1) that the FTC lacked the authority to require "affirmative disclosure," (2) that the long-term effects of advertising were minimal, and (3) that affirmative disclosure, if adopted as a remedy by the FTC, would be injurious to the process of competition.

The Federal Trade Commission[1]

The FTC was established in 1914 as an independent regulatory agency. The FTC's primary responsibility was to enforce certain provisions of the antitrust laws, especially with regard to "unfair methods of competition in commerce." Since the meaning of the provisions in question was somewhat unclear, the FTC was intended to serve as a "forum" for the interpretation of the law as well as an enforcement agency. According to most legal scholars, the FTC's authority was thus limited to the issuance of cease and desist orders, which required that a party charged with specific "unfair practices" not engage in those unfair practices in the future. The FTC did not have the authority to impose penalties or sanctions unless one of its cease and desist orders was disobeyed.

Throughout its history, there had been considerable controversy concerning the scope of its authority and jurisdiction. During the 1920s, for example, the FTC became increasingly involved in consumer protection on the grounds that deceptive trade practices were a form of unfair competition. In 1931, the U.S. Supreme Court ruled that deceptive trade practices did not necessarily fall under the FTC's jurisdiction, since deceptive practices were not injurious to competition in an industry where most major competitors engaged in such practices. In 1936, however, Congress amended the Fair Trade Commission Act to give the FTC explicit jurisdiction over "unfair or deceptive acts or practices in commerce."

The FTC consisted of a Chairman and four commissioners appointed for staggered 7-year terms. In 1970, the Commission staff included

[1]This section of the case is based on the *Report of the ABA Commission to Study the Federal Trade Commission,* September 1969; E. Cox et al., *The Consumer and the Federal Trade Commission* (the "Nader Report"), 1969; G. J. Alexander, *Honesty and Competition,* Syracuse University Press, Syracuse, N.Y., 1967; and John Osborne, "Reform at the FTC," *New Republic,* October 2, 1971.

approximately 400 lawyers and 200 economists and other professionals. In general, the staff was expected to identify and investigate "unfair or deceptive practices in commerce" and bring them to the attention of the five commissioners. If the commissioners agreed that the practices in question were in fact either unfair or deceptive, the FTC staff could seek their curtailment through either formal or informal means. If the formal procedure were followed, the FTC staff would issue a formal complaint and a proposed "order" or "remedy." The party against whom the complaint had been issued could then either agree to cease and desist from the practices in question or demand a formal hearing before a hearing examiner. At such a hearing, the FTC staff and the respondent each presented briefs and oral arguments to the hearing examiner, who then reached a decision and issued an order. Either party could then appeal the hearing examiner's decision to the five commissioners. If dissatisfied with the commissioners' decision, the respondent could appeal to the federal courts.

During the 1960s, the FTC placed increased emphasis on informal procedures, none of which had the force of law. Among the more important of these procedures, as summarized by the American Bar Association, were the following:

1. Industry Guides. *These constitute advice to the business community of the FTC's views of the legality of specific conduct in selected areas. . . .*
2. Advisory Opinions. *These opinions are rendered in response to individual inquiries concerning the legality of a proposed course of action. Opinions can be requested, for example, with respect to proposed advertising claims. . . . While the FTC may reconsider its advice, particularly in light of changed circumstances, the advice affords a businessman a dependable assurance that the agency will not move against the business conduct in question.*
3. Trade Regulation Rules. *These rules are pub-*

lished after hearings, at which all businessmen who are likely to be affected have an opportunity to present their views. . . .

4. Assurances of Voluntary Compliance and Informal Corrective Actions. *"Assurances" are written agreements to discontinue objectionable practices, which now include a provision for the submission of a subsequent compliance report by the business unit.*

In the late 1960s, the FTC began to receive very strong criticism from a number of sources. In early 1969, for example, a group of law students working with consumer advocate Ralph Nader issued a report entitled *The Consumer and the Federal Trade Commission.* This report concluded that:

> Among other failings, the agency's methods of detecting statutory violations were inadequate, its consumer protection program (particularly in the area of false advertising) was largely ineffective in coping with modern forms of deceptive advertising, its heavy reliance on voluntary enforcement techniques was failing to secure real compliance with the law, [and] the overall performance of the FTC was "shockingly poor."

Later in 1969, a special commission of the American Bar Association issued a report on the FTC.[2] While somewhat more temperate than the Nader group's report, the ABA commission's report was also highly critical of the FTC, especially in the area of consumer protection. For example, the ABA commission was not favorably impressed with the methods used by the FTC to detect deceptive advertising:

> The FTC's monitoring program is limited almost exclusively to examination of commercial advertising on national television. . . . Although vast amounts of material are accumulated dealing with national and local magazine advertising, national and regional radio scripts, regional television, and local newspaper advertising, no personnel have been assigned to screen this material. . . .

[2]This study had been undertaken at President Nixon's request shortly after the publication of the Nader report.

The commission was extremely critical of the FTC's enforcement procedures:

> The failure to put some bite into enforcement is illustrated by the long history of the FTC's dealings with the J. B. Williams Company over advertising compaigns for Geritol. After more than three years of investigation, the FTC, in December, 1962, directed the issuance of a complaint in which it alleged, among other things, that respondents had misrepresented the efficacy of Geritol in the treatment of tiredness, nervousness, loss of strength and irritability. No preliminary injunction was sought. About three years later a cease and desist order was entered which was eventually affirmed with slight modification by the Court of Appeals. . . . In March, 1969, almost 10 years to the day after the beginning of the investigation, the FTC found that certain of Geritol's commercials still violated the cease and desist order. . . . No further action has been taken.

The ABA commission charged that the FTC had done a poor job of allocating its admittedly limited resources. A great deal of effort seemed to be going into relatively trivial matters (e.g., that "Navy shoes" were not made by the Navy; that "Indian" trinkets were not manufactured by American Indians) rather than into the detection and prevention of deceptive practices which had a major impact on consumers. For example, in 1969, according to the ABA commission, only 12 attorneys were assigned to work on:

> . . . misbranding of softwood lumber, cigarette advertising and labeling, fair packaging and labeling, encyclopedia and magazine subscription frauds, failure to publish or deceptive publication of gasoline octane ratings, advertising campaigns dealing with gasoline additives, promulgation of product safety standards, automobile warranty claims, and several other matters which are still confidential. . . . The predictable result is that investigations, once initiated, disappear from public view and surface, if at all, many years later.

In 1970, President Nixon appointed Mr. Miles Kirkpatrick, who had been chairman of the ABA special commission, to be chairman of the FTC.

This appointment was widely interpreted in the press as a mandate for the FTC to increase its effectiveness. In his first few months, Mr. Kirkpatrick induced a number of promising young lawyers to join the FTC staff, including Robert Pitofsky, a New York University law professor who had been counsel to the ABA commission. Mr. Pitofsky became the head of the FTC's Consumer Protection Bureau.

By July 1971, FTC activities in the field of consumer protection had increased noticeably. In recent months, for example, the FTC had obtained an injunction to prevent the insertion of razor blade samples in Sunday newspapers, asserted its authority to require affirmative disclosure, given increased attention to advertising directed at children, entered into a consent decree requiring affirmative disclosure,[3] and undertaken a major study of the processes through which television advertising affected consumer behavior.

The Firestone Complaint

The FTC had issued its initial complaint against Firestone in June 1970. This complaint was directed at Firestone advertisements which had

[3]On July 2, 1971, the FTC and ITT Continental Baking Company announced the provisional acceptance of a voluntary consent order under which Continental would devote 25 percent of the advertising expenditures for Profile bread for 1 year to affirmative disclosure of the fact that Profile was not effective for weight reduction, contrary to possible interpretations of prior advertising. Interestingly, the FTC staff had decided not to seek affirmative disclosure in a similar case against Swift Baby Food, since Swift was "an extremely weak company in this particular market (no. 4 in the four-member baby food field) and it was not thought desirable to impose an advertising requirement which might make it more difficult for Swift to become a more effective competitor in that product category. More significantly, this very weak position in the market indicated that . . . there must have been little residual effect on the consumer from the false advertising, one of the reasons for requiring corrective advertising in the first place. . . ." (Address by Gerald J. Thain, July 7, 1971.)

appeared in 1966, 1967, and 1968. According to the complaint, certain advertisements used by Firestone during this period had been deceptive with regard to pricing, product quality, and/or product safety.

Pricing

In the tire industry it was common to advertise price reductions on specified tires for limited periods of time. During the summer of 1966, for example, Firestone had run the following advertisements in a number of newspapers:

> Gigantic July 4th Offer
> 10 Day Offer Now Thru Sat. July 2
>
> TIRE JAMBOREE
>
> Low, low prices on our popular high quality nylon cord tire . . . the Firestone Safety Champion. Jamboree Prices Start at $16 Plus $1.61 per tire Fed. excise tax, sales tax and trade-in tire with recappable cord body 6.00–13 tubeless blackwall.
>
> [The advertisement includes a listing of other sizes of Safety Champion tires and the price for each.]

> * * * *
>
> Now thru Sept. 3 SAVE BIG! BUY NOW AT DISCOUNT PRICES
>
> FIRESTONE
> Pre-Labor Day
> TIRE SALE
>
> Prices slashed on
> FIRESTONE
> Safety Champions
>
> Sale Prices Start at $16 Plus $1.61 Fed. excise tax and trade-in tire off your car.
> [The advertisement includes a listing of other sizes of Safety Champion tires and the price for each.]

According to the complaint, these advertisements clearly implied that:

> The tires advertised were being offered at prices which were significantly reduced from the actual bona fide prices at which those tires had been sold

to the public at retail by respondent in the recent regular course of its business prior to the publication of the advertisement and purchasers would thereby realize bona fide savings in the amount of such reduction.

The complaint went on to allege that the tires in question were rarely sold at prices higher than those stated in the advertisements and that the advertisements were thus deceptive.

Product Quality

During 1967, Firestone had used the following advertisement:

THE SAFE TIRE—FIRESTONE
When you buy a Firestone Tire—no matter how much or how little you pay—you get a safe tire; Firestone tires are custom-built one by one. By skilled craftsmen. And they're personally inspected for an extra margin of safety. If these tires don't pass all of the exacting Firestone inspections, they don't get out.

The complaint contended that this advertisement conveyed the impression that:

A purchaser of a tire bearing the brand name "Firestone" is assured of receiving a tire which will be free from any defects in materials or workmanship or any other manufacturing defects. . . . Although [Firestone] may exercise due care in the course of manufacturing its tires, [Firestone] cannot assure that tires containing defects in materials or workmanship or other manufacturing defects will not reach the hands of the purchasing public.

Product Safety

The following statements had appeared in Firestone advertisements during 1967 and 1968:

Firestone—The Safe Tire. At 60,000 Firestone Safe Tire Centers. At no more cost than ordinary tires.

* * * *

Like the original Super Sports Wide Oval Tire. It came straight out of Firestone racing research.

It's built lower, wider. Nearly two inches wider than regular tires. To corner better, run cooler, stop 25% quicker.

According to the complaint, these statements implied that Firestone tires would be "safe under all conditions of use" and that Firestone:

. . . had established through adequate scientific tests that any car equipped with Firestone Super Sports Wide Oval tires could be stopped 25 percent quicker under typical road and weather conditions . . . when compared with the performance of the same vehicle under the same conditions when equipped with any [other] manufacturer's tires. . . .

These implications were deceptive, the FTC alleged, because (1) the safety of any tire was dependent on the conditions (e.g., inflation pressure, vehicle weight) under which the tire was used and (2) Firestone had not established the performance claims for Super Sports Wide Oval tires through "adequate scientific tests."

Remedy

The complaint concluded by requesting that Firestone be ordered to cease and desist from the allegedly deceptive practices described above.

The Hearing

At the hearing, arguments were presented concerning the pricing issue, the product quality issue, the product safety issue, and the remedy itself.

The Pricing Issue

On this issue, Firestone agreed with the complaint's allegation that the advertisements in question offered significant price reductions to consumers for specified periods of time. Arguments at the hearing thus focused on whether consumers had, in fact, been able to obtain significant price reductions during the "sale" periods.

In support of its complaint, the FTC presented a tabulation of data from a sample of 357 "sales slips" examined at Firestone stores in Washington, D.C., Philadelphia, and Baltimore. These sales slips covered sales of advertised tires during the summer of 1966. Of the 357 sales slips, 104 reflected purchases at or below advertised prices during periods when price reductions had been advertised. An additional 208 sales slips reflected purchases at prices at least 10 percent higher than advertised prices during periods when price reductions were not being advertised. According to the FTC, the remaining 45 sales slips reflected purchases either at or below advertised prices during "sale" periods.

The FTC contended that these pricing irregularities were highly significant, since price reductions played a major role in the sale of tires. Several years previously, for example, Firestone's counsel had written to the FTC:

> Our Advertising Department feels, and this is supported by surveys they have made from time to time, that the only advertising which effectively produces greater than normal sales [is that] which pertain[s] to promotions which specifically refer to price reductions.

In response, Firestone contended that 28 of the sales slips at issue were explained by special situations and that the remaining 17 sales slips represented an insignificant proportion of the total sample. According to Firestone, the 28 sales slips which reflected special situations were accounted for by employee discounts, discounts to employees' friends and relatives, tires sold after "sale" periods which had been ordered during "sale" periods, and, in one case, "a special price as a reward for [a customer's] honesty in returning the [higher-priced] tires put on his car by mistake." Firestone's allegations in these 28 cases were supported by affidavits of employees of the stores where the sales had taken place.

The Product Quality Issue

On this issue, Firestone argued that the complaint's interpretation of how consumers would perceive the advertisements was erroneous. Firestone had hired an expert consultant to conduct a survey on how prospective tire buyers perceived the advertising claims in question. According to this survey, 52.7 percent of those interviewed "thought the advertisement said that [Firestone] did all it could to use the best procedures to make its tires safe and as free as possible of defects"; 30.2 percent "understood the advertisement to say that 'almost all' of [Firestone's] tires were safe under normal conditions" or "that 'each model' of [Firestone's] tires at least met minimum Government safety standards"; and 15.3 percent "thought the advertisement said that [Firestone's] tires were absolutely safe or absolutely free from defects." On the basis of this survey, Firestone argued that "no significant segment of the tire-buying public would actually purchase its tires by construing 'The safe tire' text as alleged in the complaint."

In response, while agreeing that the survey had been conducted in "a professional and competent manner," the FTC questioned whether a structured survey of this kind could measure a consumer's true perception of an advertisement under nonsurvey conditions. Moreover, the FTC argued, 15 percent was not an "insignificant segment," especially when safety was at stake.

The Product Safety Issue

This issue was complex; it included references to advertisements which are not described in this case. Fairly typical, however, was the argument concerning the "stop 25 percent quicker" claim. The FTC contended that Firestone had not conducted scientific tests to establish this claim. Firestone alleged that its wide oval tires would, in fact, stop a vehicle 25 percent quicker than would ordinary tires on glare ice and that it had test data to support this claim. Firestone did not, however, claim to have test data which demonstrated that the wide oval would stop 25 percent quicker on ordinary surfaces. The FTC did not dispute the wide oval tire's alleged performance on glare ice and did not present evidence suggesting that the wide oval tire would not stop 25 percent quicker on ordinary surfaces. In essence, the FTC was not disputing the performance claim per se but the fact that it was being made without the support of "adequate scientific tests."

A second dimension of this issue was concerned with the brand name used by Firestone for its "second-level" line of tires prior to 1969. During the 1960s, Firestone had marketed this line of tires under the brand name *Safety Champion*. According to the FTC, this brand name implied that the tires:

> . . . had unique construction or performance features which rendered them safer than other tires; [but] the tires so designated did not have any unique construction or performance features that rendered them safer than other tires, and there were other tires available that were as safe as those designated Safety Champion.

At the hearing, the FTC counsel argued that "the literal meaning of the term 'safety champion' is that it is supreme over all competitors, unexcelled, and first rate." In support of this contention, he cited a dictionary definition of the word *champion* and argued that "it is reasonable to infer that this term represents that the tires were supreme over all competitors as to safety."

Firestone responded by citing a study it had conducted which indicated that the brand name Safety Champion did not connote a safer tire than competitive brand names such as Safety All-Weather, Safety-Traction Tread, Grip Safe, Super Safety 800, and Safety Master. Moreover, Firestone argued, it had submitted the brand name Safety Champion to the FTC for approval in September 1958 and had received an FTC staff opinion that "we would interpose no objection, provided, of course, that the tire so designated is safe under the conditions outlined

in your letter." In its letter requesting approval, Firestone had stated that "under normal driving conditions, including driving at maximum legal limits on super highways, this tire has exclusive Firestone construction features and will give excellent performance from a safety standpoint."

The Remedy

As noted above, the FTC complaint had requested that an order be issued requiring Firestone to cease and desist from the allegedly deceptive practices described in the complaint. In July 1970, Students Opposed to Unfair Practices (SOUP) had requested permission to intervene in the case on behalf of the public. In essence, SOUP had contended that a cease and desist order would not be an effective remedy in the case since the effects of the allegedly deceptive advertisements would continue to be felt long after the cessation of such advertisements. An appropriate remedy, SOUP had argued, would be for Firestone to admit its previous alleged deception in future advertisements so as to mitigate the residual effects of that deception.

After considerable debate, the five commissioners overruled the hearing examiner, and SOUP was allowed to intervene in the proceedings. SOUP's intervention was limited to the question of remedy. Shortly thereafter, the Association of National Advertisers (ANA) was also granted permission to intervene.

Soup

SOUP was an organization of law students at George Washington University. The stated purpose of SOUP was:

> . . . the protection of consumer interests, and advocacy of their interests before the federal administration agencies. . . . Incorporated as a non-profit organization, SOUP [was] totally independent [;] all decisions concerning policy, strate-

gy, and goals [were] the sole product of a majority vote of its members.

The Campbell Soup Case.

SOUP had first come to public attention in 1969 when it had attempted to intervene in FTC proceedings against Campbell Soup Company. The FTC and Campbell had agreed to a consent order under which Campbell would cease and desist from certain allegedly deceptive practices. In particular, the FTC had alleged that Campbell had exaggerated the quantity of solid ingredients in Campbell soups in certain advertisements by placing marbles at the bottom of the bowl of soup being photographed. In the proposed consent order, Campbell had agreed not to use such advertising techniques in the future.

In a lengthy brief, SOUP had argued that the proposed consent order was not adequate in this case because it did not take account of the way in which modern advertising actually worked. Citing dozens of marketing textbooks, studies of advertising effectiveness, and popular books (e.g., Packard's *The Hidden Persuaders,* McLuhan's *Understanding Media,* and Galbraith's *The New Industrial State*), SOUP argued that advertising was often most effective on a subconscious (subliminal) level and that its effects on consumer behavior often persisted long after the advertisement had been viewed. In a typical passage, SOUP contended:

> Campbell's Soup ads ensure that the message (the product) is impressed in the memory.
>
> Women, according to Francesco Nicosia (a behavioral scientist), are especially prone to learning from pictures rather than from copy.[4] Campbell exploits this proclivity by using distracting pictures, and by symbolizing the message within the picture rather than writing it. Thus, resistance to the message is broken, and the information enters the woman's memory. As described supra by Krugman, eventually the information enters the

[4]Francesco Nicosia, *Consumer Division Processes in the Behavioral Sciences,* 1966, at 165.

subconscious, where it becomes a motivating force in crisis (purchase) situations.

> Besides the fact that Campbell scenes are highly filled with identification, they are also fairly unstructured. That is, very rarely is the bowl of soup so emphasized as to overpower the rest of the scene. Often, the family—e.g., the children or the husband—are as important to the ad as the bowl of soup. The family scene is pleasant, and permits the woman to contemplate the better side of family life. While she is meditating, Campbell's central message—the superiority of its product—is learned without resistance and without consciousness. The woman learns that Campbell's Soups are superior to other soups because of the numerous vegetables (or beans or dumplings) which it contains. By serving soup with such rich garnish, the woman is truly performing well: not only is she feeding her family, she is feeding them soup (with all of its rich connotations); not only is she feeding them soup, she is feeding them the richest and most nutritious brand.

> Thus, women are consciously persuaded to choose Campbell's Soups to attain the image of the appreciated efficient important provider; and they are subconsciously persuaded that Campbell's is a superior brand, though this knowledge may not be realized until after the purchase is made. Campbell's Soup ads have accomplished a prodigious feat in mass persuasion, as verified by increasing sales and earnings.

Because of the nature of Campbell's advertising, SOUP had argued, a cease and desist order would not adequately protect the public interest. Cease and desist orders were not widely publicized, and the public thus had no practical means of learning that it had been deceived. As a result, it would continue to believe that Campbell soups contained more solid ingredients than they in fact did and would continue to buy Campbell soups on the basis of false information.

The only appropriate remedy, according to SOUP, was to inform the consumers who had been deceived. Since the FTC had limited resources, SOUP recommended that Campbell be required in a specified percentage of its advertisements for a specified time period to "affirmatively disclose" that:

> Campbell Soup Company has been charged with deceptive advertising in violation of the Federal Trade Commission Act. Pictured bowls of soup appeared to contain more solid ingredients than a bowl actually contains if prepared according to the dilution directions on the can.

Such affirmative disclosure, SOUP argued, would counteract the effects of the allegedly deceptive advertising and deter such deceptive advertising in the future.

In a split decision, a majority of the FTC commissioners denied SOUP's intervention in this case. According to the majority opinion, the alleged deception, while "tawdry," was not one which warranted the affirmative disclosure proposed by SOUP. Nevertheless, the opinion continued:

> We have no doubt as to the Commission's power to require such affirmative disclosures when such disclosures are reasonably related to the deception found and are required in order to dissipate the effects of that deception. . . . All that is required is that there be a "reasonable relation to the unlawful practice found to exist."

According to a number of observers, the commissioners had, in effect, reasserted their authority to take action which would "remedy" the effects of unfair or deceptive business practices. They had not claimed the right to "punish" a company which had engaged in unfair or deceptive practices or to use the threat of punishment to deter future unfair or deceptive practices. While it was expected that the FTC's authority to require affirmative disclosures would eventually be determined by the U.S. Supreme Court, it was generally believed that hearing examiners would now assume that the FTC had such authority until such time as the courts decided otherwise.

The Firestone Case. As noted above, SOUP had received permission to intervene in the Firestone case. In its brief, SOUP argued that the Commission had the authority to require affirmative disclosure and that affirmative disclosure was both appropriate and necessary in this case. Essentially, SOUP's position was:

> The good will created by the advertising alleged in the complaint to be false is still contributing to Firestone's tire sales.
> 1. Memory, both conscious and unconscious, of [Firestone's] 1967–1968 advertising compaign is still favorably affecting [Firestone's] tire sales.
> 2. Firestone's 1968 advertising will significantly continue to contribute to its sales through 1972 as a result of the lagged effect of its advertising.

In support of this position, SOUP relied heavily on the testimony of three expert witnesses, all of whom testified without compensation. The first to testify was Dr. Darrell B. Lucas, professor of marketing at New York University, author of numerous "standard" marketing texts and monographs, and consultant to many organizations (including ANA). Twenty years previously, Dr. Lucas had studied the ability of consumers to remember advertising claims which had appeared in a single issue of *Life* magazine. In that study, Dr. Lucas had found that at least 20 percent of those who had seen a single advertisement could remember having seen that advertisement when it was shown to them a year later. According to Professor Lucas:

> Individual advertisements differ greatly in memorability and no claim is made for the precision of this memory measurement, but the evidence tended to confirm my judgment that vivid individual advertisements, and especially whole advertising campaigns, can and do leave a lasting impression that is significant. . . .
>
> I think it is important to point out when we talk about the memory of an advertisement or campaign in the conscious sense, that advertising creative people are told to write advertisements which cause people to buy the product, not to remember the specific advertisement. . . .

Dr. Lucas also noted that both economists and advertisers increasingly viewed advertising expenditures as capital investments which were expected "to pay out" well into the future. In addition, he testified that:

> There is a growing body of evidence supporting the psychological theory that advertising has a "sleeper effect."
>
> The meaning of that ["sleeper effect"] is that the impressions which one receives from a source which he doesn't credit as being particularly reliable or important, and often advertising is in that category in the mind of the person exposed, these impressions may carry on and not be accepted fully at the time they are made. But at some later date when one has forgotten the source of the impression, he may assume that it was told to him by a more important source, like a friend or someone who is capable of giving him authentic advice. So he may then accept and act upon impressions or ideas that he would not have accepted or acted upon at the time they were made.

SOUP's second expert witness was Assistant Professor Douglas F. Greer of the University of Maryland. At SOUP's request, Dr. Greer had developed an econometric model which estimated the lagged effects of Firestone's 1968 tire and tube advertising.[5] Using this model, Dr. Greer estimated that "the lagged effect of *all* Firestone's tire and tube advertising in 1968 was approximately 35% in 1969; 12% in 1970; 4% in 1971; and 1.5% in 1972. If 1967 advertising is included, this last figure is increased to 2%." He then testified that:

> These estimates provide rough approximations of the goodwill created by Firestone's advertising in 1967 and 1968 that continued to generate sales.

[5]Under cross-examination, Dr. Greer had stated (1) that he had only a very short period of time to do the work on which his testimony was based; (2) that the model he had used was a relatively unsophisticated model which had been developed many years before for a study of the cigarette industry; (3) that the quality of his work in this case (because of limitations of time and available data) was not such that he would have submitted it to a professional journal; and (4) that Dr. Kuehn (an ANA witness—see later) was one of the world's leading experts in advanced model-building techniques.

. . . It is not possible, with the information and techniques available, . . . to estimate quantitatively the lagged effect of a specific advertising campaign for a specific line of tires.

SOUP's third expert witness was Dr. Harvey Resnik, chief of the Center for Suicide Prevention of the National Institute of Mental Health. Dr. Resnik testified that on the basis of his clinical experience as a psychiatrist specializing in suicidology and high-risk-taking patients, an undetermined but relatively small proportion of the car-driving population could be classified as high-risk takers and that this class of drivers tended to use equipment up to and beyond the limits of what it believed to be its safety. In his opinion, those high-risk takers who believed that the tires were safe and stopped 25 percent quicker could be expected to drive less carefully. In addition, Dr. Resnik testified that an undetermined number of persons who might be classified as average-risk takers and who read and believed that Firestone wide oval tires were safe and would stop 25 percent quicker could also be expected to drive less carefully.

In addition, SOUP argued that Firestone had known that its advertisements were deceptive at the time it had used them. After considerable debate, SOUP had been able to obtain access to a survey of consumer reactions to an *earlier* Firestone advertisement containing language virtually identical to that in the advertisements under consideration. According to this survey:

> 20% of the persons surveyed stated that they thought the idea of a "safe tire" "is the main idea they are trying to get across in this ad."
> When asked "what did you learn from this ad that you didn't know before," 15% stated "quicker stops."
> 93% did not find anything in the advertisement "unbelievable."
> 86% of the persons interviewed said that from this advertisement alone they derived the impression that the tire advertised was "safer than most tires."

SOUP contended that these data demonstrated

that Firestone had *knowingly* engaged in deceptive advertising and that the public should thus have the benefit of any doubt concerning an appropriate remedy.

In conclusion, SOUP asked for an order which would require that Firestone, for a period of 1 year:

> . . . cease and desist [from making] any claims, directly or indirectly, in connection with the advertisement of Firestone tires as to . . . the safety or stopping ability of Firestone tires . . . unless it is clearly and conspicuously disclosed in any such advertisements . . . that the Federal Trade Commission has found that certain of [Firestone's] previous advertisements of Firestone tires were false, misleading or deceptive . . . ; [and] the respects in which . . . [such] advertisements were false, deceptive, or misleading.[6]

ANA's Intervention

The Association of National Advertisers, Inc. (ANA), was a trade association consisting of approximately 500 manufacturers and others who advertised on a national or regional basis. As a leading professional advertising organization, it felt that it should intervene in opposition to SOUP's position, since SOUP's proposal, if adopted, would have important implications for other advertisers. In its brief, ANA essentially argued (1) that the FTC did not have the authority to require affirmative disclosure, (2) that advertising's delayed impact was considerably less than SOUP contended, and (3) that SOUP's proposed remedy, if adopted, would be detrimental to the competitive process.

On the second point, ANA relied heavily on expert witnesses.[7] Its first witness was Dr. Alfred Kuehn, a highly respected econometrician. Dr. Kuehn testified that he had:

[6]This is one of four alternative wordings suggested by SOUP.

[7]According to SOUP, ANA's witnesses were compensated at rates up to $600 per day for time spent in conducting studies, preparing to testify, and testifying.

. . . studied, analyzed, and estimated lagged effects of advertising outlays, and his total research experience establish[ed] that the direct delayed advertising effect is very small compared to the repeat purchase or habit effect . . . [having] an annual delayed effect ranging from zero to approximately 3%, but generally under 1%.

In fact, Dr. Kuehn stated, the lagged effects of advertising were "so small compared to those of other variables that [he] frequently no longer even include[d] lagged advertising as a variable factor in his market analysis and predictive models and studies." Dr. Kuehn also criticized Dr. Greer's econometric model, contending that it was greatly oversimplified and thus attributed effects to advertising which in fact were highly dependent on other variables. In this regard, Dr. Kuehn noted that Dr. Greer's model had originally been developed in a study of the cigarette industry and that advertising had a much greater effect on cigarette sales than it did on tire sales.

ANA then presented evidence through three other witnesses that the great bulk of advertising claims is quickly forgotten. Mr. Ernest A. Rockey of Gallup & Robinson (G&R), a leading marketing research firm, reported the results of a study G&R had conducted at ANA's request. G&R had access to considerable data from previous studies concerning consumers' ability to remember specific advertisements. While these data varied considerably from product category to product category and from specific advertisement to specific advertisement, Mr. Rockey claimed that they demonstrated that the vast majority of consumers could not remember the main features of advertisements they had seen on television or read in magazines the previous day. For example, only 6 to 8 percent of consumers could typically remember the "featured idea" of a television commercial for tires they had seen the night before.

Mr. Charles D. Jacobson of Daniel Starch & Staff, Inc., also a leading marketing research firm, then testified concerning a Starch study conducted in Atlanta, Georgia, in the spring of 1969. In that study, persons who had viewed a particular television channel during a specified 30-minute period had been questioned within 2½ hours concerning a commercial which had been aired during that period. Only 32 percent reported having seen the commercial, and only half of that group (16 percent) were able to identify the brand which had been featured in the commercial.

ANA's next witness was Mr. Edward G. Gerbic, who had 30 years' experience in marketing and advertising for various firms and most recently had been vice president and director of marketing for Johnson & Johnson. Mr. Gerbic agreed with Dr. Lucas that:

> In order for advertising to be profitable it must leave some impression on the respondent's memory until he has an occasion to buy . . . but . . . in actual practice, advertisers consider it pretty hazardous to buy consumer advertising at the wrong time and at the wrong place and in the wrong way. . . . [While] I think in the very nature of things it is possible for one to remember something that made a deep impression on him years ago and for no good reason . . . , such instances . . . do not represent any substantial ratio of the total advertising claims that were made during the same period as they ran. . . .
>
> [Moreover] advertising for infrequently purchased products [such as tires] commands an even lower degree of attention than other kinds of advertising. . . . If one is not in the market for an automobile, or carpeting, or a battery, or a refrigerator, he has a lot more things to do than [to] read advertising for these products. So, instead of five million people, . . . one might actually reach fifty thousand. . . . Of these, how many will remember a month later, or two months later, or three . . .?

ANA's final witness was Mr. Walter Bregman, chief operating officer of Norman, Craig and Kummel, a major advertising agency. Mr. Bregman argued that the adoption of the SOUP proposal would greatly inhibit effective advertising and thus lessen competition:

> We would lean over so far backwards, in my opinion, that much of our advertising would be what we call in the trade compliments-of-a-friend advertising. In other words, we would probably not provide the information—that, as I understand it, is one of the directions, one of the hoped-for benefits—we would not provide the information, as we probably could, because we would be afraid, we would be concerned about it, and I guess we would pull back a little too far.
>
> . . . I can see myself sitting on a creative review committee and saying to someone, I don't think we had better recommend that demonstration because it could be a problem, and I don't want to have to run this advertising for my client in the future or have him run it for himself, even though, in our judgment, that is a perfectly valid claim and we may have support for it—I mean, for example, a genuine product claim.
>
> Under the old guidelines—and I believe most of us, all of us, genuinely believe that what we were saying about a product was honest, ethical, and true—if, for some reason, the guidelines changed, or the rules changed, someone would come to you and say you can't do this anymore, a cease and desist order would be passed or given to us, and we would stop. And that would be that. In this case, if we do this thing, which we in truth believe to be absolutely correct and proper at the time, and subsequent to that time something changes, it is no longer a question of you can't say that anymore—it is now a question of not only you can't say it anymore, but you have to tell people that what you have been saying, presumably, has been found by someone to be deceitful or fraudulent, or whatever. I don't want to be put in that position. It is a great concern to me as an advertising man not to put my client in that position. That is why I would refrain probably, and perhaps incorrectly, but I would probably refrain from getting involved in that closeness to the problem.
>
> I suspect we would end up in areas of very sort of general image, this is a nice product, why don't you buy it, kind of thing. This is what I mean by compliments-of-a-friend advertising.

The Decision

Before he could write his decision, Mr. Hughes, the hearing examiner in the Firestone case, would have to reach a conclusion on four major issues:

1. Were Firestone's July 4th and Labor Day "sale" advertisements deceptive?
2. Was Firestone's "The Safe Tire" advertisement deceptive?
3. Was Firestone's "stop 25% quicker" advertisement deceptive?
4. If he found that any or all of these advertisements had been deceptive, should SOUP's proposed remedy be adopted?.

On the fourth question, Mr. Hughes had already decided to assume that the FTC had the authority to order "affirmative disclosure" if the facts of the case warranted it. While the Supreme Court might later "knock the props out from under his assumption," he believed that such questions were best left to a court higher than his.

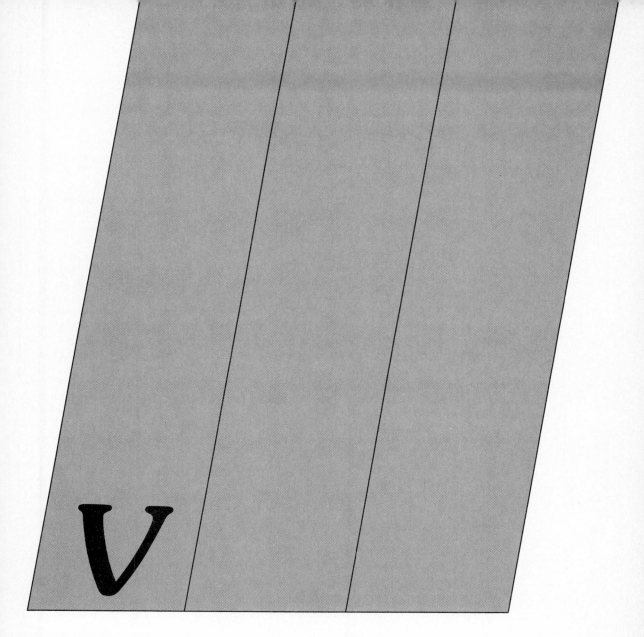

V

Marketing Research

The overall objective of the cases in this section is to provide experience in using marketing research in the design, execution, and evaluation of marketing strategy.

The marketing research process moves through at least four stages, as follows:

1. Specifying information needs
2. Determining optimal data-collection techniques
3. Analyzing data and interpreting results
4. Applying research results

The first step in the process is often the most crucial. Marketing managers must contribute to the research process by specifying information needs that are (1) clearly related to the strategic problem, (2) conceived and stated in a manner which is amenable to research, (3) clearly useful—that is, the manager knows precisely how the results will be used. Some managers avoid these conditions by requesting too much information. The result is an overload of data which have little meaning for the problems at hand. Another danger is asking a question which is so broad that it is hardly amenable to research and will end up having little impact on the marketing program. For example, a manager might wish to explore a market prior to new-product introduction. Simply asking "What makes consumers buy product X?" is not very useful. It is not possible for research to provide simple answers to exceedingly complex questions! On the other hand, the manager might believe that consumer acceptance for product X may vary by income level and that acceptance depends on favorable attitudes toward the product. If this is the case, one would want to assess attitudes toward competing or comparable existing products among various income groups in order to determine potential market acceptance. The question then becomes "What are the attitudes among low-, medium-, and high-income groups toward products which would compete with product X?" This question is considerably more focused and clear, and it is based on some a priori thinking by the manager about what information is needed and how it will be used.

A final difficulty in specifying information needs is the expectation that the "research specialist" should be able to filter and translate management's information needs into actionable and useful research. While it is true that research managers should be expected to be more familiar with research procedures, it is unreasonable to expect the researcher to provide clear and useful information if the precise information needs and their implications for marketing problems are not clearly communicated. It becomes important, then, for marketing managers and research specialists to interact in formulating information needs. Too often, communication between marketing managers and research specialists is imperfect, owing to differences in their career goals, attitudes, performance measures, and experience. Nonetheless, the relationship should be a symbiotic one, with marketing managers articulating strategic issues and related information needs and market researchers working to assure the definition of researchable problems.

The second stage involves information-gathering techniques. The options run from small-scale "qualitative" research in which individuals or small groups are asked a focused series of questions concerning attitudes toward a product or an advertising message, for example, to large-scale "quantitative" studies involving telephone, mail, or personal surveys of individual consumers. Information can be gathered, as well, from existing or "secondary" sources such as census data. There is also the option of gathering information from sales records and commercial market information services.

A third research approach is to conduct an "experiment" in a test market. This approach, which is considerably more costly, lengthy, and difficult to administer than qualitative or survey approaches, might involve, for example, the testing of two different advertising campaigns in two test markets. Just as one must take care to design surveys to avoid bias, one must be cautious with test market experiments. The cities must be reasonably "matched" in terms of characteristics which might affect responses to the test advertising. For example, they should have nearly identical levels of brand familiarity, sales, distribution, and competitive activity.

Another kind of experiment might be employed to test several versions of a product. It involves exposing target consumers to different product configurations, under different conditions. For example, the marketer might give one group of consumers price information before showing them the product, while a second group of consumers is not given price information in advance. Such data could be used to evaluate how price information affects judgments of the product.

The choice of an information-gathering technique depends on several factors. First, is the information already available from some source? For example, a marketer can purchase data on a brand's warehouse or supermarket sales from existing firms which provide periodic sales audits. A second consideration is the kind of information required. If a marketer wishes to quickly have in-depth information from target consumers regarding a new appliance feature, group interviews might be used, since these allow for qualitative in-depth analysis of consumers' perceptions and judgments. Also, consumers can actually see and try the new feature. On the other hand, if a marketer needs information from broad groups of consumers—as in a segmentation study, for example—a large-scale mail, telephone, or personal survey might be used. Such a survey involves the careful selection of a sample to be interviewed and the construction of a questionnaire which is free from bias and appropriate for quantitative analysis of the information obtained.

The third stage in the research process involves analyzing data and interpreting results. No attempt is made here to cover the range of multivariate or modeling approaches prevalent in marketing research today. Such an overview is beyond the scope of these cases. Rather, an attempt is made to familiarize students with the logic of data analysis and interpretation. Some cases in this section raise issues concerning how research results should be interpreted in the light of the way in which questions were worded, the character of the respondent group, and the setting in which the questionnaires were administered. Other cases require the assessment of information gathered by different means; they focus on the issues involved in integrating research results gathered via several different methods.

Finally, all the cases require decisions about how results should be used. Frequently, one would like more information before making strategic decisions, but it is important to realize that information needs must be evaluated against the costs that would be incurred in terms of time and money. Perhaps more important, the cases suggest that all research approaches have limitations but that the lack of "perfect" information cannot be an excuse for failing to make decisions based on the information at hand. Indeed, the goal of these cases is to provide experience in the art of blending management intuition, research results, and the manager's skills in creatively using the research process.

33 Multiple Sclerosis Society

Thomas S. Robertson • Scott Ward •
Steven L. Diamond

"I still don't see that we have the package that's going to motivate people to sit down and write us a check for $3," explained Nick Arnao, executive director of the Washington, D.C., chapter of the National Multiple Sclerosis Society, in response to the new family membership concept.

As envisioned, this membership idea was intended to provide the unifying theme for all fund-raising efforts of the Washington chapter. The family would provide the basic unit of solicitation. In return for each contribution of $3 or more, the family would receive a 1-year membership to the Multiple Sclerosis Society. The benefits of membership, in turn, would include a subscription to the chapter's quarterly newsletter reviewing its activities and progress,

Thomas S. Robertson and Scott Ward are professors of marketing at the Wharton School, University of Pennsylvania. Steven L. Diamond was formerly a research associate at the Harvard Graduate School of Business Administration.

and an opportunity to vote for the chapter's board of directors.

Arnao, along with Tom Bendorf, director of commercial and international programs for Lockheed Aircraft and a member of the chapter's board of trustees, had been in search of a vehicle for increasing the MS Society's fund-raising effectiveness in the Washington, D.C., area. "Fund raising is like any other marketing-oriented business," Arnao continued. "We have a product to sell—hope, I guess you'd call it—and we must convince our customer, the contributor, that his or her dollar is better spent here than on the Heart Fund, the Cancer Society, or some other product."

Fund raising is, in fact, a very big business. Religious, educational, health, human resource, civil, and cultural causes generated contributions totaling $17.6 billion in 1969. Of this total, $2.9 billion (or 16.2 percent) was shared by health and hospital agencies, according to the American Association of Fund Raising Council.

EXHIBIT 1
STATEMENTS OF CHANGES IN FUND BALANCES
Year Ended December 31, 1969

	General fund	Research fund	Fellowship and scholarship fund	International Federation of Multiple Sclerosis Societies fund	Total
Balances at January 1, 1969	$1,020,960	$ 12,574	$13,701	$37,478	$1,084,713
Receipts:					
Contributions from chapters	2,083,623	442,368	6,013		2,532,004
Dues and contributions from members and others	119,262	188,405	100	1,415	309,182
Legacies and bequests		208,004			208,004
Federal Services campaign for national health agencies	17,979				17,979
Interest and other	39,746				39,746
Total receipts	2,260,610	838,777	6,113	1,415	3,106,915
	$3,281,570	$ 851,351	$19,814	$38,893	$4,191,628
Disbursements and transfers:					
Program services:					
Research	$ 182,760	$1,046,653			$1,229,413
Professional education and training	180,235		$87,625	$10,000	277,860
Patient services	288,004			10,000	298,004
Community services	115,437				115,437
Public education	354,367			10,000	364,367
Total program services	$1,120,803	$1,046,653	$87,625	$30,000	$2,285,081
Supporting services:					
Fund raising	$ 310,723				$ 310,723
Management and general	275,847				275,847
Total supporting services	$ 586,570				$ 586,570
Transfers from (to) fund	$ 548,884	($ 472,884)	($76,000)		–
Total disbursements and transfers	$2,256,257	$ 573,769	$11,625	$30,000	$2,871,651
Balances at December 31, 1969	$1,025,313	$ 277,582	$ 8,189	$ 8,893	$1,319,977

Note: Expenses have been allocated to various classifications on the basis of time records and/or estimates made by the society.

Headquarters Operations

The National Multiple Sclerosis Society, head-quartered in New York, ranked eleventh among the national health agencies, having raised $7.4 million in fiscal 1969. According to the society's *Annual Report,* about 9 percent of these funds came from legacies and bequests, while the remainder was generated from the contributing public. In turn, total contributions were divided according to a standard formula whereby approximately 60 percent was shared by the local chapters and the remaining 40 percent was used by the national headquarters.

A large part of the Multiple Sclerosis Society's budget was committed to research (Exhibit 1) because of the very limited body of medical knowledge about the disease. Neither the cause, prevention, nor cure for MS had yet been identified. Educational and promotional literature regarding the disease, therefore, took on a symptomatic orientation, explaining that "Multiple Sclerosis is a continuing disabling disease of the brain and spinal cord that causes paralysis and other disturbances of nerve impulses which control such bodily functions as walking, talking and seeing." One typical brochure, which was distributed by volunteers during house-to-house fund-raising drives, is illustrated in Exhibit 2.

The Washington Chapter's Activities

While the headquarters' staff centered its concern on administrative and research-oriented activities, the focus of the local chapters was of a somewhat different nature. The Washington office, exempted from medical research activities by the society's charter, was very much involved in public education efforts and service programs for MS patients. Working with the support of national headquarters, the Washington staff issued various educationally oriented public relations and advertising materials, which were carried by local mass media at no charge. Attention in the public education field was also directed at physicians to encourage early diagnosis of MS.

Patient services, the other primary thrust of

EXHIBIT 2
MULTIPLE SCLEROSIS SOCIETY BROCHURE

"Neurological ailments add up to the leading cause of permanent disability and the third cause of death in the United States."
U.S. PUBLIC HEALTH SERVICE

What is MS?

Multiple sclerosis is a neurological disease—a disease of the central nervous system—the brain and spinal cord. It is not a mental disease, nor is it contagious.

The brain and spinal cord control such important body functions as walking, talking, seeing, hearing, eating, tying a shoe lace, opening a door. These functions are controlled by impulses from the brain and spinal cord. The impulses travel along nerves in the brain and spinal cord, then to other parts of the body. The nerves are coated by a material called myelin. When the disease hits, patches of myelin disintegrate, being replaced by scar tissue. Why this happens, or how, is a medical mystery. But when it does happen, impulses have trouble getting by the scarred spots; there is interference. And with interference come malfunctions—the danger signals of MS.

EXHIBIT 2
Continued

What to watch for

MS danger signals are many and unpredictable. They are often mistaken for signs of other disorders. Each symptom—by itself—could be a sign of other ailments.

But, warns the Society's Medical Advisory Board, a combination of three or more symptoms such as those listed below, appearing at once, or in succession, *could* be MS danger signals. Never ignore such signals—*see* your doctor at once. It may very well *not be* MS. But let your doctor tell you—don't guess.

Here are danger signals that could mean MS:

Partial or complete paralysis of parts of the body
Numbness in parts of the body
Double or otherwise defective vision such as involuntary movements of eyeballs
Noticeable dragging of one or both feet
Severe bladder or bowel trouble (loss of control)
Speech difficulties such as slurring
Staggering or loss of balance (MS patients erroneously are thought to be intoxicated)
Extreme weakness or fatigue
Pricking sensation in parts of the body, like pins and needles
Loss of coordination
Tremors of hands

Of special significance is the unexplained disappearance of one or more of these symptoms either permanently or temporarily. At times symptoms may disappear for periods of several years and occasionally may never return.

What can be done?

While no specific treatment exists, the patient can and should be treated. Good general medical care devoted to prevention of upper respiratory and other infections is recommended. Braces may be prescribed at times for stabilizing useable limbs and the physician may consider massage, passive or active exercise, and other physical measures suitable for assuring the greatest effort on the part of the patient to continue active. Nursing needs of wide variation and long duration must be expected. The early establishment of good patterns of care, fullest use of the physical and other resources available and avoidance of fatigue and emotional or physical stress is important.

What help is available?

When MS strikes, families can turn to their local chapter of the National Multiple Sclerosis Society for information, sympathetic help and guidance. Chapters can make available many specific services including aids to daily living, social, recreational and friendly visiting opportunities, professional counseling to alleviate social and psychological pressures and medical guidance through the chapter's medical advisory committee.

The progress made in the Society's programs of basic and clinical research and professional education brings hope and help through the dissemination of accurate, valid, authentic information.

Source: Multiple Sclerosis Facts, March 1969, pp. 1–4.

the chapter's efforts, covered a wide spectrum of activities. Because MS is a crippling disease, medical equipment and care cover only part of the services required by the patient. In addition, various peripheral, supportive needs relating to transportation, house design, welfare, child care, social activities, and psychiatric family problems were supported by the Washington chapter.

In 1969 the chapter allocated $292,000 in disbursements among the following activities.

Washington Chapter—Funds Usage

	Percentage of total disbursements (1969)	
Program services	27.8	
Medical and related patient services		17.1
Public and professional education and training programs		7.9
Community services		2.8
Supporting services	72.2	
Headquarters allocation		40.0
Research and development campaign (to headquarters)		3.6
Fund-raising expenditure		17.2
Management and general overhead		11.4
Total	100.0	100.0

Chapter Fund-Raising Efforts

In order to support this vast array of services, fund-raising efforts took on a paramount role in chapter operations.[1] The Combined Federal Campaign, a coordinated solicitation of federal employees performed by the Washington MS office in partnership with other health and service agencies, provided one substantial source of funding, contributing 40 percent of the chapter's income. Although this combined effort

[1]The attention of the Washington staff had traditionally been directed at individual givers because corporate contributions—common in other large cities—were only moderate in the government-dominated Washington area.

had been judged quite successful by MS management, it was determined some time ago that additional partnership arrangements were relatively ineffective. Accordingly, the idea of membership in the local United Fund Drive, for example, was rejected.

Instead, considerable emphasis had been placed on the annual residential house-to-house campaign. Because effective timing was thought to play such an essential role in the giving process, the 12 largest national health agencies had each designated a different month for their bell-ringing campaigns. The Multiple Sclerosis Society held its annual drive between Mother's Day and Father's Day, with the rationale that MS attacks people between the ages of 20 and 40—young mothers and fathers. In the Washington metropolitan area, 10,000 volunteers were canvassed by professional telephone solicitors, and each was assigned an area in which to solicit donations. This effort generated about 26 percent of the chapter's total funding.

Special gift solicitation, referring to contributions of $25 or more, was also conducted on an annual basis concurrently with the door-to-door efforts. This program was conducted primarily by mail, although Nick Arnao believed that personal follow-up efforts could raise this source of income above the 4 percent of total contributions level being generated. Similar thinking also applied to legacies and bequests, which contributed 6 percent of total income.

Additional funds came from a donor renewal campaign developed by the Washington chapter. Under this system, former contributors were reminded that they had not donated to the society within the past year and were encouraged to write checks. About 2,000 solicitations were mailed monthly out of the Washington office, and experience showed a return of approximately 20 percent. Interestingly, however, renewal contributions normally doubled so that the $3 giver of last year became the $5 or $6 giver of this year. Because of this, the chapter had succeeded in raising 14 percent of its total income, projecting current figures at an annual rate.

Finally, the chapter conducted a number of special events which provided 10 percent of its income. An annual fashion show luncheon and a children's Christmas banquet were the most successful and well known of these functions.

This combination of fund-raising efforts had proved reasonably effective in the Washington area. The National Multiple Sclerosis Society generated about 3 cents per capita on a nation-wide basis, whereas the District of Columbia chapter generated about 10 cents per person in the Washington region. While per capita dona-tions in Washington exceeded the national aver-age, MS ranked third among health agencies in dollars raised in the Washington area, compared with a ranking of eleventh nationally. Tom Bendorf and Nick Arnao believed that the critical components in a fund-raising effort included (1) the leadership, (2) the cause, (3) the volunteers, (4) the contributors, and (5) the dynamics of advertising, public relations, and other promo-tions. "Actually, it's just like any other corpora-tion," Arnao explained. "We need leadership to function effectively; we need a good cause which is our product; we need an army of volunteers who are our sales representatives; we need contributors, our customers; and we need the dynamics or the marketing package."

Motivations for Giving

In attempting to revamp its fund-raising package in search of additional contributions, the MS management team reflected on its experiences with people's motivations for giving. It identified four prime motivations which it believed seg-mented its market.

The first and most common type of motiva-tion was the *nuisance gift.* In this case, people were thought to donate solely because a volun-teer was standing at the door with a canister. The cause really did not matter here, for supposedly

if contributors were asked what organization they gave money to just an hour after donating, they would generally be unable to remember. Gifts in the nuisance category normally ranged from $1 to $5—a standard contribution which many families would hand over to any volunteer who rang the doorbell.

A second and closely related motivation for giving emanated from the fund-raising precept that *people give to people,* not to causes. Thus, the degree of need which a given charity could demonstrate really became irrelevant. Rather, the person on the poster or the volunteer at the door was thought to hold the key to effective solicitation. In order to evoke people's emotions on a personal level, the MS Society's poster featured a 25-year-old former runner-up for the Miss Kansas title. The cover of the society's *Annual Report* showed photographs of her posing in a swimsuit at the Miss Kansas competi-tion and then seated in a wheelchair after she was afflicted with MS. This approach was thought to be effective because people could sympathize with this person and in turn were led to contribute. Similarly, the giver's relationship to the solicitor was also of vital importance. "When you get a letter from a friend or a visit from a neighbor, it's much more difficult to say 'no' than it is if the letter is printed by a computer or a stranger knocks on your door," Nick Arnao explained.

Unlike the previous two motivations for giv-ing, the third motivational category was com-posed of donors who were thought to be very responsive to the nature of the cause. In this case, the so-called *"captive givers"* contributed because members of the family or friends had been afflicted by a particular disease, and they wished to aid in its prevention and cure. Neither Bendorf nor Arnao believed that these donors were especially receptive to particular types of appeals but both felt that if given the opportuni-ty, they would contribute to the cause no matter what the format of the appeal.

The final motivational category, according to

Bendorf and Arnao, was *self-interest* giving. In this case, usually found at higher income and giving levels, the donors offered their contribution in search of some direct benefit for themselves. At the upper levels, the solicitor must usually make a clear demonstration of some return for the giver. The rationale in this case could take various forms: political or business benefits, the return of a favor, the purchase of a ticket for a fashion show or a benefit.

Other Opinions on Motivations

Others had additional ideas regarding the reasons why people donated to charities. Dr. Sidney J. Levy of Social Research, Inc., reached the following conclusions,[2] based on research in this area:

> When people are asked to donate money to a worthy cause, their reactions are not based solely on whether they understand the need. They are being asked to join in a collective action, to give a sign of recognizing a common bond. Their involvement will grow out of many possible motives. These can be phrased in innumerable ways and at various levels. Being part of the group supporting a particular cause may reflect wishes for:
>
> the feeling of belonging and status
> the protection from real or fantasied threat
> the enhancement of self-esteem
> internalizing group standards in exchange for love
>   and protection received
> diverting undue aggressiveness onto real evils
>
> In more direct and personal terms, this means that people give because of a hierarchy of reasons and goals. The most intense participation and giving usually relate to an emotional awareness due to an afflicted loved one; a wish to be influential in the community; personal anxiety

[2]From Sidney J. Levy, *The Myth of Communication,* a talk presented at the national convention of the United Cerebral Palsy Organizations in Chicago on November 15, 1960. A more complete summary of Dr. Levy's findings is reprinted in the "Appendix."

about being sick or deprived; wanting approval in face-to-face relations; and finding it a convenient avenue for demonstrating competence or power-seeking.

Dr. Ernest Dichter of the Institute for Motivational Research related his interpretation of motivations for giving to action-oriented suggestions:

Practical Uses of Motivations for Giving[3]

NEEDED: TOUGHER THINKING ABOUT "SWEET CHARITY"

Most thinking about raising and dispensing money—be it charity organizations or social welfare operations—is unrealistic. Either too one-sided: "How do we get that guy to make a contribution?" Or too likely to preach conventional axioms about duty. We also assume that recipients of "charity" are sure to be made happy—while actually the unskillfully given contribution can easily backfire and have negative results. Policy-makers should consider such human motivations in giving and receiving as these:

The "disease" of poverty. Many people subconsciously fear that poverty will contaminate them. The act of giving (making one's self a little bit poorer) reminds one that, with a little bad luck, one might be as badly off as those to whom the contribution is made. Fund-raising appeals should recognize this secret fear of involvement—and, if possible, switch the emphasis from "charity" to "smart business."

Fear of embarrassment also inhibits giving. In everyday life, people are afraid of over- or under-tipping. This same fear of not behaving properly also applies to fund-raising: is one acting like too hard or too easy a mark . . . how to decide how much to give and to whom, etc.

"Psychological income taxes." Fund-raisers should point out that giving helps relieve guilt feelings. Tell people they've done some good—and now deserve to go out and enjoy themselves. Or, if they've had some good luck that doesn't

[3]Excerpted from *Findings,* vol. 4, no. 2, February 1968, pp. 2 and 3.

seem to have been earned, a contribution will allay that guilt feeling. If you've paid your "taxes."

Giving goes both ways. The donor is dissatisfied if he doesn't receive something too. What the donor really wants is approval—or self-approval, really. If he's not told he's a great guy or given some concrete symbol of his accomplishment in giving, he may not give again. For instance, we found that pictures of happy children ("Win the gift of these children's smiles") are more effective in soliciting aid than pictures of starving, miserable ones.

Competitive giving. It's possible that giving could be promoted as a way of competing and earning prestige, just as much as through job titles, buying big houses and boats.

"From a friend." Although a gift is supposed to be a result of love, too often it appears to come from a large, impersonal, nonlove sort of organization. Needed are "personalities" or symbols to establish contact between giver and receiver.

The Importance of Image as a Motivator

As the MS management team reflected further, it decided that while the cause may not be a primary determinant of giving behavior among some donors, it remained essential that the charitable organization maintain an attractive image in order to appeal to a broad spectrum of potential donors. In line with this reasoning it reviewed the components which its members considered essential for a strong image. The first element mentioned was the product itself—The National Multiple Sclerosis Society. While they believed that smaller contributions could be generated no matter what the cause, substantial mass efforts and larger gift programs were thought to require some evidence of the worthiness of the cause.

But merely having a worthwhile objective clearly was not adequate for the development of an effective image. Thus, credibility and a sound reputation constituted the second vital element in image building. Specifically, if people were to be made to feel that their contributions were

meaningful, they would first have to have reason to believe that their donations—however small—would be used wisely and effectively. "Once you give someone reason to believe that his or her money isn't being used as you said it would be, that person will never give you another penny," Nick Arnao explained.

Accordingly, Arnao operated his office with a moderate budget and low overhead and made every effort to convey a sense of administrative efficiency to the Washington community. A meal costing only $3 instead of $6 was often served as a $25-a-plate fund-raising dinner. The reasoning behind this "reverse psychology," as he called it, was that the appearance of efficiency was more important to many contributors than was the nature of the banquet. Thus, a $6-a-plate dinner might make people feel that their contributions were being squandered, while the lesser meal provided a sense of gratification for many givers.

Finally, Arnao explained his belief that even the most selfless giver is in fact selfish:

> Our job as fund raisers for Multiple Sclerosis is to sell hope. But we don't just sell hope for the patient; we also offer a motivation for the donor. Namely, we say—although not in so many words—that your contribution of $1, $10, $100 or whatever will indirectly buy you and your family a certain element of *safety*. That is, if you give to M.S., then we in turn will do everything we can through our medical research programs to prevent this disease from striking you. You can call it "hope" or "safety" or "preventability," but whatever you call it—it sells!

Gaps in the Marketing Program

In reviewing the current status of the Washington chapter's fund-raising efforts, Arnao and Bendorf recognized that their marketing package suffered two weak links. First, their product— that is, hope for a better understanding of a cause, the prevention and cure of multiple sclerosis—suffered by comparison with its competitors. Second, they noted that a decidedly imbalanced fund-raising record had developed, showing great strength in the predominantly white metropolitan Washington suburbs and a corresponding weakness in the penetration of the largely black core city.

Competitive Disadvantages

In comparing the salability of the MS cause with that of the causes of other charitable organizations, it was found that the MS Society had these disadvantages:

1. While the MS Society was selling hope just as the other national health agencies were, medical research efforts had been largely discouraging thus far. Therefore, although MS management believed that researchers might be nearing the frontiers of a major breakthrough, it was difficult to bring this message to the public year after year without producing any tangible signs of progress. On the one hand, the society boasted of its efforts to date (Exhibit 3), while on the other

it was forced to admit, "Many theories as to the cause of MS have been advanced over the years. Although some solid clues have been developed, no single fact yet explains why multiple sclerosis behaves as it does."

This lack of research progress had substantial repercussions on the society's fund-raising efforts. The Heart Fund and the Cancer Society predicated their fund-raising programs on effective public education messages. The Cancer Society, for example, could offer a prospective contributor a printed card listing the seven danger signals of cancer. This information had meaning to the prospect and was believed to increase both the number of donors and the size of contributions. The Multiple Sclerosis Society, for lack of definitive research findings, however, could not appeal along similar educational lines.

2. While heart disease affected about 21 million people and cancer struck over 1 million each year in the United States, the incidence of multiple sclerosis was substantially lower—

EXHIBIT 3
A SAMPLE OF NEWSPAPER ARTICLES ON MULTIPLE SCLEROSIS

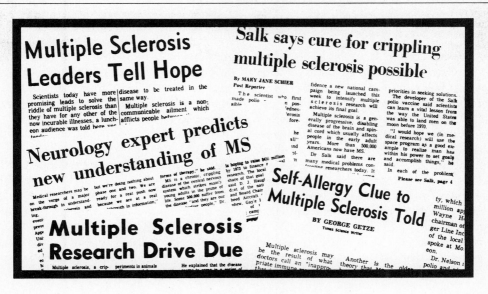

approximately 500,000 Americans had been diagnosed as having MS or related diseases. This incidence factor in and of itself meant that far fewer people knew MS victims than cancer or heart victims. In turn, public education and the elicitation of emotional and financial support became relatively more difficult for the MS Society than for other agencies.

3. It was well known that children elicited more sympathy on posters and in advertisements than did adults. Multiple sclerosis, however, did not strike until people reached the 20-to-40 age bracket. Although MS had come to be known as "the crippler of young adults," this did not evoke as much sympathy as a child in a wheelchair.

4. The emotional appeal of a health-oriented cause was heightened if the disease was a killer. Although people respond to the idea of a young man or woman going through life as a cripple, the message was not as potent as are messages which relate to terminal afflictions.

For these reasons, multiple sclerosis lost some degree of appeal as a fund-raising cause relative to other charities.

Weak Record in Black Areas

The MS Washington, D.C., chapter faced a second problem—weak penetration among Washington's black population. Studies conducted comparing various segments of the metropolitan Washington population across such lines as contributions per capita, number of MS patients per thousand people, and dollars spent on patient services per thousand people indicated that the Washington chapter had been decidedly less effective in the black communities of the core city than in predominantly white suburban areas.

The reasons for this differential, however, were unclear. "I really don't know what our image is in the black community," Nick Arnao explained. "Our recorded patient population in the central city is off in terms of total population, and so is the giving record. Maybe there's a correlation there. We know that blacks do give to charities; just look at their record of giving to churches. But I frankly can't tell you why we're not reaching them."

It was agreed that increased effectiveness among Washington's blacks should be a high-priority goal for the local chapter. First, the low MS patient population count in these areas was thought to be the result of poor diagnosis and bad communications. If the organization was to serve as intended, then clearly it would be necessary to identify the multiple sclerosis victims in the area. Providing medical and supportive services would be a second objective—a badly needed and costly one. Finally, in order to support these added efforts as well as its other functions within the metropolitan area, the Washington chapter would need to improve substantially its fund-raising effectiveness within the black community.

Because the black population constituted about 70 percent of Washington's total population and approximately one-fourth of the chapter's market, the scope of this task would be a large one. Efforts were under way to determine the image of the MS organization in the black community by talking to local black leaders. At the same time, a fund-raising strategy was being developed to generate additional funds from blacks, which could then be used in black communities for public education programs and patient services.

The Family Membership Concept

In attempting to design a program which would overcome the Multiple Sclerosis Society's intrinsic competitive disadvantages as well as its poor fund-raising record in predominantly black areas, MS management began by reviewing its past fund-raising efforts.

It was noted that much the same appeal had been used by MS and many charitable organizations over the years. Specifically, fund-raising messages had shown MS victims in pathetic roles. Possibly a more hopeful message with a greater self-interest appeal would be a welcome relief from the concentration on human suffering.

Arnao and Bendorf also reviewed giving patterns in the Washington metropolitan area. Here they found that although their market consisted of a total population of about 2 million people, only 30 percent (or 600,000) were actively contributing to health and welfare organizations. Moreover, while the total fund-raising receipts among these charities approached the $20 million level annually, about 80 percent of these dollars were generated by a far smaller "givers community" of about 50,000 people, or only 2.5 percent of the total metropolitan population. Figures for the Washington chapter closely followed this pattern. Disposable income statistics, however, indicated a much broader but thus far untapped market for fund-raising efforts.

Arnao and Bendorf conceived the idea, on the basis of these observations, of developing a marketing program geared around a family membership plan. Under this arrangement, all 500,000 families in the metropolitan area would be solicited for $3 contributions, in return for which they would be given a 1-year membership in the National Multiple Sclerosis Society. This membership concept was not a new one, but it had never before been actively sold to the giving public, nor had the approach ever been used on a broad, mass-appeal basis.

A tentative enrollment goal was set for the new program to enlist 100,000 families, a 20 percent market share, over the next 2 years. Using this plan as the basis for all fund-raising efforts, MS management hoped to reach an admittedly high goal of $500,000 in annual contributions by 1973 and $1 million in yearly donations by the late 1970s. While still cautious about the concept, Nick Arnao felt that it held an attractive appeal:

> We're no longer emphasizing the sickly and unpleasant aspects of the disease. Instead, we'll talk in terms of supporting research—a preventative approach. And in addition, we're giving something—a membership in our organization. It may not be much, but at least we're developing a two-way giving process where you give and you get at the same time.

Tom Bendorf elaborated further, talking in terms of finding a market niche:

> We're offering a good bargain charity opportunity where people can do something for somebody else without pain to themselves. The number of people who will give until it hurts is minimal; there aren't very many really charitable people. At the $3 level you don't have to demonstrate that it's painless. They understand that. Here's where you're really appealing to people's sense of charity and selflessness.

The Mechanics of the Plan

Under the new program, members would receive a quarterly publication of the Washington MS Society, geared specifically to the membership population. In addition, they would be invited to attend the chapter's annual meeting and would have voting privileges for the board of trustees. While Nick did not feel that these benefits in and of themselves would attract givers at the $3 level, he did believe that an appeal to people's sense of belonging could be effective.

The basic fund-raising vehicles—door-to-door solicitation, the Combined Federal Campaign, the annual fashion show luncheon and children's Christmas festival, the special gift campaigns—would all be employed as before. In all these cases, however, a theme would be added. That is, all fund-raising efforts emanating from the Washington office would be geared to the membership concept.

In order to reach effectively a greater number of potential contributors, Bendorf envisioned the utilization of one new fund-raising tool for the family membership plan. The chain letter concept, as he referred to it, would be used to compound solicitation results through a process by which givers would also act as solicitors. Under this plan, each member of the Washington MS Society would send out requests for $3 membership contributions to approximately 100 friends, neighbors, relatives, and business acquaintances. Included in this mailing would be additional materials which recipients would be asked to send to five more families.

The philosophy behind this process would be one of asking people to give not because the MS Society needed the money, but because someone they knew had asked them to give. Attractive envelopes, handwritten addresses, postage stamps rather than metered envelopes, and perhaps a card on which the solicitor could write a short note would be used to make the appeal more personal.

To supplement this initial chain letter mailing, additional solicitation letters would also be sent out. Neither Bendorf nor Arnao saw any need to segment their market for these purposes. They felt that given their objective of a mass appeal, their resources would be better spent in search of quantity rather than in attempts to appeal to various market segments. "We have all kinds of lists—past givers, social registers, contributions to other charities—but for our purposes here I think the telephone book will probably be our best bet," Arnao explained. "On a broad appeal such as this, we don't need to get a contribution from everyone. If we use the phone book it will be much easier to reach a greater number of families."

While door-to-door solicitations would remain an integral part of fund-raising tactics, mail efforts would play an increasingly larger role under the new program. The rationale behind this shift reflected MS management's concern that too much of the contributed dollar was being eaten up by fund-raising expenses. Specifically, the chapter's experience had shown that volunteer campaigns cost 25 cents per dollar raised, while the corresponding cost of mail solicitations was only about 20 cents. Thus, from a cost-benefit standpoint, mail solicitations appeared more attractive.

Ultimately, Arnao hoped to build a substantial listing of one-time givers and to follow up on each of these families with appeals for repeat gifts. He believed that people could be conditioned to respond to charitable solicitations and that if they were approached in the proper manner, they could be called on annually (or perhaps even more frequently). If in fact such was the case, and if his prior experience with repeat donors who sometimes doubled the size of their original contributions held true, then increasing memberships today could certainly be expected to have attractive repercussions for years to come.

The Dilemma

There was some management dissension regarding the proposed membership plan. Tom Bendorf believed that they had developed the essentials of a package which would substantially increase fund-raising results, but Nick Arnao viewed the new plan with some hesitancy. "It's a new idea, something which has never been tried by any MS chapter, or any charitable organization at all for that matter. I don't think it's a high-risk strategy because we'll still be pursuing the same types of campaigns; they'll just be oriented to a larger market and they'll carry a theme.

"I'm not sure," he continued, "that this mass-market approach is the answer. It looks awfully attractive when you talk in terms of 500,000 families, but when you get down to the costs you run into another problem. It costs us as much to process a $3 contribution as it does to process a $3,000 donation. If we spend an average of $1 on processing, solicitation efforts, pamphlets and on our magazine for members, we come up with only a $2 margin. While this margin should be increased over time, it will take an awful lot of $3 contributions for that to add up to anything significant."

Finally, Arnao was concerned about the membership concept as a motivator. He concluded on a note of skepticism: "When we talk about membership, the one part that's missing in the puzzle is the 'grabber.' That is, what's going to motivate the average guy, John Jones, who doesn't know what MS is and never knew anyone who had the disease, to sit down and write out a check for three bucks? Tom thinks we have that motivation already, but I don't see it."

Appendix
Humanized Appeals in Fund Raising[4]

What Motivates People?

An understanding of what motivates people to respond to appeals for money has application to any type of fund drive, whether for a church, a school, a health organization, a community fund or a political party. Motivation research indicates that people—either as individuals or corporations—usually are guided both by a sense of duty and by their own self-interest—often without realizing it—in deciding whether to give much, little, or not at all. And self-interest may range from an individual's unconscious (and certainly unexpressed) wish to impress the neighbors all the way to the corporation's conscious wish to affect an entire community favorably.

Other motives for giving: buying a place in heaven; repentance and forgiveness for sins; insurance for good luck; a personal sense of well-being and generosity; to do one's duty; to be kind to the underdog; to achieve membership in desired groups.

All of these motives apply to willingness to participate actively in fund-raising work and should be taken into account when volunteer committees are being organized.

Two Factors to Watch

Two corollary factors, in addition to basic motives, are bound up in the entire giving process.

1. People have been taught to give but not *how* to give. They consider charity to be a moral obligation, but find it difficult to decide how much to give and how to allocate their donations among the various causes soliciting their support. The necessity to make these decisions reduces the gratification

that otherwise goes with giving. Payroll deduction plans often are welcomed because they relieve the donor of the necessity of deciding how much to give to whom.

Corporations and upper middle class people are exceptions to the uncertainty factor. They often give consideration to income tax deductions in determining the amount they will give.

2. Patterns of giving are seldom formed on a basis of logical planning but, once established, they are likely to be continued. The majority of people (those in the middle and lower income groups) continue to give to the same five or six charities year after year, usually giving similar amounts each year.

In an economic recession period, they will be ashamed to reduce their donations and therefore may drop the charity entirely. At such times, public relations men must take care that their appeals do not arouse anxieties that would trigger this reaction. The tendency to give the same amount each year also must be taken into account when attempts must be made to increase donations to meet rising costs of charity operations.

* * * * *

People give most readily to causes that have a personal or emotional meaning to them. They feel obliged to give to other causes, much as they are obliged to pay taxes. These obligatory commitments are made because the project is considered worthy and necessary, not because the donor expects to receive any direct value or even great personal satisfaction.

The hierarchy of loyalties goes like this:

1. The church.
2. Fraternal organizations and other socially purposeful groups, such as schools, with which the donor or his family is associated.

3. Emotionally related organizations such as health groups, orphanages and old people's homes with which the donor can identify present or prospective interests.
4. Obligatory commitments, such as the Red Cross or Community Chest, which the donor feels he has to support regardless of personal considerations.

In each of the first three groups the personal motivation is extremely strong. People recognize the church emotionally. Rationally, they say that individuals are its only means of support and that its existence is essential to the family, the individual and the moral welfare of the community and the world. Socially, the church offers an important in-group, a support that is especially important for minority group members.

Fraternal organizations, schools, colleges, and, to some extent, political parties, provide a "this is mine" incentive. People support groups to which they belong as a matter of prestige, as well as for the opportunity to associate with like-minded people. A college graduate wants his alma mater to be recognized as a leader, whether academically or on the football field. He also wants his children's school to provide the best possible educational facilities.

"Preventive" Giving

Health groups receive strong support because a relative or friend has died of heart disease or cancer or polio—or because these are real threats to the individual and the public. Orphanages have a strong emotional appeal to people with many young children. Old people's homes and welfare groups are important to those nearing old age themselves.

Supporting such organizations constitutes a kind of "preventive" giving, with anticipation of concrete results that may, conceivably, save one's own life or that of others in the future.

* * * * *

Our studies indicate that the communications should emphasize feelings of individuals, rather than formal needs. The unhappiness of deprived children, their joy in freedom from sordid pressures, the sympathy of helpful adults, the happiness of a reconciled family—all are far more persuasive than a "big picture" approach based on dollar quotes and how money will be divided among agencies.

In money raising, as in vote getting, the doorbell approach is unsurpassed. People find it extremely difficult to say no to a personal request. The same person-to-person effect can be achieved by direct mail, if a solicitation letter is signed by someone known to the recipient. Even when signed by a stranger, a letter forces the recipient to make a conscious decision whether to write a check or throw the letter away. This is a situation he does not face when merely reading about a fund drive in a newspaper, although the right kind of publicity will have aroused his sympathy for the object of the drive.

* * * * *

Whether people are asked to give money or time or both to fund-raising drives, their response is conditioned by their attitudes toward the particular fund-raising group. Attitudes toward charities can be changed or strengthened, just as attitudes toward products can be changed or strengthened by applying the various techniques of public relations.

34 Wolff Drug Company: I

Stephen A. Greyser

Marketing executives at the Wolff Drug Company were examining several recent marketing research reports concerning the relative importance of different sources of drug information for doctors. They thought that the research would be particularly relevant to the allocation of promotional funds between advertising to physicians and "detailing" them, via sales representatives, as effective methods of informing and persuading doctors to use Wolff drugs.

The drug company detailer is a professional representative who calls regularly on physicians

Stephen A. Greyser is a professor of business administration at the Harvard Graduate School of Business Administration.

in their offices to provide them with information on drug products. While detailing primarily focuses on introducing new products to doctors, the detailer also distributes drug samples, literature, and reprints of articles. In addition, the detailer disseminates information on newly developed uses for drug products already in existence. Detailers do not generally sell direct to doctors. Though not doctors themselves, they typically have pharmaceutical or medical training. They are informed of current medical topics via company bulletins and journal articles and have a full knowledge of company products, policies, and practices. Their work is considered essential because in many instances the doctors must prescribe a particular drug for patient use. Detailers are viewed as respected information disseminators by physicians, although not as authorities in their own right.

Prominent among the many other known influences affecting doctors' drug selection are medical journal articles and advertising, professional colleagues, direct mail, drug product samples, and personal experience. In order to acquire data on which of these sources doctors consider most important, researchers for Wolff Drug conducted interviews of 632 physicians at two medical conventions during the previous summer. The questioning was performed without company identification, and respondents remained anonymous. The results of this survey are tabulated below.

Doctors Learn about Drugs from Many Different Sources. Which Three Sources on This List Are Most Important to You in Learning about Drugs? Which Three Are Least Important?

	Most important	Least important
Total physicians interviewed	632	632
1. Journal articles	78%	5%
2. Colleagues	75	47
Other specialists	(37)	(17)
Other practitioners	(38)	(30)
3. Detailers	53	23
4. Personal experience	52	10
5. Drug samples	23	36
6. Article reprints	19	32
7. Drug company literature	19	54
8. Journal advertising	14	49
9. Direct mail	8	76

Percentages add to more than 100 because of multiple answers.

Four hundred ninety interviews at AMA convention; 142 at West Virginia medical meeting.

While the executives realized that samples might vary widely, separate tabulations of the AMA and West Virginia results revealed an identical relative ranking of the different sources. (The AMA group was mainly an urban physician group; the West Virginia group was mostly a rural physician group.)

Shortly after receiving the results of the company-conducted survey, the marketing research director received a study performed for the American Medical Association in the same general area of investigation. The study, carried out by an independent research organization, was based on personal, structured interviews during the preceding winter with a "representative national cross section of 1,011 practicing physicians." The organization claimed that its findings were true within 1 to 2 percent of the total United States physician population.

The questions and tabulated responses follow.

I'd Like to Have You Think of the Brand Name of the Drug Which You Most Recently Prescribed for the First Time.

Where Did You Happen to Get the Information Which Led You to Prescribe It? Anywhere Else?

Total physicians interviewed	1,011
Detailer; sales representative	48%
Direct mail	20
Medical journals	17
Received sample	10
Other doctors who have knowledge of product	8
In residency training, medical meetings, conventions	3
Druggists; hospital pharmacists	2
Magazines (not medical)	1
Tested it for manufacturer	1
Patient asked about it	1
Other (all less than 1%)	5
Don't recall	18

Percentages add to more than 100 because of multiple answers.

This question was followed immediately by three related questions, which the doctor answered with the aid of a list.

So Many New Drugs Are Being Developed Today That It Is Getting Harder for a Physician to Keep Current. Which Two or Three of the Sources Listed Here Do You Find Most Important to You Personally in Familiarizing Yourself with New Drugs?

Which Two or Three Sources on the List Would You Say Are Probably Most Effective with Most Doctors?

Which Two or Three Sources on the List Would You Say Are Probably Least Effective with Most Doctors?

	Most important personally	Most effective generally	Least effective generally
Total physicians interviewed	1,011	1,011	1,011
Detailers	58%	65%	5%
Journal papers, articles	40	30	7
Medical journal ads	32	26	18
Direct mail	25	23	35
Doctor conversations	24	19	10
Drug samples	22	20	11
Staff meetings, hospital, clinic	16	12	20
National conventions	15	10	19
County meetings	4	3	32
Druggists	3	2	39
Other	4	1	1

Percentages add to more than 100 because of multiple answers.

After studying these results, the marketing research director was disturbed over the disparity in the ranking order of sources of drug information as found by the two surveys. He hoped that he would be able to reconcile the apparent conflict by a closer examination of the research material.

35 *Wolff Drug Company: II*

Stephen A. Greyser

Executives of the Wolff Drug Company were involved in designing a test to ascertain the benefits, if any, which would result from an increase in the company's detailing force. Previous research[1] had indicated that detailers played an important role in the process of drug introduction, but available evidence varied concerning the extent of that influence, both as among drug firms' own promotional methods (e.g., direct mail and medical journal advertising) and as among all information sources (e.g., journal articles and colleagues). Regardless of how great an influence detailers had on physicians' prescription behavior, there still remained the question of whether the limit of that influence might have been reached. It was hoped that answers to some of these questions would be forthcoming from the test. Research findings on doctors indicate that detailers and the information which they bring to the physician are believed and that many doctors look to the detailers for certain information. However, doctors do not regard detailers as authorities in their own right.

The drug company detailers are professional representatives who call regularly on physicians and drugstores in their assigned areas to provide them with information on drug products. Doctor detailing centers on stimulating the use of new and also, to some extent, older products. In addition to providing information directly, detailers distribute drug samples, literature, and reprints of articles appearing in medical journals. Detailers also disseminate information on new uses which have been developed for drugs already in existence. Detailers do not generally sell direct to doctors. Although detailers are not actually doctors themselves, they usually have pharmaceutical training or some medical training. They are kept informed of current medical news via company bulletins and journal articles, and they have a full knowledge of company

Stephen A. Greyser is a professor of business administration at the Harvard Graduate School of Business Administration.

[1]See "Wolff Drug Company: I."

products, policies, and practices. Because in most instances the doctors themselves determine the particular drug for patient use, the detailers' missionary efforts are considered highly important.

Wolff Drug estimated the cost of paying a detailer and supporting his or her activities in the field at approximately $2,500 a month. Because of the additional effort involved in training a new person, the cost for the first several months of detailing work would be somewhat higher.

The Wolff Drug Company divided its nationwide sales area into territories designated as Sales Control Units. Each SCU was a territory normally covered by a single detailer. The total number of SCUs was 500, and they were assigned to about 400 detailers, of whom 100 covered two territories each.[2] About 30 division managers supervised the detailing force.

Sales Control Units varied in size and by the number and types of doctors. For example, the island of Manhattan consisted of several SCUs, while a large geographic segment of a sparsely populated state constituted a single SCU. Except in places where large numbers of doctors were congregated, SCUs included some urban and some suburban or rural territory. In establishing the limits of SCUs, the company used a doctor classification system based on estimated prescription volume in order to channel the intensity of coverage along a desired pattern. Other factors, such as the specialties of the doctors and administrative convenience, were also taken into account in mapping detailing districts.

Wolff's doctor classification system embraced four categories. Physicians in category A were to be seen every 4 to 8 weeks. Those in category B were to be visited once every 8 to 12 weeks. Doctors in category C were scheduled for detailing calls every 6 months, and physicians in category D were seen once a year. Each district also included 80 to 150 drugstores, which were

also visited with varying frequency, averaging about once a month. The source of the information for categorizing doctors was the detailers themselves.

In designing the test, it had been decided after much consideration to double the detailing in the experimental situations, although obviously there existed the possibility of testing the importance of detailers by making other changes in the intensity of their coverage. Indeed, a recently circulated trade rumor was that one large drug firm had dropped a number of detailers in Long Island and "had never noticed the difference." Marketing executives at Wolff realized that "doubling the detailing" involved a number of complications regardless of how the doubling was accomplished. One suggestion that was made was to add a detailer, either experienced or new, to a territory's already established detailing force. Another plan was to reduce an established detailer's territory to one-half its former size and either add a person to cover the remainder of the district or leave it open for the duration of the test.

Wolff's current plans for the eventual expansion of its detail force programmed a gradual increase toward a one-for-one detailer-SCU relationship. However, it had not been determined whether the increase should be applied entirely to the present double-SCU territories or spread throughout the country. In developing any new detailer, either within the framework of the experimental situation or in general, it was recognized that a period of several months in the field was required before a relatively high level of proficiency would be attained by a new person.

Wolff officials also decided that the drug products involved in the experimentation should be from the two product classes in which it was most interested. Neither of these drug classes would be likely to have its sales affected appreciably by the occurrence of an epidemic during the course of the test.

The typical promotional pattern for a Wolff drug included the use of direct mail to physi-

[2]The two-SCU districts tended to be concentrated in the less populated areas.

cians, advertisements in medical journals, the distribution of samples by detailers, and specific detailing attention. Detailers usually had two or three drugs which they emphasized to doctors while making their calls during a given month. At the time of the test, roughly equal expenditures were being made on detailing activities and on all other promotional means.

Having decided on doubling the detail force for the experiment, and having determined the two drugs on which to concentrate, Wolff marketing executives were faced with the problems of what to measure, how to measure it and for how long, and in what locations to conduct the test.

Wolff factory sales figures were currently broken down on the basis of SCUs. About half of the factory shipments were sales direct to drugstores or chains; the other half went to wholesalers, who then supplied the smaller drug outlets. Sales to wholesalers whose areas of distribution extended into more than one SCU were prorated into those SCUs. No inventory adjustments were made, inasmuch as no information was available about retail inventory lagtime or on wholesale inventory fluctuation. It was known that substantial regional differences existed as to both sales per doctor and sales per capita within the same drug class and for the same drug. Moreover, individual and seasonal patterns were reasonably well known and for purposes of the experiment could be treated as known.

As for sales at retail, Wolff could purchase information from two available commercial auditing services. One was a national audit of retail drug sales. For a $90 fixed charge plus $25 per audit, Wolff Drug Company could be supplied with a drugstore's net retail sales of all products in several product classes, or with a count of the prescription volume for all products in several product classes. It was estimated that about 25 percent of the drugstores in any given SCU accounted for approximately 75 percent of total drug prescription sales.

There was also available a prescription audit service, which kept on file a card for every prescription filled by a national sample of 1,000 of the 50,000 United States drugstores. These cards were filed once monthly, within month-by-product class and within product class by product. Approximately 5,000 cards monthly were made up for prescriptions of drugs in the two product classes of major interest to Wolff. A considerable amount of work would have to be done before the available material could be put on punched cards in a form useful for analysis. The audit service owning the prescription records offered to supply the material in punched card form. However, the Wolff Drug Company would have to commit itself to this service for a 12-month period, at a cost of $4,500. Wolff Drug was not a regular subscriber to the firm's service.

A further possibility was to measure direct sales to those large drugstores which had direct accounts with Wolff. However, no information was available on the inventory lag in these stores. It was assumed that this lag would be less than in the instances of the wholesalers.

The total funds which Wolff had allocated to the detailing experiment were about $25,000, exclusive of hiring new detailers.

36 Grey Advertising Canada Dry Account

Craig E. Cline • Scott Ward • Edward T. Popper

The main topic on the agenda of the weekly management board meeting at Grey Advertising was the agency's Canada Dry Mixers account. Canada Dry had assigned the multimillion-dollar advertising account for its mixers product line 2 years ago to Grey, one of the 10 largest United States agencies in terms of client billings. Grey subsequently developed a new advertising campaign for the account, "America's Going Dry," that was built around a prohibition-era theme (see Exhibit 1). Canada Dry Ginger Ale (the primary mixer product) sales had grown by over 8 percent over the past 2 years, but this growth had been necessary just to keep pace with the expanding mixer and soft drink market. Canada Dry Ginger Ale's market share had remained stable, but both the actual volume and the

Craig E. Cline is a former research assistant at the Harvard Graduate School of Business Administration. Scott Ward is a professor of marketing at the Wharton School, University of Pennsylvania. Edward T. Popper is an assistant professor of marketing at the College of Business Administration, University of Florida.

market share for other Canada Dry mixers had declined (see Exhibit 2).

At the meeting it was agreed that Canada Dry had three basic alternatives for the future marketing and advertising strategies of its mixer line:

1. To continue to position its product line as a quality line of mixers, expand its mixer line, and continue the "America's Going Dry" campaign
2. To position Canada Dry Ginger Ale as a soft drink and compete head to head with the major soft drink producers, such as Coca-Cola, Pepsi-Cola, and Seven-Up
2. To remain a major mixer producer, but to also expand its position to include some soft drink orientation

Whichever alternative was chosen would be launched by a series of advertising spots on national television over a 4-week period, costing $2 million. But both the client and the agency agreed that consumer research was needed to develop an effective marketing campaign. The

EXHIBIT 1

CLIENT:	Canada Dry Corporation
PRODUCT:	Canada Dry Ginger Ale
COMML. NO.:	055-01-713-8
TITLE:	"Movie Set"
TIME:	60 sec

ACTOR:	Oh, please be mine, Irene. Be mine.
ACTRESS:	But, sweet sweet Prince . . . your father thinks I'm a golddigger!
DIRECTOR:	Cut! Cut! Dohling . . . that was superb . . . you were brilliant!
ACTRESS:	Yeah . . . but these lights is killin' me. Ain't the stuff come yet? I'm thirsty!
MOB GIRL:	Here you are . . . special delivery . . . Canada Dry Straight Ginger Ale.
ACTRESS:	Ooooooohh!
MOB BOSS:	Just listen to these bubbles!
ACTRESS (VO):	Rat-a-tat-tat . . . Rat-a-tat-tat . . .
ACTRESS:	It's the . . . Ginger Ale with a jolt.
BABY FACE:	Sure it's got a real bang bang flavor.
ACTOR:	The stars tell me . . . America's Going Dry!
MOB BOSS:	With Canada Dry Ginger Ale, . . . Regular or Diet.
MOB:	It's the Thirst Killer!
EVERYONE:	Canada Dry . . . Rat-a-tat . . . Rat-a-tat!
EVERYONE:	(VO) Canada Dry . . . Rat-a-tat . . . Rat-a-tat! Canada Dry . . . Rat-a-tat-tat! Rat-a-tat!

task fell to Ms. Jessica Swann, executive vice president and director of research studies.

Canada Dry Corporation

Canada Dry was a nationwide marketer of a premium line of mixers and soft drinks, with sales of 127 million cases (24 eight-ounce bottles each) in 1968. The company was one of nine major national carbonated-beverage producers but also competed against 23 regional, local, and private-label competitors. Together, these 32 carbonated-beverage producers sold more than 3.8 billion cases (24 eight-ounce bottles each) in 1968.[1] (See Exhibit 2.)

Of this total of 3.8 billion cases, 140 million cases were classified in the trade as "mixers," including ginger ale, tonic water, and soda

[1]Nationally, two-thirds of the soft drink volume generally were colas.

EXHIBIT 2
CARBONATED-BEVERAGE CONSUMPTION

	1966		1967		1968 (estimated)	
	Million cases*	SOM†	Million cases*	SOM†	Million cases*	SOM†
National						
Canada Dry Corporation						
Ginger Ale	35.0	1.1	37.0	1.0	40.0	1.1
Wink	20.0	0.6	20.0	0.6	15.0	0.4
Soda Water	18.0	0.5	16.0	0.5	15.0	0.4
Tonic and Bitter Lemon	12.0	0.4	10.0	0.3	10.0	0.3
Other‡	45.0	1.3	45.0	1.3	47.0	1.2
Total	130.0	3.9	128.0	3.7	127.0	3.4
Coca-Cola Company	1,240.0	37.6	1,380.0	39.4	1,558.0	40.7
Pepsi Company, Inc.	595.0	18.0	620.0	17.7	672.0	17.5
Royal Crown Cola Company	262.0	7.9	270.0	7.7	290.0	7.6
Seven-Up Company	200.0	6.1	200.0	5.7	226.0	5.9
Dr Pepper Company	97.0	7.6	100.0	2.9	117.0	3.1
Beverages International	80.0	2.4	96.0	2.7	115.0	3.0
Cott Corporation	61.0	1.9	68.9	2.0	83.1	2.2
Schweppes	10.0	0.3	11.0	0.3	11.0	0.3
Regional and local						
Nesbitt Food Corporation	50.0	1.5	64.0	1.8	70.0	1.8
Moxie-Monarch-NuGrade						
Company	43.0	1.3	49.0	1.4	53.2	1.4
Shasta	27.0	0.8	31.0	0.9	38.4	1.0
Dad's Root Beer Company	13.5	0.4	19.0	0.5	23.8	0.6
Frank's Beverages	14.0	0.4	19.0	0.5	21.0	0.5
Mason & Mason	18.5	0.6	19.2	0.6	21.4	0.5
White Rock Corporation	17.5	0.5	19.5	0.6	21.5	0.6
Big K (Kroger)			11.9	0.3	18.0	0.5
Double Cola					20.0	0.5
Grape Company	18.0	0.5	19.0	0.5	19.0	0.5
Yukon (A&P)			9.2	0.3	13.0	0.3
Cragmont (Safeway)			7.0	0.2	10.0	0.3
11 others	404.5	12.2	354.3	10.2	294.6	7.8
Grand total	**3,300.0**	**100.0**	**3,500.0**	**100.0**	**3,830.0**	**100.0**

*Case = 1 case of twenty-four 8-ounce bottles.
†Share of total carbonated-beverage market.
‡Includes all Canada Dry soft drinks, such as Jamaica Cola and root beer.

water; some definitions included flavored beverages such as bitter lemon and grapefruit as "mixers," although these could be classified as either mixers or soft drinks. Ginger ale was the largest in sales volume, roughly equal to the combined volume for tonic and soda water. Unlike soft drinks, which were marketed on a national basis by Coca-Cola, Pepsi-Cola, and several other companies, mixers had only one national brand—Canada Dry (although Schweppes was making a bid for national distribution and consumer recognition).

Canada Dry's mixer line[2] included Ginger

[2]Canada Dry also marketed soft drinks, including a cola product (Jamaica Cola) and other fruit-flavored soft drinks.

Ale, Soda Water, Tonic (Quinine Water), and Bitter Lemon. Wink (a grapefruit-flavored drink) was considered to be both a mixer and a soft drink. Plans were under way for expanding the mixer line to include Bitter Orange, Collins Mix, and other "premixed" cocktail mixers. Canada Dry's 1968 shares of the mixer market (based on volume) for its three major mixer products— Ginger Ale, Tonic Water, and Soda Water—were 34.7 percent, 43.5 percent, and 52.9 percent, respectively.[3] A Diet Ginger Ale was also marketed.

In 1968, Canada Dry had 170 franchised bottlers in the United States as well as eight company-owned and -operated bottling plants, each with exclusive geographic marketing areas. Bottlers were responsible for the production and distribution of their products. More than two-thirds of all soft drinks were sold through food outlets, such as supermarkets and other grocery stores. The remaining one-third was sold in nonfood outlets, such as vending machines, hotels, bars, liquor stores, and restaurants. Canada Dry's sales were equally divided between grocery stores and liquor stores. Its bottlers therefore had had to develop sales contacts in the liquor stores as well as establish more frequent deliveries, since liquor stores (typically) were not large enough to inventory large supplies of mixers. Consequently, it was difficult to obtain accurate data on liquor store sales.

On the other hand, supermarket sales data were easily obtainable. Since soft drinks and mixers were a highly profitable category for supermarkets in spite of their large shelf-space requirements (see Exhibit 3), supermarkets were prone to using these products in price promotions. Mixers were especially useful for this purpose, since soda and tonic water, as well as ginger ale, had seasonal fluctuations, with holi-

days sparking high sales periods. Consequently, mixer price promotions drew people into the store on occasions when they were likely to be making larger than average grocery purchases.

Competitive Environment

Canada Dry competed not only against other mixers and soft drinks but also against beverages such as milk, juice, coffee, beer, and tea. And, of course, because Canada Dry's products were used as mixers, its sales were directly related to liquor consumption.

The carbonated-beverage industry was a beneficiary of a life-style and eating habit change that had shifted beverage consumption patterns. Carbonated-beverage consumption had increased dramatically since the turn of the century, especially during the 1960s, when per capita consumption increased by over 50 percent:

Per Capita Consumption in the United States: 1960 and 1968 (Gallons)

	1960	1968
Carbonated beverages	17.5	28.5
Coffee	40.0	36.5
Milk	28.5	24.0
Beer	15.0	16.5
Distilled spirits	1.2	1.8

Canada Dry, however, did not benefit from these increases as much as other beverages. It owed a substantial portion of its usage to the mixer market and thus was tied to the distilled-spirit market.

The tie to liquor consumption had a significant impact on Canada Dry sales, making them seasonal and dependent on consumer drinking habits. A large portion of mixer sales occurred during the Christmas holiday period, reflecting the surge in holiday parties. Moreover, tonic tended to be tied to clear-spirits consumption

---

[3]Ginger ale accounted for approximately 3.17 percent of the total United States carbonated-beverage volume; soda and tonic water for about 1.41 percent combined.

EXHIBIT 3
SOFT DRINKS AND MIXERS: NATIONAL SUPERMARKET PERFORMANCE, 1968

	Sales		Profit			Assortment: items/brands sizes at warehouse	Average gross margin (percentage of retail)
	Percentage of department sales	Dollar volume (millions)	Percentage of department's gross profit	Gross profit dollars (millions)			
Carbonated soft drinks:							
Regular bottled	68.0	620.1	64.9	143.2		NA	23.1
Regular cans	14.7	134.1	15.2	33.6		17	25.0
Low-calorie	9.7	88.4	9.8	21.6		17	24.5
Carbonated mixers:							
Powders, presweetened	4.6	41.9	6.2	13.8		11	32.6
Powders, regular	1.7	15.5	2.0	4.4		17	28.5
Ice bar mixers	0.3	2.8	0.5	1.1		4	40.3
Syrups	0.2	1.8	0.2	0.4		4	24.2
Tablets	0.2	1.8	0.2	0.4		4	24.2
Nonalcoholic cocktail mixers:							
Liquid	0.5	4.6	0.9	2.0		7	43.6
Powdered	0.1	0.9	0.1	0.2		1	24.2
Total	100.0	911.9	100.0	220.7			24.2

Percentage of total store volume: 1.69%
Percentage of gross profit: 1.92%
NA = not ascertainable

(gin, vodka, rum), which was higher during the summer. While the total consumption of distilled spirits had been increasing gradually, changes in the composition of liquor sales volumes had also affected Canada Dry mixer sales. The decrease in the volume of blended and bonded whiskey sold had reduced the consumption of ginger ale (which, as a mixer, was primarily mixed with whiskey). The effects of this trend were somewhat offset, however, by an increase in scotch, gin, and vodka sales, which had led to increased club soda and tonic usage (Exhibit 4).

EXHIBIT 4
DISTILLED SPIRITS ENTERING TRADE CHANNELS
IN MILLIONS OF WINE GALLONS

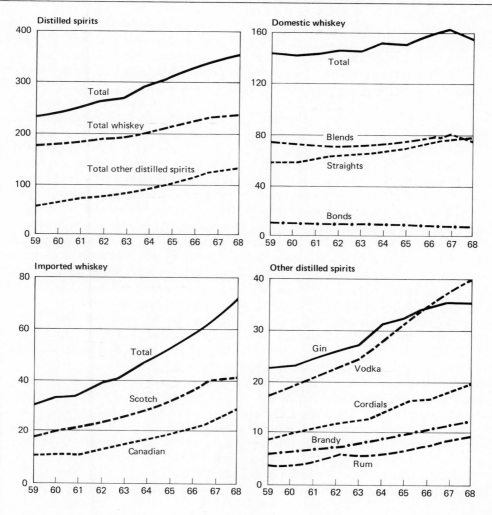

The Mixer Market

The mixer market was highly competitive, and Canada Dry had to compete nationally, regionally, and locally. Mixer usage varied geographically, with usage in the Northeast, for example, ranking higher than usage in the Midwest. But Ms. Swann felt that the largest single factor complicating the competitive environment in the mixer market was the consumer's perception of the product. In her opinion, consumers could not see or taste significant differences between competing mixer brands. Tonic and soda water resembled "water," and all mixers had their tastes diluted by the liquor added to them. The consumer, therefore, tended to consider mixers as a "commodity" and consequently bought national, regional, local, or private label brands interchangeably. The consumer, she thought, was also "very responsive" to price promotions.

Another agency executive cited several additional factors that in his view reinforced the consumer's perception of mixers as a commodity product. Since both bottler and dealer margins were high (especially for food outlets) and bottlers used little or no extract in the manufacture of mixers, the mixers were frequently the target of severe price competition. And because of the ease of manufacture, more local bottlers prepared mixers, especially for use at commercial bars where the brand name was rarely seen. Furthermore, the increased use of carbonated-beverage dispensing units behind the bar reduced commercial sales of nationally branded mixers.

In spite of these factors, agency executives felt that there was a position in the marketplace for premium quality mixers. Mr. Edward Pointsman, executive vice president and director of client services, pointed to the success of Schweppes mixers as an indication of the public's willingness to demand quality mixers as a symbol of taste and quality when entertaining in the home and as an assurance of quality when ordering mixed beverages away from home. He also thought that Canada Dry's mixers could be positioned in the market as soft drinks:

> Even though mixers are brought into a consumer's house as a mixer initially, they frequently get used as soft drinks. When people are thirsty, they will drink everything they have on hand. Canada Dry's mixers have a very small piece of a large pie. So it might be possible to position ginger ale as a soft drink without hurting its image as a quality mixer.

Advertising and Promotion

In addition to supplying extract and packaging materials to its bottlers, Canada Dry was responsible for generating a demand for its product. This was accomplished through a major national and local advertising program, which was administered by Canada Dry and funded jointly by the company and its bottlers. Each year, Canada Dry executives met with their bottlers individually and presented the national advertising and promotion campaign. Each bottler was then assessed a portion of the national advertising and promotional costs (which were prorated for the bottler's marketing area on the basis of share of national population). This cost was evenly divided between Canada Dry and the bottler. Canada Dry also presented a recommendation for local advertising and promotion that was shared equally by the bottler and the company. The dealer had the option of increasing or decreasing the local program. The company shared the cost of any local program as long as the bottler's program was an extension of the national program (each bottler was provided with an extensive selection of fully prepared advertisements and commercials to choose from). Canada Dry's national agency, Grey Advertising, was responsible for placing the ads. However, if the bottler chose to run materials other than those of the national campaign, it had to bear all the costs of its campaign.

Brand selection of beverages was highly sensitive to advertising, and so major investments in advertising and promotion were necessary simply to remain competitive in the marketplace. With the high volume of advertising and promotion being sustained by all factions of the beverage industry in 1968 (Exhibit 5), establishing a distinct brand image was essential for cutting through commercial clutter. For Canada Dry, the problem was even more difficult. Clearly, it would be difficult to compete directly for visibility as a soft drink against Coca-Cola, which outspent Canada Dry by a rate of four to one. Establishing a brand identity as a mixer was a far easier task that Canada Dry had been successfully doing since its inception. Yet, in 1965 and 1966 its position as the quality premium brand was being challenged nationally by Schweppes and regionally by White Rock for the first time.

As the largest of the mixer companies, Canada Dry might benefit substantially from a campaign to generate primary demand. Yet even that course was fraught with problems. Creating primary demand would also benefit competitors, especially local and private-label brands that could compete on the basis of price and lure customers away from Canada Dry at the point of sale.

The "America's Going Dry" Ad Campaign

The uncertainty surrounding the positioning of its mixer line had been largely responsible for Canada Dry assigning its mixer account to Grey Advertising. After evaluating the products and their competitive environment, Grey decided to strengthen the company's premium image. Grey's objectives were to convince consumers that they were not getting the best product if they were not being served Canada Dry mixers, that serving mixers other than Canada Dry was not socially acceptable, and that Canada Dry was the highest quality line of mixers on the market.

The vehicles for communicating this message were ads and commercials built around the theme "America's Going Dry." By using models dressed in styles reminiscent of B-movie versions of prohibition mobsters and molls, Canada Dry's ads and commercials were able to describe a product that was designed to be mixed with alcoholic beverages without ever mentioning the latter directly. This was pivotal to the strategy, since commercials were specifically prohibited from explicitly mentioning alcoholic beverages or their consumption. Although this requirement did not apply to print advertising, the campaign was used in all media for the sake of consistency.

Grey tested this campaign, as it tested all campaigns, to determine how successful it was in accomplishing a number of basic tasks. The agency measured a variety of responses to test commercials that were exposed to samples of respondents under clinical conditions. These responses included attention (measured by unobtrusively observing respondents' eye movements during exposure), recall and comprehension of copy points, and attitude change. The last variable was obtained by comparing respondent attitudes toward Canada Dry products before exposure to the commercial with the attitudes after exposure. The "America's Going Dry" campaign performed extremely well against all these criteria.

Ms. Swann's Research Project

As she reviewed the sales and competitive situation, Ms. Swann wondered how changing liquor consumption patterns would affect future mixer sales. In fact, what impact would the changes in life-style, eating habits, and general beverage consumption have on Canada Dry's mixer line? What was needed, Ms. Swann decided, was a full picture of Canada Dry and soft drink consumers—what they thought about Canada Dry and its products, what they thought about soft drinks and mixers, and, most important, what motivated them to purchase each. Were there different groups of soft drink consumers? How did they differ? And, how could

EXHIBIT 5
1968 CONSUMER MEDIA EXPENDITURE ANALYSIS*
Selected Soft Drink, Beer, and Liquor Companies

(handwritten annotation: "Ad $ extremely high")

	Total advertising dollars	Newspaper Dollars	% Total	General magazine Dollars	% Total	Spot TV Dollars	% Total	Other Dollars	% Total
Soft drinks									
Coca-Cola Co.	55,992,564	2,631,651	4.7	3,527,532	6.3	29,900,029	53.4	38,941	0.1
PepsiCo	38,940,890	1,557,636	4.0	1,635,517	4.2	12,850,493	33.0		
Canada Dry Corp.	13,000,000	2,080,000	16.0	4,056,000	31.2	3,068,000	23.6		
Seven-Up Co.	15,808,951	727,212	4.6	189,707	1.2	8,758,159	55.4		
Royal Crown Cola Co.	12,988,426	246,780	1.9	25,977	0.2	5,909,734	45.5		
Beer									
Jos. Schlitz Brewing Co.	17,707,628	212,492	1.2	726,013	4.1	8,127,801	45.9		
Anheuser-Busch, Inc.	15,785,072	426,197	2.7	3,078,089	19.5	2,572,967	16.3		
Falstaff Brewing Co.	9,287,061	371,482	4.0	1,263,040	13.6	4,615,669	49.7		
Pabst Brewing Co.	9,070,908	54,425	0.6			5,687,459	62.7		
Liquor									
Distillers Corp.—Seagrams Ltd.	46,353,367	12,608,115	27.2	25,077,171	54.1	1,019,774	2.2		
Heublein, Inc.	18,330,533	2,382,969	13.0	5,865,771	32.0	3,079,530	16.8		
National Distillers	16,504,682	4,340,731	26.3	8,516,416	51.6	49,514	0.3		
Hiram Walker	14,536,530	5,858,403	40.3	6,788,560	46.7				

	National TV Dollars	% Total	Spot radio Dollars	% Total	Outdoor Dollars	% Total	Business Dollars	% Total
Soft drink								
Coca-Cola, Co.	8,342,892	14.9	9,686,714	17.3	1,343,822	2.4	559,926	1.0
PepsiCo	12,149,557	31.2	8,995,346	23.1	1,285,049	3.3	428,350	1.1
Canada Dry Corp.			2,496,000	19.2	1,144,000	8.8	169,000	1.3
Seven-Up Co.	2,150,017	13.6	3,272,453	20.7	553,313	3.5	158,090	1.0
Royal Crown Cola Co.	2,104,125	16.2	4,065,377	31.3	597,468	4.6	51,954	0.4
Beer								
Jos. Schlitz Brewing Co.	4,179,000	23.6	4,302,954	24.3	159,369	0.9		
Anheuser-Busch, Inc.	3,267,510	20.7	4,840,728	31.3	1,168,095	7.4	331,487	2.1
Falstaff Brewing Co.	92,871	1.0	2,126,737	22.9	817,261	8.8		
Pabst Brewing Co.	1,886,749	20.8	8,898,020	9.9	544,254	6.0		
Liquor								
Distillers Corp.—Seagrams Ltd.					6,767,592	14.6	834,361	1.8
Heublein, Inc.	3,061,199	16.7	1,778,062	9.7	2,071,350	11.3	91,653	0.5
National Distillers					2,574,730	15.6	1,023,290	6.2
Hiram Walker					1,642,628	11.3	247,121	1.7

their differences be turned into opportunities for Canada Dry?

The executives at Canada Dry agreed with Ms. Swann's assessment of their needs for consumer research data and authorized her to proceed with a major study of the carbonated-beverage market. The project was designed to help Canada Dry answer the following questions:

What should Canada Dry's corporate strategy be, in terms of product emphasis within the existing product line?
What is the relative potential for each of the existing Canada Dry brands?
What should Canada Dry's brand strategy be?
    Positioning:
        Should Ginger Ale be positioned as a soft drink only, or as a mixer as well?
        Should Ginger Ale compete against other ginger ale brands only, or should it seek expansion against other beverage types?
        Can Ginger Ale compete against all types of beverages, or only selected ones?
        Should mixers be promoted independently or within the same framework as Ginger Ale?
    Target market:
        What group of consumers represents the best target market for each brand?
    Buying incentive:
        What appeals should be used in advertising to appeal to the target market?
    Advertising impression:
        What impression and "flavor" should advertising strive for? How does current advertising fit in with the desired direction?

The study was designed in two stages—the first a group of in-depth interviews to develop the ideas, directions, and question wording to be used in the second stage, which would be a national survey of consumers' attitudes, perceptions, and motivations. This survey would be based on a probability sample so that results could be generalized for the entire United States.

In the first stage, 20 "depth interviews" were conducted with men, women, and teenagers in the metropolitan New York area. In depth interviews, a trained interviewer meets individually with a consumer and determines the consumer's range of feelings about a product by using a relatively unstructured interview format that could last for 2 to 3 hours. The objective was to develop a "phrase list" of product associations applicable to ginger ale and other soft drink consumption that could then be reduced to a series of scale questionnaire items for use in the national survey. Over 130 phrases were generated by individuals in the depth interviews, and these were reduced to 22 clusters of phrases by means of a statistical technique known as factor analysis. This technique was used to cluster highly correlated phrases into a single evaluative dimension consumers used to judge a product—in this case, a carbonated beverage. Each of the single evaluative dimensions, or "factors," had a meaning independent of other factors. (See Appendix A of this case for an outline of Ms. Swann's study as well as a listing of the factors involved and several representative phrases that make up each of them.)

The second stage of the study involved a nationally projectable survey (using personal, in-home interviews) with 1,970 adults and teenagers. The survey gathered four types of information: (1) demographic data on consumers, such as age, income, and education; (2) consumption patterns and brand ratings—that is, information on incidence of use and consumption volume concerning the types of carbonated beverages consumed; (3) attitudinal information concerning consumer perceptions of "ideal" beverages, and Canada Dry products in particular; and (4) "psychographic" data. The latter was a general term referring to information on consumer attitudes, interests, and opinions (both general and product-related); this information was used as a basis for market segmentation.

"Psychographic" data were often used in cases in which demographics did not provide clear-cut and actionable differentiation among consumer subgroups and/or when rather detailed and subtle information was required about consumers (for example, for use in advertising appeal and product-positioning decisions). Such detailed and "subtle" information was often required for products in markets characterized by intense brand competition among competitive products that were functionally relatively similar.

Key results from phase II of Ms. Swann's study are in Appendix B of this case. Tables 1–7 in that appendix present demographic results, consumption patterns, and brand-rating results. Tables 8–11 concern the psychographic results. For this part of the study consumers completed a section of the questionnaire that asked carefully worded questions designed to measure 12 general psychological attributes.[4] Additional questions were asked to measure considerably more product-specific attributes, such as the consumer's desire for carbonated taste and concern about calories. Again through the technique of factor analysis, results from the psychographic portion of the questionnaire were reduced to a set of factors that grouped consumers who responded in similar ways to the psychographic items and who were relatively distinct from individuals in the other segments. Here, five segments of consumers were identified. These were judgmentally labeled as follows (information in Appendix B describes each factor, or segment, in detail):

		Share of population
Segment A	Adult—morally concerned	35%
Segment B	Adult—socially concerned	19
Segment C	Adult—pleasure-oriented	24
Segment D	Adult and teen— low-calorie–concerned	14
Segment E	Other teens	8
		100%

Each segment was then analyzed in terms of demographics (Table 8), beverage consumption patterns (Table 9), key attitudes concerning carbonated-beverage attributes (Table 10), and patterns of carbonated-beverage usage, ginger ale consumption, and Canada Dry awareness and usage (Table 11).

Current Situation

Ms. Swann received the results of the study in mid-March 1969. They clearly showed that areas of opportunity for mixer-line repositioning existed. But Ms. Swann also knew that her tasks of analyzing the data and making recommendations would be carefully scrutinized within the agency and by the client. A "management summary" would not suffice, since the stakes were high, and both Grey's and Canada Dry's management groups would want to know explicitly the results on which recommendations were based.

As she tried to determine what recommendations to make to Grey's management board on mixer-line positioning strategy at the next meeting, she hoped that the study had fully addressed the questions raised initially. She vividly recalled Mr. Pointsman's advice at the end of the December 12 meeting and had heard that the president of the agency was anxious to present a "winning" advertising campaign to Canada Dry when he met with its executives in mid-April.

[4]The 12 psychological attributes were abasement, activeness, cheerfulness, conscientiousness, dominance, exhibitionism, impulsiveness, masculinity, playfulness, sociability, succorance, and trust.

Appendix A
The Canada Dry Study: The Methods Employed, and Its Execution and Analysis

Method

Phase I: Exploratory Interviews (to develop phrase list for attitude measurements)

20 depth interviews with men, women, teens Metropolitan New York

Phase II: National Study

1,970 personal interviews
    1,422 adults (19 years and older)
    548 teenagers (13–18)

National probability sample of the United States, based on 145 primary sampling units

Procedure Used in Determining What Consumers Look for in Carbonated Beverages

To determine the important attitude factors in judging beverages, four steps were taken:

1. The Basic Phrase List
   A list was compiled of 125 phrases typically used by consumers to describe what they are looking for in carbonated beverages. These were generated by individual consumers in the depth interviews.
2. Desirability Ratings
   Consumers then rated the desirability of these phrases (or product associations) in carbonated beverages, using a six-point scale ranging from "extremely desirable" to "not at all desirable."
3. Factor Analysis of Phrases
   Consumers' ratings of the 125 phrases were analyzed on a computer to *objectively* group those phrases which were highly correlated by consumers. The grouping into an attitude factor means:
   > That these phrases together represent a single evaluative dimension for judging a carbonated beverage
   >
   > That this attitude factor has a meaning that is independent of other factors
4. Naming Each Factor
   Each attitude factor was judgmentally given a name which we felt best summarized the phrases in that factor.

Appendix A
Continued

General description of factors	Factor no.	The 22 attitude factors by which adults and teens evaluate carbonated beverages with representative "basic phrases" composing each

Subjective taste	1	Fresh satisfying taste
		    Has a clean taste
		    Has a crisp taste

	2	Natural flavor (adults only)
		    Has real fruit flavor
		    Has a "true" flavor

Specific taste	3	Grapefruit/lemon taste

	4	Strong/bitter/sour taste
		    Tickles your tongue (adults)
		    Has a strong taste (teens)

	5	Subtle/dry taste with no aftertaste
		    Has a light taste (adults)
		    Has no aftertaste (teens)

	6	Sweet taste (teens only)

Taste as a mixer	7	Masks the taste of liquor
		    Makes the liquor drinks less strong (adults)
		    Helps keep you from getting high (teens)

	8	Good mixer/adds to the taste of liquor (adults only) Mixes well with the kind of liquor I like

Physical effects	9	Gives you a lift
		    Is relaxing (adults)
		    Gives you a kick

	10	Thirst-quenching without bloating or filling you
		    Doesn't bloat you
		    Not syrupy

	11	Low in calories
	12	Medicinal values

Product attributes	13	Highly carbonated/long-lasting carbonation
		    It sparkles
		    It tingles
		    Has high carbonation

	14	Low carbonation (teens only)
	15	Variety of bottle sizes
	16	Easy-to-use cans
	17	Has sugar (teens only)

Associations with product	18	Drunk by modern/sociable people
		    Drunk by modern people
		    Drunk by well-educated people
		    Drunk by mature people

	19	Liked by children

Miscellaneous	20	Good to drink any time
		    Good for picnics
		    Good with meals
		    Good by itself
		    Good in hot weather

	21	Good company reputation
		    Made by leading soft drink company
		    Made by company with lively ideas

Judgmentally added	22	Good value

Appendix B
Phase II Results

TABLE 1
IMPORTANCE OF DEMOGRAPHIC GROUPS IN TOTAL SOFT DRINK CONSUMPTION
Adults and Teens*

	Population	Share of soft drink volume	Canada Dry users† in past 2 weeks
Sex:			
Males	49%	54%	53%
Females	51	46	47
Age:			
Teens (13–18)	15	17	13
19–34	28	38	30
35–49	25	23	26
50 and over	32	22	31
Income:			
Under $5,000	25	22	14
$5,000–$9,999	47	52	54
$10,000 and over	28	26	32
Occupation of head of household:			
Whitecollar:			
Professional	26	26	27
Clerical/sales	14	11	16
Bluecollar	41	52	43
Retired and other	19	11	14
Geographic region:			
West	19	18	11
South	25	31	12
Central	29	28	22
East	27	23	55
City size:			
1 million or more	39	45	66
50,000–1 million	27	23	16
Nonurban	34	32	18

*This table and all subsequent tables are based on the 85% of adult and 69% of teen consumers in the study who indicated that they had consumed carbonated beverages in the past 2 weeks.

†Any Canada Dry product (except Wink).

Appendix B

Continued

TABLE 2
BRAND AWARENESS: UNAIDED*
Percentage of Total Sample

Coca-Cola	88%
Pepsi-Cola	80
7-Up	60
Royal Crown	35
Fresca	34
Dr. Pepper	31
Tab	27
Canada Dry†	24
Sprite	24
Diet Rite	23
Diet Pepsi	22
Wink	22
Squirt	17

*Based on the question "What carbonated-beverage brand names can you think of?"
†Does not include Wink.

TABLE 3
AWARENESS OF CANADA DRY PRODUCTS: AIDED*

Ginger Ale	91%	Cherry	26%
Club Soda	69	Cola	23
Tonic Water	51	Strawberry	23
Orange	47	Tahitian Treat	15
Cream Soda	36	Raspberry	15
Grape	34	Wink	NA
Root Beer	32	Bitter Lemon	NA

*Based on the question "What Canada Dry brand beverages can you think of?"
NA=Not ascertainable.

TABLE 4
BRAND, TYPE OF CARBONATED BEVERAGES USED IN PAST 2 WEEKS

	Percentage of sample using product in last 2 weeks	Percentage (volume)* of carbonated beverages consumed in past 2 weeks by those in sample saying they used each type during past 2 weeks	
		Total sample	Children 5–12†
Colas:			
Regular colas	34	51	50
Diet colas	9	12	10
Total	43	63	60
Green-bottle items:			
Lemon-lime	14	11	5
Grapefruit	9	7	4
Ginger ale	6	4	6
Total	30	22	15
Flavors:			
Root beer	9	5	8
Orange	7	4	9
Grape	3	2	5
Cherry, strawberry	2	1	3
Raspberry	NA	NA	NA
Total	20	12	25
Club soda	4	2	
Summer mixers	3	1	
	100	100	100

*In the study, volume estimates were based on questions concerning the amounts of various beverages purchased during specified time periods.
†As reported by parents.
NA = Not ascertainable.

Appendix B
Continued

TABLE 5
SHARE OF SOFT DRINK VOLUME BY USE AND LOCATION OF CONSUMPTION

Percentage of Total Volume Per Type

	Total	Colas	Ginger ale	Lemon-lime	Grape-fruit	All green-bottle items	Summer mixers*	Club soda	Flavors
						Green-bottle items			
Typical use as soft drink vs. mixer:									
Mixer	7%	1%	38%	18%	14%	23%	73%	64%	
Soft drink	93	99	62	82	86	77	27	36	100%
At home vs. away from home (typically):									
Away from home	36	35	23	42	29	31	NB	NB	43
At home	64	65	77	58	71	68	NB	NB	57
Per capita consumption (no. of glasses)—past 2 weeks†	13	12.3	3.9	4.9	5.0	4.6	NB	NB	1.7

*Includes quinine water, bitter lemon, and bitter orange.

†Percentage of total adults and teens who indicated that they had consumed carbonated beverages in the past 2 weeks.

NB = Base too small for percentage.

TABLE 6
TYPES OF SUBSTITUTE CARBONATED BEVERAGES USED BY CARBONATED-BEVERAGE CONSUMERS WHO INDICATE A GENERALLY PREFERRED CARBONATED BEVERAGE*

Preferred carbonated beverages

Substitute type	Coca-Cola drinkers	Pepsi-Cola drinkers	7-Up drinkers	Ginger ale drinkers	Wink drinkers	Fresca drinkers	Orange drinkers	Root beer drinkers
Colas	72%†	83%	19%	18%	12%	13%	26%	61%
Green-bottle items:‡								
Lemon-lime	12	6	27	50	45	45	10	7
Ginger ale	3	2	20	8	27	23	4	2
Grapefruit	2	1	20	12	6	7	4	3
Flavors	11	7	12	7	8	10	55	26
Club soda/summer mixers	§	1	2		2	2	1	1
	100%	100%	100%	100%	100%	100%	100%	100%

*Percentage of total sample of adult and teen drinkers of each brand who gave a substitute based on this question: "You said that _(brand name given)_ was your favorite kind of soft drink. Supposing you had to pick a substitute for it. What kind of soft drink would you substitute?"

†Should be read: "72% of Coca-Cola preferers say they prefer another cola as a substitute for Coca-Cola."

‡Should be read: "17% of Coca-Cola preferers say they prefer green-bottle items (lemon-lime, ginger ale, or grapefruit) as a substitute for Coca-Cola."

§Less than 0.5%.

Appendix B
Continued

TABLE 7
IDEAL BEVERAGE ATTRIBUTES VS. CANADA DRY

The 22 attitude factors reduced from "basic phrase" list	Percentage of adults rating extremely desirable in ideal carbonated beverages	Percentage of adults rating Canada Dry excellent	
		All adults	Users*
Good value	39	20	25
Fresh satisfying taste	47	34	52
Thirst-quenching without bloating or filling you	40	25	38
Good to drink any time	38	27	37
Liked by children	38	24	27
Medicinal values	37	26	30
Gives you a lift	33	22	28
Natural flavor	31	21	31
Low in calories	25	13	15
Easy-to-use cans	25	18	36
Variety of bottle sizes	23	–	–
Good mixer/adds to the taste of liquor	22	24	40
Has sugar	–	–	–
Sweet taste	–	–	–
Drunk by modern/sociable people	19	21	31
Highly carbonated/long-lasting carbonation	19	20	28
Good company reputation	18	26	38
Subtle/dry taste with no aftertaste	15	14	18
Low carbonation	–	–	–
Masks the taste of liquor	14	12	17
Grapefruit/lemon taste	10	–	–
Strong/bitter/sour taste	7	8	13

*Adults who drank a Canada Dry carbonated beverage during the past 6 months.
†Calculated: Percentage rating Canada Dry excellent minus percentage rating factor extremely desirable.

Definitions of Psychographic Profiles

Segment A: Adult—morally concerned

Segment A adults are characterized by a puritanical and conservative personality. They are humble, compliant people who conscientiously fulfill their duties. They see themselves as moral, unpretentious, and content with their work, their families, and what they consider to be the pleasures of a simple life.

Segment A drinkers disapprove of self-seeking people and those who live for pleasure alone. They are likely to disapprove of liquor drinking.

Soft drinks represent a mild pleasure that is consistent with their simple way of life. They would be likely to favor beverages that possess the old-

Percentage of teens rating extremely desirable in ideal carbonated beverages	Percentage of teens rating Canada Dry excellent	Percentage difference between ideal and Canada Dry	
		All adults†	All teens†
41	20	−19	−21
45	31	−13	−13
41	29	−15	−12
55	35	−11	−20
30	20	−14	−10
36	26	−11	−10
29	20	−11	−14
–	–	−10	–
23	18	−12	− 7
33	27	− 7	− 6
32	–	–	–
–	–	− 2	–
22	17	–	− 5
20	16	–	− 4
19	18	+ 2	− 1
25	25	+ 3	0
25	27	+ 8	+ 2
27	15	− 1	− 4
15	8	–	− 7
16	14	− 2	− 2
11	–	–	–
11	8	+ 1	− 3

(Minus sign means ideal rated higher than Canada Dry. Plus sign means Canada Dry rated higher.)

fashioned virtue they seek. Thus, well-established brands that are made with natural ingredients would be in keeping with their personality.

Segment B: Adult—socially concerned

Segment B adults are motivated primarily by a need to be liked by their peers. They want to be seen as easy to get along with, part of the gang, and an asset in social situations. Actually socially uneasy and insecure people, they are anxious to conform, to do what is expected of them, and to fit in with what is considered to be fun and pleasurable by normal, well-rounded people.

Socializing and the pursuit of good times are very important to these consumers. They value most the feeling that they belong, that they are accepted. The purpose of the occasion, whether bowling, informal

Appendix B
Continued

home entertainment, breaks at work, etc., is less important than a shared feeling of being part of a lively group who are unmistakably enjoying themselves. Essentially unsophisticated, they would be likely to seek out the most conventionally popular pursuits.

The Segment B drinkers are more likely to look favorably upon brands or types of beverages that are "in"—not exotic or unconventional, but popular and well thought of as they themselves would like to be.

Segment C: Adult—pleasure-oriented

Segment C adults are pleasure seekers. Confident, assertive people, they see themselves as being able to achieve whatever they want. Intent on living life to the fullest, they lay great emphasis on self-gratification and on their image as leading pleasure-filled lives.

Both men and women in Segment C display an earthy, robust approach to life, particularly when it comes to pleasure. In contrast to Segment B, they care little about what others think and what is socially accepted. They harbor an ideal fantasy of unfettered freedom to enjoy all pleasures as they desire them.

Carbonated beverages fit well into the amusement and diversion-seeking orientation of Segment C individuals, as does liquor. They are likely to be heavy consumers of both. Their preferences in carbonated beverages would tend to reflect little concern for health or weight but great concern for physical gratification.

Segment D: Adult and teen—low-calorie–concerned

Results from adults and teens were highly similar, so these groups were combined for analysis. Segment D adults and teens are a self-controlled people with cheerful and altruistic outlooks on life. They tend to subordinate the material aspects of life and are motivated by the desire to engage in unselfish and constructive activity. Teens are well adjusted, desire individuality, and are "planners" for the future.

Even in their pleasures, Segment D drinkers remain in control; they have little capacity for indulging their lustier impulses or physical appetites. Their pleasures would tend to be wholesome, temperate, and refined.

To Segment D adults and teens, soft drinks are acceptable but not relished. Typically, they would like to suggest that they can take them or leave them. They are likely to look favorably upon brands or types that denote refinement, are not perceived as too gratifying, and are suggestive of control rather than indulgence.

Segment E: Other teens

Segment E teens are primarily motivated by their desire to pursue fun and pleasure as a way of life. They are characterized by physical, fast-paced and extroverted behavior. However, much of the activity that they engage in is a means of compensating for their underlying insecurities. Continuous distractions enable them to avoid self-confrontation with their own shortcomings.

Their groups of friends are very important to fulfilling their need for social acceptance and approval. They are less likely to seek out individual friendships than to want to be part of a group.

Carbonated beverages fit in with these teenagers' concept of good times within a group, and the act of drinking fulfills their need for immediate impulse gratification. They would be most likely to seek the carbonated beverage that offers the greatest amount of acceptance by the group.

Appendix B
Continued

TABLE 8
DEMOGRAPHIC SUMMARY BY ALL PSYCHOGRAPHIC SEGMENTS

Psychographic segments	Sex		Age					Presence of children			Income		
	Male	Female	19–24	25–34	35–44	45–54	55+	No. children	1–2	3+	Under $5,000	$5,000–$9,999	$10,000 plus
Segment A (Adult—morally concerned)	41%	59%	11%	14%	19%	20%	36%	51%	28%	21%	34%	46%	20%
Segment B (Adult—socially concerned)	49	51	16	22	20	20	22	43	26	31	20	50	30
Segment C (Adult—pleasure-oriented)	59	41	18	26	23	19	14	39	37	24	13	50	37
Segment D (Adult and Teen—low-calorie-concerned)	35	65	20*	21	20	13	26	43	31	26	23	33	44

Psychographic segments	Sex		Age of teen		Education of teen			
	Male	Female	13–15	16–18	6–8 grade	9–12 grade	College	Not in school
Segment E (Other teens)	59	41	66%	34%	25%	66%	6%	3%

*Age category is 13–24.

TABLE 8
Continued

Psychographic segments	Education of household head				Occupation of household head			
					Whitecollar			
	Grade school or less	Some HS	Comp- leted HS	Some college or more	Professional/ managerial	Clerical/ sales	Blue collar	Retired and other
Segment A (Adult—morally concerned)	24%	25%	30%	21%	19%	12%	39%	30%
Segment B (Adult—socially concerned)	13	25	35	27	24	10	46	20
Segment C (Adult—pleasure- oriented)	9	12	37	42	35	15	35	15
Segment D (Adult and Teen— low-calorie–concerned)	11	18	32	39	28	19	28	25
Segment E (Other teens)	14	23	35	28	25	21	47	7

TABLE 9
SEGMENT SUMMARY

	Share of population	Share of soft drink volume	Share of mixer volume	Share of total ginger ale volume
Segment A (Adult—morally concerned)	35%	35%	7%	17%
Segment B (Adult—socially concerned)	19	20	39	42
Segment C (Adult—pleasure-oriented)	24	22	44	28
Segment D (Adult and teen—low-calorie– concerned)	14	13	10	7
Segment E (Other teens)	8	10	–	6
	100%	100%	100%	100%

Region				City size		
West	South	Central	East	Non-urban	50,000–million	1 million or more
14%	38%	29%	19%	39%	30%	31%
17	19	31	33	27	23	50
25	15	28	32	28	27	45
30	12	28	30	39	22	39
15	24	30	31	35	21	44

Share of ginger ale soft drink volume	Share of ginger ale mixer volume	Share of cola volume	Share of club soda volume	Share of tonic volume	Share of diet soda volume
23%	7%	36%	8%	8%	37%
30	60	19	32	27	17
26	30	23	49	45	22
13	3	13	10	18	18
8	–	9	1	2	6
100%	100%	100%	100%	100%	100%

Appendix B
Continued

TABLE 10
DIFFERENTIATING ATTITUDES REGARDING IDEAL CARBONATED BEVERAGE RELATIVE TO OTHER SEGMENTS' AVERAGES

	Segment A (adult—morally concerned)	Segment B (adult—socially concerned)	Segment C (adult—pleasure-oriented)	Segment D (adult and teen—low-calorie-concerned)	Segment E (Other teens)
General factors					
Fresh satisfying taste	+ 6%*			−20%	
Drunk by modern/sociable people		+23%	−18%	−24	+22%
Liked by children	+ 6	+14	−14	−21	
Good value				+11	
Natural flavor	+ 5		−12	−14	
Easy-to-use cans				+11	+15
Good to drink any time	+ 5	+11		−17	
Gives you a lift				−17	
Good company reputation	+ 4	+16	−13		+15
Low in calories		+10	−14	+27	−20
Low carbonation					+13
Variety of bottle sizes		+10			
Highly carbonated/long-lasting carbonation					+21
Has sugar				−12	+14
Sweet taste					+14
Mixer factor					
Masks the taste of liquor	−11%†	+33%	− 4%		
Good mixer/adds to the taste of liquor	−31	+25	+ 8		

*To be read: "Segment A is 6% more concerned about fresh satisfying taste than the average of the other segments."
†To be read: "Segment A is 11% less concerned about masking the taste of liquor."
+ means more concerned about than average.
− means less concerned than average.

Appendix B

Continued

TABLE 11

CARBONATED-BEVERAGE CONSUMPTION BY PSYCHOGRAPHIC SEGMENT AND RELATIVE TO AVERAGE OF REMAINING SEGMENTS

As Percentage of Total Sample

	Segment A (adult—morally concerned)	Segment B (adult—socially concerned)	Segment C (adult—pleasure-concerned)	Segment D (adult and teen—low-calorie-concerned)	Segment E (other teens)
Use of carbonated-beverage drink	85%*	86%	92%	84%	
As a soft drink only	78	57	65	58	
Both	6	26	24	22	
As a mixer only	1	3	3	4	
Drank alcohol in past 2 weeks	13%	42%	48%	42%	
With mixer only	4	21	19	21	
Both	3	8	9	5	
Without mixer only	6	13	20	16	
Type of soft drink used in past 2 weeks:					
Cola incidence (volume %)	69% (70)	67% (62)	74% (66)	60% (64)	89% (68)
Lemon lime incidence (volume %)	24 (10)	33 (11)	29 (9)	20 (8)	34 (11)
Grapefruit incidence (volume %)	15 (6)	21 (8)	18 (7)	24 (12)	20 (4)
Ginger ale incidence (volume %)	8 (2)	16 (4)	11 (3)	12 (3)	11 (2)
Flavors incidence (volume %)	28 (12)	31 (13)	37 (13)	26 (10)	49 (10)
Club soda or mixer incidence (volume %)	1 (1)	2 (3)	3 (4)	5 (6)	1 (1)
Ginger ale usage:					
Total incidence ("recently")	8.6%	20.6%	14.2%	15.4%	10.9%
As a mixer only	1.0	10.0	10.0	11.0	
Both	0.8	5.6	1.5	0.6	
As a soft drink only	6.8	5.0	2.7	3.8	
Canada Dry penetration:					
Unaided awareness	19%	24%	33%	25%	16%
Knowledge of Canada Dry label products (no. of brands known)	3.5	4.3	4.7	4.9	4.4
Overall attitude (percentage rating excellent)	17%	26%	22%	27%	12%
Incidence of drinking any Canada Dry ("recently")	3%	11%	7%	12%	5%

*To be read: "85% of Segment A consumers used a carbonated beverage during last 2 weeks."

General Foods Corporation
Tang Instant Breakfast Drink

Harvey N. Singer • Gary R. Garrasi • F. Stewart DeBruicker

37

Bill King, product group manager of the breakfast beverage product group at General Foods, was faced with a most pressing and difficult decision. Sales of Orange Tang Instant Breakfast Drink[1] had been dropping significantly, and this was attributed to the declining effectiveness of the brand's present advertising.

In order to reverse the downward trend, the brand's product group management and its

Harvey N. Singer is an assistant professor of marketing at American University. Gary R. Garrasi was formerly a research assistant and F. Stewart DeBruicker is an assistant professor of marketing—both at the Wharton School, University of Pennsylvania.

Dollar and unit figures in this case have been disguised.

[1]Tang is a trademark of the General Foods Corporation. A small amount of Tang, a dry crystalline powder, added to a larger quantity of water made a beverage described by the Tang package label as "natural tasting orange flavor breakfast drink. It contains more Vitamin C and A than like amounts of orange, grapefruit or tomato juice. Tang is not a juice, juice product, or soft drink mix. Tang is a nutritious instant breakfast drink."

advertising agency, Young & Rubicam, had prepared new advertising approaches. The approaches, which had been prepared over the summer of 1972, took the form of four 30-second television commercials. Young & Rubicam had just completed the final phase of testing for the four commercials, and Frank Thomas, the Y&R account executive for the Tang account, had just completed his presentation of the findings. Mr. Thomas and Sharon Wolf, the Tang assistant product manager, had argued for the selection of one of the four candidates on the basis of qualitative research findings. Dick Jackson, the Tang product manager, disagreed with their choice on the basis of his interpretation of quantitative measures of brand-related recall. He argued instead for the selection of a different commercial on the basis of his interpretation of the research results.

Having had the benefit of hearing Messrs. Thomas and Jackson and Ms. Wolf make and defend their choices, Mr. King had to make the final decision and defend it to his strategic business unit manager. It seemed that further copy development work was inadvisable, given the sales record of Tang over the recent weeks.

Background

General Foods Corporation (GF) was a leading manufacturer and marketer of grocery products, chiefly processed foods. Its brands were among the best-selling products nationally in a variety of categories: coffee, frozen foods, gelatin desserts, puddings, soft drink mixes, syrups, semimoist and dry dog food, and cereals. Going into the last quarter of fiscal 1973, sales were expected to be over $2.5 billion and the net profit over $100 million for the year.[2]

The company's long-term strength was built on large consumer franchises for its 400 products and on some 30 of the food industry's best-known brand names, including Maxwell House Coffee, Birds Eye Frozen Foods, Post Cereals, Jell-O Desserts, Gaines Pet Foods, and Tang Instant Breakfast Drink.

In terms of GF's marketing organization, a product manager worked within a product group, which in turn was part of a strategic business unit, or SBU. Until very recently the company's marketing activities had been organized by products produced by similar technologies or by products that had developed as line extensions of a single brand. In the early 1970s, pressure on sales and profits in the highly competitive convenience foods and fast-food restaurant markets led to a major reorganization in the company's marketing organization. Individual products and brands were placed into groups according to the strategic business unit concept. This meant that all products, regardless

[2]Fiscal years began on April 1. Fiscal 1973, for example, began on April 1, 1972, and ended March 31, 1973. Operating quarters were named for the months in which they ended: June, September, December, and March.

of brand name or production technology, which were viewed in the same competitive framework by consumers in the marketplace were grouped and managed together. The goal was to encourage managers to concentrate their efforts on strategic markets as well as individual products. For example, all dessert products, whether Birds Eye frozen desserts or Jell-O gelatins, were placed in the dessert SBU. All main-meal dishes, whether Birds Eye frozen vegetables or Minute Rice or Shake & Bake seasoned coating mixes, were placed in the main meal SBU. Tang was included in the beverage SBU, along with frozen beverage products (frozen orange juice concentrate, Orange Plus, and Awake), other breakfast beverages (Start and Postum), and refreshment beverages (Kool-Aid brand products).

The SBU managers reported to the president of one of the company's major divisions. Tang was grouped in the beverage and breakfast division. Each division also had support staff personnel (staffs for finance, production, and technical R&D, and a field sales force) to service its SBUs. Division presidents then reported to General Foods's top corporate management, which included the president, executive and group vice presidents, and support staffs at that level which provided service for all the divisions—chief among them a financial staff and a market research group.

An organization chart outlining these relationships is shown in Exhibit 1.

Product managers at GF acted as both marketing and business managers for their brands. On the marketing side, they had the mission of planning and executing all advertising, promotion, pricing, and merchandising strategies for their brands. More generally, they had to compete for and coordinate all of their division's functional resources for their respective brands, which included technical inputs, marketing research, sales force programs, processing, and packaging. On the operations side, they were responsible for their brands' financial contribu-

EXHIBIT 1
GENERAL FOODS MARKETING ORGANIZATION

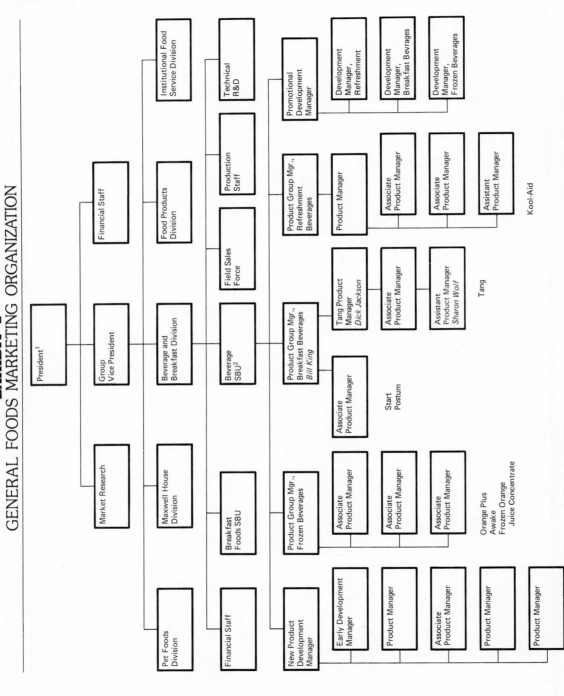

[1] Also attached to the President's office were support staffs for legal, purchasing, etc.

[2] The SBU Manager also had a supporting staff with functions similar to the divisional staffs.

tion through volume attainment, marketing spending, and pricing decisions. On the planning side, they worked with top management on setting current fiscal objectives and long-range expectations (5-year strategic plans).

Dick Jackson, Tang product manager, was assisted by an associate product manager and the assistant product manager, Sharon Wolf. They were supported by product development personnel and promotional merchandising personnel within the SBU. Mr. Jackson reported to Bill King, the product group manager with responsibility for Tang, Start, and Postum breakfast beverages. Mr. King in turn reported to the beverage SBU manager.

Tang History

Tang powdered instant breakfast drink was introduced nationally in 1958. Tang's ingredients, in descending order of weight, were sugar, citric acid (for tartness), calcium phosphates (to regulate tartness and prevent caking), gum arabic (vegetable gum to provide body), natural flavor, potassium citrate (to regulate tartness), vitamin C, cellulose gum (vegetable gum), hydrogenated coconut oil, artificial flavor, artificial color, vitamin A, and BHA (a preservative). After Tang's national introduction in 1958, its volume grew slowly but steadily. The volume seemed to plateau as the product matured by about 1962, so marketing spending was stepped up, and new copy was devised. Mr. Jackson indicated that this gave the product a "shot in the arm," and sales improved through 1968, when stagnation began again. Accordingly, marketing efforts were intensified in fiscal 1969. The product was significantly improved, and sampling efforts, advertising, and promotion spending were all increased. The brand's media copy program featured association with the United States space program through the National Aeronautics and Space Administration (NASA).

This association proved successful, as Tang sales increased 20 percent in fiscal 1969 over the fiscal 1968 level.

In fiscal 1970, this approach was continued and sales increased. Even when the price of Tang was raised, the volume continued to grow. This was due in part to the government's ban on cyclamates and the quick response of Tang advertising, which noted that no artificial sweeteners were used in Tang. Sales were up 31 percent for the year.

In fiscal 1971 the Apollo program became less active, so a new Tang campaign was introduced which was designed to enlighten and excite consumers about the "future" in space. The overall strategy of associating Tang with NASA and space was continued, but focus of the campaign shifted from actual space flights to potential space programs made feasible by the Apollo program.

Sales continued to rise, but at a slower rate; they were up only 19 percent for the year. In fiscal 1972, sales growth again slowed. Tang prices had been increased to maintain profit margins close to historical levels, although some margin erosion occurred as additional advertising was invested in support of both Orange Tang and a new grapefruit flavor extension. In fiscal 1972, competing products began to appear. One firm introduced a product offering more ounces in a package priced the same as Tang, and some store-label brands appeared which were priced as much as 40 percent below the price of equivalent Tang packages. Estimates of competitors' prices and media spending are listed in Exhibit 2. Orange Tang sales for fiscal 1972 were up only 3 percent.

It was about this time that Ms. Wolf began to question the efficacy of the existing copy themes. She contended that both the client and the agency might be putting too much faith in the campaigns that were so closely associated with the hardware and mechanics of the space program. Though the overall strategy of the

EXHIBIT 2

1. Tang price per unit (10½-lb units)—1967-1973 (first half)

	Retail
Fiscal 1967	$8.42
Fiscal 1968	8.41
Fiscal 1969	8.38
Fiscal 1970	8.71
Fiscal 1971	8.70
Fiscal 1972	9.03
Fiscal 1973 (first half)	9.08

2. Estimates of competitive prices (10½-lb units)

	Retail
Fiscal 1972	$7.49
Fiscal 1973 (first half)	7.53

3. Competitive advertising ($000)

	Borden	Lipton
Fiscal 1972	$ 59	–
Fiscal 1973 (first half)	278	$630

space theme was never in question, she believed that the brand group should consider alternative or backup campaigns.

Also about this time, General Foods began implementing a portfolio approach to its many businesses that was modeled after the Boston Consulting Group's terminology. Products were classified as "stars," which justified investment spending with the objective of high volume and market share growth; "cash cows," which had less growth potential but could provide positive cash flow that could be channeled to the stars, and which should be managed for the objective of market share stability and positive cash flow; and "dogs," which should be dropped.

Early in fiscal 1973 sales began to drop precipitously—as much as 13 percent in some bimonthly periods versus the previous years figures—and the product group became increasingly concerned over the issues of advertising copy and marketing spending. Mr. Jackson was concerned that Tang would not meet its goal of a $7 million contribution after marketing costs, as specified in GF's 1973 annual business plan. Exhibit 3 shows Orange Tang sales and marketing spending figures from fiscal 1968 through mid-fiscal 1973, as well as competing powdered orange beverages product sales and price differences between Tang and frozen orange juice concentrate (FOJC).

The Tang gross margin was about $3.15 per 10½-pound unit. Marketing costs were primarily the amounts spent on advertising and promotion. Mr. Jackson felt that a further price increase to deliver profits was unfeasible. Product line extensions (new flavors) to increase volume were no longer favored by the product group. Only one alternative to the NASA theme had been developed and tested.

The Client-Agency Relationship

There was a management hierarchy for the Tang account at Y&R that corresponded to GF's structure. Walter Roberts was the senior management supervisor for the Tang account and for a variety of other accounts handled by Y&R. Reporting to him were Jack Kelso, account supervisor, and Frank Thomas, account executive. Mr. Thomas was responsible for planning and directing the Y&R support staffs for the creative, media, and research departments, and for supervising the activities of two assistant account executives. Mr. Thomas and his staff were in regular contact with the members of the Tang product management group. It was not unusual for the agency and client management teams to meet daily when engaged in strategic planning activities. During these meetings, the agency and client managers functioned as a team, with the agency personnel often taking strong advocacy positions for points of view with which the client might disagree. Final responsi-

EXHIBIT 3

ORANGE TANG SALES AND MARKETING SPENDING, 1968–1973

Period		Orange Tang sales (thousands 10½-lb units)	Advertising ($000)	Promotion ($000)	Competitive sales (thousands 10½-lb units)	Price difference: FOJC–Tang (cents per 24 ounces)
Fiscal year	Quarter					
1968	1	530	365	289	0	−0.5
	2	511	435	338	0	0.1
	3	514	303	330	0	1.4
	4	545	188	190	0	2.2
	Total	2,100	1,291	1,147		
1969	1	579	437	1,006	0	3.3
	2	615	331	51	0	3.8
	3	664	570	129	0	4.7
	4	850	1,176	471	0	6.0
	Total	2,708	2,514	1,657		
1970	1	801	992	254	0	6.3
	2	853	771	356	0	5.1
	3	872	802	128	0	4.8
	4	1,029	988	448	0	4.0
	Total	3,555	3,553	1,186		
1971	1	1,019	1,400	710	0	3.4
	2	1,002	806	549	0	3.2
	3	1,024	843	1,011	0	2.5
	4	1,197	1,110	684	0	2.1
	Total	4,242	4,159	2,954		
1972	1	1,088	883	339	0	3.4
	2	1,070	769	1,070	22	4.8
	3	1,052	864	1,006	50	5.1
	4	1,142	430	763	89	8.0
	Total	4,352	2,946	3,718	161	
1973	1	1,044	884	576	200	7.9
	2	965	363	851	271	7.9

bility for decision making rested with the client, however. At meetings between the agency and client, it was customary for the most junior members of the agency and client staffs to offer their analyses and recommendations first; other participants joined the discussion in order of increasing management responsibility.

The relationship between the GF product management group and the agency group was unusually strong. Since Tang was one of Y&R's largest clients in terms of billings, both the agency and the product group viewed themselves as partners in the Tang business. In this regard, the agency's responsibilities encompassed not only developing advertising strategies and creating and producing copy executions but also providing marketing research and merchandising consulting services.

A number of people from the agency's account management group and creative department had worked on the Tang account for several years. Some had become very successful as a result of Tang performance. In fact, one of the agency's executive vice presidents had risen to his present position as a result of Tang success. Additionally, members of the agency groups and the GF product group had had continuous professional contact with each other over the years on accounts other than Tang. This continuity of service on the part of both groups was considered to be one of the Tang marketing program's major strengths.

Orange Tang Positioning and Message Strategy

Since the Tang introduction in 1958, the product group and agency representatives had gone to great lengths to design strategy and copy that would portray Tang as a highly nutritional and flavorful breakfast drink substitute for fresh frozen orange juice concentrate. Over the years the product had been upgraded by increasing its vitamin content and improving its flavor. The issue of the legitimacy of Tang as a substitute for frozen orange juice concentrate had been of continuous concern to both the product group and the agency.

The NASA testimonials used in the Tang media strategy throughout the late 1960s had provided a strong sense of legitimacy for the product, differentiating it from children's beverage mixes. Studies conducted by both GF and Y&R had confirmed that Tang consumers felt that if the product was nutritional enough to be selected by NASA to be included in the Apollo astronauts' diets when they traveled to the moon, then it must be nutritional enough to serve to their entire families.

Though sales in the fourth quarter of fiscal 1972 had declined compared with sales in the same period 1 year earlier, the Tang basic message strategy was confirmed in an April 1972 meeting of the brand management team and members of the account team from Y&R. The product would continue to be positioned against fresh and concentrated frozen orange juice; private-label and "me-too" competition would not be discussed in any way. The target audience would continue to be married women between the ages of 18 and 44 with two or more children and at least a high school education. The copy development guidelines were that the nutritional story would continue to receive the major emphasis and that secondary emphasis on flavor and the brand's NASA connection would be continued.

There was to be one noteworthy change in the copy strategy. While the NASA themes had always associated the brand with the space program, the management group felt that space was too "sterile" an environment to be realistic for many present users of the product. Therefore, the agency sought to develop thematic approaches that placed the product in more conventional consumption environments. Mr. Jackson decided, with the approval of both Mr. King and the SBU manager, that until satisfactory new copy approaches were developed, the planned annual media spending on Tang would be reduced for the remainder of fiscal 1973 from $4.5 million to only $3.0 million, and consumer promotional expenditures would be increased by $800,000.

Sales in the first quarter of fiscal 1973 declined slightly from the level of the same period in 1972, but as the second quarter began, sales declines of over 10 percent from the previous year's levels were becoming evident nationwide. In order to hasten new advertising copy development, some of the normal procedures were suspended, and a major econometric analysis of the historic sales effects of advertising and promotion spending was begun. The agency forwarded to Mr. Jackson a creative work plan, which described a so-called "authority strategy" aimed at further legitimatizing Tang.

Mr. Jackson approved the work plan, which is presented in Exhibit 4. In late June, Mr. Jackson decided to cancel the September quarter's planned advertising until more effective copy could be developed, thus vividly demonstrating to the agency the product group's dissatisfaction with the performance of the then available advertising copy. This cancellation was approved by the SBU manager.

The Search for New Copy Executions

Ordinarily, the typical advertising creative process involved the creation of a large number of copy executions by the agency's creative teams, with the executions then being reviewed by the agency's creative supervisor. The executions would then be forwarded to Y&R's associate creative director, who would either send the copy back to the creative supervisor for reworking by the creative teams or, if satisfied, present it to Carol Alexander, the agency creative director, for inspection. If Ms. Alexander approved the copy, she would authorize the associate creative director to forward the executions to the account

executive, Frank Thomas. Mr. Thomas would closely examine the copy executions for consistency with the product's strategy, and if the executions were satisfactory to him, he would present them to Dick Jackson at GF.

The product manager would examine the copy executions with the account executive and would often request that revisions be made by the agency's creative team. After the revisions had been made, the account executive would review the executions with the product manager, who would then present the executions to Bill King, the product group manager. Mr. King usually requested further revisions, and when they had been made to his satisfaction, he would present the executions to the SBU manager for final approval. Normally six to eight executions, in rough storyboard form, survived at this point.

After the SBU manager was satisfied with the copy executions, the agency and product management groups would meet and decide which executions should be rough-produced on 16-mm film. The rough commercials would be tested for their intrusiveness—i.e., recall or memorability—and sales point communication. On the basis of test results and agency recommendations, the product management group would select one or more of the commercials for finished production, using 35-mm film or videotape. Spot and/or network television time would then be purchased, and the commercial would be televised nationally.

Both the agency and the client viewed this stepwise development process as an opportunity to provide the more junior members of their organizations with a valuable learning experience regarding the preparation of a product for market and the mechanics and intricacies of the agency-client relationship. The severity of the present situation did not permit the luxury of the normal procedures, however. It was decided that the number of formal copy presentations would be reduced, and the initial presentations would be made to Dick Jackson and Sharon Wolf so that the product manager and his

EXHIBIT 4
CREATIVE WORK PLAN
"Authority Strategy"

Key fact

Orange Tang prime prospects, both regular and infrequent users, reflect a positive interest in the brand, yet are concerned about its legitimacy as a food product due to its powdered form.

Problems advertising must solve

Due to OT's powdered form, most people believe it not to be a legitimate substitute for FOJC at breakfast and, therefore, not as "healthy" and "good" for their families.

Advertising objective

To reassure current users and convince infrequent users that OT is a legitimate substitute for FOJC and, consequently, is good for their families at breakfast.

Prospect definition

Women who are characterized as mothers aged 18–44 with two plus children under 12 years of age with income of $10,000 plus living in A&B counties and users of FOJC and/or IBD. Attitudinally, these women are somewhat self-indulgent and have respect for authority. They are concerned with the well-being of their families and try to provide (not necessarily feed) them with a nutritionally adequate diet.

Principal competition

FOJC is considered OT's primary competition and major source of volume. Lower priced IBD's are OT's secondary competition.

Promise

OT is a good-tasting, legitimate food product that helps you fulfill your role as the supplier of nutrition and health to your family by serving it at breakfast.

Reasons why

1. Nutritious OT has a full day's supply of vitamin C plus vitamin A.
2. OT has a taste that can be enjoyed by the entire family and is especially liked by kids.
3. OT has been selected for use by the NASA astronauts.

Tone and manner

The advertising must establish a sense of authority in support of the posture that Tang is a legitimate, serious food product. It must be consistent with the stature relationship between Tang and NASA.

Constraint agreement

A consent agreement between GF and the Federal Trade Commission prohibits statements "disparaging" to any natural fruit juices.

assistant could comment on the copy and begin winnowing out some of the weaker executions immediately. In the summer of 1972 the Tang associate product manager was on special assignment elsewhere at GF and was not a part of the decision-making process.

By the end of June 1972, the agency had produced 16 storyboard executions for the product manager's consideration. At the initial presentation of the copy executions at the agency, the product manager and his assistant made several suggestions regarding copy content. The agency quickly revised the copy according to the client's suggestions and made a second presentation at the agency to Mr. Jackson and Ms. Wolf. This time only eight of the executions were selected for further development. A third presentation was convened, this time at GF's White Plains, New York, offices during the first week of July. This presentation was attended by the entire product management group as well as by the agency account manage-

---

EXHIBIT 5
"ANDROMEDA" PHOTOSCRIPT

YOUNG & RUBICAM INTERNATIONAL, INC.

CLIENT: GENERAL FOODS CORP.
PRODUCT: ORANGE TANG
TITLE: "ANDROMEDA"

LENGTH: 30 SECONDS
COMM. NO: GFOT2518

 1. (SFX: TYPEWRITER)

 2. (SFX: TYPEWRITER)

 3. (SFX: TYPEWRITER)

 4. (SFX: TYPEWRITER)

 5. (SFX: TYPEWRITER)

 6. (SFX: TYPEWRITER)

 7. (SFX: TYPEWRITER)

 8. (SFX: TYPEWRITER)

 9. (SFX: TYPEWRITER)

 10. (SFX: TYPEWRITER)

EXHIBIT 6
"FOOD SELECTION" PHOTOSCRIPT

YOUNG & RUBICAM INTERNATIONAL, INC.

CLIENT: GENERAL FOODS CORP.
PRODUCT: ORANGE TANG
TITLE: "FOOD SELECTION"

LENGTH: 30 SECONDS
COMM. NO: GFOT2517

1. (MUSIC THROUGH-OUT)

2. ANNCR: (VO) The Nutrition Team at the NASA Space Center

3. worked long and hard to come up with breakfast for outer space.

4. They looked at 28 versions of the scrambled egg ...

5. Spent months getting bacon crispy ...

6. Then they decided on an orange-flavored instant breakfast drink

7. straight from the super-market...

8. Tang. With a full day's supply of Vitamin C.

9. Good, nutritious Tang.

10. It passed the test.

ment group. The agency presented six copy executions to the product group (two others had been eliminated since the second presentation) and recommended that the product group produce the executions entitled "Andromeda," which was the agency creative director's favorite; "Food Selection"; and "Packing."

After some discussion of the agency's copy analyses and recommendations, the product group management authorized the agency to produce those three executions. The client group also requested that the agency produce "Lady Ph.D." as well. Sharon Wolf argued for this inclusion rather persuasively, even though no research had yet been conducted on any of the executions. Ms. Wolf contended that there was something persuasive about a real mother with an authentic scientific background serving her children Tang for breakfast. It seemed to overcome the legitimacy obstacle while depicting a situation to which the target audience could readily relate.

EXHIBIT 7
"PACKING" PHOTOSCRIPT

YOUNG & RUBICAM INTERNATIONAL, INC.

CLIENT: GENERAL FOODS CORP.
PRODUCT: ORANGE TANG
TITLE: "PACKING"

LENGTH: 30 SECONDS
COMM. NO: GFOT2516

1. (MUSIC THROUGH-OUT) WOMAN: (VO) If you were leaving for a day on the moon,

2. you'd have to pack a little differently.

3. You'd need a helmet, so you could breathe...

4. an extra-vehicular suit...

5. something special in the way of footwear...

6. and protective gloves.

7. But there's one scientific miracle that you could pack right from your kitchen table...

8. Tang. The orange-flavored instant breakfast drink

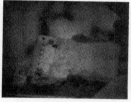

9. with a full day's supply of Vitamin C.

10. Tang. Good no matter where you're having breakfast.

At the conclusion of this meeting, the client authorized the agency to go directly to 35-mm production of the choices. This was a rather expensive procedure, since the services of both professional production crews and professional actors and actresses had to be contracted. And the cost of 35-mm production was charged directly to the client. Due to the urgency of the present situation, Dick Jackson considered the cost of 35-mm production of all four executions to be a necessary and unavoidable expense.

Filming of the four commercials was contracted out to independent production companies and was completed at the end of July. Photoscripts of the completed commercials are presented in Exhibits 5 through 8.

Copy Strategy Research

The commercials were immediately put into a program of research designed to develop data to

EXHIBIT 8
"LADY Ph.D." PHOTOSCRIPT

YOUNG & RUBICAM INTERNATIONAL, INC.

CLIENT: GENERAL FOODS CORP.
PRODUCT: ORANGE TANG
TITLE: "LADY P.H.D."

LENGTH: 30 SECONDS
COMM. NO. GFOT2520

1. MARY ETHIMION: I'm a mother of two children.

2. And I have a PHD in biological science.

3. You know a woman involved with science

4. wants to be sure her family gets their breakfast vitamins.

5. I know the astronauts use Tang,

6. and I am sure NASA took a lot of time and trouble to find good things for them.

7. Things that would maintain

8. their vitamin supply.

9. And Tang is a good source of Vitamin C and A.

10. We drink it all the time.

11. Mm. It really tastes

12. great.

help management choose the most effective execution for use in the fall media period, and to use as a basis for developing more refined executions of the winning concept later in the fall. The commercials were tested by using focus-group interviews and sample surveys of recall of televised commercials in test markets. The focus-group interviews were conducted by the agency in several shopping malls in early August. In the interviews, small groups of women typical of the target audience were invited to an informal screening of several commercials; then they were interviewed in groups to determine their feelings as to the commercials' intentions and effectiveness. The results of the interviews provided qualitative guidance, but due to their subjective nature, they were considered only one ingredient in the mix of data and judgments used to make final decisions on a set of executions.

Mr. Thomas, the account executive, noted that most of the respondents did not seem to like the spokesperson used in the "Lady Ph.D." commercial, but they did seem to respect her judgment in matters of choosing nutritious foods for her family. He believed, however, that unless that element of respect could be demonstrated in the sample surveys used in the television recall testing procedures, he would have a difficult time selling the "Lady Ph.D." execution to management. Interview summaries for "Lady Ph.D." and "Food Selection" are presented in Exhibits 9 and 10.

The television recall tests were designed to develop data of a quantitative nature on large samples of viewers of the four commercials in a realistic, in-home setting. These tests were conducted by GF's corporate marketing research group, using standardized procedures that had been used to test past Tang advertisements. The procedures involved "cutting" each of the four candidate commercials into the normal network commercial period on a nationally televised program. Next-day telephone interviews were then conducted in some market areas within 24 hours of the airing of the test commercials, and questions were asked to determine their memorability and copy-point playback performance. The commercial which achieved the highest level of memorability over the historic Tang norm and which best communicated the strategic copy points would be selected for airing. Arrangements were made for the commercials to be inserted into the 9:24 P.M. slot in the CBS Thursday night movie *Night Gallery* on September 7, 1972, in the following cities:

Execution	Length (sec)	Cities
"Andromeda"	30	Atlanta, Hartford, Sacramento
"Food selection"	30	Buffalo, Indianapolis, San Diego
"Lady Ph.D."	30	Cincinnati, Denver, Omaha, Syracuse
"Packing"	30	Minneapolis, Phoenix, Portland, Youngstown

The cost of the TV recall studies was approximately $14,000 in out-of-pocket charges to the Tang budget.

The recall measurement procedure was a standard GF methodology which involved asking a hierarchy of questions to determine whether or not the respondent had in fact seen the commercial being tested and, if so, what level of

EXHIBIT 9
"LADY Ph.D." GROUP INTERVIEW SUMMARY

Communication of product messages

In both sessions, it was quite clear that virtually all of the respondents seemed to understand what was being said in the "Ph.D." commercial and all of the women played back the messages that Tang is "good for you" because of its vitamin contents. In addition to pointing out that Tang is rich in vitamins C and A, the women came away with the impression that Tang is a "well researched product" that is scientifically accepted as being nutritious. The NASA reference seemed to be picked up by many of the women too, and the women seemed to realize that if Tang is being sent to the moon with the astronauts, it must be a nutritionally superior product. Consequently, the NASA reference, plus the presence of a Ph.D. endorsing the product, seemed to convey the intended claim that Tang is a "good product" for spacemen and earth families.

EXHIBIT 9
Continued

Reactions to the commercial

In reacting to the commercials and its messages, there was a mixed response, with users of Tang, interestingly enough, being particularly inclined to react favorably to the Ph.D. theme and to the idea that this knowledgeable "authority" was endorsing the product (which, incidentally, is a product they themselves use). These women seemed to accept the commercial as being both believable and convincing in conveying the idea that Tang is nutritionally "good for you." Spontaneously, several volunteered that Tang has apparently been well researched by scientists and many of the women seemed to be impressed with the idea that a "mother with her doctorate in science" believed in the product enough to integrate it into her family's diet. It is important to note that, in the course of discussing this commercial, several of the women latched on to the "mother/scientist" role of the presenter and the respondents reacted positively to the fact that this woman thinks enough of Tang, from a professional vantage point, to use the product in her home. As one woman remarked, "her children are first in her mind and she wants to take good care of them." Virtually all of the users in the session, as well as several nonusers of the product, spontaneously commented that a scientist obviously has more "authority" and "knowledge" about the product than the average housewife and yet, at the same time, she is a mother of two children who naturally wants the best for her family. In a sense, the women seemed to feel that the commercial combined "the business and home life together."

A number of these women went on the describe "Lady Ph.D." as being a "capable" woman whose first concern is her children's health and well-being. The respondents seemed to feel that this spokesman was "happy and healthy" looking, "neat and attractive" and "realistic" in that she isn't the typical model type but rather an ordinary housewife who is the mother of two children. A few of the respondents volunteered that they could "relate to her" on a personal level because of her age and her appearance. In total, it should be recognized that the differences in the reactions of users and nonusers can possibly be attributed to the fact that the Ph.D. mother, as the spokesman for the product, seemed to reinforce for the users the idea that they are "good mothers" in that they are concerned about their children's health and diet and, at the same time, to offer them additional rebuttal for the reservations they themselves might have had about the product.

Among the nonusers, however, the reactions to the commercial were somewhat different. While some of the women seemed to respect the opinion of a "mother/scientist" as being an authority on nutrition, others in the session, upon being directly probed, indicated that they couldn't really relate to or identify with "Ph.D." in spite of the fact that they respect her educational background. On a more personal level, they seemed to perceive the woman as being "cold," "stiff" and somewhat "distant." One or two of the respondents commented that she didn't seem like a "homey" person, but rather, like an "efficient" person who is more "executive" than motherly.

Yet, despite their tendency to disassociate themselves from the presenter, the nonusers also agreed that her education makes her a qualified person to speak about the nutritious elements of Tang and, at least on an intellectual level, they too were able to take away the essential "nutrition" message of the commercial.

EXHIBIT 10
"FOOD SELECTION" GROUP INTERVIEW SUMMARY

Communication of product messages

In both the sessions with users and nonusers, there seemed to be some confusion on the part of the respondents as to what the "Food Selection" commercial was saying about the product. Those who seemed to understand the commercial, played back the idea that the astronauts' menu is carefully planned and selected and that Orange Tang has been chosen over other orange drink products because of the superior taste and nutritional value. The women, who seemed to grasp the idea that selectivity has gone into making Tang the drink of the astronauts, pointed out that nutritionists have sampled and evaluated many foods and came up with Tang as the best in the orange drink category. The nutritional quality of the product, rich in vitamin C, was played back frequently by these respondents and the astronaut association seemed to confirm the fact that Tang must be nutritious. Several of the women seemed to say, "If it is good enough for the spacemen, then it should be good enough for us."

Others in the session were baffled as to what point the commercial was trying to make. Some of the women were confused as to why the eggs and bacon were being rejected. Interestingly enough, because of their lack of understanding, they played back the message that Tang is a complete breakfast drink . . . "a product that can replace bacon and eggs." These respondents failed to understand the intended idea that NASA is highly selective in choosing food that is suitable for the astronauts and, consequently, they got the impression that Tang will take the place of a full course breakfast.

Interestingly enough, some of the respondents found the commercial confusing because they could not understand the purpose of showing bacon and eggs. A few of the women added that Tang contains vitamins whereas bacon and eggs are protein foods and they could not see the connection or purpose for showing both kinds of foods. Thus, it was apparent that a number of the women were confused about what the commercial was trying to say about Tang.

Reactions to the commercial

On the whole, the respondents in both Denver as well as St. Louis seemed to react negatively to the way in which this commercial was presented. In fact, it appeared that the "Food Selection" commercial seemed to antagonize many of the consumers interviewed, which in effect, caused many of the respondents to disbelieve the product claims.

A number of the respondents specifically commented that they were "turned off" by the actors in the commercial who were portraying the researchers. As one woman put it, "I would expect a little boy to react this way over eggs but not an adult." Others also seemed to disapprove of the way in which NASA was represented in the commercial, and here too, the women commented that "researchers would never look or act like the people in the film." Furthermore, because the women seemed to perceive the commercial as being "cartoon-like" and "spoofish," it was difficult for them to relate to the product messages as being real and credulous. In a sense, science and research seem to be a matter taken more seriously by the respondents and they seemed to resent the way it was portrayed in the commercial. By parodying NASA in a "Mickey Mouse" way, many of the women immediately seemed to discredit what was being said.

EXHIBIT 10
Continued

In light of this objection to the commercial, the respondents went on to object to the hard sell approach of the commercial. These consumers from the midwestern states complained that the pace of the commercial was "too fast" and "pushy." One woman in particular objected to the "driving tempo" that was constant throughout the commercial. Several women in each of the sessions mentioned that they resent being told to use a product because "the astronauts use it" and these women went on to say that they feel quite qualified to judge for themselves whether a product is good or not. In a sense, they seemed to feel "put down" by the commercial and tended to feel that it was "stupid" and "insulting."

Consequently, in spite of the fact that some of the women were getting the message that Tang is a nutritious orange drink, the claim itself seemed to be ignored in light of the presentation. Surprisingly, even those women who were using Tang commented that a commercial like "Food Selection" would never motivate them to buy the product.

awareness the commercial had generated for the respondent. There were two measures, not necessarily independent of one another, which were used to classify respondents into a hierarchical order that was roughly equivalent to the commercial's ability to promote accurate retention of intended copy points. The first measure was related to the level of cueing, or prompting, that was necessary in order to stimulate the respondent's memory of having seen (or not seen) the commercial.

As described in Exhibit 11, which is a flow diagram of the questioning procedure, three levels of prompting were employed. The first level was the category prompt; only the product category—orange breakfast drink—was used as a memory cue. The second level was the brand prompt; the respondent was asked directly whether or not he or she saw a Tang commercial last night on TV. The final level was the commercial prompt; the respondent who claimed to have seen the program in which the commercial was shown but couldn't recall the commercial was cued by prompts drawn from the dramatic story line of the program before and after the airing to the Tang commercial. The hierarchy of cues, then, was as follows:

Level of prompting	Type of prompt
Unaided	Category: "Did you see a commercial for a brand of orange breakfast drink?"
Aided	Brand: "Do you remember seeing a commercial for Tang last night?"
Prompted	Commercial: "Right after this scene, there was a commercial for Tang. Do you recall seeing this commercial?"

The second measure of the quality of awareness which each commercial promoted was based on the verbatim responses of the respondents when directly questioned about the commercials which they claimed they had seen. Seven questions, listed in Exhibit 12, were asked of each person claiming to have seen the commercial being tested. On the basis of whether or not the verbatim responses described the actual content of the commercial, respondents were classified as falling into one of three categories. "Proven" recallers had the highest levels of recall with respect to the message and format of presentation of the commercial. "Re-

EXHIBIT 11
FLOW OF QUESTIONS TO DETERMINE THE LEVEL OF PROMPTING REQUIRED TO STIMULATE RECALL

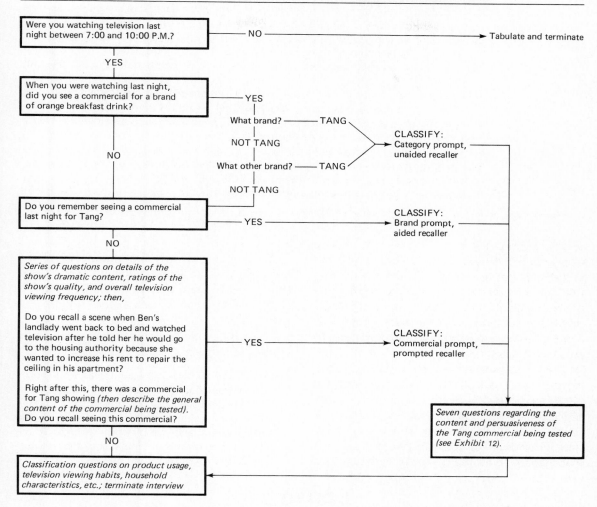

lated'' recallers showed a grasp of the basic content of the commercial, though they were often less certain of the details of presentation. "Incorrect" recallers were those respondents who claimed to have seen the commercial but whose verbatim descriptions of the commercial's content were highly inaccurate. "Incorrect" re-

callers were usually eliminated from the tabulations of results prepared in management summary form by the GF marketing research department, while "proven" and "related" recallers were reported both separately and in the aggregate.

The verbatim responses to the seven ques-

EXHIBIT 12
OPEN-ENDED QUESTIONS USED TO DETERMINE WHETHER A RESPONDENT WAS A PROVEN RECALLER, A RELATED RECALLER, OR AN INCORRECT RECALLER

1. Please tell me anything at all you remember about the Tang commercial you saw last night. (PROBE FOR DETAIL, RECORD VERBATIM)
2. In addition to what you already told me, what did the commercial look like? What did you see in the Tang commercial last night? (PROBE, RECORD VERBATIM)
3. What (else) did they say about Tang in last night's commercial? (PROBE, RECORD VERBATIM)
4. What ideas about Tang were brought out in the commercial last night? What other ideas were brought out? (PROBE, RECORD VERBATIM)
5. Advertising generally tries to tell you what is good about a product and tries to convince you to buy it. What did the advertising for Tang tell you in order to convince you that it is good or that you should buy it? (PROBE, RECORD VERBATIM)
6. Did the commercial make Tang seem different from other brands? (If yes, in what ways did it make it seem different?) (PROBE, RECORD VERBATIM)
7. Have you ever seen this very same commercial before?

tions regarding the test commercial's content were coded by specific copy points and reported in the quantitative summary of the test. Finally, the verbatim responses were reported in a qualitative supplement to each test commercial's research report and were often used by management to enrich its insight into the commercial's audience impact.

The GF marketing research department summarized the results of the TV recall tests (Exhibit 13) in a brief memo that accompanied the four separate reports, each numbering about 18 pages of tabulated findings and about a like number of pages of verbatim transcripts. In the management summary, the research depart-

ment concluded, "The total proven and related recall was above the Tang norm for Food Selection and Packing, at the norm for Lady Ph.D., and below the norm for Andromeda."

Additional recall tabulations are reported in Exhibit 14.

The marketing research summary went on to report the following:

Playback of all major copy points was below norm for "Andromeda." "Food Selection" had superior playback on taste/flavor and convenience. "Lady Ph.D." had superior playback on space association, vitamins and taste/flavor. "Packing" had superior playback on vitamins and convenience and average playback on nutrition.

EXHIBIT 13
SUMMARY RESULTS OF RECALL TEST

Measure	*Percentage of Commercial Audience (Unaided + Aided)*				
	Tang norm	"Andromeda"	"Food Selection"	"Lady Ph.D."	"Packing"
Proven recall	11	7	19	7	18
Related recall	8	3	9	12	3
Proven and related combined	19	10	28	19	21

EXHIBIT 13

Continued

Percentage of Commercial Audience (Unaided + Aided + Prompted)

Copy point	Tang norm	"Andromeda"	"Food Selection"	"Lady Ph.D."	"Packing"
Space association	63%	46%	59%	66%	55%
Vitamins	53	23	43	66	74
Nutrition	29	8	20	24	29
Taste/flavor	49	23	70	55	23
Convenience	37	15	48	34	45

The research department's summary concluded:

> Responses to special questions directed to recallers of "Lady Ph.D." to elicit attitudes toward the presenter were generally positive and indicated that she was believable, convincing and seemed to lend an air of authority to the message. Responses to special questions to recallers of "Andromeda" to elicit attitudes toward the unique execution were generally negative.

The copy-testing studies were completed in about half the normal time, and by mid-September the findings had been reported to both the brand group and the agency. Mr. Thomas, as the head of the administrative center for the copy development program, had prepared an analysis of the findings with his colleagues from the creative and account groups. He went to what was to be the final decision-

EXHIBIT 14
RESULTS OF RECALL TEST

	"Andromeda"		"Food Selection"		"Lady Ph.D."		"Packing"	
Number of contacts	2,266		4,048		3,745		3,470	
Number of program viewers	170		249		206		214	
Size of commercial audience	128		160		148		146	
Proven recallers								
Unaided (category prompt)	9	7%	34	15%	6	4%	11	8%
Aided (brand prompt)	2	2	7	4	1	1	15	10
Prompted (commercial prompt)	0	0	1	1	3	2	8	5
Total	11	9%	42	20%	10	7%	34	23%
Related recallers								
Unaided (category prompt)	3	2%	5	3%	3	2%	2	1%
Aided (brand prompt)	1	1	8	5	16	11	3	2
Prompted (commercial prompt)	1	1	6	4	7	5	5	3
Total	5	4%	19	12%	26	18%	10	6%
Incorrect recallers								
Unaided (category prompt)	5	4%	7	4%	5	3%	2	1%
Aided (brand prompt)	4	3	8	5	6	4	4	3
Prompted (commercial prompt)	3	2	3	2	2	1	1	1
Total	12	9%	18	11%	13	8%	7	5%
No claimed recall	100	78%	91	57%	99	67%	95	65%
Grand total	128	100%	160	100%	148	100%	146	100%

making meeting in White Plains in September.

At this meeting the agency group first presented and discussed the results of the TV recall scores and verbatim responses. This was followed by a qualitative analysis of the strengths and weaknesses of each of the four commercial copy executions. Frank Thomas concluded his presentation with a recommendation that the client use the "Lady Ph.D." commercial to launch the new advertising campaign. Mr. Thomas explained that although "Food Selection" scored highest on the TV recall tests, "Lady Ph.D." seemed to be communicating the sales message better, as indicated by the quality of the verbatim responses associated with this particular commercial. (The verbatim reports of the individual telephone interviews for "Lady Ph.D." and "Food Selection" covered over 54 pages of material and are not reproduced here for reasons of length. The subjective content of the verbatim reports is imperfectly but adequately conveyed by the focus group interview summaries listed in Exhibits 9 and 10.)

Dick Jackson, the product manager, disagreed with the line of reasoning at the meeting by contending that the quality of the verbatim responses should not be given as much weight in this particular instance as it normally would receive because of the rather large margin in recall scores in favor of "Food Selection." The product manager argued that although the "Lady Ph.D." verbatim reponses were indeed richer qualitatively than those of "Food Selection," the latter's recall scores were nearly 1½ times greater than those of "Lady Ph.D." Further, Mr. Jackson stated that the quality of the "Lady Ph.D." verbatim reports would mean very little if consumers were unable to recall that "Lady Ph.D." was specifically associated with Orange Tang.

At that point of apparent impasse between the assistant product manager and the account executive on one hand and the product manager on the other, Bill King, the product group manager, began his review of the situation. Everyone in the meeting was well aware that the shipments of Tang in the second quarter of fiscal 1973 had dropped well below the previous year's level, and further declines seemed likely in the absence of effective, fresh advertising copy.

38 General Motors Corporation

Craig E. Cline • Scott Ward

In the summer of 1977 Secretary of Transportation Brock Adams announced that passive restraints[1] would be required for all new cars by the 1984 model year.[2] The federal program

Craig E. Cline was formerly a research assistant at the Harvard Graduate School of Business Administration. Scott Ward is a professor of marketing at the Wharton School, University of Pennsylvania.

Note: The data provided in this case have in part been altered and do not reflect the actual results of the study.

[1]Passive restraints were defined as any occupant protection system that required "no action by vehicle occupants" to activate. Leading passive restraint designs in 1978 were variations on two systems: (1) air cushion (inflatable) restraint systems, or "air bags," automatically inflated on impact to protect front-seat passengers from the force of a frontal collision and then deflated (in less than several seconds) to permit quick egress from the vehicle; and (2) automatic safety belt systems which automatically positioned the belts around the front-seat passengers when doors were shut.

[2]"Model year" was defined as the automaker's annual production period. For example, the 1979 model year commenced on October 1, 1978, and was scheduled to terminate September 30, 1979.

specified a 3-year transition period, starting with the 1982 model year family-size cars. The remainder of the program was to be implemented as follows:

1983 model year—All intermediate and compact cars must be equipped with passive restraint systems.

1984 model year—All cars must be equipped with passive restraint systems.

Secretary Adams's ruling did not apply to trucks or vans.

In July 1978, Ms. Regina Lipsky, manager of General Motors's (GM's) Corporate Product Planning Group, received a memorandum from the Product Policy Group. In it, she was requested to:

1. Assess consumer preferences for each of the restraint system designs, determine which system would be most appropriate for each car line, and provide a production/capacity

forecast for each system chosen. These systems were:

a. *Two-point passive system*, in which the belt was anchored at two points on the car frame. (This system also included an "active" lap belt—that is, one which the person must manually buckle.)

b. *Three-point passive system*,[3] in which the belt was anchored at three points on the car frame. This system would be made available in either a "base" or "deluxe" version, the latter being somewhat more attractive and less cumbersome to use.

c. *Three-point power passive*, in which a motor automatically positioned the belt around the driver.

d. The *air bag* (which also included an active lap belt system).

The systems were to be compared with the current-production three-point active system.

2. Develop production forecasts for air bag systems that could be used as the basis of a make/buy decision. Engineering stated that if air bag production for intermediate and standard cars were to exceed 1 million units in model year 1982, a make decision would most likely be indicated.

The results of her analysis were to be presented in a report to the Product Policy Group on November 1, 1978. Subsequently, her report and the Product Policy Group's recommendations would be passed on to the GM executive committee for final approval. The memorandum concluded with a handwritten addendum from the group's chairperson:

> As you know, Reggie, this is a government-mandated program—which means it has high visibility everywhere. Therefore, we want to make certain that our customers get the best system at an

affordable price. But we also need to know how the price of each system affects the customers' preference for each. So I hope you can factor price sensitivity into your analysis somehow. We are going to base our final decisions heavily on the results of your report, so it is imperative that it be good.

The Corporate Product Planning Group, which Ms. Lipsky managed, reported to the executive vice president in charge of the functional area groups, such as marketing, engineering, and industrial relations. The Product Policy Group was one of a dozen policy groups that reported to the executive committee, which formulated the operating policy for General Motors. It was composed of the top executives from the major operating divisions, as well as the various functional groups and financial staff. The Corporate Product Planning Group was responsible for long-range product forecasting and planning, with strong emphasis on market and consumer research.

The Current Situation

After meeting to discuss the implications of the federal program, General Motors Corporation's Product Policy Group had decided that GM would offer to the public both air bag and automatic safety belt options on selected models in advance of the proposed federal requirements. The Product Policy Group felt that an early introduction of the two basic passive restraint systems under consideration (two- and three-point systems) was necessary to enable GM to (1) measure customer acceptance and (2) gain production and field experience with these systems. GM subsequently announced that it expected to offer optional air bags in some 1981 model year family-size cars, 1 year in advance of the requirements. Further, it planned to offer two-point passive systems as options on certain car lines, with the first system to be available on Chevrolet's Chevette (a subcompact) in model year 1978.

---

[3]As opposed to two-point passive systems, three-point passive systems have an additional belt which goes over the lap, as well as a belt going over the shoulder, across the chest.

In the summer of 1978, prior to the beginning of the 1979 model year, GM had developed four separate passive safety belt systems—one of which was currently being offered on the Chevette—and one air bag system. Each system was designed to meet the requirements of the federal passive restraint regulations. With the exception of the air bag system,[4] all were judged by GM engineers to be "more or less equally safe." Air bag restraint systems, which had been the focal point of a decade-long debate on the merits and costs of passive restraint systems, were extremely complex technologically. One GM official observed that air bag systems had to work "with greater reliability than equipment in the space program" and thus were less favored by automakers than the simpler automatic, or passive, safety belt systems currently available.

Cost was also a factor in the automakers' preference for automatic safety belts. According to an article in the *Detroit News*, "air bags have been estimated to cost the manufacturer about $200 if mass produced, while automatic belts are expected to cost about $50–$100. Replacing deployed air bags currently costs more than $600 and is expected to remain about three times higher than initial production costs."[5] However, more recently, industry observers had indicated that air bags might initially cost between $450 and $600.

General Motors Corporation

With 1977 sales of almost $55 billion, General Motors was the largest manufacturing company

in the world. Worldwide retail sales of 8.9 million GM passenger cars and trucks were 7 percent above 1976 sales and 6 percent over the previous record, set in 1973. GM accounted for 24 percent of the estimated 36.6 million passenger cars and trucks sold worldwide in 1977. In the United States, retail sales of 5.3 million GM passenger cars in 1977 set a new record, exceeding 1976 sales by 8 percent and the previous 1973 record by 1 percent. Other major product groups were diesel locomotives, diesel engines, automotive and truck parts, aircraft engines, and gas turbines. GM operated over 100 plants in the United States and Canada and had assembly, manufacturing, and/or warehousing locations in more than 20 other countries. Selected operating and financial data are presented in Exhibit 1. Exhibit 2 contains data on GM car production.

The General Motors organization was decentralized, with profit responsibility at the division level. There were 33 operating divisions—7 automotive divisions; 17 automotive body, components, and assembly divisions; and 9 nonautomotive products divisions. Central engineering and research functions existed for the company as a whole; however, new products or automotive system projects had independent engineering and research staffs, organized into "project centers." For example, the air bag was developed and tested by the Air Bag Passive Restraint System project center (with the aid of the divisions), which was responsible for overseeing the air bag restraint system from initial design to final implementation, whereupon responsibility for it would be transferred to the appropriate operating division or outside vendor.

Capital Investments

In the 5-year period ending in 1980, investment by GM was expected to exceed about $15 billion to $20 billion for plant facilities and special tools. The great bulk of this spending would be to resize virtually the entire product line to be sold in the United States. This was being done to

---

[4] Due to other impacts, such as side, rear, and roll-over, and because of the possibility of a second collision after the primary one—which would occur after the air bag had already deflated—GM engineers recommended that a lap belt be worn in air bag–equipped cars. (In fact, the use of a lap belt was required to meet federal standards.) With the use of a lap belt, the air bag was judged to be as safe as the automatic safety belt options. GM's air bag system, with lap belts, was to be offered to customers as an alternative to the automatic safety belt option.

[5] "Car Safety Rules Win Public Nod," *Detroit News*, Aug. 31, 1978.

EXHIBIT 1
OPERATING AND FINANCIAL HIGHLIGHTS

Dollars in Millions Except Per Share Amounts	1977	1976	1973*
Sales of all products			
United States operations:			
Automotive products	$44,317.0	$37,069.6	$28,116.6
Nonautomotive products	2,795.2	2,277.0	1,938.8
Defense and space	438.8	438.1	316.4
Total United States operations	47,551.0	39,784.7	30,371.8
Canadian operations	5,743.9	5,263.0	3,116.0
Overseas operations	8,399.1	7,495.2	5,779.0
Elimination of intercompany sales	(6,732.7)	(5,361.9)	(3,468.5)
Total	$54,961.3	$47,181.0	$35,798.3
Worldwide factory sales of cars and trucks			
(units in thousands)	9,068	8,568	8,684
Net income			
Amount	$ 3,337.5	$ 2,902.8	$ 2,398.1
As a percent of sales	6.1%	6.2%	6.7%
As a percent of stockholders' equity	21.2%	20.2%	19.1%
Earned per share of common stock	$11.62	$10.08	$8.34
Dividends per share of common stock	$ 6.80	$ 5.55	$5.25
Taxes			
United States, foreign and other income taxes	$ 2,934.2	$ 2,567.8	$ 2,115.0
Other taxes (principally payroll and property taxes)	1,809.7	1,492.0	1,090.7
Total	$ 4,743.9	$ 4,059.8	$ 3,205.7
Taxes per share of common stock	$16.58	$14.16	$11.21
Investment as of December 31			
Working capital	$ 7,630.3	$ 7,556.6	$ 6,196.9
Stockholders' equity	$15,766.9	$14,385.2	$12,566.8
Book value per share of common stock	$53.82	$49.02	42.71
Number of stockholders as of December 31			
(in thousands)	1,245	1,251	1,306
Worldwide employment			
Average number of employes (in thousands)	797	748	811
Total payrolls	$15,270.8	$12,908.5	$10,308.5
Property			
Real estate, plants and equipment—Expenditures	$ 1,870.9	$ 998.9	$ 1,163.4
—Depreciation	$ 974.0	$ 939.3	$ 902.9
Special tools—Expenditures	$ 1,775.8	$ 1,308.4	$ 941.0
—Amortization	$ 1,406.4	$ 1,296.9	$ 1,081.0

*For comparative purposes, results are shown for 1973 when the previous record for factory unit sales was established.

What Happened to the Revenue GM Received During 1977 Total 100.0%

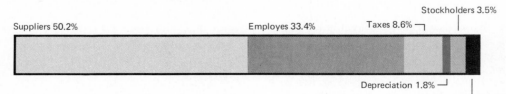

Suppliers 50.2%   Employes 33.4%   Taxes 8.6%   Stockholders 3.5%

Depreciation 1.8%

Use in the Business 2.5%

Source: General Motors *Annual Report,* 1977.

make GM vehicles more fuel-efficient and in conformity to federal safety requirements. During 1977, GM spent a record $3.6 billion on plants and retooling, 43 percent above the previous peak established in 1974 and 65 percent above the 1972 to 1976 average. The high cost of GM's capital investment program, coupled with the effects of inflation on product costs not fully recovered by increased prices, had had an adverse effect on profit as a percent of sales. As GM's chairman and president noted in the 1977 *Annual Report,*

> Measured simply in the dollars it costs—whether inflated or real—this redesign of the American automobile will exceed even the Apollo space program that carried men to the moon. This dramatic overhaul of already successful products in the hope of satisfying the changing demands of millions of individuals—and at the same time meeting ever-tightening governmental standards—has been called the biggest and most expensive new-product program in industrial history.

Automobile Restraint Regulations

Automobile restraint requirements, some form of which had been in effect since 1966, were intended to help reduce what Ralph Nader termed the "horrible carnage on our nation's highways." Every week, about 900 people were killed in motor vehicle accidents; 10,000 others were injured every day. As a result of studies which showed that safety belts were effective in reducing accident injuries and fatalities, lap belts—and later lap-shoulder belts—were made mandatory for all vehicles produced or sold in the United States, including light trucks up to 10,000 pounds GVW. Subsequent studies had demonstrated that *when used,* lap belts were 31 percent effective and lap-shoulder belts 57 percent effective, in preventing injury or death in motor vehicle accidents.

Despite the massive publicity surrounding the safety belt issue, including the "buckle up your seat belt" campaigns sponsored by the government in national and local media, it had been generally reported in the press that no more than 15 to 30 percent of the population used safety belts "regularly." Many people reported that they only wore safety belts for long trips at high speed, even though it had been widely publicized that (reflecting normal automobile usage patterns) 75 percent of all accidents occur within 25 miles of home and that 80 percent occur at speeds less than 40 mph.

Standard 208

In attempts to improve usage of safety restraints, the National Highway Traffic Safety Administration (NHTSA) had issued additional requirements for warning buzzers, and later starter-interlock devices,[6] on all passenger cars. Faced with consumers' complaints about the inconvenience and discomfort of safety belts, coupled with widespread consumer attempts to circumvent the buzzer and starter-interlock systems, the NHTSA in 1972 amended Standard 208, which called for a passive restraint system of either the air bag or automatic belt type to be installed in all passenger automobiles. Delays caused by court challenges and congressional hearings, primarily concerning the nature and scope of the standard, postponed the implementation of Standard 208 until the summer of 1977, when Secretary of Transportation Adams announced the timetable described earlier.

Meanwhile in 1974 Congress had revoked the starter-interlock requirement in response to what was perceived to be a widespread revolt against the interlock system. One newspaper had reported that "hundreds of thousands" of new-automobile owners had already disconnected the system. At the same time it revoked the

---

[6]In starter-interlock systems, the driver could not start the car until the driver's seat belt was fastened.

EXHIBIT 2
GM CAR PRODUCTION BY MODEL LINES, 1972–1977

	1977		1976		1975	
	Units	Percentage of total*	Units	Percentage of total*	Units	Percentage of total*
Chevette	133,468	1.47	187,830	2.31	–	–
Acadian	3,299	0.04	7,523	0.09	–	–
Vega	78,402	0.86	160,592	1.98	207.843	3.17
Monza	6,230	0.07	37,396	0.46	66.622	1.02
© Corvette	49,213	0.54	46,558	0.57	38,465	0.59
Nova	365,269	4.01	334,728	4.13	273,014	4.17
Corvair	–	–	–	–	–	–
Camaro	218,854	2.40	182,981	2.25	145,775	2.23
Sportvan	37,595	0.41	23,332	0.29	18,653	0.28
⑧ Malibu (Chevelle)	291,955	3.21	307,970	3.80	280,911	4.29
Ⓐ Monte Carlo	374,749	4.12	328,169	4.04	258,921	3.95
Ⓐ Chevrolet	561,658	6.16	333,976	4.12	352,021	5.37
Total Chevrolet	2,120,692	23.29	1,951,055	24.02	1,642,225	25.07
Astre	32,788	0.36	50,384	0.62	64,601	0.99
© Sunbird	7,014	0.08	24,803	0.31	–	–
Ventura	90,764	1.00	74,116	0.91	66,554	1.02
Firebird	155,736	1.71	110,775	1.37	84,063	1.28
⑧ LeMans (Tempest)	69,944	0.77	96,229	1.19	97,058	1.48
Grand Prix	288,430	3.16	228,091	2.81	86,582	1.32
Ⓐ Pontiac	202,453	2.22	137,216	1.69	126,555	1.93
Total Pontiac	847,129	9.30	721,614	8.90	525,413	8.02
© Starfire†	–	–	12,278	0.15	–	–
Omega	63,982	0.70	58,159	0.72	41,807	0.64
⑧ Cutlass/F-85	632,742	6.95	500,129	6.16	319,531	4.88
Toronado	34,261	0.38	24,444	0.30	23,333	0.35
Oldsmobile	385,833	4.24	279,608	3.45	213,150	3.25
Total Oldsmobile	1,116,818	12.27	874,618	10.78	597,821	9.12
© Skyhawk†	–	–	15,768	0.19	–	–
Skylark (Apollo)	113,472	1.25	114,491	1,41	63,133	0.96
⑧ Century (Skylark/Special)	328,196	3.60	305,085	3.76	183,458	2.80
Ⓐ Riviera	26,138	0.29	20,082	0.25	17,306	0.26
Buick	377,428	4.14	217,871	3.48	217,871	3.33
Total Buick	845,234	9.28	737,466	9.09	481,768	7.35
⑧ Seville‡	45,060	0.50	43,772	0.54	16,355	0.25
Ⓐ Cadillac	266,083	2.92	216,183	2.66	203,624	3.11
Eldorado	47,344	0.53	49,184	0.61	44,752	0.68
Total Cadillac	358,487	3.94	309,139	3.81	264,731	4.04
Total General Motors Corp.	5,288,360	58.08	4,593,892	56.60	3,511,958	53.60

EXHIBIT 2
Continued

	1974 Units	1974 Percentage of total*	1973 Units	1973 Percentage of total*	1972 Units	1972 Percentage of total*
Chevette	–	–	–	–	–	–
Acadian	–	–	–	–	–	–
Vega	369.407	4.55	395,792	4.0	390.478	4.5
Monza	–	–	–	–	–	–
© Corvette	37,504	0.46	30.464	0.3	27,004	0.3
Nova	391,454	4.80	369,511	3.7	349,733	4.1
Corvair	–	–	–	–	–	–
Camaro	151,021	1.86	96,752	1.0	68,651	0.8
Sportvan	22,059	0.30	21,641	0.3	18,266	0.2
® Malibu (Chevelle)	291,772	3.59	328,533	3.3	357,820	4.2
Monte Carlo	224,600	2.77	233,689	2.4	163,085	1.9
Ⓐ Chevrolet	630,861	7.77	941,104	9.5	906,541	10.5
Total Chevrolet	2,118,678	26.09	2,417,486	24.5	2,281,578	26.5
Astre	–	–	–	–	–	–
© Sunbird	–	–	–	–	–	–
Ventura	81,799	1.01	96,500	1.0	72,787	0.8
Firebird	73,729	0.91	46,313	0.5	29,951	0.3
® LeMans (Tempest)	129,105	1.59	232,600	2.3	169,993	2.0
Grand Prix	99,817	1.23	153,899	1.5	91,961	1.1
Ⓐ Pontiac	175,766	2.16	365,134	3.7	274,081	3.2
Total Pontiac	560,216	6.90	894,446	9.0	638,773	7.4
© Starfire†	–	–	–	–	–	–
Omega	50,280	0.63	60,363	0.6	–	–
® Cutlass/F-85	333,241	4.10	405,519	4.1	334,582	3.9
Toronado	27,600	0.34	56,226	0.6	48,900	0.6
Oldsmobile	208,276	2.56	417,522	4.2	374,702	4.3
Total Oldsmobile	619,397	7.63	939,630	9.5	758,184	8.8
© Skyhawk†	–	–	–	–	–	–
Skylark (Apollo)	56,709	0.70	32,793	0.3	–	–
® Century (Skylark/Special)	190,607	2.35	298,468	3.0	225,346	2.6
Ⓐ Riviera	20,129	0.25	34,080	0.4	33,728	0.4
Buick	227,618	2.80	455,824	4.6	420,847	4.9
Total Buick	495,063	6.10	821,165	8.3	679,921	7.9
® Seville‡	–	–	–	–	–	–
Ⓐ Cadillac	201,918	2.48	253,388	2.6	227,713	2.6
Eldorado	40,412	0.50	51,451	0.5	40,074	0.5
Total Cadillac	242,330	2.98	304,839	3.1	267,787	3.1
Total General Motors Corp.	4,035,684	49.70	5,377,566	54.4	4,626,243	53.7

*Percentage of total United States–Canadian car production.

†Built in Canada for sale in Canada.

‡Includes United States production only; 1,152 Sevilles built in Canada are not shown in the tabulation.

Note: Ⓐ, ®, and © refer to car body types used for classification in the passive restraint system study. See discussion on pp. 583–585.

Source: Ward's Automotive Yearbook 1978.

starter-interlock requirement, Congress set ground rules affecting any future requirements for passive restraints. The NHTSA in future rule making had to submit to Congress all passive-restraint-related regulations for a 60-day period; a regulation would take effect if Congress did not disapprove of it by concurrent resolution within that time.

Ms. Lipsky, of General Motors, noted that continuing debate lingered within Congress between a faction opposing the implementation of Standard 208 and senators and representatives supporting the Standard. The latter were supported by a broad-based coalition of labor, consumer, insurance, and public interest groups. Thus far, no move to kill the legislation had succeeded. Nevertheless, the possibility existed that Congress or the NHTSA would delay or revoke Standard 208 at some future date.

The Passive Restraint Study

Given the necessity of recommending which passive restraint systems would be most appropriate for which GM cars, Ms. Lipsky and her colleagues decided to hold a passive restraint "clinic" that would simulate the climate of the 1984 model year, when passive restraint systems would be mandatory. "Clinics" refer to GM's characteristic approach to consumer research. Consumers are exposed to proposed new models and features in advance of their actual production, and attitudinal and behavioral (choice) data are gathered. Across all GM divisions, about 25 to 30 such clinics might be held in a year. Participants in the passive restraint clinic would consist of GM-car owners, and the clinic would be designed to afford individuals an opportunity to experience the use of the various safety belt passive systems (compared with the existing three-point active belt system—see page 568). Although it was decided that it would not be possible to have individuals actually test the

air bag system, they would be queried concerning their preferences for air bags compared with the other systems on the basis of an explanation of the former's features.

Available Demographic and Attitudinal Data

Before designing the questionnaire that would be used to record individuals' responses in the clinic, Ms. Lipsky and her colleagues decided to survey relevant previous studies on car buyers and their attitudes toward safety restraints. Although meaningful data on consumer attitudes toward, and usage of, seat belts were scarce, members of the study team were able to find some data that they thought could be helpful.

Demographic data on the age, sex, and income levels of car owners and drivers were readily available from industry publications (see Exhibit 3). Ms. Lipsky discovered, for example, that 75 percent of domestic cars were registered to males but that over 42 percent of the principal drivers of these vehicles were female. Car ownership was greatest among people aged 25 to 35. And nearly 70 percent of families with before-tax incomes of at least $4,000 to $5,000 owned at least one vehicle.

In addition to demographic data, Ms. Lipsky had available a survey of the existing literature on joint decision making within families that had been commissioned by the Corporate Product Planning Group in 1976 (see Exhibit 4). At the time she had been investigating the relative influence of both the husband and the wife in the decision to purchase an automobile. She felt that the joint decision-making process might also be a significant factor in selecting an auto restraint system and thus decided to build it somehow into the Automobile Restraint Study.

While preparing the final research design of the Automobile Restraint Study in August 1978, Ms. Lipsky received a summary report, *Public*

EXHIBIT 3
DEMOGRAPHIC DATA ON AUTOMOBILE OWNERS AND DRIVERS

Automobile Owners and Drivers

Characteristic	Domestic Cars		Imported Cars	
	Registered Owner	Principal Driver	Registered Owner	Principal Driver
Sex				
Male	75.8%	57.4%	69.7%	56.8%
Female	24.2	42.6	30.3	43.2
Total	100.0%	100.0%	100.0%	100.0%
Age				
Under 18	0.2%	0.8%	0.3%	1.1%
18-24	9.7	11.6	20.1	23.5
25-34	22.8	23.5	37.4	38.0
35-39	9.3	9.8	10.5	10.2
40-44	8.8	8.5	7.7	7.0
45-49	9.7	8.9	6.6	5.6
50-54	11.9	10.7	6.4	5.1
55-64	16.4	15.6	7.8	6.7
65 and Over	11.3	10.6	3.2	2.9
Total	100.0%	100.0%	100.0%	100.0%

Note: The above data are from a study of a sample of buyers of new domestic and imported automobiles registered during January and February 1977.

Source: Buyers of New Domestic Cars, 1977 and *Buyers of New Imported Cars, 1977.* Copyright 1977, Newsweek, Inc. Reproduced with permission.

Buyers of New Domestic Cars, 1977

Item	Percent of New Cars Purchased
List Price Including Options	
Under $4,000	3.2%
$4,000-$4,999	9.3
$5,000-$5,999	19.1
$6,000-$6,999	29.9
$7,000-$7,999	20.1
$8,000-$9,999	11.3
$10,000 and Over	7.0
Total	100.0%
Principal Usage of New Car	
To and From Work	42.0%
Business	11.1
Pleasure Trips	16.8
Local Transportation in Community	35.9
School	1.9
Total	100.0%(1)
Car Disposed of When Purchasing	
Yes	81.1%
No	18.9
Total	100.0%
Year Model of Car Disposed	
1977	0.8%
1976	8.5
1975	10.7
1974	15.6
1973	15.5
1972	14.9
1971	9.7
1970	9.4
1969	6.2
1968	4.3
1967 & Earlier	11.1
Total	100.0%(1)

(1) Detail adds to more than 100 percent due to multiple mentions.

Source: Buyers of New Domestic Cars, 1977 and *Buyers of New Imported Cars, 1977.* Copyright 1977, Newsweek, Inc. Reproduced with permission.

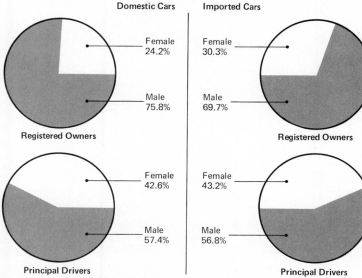

Sex of Passenger Car Owners and Drivers

Domestic Cars — Imported Cars

Registered Owners: Domestic — Female 24.2%, Male 75.8%; Imported — Female 30.3%, Male 69.7%

Principal Drivers: Domestic — Female 42.6%, Male 57.4%; Imported — Female 43.2%, Male 56.8%

Source: MVMA Motor Vehicle Facts & Figures, 1978.

EXHIBIT 3
Continued

Age	Male (000)	Female (000)	Total (000)
Under 16	78	60	138
16	1,072	859	1,931
17	1,669	1,365	3,034
18	1,880	1,568	3,448
19	2,016	1,707	3,723
Under 20	6,715	5,559	12,274
20-24	9,935	8,818	18,753
25-29	9,471	8,594	18,065
30-34	7,850	7,181	15,031
35-39	6,338	5,797	12,135
40-44	5,536	4,944	10,480
45-49	5,505	4,838	10,343
50-54	5,441	4,764	10,205
55-59	5,075	4,302	9,377
60-64	4,189	3,396	7,585
65-69	3,490	2,578	6,068
70 and over	4,650	2,935	7,585
Total	74,195	63,706	137,901

*Number of Drivers, 1977**

*Estimated
Source: U.S. Federal Highway Administration.

Average Annual Miles Driven

Age	Male	Female	All
16-19	5,461	3,586	4,633
20-24	11,425	5,322	8,260
25-29	13,931	5,539	9,814
30-34	14,496	5,752	10,274
35-39	13,035	6,232	9,878
40-44	13,133	5,950	9,833
45-49	12,818	6,271	9,875
50-54	12,345	5,454	9,447
55-59	11,495	5,439	9,009
60-64	9,710	5,291	8,112
65-69	6,915	4,173	5,850
70 and over	5,302	3,183	4,644
All ages	11,352	5,411	8,685

Source: Based on unpublished data from National Personal Transportation Survey conducted by Bureau of the Census for the Federal Highway Administration 1969-70.

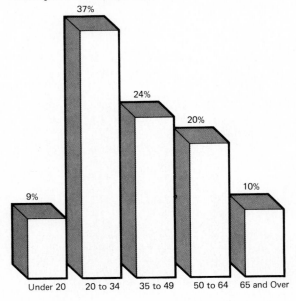

Percentage of Drivers by Age, 1977

Source: U.S. Federal Highway Administration.

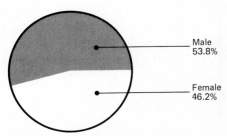

Percentage of Drivers by Sex, 1977

Source: U.S. Federal Highway Administration.

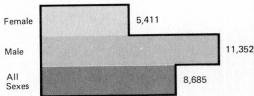

Average Miles Driven by Sex

Source: Based on unpublished data from National Personal Transportation Survey conducted by Bureau of the Census for the Federal Highway Administration 1969-70.

EXHIBIT 3
Continued

Family Ownership of Vehicles, by Selected Family Characteristics — 1972-1974

	Number of Families (000)	Average No. of Vehicles Owned	Percent Owning at Least One Vehicle		Number of Families (000)	Average No. of Vehicles Owned	Percent Owning at Least One Vehicle
Family Income Before Taxes				**Occupation of Family Head**			
Under $3,000	10,277	.5	38%	Self-employed Workers	5,304	1.8	93%
$3,000 to $3,999	3,890	.7	57	Salaried; Wage Earners	46,294	1.5	89
$4,000 to $4,999	3,680	.9	71	Professionals			
$5,000 to $5,999	3,365	1.0	80	and Managers	13,467	1.6	94
$6,000 to $6,999	3,574	1.2	83	Clerical and Sales			
$7,000 to $7,999	3,302	1.2	87	Workers	7,517	1.3	85
$8,000 to $9,999	6,449	1.4	91	Craftsmen and			
$10,000 to $11,999	6,524	1.5	94	Operatives	16,937	1.6	92
$12,000 to $14,999	7,659	1.7	96	Laborers and Service			
$15,000 to $19,999	7,847	1.8	97	Workers	8,372	1.1	77
$20,000 to $24,999	3,461	2.0	98	Armed Forces			
$25,000 and Over	3,372	2.1	98	Personnel	855	1.5	96
Not Reported	8,331	1.2	72	Retired	11,667	.7	56
				All Other and Not			
Family Size				Reported	7,611	.6	45
1 Person	17,080	.6	53%				
2 Persons	20,403	1.2	84	**Education of Family Head**			
3 Persons	11,563	1.5	87	Elementary 1 to 8 Years	16,148	1.0	66%
4 Persons	10,471	1.7	91	High School:			
5 Persons	6,392	1.8	92	1 to 3 Years	11,524	1.3	79
6 Persons or More	5,822	1.7	88	Graduate 4 Years	20,781	1.4	87
				College:			
Age of Family Head				1 to 3 Years	9,800	1.4	89
Under 25	6,478	1.0	77%	Graduate 4 Years	5,957	1.5	91
25-34	14,457	1.4	87	More than 4 Years	4,726	1.5	93
35-44	11,590	1.6	88	No School and Not			
45-54	13,227	1.6	87	Reported	2,797	.3	19
55-64	11,551	1.3	81				
65 and Over	14,428	.8	58	**All Families**	71,731	13.0	79%
Region							
Northeast	17,103	1.1	74%				
Northcentral	19,780	1.3	82				
South	21,979	1.3	79				
West	12,869	1.4	83				
Housing Tenure							
Homeowner	43,135	1.6	90%				
Renter	25,587	.9	67				
Not Reported	3,010	.3	27				
Urbanization Group							
Total Inside SMSA	50,076	1.2	78%				
Urban	44,868	1.2	76				
Central City	23,541	1.0	67				
Other Urban	21,326	1.4	87				
Rural	5,209	1.7	92				
Outside SMSA	21,655	1.4	82				
Urban	9,082	1.2	78				
Rural	12,573	1.5	85				

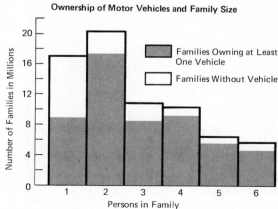

Ownership of Motor Vehicles and Family Size

Source: U.S. Bureau of Labor Statistics, *Consumer Expenditure Survey: Diary Survey, July 1972-June 1974 Bulletin 1959.*

EXHIBIT 4
A STUDY CONDUCTED FOR GENERAL MOTORS CORPORATION: JOINT DECISION MAKING IN CONTROLLED CIRCUMSTANCES
by Lorna Middendorf

The recent energy crisis had a profound effect on the automobile market. The sudden reality of fuel shortages generated a ripple effect with resultant reduced car purchases and shifts in new car requirements. Concurrently, market research had begun to delineate the importance of joint purchase decisions and the household as a purchasing unit. This paper reports the results of studies that have made an attempt to obtain information during an especially dynamic period about new automobile customer requirements.

Background studies of joint purchase decision making

With increased economic pressures on the household today and attention given to the changing roles of women in society, an increasing number of market researchers are calling for new research models. In an extensive review, Davis (1975) criticizes the pervasive focus on the individual when the household is logically the consumption *and* the decision-making unit. Haley, Overholser and Associates (1975) have demonstrated by their national study that husband and wife members of households contribute both *indirect* and direct influences in product decisions. Other studies reflect similar findings and are summarized in the following tables.

Conclusions

It seems clear from this review that combined social and economic forces are changing both consumer purchase patterns and the ways in which consumers make decisions about those purchases. While relative influence of husband and wife shifts according to particular product, consideration should be given to both spouses in product planning, merchandising, sales, and advertising. In marketing research, studies may have to be expanded to include probable influences from both spouses in the manner of Haley and Overholser; that is, a constant sum scalar technique and the determination of spouse influence weights.

Many of the studies reviewed here were based on questionnaire data and recall methods. As a consequence, it should be recognized that these approaches give rise to questions about error sources due to socially acceptable responses, faulty memory, and the partitioning of influence units when both spouses are not present.

Summary of Background Studies of Joint Purchase Decision-Making

Study	Study group	Focus	Results and implications
Haley, Overholser and Associates, *Purchase Influence Measures of Husband/Wife Influence on Buying Decisions*, New Canaan, CT, 1974–1975.	2,480 Households National Probability Sample	Direct and indirect product influence to assign weights to market targets for 108 package products and durable goods and services.	Three purchase decision influence patterns mark product and brand selections for packaged products and durable goods: 1. spouse dominant, 2. spouse independent, and 3. joint spouse influence. Buying influence (direct and indirect) exerted by husband and wife varies by time and circumstances.

EXHIBIT 4
Continued

Green and Cunningham, "Feminine Role Perception and Family Purchasing Decisions," *Journal of Marketing Research*, XII (August 1975).	257 Married Women in Houston, Texas	Change in husband-wife purchasing roles by age, income, and attitude groups for 10 products and services.	Purchasing behavior changes are a function of the emerging social female role and income and age factors. For automobiles there were significantly more joint and wife decisions among liberals.
Davis, *Decision Making within the Household*, Project: Synthesis of Knowledge of Consumer Behavior, Rann Program, NSF, April 1975.	100 Published Sources of Purchase Decision-making	The family as the primary consumption and decision-making unit. Variable involvement by family members in economic decisions. Changes in decision-making processes as function of environment, needs, and customary strategies. Consequences of husband/wife involvement and different decision strategies.	Husband/wife involvement varies widely by product category. Need good product studies, consideration of both spouses. H/W involvement varies by specific decisions and decision stages. Looking for one dominant spouse is poor approach, too simplistic. H/W involvement for any consumer decision is likely to show considerable variability among families. Families should be classified in more meaningful terms. Variable decision-making for cars. Davis (70) found H/W equal in gathering information, shopping and car use.
Cox, "Family Purchase Decision-making and the Process of Adjustment," *Journal of Marketing Research*, XII (May 1975).	93 Midwest Couples	Family product decision-making in context of goal-oriented small group.	Rankings of family car preferences and attributes showed family life cycle (Hill: *Establishment to Childless Family*) to give better explanation than marriage length or age.
Munsinger, Weber, and Hansen, "Joint Home Purchasing Decisions by Husbands and Wives," *Journal of Consumer Research*, I (March 1975).	138 Husband-Wife Dyads	Study of 7 elements in making house purchase following purchase.	Considerable variance in roles played by H/W in different elements of the housing decision. In every element majority of H/W reported equal influence.
Green and Langeard, "A Cross-National Comparison of Consumer Habits and Innovator Characteristics," *Journal of Marketing*, 39 (July 1975).	193 Texas US Women 222 French (Aix-en-Provence) Women	Study to generate French-American consumer profiles for grocery products and retail services.	Significant differences in cross-national personal habits and consumption behaviors. Biggest differences were social habits and environmental factors.

EXHIBIT 4
Continued

Wilkes, "Husband-Wife Influence in Purchase Decision," *Journal of Marketing Research*, XII (May 1975).	60 Middle Income Black Husbands, Wives	Identification of purchase influence from problem recognition through actual purchase.	Both spouses had considerable influence over all phases of decision processes. Relative influence varies across decision processes.

Attitudes Toward Passive Restraint Systems, that had just been issued in Washington by the NHTSA. Excerpts from the report are included in Exhibit 5. Ms. Lipsky was particularly interested in information in the report on the frequency of usage (Figure 2), choice of passive restraint system (air bag or automatic belt) at various price levels (Figure 4), and perceived quality of various restraint systems (Figure 5).

EXHIBIT 5
PUBLIC ATTITUDES TOWARD PASSIVE RESTRAINT SYSTEMS: SUMMARY REPORT, AUGUST 1978*

Introduction

Under the sponsorship of the National Highway Traffic Safety administration, Peter D. Hart Research Associates, Inc., has conducted a nationwide study of public attitudes toward automobile safety. Hart Research interviewed a scientifically selected sample of 2,016 adult Americans who are either licensed drivers or who live in households with at least one automobile. Interviews were conducted across the country between May 17 and May 27, 1978. Each interview lasted approximately 50 minutes and was administered personally in the homes of the respondents.

This survey explored a broad range of subjects relating to automobile safety including:

Public concern about automobile safety and perception of the need to protect automobile passengers from crash injury,

Public attitudes toward currently available safety equipment, particularly the active safety belts,

Attitudes toward new rules requiring passive restraint systems in new automobiles for crash protection, and

Public expectations about the technology and use of new passive restraint systems.

Summary of key observations

1. The American public expresses considerable concern about the possibility of being injured in an automobile accident. In fact, people show greater concern about injuries from auto crashes than from a variety of other accidents with which they were compared.
2. Only a quarter of the population report that they use seat belts all or most of the time. Seat belts in cars currently in use are perceived to be very uncomfortable and, to a lesser extent, difficult to use.

EXHIBIT 5
Continued

3. By a two to one margin, Americans believe that the government should require automatic crash protection in new cars rather than encourage greater seat belt use. A majority of Americans strongly oppose laws that would require belt use.

4. The public generally agrees with the Secretary of Transportation's decision to require passive restraints in new automobiles. Agreement remains high after people have been briefed on the systems—air bags and automatic belts—that will be used to meet the requirement.

5. Air bags are much better known than automatic seat belts. Nevertheless, the public wants much more information about air bags, their operation, and dependability, while automatic belts seem readily understood when they are explained.

6. When asked to choose between air bags and automatic belts, the public divides its preference with price being only a marginal consideration. There is a constituency for each system with younger people tending to prefer air bags to a greater degree than older people.

7. The public rates air bags above automatic or active belts for their safety protection, comfort, appearance, and ease of use. People who rarely or never use active belts transfer their dislike for active belts to automatic belts. A majority of these people say that they would try to disconnect their automatic belts if they owned a car with them.

8. The public is generally favorable to government auto safety regulation, and believes that government regulators have the public's interest at heart. The public tends to trust government auto safety officials somewhat more than auto manufacturers on questions of safety.

9. The public believes that many major industries should have a great deal of regulation to protect public safety. The auto industry is similarly regarded as needing regulation, but is not singled out as needing much more than other industries. Under current conditions, however, the public perceives that auto makers are doing a responsible job with auto safety and are generally responsive to consumer desires.

Excerpts from the report published by the U.S. Department of Transportation, National Highway Traffic Safety Administration, Washington, D.C.

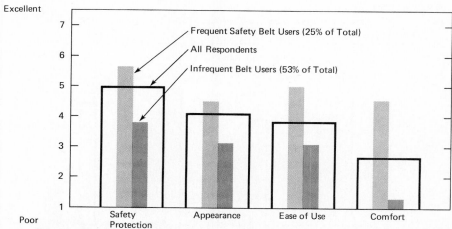

Figure 1   Median scores on a seven-point scale of the quality of seat belts perceived by respondents classed according to their seat belt use habits.

EXHIBIT 5
Continued

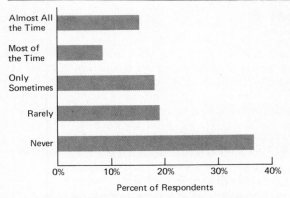

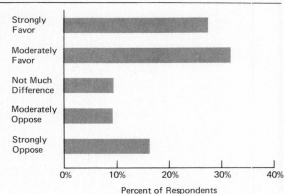

Figure 2 Frequency with which people report that they wear seat belts in automobiles.

Figure 3 Attitudes toward the Secretary of Transportation's requirement that new cars must have passive restraints (air bags or automatic seat belts) beginning in the 1982–1984 model years.

	Prefer Air Bag	Not Sure	Prefer Automatic Belt
Air Bags at $350 More than Automatic Belt	35%		50%
Air Bag at $200 More than Automatic Belt[1]	38%		46%
Air Bag at $100 More than Automatic Belt[2]	44%		41%
Air Bag Price the Same as Automatic Belt	50%		37%
Automatic Belt at $100 More than Air Bag	52%		31%

[1] Total air bag percentage calculated by adding air bag preference at $350 and air bag preference at $200.

[2] Total air bag percentage calculated by adding air bag preference at $350, air bag preference at $200, and air bag preference at $100.

Figure 4 Choice of passive restraint system—air bag or automatic belt—at various relative prices.

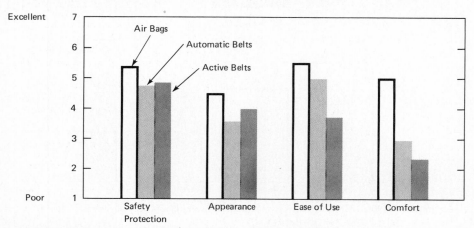

Figure 5 Median scores on a seven-point scale for perceived quality of various restraint systems: air bags, automatic seat belts, and conventional active seat belts.

EXHIBIT 5
Continued

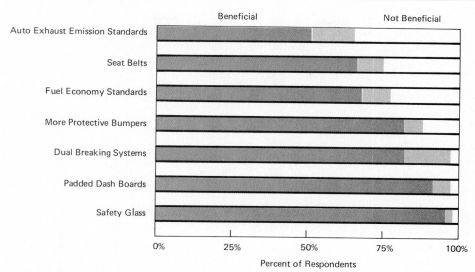

Figure 6 Attitudes of the public toward improvements that have been made in response to federal requirements for new cars.

St. Paul Passive Restraint Clinic

GM's passive restraint clinic was conducted in St. Paul, Minnesota, from September 18 to 23, 1978. St. Paul was chosen because GM had found that it tended to be one of the few GM markets that scored close to the national average in many other market research studies GM had conducted over the years.

For purposes of the clinic, GM divided its total product line into three main categories based on automobile body type (table at right).

Participant Selection. The sample for the passive restraint clinic consisted of General Motors car owners who intended to buy another new GM Ⓐ- or Ⓑ-type car within the next 2 to 3 years. The Ⓒ-type car segment of the sample was qualified solely on the basis of ownership; that is, Ⓒ-type car owners were not asked about future buying intentions. The sample was recruited by

Body Type	1978 Model wheelbase	General Motors car line examples
Ⓐ	116″	Chevrolet Impala, Pontiac Catalina, Oldsmobile 88, Buick LeSabre
(Family size and luxury)	119″	Oldsmobile 98, Buick Electra 225, Cadillac DeVille
Ⓑ	108″	Chevrolet Malibu, Pontiac LeMans, Oldsmobile Cutlass, Buick Century
(Intermediate size)	108″	Pontiac Grand Prix, Oldsmobile Cutlass Supreme, Buick Regal
Ⓒ	108″	Chevrolet Camaro, Pontiac Firebird
(Compact and subcompact)	94″	Chevrolet Chevette

Amrigon, Inc.,[7] from the R. L. Polk Registration lists drawn randomly from selected zip codes in the Minneapolis–St. Paul area on the basis of proximity to the clinic site; it excluded the central city. The ownership lists consisted of owners of 1976–1978 model year GM vehicles that were purchased new.

A random sample was drawn from these lists, and letters were sent to the selected owners. The letters described the purpose of the study and extended an invitation to participate. Participants would be paid $15 each. Owners were invited to bring their spouse (or some other person who was either the principal driver or normally a front-seat passenger),[8] but this was not required. If both the "principal driver" (most often, the husband) and the "front-seat passenger" (most often, the wife) arrived, both were given individual questionnaires, and both were taken through the study in the exact same way (although not at the same time to minimize interaction and influence which might inhibit gathering independent opinions). The sample size eventually was as follows:

Owner/Intender Groups	Participants[9]		
	Principal driver	Front-seat passenger	Total
Ⓐ	209	128	337
Ⓑ	249	122	371
Ⓒ	92	48	140
Total	550	298	848

[7]Amrigon Inc., was an independent market research company which handled the actual details of setting up and running the clinic. Amrigon—which was previously known as Addidas Market Research until Addidas, the running shoe company, forced a name change (hence, Addidas *market research is gone*)—was frequently employed by GM to conduct market research studies.

[8]If two people arrived at the clinic (normally, husband and wife), they were questioned to classify each as either "principal driver" or "front-seat passenger."

[9]Eighty percent of those initially contacted actually participated in the study. Analysis of nonrespondents indicated that they did not differ in significant ways from respondents, so it was reasonable to conclude that the sample was unbiased.

Participants in the passive restraint clinic were not told of GM's connection with the study, and none of the cars used in the clinic was identified by brand name or logo.

Clinic Methodology. Prior to attending the passive restraint clinic, participants were mailed invitations that gave the location (the St. Paul Arena) and the times of their appointments (which had been prearranged with them during the initial telephone interview). Coded on each invitation was the car body type classification (i.e., body type Ⓐ, Ⓑ, or Ⓒ). Thus, a consumer with an Ⓐ invitation was a person owning a full-size car and intending to purchase another full-size car in the future. At the clinic, Ⓐ consumers were shown Ⓐ-type automobiles with the various systems, Ⓑ consumers were shown Ⓑ-type cars, and Ⓒ consumers were shown Ⓒ-type cars.

At the door each participant was handed a questionnaire which was divided into four principal sections, corresponding with the sequence of activities at the clinic:

Section I:	About You (demographic questions)
Section II:	Future Buying Intentions and Current Seat Belt Use
Section III:	Evaluation of Automobile Restraint Systems
Section IV:	System Preference (under three scenarios)

Scenario 1 asked each participant to look back over the six systems to which he or she had been exposed and make a summary judgment as to which one he or she would prefer.

Scenario 2 gave price points for each system and asked for a rejudgment now that price information was included.

Scenario 3 asked each participant to make another choice, this time assuming it was 1984 and the current three-point active system was not available, by law.

After registering for the clinic and receiving the questionnaire, participants were given time to complete sections I and II. They were then shown a slide presentation that explained the passive restraint regulation and its effect on model years 1982, 1983, and 1984. The first phase of the test concluded with a description of the clinic's procedures. This presentation was intended to ensure that the participants were equivalent in terms of knowledge of the regulation and its effect on each model year's offerings. Another objective was to encourage participants to be candid.

Participants were next divided into groups according to their car body type classification. They then proceeded with the evaluation of the restraint systems available for their particular car body type (Ⓐ, Ⓑ, or Ⓒ).

Procedures for Evaluating Automobile Restraint Systems. Participants evaluated either five (Ⓑ

and Ⓒ models) or six (Ⓐ cars) restraint systems that were installed in the cars on display. Since evaluating all five or six restraint systems would require a great deal of time, the research procedure was modified so that while every system was evaluated, not all participants evaluated every system. Some participants evaluated three or four of the systems.

All the cars used in the clinic by each participant were identical in design, color, and interior. Only the restraint system installed in each differed. A list of the restraint systems evaluated in each car body type, along with their letter code designations and prices, is presented in Exhibit 6.

The sequence of events involved in the rating of each restraint system was as follows.

At the start, the participant (either singly or with a companion) approached the first car designated in the questionnaire.

Stationed at each car was a hostess. She welcomed the participant and, using a chart (Exhibit 7), described the system's function. Then she entered the car and demonstrated the use of the restraint system while a taped expla-

EXHIBIT 6
ST. PAUL PASSIVE RESTRAINT CLINIC PRICING SUMMARY*

	Body type Ⓐ (Bonneville)†		Body type Ⓑ (Monte Carlo)†		Body type Ⓒ (Chevette)†	
Current three-point active belt	Car Z	$ 45‡	Car M	$ 35‡	Car L	$25‡
Two-point passive belt	Car H	50	§		Car G	30
Three-point passive belt (base)	Car B	70	Car P	60	Car Y	50
Three-point passive belt (deluxe)	Car W	80	Car X	70	Car N	60
Three-point power passive belt	Car S	95	Car F	85	Car D	75
Air bag	Car C	600	Car V	550	§	

*Participants in the clinic received the pricing summary for their car body type only. For example, a body type Ⓐ individual received the price list under "Body Type Ⓐ."

†The actual production models used in the clinic.

‡Each system's price also represented GM's cost. These prices differed slightly for each of the car body types because of variations in product design necessitated by each car's size.

§The designated system was either not appropriate for or not available in the body type indicated.

Note: The prices listed above are artificial and do not reflect GM's actual costs or prices.

EXHIBIT 7
RESTRAINT SYSTEM INTRODUCTORY CHART

DRIVER

Normal Position

Occupant Being Restrained During Impact

PASSENGER

Normal Position

Occupant Being Restrained During Impact

System	Active Lap and Shoulder Belt
Front Seat Capacity	3
Comfort Adjustment	Yes
Warning System	Buzzer and Light
Availability	Current System

nation played in the background (Exhibit 8). (The same format was followed for the subsequent systems each participant evaluated.) In addition, Amrigon representatives were available on the floor to answer questions.

Exhibit 9 shows the sequence of events that followed. The hostess next asked the participant who was the principal driver to enter the car and then adjust the seat to his or her normal driving position. She then asked him or her to exit from the car and then get back in. Subsequently, she took the participant's questionnaire and ex-

plained that she would be asking him or her to rate the system on the following characteristics:

1. Ease of entry
2. Comfort
3. Convenience
4. Front seat roominess
5. Ease of exit

The participant then reentered the car with the door opened partially, not fully, to simulate entry conditions one might encounter in a parking lot, in which cars are parked close to

EXHIBIT 8
RESTRAINT SYSTEM INTRODUCTORY RECORDED MESSAGE
Current System (Three-Point Active Belt System)

This car is equipped with the current occupant restraint that provides a lap and shoulder belt combination. This system is called an "active" system because it requires the occupants to "actively" buckle the belts themselves.

This system allows three passengers to sit in the front seat, making this car capable of carrying six occupants. The center front seat passenger has a lap belt only.

A buzzer and light come on when the car is started and the seat belt is unbuckled. The buzzer and light combination remain on for 4 to 8 seconds to remind you to buckle up.

The front seat belts in this vehicle are equipped with "Vehicle Sensitive Retractors" which are designed to grip the belt during a sudden stop or impact. Under normal driving conditions, the belts are designed to move freely with the occupants.

For the most effective use of the restraint, a slight tension on the belt retractors is desirable. Shoulder belt tension can be adjusted by simply giving the belt a slight tug to achieve a comfortable position.

Now review the graphics that summarize the use and function of this system. Please enter the car, close the door, adjust the seat to a comfortable driving position and secure the belt system just as your guide has demonstrated. Exit the car and continue to complete this section of your questionnaire.

Remember, this is the *current* belt restraint system.

---

each other. Subsequently, two more ratings were obtained:

6. Ease of entry with door at first door stop
7. Ease of exit with door at first door stop

The participant then exited from the car and was asked to think about the entire system and rate it concerning:

8. Overall appearance
9. Overall system

In the case of (A) and (B) owners (not (C) owners), two additional ratings were obtained. These participants were given an object to simulate a briefcase or a bag of groceries and asked to reenter the car for a fourth time. Then they were asked to provide ratings concerning:

10. Accessibility (with object)
11. Ease of exit (with object)

The participant then moved on to the next car in the sequence listed in the questionnaire and repeated the evaluation procedures described here (Exhibit 10). The average elapsed time for a participant in the study was 2.5 hours.

System Preferences. Finally, the participant arrived at a "decision desk"—the third and last stage of the study, which corresponded to section IV of the questionnaire in the appendix

EXHIBIT 9
FLOW DIAGRAM:
SYSTEM EVALUATION PROCEDURE
FOR EACH CAR*

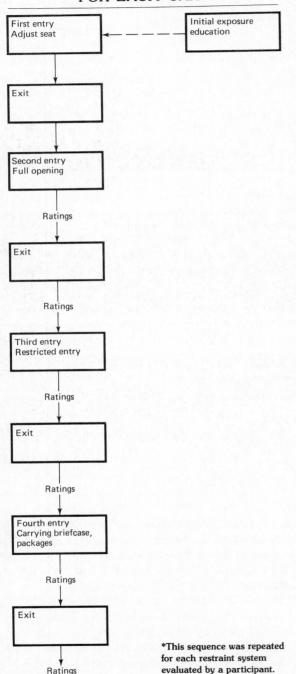

*This sequence was repeated
for each restraint system
evaluated by a participant.

to this case—and was asked to give his or her first, second, third, and last choices under two scenarios (Exhibit 11). In this final stage, the participant was asked first to evaluate each system individually, indicating the probability of purchase assuming all systems were available and passive restraints were *not* mandatory. Second, prices for each system were given (see Exhibit 6), and the participant was asked to rank-order his or her preferences again. Third, the participant was asked to state rank-order preferences assuming the current production system (the three-point active belt) was not available, thus replicating the environment as it might exist in 1984. Short group sessions, each composed of 10 to 15 people having the same car body type classification, were then held. At these sessions, participants were able to ask questions about the clinic, each restraint system, and passive restraint regulations. The participants were subsequently thanked and paid, and then they left.

Planning the Analysis

Ms. Lipsky began to organize her plans for assessing the data. She knew that consumer preferences for the passive restraint system might vary by owner/intender characteristics, price level, and availability of the current three-point active system (the 1984 scenario). She also wondered which measures of consumer preference she would trust the most: those given while evaluating the different car system combinations, or those given after all the car systems had been experienced. She knew that she would have to give specific recommendations based on her analysis, and she began to think carefully about the most useful analyses for management's decisions.

EXHIBIT 10
FLOW DIAGRAM: EVALUATION SEQUENCE FOR EACH CAR BODY TYPE

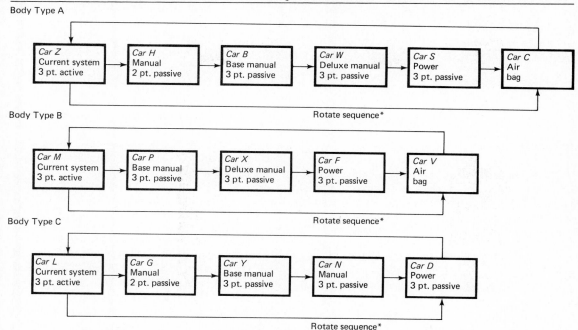

*The sequence of exposure to each system was rotated randomly for each participant in the clinic to counterbalance participants' responses to the order of exposure to each system.

EXHIBIT 11
FLOW DIAGRAM: SYSTEM EVALUATION PROCEDURE AFTER THE LAST WAS EVALUATED

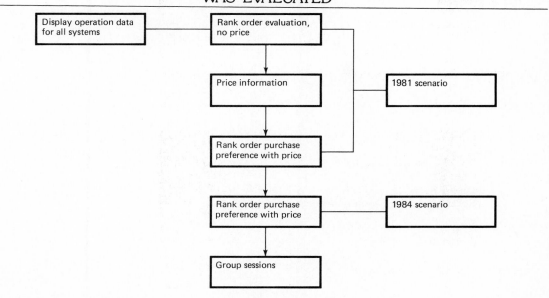

Appendix A

Automobile Restraint Study Questionnaire

Introduction

Welcome to our Automobile Restraint Study. As you have previously been advised, the purpose of this preview is to obtain consumer reaction to various restraint systems for future automobiles. These systems may or may not be available in the future.

You will in no way be subjected to any sales solicitation as a result of your participation in this study. We are only interested in your personal reactions to the restraint systems that will be displayed today.

By sampling public attitudes toward restraint systems, manufacturers are better able to bring to market products which will both satisfy the consumer as well as meet government regulations. You were selected because you match a particular buying group, so your personal opinion is important.

We are interested in each individual's personal reaction. Please do not discuss your answers to any of the questions, nor make any comments about the systems with other participants.

As you go through this review, you will occasionally have questions about the vehicles or some aspect of your questionnaire. DO NOT HESITATE TO ASK FOR HELP FROM A HOSTESS.

THANK YOU. We think you will find this an interesting experience. As you have been told, we are vitally interested in your opinions of these automobile restraint systems.

Section I

About You

> FOR THE PURPOSE OF CLASSIFICATION AND STATISTICAL ANALYSIS,
> PLEASE ANSWER THE FOLLOWING QUESTIONS.

Variables*

1   Respondent number:
2   Respondent type: 1 = principal driver; 2 = front-seat passenger
3   1. What is your sex?   MALE   FEMALE

4   2. What is your approximate age?
      1 Under 25 years   4 35–39   7 50–54   9 60–64
      2 25–29   5 40–44   8 55–59   10 65 & Older
      3 30–34   6 45–49

5   3. What is your marital status?
      1 Married   2 Single   3 Divorced   4 Widowed

*Variables (italic numbers) refer to computer exercise.

6   4. What is your degree of education?
       1 Grammar school   3 Trade or technical school   5 College graduate
       2 High school   4 Some college   6 Post graduate study

7   5. What is your occupation? (DESCRIBE) _____ . Please check the category
       below that best describes your occupation.
       1 Skilled labor   4 Retired   7 Professional   10 Other _____
       2 Unskilled labor   5 Managerial   8 Scientific/technical   (specify)
       3 Housewife   6 Service, farmer,   9 Clerical
                           merchant

8   6. What is your approximate family income?
       1 Under $6,500   4 $12,500–$14,999   7 $25,000–$29,999   9 $35,000–$39,999
       2 $ 6,500–$ 9,999   5 $15,000–$19,999   8 $30,000–$34,999   10 $40,000 & over
       3 $10,000–$12,499   6 $20,000–$24,999

9   7. What is your position in your household?
       1 Husband   3 Son   5 Single male   7 Other male
       2 Wife   4 Daughter   6 Single female   8 Other female

10   8. How many people are in your household?
       1 One   3 Three   5 Five   7 Seven or More
       2 Two   4 Four   6 Six

(Question 9 omitted.)

Section II
Future Buying Intentions and Current Seat Belt Use

11   10. Approximately when do you plan to make your next new car purchase? (CHECK ONLY ONE)
        1 Within one year   2 Within two years   3 Three or more years

12   11. What is the maximum number of people you expect to carry in the front seat of this new car? In
       rear seat? RECORD ANSWERS IN THE APPROPRIATE BOXES BELOW.

       Front seat   ☐
13   Rear seat   ☐

14   12. Generally, when you are driving, how often do you wear seat belts?
        1 Always (100%)
        2 Most of the time (approx. 75%)
        3 Quite often (approx. 50%)
        4 Some of the time (approx. 25%)
        5 Never (0)

15   13. There has been much discussion lately about passive restraint systems. One type is the *passive belt system*. How much knowledge do you feel you have about how passive belt systems would work?
        1 A great deal of knowledge   3 Not very much knowledge
        2 Some knowledge   4 None

16 14. In general, do you favor passive belt systems?
    1 Yes, I do.   2 I'm not sure.   3 No, I don't

17 15. The air bag system is another type of passive restraint system. How much knowledge do you feel you have about how the air bag system works?
    1 A great deal of knowledge   3 Not very much knowledge
    2 Some knowledge   4 None

18 16. In general, do you favor the air bag system?
    1 Yes, I do.   2 I'm not sure.   3 No, I don't.

19 17. How often do you place a briefcase in the front seat area of the car?
    1 Always (100%)
    2 Most of the time (approx. 75%)
    3 Quite often (approx. 50%)
    4 Some of the time (approx. 25%)
    5 Never (0)

20 18. How often do you place a shopping bag containing a small amount of groceries in the front seat area of the car?
    1 Always (100%)
    2 Most of the time (approx. 75%)
    3 Quite often (approx. 50%)
    4 Some of the time (approx. 25%)
    5 Never (0)

Last summer, Secretary of Transportation, Brock Adams, announced that the Government will require passive restraint systems in full size cars by 1982, and in all cars by 1984. This order would require the auto makers to equip their cars with either air bags or passive belts.

In an effort to aid in the design of passive restraint systems, we are asking you to evaluate various automobile restraint systems.

THERE ARE NO "RIGHT" OR "WRONG" ANSWERS! It is *your* opinion that is important to us. Please take the time necessary and give us your frank and honest opinions about the systems.

Section III
Evaluation of Automobile Restraint Systems

Read Carefully

PLEASE REMEMBER THAT WE ARE ONLY ASKING ABOUT YOUR LIKES AND DISLIKES IN REFERENCE TO THE VARIOUS ALTERNATIVE RESTRAINT SYSTEMS. PLEASE, TRY NOT TO LET SUCH THINGS AS EXTERIOR AND INTERIOR COLORS, UPHOLSTERY APPEARANCE, MAKE OF CAR, ETC., INFLUENCE YOUR OPINIONS!

Rate each vehicle you examine using a ten point rating scale shown below to indicate how you feel about a particular restraint system.

	Dislike			Neither Like Nor Dislike		Like			
Very Much		Somewhat				Somewhat		Very Much	
1	2	3	4	5	6	7	8	9	10

We want you to describe each feature in terms of "Dislike Very Much" or "Like Very Much." If you like a particular restraint system *very much* (that is, it meets your particular needs), you should select a number to the extreme right of the scale (9 or 10).

On the other hand, if you strongly dislike a particular system (that is, it does not meet your particular needs), you should select a number to the extreme left of the scale (1 or 2).

If you feel somewhere in between, you should select the middle numbers between the two extremes.

> A GOOD "RULE OF THUMB"—THE HIGHER THE NUMBER, THE MORE YOU LIKE THE FEATURE.
> PLEASE WAIT FOR THE GUIDE TO GIVE YOU FURTHER INFORMATION.
> PLEASE WAIT.

Current Production Three-Point Active Belt

[NOTE: These exact questions (11 variables) were asked for *each* system rated by each respondent. To save space, the questions for each system are *not* reproduced here, but the variable numbers for each system are noted on page 594.]

> PLEASE LISTEN CAREFULLY TO THE TAPE RECORDER AND WATCH AS THE GUIDE DEMONSTRATES THE PROPER ENTRANCE AND EXIT FROM THE CAR.

Now, please enter the driver's seat. Adjust the seat to a comfortable driving position and exit from the car.

> ENTER AT FULL DOOR OPENING.

Please circle the number that best describes your feelings about each of the following characteristics.

Variables		Dislike		Neither Like nor		Like			
		Very Much	Somewhat	Dislike		Somewhat		Very Much	
21	Ease of Entry	1 2	3 4	5 6		7 8		9 10	
22	Overall Comfort	1 2	3 4	5 6		7 8		9 10	
23	Overall Convenience	1 2	3 4	5 6		7 8		9 10	
24	Overall Front Seat Roominess	1 2	3 4	5 6		7 8		9 10	

EXIT AT FULL DOOR OPENING.

25 Ease of Exit   1 2 3 4 5 6 7 8 9 10

RE-ENTER WITH DOOR OPEN TO FIRST DOOR STOP *ONLY*.

26 Ease of Entry   1 2 3 4 5 6 7 8 9 10

EXIT AT FIRST DOOR STOP POSITION.

27 Ease of Exit   1 2 3 4 5 6 7 8 9 10

PLEASE THINK ABOUT ENTIRE SYSTEM.

28 Overall Appearance of Restraint System   1 2 3 4 5 6 7 8 9 10
29 Overall System   1 2 3 4 5 6 7 8 9 10

STOP—PLEASE SEE THE GUIDE.

Please take the object that the Hostess provides and enter the driver's seat as you normally would at full door opening. Place the object in the front seat area and circle the number that best describes your feelings.

Variables	Dislike		Neither Like nor Dislike	Like	
	Very Much	Somewhat		Somewhat	Very Much
30 Accessibility	1 2	3 4	5 6	7 8	9 10

EXIT AT FULL DOOR OPENING, REMOVING THE OBJECT.

31 Ease of Exit   1 2 3 4 5 6 7 8 9 10

Car Ⓐ (large) variables:	AC 21–31	AZ 32–42	AH 43–53	AB 54–64	AW 65–75	AS 76–86
Car Ⓑ (medium) variables:	BM 21–31	– 32–42	BP 43–53	BX 54–64	BF 65–75	BV 76–86
Car Ⓒ (small) variables:	CL 21–31*	CG 32–42*	CY 43–53*	CN 54–64*	CD 65–75*	76–86*
	*Ignore vars. 30–31	*Ignore vars. 41–42	*Ignore vars. 52–53	*Ignore vars. 63–64	*Ignore vars. 74–75	*Ignore vars. 85–86

Section IV

System Preference

Current Production Three-Point Active Belt	Two-Point Passive Belt	Three-Point Passive Belt (base)	Three-Point Passive Belt (deluxe)	Three-Point Power Passive	Air Bag

> PLEASE REVIEW THE DISPLAY BOARDS SUMMARIZING THE OPERATION OF ALL SYSTEMS.

After you evaluate all these systems individually, we would like you to indicate your probability of purchase for each system. Please use the scale shown below. A high number (9 or 10) would mean you would *DEFINITELY PURCHASE* the system and a low number (1 or 2) would mean you would *DEFINITELY NOT PURCHASE* the system. Please rate *all* systems.

> CIRCLE THE NUMBER THAT BEST DESCRIBES YOUR PROBABILITY OF PURCHASE.

Car (A)	Car (B)	Car (C)	Variables	Would Not Purchase Definitely	Probably	Possibly Purchase	Would Purchase Probably	Definitely
AC	BM	CL	87	1 2	3 4	5 6	7 8	9 10
AZ	–	CG	88	1 2	3 4	5 6	7 8	9 10
AH	BP	CY	89	1 2	3 4	5 6	7 8	9 10
AB	BX	CN	90	1 2	3 4	5 6	7 8	9 10
AW	BF	CD	91	1 2	3 4	5 6	7 8	9 10
AS	BV	–	92	1 2	3 4	5 6	7 8	9 10

Now, please give us your first, second, third and *last* choice for these systems. Use the letter designation for each choice.

First Choice   Car: _____
Second Choice   Car: _____   **Variables**
Third Choice   Car: _____   *93–98*
Last Choice   Car: _____

> PLEASE SEE YOUR GUIDE FOR PRICE INFORMATION.

> GO TO THE NEXT PAGE.

System Preference with Price

Current Production Three-Point Active Belt	Two-Point Passive Belt	Three-Point Passive Belt (base)	Three-Point Passive Belt (deluxe)	Three-Point Power Passive	Air Bag

Keeping in mind the price information for these various systems, we would like you to rate these systems for *probability of purchase* again. Please use the same procedure as you did on the previous page.

> CIRCLE THE NUMBER THAT BEST DESCRIBES YOUR PROBABILITY OF PURCHASE.

Car (A)	Car (B)	Car (C)	Variables	Would Not Purchase Definitely		Probably		Possibly Purchase		Would Purchase Probably		Definitely	
AC	BM	CL	99	1	2	3	4	5	6	7	8	9	10
AZ	–	CG	100	1	2	3	4	5	6	7	8	9	10
AH	BP	CY	101	1	2	3	4	5	6	7	8	9	10
AB	BX	CN	102	1	2	3	4	5	6	7	8	9	10
AW	BF	CD	103	1	2	3	4	5	6	7	8	9	10
AS	BV	–	104	1	2	3	4	5	6	7	8	9	10

Now, please give us your first, second, third and *last* choice for these systems. Use the same letter designation as on the previous page.

First Choice   Car:_____
Second Choice   Car:_____   } **Variables**
Third Choice   Car:_____   *105–110*
Last Choice   Car:_____

> GO TO NEXT PAGE.

Preference Without Current System

Now, suppose the current system is not available, and in fact, beginning in 1984, only passive systems will be available on new cars.

> NOW, INDICATE YOUR OWN INDIVIDUAL PREFERENCE FOR EACH OF THE REMAINING SYSTEMS.

Please use the same ranking procedure as before.

| Two-Point Passive Belt | Three-Point Passive Belt (base) | Three-Point Passive Belt (deluxe) | Three-Point Power Passive | Air Bag |

First Choice   Car:_____
Second Choice   Car:_____   **Variables**
Third Choice   Car:_____   *111–116*
Last Choice   Car:_____

> REFER TO YOUR "FIRST CHOICE" FROM THE PRECEDING PAGE.

An alternative to the proposed systems you have seen here today . . . passive belts or air bags . . . is a mandatory seat belt law. Such a law would require the occupants to *use* the current production system or be subject to a traffic violation if they did not. Which do you favor?

Variable
117
    1 Passive belts or air bags
    2 Mandatory seat belt law

If you were to buy the passive restraint system for your next new car, would you eliminate another option to make up for the added cost of the restraint?

Variable
118
    1 Yes   2 No

| Two-Point Passive Belt | Three-Point Passive Belt (base) | Three-Point Passive Belt (deluxe) | Three-Point Power Passive | Air Bag |

Thinking a moment about all the possible alternative restraint systems you have seen today, which one of these systems might your neighbor choose as his or her first choice if they were attending?

Variable
119
    Car:_____

One car presently sold in this country offers a passive restraint system in combination with a deluxe option package (including deluxe exterior chrome trim, radial tires, custom wheels, interior plush carpeting, sport steering wheel, etc.). How interested would you be in purchasing a passive restraint system that was part of an option package? Would you be . . .

Variable
120
    1 Very interested   3 Not too interested
    2 Somewhat interested   4 Not at all interested

> PLEASE SEE YOUR GUIDE

39 Parkland Foods Corporation

Scott Ward

Dan Wackman, manager of public affairs of the Parkland Foods Corporation, began to prepare an important presentation for a United States Senate subcommittee investigating advertising practices affecting children. Parkland was one of several food and toy companies with significant advertising billings ($13 million) on television directed at children (primarily Saturday mornings, with some after-school-hour programming). The Senate subcommittee wished to know how Parkland designed and evaluated TV ads for children, what safeguards were employed to ensure that advertising was not false and/or misleading, whether Parkland Foods Corporation considered what it was now doing in this area adequate, and what the corporation's strategic posture was for the future regard-

Scott Ward is a professor of marketing at the Wharton School, University of Pennsylvania.

ing advertising directed at children. The Senate subcommittee had requested that Mr. Wackman show commercials for Parkland Foods Corporation products to the committee and comment on them in terms of their objectives and in terms of their possible capacity to deceive children. The ads he would show were current campaigns for Crunch-O, K-K, Parkland's Smacks, and Moo-Cow (a milk additive). See Appendix A at the end of this case.

Mr. Wackman also had to report to Mr. Richard Marks, president of Parkland Foods and chairman of the board of directors. Mr. Marks wished to know Mr. Wackman's *strategy* recommendations regarding the corporation's advertising directed at children. It was agreed that TV advertising could not be eliminated altogether, but the budget could be reduced, if that was a viable alternative. But the Marketing Department made it quite clear that TV advertising directed at children must continue, or significant losses in market share would result.[1]

Mr. Wackman's problem was particularly severe owing to the major consumerism controversy surrounding advertising practices affecting children; moreover, raw material costs for Parkland Foods Corporation products had all increased dramatically. Even with the recent increase in candy bar retail prices to 15 cents, financial considerations were acute, and a decision had been made that further reductions in the size of the bar products would not be made.

The Children's Advertising Controversy

Recent public opinion polls show that a majority of American adults disapprove of television advertising directed at children. Many industry observers feel that the roots of these negative attitudes can be traced to the testimony of consumerist Robert Choate before a Senate committee in the summer of 1970. Mr. Choate lambasted breakfast cereals, calling them "empty calories," and charged food companies with making misleading energy claims in ads directed at children. Groups such as Action for Children's Television have mounted vigorous public relations campaigns and have found receptive politicians.

[1]Parkland had experimented with reducing and eliminating advertising, but loss of share resulted. Market research had shown that virtually all United States children eat candy, and most of them cite chocolate (68 percent) as the candy most often eaten. Preteenage children eat an average of 28 chocolate bars per month, and 20 percent of children accounted for 35 percent of chocolate bar volume. Children eat 3.2 different brands of chocolate bars, and the main chocolate bar competition is between Parkland Foods Corporation, Hershey, Nestle, and M&M Mars.

"Chocolate bar" is loosely defined in marketing research to include products such as bags of Parkland Smacks and Peanut Butter Cups. These are distinct from hard sucking candies, caramels and toffies, and jellied candies.

Mr. Wackman believed that the major issues were as follows:

1. Whether advertising misleads preteenage children, particularly "preoperational" children (see appendix B at the end of this case).
2. Whether specific techniques (camera angles, etc.) in ads directed at children contribute to their being misleading.
3. Whether there is too much advertising directed at children.
4. Whether children can understand the "puffery" characteristic of much of the advertising directed at adults and children.
5. Whether advertising should be permitted for products which are not "good" for children. (Mr. Wackman knew that dental and medical research was not conclusive regarding chocolate candy's role in causing dental cavities and/or digestive and heart ailments, but he knew that most people worried about these "effects" of candy consumption, in any case.)
6. Whether children irritate their parents by urging them to buy advertised products.
7. Whether advertising has great potency in affecting children's purchase desires, attitudes, etc., and whether the effects are particularly strong among disadvantaged children.

The importance of these issues—and the controversy as a whole—was that consumerism pressure might force advertising directed at children off the air. The Federal Trade Commission was currently considering a trade rule which would ban advertising directed toward younger children and/or require disclosures or warnings in advertising for products containing high amounts of sugar. The latter requirement would apply to Parkland's products. There was great industry resistance to this proposal, since it would mandate advertising practices and possibly reduce the effectiveness of commercials.

Corporate and Industry Responses to the Controversy

To date, industry's responses to the controversy on advertising directed at children had seemingly been to hire good Washington lawyers and lobbyists to forestall congressional or regulatory agency action. However, the controversy was an appetizing one for politicians, for obvious reasons, so normal routes of political pressures were proving ineffective. The political climate was well expressed by the Chairman of the Federal Trade Commission: "If business doesn't regulate itself in this area [advertising directed at children] we will have to step in and impose regulations."

The primary industry defense agent was the Association of National Advertisers, an industry association consisting of major advertisers for national brands. The ANA produced a set of guidelines for advertising practices to be used in appealing to children (Exhibit 1). The guidelines had been modified by a panel of child development experts, recruited for the task by the National Council of Better Business Bureaus. Parkland Foods Corporation also had an advertising philosophy (Exhibit 2), and Mr. Wackman wondered about how the ANA guidelines (which Parkland supported) and the advertising philosophy would be received in the hearing room.

Parkland had taken some action of its own by employing behavioral scientists to evaluate Parkland Foods Corporation advertising for several of its products (Exhibit 3). Essentially, the research consisted of carefully probing children's reactions to the commercials which they saw in a laboratory test environment. Additionally, these researchers probed the opinions of mothers of children ages 4 to 9 toward the commercials, and the judgment of the children themselves. (See Exhibit 4, which contains key results.) The

---

EXHIBIT 1
ASSOCIATION OF NATIONAL ADVERTISERS: CHILDREN'S TELEVISION ADVERTISING GUIDELINES
(Excerpts)

Preamble

Advertising directed to children, for products and services which are used or consumed by children, is appropriate in a society and economy such as ours. Such advertising serves to bring information to children and helps prepare them for maturity. Advertising to children is also the economic base for children's programming with all of its potential for education and entertainment. Without such advertising, continued and improved children's programming would be jeopardized.

At the same time, children are a unique audience as they are in their most formative development period, may be more easily influenced than are adults, and because of their limited experience are not fully equipped to make comparative judgments.

Heretofore, parents, school and church have been the primary guiding forces in shaping values and judgments. However, the amount of time spent with TV today adds it as a fourth major influence. Special responsibilities are therefore placed upon advertisers and broadcasters to deal protectively with children, to help them better understand the world and how to live in it, and to respect and complement the parental role.

These Guidelines, recognizing the uniqueness of children's audience, are designed to assist advertisers in the preparation of advertising that fulfills the special standards that are desirable in advertising to children.

EXHIBIT 1
Continued

Principles

While the process of communication with children through television must be continually responsive to changing times, four basic principles underlie these Guidelines:

I. Advertisers should always take into consideration the level of knowledge, sophistication and maturity of the audience to which the message is primarily directed. Since younger children have limited capabilities for discerning the credibility of what they watch, they pose a special responsibility for advertisers and broadcasters alike to protect them from their own susceptibilities.

II. Realizing that children are limited in their ability to distinguish between fact and fantasy, advertisers should exercise care not to stimulate (directly or by implication) unreasonable expectations of performance. A child's imagination should be respected rather than exploited.

III. Recognizing that advertising may play an important part in educating a child to become a member of society, product information should be communicated in a truthful and tasteful manner.

IV. Advertisers are urged to capitalize on the potential of television to communicate and impart knowledge and understanding by sponsoring children's programs that provide value beyond entertainment alone, and by developing advertising that, where possible, addresses itself to social standards generally regarded as positive and beneficial (such as friendship, equality, kindness, honesty, and generosity).

Presentation

Children, especially in their pre-school years, have vivid imaginations. Use of imagination enables a child to project himself beyond his immediate capacities and reach for his future potential. Advertisers should, therefore, always respect a child's imagination.

The use of imaginative situations relevant to the audience concerned is an acceptable and normal communications practice. Implicit in the foregoing is the concept of fantasy, including animation, as an appropriate form of communications to any audience, including the very young. However, the use of special situations and fantasy in advertising directed to children should assure that the advertisement will not suggest unattainable expectation of performance.

To this end:

a. Any form of presentation which capitalizes on a child's difficulty in distinguishing between the real and the fanciful should be positively guarded against.

b. In the use of fantasy, advertisers should seek to channel a child's imagination toward healthy and constructive growth and development.

In more specific terms, particular control should be exercised to be sure that:

a. Copy, sound and visual presentation—as well as the commercial in its totality—do not mislead the audience to which it is directed on such performance characteristics as speed, size, color, durability, nutrition, noise, etc.; or on perceived benefits such as the acquisition of strength, popularity, growth, proficiency, intelligence, and the like.

b. The advertisement clearly establishes what is included in the original purchase price of

EXHIBIT 1
Continued

the advertised product, employing where necessary positive disclosure on what items are to be purchased separately. All advertising for products sold unassembled should indicate that assembly is required.

c. A clearly depicted representation of the advertised product will be shown during the advertisement. When appropriate in assisting consumers to identify the product, the package may be depicted, provided that it does not mislead as to product characteristics or content.

d. Advertising demonstrations showing the use of a product or premium can be readily duplicated by the average child for whom the product is intended.

Promotion by Program Character and Personal Endorsements

It is recognized that very young children may not fully recognize differences between commercial messages and program content. Hence, product endorsements by personalities may exert undue influence upon the rationalization process of children. Therefore:

a. Program personalities or program characters (live or animated) on children's programs should not be used to promote products, premiums or services in or adjacent to any program where the personality or character appears.

b. Subject to paragraph *a* of this section, "product characters"—personalities (real or fanciful) which are closely associated and identified with the product—may be used as presenters for the advertised product or service, provided they do not perform acts, which children might be expected to emulate, which would be misleading as to the attributes of the product or service concerned.

c. Nationally known persons may be used to attribute a characteristic or quality to a product (including a premium) or service when they are generally recognized as qualified to speak to the subject, and their statements represent their good-faith evaluation.

Claim Substantiation

In accordance with the basic principle of "dealing fairly and honestly" with children:

a. Advertising to children shall not claim or imply any product or premium performance characteristics which are not supportable by factual data or research which conforms to sound professional practices. Exceptions are those claims recognized to be generic to products in a category.

b. Puffery (defined as "flattering publicity" or "extravagant commendation") is not acceptable support for an objective product claim. Advertising claims which might be construed as literally true must be literally true. If there is doubt, the burden will be on the advertiser to document the claim.

Adopted May 13, 1972, by the board of directors of the Association of National Advertisers, Inc.
(Omitted sections concerned comparative and competitive claims, pressure to purchase, and safety.)

EXHIBIT 2
PARKLAND'S ADVERTISING PHILOSOPHY

Simply stated, Parkland's advertising philosophy will observe the following guidelines:

1. *Honest*
   Our advertising will maintain the highest standards of integrity and honesty. We will make no false or devious claims.
2. *Ethical*
   We will advertise in good taste. We will not degrade competition. We will not produce advertising whose tone or claims would offend or mislead.
3. *Respectful of Consumers' Intelligence*
   We can entertain and amuse, but never at the expense of truth. We will inform consumers of the merits of our products, but we will not take unfair advantage of the trust or lack of technical expertise of our audience in presenting those merits.
4. *Effective*
   While adhering to the above criteria, Parkland's advertising must effectively contribute to the achievement of the Company's growth and profit goals.

Our intent is not just to be within the law but to be as honest and ethical in our dealings with our unseen audience as we are with our direct customers—and as we would expect others to be with us.

EXHIBIT 3
CLINICAL SURVEY OF SELECTED
PARKLAND FOODS COMMERCIALS:
SAMPLE CHARACTERISTICS

1. Education

| | Total sample (n = 500) | | Social class | | | |
| | | | Lower (n = 250) | | Upper middle (n = 250) | |
	Wife	Husband	Wife	Husband	Wife	Husband
9–11 years	9%	5%	15%	10%	4%	0%
High school graduate	46	29	75	60	23	4
Some college	15	23	5	30	27	19
Bachelor's degree	28	21	5	–	39	37
Graduate or professional degree	2	20	–	–	8	31
Other	–	2	–	–	–	10

2. Age

Median age	
Wife	Husband
37	38

EXHIBIT 3
Continued

3. Total family income

	Total sample	Social class	
		Lower	Upper middle
Under $7,000	7%	5%	0%
$ 7,001–$9,000	2	5	0
$ 9,001–$11,000	15	25	12
$11,001–$13,000	20	20	22
$13,001–$15,000	20	30	15
$15,001–$20,000	21	15	33
Over $20,000	14	–	17

EXHIBIT 4
MOTHERS' RESPONSES TO COMMERCIALS BY CHILD'S AGE

	Child's age							
	4–5				7–9			
		Objectionable				Objectionable		
	Nothing	Little	Somewhat	Very	Nothing	Little	Somewhat	Very
Bits ("Curtain")	78%	17%	6%	0%	86%	5%	9%	–
K-K	56	22	22	0	77	9	5	9%
Moo-Cow	61	11	27	0	77	18	5	–
Smacks ("Boy")	67	17	11	6	77	18	5	–
Crunch-O	77	12	0	12	64	18	14	5
Smacks ("Girl")	67	22	6	6	82	9	9	–
Bits ("Dancing")	78	22	0	0	91	5	–	5

MOTHERS' RESPONSES TO COMMERCIALS BY SOCIAL CLASS

	Social class							
	Lower				Upper middle			
		Objectionable				Objectionable		
	Nothing	Little	Somewhat	Very	Nothing	Little	Somewhat	Very
Bits ("Curtain")	100%	–	–	–	74%	15%	11%	–
K-K	90	10%	–	–	59	15	19	7%
Moo-Cow	65	20	10%	5%	74	11	15	–
Smacks ("Boy")	95	5	–	–	63	22	11	4
Crunch-O	100	–	–	–	54	23	12	12
Smacks ("Girl")	95	5	–	–	67	19	11	4
Bits ("Dancing")	100	–	–	–	78	15	4	4

EXHIBIT 4
Continued

MOTHERS' RESPONSES TO PARKLAND'S COMMERCIALS
Total Sample (n = 500); Data from Questionnaire Given to Mothers*

	1	2	3	4	5
Bits commercials					
Understandable (1)†–not understandable (5)	72%	13%	11%	2%	2%
Better than most commercials (1)–worse (5)	28	19	32	13	9
Child can fairly evaluate (1)–not fairly evaluate (5)	62	11	23	4	–
Enjoyable for child (1)–not enjoyable (5)	70	15	9	4	2
Unlikely child misled (1)–likely child misled (5)	57	13	9	11	11
K-K					
Understandable–not understandable	53%	28%	9%	6%	4%
Better than most commercials–worse	17	17	43	19	4
Child can fairly evaluate–not fairly evaluate	49	26	15	9	2
Enjoyable for child–not enjoyable	47	17	23	6	6
Unlikely child misled–likely child misled	49	19	19	11	2
Moo-Cow					
Understandable–not understandable	64%	21%	6%	4%	4%
Better than most commercials–worse	32	17	32	9	11
Child can fairly evaluate–not fairly evaluate	55	19	21	2	2
Enjoyable for child–not enjoyable	70	6	19	2	2
Unlikely child misled–likely child misled	51	13	17	11	9
Smacks ("Girl")					
Understandable–not understandable	55%	19%	15%	9%	2%
Better than most commercials–worse	28	17	36	15	4
Child can fairly evaluate–not fairly evaluate	45	21	19	13	2
Enjoyable for child–not enjoyable	72	13	11	2	2
Unlikely child misled–likely child misled	53	11	9	17	11
Smacks ("Boy")					
Understandable–not understandable	68%	15%	6%	11%	5%
Better than most commercials–worse	30	19	30	13	9
Child can fairly evaluate–not fairly evaluate	55	17	21	6	–
Enjoyable for child–not enjoyable	75	13	9	2	2
Unlikely child misled–likely child misled	57	15	17	6	4
Crunch-O					
Understandable–not understandable	64%	11%	17%	4%	4%
Better than most commercials–worse	28	21	28	11	13
Child can fairly evaluate–not fairly evaluate	47	21	17	13	2
Enjoyable for child–not enjoyable	49	17	15	15	4
Unlikely child misled–likely child misled	68	9	19	2	2

*The sample size was 500. While the sample was not a national, projectable sample, the data were reliable. The purpose was not to generalize results to the national scene but to gain insight. Marketing research used even smaller samples in some cases. In any event, Senate staff workers indicated that the data would be accepted, given their purposes, as long as they weren't "oversold," i.e., generalized to *all* children.

†Scale:
1 ("understandable") to 5 ("not understandable")
1 ("better than most commercials") to 5 ("worse than most")
1 ("child can fairly evaluate") to 5 ("not fairly evaluate")
1 ("enjoyable for child") to 5 ("not enjoyable")
1 ("unlikely child misled") to 5 ("likely child misled")

EXHIBIT 4
Continued

SUMMARY OF MOTHERS' RESPONSES TO PARKLAND'S COMMERCIALS
*Average Ratings Across the 5 Dimensions for Each Commercial, by Child's Age and by Social Class**

	Child's age		Social class	
	4–6	**7–9**	**Lower**	**Upper middle**
Bits commercials	10.89	7.90	7.90	10.37
K-K	11.83	8.95	8.95	11.70
Moo-Cow	10.50	9.55	9.55	9.67
Smacks ("Boy")	9.78	7.70	7.70	10.30
Crunch-O	10.44	8.20	8.20	11.44
Smacks ("Girl")	10.78	8.50	8.50	11.30

*For each commercial, an overall scale (positive–negative) was constructed by summing each mother's scores for the five dimensions. Thus, a mother could have a total score ranging from 5 (if she gave a "1" to each dimension) to 25 (if she gave a "5" to each dimension). Since there are five dimensions for each commercial, scale values range from 5.00 to 25.00.

CHILDREN'S JUDGMENTS ("TRUE" OR "FALSE") OF STATEMENTS ABOUT COMMERCIALS FOR PARKLAND'S PRODUCTS (*n* = 500)

	Total sample	
	% true	**% false**
1. Bits candy bars are a lot bigger than other candy bars.	5%	95%
2. If you gave a real live animal a Parkland's Smack, he would stop chasing you.	9	91
3. If you eat one K-K candy bar, you have to eat a second one, too.	3	97
4. Bits candy bars are about as big as other candy bars.	42	59
5. In the commercial for Parkland Smacks, they are just kidding when they show the kids feeding the animals Smacks—it's not like that in real life.	79	21
6. Milk is just as good for you *without* Parkland's Moo-Cow in it, as it is with Moo-Cow in it.	70	30
7. In the commercial for Moo-Cow the boy puts it in his milk and that makes it more nutritious.	28	72
8. In the commercial for Crunch-O candy bar the boy is real but the chicken is a cartoon.	96	4
9. Milk tastes better if you put Moo-Cow in it.	79	21
10. They want you to think that K-K candy bars are so light you want to eat two, but you can enjoy eating one just as much.	81	19
11. Milk is better for you if you put Moo-Cow in it.	19	81
12. Those were real animals in the Parkland Smacks commercial.	6	94

EXHIBIT 4
Continued

CHILDREN'S EXPERIENCE WITH PARKLAND'S PRODUCTS
By Total Sample and Social Class

Question: Have you ever tried (product name)?

	Social class					
	Lower			Upper middle		
	A lot	Some-times	Never	A lot	Some-times	Never
Moo-Cow	8%	39%	54%	40%	40%	20%
K-K	7	43	50	13	53	33
Smacks	36	43	21	47	40	13
Crunch-O	21	29	50	7	47	47
Bits	0	21	79	13	40	47

CHILDREN'S ATTITUDES TOWARD PARKLAND'S PRODUCTS
Total Sample

Question: How much do you *like* each of these things?

	Social class							
	Lower				Upper middle			
	A lot	A little	Don't like	Don't know	A lot	A little	Don't like	Don't know
Moo-Cow	15%	39%	0%	46%	53%	20%	7%	20%
K-K	39	39	8	15	60	13	7	20
Smacks	62	31	–	7	67	27	7	–
Crunch-O	29	31	–	30	40	20	–	40
Bits	39	8	8	46	40	20	–	40
Choc-Bar	62	23	8	8	87	13	–	–

commercials tested were the same ones Mr. Wackman planned to show to the Senate subcommittee. Marketing informed Mr. Wackman that the advertising agency only tested ads via traditional copy research techniques—measuring copy point recall, attitudes, etc. Mr. Wackman felt that these copy research results would be of use, given the Senate subcommittee's interest.

The Purchase Process Among Children for Chocolate Candy Bar Products

Mr. Wackman was discouraged by the lack of hard information about how children make decisions to buy chocolate bar products and brands. There was no time for original research, but he did find some information in his files

EXHIBIT 5
ATTITUDES TOWARDS CHILDREN'S EATING CANDY

Perception by	Percent of children	Percent of teenagers	Percent of adults*
No limit set by parent	11	29	12
Doesn't mind, within reason	66	57	57
Likes child to have only what parent gives	14	5	23
Would not like child to have any	8	8	6

*Parents only. Based on national sample market research study.

regarding parental attitudes toward children's eating candy (see Exhibit 5) and areas of candy concern among children, teenagers, and adults (Exhibit 6). He was also interested in research which examined how often children ask for various products, including candy, and how often mothers yielded to these requests (Exhibit 7). Finally, he noted some correlations between a number of factors and children's purchase influence attempts and parental yielding (Exhibit 8).

Just before he set about to outline his testimony, Mr. Wackman contacted a team of Boston-area researchers. They gave him some prelimi-

nary results from a diary study of children's purchase requests (Exhibit 9). He wondered if these data would corroborate the earlier published research (Exhibits 7 and 8). If they did not, should he try to use the diary information? He wondered if the data in the diary study were different; *why* would the data be different?

Mr. Wackman did estimate that about 50 percent of candy bar volume was attributable to preteenage children. Television is obviously the dominant medium for reaching large audiences of children. Recent data showed that children viewed, on the average, over 3 hours of television per day and that they watched a wide variety of programs (see Exhibit 10). Interestingly, only about 10 percent of children's viewing occurred on weekend mornings—the prime target of many consumer groups. Most children's viewing took place during prime-time hours (see Exhibit 11).

Preparing for Subcommittee Appearance

Mr. Wackman outlined his presentation to the Senate subcommittee as follows:

1. Give brief history of Parkland Foods Corporation[2]
2. Describe children's decision processes regarding candy buying and consumption
3. Show commercials
4. Discuss commercials in the light of the behavioral scientists' research findings
5. Outline Parkland Foods Corporation's strategic plans regarding future television advertising directed at children

A number of things still bothered Mr.

---

[2]He would point out that Parkland had only recently begun mass media advertising, necessitated by its eroding market share among preteenage children, the Confectionery Division's most important single market segment.

EXHIBIT 6
AREAS OF CANDY CONCERN
*Mean Values—6-Point Scale**

	Children		Teenagers		Adults	
	Rank	Mean score	Rank	Mean score	Rank	Mean score
Causes cavities	①	4.70	①	4.34	②	3.85
Sticks to teeth	②	4.09	③	4.07	①	4.07
Upsets stomach	③	4.00		2.81		2.07
Doesn't look good eating in front of people	④	3.88		3.23		2.45
Messy to eat	⑤	3.84	④	3.60		3.04
Costs too much		3.72		2.93		2.14
Bad for skin		3.69	②	4.21		3.00
Spoils appetite		3.57		2.86		2.87
Fattening		3.49		3.15	⑤	3.17
Too sweet		3.41	⑤	3.54	③	3.30
Too rich		3.39		3.42	④	3.18
Can't stop eating		3.14		2.56		2.15
Artificially flavored		2.79		2.60		2.62
Don't like to be too good to myself		2.73		1.96		1.74
Have to share with others		2.62		2.00		1.49

*Highest rating indicates greatest degree of concern. Based on national sample market research study.

Wackman. Should he use the corporate advertising philosophy? And how should he use the ANA guidelines? How should he address each of the issues surrounding the controversy, and were there any further issues he had not thought about?

Finally, Mr. Wackman realized that upon his return from Washington, he faced the formidable tasks of reporting to Mr. Marks and the board of directors and making strategic suggestions to them regarding Parkland Foods Corporation's future advertising to children. He knew that Parkland Foods Corporation would continue to advertise, but he also knew that Mr. Marks would insist that the corporation do everything in its power to avoid becoming embroiled in the controversy—i.e., becoming the target of activist groups such as Action for Children's Television or being called before the Federal Trade Commission or the Better Business Bureau's powerful National Advertising Review Board.[3]

Mr. Wackman knew that his specific suggestions would be evaluated by Mr. Marks and the board in terms of (1) how adequately they overcame the controversy issues and (2) how adequately marketing could still carry on its task of effectively promoting Parkland Foods Corporation products to children.

[3]In fact, a candy manufacturer had recently been called before the NARB regarding a 10-second ad showing a boy biting into the candy bar. The sound effects were quite loud when the boy bit into the bar. The NARB's complaint charged that the biting sound was unnaturally loud and hence might be misleading to children. The company withdrew the ad at considerable expense.

EXHIBIT 7
FREQUENCY OF CHILDREN'S ATTEMPTS TO INFLUENCE PURCHASES AND PERCENTAGE OF MOTHERS' "USUALLY" YIELDING

Products	Frequency of requests*				Percentage of yielding			
	5–7 years	8–10 years	11–12 years	Total†	5–7 years	8–10 years	11–12 years	Total†
Relevant foods								
Breakfast cereal	1.26	1.59	1.97	1.59	88	91	83	87
Snack foods	1.71	2.00	1.71	1.80	52	62	77	63
Candy	1.60	2.09	2.17	1.93	40	28	57	42
Soft drinks	2.00	2.03	2.00	2.01	38	47	54	46
Jell-O	2.54	2.94	2.97	2.80	40	41	26	36
Overall mean	1.82	2.13	2.16	2.03				
Overall percentage					51.6	53.8	59.4	54.8
Less relevant foods								
Bread	3.12	2.91	3.43	3.16	14	28	17	19
Coffee	3.93	3.91	3.97	3.94	2	0	0	1
Pet food	3.29	3.59	3.24	3.36	7	3	11	7
Overall mean	3.45	3.47	3.49	3.49				
Overall percentage					7.6	10.3	9.3	9.0
Durables, for child's use								
Game, toy	1.24	1.63	2.17	1.65	57	59	46	54
Clothing	2.76	2.47	2.29	2.52	21	34	57	37
Bicycle	2.48	2.59	2.77	2.61	7	9	9	8
Hot wheels	2.43	2.41	3.20	2.67	29	19	17	22
Record album	3.36	2.63	2.23	2.78	12	16	46	24
Camera	3.91	3.75	3.71	3.80	2	3	0	2
Overall mean	2.70	2.58	2.73	2.67				
Overall percentage					25.6	28.0	35.0	29.4
Notions, toiletries								
Toothpaste	2.29	2.31	2.60	2.39	36	44	40	39
Bath soap	3.10	2.97	3.46	3.17	9	9	9	9
Shampoo	3.48	3.31	3.03	3.28	17	6	23	16
Aspirin	3.64	3.78	3.97	3.79	5	6	0	4
Overall mean	3.13	3.09	3.26	3.16				
Overall percentage					16.8	16.3	18.0	17.0
Other products								
Automobile	3.55	3.66	3.51	3.57	2	0	0	12
Gasoline brand	3.64	3.63	3.83	3.70	2	0	3	2
Laundry soap	3.69	3.75	3.71	3.72	2	0	3	2
Household cleaner	3.71	3.84	3.74	3.76	2	3	0	2
Overall mean	3.65	3.72	3.70	3.69				
Overall percentage					2.0	0.75	1.50	1.75

*On a scale from 1 ("often") to 4 ("never").

†5–7 years, $n = 43$; 8–10 years, $n = 32$; 11–12 years, $n = 34$; Total, $n = 109$.

EXHIBIT 8
CORRELATIONS BETWEEN CHILD'S PURCHASE INFLUENCE ATTEMPTS, PARENTAL YIELDING, AND THE INDEPENDENT VARIABLES

Independent variables	Child's purchase influence attempts	Parental yielding
Demographics		
Child's age	−.13	.20*†
Number of children	−.00	−.00
Social class	−.01	.00
Interpersonal variables		
Parent-child conflict	.18‡	−.00
Restrictions on viewing	−.01	−.24§
Communication variables		
Mother's time spent with television	.18‡	−.23*
Recall of commercials	.26*	.04
Attitudes toward advertising	−.00	.16‡

*$p < .01$.

†Should be read: The greater the child's age, the greater the incidence of parental yielding to purchase influence attempts (or vice versa), and the correlation coefficient (.20) could only have occurred by chance once in 100 times.

‡$p < .05$.

§Should be read: The more parents put restrictions on children's television viewing, the less likely they are to yield to children's purchase influence attempts (or vice versa), and the correlation coefficient (−.24) could only have occurred by chance once in 100 times.

Source: S. Ward and D. B. Wackman, "Children's Purchase Influence Attempts and Parental Yielding," *Journal of Marketing Research,* vol. 9, August 1972, pp. 316–319.

EXHIBIT 9
PRELIMINARY RESULTS OF DIARY STUDY OF CHILDREN'S REQUESTS FOR PRODUCTS AND SERVICES

In order to assess the frequency and kinds of requests children make in the natural home environment, a team of Boston-area researchers had recently completed a diary study involving 389 mothers of children aged 4 to 5 and 7 to 9 in upper-middle- and lower-middle-income areas in Boston. The table below presents preliminary results, as their analyses of the data were just beginning.

Each mother was trained to keep a diary of each day for 30 consecutive days (during the months of April and May). Each mother was trained to indicate everything her child asked for each day which would involve an economic transaction. She also checked appropriate spaces in the diary to indicate her response to the child's request and her child's subsequent response. Finally, she was asked to give an opinion (or indicate "don't know") concerning where she thought the child got the idea to want to buy the product.

Careful controls were used to maximize reliability: Mothers were individually trained to fill out the diaries, and a "hot line" was installed for questions.

The total number of requests across all product categories over the 30-day period was 3,632; the average number of requests per family was about 13. Thirty-nine percent of the children made 15 or more requests during the month, Mr. Wackman was told. Age and social class differences were not yet analyzed.

EXHIBIT 9
Continued

Summary of Preliminary Results from Diary Study

Product categories	Percentage of requests	Response to child's request				
		Yes, didn't mind	Yes, discuss, or change	No, period	No, discuss	No, change, or stall
Cereal	6.8*	66†	10	3	10	12
Candy	16.7	55	15	10	12	8
Toys	15.2	20	14	10	22	33
Clothing	10.1	46	21	3	9	22
Sporting goods	5.2	21	17	6	23	34
Snack foods	23.7	64	13	4	12	8
Other foods	6.5	70	12	3	8	8
Other (miscellaneous, fruits, vegetables, fast foods, OTC medicines, toothpaste)		55	15	5	11	14
OTC medicines	<1					
Toothpaste	<1					
Fruits and vegetables	3.6					
Fast foods	3.5					
Miscellaneous	6.4					
Average		49.6	14.6	5.5		15.4

*Should be read: Of the 3,632 requests in one month, 6.8% were for cereals.

†Should be read: Of all responses to children's requests for cereals, 66% were "Yes, didn't mind."

‡Should be read: Of the 25% of responses to child's requests for cereals which were "no, period," "no, discuss," or "no, change child's request, or stall" (see preceding 3 columns), 14% indicated that the child "took it OK."

§Should be read: 31% of the mothers indicated that they felt the main reason the child asked for cereal was that he or she saw it in a store. (Note that responses across this question do not add to 100% because some mothers indicated more than one perceived reason.)

EXHIBIT 9
Continued

Summary of Prelimary Results from Diary Study
Continued

	Child's reaction to "no"			Mothers' perception of "main reason" child asked					
Took it OK	Disap-pointed	Argue		Saw in store	Saw on TV	Brother, sister, friend	Saw ad for it	Don't know	Other
		A little	A lot						
14‡	5	4	2	31§	31	9	4	7	33
13	7	8	2	41	12	17	3	10	23
35	15	8	7	23	45	26	5	3	10
12	11	7	3	26	7	39	2	6	36
32	20	7	4	14	9	41	5	4	37
10	4	4	6	24	8	15	4	12	39
11	3	3	2	21	29	5	3	6	40
14	10	5	1	22	18	14	4	7	40
17.5	9.0	4.3							

ADDENDUM TO EXHIBIT 9
Explanation of Response Categories in Diary Study

I. Response to child's request
Mothers could check one space to indicate their response, from "Yes, didn't mind" (buying what the child asked for) to "No, change, or stall" (that is, said "no" to the child's request, but either tried to change the child's mind about what was wanted or stalled). The category "Yes, discuss, or change" means that the mother agreed to the requested purchase but discussed it first and/or tried to change the child's mind about what was wanted. "No, period" means a flat *no*, with no discussion, while "No, discuss" means that the mother said "no" but discussed her reasons with the child.

II. Child's reaction to "no"
For each purchase request to which a mother said "no" (any of the three "no" response categories), she also had to check a space to indicate her child's reaction to the "no." The categories under this heading are self-explanatory.

III. Mothers' perception of "main reason" child asked
For each purchase request, mothers were also asked to check a space to indicate *what they thought* was the main reason or influence on the child leading to the purchase request. Some mothers checked more than one influence. The headings under this category are self-explanatory.

EXHIBIT 10
AVERAGE NUMBER OF HOURS PER DAY SPENT WATCHING TELEVISION, BY AGE GROUP

	Ages 2 to 5	Ages 6 to 11
November 1966	3.14	2.59
November–December 1969	4.04	3.22
January–February 1970	4.20	3.38

Source: A. C. Nielsen Company. (Data are from diaries and are highly consistent with data gathered by others, by other methods.)

EXHIBIT 11
TYPES OF PROGRAMS WATCHED BY CHILDREN* (1975)

	Total viewers 2–11 years old (millions)
"Brady Bunch"	12.08
"Partridge Family"	11.73
"Wonderful World of Disney"	11.02
"All in the Family"	8.89
"Emergency"	8.89
"Waltons"	8.89
"Adam 12"	7.47
"Sonny and Cher"	7.11
"Sanford and Son"	6.75
"Room 222"	6.40

*All are "prime-time" (i.e., 7–10 P.M.) shows.

Appendix A

Client: Parkland Foods Corporation
Product: Chocolate Smacks
Title: "Boy" (Hippo)

MUSIC & SOUND EFFECTS
ANNCR. (VO): If a hippo
follows you home from
school . . .

kiss him quick (SFX-KISS)

with a Parkland's smack!

When a crocodile gives you
a smile and says "won't
you wait just a little while . . ."

kiss him quick (SFX-KISS)

with a Parkland's smack!

Parkland's Chocolate
Smacks.

Lots to a bag. So you can
spare one or two.

What do you do when a Kangaroo
puts his foot on the end of
your shoe? . . .

BOYS AND GIRLS (VO): Kiss
him quick (SFX:KISS)

with a Parkland's smack!

ANNCR: Parkland's Chocolate
Smacks.

Appendix A
Continued

Client: Parkland Foods Corporation
Product: Moo Cow
Title: "Cow in Apartment"

(SFX: MUSIC IN--UNDER &
THROUGHOUT)

(SFX)

(SFX)

MOTHER'S VOICE: Finish
your milk, George!

LITTLE BOY: There's a cow
in the kitchen.
MOTHER'S VOICE: Finish
your milk.

LITTLE BOY: Hey, what's
that?

SINGERS: Moo Cow.

Gives milk that super
Moo Cow taste.

That Moo Cow taste.

LITTLE BOY: A cow brought
it!

COW (VO): MOOO!

SINGERS: Moo Cow.
Gives milk that super
Moo Cow taste.

Appendix A

Continued

```
Client:    Parkland Foods Corporation
Product:   K-K
Title:     "Two Lions"
```

NATURAL NOISES. BOY: Wherever I go, I always take along a couple of K-K.

What's a K-K?

A chocolate bar.

How come I take along two?

Well, on the outside, a K-K's so delicious and chocolatey. . .

CRUNCH

. . . you want to eat two.

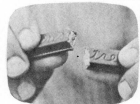

CRUNCH

And on the inside it's so light and crispy and crunchy,

CRUNCH . . . you can eat two.

Chocolatey crispy Kit Kat. It's so light you can eat two?

ROAR, ROAR

Appendix A
Continued

Client: Parkland Foods Corporation
Product: Bits
Title: "Dancing Bits: 30"

ANNCR: Bits candy brings you.

Lots of chewy Bits in every roll.

JINGLE: There are lots of chewy Bits in a roll for you.

If you're choosey 'bout what you chew . . . Real milk chocolate and caramel too . . .

To chew chew chew . . . chew chew chew!

ANNCR: Choosey chewers can choose and chew

dee-licious chocolate covered caramels . . . Bits!

So choose the chews

choosey chewers choose!

Bits!

Lots of Bits in a roll for you!

Bits!

Appendix A
Continued

Agency: Ogilvy & Mather Inc.
Product: Crunch-O
Title: "Boy & Chicken Rev. 2"

BOY: Alright, Mildred.

Tell me the name of the
chocolate bar with the
krackelly chocolate taste.
MILDRED: Kaackel!

BOY: No! Here it is. The
chocolate bar with the krackelly
chocolate taste.

Now what is it?
MILDRED: Kaackel!

BOY: No. Crunch-O!

(SFX: BITE) Crunch-O is full
of little crispies surrounded
by Parkland's milk chocolate.

So what's the chocolate bar
with the krackelly chocolate
taste?

MILDRED: Kaackel!
BOY: Crunch-O!

MILDRED: Kaackel.

BOY: Crunch-O.
MILDRED: Kaackel.

BOY: Crunch-O.
MILDRED: Kaackel.

BOY: Crunch-O.
MILDRED: Kaackel . . .

Appendix A

Continued

Client: Parkland Food Corporation
Product: Bits
Title: "Curtain Going Up-Rev."

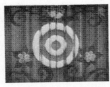   

1. ANNCR: (VO) Ladies and gentlemen: Bits candy presents the Chewy Bits.

2. (MUSIC UNDER) CHORUS: (VO) There are lots of chewy Bits . . .

3. . . . in a roll for you.

4. If you're choosy 'bout what you chew

  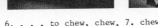 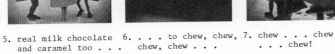

5. real milk chocolate and caramel too . . .

6. . . . to chew, chew, chew, chew . . .

7. chew . . . chew . . . chew!

8. ANNCR: (VO) Bits.

9. Chewy caramel surrounded by rich milk chocolate.

10. Delicious. And you get lots in every roll.

11. CHOROUS: (VO) To chew, chew, chew, chew, chew, chew!

12. ANNCR: (VO) Bits! (MUSIC OUT)

Appendix A
Continued

```
Client:    Parkland Foods Corporation
Product:   Chocolate Smacks
Title:     "Kiss Him Quick Girl"

           575-044
```

1. ANNCR. (VO): If you hear a little laugh,

2. and turn to find a big giraffe . . .

3. kiss him quick (SFX: KISS)

4. with a Parkland's smack!

5. If you hear a sound like a vacuum cleaner and it turns out to be a giant ant-eater . . .

6. kiss him quick (SFX: KISS)

7. with a Parkland's smack!

8. Parkland's Chocolate Smacks. Lots to a bag.

9. So if you suddenly see a big green caterpillar swinging from a tree . . .

10. BOYS AND GIRLS (VO): Kiss him quick (SFX: KISS)

11. with a Parkland's smack!

12. ANNCR: Parkland's Chocolate Smacks.

Appendix B
Child Psychology Concepts[1]

The term "preoperational" was coined by the eminent child psychologist Jean Piaget. Piaget is generally recognized as the leading psychologist studying "cognitive development," i.e., processes by which children form attitudes and behavior patterns and gain knowledge relevant to their functioning in the world. "Preoperational children" (aged about 3 through 7) are characterized by their tendency to focus on perceptual aspects of stimuli (what they see is what is real for them) and by their lack of ability to abstract from what they see in the immediate environment, relative to older children. Research on responses to advertising has shown that preoperational children often do not fully understand the concept of advertising—what commercials are and what they try

to do. Moreover, they recall less advertising content; i.e., they focus on a few elements of commercials. Finally, they use fewer dimensions to compare advertised brands of the same product, and these are often perceptual attributes (e.g., "one is bigger than the other").

"Concrete operational" children (aged about 7 or 8 to about 12), on the other hand, can engage in abstract thought, use more dimensions to compare brands, recall more elements in commercials, and are more likely to understand the concept of advertising and its intent than are younger, "preoperational" children.

As an example of the differences in the abilities of children in these two age groups to process information, research has shown the following typical kinds of responses to questions about how to compare certain objects. Note that preoperational children are most likely to compare the objects on the basis of perceptual cues, while concrete operational children can abstract and compare the objects on the basis of their different functions.

[1]For further information, see E. Zigler and I. L. Child, "Socialization," in G. Lindzey and E. Aronson (eds.), *The Handbook of Social Psychology*, 2d ed., vol. 2: *The Individual in a Social Context*, Addison-Wesley Publishing Company, Inc., Reading, Mass., 1969.

	Responses	
Objects compared	Preoperational	Concrete operational
Car–truck	"One is small; the other is big."	"Cars carry people; trucks haul a lot of things."
	"Trucks go faster."	"Cars are used by families; trucks are used by businesses."
School–house	"School is a big building; a house is smaller."	"Schools are where you go to learn; homes are where you live."
	"Schools are red."	

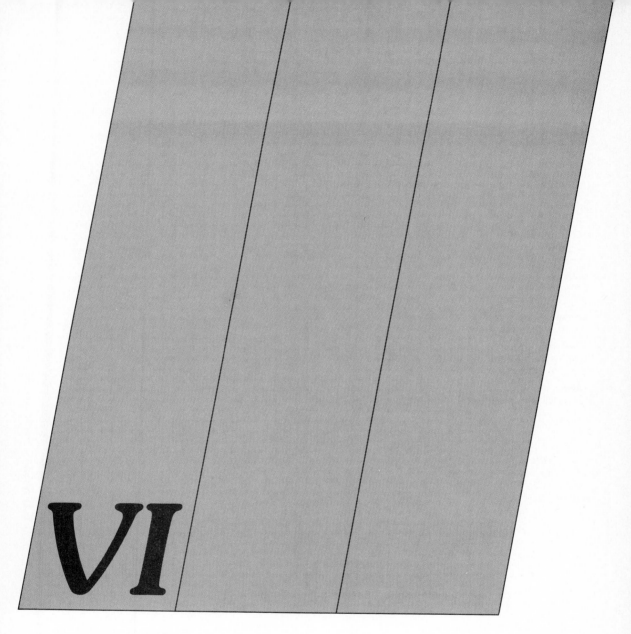

VI

Pricing Strategy

The three basic reference points in pricing are (1) the value of the product to the customer, (2) the costs the seller must incur in manufacturing and/or marketing the product, and (3) competitive pricing behavior. The first is the most important reference point; competitive prices and costs tend to set upper and lower bounds, respectively, to the degree of freedom one has in setting a price. Ideally, price should be a monetary expression of what the product is worth to the buyer as against the value of any other options he or she may have for satisfying a particular need. Pricing is an art. It is based largely on making qualitative judgments and predictions about a wide range of factors that influence the behavior of customers and competitors both.

With regard to *customer value* the questions the marketing manager must often ask are these: For what particular customer set is the product intended? What *is* the product to this group? How does it fit the patterns of use of these potential customers? Their life-styles? What other options do they have, and how are they likely to evaluate these alternatives against our product? How can we educate customers as to the values our product offers? Why and how does perceived value shift over the product life cycle, and how can we take that factor into account? If, as often happens, there are several market segments for the product and the product has different perceived values for each, can we sell at different prices in different markets? Will lowering prices significantly lead to proportional increases in demand for the product? And will price increases result in significant reductions in sales? Or is demand relatively insensitive to price?

Manufacturing and selling *costs* usually establish a bottom limit to the range within which the manager can set prices. In that area, the questions he or she will raise are these: What components of cost are relevant for pricing purposes? What is the significance of the ratio of fixed costs to variable (or out-of-pocket) costs in setting prices? How much do we have to sell to break even? How will costs behave over the product life cycle and at different volume levels? How will costs vary with the quantity purchased at any one time? Under what circumstances is it feasible to set prices at less than cost for strategic reasons?

If pricing is an art, it is also a game, one that is played often for high stakes against *competitors* whose strategies may be clearly understood or, alternatively, whose behavior is quite unpredictable. In this domain the marketing manager learns to ask: Who are the competitors, both existing and potential, in the market segments we serve? How and to what extent are our product lines differentiated from theirs? What are their cost structures? Their market shares? Their strengths and weaknesses? How do the accounts for which we all compete perceive each competitor as a potential source of supply? How can we anticipate and react to their price moves? Can we in any way legally influence their pricing behavior in a manner that helps us and the industry of which we are a part? In this regard, what is price leadership? How does it work?

Pricing Structures

We are not only concerned with establishing a selling price to buyers for any given product. More often than not, the manager is concerned with establishing *price structures* of two sorts. The price structure for a single product may provide margins for resellers such as wholesalers and retailers to allow for percentages taken off some suggested price to consumers. The structure may also make allowances for different quantities—the larger the quantity purchased, the lower the unit price. It may, and often does, provide for credit terms and means of payment.

The second type of price structure covers all the items in a line of related products. The line might include products of different sizes such as electric motors or packaged foods. Alternatively, the products in a line may relate to each other along a quality dimension—e.g., a good-better-best product offering. In these circumstances, the marketing manager will seek to set the price of each item relative to the others in the line so as to preserve demand for the item and at the same time maximize profits across the total line. Different sizes, different quality levels, and different specifications tailored to discrete product uses may appeal to different market segments. Even the competitive milieu might vary somewhat from one end of the product line to the other, and costs, too, are likely to vary considerably across the range.

The pricing process—that is, the process by which prices are set and readjusted—requires constant attention. Essential to the process is an intelligence system for monitoring customer behavior, competitive actions, and changing cost structures. It is important to constantly gather and assess information on the way customers respond to price moves in terms of aggregate demand levels and on the impact of price adjustments on the market shares of individual competitors. The pricing process is a dynamic process which constantly tests the value of what one offers to the markets one seeks to serve. It also tests the skills of the marketing manager.

40 United States Postal Service

Christopher H. Lovelock • L. Frank Demmler

Robert F. Jordan, director of product management at the United States Postal Service (USPS), was reviewing a proposal from the Retail Products Division to standardize the fee for Postal Service money orders at 35 cents.[1]

On the basis of the proposal before him, as well as the dissenting views of the Finance Department, Mr. Jordan had to prepare a marketing recommendation for transmittal to the assistant postmaster general for customer services, William D. Dunlap. In making his evaluation, he was mindful of the fact that the money order business, a profitable one for the Postal Service, not only faced direct competition from several sources but also had been plagued in recent years by a steadily shrinking market (Exhibit 1).

Christopher H. Lovelock is an associate professor at the Harvard Graduate School of Business Administration. L. Frank Demmler was formerly a research assistant at the Harvard Graduate School of Business Administration.

[1]A money order is a printed, nonnegotiable order that guarantees payment of a specified sum of money to a designated individual or organization. This payment can be obtained in a different location from that where the money order was issued.

Background

The United States Postal Service (USPS) is one of the oldest, largest, and most visible federal agencies in the United States. In fiscal year (FY) 1974, the USPS operated some 31,000 post offices (including contract stations) and had 710,000 employees. Total revenues that year were $9.0 billion, and total operating expenses were $11.3 billion.

Services offered by the USPS included several distinct categories of mail service, postal money orders, and Mailgrams (a joint venture with Western Union). First-class mail was the principal service offered, and the 51 billion pieces sent in FY 1974 yielded revenues of $5.0 billion.

The Office of Product Management was one of eight marketing-related organizational groupings in the Department of Customer Services. As director of product management, Mr. Jordan

EXHIBIT 1
POSTAL MONEY ORDER SALES, 1935–1974
(DOMESTIC TRANSACTIONS ONLY)

FY	Transactions, thousands	Average fee	Value of sales, millions	Average value per transaction to nearest $0.10
1935	213,351	9.3	1,829	8.60
1940	255,502	9.4	2,103	8.20
1945	282,421	14.0	4,827	17.10
1950	302,848	17.7	4,641	15.30
1955	349,273	18.6	5,865	16.80
1956	346,505	18.6	5,926	17.10
1957	334,882	18.9	5,880	17.60
1958	311,025	22.6	5,442	17.50
1959	286,647	23.2	5,158	18.00
1960	273,633	23.4	5,031	18.40
1961	264,267	23.5	4,958	18.80
1962	251,842	25.3	4,787	19.00
1963	242,871	25.4	4,709	19.40
1964	235,414	25.6	4,719	20.00
1965	220,045	25.8	4,551	20.70
1966	215,361	27.5	4,734	22.00
1967	204,950	31.2	4,724	23.00
1968	196,763	31.3	4,707	23.90
1969	188,569	31.6	4,733	25.10
1970	181,750	30.9	4,723	26.00
1971	179,439	30.3	4,268	23.50
1972	176,089	31.0	4,340	24.60
1973	170,776	31.4	4,400 (est.)	25.70
1974	164,491	31.5	NA	NA

Source: USPS Records

was responsible for five product-related divisions (including Retail Products) and also for the Market Research Division.

The Money Order Market

Postal money orders, which came under the Retail Products Division, had a long history. The Post Office had first started selling them in 1864, at which point it had a near monopoly of the money order business. Over time, the size of the market grew rapidly. However, many competitors, notably banks and express companies, entered the field and gradually obtained a sizable market share for themselves.

While industry data were not available, postal officials estimated that the money order market totaled in excess of 500 million transactions in fiscal year 1972. At an estimated average service fee of 30 cents, this transaction level would generate over $150 million in fee revenues.

The market was thought to be divided into three segments of roughly equal size. The USPS controlled one segment, national money order brands and major banks a second, and other financial institutions (such as savings and loans) a third. The total market was believed to be declining at a 2 percent annual rate. This was ascribed primarily to the growing use of personal checks, reflecting lower charges, greater convenience, and a more sophisticated attitude toward personal money management among the population at large.

The most significant competition to the USPS came from national money order companies, of which the two leading firms were Travelers Express (a subsidiary of Greyhound Corporation) and American Express. The value limit of their individual money orders was typically $200, while the fee varied according to the market involved. By contrast, the third market segment—sales through local financial institutions—was seen as rather disorganized. Institutions in this segment typically charged a flat fee for all values of money order, but the fees varied widely from place to place, ranging from free to 50 cents each. Value limits were at least $200 and often higher.

USPS Money Orders

Prior to 1974, USPS money orders were issued nationally in denominations up to $100. The fees were 25 cents for orders with a face value under $10, 35 cents for orders from $10 to $49.99, and 40 cents for $50 to $100. Exhibit 2 details changes in postal money order fees since 1944. The most recent fee increase had been in March 1966.

The USPS money order business was divided into three basic categories: domestic (96.8 percent of total volume), military (3.0 percent), and international (0.2 percent). While the number of transactions, 165 million per year, paled in comparison with the volume of first-class mail, money orders were still a very significant business. In addition to the revenues derived from fees, the high face values of money orders, averaging $30, provided a daily cash flow estimated at over $100 million. In FY 1974, the income from fees and float interest generated $57 million in revenues. By postal accounting standards, the money order business was very profitable for the Postal Service, with attributable costs[2] of only $2.6 million annually. Consequently, postal executives were concerned at the

[2]The Postal Service differentiated between the costs of running the system and those which were directly traceable to providing a specific product or service. The former were termed *institutional costs*; the latter *attributable costs*. This procedure was an outgrowth of recommendations made by the Kappel Commission. In the case of money orders, the variable costs of paper, printing, processing, and the like plus direct overhead were charged as attributable costs. However, lobby facilities and the window clerk were charged as institutional costs. Postal products and services were expected to cover their attributable costs and also make a contribution to institutional costs.

EXHIBIT 2
POSTAL MONEY ORDERS: DOMESTIC FEES SINCE 1944

Money order value	Nov. 1 1944	Jan. 1 1949	July 1 1957	July 1 1961	Mar. 26 1966
$0–$2.50	6¢	10¢	15¢	20¢	25¢
$2.51–$5.00	8	10	15	20	25
$5.01–$10.00	11	15	20	20	25
$10.01–$15.00	13	25	30	30	35
$15.01–$20.00	13	25	30	30	35
$20.01–$30.00	15	25	30	30	35
$30.01–$40.00	15	25	30	30	35
$40.01–$50.00	18	25	30	30	35
$50.01–$60.00	18	35	30	35	40
$60.01–$70.00	20	35	30	35	40
$70.01–$75.00	20	35	30	35	40
$75.01–$80.00	20	35	30	35	40
$80.01–$100.00	22	35	30	35	40

Source: **USPS Records**

falling volume of business, which in the past 5 years had continued the steady decline begun in the early 1950s.

The weak market performance of postal money orders was ascribed to several factors, notably aggressive marketing by competitors. Brands such as American Express and Travelers Express had achieved good distribution, particularly in retail outlets situated in high-traffic areas and offering lengthy business hours (for example, 7–11 stores, supermarkets, and drugstores). Many banking institutions were offering money orders "fee free" for the purpose of attracting new savings, checking, and loan accounts.

Postal Service executives speculated that certain actions taken in recent years by the USPS might also have contributed to the decline of its money order business. Such actions included shortening the weekly hours (due to Saturday closings of post offices) and allowing contract stations (commercial retail outlets which provided post office services on a contractual basis for the USPS) to sell competitive money orders. Compounding the postal money order's competitive difficulties was the stipulation, in most instances, that USPS money orders only be sold in contract stations during the local post office's standard opening hours.

Marketing Activities on USPS Money Orders[3]

Concern among USPS executives over declining postal money order sales and fee revenues led to a series of actions designed to counteract this trend.

Starting in FY 1972, the product and its market were carefully analyzed by the Office of Product Management to identify opportunities for expansion over a 2-year period. Additionally, market research studies and test markets were

[3]Some of the market research data on money orders has been disguised.

conducted to upgrade the money order form itself and to ascertain the best advertising and promotional mix to use in merchandising the line to customers.

After several years of study and research, originally initiated by the old Post Office Department, a new money order form was introduced nationally in October 1973. The Postal Service completely revised both the aesthetics and the function of the form. The new one included (1) a full-size four-color receipt, (2) a full-information money order, and (3) a voucher for increased internal control. Product management executives felt that this new form was competitively superior to any form in the industry and would contribute to greater customer acceptance, as well as improve the efficiency and security of USPS money order operations. Posters were hung in post offices (Exhibit 3) to announce the change.

Promotional Tests

The effectiveness of advertising and promotional activity directed at USPS money orders was tested, with three cities being selected as test markets and each matched against a control city. The money order market development plan was highlighted by the following promotional elements:

1. *Media advertising.* A television advertising campaign was aired in each city beginning in November 1972. Thirty-second commercials featured a construction worker going about his dangerous job and stressed the safety of USPS money orders as a method of sending money (Exhibit 4).
2. *Sales promotion.* Three unique, direct-mail sales promotion efforts were developed and targeted at high-potential, money order–using households in each test market. The basic format was a color-printed self-mailer offering a coupon with one of the following purchase incentives:

EXHIBIT 3
POST OFFICE LOBBY POSTER
FOR USPS MONEY ORDERS

EXHIBIT 4
TV COMMERCIAL FOR USPS MONEY ORDERS

Needham, Harper & Steers, Inc.
909 Third Avenue, New York, New York 10022
(212) 758-7600

CLIENT: U.S. POSTAL SERVICE
PRODUCT: U.S. POSTAL SERVICE
AS FILMED TV COMM'L NO: UPMO2083
TITLE: "MALE RISK"

DATE: 12/8/72
LENGTH: 30 SEC.

1. MAN: Me and Marge ... the way we feel,

2. there's too many risks in life as it is.

3. Now, when it comes to paying bills,

4. me and Marge, we pay by safe Postal Money Orders.

5. You lose them or they get stolen from you,

6. you get a refund and nobody can say you didn't pay a bill when you did.

7. Because with U.S. Postal Money Orders,

8. you get a receipt from Uncle Sam to prove you did.

9. I get them down at the Post Office, or Marge does.

10. Postal Money Orders,

11. they're safer than money.

Promotional incentive	*Purchase requirement*
1 free stamped envelope	1 money order[4]
2 free stamped envelopes	2 money orders
1 fee-free money order	4 money orders

The results of the test showed a modest increase in money order sales volume for each of the promotions, with free stamped envelopes generating a larger sales increase than the offer of four money orders for the price of three. However, it was decided not to expand the program nationally at this point, since the sales increases resulting fell slightly short of the level needed to make such a program economically viable. It was concluded that further testing should be undertaken.

Special materials were developed to communicate the promotion to key field personnel, from management to window clerks. Field exe-

[4]This promotion is shown in Exhibit 5.

EXHIBIT 5
DIRECT-MAIL PROMOTION FOR USPS MONEY ORDERS

cution of the promotion was held to be very satisfactory, and excellent cooperation was obtained from local post offices.

Test of Alternative USPS Money Order Fees

Another area of analysis and planning concerned the fees charged for different denominations of postal money orders. These fees had remained unchanged since March 1966, despite steadily rising costs in overall Postal Service operations. USPS product management believed that an opportunity existed to revise and improve the existing money order pricing structure.

Related to this issue was the decision to raise the maximum face value in which the money orders could be sold from $100 to $300. It was recognized that initially this would lead to a reduction in unit volume (and therefore in fee revenues), since sums of $100.01 to $300 would henceforth require only one money order instead of two or three. However, the change was expected to provide a competitive advantage and lead to a long-run sales increase.

An 18-month market test of alternative value-fee combinations was initiated. The primary objective of this test was to determine the impact of alternative fee structures on both postal revenues and money order purchasers. A secondary objective was to develop a price for money orders in the $100 to $300 range, the higher-value ceiling established for the new money order system.

Three different value-fee combinations were tested. In all cases, the value ceiling was increased to $200. This was felt to be responsive to the needs of customers for higher-value money orders; it also eliminated the pricing disadvantages associated with having to buy two money orders for a value between $100 and $200 and placed the USPS ceiling at parity with that of key competition. It was not feasible to test the higher $300 limit for the new money order

system at that time due to the mechanical limitations of existing hardware.

Two flat-fee schedules, one at 35 cents and the second at 25 cents, were tested along with the higher-value ceiling. The flat-fee approach was expected to eliminate many customer communications and operations disadvantages. The 35-cent price (tested in cities C and D) was close to current pricing and at parity with the prices set by national competition. The more aggressive 25-cent price (tested in cities A and B) would, it was anticipated, yield a competitive price advantage.

A third alternative was tested in cities E and F. The then-current variable-fee schedule was kept, and there was a 50-cent fee for values in the $100 to $200 range. Sales trends in the remainder of the country served as the control for the three test markets.

The results of these tests, shown in Exhibit 6, suggested that the 35-cent flat fee was the best revenue-producing alternative of the three tested. Meantime, money orders in the $100.01–$200 range were found to account for approximately 5 percent of all sales transactions, as shown in Exhibit 7.

Customer Survey Findings

The Market Research Division then initiated a study to identify consumer attitudes toward money orders. A nationally projectable quota sample was employed. Individual interviews were conducted to screen for money order or cash users in 13 towns and cities, including several of the test cities where the alternative fee structures were being test-marketed.

The objectives of this study were to:

1. Identify consumer behavior patterns in buying and using money orders.
2. Assess attitudes toward money orders in general and the USPS brand in particular.
3. Determine attitudes toward a flat-fee struc-

EXHIBIT 6
MONEY ORDER TEST MARKETS

Percentage change in transaction volume and dollar revenue versus previous year

Period	25¢ flat-fee test (cities A and B)		35¢ flat-fee test (cities C and D)		Old pricing to $100, 50¢ fee for $100–$200 (cities E and F)		Control (rest of U.S.)	
	Transactions	$ revenue	Transactions	$ revenue	Transactions	$ revenue	Transactions	$ revenue
1972:								
Qtr. 3	− 2.1%	−21.3%	−4.2%	+ 6.0%	−0.1%	+0.9%	−1.4%	−1.2%
Qtr. 4	+11.2%	−12.6%	+0.4%	+10.1%	+1.1%	+0.7%	+3.0%	+4.1%
1973:								
Qtr. 1	+17.6%	−14.1%	+0.7%	+ 2.3%	+0.8%	+0.4%	−2.3%	−1.9%
Qtr. 2	+11.3%	−17.5%	−1.1%	+ 4.1%	NA	NA	−1.7%	−1.1%
12-month total	+10.4%	−15.2%	−0.9%	+ 5.1%	NA	NA	−0.7%	−0.1%

Source: USPS records.

EXHIBIT 7
PERCENTAGE OF SALES TRANSACTIONS (BEFORE/AFTER INTRODUCTION OF $200-VALUE CEILING)

Money order value	Before	After
$0–$10.00	30%	30%
$10.01–$50.00	50	50
$50.01–$100.00	20	15
$100.01–$200.00		5

ture versus a variable-fee structure. (A small survey of postal clerks was also undertaken on this topic.)

Each respondent was exposed to only a fixed-fee concept (35 cents) or a variable-fee concept (either 25–40 cents or 25–50 cents). The respondents were asked a number of open-ended questions designed to discover perceived likes and dislikes for the specific fee concept presented and to evaluate perceived cost-value relationships for different-valued money orders.

By those who used them, money orders were seen as a safe, practical, and easy method of giving and sending money and as fair value for what they cost. Postal money orders tended to be viewed as better than money orders in general, reflecting the fact that they were sold by one of the largest and most conspicuous institutions of the federal government.

Cash users were somewhat less anxious about postal money orders than about other brands, but not enough to change their primarily cash-using behavior. This group appeared to view the idea of using money orders as strange and somewhat disconcerting, regarding them as hard to find, handle, fill out, and cash. However, despite a preference for cash transactions, one-third of this group had checking accounts, and half had savings accounts.

The survey found that the principal purposes for which respondents purchased money orders were to pay bills (including rent, mortgage, and insurance), to repay loans, to pay for mail-order purchases, and to send money to friends and relatives. Compared with the general population, money order users tended to have below-average incomes and were somewhat more likely to reside in either rural areas or central cities.

Not surprisingly, most respondents buying USPS money orders reported doing so in a post office, whereas users of other money orders tended to buy theirs in a grocery store or drugstore or in a bank. The main reasons given among other money order users for not buying the USPS brand related to the relative inconvenience of post office hours and location. Some also cited the cost of USPS orders.

Concerning the different fee alternatives, a higher percentage of positive comments concerning the fee structure were made by those exposed to the fixed-fee concept than by those in the variable-fee groups. On the other hand, when asked what fee they expected to pay for various values of money orders, respondents in both variable- and fixed-fee groups clearly expected to pay more for higher-value orders. They also indicated that higher-value money orders would be worth a higher fee to them.

Recommendations for Action

After examining the results of the market test and consumer survey, Mr. MacInnes, product manager for money orders, drafted a proposal for his superior, Mr. Vandegrift, recommending the adoption of a flat 35-cent fee for all USPS money orders. This recommendation was based on the following conclusions:

1. The flat-fee structure was preferred by customers, principally because of its simplicity. This was confirmed both by the survey findings and by the fact that not one com-

plaint had been received during the 18-month market test.

2. On the basis of the market test results, the flat fee was expected to result in an increase in money order revenues of at least 5 percent.
3. It would strengthen the Postal Service's competitive position, as the flat fee was preferred by competitive users as well as by postal users. Additionally, the 35-cent fee would, on the average, be lower than many current competitive rates.
4. A flat-fee structure would streamline postal operations by cutting back on clerk errors and increasing productivity. Additionally, a small survey of postal clerks had shown that they preferred the convenience and simplicity of a flat-fee structure.

The Finance Department's Position

Mr. Vandegrift had then circulated the proposal for a flat 35-cent fee to other organizations within the Postal Service, both at headquarters and in the field, for their review. A number of these had made comments and asked questions. Concurrence was eventually received from, among others, the Law Department, Government Relations, the Consumer Advocate, Retail Operations, and all the regions. One important organization, however, did not agree—the USPS Finance Department.

The Finance Department was responsible for the financial policies, practices, and operations of the Postal Service. This department had a separate money order branch and had been the only organization within the Postal Service with a major interest in money orders before the marketing function was established. In fact, many of the functions and interests normally associated exclusively with marketing in other organizations had fallen historically to the Finance Department.

Much internal correspondence passed between Product Management and Finance. A number of meetings were held and additional research and testing undertaken. Nevertheless, the differences between the two groups on the issue remained unresolved.

The department's final position included the following points.

1. While it was conceded that a flat fee was admittedly simpler, it was argued that customers would have to pay too high a price for simplicity. The proposal was unfair to those purchasing money orders for less than $10 in that they would have to pay 10 cents more than at present.
2. It was pointed out that many competitors in the money order business, notably banks, already charged lower fees than the Postal Service. An increase in USPS fees would, therefore, please the competitors. However, the Postal Service's chief function was to service its customers, not raise a price umbrella over the competition.
3. There was no evidence that a flat fee would build business for the USPS. In fact, American Express, which presumably watched the market closely, had recently returned to a variable-fee structure. Sales were more likely to be decided on the basis of factors such as convenience of location and service hours and whether or not the customer felt "at home" on the premises.
4. The Finance Department emphasized that money order users typically included the less-well-educated, less-prosperous elements of society, such as minority groups and blue-collar workers.

Mr. Vandergrift's Memorandum

Mr. Vandegrift felt that the Finance Department's objections to the memorandum were not sufficient to withdraw the recommendation. He summarized his division's viewpoint in a covering memo to Mr. Jordan accompanying the formal proposal.

EXHIBIT 8
USPS AND COMPETING MONEY ORDER FEE STRUCTURES, NOVEMBER 1974

Money order face value	USPS fees	
	Actual	Proposed
$ 0–$10.00	25¢	35¢
$10.01–$50.00	35¢	35¢
$50.01–$300.00	40¢	35¢

Money order face value	Average fees for competitive brands*					
	American Express		Travelers Express		Minor brands	
	Range	Average	Range	Average	Range	Average
$ 5.00	35–50¢	42.5¢	25–45¢	34.2¢	15–50¢	30.6¢
$ 25.00	35–50¢	43.1¢	35–45¢	41.9¢	15–50¢	36.2¢
$100.00	35–50¢	47.2¢	35–50¢	43.9¢	35–100¢	38.8¢

*Fees charged varied by market. Minor brands often offered fee-free money orders as a promotional incentive to account holders.
Source: USPS Office of Product Management.

In his memo, Mr. Vandegrift emphasized that most purchasers bought money orders of varying amounts, and so the proposed change would be essentially a wash for these people. Research showed that a small minority bought exclusively low-value orders. He also pointed out that a majority of this group, when surveyed, had indicated a preference for the flat-fee concept. Particularly significant, in his view, was the fact that not one complaint had been received from the test markets during the 18-month period when the fixed fee was being tested. Indeed, survey results showed that the majority of consumers had not even noticed any change in the fee structure.

Finally, he included data on the fees charged for USPS money orders and for competitive brands (Exhibit 8). He indicated that there was good evidence for believing that American Express had returned to a variable-fee structure to provide flexibility for pricing its money orders in response to local market conditions.

A Decision to Be Made

Mr. Jordan finished reading all the materials in the folder which Mr. Vandegrift had sent him and leaned back in his chair. What action should he recommend at this point to Assistant Postmaster General Dunlap, he wondered. As he saw it, there were basically three options open to him. One was a recommendation to go ahead, carefully documenting the arguments in favor of this move and countering as many as possible of the Finance Department's objections. A second was to specify an additional program of research and testing, while a third was to recommend retaining a variable-fee structure, in which case a decision still had to be taken on what fee to charge for the new $300 money order. Whichever of these alternatives he selected would have to be accompanied by a general marketing proposal for improving the Postal Service's share of the money order business.

41 Scripto Pens Ltd.

Albert H. Dunn • Ralph Z. Sorenson, II

Mr. Paul J. Brown, managing director of Scripto Pens, Ltd., of London, England, was evaluating his company's current competitive situation in the British ball-point pen industry. He was particularly concerned about a recent pricing move by Biro-Swan Company, Limited, Scripto's largest competitor, and was wondering what, if anything, Scripto should do in response to the move.

Background

In 1956, the Scripto Pen Corporation of Atlanta, Georgia, U.S.A., purchased the Scroll Pen Company of London and renamed the new company Scripto Pens, Ltd. Prior to its acquisition by

Scripto, Scroll had traditionally concentrated on the manufacture and sale of ball-point pens in the "medium" price range. Ball-point pens in this range usually sold at retail for a price somewhere between 2s. 6d. and 6s. 6d.[1] These pens were designed so that the original ink cartridge, when empty, could be replaced by a refill cartridge, which Scroll had also manufactured.

After the 1956 acquisition, Scripto Pens, Ltd., continued to manufacture a medium-priced line of ball-point pens and ink refill cartridges under the Scroll brand name. At the same time, however, the company brought out a line of ball-point pens which it marketed under its own brand name of Scripto. Most of the models in this line were also in the medium price range, although the line did include a few higher-priced

Albert H. Dunn is a professor at the University of Delaware School of Business Administration. Ralph Z. Sorenson, II, is the president of Babson College.

[1]The British currency system at that time consisted of pounds (£), shillings (s.), and pence (d.). There were 12 pence in a shilling and 20 shillings in a pound (i.e., £1=20s.=240d., and 1s.=12d.). The exchange rate at that time was £1=US$2.80 (thus, 1s.=14¢, 1d.=1.2¢).

models. As time went on, the company began to place major emphasis on the Scripto brand and gradually phase out the Scroll brand. As of late 1959, the old line of Scroll pens was still being manufactured, but only on a limited scale.

Scripto manufactured the ball-point pens which it supplied to the domestic British market in a plant adjacent to its offices in London. The manufacturing process was one of mass production, utilizing much specialized machinery. In 1956 the plant had an annual production capacity of 12.5 million ball-point pens and ink refill cartridges and employed over 450 workers.

To sell its products, Scripto maintained a force of 24 full-time sales representatives, who sold about two-thirds of the company's total volume to 1,000 wholesalers. Wholesalers, in turn, sold Scripto and Scroll pens to thousands of retailer dealers located throughout the British Isles. These retail dealers included stationers, department stores, drugstores, news agents, tobacconists, and other miscellaneous outlets. The remaining one-third of the company's sales volume was generated by Scripto sales reps selling directly to 15,000 retailers and to five or six large chain organizations. Generally speaking, both the wholesalers and retailers through whom Scripto sold its pens also carried the pens of competing manufacturers.

Scripto allowed all wholesalers a 25 percent markup on the price at which they sold to retailers. Retailers, in turn, were granted an average markup of 30 to 35 percent (depending on the model), regardless of whether they purchased from wholesalers or from Scripto's direct sales reps. Neither wholesalers nor retailers were granted additional discounts for volume purchases.

Despite the fact that Scripto sold direct to a number of retail outlets, the company made an effort to protect its wholesalers as much as possible so as to ensure that these wholesalers would devote maximum effort to the sale of Scripto's products. Thus, Scripto made it a practice never to sell directly to retailers at a price below that being charged by the wholesalers. Moreover, direct sales reps tried not to visit retailers who were already being adequately serviced by wholesalers. In most cases, wholesalers did not seem to mind the fact that Scripto sales reps were selling direct to some retailers. Mr. Brown, Scripto's managing director, felt this was due to the fact that even when Scripto sales reps did visit retailers directly, they did so only about once every 6 weeks; consequently, their efforts very often resulted in repeat orders for pens or refills for the wholesalers who visited these retailers in the interim. On the whole, Mr. Brown felt Scripto's wholesaler relationships were quite satisfactory.

The retailers whom Scripto sales reps visited, in turn, generally welcomed the opportunity to deal directly with the company, the main advantages being that reps offered on-the-spot delivery, in-store display service, and immediate attention to retailer or customer complaints.

To back up the sales plan, Scripto annually budgeted an amount equal to approximately 15 percent of total factory sales for advertising and promotion. Of this amount, about 12½ percent was allocated to newspaper and television advertising, and the remainder was set aside for promotion of Scripto's products to wholesalers and retailers. Prior to 1959 the company had never used up the total amount of its annual advertising and promotion budget. Approximate actual expenditures since 1957 were as follows:

1957:	£55,000
1958:	£65,000
1959:	£75,000 (estimated)

Trends in the Sales of Ball-Point Pens

The British ball-point pen industry had been expanding at an extremely rapid rate for several years prior to 1959. From sales of approximately 11 million ball-point pens in 1952, the industry had grown to the point where, in 1959, sales were estimated at 86 million units, reflecting a 7-year increase of almost 800 percent. Meanwhile, sales of fountain pens had remained fairly constant (Exhibit 1).

In pounds sterling, industry-wide sales of ball-point pens and ink refill cartridges had risen from about £930,000 in 1952 to an estimated £3,500,000 in 1959, reflecting an increase of about 375 percent (Exhibit 2).

During this same period, the average factory price of an individual ball-point pen dropped from 1s. 8d. (20 pence) to 8 pence.

Mr. Brown had conducted some informal market research into the public's pen-buying habits and had reached some tentative conclu-

EXHIBIT 2
TRENDS IN BALL-POINT PEN SALES IN POUNDS STERLING— UNITED KINGDOM

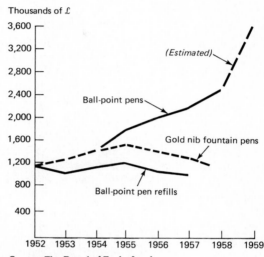

Source: **The Board of Trade, London.**

EXHIBIT 1
TRENDS IN UNIT PEN SALES— UNITED KINGDOM

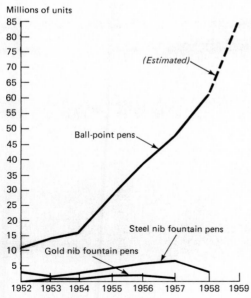

Source: **The Board of Trade, London.**

sions. He felt that the primary reason for the tremendous increase in the popularity of ball-point pens was that people felt that they represented an ideal compromise between the permanence and attractiveness of an ink-writing instrument and the convenience, cleanliness, and inexpensiveness of a lead pencil. Generally speaking, Mr. Brown felt that a ball-point pen was an impulse purchase. To most people, a ball-point was neither a large enough nor an important enough purchase to demand much forethought. Finally, Mr. Brown believed, on the basis of his experience, that the following factors, in order of importance, most influenced the sales of a particular brand of ball-point pens: (*a*) quality of pen, (*b*) availability of brand in large number of retail outlets, (*c*) price, (*d*) appearance and attractiveness of pens and retail display material, (*e*) media advertising.

Composition of the Industry

As of 1956, when Scripto bought out the Scroll Pen Company, there was one other major manufacturer of ball-point pens in the United Kingdom. This company, Biro-Swan, Limited, was the largest in the industry. Biro-Swan had about 45 percent of the 1956 sterling sales volume of ball-point pens and ink refill cartridges.[2] Scroll had about 22 percent, and a number of other small manufacturers together accounted for the remaining 33 percent of the market.

At the time of Scroll's acquisition by Scripto, all the above companies concentrated their major efforts on the manufacture of ball-point pens which sold at retail in the medium (2s. 6d. to 6s. 6d.) or high (6s. 6d. and up) price range. They also manufactured refill cartridges for these pens.

In September of 1957, a controlling interest in Biro-Swan, Ltd., was acquired by the BIC Pen Company of France.[3] Following this transaction it was rumored within the trade that an overall internal management reorganization occurred within the ranks of the Biro-Swan company. At the same time it was also rumored that Biro-Swan had begun a program to expand significantly its production capacity for ball-point pens. This management reorganization and expansion of production capacity had supposedly continued for about a year.

Introduction of a Low-Priced Line of Ball-Point Pens by Biro-Swan

Following this year of preparation, Biro-Swan made a move which marked the industry's first large-scale departure from its traditional emphasis on marketing pens in the medium price range. Thus, in August of 1958, Biro-Swan introduced the first low-priced line of ball-point pens to be seen in the U.K. This new line of pens, which was initially launched in the Midlands region of England and then quickly expanded nationwide, was sold under the "BIC" brand name. Three pen models made up the line: the nonrefillable[4] BIC Crystal retailing at 1s., the nonrefillable BIC Clic retailing at 1s. 6d., and the refillable BIC Coronet retailing at 2s.

To announce the introduction of its new low-priced line of ball-point pens, Biro-Swan made heavy expenditures on consumer advertising. Throughout the nation extensive use was made of both spot television commercials and advertisements in local newspapers. In this widespread advertising campaign, the company placed major emphasis on trying to create heavy public demand for the 1-shilling BIC Crystal. To achieve this goal, the company's advertising strongly stressed the price appeal of the new 1-shilling pen.

Biro-Swan had little difficulty getting retailers to carry the new low-priced line. In attempting to achieve intensive distribution for the new line, Biro-Swan followed its traditional policy of selling both through wholesalers and direct to the retail trade. For its selling activities, the company employed a force of "van salesmen" who operated more in the capacity of "order takers" than as sales representatives. Thus, they visited wholesalers and retailers, took orders, and immediately filled these orders from the supply of merchandise which they carried in their vehicles.

One fundamental difference existed in the pricing policies of Biro-Swan and Scripto. Whereas Scripto's direct sales reps made it a point never to undersell the company's wholesalers when visiting a retail account, Biro-Swan

---

[2]Refill cartridges manufactured by one company, generally speaking, could not be used in the ball-point pens made by other manufacturers.

[3]BIC was the largest French manufacturer of ball-point pens and had almost 80 percent of France's annual 100-million-unit market.

[4]"Nonrefillable" meant that once the original ink cartridge went dry, it was not possible to replace it with a refill cartridge. Nonrefillable ball-point pens were sometimes also known as "throw-away" pens.

sales reps would grant an additional "wholesale" discount to any retailer who ordered in sufficient quantity.

Biro-Swan's venture with the 1-shilling throwaway pen proved to be extremely successful. As of August 1959, 1 year after its introduction to the public, production of the BIC Crystal had grown to the annual rate of 53 million units. This figure compared with the annual production rate of the Biro medium-priced ball-point pen line of 7 million units.

Scripto's Reaction to the Introduction of the 1-Shilling BIC Crystal

Biro-Swan launched its 1-shilling BIC pen shortly after Mr. Brown arrived from the United States to take over as managing director of Scripto Pens, Limited. By coincidence, Mr. Brown happened to be traveling in the Midlands at the time that the BIC Crystal was introduced to the public there in August 1958. Upon noticing the apparent initial success of this low-priced competitive pen, Mr. Brown hurried back to London to assess the overall situation and decide what, if anything, Scripto should do in response to Biro-Swan's move.

As soon as it became evident that 1-shilling ball-point pens were going to become tremendously popular with the British buying public, Mr. Brown decided that Scripto must also introduce a comparable low-priced line in order to protect its overall interest in the ball-point pen industry. At the same time, however, Mr. Brown felt that the introduction of a 1-shilling Scripto pen should be viewed primarily as a defensive move. In other words, although he felt that it was essential that Scripto eventually market a pen in the low-priced field, he thought that the company should continue to place primary emphasis on its medium-priced line of pens. Mr. Brown felt that there would continue to be a strong market for medium-priced ball-point pens; consequently he thought that the medium-priced line could continue to be the most profitable segment of Scripto's business. He therefore decided that Scripto's strategy should be to "knock the pins out from under the BIC Crystal" by introducing a 1-shilling Scripto pen, while at the same time attempting to keep sales of Scripto's regular line of medium-priced pens at a normal level.

Before Scripto could come out with a 1-shilling ball-point pen, Mr. Brown felt it would be necessary to increase the company's production capacity. If demand for a 1-shilling Scripto were high, it might easily surpass the factory's 1958 capacity of 12.5 million pens annually. Therefore, in September 1958, Mr. Brown initiated steps to increase plant capacity by designing and installing a number of new high-speed, special-purpose machines that automated various stages of the production process which were previously performed by hand. By early 1959, this program of expansion through automation had enabled Scripto to cut its factory force from 450 to 400 employees, while at the same time increasing production capacity from 12.5 million units to 40 million units.

Simultaneously with his program to increase production capacity, Mr. Brown made an effort to "add more value" to Scripto's medium-priced pens. The quality of these pens was improved by increasing the ink supply in each cartridge 50 percent, installing a new metal tip on one end of the pens, and introducing more stringent quality control. This program of increased quality was in line with Mr. Brown's desire to continue to place major emphasis on medium-priced pens. By making the above improvements, he felt that Scripto's competitive position in the field would be strengthened.

Finally, Mr. Brown embarked on a project to design a new 1-shilling pen. In undertaking this project, Mr. Brown felt that, if possible, Scripto should come out with a 1-shilling pen which would be superior in quality to the 1-shilling BIC Crystal and yet which still could be sold at a satisfactory profit to Scripto. The quality of the first pen that was designed seemed to be equal, but not superior, to the quality of the BIC Crystal. Like the BIC, it was nonrefillable and did not have a retractable point. In spite of the fact that this pen had no substantial quality advantages, Mr. Brown decided to introduce it to the trade as an interim competitive measure to help arrest the gains being made daily by the BIC Crystal. Consequently, in April of 1959, Scripto's wholesalers and dealers were offered the opportunity to stock the new 1-shilling pen and sell it as the Scroll Longline. Despite the fact that the introduction of the Longline was not backed up by any consumer advertising, total sales of the new pen reached the 5 million mark by the beginning of September.

Meanwhile, Mr. Brown succeeded in developing a second ball-point pen model which Scripto could profitably sell at retail for 1 shilling and which had the added advantage of a retractable point. Because of this added feature, Mr. Brown felt that the new model was just what was needed to compete successfully against the BIC Crystal.

Accordingly, Mr. Brown named the new model the Scripto Bobby and made plans to introduce it to the public. During the beginning of August, Scripto sales representatives made a concerted effort to sell advance supplies of the Scripto Bobby to wholesalers and retailers throughout the United Kingdom. In selling the new pen, the sales reps emphasized the fact that Scripto had plans to promote its introduction to the public by means of a widespread television and newspaper advertising campaign. By the first of September, Scripto had lined up a 5-week schedule of frequent spot TV commercials devoted solely to the Bobby. Following this period of intensive TV advertising, Mr. Brown planned to promote the new pen through a series of advertisements in local newspapers all over the nation during the remaining months of 1959.

In anticipation of this year-end advertising campaign to introduce the Bobby, Mr. Brown had conserved on advertising expenditures early in the year. Up until the beginning of September he had spent only about £17,000 of his £75,000 advertising budget. Consequently, he planned to spend about £60,000 on the introductory advertising campaign for the Bobby.

Mr. Brown had designed the format of this campaign with the idea of directing it almost as much toward wholesalers and retailers as toward the general public. This strategy was in line with Scripto's policy of maintaining strong wholesaler and retailer relationships. Thus it was with the feeling that wholesalers and retailers would be favorably impressed by the prestige of TV that Mr. Brown had decided to make such heavy use of this medium.

As a result of the August selling efforts of Scripto's sales reps, about 1,750,000 Bobby pens had been distributed to the trade by the beginning of September. Although Mr. Brown did not, as yet, have any specific figures, he thought that these Bobby pens had already begun to move off the retailers' shelves at a fairly brisk rate in spite of the fact that the consumer advertising program had not yet commenced. Meanwhile sales of Scripto's medium-priced ball-point lines had continued at what Mr. Brown considered to be a "normal" level.

The Situation in August 1959

As of August 1959, Scripto was marketing a full line of ball-point pens with models in every price range. Sales of the 1-shilling line in pounds sterling were still less than sales of the medium-priced line. However, the company was poised to launch its £60,000 introductory advertising campaign for the Bobby in September.

A list of the company's most important ball-point pen models, along with the price schedule at which each pen was sold, is shown in

EXHIBIT 3
SCRIPTO PENS, LTD., PRICE LIST AS OF AUGUST 15, 1959

	Price to wholesalers (doz)	Price to retailers (doz)	Purchase tax (doz)	Retailer's margin (doz)	Retail price (each)
Scripto line					
Low-priced pens					
Bobby	5s. 0d.	6s. 8d.	1s. 8d.	3s. 8d.	1s. 0d.
Medium-priced pens					
250	12s. 6d.	16s. 8d.	4s. 2d.	9s. 2d.	2s. 6d.
490	23s. 7d.	31s. 6d.	7s. 10d.	16s. 8d.	4s. 8d.
T200	32s. 6d.	43s. 4d.	10s. 10d.	21s. 10d.	6s. 4d.
High-priced pens					
T650	38s. 6d.	51s. 4d.	12s. 10d.	25s. 10d.	7s. 6d.
Satellite	87s. 6d.	116s. 8d.	29s. 2d.	58s. 2d.	17s. 0d.
Refills	8s. 9d.	11s. 8d.	2s. 11d.	6s. 5d.	1s. 9d.
Scroll line					
Low-priced pens					
Longline	5s. 0d.	6s. 8d.	1s. 8d.	3s. 8d.	1s. 0d.
Medium-priced pens					
320	17s. 6d.	23s. 4d.	5s. 10d.	11s. 10d.	3s. 5d.
420	20s. 0d.	26s. 8d.	6s. 8d.	13s. 8d.	3s. 11d.
520	28s. 9d.	38s. 4d.	9s. 7d.	20s. 1d.	5s. 8d.
Refills	8s. 9d.	11s. 8d.	2s. 11d.	6s. 5d.	1s. 9d.

Exhibit 3. Exhibit 4 presents an abbreviated income statement for 1958; Exhibit 5 contains cost and unit sales information for various models in the Scripto line.

EXHIBIT 4
ABBREVIATED PROFIT AND LOSS STATEMENT FOR 1958*

Company sales		£620,000
Cost of goods sold		372,000
Gross margin		£248,000
Less selling and administrative expenses:		
Advertising and promotion	£65,000	
Other marketing costs	52,000	
Administrative costs	60,000	
Subtotal		177,000
Net operating profit		£ 71,000

*Disguised data.

Biro-Swan, meanwhile, was also marketing a full line of ball-point pens, its low-priced line being sold under the "BIC" brand name and its medium- and high-priced lines under the "Biro" brand name. Biro-Swan was currently producing BICs at the rate of 53 million units per year and Biros at the rate of about 7 million units per year. Biro-Swan's August 1959 price list is shown in Exhibit 6.

Announcement of Biro-Swan's Price Change

On August 26, the management of Biro-Swan suddenly announced to the trade that effective September 1, big price cuts would be made on all pens and refill cartridges in the medium-priced Biro line. Pen reductions were to range from 33⅓ percent off on the Biro Minor (old retail price: 3s., new price: 2s.) to 7½ percent off

EXHIBIT 5
SCRIPTO PENS, LTD.: SALES, COST, AND CONTRIBUTION INFORMATION*

	Average revenue per pen† (pence)	Average variable cost per pen‡ (pence)	Average contribution per pen‡ (pence)	Average contribution per pen (percentage)	Approximate units sold in 1958 (thousands)	Sales revenues in 1958 (£ thousands)
Low-priced pens						
Scripto Bobby	5.7	2.3	3.4	60	–	–
Scroll Longline	5.7	2.2	3.5	61	–	–
Medium-priced pens						
Scripto 250	14.0	4.5	9.5	68	3,400	197
Scripto 490	26.0	7.6	18.4	70	600	65
Scripto T200	36.5	10.2	26.3	72	300	45
Scroll 320	19.3	6.2	13.1	68	1,800	145
Scroll 420	22.3	7.1	15.2	68	450	42
Scroll 520	32.0	9.0	23.0	72	250	33
High-priced pens						
Scripto T650	42.5	12.1	30.6	72	150	27
Scripto Satellite	97.5	27.5	70.0	72	50	20
Total pens					7,000	574
Refills	9.7	2.7	7.0	70	1,140	46
Total company						620

*Disguised data.

†Approximate figures based on two-thirds sales through wholesalers and one-third sales direct.

‡Estimates made in early 1959 following factory expansion program.

EXHIBIT 6
BIRO-SWAN, LTD., PRICE LIST AS OF AUGUST 15, 1959

	Price to wholesalers (doz)	Price to retailers (doz)	Purchase tax (doz)	Retailer's margin (doz)	Retail price (each)
BIC line					
Low-priced pens					
Crystal	5s. 0d.	6s. 8d.	1s. 7½d.	3s. 8½d.	1s. 0d.
Clic	7s. 6d.	10s. 0d.	2s. 5½d.	5s. 6½d.	1s. 6d.
Coronet	9s. 9d.	13s. 0d.	3s. 2½d.	7s. 9½d.	2s. 0d.
Refills (Coronet only)	3s. 9d.	5s. 0d.	1s. 3d.	2s. 6d.	9d.
Biro line					
Medium- and high-priced pens					
Minor	14s. 7d.	19s. 6d.	4s. 10d.	11s. 8d.	3s. 0d.
Citizen	19s. 0d.	25s. 4d.	6s. 2d.	13s. 6d.	3s. 9d.
Retractable	22s. 2d.	29s. 6d.	7s. 4d.	17s. 2d.	4s. 6d.
Stylist	28s. 9d.	38s. 4d.	9s. 4d.	21s. 4d.	5s. 9d.
Deluxe	52s. 6d.	70s. 0d.	17s. 0d.	39s. 0d.	10s. 6d.
Squire	7s. 3d. each	9s. 8d. each	2s. 5d. each	5s. 5d. each	17s. 6d.
Magnum	7s. 10d. each	10s. 7d. each	2s. 7d. each	5s. 10d. each	19s. 0d.
Refills					
Recharge	7s. 6d.	10s. 0d.	2s. 5½d.	5s. 6½d.	1s. 6d.
Magnum	8s. 9d.	11s. 8d.	3s. 0d.	6s. 5d.	1s. 9d.
Insert	9s. 9d.	13s. 0d.	3s. 2½d.	7s. 9½d.	2s. 0d.

EXHIBIT 7
BIRO-SWAN, LTD.: PRICE LIST AS OF SEPTEMBER 1, 1959

	Price to wholesalers (doz)	Price to retailers (doz)	Purchase tax (doz)	Retailer's margin (doz)	Retail price (each)
BIC line					
Low-priced pens					
Crystal	5s. 0d.	6s. 8d.	1s. 7½d.	3s. 8½d.	1s. 0d.
Clic	7s. 6d.	10s. 0d.	2s. 5½d.	5s. 6½d.	1s. 0d.
Coronet	9s. 9d.	13s. 0d.	3s. 2½d.	7s. 9½d.	2s. 0d.
Refills (Clic and Coronet only)	3s. 9d.	5s. 0d.	1s. 3d.	2s. 6d.	9d.
Biro line					
Medium- and high-priced pens					
Minor	9s. 9d.	13s. 0d.	3s. 2½d.	7s. 9½d.	2s. 0d.
Citizen	13s. 10d.	18s. 6d.	4s. 6½d.	9s. 11½d.	2s. 9d.
Retractable	17s. 3d.	23s. 0d.	5s. 7½d.	13s. 4½d.	3s. 6d.
Stylist	23s. 8d.	31s. 6d.	7s. 8½d.	17s. 9½d.	4s. 9d.
Deluxe	37s. 6d.	50s. 0d.	12s. 2½d.	27s. 9½d.	7s. 6d.
Squire	6s. 3d. each	8s. 4d. each	2s. 0½d. each	4s. 7½d. each	15s. 0d.
Magnum	7s. 3d. each	9s. 8d. each	2s. 5d. each	5s. 5d. each	17s. 6d.
Refills					
Recharge	3s. 9d.	5s. 0d.	1s. 3d.	2s. 9d.	9d.
Magnum	5s. 0d.	6s. 8d.	1s. 7½d.	3s. 8½d.	1s. 0d.
Insert	5s. 0d.	6s. 8d.	1s. 7½d.	3s. 8½d.	1s. 0d.

on the Biro Magnum (old retail price: 19s., new price: 17s. 6d.). Retail prices of refill cartridges were to be cut in half. Prices of the low-priced BIC line were to remain unchanged. Exhibit 7 shows Biro-Swan's new price list.

Dealer margins on each unit in the Biro line were to remain the same from a percentage point of view but would be reduced in absolute money terms. To compensate for the resulting devaluation of stocks presently in the hands of wholesalers and retailers, Biro-Swan proposed a special "bonus" offer. Excerpts from the letter which Biro-Swan's management sent to the trade to announce the forthcoming price cuts are in Exhibit 8.

A *London Financial Times* newspaper article announcing the price change also indicated that Biro-Swan had plans to launch a £250,000 advertising campaign to introduce the price cuts to the public.

EXHIBIT 8
EXCERPTS FROM LETTER FROM BIRO-SWAN MANAGEMENT TO BIRO-SWAN WHOLESALERS AND RETAILERS

26th August, 1959

Dear Sirs:

On September 14th, we are announcing to the public the most-important-ever news concerning the genuine Biro range.

All Biro prices will be substantially reduced from 1st September; all pen prices will be down by at least one shilling; most refill prices will be slashed by half. . . .

Advanced techniques backed by new, ultra-modern machinery have enabled us to make significant reductions in our production costs, at the same time as increasing the quality of them.

The new prices will give the Biro range a far wider appeal than ever before. Enormous demand is anticipated, and with it will come greatly increased turnover, and larger profits for you. Trade margins remain, as they always have been, the most generous in the ball-pen field. The terms on which you buy the Biro range coupled with our Super Discount scheme give you really worthwhile profits on fast-moving merchandise.

We fully appreciate that your existing stocks are devalued by this operation, and we are therefore giving you this advance notice, together with the opportunity to claim a free special bonus during the month of September. All orders received by us between September 1st and September 30th inclusive, for pens and refills in the genuine Biro price range will be invoiced at the new trade price. All orders must be for immediate delivery. The goods will be delivered to you, plus a free bonus of the same goods ordered by you equivalent to the difference between the old and the new retail value of your order. We feel that you will appreciate that this method of adjustment causes you the least effort, and is absolutely straightforward and fair to you and all our customers. . . .

The national advertising starts on September 14th and continues until Christmas. We know that it will create enormous demand for the genuine Biro ball-pen, and at the same time ensure repeat business in refills. You can save in this demand simply by stocking up, displaying, and selling the genuine Biro range.

Yours faithfully,

Sales Manager
Biro-Swan Limited

42 Southwest Airlines: II

Christopher H. Lovelock

"BRANIFF'S 'GET ACQUAINTED SALE': HALF PRICE TO HOUSTON'S HOBBY AIRPORT" trumpeted the headlines on the full-page advertisement in the February 1, 1973, edition of *The Dallas Morning News.*

M. Lamar Muse, president of Southwest Airlines, held up the advertisement for members of the airline's management team and advertising agency executives to see, commenting as he did so:

> OK, gentlemen, at least we now know what Braniff's response to our San Antonio promotion will be. They are hitting us hard in our only really profitable market. Every decision they have made to date has been the wrong decision, so how can we turn this one to our advantage?

Christopher H. Lovelock is an associate professor at the Harvard Graduate School of Business Administration.

Southwest and Its Competition

Southwest Airlines Co. had been organized as a Texas corporation in March 1967 with the objective of providing improved quality air service between the cities of Dallas, Houston, and San Antonio. These cities, each 190 to 250 miles apart, formed a triangular route structure in eastern Texas. Southwest had been certified as an intrastate carrier on these routes by the Texas Aeronautics Commission in February 1968, but lawsuits by Braniff International Airways and Texas International Airlines (TI) had delayed the initiation of service until June 1971.

The Dallas-Houston market, the largest of the three, was dominated by Braniff, which carried some 75 percent of the local traffic on that route during the first half of 1971 (Exhibit 1). A major international carrier with an all-jet fleet of 74 aircraft, Braniff had systemwide revenues in

EXHIBIT 1
SOUTHWEST AIRLINES AND COMPETITORS: AVERAGE DAILY LOCAL PASSENGERS CARRIED IN EACH DIRECTION, DALLAS-HOUSTON MARKET

	Braniff*		Texas Int.*		Southwest		Total local market† (one direction)
	Psgrs.	% of mkt.	Psgrs.	% of mkt.	Psgrs.	% of mkt.	passengers
1967	416	86.1	67	13.9			483
1968	381	70.2	162	29.8			543
1969	427	75.4	139	24.6			566
1970							
1st half	449	79.0	119	21.0			568
2d half	380	76.0	120	24.0			500
Year	414	77.5	120	22.5			534
1971:							
1st half	402	74.7	126	23.4	10	1.9	538
2d half	338	50.7	120	18.0	209	31.3	667
Year	370	61.4	123	20.4	110	18.2	603
1972:							
Jan.	341	48.3	105	14.9	260	36.8	706
Feb.	343	47.6	100	13.9	277	38.5	720
Mar.	357	47.5	100	13.3	295	39.2	752
Apr.	367	48.3	97	12.8	296	38.9	760
May	362	48.5	84	11.3	300	40.2	746
June	362	46.8	81	10.5	330	42.7	773
1st half	356	48.0	93	12.5	293	39.5	742
July	332	48.1	74	10.7	284	41.2	690
Aug.	432	53.7	56	6.9	317	39.4	805
Sept.	422	54.9	55	7.2	291	37.9	768
Oct.	443	53.1	56	6.7	335	40.2	834
Nov.	439	50.6	55	6.3	374	43.1	868
Dec.	396	52.1	56	7.4	308	40.5	760
2d half	411	52.1	59	7.5	318	40.4	788
Year	384	50.1	77	10.0	306	39.9	767
1973:							
Jan.‡	443	51.5	62	7.3	354	41.2	859

* These figures were calculated by Mr. Muse from passenger data which Braniff and TI were required to supply to the Civil Aeronautics Board. He multiplied the original figures by a correction factor to eliminate interline traffic and arrive at net totals for local traffic.

† Excludes figures for another carrier which had about 1 percent of the local market in 1969 and 1970.

‡ Projected figures from terminal counts by Southwest personnel.

Source: Company records.

1970 of $325.6 million, and it carried 5.8 million passengers. Southwest's other principal competitor, Texas International, served the Southern and Southwestern United States and Mexico. In 1970 TI had a fleet of 45 aircraft, carried 2.2 million passengers, and generated $77.8 million in total revenues. There was considerable public discontent with the quality of service provided by these two carriers on intrastate routes within Texas—a fact which Southwest hoped to exploit.

After carefully assessing costs, Southwest settled on a $20 fare for each route. This compared with existing Braniff and TI coach fares of $27 from Dallas to Houston and $28 from Dallas to San Antonio. Management hoped Southwest could anticipate an initial price advantage, although expected Braniff and TI would probably reduce their own fares promptly.

Southwest executives had calculated that an average of 39 passengers per flight would be required to break even. They considered this level of business (and better) a reasonable expectation in the light of the market's estimated potential for growth and the frequency of flights which Southwest planned to offer. Nevertheless, they predicted a period of deficit operations before this break-even point was reached.

Operating Experience

Southwest finally inaugurated scheduled revenue service with a blaze of publicity on June 18, 1971. The airline offered all-coach-class flights and introduced a number of innovations and attractions, including new Boeing 737 twin-jet aircraft, fast ticketing, glamorous hostesses, and inexpensive, exotically named drinks.

Despite extensive promotion, the initial results were hardly spectacular. Between June 18 and 30, 1971, Southwest had an average of 13.1 passengers per flight on its Dallas–Houston service and 12.9 passengers on the Dallas–San Antonio route; passenger loads during the month of July showed only marginal improve-

ment (Exhibit 2). Both competitors had met Southwest's lower fares immediately, and they had also improved the frequency and quality of their services on the two routes served by the new airline and heavily promoted these changes.

Management concluded that it was essential to improve schedule frequencies to compete more effectively with those of Braniff and TI. This became possible with the delivery of the company's fourth Boeing 737 in late September 1971, and on October 1, hourly service was introduced between Dallas and Houston and flights every 2 hours between Dallas and San Antonio.

Surveys of Southwest passengers departing from Houston showed that a substantial percentage would have preferred service from the William P. Hobby Airport, 12 miles southwest of downtown Houston, rather than from the new Houston Intercontinental Airport, 26 miles north of the city. Accordingly, arrangements were completed in mid-November for 7 of Southwest's 14 round-trip flights between Dallas and Houston to be transferred to Hobby Airport (thus reopening this old airport to scheduled commercial passenger traffic). Additional schedule revisions included the elimination of the extremely unprofitable Saturday operation on all routes.

These actions contributed to an increase in transportation revenues in the final quarter of 1971 over those achieved in the third quarter, but Southwest's operating losses in the fourth quarter fell only slightly, from $1,006,000 to $921,000 (Exhibit 3). At the end of 1971, Southwest's accumulated deficit stood at $3.75 million (Exhibit 4).

Although the majority of ticket sales were made over the counter at the airport terminals, sales were also made through travel agents and to corporate accounts. Travel agents received a 7 percent commission on credit card sales and 10 percent on cash sales. Corporate accounts—companies whose personnel made regular use of Southwest Airlines—received no discount but

EXHIBIT 2
MONTHLY FLIGHTS AND PASSENGER COUNTS
ON EACH ROUTE BY TYPE OF FARE

| | Dallas–Houston | | | | Dallas–San Antonio | | | |
| | Full fare | | Discount | | Full fare | | Discount | |
Month	Psgrs.*	Flights	Psgrs.*	Flights	Psgrs.*	Flights	Psgrs.*	Flights
June 1971†	3.6	276			1.9	148		
July	10.3	642			5.2	346		
Aug.	11.3	672			4.8	354		
Sept.	11.7	612			4.8	327		
Oct.	14.6	764			6.5	382		
Nov.	14.0	651	0.1	3	4.2	240		
Dec.	14.5	682	0.2	5	4.0	165		
1971 total	80.0	4,299	0.3	8	31.4	1,962		
Jan. 1972	16.0	630	0.2	4	2.8	141		
Feb.	15.9	636	0.2	4	2.8	142		
Mar.	17.9	664	0.4	5	3.9	204	0.3	5
Apr.	17.4	601	0.3	4	4.3	185	0.3	4
May	17.1	554	1.5	30	3.5	177	0.7	21
June	16.5	474	3.3	47	3.8	170	1.4	31
July	13.6	447	4.0	47	3.3	162	1.8	31
Aug.	15.7	496	4.0	50	3.2	177	1.8	31
Sept.	13.7	436	3.8	53	3.1	154	1.6	30
Oct.	16.0	474	4.8	71	3.4	173	1.8	27
Nov.	15.1	403	7.4	104	2.4	122	4.2	77
Dec.	12.8	377	6.3	91	2.4	117	3.9	69
1972 total	187.7	6,192	36.2	510	38.9	1,924	17.8	326
Jan. 1973‡	15.1	404	6.8	101	1.4	75	6.3	122

| | San Antonio–Houston | | | | | |
| | Full fare | | Discount | | Total: all routes | |
Month	Psgrs.*	Flights	Psgrs.*	Flights	Psgrs.*	Flights
June 1971†					5.5	424
July					15.5	988
Aug.					16.1	1,026
Sept.					16.4	939
Oct.					21.0	1,146
Nov.	0.9	72			19.1	966
Dec.	1.7	134			20.4	986
1971 total	2.6	206			114.0	6,475

* In thousands.
† Part-month only.
‡ Estimated figures.

EXHIBIT 2
Continued

Month	San Antonio–Houston Full fare Psgrs.*	Full fare Flights	Discount Psgrs.*	Discount Flights	Total: all routes Psgrs.*	Total: all routes Flights
Jan. 1972	2.0	128			20.9	903
Feb.	2.1	134			20.9	916
Mar.	2.8	146			25.4	1,024
Apr.	2.3	130			24.7	924
May	2.5	138			25.3	1,020
June	2.6	140			27.6	862
July	2.1	131			24.7	818
Aug.	2.4	146			27.0	900
Sept.	2.2	127			24.4	800
Oct.	2.5	139			28.5	884
Nov.	2.3	123	0.5	16	32.0	845
Dec.	2.0	110	0.5	16	27.8	780
1972 total	27.8	1,592	1.0	32	309.2	10,676
Jan. 1973‡	2.4	120	0.5	16	32.5	838

* In thousands.
† Part-month only.
‡ Estimated figures.
Source: Company records.

EXHIBIT 3
QUARTERLY INCOME STATEMENTS*

	1971 Q3	1971 Q4	1972 Q1	1972 Q2	1972 Q3	1972 Q4
Transportation revenues†	887	1,138	1,273	1,401	1,493	1,745
Operating expenses:						
Operations & maintenance	1,211	1,280	1,192	1,145	1,153	1,156
Marketing & gen. admin.	371	368	334	366	313	351
Depreciation & amortiz.	311	411	333	334	335	335
Total	1,893	2,059	1,859	1,845	1,801	1,842
Operating profit (loss)	(1,006)	(921)	(586)	(444)	(308)	(97)
Net interest revenues (costs)	(254)	(253)	(218)	(220)	(194)	(204)
Net income (loss) before extraordinary items	(1,260)	(1,174)	(804)	(664)	(502)	(301)
Extraordinary items	(571)‡	(469)‡		533§		
Net income (loss)	(1,831)	(1,643)	(804)	(131)	(502)	(301)

* In thousands of dollars.
† Includes both passenger and freight business. Freight sales represented 2 percent of revenues in 1972.
‡ Write-off of preoperating costs.
§ Capital gain on sale of one aircraft.
Source: Company records.

EXHIBIT 4
BALANCE SHEET AT DECEMBER 31, 1972, 1971, AND 1970

	1972	1971	1970
Assets			
Current assets:			
Cash	$ 133,839	$ 231,530	$ 183
Certificates of deposit	1,250,000	2,850,000	
Accounts receivable:			
Trade	397,664	300,545	
Interest	14,691	35,013	
Other	67,086	32,569	100
	479,441	368,127	100
Less allowance for doubtful accounts	86,363	30,283	
	393,078	337,844	100
Inventories of parts and supplies, at cost	154,121	171,665	
Prepaid insurance and other	75,625	156,494	31
Total current assets	2,006,663	3,747,533	314
Property and equipment, at cost:			
Boeing 737-200 jet aircraft	12,409,772	16,263,250	
Support flight equipment	2,423,480	2,378,581	
Ground equipment	346,377	313,072	9,249
	15,179,629	18,954,903	9,249
Less accumulated depreciation and overhaul allowance	2,521,646	1,096,177	
	12,657,983	17,858,726	9,249
Deferred certification costs less amortization	371,095	477,122	530,136
	$15,035,741	$22,083,381	$539,699
Liabilities and stockholders' equity			
Current liabilities:			
Notes payable to banks (secured)	$ 950,000	$	$
Accounts payable	124,890	355,539	30,819
Accrued salaries and wages	55,293	54,713	79,000
Other accrued liabilities	136,437	301,244	
Long-term debt due within 1 year	1,226,457	1,500,000	
Total current liabilities	2,493,077	2,211,496	109,819
Long-term debt due after 1 year:			
7% convertible promissory notes		1,250,000	
Conditional purchase agreements—Boeing Financial Corp. (1½% over prime rate)	11,942,056	16,803,645	
	11,942,056	18,053,645	
Less amounts due within 1 year	1,226,457	1,500,000	
	10,715,599	16,553,645	
Contingencies:			
Stockholders' equity			
Common stock, $1.00 par value, 2,000,000 shares authorized, 1,108,758 issued (1,058,758 at Dec. 31, 1971)	1,108,758	1,058,758	372,404
Capital in excess of par value	6,062,105	6,012,105	57,476
Deficit	(5,343,798)	(3,752,623)	
	1,827,065	3,318,240	429,880
	$15,035,741	$22,083,381	$539,699

Notes to financial statement not shown here.
Source: Southwest Airlines Co. *Annual Reports,* 1971 and 1972.

benefited from the convenience of having their own supply of ticket stock (which they issued themselves) and receiving a single monthly billing.

Between October 1971 and April 1972, average passenger loads systemwide increased from 18.4 passengers per flight to 26.7 passengers. However, this was still substantially below the number necessary to cover the total costs per trip flown, which had been tending to rise (Exhibits 2, 3, and 5).

It had become evident that the volume of traffic during the late morning and early afternoon could not realistically support flights at hourly intervals. It was also clear that most Houston passengers preferred Hobby Airport to Houston Intercontinental, so the decision was made to abandon the latter airport altogether.

On May 14, 1972, Southwest reduced the total number of daily flights between Dallas and Houston from 29 to 22. Eleven flights daily continued to be offered on the Dallas–San Antonio route and six between San Antonio and Houston (Hobby). Braniff quickly retaliated by introducing its own commuter service from Dallas to Hobby, promoting it extensively. The new schedule enabled Southwest to dispose of its fourth Boeing 737. The company had no trou-

EXHIBIT 5
INCREMENTAL COSTS PER FLIGHT
AND PER PASSENGER, 1971–1972*

Category	Last half 1971	First half 1972	Last half 1972
Incremental costs per flight			
Crew pay	$ 46.62	$ 50.61	$ 56.82
Crew expenses and overnight	5.28	4.24	4.93
Fuel	93.50	93.35	94.91
Airport landing fees	10.44	12.87	12.37
Aircraft maintenance	69.98	69.51	75.19
	$225.82	$230.58	$244.22
Variable costs per passenger			
Passenger-handling personnel	$1.09	$0.88	$0.80
Reservation costs†	0.92	0.11	0.10
Ramp, provisioning, and baggage handling‡	0.98	0.40	0.29
Baggage claims and interrupted-trip expenses	0.01	0.01	0.01
Passenger beverage and supplies	0.25	0.13	0.43
Traffic commissions and bad debts	0.61	0.62	0.74
Passenger liability and insurance§	0.90	0.38	0.43
	$4.76¶	$2.53	$2.80

  * Includes all costs treated as variable by Southwest management for the purposes of planning and analysis.

  † Initially, Southwest contracted out its reservation service to American Airlines; after October 1, 1972, Southwest's own employees handled this task.

  ‡ Initially contracted on a minimum cost-per-flight basis, subsequently used own employees on a phased schedule as facilities permitted.

  § During the last half of 1971, Southwest paid a minimum total premium for passenger liability insurance due to the low number of passengers carried.

  ¶ Comment by management: "The high figure for costs per passenger during the last half of 1971 represents the effect of minimum staffing with very few passengers. The minimum-staffing effect declines substantially in later periods, and begins to represent a true variable."

ble finding a ready buyer for this aircraft and made a profit of $533,000 on the resale.

Changes in Pricing Strategy

June 1972 saw Southwest Airlines celebrating its first birthday. This provided an opportunity for more of the publicity stunts for which the airline was already becoming renowned. Posters were hung inside the aircraft and in the waiting lounges; the aircraft cabins were decorated; and there was an on-board party every day for a week. This activity, promoted by newspaper advertising, generated considerable publicity for the airline and, in management's view, reinforced Southwest's image as the plucky, friendly little underdog which had now survived an entire year against powerful, entrenched competition.

At this point, Southwest management decided it was time to take a hard look at the fare structure and its relationship to costs and revenues. For some months, Southwest had been experimenting with a $10 fare on Friday evening flights after 9 P.M. In May this reduced fare was extended to post–9 P.M. flights on a daily basis. The result was sharply higher load factors on these discount flights relative to the average achieved on full-fare flights (Exhibit 2).

But management concluded that the airline could no longer afford a $20 fare on daytime flights. New tariffs were therefore filed with the Texas Aeronautics Commission, effective July 9, 1972; these raised Southwest's basic one-way fare from $20 to $26, established a round-trip fare of $50, and offered a $225 Commuter Club Card entitling the purchaser to unlimited transportation on all routes for 30 days.

The key consideration was how the competition would react. "For a few days," admitted the vice president-marketing, "we were really sweating." Braniff's initial response was to devote an additional aircraft to its Dallas–Hobby Airport flights on July 11, thus offering on-the-hour service most hours of the business day. However, on July 17, Texas International increased its fares to the same level as Southwest's; then, on July 21, Braniff met all aspects of the fare and on-board service changes, also adding a $10 Sundowner flight to Hobby at 7:30 P.M. As a result of Braniff's increased service and the higher fares, Southwest's patronage fell back by 2 percent between the second and third quarters of 1972, but transportation revenues increased.

During September new advertising was launched, based on the slogan "Remember What It Was Like Before Southwest Airlines?" Southwest's advertising agency saw this as a war cry to rally consumers. The principal media used in this campaign were billboards and television. TV commercials cited the advantages of flying Southwest, notably its dependable schedules.

At the end of October, another major change was made in pricing strategy. The $10 discount fares, which had never been advertised, were replaced by half-fare flights ($13 one way, $25 round trip) on the two major routes each weekday night after 8 P.M. Saturday flights were reintroduced, and *all* weekend flights were offered at half fare. An intensive 3-week advertising campaign accompanied these new schedules and price changes, using 1-minute radio commercials on country and western stations, top forty stations, and other similar stations[1] (Exhibit 6). The response was immediate, and November 1972 traffic levels were 12 percent higher than those in October—historically the best month of the year in Southwest's commuter markets.

In the new year, management turned its attention to its largest single remaining problem. The company was now actually making money on its Dallas-Houston flights but still incurring substantial losses in the Dallas–San Antonio market. Southwest offered only 8 flights a day on this route versus 34 by its major competitor (Exhibit 7) and in January was averaging a mere

---

[1] A top forty station is one which specializes in playing currently popular rock music recordings.

EXHIBIT 6
SAMPLE RADIO COMMERCIAL FOR HALF-FARE, OFF-PEAK FLIGHTS, FALL 1972

NUMBER: 98–23–2
LENGTH: 60 sec (Dallas version)
DATE: 10/13/72

MUSIC:	Fanfare
ANNCR:	Southwest Airlines introduces the Half-Fare Frivolity Flights.
HOSTESS:	Now you can afford to fly for the fun of it.
SFX:	LAUGHTER OF ONE PERSON BUILDING FROM UNDER, WITH MUSIC
ANNCR:	Now you can take any Southwest Airlines flights any week night at eight o'clock and all flights on Saturday or Sunday for half-fare. Just $13 or $25 round trip.
SFX:	LAUGHTER, MUSIC OUT. STREET SOUNDS UNDER.
MAN:	You mean I can visit my uncle in Houston for only $13?
ANNCR:	Right.
MAN:	That's weird. My uncle lives in St. Louis.
MUSIC:	MEXICAN FIESTA SOUND
CHICANO:	Take your wife or lover on a Southwest Airlines Half-Fare Frivolity Flight to San Antonio this weekend. Float down the river while lovely senoritas strum their enchiladas and sing the beautiful, traditional guacamoles.
SFX:	ROCKET BLASTING OFF
ANNCR:	Take a Southwest Airlines Half-Fare Frivolity Flight to Houston and watch astronauts mow their lawns.
SFX:	FOOTBALL CROWD NOISES
ANNCR:	Take a Southwest Airlines Frivolity Flight to Dallas and watch Cowboys hurt themselves.
SXF	OTHERS OUT. RINKY-TINK MUSIC UP.
HOSTESS:	Half-Fare Frivolity Flights, every week night at eight o'clock and *all* weekend flights. Only $13. Almost as cheap as the bus. Cheaper than your own car. So relax with me, and stop driving yourself.
ANNCR:	Southwest Airlines' Half-Fare Frivolity Flights.
HOSTESS:	Fly for the fun of it.

EXHIBIT 7
ANALYSIS OF WEEKLY FLIGHT SCHEDULES BY SOUTHWEST AND COMPETING CARRIERS, JANUARY 1973

	Dallas–Houston*							Houston*–Dallas							Total no. flights (both directions)	
	Mon-Fri total		Sat		Sun		Total week	Mon-Fri total		Sat		Sun		Total week	Full fare	Discount
	I	H	I	H	I	H		I	H	I	H	I	H			
Braniff	80	35	8	5	12	7	147	70	45	9	7	12	7	150	297	
Texas Intl.	45		6		9		60	49		6		10		65	125	
Southwest		55		2		5	62		55		4		3	62	100	24
Total	125	90	14	7	21	12	269	119	100	15	11	22	10	277		

	Dallas–San Antonio				San Antonio–Dallas				Total no. flights (both directions)	
	Mon-Fri total	Sat	Sun	Total week	Mon-Fri total	Sat	Sun	Total week	Full fare	Discount
Braniff	85	16	15	116	85	14	17	116	232	
Texas Intl.	10	1	2	13	5	1	1	7	20	
American	10	2	2	14	10	2	2	14	28	
Southwest	20	1	3	24	20	2	2	24	30	18
Total	125	20	22	167	120	19	22	161		

	San Antonio–Houston†				Houston†–San Antonio				Total no. flights (both directions)	
	Mon-Fri total	Sat	Sun	Total week	Mon-Fri total	Sat	Sun	Total week	Full fare	Discount
Braniff	5		1	6	10	2	1	13	19	
Texas Intl.	10	2	2	14	15	3	3	21	35	
American	5	1	1	7	5	1	1	7	14‡	
Continental	45	9	9	63	45	9	9	63	126‡	
Eastern	20	4	4	28	20	4	4	28	56‡	
Southwest	15	1	1	17	15	1	1	17	30	4
Total	100	17	18	135	110	20	19	149		

* I = flights to/from Houston Intercontinental; H = Houston/Hobby.

† Southwest flights on this route used Houston-Hobby Airport; all other airlines used Houston Intercontinental.

‡ Some flights offered thrift or night fares with savings of $3–$5 over regular fare.

Source: *World Airline Guide*, North American edition, January 1973.

EXHIBIT 8
ESTIMATED MARKET SIZE, DALLAS-HOUSTON AND DALLAS-SAN ANTONIO ROUTES*

	Local passengers carried annually (both directions)			
	1969	1970	1971	1972
Dallas–Houston:				
Braniff	268,630	265,910	246,170	300,780
Texas Intl.	91,690	70,950	69,790	51,010
Other	4,390	4,790	1,830	1,910
Southwest			80,187	223,581
	364,710	341,650	397,977	577,281
Dallas–San Antonio:				
Braniff	144,010	124,690	135,660	177,020
Texas Intl.	10,400	15,040	5,290	1,800
American	4,100	4,120	3,600	2,580
Other	520	560	380	330
Southwest			31,302	56,653
	159,030	144,410	176,232	238,383

* These estimates were made by Southwest Airlines' economic consultant in New York.
Source: Company records.

17 passengers on each full-fare flight. The Dallas–San Antonio market had not grown as rapidly as had Dallas–Houston, and Southwest held a smaller market share (Exhibit 8).

Management concluded that unless a dramatic improvement in patronage was quickly achieved on this route, they would have to abandon it. They decided to make one last attempt to obtain the needed increase and on January 22, 1973, announced a "60-Day Half-Price Sale" on *all* Southwest Airlines flights between Dallas and San Antonio. This sale was promoted by TV and radio advertising. If this was successful, it was Lamar Muse's intention to make the reduced fare permanent, but he felt that by announcing it as a limited-period offer, it would stimulate consumer interest even more effectively while also reducing the likelihood of competitive response. Exhibit 9 shows a sample radio script.

The impact of these half-price fares was even faster and more dramatic than the results of the evening and weekend half-price fares introduced the previous fall. By the end of the first week, average loads on Southwest's Dallas–San Antonio service had risen to 48 passengers per flight, and they continued to rise sharply at the beginning of the following week.

On Thursday, February 1, however, Braniff employed full-page newspaper advertisements to announce a half-price "Get Acquainted Sale" on all flights between Dallas and Hobby, lasting until April 1 (Exhibit 10). However, fares for Braniff's flights between Dallas and Houston Intercontinental remained at the existing levels.

Lamar Muse immediately called an urgent management meeting to decide what action Southwest should take in response to Braniff's move.

EXHIBIT 9
SAMPLE RADIO ADVERTISING FOR HALF-FARE
SAN ANTONIO FLIGHTS, JANUARY 1973

NUMBER: 118–23–2
LENGTH: 60 sec (Dallas version)
DATE: 12/21/72

WOMAN:	Harold, this is your mother in San Antonio talking to you from the radio, Harold. I want you to know that Southwest Airlines is having a half-price sale, Harold. For 60 days you can fly between San Antonio and Dallas for half price. Only $13, Harold. I expect to see a lot of you for those 60 days. Are you listening, Harold? Harold! (STATION WIND) I'm talking to you!
MUSIC:	LIGHT, HAPPY
HOSTESS:	Southwest Airlines half-fare flights. Every flight between San Antonio and Dallas every day. Only $13.
SFX:	STREET NOISES
IRATE MALE VOICE:	Hey! You people fly Southwest Airlines during this half-price sale, you're gonna have a lonely bus driver on your conscience. Take the bus. It only costs a little more, but it's four hours longer! You'll have a lot more time with me, won't you? (FADE) Well, won't you?
SFX:	STREET NOISES
MAN:	There is a cheaper way than Southwest Airlines. Put on roller skates, tie yourself to a trailer truck . . .
MUSIC:	LIGHT, HAPPY
HOSTESSES:	Fly Southwest Airlines. Half price between Dallas and San Antonio on every flight every day. Why pay more?
VOICE:	Half price? Can they do that?
SECOND VOICE:	They did it!

43 Optical Distortion, Inc.

Darral G. Clarke

*ODI lens →
good behavior of
chicken*

Mr. Daniel Garrison, president and chief executive officer of Optical Distortion, Inc. (ODI), had asked Mr. Roland Olson, marketing vice president of ODI, to develop a marketing plan for the firm's new (and only) product—a contact lens for chickens.[1] While contact lenses served the purpose of improving human eyesight, the purpose of the lens developed by ODI was partially to blind the chickens.

Mr. Garrison explained:

> Like so many other great discoveries, our product concept was discovered quite by accident. A chicken farmer in Arizona had a flock of chickens that developed a severe cataract problem. When he became aware of the problem, he separated the afflicted birds from the rest of the flock and subsequently observed that the afflicted birds

seemed to eat less and were much easier to handle. So dramatic was the difference that a poultry medical detailman visiting the farm, rather than being asked for a cure, was asked if there was any way to similarly afflict the rest of the flock. It has not proved possible chemically or genetically to duplicate the reduced vision of the chickens resulting from the cataracts, but a chicken wearing the ODI lenses has its vision reduced enough to obtain the good behavior the Arizona farmer observed. This behavior has important economic implications for the chicken farmer.

By late 1975, the ODI lens had been tested on a number of farms in California and Oregon with satisfactory results, and Mr. Garrison was convinced that "the time has come to stop worrying about the product and get this show off the ground." While his timetable was "tentative," he hoped that the ODI lens could be introduced in at least one region during the spring of 1976 and that national distribution would be achieved by the end of 1978 (at the latest). As he explained:

Darral G. Clarke is an associate professor at the Harvard Graduate School of Business Administration.

[1]Throughout the case *chicken* is used as a technical term to describe the female bird (3 months old or older) raised for the purpose of egg production. Male birds are referred to as *friers* or *broilers*.

Our patent and license protection [see below] should hold off competition for at least three years, but—if we have the success I believe we will—I would expect the large agricultural supply firms to find a way around our patent. By 1981, I would expect the big boys to have come in, and competition to be fierce. If we are to gain the fruits of our development work, we will have to be strong enough to fight them on their own terms. To do this, we will have to be a multi-product multi-market company which can provide effective service anywhere in the country.

Company Background

The ODI lens had been invented by Robert D. Garrison (Daniel Garrison's father), working with Mr. Ronald Olson, the owner of a large chicken farm in Oregon. Mr. Robert Garrison had conceptualized and designed the original product and had then worked with Olson to test and refine the lenses on Olson's chicken farm. Their efforts attracted the attention of Mr. James Arnold, a local businessman, who invested approximately $5,000 in the venture. The three men subsequently formed a corporation to exploit Garrison's invention.

Further testing of the lens on Olson's chicken farm, however, had identified several technical difficulties with the product. In particular, the early prototypes did not always remain in the chicken's eyes after insertion and frequently caused severe irritation by the later months of the chicken's 12-month laying life. Both problems had been quite serious because, as Daniel Garrison explained, "No farmer is going to spend time looking into the eyes of his chickens to make sure the lenses are still there and the eyes are not bloodshot."

The retention problem was solved by modifying the size of the lens, and ODI was issued a United States patent on the lens. ODI found that the irritation problem could be essentially eliminated by making the lenses of a soft plastic called a *hydrophilic polymer*. The patents for hydro-

philic polymer, the same material used by Bausch and Lomb to produce soft contact lenses for human use, were controlled by New World Plastics of Baltimore, Maryland. New World Plastics' hydrophilic polymer could not be injection-molded, however, and the manufacturing costs for using alternative production processes were far too high for the chicken market. Since New World Plastics' hydrophilic polymer was the only such material known at the time, ODI had reached an impasse, and the company became dormant.

In 1974 Robert Garrison asked his son Daniel Garrison to contact New World Plastics and see if any progress had been made in the hydrophilic polymer. Daniel Garrison found that the hydrophilic polymer could now be injection-molded and became enthusiastic about the potential of the product. With the approval of the owners, Daniel Garrison obtained a long-term license from New World Plastics for the exclusive use of hydrophilic polymer for nonhuman applications.

Under the terms of the license, New World agreed not to produce the polymer for other firms seeking nonhuman markets and not to carry out development work on related polymers for such firms. ODI, in turn, agreed to pay New World Plastics $50,000 ($25,000 per year for the first 2 years) and to purchase its lenses exclusively from New World. New World would manufacture the lenses and sell them to ODI at a price of $0.032 per pair (in bulk), regardless of quantity. ODI was to supply New World with injection molds (at a cost of $12,000 each). Each injection mold had an annual capacity of 7.2 million pairs and an expected life of 15 million pairs.

During the negotiations with New World Plastics, Daniel Garrison purchased 25 percent of the stock of ODI from the previous owners and was elected president and chief executive officer of the firm. Having completed the license agreement with New World, he was able to raise $200,000 in the venture capital markets. About this time, Mr. Ronald Olson became vice president–marketing, and the two men began devoting a substantial portion of their time to ODI. As of late 1975, Daniel Garrison and Olson were the only reasonably full-time employees of the firm, although Robert Garrison and James Arnold remained active stockholders and board members.

The Poultry Industry

Poultry and egg production had its beginnings in the family barnyard. As late as 1900, it was not unusual for a family to have its own chickens or to buy eggs fresh from a small local farmer, even in urban areas. In 1921, the largest commercial egg farm in the United States was in Petaluma, California; it boasted a flock of about 2,000 hens. The hens were not housed but ran loose in a large pasture with small roosting and laying houses nearby. The eggs were picked up twice daily and loaded into a horse-drawn wagon.

In an effort to increase the efficiency of egg production, some California farmers began confining the birds in large henhouses during the 1930s and 1940s. In other parts of the United States, eggs were still being collected from haystacks until the 1940s, when henhouses became common in other areas of the country. Continuing their innovation, California poultry raisers began to increase the utilization of henhouse space by further confining the birds in groups of three or four within multitiered 18×12 inch wire cages. By the 1950s, these innovations had spread widely throughout the United States and had led to considerable concentration in the poultry industry.

By the mid-1970s the largest commercial flock of laying hens in the United States was 2.5 million birds, and 80 percent of the laying hens in the United States were housed on 3 percent of the known chicken farms. California, North Carolina, and Georgia accounted for 25 percent of the nation's chickens, while nine additional states (mostly in the South and Northeast) accounted for an additional 36 percent of the

chicken population. Two counties in southern California contained 20 farms which housed 21 million chickens. Further details on the distribution and characteristics of chicken farms in the United States are given in Exhibits 1, 2, and 3. Data on the economics of chicken farming are shown in Exhibit 4.

As might be expected from the changes in the size and number of chicken farms, the business of running a large chicken farm had changed a great deal since the 1920s. Daniel Garrison characterized the problem of managing chicken farms of various sizes as follows:

1. *Small farms (10,000 or fewer birds).* These small farms are usually family operated. They could possibly contract their production to a larger producer, but more probably, they sell their eggs locally through small grocery or milk and egg stores or at their own farm. A farmer of this size probably purchases starter pullets only once or twice a year. The birds would be housed in hen houses of about 1,000–2,000 birds. The number of such farms has recently been declining at a rate of about 25% per year.
2. *Medium farms (10,000–50,000 birds).* A chicken farm of this size is typically operated professionally. Such farms are usually still owned and managed by the farmer. The farmer-owner performs administrative tasks and makes most decisions regarding the operation of the farm himself. A farm of this size requires considerable business as well as agricultural skill. Such an owner would have yearly cash flows on the order of $375,000 to manage. He would deal with large corporate suppliers such as hatcheries, feed companies, and equipment manufacturers. He most probably also negotiates with a large corporate purchaser of his egg production. Individual cash transactions can be as large as $35,000.
3. *Large farms (over 50,000 birds).* A chicken farm of this size is, in many ways, like a small manufacturing firm. Administration of the farm is sufficiently complex to require the skills and efforts of several people. The farm could employ 100 or more people and have an annual cash flow of $12 million. Such farms may mix their own feed in facilities costing up to

EXHIBIT 1
DENSITY OF UNITED STATES CHICKEN POPULATION, 1969

Chicken 3 Months Old or Older, 1969

UNITED STATES
TOTAL
371,008,459

1 DOT - 50,000

Department of Commerce
Social and Economic Statistics Administrator
Bureau of the Census

$500,000. Their egg production may be sold through complex negotiated contracts with regional offices of large grocery chains. Some may convert waste into fertilizer in their own conversion plants as a by product. The farmers would purchase starter pullets (or grow their own) at least 4 times a year in order to smooth labor demands on the farm. On a farm of this size, a hen house would typically house from 5,000–10,000 birds.

On the basis of various government surveys, Garrison estimated that the United States chicken population would grow very slowly during the rest of the decade:

1975	457.0 million birds
1976	461.6 million birds
1977	466.2 million birds
1978	470.8 million birds
1979	475.6 million birds

Eighty percent of these chickens would be on the 3 percent of United States chicken farms having 10,000 or more chickens. Garrison believed that a farm would have to have at least 10,000 birds to be sold profitably by ODI but that 50 percent penetration of such farms within 5 years was a realistic projection.

Problem

Cannibalism among Chickens

Like many other fowl, chickens are social birds, and chicken societies have a definite social structure. A self-selected ranking of chickens begins when chickens are about 8 to 10 weeks of age and results in a complete peck order by the time the birds reach sexual maturity. According to Mark O. North, a poultry consultant, "This order is the result of the birds being able to identify other birds in the group, and through fighting and pecking, establish a hierarchical type of social organization."[2]

[2]*Poultry Digest*, December 1973.

EXHIBIT 2
CHARACTERISTICS OF UNITED STATES CHICKEN FARMS, 1969*

State	Total farms (sales over $2,500)	Chickens on total farms	20,000–49,999			50,000–99,999			100,000 and over		
			# of farms	# of farms reporting flock size	# of chickens†	# of farms	# of farms reporting flock size	# of chickens†	# of farms	# of farms reporting flock size	# of chickens†
Pacific:											
Washington	1,929	5,230,575	40	20	1,090,102	11	11	663,378	10	10	2,085,936
Oregon	1,825	2,249,752	13	13	414,220	3	3	229,000	6	6	848,705
California	3,023	46,203,988	320	320	9,517,453	114	114	7,459,944	87	87	22,952,283
Alaska	25	25,617	0	0	‡	0	0	‡	0	0	‡
Hawaii	90	1,069,618	8	8	255,000	4	0	‡	12	0	‡
	6,892	54,779,550	381	381	11,276,775	132	128	8,352,322	105	103	25,886,924
New England	2,621	17,265,305	135	128	3,660,578	31	20	1,320,796	15	13	2,974,242
Middle Atlantic	12,867	31,036,554	240	240	6,969,792	55	55	3,419,870	29	29	5,239,990
East North Central	54,429	46,650,039	339	339	9,267,919	57	39	2,631,736	22	20	3,461,252
West North Central	112,119	41,213,868	156	156	4,372,320	34	27	1,808,508	21	16	2,480,555
South Atlantic	29,971	82,176,127	860	860	24,221,265	168	155	10,085,341	70	66	12,065,486
East South Central	29,045	36,617,712	317	317	8,854,258	62	58	3,795,730	27	25	5,661,485
West South Central	31,101	46,450,783	412	412	11,876,032	77	75	5,111,151	42	39	11,264,948
Mountain	14,295	7,018,828	28	23	682,444	15	0	‡	14	3	806,350
Total U.S.	293,340	363,208,766	2,870	2,856	81,547,775	631	557	41,566,445	345	314	74,856,267
Percent of total	100%	100%	1%		22.4%	0.2%		11.4%	0.1%		20.6%

* The data in Exhibit 2 are not fully consistent with those in Exhibit 3 because of differences in sources and definitions.
† The number of chickens for which flock size was reported.
‡ Not reported to preserve the confidentiality of individual farm flock sizes.

EXHIBIT 3
CHICKEN FARM TRENDS, 1964–1969*

Flock size	Number of farms			Chickens		
	1964, %	1969, %	% change	1964, %	1969, %	% change
Under 3,200	98.5	93.8	−61	22.9	13.0	−61
3,200–9,999	1.1	3.2	−28.9	21.0	14.9	−23.4
10,000–19,999	0.3	1.7	+35.6	14.1	18.0	+38.2
20,000–49,000	0.1	1.0	+82	18.1	22.4	+81.2
50,000–99,999	0.001	0.2	+83	6.4	11.2	+89.7
100,000 and over	0.05	0.1	+50	7.5	20.6	+189.7
Total			−61			+6.1

* The data in Exhibit 3 are not fully consistent with those in Exhibit 2 because of differences in sources and definitions.

Mr. North believed that the recognition of the comb on the head of the chicken was a means of preserving the peck order, as was the position of the head. Dominant-type chickens carried their heads high, while submissive birds maintained a low head level. If a submissive bird raised her head too high, she was immediately pecked by one or more of her superiors until the head was lowered. Pecking could increase until the birds became cannibalistic. Submissive birds were also pecked if they entered the "territory" of a cage claimed by a more dominant bird. Thus cannibalism also varied with the breed of the chicken, and, unfortunately, the more productive strains

EXHIBIT 4
AVERAGE COST PER DOZEN EGGS PRODUCED, 1975

	Cost/dozen eggs*	
Laying stock:		
Purchase cost per hen	$2.40	
Allocation for replacing dead birds	0.21	
	$2.61	11.9¢
Annual feed costs per hen	$7.04	32.0¢
Labor		2.4¢
Supplies, taxes, utilities, etc.		1.8¢
Miscellaneous adjustments:		
Cull sales per dozen (credit)		(0.3¢)
Laying stock value adjustment (credit)		(1.7¢)
Net cash and labor cost per dozen		46.1¢
Depreciation (15% average value of buildings and equipment)		1.2¢
Interest (8% on land, laying stock, and average value of buildings and equipment)		1.4¢
Management per dozen		1.3¢
Total costs per dozen		50.0¢
Average price per dozen		53.0¢
Average profit per dozen		3.0¢

* Assuming 22 dozen eggs per hen-year.

tended to be more cannibalistic. According to Daniel Garrison, a major United States breeder had developed an extremely productive chicken, but "you had to put a sack over her head to keep her from killing her penmates."

Besides the obvious loss to the farmer when a bird was killed by her penmates, submissive birds got less time at the feeding trough and thus produced fewer eggs than the more dominant birds. Also, once the peck order was established, replacing a dead bird seriously disturbed the peck order.

Debeaking had been the major means of combating cannibalism for nearly 50 years. The debeaking process did not interfere with the formation of the peck order but reduced the efficiency of the beak as a weapon. The debeaking operation was simple in concept: Through the use of a hot knife and an anvil, the upper and lower mandibles of the chicken's beak were cut off at different lengths. The beak was then pressed against the hot knife to cauterize the wound and prevent excess bleeding. In the debeaking operation, the chickens were subjected to considerable trauma, and this resulted in a temporary weight loss and the retardation of egg production for at least a week; at this age, the loss was only one egg. If the beak were cut too short, a chicken could enter a permanent regression; if left too long, the beak would grow back and become a deadly weapon again. The establishment of the peck order among debeaked chickens took a longer time and involved greater social stress than it did among chickens with their full beaks, since clear victories were rare.

Experience had shown that debeaking reduced mortality due to cannibalism. The rate was as high as 25 percent for flocks of birds with full beaks and about 9 percent for debeaked flocks.

Debeaking was usually done during the first few weeks after the 20-week-old hens were purchased. The farmer's own employees or a service company could be hired to provide the debeaking crews, depending on the size of the farm. The cost of the debeaking operation was almost entirely a labor cost. An experienced crew of three, each earning about $2.50 per hour, could debeak approximately 220 birds per hour. $\frac{220}{3} = 73\frac{1}{3}$ birds $= \$2.50$ per hr

The ODI Lens

farmers will favor product a it confronts cannibalism problem

Daniel Garrison felt that the ODI contact lens was the first product to actually confront the cause of cannibalization rather than just minimize its effects. A bird wearing the ODI lens had its depth of perception reduced to about 12 inches and its visual acuity greatly reduced through an induced case of astigmatism. Thus, the ability of one bird to recognize the comb of another was seriously impaired, and in order to feed, the chickens had to walk around with their heads lowered. Thus the main visual cues for the peck order were removed, no peck order emerged, and cannibalism was reduced significantly.

The ODI lens was much like the soft contact lenses worn by humans except that it was slightly larger, had a red tint, and had a distortion built into the crown. When asked why the lenses were colored, Daniel Garrison responded:

> It may sound like rubbish to many people but chickens, like humans, respond psychologically to the color of their environment. We have found that changing the color of the birds' environment will affect the birds in many different ways such as altering their appetites or rate of sexual maturity, as well as affecting their cannibalistic tendencies. When birds are placed in a red colored environment, deaths due to cannibalism are reduced. This red color, together with the distortion of the lenses, affects the chicken's ability to act out her aggressions. Our tests have shown that flock mortality is reduced to an average of 4.5% when contact lenses are used instead of debeaking.

The lens was larger than the eye opening so that when it was in place, the rim of the eye opening and the outer eyelid acted as retainers, keeping the lens in place. The inner eyelid, or nicitating membrane, a semitransparent membrane that flicked back and forth across the eyeball to keep it moist and clean, was under the lens and thus could perform its natural function.

Daniel Garrison estimated that a trained crew of three men, similar to the debeaking crews, could install the lenses in about 225 chickens per hour. The insertion of the lenses did not result in great trauma to the birds as debeaking did. The chickens were up and about within a few hours, and neither weight loss nor reduction in egg production was noticeable.

Daniel Garrison doubted that the lenses could be reused.

The lenses are harder to take out than they are to put in, and a further problem in reusing them is the fact that the melting point of the hydrophilic polymer is very close to the sterilization temperature. You could end up with a mass of hydrophilic polymer rather than a pot full of contact lenses very easily.

Besides reducing chicken mortality due to cannibalism and egg production loss due to trauma, the ODI lens had the potential of reducing a farmer's feed cost. A debeaked chicken could only eat if the feed in her trough was at least ⅜ inch deep (the difference in length between the upper and lower mandibles of her remaining beak). Presumably, therefore, a farmer using ODI lenses instead of debeaking the chickens would be able to reduce the depth of the feed in the troughs by approximately ⅜ inch or more. A University of Maine poultry extension specialist had conducted a study which suggested that food disappearance per 100 birds per day was reduced from 24.46 pounds when the feed in the trough was 2 inches deep to 23.68 pounds when the feed in the trough was only 1 inch deep. In other words, a farmer with a 20,000-bird flock could save 156 pounds of feed per day by reducing the depth of feed in the troughs from 2 inches to 1 inch. At $158 per ton for chicken feed, this would represent considerable annual savings, especially for large flocks. According to Mr. Garrison, ODI lenses would permit a farmer to reduce the depth of feed in the troughs by at least ⅜ inch (probably to a depth of 1 inch) and would result in further savings because "a bird with a full beak *and* the ODI lenses can't see well enough to be fussy so she doesn't bill much at all [billing throws feed out of the trough], and she doesn't drool in her food as debeaked birds do."

Although he was unaware of any broad-scale research that measured the loss of feed due to billing, Daniel Garrison felt that a farmer would find that maintaining a 1- or 1½-inch food level for debeaked birds would be impractical due to more frequent trough refilling.

Developing a Marketing Strategy

As he began to develop the marketing plan requested by Daniel Garrison, Olson was acutely conscious of "the need to think big while recognizing that our assets are, after all, rather limited. There's no question this product has a whale of a future," he explained. "The problem is to achieve that potential as rapidly as is practical without too much strain on our limited managerial and financial resources." (See Exhibit 5 for ODI's balance sheet).

In discussions with Mr. Garrison, Olson had come to a number of tentative conclusions. First, it was virtually certain that ODI would enter the market via a region-by-region roll-out, beginning in California. On a rough basis, he estimated that the annual cost of a West Coast regional office and warehouse would be about $196,000 (see Exhibit 6), plus about $40,000 for each salesperson (including expenses) and $35,000 for each technical representative. He felt that, initially at least, each salesperson should cover no more than about 80 farms and that there should be one technical representative for every five sales-

EXHIBIT 5
BALANCE SHEET, SEPTEMBER 30, 1974

Current assets:		
Cash		$200,025
Patent*	$103,000	
Less accumulated depreciation	28,000	
		75,000
Total assets		$275,025
Current liabilities		$ 0
Long-term debt		0
Stockholders' equity		275,025
Total liabilities and equity		$275,025

*ODI, at incorporation, valued the contact lens for chickens patent at $103,000 and depreciated it over its 17-year life.

people. The technical representatives would follow up all major sales to make sure that the lenses were being used in such a way as to maximize benefits to the farmer.

Second, he and Mr. Garrison had agreed that the minimum price which they should consider was $20 per box[3] of 250 pairs, or $0.08 per pair. While this price would represent an incremental

[3]The plastic boxes would cost $0.10 each and could be filled by ODI at $0.14 per box. Order processing and shipping charges were estimated at $0.18 per box.

cost for the farmer (the labor cost for debeaking and that for the insertion of lenses were approximately the same), the farmer would presumably obtain benefits much greater than $0.08 per chicken because of reduced cannibalization, less trauma, and greater feeding efficiency. Such benefits would justify a much higher price, Olson felt, but he wasn't sure it would be possible to convince farmers that there were such benefits before they had had considerable experience with the lenses. It was probable, he thought, that a higher price would require more intensive sales

EXHIBIT 6
PROJECTED COSTS OF CALIFORNIA REGIONAL OFFICE AND WAREHOUSE

Office expense:		
Rent, utilities, etc.		$ 36,000
Personnel:		
Regional manager	$30,000	
Administrative assistant	15,000	
Regional technical manager	22,000	
3 secretaries (@ $10,000)	30,000	
Shipping clerk	10,000	
		107,000
Other expenses		53,000
Total projected annual costs		$196,000

and technical coverage, which would considerably increase ODI's fixed costs. Nevertheless, he was hesitant to introduce the lenses at a low price initially in the hope of raising it later. His reasons were: (1) "Chicken farmers, even the big ones, are an independent-minded breed of men, who might react very unfavorably if they get the idea that they have been taken," and (2) "Because of our limited resources, we have to try to obtain maximum contribution as soon as possible."

High contribution, Olson reasoned, was critical to support the headquarters, regional office, and advertising and promotional costs inherent in a "think big" strategy. He and Daniel Garrison had agreed that ODI should be marketing on a national basis within 2 to 3 years, which would require four to five regional offices. Monthly advertising in the eight leading poultry industry publications would cost approximately $100,000 per year, as would participation in the most important industry trade shows. Headquarters expenses, Mr. Garrison had forecast, would rise from $184,000 per year at a volume of 20 million pairs to $614,000 at 60 million pairs and $1.2 million at 120 million pairs. Moreover, Mr. Garrison's strategy of becoming "much more than a one product company" called for an investment of at least $250,000 per year in research and development as soon as the company could generate the funds or become large and profitable enough to be able to obtain additional capital on favorable terms from the equity market.

As he sat down at the already cluttered desk in the corner of his den, Olson thought:

It's really a tough problem. There's a lot at stake here; more than enough potential for a big company to put fifty people on the project. There are only four of us, and none of us can yet put full time into the company, although Daniel and I are each spending at least 50 hours per week on ODI. Still, we've got to do as good a job as a big company would, and I think we can. . . . If we pull it off, we will have revolutionized the business of animal behavior in much the same way as IBM revolutionized the processing of data.

44 Computron, Inc.

Ralph Z. Sorenson, II

Mr. Thomas Zimmermann, manager of the European Sales Division of Computron, Inc., was trying to decide what price to submit on his bid to sell a Computron 1000X digital computer to König & Cie., A.G., West Germany's largest chemical company. Were Mr. Zimmermann to follow Computron's standard pricing policy of adding a 33⅓ percent markup to factory costs and then including transportation costs and import duty, the bid he would submit would amount to $311,200. Mr. Zimmermann was afraid that a bid of this magnitude would not be low enough to win the contract for Computron.

Ralph Z. Sorenson, II, is the president of Babson College.

Note: The names of all individuals and companies have been disguised.

The original version of this case was written for 1'Institut pour 1'Etude des Methodes de Direction de 1'Entreprise (IMEDE), Lausanne, Switzerland, copyright 1965. It has been revised, with permission, by Professor Benson P. Shapiro, Harvard Graduate School of Business Administration.

Four other computer manufacturers had been invited by König to submit bids for the contract. Mr. Zimmermann had received information from what he considered to be a "reliable trade source" which indicated that at least one of these four competitors was planning to name a price somewhere in the neighborhood of $218,000. Computron's normal price of $311,200 would be $93,200, or approximately 43 percent, higher than this price. In conversations which he had had with König's vice president in charge of purchasing, Mr. Zimmermann had been led to believe that Computron would have a chance of winning the contract only if its bid were no more than 20 percent higher than the bid of the lowest competitor.

Inasmuch as König was Computron's most important German customer, Mr. Zimmermann was particularly concerned about this contract and was wondering what strategy to employ in pricing his bid.

Background on Computron and Its Products

Computron, Inc., was an American firm which had, in the winter of 1976, opened a European sales office in Paris with Mr. Zimmermann as its manager. The company's main product, both in the United States and in Europe, was the 1000X computer, a medium-size digital computer designed specifically for process control applications.

In the mid- to late 1970s, the market for digital process control computers was growing quite rapidly. These computers were substantially different from the computers used for data processing and engineering calculation. They also were generally produced by companies which specialized in digital process control computers, not by the manufacturers of office and/or calculation-oriented digital computers. The companies also were different from those companies which had produced analog process control computers—the traditional units used for process control.

Digital computers were classed as small, medium, or large, depending on their size, complexity, and cost. Small computers sold in the price range up to $80,000; medium computers in the price range $80,000 to $600,000; and large computers in the price range $1 million to $6 million.

The Computron 1000X had been designed specifically for process control application. It was used in chemical and other process industries (oil refining, pulp and paper, food manufacture, etc.) as well. as in power plants, particularly nuclear power plants.

In addition to its 1000X computer, Computron manufactured a small line of accessory process control ·computer equipment. These accessories, however, constituted a relatively insignificant share of the company's overall sales volume.

During the first 6 months after its opening, the European sales office did only about $1,100,000 worth of business. In the 1977–1978 fiscal[1] year, however, sales increased sharply, the total for the year being $5 million. Computron's total worldwide sales during that same year were roughly $44 million. Of the European countries, Germany was one of Computron's most important markets, having contributed $1,200,000, or 24 percent of the European sales total in 1977–1978. Britain and Sweden were likewise important markets, having contributed 22 percent and 18 percent respectively, to the 1977–1978 total. The remaining 36 percent of sales was spread throughout the rest of Europe.

Computron computers sold to European customers were manufactured and assembled in the United States and shipped to Europe for installation. Because of their external manufacture these computers were subject to an import duty. The amount of this tariff varied from country to country. The German tariff on computers of this type sold by Computron was 17½ percent of the United States sales price.

Prompted primarily by a desire to reduce this importation duty, Computron was constructing a plant in Frankfurt, West Germany. This plant, which would serve the entire European Common Market, was scheduled for opening on September 15, 1978. Initially it was to be used only for the assembly of 1000X computers. Assembly in Germany would lower the German importation duty from 17½ percent to 15 percent. Ultimately the company planned to use the plant for the fabrication of component parts as well. Computers which were completely manufactured in Germany would be entirely free from the importation duty.

The new plant was to occupy 10,000 square feet and would employ 20 to 30 people in the first year. The initial yearly overhead for this plant was expected to be approximately $300,000. As of July 1978, the European sales office

---

[1]Computron's fiscal years were July 1 to June 30.

had no contracts on which the new plant could begin work, although it was anticipated that the training of employees and the assembly and installation of a pilot model 1000X computer in the new plant could keep the plant busy for 2 or 3 months after it opened. Mr. Zimmermann was somewhat concerned about the possible risk that the new plant might have to sit idle after these first 2 or 3 months unless Computron could win the present König contract.

Company Pricing Policy

Computron had always concentrated on being the quality, "blue-chip" company in its segment of the digital computer industry. The company prided itself on manufacturing what it considered to be the best all-around computer of its kind in terms of precision, dependability, flexibility, and ease of operation.

Computron did not try to sell the 1000X on the basis of price. The price charged by Computron was very often higher than that being charged for competing equipment. In spite of this fact, the superior quality of Computron's computers had, to date, enabled the company to compete successfully in both the United States and Europe.

The European price for the 1000X computer was normally figured as follows:

United States "cost"	(Includes factory cost and factory overhead)
plus	
Markup of 33⅓ percent on "cost"	(To cover profit, research and development allowances, and selling expenses)
Transportation and installation costs	
plus	
Importation duty	
Total European price	

Prices calculated by the above method tended to vary slightly because of the country-to-

country difference in tariffs and the difference in components between specific computers.[2] In the case of the present König application, Mr. Zimmermann had calculated that the "normal" price for the 1000X computer would be $311,200. Exhibit 1 shows his calculations.

The 33⅓ percent markup on cost used by the company was designed to provide a before-tax profit margin of 15 percent, a research and development allowance of 10 percent, and a selling and administrative expense allowance of 8 percent. The stated policy of top management was clearly against cutting this markup in order to obtain sales. Management felt that the practice of cutting prices "not only reduced profits, but also reflected unfavorably on the company's 'quality' image." Mr. Zimmermann knew that Computron's president was especially eager not to cut prices at this particular moment, inasmuch as Computron's overall profit before taxes had been only 6 percent of sales in 1977–1978 as compared with 17 percent in 1976–1977. Consequently, the president had stated that he not only wanted to try to maintain the 33⅓ percent markup on cost; he also was eager to raise it.

In spite of Computron's policy of maintaining prices, Mr. Zimmermann was aware of a few isolated instances when the markup on cost had been dropped to the neighborhood of 25 per-

[2]Depending on the specific application in question, the components of the 1000X varied slightly so that each machine was somewhat different from the rest.

EXHIBIT 1
CALCULATED "NORMAL" PRICE FOR THE 1000X COMPUTER FOR KÖNIG

Factory cost	$192,000
33⅓% markup on cost	64,000
U.S. list price	$256,000
Import duty (15% of U.S. list price)	38,400
Transportation and installation	16,800
Total "normal" price	$311,200

cent in order to obtain important orders in the United States. In fact, he was aware of one instance in the United States when the markup had been cut to 20 percent. In the European market, however, Computron had never yet deviated from the policy of maintaining a 33⅓ percent markup on cost.

The Customer

König & Cie., A.G., was the largest manufacturer and processor of basic chemicals and chemical products in West Germany. It operated a number of chemical plants located throughout the country. To date it had purchased three digital computer process control systems, all from Computron. The three systems had been bought during 1977–1978 and had represented $1 million worth of business for Computron. Thus König was Computron's largest German customer and had alone accounted for over 80 percent of Computron's 1977–1978 sales to Germany.

Mr. Zimmermann felt that the primary reason König had purchased Computron computer systems in the past was their proven reputation for flexibility, accuracy, and overall high quality. So far, König officials seemed well pleased with the performance of their Computron computers.

Looking ahead, Mr. Zimmermann felt that König, in contrast to any other single German customer, would continue to represent more potential future business. He estimated that during the next year or two König would have a need for another $1 million worth of digital computer equipment.

The computer on which König was presently inviting bids was to be used in the training of operators for a new chemical plant. The training program was to last approximately 4 to 5 years. At the end of the program the computer would be either scrapped or converted for other uses. The calculations which the computer would be called upon to perform were highly specialized

and would require little machine flexibility. In the specifications which had been published along with the invitation to bid, König management had stated that in buying this computer König was primarily interested in dependability and a reasonable price. Machine flexibility and pinpoint accuracy were listed as being of very minor importance, inasmuch as the machine was to be used primarily for training purposes and not for on-line process control.

Competition

In West Germany, approximately nine companies were competing with Computron in the sale of medium-priced digital process control computers. Exhibit 2 shows a breakdown of sales among these companies for 1 year. As can be seen from this exhibit, four companies accounted for 80 percent of industrywide sales in 1977–1978.

Mr. Zimmermann was primarily concerned with the competition offered by the following companies:

Ruhr Machinenfabrik, A.G. A very aggressive German company which was trying hard to expand its share of the market. Ruhr sold a

EXHIBIT 2
1977–1978 MARKET SHARES FOR COMPANIES SELLING MEDIUM-PRICED DIGITAL COMPUTERS TO THE WEST GERMAN MARKET

	Dollars	**%**
Computron, Inc.	1,200,000	30.0
Ruhr Machinenfabrik, A.G.	800,000	20.0
Elektronische Datenverarbeitungsanlagen, A.G.	500,000	12.5
Digitex, G.m.b.H.	700,000	17.5
Six other companies (combined)	800,000	20.0
Total	4,000,000	100.0

medium-quality, general-purpose digital computer at a price which was roughly 22½ percent lower than the price which Computron charged for its 1000X computer. Seventeen and one-half percentage points of this price differential was attributable to the fact that there was no import duty on the Ruhr machine, inasmuch as it was manufactured entirely in Germany. Though to date Ruhr had sold only general-purpose computers, reliable trade sources indicated that the company was presently developing a special computer in an effort to win the König bid. The price which Ruhr was planning to place on the special-purpose computer was reported to be in the neighborhood of $218,000.

Elektronische Datenverarbeitungsanlagen, A.G. A relatively new company which had recently developed a general-purpose computer of a quality comparable to that of the Computron 1000X. Mr. Zimmermann felt that Elektronische Datenverarbeitungsanlagen presented a real long-range threat to Computron's position as the "blue-chip" company in the industry. In order to get a foothold in the industry it had sold its first computer "almost at cost." Since that time, however, it had undersold Computron only by the amount of the import duty to which Computron's computers were subject.

Digitex, G.m.b.H. A subsidiary of an American firm, this company had complete manufacturing facilities in Germany and produced a wide line of computer equipment. The Digitex computer which competed with the Computron 1000X was only of fair quality. Digitex often engaged in price-cutting tactics, and the price which it charged for its computer had sometimes, in the past, been as much as 50 percent lower than that charged by Computron for its 1000X. In spite of this difference, Computron had usually been able to compete successfully against Digitex because of the technical superiority of the Computron 1000X.

Mr. Zimmermann was not overly concerned about the remaining competitors, inasmuch as he did not consider them significant factors in Computron's segment of the computer industry.

The West German Market for Medium-Priced Digital Computers

The total estimated West German market for medium-priced digital process control computers of the type manufactured by Computron was presently running at about $4 million per year, Mr. Zimmermann thought that this market could be expected to increase at an annual rate of about 25 percent for the next several years. For 1978–1979 he already had positive knowledge of about $1,300,000 worth of specific new business. This new business was broken down as follows:

König & Cie., A.G.	
Frankfurt plant	$ 300,000
Düsseldorf plant	250,000
Mannheim plant	150,000
Central German Power Commission	440,000
Deutsche Autowerke	160,000
	$1,300,000

The above business was in addition to the computer which König was presently seeking for its new experimental pilot plant. None of this already known business was expected to materialize until late spring or early summer.

Deadline for Bids

In the light of the various facts and considerations discussed above, Mr. Zimmermann was wondering what price to bid on the König contract. The deadline for the submission of bids to König was August 1, 1978. Since this was less than 2 weeks away, he knew he would have to reach a decision sometime during the next few days.

45 Polyfiber Plastics Group

Stanton G. Cort • Walter J. Salmon

Mr. Herbert Wilson, product manager of Zytene, was drafting his 1968 marketing plan. Zytene was a relatively new nucleopolyamide plastic material with performance characteristics which made it a potential replacement material, in many applications, for zinc, aluminum, brass and copper. Zytene was currently being sold at a relatively high price and with considerable technological support from the Polyfiber Plastics Group's technical and R&D staffs.

Recent analysis of Zytene's 1967 sales performance had shown the plastic to be sensitive to the business slowdown in late 1966 and early 1967. This fact had led Mr. Wilson to initiate a reexamination of Zytene's potential in replacing metals and in competing with other plastics. He was anxious to determine what specific changes, if any, should be made in the current Zytene marketing strategy to overcome the recent unsatisfactory sales situation and to maximize the product's success in the long-range (5-year) future. He was particularly interested in whether a change in selling strategy or a price reduction could help achieve these objectives.

Stanton G. Cort is an associate professor of marketing at the Case Western Reserve School of Management. Walter J. Salmon is the Stanley Roth, Jr., Professor of Retailing at the Harvard Graduate School of Business Administration.

Polyfiber Industries, Inc.

Polyfiber Industries, Inc. (Polyfiber), originally a manufacturer of synthetic fibers, had grown into a diversified corporation with sales of approximately $1.6 billion and earnings of $152 million after taxes.

The corporation was organized by product class into seven groups: fiber materials, chemicals, paper, silicones, cellulose products, plastics, and consumer products. An eighth group, the Polyfiber Central Research Laboratories, conducted exploratory research for the corporation. Each group was headed by a group president and was virtually autonomous in terms of manufacturing and marketing. Nevertheless, the groups were strongly related by virtue of their vertical integration. For example, the cellulose products group helped to supply the other groups with raw materials, and the plastics group was a captive market for many of the products of the chemicals group.

In 1966, the Polyfiber Plastics Group (PPG), whose sales had increased 25 percent since 1965, accounted for about 10 percent of corporate sales. The PPG was divided into three companies, each headed by a general manager. These were Bulk Plastics, which concentrated on the production and marketing of raw plastics materials; Consumer Products; and Industrial Products. The latter two were fabricating operations which purchased some of their raw materials from the Bulk Plastics operation.

The Bulk Plastics Company

Mr. Larry Greene was the vice president and general manager of the PPG's Bulk Plastics Company (BPC), whose sales were $81.5 million in 1966. BPC manufactured five basic resins, each of which had a distinct position in the thermoplastics market: high-density polyethylene, phenoxies, styrenes, paralenes, and Zytene, a nucleopolyamide. BPC's organization was composed of a manufacturing manager, a staff of four product managers, and a general sales manager who headed the field sales organization.

The product managers and their assistants shouldered the principal responsibility for the marketing of their respective product lines. They developed sales, inventory, and profit forecasts and developed detailed marketing plans for their products. This involved identifying and evaluating potential markets and applications, planning and justifying R&D efforts to develop new uses, determining product pricing strategy, deciding the amount and kind of selling effort required, and supervising industrial advertising and promotion.

Direct-selling efforts for all of BPC's products were the responsibility of a single sales force directed by a general sales manager. The general sales manager was assisted by six district sales managers located in Atlanta, New York, Cleveland, Detroit, Houston, and San Francisco; they had both supervisory and direct-selling responsibilities. The district sales managers were remunerated on a straight salary basis and received $25,000 to $30,000 annually. The New York and Cleveland district sales managers were assisted by junior district sales managers. Two were located in New York and one in Cleveland.

Under the district managers was a 41-person sales force: 25 field salespeople, all of whom sold all BPC products; 6 product specialists, who sold only polyethylene; and 10 applications engineers (AEs), who called only on end users of plastic parts.

The 25 field sales representatives called on all types of customers. They covered approximately 3,625 accounts (145 per salesperson). Approximately 94 percent were independent molders (firms which manufactured plastic parts for use in the products of other firms), 5 percent were captive molders (molders which were owned by end users), and 1 percent were nonfabricating end users (firms which bought parts from independent molders).

The six polyethylene product specialists were the least technically oriented people on the sales force. They called only on molders. The general sales manager described their job as primarily commodity selling rather than end-use or application development. They handled 720 accounts, or 120 per person.

The 10 AEs, on the other hand, were the most technically oriented salespeople. They called only on end users of plastic resins or parts to help develop new uses for resins by reevaluating the end users' materials specifications. Nine of these AEs were graduate engineers, and the tenth, while not a graduate engineer, had had extensive engineering experience. Three of them were automotive industry specialists, while the rest called on end users in many industries (e.g., appliance, plumbing, and communications industries).

All sales representatives were remunerated on a straight salary basis, ranging from approximately $8,000 per year for the trainee to $15,000 to $16,000 per year for seasoned, senior salespersons.

The total cost of operating this sales force, including administrative and salary expenses, was $2.33 million in 1966. This cost was allocated to each product according to the budget for sales calls for that product. For example, if the 1968 budget set a goal of 20,000 product calls and 10,000 were to sell Zytene, 50 percent of the selling expense would be allocated to Zytene. A product call was defined as an attempt to sell a product during a visit to a customer. Since selling more than one product could be attempted during a single visit, the number of product calls exceeded the number of visits.

The total number of annual product calls was determined by negotiations among the general sales manager and the four product managers. Each product manager forecasted the number of calls desired for his or her product. The general sales manager accumulated these forecasts, compared them with sales force capacity, and negotiated with the product managers to bring their sales requirements into balance with the amount of total selling time available. Selling costs were then allocated by product.

Two research and development groups were available to provide technical support for the sales force. One, the Development Research Group (DRG), which reported to the technical vice president of the Polyfiber Plastics Group, was concerned with long-range (more than 1 year) problems involving the exploitation and commercial application of technology which had been developed by the Polyfiber Central Research Laboratory. The product managers would analyze the market potential for an application of their products, formulate specific marketing goals, budget funds from their re-

sources, and request DRG to do the technical work required to formulate a product which would meet the requirements of the application.

The other technical support program, the Customer Services Lab, reported to the BPC general sales manager and was responsible primarily for helping customers to solve existing performance and fabricating problems. In addition, Customer Services worked on short-range (less than 1 year) molding, product design, and applications development projects.

The Resins Market

End users of injection-molding plastic parts, some of whom maintained molding operations of their own, and independent molders, or fabricators, were the two targets of resins manufacturers' marketing efforts. Although there were also a few plastics distributors, they were an unimportant market factor. Their business accounted for less than 1 percent of sales.

End users of engineering thermoplastics[1] typically incorporated a plastic part into a larger piece of equipment. Mr. Wilson estimated that there were approximately 3,000 such firms in the United States. Although plastics were sold to all industries, traditionally automobile and appliance manufacturers were large-quantity consumers of plastics.

Studies had shown that two fundamental motivations underlay most purchasing decisions. They were a desire to reduce the overall costs of finished parts and, even more important, a desire to improve products. The use of a resin could reduce end users' costs in two ways. First, savings could be realized on raw-materials pur-

---

[1]All BPC resins were thermoplastics. That is, they could be remelted and re-formed, as opposed to thermosets, which were not re-formable after having been fabricated. Engineering thermoplastics such as fluorocarbons, nylon, and nucleopolyamides, like Zytene, had high performance specifications, high product and applications development costs, high margins, high prices, and small markets.

chases. This was typically the most important cost criterion, when substitution of one resin for another was being considered. Cost reduction could also result from savings in the fabricating, machining, handling, and assembly of parts.

The time a purchaser took to arrive at a firm decision on a change in material specifications varied greatly. The newness of the materials, demanding applications requirements, and rigorous design and testing standards extended the decision process. With a new engineering resin, such as Zytene, BPC personnel estimated that the time from initial contact to initial purchase averaged 27 months, but there were wide variations in this average. For general industrial use the average was 1 to 2 years; for the appliance industry about 2 years; for the automotive industry, 3 years; and for some special applications it took more than 5 years to secure the first order.

time to secure order

Once end users decided to use a specific material, they typically purchased molds and drew up specifications such as dimensional tolerances of the material to be used. The molds and the specifications were turned over to captive molders, maintained by approximately 7 percent of plastics end users, and/or to independent molders. Independent molders were typically paid on a price-per-finished-part basis.

Independent molders maintained molding processing equipment with which many different molds could be used. The molders' job was to produce the items required by a specific contract. Although the specifications generally reflected the end user's concern for reliability of supply, molders were responsible for the procurement of materials as well as the maintenance and operation of processing equipment. Nevertheless, the end user's specifications frequently constrained molders to use a specific brand of plastic materials, particularly on new or engineering types of resins. When only the *type* of plastic was specified, which was common in applications using commodity plastics, molders usually shopped for the best price and supply.

Currently there were approximately 3,500 molders in the United States. Roughly 60 were large-scale operations (50–60 machines), 600 were medium-size (20–30 machines), and the balance were small operations. Generally the larger firms sought technically complex, long-range projects. The large firms typically maintained engineering staffs to explore applications of new and old materials. These staffs frequently worked directly with end users in these endeavors. Small molding operations, however, which frequently were economically unstable, could not support these kinds of activities.

When working with end users, large molders could exert substantial influence on the end users' initial choice of materials. Moreover, after the initial choice, large molders as well as small could exert pressure on an end user to reexamine specifications if difficulty was encountered in procuring or molding a certain material, or if the molders believed a change in materials could result in a reduction in fabrication costs.

To determine what changes, if any, he should make in the strategies for Zytene, Mr. Wilson decided to review the position of nucleopolyamides in the resins market, Zytene's current performance, and the future sales and profit potential for his product.

Nucleopolyamides and the Nucleopolyamide Market

Nucleopolyamides (NPAs) were a relatively new development in the resins market. The Thermoplastic Department of the Pyramid Chemical Corporation had introduced the first NPA, Nuclan, to the market in 1957, after 5 to 10 years of research and development, including about 2 years of test marketing. In 1967 only Pyramid and Polyfiber were manufacturing NPA.

Situated at the engineering end of the thermoplastic performance spectrum, NPAs had predictable stress/strain characteristics, with properties maintained at continuous dry temperatures up to 215°F and at intermittent peaks up to 275°, and performed in many ways like metal. Therefore NPAs were able to satisfy some of the end uses for which formerly only die-cast zinc, aluminum, or sand-cast brass and copper were used.

In these end uses, NPAs had several advantages over metal. They were lighter in weight and easier to fabricate than cast-metal parts. Unlike cast-metal parts, NPA parts seldom needed trimming and finishing after fabrication and were usable as molded. Holes, threads for male and female fittings, bosses, etc., with a mirror finish or a variety of textures could be obtained through molding. Where machining was necessary, NPAs could be machined as easily as zinc. Furthermore, at current raw material prices per cubic inch of material (the volumetric price), finished NPA parts offered an economic advantage in material cost over metal parts requiring finishing.

The prime disadvantage of NPAs as a replacement for metal was the cost of retooling for injection-molding fabrication. Mr. Wilson estimated that injection-molding equipment for most contemplated applications cost $30,000 to $70,000, while the molds themselves cost $10,000 to $30,000 each.

Potential end-user customers who maintained captive metal-casting facilities also had to consider the question of casting capacity made idle by a switch to plastics. Auto makers casted about 60 percent of the zinc and 70 percent of the aluminum they used. Appliance manufacturers casted 40 to 45 percent of their zinc requirements and 60 percent of their aluminum needs. According to BPC sales personnel, this problem was most easily overcome when expansion of the customer's need for other cast parts took up the slack produced by the change to NPAs. In most cases, however, it was necessary to demonstrate the advantages of the switch to NPAs, in spite of the captive casting capacity which would be idled.

The end-user market for NPAs was composed primarily of automobile, appliance, and industrial machine tool manufacturers who could use large quantities of the resin. Exhibit 1 shows NPA use by industry from 1963 to 1967. The relatively high initial costs of molds and/or injection equipment more or less restricted the market to such large users. Because of their size, most end users of NPAs engaged in extensive research and development efforts directed toward product development and improvement.

In contrast with end users, independent molders were primarily interested in the profitability of fabrication. Their principal concern was with different types of resins or brands of NPAs to determine whether one or another molded

EXHIBIT 1
UNITED STATES NUCLEOPOLYAMIDE
USE BY INDUSTRY

Millions of Pounds

Industry	1963	1964	1965	1966	1967
Automotive	3.6	6.1	8.6	11.3	11.4
Appliance	1.9	2.9	3.7	4.8	3.7
Communications	3.0	3.8	4.7	5.5	5.2
General industrial	4.1	5.5	7.0	8.4	8.4
Plumbing and hardware	2.3	3.6	4.8	6.2	5.6
Other	3.1	5.6	8.4	11.5	10.7
Total	18.0	27.5	37.2	47.7	45.0

Source: Zytene 1968 marketing plan.

faster, made molds last longer, or reduced machine maintenance.

History of Nucleopolyamide Marketing

Nuclan was introduced by Pyramid in 1957 at $1 per pound. With a marketing strategy emphasizing technological application and engineering support, Pyramid engineering personnel worked closely with product development engineering groups in potential end-user companies. They concentrated on areas where Nuclan could be substituted for die-cast zinc. Zinc then was thought to be trending upward in price, thereby giving NPAs an increasing economic advantage.

Upon realizing that Nuclan NPA was made by technical processes with which it was most familiar, Polyfiber Industries relatively quickly developed its own NPA, which it named Zytene. The Bulk Plastics operation was given responsibility for manufacturing and marketing the new product. Upon Zytene's introduction in 1960, Pyramid lowered Nuclan's selling price to 75 cents per pound. The price of NPAs had remained at this level through 1967.

Zytene was slightly less flexible than Nuclan. This property was advantageous in some applications and disadvantageous in others. BPC's initial strategy was to follow in Pyramid's footsteps and capture Nuclan business primarily at the molder level. There BPC field sales representatives could stress molding advantages. Zytene set faster than the original Nuclan, thus enabling molders to reduce molding time by 5 to 40 percent and increase the profitability of molding NPAs. Because of the economic benefits Zytene offered to molders and BPC's sales force strength at the molder level, BPC was relatively successful with this strategy.

Pyramid proceeded to reduce the molding time for Nuclan, however, and end users increasingly specified Nuclan or Zytene by name. Therefore, BPC embarked on its own technical

missionary work with end users. In 1963 the applications engineers (AEs) were added to the BPC sales force specifically to develop applications for new products such as Zytene.

Thus by 1968 Polyfiber had almost duplicated Pyramid's strategy, and both were selling NPAs at the relatively high price of 75 cents per pound to cover their R&D and applications engineering expenses.

Zytene's Current Position in the Domestic Nucleopolyamide Market

Worldwide NPA sales by Pyramid and Polyfiber totaled 90 million pounds in 1966. United States sales, which had been growing at an annual rate of 33 percent since 1963, accounted for approximately 53 percent of worldwide sales. In 1966 Zytene accounted for 33 percent or 15.5 million pounds of United States NPA resin sales.

Mr. Wilson said the market for Zytene included end users in the automotive, general industrial, appliance, plumbing and hardware, and communications fields, as well as end users in other fields. Ninety percent of the applications in which Zytene was used were in the prime specification markets. That is, the material used had to meet rigid specifications and pass exhaustive performance tests. Although one application consumed 1.6 million pounds per year, most of the hundreds of Zytene applications used small volumes of resin. A typical application would require 15,000 to 20,000 pounds per year.

Eighty-five percent of the parts made of Zytene were fabricated by injection molding. Stamping and extrusion accounted for the remainder. Results from the latter processes were comparatively inferior, however, because the stamping created internal stresses in the part and because Zytene's composition made the extrusion of shapes other than rods difficult.

Since the primary uses for Zytene were in functional, as opposed to decorative, applications, 60 percent of the poundage sold was natural-color resin (a translucent gray). To meet the requirements of customers who specified colored resins, BPC had formulated 500 color combinations. These pigmented resins sold at a 7-cents-per-pound premium over natural resin. Recently color concentrate capsules, which lowered the premium to 3 cents per pound, had been developed. The customer added the capsules to the natural resin to make colored resin. Mr. Wilson hoped that the eventual production of a variety of these concentrates would allow the end user or molder to mix any color needed and alleviate BPC's problem of selling a large variety of pigmented resins in very small quantities. Furthermore, since no such concentrates were available, or currently feasible, for Nuclan, Zytene would have a 4-cents-per-pound price advantage in pigmented resins.

The current customers for Zytene included 1,000 buying accounts. Ten percent of these, who purchased more than 60,000 pounds per year, accounted for 50 percent of Zytene's sales. Mr. Wilson believed that Nuclan's situation was similar, in that only 150 Nuclan accounts consumed over 60,000 pounds per year. The remaining 90 percent of Zytene's 1,000 customers bought in relatively small quantities. An average customer purchased 15,000 pounds per year, and the average order size was 3,600 pounds.

Field sales reps served 250 accounts who were molders and generated about 35 percent of the new Zytene business in a typical year. This new volume was primarily Nuclan replacement business.

The AEs, who made 90 percent of their calls on end users, generated the remaining 65 percent of new Zytene business. This business, secured during calls on Zytene's 750 end-user customers, included the replacement of Nuclan, conventional nylon polyacetals, and other plastics, as well as the replacement of metals. In 1967, AEs made 5,400 Zytene product calls on end users. About 60 percent of this effort was aimed at the automotive industry, 15 percent at the general industrial field, 10 percent at the appliance industry, and 4 percent at the plumbing and hardware industry. The remaining 11 percent of the effort went to seeking communications, military, and other applications. Of the total calls to all industries, AEs spent 70 percent of their effort attempting to secure metal replacement business, 15 percent trying to secure Nuclan replacement, and 15 percent selling other BPC products.

The AEs' leads were produced by field sales reps, who saw Nuclan in use by molders but could not convert these molders to Zytene because Nuclan was specified by name; by inquiries from interested design engineers; by the BPC marketing group's studies of metals and plastics markets; and by the AEs' own prospecting.

To cover the cost of these long-term selling efforts as well as the work of the Customer Services Lab and the DRG, Zytene's MAT (marketing, administration, and technical) overhead was three to four times that of any other Polyfiber Plastics Group product. Manufacturing and overhead costs for Zytene are shown below.

Zytene Cost Structure

Cost element	1966 ¢ / lb	1966 %	1967 (est.) ¢ / lb	1967 (est.) %
Cost of goods sold:				
Fixed	12.5	27.8	12.5	29.1
Variable	8.3	18.7	8.3	19.4
Total	20.8	46.5	20.8	48.5
MAT				
Marketing	10.4	23.3	10.2	23.7
Technical	10.5	23.4	9.6	22.5
Administration	3.1	6.8	2.3	5.3
Total MAT	24.0	53.5	22.1	51.5
Total cost	44.8	100.0	42.9	100.0

Based on a selling price of 75 cents per pound, Zytene was earning 40 percent before taxes in 1966 and 43 percent in 1967. The MAT was 32 percent and 29.4 percent of sales, respectively, for the 2 years. Mr. Wilson believed that Zytene's ratio of fixed to variable manufacturing costs was similar to that of other engineering thermoplastics. His cost estimates for selected competing plastics are shown in Exhibit 2. The MAT or equivalent overhead for these competitors was more difficult to estimate but probably varied with the material price. Thus, polycarbonates and polyacetals probably required more MAT efforts and higher MAT expenditures than ABS.

In formulating the 1968 Zytene pricing strategy, Mr. Wilson was considering whether to maintain Zytene's price as long as possible to cover MAT overhead at current levels and return maximum profits, or whether to make deep price cuts in an attempt to capture business from less expensive plastics like ABS. Capturing business from the competitors, Mr. Wilson alleged, required reducing Zytene's volumetric price to the equivalent of that of the competition. To compete with ABS at its 1967 price of 35 cents per pound, for example, Zytene would have to be priced at 32.4 cents per pound.

The Polyfiber plant capacity for Zytene was 30 million pounds.[2] It was estimated that each additional 10 million pounds of capacity would

_____

[2]This capacity was being used only to supply the domestic markets for Zytene.

require $5 million in plant investment and $1.5 million in working capital.

1967 Zytene Sales Performance

Mr. Wilson was disappointed with Zytene's sales performance in the first 9 months of 1967. Domestic sales would be approximately 15.2 million pounds, or about 1.9 percent below the 15.5 million pounds sold in 1966. The net loss in Zytene sales resulted from gains in Zytene usage of more than 3.7 million pounds being more than offset by losses of approximately 4.1 million pounds.

Mr. Wilson identified three sources of new Zytene volume. The commercialization of new applications and replacement of Nuclan business had accounted for 64 percent and 28 percent, respectively, of the total gains. The remaining 8 percent was the result of the expansion of existing business. Although the proportions of these gains varied by industry, new applications were the key factor across the board. Mr. Wilson thought these gains had been reduced by the general business slowdown, but the percentages attributable to the various sources of new business were typical.

Of the several reasons for lost volume, the most significant had been the business slow-

---

EXHIBIT 2
PRICE AND COST STRUCTURE OF SELECTED COMPETING PLASTICS AT 1967 PRICE AND COST LEVELS*

Plastic	Selling price (¢ / lb)	Full manufacturing cost (¢ / lb)	Variable costs† (%)	Fixed costs (%)
Nylon	75.0	20.0	50	50
Noryl	70.0	19.0	40	60
ABS	37.0	20.0	40	60
Zytene	75.0	20.8	40	60

Zytene 32.4¢ ←ABS

*Estimated by Bulk Plastics Company management.
†The variable costs of producing these plastics were almost entirely raw material costs. Direct labor accounted for a very small portion.

down, which had accounted for 42 percent of the total. Customers had decided not to increase the production of products already incorporating Zytene and had delayed introducing new products. The obsolescence factor (38 percent of the total losses), which was defined as the end users' discontinuance of obsolete products in which Zytene was used, was unusually large in 1967 because a sporting goods company had withdrawn several unsuccessful products in 1966. This company, which accounted for 46 percent of the loss ascribed to obsolescence, had reground and reused the material molded for the unsuccessful products instead of buying new Zytene in 1967. Seventeen percent of the losses were to cheaper competitive plastics, primarily in the plumbing and hardware, appliance, and general industrial fields, which, according to Mr. Wilson, was about 50 percent higher than normal.

Market Opportunities

The replacement of metal in cast-metal parts had consistently been the primary source of growth of NPA sales. The largest end users of metals suitable for replacement, such as die-cast zinc, aluminum, brass, and magnesium, were the automotive and appliance industries. The plumbing and hardware industries accounted for the majority of cast brass used. Each of these end-use markets was highly specification-oriented. Thus, extensive laboratory and field testing of a new material was required prior to use.

Use of NPAs to Replace Die-Cast Zinc

Zinc was the primary die-casting metal, accounting for over 50 percent of all die castings on a poundage basis. In 1966, 968 million pounds of zinc were used for this purpose. The automotive, appliance, and industrial machinery and tools markets consumed 59 percent, 14 percent, and

10 percent of this total, respectively. In all three markets, many applications were vulnerable to penetration by NPAs.

Die-cast zinc's vulnerability in specific applications was based on NPAs lower cost per finished part. Although variability of conditions warranted individual analysis of particular applications, some cost generalizations had been developed.

One study of 32 die-cast zinc parts indicated that the cost to the end user of cast and trimmed parts[3] and cast, trimmed, and painted parts procured from independent casters ranged from 32 cents to 48 cents per pound. Two-pound parts could then be expected to cost 64 cents to 96 cents. A further study of finished and shipped parts showed the following costs for a 1-pound finished part selling to the end user for 45 cents:

Component	¢	%
Raw material	14.8	33
Casting and trimming	17.1	38
Machining and finishing	11.3	25
Packing and shipping	1.8	4
Total	45.0	100

Two sources of savings resulted from using NPAs like Zytene: the need for less raw material and the avoidance of finishing. Because of a difference in density, zinc at 16.75 cents per pound cost 4.02 cents per cubic inch[4] while Zytene at 75 cents per pound cost 3.19 cents per cubic inch.

Zytene also required no trimming and a minimum of machining and finishing because no "flash" was produced in the injection molding

---

[3]Die casting involved two processes. First, the part was cast; then the "flash" (the thin residue of metal which had flowed between the halves of the die) was trimmed by a cutting die or by hand. Any finish machining required was accomplished in subsequent machining operations.

[4]In order to account for the different densities of various materials, prices per pound of material were adjusted to prices per cubic inch of material. These were referred to by the industry as the volumetric prices.

process, and the surfaces produced were very smooth. Thus, savings in finishing would be far more significant than materials savings in a two-barrel carburetor weighing 3.5 pounds in zinc and costing $12, since zinc itself was only 4 percent of the total cost.

On a poundage basis, complete chrome plating accounted for approximately 50 percent of the automotive industry's use of zinc die castings, and an additional 20 percent to 25 percent were partially plated or painted. In the appliance industry, 70 percent of the zinc castings were chrome-plated.

BPC management believed that Zytene could not compete in the major portion of the fully plated castings market because lower-priced plastics such as polypropylene and ABS, at 65 cents per cubic inch and 1.38 cents per cubic inch, respectively, could function satisfactorily in about 95 percent of the applications. Significant penetration of the partially plated castings market was also doubtful.

Competition from lower-priced plastics also limited other potential applications for Zytene to replace die-cast zinc. In the automotive field 90 percent of the resins used in 1966, including those for plated parts, sold for 75 cents per pound or less. Similarly, almost 95 percent of the resins used by the appliance industry sold for less than 50 cents per pound, and nearly 70 percent, including those for plated parts, cost less than 40 cents per pound.

Given these limitations on price competition, Mr. Wilson believed that Zytene's best potential was in functional applications where its performance characteristics were required. These applications had the further advantage of not being susceptible to the year-to-year design changes experienced by decorative parts.

Analysis of the automotive industry indicated that 100 million pounds of zinc castings, the equivalent of 26.6 million pounds of NPA, fit into this kind of functional category. This 26.6 million pounds was in addition to the 11.4 million pounds the industry was already consuming in 1967. Of the 26.6 million pounds, applications which would consume 6.1 million pounds of NPA were either not technically feasible or not economical. Of the remaining 20.5-million-pound potential, 9.7 million pounds were already under development in Zytene. These applications were the intake manifold, distributor cap, radiator valves, and fuel pump parts. Mr. Wilson estimated that applications which would consume 10.8 million pounds of NPA were open for development.

A similarly detailed analysis of the appliance applications had not yet been accomplished. Indications were, however, that the gross potential of NPAs was probably less than 1.8 million pounds.

Replacement of Die-Cast Aluminum

Aluminum was a close second to zinc as the most important die-casting metal on a poundage basis. The automotive, appliance, and industrial machinery and tools markets also consumed the lion's share of aluminum castings (48 percent, 12 percent, and 11 percent, respectively, of the total).

Aluminum had a high strength-to-weight ratio, maintained its properties at a continuous operating temperature of 400°F, and was light. Because of its low density, its volumetric price was 1.59 cents below that of zinc.[5] Therefore, aluminum could be used to produce strong, light parts at a relatively low cost.

Aluminum, however, was difficult to cast and particularly difficult to machine. Consequently, aluminum castings were used primarily in functional applications which did not require extensive machining and finishing. For example, in an aluminum transmission case weighing about 14.5 pounds and requiring medium finishing, raw materials accounted for 40 percent of the total cost. Major uses were in transmission cases

---

[5]Some evidence of price discounting (to 22 cents per cubic inch) for high-volume users was noted in 1967.

and components (55 to 65 percent of all aluminum die castings used in 1966 passenger cars), flywheel housings, brake drum assemblies, starter motor housings, and timing chain covers.

Die-cast aluminum applications in other industries were similar to applications in the automotive industry. The metal was used where its strength and heat resistance were required and where machining was minimal.

Under these circumstances, Mr. Wilson felt that Zytene's potential for replacing aluminum was limited by its price as well as by functional limitations. Transmission parts, for example, had to work under a continuous temperature of 300°F, which was near Zytene's melting point of 305°F. The castings had to resist extreme shock stresses, which would require special Zytene formulations. Assuming that a plastic could meet these requirements and weigh half as much as aluminum, it would have to sell at about 43 cents per pound to be competitive with aluminum for the transmission case application.

Replacement of Cast Brass

Because of the critical shortage of copper and brass in 1966 and 1967, many brass and copper users had begun to investigate plastics. Nevertheless, the plumbing and hardware industry, which consumed 66 percent of all brass castings on a poundage basis, had limited the commercial use of NPAs to noncritical applications (e.g., cold water valves and shower heads). Major producers in the industry had traditionally required years of field testing prior to acceptance of a new material. Substantial brass casting facilities which they didn't want to be idle augmented their normal inertia. Furthermore, producers didn't want to expand the effort to gain acceptance of new materials in varying and exacting local building codes. No regional or nationwide code acceptance procedures existed. The need to persuade local plumbers that the installation of the new material rather than brass was advantageous to them compounded this

problem. Mr. Wilson admitted that to date, however, no plastics manufacturers had expended the selling effort to penetrate the plumbing market.

Mr. Wilson believed that Zytene's significant cost advantages over brass warranted further penetration efforts. At current prices Zytene was 75 percent less expensive than brass on a volumetric basis. Furthermore, potential savings in fabrication, machining, and assembly work meant differences in finished-part costs which were even more impressive than raw material savings, as illustrated below.

BRASS VS. ZYTENE COST COMPARISON*
Two-Valve Diverter Assembly

	In brass ($/part)	In pigmented Zytene ($/part)
Material cost	1.45	0.41
Fabrication and assembly	5.00	1.11
Total	6.45	1.52

*Based on the production of 200,000 parts and full amortization of molds and patterns. Packing and shipping costs are not included.

Replacement of Extruded Aluminum and Brass

BPC was currently unable to enter the market for extruded metal shapes because the plasticizers in Zytene made the extrusion of shapes impossible.[6] Zytene could be extruded into rod, however, and an average of 500,000 pounds of rod had been sold in 1966 and 1967. These sales were primarily for test applications and for the screw machine market.

[6]In the injection molding process, the part remained in the mold until the resin had set. The shape of the part was maintained by the mold. The extrusion process, however, was continuous, so the resin had to hold its shape and set after it left the extruding die. Zytene could be formulated so that it would flow through the die. When extruded into thin-walled shapes, like window frame channels, however, Zytene did not hold its shape while the resin set.

Recent analysis had indicated that a significant potential for Zytene might exist in the extruded metals market. Shown below are 1966 sales of extruded aluminum and brass and the equivalent of these sales in Zytene.

	Millions of pounds		
	Aluminum	**Brass**	**Zytene equivalent**
Extruded shapes	1,861	–	1,145
Rod	–	797	197
Total	1,861	797	1,342

Mr. Wilson realized that the development of an extrudable resin and extensive market research had to precede penetration of the extruded metals market. The DRG had already been instructed to work on the technical problems, but the market research also posed a problem. Extruded Zytene rod sales had been through plastics distributors, so data on end users and their use for Zytene were unavailable.

Replacement of Pyramid's Nuclan

The replacement of Nuclan was a quick and attractive way of increasing Zytene's volume and market share without extensive testing and applications research. The only task was to convince Nuclan users to switch to Zytene. Zytene's advantage over Nuclan in retaining its original properties and capabilities over 5 to 10 years facilitated this task.[7] Independent and captive molders were also likely to prefer Zytene because it was still slightly easier to mold than Nuclan and left fewer deposits in the mold. On the other hand, Nuclan had greater tensile strength than Zytene, so it was better suited for applications involving very high stress.

Since the introduction of the AEs and the technical support groups, however, there had

been less emphasis on Nuclan replacement than on developing new applications. In early 1967, only about 10 percent of the AEs' time was spent on replacing Nuclan, and only 3 percent of the prospective new volume which they reported was in Nuclan replacement.

Some AEs reported that the close relationships developed between Pyramid and the end users and molders made Nuclan business difficult to secure. If customers were happy with Nuclan and with their relations with Pyramid, the AEs had difficulty contacting the proper people in the customers' organizations.

Zytene's Position vis-à-vis Competitive Plastics

Mr. Wilson identified three other plastic materials, two of which, nylon and Noryl, were especially competitive in certain applications with Zytene. The third one, ABS, was of interest because it had a large market, one for which Zytene could compete if its price was lowered significantly.

Conventional nylon was Zytene's major competitor among the thermoplastics. Du Pont had reduced the price of virgin nylon from 82 cents per pound (3.40 cents per cubic inch) to 70.5 cents per pound (2.91 cents per cubic inch) in October 1967. The result was that it sold for about 8.7 percent less per cubic inch than Zytene. A further decline to 63 cents per pound (2.59 cents per cubic inch) was expected by 1970 as a result of competition from at least three new manufacturers. Vendors of upgraded nylon fiber scrap, a blend of scrap and virgin nylon, were expected to exert additional pressure on prices.

Mr. Wilson estimated that during 1968 and 1969, at current prices, a total of 1.5 million to 2.3 million pounds (10 to 15 percent of Zytene's domestic volume) could be vulnerable to nylon. Conventional nylon's inadequate performance at high temperatures and in liquids would prevent further penetration of the Zytene market.

[7]Nyclan's heat resistance and strength deteriorated more rapidly than Zytene's, so parts under continued stress were more likely to fail.

ABS did not have the strength, heat resistance, or chemical resistance of Zytene but was inexpensive compared with other engineering resins and could be chrome-plated or painted easily. ABS was most suitable for decorative, rather than functional, uses and was unlikely to threaten Zytene in functional applications.

Sales of ABS in 1967 totaled 240 million pounds (see Exhibit 3). ABS manufacturers were producing at capacity and, toward the end of the year, were selling on an allocation basis. They managed to fill their best customers' needs and allocated the remaining material to other customers.

Zytene's properties were suitable for all ABS

applications. For Zytene to compete on a volumetric price basis, however, prices would have to be cut to 32.4 cents per pound. Mr. Wilson believed that some offsetting savings in MAT expenses might be realized, since ABS was being sold like a commodity plastic with a minimum of technical support.

Noryl, a blend of polyphenylene oxide and polystyrene, had short-term properties similar to those of Zytene but did not maintain them over the long term as well. Noryl was subject to deterioration in solvents and gasoline, had poor abrasion resistance, and had a high friction coefficient. It was not likely, therefore, to be a threat in automotive, appliance, plumbing, or mechanical applications.

Noryl's advantages were its price—69 cents per pound (2.63 cents per cubic inch), which was about 17.5 percent less than the price of Zytene on a volumetric basis—and its superior self-extinguishing characteristics.[8] Noryl's price advantage was practically negated by its higher processing cost. Its self-extinguishing property, on the other hand, gave it a significant advantage over Zytene in some electrical and communications applications. BPC was continuing its heretofore unsuccessful attempts to develop more satisfactory self-extinguishing properties in Zytene in order to counter this advantage. For 1968, however, Mr. Wilson thought that his strategy would have to be to stress Zytene's other properties (e.g., "processability," resistance, and toughness) in order to counter Noryl's advantages.

EXHIBIT 3
PRICE/DEMAND RELATIONSHIP FOR SELECTED PLASTIC MOLDING MATERIALS

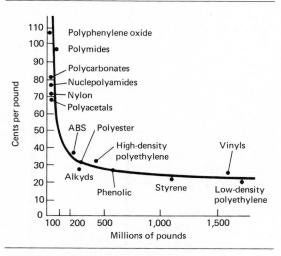

Source: **BPC compilation of trade statistics.**

[8]Self-extinguishing materials, when ignited, produced chemicals or gases which put out flame. In communications and electrical applications, in which the materials could be exposed to sparks, this property was very important.

46 The Information Bank

Nancy J. Davis • Steven H. Star

Mr. Carl Keil, director of marketing, was formulating a pricing strategy for The Information Bank, a computerized system for the storage and retrieval of general information drawn from about 60 publications. Since joining The Information Bank in December 1974, Keil had reorganized sales territories, changed the compensation system for salespeople, and begun to concentrate on specific geographic areas and vertical selling within industries. He had also taken significant steps toward securing less costly hardware and telecommunications systems. Now, however, he had to construct a consistent pricing policy which would allow the company to improve its financial position. "We currently have rate structures ranging from no charge at all to a flat rate of $1,350 per month for unlimited usage," he thought. "Our average per hour access revenue is about $20. If we retain

Nancy J. Davis was formerly a research associate at the Harvard Graduate School of Business Administration. Steven H. Star was formerly an associate professor at the Harvard Graduate School of Business Administration.

this structure, we will never have a manageable billing system."

Description of the Service

The Information Bank, a subsidiary of The New York Times Company, maintained and marketed a fully automated system for the storage and retrieval of general information. The computer in which the information was stored was located in the Times Building in New York City. It contained about one million abstracts of articles, 60 percent of which were from 6 years of *The New York Times* material and 40 percent from 3 years of 60 other publications. Approximately 20,000 abstracts were added per month, half from *The New York Times* and half from the other publications. New entries were usually added within 72 to 96 hours of receipt of the source publications (See Exhibit 1 for a list of publications abstracted.)

The abstracts were tersely written summaries

EXHIBIT 1
PERIODICALS INCLUDED IN THE BANK

THE
INFORMATION
BANK®   # Data Base

 A SUBSIDIARY OF THE NEW YORK TIMES COMPANY

I. THE NEW YORK TIMES

Input into the data base comprises virtually all news and editorial matter from the final Late City Edition, including Sunday feature sections and daily and Sunday regional material not distributed within New York City. Current issues are normally processed four or five working days after publication. At present, New York Times material extends back to January 1, 1969.

II. OTHER PUBLICATIONS

General Circulation Newspapers:

Atlanta Constitution
Chicago Tribune
Christian Science Monitor
Houston Chronicle
Los Angeles Times
Miami Herald
National Observer
New York Times
San Francisco Chronicle
Washington Post

Foreign Affairs:

Atlas
Economist of London
Far Eastern Economic Review
Foreign Affairs
Foreign Policy
Latin America
Latin America Economic Report
Manchester Guardian
Middle East
Times of London

Newsweeklies, Monthlies, Quarterlies:

American Scholar
Atlantic
Black Scholar
Commentary
Commonweal
Consumer Reports
Current Biography
Ebony
Harpers
Nation (The)
National Journal
National Review
New Republic
New York
New York Review of Books
New Yorker
Newsweek
Psychology Today
Saturday Review
Sports Illustrated
Time
US News and World Report
Variety
Village Voice
Washington Monthly

Business Publications:

Advertising Age
American Banker
Automotive News
Barron's
Business Week
Editor and Publisher
Forbes
Fortune
Harvard Business Review
Journal of Commerce
Wall Street Journal

Science Publications:

Astronautics
Bulletin of Atomic Scientists
Industrial Research
Science
Scientific American

Material selected from the magazines and newspapers listed above is being processed at varying rates according to priorities established in consultation with subscribers. At present, top priority is being given to Business Week, Los Angeles Times, The Wall Street Journal and The Washington Post. However, current selections from most of these periodicals are now available. Back files for most of these publications extend back to January 1, 1973, and for many to early 1972.

Selection Criteria

Normally **included** are:

Significant news items, interpretive articles, and articles of opinion or commentary originating with or exclusive to the source periodicals.

Biographical material.

Business and financial news and interpretive items on business and financial subjects unless of interest only on a very short-term basis or only to a narrow, highly specialized group.

Editorials.

Surveys, background or chronological reviews, and similar descriptive material on subjects of general interest.

Items by or about people of substantial general interest, regardless of content.

Commercial and political advertising when of research value.

headed by bibliographic citations that gave the journal titles, dates, pages, and, when applicable, columns. The abstracts were "manufactured" by a highly skilled group of editors and writers. Editors who specialized in particular areas—the United States economy, for example—read all the incoming articles about this subject and marked critical passages. The articles then went to a writer who also specialized in that particular area, and he or she wrote the abstract. Abstracts ranged in length from one or two sentences up to 300 or 400 words.

Customers of The Information Bank received information from the Bank's computer by means of a cathode-ray-tube (CRT) video terminal located at their offices. Connections between the CRT and the computer were made through regular telephone lines or through other telecommunications channels. Customers could also purchase a high-speed printer which operated at up to 165 characters per second. The auxiliary printer provided a hard-copy capability to the customers. If the customers did not have a printer but wanted printed abstracts, they could request that The Information Bank print the abstracts and mail them to them. It normally took several days to receive the abstracts.

The Information Bank's system was designed so that the user need not be an information scientist, a computer specialist, or a librarian. Each step was conducted in plain English. Messages to and from the computer could be spelled out completely, though a set of abbreviations had been developed which an experienced researcher could use to save time. If researchers became confused about what was going on with the system, they could press a special key which flashed an explanatory message on the CRT screen. If the explanation was not adequate or if the system malfunctioned, they could telephone a specially trained person at the New York office. To use the system, the researchers typed in descriptors—i.e., subject headings or index terms comparable to subject headings in a card catalog—and the computer scanned the Bank

and printed the relevant abstracts onto the CRT. On the average, an abstract had about 10 descriptors. If the researchers typed in a very general descriptor, the computer suggested more specific terms and asked if they would like to use any of them instead of or in addition to the one they first entered. If the descriptor entered matched two or more terms in the Bank, the computer displayed all the terms so the researchers could select the one most appropriate for their search. If the descriptor entered had a widely used synonym which Information Bank editors had chosen for filing entries, the computer usually automatically switched to the synonym. The system was designed to allow the combining of terms through Boolean logic for more complex searches. For example, the terms *Great Britain* and *labor contracts* could be entered and combined, and only those abstracts about both Great Britain and labor contracts would be retrieved.

Because of the volume of material available on many subjects, the computer could conceivably provide hundreds of abstracts if the researchers did not somehow restrict the search. To do this, they used modifiers, words which directed the search in a highly specific fashion. Only one modifier could be used, or several could be used simultaneously. The principal modifiers were:

Byline. A term which limited material to that by a given person. If the researchers did not use the byline, they got material both *by* and *about* the person.

Sketch material. A term which selected material primarily of biographical interest.

Date of publication. A term which limited material to that which appeared on a single date, on several dates, or during any given time period(s) such as a month or a year.

Journal. A term which limited material to that published in one or more of the newspapers and magazines the Bank contained.

Source. A term which limited the material to that

·received from a specific wire service or some other credited source.

Type of material. A term which limited the abstracts to specific types, such as editorial, letters to the editor, news analysis, obituary, or critical review.

Graphics. A term which limited the abstracts to those accompanied by specific illustrations, such as maps, charts, and photographs.

In addition to the regular storage and retrieval system, The Information Bank offered *The New York Times* on microfiche. Microfiche was similar to conventional-roll microfilm, but it was easier to use and could be produced more frequently. A fiche consisted of a 4 × 6 inch negative which contained 98 frames. Each frame was a microphotograph of a 9 × 12 inch sheet on which The Information Bank personnel had mounted clippings. The contents of a daily *Times* could be printed on a single fiche, while Sunday editions required four fiche. Except for items of no discernible research value, *Times* fiche contained virtually all the news and editorial material published in the paper. Advertisements of potential research value were included. A clipping on fiche was located by the regular procedure of entering descriptors and modifiers into the CRT terminal. The fiche file number and the specific frame number for the clipping were included in the abstract's bibliographic citation. Fiche of current material were mailed to customers twice a week, and customers could obtain fiche of back issues of the *Times*. Keil thought that as copyright agreements were made with other publishers, material from their publications could also be issued on microfiche. While 80 percent of The Information Bank's customers said they were satisfied with the abstracts, 50 percent still subscribed to the microfiche service. To use the microfiche, a customer had to have a microfiche reader. Readers available ranged from very inexpensive, small units to large readers with printers which produced printed copies of any article on the fiche.

The Market and Competition

In February 1975, a few companies in addition to The Information Bank offered computerized information storage and retrieval systems. However, most of these concentrated on highly specialized information such as that needed by lawyers or doctors. Four of the major companies in this business were Mead Data Central, Inc., System Development Corporation (SDC), Predicasts, Inc., and Bunker Ramo. Mead's system, known as LEXIS, supplied legal information for law offices. SDC offered a system for 10 different fields—life sciences, engineering, geosciences, business management, chemistry, government research and development, agriculture, education, medicine, and petroleum. While SDC's system contained almost 4 million citations, it did not provide abstracts of the periodicals covered. Predicasts specialized in domestic and international statistics and major indexing services. Bunker Ramo's information base went back only 90 days, and the information was categorized into only 10 general areas. None of these companies supplied the wide variety of general information which The Information Bank supplied.

Eight companies, some of which were small businesses that needed information but had limited financial resources, had begun to subscribe to The Information Bank and to resell it at retail. The Information Bank had made only short-term arrangements with these companies.

Keil had no idea what the sales volume of Mead, SDC, Predicasts, Bunker Ramo, and other companies in the field might be, but industry sources estimated that by 1980 the information storage and retrieval business would be a billion-dollar industry. Keil expected numerous companies to enter the field in the next few years, but he thought that they might concentrate on one specific area of information. Satellite transmission was lowering communication costs to the point where worldwide access to data bases would soon be both technically and economically feasible.

Keil stated that in the United States, federal, state, and local government agencies probably accounted for about 30 percent of the potential market for The Information Bank's services. He noted, for example, that in Washington the Library of Congress was trying to make its services more readily accessible to the Senate and House of Representatives and that it had been instrumental in installing several terminals at the Senate and the House, as well as in its own buildings. Keil thought college, university, and public libraries probably constituted another 25 percent of the total potential market. He felt this market segment would be difficult to develop, however, because its funding was very erratic and locating the appropriate decision makers was difficult. Another 25 percent of the potential market consisted of corporations, Keil thought. He said that large corporations such as those included on the *Fortune 500* list were setting up information centers which should be a prime market for The Information Bank. The final 20 percent of the potential market, Keil thought, comprised the intelligence community and foreign embassies.

History of the Information Bank

The development of The Information Bank began in 1966. Initially, management thought it would be used as a service for *The New York Times's* news and editorial department, with future commercial development to follow after a thorough test period. Issues of the *Times* going back to the turn of the century would be abstracted and included in the Bank so that writers would have quick, easy access to any historical data they needed when writing a story. Not until the early seventies, however, did management try to market the system to organizations outside the *Times*. Though various salespeople were hired and the information base was expanded to include publications other than the *Times*, a major unified marketing program did not get under way until Mr. Carl Keil joined the company in December 1974. Keil had previous work experience with Mobil Oil, IBM, and the United States Postal Service.

The situation Keil inherited offered significant opportunities for improvement. The 1974 annual report of The New York Times Company stated, "A full-scale marketing program, and the continuing costs of expanding the data base, caused The Information Bank to incur larger expenses than in prior years." To be more specific, the company had spent about $3 million on the system in 1974, while total revenues had been about $240,000. About $1 million had been spent to abstract data, $600,000 to rent the IBM computer, and $200,000 on trade shows and media advertising, primarily newspaper ads. The remaining $1.2 million had been spent on administrative costs, systems supports, and trainers' and salespeople's salaries and expenses. Since 1966, The New York Times Company had spent about $9 million developing the system.

The sales organization Keil inherited consisted of four salespeople and two trainers who taught customers to use the system. One salesperson had previously been a broker; one had been an administrative assistant in a large company; the third had just finished a master's degree in information science; and the fourth had been a time-sharing salesperson for a computer company. Only the last had any related selling experience before joining The Information Bank. The salespeople were paid a straight salary of about $21,000. No commissions or other special incentives were offered, but the company did pay all their selling expenses. This constituted a very large sum because the salespeople all operated out of the New York office, and there was no clear geographic definition to their territories. There was some specialization by industry, but for the most part, the salesperson who answered the telephone when a response to an advertisement came in got that account. In addition to the sales staff, Keil had one secretary and one billing clerk. All billing was done manually.

In February 1975, The Information Bank had 38 customers. They were scattered all over the United States, and one was located in Canada. (See Exhibit 2 for a list of customers as of February 1975.)

According to the company's records, a customer currently used the system about 15 hours per month on the average, and this figure was reached about 3 months after the system was installed.

The Information Bank's usage pattern closely paralleled that of an interactive time-sharing operation. People began using the system around 9 A.M., and the number of users increased steadily until about 11:30 A.M. A slight lull occurred during lunchtime, then usage increased more rapidly until it reached a peak between 2 and 2:30 P.M. From then until 5 P.M.,

EXHIBIT 2
INFORMATION BANK SUBSCRIBERS

	Location
Royal Canadian Mounted Police	Canada
Library of Congress	Washington, D.C.
U.S. Army War College	Carlisle, Pa.
State Department	Washington, D.C.
Gruner & Jahr	New York City
Army Library	Washington, D.C.
National Broadcasting Company	New York City
Enoch Pratt Memorial Library	Baltimore, Md.
Kansas City Public Library	Kansas City, Mo.
Brooklyn Public Library	New York City
New York State Library	Albany, N.Y.
United Nations	New York City
Connecticut State Library	Hartford, Conn.
IBM	White Plains, N.Y.
Hill & Knowlton	New York City
Mobil Oil	New York City
General Foods	White Plains, N.Y.
Exxon	Linden, N.J.
Detroit Free Press	Detroit, Mich.
Shell	Houston, Tex.
B. F. Goodrich	Akron, Ohio
General Mills	Chicago, Ill.
Reuters	New York City
Chase Manhattan	New York City
New York Public Library	New York City
Philip Morris Incorporated	Richmond, Va.
Gulf	Houston, Tex.
Dentsu	New York City
U.S. Academy at West Point	West Point, N.Y.
Voice of America	Washington, D.C.
University of Pennsylvania	Philadelphia, Pa.
Time Incorporated	New York City
Louisville Courier Journal	Louisville, Ky.
Adelphi University	Garden City, N.Y.
Philadelphia Free Library	Philadelphia, Pa.
Secretary of the Air Force	Washington, D.C.
Environmental Protection Agency	Raleigh, Durham, N.C.
University of California at Berkeley Library	Berkeley, Calif.

it dropped steadily and then leveled off. While The Information Bank's computer could, theoretically, handle as many as 400 terminals, Keil's experience suggested that response time would be slow and customers would lose interest if more than approximately 300 terminals were in use at one time. By spreading usage across the various time zones, he reasoned, it would be possible to increase capacity by 25 percent (i.e., from 300 to 375 terminals), since it would be unlikely that all terminals would be in use at the same time.

Customer Visits

Keil decided to visit several customers to see if there was a "typical" customer profile. In the industrial segment, he visited a major oil company and a major bank. He called the oil company an "ideal user." The Information Bank's terminal was located in the company's "public affairs secretariat," which serviced the top level of the organization. In addition to The Information Bank, this department subscribed to UPI, API, Reuters, and a data base oriented to the oil industry. It had four video-tape recorders, three television monitors, and a large file of clippings. It was run by two people who had Ph.D.'s in philosophy. They said they used The Information Bank to find out what various people had said about issues affecting the oil industry, to determine what other oil companies were doing, to determine what was being said about their company, to provide material for executives' speeches, to anticipate questions executives were likely to be asked, and to determine how to position the company's advertising. It took these researchers 5 to 10 minutes to do a typical search, and they normally used the Bank 10 to 20 hours a month. Records were not kept of who requested what information, and the people in charge said they were not called upon to justify their expenses. They suspected that other oil companies had comparable departments.

At the bank which Keil visited, he found what

he called "an excellent example of a bad placement." The Information Bank's terminal was located in and charged to the bank's library, though it was used primarily for credit checks on companies which approached the bank for loans. Credit officers sent requests to the librarian, who actually did the search. A logbook was kept, but usage of the system was not charged back to the credit department. The librarian was not anxious for other people to learn about the system because additional requests would mean additional expenses for her department, and this might soon necessitate the hiring of another librarian. This bank used the system between 17 and 18 hours a month. Keil thought usage would be much higher if the system were placed in the commercial loan department and credit officers were trained to use it, or in the international and investment departments.

Keil visited three government agencies which subscribed to The Information Bank. At the State Department, The Information Bank's terminal was located in the library, but a large number of employees had been trained to use it, and it was extremely accessible. There was a logbook for the user to register his or her name, department, and request, but usage of the Bank was not charged back to specific departments. The average search here took at least 10 minutes, and the system was used approximately 25 hours a month. Someone apparently considered this usage to be rather high because the librarian had recently been requested to do searches for untrained people rather than train new people to use the system. However, the librarian stated that she was not under substantial pressure to decrease usage of the system or overall costs in her department.

At the office of the Secretary of the Air Force, The Information Bank's terminal was located in the library and was used by four very skilled librarians, normally for information regarding military and foreign affairs. Though they maintained several files on a wide variety of topics, they said they went first to The Information Bank when requested to research a subject. The average time of a search was 5 minutes, and the Bank was used about 15 hours per month. One librarian said she had been asked to supply a copy of a speech, but the person making the request gave an incorrect date for the speech. She said she located the speech in about 15 minutes using The Information Bank but that it would probably have taken 1½ days for her to find it through regular research methods. This was the closest anyone came to quantifying the benefits of the Bank.

The Environment Protection Agency (EPA) initially had a terminal located in Washington and another in North Carolina. However, the head librarian, who kept the terminal in her office and was its sole user, said she was not getting many requests for information she thought the Bank was likely to contain, and so she had eliminated one terminal. Keil said she was generally negative about the system and that she felt the EPA didn't need it. She said she used it about once a week.

In the library segment, Keil visited publicly funded libraries as well as college and university libraries. The Philadelphia Free Library, a public library system consisting of a main library and 55 branches, offered The Information Bank to the general public. About 50 percent of its inquiries came from the business community (about half of these were from news media), about 30 percent from the educational community, and about 20 percent from miscellaneous sources. Fifteen to twenty percent of the users were referred to the Bank by library personnel. The system was operated by two highly skilled librarians, and their average search lasted 6 to 8 minutes. The librarians averaged about 250 searches per month, which amounted to 25 to 35 hours on-line. This number seemed to be increasing as word of the system spread throughout the greater Philadelphia area as a result of newspaper articles and talk show appearances by the librarians who ran the system. For any given inquiry, the library would do 15 minutes of

searching for free, but after that, it charged $1 per minute. Most of the searches which lasted more than 15 minutes were done for the business community. The librarian in charge of the Bank said it was quite expensive but that it had generated so much goodwill within the local business and academic communities that there would be a tremendous uproar if the city tried to cut it out of the library's budget. He said further that comparisons could not be made between the cost of the Bank and the cost of a skilled researcher doing the task manually because the Bank was infinitely faster and generated far more data than a person using printed indexes ever could.

The Connecticut State Library used The Information Bank in a manner similar to that of the Philadelphia Free Library. The terminal was located in a special department which had been set up in 1973 to function as a free telephone information service for anyone in Connecticut. It was staffed by six full-time and three part-time librarians. The head librarian said they had been unable to categorize their customers. Their average search took 3.4 minutes, and they averaged 245 searches a month. September, December, and January were their heaviest months, and the number of searches per month appeared to be increasing. There was no charge for the first 10 minutes of a search, but the department charged 75 cents per minute after that. The department was financed by federal funds distributed by the New England Library Board. Each library which received these funds decided how to use them.

College and university libraries usually faced more budgetary restraints than did public libraries who had the system. Adelphi University had an Information Bank terminal located in its reference department, and it was operated by seven reference librarians. For anyone affiliated with Adelphi the library charged $3 per search for the first 30 citations, then 25 cents for each additional citation. Adelphi also offered the system to businesses on Long Island. By paying

$100 a year, a company gained access to the service and got two free searches. After that, the subscribing company paid $25 for the next 20 abstracts and 50 cents for each additional abstract. A typical search at Adelphi took about 6 minutes. One librarian estimated that she and the other six librarians together might do anywhere from 8 to 80 searches a month. She said further that the library had publicized the Bank heavily within the university and that it was used by students, faculty, and administrators alike. This library also offered SDC's systems.

At the University of California at Berkeley, the head librarian said that during the first 6 months when the library offered The Information Bank free of charge, students made most of the inquiries. In order to cover out-of-pocket costs, however, the library had begun to charge for the system, and the chief users now were faculty members and graduate students, especially those from departments such as the graduate school of public policy which subsidized the program. The charge was $25 for the first 15 minutes and $25 for each 15 minutes thereafter. In addition to the 15 minutes of search time, the user received up to 50 abstracts by deferred print. Four librarians operated the system, and their typical search took between 10 and 15 minutes. They now used the system between 3 and 5 hours a month. The library no longer advertised the Bank for the total community because management felt it was too expensive for most students. When requests came in, the librarians tried to steer students to other resources which could meet their needs. This library also had systems by Lockheed, SDC, and Medline.

Keil did not visit customers in the intelligence community, but he thought these customers used the Bank in their training programs and in the normal course of their intelligence work. Most of their searches, he thought, were simple name checks which probably took no more than 3 or 4 minutes. He thought a typical customer in this segment would probably do 350 to 400 searches a month.

Keil's Objectives for the Information Bank and Changes Instituted as of February 1975

In the business plan which Keil presented to top management in January 1975, he listed the following business and marketing objectives:

Business Objectives
1. Within the next 24 months have The Information Bank operating as a profitable business.
2. Establish a dominant marketing position over the next 24 months in general data base retrieval companies who are marketing on a commercial basis.
3. Organize and develop a professional marketing team capable of carrying out objectives one and two.
4. Insure that both EDP systems and communications are capable of supporting an expandable and reliable service consistent with the high standards of The New York Times Company.
5. Establish a measurement system which will track usage of the base and produce statistics that will be used in evaluating journal entries, as well as producing marketing information. This system will be used to determine system performance, billing, and commission information.

Marketing Objectives
1. Formulate a pricing policy which will hit a breakeven point at 60 percent of system capacity.
2. Formulate a compensation plan for the sales staff that will motivate them to higher productivity levels.
3. Establish revenue benchmarks on a monthly basis which total an annual revenue of $1.1 million.
4. Hire in 1975 a sales manager and trainer for the Washington office.
5. Hire two new salespeople and a trainer for the New York office.
6. Create and establish an identity for The Information Bank.
7. Formulate a sales strategy through industry penetration, application selling and geographical concentration that will optimize our sales resources.
8. Through development of a professional marketing team, newsletters, and promotional piec-

es, demonstrate to our customers and prospects that The Bank is a sound, viable business.

Keil first addressed the issue of the geographic spread of customers. Geographic concentration would enable the company to take advantage of wide-band leased telephone lines which could accommodate several users at one time, thereby lowering costs. Furthermore, it would allow the company to build a local staff of salespeople and trainers and to concentrate its advertising and promotional activities. Keil's first target market was the Northeast. However, he did not want to neglect opportunities beyond this area. Therefore, in organizing the sales force, he assigned salespeople to specific geographic areas in the Northeast plus specific industries in other parts of the United States. (See Exhibit 3 for the new sales responsibilities.)

Within the Northeast, the Washington market was selected for maximum attention. Keil leased office space there and hired a sales manager and a trainer.

Keil also changed the compensation system by formalizing a commission plan for the salespeople. The plan emphasized the generation of new net revenue from both existing accounts and new accounts. However, a $100 bonus for opening a new account was also offered. Keil estimated that salespeople's salaries and commissions would amount to about 15 percent of the total revenue generated, an amount typical of the data-processing industry. His goal, which he thought would be reached by June 1976, was to have each salesperson handling 20 to 25 customers, each of whom would spend between $900 and $1,000 a month on The Information Bank. The salespeople should eventually be earning between $25,000 and $30,000 each year, Keil thought.

To support the personal sales effort and build product awareness, Keil used a limited amount of media advertising and direct mail. He hired Mr. William Saxon to create cartoons for the ads, and he ran a few ads in *The Washington Post, The Wall Street Journal, The New York Times,*

EXHIBIT 3
INFOBANK TERRITORY ASSIGNMENTS

Smith

1. **Geography: Northern New Jersey**
2. **Colleges and universities: West**
3. **Banking, accounting, diversified financial services, brokers, law firms, law enforcement agencies, New York City government, ethical drugs, automobiles, trucks and farm implements, oil, gas, coal and other energy companies**

Jones

1. **Geography: Philadelphia**
2. **Colleges and universities: Midwest**
3. **Broadcast and print media, advertising and public relations agencies, consumer personal products and services, consumer durables and household products, leisure time products and services, apparel, textiles, transportation products and services**

Randolph

1. **Geography: Boston**
2. **Insurance, real estate, utilities, metals, mining (non-coal), chemicals, electronics, office products and services, rubber, machinery, construction and construction products, consultants, think tanks and research organizations, foundations**

Bachelder

1. **Geography: Pittsburgh**
2. **Colleges and universities: East**
3. **Municipal public libraries, state, county, and regional library systems, colleges and universities**

Franke

Washington, D.C., area

and some association magazines aimed at the Washington market. He sent direct-mail pieces to the chief executive officers, advertising vice presidents, and marketing vice presidents on the *Fortune* magazine list of the 1,000 largest corporations, to association executives, and to people designated by the Bank's salespeople as potential customers. He budgeted approximately $50,000 for the advertising and direct-mail campaign for 1975. (See Exhibit 4 for sample advertisements.)

EXHIBIT 4
SAMPLE ADVERTISING

SPARKLE WITH STATISTICS!

The Information Bank: your personal source of comprehensive, accurate data on thousands of subjects.

 Computerized information retrieval has come of age with The Information Bank. This on-line, interactive system gives you the opportunity of searching for the specific data you need—from 60 worldwide sources at the same time! No need to check through individual indexes or reference files. No need to set up special research projects. No need to learn a computer language. The Information Bank is designed to serve you, the end-user... with speed and accuracy on a routine day-to-day basis. In response to inquiries you type in, fully informative "abstracts" appear on your terminal screen *in seconds*. Using an optional printer, you can also obtain printed copies of whatever material you've retrieved.

A proven system—based on years of testing, development, and the refinement of an unmatched data base.

At the heart of The Information Bank's data base is material from The New York Times—daily and Sunday editions

dating back to 1969. Supplementing this vast resource are "abstracts" from 59 other journals—published in this country and abroad. The scope is extensive, ranging from the Los Angeles Times to The Times of London. You can look into every conceivable subject, requesting specific material as indicated in this chart:

Here are just a few ways The Information Bank can help you in fulfilling objectives.

■ Provides current (and historical) background material for those involved in Congressional liaison work.
■ Managers and directors of associations utilize the system in compiling reports and articles for membership; also in preparing speeches and panel-discussion data.
■ Helps you stay responsive to status of legislative hearings, budgets, committee action—affecting your own department and others.

■ Business and industrial management groups use the system as a "barometer" of consumer and political opinion...in economic and public-affairs work...as an updating service for executives.
■ Full source of economic, financial and appropriations data—useful in forecasting, planning, analysis and review of budgets.
■ In presentations to regulatory agencies, trade association legal and management groups use Information Bank as source of supporting data.

A simple-to-operate system: key factor in The Information Bank's wide acceptance in government, industry, libraries.

New subscribers, under our start-up plan, get comprehensive on-site training plus 200 hours of computer time for the first 60 days. This usage is charged at our flat rate. Thus, you have a unique opportunity to discover the full potential of this system.

THE INFORMATION BANK   The New York Times Company

Mr. Carl Keil, Director of Marketing
The New York Times Information Bank
229 West 43rd Street
New York, N.Y. 10036
(212) 556-1111

Please have your Washington office contact us regarding:
☐ description of system: ☐ demonstration.

Name_____
Title_____ Phone_____
Agency or Organization_____
_____
Address_____
City, State, Zip_____
☐ Send literature only

EXHIBIT 4
Continued

Presenting a computerized information-retrieval system that brings you the specific data you need...from over 60 worldwide sources.

THE INFORMATION BANK

The Information Bank represents computerized information-retrieval at its most productive. Designed to serve the end-user directly—this on-line, interactive system "guides" you to the specific data you need on virtually *any* subject of current or historical interest. The Information Bank pinpoints your desired data by searching through its *entire* data base in a matter of seconds. System is fully operational across the U.S., following almost a decade of testing, development and the refinement of an unmatched data base.

The Information Bank is a service of The New York Times Company. **NYT**

Designed for routine, day-to-day use:

At long last, the time-consuming process of checking through individual indexes, reference files and clippings is eliminated. So is the need for special task-force research. In response to inquiries you type in, fully informative "abstracts" appear almost instantly on your terminal screen. Thus, you can scan and bypass unwanted pieces quickly. Selected material can be arranged in chronological (or reverse-chronological) order at the touch of a button. As you'll see in chart "A" the system allows you to select material by publication, date, type of article, etc. Further, an optional printer can provide hard-copy of whatever data you've retrieved. All steps are in plain English, no computer language to learn.

A. Four simple steps in typical search:

Data base grows at rate of 20,000 items monthly:

No other computerized system—anywhere in the world—can match the remarkable scope and size of this data base. Over one million abstracts are "stored" in The Information Bank's disk memory, and the

expansion process constantly enriches this data base. Prime source of Information Bank material is The New York Times, daily and Sunday editions dating back to 1969. Additionally, the system contains items from more than 60 other leading journals—published in this country and abroad. The following chart breaks down the data base by *type* of article...

23.0% from special-interest journals and magazines.

13.1% from overseas publications.

54.8% from U.S. newspapers.

9.1% from U.S. general interest magazines.

As the next chart demonstrates, when you access The Information Bank for data on a desired subject—you can request almost *any* type of article...

Elections
Legislation
Litigation
Labor/Management

Energy
World trade
Finance
Science

Companies
Organizations
Foundations
Industries

20K ABSTRACTS ADDED MONTHLY

News articles
Forecasts
Analyses

Surveys
Summaries
Biographies

By-line pieces
Features
Columns
Editorials

Maps
Charts
Diagrams

Subscriber list covers many fields:

- University libraries
- State and local libraries
- Government agencies/departments
- Law enforcement
- Research centers
- Foundations
- Communications/Publishing
- Advertising/PR
- Industrial companies
- Consumer-products firms

EXHIBIT 4
Continued

- Conglomerates
- Plus subscribers in Canada, Mexico

Generally speaking, The Information Bank's basic computer-usage charge to such subscribers averages between $45/50 per hour.

Communications charges and equipment rental are additional and separate. Most new subscribers now make their own arrangements for communications and "hardware," through direct contacts with suppliers. In certain cases, however, The Information Bank will assist in such matters.

A few technical details:

- Subscribers receive comprehensive on-site training at no charge for designated individuals and groups.
- New subscribers, under our start-up plan, get comprehensive on-site training plus 200 hours of computer time for the first 60 days. This usage is charged at our flat rate. Thus, you have a unique opportunity to discover the full potential of this system.
- Subscribers with existing compatible CRTs simply access our computer on a telephone "dial-up" basis.
- With multiple CRTs available, the system can readily function on a multi-department basis, as a central-library tool, *and* for individual searches.
- Microfiche reader-printer available as an option—for viewing or copying the full New York Times article from which an "abstract" is taken.
- To assure continuous, smooth performance of system, subscribers can reach the "Systems Monitor Office" in New York by using a special toll-free number.
- Information Bank supplies an informative Newsletter for its subscribers—covers latest developments in the system, new "descriptor" terms, tips and advice for

gaining optimum performance. We try to share with you the experiences gained over our *entire* subscriber network.

How the system helps you fulfill objectives...

Provides current (and historical) background material for those involved in Congressional liaison work.

Managers and directors of associations utilize the system in compiling reports and articles for membership; also in preparing speeches and panel-discussion data for meetings.

In communications or media-liaison work, The Information Bank gives overview of public and press reactions to current situations.

Helps you stay responsive to status of legislative hearings, budgets, committee action—affecting your own department and others.

Provides comparative benchmarks with the private sector, in such matters as recruiting, employment, transfers, job benefits, etc.

Full source of economic, financial and appropriations data—useful in forecasting, planning, analysis and review of budgets.

In dealing with regulatory agencies, trade association legal and management groups find Information Bank an invaluable source of supporting data.

Serves the needs of agencies whose overseas bureaus and personnel need up-dating from key U.S. sources.

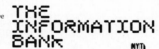

THE INFORMATION BANK

A service of The New York Times Company

The New York Times Information Bank
229 West 43rd Street
New York, N.Y. 10036
(212) 556-1111

EXHIBIT 4
Continued

DAZZLE THEM WITH YOUR DATA

The Information Bank: your personal source of comprehensive, accurate data on thousands of subjects.

Computerized information retrieval has come of age with The Information Bank. This on-line, interactive system gives you the opportunity of searching for the specific data you need—from 60 worldwide sources at the same time! No need to check through individual indexes or reference files. No need to set up special research projects. No need to learn a computer language. The Information Bank is designed to serve you, the end-user... with speed and accuracy on a routine day-to-day basis. In response to inquiries you type in, fully informative "abstracts" appear on your terminal screen *in seconds.* Using an optional printer, you can also obtain printed copies of whatever material you've retrieved.

A proven system—based on years of testing, development, and the refinement of an unmatched data base.

The Information Bank is currently operating for subscribers across the U.S.—and in Canada and Mexico as well. Among these are government agencies, libraries, universities and research centers, communications firms and leading companies on the Fortune 500 list. In many cases, subscribers use their existing CRTs and access our computer on a telephone "dial-up" basis. Others lease CRTs from major suppliers (or through The Information Bank) to receive the service.

Data base almost one million items; continues to grow at the rate of over 20,000 items monthly.

At the heart of The Information Bank's data base is material from The New York Times—daily and Sunday editions dating back to 1969. Supplementing this vast resource are "abstracts" from 59 other journals—published in this country and abroad. The scope is extensive, ranging from the Los Angeles Times to The Times of London. You can look into every conceivable subject, requesting news articles, columns, editorials, analyses, surveys, biographies, illustrated items (maps, charts, diagrams, etc.), and reviews.

DATA-BASE BREAKDOWN BY INPUT OF ARTICLES (1974)

23.0% from special-interest journals and magazines. **54.8%** from U.S. newspapers. **13.1%** from overseas publications. **9.1%** from U.S. general-interest magazines.

Functions on a multi-department basis, as a central-library tool, for individual searches.

Here are just a few ways The Information Bank can help you ...

■ Provides current (and historical) background material for those involved in Congressional liaison work.
■ In communications or media-liaison work, The Information Bank gives overview of public and press reactions to current situations.
■ Helps you stay responsive to status of legislative hearings, budgets, committee action—affecting your own department and others.
■ Provides comparative benchmarks with the private sector, in such matters as plant and operations, management training and services, employee benefits, etc.
■ Full source of economic, financial and appropriations data—useful in forecasting, planning, analysis and review of budgets.

You get comprehensive on-site training, plus unlimited computer time for the first two months to help you discover the full potential of this system. Next step: for complete descriptive material, or better yet, a private demonstration—use the coupon below.

THE INFORMATION BANK The New York Times Company

Mr. Carl Keil, Director of Marketing
The New York Times Information Bank
229 West 43rd Street
New York, N.Y. 10036
(212) 556-1111

Please have your Washington office contact us regarding:
☐ description of system; ☐ demonstration.

Name
Title_____ Phone_____
Agency or Organization_____
Address_____
City, State, Zip_____
☐ Send literature only

The Pricing Issue

A financial price schedule for the Information Bank had been published in June 1973, but another set of rates had been drawn up early in 1974. (See Appendix A for these two price schedules.) Salespeople might use either schedule and were free to offer special terms. Some customers, in fact, were getting the system free. The amount customers paid was seldom based on the amount of time they spent using the system. In some cases, the customers paid the telephone charges, while in others the charges were paid by The Information Bank.

Keil broke down the cost to the customers into three components—the CRT terminal and other equipment, lines of communication between the terminal and the central computer, and usage of the system. With regard to the hardware, he found that the average customer was paying about $400 a month for a CRT terminal, a modem,[1] and an abstract printer. Some customers were using an Incoterm CRT, a very expensive terminal which had been customized for The Information Bank. From his experience in the data-processing industry, Keil knew that terminals not customized for the Bank could perform the necessary functions perfectly adequately at a substantially lower cost and that if all the equipment were purchased or leased from one source, the total cost would probably be less. Therefore, he arranged for a computer hardware company to supply customers with a CRT terminal, a modem, and a high-speed abstract printer for only $280 a month. The company billed The Information Bank, not the Bank's individual customers, for the hardware. Keil thought the Bank would probably charge customers the amount it paid for the hardware rather than mark it up by any amount. If customers wanted a microfiche reader or reader-printer, they could purchase it from several sources. Prices ranged from $20 to $2,000.

To communicate with The Information Bank's computer, most customers used either regular direct-dial connections or WATS lines which the company already leased. On the average, customers located outside the greater New York City metropolitan area who did not have access to a company-leased WATS line paid $15 to $30 per hour in communications charges. Not only were these the most expensive communication methods, but line noise often interrupted the communication.

Keil thought The Information Bank should begin to use leased lines which provided higher-quality communication. Once it secured an adequate number of customers within a city for a leased line to be cost-effective, The Information Bank could use a time-division multiplexing line, i.e., a line which could be split into different channels to handle more than one customer simultaneously. The cost of an eight-channel line between Washington and New York was $315 per month, while the cost of a comparable line between New York and San Francisco was $2,300 per month. Each multiplexer cost $4,500. Keil had to decide whether the cost of the lines and the multiplexers would be covered by the customer or The Information Bank.

With regard to usage of the system, Keil had to decide whether The Information Bank should charge a fixed monthly fee or a fee tied to hourly usage. If he chose the latter option, he would have to decide whether the fee would be determined by the amount of use, by the time of the day the system was used, or by some combination of the two.

Unfortunately, he had very few guidelines as to which option to choose and what prices

---

[1] The type of signal produced and processed by the computer and the CRT terminals was known as a *digital* signal, while the signals transmitted over telephone lines were *analog* signals. To convert one type of signal into the other, a modem (*modulator-demodulator*) was used. Therefore, The Information Bank's computer would generate messages using digital signals which would pass through a modem before entering the telephone lines. At the customer's office, the signals would again be processed through a modem which converted them from analog to digital for use by the CRT.

would be acceptable. He noted that the Bank currently had some customers paying more than $50 per hour who apparently did not consider the price exorbitant. Other customers, however, were paying flat monthly rates for unlimited usage, while still others were paying virtually no usage fee at all. He had spoken with staff members of a commercial time-sharing service which marketed similar interactive computer time for $100 per hour. Since the service used time-division multiplexing lines, its customers did not have to pay large communications charges, however. Keil had the pricing schedules of LEXIS, SDC, and Predicasts, but since they were not really direct competitors, he was not sure how applicable their pricing schemes were to The Information Bank's situation. (See Appendix B for LEXIS's SDC's, and Predicasts's price lists.)

In deciding how to price the microfiche, Keil noted that only half the Bank's current customers subscribed to microfiche, probably, he thought, because of its high cost—$900 per year—and the widespread availability of less costly microfilm. He thought a reduction in microfiche prices would be a good marketing tactic if he decided to raise usage prices of the total system. It cost The Information Bank about $4.80 to produce a master of a fiche, and it produced about 500 masters per year. To produce a copy of a master cost about 21 cents, and the cost of handling and mailing a copy was about 75 cents. The copies (i.e., the items that were sent to the customers) were sent out 110 times a year.

Keil estimated that in 1975, the total operating costs to be incurred by The Information Bank would be about $2.5 million:

Computer lease (flat rate)	$600,000
Marketing expenses	$925,000
System improvements	$150,000
Indexing and abstracting	$700,000
Miscellaneous office expenses	$125,000

These expenses did not include the costs of any terminals, customers' modems, or other equipment because Keil assumed that these equipment costs would be passed along to customers. The $150,000 budgeted for system improvements included provisions for modifications or additions to the system's hardware and software which would be required as additional customers were brought onto the system.

Plans for the Future

Keil felt that the future of The Information Bank was extremely bright. He mentioned several products which the Bank could furnish at a minimal cost. It already offered a daily news summary, which an editor wrote from the earliest edition of the *Times*. Customers could simply call up the summary on their CRT and scan the major news events. Keil had not tracked usage of the news summary, but one day the editor who wrote it was sick, the summary was not written, and Keil's office was flooded with calls. Keil thought the Bank would soon also offer a summary of each day's business news. Another possible spin-off product was books of abstracts on particular subjects. It would cost very little to print the abstracts, and another subsidiary of The New York Times Company would actually publish the books. Finally, Keil thought that the Bank might start providing corporate profiles which gave the names, titles, and addresses of leading officers of major corporations and that it would eventually offer proprietary data to various customers.

Appendix A
Price Schedule, June 15, 1973

The following price schedule has been formulated to provide several classes of service to suit the varying needs of our customers most economically. For example, a corporate library which uses The Information Bank to produce a large volume of current awareness searches for corporate divisions and departments could achieve the lowest per-search costs by subscribing to a Class IV subscription giving unlimited use during morning hours. Conversely, a medium-sized newspaper requiring only a few searches per day, but needing the availability of the system throughout the day, would best be served by a Class I and II subscription providing limits on total hours used but fewer restrictions on when this use is made.

1. Minimum subscription duration is 4 months. Subsequent service is sold on a monthly basis. Service may be canceled following 1 month's prior written notice.
2. Training period. During the first 2 months of service, while a subscriber's staff is learning to use The Information Bank, service will be supplied on an unlimited basis during all hours of system operation for the minimum monthly subscription rate of $675. Following this period the subscriber may choose the class of service best suited to his needs.
3. Equipment and communications. Prices shown in the following list do not include CRT terminals, printers, microfiche readers, or communications services or equipment.

   However, CRT terminals and printers may be leased for up to a year on a monthly basis from The Information Bank at the rate of $163 per month for one CRT terminal plus $30 monthly maintenance and $120 per month for one hard-copy printer plus $30 maintenance. At the end of the year, the equipment may be purchased, with partial credit given for lease payments, or the lease continued with the equipment manufacturer. If the service subscription is canceled before the lease has run, The Information Bank will terminate the equipment lease at return freight cost only.

   Communications services are normally obtained for subscribers by *The Times* Communications Department and billed to them at cost.
4. Use of Information Bank data by third parties. Use of The Information Bank is normally limited to a subscriber's own organization. However, special arrangements may be made to use service in Classes I and II to supply searches to nonsubscribers. An extra charge of $250 per month is made under such arrangements.

CLASSES OF SERVICE

I

Hours of availability: 9 A.M. to 6 P.M. Monday through Friday.
Type of access: up to a total of 25 hours of on-line use per month.
Price: $675 per month (extra access is available at $20 per hour).

II

Hours of availability: 8 A.M. until system shutdown Monday through Sunday.
Type of access: up to a total of 25 hours of on-line use per month.
Price: $775 per month (extra access is available at $20 per hour).

Appendix A
Continued

III

Hours of accessibility: 8 A.M. until system shutdown Monday through Sunday.
Type of access: unlimited.
Price: $1,350 per month.

IV

Hours of accessibility: 8 A.M. to 1 P.M. Monday through Friday.
Type of access: unlimited during hours specified.
Price: $675 per month (emergency service in afternoons is available on a spot basis at
$50 per afternoon).

V

Hours of accessibility: 1 to 6 P.M. Monday through Friday.
Type of access: unlimited during hours specified.
Price: $850 per month (emergency service in mornings is available on a spot basis at $50
per morning).

THE NEW YORK TIMES ON MICROFICHE

Microfiche of the news and editorial contents of *The New York Times* on 4 × 6 inch fiche,
25× reduction. Mailed to subscribers on a weekly (Wednesday to Tuesday) basis on the
Friday after the last Tuesday of each week's group. $900/year.
(Written agreements will be entered into with *The New York Times* Sales, Inc.)

SUBSCRIPTION RATES AND OTHER TERMS, EARLY 1974

I. TERM

If subscriber provides his own terminal, the subscription is for a minimum of 6 months. After
6 months, the subscription continues automatically unless canceled. Thirty days' prior
written notice is required for cancellation.

If subscriber has *The Times* lease the terminal for him, the subscription must be for a
minimum of 1 year. Renewals will be automatic, and also for a period of 1 year, unless 30
days' prior written notice of cancellation is given.

II. START-UP PERIOD

The start-up period is defined as the first 2 months of a subscription, starting when the
installation is certified to be operational.

Appendix A
Continued

Unlimited access is permitted during the days and hours of normal operation (Monday through Friday, 8 A.M. to 12 midnight, eastern time, major holidays excepted; also most Saturdays, 9 A.M. to 5 P.M.).

A flat amount of $625 per month is charged to cover costs of installation, start-up, and training.

III. TERMINALS AND OTHER EQUIPMENT

Terminals may be selected from among the models specified by *The Times* as compatible with The Information Bank system.

Terminals may be purchased or leased by subscriber, or leased by *The Times* on behalf of subscriber.

Typical costs are:	
Incoterm CRT terminal SPD 10/20 monthly rental	$163.00
Centronics printer monthly	133.00
Maintenance for each of the above monthly	30.00
Telephone data sets (modems):	
For leased-line connections monthly	55.00
For dial-up connections monthly (approx. figure)	115.00

Microfiche readers or reader-printers are not marketed by *The Times*. A variety of models ranging in price from $100 to over $2,000 are available.

IV. COMMUNICATIONS

May be provided by subscriber

May be arranged with a common carrier through *The Times*

May be provided by The Information Bank through its network as part of the service. However, *The Times* reserves the right not to provide network service to a given location, or to discontinue service to a given location upon adequate notice. Network communications are available only in the continental United States.

V. SUBSCRIPTION RATES

Rates are effective at the start of the third month of subscriptions (*see* Section II) and do not include costs of terminals and other equipment (*see* Section III), communications costs (unless communications are provided through The Information Bank network as part of the service), and the costs of microfiche.

Rates for service including communications vary with the subscriber's distance from New York City, as follows:

Appendix A
Continued

- Zone I: 0–75   miles
- Zone II: 75–250   miles
- Zone III: 250–500   miles
- Zone IV: 500–1,000 miles
- Zone V: 1,000–1,500 miles
- Zone VI: 1,500–3,000 miles

Rates vary with the number of hours of usage (connect time) according to Table 1. Future communications rates may be adjusted downward if warranted by increased use of the system.

Table 1

Hours per month	All zones	Zone I	Zone II	Zone III	Zone IV	Zone V	Zone VI
	Without communications, per minute	With communications, per minute					
First 10	$0.75						
Second 10	0.68						
Third 10	0.63		*To be determined*				
Fourth 10	0.58						
Fifth 10	0.54						
Over 50	0.50						

Table 2

Without communications	With communications	
$875.00	Zone I:	$1,025.00
	Zone II:	1,175.00
	Zone III:	1,325.00
	Zone IV:	1,475.00
	Zone V:	1,625.00
	Zone VI:	1,775.00

Access is at any time that the system is in operation.
Subscribers will be billed a minimum of 4 hours of service per month.

FLAT-RATE OPTION. Subscribers may contract for up to 25 hours of service per month at a flat rate, as shown in Table 2. Additional hours may be purchased on a connect-time basis in accordance with the rate schedule shown in Table 1.

VI. MULTIPLE SUBSCRIPTIONS

On second and subsequent subscriptions by the same subscriber, whether or not for the same locations, hours logged on all terminals will be pooled for billing purposes.

Appendix A
Continued

VII. RESALE OF SERVICE

Special terms may be arranged for subscribers wishing to resell Information Bank materials.

VIII. MICROFICHE

Microfiche of *The New York Times* is available to subscribers at $75 a month. Sets for past years (1969–1973) are available at $600 a year.

Appendix B
Pricing Schedules of Three Major Information Storage and Retrieval Companies

LEXIS (Mead Data Central, Inc.)	**Systems Development Corporation**		
	Equipment		
$500/mo for the initial research terminal (i.e., a video display unit, a printer, and communications equipment) and all communications costs between that terminal and Mead Data Central's computer in Dayton, Ohio.* $375/mo for each additional terminal installed in same city.* $450/mo for each additional terminal installed in another city.*	Charges not available in company promotional literature.		
	Communications		
Included in equipment charges.	$10/hr via TYM-share communications plus any locally incurred charges to the nearest TYM-share city.†		
	Usage		

There are two classes of subscription. Schedule A has a minimum monthly use commitment of $1,000; schedule B has a minimum monthly use commitment of $2,500. Use charges in each class are divided into three categories: 1. Research time (peak hours) 2. Research time (off-peak hours) 3. Search time Research time is the total time a user is in contact with MDC's central computer, from the time he transmits his identification number until he terminates communications with the computer.	Data base	Hourly rate	Off-line printing per citation
	Life Science	$90	$.25
	Engineering	90	.20
	Geosciences	60	.15
	Business mgt.	45	.10
	Chemistry	45	.08
	Govt. R & D	45	.10
	Agriculture	30	.08
	Education	25	.08
	Petroleum	35	.05

Appendix B

Continued

Predicasts

Charges not available in company
promotional literature.

$10/hr via TYM-share
  communications in N. America.
$15/hr in Europe.
WATS lines and regular direct dial to
  Palo Alto could also be used.

$90/hr of connect time
$425 annual access fee for market abstracts
$360 annual access fee for F & S indexes
$500 annual access fee for domestic statistics
$500 annual access fee for international statistics

Appendix B

Continued

LEXIS (Mead Data Central, Inc.)	**Systems Development Corporation**

Search time is that small portion of research time beginning with the transmission of a search request to the central computer and ending with the appearance on the research terminal of a statement that a certain number of documents (e.g., cases) satisfy the request. Search time does not include the time when messages, replies, or documents are displayed on the terminal screen; when the user is typing requests or instructions, or reading or thinking; and when the hard-copy printer is operating.

Use charges in each category are measured to the nearest second as follows:

Schedule A

Research time (peak hours)	$97/hr
Research time (off-peak hours)	48/hr
Surcharge for search time	195/hr

Schedule B

Research time (peak hours)	$77/hr
Research time (off-peak hours)	48/hr
Surcharge for search time	195/hr

To eliminate inequities, any unused portion of the minimum monthly use commitment or any use above the minimum monthly commitment is accumulated and carried forward within each calendar quarter. There is no carryforward from one calendar to the next.

There is no additional use commitment for additional terminals.

Installation and training

$2,500 for the first terminal installed.
$200 for each additional terminal installed.
  (Covers training of all users plus written instructional and reference materials.)

Charges not available in company promotional literature.

---

*These charges apply to terminals installed in the states of Illinois, Missouri, New York, Ohio, and Texas, the District of Columbia, and some other large metropolitan areas, a list of which can be obtained from an MDC representative. Installation of LEXIS research terminals elsewhere must be by special arrangement and possibly at a special charge.

†SDC had TYM-share-entry points in 50 United States cities and three European cities.

Appendix B

Continued

Predicasts

Private instruction at
   customer's site = **$200** plus expenses
Scheduled seminar = **$50**/person or
   $100/company

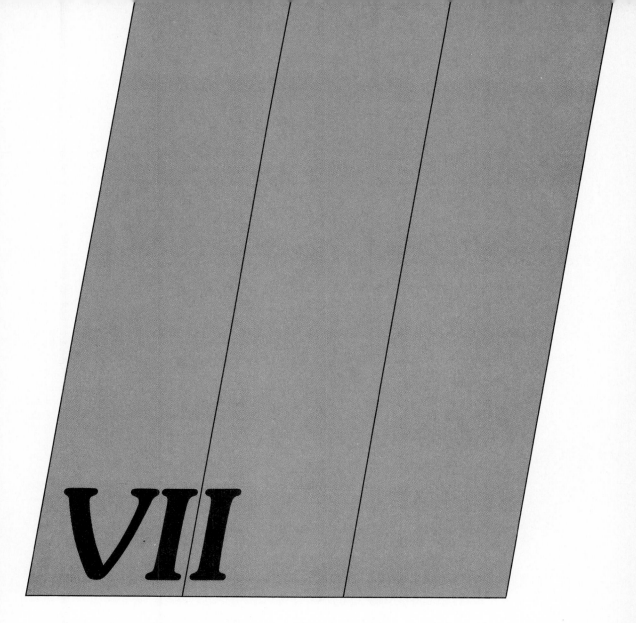

VII

Marketing Organization

A way to think about marketing organizations is that they are the houses in which marketing strategies live—and often are born. We can visualize a house in which there are spaces for each of several strategies and some common facilities that serve all spaces. As the occupants of each space grow and change in response to changes in the market environments and as new strategies are added, changes are needed in the structure if it is to continue to serve the needs of an evolving business. The firm may add new products going to different customer groups. It may shift strategic directions for some existing product lines as their markets mature. It may expand its operations geographically to become multinational in scope.

Because strategies are constantly evolving, marketing organizations must evolve as well. Not to do so is to risk losing a market position against more alert competitors.

Product, Market, and Geography

There are three basic dimensions to any marketing organization—product, market, and geography—and there are managers whose work is defined along each of these dimensions. For instance, in the IBM Data Processing Division, which is the marketing arm of IBM's intermediate-to-large computer business, there are *product managers* for each computer system in the various lines, e.g., the 4300 Series, the 303 Series, and the System/360 and System/370 computer families. Each product manager is responsible for working with IBM's development engineers to assure that the product is designed to meet user needs, identifying market applications for his or her product line, and training field sales personnel so that they can effectively represent the line to potential customers. In addition, product managers become involved in preparing sales literature, advertising, and technical service manuals. They contribute to pricing decisions. Each is responsible for doing all that he or she can to maximize sales revenue and profits for the product.

IBM's Data Processing Division also provides for *industry (market) managers*. For this purpose IBM identified eight separate markets for large computers and the software that goes with them. These are utilities, finance and securities, process, insurance, distribution, manufacturing, transportation, and public sector. Each industry group is distinguished from the others in the way it purchases and/or uses computers and the software programs designed for its applications.

Market managers are responsible for planning the strategies for these several market segments. What products will go into each market? What communications programs will be planned for each? How much field sales time will be required to reach potential new customers and to serve existing accounts? What systems design and field service resources will be required? What new product development work must be done to meet identified customer needs and to maintain a technical lead against competition?

Market managers, like product managers, work through and with others in the organization—the field sales force, the development engineering group, and the manufacturing plants, for example—to develop their plans and get them carried out.

In designing marketing organizations it is critically important that the market management dimension be based on a clear and explicit market segmentation scheme because each market management position becomes a center for formulating and implementing strategy. That means segmenting the market in a way that groups potential customers according to the way they perceive the product, value it, purchase it, and use it.

Inevitably the characteristics of any market change over the product life cycle. New segments emerge, and the key factors distinguishing one from another will change both with product technology and market maturity. Organizations need to be adapted to reflect evolving segmentation patterns, especially along the market management dimension.

IBM's Data Processing Division also has a geographic dimension. In the field, it is organized into 14 marketing regions, each headed by a *regional manager*. Within each region are 8 to 12 branch offices, each one responsible for defined territories and certain groups of customers. The manager of any given branch is responsible for developing, organizing, and managing field sales and customer service personnel in their assigned geographic areas. The branch manager is also responsible for the customer interface, for contributing field intelligence to the formulation of product and market strategies, and for carrying out these strategic programs.

The discussion thus far has described three facets of a marketing organization: product, market, and geography. It may be noted parenthetically that in many companies, especially in the consumer goods industries, product and market are combined organizationally. This is because these companies implicitly recognize only one market segment. That segment might be defined for some of the companies as "the homemaker shopping in a supermarket." At Sears, Roebuck the market is defined simply as "middle America." In such cases the organization structure typically provides for product management and area management.

Marketing organizations also include certain kinds of staff resources. There may be market research managers who make studies of buyer behavior, often using outside market research firms. Often the marketing organization will have advertising managers who work with agencies in designing advertising copy and planning media campaigns. There may also be specialists for planning promotions, for package design, and for direct-mail advertising. These resources typically work with product and market managers as staff specialists.

Allocating Resources to Programs

At a general management level a key concern is how to allocate resources to product and market programs. For this purpose, the field sales force is a resource, as are the production facilities, the R&D laboratories, and the field service units. Each represents a body of human skills and capacities, equipment, and capital.

The general manager has several options. He or she may elect to serve all product and/or market programs through a single set of "pooled" resources. At the other end of the scale, he or she may elect to give each program its own resources—e.g., its own field sales force, its own manufacturing facilities, and its own R&D laboratories. Under the latter option each program becomes a functionally integrated business.

A third possibility is to pool some resources but not others. At General Electric, for example, several product departments share a common field sales organization, but in every other respect each is an independent business with its own resources. There are a number of pooled sales organizations at GE, each selling to such different markets as utilities, OEMs, and resellers. Any one sales organization may carry the products of a large number of product departments; any product department may sell through several pooled sales forces.

A fourth possibility is to utilize pooled resources, each centrally managed, but specialize within each resource by market program. For example, IBM's Data Processing Division has program-specialized field branches in the larger cities. There are branches which serve only customers in the finance and securities fields, branches that specialize in selling to public sector organizations, and branches that deal only with manufacturing companies. Specialization of this sort may be advantageous if it is important for field sales personnel to develop expertise in how a customer set purchases and uses the product. Specialization may be practical to undertake if the base of business in terms of current and potential sales volume in a geographic area is large enough to support it.

This introduction has described the basic dimensions of marketing organizations and suggested some of the questions that are posed for managers. The cases which follow describe problems in marketing organization in consumer goods and industrial companies, in domestic and multinational corporations. Taken all together they suggest that one of the most critical and difficult tasks of the manager is designing market-oriented organizations and adapting them continually to changes in strategy and in response to changing market conditions and evolving technology. How to segment markets for organizing purposes; how to relate strategic programs to business resources; how to preserve a healthy balance among the product, market, and geography dimensions of the organization—these are key concerns for both marketing managers and general managers. And the most successful firms are the ones in which considerable attention is paid to the task of organizing the business to serve its several markets.

The Architects Collaborative, Inc.

Ralph Biggadike • Ulrich Wiechmann

Peter Holmes, in charge of job development for The Architects Collaborative (TAC), Cambridge, Massachusetts, was reflecting on the news that his firm had failed to win a $20 million hospital job in Salisbury, Maryland. He and his colleagues had been surprised by this decision. They had gained the impression from the medical planning consultants advising the hospital board that the selection process would be rational, and they had expected TAC to benefit from such a process. Now, early 1974, Holmes was wondering about the implications of this failure for his job development activities. Some of the questions running through his mind were: Just how appropriate was TAC's method of obtaining jobs? Could the distinctive features of TAC's operating style be used to obtain more jobs? Ought TAC to change its client presenta-

Ralph Biggadike is a professor of marketing at the Colgate Darden Graduate School of Business Administration, University of Virginia. Ulrich Wiechmann is an associate professor of business administration at the Harvard Graduate School of Business Administration.

tions? What was the most useful role he could play in TAC's future? Finally, he recalled the words of the TAC partner in charge of the Salisbury project, Roland Kluver. On the flight back to Cambridge after the presentation, Kluver had commented:

> I wonder if I should have emphasized the fact that the partners and professionals representing TAC at a client presentation are the *actual* people who will do the job. We are not like some companies who have a special presentation force consisting of super-salesmen dressed in $300 suits. Those people make the pitch but have probably not designed a hospital for years and will not be seen in Salisbury again. With TAC, the client sees at the presentation what he'll get later on.

The Architects Collaborative

The Architects Collaborative, Inc., was founded in 1945 by eight architects who were committed to the collaborative problem-solving approach introduced by one of the founders, Walter Gropius, at the Bauhaus during the 1920s and, later, at the Harvard Graduate School of Design. By early 1974, the staff numbered 272 employees. The number of professional employees stood at 217, including 12 partners (four of the original eight founding partners were still active) and 28 associates. Among the professional employees, there were 156 architects and 5 registered landscape architects, plus 18 people in a landscape architecture and planning department, 5 engineers, 16 people in an interiors and space planning department, 12 people in a construction supervision department, and 5 people in a graphics department. Billings had risen over the years but had been on a plateau during the last 4 years.

TAC's rank among the *Engineering-News Record* (ENR) Top 500 Design Firms in 1973 was 81, and it was in the $5 million–$7.5 million billings category.[1] Its rank and billings since 1964 (when ENR first began its 500 listing) are shown in Exhibit 1. TAC classified itself for ENR's

[1] Billings were defined by ENR as "fees, reimbursables, staff loans, or temporary staff transfers." (Reimbursables are fees paid by the architect to a consultant or subcontractor and passed on to the client.)

EXHIBIT 1
TAC RANK AND BILLINGS AMONG TOP 500 DESIGN FIRMS, 1964–1973

	Billings category (million $)	Rank
1964	1.0–2.49	92
1965	2.5–4.9	78
1966	2.5–4.9	88
1967	2.5–4.9	100
1968	2.5–4.9	83
1969	5.0–7.49	77
1970	5.0–7.49	67
1971	5.0–7.49	66
1972	5.0–7.5	75
1973	5.0–7.5	81

Source: Compiled from *Engineering-News Record,* 1964–1973.

EXHIBIT 2
BREAKDOWN OF TAC BILLINGS BY TYPE OF PROJECT, 1973

Health institutions	33%
Business, government, industrial	22
Educational institutions	19
Tourism	12
Housing	10
Urban Development	2
Other	2

Source: Company records.

survey as an architectural firm. (Other choices were architect-engineers, engineer-architects, engineers, planners, and various combinations of these.) In 1973, TAC was the largest architecture-only firm. Its practice mix included jobs in health, business, government, education, tourism, housing, and urban development. Exhibit 2 shows a breakdown of 1973 billings by type of project. TAC's mix was considered quite diverse and stemmed from the generalist orientation that was a characteristic of its collaborative approach.

The Gropius collaborative method, as developed at TAC, had two hallmarks: final design decisions rested with individual partners (although all partners would comment upon and criticize all projects); and project teams consisted of "rounded" architects—architects who had similar skills and who were interested in all aspects of architectural practice—rather than complementary specialists. The attempted result was a team of generalists who collaborated on a project as equals. Collaboration was achieved when the objectivity of the project task instead of the personal ambitions and viewpoints of individual members dominated team interaction. To the founding partners, collaboration was a way of life and an attitude of mind. They expressed their understanding of collaboration as follows:

Louis McMillen: "We realized that we had to recognize the virtues and tolerate the weaknesses in each other and acknowledge our own shortcomings. With the group firmly established on this base, we were able to achieve the most important aspect of collaboration—effective intergroup criticism."

Walter Gropius: "It describes . . . the attitude of a man who has been able to empty his mind of prejudice and all non-considerations and has thereby arrived at a state of new innocence which allows him to penetrate to the very core of his task."

Sarah Harkness: "A world that believes only in survival through competition must always be at war. And if the winner is preoccupied with winning he may find himself on a mountain he never would have climbed."

The collaborative concept was a direct influence on the design attitudes of TAC professionals. One founding partner, John Harkness, described a common denominator in TAC buildings as follows:

> . . . a specific attitude in the handling of space, both within and between buildings, an attitude which looks for dynamic spaces, flowing one to another, thereby producing the sense of involvement.

Walter Gropius had felt collaboration as a stimulus to consider the *user* of buildings:

> . . . we believe that the potential user of a building should be studied first, for his practical and spiritual needs, which vary with the customs and climate of the region and with each category and purpose of a building, determine the design of the plan and its three-dimensional appearance.

And to Roland Kluver, there was an emphasis at TAC on an architect's responsibility to society:

> An architect's greatest role is as a public servant because, after all, we're changing the physical environment.

TAC members believed that the avoidance of a partnership of specialists had been their greatest source of strength. More recently, however, some specialism had crept in with the introduction of support services such as interior design, landscaping, and specifications, although none of these services had representation on the board of management. Also, there were some signs of partners beginning to concentrate on building types such as medical facilities and the related problems of the financing and supply of medical services. Roland Kluver, for example, was particularly interested in the medical building field. One small group was developing a specialty in design for the physically handicapped user. Another group was experimenting with office landscaping. Administration, too, had brought in its crop of specialists: apart from the computerization of payrolls, TAC's programmers and an outside consultant had developed the Facilities Information System. This system recorded information on every single room in a building and provided a variety of printouts to help designers. It had proved particularly useful for design work on complex projects such as hospitals.

Collaboration and Organization at TAC

Originally, collaboration at TAC involved equal salaries and profit sharing among the partners because equality was considered to be the very basis of TAC's teamwork. Even fees for outside work, such as teaching, were at one time considered to be income of the partnership. In more recent times, these points of collaboration had been dropped. TAC's practice of not offering personal rewards for securing a job or running a project efficiently continued. Profit sharing and pension plans included partners and associates.

The principal organizational mechanism was a weekly meeting of partners and associates. Both design and business matters were discussed at the meetings, which were known internally as the design review process. Project leaders and their assistants presented drawings, models, and other information at the meetings for thorough consideration and criticism. No new design was "frozen" until it had received the attention of the entire group. Project leaders were free to accept or reject suggestions because to maintain the integrity of original conception, it was considered important that one person should have final authority.

Only partners could be project leaders at TAC. The founding partners had believed strongly that the client had a right to expect a partner to be in charge of a project from start to finish. Accordingly, the partner who would handle the project supervised the preliminary interviews, the preparation of submissions required by clients to evaluate competing clients, and control of the project if TAC obtained it.

Project control in a TAC team was the responsibility of the partner in charge, assisted by the associate and the job captain (often, these latter two were the same person). Two years before, project control procedures had been computerized, and job captains could now obtain printouts showing the percentage of the work completed and whether the project was ahead or behind budgeted time and expenditures. Responsibility for keeping this information current lay with the job captains. Every 2 weeks, they were supposed to submit job captains' report forms giving details about the progress of projects. The return rate for these report forms, however, had never reached 100 percent, and some forms continued to show no changes in a project for several weeks. The system also included a printout summarizing the status, earnings, expenses, and profit to date for all TAC projects, as well as what billings had been mailed. While it was possible to tell from this form who was running unprofitable projects, it had never been used as an internal management tool because such procedures were considered inappropriate in a collaborative effort devoted to quality design.

The organization after incorporation in 1963, which necessitated the appointment of a president and directors, was adjusted to enable collaboration to continue. Since a "frozen" hierarchy did not fit the collaborative concept, the responsibilities of president and director were rotated. Formal voting was used only for legal decisions; the TAC tradition of design decisions being made by the sense of the meeting rather than by vote continued.

One founding partner described TAC's way of working as "motivated anarchy." This description, he suggested, captured the excitement and involvement generated by the collaborative approach at TAC. He emphasized:

> We try to avoid formality, hierarchy, and rigidity. We do have system—for example, the design review process at the weekly meetings—but system must never be allowed to take priority over the work, even if office inefficiency and costs rise.

To this partner, the choice was between the more common and economically rewarding collaboration of specialists and the more demanding but creatively productive collaboration of equals. He commented:

> I'm proud to say that TAC has chosen the "equals" alternative. And we try to protect personal identity while obtaining consensus.

The "demanding" aspects of the "equals" alternative were primarily caused by its lack of structure. Kluver, a more recently appointed partner, commented:

> Lack of structure can also mean that individuals don't know where they stand, what their incentives are, and what their motivation should be directed towards. The impact can be severe too on job development, because new jobs are not assigned to partners on the basis of expertise or experience but who is light on work and interested. "Anybody can do anything" may have been O.K. in earlier days, but is it O.K. now in these technological times? Surely, collaboration can apply to a team of specialists, where each member respects the others for what they can do and he cannot, just as much as it can apply to a team of equals.

Recent Developments

Several trends in the external environment had begun to affect TAC. First, its New England location meant that it was some distance from the growth areas of the South and West. Exhibit 3 shows the receipts of architectural, engineering, and land surveying firms by region, as recorded in the 1967 and 1972 *Census of Business*. Exhibit 4 shows the value of buildings signed up by region for 1970 and 1973, in actual and real dollars, as estimated by *Engineering-News Record*.

Second, the administration's plans for revenue sharing between federal and local governments might favor local architectural firms over national architects. Revenue sharing consisted of a transfer of money to local governments, some of which was to be spent in specific fields and the remainder as local authorities desired. The fields primarily affected were education, urban community development, law enforcement, and personnel training. Many buildings which would previously have been competed for in Washington would now be fought for locally, and the local government would select the winning architect.

Third, client needs were becoming more diversified, and some architects argued that architectural firms had to recruit specialists and offer more services to clients. They contended that modern-day community and social planning involved economists, sociologists, systems analysts, engineers of all kinds, and ecologists and that many firms had already added these services. Some knowledgeable observers of the construction industry even went so far as to suggest that the role of the traditional architect was increasingly subordinate to that of these specialists. Furthermore, these specialists could also form separate revenue-producing departments. For example, some architects had departments for environmental design and planning, interior space design, graphics, and construction management which served their employers as support departments, and they marketed themselves separately as specialists in their field. Other observers argued that most clients still thought in terms of specialists and preferred to hire a specialist for a specialist job. This view represented the traditional view in the profession. It held that the combination of owner-architect-constructor was the best means of getting quality design and quality construction. Peter Holmes held this view firmly:

> As an architectural firm, as opposed to an architectural-engineering firm, we have much more flexibility over choosing engineers. We can evaluate engineering firms on their current work load and their specialty and choose the most suitable for the job we have to do. Furthermore, we believe that the truly innovative engineers, and this applies particularly to structural engineers, are independent, not part of some design conglomerate.

Some idea of trends in the growth of the multiprofessional firm can be gained from studying the ENR 500 for 1969 and 1973. These appear in Exhibit 5.

The addition of services was an important issue for firms pursuing a growth objective. Income from fees[2] increased as the firm's product-service mix broadened. Another way of increasing revenues was to widen the range of building types handled by the architectural firm. A broad range of building types also enabled a firm to obtain greater stability in its growth. For example, when housing was down, government building activity might be up.

Fourth, the lack of land and the growing complexity of buildings was leading some clients to expect studies on land use, zoning, and financial feasibility from their architects. Such activities, which might be termed "prearchitectural" work, could enable a firm to increase its chances of winning a job.

Finally, the profession seemed to think that "times were getting tougher." The professional journals during the '70s had been filled with comments about "escalating building costs and

---

[2]Fee income is different from billings. Fees are flat percentages of some value (usually construction value) for services rendered, whereas billings include reimbursables—money paid to subcontractors (consulting engineers, landscape architects, etc.). Therefore, adding services does not change a firm's billings but does change its fees received.

EXHIBIT 3
RECEIPTS OF ARCHITECTURAL, ENGINEERING, AND LAND SURVEYING FIRMS (WITH PAYROLL)

Regional comparison

	Number of firms		Receipts ($000)		Change of receipts, 1967–1972 (%)
	1967	1972	1967	1972	
Northeast	1,491	1,768	$248,054	$ 416,719	+68
Middle Atlantic	3,861	4,284	993,202	1,514,738	53
East North Central	3,632	4,142	791,959	1,096,105	38
West North Central	1,454	1,638	256,284	397,523	55
South Atlantic	3,191	4,297	590,689	1,038,557	76
East South Central	1,087	1,331	115,236	225,151	95
West South Central	2,430	2,855	305,417	618,517	103
Mountain	1,188	1,535	128,041	205,692	61
Pacific	3,669	4,350	806,789	1,211,347	50
U.S. total	21,953	26,200	$4,235,671	$6,724,349	
			Building cost index =100.0	=160.0	

Top 10 mainland states according to percentage receipts increase

	1967	1972	Change (%)
1. Florida	$ 98,701	$304,816	+209
2. Maryland	77,674	212,409	174
3. Colorado	41,431	100,484	143
4. Texas	177,606	410,991	131
5. Washington	72,597	166,662	130
6. Tennessee	39,717	86,594	118
7. Arizona	36,284	77,564	114
8. Alaska	7,939	16,974	114
9. North Carolina	46,154	94,585	105
10. Georgia	68,986	139,701	103

Selected other states

	1967	1972	Change (%)
California	$673,581	$907,898	+35
Illinois	287,700	426,109	48
Massachusetts	162,493	276,069	70
Michigan	215,125	276,602	30
New Jersey	185,249	277,101	50
New York	523,626	802,891	54
Pennsylvania	284,327	434,746	53

Source: Compiled from 1967 and 1972 *Census of Business*, SIC 891, U.S. Department of Commerce.

EXHIBIT 4
ACTUAL AND REAL DOLLAR VALUE OF BUILDING PROJECTS
Construction Dollars—$000

	1970	1973	Change (%)
U.S. total	$38,547	$52,980	+37
U.S. building cost index (1967=100)	124.4	169.3	
U.S. total real dollars	$30,986	$31,294	+ 1
Regional breakdown			
New England	$2,438	$3,315	+36
Boston BCI (1967=100)	119	175	
New England real dollars	$2,049	$1,894	− 8
Middle Atlantic	$9,691	$10,043	+ 4
New York BCI	125	172	
Middle Atlantic real dollars	$7,753	$5,839	−25
South	$6,551	$12,274	+87
Atlanta BCI	127	173	
South real dollars	$5,158	$7,095	+38
Middle West	$6,978	$9,146	+31
Chicago BCI	125	165	
Middle West real dollars	$5,582	$5,543	− ½
Mississippi to Rockies	$7,241	$9,560	+32
Denver BCI	124	167	
Mississippi to Rockies real dollars	$5,840	$5,725	− 2
Far West	$5,648	$8,643	+53
Los Angeles BCI	122	173	
Far West real dollars	$4,630	$4,996	+ 8

Source: Compiled from *Engineering-News Record,* January 1971 and 1973.

EXHIBIT 5
TRENDS IN MULTIPROFESSIONAL FIRMS, 1969 AND 1973
Self-Description of Firms Listed among the Top 500 Design Firms

	1973	1969
Architects	41	52
Architects-engineers	86	104
Architects-planners	10	6
Architects-engineers-planners	26	18
Engineers-architects	87	83
Engineers-architects-planners	14	7
Engineers	143	160
Engineers-planners	13	6
Engineers-soils	11	11
Soils/geotechnical engineers	9	6
Multiple combinations of above	5	7
	445	460
Top design constructors	55	40
	500	500

Source: Compiled from *Engineering-News Record,* 1964–1973.

shrinking budgets," "more legislation, particularly environmental, which was lengthening the time from drawing-board to building site," "reduced fee percentages," and "investigation by the Department of Justice for violations of the Sherman Act." There were signs, in the journals at least, that attention was turning to management issues and the exploration of the question "Should architects become more businesslike?"

Job Development at TAC

Until recently, TAC had not attempted to systematize and coordinate its job development activities. Such an approach was not considered appropriate to the collaborative concept. TAC had always relied on repeat clients and word-of-mouth recommendations. This policy had been successful in the past because within the architectural community there was no doubt that TAC's reputation for design was of the very highest. Typically, a client or a client representative asked TAC if it was interested in a particular project and whether it would send someone for an interview. If one of the partners was interested in the building type, then he or she would attend the interview. The recent billings pressure had, however, led to the appointment of Peter Holmes to begin some job development, although he was requested to avoid the use of that term whenever possible. In talking about his job, Holmes said he had three main duties:

> First, I must seek out ways of finding out about jobs—just how do you learn of an opportunity? Second, I have to persuade the partners to pick up the ball on a job. I do this by matching the design potential of a project with the design interests of the partner. Third, I must try to promote our thinking about marketing: what should we be doing in marketing—our strategy, points we stress, the nature of our product or service and the design of promotional materials, etc.

Holmes emphasized that his work was still in the early days and that he had to proceed most cautiously. Just the other day, a founding partner grumbled to him:

> I don't know why we are doing job development any more. I'm too busy now.

Holmes believed that every TAC partner was a designer, first and foremost. No partner allocated time to marketing because it would take time away from what they felt they ought to be doing—designing buildings. Holmes commented:

> Any time spent on marketing is an intrusion. Every partner in this office would be happy with just being given enough challenging and interesting work.

TAC did have some promotional materials which presented photographs and displays of past TAC award-winning designs. Holmes had also thought about a newsletter but had been

told that this would not be appropriate for TAC. TAC also, of course, prepared folders for each client presentation which contained details about the TAC collaborative approach and previous projects completed, as well as details about the partner and staff who would handle the project. Holmes was not happy with some of these materials and TAC's approach to presentations. He explained:

> We don't spend enough time on analyzing what clients need and what they want to hear: we tend to assume clients want visually superior architecture, and so we show this in our presentations.

Holmes also experienced trouble in getting partners to commit themselves for client presentations:

> Sometimes I turn down job opportunities because I cannot get a partner to go to the interview.

Another problem on Holmes's mind was TAC's ability to compete nationally. He explained:

> If we are to grow, then we'll have to go for more and more jobs outside New England. I must think through why any clients outside Massachusetts would choose us. What can we offer him? A related question is, should we introduce branch offices? The founding partners have always been against it, but is this view appropriate now?

As he mused over these aspects of TAC and the recent loss of the Salisbury hospital project, Holmes thought it might help to reconstruct the chain of events in this project and analyze the competition.

The Salisbury Hospital Project

In the middle of January, Roland Kluver received a call from Jack Solovoy, a health and financial planning consultant working for Health Facilities Corporation (HFC) of Northbrook, Illinois. He invited TAC to preliminary interviews for the $20 million new hospital in Salisbury, Maryland. Five other firms had also been invited. After the preliminary interviews, the group was to be narrowed to three, and then a more complete interview would take place. Kluver accepted the invitation, and the preliminary interview was set for January 28.

Kluver and Holmes flew to Salisbury for the preliminary interview. They arrived well before the scheduled time for the interview and spent the time looking around Salisbury, as well as taking a 2-hour tour of the hospital's existing facilities and the site for the new hospital. Both were impressed with the town, the existing hospital, and the site. Kluver recalled:

> Salisbury is a farming community, and the people had those healthy and persevering qualities that this country admired so much. In fact, I was reminded of my own folks and upbringing in the Midwest. The new site was clean and pleasantly situated. All in all, I think both of us agreed that this was a project TAC would like to be associated with.

The first part of the interview was with Jack Solovoy and Ed Grube, a medical planning consultant who had been retained to advise on medical details. Solovoy explained that he was working out the financing of the hospital and needed an architect as soon as possible to give greater definition and certainty to the hospital. The conversation then turned to TAC's previous work in hospitals. Kluver emphasized that TAC had substantial experience in the complexities of hospital financing; he cited the $40 million Lahey Clinic in Boston as a most recent example.

Holmes and Kluver recalled that they both obtained the impression that Solovoy and Grube were looking for an architect who would provide a complementary relationship to them rather than a competitive one. They judged the meeting to have gone very well for TAC on this criterion. They also thought Kluver's experience with both medical architecture and medical financing had made a favorable impression. The

second half of the meeting included the Salisbury Hospital administrator, his assistant, and a trustee. It largely duplicated the first half of the meeting.

Two days later, Solovoy called Kluver and told him that TAC was in the final threesome, along with RTKL and Caudill, Rowlett and Scott (CRS). He also asked if he and Grube could visit TAC offices to "prime you for the final interview," in his words, and a visit in the following week was arranged. Solovoy indicated that they did not plan to visit the offices of RTKL and CRS.

After the usual tour around the office, Solovoy asked for a discussion on the fee and the contract. They agreed that the standard AIA contract should be used. Regarding the fee, Solovoy and Grube said that size of fee should not be an issue in the selection process. So Solovoy suggested that the fee be set now and at ½ percent lower than usual—that is, 6½ percent as opposed to 7 percent. He added that the other two finalists had already agreed on 6½ percent. After establishing that the percentage would be calculated on the combined construction-equipment cost and that fixed payment intervals were acceptable, Kluver agreed to 6½ percent.

Grube then explained how they proposed that the actual selection be made. He expressed the view that the selection of an architect should follow a rational process. A selection decision was not only extremely important, he explained, but also surrounded by risk and uncertainty because the selection committee was composed of individuals with varying levels of hospital sophistication. Furthermore, the interview process itself was inherently intensive and often lacking in unity of analysis of each competing architect. Consequently, he planned a selection process that would uniformly apply to three architects, as follows:

> Your formal presentation should take no longer than 45 minutes, thus leaving you 30 minutes for questioning. Use the graphics with which you feel

most comfortable and which suit your presentation format. We do *not* want you to invest in special presentation forms for this interview; rather we want you to have a *minimum* monetary investment. More importantly, we want to learn about your firm and its capabilities in the hospital field, and in the most simple context possible.

After all of the interviews, the entire Executive Committee will score the candidates, utilizing the "Factor Analysis—Architect Selection" which has been recast and reweighted for the Executive Committee. [See Exhibit 6.]

We are also asking each firm to fill in a standardized pre-interview form. This consists of a letter from you to the Hospital Administrator explaining how you would approach the planning process [extracts from TAC's letter appear in Exhibit 7], background details on your firm and a record of your previous hospital work [Exhibit 8]. Don't include any photographs or other graphics; just follow the standardized format.

Both Solovoy and Grube emphasized that the final interview would be informal and with an emphasis on substantive matters in a thorough but relaxed way. Extravagant presentations would be inappropriate.

Holmes and Kluver were pleased with these arrangements. Holmes recalled:

Although we don't think the interview method is the best method of selecting an architect, because of the showmanship that is involved, I recall thinking that Grube's method was a big improvement and one that would help us.

Kluver remembered that he had been particularly enthusiastic about the "Factor Analysis" sheet:

I told Grube this was exactly how architects should be evaluated and that I would like to see the scores afterward because they could be helpful.

A few days later, all the final interview arrangements discussed above were confirmed by letter from Grube. The interview was set for Tuesday, February 19, and the order of firms, determined by lottery, was as follows:

12:45 P.M.	RTKL
2:00 P.M.	Break
2:15 P.M.	CRS
3:30 P.M.	Break
3:45 P.M.	TAC
5:00 P.M.	Interviews concluded

About a week before the final interview, Solovoy called Holmes and told him that a

EXHIBIT 6
FACTOR ANALYSIS—ARCHITECT SELECTION
Evaluation for Salisbury Hospital Project

Factors	Weight	RTKL	CRS	TAC
Hospital related (past 5 years)				
Prior health field experience	10			
Site master planning experience	5			
Innovation and creativity	2			
Demonstrated willingness to involve hosp. personnel*	7			
Understanding of role of consultant	4			

EXHIBIT 6
Continued

Factors	Weight	RTKL	CRS	TAC
Design related				
Ability to relate functional program to design concept	5			
Flexibility in design concepts	4			
Aesthetic appearance	2			
Understanding of transport/distribution systems	3			
Landscaping design capability	1			
Technical related (hospital)				
Experience in monitoring construction progress	5			
Capability in handling parking requirements	1			
Control of structural, mech., and elec. system design process	5			
Fast track construction				
Hospital experience	5			
Method of work with contract manager	2			
Ability to negotiate contracts to a guaranteed minimum	3			
Use of CPM	1			
Method of scheduling working drawings concurrent w. const.	2			
Administrative				
Control and supervision of design development	4			
Method of estimating project costs	2			
Method of scheduling project progress	3			
Fee structure	5			
Total score				

*And medical staff.

1. Assign a score for each factor for each candidate. Score depends on the factor. For example: if factor is five, score on a scale of 1 to 5.
2. Multiply the score in each factor by the weight given it. This yields a factor score weight.
3. Add the total score weights to determine a total.
4. The candidate with the highest score is the one selected.

Source: TAC records.

EXHIBIT 7
EXTRACTS FROM TAC'S TRANSMITTAL LETTER TO THE SALISBURY HOSPITAL ADMINISTRATOR DESCRIBING ITS PLANNING PROCESS

TAC's approach to Hospital Planning, as with all complex planning projects, begins from two basic principles. First, each planning effort is different and special (notwithstanding the commonalities also to be found and compared). Second, the most appropriate and flexible planning unit is the collaborative team. The *individuals* of the team are selected for their experience in the general building type; the *composition* of the team is made to respond to the uniqueness of the problem.

At the outset of work, the planning needs of Peninsula General Hospital, in both their normal and special aspects, will be thoroughly evaluated by the principal-in-charge from TAC, the consultants from Tribrook and HFA and the key trustees and administrators. From this evaluation, TAC will compose the architectural design team. The TAC design team, the "Architect," thus becomes an integral unit of the larger project team composed of the Owner-User, Financial Consultant, Health Facilities Programmer, Architect, and Construction Manager and/or Contractor.

The successful planning enterprise requires a process that is mutually agreed upon by the participants; a game plan, as it were, that is laid out sensibly and practically and followed through conscientiously. Such a game plan might be comprised of the following activities:

Goal Setting—The desire to renew, to grow, and to excel as a health care facility.

Statement of Need—The "how" of reaching the long-term goals; the articulate, statistical and definitive functional program.

Assessment of Resources—The realistic statement of available capital and of the ability to carry debt. Land holding is also a resource, as are professional skills to deliver health care.

Assessment of Constraints—The recognition that there are always "conditioners" of planning action such as the geometry of land holding, timing constraints, and local conditions.

Posing of Alternatives, Evaluation and Selection—This is the "design" phase of the architectural work and involves master planning and analysis of growth concepts.

Implementation—Specific building design, including overall configuration, space planning, and building systems design, construction, and furnishings and equipment.

It does not really matter that these activities often overlap and that the team members play a smaller or more dominant role at different times. What is important is that, although the process is complex, it is quite amenable to understanding and management. TAC can contribute in all of the activities and would hope to participate in the management of the process as well.

Clearly, much of the early work would need to be done in Salisbury. For certain periods of time, the design team, including engineering consultants as vital members of the team, would virtually "encamp" at or near the Hospital. As a parallel early activity, a contractor with hospital building experience, reasonable size, and local knowledge should be engaged to undertake cost verification and prediction with the architect and other consultants, and all subsequent design activity would thus be tested against the prediction.

With architectural input, Tribrook's functional program would be evolved into a detailed architectural program. From this, departmental adjacencies would be developed, then floor

EXHIBIT 7
Continued

configurations, circulation patterns for personnel and goods; then on to stacking concepts and finally building and site alternates for functional and cost evaluation. This process leads to the development of the preliminary design solution for the proposed facility. With the agreement of all the members of the Project Team, this design is then elaborated and the details of all the architectural elements are developed, ultimately leading to construction documents and, finally, construction.

In summary, The Architects Collaborative is committed to the collaborative team approach to planning physical facilities, has extensive experience in the development of medical projects, and is most interested in providing the highest level of professional service for your program at Peninsula General Hospital. We look forward to meeting again with you on February 19th and hope at that time to elaborate on our capabilities and experience and answer any remaining questions that you might have.

Source: TAC records.

EXHIBIT 8
BACKGROUND DETAILS FORM GIVEN TO TAC FOR THE SALISBURY HOSPITAL PROJECT

HISTORY: Describe the history of your organization, when it was founded and by whom. State the number of professionals, their description as well as the number of support employees.

(one-half page)

PRACTICE: Briefly describe your professional practice.

(one-half page)

ENGINEERING: Do you have in-house engineering capability? If so, please describe that capability. If not, state the firm or firms with whom you would associate on *this* project; describe the scope of their practice, your previous association with them, and their previous hospital experience.

(one page)

COST CONTROL: Describe the method of cost control utilized during the design stages.

(one-half page)

AWARDS: List all awards received during the course of your firm's professional practice in two separate categories:

1. Health care related
2. Other

CLIENTS: List major non-hospital clients.

EXHIBIT 8
Continued

FORM ON WHICH TO PROVIDE DETAILS OF PREVIOUS HOSPITAL WORK

1. Number client beds	2. Project scope	3. Const. cost	4. Project status	5. Contract methodology

1. **CLIENT:**   List hospital clients only; those you have served from January 1, 1969, to the present time; state name and address of clients as well as the person whom we may contact as a reference in your behalf.
2. **PROJECT SCOPE:**   Indicate the type of project: addition, replacement, renovation or new, whether project consisted of nursing units, ancillary departments, research, etc. If master planning was included, please state.
3. **CONSTRUCTION COST:**   Actual or anticipated. State in millions, e.g., $12M.
4. **PROJECT STATUS:**   State date your work was initiated, present status and/or date construction was completed.
5. **CONTRACT METHODOLOGY:**   Use of CM, CM/General Contractor, guaranteed max., fast tracking, standard bidding, etc.

Source: TAC records.

developer on the Executive Committee flatly refused to pay any architect 6½ percent and that the fee was to be dropped to 6 percent. The other two architectural firms had already agreed, and he wanted to know if 6 percent was acceptable to TAC. Kluver was on the West Coast, and Holmes eventually got this news to him. Kluver recalled that he was extremely annoyed at this development and nearly dropped the project there and then. He commented:

> In fact, I should have followed TAC's normal policy of not discussing the fee before the job. Apart from this, however, it conflicted with their intention to make the selection process rational: after all, fee haggling should not influence the choice of an architect and, anyway, we'll deliver more than a ½ percent in extra quality. Consider, too, that half a percent on six and a half is one part in thirteen, and that is probably our net profit.

After discussion with the treasurer, Kluver reluctantly accepted the 6 percent fee.

On the morning of the nineteenth, Kluver, Ed Summersby—the project architect—and Holmes flew to Washington. There they met up with Dick Brooker, another TAC partner, and Marvin Mass, a mechanical engineer from Cosentini Associates of New York City, whom Kluver had asked to join the presentation because he had heard that some Executive Committee members were particularly worried about mechanical aspects. The presentation team had not met before the nineteenth, as Kluver, Brooker, and Summersby had all been out of the office for several days. On the plane journey to Washington, Holmes detailed to Kluver the 20 or so slides he had brought along. The first few presented some general shots of TAC buildings for a variety of uses, and the majority showed recent hospital projects such as the $98 million University of Minnesota Health Services Expansion, the $40 million Lahey Clinic and Hospital, and the $10 million Montego Bay, Jamaica, Hospital.

In order to get from Washington, D.C., to Salisbury, Maryland, the team had to charter a small plane. After a somewhat bumpy ride, they arrived just in time for the interview. When they entered the interview room, Kluver was surprised to see a chairperson with a gavel and the

Executive Committee facing them in a row of chairs. The chairperson brought the meeting "to order" and introduced Kluver. "Suddenly," Kluver reminisced, "the presentation was on and in a much more formal manner than any of us had expected."

Kluver was familiar with all the slides brought by Holmes and presented them one by one. He then presented the members of the TAC team who would actually work on the project (although, as he had recalled earlier, he felt that perhaps he did not emphasize this sufficiently). Kluver spent some time on TAC's experience with the Lahey Clinic because, as noted, it had involved participation in the financing and provision of medical services. These aspects also were important in the Salisbury Hospital project, and Kluver believed it was important to stress TAC's understanding of them. He also covered TAC's concern for the user of medical facilities as well as for the owner, and he promised that the design team would "encamp" at or near the hospital during the early stages of the project.

After the completion of the presentation there were no questions, and the members of the board did not seem too animated. Grube asked Kluver and his team to wait, as he thought that a decision would be available in about an hour.

Eventually, Grube emerged from the interview room and told Kluver that CRS had won the contract. Kluver asked him why and was told, "Your presentation was a little disjointed, and some felt you may not be able to solve the problems of a small hospital." Kluver asked him about the "Factor Analysis" sheet. Grube replied, "They didn't fill it in; what can I say?"

The Winner—Caudill, Rowlett and Scott

From published materials, it was possible to put together the following description of the strategy and structure of the winner of the Salisbury project—CRS, Houston, Texas.

CRS was formed in 1949 by William Caudill and John M. Rowlett on the philosophy that the complexity of client needs demanded a team of specialists. In 1971, the firm employed 250 professionals, including 125 architects, 38 engineers (mechanical, civil, structural, and electrical), and 87 people in specialist and support services (landscaping, interior design, computing services, construction management, planning, and graphics). CRS's rank among the *Engineering-News Record* Top 500 Design Firms in 1973 was 25, and its billings were in the $20 million–$24.9 million category. Rank and billings category since 1964 are shown in Exhibit 9. CRS classified itself as an architectural-engineering firm; it was the fourth largest architectural-engineering firm in 1973 and the twenty-third largest in 1969.

Building Design and Construction (January 1971) reported that CRS's practice revenue was split 90 percent from building services and 10 percent from nonbuilding services, and 70 percent from educational facilities, 23 percent from

EXHIBIT 9
RANK AND BILLINGS OF CRS AMONG TOP 500 DESIGN FIRMS, 1964–1973

	Billings category (million $)	Rank
1964	1.0–2.49	129
1965	2.5–4.9	98
1966	2.5–4.9	66
1967	2.5–4.9	80
1968	2.5–4.9	78
1969	5.0–7.49	73
1970	7.5–9.9	62
1971	7.5–9.9	52
1972	10.0–14.9	34
1973	20.0–24.9	25

Source: Compiled from *Engineering-News Record,* 1964–1973.

health facilities, 4 percent from commercial projects, and 3 percent from miscellaneous activities. This journal expressed the opinion, after surveying the company, that "it is clear that, insofar as any firm can know the future, CRS knows where it is going and how it will get there." The firm's goals were reported in the *AIA Journal* (August 1969) and these appear in Exhibit 10.

The team approach was emphasized because, in the view of CRS members, it represented the best means of delivering the ever-increasing degree of expertness or specialization while still achieving integration. CRS executives seemed to believe firmly that industrialization of the building process, technological breakthroughs in materials, increased legislation, and tighter budgeting were here to stay. The only

---

EXHIBIT 10
THE 12 GOALS OF CAUDILL, ROWLETT AND SCOTT

CRS is committed to the multioffice form of practice with total firm unity. Concentrated effort should be made to search for methods of unifying decentralization and diversified situations with special consideration given to the "circuit manager," revolving design board, etc.

CRS is committed to both socially significant architecture and great-example architecture.

CRS is committed to nonbuilding services—programming, surveys, feasibility studies, computer applications, research and planning. An effort to promote programming and research should be accelerated. CRS must have more superconsultants and nationally known experts.

CRS is committed to a diversified practice. Hardly any building type will be off-limits, for future schools will be mixed with housing, offices, stores, and civic centers.

CRS is committed to a serious study of urbanization in keeping with the nation's effort to solve the problems of the inner city.

CRS is committed to setting up an aggressive recruiting program.

CRS is committed to a thorough personnel evaluation process. In order to judge individual performance, this is essential, especially in periods of fast growth.

CRS is committed to developing professional growth. The idea of a "CRS school" has been discussed for years. Now we must set one up in order to keep up with technological, procedural and even philosophical changes. In addition, a CRS sabbatical for professional growth must be established.

CRS is committed to making a profit and practicing architecture in a businesslike manner.

CRS is committed to further exploration and refinement of the design board and the separate design groups concept. Past performance indicates that design is improving and promotion is benefiting. The design board also has great worth as a coordinating device for giving unity to the separate and scattered design groups, but serious consideration should be given to returning to the broader scope of the quality control board issue.

CRS is committed to a spirit of openness—sharing CRS developments with all people, including the profession.

CRS is committed to the development of national leaders with the capability and dedication to make a significant contribution in all facets of architecture.

Source: "Forward-Geared People and Processes," a practice profile of CRS in *American Institute of Architects Journal*, August 1969.

way, claimed CRS directors, in which projects could be efficiently completed, and without major mishaps occurring, was for each team member to have a specialty. Concentration would enable each member to keep on top of developments in his or her field and ensure that the project team had the latest information on all the many aspects of construction and building. CRS teams consisted of architects who specialized in aspects of architecture and nonarchitects who contributed specialized skills in urban affairs, systems analysis, and behavioral science. William Caudill described his view of the team in his book,[3] *Architecture by Team*, as follows:

> The idea of architecture by team has three underlying secondary ideas: (1) the team is a genius; (2) the client/user is a member of the team; and (3) the team is an ever-expanding unit, not limited to the design profession.

The CRS team of specialists approach was an explicit rejection of the prima donna concept where a building was one person's personal statement and the generalist view of an architect. Caudill commented in the *Building Design and Construction* article:

> We feel one man can't design a building—it'll take at least three, usually more. The process involves integrating people from management, design, and technology into a team we call a "task troika."

In addition to the team approach, company literature and journal articles emphasized three other characteristics about CRS's strategy. These were control techniques, the provision of services, and an attention to design.

In control techniques, CRS emphasized systems building, fast-track construction scheduling, computer-generated cost estimating, and critical path scheduling. Systems building was described as "a concentration on the traditionally expensive components of buildings in an effort to identify and develop those elements of a project

that can be used universally."[4] Fast-track scheduling enabled overlaps among the four phases of building. Usually, "programming precedes design, bidding and construction phases. Each phase has to be completed before the next one can begin. This traditional process wastes time and money."[5] Fast-track sorted out those elements of each phase which could be handled concurrently or overlapped and often enabled reductions in design and construction time 25 to 50 percent.

The provision of services stemmed directly from a CRS perception that client needs had changed. Increasingly, CRS representatives commented in an *AIA Journal* (August 1969) article, the client demanded programming,[6] planning, and feasibility analyses. Furthermore, it was in these areas that outside experts offered tough competition to traditional architects. Consequently, providing services both delivered a better product to the client and dealt with encroachers.

CRS executives emphasized their attention to design. A CRS brochure commented:

> A money-making building doesn't make money lying on the drafting boards. Design, however, is our business—not racing. Our reputation has been built on design quality, so we have always been faced with the problem of quality versus speed.

One technique used to get quality design and speed was "squatting." The project team literally moved to the client's premises or a nearby motel to solve problems and design the project on the spot. A CRS executive commented in *Building Design and Construction* (January 1971):

---

[3]William Caudill, *Architecture by Team*, Van Nostrand Reinhold Company, New York, 1971.

[4]James R. Cagley, John Almont Pierce, and Paul N. Detz (CRS staff members), "Systems Building: Need and Response," *Building Systems Design*, November 1971.

[5]Malcolm T. Tengler and Jack W. Smith, "A Fast-Track to Quality, Speed and Economy in Hospital Construction," *Building Systems Design*, November 1971, pp. 19–23.

[6]Some clients now expected their architect to advise on what should be built—and, indeed, on whether they should build at all—as well as provide design skills.

If we send a team to the mountains of Colorado to design a building, there is a lot better chance of achieving an indigenous flavor than if we were to design that building in Houston.

Another advantage is that clients participated in the excitement of the design stage of their project. This involvement could encourage their commitment to the building and settle details rapidly so that planning time was saved.

Organization at CRS

To implement its strategy, CRS had adopted a divisionalized organizational structure. Each division manager was responsible for the profitability of his or her division. Fees were allocated by central management to the various divisions according to their proportionate role in the project. A company publication explained that the CRS divisions were structured as a system known as CRS Design Associates in such a way that the system:

> . . . melds together the special types of expertise of its member firms, and brings to its clients a total services package that is markedly stronger than the sum of its parts.

CRS Design Associates (known as CRSDA) consisted of CRS Development, CRS Computing Research Systems Corporation (known as CRS2), and CRS Construction Management, Inc. (known as CRS/CM). The organization chart for the main company, CRS (and CRS Development), is shown in Exhibit 11. The function of each of the member companies of CRSDA was as follows.

CRS—as noted, the main company— provided a full range of services in the programming and design of buildings and the master planning of building complexes. As seen in Exhibit 11, this member company had three major components: corporate management, central services, and operating divisions. The operating divisions were of three types: geo-graphic, health, and services. The geographic divisions (based in Houston, New York, and Los Angeles) offered project management, design and planning skills, and construction management. The health division was formed to quicken the development of specialist knowledge. The service divisions were Construction Documents, Engineering, Interiors and Graphics, and Management Planning Services. The service divisions were primarily support divisions, but it was expected that they would generate some outside income.

Quality control was personally headed by William Caudill. It consisted of an employees' jury, which scored each CRS project by answering questions about its function, form, and economy. To Caudill, function "concerns the task—the way people move about to do the job they have to do. . . . Form is not only what it looks like but also what it feels like. . . . Economy concerns the principle of maximum effect with minimum means." The final score was a "quality quotient"—a summation of the project's performance on these three criteria.

Job development and client presentations were handled by *CRS Development* (CRSD)—a separate division within CRSDA (see Exhibit 11) staffed with generalists and building-type specialists. The role of CRSD was to promote the total firm, and its formation was another example of the group's commitment to specialization. A potential client's first contact was with two CRSD representatives: an appropriate specialist and a CRS vice president, who explained the firm's overall capabilities. These *CRS Development* representatives stayed with the client until the final decision on which firm of architects was to obtain the project had been made.

Geographic expansion also came under *CRS Development* because it was the firm's strategy to first create the clients through promotion, before staffing an office with designers. For example, a recently opened office in Chicago had no designers but did have an office manager

EXHIBIT 11
CRS ORGANIZATION CHART

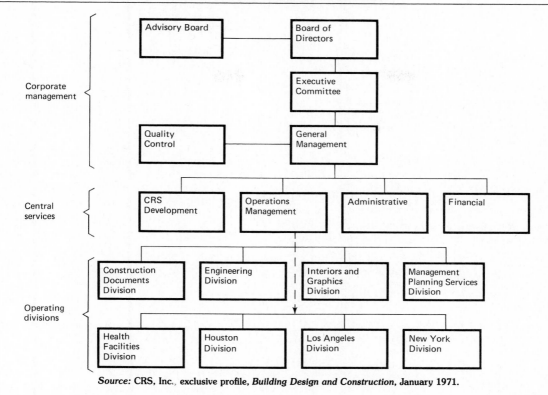

Source: CRS, Inc., exclusive profile, *Building Design and Construction*, January 1971.

and a promotional team. When the promotional team had generated enough work to justify designers being based in Chicago permanently, the office would be staffed with professionals and become a geographic division, and a profit center, in its own right. Meanwhile, any work created by the Chicago promotional team was handled in Houston.

When CRSD won a project, it was transferred to the appropriate geographic or specialized operating division. C. Herbert Paseur, CRS vice president, commented to *Building Design and Construction*:

We balance work between the divisions. We don't observe strict geographic boundaries—we can flex those to meet the demands of a specific project or to balance the division work load.

The operating division appointed a project manager, who in turn built the "task troika" team, coordinated the service divisions, and managed the allocation of CRS resources to the project.

CRS2 and CRS/CM, the other two companies in the CRSDA system, dealt with computing services and construction management, respectively. Both also marketed their services to outside clients.

Conclusion

In discussing the loss of the Salisbury contract, Roland Kluver commented:

> Salisbury is a farming community, and I wonder if I came across as an Ivy League, Northerner. Of course I'm not, but maybe they thought I was selling them. Perhaps I should have thought out how to handle the client more thoroughly and planned to allay any fears and apprehensions of the people.

As for the "Factor Analysis" sheet, Kluver commented:

> TAC would benefit under a rational selection process. It is obvious, therefore, that as the sheet was not used, TAC did not show up well. Why could they not spend another 15 minutes or so filling in the form? As it turned out, it was just the same old popularity contest.

Holmes agreed that it was a great shame for TAC that the "Factor Analysis" sheet was not used.

> I really believed that Grube and Solovoy were as close as one can get to professionalizing the interview method for selecting an architect. Personally, I think interviews are poor because all finalists tend to look similar in a final presentation and so the final decision has to be based on showmanship. I would really like to change the whole process to one where the client inspects other buildings constructed by the competing architects and talks to the owners and users.

Holmes continued:

> As I think about what my job should be and how TAC gets jobs, I think about our style. I wonder, can we do a better job of marketing our style?

48 Sears, Roebuck and Co.

Steven H. Star • E. Raymond Corey

Sears, Roebuck and Co. was the world's largest general merchandise company, with 1966 sales of slightly more than $6.8 billion. Approximately 77 percent of this sales volume was derived from Sears retail stores; the remaining 23 percent represented sales through the Sears catalog.

In January 1967, Sears operated 801 retail stores in the United States. The Sears 1966 *Annual Report* segregated these stores into three categories:

Complete department stores	199
Medium-size department stores (carrying extensive assortments of general merchandise)	363
Hard lines stores (carrying major household appliances, hard lines, sporting goods, and automotive supplies)	<u>239</u>
	801

Steven H. Star was formerly an associate professor at the Harvard Graduate School of Business Administration. E. Raymond Corey is the Malcolm P. McNair Professor of Marketing at the Harvard Graduate School of Business Administration.

The Sears catalog order business was serviced by 11 catalog order plants, each serving a geographic area. A considerable number of catalog orders were placed at catalog, retail, and telephone sales offices rather than being sent through the mail. Sears operated 1,653 such offices. This number represented an increase of 60 percent since 1961, and an increase of over 20 percent from the previous year.

Organization

A simplified organization chart showing reporting relationships as they existed in early 1967 is presented in Exhibit 1.[1] The company was headed by a chair and president, to whom reported the vice presidents of merchandising,

[1]This organization chart and all other charts included in this case were prepared by the casewriters. Since the founding of the company, Sears managemenťs had made it a point *not* to have formal organization charts.

EXHIBIT 1
CORPORATE ORGANIZATION CHART (1967)

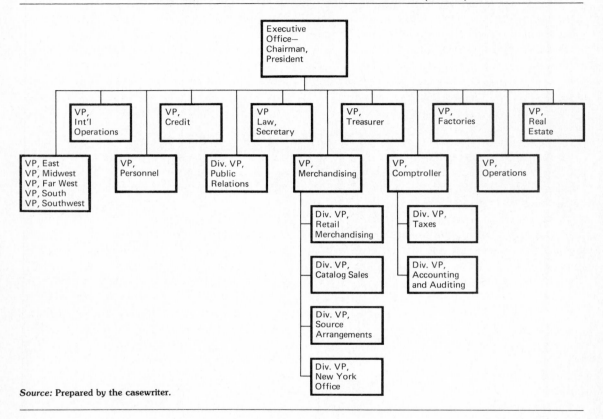

Source: **Prepared by the casewriter.**

personnel, public relations, credit, law factories, real estate, and operations; the corporate controller and treasurer; five territorial vice presidents; and a vice president of international operations.

All field operations in the United States were under the control of the five territorial vice presidents. Each territory was divided into retail groups, zones,[2] and catalog order regions. A

group consisted of the stores in a major metropolitan market. A zone covered a fairly wide area and included the stores in that area which were not assigned to groups. A catalog order region covered the area served by a catalog order plant and included the catalog order offices located in that area. In the eastern territory, for example, there were 14 groups (containing 113 stores), three zones (containing 91 stores), and two catalog order regions.

Each group was headed by a group manager,

[2]A group generally consisted of a number of stores in a single metropolitan market, while a zone consisted of stores in smaller one-store cities and towns. The key difference, according to Sears executives, was one of media usage. In a metropolitan market, where all customers could be reached by metropolitan newspapers, it was considered essential that

all stores have the same merchandise available at common prices. In a zone, however, there was much less of a need to coordinate the pricing policies of individual stores.

and each zone was headed by a zone manager. The managers reported to the territorial vice presidents. Retail store managers reported to the group and zone managers. The catalog order plants were headed by plant managers, who also reported to the territorial vice presidents. The managers of the catalog order offices reported to the plant managers, generally through several layers of field administration.

Each territory, group, zone, catalog order plant, and store was operated as a profit center. Managers at each level had considerable freedom to operate their organizational units as they wished, subject to policies established by the headquarters departments or higher levels of territorial management.

Sears employees generally made a distinction between the "parent" and the "field" when discussing the company's organization. The field consisted of the five territories, while the parent included the various headquarters departments.

The largest parent department was the merchandising department, which was responsible for the development, procurement, and promotion of all merchandise sold in Sears stores or catalogs. The merchandising department included 51 buying departments, a retail merchandising department, a catalog merchandising department, a merchandise control department, and the sears merchandise laboratory.

Each buying department was headed by a national merchandise manager, who reported to the vice president of merchandising. The retail divisions were headed by division managers, who reported to their store managers (generally through one or two layers of store management).

The national merchandise managers had no authority over the field. While the stores generally did not sell merchandise which had not been bought by a buying department, they were not required to order particular merchandise items. If a buying department purchased 100,000 pink toasters, for example, and the division managers did not wish to order pink toasters, the buying department found itself with an inventory of 100,000 pink toasters.

Two important exceptions to this pattern should be noted. Each buying department received a specific number of pages in each Sears catalog. Having received these pages, the buying department was free to place whatever items it wished in that catalog, subject only to page limitations and catalog staff approval. The catalog thus differed from retail stores in that a buying department could select the merchandise which would be displayed in a catalog but could not specifically do so in the retail stores.

The other exception concerned merchandise items designated as "basic-basic items." If a buying department designated a line as "basic-basic," all retail stores with over 32,500 square feet of selling space were required to carry that line. "Basic-basic" items accounted for more than 46 percent of Sears retail sales but a much smaller percentage (6 percent) of the items sold by Sears. Even in the case of "basic-basic" items, the division managers had considerable autonomy. One division manager might order 12 of a "basic-basic" item, for example, while another division manager in a similar store might choose to order 12 dozen in expectation of a different rate of sales.

One Sears executive commented on the concept of field autonomy as follows:

> It is impossible to understand Sears' organization without fully understanding our concept of autonomy. Everything we do at parent takes the form of a recommendation when sent to the field. We spend a lot of money on advertising mats for use by the field, for example, but a group or store is perfectly free to prepare its own advertising if, taking the costs of local advertising preparation into account, it feels it can make more money that way.
>
> In practice, the field does follow most parent recommendations. With few exceptions, it orders the merchandise selected by the buying departments, uses parent-prepared advertising in one way or another, and follows the procedures established by the various parent departments.
>
> You should not, however, allow this willingness

to follow parent recommendations mislead you. The important thing about autonomy is that it exists—as a right!—not that it is used. The right of the field to reject our recommendations is the best possible way to insure that our recommendations are correct and practical. There is no critic more severe than a retail store executive!

Recent Developments

In discussing the company's organization, Sears executives cited two developments as having particular significance for the future. The first was a fundamental change in the nature of the catalog order business, bringing it much closer to the retail store business. The second was related to fundamental changes in consumer buying behavior—from "need" buying to "want" buying.

The Catalog Order Business

Sears had historically operated the retail stores and the catalog as two separate businesses. In general, the catalog customer had lived in a small town or on a farm and had not had access to a Sears retail store. He or she had received a Sears catalog in the mail and had then mailed an order to the catalog order plant serving the area. The catalog order plant had then shipped the merchandise, generally by mail. With the access to Sears retail stores, by 1967, these trends had gone so far that Sears executives believed that it was no longer possible to differentiate between retail customers and catalog customers. As one executive explained:

> They are really the same people. The same customer will buy some items from the catalog; others from a retail store. It depends on the kind of item, how busy she is when she decides to "shop," local traffic conditions, and a host of other factors.

The change in the characteristics of the catalog order customer contributed to a major change in the nature of catalog order shopping.

By 1967, only 10 percent of catalog sales were carried out through the mail. The remaining 90 percent of catalog sales were transacted in one of three ways:

1. At catalog order desks in retail stores. These desks had all the Sears catalogs available, and merchandise not available in the store could be provided. The large Sears general catalog, it should be noted, contained approximately six times as many items as were stocked by the largest Sears stores.
2. At catalog order offices, which were essentially like catalog order desks, except that they were in separate facilities (generally in small towns) rather than in Sears retail stores. A customer typically came into a catalog order office to place an order and then picked up the merchandise at the office approximately 48 hours later.
3. By calling a telephone sales office. A customer ordered merchandise from a catalog in his or her possession.

The Boston Experiment. One unmistakable effect of these developments was that the catalog order plants were now in the retail business. In 1967, there were twice as many catalog and telephone sales offices (under catalog plant management) as there were retail stores. In many ways, operating catalog and telephone sales offices was more like operating retail stores than like operating catalog plants. It seemed possible, therefore, that it might be more appropriate for the catalog and telephone sales offices to report to the retail organization than to the catalog plants.

In an attempt to test this possibility, all catalog and telephone sales offices in the Boston catalog order region were assigned to the groups and zones in whose territories they were located. This organizational change permitted the Boston catalog order plant to dispense with its field sales organization and was intended to facilitate coordination between retail stores and catalog and telephone sales offices in the same geographic area.

In early 1967, the experiment had been in progress for less than a year, and Sears executives believed that it was still too early to assess results. While sales had been encouraging and expenses had been reduced somewhat, many executives believed that the critical factor was the separate identity of the catalog order business. As one executive explained:

> It really comes down to a single issue. The catalog stores would undoubtedly benefit from professional retail management and closer coordination with the retail stores. On the other hand, they presently benefit from a specialized field organization, whose performance is measured solely on the basis of catalog sales. We are trying to find out which of these considerations is more important. The Boston experiment is an attempt to answer this question.

"Need Buying" versus "Want Buying"

The other major change in Sears's way of doing business was related to a fundamental change in consumer purchasing behavior. With greater affluence, a growing proportion of United States consumer expenditures was for merchandise the consumer "desired," or "wanted," rather than merchandise that she "needed." According to Sears executives, the consumer engaged in "want buying" was susceptible to a different merchandising approach than the customer engaged in "need buying." If a customer "needed" an item, these executives reasoned, she would scan advertisements and/or search for it in a catalog or in a store. If she only "wanted" it, however, she was unlikely to make a purchase unless the item was brought dramatically to her attention. In merchandising to the "want" market, therefore, it was necessary to present the consumer with advertising and displays which themselves drew her attention. Having seen the advertisement, or having entered the selling area, she was likely to purchase the item which

she found that she wanted; she would not, however, search for that item, as she would in the case of "need" merchandise.

Serving the "want" market gave Sears an opportunity to move toward higher price points in its merchandising lines with concomitant increases in gross margins. It also had significant implications for merchandising, advertising, branding, in-store display, and organization. Merchandising was affected in that serving the "want" market would mean offering more items with style appeal. Since style or fashion cycles tended to be short, there would be a clear need to manage inventories well and to plan promotions and markdowns in a timely way.

"Want" item marketing, too, could mean higher levels of advertising relative to sales, national in scope, and featuring clusters of related items. Sears advertising had traditionally been single-item-oriented and largely local in nature. A single page of newspaper advertising, for example, might contain advertisements for lawn mowers, clothes washers, children's underwear, brassieres, and kitchen furniture, to use an extreme example.

A further implication concerned branding. "Want" marketing would require adding new Sears brands, some national brand names, and some brands identified with leading personalities in fields such as sports and entertainment.

Finally, changes would be needed in the way Sears organized its vast buying organization. Each of Sears's 51 buying departments was highly independent, procuring and merchandising its product line with little regard for the activities of related buying departments. In women's clothing, for example, separate buying departments were responsible for lingerie (Department 638), brassieres and girdles (Department 618), and nylon hosiery (Department 675). While the national merchandise managers heading these departments often met in the corridors or at lunch, they rarely conducted business together. In at least one case, two national merchandise managers in a single category had never been in each other's offices, even though both had been in their present positions for several years.

Coordination, where it existed, had been largely due to the efforts of personnel in the retail general merchandising office. A number of category merchandisers reported to the divisional vice president of retail merchandising. These category merchandisers had each been responsible for overseeing (but *not* directing) the advertising and promotional programs of several related buying departments. In many cases, they had worked with the buying departments assigned to them, and with the advertising and sales promotion staffs, to develop programs featuring merchandise from several buying departments.

In early 1967, Mr. James Button, vice president of merchandising, undertook to establish 15 merchandise categories: home fashions, home appliances, automotive, recreation, men's apparel, shoes, notions and fashion fabrics, women's apparel, intimate apparel, children's apparel, hardware store, home improvement (installed), toys, candy, and specialties (miscellaneous).[3]

Each category consisted of several related buying departments. A senior national merchandise manager was elected chair of each category. The categories were expected to develop joint category plans for presentation to parent executives and the field. To aid them in this task, several parent departments (e.g., advertising, display, retail merchandising) realigned their organizations to assign specific individuals or work groups to each category.

In commenting on this change, the vice president of merchandising explained:

Category merchandising began in parent in our marketing effort directed by our retail merchandise staff. What I am trying to do is to modify our organization and procedures to conform to what has already happened to maximize the value of what we offer the field, and—ultimately—the consumer.

I am trying to do this without changing our basic structure. While we have category chairmen, they have no authority over the other national merchandise managers in their categories. In fact, the chairman is elected by the other national merchandise managers in the category. All national merchandise managers still report to me! The job of the category chairman is to preside at meetings, and to give me one person to talk to when I want to know what is happening in a particular category.

Although Sears had moved in the early 1960s toward serving the "want" markets with such lines as Ted Williams[4] sporting goods, the new strategy became closely identified with Mr. Button. Mr. Button had joined Sears in 1939. Two years later he was named as General Wood's office assistant. He then rose rapidly in the Sears buying organization as a buyer, assistant in buying to the merchandising vice president, and general manager of the Sears fashion buying offices in New York. From 1962 to 1966 Mr. Button served as president of Simpsons-Sears Limited, Sears's Canadian affiliate. In this assignment, he made effective use of market research to identify consumer preferences and buying behavior. Then, finding that traditional newspaper media were not effective in developing markets for new line additions, he turned increasingly to national media, particularly television.

It was with this background that he came in 1966 to his new post as vice president of merchandising and began vigorously implementing the new Sears "want" marketing strategy. According to Mr. Button:

Markets for products with better function, better design, higher styles, higher prices, are just waiting to be served at full margins and do not necessarily lend themselves to unadulterated price exploita-

---

[3]Actually, five such merchandise category organizations were put in place, and then, at the direction of Sears's chair, no further groupings were established.

[4]Ted Williams was famous as a baseball player for the Boston Red Sox.

tions. The appeal must be to the fancy of the consumer in the infinite variations of their tastes, desires, and wants.[5]

Under this program, Sears eventually introduced a long list of brands, including Road-Handler tires, DieHard batteries, Toughskins jeans, Ah-Bra brassieres, Winnie-the-Pooh children's clothes, Doesn't Slip slips, Traveller knit suits, Thumbs Up pants, Easy Living paint, and Power Mite vacuum cleaners.

Merchandising

On November 8, 1966, the newly appointed vice president of merchandising called a meeting of all Sears buying personnel. No such meeting had been held for some time. In his remarks to the buyers, the vice president of merchandising described the buyers' responsibilities:

You, the buyer, are responsible for everything that has to do with your lines of merchandise. As buyers you have been assigned to the narrowest product line responsibilities possible commensurate with the known potentials of those lines.

This structure enables *you* to learn and master *your* lines and be responsible for an understanding of your consumer—your market—the product, research and development—where to have it made—what costs you generate—under what contractual arrangement it will be produced—what assortments you will have—what prices—what packaging—when it will be offered—what type of display and advertising—what guarantee—how it will be promoted—what training, servicing, etc., is required.

There is nothing as it relates to a line that the buyer is not responsible for, including the inventory (old and new)—sales—the growth—and, above all, the profit.

This is an overwhelming responsibility—an awesome assignment.

But interestingly enough I have never known the perfect buyer—that buyer who incorporates in

his education, experience, or aptitudes, all of the characteristics necessary for the perfect buyer. I have met, and have personally known, some who indulge themselves with the fantasy that somehow they were blessed with special powers—not so for those of us less gifted.

Do our talents lie in creativity—that sensitive area which transforms a consumer want, desire, or need into physical product?

Do they lie more in the economic structure of the buying arrangement, or perhaps in the special gifted area of selling and promoting? Usually our aptitudes include one or two of the areas, but I have yet to see, for example, the strong figure-oriented aptitude be creative in merchandise, or vice versa.

Each of us has talents that predominate, and each of us has weaknesses that are evident.

Fortunately, we, in Sears, do not have to be perfect, *but we do have to be good administrators*—because for every talent we might lack—the company, in its infinite wisdom, has made up for it—there is—today—no area of your responsibility that the company does not provide the services of a gifted specialist to advise and counsel you. From industrial engineers to any fanciful named designer, to the most exotic testing equipment . . . from cost accountant to home economist . . . to controller . . . from attorney to promotional specialist . . . services have been and are available to the buyer.

The Buying Departments

Each of Sears's 51 buying departments was headed by a national merchandise manager. Reporting to each national merchandise manager were a retail sales manager, a catalog sales manager, a merchandise controller, and 6 to 25 buyers. The retail sales manager and catalog **sales manager developed programs to promote their departments' merchandise through their** respective channels of distribution. The merchandise controller was responsible for preparing inventory budgets and for keeping track of commitments to sources, inventories, and other control-oriented data.

The buying departments arranged for the

---

[5]Excerpt from a speech to security analysts at Goldman Sachs & Co., December 15, 1969.

availability of products which the stores could then order; they were not able to place the merchandise automatically in the stores.[6] The method used to inform the stores of product availability was the use of "merchandise lists," which contained all the necessary information as to how to merchandise a line. These lists were issued seasonally, yearly, or at least every 2 years. Division managers in the stores ordered merchandise from these lists, generally directly from manufacturing sources.

In addition, each buying department offered merchandise in the monthly "Combo." The Combo listed merchandise which would be promoted during the month in question, generally at reduced prices to both the stores and consumers. An advertising layout book and display recommendations were sent to the stores at the same time as the Combo; they were to be used in support of the promotions planned for the month.

Merchandise was placed in the catalog through a different process. Each buying department was allotted a specific number of pages which it was relatively free to use as it wished. In practice, however, the amount of space allotted to a department was at least partially determined by what the department planned to do with it.

A significant percentage of Sears's merchandise was bought on a basic known-cost basis. Under this type of arrangement, Sears specified the quantity and type of merchandise it wished to receive over a relatively long time period, and the source agreed to supply Sears with cost data, which were subject to an audit. Sears then paid the source the cost, plus an agreed-upon profit margin. In these cases, Sears absorbed certain costs directly, such as the cost of tooling or R&D,

and sometimes procured materials (such as fabrics) for the source concerned.

On the basis of the theory that the Sears merchandising department, as a large and highly professional organization, could buy more effectively than competing retailers, buyers accumulated credits in a so-called 599 account, which represented the margin of difference. Goods purchased from Sears's sources at one price were transferred to the retail stores at a higher "market" price. This practice was known as "overbilling." The transfer price for any item was based on the buyer's estimate of what competing retailers would have to pay to independent sources for the same item. The differences between purchase cost and transfer price, credited to each buying department's 599 account, could be used by that department for a range of purposes. Charges to the account, for example, were made to finance suppliers' tool-and-die costs, new-product development, national advertising, sales contests, field promotions, and the costs of extra sales personnel on the selling floor. The field could also charge markdowns against the 599 account.

Although it was not explicitly stated, buyers believed that the extent of their contributions to the 599 account through overbilling was perceived by their superiors as a key measure of buying performance. This perception took on particular meaning because buying department personnel received a significant portion of their compensation in the form of bonuses, the amounts of which were closely (although not systematically) related to an estimate of contribution to sales and profits.

Department 609

The hardware buying department (Department 609) bought and merchandised power tools, hand tools, lawn and garden tools, lawn mowers, snow blowers, welders, cabinet hardware, builders' hardware, and a wide variety of general hardware ranging from nails and screws to

---

[6]In most retail merchandising chains, the buyers purchased merchandise for shipment to specific stores and thus had considerably more authority than Sears buyers. Most Sears executives believed that this procedure would not be practicable for Sears because of the large number of stores in the chain.

mailboxes. Department 609 was one of Sears's largest departments in sales, number of stock-keeping units (6,372), and number of sources (411).

At one time, the hardware department had been responsible for product lines presently assigned to Departments 606 (recreation and sporting goods), 611 (housewares), 630 (paints), 634 (small electrical appliances), 642 (plumbing, heating, and cooling), and 664 (building materials), but these departments had been spun off from Department 609 as the hardware business grew.

Department 609 had 11 buyers, each assigned a reasonably narrow product line. (See Exhibit 2 for illustrations of buying assignments.) The retail sales office consisted of a sales manager and five assistant retail sales managers. Each assistant retail sales manager had functional responsibilities (e.g., shopping reports and sales contests), a product line assignment (e.g., hand tools), and responsibility for liaison with one of Sears's five territories. The department also included a catalog sales manager, a merchandise controller, and approximately 65 clerical personnel. The catalog sales manager, besides being responsible for the selection of merchandise and preparation of copy for the catalog, prepared the retail merchandise lists and retail catalogs for hand and power tools.

EXHIBIT 2
HARDWARE DEPARTMENT BUYING ASSIGNMENTS (ILLUSTRATIVE)
Merchandise Lines of Three Buyers in Department 609

Buyer A

Line 1—Electric motors and electrically driven hand tools

1. Electric hand saws
2. Electric hand saw accessories
3. Electric drill kits
4. Electric drills
5. Electric drill accessories and attachments
6. Drills, twists and stands, jigs and sharpening stands
7. Circle and gasket cutters
8. Power wood bits and accessories
9. Electric impact wrenches
10. Pneumatic tools
11. Pneumatic tool accessories
12. Saber saws
13. Saber saw accessories and blades
14. Electric sander/polishers
15. Electric sander/polisher accessories
16. Electric grinder (no. 2584)
17. Electric grinder accessories
18. Electric routers
19. Electric router accessories
20. Electric planers
21. Tool cases

Line 2—Power tools and accessories

26. Roto trowels and midget vibrators

Line 7—Lawn and garden tools

16. Electric edgers and accessories
17. Electric hedge trimmers and accessories

EXHIBIT 2
Continued

Buyer B

Line 1—Electric motors and electrically driven hand tools

22. Motors
23. Electric bench grinders

Line 2—Power tools and accessories

1. Bench and floor model saws
2. Bench and floor model saw accessories
3. Radial saws
4. Radial saw accessories
5. Band saws
6. Band saw accessories
7. Jigsaws
8. Jigsaw blades
9. Drill presses
10. Drill press accessories
11. Thickness planers, jointer planers, and accessories
12. Sanders
13. Wood lathes
14. Wood lathe accessories
15. Wood shapers, cutters, and accessories

Line 2—Power tools and accessories

16. Belt-driven grinders, mandrels, and polishing heads
17. Metal lathes
18. Metal lathe accessories
19. Metal lathe chucks
20. Machine stands and accessories
21. 6″–12″ circular blades
22. Dado sets
23. Molding heads and cutters
24. Power hacksaws
25. Line shafts, shaft hangers, coupling, etc.
27. Tool lights
28. V-belts and accessories
29. V-pulleys
30. Flexible shafts and accessories
31. Publications
34. Furniture kits

Line 3—Carpenters' and masons' tools

33. Workbenches

Line 5—Shop tools and supplies

1. Shop vacuums
2. Shop vacuum accessories

EXHIBIT 2

Continued

Buyer C

Line 1—Electric motors and electrically driven hand tools

24. Arc welders
25. Arc welder accessories

Line 2—Power tools and accessories

32. Gem makers and accessories
33. Miscellaneous hobby supplies and publications

Line 3—Carpenters' and masons' tools

30. Surveying instruments
31. Brushes, wire
32. Hand grinder and grinding wheel dressers

Line 5—Shop tools and supplies

3. Oxyacetylene welders
4. Oxyacetylene welder accessories
5. Buffs, buffing wheels, and compound
6. Sanding discs
7. Wire wheel brushes
8. Sanding belts
9. Glue and adhesives
10. Coated abrasive products
11. Karbo grit products
12. Steel wool
13. Stones, grinding wheels, and points
23. Dowels
24. Respirators, goggles, glasses, and shields

One of Department 609's 11 buyers was responsible *essentially* for buying flat wrenches and socket wrenches (*not* adjustable wrenches). He described the buying function as follows:

Source relationships. I took over this line 2½ years ago. When you come onto a line, there are existing products and sources. You constantly look at these sources, to make sure that product quality and service of supply are what they should be. Price is also important, but it is really secondary to the other two factors.

I work with five sources. We take about 50 percent of one source's production; about 10 percent of another's. Several other Department 609 buyers are dealing with these same sources.

Commitments. I decide how much production to contract for. My lines are pretty much staples, and I can learn a lot from last year's sales pattern. I read a lot of business periodicals concerning the state of the economy and watch our monthly sales figures pretty closely. We are currently on an uptrend; I'm looking for a 15 percent to 20 percent sales increase.

Product development. I have full responsibility for selecting items within my line responsibility. I watch the trade journals and automotive magazines; I go out and talk to automotive mechanics concerning what they would like if they could get it. Inventors come to us with ideas for new products; if an idea seems promising we send it to a source for a cost evaluation, and to the Sears laboratory for testing.

The national merchandise manager of Department 609 had been in his present position for many years. He commented on his department, and its organization, as follows:

Our buyers all have full responsibility for the lines assigned to them. It is up to them to make sure that we have the right quantities of the right products at the right time. Our retail sales manager, catalog sales manager, and I are then responsible for pulling the whole thing together.

Retail promotions. Because most of our products are staple items, we are able to freeze our retail promotions six months in advance. We set our targets for a season, and ask the buyers to give us their candidates for promotion. The buyers send their spec sheets to me and the retail sales manager. We both review them and then call each buyer in individually, and do all that we can to get him or her to do an even better job.

We then call all the buyers together and vote on what to include in the promotion. This is better than the retail sales manager and I just choosing.

The catalog. Our catalog sales manager then develops catalog pages which are compatible with what retail has decided to do. The catalog is very good for us on some items, because it allows us to describe an item fully. The average retail salesperson does not want to sell electric arc welders, for example. A customer who wants an electric arc welder probably knows more about the product than the salesperson does, which makes that individual feel insecure. In the catalog we can say, "Here it is; here are its specifications; here's what it can do." Hand tools and other impulse items do better in the retail stores, of course.

Store relations. I cannot put enough stress on internal selling. We have great products (a totally new kind of lawn mower, for example), but just don't get through to the customer. In 1964 we visited all Sears retail stores. I personally was on the road 80 percent of the year. We spent 8–12 hours on a thorough analysis of our department in each store. We presented a written report to the division manager and the store manager, and a summary to the territorial office. But I don't think you can do what we are trying to do with paper. We need belly-to-belly confrontations with the division managers and store managers.

I have also instituted a "work-a-week" program. All Department 609 personnel (except the clerks) spend one week a year in a store selling. Besides selling, they are to handle all customer complaints concerning our products. It's just a device, but a darn effective one!

I participate in the selection of Department 609 control buyers (in the catalog plants) and try to influence the choice of Division 9 managers in the retail stores. On my store visits, I do not hesitate to call attention to a weak division manager, or to point out to the store managers that they should have strong people in the hardware area, since it produces so many profit dollars.

Junior Clothing

The junior clothing department (Department 619) was one of 10 buying departments located in New York City. These buying departments were responsible for buying women's and girls' clothing and accessories, luggage, and jewelry. They were located in New York rather than Chicago because these particular industries were concentrated in New York City to such a great extent that it would have been impractical to operate out of Chicago.

The New York office was headed by a divisional vice president, who reported to the vice president of merchandising. In addition to the 10 buying departments, representatives of other parent departments (e.g., Chicago-based buying departments, retail merchandising, catalog merchandising, merchandise control, merchandise comparison, operations, and merchandise laboratory) were located in the New York office. While these personnel reported functionally to their respective parent departments, it was generally understood that they were under the administrative control of the divisional vice president–New York.

Department 619 was responsible for buying and merchandising junior clothing. *Junior* was a term which had been used by the fashion industry for many years to describe a range of sizes and styles oriented primarily toward teen-age girls and women "with a young outlook."[7] In recent years, the junior category had been increasingly associated with "mod" styles and exciting, brightly colored fashion merchandise. The so-called "junior look" had become extra-odinarily popular in the mid-1960s, with the result that junior merchandise was accounting for a steadily increasing share of the women's ready-to-wear market.

Department 619 had been established late in 1965. Prior to this time, junior merchandise had been bought by Department 607 (women's sportswear), Department 617 (ladies' coats and suits), Department 677 (girls' and teens' wear), and Department 631 (women's dresses). While each of these departments had been moderately active in the junior field, Sears had never really tried to go after the junior customer in a big way. An exception was Department 677, which had begun to "push" juniors about 1963, primarily in an effort to make up for the vanishing subteen market.[8] Department 677 had had unusual success with its junior program, which represent-ed 25 percent of departmental volume in 1965. It had begun to work with the leading manufac-

turers of junior merchandise and had made significant inroads into the women's sportswear and dress fields. The decision to establish a separate junior department was made by top management "to bring Sears into line with what had happened in the department stores five years before."

The national merchandise manager of Department 619 had been in charge of the girls' department during the period when it had begun to "push" junior merchandise (1963–1965). When he took over the girls' department, he said, "I will have succeeded when this department is split in two." As the driving force behind the junior program, he had, according to Sears executives, been the logical choice to head the new department. Early in 1967, he commented on his department as follows:

Ours is a fast-moving fashion business. Dress manufacturers are coming out with new styles every day of the week. While we plan ahead as much as we can on our relatively more stable merchandise (e.g., outerwear), we have to retain considerable freedom to be where the action is. A young designer in a loft down the street can revolutionize this business overnight.

That is actually an overstatement. A certain amount of lead time is required before an item can really take off, particularly with regard to fabrics. There is sort of a pulse in this industry: textile mills, fabric houses, manufacturers, designers, and buyers somehow all get moving in the same direction at more or less the same time, but a certain number of items—the items that give you a fashion image—do have an aura of spontaneity about them.

Buying assignments. We have 10 buyers, most of whom are responsible for a particular type of product (e.g., outerwear, or skirts, blouses, and sweaters). There are two major exceptions to this pattern. We have three dress buyers, each responsible for a particular price range. This is the way the industry is organized; one manufacturer makes lower price dresses, another makes higher price dresses, and so forth.

We also have one buyer who buys all dresses

---

[7]Sears executives estimated that the junior market was divided according to age as follows:

Age	Percentage of junior customers
12–15 years	33%
16–19 years	36
20–24 years	14
25–29 years	5
30–39 years	8
40 and over	4
	100%

[8]According to Sears executives, the subteen market was disappearing because girls were going directly from children's clothing to teenage clothing, without passing through a subteen style phase.

for the catalog. This is a high-risk business. We need to buy nine months ahead, and yet be right with regard to fashion. We buy for the Christmas catalog in March; for the retail Christmas season in September and October.

Logistics. With very few exceptions (mainly staple items and coordinated separates), our products are merchandised and distributed through the fashion centers.[9] These fashion centers handle merchandise for all the New York departments except luggage and jewelry, and a few items for the children's department in Chicago.

We have a fashion merchandiser for our department in each fashion center. While he/she works for the territory, he/she is concerned only with our lines of merchandise.

The division managers in the stores do not order merchandise, although they do help to establish the merchandising program for their division. All of our fashion center merchandise is ticketed with punched tickets. When an item is sold, the punched ticket is torn off and retained by the person writing up the sale. These tickets are collected, and mailed to the fashion center daily. At the fashion center, they are run through a computer which prepares a sales summary for a week. The fashion merchandiser then uses this summary to determine how much merchandise to ship to the store during the following week. The division managers can, of course, shortcut the system when necessary. They might enclose a note with their tickets, for example, saying, "For God's sake, don't send me any more red dresses."

Central merchandising of fashion merchandise makes a lot of sense. We feel that we have a better understanding of the direction styles are likely to take than our division managers do. If nothing else, we have learned that *our* taste (as compared with the customer's) is relatively unimportant. If we let

[9]There were five fashion centers, one in each territory. The fashion centers were intermediate warehousing facilities; they ordered and received merchandise from manufacturing sources and then shipped the merchandise to the stores.

Each fashion center was headed by a manager, who reported to the territorial vice president. Within each fashion center, a fashion merchandiser was assigned to each buying department using the fashion centers. The fashion merchandiser was responsible for placing orders with the sources and for distributing merchandise to the stores.

the division managers do the ordering, we would run into situations where a key store would not be stocking pants dresses because the division manager didn't like pants dresses.

Promotion. In the promotional area we have not yet really made our mark. I am convinced that cut-price advertising, "Combos," and newspapers in general are just not the way to move our lines of merchandise. Our customers read the teenage fashion magazines; that's where they get their ideas and that's where we ought to advertise.

We have been held back from doing as much of this sort of thing as we should by a couple of factors. There are still a lot of people in Sears who refuse to let go of the price impression approach, for example. One of the territories still insists on stocking $5.98–$7.98 dresses, even though we have dropped these price points in the other territories.

Retail Merchandising

The retail merchandising function was described by one Sears executive as follows:

> The buying departments are responsible for selecting the merchandise which will be sold in the stores. The territories are responsible for assuring that we have an adequate number of well-run stores in the proper locations. And the Retail Merchandising Department is responsible for providing the stores with advertising, promotions, and displays which will bring customers into the stores and motivate them to buy.

The retail merchandising function was headed by the divisional vice president of retail merchandising. Reporting to the divisional vice president of retail merchandising were eight category retail merchandisers, and the heads of the visual merchandising department (display and packaging), the retail merchandise lists department, and the retail sales promotion and advertising department.

The major task of the departments and individuals reporting to the divisional vice president of retail merchandising was to prepare the monthly Combo. As noted above, the Combo consisted of special merchandise offers to the stores (i.e., opportunities to buy merchandise at reduced prices), an advertising mat service, a display recommendation service, and various kinds of historical sales data to be used as a planning aid at the local level.

Planning for a particular Combo began approximately 13 months prior to the month in question, with a preliminary seasonal calendar review. Based largely on extrapolations from detailed historical sales data, this review was used to highlight the types of merchandise which were likely to be susceptible to promotional support during the month in question.

The buying departments used the data to select merchandise for promotion. After a series of meetings with the divisional vice president of retail merchandising, the retail merchandisers, and the visual merchandising and advertising and promotion departments, tentative promotional offerings (with promotional themes) were presented to representatives from the field at "tote board" meetings.

Catalog Merchandising

The catalog merchandising office and its subordinate departments were responsible for the planning, execution, and distribution of Sears catalogs. The divisional vice president of catalog merchandising management supervised a group of catalog merchandisers (essentially responsible for planning), an advertising department (layouts, artwork, copywriting), and a department which planned and did research in the fields of catalog circulation and distribution. In addition, he worked closely with the 11 catalog order plants, even though they reported to the territorial vice presidents. The divisional vice president of catalog merchandising explained that he was able to work quite directly with catalog management in the field, as there were only 11 catalog order plants, which facilitated direct personal contact.

The task of catalog planning began with the appropriation of funds for the catalog by corporate management. In making this appropriation, management compared the probable return on investment in the catalog with other investments available to it (e.g., new stores).

Once the budget had been established, the catalog merchandising office determined how it should be spent. In simple terms, there were three major considerations:

1. How many separate catalogs should there be?
2. How many pages (and how many color pages) should each catalog contain?
3. How many copies of each catalog should be distributed?

Once these decisions had been made, it was necessary to allocate pages to the buying departments. The spring and fall general catalogs each contained 1,600 pages. The buying departments were charged with the cost of each page they used, and in practice, virtually all departments wanted more pages than were available to them.

The catalogs were distributed to Sears customers who had met criteria concerning such factors as total purchases, number of purchases, and use of credit during the previous year. These criteria were changed frequently, and they varied among geographic areas and types of catalog. In some cases (e.g., the opening of a catalog order store in a town where Sears had not previously had an outlet), catalogs were sent to persons who were not presently Sears customers.

The Field

The "field" was divided into five territories, each headed by a vice president who was a member of the Sears board of directors. The territories, in turn, were divided into groups, zones, and catalog regions (each containing one catalog order plant). In general, individual stores were part of either a group or a zone, while catalog sales offices reported through several layers of field administration to the manager of the catalog order plant in their region.

This section of the case describes the organization and activities of the eastern territory. It begins by describing the territorial office and then describes a group (Boston) and a zone (mid-Atlantic).

The Eastern Territory

The eastern territory included the states of Maine, New Hampshire, Vermont, Massachusetts, Rhode Island, Connecticut, New York, New Jersey, Pennsylvania, Delaware, Maryland, and West Virginia, the District of Columbia, and portions of Ohio and Virginia. This geographic area contained approximately 40 percent of the population of the United States but represented a considerably smaller percentage of Sears's sales volume. According to Sears executives, the company's relative weakness in the East was attributable to two major factors: (1) Sears had fewer stores (and less square feet of floor space) per capita in the East than it did in its stronger territories and (2) Sears had not yet overcome its hard-goods image in the East to the extent it had in the newer territories.

In this territory there were 14 groups, three zones, and two catalog order regions. At the end of 1965, the territory contained 204 retail stores, 113 'of which were in groups and the rest in zones. The largest group (New York) consisted of 37 stores (of which 10 were large stores).

Catalog order sales represented 25 percent of territorial sales. There were two catalog order plants in the territory, one in Philadelphia and one in Boston. Each catalog order plant served a catalog order region; the regional boundary was a more or less straight line between lower Connecticut and Rochester, New York.

Individual retail store, group, zone, and catalog order plant operations were measured in terms of sales and profits. As in the parent merchandising department, managers at all these levels received a significant por-

tion of their compensation in the form of incentive bonuses.

The territorial office was located in Philadelphia in an office building adjacent to the Philadelphia catalog order plant. Reporting to the territorial vice president were an administrative assistant and 12 managers of staff departments. The 14 group managers, the three zone managers, the two catalog order plant managers, and the fashion center manager also reported to the territorial vice president, but they were not considered part of the territorial office.

The territorial vice presidents had virtually unlimited authority to make operating and policy decisions for their territories. As one executive explained:

> The territorial vice presidents are really like presidents of their own companies. Each territory, by itself, would easily make *Fortune*'s 500, and our territorial vice presidents are equal to their counterparts [i.e., the presidents of other large companies] in compensation, responsibility, and authority. At Sears, there's no question that the territorial vice presidents run the show.[10]

In practice, the territorial vice presidents generally operated within policies, guidelines, and procedures established by the various parent departments. In theory, they were free to reject or alter[11] most of these policies, but in fact they rarely did so.

A key department in the territorial headquarters office was merchandising. It consisted of a manager, a merchandise controller, and approximately 20 territorial merchandisers. The merchandise controller worked with the groups, zones, and stores to prepare "sales and inventory budgets."

---

[10]All five territorial vice presidents were members of the Sears board of directors. Also, of Sears's four chairs and presidents in recent years, three had been territorial vice presidents immediately prior to their promotions to top management.

[11]Limitations on the territorial vice presidents' authority concerned budgets and the buying of merchandise, which had to be approved by the parent; capital expenditures, which required a parent allocation of funds; and accounting and personnel policies, which were closely administered by the parent.

Each territorial merchandiser was responsible for one or more divisions. These assignments did not generally correspond to the new category breakdown but would probably be brought into line with the category concept in the near future.

The territorial merchandisers were primarily responsible for reviewing parent-sponsored programs and tailoring them to meet the needs of their territory.

The merchandisers also worked with the parent to develop local promotions tailored to the eastern territory (e.g., a Washington's Birthday sale). The merchandisers asked the buying departments for "special deals" on merchandise for such sales and arranged for the parent advertising department to prepare advertising mats. While many of Sears's promotional efforts were national in scope, it was generally believed that local promotions (at the territory, group *and* store levels) were necessary to give field personnel "a feeling of belonging to something a little bit smaller than a $7 billion plus corporation."

The parent buying departments used the territorial merchandisers as sounding boards for new products and promotional programs. The merchandisers visited Chicago (or New York) frequently, at the request of the parent departments, and attended all category "totes."

The Boston Group

The Boston group contained 17 stores at the end of 1965. Of these, four were "A" stores, five were "B1" stores, one was a "B2" store, and seven were "B3" stores.[12] These stores were located within a geographic area circumscribed

---

[12]Sears stores were classified as A, B1, B2, B3, and C stores according to several criteria. An "A" store was the largest type—a full-line department store, usually located in a large city. A "B1" store was the smallest type to include all selling divisions. A "B2" store carried fewer lines of merchandise than a "B1" store and was usually located in a small town. A "B3" store carried hard lines and appliances on a broader scale than a "C" store and was usually located in or near a metropolitan area. "C" stores, which were the smallest type, carried hard lines and appliances and were usually located in small towns in rural areas.

by a highway network which formed the limits of what was generally known as "Boston and its suburbs." As highway facilities had improved in recent years and the suburbs had "moved outward," the group's boundaries had been broadened to include outlying stores which had previously been part of the New England zone.

The group office consisted of the group manager, the controller, the operating manager, the sales promotion manager, the service manager, the personnel manager, the advertising manager, three group merchandisers (responsible for soft lines, hard lines, and "big tickets," respectively), and about a dozen merchandising assistants (responsible for narrower product lines, such as home fashions or men's and boys' wear).

Most merchandising decisions for the stores in the group were made by the group office. The group merchandisers (in consultation with store merchandisers and/or division managers) determined which specific items were to be stocked by each store and at what prices they should be sold. The group advertising department prepared and placed all advertising for the group. The division managers in the stores were thus responsible for ordering the merchandise selected for them at the group level and for making certain that it was displayed and sold effectively.

The group operated a "pool stock" and a number of central repair service facilities. The pool stock delivered all major appliances directly to customers from its central warehouse, thus relieving the stores of the need to maintain inventories of these items. Similarly, a customer requiring repair service for a Sears product telephoned a central repair service office, which scheduled the service call, thus relieving the local store of responsibility for repair service.

The Mid-Atlantic Zone

The operation of a *zone* was quite different. By definition, a zone comprised a number of stores which were *not* linked together by common media, and road networks. Consequently, individual stores in a zone operated with considerably more autonomy than stores in a group. The division managers, for example, not only ordered merchandise but also selected the items which they would sell and established the retail price at which they would be sold. The zone managers and their staffs (which were smaller than group staffs) visited most of the stores in their zone regularly and tried to provide as much direction as their group counterparts did.

Product Development

In early 1967, Mr. Button was particularly concerned with Sears's efforts in the area of product development. As he explained:

> Our chairman has publicly stated the goal of $10 billion in sales by 1970, a $3 billion increase in three years. Some of this increase will come from new facilities, but only a relatively small part of it. If we are to achieve our goal, we must develop new

> products—unique to Sears—which will draw new customers into our stores, and motivate them to spend a larger share of their disposable income with us.

> Speaking frankly, I must admit that we have not done all that we should in this area. Our buyers, merchandise laboratory, and sources have developed a great many new or superior products, but, considering the number of products we carry, we have really only scratched the surface.

> Historically (with some very major exceptions), we have let the leading manufacturers of branded consumer goods develop new products, and introduce them to the public. We have then refined their developments, to give the consumer a higher quality product for less money.

> I strongly believe that product development is the area of greatest potential growth for Sears. The buyers are responsible for product development—let there be no doubt of that!—but we will review their lines more frequently (asking continually, "What's new?") and give them more help. I hope that the new product categories, with more resources than the individual buying departments, will be able to increase our efforts in this area.

49 Pfizer International: I

Steven H. Star • E. Raymond Corey • Cedric L. Suzman

Chas. Pfizer & Co., Inc., was one of the world's leading pharmaceutical companies. While sales had been only $60 million in 1950, they had grown to almost $500 million in 1964. Profits of $44.7 million in 1964 represented an increase in earnings of 10 percent over 1963 and almost 300 percent over 1955 (Exhibit 1).

The rapid growth of Pfizer during the 1950s and early 1960s was attributed to a number of factors. Several important product developments (Terramycin was perhaps the most notable) had a significant effect on company sales and earnings, as did acquisitions, which were believed to be responsible for about 20 percent of Pfizer's 1964 sales. During this period the

company also accelerated the process of diversification, with pharmaceuticals (human antibiotics and other ethical prescription drugs) accounting for only 47 percent of sales in 1964. Pfizer's other major product lines and their shares of 1964 sales were chemicals (25 percent), agricultural products (13 percent), and consumer products (15 percent).

A large amount of Chas. Pfizer's business was conducted outside the United States. In 1964, Pfizer International[1] sales reached $233 million, almost 50 percent of the Pfizer total. Manufacturing plants for pharmaceutical, chemical, agricultural, and consumer products were operated in 27 countries, while 17,000 employees worked for the international company (as compared with 11,000 for the domestic company).

Steven H. Star was formerly an associate professor at the Harvard Graduate School of Business Administration. E. Raymond Corey is the Malcolm P. McNair Professor of Marketing at the Harvard Graduate School of Business Administration. Cedric L. Suzman is the director of research at Georgia State University.

[1]In this case series, Chas. Pfizer's various foreign subsidiaries will be treated as a single company, "Pfizer International."

EXHIBIT 1
CHAS. PFIZER & CO., INC., AND SUBSIDIARY COMPANIES: 10-YEAR FINANCIAL SUMMARY
All Amounts in Thousands Except Per Share Data

	1964	1963	1962	1961
Net sales	$480,144	$414,290	$383,573	$312,433
Other income	8,425	8,500	8,710	7,534
	$488,569	$422,790	$392,283	$319,967
Cost of goods sold and research expenses	$242,816	$203,923	$188,150	$150,836
Selling, general, and administrative expenses	156,051	136,186	131,455	109,279
Other deductions	11,706	13,074	8,984	6,209
	$410,573	$353,183	$328,589	$266,324
Earnings before taxes	$ 77,996	$ 69,607	$ 63,694	$ 53,643
Taxes on income	33,300	29,300	27,200	22,200
Net earnings	$ 44,696	$ 40,307	$ 36,494	$ 31,443
Preferred stock dividends	–	–	–	24
Common stock earnings	$ 44,696	$ 40,307	$ 36,494	$ 31,419
Fixed assets net of depreciation	$175,261	$154,988	$148,103	$121,348
Working capital	$110,882	$101,040	$ 98,467	$ 86,502
Share owners' equity	$301,448	$275,120	$244,137	$199,647
Average number of common shares outstanding*	19,666	19,362	18,881	17,979
Earnings per share of common stock*	$2.27	$2.08	$1.98	$1.74
Dividends per share of common stock*	$1.15	$1.05	$0.95	$0.85

Pfizer International

Pfizer International was responsible for marketing all Pfizer products outside the United States, and it conducted extensive development and manufacturing operations abroad. Pfizer International had its own board of directors and officers and operated, for the most part, independently of the parent company. While it purchased part of its raw materials from Chas. Pfizer and generally marketed products which were part of the Chas. Pfizer product line, its executives were free to run the international business as they saw fit, with only general policy guidance from the parent company.

Product Lines

Like the parent company, Pfizer International was engaged in the development, manufacture, and sale of pharmaceutical, agricultural, chemical, and consumer products. While there was some overlap among product lines, they differed markedly in development, manufacturing, and marketing characteristics.

Pharmaceutical Products

The pharmaceutical product line consisted of antibiotics and other ethical drugs (sold only by prescription) and proprietary drugs (sold without

EXHIBIT 1
Continued

	1960	1959	1958	1957	1956	1955
Net sales	$269,376	$253,673	$222,726	$207,152	$178,362	$163,795
Other income	5,715	7,189	6,484	7,121	5,820	3,087
	$275,091	$260,862	$229,210	$214,273	$184,182	$166,882
Cost of goods sold and research expenses	$140,283	$138,802	$116,966	$101,142	$ 91,440	$ 87,017
Selling, general, and administrative expenses	89,684	81,820	71,359	65,083	57,308	50,980
Other deductions	6,271	5,027	4,020	5,095	3,006	2,314
	$236,238	$225,649	$192,345	$171,320	$151,754	$140,311
Earnings before taxes	$ 38,853	$ 35,213	$ 36,865	$ 42,953	$ 32,428	$ 26,571
Taxes on income	12,670	10,350	12,900	20,044	14,174	11,244
Net earnings	$ 26,183	$ 24,863	$ 23,965	$ 22,909	$ 18,254	$ 15,327
Preferred stock dividends	128	150	165	192	497	739
Common stock earnings	$ 26,055	$ 24,713	$ 23,800	$ 22,717	$ 17,757	$ 14,588
Fixed assets net of depreciation	$111,503	$ 97,768	$ 75,056	$ 44,438	$ 36,413	$ 38,134
Working capital	$ 78,464	$ 79,405	$ 69,366	$ 74,896	$ 72,590	$ 63,384
Share owners' equity	$170,462	$154,849	$138,434	$127,081	$115,051	$105,263
Average number of common shares outstanding*	16,456	16,232	16,116	16,079	15,385	14,770
Earnings per share of common stock*	$1.58	$1.52	$1.47	$1.41	$1.15	$0.98
Dividends per share of common stock*	$0.80	$0.80	$0.75	$0.70	$0.58	$0.51

*Earnings and dividends per common share are based on the average number of shares of common stock outstanding during each year (excluding shares reacquired and held in the treasury) and are restated for comparative purposes on the basis of the 3-for-1 stock split, April 20, 1959.

a prescription). In FY 1964, pharmaceutical sales represented 59.5 percent of Pfizer International's sales volume and an even larger percentage of its profits.

Pharmaceutical Research and Development. A great deal of laboratory research and development work was needed in the pharmaceutical field in order to ensure a continuing flow of new products. In 1965, Chas. Pfizer had a number of basic new drugs in various stages of clinical evaluation in the United States and overseas.

The bulk of Pfizer International's development work was carried out in its research and development laboratories in Sandwich, England. In addition, each pharmaceutical manufacturing plant had laboratory facilities, which were necessary for quality control. These laboratory facilities were also used to develop new dosage forms and to adapt products to local market conditions.

Pharmaceutical Manufacturing. There were two major phases in the pharmaceutical manufacturing process. In the initial basic manufacturing phase, the active ingredients in a given pharmaceutical product were produced in bulk form. In some cases this was done through fermentation; in others the basic process was one of chemical synthesis, or a combination of fermentation and synthesis. Whichever process was used, carefully controlled conditions and exceptional safeguards against impurities were required. The basic manufacturing process produced a basic ingredient, which was then packaged in bulk form for bulk sale or further processed into finished goods.

The second phase of the pharmaceutical manufacturing process was carried out in pharmaceutical manufacturing plants. In these plants, the bulk pharmaceuticals were transformed into final dosage forms such as tablets, capsules, ointments, syrups, liquids, and injectables. Prescribed dosages were often as small as 1 mg, and in final dosage form the drug was mixed with a base so that it could be administered safely and conveniently in a form acceptable to the patient. As in the case of bulk manufacture, exceptionally sanitary conditions were essential.

Pharmaceutical Marketing. In general, pharmaceutical products were sold at the retail level by pharmacies. While there was wide variation in channels of distribution among the many countries in which Pfizer International sold its products, Pfizer generally sold its products either to drug wholesalers or directly to pharmacies. As national health plans proliferated, increasing sales were made directly or indirectly to governmental agencies. In some areas, moreover, pharmaceuticals were sold to practicing physicians, who then supplied them to their patients.

Pfizer's pharmaceutical marketing effort was directed toward physicians. Detailers, who were often professionally trained, called on doctors to familiarize them with Pfizer drugs so that they would prescribe or recommend Pfizer products for their patients. On detailing calls, the detailer generally pointed out the advantages of Pfizer products and left product samples and informative literature with the doctor.

Expenditures on advertising (not including the cost of samples and materials used by the detailers) represented a relatively small marketing expense. While advertisements were placed in medical and pharmaceutical professional journals, consumer advertising was rarely used by the pharmaceutical industry. In almost all countries, it was believed that doctors would not prescribe pharmaceuticals which had been advertised directly to the consumer.

Agricultural and Veterinary Products

Pfizer International's agricultural and veterinary product line consisted essentially of three categories of products: (1) *animal feed supplements*, which primarily consisted of various vitamins and antibiotics, in crude form, which were added to proteins and minerals and then to a basic grain, such as corn or wheat, to provide a balanced animal ration; (2) a range of *veterinary products* such as antibiotic injectables, soluble powders, boluses, and animal vaccines; and (3) *pesticides* (formulations of standard compounds marketed in France, Canada, Rhodesia, South Africa, and Brazil). In FY 1964, agricultural and veterinary products accounted for 13.5 percent of Pfizer International's total sales. Western Europe accounted for one-third of this total.

Development. The development of animal feed supplements and veterinary antibiotic formulations was generally carried out in Pfizer pharmaceutical laboratories. While procedures for product testing and obtaining government approval differed somewhat from those for human pharmaceuticals, the actual development processes were essentially similar. In many cases, Pfizer human pharmaceuticals were adapted to agricultural needs. Terramycin, for example, was the basic ingredient in a large number of Pfizer antibiotic animal health products.

Animal vaccines were generally developed in the areas where they were marketed. Since strains of disease-producing organisms were usually confined to particular geographic areas, each area generally had to develop its own vaccines.

Manufacturing. The active ingredients, when manufactured by Pfizer, came from the same basic manufacturing plants as the pharmaceutical ingredients. Animal feed supplements were then manufactured for the most part at local blending plants through processes involving the blending of the active ingredient(s) with diluents to facilitate addition to feed formulations. These supplements were then generally sold to feed millers, who blended the supplements into finished feeds for sale to farmers. In a few countries where farm mixing was the practice (e.g., Brazil), sales were direct to farmers. In Nigeria, Pfizer International produced the finished feed for sale to farmers.

Veterinary products were produced in Pfizer's basic pharmaceutical plants. While purity dosage and packaging may have differed from those for human pharmaceuticals, the manufacturing processes were basically similar. Animal vaccines were also manufactured locally, since these products frequently had applications restricted to limited geographic areas corresponding to locally specific disease-causative organisms.

Marketing. Feed supplements were generally sold to feed millers, who mixed them with other ingredients and basic animal feed stuffs and then sold the resulting balanced "mix" to farmers through retail feed stores. Pfizer sales representatives usually placed major emphasis on convincing millers of the benefits of Pfizer feed supplements, including antibiotics, vitamins, and custom mixes, and, when necessary, the sales representatives helped the millers to determine proper formulas for their markets. In recent years stress had also been laid on visiting the larger farmers and urging them to specify feed containing Pfizer supplements. Product excellence, technical service support, and competitive pricing enabled Pfizer to maintain a favorable position against constant competitive pressure.

Pfizer also sold direct to the farmer in some markets. In Nigeria, Pfizer operated as a feed miller and marketed a variety of animal feeds. In Italy and certain other markets, Pfizer sold "custom premixes," which allowed the farmers to mix their own feed. Custom premixes were particularly successful in markets where large modern farms could achieve significant economies by mixing their own feeds and in less developed areas where feed manufacturers were not a significant factor (e.g., Brazil).

Animal health products sales reps generally called on veterinarians and tried to convince them to prescribe Pfizer products for the farmers in their area or, in some cases, to sell Pfizer products themselves. In some countries, where regulatory and marketing practices permitted, Pfizer promoted its products directly to the farmer. This practice was particularly prevalent in proprietary marketing areas in which veterinary medicine was still relatively undeveloped.

Chemical Products

Pfizer International's chemical product line consisted of three categories of products: (1) fine chemicals, (2) petrochemicals and plastics, and (3) bulk pharmaceuticals. The chemical product line had experienced rapid growth in recent years and represented 14 percent of Pfizer International's sales in 1964. About 27 percent of Pfizer International's chemical sales were in the United Kingdom, and about 28 percent were in the rest of Europe.

Fine Chemicals. These were distinguished from other industrial chemicals in that they were usually of higher purity and price and required relatively complex manufacturing processes involving organic chemistry.

Pfizer's line of fine chemicals was extremely diverse with regard to manufacturing processes, uses, and channels of distribution. Citric acid, oxalic acid, and gluconic acid were produced by a fermentation process. Pfizer International's fine chemicals were sold directly to food processors and other industries, as well as to other pharmaceutical companies.

Fine chemicals were sold with little product differentiation among suppliers and at published, well-established prices. Pfizer International's competitors in the chemical field were mostly large chemical companies, many of which produced fine chemicals as well as basic chemicals. Competition, in Europe in particular, was becoming quite severe.

Petrochemicals and Plastics. Pfizer International's activity in the petrochemical field was limited to the manufacture of polyethers in the United Kingdom and the manufacture of polyurethane foams in Belgium and France.

The polyether produced by the U.K. plant was one of the basic ingredients in the manufacture of polyurethane foams. These foams were used as insulation in a variety of construction applications and as cushioning in furniture and automobile seats.

Polyurethane foams were manufactured by "foamers." Foamers were generally small companies, since distribution of their product was economic only within a radius of 200 to 300 miles. Foamers sometimes purchased polyethers on long-term contracts, with price and consistent quality the key elements in their buying decisions. Most of the polyether production of Pfizer's U.K. plant was sold to British foamers.

Pfizer owned two foamers in continental Europe, one in Belgium and one in France. While these foamers received some of their polyether from the Pfizer plant in the United Kingdom, tariff considerations forced them to buy most of their polyether locally. Pfizer sold its polyurethane foam to a large number of furniture manufacturers located near its plants. Furniture manufacturers generally purchased polyurethane each month, largely on the basis of price. When furniture manufacturers were ready to add to their polyurethane foam inventories, they generally asked several foamers for price quotations.

Bulk Pharmaceuticals.[2] Pfizer International sold several pharmaceutical products in bulk form to other pharmaceutical manufacturers. These manufacturers then packaged the pharmaceuticals in final dosage form and sold them under their own labels. Most of the bulk pharmaceuticals which Pfizer sold to other pharmaceutical manufacturers were the so-called "narrow-spectrum" antibiotics,[3] which were no longer patentable and were thus sold in much the same way as fine chemicals, with low margins, commodity pricing, and little product differentiation among suppliers. Also included in the chemical product line were a few Pfizer patented ethical drugs. These were sold in bulk form to a limited number of manufacturers, who manufactured them into final dosage form and sold them under their own labels.

Consumer Products

Pfizer International's consumer product line included three categories of products: (1) selectively distributed cosmetics and toiletries, (2) mass-marketed toiletries and other consumer products, and (3) door-to-door cosmetics. In the cosmetics and toiletries field, Pfizer's major entries were the Coty line of cosmetics (acquired by Pfizer late in 1963) and the Pacquin line of

---

[2]Bulk pharmaceuticals were considered part of the chemical rather than pharmaceutical business and were the responsibility of country chemical managers. This assignment was intended to provide maximum incentive for bulk pharmaceutical sales. It was believed that pharmaceutical managers would lack enthusiasm for bulk pharmaceutical sales to their competitors.

[3]Narrow-spectrum antibiotics were effective against a narrow range of disease-producing organisms, while broad-spectrum antibiotics were effective against a wider range of organisms. Terramycin, Pfizer's most important patented pharmaceutical, was one of the first broad-spectrum antibiotics.

women's hand creams and lotions. Pfizer International's consumer products included vitamins, cough and cold remedies, analgesics, antacids, dietary products, baby formulas, and a line of health "tonics" sold only in Germany and Austria. Cosmetic and consumer products together accounted for 13 percent of Pfizer International's 1964 sales.

Pfizer did not make the basic raw materials for its consumer products, and supplies were often obtained from local suppliers in the countries where the products were produced. The manufacturing process required mixing and filling operations but was complicated by frequent changes in package design and product features. It was customary, for example, to introduce new lipstick shades each season.

The cosmetic and general health products were sold through separate sales forces to drug wholesalers and direct to pharmacies and other retail outlets. They were rarely sold by the sales rep who sold Pfizer's pharmaceutical products. Relatively heavy consumer advertising and promotional expenditures differentiate the marketing of these products from the marketing of pharmaceuticals. Moreover, Pfizer was beginning to experiment with door-to-door sales of cosmetic products, particularly in the U.K.

Geographic Location of Pfizer International Activities

In early 1965, Pfizer products were sold in more than 100 countries and manufactured in 27 countries. In addition, Pfizer operated bonded warehouses (which were used as supply points) in Belgium, Hong Kong, and Panama and had extensive research and development laboratories in the United Kingdom.

Pfizer's foreign operations took a variety of legal forms. In 13 countries, Pfizer operated through branches, which were legally considered local offices of a foreign company. In most cases, however, Pfizer operated through subsidiaries, which were locally domiciled corporations in the countries in which they operated. In early 1965, Pfizer had 84 foreign subsidiaries, a few of which were partially owned locally. In several countries, Pfizer operated through several different subsidiaries, some of which were subsidiaries of still other subsidiaries.

In general, the legal form of a given operation was dictated by financial and fiscal considerations and had little relevance to the way in which it functioned. Some countries, for example, had different tax rates for branches of foreign companies and locally incorporated subsidiaries. Moreover, there might be different policies concerning the remission of profits and the reporting of financial data. In the case of partially owned subsidiaries, however, the local owners sometimes took part in the management of the company.

Manufacturing Plant Locations

Manufacturing operations differed markedly among countries and product lines. Bulk pharmaceutical fermentation plants were located in Argentina, Brazil, Japan, India, Spain, France, and the United Kingdom. The plants in France and Japan were only 50 percent owned by Pfizer. In general, the foreign bulk pharmaceutical plants produced only for their own national markets; other countries received bulk pharmaceuticals (through the three bonded warehouses) from Chas. Pfizer bulk pharmaceutical plants in the United States. In some cases, however, bulk pharmaceuticals were shipped from the foreign plants to the supply points for eventual shipment to other countries.

Pharmaceutical manufacturing plants (where bulk pharmaceuticals were manufactured in dosage form and packaged) were located in 24 countries. In addition, operations limited to pharmaceutical packaging were carried out in Puerto Rico and South Africa. The pharmaceutical manufacturing plants generally received bulk pharmaceuticals from one of the supply points or directly from a bulk pharmaceutical plant if one was located in the same country. The output of these plants was transferred to warehouses which supplied the local market. Occasionally, finished goods were sent to one of the supply points for later shipment to other countries.

Pfizer executives gave several reasons for the relatively large number of pharmaceutical manufacturing plants (as compared with the number of bulk pharmaceutical plants). The reasons fell into three categories: economic, political, and marketing. On the economic side, the capital investment required for a pharmaceutical manufacturing or packaging plant was far less than for a basic fermentation plant; transportation costs for dosage forms were greater than those for bulk pharmaceuticals (the former included inert materials, which were often purchased locally, and packaging materials); economies of scale were far more significant in bulk production than in dosage production; and tariffs were usually higher on dosage forms than on bulk pharmaceuticals. On the political side, there was considerable pressure for at least some manufacturing to take place in the country where a drug was marketed. Moreover, differences in national regulations concerning dosages and labeling often made local dosage manufacture almost a necessity. From a marketing point of view, Pfizer International found that medical and patient practices and tastes varied widely from country to country, and the ability to satisfy them under local management was a big advantage.

Argicultural and/or veterinary products were manufactured in Canada, Mexico, Brazil, Colombia, Argentina, Chile, the United Kingdom, France, Sweden, Germany, Italy, Spain, Belgium, Greece, Turkey, Egypt, Nigeria, Venezuela, Japan, India, Pakistan, the Philippines, and Australia. In addition, they were manufactured in plants owned by third parties in Denmark and Yugoslavia. In general, the bulk pharmaceuticals used in these products were produced at the basic manufacturing plants and shipped to the agricultural and/or veterinary product-manufacturing facilities through the three supply points. As in the case of the pharmaceutical manufacturing plants, the finished agricultural and veterinary products produced abroad were almost always sold in the same country in which they were manufactured.

Pfizer International chemical manufacturing plants were located in Australia, Canada, Argentina, Belgium, France, and the United Kingdom. These plants generally represented a large capital investment and were limited by high tariffs and transportation costs to sales in their national markets. Some chemicals and bulk pharmaceuticals were exported from the United States and the United Kingdom, however.

Cosmetics and/or other consumer products were manufactured in Argentina, Mexico, Canada, Brazil, Chile, South Africa, France, Germany, Italy, Sweden, Venezuela, Uruguay,[4] and the United Kingdom. While the factories in these countries produced consumer products primarily for their local markets, there was a considerable temporary movement of these products across national boundaries, as this was still a relatively new business and volumes were not yet high enough to justify all desirable plants. This was particularly true of the Coty cosmetics line, a large part of which, for Europe, was manufactured in France.

Decisions as to which manufacturing facilities or supply points were to supply which markets were made by the operations services department in New York under policies set by the president. In making these decisions, the department took into account differences in manufacturing costs, tariffs, transportation expenses, and utilization of capacity. In general, a given logistics pattern, once established, was not changed unless a major development occurred. A new plant or above-capacity demands on an existing facility were typical reasons for making changes.

[4]Under license.

In early 1965, as a considerable number of Pfizer's United States manufacturing facilities were reaching capacity levels, the operations services department requested foreign manufacturing facilities with excess capacity to estimate unit costs at higher production levels. On the basis of these estimates, future logistics patterns were to be established. A typical problem was whether to increase the size of a plant then operating at capacity or increase the production level of a plant operating below capacity. According to the manager of the operations services department, decisions of this sort required not only complex economic analysis but also consideration of the economic policies and trading patterns of the countries in which Pfizer did business.

Geographic Distribution of Sales

Pfizer International sales varied considerably from country to country and among product lines. Exhibit 2 presents sales data for each business in a number of representative countries.

Organization

The basic organizational concept under which Pfizer International operated was that the key operating entity was the country business. There was a direct-line relationship between 10 geographic area managers and Pfizer International President Richard C. Fenton. Area managers

EXHIBIT 2
NET SALES BY COUNTRY AND BUSINESS (FY 1964)*
In Thousands of Dollars

Country	Pharmaceutical products	Agricultural and veterinary products	Chemical products	Consumer products
France	5,000	400	3,400	2,400
Germany	9,200	1,800	400	9,000
Italy	10,000	5,000	800	900
U.K.	23,000	4,000	5,200	1,500
Benelux	11,000	1,600	1,800	280
Sweden	2,800	400	440	140
Norway	520	100	60	280
Finland	480	350	240	140
Greece	2,000	300	30	–
Iran	900	300	35	–
Spain	4,800	900	400	35
Egypt	920	200	200	–
Mexico	9,600	1,600	500	360
Brazil	6,800	3,200	170	1,600
Argentina	11,000	2,400	900	700
Guatemala	550	70	70	8
Colombia	3,200	700	600	140
Chile	2,400	1,200	100	2
Australia	3,000	800	3,200	2,000
Japan	2,400	30	2,200	200
Philippines	2,400	600	250	–
India	28,000	1,400	1,850	65

*Financial data not publicly available have been disguised.

were responsible for the Pfizer businesses in the countries under their jurisdiction and exercised direct-line authority over the country managers located in their areas.

In addition to the line organization, a number of staff departments reported to Mr. Fenton. The headquarters staff, consisting of about 250 persons in early 1965, provided staff services in such areas as accounting, legal counsel, personnel, and public and government relations. In addition, it coordinated (by disseminating information) worldwide Pfizer activities in the fields of product development, long-range planning, and production and advised Mr. Fenton (for line implementation) about transfer prices, logistics, and capital budgeting.

Members of the Pfizer International organization believed that decentralization of line authority to as great an extent as possible to the country business level was a major factor in the company's success. While executives on the headquarters staff traveled frequently and had close working relationships with members of the line organization located in the field, their role was limited to making suggestions to line managers or policy recommendations to Mr. Fenton.

Historical Development of Pfizer International's Organization

The Pfizer International organization, as it existed in early 1965, was the outgrowth of a series of organizational changes. In the early 1950s, Chas. Pfizer had an export department which sold fine chemicals (Pfizer's original product line) to distributors in a number of foreign countries. As Pfizer entered the pharmaceutical field (1950), the export department sold some pharmaceutical products to the same distributors who handled the fine chemicals line.

Then, in 1951, Pfizer decided to export Terramycin, the broad-spectrum antibiotic which was to play such a significant part in the company's future growth. At this time, the company concluded that fine chemicals distribu-

tors would not be an effective channel for marketing Terramycin and decided to set up branches in the key foreign markets. As the result of a consultant's study, Pfizer decided to establish international subsidiaries to operate these foreign branches.

These subsidiaries soon became known as "Pfizer International." They had their own boards of directors, drawn from Chas. Pfizer and Pfizer International executives. Mr. John J. Powers, who had previously been a member of the Chas. Pfizer board of directors and corporate secretary, became president and chairman of the board of Pfizer International.

In the early 1950s, Pfizer International operated as a highly centralized organization. At New York headquarters, four regional directors, responsible respectively for Europe, Latin America, the Middle East, and the Far East, reported to the president of Pfizer International. Territorial managers, who were also located in New York, were each responsible for several countries (whether branches or independent distributors). These territorial managers reported to the regional directors.

During this period, Pfizer International attempted to manage its growing foreign operations from New York. Advertising and promotional brochures were prepared at headquarters and sent out to the branches. Territorial managers made many operating decisions, particularly in the area of marketing. New York headquarters attempted to plan foreign activities in detail, and the regional directors spent most of their time traveling.

By 1956, as the business grew, it became clear that extreme centralization was an inefficient way to run Pfizer's international business. After considerable analysis, Mr. Powers decided to send the regional directors abroad and eliminate the territorial managers altogether. The regional directors were designated as area managers, and area headquarters were established in the United Kingdom (Europe, the Middle East, Africa), Hong Kong (the Far East), and Buenos

Aires (Latin America). The managers in the various countries, who were now more likely to be managing subsidiaries than branches or distributors, were given increased responsibility, particularly in the marketing area, and were called country managers. These people reported to the appropriate area manager.

The 1956–1957 reorganization resulted in a highly decentralized organization. Mr. Powers's staff was limited to technical specialists, and there was no way for him to follow the operations of the regions and countries closely. The area managers developed their own headquarters organizations. The country managers had considerable autonomy in running their countries and complete responsibility for local marketing activities.

While an organizational philosophy based on decentralization was firmly established in the late 1950s, Pfizer International's rapid growth suggested some changes. In particular, Mr. Powers felt that he needed assistance in New York and that more areas should be established. As a result, he decided to divide the old areas, which had grown from three to four, into eight new areas, each under an area manager. The former area managers returned to New York. Richard Fenton, who had been in charge of the European area, became an operational vice president and was responsible for the area managers located in Europe, Africa, the Middle East, and Canada. The former area manager for southern Latin America became an operational vice president and supervised area managers in Latin America and the Far East. The Far East area manager became vice president in charge of the New York administrative staff.

In late 1963, Mr. Powers was promoted to vice chairman of Chas. Pfizer & Co., and Mr. Fenton became president of Pfizer International. Under Mr. Fenton, the organization remained much as it had under Mr. Powers, except that the positions of the operational vice presidents were eliminated. As a result, the area managers reported directly to the president.

The Line Organization in Early 1965

In early 1965, 10 area managers reported directly to Mr. Fenton. The 10 areas and the countries under area managers' jurisdiction are shown in Exhibit 3.

According to a Pfizer International position description, it was "the responsibility of each Area Manager to plan, develop, and carry out Pfizer International's business in the assigned foreign area in keeping with company policies and goals. This involves, for the area assigned, the managerial planning and integration of products imported from established plants located elsewhere; location and recommendation of potentialities of local manufacture; acquisition or establishment of plants or businesses; and direction of manufacture (where applicable) and marketing of products."

The memorandum went on to list a number of specific responsibilities charged to the area managers. The area manager:

1. Participates in top-level consideration of overall Pfizer International policies. Establishes area policies within limits of company general policies.
2. Initiates, evaluates, and determines long-range planning and annual and interim product plans for the area. Administers area's operations through delegation of responsibility to staff members and country managers (if applicable) for timely accomplishment of objectives. Guides and directs specific action, as required by emergency or change of conditions. Continually reviews and evaluates area's status and trends with the president, and recommends solutions to major problems.
3. Determines and establishes organization structure for the area's needs and objectives. Develops key personnel through example, counsel, job assignment, and establishment of standards of leadership at managerial levels. Assures conduct of development and training programs at lower levels.
4. Represents the company through participation in major negotiations in such matters as acquisi-

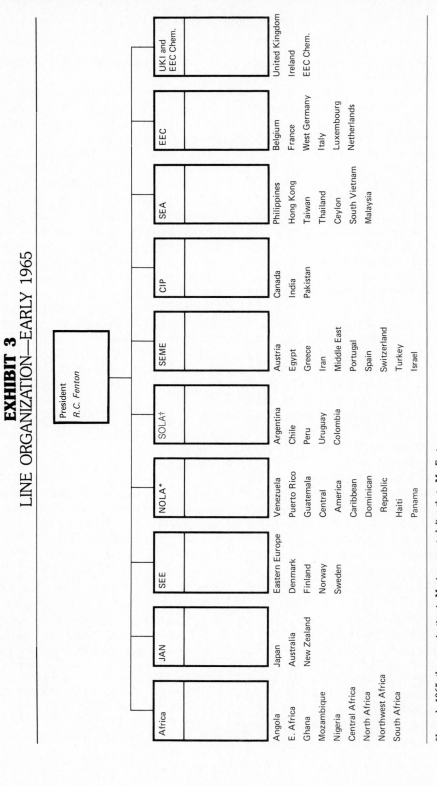

EXHIBIT 3
LINE ORGANIZATION—EARLY 1965

President
R.C. Fenton

Africa

Angola
E. Africa
Ghana
Mozambique
Nigeria
Central Africa
North Africa
Northwest Africa
South Africa

JAN

Japan
Australia
New Zealand

SEE

Eastern Europe
Denmark
Finland
Norway
Sweden

NOLA*

Venezuela
Puerto Rico
Guatemala
Central
  America
Caribbean
Dominican
  Republic
Haiti
Panama

SOLA†

Argentina
Chile
Peru
Uruguay
Colombia

SEME

Austria
Egypt
Greece
Iran
Middle East
Portugal
Spain
Switzerland
Turkey
Israel

CIP

Canada
India
Pakistan

SEA

Philippines
Hong Kong
Taiwan
Thailand
Ceylon
South Vietnam
Malaysia

EEC

Belgium
France
West Germany
Italy
Luxembourg
Netherlands

**UKI and
EEC Chem.**

United Kingdom
Ireland
EEC Chem.

*In early 1965, the organization in Mexico reported directly to **Mr. Fenton.**
†In early 1965, the organization in Brazil reported directly to **Mr. Fenton.**

768

tions of businesses or plants, securing necessary clearances from foreign governments or international operators.

5. As applicable, assures that country managers:
   a. Maintain balanced product lines, determining product additions or deletions.
   b. Look after foreign-language labeling and packaging requirements.
   c. Establish selling prices and agency discounts and terms—requesting the N.Y. office approval when required by existing policies.
   d. Analyze sales volume and profit contribution of each product variety.
   e. Direct sales promotional plans, adapting domestic or other overseas promotions when feasible.
   f. Develop and maintain a field sales organization.

Area managers were generally located in the area for which they were responsible. Exceptions to this rule in early 1965 were the CIP (Canada, India, and Pakistan) area manager, who was temporarily located in New York, and the SEE (Scandinavia and Eastern Europe), SEME (Southern Europe and the Middle East), and EEC (European Economic Community) area managers, all of whom were located in Brussels, where they shared a common staff.

The size and functions of the area staff varied widely among the various areas. While all areas had staffs operating in the fields of control, personnel, and finance, some areas also had staffs concerned with production coordination and legal matters. Differences among areas in this regard were generally accounted for by differences in the complexity of their activities in these fields.

By early 1965, some areas with extensive nonpharmaceutical businesses were also beginning to set up product-oriented staff departments at the area level. While no such staffs had yet been set up in Brussels, chemical product specialists were operating in the SOLA (Southern Latin America) and JAN (Japan, Australia, and New Zealand) areas. In Europe, the UKI (United Kingdom and Ireland) area manager

had line responsibility for chemical sales and manufacture in the EEC area. A member of his staff was located in Brussels, with responsibility for chemical activities in the EEC.

At the country level, one or more managers had profit responsibility for Pfizer activities in each country. In most cases, a single country manager had responsibility for all Pfizer activities in that country. In the EEC, however, the country manager was responsible only for the pharmaceutical and agricultural products businesses. Separate general managers, who reported to area management, were responsible for the chemicals and consumer products businesses. In countries where the businesses were divided, the country manager generally retained administrative responsibility for staff services which were shared and represented Pfizer International on occasions requiring a representative of the company as a whole. Organizationally, however, country managers and general managers in the EEC area were at the same level and reported directly to the area managers.[5]

Pfizer Organization in Europe. In early 1965, the chief exception to this organizational pattern was Pfizer's line organization in Europe, where three area managers (EEC, SEE, SEME) shared a common staff and a fourth area manager (UKI) was responsible for chemical operations in the EEC area (see Exhibit 4, organization chart).

Pfizer's European organization took this form for a variety of reasons. The decision to bring the three area managers together in Brussels had been made in 1963 as part of a wider realignment of areas intended to reflect the growing importance of the European Economic Community. Once the three areas had been brought together, it had seemed logical to have them

[5]In the EEC area (which was made up of Belgium, France, Italy, Luxembourg, the Netherlands, and West Germany), the area manager had written a memorandum setting forth the relationship between country and business managers. See appendix A at the end of this case for excerpts from this memorandum.

EXHIBIT 4
ORGANIZATION IN EUROPE—EARLY 1965

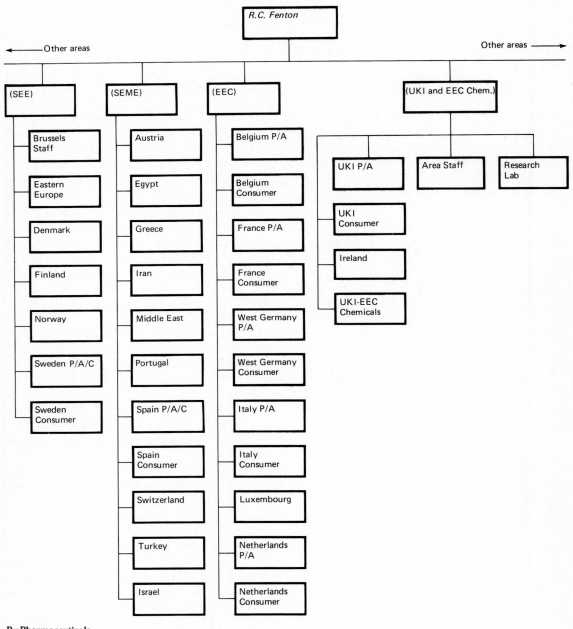

R.C. Fenton

←—— Other areas

Other areas ——→

(SEE)

Brussels Staff

Eastern Europe

Denmark

Finland

Norway

Sweden P/A/C

Sweden Consumer

(SEME)

Austria

Egypt

Greece

Iran

Middle East

Portugal

Spain P/A/C

Spain Consumer

Switzerland

Turkey

Israel

(EEC)

Belgium P/A

Belgium Consumer

France P/A

France Consumer

West Germany P/A

West Germany Consumer

Italy P/A

Italy Consumer

Luxembourg

Netherlands P/A

Netherlands Consumer

(UKI and EEC Chem.)

UKI P/A

UKI Consumer

Ireland

UKI-EEC Chemicals

Area Staff

Research Lab

P=Pharmaceuticals
A=Agricultural
C=Chemicals

share a common staff, which was put under the administrative direction of the SEE area manager.

The decision to have the UKI area manager direct the EEC chemical operations as well as the UKI area from the United Kingdom was also due to a number of factors. The UKI area manager had not been moved to Brussels because of the magnitude of the U.K. operations and the location of Pfizer International's research laboratories in England. This manager had also taken the lead in establishing Pfizer International's chemical business, most of which was located in the United Kingdom. Since he had had far more experience with chemicals than the EEC area manager, he had been given responsibility for chemical operations in the EEC. Chemical business managers in the six EEC countries reported to an EEC chemical manager, who reported to the UKI area manager.

This arrangement caused some problems in the field of bulk pharmaceutical sales and licensing. As previously noted, bulk pharmaceutical sales were considered part of the chemicals business so that pharmaceutical managers would not have to face conflicts between marketing Pfizer pharmaceutical products to the trade and selling or licensing Pfizer patented products to competitors. If a chemicals manager wished to make such a sale or licensing arrangement, the pharmaceuticals manager could present opposing arguments to the area manager, who would make the final decision. This procedure was followed in the SEE and SEME areas, where chemical and pharmaceutical managers reported to the same area manager. In the EEC area, however, such conflicts had to be resolved by Mr. Fenton, since chemical and pharmaceutical managers reported to different area managers.

The Headquarters Staff in Early 1965

In early 1965, Pfizer International maintained a headquarters staff of about 250 persons in New York City. Most of these personnel (193 persons) were located in eight staff departments, the managers of which reported to Mr. R. D. Royer, Pfizer International vice president of administration. Mr. Royer reported to Mr. Fenton. (See Exhibit 5, Pfizer International headquarters organization.)

The administrative departments which reported to the vice president of administration were responsible for such functions as employee relations, long-range planning, production, control, legal matters, purchasing, pricing, shipping, and finance. The managers of these departments had no line authority but influenced field activities through policy recommendations submitted to Mr. Fenton. In addition, these departments reviewed plans, budgets, and operating results of the field organizations and submitted their analyses to Mr. Fenton, who met with area managers several times a year. Moreover, the administrative department managers visited most of the larger countries on a regular basis in order to meet with the area and country managers and their functional counterparts. On these occasions, they explained new policies and guidelines established by Mr. Fenton and made certain that existing policies were being implemented effectively.

The staff departments which reported directly to Mr. Fenton were government relations, public relations, product development, and projects. The government and public relations departments were responsible for Pfizer International's efforts in these areas in the United States and also had advisory relationships with their functional counterparts in the field organization. The product development department was responsible for coordinating the development activities of the areas and countries with those of the Pfizer International research laboratories in England and the Chas. Pfizer & Co. Laboratories in the United States. In addition, it made policy recommendations to Mr. Fenton concerning long-range development projects and was responsible for making certain that Pfizer International made

EXHIBIT 5
PFIZER INTERNATIONAL HEADQUARTERS ORGANIZATION—EARLY 1965

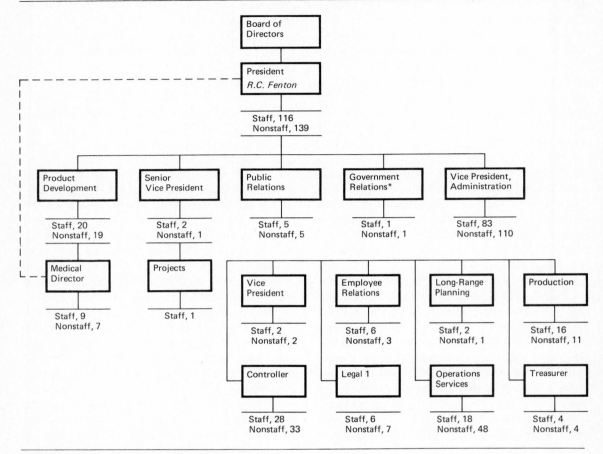

*Also reports to J. J. Powers, Jr., president, Chas. Pfizer & Co.

adequate use of product developments originating in the United States. Finally, a projects committee appraised the merits of capital investment proposals (investments of more than $20,000 [US]).

Profit Centers and Budgets

The cornerstone of Pfizer International's reporting and control system was a large number of decentralized profit centers (about 200 in early 1965). Each geographic area was a profit center and prepared annual area budgets. Within each area, the countries were also profit centers, preparing annual budgets for review and consolidation at the area level. In the larger countries, each business (i.e., pharmaceutical, agricultural, consumer, and chemical) was treated as a separate profit center.

Area budgets were reviewed, modified, and approved by Mr. Fenton at annual budgetary meetings held in New York each fall. In preparing their budgets, the area managers followed "guideposts" established by Mr. Fenton. For an example of such guideposts, see appendix B at the end of this case.

Differences in customs regulations and fiscal policies among the countries in which Pfizer did business often required that external transfer prices be calculated individually for each country. If these external transfer prices were used in measuring the performance of each profit center, meaningful evaluation of operating results would have been virtually impossible.

For this reason, results for each profit center were measured by reference to an "internal" transfer price. A primary source of supply was established for each product, and the cost of manufacturing at the source of supply was used as the "internal" transfer price. While secondary sources of supply were sometimes used, the internal transfer price could not be higher than that used for shipments from the primary source of supply so as not to penalize those profit centers which were supplied by relatively high-cost manufacturing facilities. This latter modification was particularly important, since decisions as to which manufacturing facility or supply point would supply a particular country were made in the operations services department in New York.

New York headquarters received interim financial reports from the profit centers each month. In addition, a number of standard operating reports were submitted to New York on a regular basis. Among these were reports dealing with production efficiency and inventory levels. The New York headquarters staff used these reports to discover significant trends before they began to show up in the profit centers' financial statements.

Pfizer International's growing diversification had significant implications for the company's reporting and control procedures. By early 1965, separate financial statements were being prepared for each of the four businesses so that management could appraise the performance of each product line as well as each geographic area. Nevertheless, there were increasing complaints from consumer products managers; they contended that Pfizer's account structure at the market level was oriented to the pharmaceutical business and did not provide them with sufficiently detailed data. For example, the Pfizer accounting manual contained the category "advertising expenses." This category was not broken down into types of media, since consumer advertising was a relatively insignificant expense in the pharmaceutical business.

Pricing

New York headquarters exercised differing degrees of control over the to-the-market price of each of the four categories of products. While there were variations within each of the four businesses, the following generalizations give an indication of the differences.

In general, New York headquarters exercised the most control over pharmaceutical prices. When a pharmaceutical product was first introduced, basic price levels were determined by the operations services department, with approval by Mr. Fenton. This procedure was necessary because of the broad international nature of most of the basic products.

For agricultural and chemical products, the area managers generally had final responsibility for pricing. Strong competition in most markets, considerable product variety by country, and the commodity nature of many of these products made this policy necessary. In some cases, however, floor prices were established by New York headquarters. Area managers could not go below these floor price levels without headquarters approval.

In the consumer products field, country managers had considerably more autonomy because of the distinctly national character of the consumer goods business. While area managers had to approve all major price changes, country managers and consumer products general managers were relatively free to respond to local marketing conditions.

Appendix A

Extracts from an Interoffice Memorandum, Brussels Headquarters

TO: EEC country managers and consumer products general managers

FROM: EEC area manager—Brussels

SUBJECT: Relationship between country manager and consumer products general manager—EEC Area

DATE: November 9, 1964

. . . in the EEC Area, both the Country Managers and the Consumer Products General Managers are at the same level of operational authority and responsibility, which is the country manager level. The authority and responsibilities of a country-manager-level operational position is defined in more detail in the Pfizer International Accounting Manual as well as the Pfizer Europe Procedures Manual. Thus, in the EEC Area, the Country Manager and the Consumer Products General Manager have complete profit and loss responsibility for their respective operations, complete budget responsibility, capital appropriations responsibility, pricing and new product development responsibility, to mention only a few of the most obvious criteria. There are, however, certain differences in the administrative and organizational responsibilities of the Country Manager versus the Consumer Products General Manager, as outlined in the following paragraphs.

Country Manager

The Country Manager has complete responsibility for our Pharmaceutical and Agricultural operation in his country, reporting directly to the EEC Area Manager. The Pharmaceutical and Ag/Vet Division Managers report to him. In addition, the managers of the service divisions, Technical, Finance and Medical, report to him administratively. In addition to providing appropriate services for the pharmaceutical and agricultural operations, the service division managers, under the Country Manager, have responsibility, likewise, for providing services to the consumer products operating divisions in their country. In addition to this operational responsibility for our pharmaceutical and agricultural activities and his administrative responsibility for the service functions, the Country Manager is also expected to exercise over-all cognizance concerning governmental, community, legal and social problems affecting Pfizer interests in the country as a whole.

Consumer Products General Manager

The Consumer Products General Manager has complete responsibility for all consumer products operations in his country, reporting directly to the EEC Area Manager. The consumer products operating divisions report to him. He obtains services as a requirement from the Finance, Technical and Medical Divisions in order to ensure the proper functioning of these operating divisions. In matters related to the consumer products operating divisions he is the final authority on finance, technical, medical and personnel issues at the local country level. If consumer products operations affect our ethical pharmaceutical activities he would consult the Country Manager, and if local agreement cannot be reached the matter would be referred to the Area Manager.

Use of Service Divisions

If the organization as defined above is to function smoothly, managers must ensure that there is direct

774

liaison between the service divisions and the operating divisions at all levels. The Country Manager and Consumer Products General Manager must not act as bottlenecks to the normal routine functioning of staff and service activities. Most routine activity must be accomplished by horizontal contact between division managers, department heads and section heads down through the entire organization, consistent with proper operating procedure. Any important problems of policy and priorities would be resolved as necessary between the Country Manager and the Consumer Products General Manager.

Decentralization of Authority to Division Managers

The proper functioning of the above organization is certainly dependent upon one aspect of good management practice which we assume is carried out in all of our countries. This is the policy of decentralizing authority to the managers for both operating and service divisions. Essentially, this means that the country should run properly without the interference of the Country Manager or Consumer Products General Manager. This is particularly important in the operating divisions where the division manager must have complete profit and loss responsibility for his operations. This may involve only giving him responsibility for the *local* profit and loss situation; however, the basic principle is essentially the same. We would also hope that eventually all division managers could have the consolidated profit and loss responsibility.

In any event, it means that the Operating Division Manager must be cognizant not only of sales and promotional expenses, but the financial, technical and all other business aspects affecting his division as well. This does not give the Operating Division Manager direct authority over the Service Division Manager. For example, the Pharmaceutical Division Manager obtains services and has essentially the same relationship with the Finance and Technical Divisions as the Consumer Products General Manager, and, under him, the Coty or other consumer products division managers.

Charges for Services

The operating divisions, whether they be pharmaceutical, agricultural, or consumer products, are charged their proportion of the expenses of the service divisions in accordance with the general policy in Pfizer International of direct and indirect charges. Direct charges are those which can be positively and exclusively identified with the activity of a particular operating division. After these direct charges have been allocated, the remainder of the expenses of the service divisions are allocated to the operating divisions in direct proportion to the sales volume of each division. In a particular country, the system of effecting direct charges to the operating divisions is the responsibility of the Finance Division Manager under the control of the Area Controller. The Country Manager and the Consumer Products General Manager must be cognizant of and approve the system of allocating direct expenses which is in use. The most important point is that this system must be defined in detail at the time of preparation of the budget and thereafter can only be changed with the approval of the Area Controller and the Area Manager.

Chemical Divisions

The service division managers under the administration of the Country Manager are responsible for providing service to the Chemical Division in each country in a manner similar to that provided for the consumer products activities as outlined above.

Dissemination of Above Procedure

Country Managers and Consumer Products General Managers should ensure that their division managers as well as other appropriate staff personnel are informed of the above procedures as they apply to their particular country.

Appendix B
Guideposts for 1966 Budget

The following is a memorandum from Mr. R. C. Fenton in New York to PI area managers:

> With some of you, I have been able to discuss this subject during my recent trips, but this has not been the case with all of you. So, I am setting down in writing the main points that I can think of. These are not intended to be rigid rules, and, if you have good reasons for breaking them and doing something different, you should, by all means, follow your own view in preparing the budget, but you should know that I will have to be convinced by you during your visit to New York. Therefore, it would be wise for you to give your reasons for departing from these principles in writing when you submit the budgets.

Pharmaceutical and Agricultural Business:

If the total expenses of promotion and S.&G.A. exceed 20% of sales, there should be some reduction in the percentage. There should not be any increase in the percentage whatever the present percentage may be.

Consumer Products Business:

I will not be prepared to approve any budget showing a significant loss unless a 5-year plan is presented at the same time which indicates when we will get into profit. There should be no significant expenditure in any country where a consumer products general manager has not been appointed. The emphasis should be on Coty unless we already have another major activity. Our long-range aim should be to achieve at least as good a percentage of the cosmetics market as we have of the pharmaceutical market, and, in any country where we are concentrating on consumer products, the budget for 1966 should be framed as part of a program in this direction.

Personnel:

Adequate provision should be made for the management training programs discussed at the last Area Managers' meeting.

Public Relations:

Adequate provision should be made for serious industry programs in all major countries.

Net Income:

Generally, I will expect the net income after taxes of each country to grow by at least 10% unless there are good explanations as to why this cannot be done. The countries where we are making substantial effort with investment and people should, of course, be growing at a greater rate than this. We will always have problems in one part of the world or another which have to be absorbed by greater than average growth where it is within our power. Our over-all aim is for our net income after all taxes to grow by substantially more than 10%, so many countries must do better than this—after absorbing the losses which we will certainly have in opening up new markets for consumer products.

50
Pfizer International: II

Steven H. Star • E. Raymond Corey • Cedric L. Suzman

In June 1965, Mr. Richard Fenton, president of Pfizer International, announced that the EEC, SEE, and SEME[1] areas were to be combined in a new regional grouping, Pfizer Europe. The former manager of the EEC area, Mr. James Green, was appointed senior vice president of Pfizer Europe (and a vice president of Pfizer International). He would continue to report directly to Mr. Fenton, but the SEE and SEME area managers would now report to him.

According to Mr. Fenton, the establishment of Pfizer Europe as a "management center" represented a step in the direction of further decentralization. At some time in the future, he

Steven H. Star was formerly an associate professor of business administration at the Harvard Graduate School of Business Administration. E. Raymond Corey is the Malcolm P. McNair Professor of Marketing at the Harvard Graduate School of Business Administration. Cedric L. Suzman is the director of research at Georgia State University.

[1]EEC = European Economic Community; SEE = Scandinavia and Eastern Europe; SEME = Southern Europe and the Middle East.

expected to set up similar management centers for Asia and Latin America. Eventually, three management center heads would report to him, each responsible for several of the old areas.

Mr. Fenton had decided to begin with Pfizer Europe for several reasons. Europe was the largest and most sophisticated market for Pfizer International products and thus was able to support an extensive headquarters staff sooner than other parts of the world. The growth of the EEC, the diversification of the product line, and the tendency of competition to view Europe as a single market had all contributed to the decision.

Pfizer Europe Organization

When Mr. Green became senior vice president of Pfizer Europe, he added responsibility for the combined Brussels staff and the SEE and SEME areas to his previous responsibilities as manager of the EEC area. Initially, he would retain responsibility for managing the EEC area, whose five pharmaceutical agricultural country business managers and four consumer products country business managers would continue to report to him. Temporarily, the SEE and SEME areas would remain intact, and country business managers in these areas would continue to report to their respective area managers, who would report to Mr. Green. The manager of the SEE area would continue to supervise the headquarters staff, and the manager of the separate United Kingdom and Ireland (UKI) area would continue to have line responsibility for chemicals and basic research.

During 1966 and 1967, however, Mr. Green expected to begin making changes in the organization of Pfizer Europe. While he was not yet certain what form these changes would take, he outlined certain possibilities in the late fall of 1965.

As a first step, the UKI area might be brought into Pfizer Europe. This move would add a major market to Mr. Green's responsibility and bring UK/EEC chemicals and European basic research, which were presently under the UKI area manager, into Pfizer Europe.

If the United Kingdom were added, Pfizer Europe would then have seven countries which were large enough to have separate managers for the various businesses conducted in each (i.e., UK, France, Italy, Benelux, Germany, Sweden, and Spain). In each of these countries, for example, separate country business managers might be appointed for (1) the pharmaceutical–agricultural/veterinary business, (2) the chemicals business, (3) the consumer products business, and (4) a door-to-door cosmetics business. While these separate managers would probably share some staff services, each would have profit responsibility for his or her business and report directly to Pfizer Europe headquarters.

With this in mind, Mr. Green was considering a top organization which would ultimately consist of six vice presidents at Pfizer Europe headquarters. Three of these vice presidents would be responsible for product lines: (1) the vice president of pharmaceuticals (including agricultural products), (2) the vice president of consumer products, and (3) the vice president of chemicals. Each of these product line vice presidents would have line authority over the country business managers responsible for his or her particular product line in each of the seven large countries indicated above. The other three vice presidents would be (1) the vice president of administration, with responsibility for staff activities at the Pfizer Europe headquarters; (2) the vice president of country organizations, with responsibility for those smaller markets essentially involved in the pharmaceutical business with small agricultural and chemical operations; and (3) the vice president of scientific affairs, with responsibility for basic research in the British and Belgian research centers. The vice president of country organizations would function in much the same way as the old area managers had, except that he or she would report to Mr. Green and work closely with the product line vice presidents (see Exhibit 1).

Pfizer International Staff Vice President—New York

In early September 1965, Mr. Fenton announced the establishment in New York of four new vice presidential positions in a memorandum to Pfizer International area managers and New York division heads (see Exhibit 2):

> We are creating four positions of Vice President for Development, each concerned with one of our separate businesses on an international basis and each reporting directly to me. These positions will be International staff positions, not line. That is to say, they will not intervene in the direct line of authority between me and Senior Vice President Green of Pfizer Europe or the Area Managers in other parts of the world, nor will they take responsibility away from these men. They will be

EXHIBIT 1
POSSIBLE PFIZER EUROPE ORGANIZATION

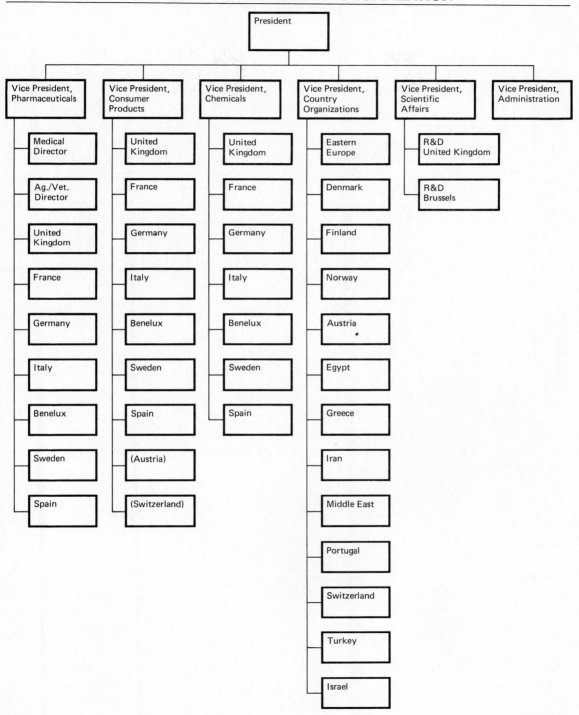

EXHIBIT 2
N.Y. HEADQUARTERS—ORGANIZATION CHART

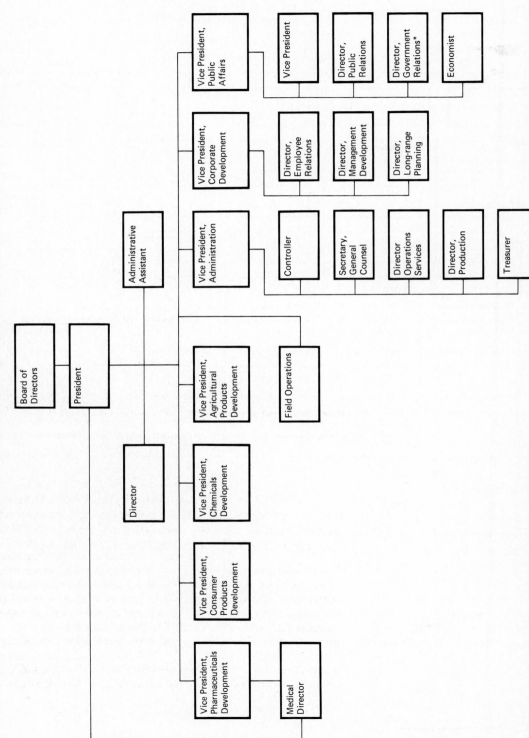

*Also reports to J. J. Powers, Jr., Chas. Pfizer & Col, Inc. Jan. 31, 1966.

responsible, in consultation with operating managements abroad, for formulating and recommending to me strategic policies for the International business with which they are concerned, and for ensuring that such policies, when agreed, are implemented through operating managements abroad. They will also be responsible for maintaining liaison with the Managers of the corresponding businesses in the United States with a view to ensuring that there is a free flow of technological and other information in both directions between the U.S. businesses and the businesses abroad, and also between our organizations in different parts of the world.

In describing the duties of the new vice presidents, Mr. Fenton pointed out that each would have a somewhat different role to play. Since each of the four Pfizer businesses was at a different stage in development, the line organization would require differing degrees of assistance in policy formulation and implementation.

At one extreme, the Pfizer pharmaceutical business was highly developed, and the field organization had adequate experience and resources to deal with most of its problems. For this reason, the vice president for pharmaceutical development would be primarily responsible for coordinating the flow of information between Chas. Pfizer research and development and the country pharmaceutical business managers and for ensuring that information concerning successful marketing approaches in one country was disseminated to the other countries. According to Mr. Fenton, the vice president for pharmaceutical development would largely confine planning activities to the fields of logistics and new plant construction.

The vice president for agricultural development would also be involved with dissemination of information and logistics planning. In contrast to pharmaceuticals, however, there were still several major strategic issues for Pfizer to resolve in the agricultural field. In Nigeria, Pfizer had integrated forward into the manufacture of finished feeds instead of concentrating on the sale of feed supplements to independent millers, as it had done in most other countries. Mr.

Fenton expected the new vice president for agricultural development to study these and other strategic alternatives and make recommendations as to what Pfizer's long-range strategy should be for the development of this business.

The vice president for consumer products development, who had been head of international marketing for Avon Cosmetics, would devote a large part of his time to the establishment of a Pfizer International door-to-door sales organization.

The new vice president for chemical development had previously been an executive with a major international chemical company. Because Pfizer International was still relatively inexperienced in the chemical business,[2] the vice president for chemical development would have a somewhat broader assignment than the other new vice presidents. According to an internal memorandum:

> The Vice President of Chemical Development will be responsible, in consultation with operating managements abroad, for formulating and recommending to the President strategic policy for the company's worldwide chemical business outside the United States and for insuring that such policies when agreed by the President are implemented through operating managements abroad.

The Future

In late December 1965, Mr. Fenton made the following comments on the future of Pfizer International's organization:

> It is difficult to predict what type of organization will be appropriate to our needs in the 1970s. We might want to go to line product divisions, as so many companies have done. Conversely, we might find that modern management techniques make it possible for geographic managers to operate a number of different businesses. After all, this is what I try to do for the company as a whole.

[2] Pfizer International chemical sales were only $28 million in 1964 (excluding bulk pharmaceuticals).

51 Bergman Wire and Cable Company

Ralph G. M. Sultan • E. Raymond Corey

The 8 o'clock Eastern Shuttle to New York was filled as Gordon Churchill settled into one of the remaining seats, loosened his necktie, and opened his briefcase. It was February 16, 1971. Churchill, president of the Bergman Wire and Cable Company, had a 10 o'clock appointment that day with the company's chairman of the board. The meeting was being held to discuss proposals for reorganizing the Bergman sales organization.

For the past 8 years, Bergman had sold its three major product lines (conduit products, wire and cable, and wiring devices) through one common sales division. The vice presidents of the three product divisions had expressed dissatisfaction with the arrangement almost since the day it was set up. On several occasions they had

Ralph G. M. Sultan was formerly an associate professor of business administration at the Harvard Graduate School of Business Administration. E. Raymond Corey is the Malcolm P. McNair Professor of Marketing at the Harvard Graduate School of Business Administration.

requested permission to withdraw from the pooled sales organization.

Churchill had been on the job as president for 1 year, and during that time he had familiarized himself with all phases of Bergman's business operations. The sales organization problem was a particularly vexing issue, and Churchill was determined to review all the facts once more to make sure he was making the right recommendation to the chairman of the board.

The Bergman Wire and Cable Company

The Bergman Wire and Cable Company was a publicly held company; its corporate offices were located in Cohasset, Massachusetts. Representative products sold by the company are pictured in Exhibits 1, 2, and 3. Other information about the three major product lines is shown in Exhibit 4.

EXHIBIT 1
PRODUCTS OF THE WIRING DEVICES DIVISION

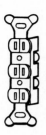

Triple
Outlet

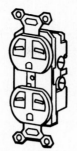

Double
Outlet

4-way
Switch

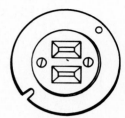

Single
Outlet

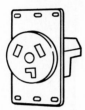

Dryer
Outlet

Porcelain
Lampholder

Porcelain
Lampholder

Mercury
Switch

Cable Set

Fuse

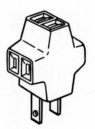

Cube Tap

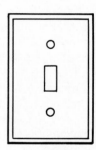

Wall Plate

Appliance
Connector

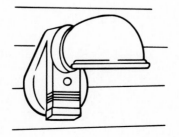

Wall
Fixture

Pilot
Lamp

Pull-Chain
Lampholder

783

EXHIBIT 2
PRODUCTS OF THE CONDUIT PRODUCTS DIVISION

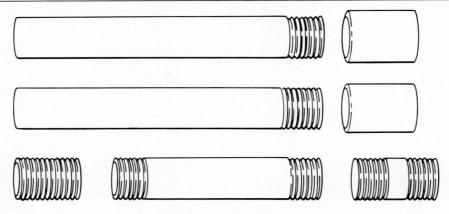

Close Nipples   Meter Service Nipples   Short Nipples

RIGID STEEL CONDUIT

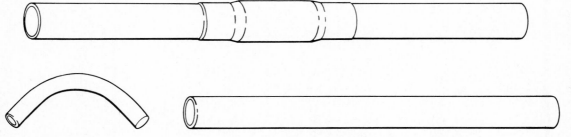

Long Radius Elbow,
90 deg

EMT is furnished in 10-foot lengths

ELECTRICAL METALLIC TUBING (EMT)

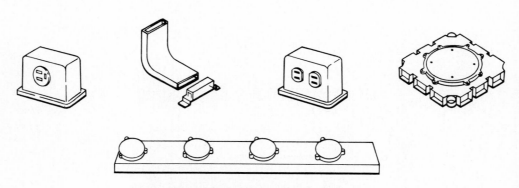

UNDERFLOOR DUCTS AND RACEWAYS

EXHIBIT 3
PRODUCTS OF THE WIRE AND CABLE DIVISION

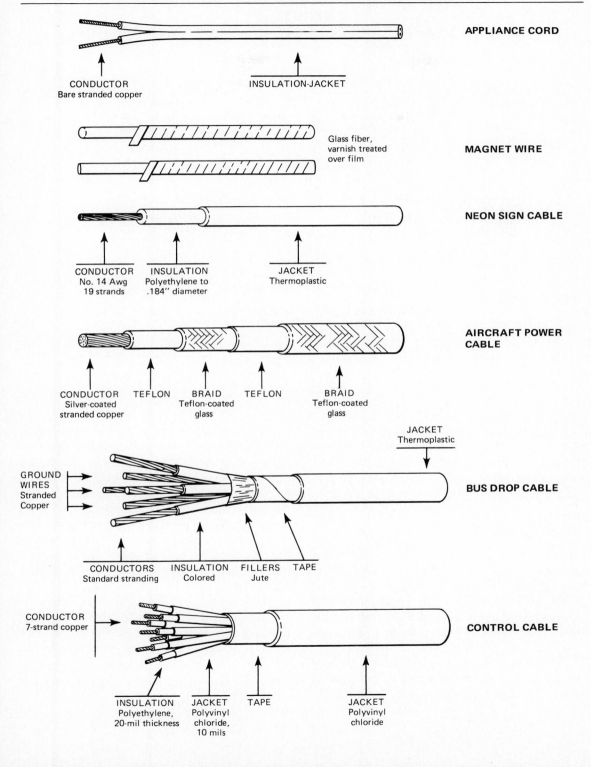

APPLIANCE CORD

CONDUCTOR
Bare stranded copper

INSULATION-JACKET

MAGNET WIRE

Glass fiber,
varnish treated
over film

NEON SIGN CABLE

CONDUCTOR
No. 14 Awg
19 strands

INSULATION
Polyethylene to
.184″ diameter

JACKET
Thermoplastic

AIRCRAFT POWER CABLE

CONDUCTOR
Silver-coated
stranded copper

TEFLON

BRAID
Teflon-coated
glass

TEFLON

BRAID
Teflon-coated
glass

BUS DROP CABLE

JACKET
Thermoplastic

GROUND
WIRES
Stranded
Copper

CONDUCTORS
Standard stranding

INSULATION
Colored

FILLERS
Jute

TAPE

CONTROL CABLE

CONDUCTOR
7-strand copper

INSULATION
Polyethylene,
20-mil thickness

JACKET
Polyvinyl
chloride,
10 mils

TAPE

JACKET
Polyvinyl
chloride

EXHIBIT 4
PRODUCTS OF THE BERGMAN WIRE AND CABLE COMPANY

	Product line		
	Wiring devices	**Conduit products**	**Wire and cable**

Products	Consumer line
	Contractor line
	Standard line
		Conduit
		  Rigid conduit
		  EMT
		  Underfloor duct
			Power cable
			Appliance wire
			Mining cable
			Transportation cable
			Supply cord
			Magnet wire
			Electronic cable

1970 national sales (millions)	$26*	$42	$72
1970 national market share	About 10%*	About 10%	About 10%

1970 profits
  (before taxes)
  as a percentage
  of sales
	15%	6%	1.5%

Division headquarters	Woonsocket, R.I.	Sandusky, Ohio	Cohasset, Mass.
Manufacturing plants	Woonsocket, R.I.; New London, Conn.; Savannah, Ga.	Sandusky, Ohio	Cohasset, Mass.

*Excluding consumer line.

Bergman products handled by the sales division were sold exclusively through franchised distributors, with the exception of wire and cable, which was sold both direct and through distributors.

Wiring Devices

The wiring devices division manufactured the following types of products: electrical outlets, caps, connectors, plugs, switches, lamp holders, thermostat controls, heating cable sets, fuse holders, cable terminals, wall plates, and many other miscellaneous electrical fixtures. The products were divided roughly into three lines.

The *consumer line* consisted of inexpensive wiring devices which were sold to the general public through hardware stores, food stores, chain department stores, and other retail outlets. Most of these outlets were serviced by rack jobbers and hardware wholesalers. The wiring devices division handled all sales of this line with its own selling organization, consisting of a consumer products sales manager and 12 sales representatives. The sales division was therefore not involved in the promotion of the consumer line. Sales of the consumer line were approximately equal to sales of the other two lines combined.[1]

The *small building contractor line* was sold for installation in residential and small commercial buildings. It was one of the most complete lines in the industry and superior in quality to the

---

[1]All sales data in this case exclude the consumer line of wiring devices.

consumer line. The contractor line was sold to lumberyards, hardware stores, and electrical contractors. The most important customers, small electrical contractors, were referred to as "basket contractors," since they usually purchased a "basket" of miscellaneous wiring devices as required during the construction of a building.

The *standard line* consisted of heavy-duty wiring devices for commercial, industrial, and institutional applications. These wiring devices were sold for both new construction and building maintenance purposes through wholesale distributors. Some devices were sold through retail outlets to the general public.

The Bergman wiring devices line was an industry leader in quality and design. Most devices manufactured by Bergman had a high assembly labor content and a high value added during manufacture.

Conduit Products

The conduit products division manufactured two lines of products: conduit and underfloor duct.

Conduit. The conduit line, by far the most important in terms of sales volume, was in turn composed of two products: rigid conduit and electrical metallic tubing (referred to simply as EMT).

Rigid conduit was galvanized steel pipe which was used in building construction to convey and to protect electrical wiring. It resembled ordinary water pipe. EMT was also used to carry electrical wiring in buildings, but it was of light tubular steel construction.

The conduit products division manufactured rigid steel conduit from steel pipe which it purchased from primary steel producers. The principal manufacturing operations consisted of cleaning, galvanizing, threading, and labeling. Approximately 80 percent of the total value of rigid conduit was the raw material cost. EMT was manufactured by induction welding of steel strip

which was purchased from primary steel producers.

Conduit was installed in a building by attaching it to the walls and ceilings with brackets or by embedding it in concrete during construction. The electrical wiring was threaded through the conduit after it was in place and was purchased separately from the conduit. Most conduit was purchased by building and electrical contractors for installation in new construction.[2]

Underfloor Duct. The other product manufactured by the conduit products division, underfloor duct, accounted for about 1 percent of the division's sales. The underfloor duct line consisted of systems of channels and raceways designed to carry power, telephone, and signal wiring under the floors of commercial and industrial buildings. Underfloor duct was of metal tubular construction, with special fittings for junctions and outlets. When underfloor duct was installed in a building, the electrical services could be tapped through special outlets at any location, thus permitting a flexible and easily modified layout of offices and machinery. The installation of underfloor duct had to be planned during the design stage of a new building. It was normally specified in the drawings of the architect or consulting engineer.

Wire and Cable

The various cable products manufactured by the wire and cable division covered a broad range of applications and customers, as shown in Exhibit 5.

Altogether, Bergman stocked several hundred types of wire and cable and regularly manufactured many other types upon special order. Two big markets which Bergman did not

[2]Conduit was usually purchased by the carload. One carload of conduit weighing 40,000 pounds sold for approximately $6,000. A large construction project of the magnitude of the Boston Prudential Center could consume about 100 carloads of conduit.

EXHIBIT 5
WIRE AND CABLE PRODUCTS

Cable type and applications	Selling channels	Customers	Percentage of sales
Power cable: Heavy power distribution to factories or machinery	Mostly through distributors	Plant maintenance organizations, electrical contractors, and utilities	35%
Appliance wire: Light wire for home appliances, machine tools, etc.	Mostly direct	OEMs manufacturing washing machines, radios, light power tools, etc.	10
Mining cable: Power supply to underground mine cars, excavating shovels, etc.	Mostly direct	Mining and quarrying companies	2
Transportation cable: Power supply to locomotives, subway cars, municipal transport, etc.	Mostly direct	Railways and transport companies; OEMs of transportation equipment	5
Supply cord: In buildings, houses (flexible BX cable and service entrance wire)	Through distributors	Home builders and electrical contractors	12
Magnet wire: Windings on electrical motors and servomechanisms	Direct / Through distributors	Electric motor OEMs and electronic OEMs / Motor repair shops	8
Electronic cable: Harness and hookup wire for computers and military applications	Direct	Electronic OEMs	28 / 100%

cover were (*a*) building wire used in house construction and (*b*) paper-insulated and uninsulated power cable used by utilities. Bergman had been in the building wire business at one time, but price competition had been too severe.[3] The paper-insulated and uninsulated cable market was dominated by primary copper and aluminum producers.[4]

The wire and cable division purchased copper wire from primary copper producers and then subjected it to various operations, such as bunching, wrapping, stranding, and extrusion.

[3]Of the cable products handled by wire and cable distributors, building wire had the largest volume.
[4]Paper-insulated and uninsulated power cable constituted 60 percent of utility purchases of wire and cable.

A large fraction of the total cost of a cable was represented by raw materials, particularly copper.

The Sales Organization

The Bergman sales division sold all products manufactured by the company, with the exception of the consumer wiring devices line, which was sold directly by the wiring devices division. It was an autonomous organization, completely responsible for organizing field selling activities and maintaining distributor relations. At the head office of the sales division in Cohasset, certain advertising, accounting, and market research functions were carried out. The sales division employed 120 district representatives in 11 districts across the United States. Each district was under the supervision of a district manager.

The three product divisions also maintained marketing organizations under the direction of marketing managers. Within the marketing organizations, sales managers were appointed for each major product or customer group. For example, the wiring devices division had (in addition to the consumer products sales manager) a construction products sales manager, who was responsible for sales to the construction industry. The conduit products division had sales managers for underfloor duct and for conduit. The wire and cable division had five sales managers responsible for government and transportation cable sales, distributor and contractor sales, OEM sales, utility and direct sales, and magnet wire sales. The product divisions also employed various marketing administrators, advertising managers, and market research managers.

While the marketing organizations within each product division were expected to maintain and increase Bergman sales, they had to work through the sales division in executing their programs at the field level. The principal point of contact between the sales division and a product division was at the district manager level in the sales division and the product sales manager level in the product division.

Exhibit 6 shows the division of responsibilities that existed between the three product divisions and the sales division.

As indicated above, ultimate pricing authority was held by the product divisions. For wiring devices, the district managers in the sales division were permitted to meet the lowest published list price of competitors, but quotations below any published price had to be approved by the product sales manager. For wire and cable, the district managers were sometimes allowed to adjust list prices by 5 to 7 percent on certain items in response to competition; for greater adjustments they had to request permission from the product sales manager. For conduit products, the district managers had to call the product sales managers for clearance on virtually every quotation. Requests for price cuts in response to genuine competition were seldom refused unless the factory was operating at capacity.

In an accounting sense, the three product divisions leased the services of the sales division. The share of the total operating expense which was paid by each product division was negotiat-

EXHIBIT 6
DIVISION OF MARKETING RESPONSIBILITIES

Responsibility of	**Wiring devices**	**Conduit products**	**Wire and cable**
Product divisions	Pricing	Pricing	Pricing
	Inventories	Inventories	Inventories
	Scheduling	Scheduling	Scheduling
	Product planning	Product planning	Product planning
	Promotions	Promotions	Promotions
	Market research	Order processing	
	Order processing		
	Advertising		
Sales division	Field selling	Field selling	Field selling
	Market research	Market research	Market research
	Sales accounting	Sales accounting	Sales accounting
		Advertising	Advertising
			Order processing

ed annually between the divisions and was apportioned roughly in accordance with the sales volume of each of the product divisions.

Sales quotas were established by the product divisions annually, in conjunction with the sales division. Each September the district managers in the sales division made a 1-year forecast of sales for their territories on the basis of visits to important customers and local economic forecasting agencies. This forecast was checked against national forecasts prepared by the sales division's market research unit. In November the reworked forecast was forwarded to the market research groups in the product divisions for further analysis. Gross quotas were finally established by negotiation between the sales division and the product division. These gross quotas were divided into district quotas by the sales division top management, and the district quotas were divided into individual sales reps' quotas by the district managers.

All district managers and district representatives were paid a straight salary, with a 10 percent bonus for reaching 100 percent of the sales quota. If individual quotas were exceeded, the district managers and representatives received further bonuses, up to a maximum of 40 percent of the base salary. For purposes of bonus determination, performance on each of the three product lines was considered separately; hence, one-third of the bonus was given if the sales quota was achieved in only one product line. All expenses incurred by the district representatives were paid by the company.

Many of the district representatives were responsible for selling all three product lines. Over a period of several years, a trend toward specialization on one or two product lines had become discernible. Product specialists were assigned to each district. These people had a specialized knowledge of a single product line and were expected to provide both technical assistance and sales leadership for the other sales reps in the district. Product specialists received an override bonus based on total sales for their product in the district.

Field Selling Activities

Many Bergman products were used in the construction industry. Often all three lines were sold through the same channels of distribution to the same customers. One 20-story office building, for example, utilized approximately $10,000 worth of wiring devices, $100,000 worth of conduit products, and $125,000 worth of wire and cable.

In order to have Bergman products used in a large construction project, such as a school or office building, it was necessary to have the Bergman name included in the list of approved suppliers drawn up by the architect or consulting engineer.[5] If Bergman was left off the list, it could not submit bids during construction to the contractor. Bergman district representatives therefore were expected to call on specifiers, such as architects or consulting engineers, whenever a project was in the design stage. Architects and engineers usually finished all specification work involving wire and cable and conduit products much earlier than the specification work involving wiring devices.

Architects or consulting engineers who did not call a Bergman representative for assistance were regularly called on by a representative. Most representatives were instructed to call at least once a month on important architects and consulting engineers in the territory. Bergman could not rely upon its distributors to do this type of work.

Once Bergman was specified, it was still necessary to compete with other suppliers for the actual order from the construction contractor

---

[5]Architects usually split their fees with consulting mechanical engineers who did the layout and specification work on mechanical and electrical services.

or electrical contractor. Whenever a major contract was being subcontracted, Bergman representatives called once a week on the contractors until the order was placed. At other times they called on contractors about once a month.

Conduit products were purchased early in a construction project; wire and cable were purchased somewhat later; and wiring devices were purchased at the very end of construction. The three types of products were almost never purchased as a single package; it was necessary to bid separately on each product line. Contractors expected delivery of wire and cable within 2 to 10 weeks, conduit products in less than 2 weeks, and wiring devices also in less than 2 weeks.

Apart from the construction industry, many Bergman sales originated with utilities, industrial companies, and original equipment manufacturers. The Bergman district representatives attempted to call on these accounts about once a month—more frequently if they were prime accounts.

A great deal of selling effort was expended upon the Bergman distributors. District representatives usually called on every major distributor once a week; less important distributors every 2 or 3 weeks; and small, marginal distributors approximately two or three times a year. During these visits the Bergman representatives checked stocks and suggested quantities for ordering. It was also necessary to hold sales meetings with the distributors' sales reps in order to train new reps, explain product features, and introduce new products. Bergman representatives also traveled with distributors' sales reps in order to stimulate interest in the Bergman product line.

It may be noted that about half of Bergman's distributors carried only one of the three lines, and in three-fourths of these cases it was the wiring devices line. Another 45 percent carried all three lines, and about 5 percent carried wiring devices plus wire and cable.

Early History of the Bergman Wire and Cable Company

The Bergman Wire and Cable Company had been one of the industry pioneers in designing, manufacturing, and marketing "connecting links" (e.g., lamp holders, fuses, conductors, and raceways) for electrical distribution systems. The early Bergman apparatus was designed to provide complete distribution systems, and the company consequently became active in three related product lines (wire and cable, metal conduit, and wiring devices), each of which was a necessary part of a complete system.

In 1928, a consolidated field sales organization was established to facilitate the marketing of these products. The sales organization sold almost entirely to electrical distributors, the exception being the case of certain equipment that was sold direct to other original equipment manufacturers. By 1936 Bergman was depending primarily upon 40 large supply houses plus certain of their branch operations to move merchandise. These same distributors also sold small appliances, major appliances, and radios. During the late 1930s the number of Bergman distributors expanded to 86.

One Bergman manager, in reflecting back upon the situation prior to World War II, commented:

> This large, well-financed group of independent distributors had a very strong jobber trade association. I can remember that this group always met at Palm Beach every year, and in the interim periods had various meetings that they conducted very much as a militant union, making various demands on Bergman as to how they would sell their merchandise, how they should be franchised, and numerous other requests that would serve their own interests.
>
> In retrospect, I think we became the captive of this large, influential, and highly selective distribution system, while outside this group the electrical construction materials industry was growing at a

very rapid rate. The result was that our competitors were growing much faster with the outside distribution, which by 1940 had become something over 2,000 wholesalers. The Bergman people in the lower echelons who tried to expand our distribution to match the outside growth of the industry had the obstacle of getting a new distributor approved by a high-level company committee called the distribution committee. The distribution committee was a phantom-type operation as far as our prospective customers were concerned since no outsider could for sure find out who composed its membership. Management could hide behind this committee's decisions when it served its purpose to do so.

Rebuilding Distribution in the Postwar Period

In the words of another Bergman sales manager, the company's distribution "was decimated" during World War II. Many of the large, prosperous distribution houses of the prewar period went out of business or changed the emphasis of their business away from electrical construction materials. The sons of certain pioneer Bergman distributors had no desire to continue in business when their fathers retired. New distributing companies sprang into existence after the war, many of them operated by aggressive young war veterans.

In 1953 David Fulton, who had started with Bergman as a field sales representative in 1935, was made manager of the marketing department. The position was nominally a staff job, but Fulton directed the entire marketing program of the company and was directly in charge of the field sales organization. Under Fulton, the marketing department was expanded from 30 to 140 persons. An organization chart for the Bergman Wire and Cable Company during this period is shown in Exhibit 7. The staff department managers holding positions equivalent to Fulton's position (e.g., in engineering and manu-

facturing) made most of the operating decisions for the company.

Bergman's effort to expand its distribution met with some resistance. The distribution committee was not permanently abolished until 1963. On the customer front, Bergman encountered protests from its old-line distributors, who did not want increased competition, and also from prospective new distributors who had built existing strong positions without Bergman support. Bergman also discovered that many competitors were taking their materials directly to the end users through specialized field selling organizations, with fast-moving manufacturing and engineering support. Furthermore, many competitors introduced new special-purpose products which met the needs of select customer groups better than equivalent Bergman products. Few competitors emphasized the overall systems approach in selling connecting links for electrical installations, and Bergman found that it was progressively more difficult to provide competitive products across the increasingly wide spectrum of electrical devices which were offered for sale.

Decentralization of the Company in 1963

In 1963, in a major decentralization move aimed at increasing competitive strength, the powerful "staff" department manager positions were liquidated, and the autonomy of the three product departments (hereafter designated as divisions) was increased. Also, a fourth division was created: the sales division. Jack Monteith, former manager of marketing in the wiring devices department, was named vice president of the sales division. Monteith, an excellent golfer and bridge player, had developed a wide circle of friends in the management of the company. Fulton, former manager of the marketing department, was named vice president of the wiring

EXHIBIT 7
ORGANIZATION CHART: 1948–1962

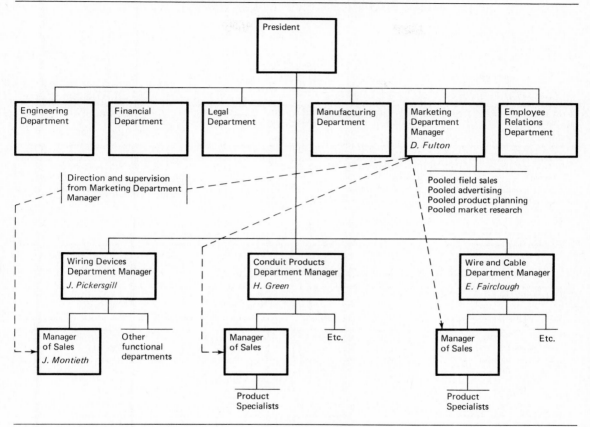

devices division. Exhibit 8 is an organization chart which shows how the company looked after 1963.

The sales division was assigned many of the responsibilities of the old marketing department. The sales division acted as the marketing outlet for the three product divisions on a pooled basis.

One exception to the pooled-sales policy existed. In April 1963, the Bergman Wire and Cable Company strengthened its position in the wiring devices field by purchasing the Kreuger Corporation, a thriving independent electrical manufacturer which sold low-priced consumer-type wiring devices through chain stores. Kreuger had a well-organized sales department, and the market it served, the retail consumer market, was largely separate and distinct from the higher-priced industrial and construction market served by the Bergman wiring devices department.[6] The Kreuger Corporation was merged

[6]Bergman and Kreuger did sometimes compete for distribution through hardware stores, and certain parts of their respective product lines overlapped.

EXHIBIT 8
ORGANIZATION CHART—1963

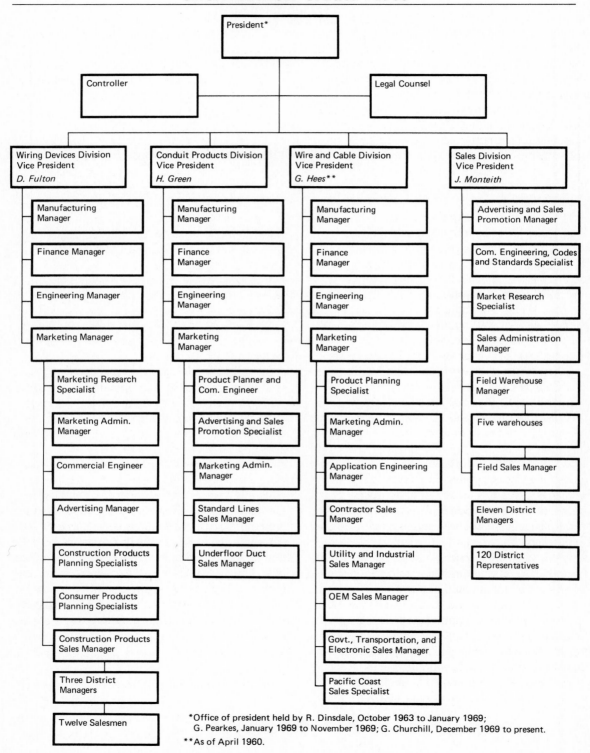

President*

Controller

Legal Counsel

Wiring Devices Division Vice President
D. Fulton

- Manufacturing Manager
- Finance Manager
- Engineering Manager
- Marketing Manager
  - Marketing Research Specialist
  - Marketing Admin. Manager
  - Commercial Engineer
  - Advertising Manager
  - Construction Products Planning Specialists
  - Consumer Products Planning Specialists
  - Construction Products Sales Manager
    - Three District Managers
      - Twelve Salesmen

Conduit Products Division Vice President
H. Green

- Manufacturing Manager
- Finance Manager
- Engineering Manager
- Marketing Manager
  - Product Planner and Com. Engineer
  - Advertising and Sales Promotion Specialist
  - Marketing Admin. Manager
  - Standard Lines Sales Manager
  - Underfloor Duct Sales Manager

Wire and Cable Division Vice President
G. Hees**

- Manufacturing Manager
- Finance Manager
- Engineering Manager
- Marketing Manager
  - Product Planning Specialist
  - Marketing Admin. Manager
  - Application Engineering Manager
  - Contractor Sales Manager
  - Utility and Industrial Sales Manager
  - OEM Sales Manager
  - Govt., Transportation, and Electronic Sales Manager
  - Pacific Coast Sales Specialist

Sales Division Vice President
J. Monteith

- Advertising and Sales Promotion Manager
- Com. Engineering, Codes and Standards Specialist
- Market Research Specialist
- Sales Administration Manager
- Field Warehouse Manager
  - Five warehouses
- Field Sales Manager
  - Eleven District Managers
    - 120 District Representatives

*Office of president held by R. Dinsdale, October 1963 to January 1969;
G. Pearkes, January 1969 to November 1969; G. Churchill, December 1969 to present.

**As of April 1960.

intact with the Bergman wiring devices department, and Kreuger personnel took over many of the management positions in the new wiring devices division. The Kreuger sales department became part of the division and functioned as a separate autonomous organization.

The principal argument used in keeping the consumer sales organization (Kreuger) out of the sales division was the specialized nature of the consumer products selling job. Fulton explained, "The consumer salesman fights his way into a 15-cent store and sells programs, plans, advertising, national copy, and displays. He will commit murder for eight inches of shelf space. The industrial sales job is just the opposite."

The wiring devices division thus came to sell its products through two separate marketing organizations. The retail consumer market was covered by the consumer sales organization directly, while the industrial and construction market was covered by the pooled sales organization, the sales division. Pointing to the problem of meshing activities on the consumer and industrial lines, the wiring devices division vice president, Fulton, argued successfully for the retention of all advertising, market research, and sales promotion activities. The other two product divisions turned over these functions to the sales division.

Postwar supply shortages which had characterized the industry carried over into the early 1950s and many customers were supplied by allocation. This situation had continued until the mid-1950s, when the stimulus provided by the Korean boom reached its peak. Thereafter, industry capacity exceeded demand, materials were in free supply, and the competitive situation changed markedly.

As competition in the industry became more intense, Bergman dropped, one by one, certain unprofitable segments of the market, including paper-insulated cable, circuit breakers, panel boards, flexible conduit, conduit fittings, terminal boxes, building wire, and cartridge fuses.

From the outset, the relationships between the product divisions and the sales division were not without some antagonism and friction. Reginald Dinsdale,[7] the president of the company, was a staunch supporter of the sales division and its vice president, Jack Monteith. (Monteith's office was across the hall from Dinsdale's office, and the two conferred often.)

Planning and Performance Appraisal in the Company

Prior to the 1963 decentralization, department managers were not held directly responsible for profits. With decentralization, the three product divisions became separate profit centers, and the product division vice presidents were held accountable for the performance of their divisions. Performance was appraised with respect to each division's return on investment, market share, and percentage profit on sales. Much emphasis was placed on the profit performance of the product divisions.

The sales division was appraised under slightly different criteria. Since it operated solely with funds provided by the three product departments, it was evaluated most heavily on the percentage of the sales quota achieved and on expense-to-sales ratios.

District managers in the sales division were evaluated on the percentage of the sales quota achieved. They received bonuses for meeting their district quotas. The district sales representatives or salespeople in the sales division were similarly evaluated on their percentages of the sales quotas achieved. They received three separate bonuses for meeting their sales quotas in each of three product lines.

Sales plans for the company were formalized in November of each year at the sales division's budget review meeting with the president. The three product division vice presidents were

---

[7]Prior to becoming president, Dinsdale had been part of the engineering management of the company.

invited to attend this meeting. Working within the sales targets established by the product divisions, the sales division presented its program for the following year. The product division vice presidents had an opportunity to comment on the plans and request changes.

The agenda for a typical budget review meeting read as follows:

1969 Plans and Budget Review Meeting
November 28, 1968
9:00 A.M.

Sales objectives and major changes in 1969 budget	J. Monteith
Field sales plans	R. Harkness
Application of sales analyses and indexes	E. Holt
Industry trends	J. Mosby
Field warehousing plans	R. Molson
Administration plans	W. Lippincott
Summary	J. Monteith

Luncheon at 12:30 in Rose Room

Typically, the sales division's plans were prepared with little consultation with the product departments. In fact, the product vice presidents seldom discussed anything with the sales vice president, except at bimonthly meetings with the president of the company. At these meetings, any deviations in performance from the sales plans were discussed.

The sales division was not usually open to criticism for failing to operate within budgeted expenses. However, sales revenue targets were frequently not met, and personnel in the sales division and the product divisions usually shrugged off responsibility, blaming one another. It was difficult to ascertain exactly who was to blame if sales quotas were not achieved. Sometimes new products were not available for sale when planned, and sometimes poor product performance was blamed by the sales division vice president for lack of sales volume.

Although it was hard to "pin down" just whose fault it was when sales budgets weren't met, the product division vice presidents believed they were ultimately held responsible, since profits were affected adversely. The product division vice presidents came to believe that while they were held accountable to very strict profit standards, the sales division was measured on a very subjective basis at best.

Requests to Withdraw from the Pooled Selling Arrangements

Dissatisfaction with the pooled selling arrangements among the product divisions led to attempts to withdraw. The first request was made by the wire and cable division in 1964. It was refused by President Dinsdale. The next request came from the wiring devices division in 1965. President Dinsdale took a very firm stand at this time, refused the request, and requested that the vice president of the wiring devices division not bring up the subject again. Subsequently, the conduit products division also asked to be released from the pooled selling organization and was turned down. Thereafter, similar requests to withdraw were made every 1 or 2 years and were refused.

The reasons given by the product divisions for their dissatisfaction with the pooled selling arrangements were diverse. The following comments were typical of the feelings of a sampling of managers in the three product divisions:

Comments from Various Managers in the Wire and Cable Division

The sales division's main objective is sales dollars. We have to worry about profits. The sales division pushes low-profit commodity-type products in order to get total sales volume up. We want to push complicated products which are in the development stage, so that our profits won't suffer in the long run.

The sales division can shift expenses and we can *never* track them down! They always make sales-expense ratios look all right. At the end of the year we have to talk assessments nevertheless. We try to watch, but we can't keep our finger on them.

How do you rebalance personnel when selling emphasis is changed? If Seattle is served by a 50–50 worker on cable and conduit, and if cable wants to cut back, who gets the worker's extra time? It can only be done by shifting assignments around from city to city. For two years running, on January 1 when the new budgets came down, 25 percent of our customers had a different rep calling on them. In the third year, 30 percent of our customers had a different rep. A district representative needs time in a territory before paying off. Constant change leads to chaotic customer relations.

Lines of communication are clumsy between the product divisions and the field organization. In part, this is because the levels of organization in the sales division are one step higher than they should be. For example, the district managers take direction in an administrative sense from the Sales Division, but they take direction in a sales sense from the product specialists in the product divisions. Now, if the sales managers (product specialists) for utility wire and cable (in the wire and cable division) want to issue instructions to the Chicago district manager, they first have to go through the manager, field sales, in the sales division. In other words, they have to first go up before they can go down. This is circuitous. It would be better to recognize the fact that the sales manager for utility wire and cable is organizationally on par with the manager, field sales, in the sales division. Then our product specialists could communicate freely downward to the district managers.

We have been accused of making derogatory comments about the sales division to the district representatives. Of course, if the DR's ask our visiting product specialists if it would be better to drop the pooled selling arrangement, our people tell them what they think. This gets back to the top in the sales division. We are accused of spreading propaganda in the sales division. It's a life of diplomacy. We want to be able to lay things on the line.

Comments from Various Managers in the Wiring Devices Division

In wiring devices we have a comparison between our direct sales organization, and the pooled-sales organization. The striking difference is in attitude. For example, when we want to bring a sales division rep into the factory for a meeting, we might be told "not this month." Our direct sales force, on the other hand, gets damned involved.

The field sales manager tells me that he has to tell his reps to *ask* for a wiring devices order before they leave a customer! In other words, wiring devices is on the tail end of every call, and often is left out completely. The sales reps admit that the first thing they talk about is wire and cable. Then comes conduit. Last comes wiring devices, if there is time.

The typical wiring devices order is small in comparison to wire and cable and conduit products. A Bergman sales rep who gets the conduit products order on a construction job will leave the wiring devices business to someone else. Furthermore, contractors always want to split up their business—to have lots of friends—so wiring devices gets left out.

Our competitors are selling by pull-through tactics. They are selling beyond the distributors. Our reps make most of their calls on distributors. If we had control, we could direct their calls into more productive channels.

Each sales rep has three budgets to meet. If they get a lucky break on wiring devices, and fill their quotas, they then concentrate on the other two products exclusively. We can *never* get any better than budget. We don't realize the full potential of the wiring devices market.

We are very conscious of product planning. For good planning we need good feedback from the field. All we get from the field are a bunch of alibis. They say, "We can't sell this" or "We can't sell that." We ask them what they want, and they can't tell us. We can send out a new product and never hear what happens to it for months! We finally resorted to attaching post cards to the samples, with instructions for the sales rep to follow: "When you give this to the customers, write what they say on the card and mail it in." This sort of thing shouldn't be necessary.

We feel we need more people in the field, and we are willing to pay for them. So what do we get from the sales division: 65 percent of one person in St. Louis instead of 45 percent. As far as we're concerned, we still have one person working for us in St. Louis, except that now we're paying more!

In wiring devices, our sales run contracyclical to sales of the wire and cable division and the conduit products division. When money is tight, housing starts go up and industrial construction goes down. This places us in an untenable position. When the other divisions are down, we are up, and they want us to take over their manpower in the sales division. This results in juggling accounts, and a constant movement of personnel. Too many moves are made on the basis of expediency.

Comments from Various Managers in the Conduit Products Division

These large construction jobs are field days for purchasing agents. They drive prices down to extreme. Nevertheless, our salespeople cave in too easily. They sell only on price. A smart salesperson can do better than that. We must sell on more than price!

This is what happens when we have pooled selling: if wiring devices gets into trouble, and can't pay for more than, say, 40 sales reps, then Monteith will say "OK, pay for 38 people." Then he shuffles the percentages, and moves the reps over to the conduit products or wire and cable payrolls. Nobody leaves. There really isn't any cutback. It all depends upon who is putting on the pressure at the moment.

The system concept is out of date. We really have little in common with the other product departments. The industry is sophisticated, and doesn't need to buy a packaged system any longer. All three products are purchased at different stages in a construction project.

Once we wanted to get all the people in the sales division together at the factory. The sales division said that while they were gone, the conduit products division had to pay their salaries and expenses. This totaled $30,000 for 70 people for a week. In effect, conduit products was paying twice for these people. It's an accounting mess!

Last year the sales division set the quota for one district representative *lower* than the year before. When we asked why, they explained that it was all that was left over after splitting up the district quota among the other district representatives. We need control over this sort of thing.

We don't want to dissolve the sales division. We just want to pull out.

Pearkes Takes Over as President

On January 1, 1969, R. Dinsdale retired as president of Bergman Wire and Cable. His position was taken over by G. R. Pearkes, who was hired from outside the Bergman organization. Pearkes had previously held high-level marketing positions in other companies. An extremely dynamic person, Pearkes openly encouraged all division vice presidents to present with vigor their views on the ideal marketing organization needed by the company. The product division vice presidents found him more receptive to their point of view than Dinsdale had been.

Pearkes was concerned with the discord which he found between the product divisions and the sales division, and he resolved to settle matters without delay. In order to obtain an independent view of the pros and cons of the pooled selling organization, he called in the management consulting firm of McNeuter Associates Incorporated. A team of consultants from the McNeuter organization began studies at Bergman on September 30, 1969, headed by a McNeuter senior partner, R. Frost. McNeuter, and R. Frost in particular, had performed studies for Bergman Wire and Cable in the past, and Frost had become a good friend of J. Monteith, vice president of the sales division. It was known that Frost was leaving McNeuter at the end of this assignment.

One manager said that he believed that the new president, Pearkes, had decided after a few months on the job to disband the sales division and that he had brought in the McNeuter consultants only to confirm this decision.

The Frost Report

The McNeuter consultants spent 2½ months on the study. The objective of the study, as defined by McNeuter and Bergman personnel, was "to determine the impact on market position and costs of selected alternative marketing organization structures, and to make recommendations as to the form the organization structure should take to achieve a primary objective of a stronger industry position."

The final report of the consulting team became known as the *Frost Report*, after the author. Among the major findings of the report were the following:

1. Bergman is losing industry position.
2. The technical competence of Bergman sales reps is better, on the average, than the technical competence of competitors' sales reps, and Bergman sales reps are better than competitors' sales reps.
3. There is not a clear understanding of the division of responsibility between the sales division and the product divisions.
4. The sales division has not been set up as a true pooled-work organization component.
5. The most profitable sales operation is not measured by the largest dollar orders per sales rep.

Contrary to the expectation of many persons in the company, the *Frost Report* did not recommend dissolving the sales division. The *Frost Report* stated that the many advantages of a pooled sales organization outweighed its disadvantages. The report seemed to suggest that much of the difficulty had arisen in the past through a mutual misunderstanding of duties and responsibilities and that, as a result, the sales division had not actually operated as a pooled organization. The report recommended that the sales division be reconstituted as a "true pooled-work organization," with a charter written by the product divisions. With wholehearted support of this decision, the report said, the full benefits of the pooled sales organization could be realized. A sentence in the recommendations which was written in capital letters was "IF THIS CANNOT BE OBTAINED IT WOULD BE BETTER TO DECENTRALIZE."

Reactions to the Frost Report

When the final draft of the *Frost Report* was submitted on December 15, 1969, Pearkes was no longer with the company. He had been hired away in the autumn of 1969 at a substantial increase in salary to head a group of companies in a related industry. To replace him, the board of directors hired an electrical engineer with impressive technical and management qualifications, Gordon Churchill.

Churchill felt that he should receive the advice of as many informed persons as possible before making a decision on the recommendations of the *Frost Report*. He therefore sent copies of the report to the division vice presidents, asking for their comments. Some of their remarks, as abstracted from letters which Churchill received in reply, are shown below and on the next page.

From the Vice President of the Wire and Cable Division

The recommendation against separating the sales function hinges strongly on the implied similarity of the products of the three divisions, which does not have support in the investigations conducted. While it is true that certain segments (15 percent) of wire and cable business fall into the "commodity" pattern, this cannot be accepted as an over-all long-term direction in sale of all of our products if our growth is to continue. . . .

If for any reason you feel the sales function should not be decentralized I would appreciate an opportunity of reviewing the subject with you before such a decision is made.

From the Vice President of the Conduit Products Division

It has proven difficult, if not impossible, to get the sales division to respond to our division's goals except to get volume business and always with constant pressure for lower prices. . . .

. . . a disjointed and confusing report. . . .

The recommendation to reconstitute the sales division as a true pooled-work organization cannot be done without a major unheaval of personnel in key positions in the present sales division and without taking an excessive amount of time. Even if this could be done, we believe there would still be too many problems, frictions, and disagreement to make it an efficient working relationship. . . .

From the Vice President of the Wiring Devices Division

I fully realize that the time allotted and the personnel assigned to the study job was probably far too scant to produce the document that I hoped would be produced for presentation to you. . . .

It seems to me that when the choice is between maintaining old relationships and getting the job done, it is time we decided in favor of the job. . . .

From the Vice President of the Sales Division

I believe this report represents a fairly thorough and unbiased study of alternate marketing organization structures for Bergman products. . . .

It is very difficult for me to discern in the comments of the product divisions any significant improvement that they anticipated from decentralization. I, therefore, reiterate my concurrence with the findings and recommendations of the study team. . . .

The Suggestion for Independent Studies

In July 1970, while eliciting advice from personal friends in top management positions outside the company, Churchill received this suggestion:

Because the preferred solution is to let each division do its own selling if it is feasible, start the investigation from this point. Probably most of the people in the divisions have never operated a sales force. Very likely they need a great deal of help in translating their customers and marketing channels into required calls and then to sales reps, districts, overheads, and reliable costs.

Insist that they do a thorough, unbiased job, and that they *prove* it. Insist that they show that they have considered the interests of the other divisions and the company and that they prove that too. Insist that they show that they have considered *all* alternatives.

Then if they do make these studies—and if all those divisions still want their own sales organizations they should have them. They should have them, however, with the clear understanding that they have made the studies and the decisions and it is their necks if it does not work.

Churchill believed that this was very practical advice. In a letter dated August 24, 1970, he instructed the three product division vice presidents to select from among all reasonable alternatives the field sales organization most likely to realize the long-range sales and profitability goals of the respective divisions and to prepare detailed plans for implementing their organizational proposals.

The three vice presidents submitted their plans in the late fall of 1970. Summarizing these plans, Churchill was particularly interested in their implications for marketing personnel levels. The comparison between existing and proposed staffing is shown in Exhibit 9.

Bergman Strategy

Finally, as he reflected broadly on the options that might be open to him, Churchill recognized that Bergman had fallen behind significantly over the previous decade in market position and profitability and that there were certain strategic factors that would have to be considered before he made any moves. While Bergman's position

EXHIBIT 9

PERSONNEL SUMMARY FOR THE PROPOSED REORGANIZATION OF THE SELLING FUNCTION

Position	Present					Proposed			
	Conduit products	Wire and cable	Wiring devices	Sales	Total	Conduit products	Wire and cable	Wiring devices	Total
Sales manager and section manager	3	2	6	4	15	2	3	6	11
Application engineering	–	7	2	1	10	–	6	2	8
Market research and product planning	1	1	6	2	10	1	3	6	10
Market administration	8	9	51	7	75	9	8	52	69
Advertising and sales promotion	1	–	14	9	24	2	6	14.4	22.4
Field warehousing	–	–	–	126	126	11	65.4	49.6	126
Field sales									
District managers and representatives	–	–	15	146	161	21*	63	66	150
Sales service and district clerical	–	–	3	84	87	–	58.6	8	66.6
Staff or home office sales	6	22	4	–	32	7	20	4	31
Total number of people	19	41	101	379†	540	53	233	208	494

*This sales force would be managed centrally from the conduit products division headquarters, and the field warehousing function would be transferred to key distributors.
†These sales division personnel were allocated as follows to the product divisions on the basis of work performed: conduit products, 60.1 people; wire and cable, 201.1 people; wiring devices, 117.8 people.

on wiring devices was relatively strong, the other two lines showed weaknesses.

Wiring Devices. This line was competitive in price, quality, and service. It had very good acceptance among builders and electrical contractors for residential construction. Consulting engineers and architects knew it as having a decided edge in product innovation. Bergman wiring devices, however, did not have a competitive edge in the industrial market.

Conduit Products. Price leadership in this market was held by the large steel companies. At the same time steel was being challenged strongly in this application by aluminum. Hence, the market was extremely price-competitive, and buyers were very price-sensitive. Bergman was not an integrated producer of conduit, and approximately 80 percent of the total cost of producing conduit was the cost of the material. The return on sales for conduit was 6 percent before taxes, although the return on investment was considered adequate. Little opportunity existed here, thought Churchill, for product innovation or differentiation.

Over 80 percent of Bergman's conduit orders were negotiated by Bergman district representatives and delivered directly to the job site (although the distributor still received a commission). The remainder was delivered to distributor inventory, where it was sold to "pickup" customers. The conduit line was a very-low-profit item for the distributors, and they had little incentive to do promotional work. As a result, Bergman district representatives had to maintain most of the selling contact with the construction industry. It was estimated that without district representatives' sales support, about one-half of the distributors would drop the Bergman conduit line.

Wire and Cable. Competition in the wire and cable market was intense among the 275 manufacturers of these products in the United States. Ten of these companies competed with Bergman across its full line. Price leadership was held on many products, however, by small, narrow-line producers.

Bergman was in a strong position in the power cable field, where engineering and quality were important selling factors. With supply cord, which was almost a commodity, Bergman was frequently high in price.

Bergman's foothold in the electric cable market was threatened by many small manufacturing firms which had sprung up to provide unusual service for the electronic manufacturers. The electronic cable market required unusual technical competence on the part of the cable manufacturer, since many of the designs had special high-temperature, electrical, or dimensional characteristics. Extensive development work with electronic design engineers was a necessary part of selling in the electronics market. While Bergman had competed primarily on a price basis in the wire and cable market, Churchill thought that in some market segments it might be able to compete more effectively by stressing new-product development for specific applications.

For other segments, those reached largely through distributors, it was essential for sales reps to make calls in support of distributors in order to retain their loyalty. It was necessary then to concentrate selling effort on consulting engineers, utility engineers, industrial plant engineers, purchasing agents, and large electrical contractors, as well as on distributors.

Churchill knew that many persons in the company believed that a decision was imminent. He was convinced that further delay would be pointless; the morale of the organization had already suffered as a result of the many disputes over the sales organization. Churchill was determined to resolve the matter once and for all in New York on February 16, 1971, and to announce his final decision to his managers by February 22.

Appendix: Economic Analysis

Economic Analysis

Marketing managers find themselves engaging in both quantitative and qualitative types of analysis as they evaluate market opportunities and seek to develop appropriate marketing programs.

Some of the quantitative tools and techniques used in marketing are highly sophisticated and require a significant level of statistical and mathematical expertise. Others, involving relatively simple concepts and computations, represent fundamental skills which every marketing manager should possess. In almost all instances, it is necessary to determine the economic consequences of alternative courses of action and of adopting alternative sets of assumptions. This appendix discusses some of the basic terminology and calculations used in analyzing marketing problems, beginning with the concept of *contribution* and how it is calculated.

Contribution

Contribution refers to the funds available to the seller of an item after subtracting the variable costs associated with it. The commonly used term *unit contribution* refers to the contribution yielded by item sold. Assume, for example, that we sell a unit of a particular product to wholesalers at a price of $100 and that the *variable* manufacturing costs of that unit are $30. In addition, it costs us $3 per unit to ship the product to wholesalers, and we pay a 5 percent commission to our salespeople ($5 per unit). Under these circumstances, the variable costs associated with each unit of this product are $38 ($30 + $3 + $5). Since we receive $100 revenue for each unit we sell, our unit contribution is $62 ($100 − $38).

This $62 unit contribution is available to cover the fixed manufacturing expenses, overheads, and marketing costs associated with the product and, it is hoped, to provide a profit. *Fixed costs* are costs which remain fixed regardless of the volume of production. Thus, whether we produce 1,000 or 5,000 items, the cost of executive salaries remains fixed, as does rent, insurance, and other so-called overhead expenses. Fixed costs remain unchanged over some reasonable range of activity of the firm. *Variable costs*, on the other hand, are costs which are directly traceable to the volume of activity—the more we sell, the more raw material we need, usually the more assembly workers we need, the more sales commission we pay. Variable costs are directly traceable to variations in volume of activity.

Break Even

Break even means that our revenue is just enough to pay for both the variable and the fixed costs incurred. But only just that. We have no profit; we have no losses. We have only broken even.

As a bare minimum, most companies expect a product to break even, i.e., not to lose money. Depending on the situation, the appropriate time within which a product should break even may be short (a year, or a season) or long (perhaps as much as 5 years). For the sake of simplicity, we will assume that the appropriate time period for break even is 1 year.

One way to talk of break even is to say it occurs when the number of units we sell, multiplied by the unit contribution, is equal to the fixed costs. Thus we calculate break even as follows: BE = total fixed costs divided by unit contribution. If unit contribution is $62, for example, and fixed costs are $100,000, break even will occur when we produce and sell 1,613 units (that is, $100,000 ÷ $62). If we expect to produce and sell 1,613 units, we expect to break even. But if we produce 2,000 and sell 1,613, we have not broken even. We have incurred losses because our total variable costs are now $38 × 2,000, not $38 × 1,613.

Profit Impact

Few companies are content to operate at break even. Normally, companies require that each product produce a positive impact on company profits. The impact which a particular product will have on company profits is easily calculated, as follows, using the same figures we have been using:

$$(Unit\ contribution \times units\ prod.\ and\ sold) \quad - \quad fixed\ costs = profit\ impact$$
$$(\quad \$62 \quad \times \quad 2,000 \quad)$$
$$\$124,000 \quad\quad\quad - \$100,000 = \$24,000$$

Why do we call this $24,000 *impact on profit* (or *profit impact*) and not just plain *profit*? The answer is that there may be a few other costs yet to be charged against the product, such as corporate headquarters overhead, not just product-related overhead.

Suppose we have a certain profit target in mind—say we want to have a profit impact of $50,000. What will our production and sales have to be to achieve this target? The calculation is the same as the above, except that we add the $50,000 profit target to the fixed costs. With fixed costs now at $150,000 instead of $100,000, the resulting calculation gives us 2,419 units.

When the demand for a product is not static (as we have assumed in this example), the calculation of the probable effect on market share is more difficult. If we increase advertising by $50,000, for example, the total demand for the product may increase. If this happens, some of our sales increase may come from increased market share, but some may also come from increased demand. Would the competition then be as likely to retaliate?

Computation of Margin

When manufacturers produce an item for sale, or when retailers buy an item for resale, they decide on the price for which they hope to sell it. This price exceeds the manufacturing cost, or the cost paid by the merchant, by an amount termed the *margin*. (The terms *markup* and *markon* are also often used interchangeably with margin.) The margin is similar to, though not necessarily the same as, *unit contribution*—a distinction we shall not attempt to clarify here.

Margin, cost, and selling price are related to each other in the following manner:

$$\text{Selling price} = \text{margin} + \text{cost}$$
$$\$1 \quad = \$0.40 + \$0.60$$

Thus, we say that the retailer's selling price of an item consists of the cost to the retailer plus the margin. For many purposes it is useful to express the margin as a percentage. Theoretically, the 40-cent margin might be expressed either as a percentage of the cost or as a percentage of the selling price. If it were expressed as a percentage of the cost, the margin would be 66.67 percent, i.e., the 40-cent margin divided by the 60-cent cost equals 66.67 percent. When it is expressed as a percentage of the selling price, the margin is 40 percent—$\$0.40 \div \$1$. The commonly accepted practice is to express percentages (regarding both margins and costs) with net sales as the base. While this is the "commonly accepted" practice, some industries, firms, and individuals depart from that practice. We will follow the common practice.

If the cost is known and the percentage of margin on selling price is given, it is a simple matter to compute the selling price. Suppose, for example, that a retail merchant buys goods at a cost of $10 and wants a margin of 33⅓ percent to cover expenses and have some chance of making a net profit. What should be the selling price? Since 100 percent of the selling price is made up of two parts (the cost and the margin), this means that $10 + 33⅓ percent = 100 percent. It follows that the $10 cost must be 66⅔ percent of the selling price. What is 100 percent—the selling price itself?

We have said that

$$\text{Then: } 66\tfrac{2}{3}\% \times \text{selling price} = \$10$$
$$\text{Selling price} = \$10 \div 66\tfrac{2}{3}\%$$
$$= \$15$$

Similarly, if a wholesaler buys an article for 60 cents and wants a margin of 20 percent, the selling price is 60 cents ÷ 80 percent, or 75 cents.

A similar technique may be used to calculate the effects of a change in our marketing program. Assume that with our present program we expect to make and sell 2,000 units of a product with a $62 unit contribution. With our fixed costs of $100,000, we saw that this yields a $24,000 profit impact. We now consider raising our advertising expenditure by $50,000, which would increase our fixed costs to $150,000. If we do so, how much volume would the new marketing program have to achieve to generate the same profit impact ($24,000) as our present program?

The calculation is as follows:

Present fixed cost	+	present profit impact	+	add'l. fixed cost	÷	unit contrib.	=	required vol.
$100,000	+	$24,000	+	$50,000	÷	$62	=	2,806

We would have to make and sell 2,806 units in order for the new program to yield the same profit impact as the old one, which required sales of only 2,000 units. There are other ways to come up with the same answer, of course, but this way has at least the virtue of simple clarity for the amateur.

Suppose we improve our product by adding $3 per unit of variable cost. This cuts our unit contribution to $59. If all other costs, as well as prices, remain unchanged, how much would we have to sell to maintain our current profit impact of $24,000? The answer is ($100,000 + $24,000) ÷ $59 = 2,102 units.

In calculating the economic effects of a marketing program, one is generally forced to make a number of assumptions. The sales forecast is generally the most critical, but fixed costs, variable costs, and selling prices may also be uncertain. Under these circumstances, it is generally useful to calculate the profit impact of a marketing program under varying sets of assumptions.

Obviously, one can make break-even points or expected profit impact come out any way one wishes by making the appropriate assumptions about sales volumes and costs. For this reason, the marketing manager should become adept at appraising the realism of the assumptions on which calculations of these types are based.

Market Share Analysis

One way of assessing the realism of a sales forecast is to calculate its implications for a firm's market share. Assume, for example, that the total market for the product mentioned in the previous examples is 10,000 units, that the market is not expanding, and that we presently sell 2,000 units. We therefore have a market share of 20 percent. The product manager recommends that we raise our advertising budget by $50,000, which means that we would have to make and sell 2,806 units to maintain our current profit impact. We shall have to make and sell 806 units above the present level, raising our market share from 20 to 28.06 percent. How likely is this? Can $50,000 of additional advertising accomplish that? Will our competitors give up an 8 percent market share without fighting back?

Margin percentages are figured on the selling price at each level of business. If it costs a company 75 cents to manufacture an item and it wants a 25 percent margin, the selling price must be $1. If the wholesaler to whom the manufacturer sells the item for $1 wants a margin of 16⅔ percent, the selling price will be $1.20. And if the retailer who buys it from the wholesaler for $1.20 resells it to consumers at $2, the margin will be 40 percent.

Since some firms and industries use cost rather than selling price as the base for their percentage calculations, it is useful to know how to convert from one base to the other. On merchandise costing $6 and selling for $10, the margin is $4. This margin, which is 40 percent of the selling price, would be 66⅔ percent if computed on the basis of the cost. To make the conversion, from either the cost base or the selling-price base to the other, it helps to understand once more that selling price is composed of two parts, the margin and the cost, as follows:

$$\text{Cost} + \text{margin} = \text{selling price}$$
$$\$0.60 + \$0.40 = \$1$$

$$\text{Margin as percentage of selling price} = \frac{\$0.40}{\$1.00} = 40\%$$

If we want quickly to convert this margin, expressed as a percentage of selling price, into a margin expressed as a percentage of cost, we say:

1. If 40 percent is the margin on selling price
2. Then the remaining 60 percent must be the cost
3. 40 percent ÷ 60 percent = 66⅔ percent = margin based on cost

The following formula invariably gets this conversion right:

$$\frac{\text{Percentage margin on price}}{100\% - \text{percentage margin on price}} = \text{percentage margin on cost}$$

$$\frac{40\%}{100\% - 40\%} = \frac{40\%}{60\%} \qquad = \qquad 66\frac{2}{3}\%$$

Suppose we have the opposite question: How to express a margin figured as a percentage of cost into one figured as a percentage of selling price? We say:

1. Cost is 100 percent, i.e., the denominator on which the margin was figured
2. Since the margin on cost (in the above example) is $66\frac{2}{3}$ percent
3. Then the selling price must be

$$\text{Cost} + \text{margin} = \text{selling price}$$
$$100\% + 66\frac{2}{3}\% = 166\frac{2}{3}\%$$

4. Margin on percentage of selling price = $66\frac{2}{3}$ percent ÷ $166\frac{2}{3}$ percent = 40 percent

The following formula invariably gets this conversion right:

$$\frac{\text{Percentage margin on cost}}{100\% + \text{percentage margin on cost}} = \text{percentage margin on selling price}$$

$$\frac{66\frac{2}{3}\%}{100\% + 66\frac{2}{3}\%} = \frac{66\frac{2}{3}\%}{166\frac{2}{3}\%} \qquad = \qquad 40\%$$

Discounts and Chain Discounts

A common practice is for the manufacturer to suggest at what price the product should be sold by a retailer. If the "suggested retail price" is $100 while selling the item to the retailer for $60, the manufacturer is, in effect, proposing a "suggested retail margin" of 40 percent; that is ($100 − $60) ÷ $100 = 40 percent. In common usage it will be said that the manufacturer is offering a "trade discount" of 40 percent. Indeed, the manufacturer may actually quote the price to the retailer as "$100 less 40%." If the retailer chooses to sell the item for, say, $90 instead of $100, the retailer will still have to pay "$100 less 40%," or $60. The retail margin will be $30 ÷ $90, or $33\frac{1}{3}$ percent.

Occasionally, discounts from a suggested resale price will be computed in two or more increments. For example, a manufacturer might offer discounts of 40 percent + 5 percent on a product priced to be resold at $100. This means that in addition to the original discount (suggested margin) of 40 percent (i.e., $40), the manufacturer has allowed an additional 5 percent. This does not mean 40 percent plus 5 percent, or 45 percent. It means $100 − 40 percent less 5 percent of $100 − 40 percent. Thus the retailer pays ($100 − $40) − 5% × ($100 − $40) = $60 − $3 = $57. The 40 percent + 5 percent is called a *chain discount*. In chain discounts the specific percentage link in the chain that is referred to (say, 5 percent, as in the present example) is calculated on the price that is derived after the application of the prior link or links to the suggested retail price. This rather cumbersome practice of stating discounts (or margins) probably arose originally to advise customers of changes in a discount structure. Over the years, the method has become traditional in certain industries.

Terms of Sale

When a manufacturer sells to a wholesaler or distributor, who then in turn sells to a retailer, prices are also generally listed as discounts from a suggested retail price. A product suggested to sell for $100 at retail, with a suggested retail margin of 40 percent and a suggested wholesale margin of 20 percent, will be sold by the wholesaler to the retailer at a price of $60 (i.e., $100 less 40 percent) and will be purchased by the wholesaler from the manufacturer for $48 (i.e., $60 less 20 percent). Once again, the margin for a particular institution in the channel of distribution is applied to the price at which the institution sells its goods and services.

Terms of sales are a shorthand method of setting forth the conditions under which a company offers to sell its goods or services. They include, in addition to price, a statement of trade discounts, the date by which the amount is to be paid, and shipping responsibilities.

For example, terms of sale of "$50 per unit, 2/10 e.o.m., 60 days net, f.o.b. seller's plant" indicate that (1) the price for which the product is being sold is $50, (2) a 2 percent trade discount off the price (i.e., $1) will be offered if the bill (or "invoice") is paid within a period ending 10 days after the end of the month in which the invoice is issued, (3) the total amount of the bill is due within 60 days of the invoice date, and (4) the title and responsibility for the subsequent transportation of the product pass from the seller to the buyer at the plant of the former.

Here, the letters *e.o.m.* stand for *end of month*. In their absence, to qualify for receipt of the 2 percent special discount would require paying the bill within 10 days after the date on the invoice. The letters *f.o.b.* stand for *free on board*, traditional means of expressing the physical location at which certain responsibilities for transportation and damage-claim litigation pass from seller to buyer. While these are just two of many different discount and shipping terms, they are perhaps the most commonly used in business today.

Summary

When analyzing marketing problems, it is important to determine the economic consequences of alternative strategies, as well as of variations in the assumptions underlying production, marketing, and market data.

This appendix has reviewed several key concepts in economic analysis, including those of contribution, fixed and variable costs, break even, profit impact, and margins. It has also highlighted the basic arithmetical computations involved in undertaking economic analysis for marketing decisions.

Exercises

Horatio Alger has just become the product manager for brand X. Brand X is a consumer product with a retail price of $1. Retail margins on the product are 33 percent, while wholesalers take a 12 percent margin.

A total of 20 million units of brand X and its direct competitors are sold annually; brand X has 24 percent of this market.

Variable manufacturing costs for brand X amount to $0.09 per unit. Fixed manufacturing costs amount to $900,000.

The advertising budget for brand X is $500,000. The brand X product manager's salary and expenses total $35,000. Salespeople are paid entirely by commission; this is 10 percent. Shipping costs, breakage, insurance, etc., amount to $0.02 per unit.

1. What is the unit contribution for brand X?
2. What is brand X's break-even point?
3. What market share does brand X need to break even?
4. What is brand X's profit impact?
5. Industry demand is expected to increase to 23 million units next year. Mr. Alger is considering raising his advertising budget to $1 million.
   a. If the advertising budget is raised, how many units of brand X will have to be sold for it to break even?
   b. How many units of brand X will have to be sold for it to achieve the same profit impact that it did this year?
   c. What will brand X's market share have to be next year for its profit impact to be the same as this year's?